W9-CAB-170

MAGILL'S
LITERARY ANNUAL
2004

MAGILL'S LITERARY ANNUAL 2004

*Essay-Reviews of 200 Outstanding Books
Published in the United States during 2003*

With an Annotated Categories List

Volume Two
M-Z

Edited by
JOHN D. WILSON
STEVEN G. KELLMAN

SALEM PRESS
Pasadena, California   Hackensack, New Jersey

LIBRARY OF CONGRESS CATALOG CARD NO. 77-99209
ISBN 1-58765-158-0

FIRST PRINTING

PRINTED IN THE UNITED STATES OF AMERICA

MAGILL'S
LITERARY ANNUAL
2004

MONSTER OF GOD
The Man-Eating Predator in the Jungles of History and the Mind

Author: David Quammen (1948-   )
Publisher: W. W. Norton (New York). 515 pp. $26.95
Type of work: Environment and natural history
Time: The 1990's
Locale: Western India, Romania, Australia, and the Russian Far East

Quammen traveled to the Kathiawar Peninsula of western India to study the remaining Asian lions, to Arnhem Land in northern Australia to learn about crocodiles, to Romania's Carpathian Mountains for a look at brown bears, and to Russia's Far East to go snowmobiling in the habitat of the Siberian tiger

Principal personages:

> RAVI CHELLAM, a naturalist with the Wildlife Institute of India and Quammen's lion guru
> JACKIE ADJARRAL, Quammen's intrepid Aboriginal guide to crocodile habits and habitats
> ION MICU, the author of *Ursul Brun* and one of Quammen's tutors on *Ursus arctos*, the brown bear
> DMITRI PIKUNOV, a "burly, impetuous" biologist in his sixties who takes Quammen on the coldest snowmobile ride of his life

David Quammen announces his interests immediately:

> What I'm asking you to contemplate are the psychological, mythic, and spiritual dimensions (as well as the ecological implications) of a particular sort of relationship: the predator-prey showdown between one dangerous, flesh-eating animal and one human victim. That relationship, I believe, has played a crucial role in shaping the way we humans construe our place in the natural world.

After a prelude in which he surveys some of the alpha predators, as he calls them, in world myth and literature, Quammen goes directly to the Gir forest of India's Gujerat Province, where forty-five million people live in an area roughly the size of Nebraska. In the Gir Wildlife Sanctuary and National Park of Gujerat's Kathiawar Peninsula, about 350 Asiatic lions, the last survivors of *Panthera leo* still to be found in Asia, live in a sometimes uneasy truce with the Maldharis (*mal* = livestock, *dhari* = guardian) an indigenous pastoral people of the region who live in acre-size, thorn-enclosed camps with iron doors that shut out lions and leopards at nights.

Panthera leo persica has persisted in Kathiawar, a historically semi-lawless area, probably because of the peninsula's relative remoteness from dominance by the raj, whose functionaries reveled in "well-catered" lion hunts in eastern and central India.

David Quammen won the John Burroughs Medal for natural history writing for his book The Song of the Dodo *(1996), and he writes on assignment for* National Geographic, Harper's, *and other magazines. He lives in Montana.*

Lions' boldness around people and preference for open habitat made them easy targets for sportsmen like Colonel George A. Smith, reputed slayer of three hundred of the animals. Depletion of the lion population in Kathiawar was slowed by Lord Curzon's ban on shooting in the mid-1800's, but as their numbers grew the lions preyed on livestock, and in 1899-1900 a severe drought killed off the ungulates they lived on, drawing the lions into the villages for food and ending the ban. Weather and ecopolitics kept the lions' numbers in flux during the twentieth century. For the most part, the Maldharis and the lions have achieved "a degree of compatibility," but not without 193 attacks on humans, 28 of them fatal, between 1978 and 1991.

Quammen interlards his account of his travels in the Gir Sanctuary with Ravi Chellam from the national Wildlife Institute with reflections on leopards and conversations with Maldharis who have encountered lions up close. His consideration of the toll of large predators on humans leads him to the studies of Paul Errington, an American small-animal ecologist, who learned that muskrats hate overcrowding and, in effect, sacrifice to the mink, their chief predator, the old, the sick, the handicapped—all the "wastage parts." From this observation Quammen derives his "Muskrat Conundrum": "that the costs exacted by alpha predators be borne disproportionately by poor people . . . while the spiritual and aesthetic benefits of these magnificent beasts are enjoyed from afar."

Quammen turns to A. D. Graham's 1973 book *Eyelids of Morning: The Mingled Destinies of Crocodiles and Men* for some horrible instances of humans eaten by the large (up to half a ton) crocodiles in Kenya's Lake Rudolf (now Lake Turkana). Quammen stresses the "dour animist theology" of the Turkana, which leads them to understand *Crocodylus nilotica* as "the punishing agent of a capricious God who was by turns benevolent and vindictive" and, in Graham's words, "indistinguishable from the devil." This perverse theodicy assures Turkana that they can wade in crocodile waters with impunity if their consciences are untroubled. Quammen rejects Graham's thesis about parallels with cannibalism and his view that for Turkana "to be eaten by a croc is to be consumed forever *by evil*," suggesting instead that the dread of being consumed by a predator reflects ancient concerns about proper funeral rites.

From Graham's studies, Quammen turns to the largest crocodile of all, *Crocodylus porosus*, up to twenty feet long and found in small but growing numbers (190 in 1995) in eastern India's Orissa Province. In the village of Khamar Sahi, Quammen hears tales of death and mangling by *C. porosus* and learns of the villagers' bitterness that the forestry department takes no action against the animals. There is no romantic feeling in Khamar Sahi about animals and humans living in natural harmony. Quammen concludes, "The very subject of crocodiles, for this community, is a sort of collective psychic abscess."

The other haunt of *C. porosus* is northern Australia, in Arnhem Land, just east of Darwin, where Crocodylus Park conducts research and allows some hunting for skins, all part of a philosophy that treats wildlife as a renewable resource. Quammen finds his guide to crocodile life in the dusty village of Maningrida: He is "the Professor," Jackie Adjarral, "a tiny black man of indeterminate middle age" whose "rooster confidence" reminds Quammen of singer Chuck Berry. After a tour of some nasty, dangerous terrain with Jackie, Quammen moves on to Nhulunbuy, an obscure village on the Gulf of Carpenteria populated by an ancient people called the Yolngu. Among the Yolngu, Quammen hears stories of crocodile encounters, such as that of a man named Dulu and his brother who fought off an attack, killed their assailant with two shotgun blasts, and then baked the animal up in an earth oven and ate it. Dulu explains, "If we kill something, we eat it." In a remote crocodile nesting ground called Garrangali, Quammen learns with surprise of tunnels under the banks that crocodiles follow.

In a tour of crocodile country, Quammen visits Dhuruputjpi, near Garrangali, to interview MänMan Wirrpanda, a local leader who has complained to the federal officials about crocodile attacks. MänMan's Djapu clan takes Mäna, the Ancestral Shark, not Bäru, the Ancestral Crocodile, as its totem, and, unlike other clansmen of Arnhem Land, MänMan feels no reverence for *C. porosus*. Eight months later, back in Maningrida for the crocodile egg harvest, Quammen has eggs hatch in his hands and witnesses Jackie Adjarral harpoon an angry mother crocodile and play her "like a five-hundred pound catfish." Quammen's education in crocodiles ends, later, in the bush compound of Humpty Doo, where he interviews Andrew Cappo, a taxidermist who does occasional pickled crododile heads and other "croc schlock" for "bikies," the Darwin area's "leather-clad, Harley-Davidson-riding gentlemen." The technology of Cappo's crocodile work holds the reader's attention.

There are no crocodiles in Romania's Carpathian Mountains, but for several decades a monster just as slimy prowled the forests: Nicolae Ceaušescu, the Conducător, or supreme leader, as he designated himself. In one of the many facets of his megalomania, this "tin-pot dictator" fancied himself a hunter. He was himself a good shot with a rifle. After his execution, by firing squad in 1989, he was known as Împuşcatul, "the Shot One." Thanks to Ceaušescu's intense desire to shoot brown bears, Romania's forests were divided into hunting areas carefully managed to maintain plenty of targets for Ceaušescu and his two Holland & Holland .375 rifles. On October 15, 1983, Ceaušescu arrived by helicopter at a hunting lodge called Dealul Negra in the Bistriþa district, and with four hundred local people acting as beaters he shot—from a high stand—twenty-four bears and posed for photographs with them. Vasile Crišan, author of *Ceaušescu: Hunter or Butcher?*, describes this bloody day as the Massacre of Bistriþa.

Quammen enjoys his mountain hikes with shepherds, drinking *palinca* (plum brandy) and eating *mamaliga* (polenta sliced like meatloaf) and a favorite Romanian cheese called *brânzā de burduf*, which a peasant named Nicu tells him works miracles for a man's virility: *"Viagra? Nu. Brânzā!"* The bear biologist Ion Micu recounts for Quammen the story of an experiment in bear management instigated by politicians of the Argeš region seeking to curry favor with the Conducător. The project entailed kidnapping bear cubs and raising them in "a concentration camp for cubs" located in Râušor. Of the 227 kidnapped cubs raised between 1974 and 1981 and released into the wild, none was ever shot by Ceaušescu, and they suffered a variety of sad fates, unable to cope with challenges for which their nursery life never prepared them. Quammen states a general principal illustrated in this dismal tale: "Planting hatchery-raised animals into habitat already occupied by a wild population is nowadays recognized to be futile at best, and more likely counterproductive."

Although it does not apply to Romania, Quammen offers a "small theory" about the extermination of the big predators—that it is "fundamental to the colonial enterprise." He opines that the hatred for grizzlies felt by ranchers (of European descent) in Idaho, Wyoming, and Montana, where Quammen lives, is a residual feature of colonialism and that killing off the "resident monsters" is all part of subduing new territories. These ruminations lead Quammen to a survey of monsters in myth and literature and their national associations. Beowulf's defeat of Grendel and Theseus's encounter with the Minotaur are well known, but allusions to Minamoto-no-Yorimasa versus Nue and to Tishpak versus the Labbu do not extend Quammen's thesis noticeably.

A digression on teeth—their shapes, sizes, functions—inevitably leads to a meditation on sabertooth cats and finally to *Panthera tigris altaica*, the Siberian (or Amur) tiger, now well confined to the Sikhote-Alin region of southeastern Russia just across the Sea of Japan from Hokkaido. Quammen's guide to Bikin, the most "northerly, isolated, and pristine" of the Sikhote-Alin valleys, is Dima Pikunov, who has worked many years in the region, "following signs, reading clues from the prints and the scrape marks and the fed-upon kills," but hardly ever seeing a live tiger. The human population of the Bikin consists of about eight hundred members of the Udege tribe, now transformed by Soviet planning into professional hunters and too fond, complains Dima, of holing up in town during the winter with a bottle of vodka. Quammen enjoys being introduced by Dima to such locals as Su-San Tyfuivich Geonka, who began professional hunting in 1934, and Nikolai Alexsandrovich Semonchuk, who gave up hunting in 1993 and does not share Su-San's feelings about the tiger as an "enchanter." Ivan Gambovich Kulindziga is even less willing than Nikolai "to sacralize *Panthera tigris altaica* as some mystic spirit of the forest."

An irony of the tiger's fate in Russia bears an analogy to Ceaušescu's role in supporting Romania's bear population. Soviet leader Joseph Stalin in 1935 designated seven thousand square miles of the Sikhote-Alin range as a nature reserve, and three years later he banished around nineteen thousand Chinese and Korean hunters. That act, think some of the oldsters, explains why there are still a few Amur tigers in Russia.

In a windup chapter he calls "Science Fiction Ending," Quammen tells the truly exciting story of the discovery in 1994 in southeastern France of La Grotte Chauvet, a series of caves featuring the illustrations of the so-called Lion Panel. Scientists were stunned when radiocarbon tests indicated some of the lion images were thirty-five thousand years old. Quammen ponders these ancient drawings with gloom, predicting the virtual extinction of big flesh-eaters by 2150 and elaborating on the key ideas of keystone species and trophic cascades. Take out the big killers at the top, and a cascade of ecological changes will follow.

The science-fiction bit of the chapter comes in Quammen's analysis of the *Aliens* film series. Whether his readers agree that these motion pictures succeed for their "vivid portrayal of predation on human victims" and the human "need and desire" for homicidal monsters like Grendel, they will appreciate Quammen's serious research, his physical courage and energy, and the great wealth of anecdotes he has stuffed into this compelling story of monsters—maybe of God, maybe of Satan.

Frank Day

Review Sources

American Scholar 72, no. 4 (Autumn, 2003): 144-146.
Booklist 99, no. 21 (July 1, 2003): 1853.
Discover 24, no. 10 (October, 2003): 75-76.
Kirkus Reviews 71, no. 12 (June 15, 2003): 849-850.
Library Journal 128, no. 13 (August 15, 2003): 126.
Natural History 112, no. 7 (September, 2003): 60-61.
The New York Review of Books 50, no. 15 (October 9, 2003): 13-14.
The New York Times, August 26, 2003, p. E6.
The New York Times Book Review, August 31, 2003, p. 7-9.
Publishers Weekly 250, no. 25 (June 23, 2003): 57.
Scientific American 289, no. 3 (September, 2003): 110-111.
The Wall Street Journal, September 24, 2003, p. D9.

THE MURDER ROOM

Author: P. D. James (1920-   )
Publisher: Alfred A. Knopf (New York). 415 pp. $25.95
Type of work: Novel
Time: 2002
Locale: London and its suburbs

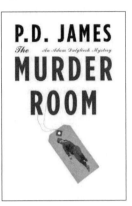

Commander Adam Dalgliesh of Scotland Yard investigates a series of interconnected murders occurring at a little-known museum in a fashionable section of the London suburbs

Principal characters:
> COMMANDER ADAM DALGLIESH, an investigator of high-profile murders for Scotland Yard
> CONRAD ACKROYD, his friend and frequent visitor to the Dupayne Museum collection
> MARCUS DUPAYNE, one of the owners of the Dupayne Museum
> CAROLINE DUPAYNE, another owner of the museum
> NEVILLE DUPAYNE, a third owner of the museum
> JAMES CALDER-HALE, the museum curator
> MURIEL GODBY, the museum receptionist
> TALLULAH (TALLY) CLUTTON, the museum housekeeper
> RYAN ARCHER, the museum groundskeeper
> CELIA MELLOCK, a young woman who participates in a sex club operated at the museum
> LORD MARTLESHAM, a British peer who frequents the sex club

Having taken up writing as a second career, P. D. James has proved that it is possible to achieve renown at an age when many writers have burned out. Additionally, her novels demonstrate that one can write first-rate literature within the genre of the mystery novel, a class of fiction not normally known for its sensitive examination of character or its complex analysis of modern society. Like James's other mysteries, *The Murder Room* demonstrates that she is able to work within the conventions of her chosen genre to portray the world not in black-and-white but in subtle shades of gray.

Like all good mysteries, *The Murder Room* has a strong story line filled with suspense and containing numerous plot twists. Whereas many mystery novelists open their narrative with an account of a murder, James takes a different approach. In the opening scenes, Commander Adam Dalgliesh, chief of the Scotland Yard team that investigates high-profile murders, is taken for a visit to the Dupayne Museum by his eccentric friend Conrad Ackroyd. Located in the London suburbs, the museum is a little-known place where a limited number of specialists and curiosity seekers come to explore the collection assembled by its founder, Max Dupayne, celebrating British culture of the 1920's and 1930's.

A chief attraction of the museum is the Murder Room, in which are stored artifacts from celebrated homicides committed during the period between the two world wars. Ackroyd takes great pleasure in explaining to his friend the unusual nature of three particularly gruesome crimes. These are chiefly of academic interest, Dalgliesh thinks, until he is called to investigate a series of new murders on the grounds of the museum. When Dalgliesh realizes that circumstances surrounding the new crimes are eerily similar to ones described by Ackroyd, he begins to believe otherwise.

After retiring from a career in the British civil service, P. D. James has authored seventeen novels, most featuring Detective Adam Dalgliesh. A number of her works have inspired successful television shows in the United States and Britain.

James skillfully delays the commission of the first crime until she has had a chance to introduce readers to her cast of characters; their troubled lives make it not surprising that some sort of conflict could occur. The catalyst for such conflict involves everyone associated with the museum. The lease on the building and grounds where the Dupayne collection is housed is up for renewal. The terms under which the children of the late Max Dupayne operate the facility require that they all agree to continue operations; otherwise the collection must be sold. Marcus and Caroline Dupayne want to keep the facility open; their younger brother, Neville, wants it to close. Marcus, recently retired from a civil service position, wants to assume more direct control over the museum's operations. If he does, though, he will jeopardize the security of the current curator, James Calder-Hale, and that of his sister, Caroline, who lives on the premises. Other employees, such as Muriel Godby, the receptionist, and Tallulah "Tally" Clutton, the housekeeper, worry as well. They know their jobs are at stake, and they make no secret of their concern for the facility's future. Before anyone meets a sinister fate, readers understand—and in some cases might sympathize with—the men and women whose livelihoods depend on the continuance of the museum's operations.

When Neville Dupayne is burned to death in a sports car he keeps in the museum's garage, Dalgliesh returns to the museum to find the culprit. Unfortunately, he and his team are stymied at every turn. Virtually everyone who might be able to help them seems reluctant to cooperate. Early intimations of dark secrets make the commander and his associates suspect that there is more going on at the Dupayne Museum than seems apparent. Not only are the Dupayne siblings unwilling to speak openly about their relationships with each other, but each is also clearly hiding something about his or her private life. In the course of his inquiry, Dalgliesh learns that Calder-Hale seems to be using the museum as a front to continue his activities for the British secret service, from which he had ostensibly retired some years earlier. Caroline Dupayne and Muriel Godby appear to be hiding something sinister as well. Suspicion is cast on all of these people, even the young groundskeeper, Ryan Archer, who has been cagy about his relationship with a middle-aged bachelor and his gay lifestyle.

The plot takes an unexpected turn when Dalgliesh and his associates discover a second murder on the grounds. The corpse is that of Celia Mellock, a young woman with no apparent connection to the museum. Clever detective work reveals, however, that she had attended the school where Caroline Dupayne is assistant headmistress and Muriel Godby was once employed. When the trail of clues leads to Lord Martlesham, a prominent member of Parliament, Dalgliesh finds the missing link that makes the connections clear: An unusual sex club is being operated clandestinely at the museum, and making its existence public could ruin the reputations of a number of those associated with the Dupayne.

To reveal the ending of a mystery novel is inappropriate, but it is worth noting that James performs no extraordinary tricks to bring her story to a conclusion. The culprit is, indeed, one of those associated with the museum, and the motive for the crimes makes sense once all the details are revealed. Furthermore, key clues are interspersed throughout the narrative so that attentive readers might arrive at the solution before Dalgliesh nabs the perpetrator, just as another murder is about to be committed. One might be put off by the rather trite sobriquet the Scotland Yard crew uses to designate the murderer—"Vulcan," in deference to the method by which the murderer dispatches Neville Dupayne—but such small blemishes hardly affect the overall impact created by this well-crafted thriller that operates on more than one level to satisfy even the most demanding readers.

It is precisely because this novel, and others in the James canon, appeal to an audience broader than those who regularly read mysteries that James has achieved recognition as one of the finest writers of her time. Certainly the suspense she creates in narrating her tale would be sufficient to make *The Murder Room* a superb mystery novel. There is more, however, for readers who are not satisfied simply with finding out "whodunit." The novel is rich in description, and throughout there are oblique allusions to the works of writers such as William Shakespeare, Charles Dickens, Jane Austen, and T. S. Eliot, giving *The Murder Room* a texture similar to the works of James's contemporaries A. S. Byatt and Margaret Drabble. Unlike so many mystery writers, James is as interested in exploring the inner motivations of both suspects and detectives as she is in weaving a complex plot with many false leads and tempting false solutions.

Furthermore, few writers in this genre would devote attention to the contemporary social and intellectual scene. James does so with great skill, giving readers significant insight into life in England at the start of the twenty-first century. Beneath the strong story line, the novel offers a critique of a society in which social mores are shifting, people tend to equate success with material possessions, and psychological dysfunction runs rampant. As Adam Dalgliesh tries to find the murderer of Neville Dupayne and Celia Mellock, he encounters people trying to save failed marriages, evaluate their own self-worth, and gain acceptance by those whom they love but with whom they cannot seem to communicate.

Ultimately, what sets James apart from run-of-the-mill mystery writers is her ability to create complex characters within the context of the genre in which she has chosen to practice her craft. This will not be surprising to those who have read widely among writers of mystery and detective fiction. Great mystery writers do not simply create a hero or heroine who solves crimes. Instead, they fashion detectives (and sometimes villains) whose personalities transcend individual story lines. Sir Arthur Conan Doyle, Dorothy Sayers, and Agatha Christie created memorable figures whose ability to sift through the many false clues to arrive at the solution to murders, robberies, and other felony offenses was only one part of their enduring charm. Over a series of books figures such as Sherlock Holmes, Sir Peter Wimsey, Hercule Poirot, and Miss Marple are developed as complex personalities with personal idiosyncrasies and weaknesses of character that allow readers to identify with them on a personal level. Few who have read the Holmes stories have missed the difficulties Dr. Watson has with Holmes's cocaine addiction. Similarly, few familiar with Poirot's exceptional mental abilities at detection have not also been alternately attracted or put off by the Belgian sleuth's fastidious personal habits.

James follows in this tradition by creating one of the most complex of all popular investigators. Commander Adam Dalgliesh is a published poet who is repulsed by murder and saddened at the brutality he witnesses on a daily basis. He is sometimes aloof from his subordinates, often detached from his work, and frequently conflicted as he tries to balance his career with his personal life. As readers familiar with earlier James novels featuring Dalgliesh know all too well, the inspector is seldom as successful in love as he is in solving crimes.

In *The Murder Room*, he is once again attempting to make a relationship work, this time with Cambridge University professor Emma Lavenham. Early in the story his work prevents him from keeping an engagement with her, bringing upon himself opprobrium from her roommate and a gnawing sense of anxiety that recurs as he pursues the culprit in the Dupayne Museum murders. The novel ends not with the apprehension of the criminal but with a scene in which Dalgliesh finally professes his love for Lavenham and proposes marriage. Will they marry? If they do, how will their marriage affect Dalgliesh's work? The answers will certainly come in another novel, in which James will weave the ongoing tale of a complex servant of law and order together with a tale of murder that will keep readers engaged from the first page to the last.

Laurence W. Mazzeno

Review Sources

Booklist 100, no. 2 (September 15, 2003): 180.
Kirkus Reviews 71, no. 16 (August 15, 2003): 1048.
Library Journal 128, no. 16 (October 1, 2003): 122.
New Statesman 16, no. 4648 (July 28, 2003): 38-39.
The New York Times Book Review, December 7, 2003, p. 43.
Publishers Weekly 250, no. 37 (September 15, 2003): 47.
The Spectator, June 21, 2003, p. 59.
The Wall Street Journal, November 28, 2003, p. W4.

MY LIFE AS A FAKE

Author: Peter Carey (1943-   )
Publisher: Alfred A. Knopf (New York). 266 pp. $24.00
Type of work: Novel
Time: 1943, 1972, and 1985
Locale: Kuala Lumpur, Malaysia; Sydney, Australia

The editor of a British literary magazine is told the story of a poet haunted by an invented poet who takes on a life of his own

Principal characters:
SARAH WODE-DOUGLAS, the editor of a
   British literary magazine
JOHN SLATER, a rakish best-selling British
   writer
CHRISTOPHER CHUBB, an Australian poet
BOB MCCORKLE, a poet invented by Chubb as a hoax, who assumes real
   life
DAVID WEISS, the editor of an Australian literary magazine

In his author's note at the conclusion of his first novel since *True History of the Kelly Gang* (2000) won England's Booker Prize, Australian writer Peter Carey makes it clear he is not trying to fool anyone here. He acknowledges that *My Life as a Fake* is based on a real-life incident familiar to many Australians. The event took place in 1943, when Harold Stewart and James McAuley, two conservative Australian soldiers who fancied themselves poets and who hated the early twentieth century modernist movement, perpetuated a hoax on the pretentious editor of an avant-garde Australian literary magazine, *Angry Penguins.*

According to the legend that has sprung up around the hoax, Stewart and McAuley spent a weekend creating a batch of eighteen bogus surrealist poems by cutting and pasting words from the works of William Shakespeare, the dictionary, and other miscellaneous sources, even throwing in some quotes from a report on mosquito breeding grounds. They then invented a young garage mechanic/insurance salesman named Ern Malley as their author, who supposedly had died young, tragic, unpublished, and unappreciated. They also dreamed up a sister for Malley, who supposedly sent the poems to the editor, Max Harris, saying she had found the typescript when she was going through Malley's things after his death.

Harris was so enthusiastic about the fake poems that he devoted thirty-five pages of his magazine to them under the title "The Darkening Ecliptic." In an introduction, Harris wrote that he was convinced Malley was one of the most outstanding poets Australia had ever produced. As Australian literati had long labored in the shadow of Great Britain, lamenting that the country had never produced a prodigious talent with far-reaching influence, there were those who were quite willing to welcome this bril-

liant new poet, complete with a romantic story of
having languished unknown and unappreciated
until he died, perhaps of a broken heart.

Although Harris was mocked and ridiculed
by the press and the Australian literary establishment when the hoax was revealed, he held fast to
his original conviction that the poems were brilliant works of art. To make matters worse, when
the poems were called indecent publications for
their references to sex, Harris was further humil-

Peter Carey, an Australian, won the prestigious Booker Prize for his novel Oscar and Lucinda *(1988) and then again for* True History of the Kelly Gang *(2000). He has also won the Commonwealth Prize and the Miles Franklin Award.*

iated by being dragged into court to defend the nonexistent Ern Malley against obscenity charges. Harris was fined and released, vowing to appeal the conviction, but
he never did. Carey, who has said he was always fascinated by the story of the hoax,
seems to have been particularly inspired by the fact that years after the event, Harris
still insisted that he believed in Ern Malley, not as a real person, for he knew he had
been hoaxed, but as an embodiment of the pathos of his time. He said he imagined him
as a kind of combination of Franz Kafka and Rainer Maria Rilke, lamenting that
somewhere in the streets of every city is a brilliant but unrecognized Ern Malley.

The final irony of the hoax is that the poems of the imaginary Ern Malley have
turned in up in subsequent anthologies of Australian poetry and have been said to
have influenced younger poets since then. As Carey has noted as a sort of justification
for his fantastic take on the hoax story, Malley did assume a sort of independent life.
On the surface, Carey's novel manages to poke some fun at the provincial nature of
Australian culture, while simultaneously refusing to take seriously the pompous
stance of British high culture. However, as is usual with Carey's fiction, he has more
serious intentions in mind than an easy satire on colonial culture and British literary
imperialism.

Carey's novel is based on the premise that if an invented poem can take on a mysterious sense of reality, then perhaps an invented poet can also. Consequently, although part of the plot structure of the book comes from the real-life story of the Ern
Malley hoax of 1943, another important part of its foundation comes from Mary Shelley's 1818 novel *Frankenstein*. For in *My Life as a Fake*, the make-believe poet,
named Bob McCorkle, invented by struggling poet Christopher Chubb, becomes a
hulking physical presence who comes to haunt his creator, chastising him for making
him an anonymous and lonely creature with no childhood and no family. The basic
plot ambiguity of the book is the uncertainty whether Bob McCorkle is a Frankenstein
monster who has come into being as a result of Chubb's imaginative construction, or
whether some poor, unappreciated hulk of a poet has been so influenced by the hoax
that he imagines himself to be Bob McCorkle, that the poems are his, and that he is
able to take on the McCorkle persona and write additional poems of possible artistic
merit.

Carey has said that he began writing the novel from the point of view of the invented poet McCorkle but that he got stuck and changed it to the voice of Sarah
Wode-Douglas, who encounters Chubb thirty years after the hoax while on vacation

in Kuala Lumpur with a family friend, John Slater, and then recounts her encounter thirteen years later. Wode-Douglas's reason for going to Malaysia has a certain plot shakiness to it—her old family friend Slater, an "unapologetic narcissist" and a notorious rake, begs her to go with him so they can talk, although what they need to talk about is not clear. Perhaps Slater wants her to meet Chubb. Perhaps it is just a plot device. Whatever. By getting Wode-Douglas to Malaysia, Carey (who has said that after spending some time there he loves the area) gives himself the opportunity to make use of his knowledge of Malaysia to describe many exotic locales and to play around with the native patois. After Wode-Douglas sees Chubb reading a book in a bicycle shop, she takes him a copy of her literary magazine, which she just happens to have with her. When Chubb shows her the tattered manuscript of the fictional Bob McCorkle and Wode-Douglas realizes who he is, she is outraged that he would try to deceive her as he deceived the unfortunate editor David Weiss thirty years before.

However, after reading one of the poems (Carey uses an actual poem of the fictional Ern Malley), Wode-Douglas is smitten by the occupational hazard of all editors—the desire to publish a new and brilliant discovery. She is intrigued enough to sit still and transcribe Chubb's endless, fantastic adventures of chasing McCorkle across Malaysia. She is also ambitious enough for an editorial coup to believe Chubb's story that McCorkle has left another manuscript of brilliant poetry, which is jealously guarded by McCorkle's native wife and Chubb's own kidnapped daughter. However, *My Life as a Fake* ends with Wode-Douglas's failure to publish the manuscript, leaving her to ponder the mystery of the imagination and the truth of what really happened.

According to Chubb's story of the hoax, his monstrous creation first appears in the flesh at the obscenity trial of Weiss, who recognizes him as the figure in a forged photograph sent with the poems. After Weiss commits suicide, the McCorkle figure begins chasing Chubb, finally kidnapping his adopted infant daughter, born to his mistress, at which point the chase reverses, and Chubb pursues McCorkle to Kuala Lumpur thirty years later, where he is discovered by Wode-Douglas. The notion of a created offspring of the imagination chasing its creator and then being chased in turn is taken directly from Shelley's famous book. In both cases, the "monster" seeks revenge on his creator for depriving him of a past, an identity, companionship, and love.

Although the Ern Malley hoax and the Shelley novel provide a fairly straightforward bone structure for *My Life as a Fake*, Carey manages to keep the reader constantly off balance. First, he creates so many stories-within-stories that one is not always sure who is speaking, a technique further complicated by Carey's refusal to identify dialogue with quotation marks. Then he creates an elaborate chase scenario in the second half of the novel that has Chubb pursue his monster creation throughout Malaysia, complete with kidnappings, imprisonment, machete attacks, and other bits of nineteenth century Far Eastern melodrama and Kiplingesque exotic local color.

Both techniques seem calculated to catch the reader up in the basic techniques of fiction itself, as the ambiguous relationship between fiction and truth lies at the very heart of the novel. Another mysterious aspect of fictional creation the book raises is the haunting possibility that the product of a writer's imagination can actually exceed and transcend his intentions, that once he has created it, the writer has no control over what he has let loose on the world. Finally, of course, the book has fun with the possibility that critical judgment of a work of art is not an exact science but often a matter of subjective opinion and clever marketing. Ultimately, the book suggests, it is difficult, if not impossible, to justify one's judgment of what is good or bad, brilliant or nonsense.

Carey has said in interviews that in *My Life as a Fake* he was not so much interested in the Ern Malley hoax as he was in the mysterious nature of the imagination. In fact, he has expressed some exasperation that reaction to the book in England and Australia has focused more on the historical hoax than on his novel. However, this reaction is to be expected. One of the first responses that children make after hearing a story is, "Did that really happen?" and the popularity of so-called reality television in the United States in the first decade of the twenty-first century suggests that audiences like to feel they are reacting to the "real thing," even though such entertainment "reality" shows are often highly scripted and elaborately staged.

Carey perhaps tries to keep the focus on fiction rather than on historical truth, whatever that might be, by shifting the emphasis halfway through *My Life as a Fake* from fairly straightforward realism to the wildly extravagant stuff of fantastic fiction, thus provoking the reader with questions about the very nature of fantasy and reality. One is never quite sure whether McCorkle is a double for Chubb and, if so, why Chubb cannot write poetry as good as McCorkle's. The reader cannot know for sure whether McCorkle has, in Frankenstein fashion, actually physically come alive, or whether the hulking McCorkle is just some poor poet who has become so obsessed with the hoax that he actually thinks he is the "real" McCorkle. By such artistic sleight of hand, Carey makes not only his narrator, Wode-Douglas, doubt what is meant by the word "real" but also the reader.

Charles E. May

Review Sources

Booklist 100, no. 1 (September 1, 2003): 5.
The Christian Science Monitor, October 23, 2003, p. 14.
Kirkus Reviews 71, no. 17 (September 1, 2003): 1086-1087.
Library Journal 128, no. 18 (November 1, 2003): 122.
New Statesman 132, no. 4656 (September 22, 2003): 52-54.
The New York Times, November 6, 2003, p. E9.
The New York Times Book Review, November 9, 2003, p. 12.
The New Yorker 79, no. 36 (November 24, 2003): 100-102.
Newsday, November 6, 2003, p. B04.
Publishers Weekly 250, no. 41 (October 13, 2003): 56.
San Francisco Chronicle, November 4, 2003, p. D1.
The Times Literary Supplement, September 12, 2003, p. 23-24.

THE NAMESAKE

Author: Jhumpa Lahiri (1967-   )
Publisher: Houghton Mifflin (Boston). 291 pp. $24.00
Type of work: Novel
Time: 1968-2000
Locale: Calcutta, India; Boston; and New York City

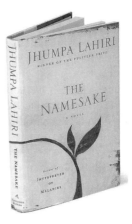

*The story of Ashoke and Ashima Ganguli, immigrants
from India, and their son Gogol, whose search for his identity is the focus of the novel*

> *Principal characters:*
> GOGOL GANGULI, born in the United States
> to Indian parents
> ASHOKE GANGULI, his father, who emi-
> grates from India to earn his degree and
> becomes a teacher of engineering
> ASHIMA GANGULI, his mother, the wife of Ashoke through an arranged
> marriage
> MAXINE RATLIFF, his lover, a sophisticated young woman
> SONALI GANGULI (SONIA), his younger sister
> MOUSHUMI MAZOOMDAR, his wife, whom he divorces

Gogol Ganguli, the protagonist of Jhumpa Lahiri's first novel, is on a quest: He is
compelled to reinvent himself, to achieve a sense of dignity that will overcome the
embarrassment of his name. Born in the United States, he is the son of Ashima and
Ashoke Ganguli, who were married in India in the traditional way, by parental arrangement. They strive to preserve their Bengali culture while freeing their children
to become successful Americans. Unlike immigrants of earlier generations who
turned their backs on the old country, knowing they could never return, the Ganguli
family travels frequently and with fluid ease between the United States and India,
fully at home in neither place.

Gogol's name is a bizarre accident of fate. Ashoke, as a young man in India, survives a terrible train accident and is saved only because the rescuers notice the crum-
pled page of a book falling from his hand. This book is the collected short stories of
Russian writer Nikolai Gogol. This accident marks Ashoke physically with a lifelong
limp and emotionally with a sense of mystery about his survival when all others in the
same railroad car perished.

When his son is born in Boston, Ashoke must name the child on the birth certifi-
cate before the infant is released from the hospital. Indian children are given a pet
name for the family, with the formal or "good" name chosen later, when the child's
personality has been formed. The grandmother in India has been chosen to name the
boy, but her letter has not yet arrived. Ashoke names his son for the author whose
book saved his life.

This name is, for Gogol, a despised symbol of his cultural alienation, neither Indian nor American but Russian. Worse still, as he learns in high school, the author, although a genius, was mentally disturbed and suicidal. The narrative spans the first thirty-two years of Gogol's life, following him as a young child, then a schoolboy, continuing through his college years and his early career as an architect. While Gogol is the focus of the story, the narrator, writing in the third person as a distant observer, departs from this position at times to explore the lives of other major characters who are on their own journeys, trying to make sense of their lives.

Jhumpa Lahiri was born in England in 1967 and later emigrated to the United States with her parents. The Interpreter of Maladies *is a short-story collection that won the* Pulitzer Prize in 2000. The Namesake *is her first novel. She won a Guggenheim Fellowship in 2002.*

Ashoke earns his degree in engineering and becomes a tenured professor at a small-town New England college, and the family establishes a home on Pemberton Road. A man of the working world, Ashoke successfully adapts to American ways in his public life. However, he and Ashima socialize only with their Bengali friends, immigrants who share their traditions. Ashoke and Gogol are outwardly respectful to each other, but Ashoke is puzzled and saddened by his son's emotional distance. Ashima, a homemaker in the old world tradition, is torn between the old ways and the new. She wears the sari throughout her life and cooks Indian food but adopts American customs for the sake of her children. Her Thanksgiving turkey is seasoned with garlic and cumin, and she decorates an artificial Christmas tree.

The scenes in the novel are fraught with the tension between the two cultures which causes conflict in the family life. Ashima often accedes to her son's wishes but sometimes stands her ground with indignation. When Gogol returns from a grade-school field trip with a grave rubbing from a Puritan cemetery which he intends to display on the refrigerator, Ashima is horrified. In Hindu tradition, the body is burned; she finds it barbaric that Americans display artifacts of the dead in the place where food is cooked and consumed.

Ashoke, in a poignant scene, presents his son with a hardcover volume of Gogol's short stories for his fourteenth birthday, a special edition ordered from England and intended to commemorate the significance of his name. Gogol, a thoroughly Americanized teenager preoccupied with his favorite Beatles recording, is indifferent to his father's gift. Ashoke quietly leaves the room, where he is not welcome. Although Gogol will eventually learn this story, the author conveys a powerful sense of loss for a moment of love that might have united father and son.

The Gangulis maintain close ties with their families in India by telephone. The middle-of-the-night overseas calls invariably bring news of serious illness or a death in the family, revealing Ashimi's sense of loss and separation from loved ones and her native traditions. Only on her return to India does she feel secure. However, Gogol and his younger sister, Sonia, are bored and annoyed by their noisy, intrusive Bengali relatives. They crave their hamburgers and pizza and hot showers. When they return to the United States, they purposely forget their Indian experience—it seems irrelevant to their lives.

Although Gogol is enrolled in school under his formal name, Nikhil, it seems strange to him, and he continues to call himself Gogol, much as he hates the name. His sister calls him by the unfortunate nickname of Goggles. When he is eighteen and a freshman at Yale University, he changes his name legally to Nikhil. His roommates, and later his adult friends, know him as Nikhil, but occasionally a family member calls him Gogol, and this requires an embarrassing explanation.

Gogol's headlong affair with Maxine Ratliff in New York City, where he works as an architect, illuminates the clash between the two cultures that is at the heart of this story. Maxine is an editor of art books, and she and her parents are upscale Americans whose lifestyle would make a good feature story in a trendy magazine. Maxine's mother is a textile curator at the Metropolitan Museum, and her father is a lawyer. The Ratliffs are as different from the Gangulis as it is possible to imagine. Where Gogol's parents refuse to acknowledge that he might have a sex life, the Ratliffs are at ease with Maxine and Gogol's affair, conducted casually in their home. The Ratliffs have frequent dinner parties, featuring small portions of elegantly prepared food. They are wine connoisseurs and often appear to be mildly intoxicated. The Gangulis are teetotalers, and Gogol has never seen them display physical affection. They entertain their Bengali friends in large, noisy gatherings with an overabundance of food, which they chew with their mouths open.

Seduced by their contrasting lifestyle and infatuated with Maxine, Gogol moves into the Ratliffs' tastefully decorated Manhattan town house. In one scene, Gogol and Maxine stop briefly at the house on Pemberton Road on their way to a vacation in New Hampshire. Ashima is hurt that they will spend the holiday with Maxine's family but responds with polite hospitality. Gogol sees that his mother is overdressed and has cooked too much food. Ashima is deeply offended when the young woman calls her by her first name but suffers the insult without comment.

The death of Ashoke is a wrenching experience for Gogol and a turning point in his life. During a visiting professorship at an Ohio university, Ashoke is felled by a fatal heart attack. Ashima, who has remained in the family home, is notified by telephone from the hospital; she finally reaches Gogol at the Ratliff home. Gogol must identify his father's body in the morgue and clear out the apartment where his father had lived temporarily. The precisely detailed description of Ashoke's body, the hospital rooms, and the bare furnishings of the apartment are a stark reminder to Gogol of his loss, his discovery that he has never truly known his father. These scenes recall an earlier event when young Gogol and his father had walked on the sands at Cape Cod to the lighthouse, as far as they could go. Ashoke said, "Remember that you and I made this journey, that we went together to a place where there was nowhere left to go."

After Ashoke's death, Maxine and Gogol gradually drift apart. Gogol's reaction seems remote and puzzling: "His time with her seems like a permanent part of him that no longer has any relevance, or currency. As if that time were a name he'd ceased to use." After the period of mourning for Ashoke, Gogol agrees, at his mother's request, to meet Moushumi, the daughter of Bengali friends whom he has known since childhood. The two are attracted to each other, begin an affair, and marry in a traditional Indian ceremony. Moushumi, however, has had previous affairs and a troubled history of mental breakdowns. She inexplicably sabotages her marriage through an affair with an older, less attractive man.

The conclusion reaches for a symmetry that resolves the conflicts in the narrative. Ashima sells the family home and will spend half the year in Calcutta with her friends and relatives, the other half with her children in the United States. Sonia is engaged to Ben, a man of mixed Jewish and Chinese ancestry, and this promises to be a successful union. Gogol, as he helps to dismantle the home on Pemberton Road, rediscovers the volume of short stories, his father's birthday gift, and begins to read.

Lahiri's first book, *The Interpreter of Maladies*, is a collection of short stories which won the Pulitzer Prize in 2000. *The Namesake*, her first novel, has raised high critical expectations. Her style, often described as luminous and graceful, is accomplished, especially in the precisely detailed word choices and descriptions of ordinary life that draw the reader into the narrative. Lahiri grounds the reader with a sense of time and place by frequent mentions of historical events, such as the assassinations of the 1960's. She is a shrewd, often ironic, observer of the nuances of both Indian traditions and American pop culture. The Gangulis, for instance, are baffled by teenage Sonia's disruption of the household when she dyes her entire wardrobe black, and they find it incredible that the president of the United States is addressed as Jimmy.

Critics have high praise for Lahiri's richly sensuous, epicurean descriptions of the preparation and consumption of food. The author says that she is an enthusiastic cook. Like food, train travel, both in India and the United States, is a recurring motif. In an interview, Lahiri said that she sees her narrative as resembling the incomplete glimpses of the passing scene through the window of a train.

Several critics find that the gaps in the narrative give the impression of incompleteness. Others say that the third-person, distant narrative voice creates a flat, unemotional tone. However, *The Namesake* has received enthusiastic popular acclaim, and most critics agree that it fulfills the promise of her earlier, highly praised work.

As a portrait of immigration and a personal quest for identity, the novel raises interesting questions. Given the genuine pain that Ashima and Ashoke suffer in attempting to reconcile their cultural heritage with the American dream, it is worth considering whether Gogol's angst over the oddity of his name should evoke the reader's sympathy. Ashoke's common-sense interpretation of Gogol's complaints when he announces he will change his name is instructive: "The only person who didn't take Gogol seriously, the only person who tormented him, the only person chronically aware of and afflicted by the embarrassment of this name . . . was Gogol." As Gogol takes up his father's gift and begins to read, there is hope that he has reached a mature resting place between the two cultures that are his heritage.

Marjorie J. Podolsky

Review Sources

Booklist 99, nos. 19/20 (June 1, 2003): 1710.
Kirkus Reviews 71, no. 11 (June 1, 2003): 773.
Library Journal 128, no. 12 (July 15, 2003): 123.
The Nation 277, no. 13 (October 27, 2003): 36-38.
New Leader 86, no. 5 (September/October, 2003): 31-32.
The New York Times Book Review, September 28, 2003, p. 11.
Publishers Weekly 250, no. 27 (July 7, 2003): 48-49.
San Francisco Chronicle, September 14, p. M1.
Time 162, no. 12 (September 22, 2003): 76.
The Washington Post, September 14, 2003, p. BW10.

THE NATURE OF ORDER
An Essay on the Art of Building and the Nature of the Universe

Author: Christopher Alexander (1936-   )
Publisher: The Center for Environmental Structure
(Berkeley, Calif.). 4 volumes. Book 1: 476 pp. $75.00;
Book 2: 636 pp. $75.00
Type of work: Fine arts, science, environment, philoso-
phy, and psychology
Time: From antiquity to 2003
Locale: The world

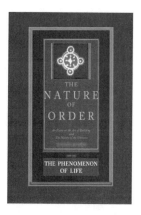

*These volumes set forth Alexander's ideas about restor-
ing integrity and beauty to the built environment through
an understanding of the nature of order and the geometrical unfolding of wholeness*

At the beginning of the twenty-first century, many people have identified significant problems with modern culture, ranging from superficiality, materialism, and
greed and dehumanizing forces of technology to rampant destruction of humanity and
the environment. A substantial body of literature has arisen that offers solutions to
these problems and visions of how to return to the "real," to basic values that emphasize respect for the self, for others, and for the world.

In *The Nature of Order*, Christopher Alexander presents another voice of criticism
and distress. As an architect, his main concern is the built environment, which includes not only the structures one inhabits but also one's communities with all their
infrastructure and the surrounding natural environment. He levels strong criticism at
most twentieth century architecture, which he characterizes as ugly, banal, pretentious, "almost unimaginably bad." He says that many modern architects have "altogether poisoned the earth with an abundance of terrible and senseless designs" and
have failed to create a built environment which is nourishing and in which structures
become "vehicles for our sacred human life." He asks: "Has there ever been a time in
the history of the earth when a group of people, entrusted by society with the creation
and preservation of our physical world, have so sadly undermined it?"

The Nature of Order is Alexander's solution to this great dilemma. What makes his
approach so different is that his answer goes deeply to the fundamental basis of life, in
fact, the nature of order itself. Alexander is a mathematician and architect with advanced
degrees from Trinity College and Cambridge and Harvard Universities. *The Nature of
Order* is a projected four-volume summa of many of years of thinking about these issues from a scientific standpoint. The subtitle, *An Essay on the Art of Building and the
Nature of the Universe*, indicates the encompassing inquiry that Alexander undertakes.

Alexander begins by challenging the modern mentality which views order as mechanism. He traces the origin of this worldview to the seventeenth century, as stated
most clearly by the French mathematician and philosopher René Descartes (1596-

〜

Christopher Alexander, an architect and mathematician, is professor emeritus of architecture at the University of California at Berkeley and the founder of the Center for Environmental Structure. The recipient of numerous awards in architecture and architectural research, he is the author of many books and articles on architectural theory, the best known of which is A Pattern Language: Towns, Building, Construction *(1977).*

〜

1650), who espoused the idea of using a mechanical analogy to aid in understanding how things work. Much of the scientific method since that time has been based on this mechanistic approach. However, Alexander identifies a major mental shift in the twentieth century, when the mechanical model or method came to be regarded as veritable reality. As a consequence, "the idea of order fell apart."

Alexander's approach is to develop a more fundamental concept of order. A deeper understanding of order not only would rectify problems with architecture, an inherently "order-creating process," but also would illuminate the very nature of "life." Alexander states: "It is this very general life—formal, geometric, structural, social, biological, holistic—which is my main target."

Much of book 1, titled *The Phenomenon of Life*, is concerned with explaining, analyzing, and proving in mathematical terms the geometrical structure of "wholeness" (W) in space which forms the essence of life and order. The character of wholeness resides in "centers." From a mathematical standpoint, centers are recursive: "*Centers are always made of other centers.*" A center "functions as an organized field of force in space"; the wholeness of an entity comes from the field-like interaction among its composite centers.

In an optimal situation where the greatest degree of life or wholeness exists, the centers help and intensify one another. Alexander identifies fifteen fundamental properties, "recurrent geometrical structural features," that form the main ways that centers create coherence and life in a given entity. He describes and analyzes these properties first in things made by human agency and then in nature. The examples on which he draws to illustrate these fifteen fundamental properties are vast. Built structures and objects come from all cultures and all periods, while in nature examples range from cells and molecules to systems of galaxies. The fifteen fundamental properties are levels of scale, strong centers, boundaries, alternating repetition, positive space, good shape, local symmetries, deep interlock and ambiguity, contrast, gradients, roughness, echoes, the void, simplicity and inner calm, not-separateness (connectedness).

Most of these properties are basic elements of design (roughness, for instance, generally corresponds to texture) that have long been recognized in the arts and in nature. Where Alexander breaks new ground is in the way that these properties function together to create a system united through a geometrical articulation of space. He envisions the possibility that "*the unfolding of wholeness might one day be understood as a single law which underlies the entirety of everything we know as nature.*"

For Alexander, seeing the nature of order as this "dazzling geometrical coherence" leads to two important aspects that go beyond what the modern view would consider scientific or mathematical. First, the deep feeling that one experiences when one recognizes order, wholeness, or life is an inherent, real, and objective part of the nature of order. Second, the degree of life or wholeness is also real, measurable, and objective. Thus, value and value judgments are essential to the concept of order or wholeness. In sum, "living structure is at once both structural and personal."

In Alexander's view, the nature of order, this wholeness created by the field-like interaction of centers, does not exist only as some recognizable structure or entity in the external world. It is intrinsically connected to the inner self. One *feels* when this order is present. Alexander states that "profound order makes us feel our own existence." This connection between inner feelings and the external world seems alien to a Cartesian mechanistic world view in which only "facts" based on mechanical operations are "objective." Sophisticated observation of inner states and feelings is well-known and accepted in Eastern thought, however, and Alexander discusses some examples such as the Visuddhimagga from the Buddhist canons. Furthermore, when people are trained to focus on the inner self and recognize "deep liking" (in contrast to superficial preferences), this experience has objective validity which is reliable, replicable, and can be used as "a fundamental measuring instrument *about the structure of the real world outside the observer.*" In turn, value judgments about the degree of life or wholeness can be made with accuracy and predictability. Alexander does not exclude the mechanical Cartesian method; rather, he combines it with this second method of internal observation to achieve a multilayered view in which the self is enfolded into the nature of order.

The geometrical structure of order in space discussed in book 1 is a constantly changing and interacting field. The title of book 2 is *The Process of Creating Life.* Its topic, process (that is, living structure unfolding in time), is both more dynamic and more practical, especially for architects and others with interests in building. Alexander first presents several scientific theories about how form emerges. While each of these theories offer partial explanations of morphogenesis, the creation of form in nature, none of them provide a completely satisfying picture. Alexander proposes a "principle of unfolding wholeness," a geometrical principle similar to the principle of least action but one which underlies all of the theories. This principle states that "*the evolution of any natural system is governed by the transformations of the mathematical wholeness and by a tendency, inherent in these transformations, for the whole to unfold in a particular direction.*"

In examining this process of creating living structure, Alexander looks at the character of transformations, focusing on the direction in which they unfold, either toward structure-preserving or toward structure-destroying. First, he looks at the principle of unfolding wholeness in nature where, almost without exception, each transformative stage moves toward structure preservation, enhancing the degree of life by means of the fifteen fundamental properties. The process even includes some cleaning out of unnecessary centers through properties such as the void to achieve the simplicity and calm of "deep structure."

While nature constantly seeks structure-preserving transformations, only humans, whose actions can be governed by mental images, concepts, and constructs, have the capacity to "violate the wholeness." Thus, the built environment can easily be taken in the direction of structure-destroying transformations. Most of book 2 discusses in detail how architects specifically and everyone who participates in building and creative acts can follow processes that will preserve structure and enhance life. The key is that the process is generative, not additive, fabricated, or random. This generative process proceeds step by step.

For a large building project, for example, the number of steps can be in the thousands. For each step, the person makes a decision based on knowledge of the nature of order and the operation of the fifteen fundamental properties in a living structure about what direction will preserve the essential life, the deep inner structure of wholeness, while bringing about a positive transformation. Each decision is also based on the objective value judgment that a person is able to make if he or she is attuned to that fundamental connection between the inner self and the geometric dynamic of wholeness in a structure. The generative process is simultaneously conservative and creative. When successful, it has the capacity to "propagate beauty with enormous force."

Alexander's ideas about the nature of order have aroused controversy and strong reactions, both positive and negative. Like the very process he advocates, his views are both conservative and creative in putting together ideas and information in new ways. As he points out, the ideas he sets forth are not in conflict with contemporary thinking in science and mathematics, but he extends his scope by drawing on many diverse fields, including architecture and the visual arts, ecology, and psychology. His holistic view of living structure and creative process indeed becomes a philosophical statement about the nature of life that unites objective and subjective. As Alexander asserts: "It can lead to a mental world where art, form, order, and life unite our feeling with our objective sense of reality, in a synthesis which opens the door to a form of living in which we may be truly human."

In addition, by placing the idea of value in the realm of an objective, shared experience, Alexander's perspective promotes community, consensus, and mutual responsibility for preserving and nurturing life. He calls the generative process "a startling and new conception of ethics and aesthetics" that "dignifies our respect for what exists and treasures that which grows from this respect." Although architecture, the "mother art," is his primary focus, the implications of Alexander's thought extend to every aspect of life, including the spiritual dimension to be examined in book 4, *The Luminous Ground*. (Book 3, titled *A Vision of a Living World*, will present hundreds of buildings as examples of his theories.) Eventually, Alexander's ideas about the nature of order must stand the test of time, but his far-reaching views are a major contribution toward a new understanding of the essence of life and offer the potential for addressing pressing issues about the quality of life and the built environment that merit serious thought and consideration.

Karen Gould

Review Sources

Architectural Record 190, no. 5 (May, 2002): 93-95.
Whole Earth 106 (Winter, 2001): 73.

NATURE VIA NURTURE
Genes, Experience, and What Makes Us Human

Author: Matt Ridley (1958-   )
Publisher: HarperCollins (New York). 326 pp. $25.95
Type of work: Science

Ridley rejects the premise that human nature is primarily determined either by genetic inheritance or by environmental influences. He argues that nature and nurture are not competitors but partners which collaborate to create a human being

Through much of the twentieth century, biologists and social scientists debated whether human behavior was governed primarily by inherited characteristics or by the environment in which a person grew up. Biologists stressed the role of genes in controlling the development of living things, while psychologists and sociologists investigated the impact of subjective experience and the social milieu upon individuals. Each discipline found convincing evidence for its view and concluded that the other approach was mistaken.

Matt Ridley objects to this either/or dichotomy and argues that proving one belief correct does not necessarily prove the other concept wrong. He maintains that recent studies demonstrating how the environment affects the ways in which genes are expressed, combined with data showing how genes influence behavior, provide an understanding of how heredity and environment actually cooperate in producing human behavior.

"Learning," Ridley states, "could not happen without an innate capacity to learn. Innateness could not be expressed without experience. The truth of each idea is not proof of the falsehood of another." He concludes that "the more we discover genes that influence behavior, the more we find that they work through nurture; and the more we find that animals learn, the more we discover that learning works through genes."

Ridley is hardly the first to suggest that both genetic and environmental factors govern individual development. Many scientists have tried to find a balanced position providing a just consideration of the way nature and nurture interact. Ridley, however, brings to his task both a familiarity with the latest genetic research and an engaging writing style that has made him an outstanding popularizer of biological science.

Modern studies of human twins show how genes can triumph over environment. Identical twins sharing the same genes, when separated at birth and raised in very different families, behave in amazingly similar ways. In contrast, fraternal twins, experiencing the same prenatal experiences and raised together, usually behave in very individualistic manners. Studies of primate behavior, however, demonstrate the powerful effect of environment in modifying the expression of comparable genetic endowment.

Matt Ridley is a British scientist and journalist who earned a Ph.D. in biology from Oxford University and was science editor of The Economist *for nine years. He also wrote* The Red Queen: Sex and Evolution in Human Nature *(1993).*

Of the approximately thirty thousand human genes transcribed by the Human Genome Project, from 95 percent to nearly 99 percent are identical with those of the great apes. One of the few sharp distinctions between humans and other primates is that humans possess one less chromosome. At some point in the past, two middle-sized ape chromosomes fused to form the exceptionally large human chromosome 2. The source of the divergence between humans and apes, Ridley stresses, lies not in different genes but in the same set of genes being used in a different pattern. The consequence of the genetic similarity of the great apes is that they all resemble one another physically—skeletons of large chimpanzees have been mistakenly identified as small gorillas and gorillas as large chimpanzees.

Ridley uses examples drawn from ethological research on primates to show that, despite the physical resemblance, some behavior can be affected more by environment than by genes, even when involving as universal an instinct as sexual behavior. The genetic basis for sex would be very similar in gorillas and chimpanzees, but expression of such genes is heavily influenced by different habitats and food-gathering practices. Gorillas are herbivores. Plants are abundant in the African jungle but not very nutritious. The gorilla must eat almost continuously but need not move very far; therefore, a group of gorillas can easily be defended. A male gorilla that grows to great size can assemble a harem of females and effectively hold off competitors. Chimpanzees eat fruit primarily—supplemented with insects and monkey meat, when they can get it. Because fruit is widely disseminated, the chimpanzee needs a large range, which is easier to defend by an alliance of males sharing the favors of their associated females. There is no great advantage for chimpanzees in being much larger than average. Adapting to their environment, chimpanzee males are only slightly larger than females, while gorilla males are nearly twice as large as females.

As Ridley examines various aspects of the interaction of nature and nurture, he provides many acute observations. He cites the paradox that the more equal society is, the more heritability matters, and the more genes affect outcomes. In a true meritocracy, in which all receive equal opportunity and equal training, the outstanding athletes would be the ones whose genes are best adapted to physical activity. In a society where only a privileged few get sufficient food and the chance to train, background and opportunity would determine who wins races. "Ironically, the more egalitarian a society is, the more innate factors will matter."

In a chapter devoted to schizophrenia, Ridley examines various attempts to discover the cause of this disease, stressing the difficulty of disentangling the possible roles played by various factors. He remarks:

> The cause of schizophrenia is still very much an open question, with many rival explanations covering all possibilities. You can still plausibly say that genes, viruses, diets, or accidents are the first cause of psychosis. But the confusion goes deeper than that, for the

closer science gets to understanding schizophrenia—and it is very close—the more it is blurring the distinction between cause and symptom. Environmental and genetic influences seem to work together, to require each other, until it is impossible to say which is cause and which is effect.

An excellent chapter discusses the phenomenon of imprinting, made famous by Konrad Lorenz. Ridley examines later work with animals, describing research devoted to discovering the molecular changes within the brain during imprinting. Applying these ideas to humans, Ridley describes research on children's language acquisition. He describes the difficulty of acquiring a new language, or learning to speak it with a native accent, after early adolescence, when the brain is no longer rapidly forming new connections. He notes, in passing, that Lorenz carefully concealed the articles he wrote during the 1930's, claiming that his science supported the racist ideas of Nazism. Although Ridley thereby raises the question of whether, or to what degree, Lorenz's theories on inherited instincts were essentially racist, he never fully analyzes this intriguing issue.

Unlike many commentators who objected to Edward O. Wilson's massive *Sociobiology* (1975), in which he extended his analysis of animal social behavior to human society, Ridley sides with Wilson. Other readers, fully willing to accept Wilson's portrayal of the role of instinct in controlling ant behavior and social organization, were repulsed when Wilson's final chapter examined the role of inherited instincts in human behavior and society. The idea that a small segment of DNA could shape human social attitudes seemed intuitively wrong as well as humiliating. Some critics accused Wilson of postulating specific genes for all social behavior patterns and of justifying war, male supremacy, and racism as natural phenomena. Ridley is not impressed by such disparagement, arguing that terming behavior natural does not necessarily mean one believes it is moral or desirable or even healthy—disease is also natural.

When discussing human intelligence, Ridley judiciously tries to be even-handed concerning the role of genes and environment. He asserts that recent studies concerning the role of intelligence quotient (IQ) heritability in twins and adoptees indicate that IQ is approximately 50 percent genetic, 25 percent influenced by a shared environment, and 25 percent influenced by factors unique to the individual environment. How these precise numbers were arrived at is not clear.

Ridley believes that the human ability to accumulate and transmit culture across generations, rather than a tiny percentage of unique DNA, is what truly distinguishes humans from other animals and also explains why humanity dominates the earth. He cites ethological studies which demonstrate other large-brained animals' capacity for culture but insists that only humans have shown a pattern of cumulative innovation. The basis for this ability, Ridley claims, lies within the human genetic endowment. Genes are at the root of cultural development, he states, not as simple causes but as empowering mechanisms that respond to the environment. "What we celebrate about our brain," he writes, "has nothing to do with culture. Our intelligence, imagination, empathy, and foresight came into existence gradually and inexorably, but with no help from culture. They made culture possible, but culture did not make them."

The previous quotation illustrates the difficulty Ridley faces when treating heredity and environment as equal partners in determining human behavior. His earlier book, *Genome: The Autobiography of a Species in Twenty-three Chapters* (1999), in which he discussed genes from each of the twenty-three human chromosome pairs, celebrated the decipherment of human DNA. In the present volume Ridley continually assigns a dominant role to genetic endowment—nurture, he asserts, is reversible, nature is not. He typically considers differences in genetic makeup more important than differences in familial or social circumstances. Ridley insists that while small genetic differences can have significant effects, small environmental differences are of little consequence.

At times Ridley indulges in gross oversimplifications. He attributes gender roles to genetically controlled instincts modified by the particular cultural environment in which an individual grows up. As a result, he tells the reader that women and gay men are more interested in people than football, while heterosexual men are more interested in football than people. Women, he says, are most interested in a man's financial prospects when seeking mates; men stress youth and physical beauty. Ridley is uninterested in examining exceptions to his generalizations.

Ridley objects that equating a single gene with a single effect is an oversimplification. He is uneasy with calling a single mutant gene the cause of a disease, arguing that a single gene can be associated with many diseases and a single disease with many genes. He then surprises the reader by finding a single gene for so complex a phenomenon as maleness:

> Given a typical middle-class upbringing, all the vast details of masculinity, as expressed in the modern environment—from testes to baldness to a tendency to sit on the couch drinking beer and flipping between channels on the television—stem from this single gene, SRY. It is surely not absurd to call it the gene "for" maleness.

The discovery that defective versions of a gene identified as FOXP2 cause speech and language disorders leads Ridley to an astounding speculative leap—although he admits that no one knows what the gene actually does, he asserts that the gene mutated some 200,000 years ago, thereby enabling the development of speech and language.

Ridley explicitly accepts the Darwinian idea that the course of evolution is random, yet he frequently resorts to the language of intentionality in clarifying his explanations of how genes work, going so far as to use the metaphor of a "Genome Organizing Device, or GOD for short" in describing how complex genetic interactions occur.

Despite its flaws, *Nature via Nurture* is an excellent example of successful scientific popularization. Ridley's enthusiasm for his field illuminates every chapter. He enlivens his text with intriguing examples and humorous anecdotes as he presents the latest findings of genetic research. His tendency to portray nature as mostly, though not entirely, dominant over nurture, is not always convincing. Ridley is deliberately thought-provoking, and his controversial and sometimes overly simple statements should stimulate critical responses from his readers.

Milton Berman

Review Sources

Booklist 99, no. 14 (March 15, 2003): 1251.
The Economist 367, no. 8319 (April 12, 2003): 73-74.
Kirkus Reviews 71, no. 7 (April 1, 2003): 525.
Library Journal 128, no. 8 (May 1, 2003): 151.
Los Angeles Times, June 16, 2003, p. E10.
National Review 54, no. 11 (June 16, 2003): 46-47.
The New York Times Book Review, July 20, 2003, p. 11.
Publishers Weekly 250, no. 15 (April 14, 2003): 57.
Science News 164, no. 3 (July 19, 2003): 47.
Scientific American 289, no. 1 (July, 2003): 89.
The Washington Post Book World, July 6, 2003, p. 7.

NEHRU
The Invention of India

Author: Shashi Tharoor (1956-   )
Publisher: Arcade (New York). 282 pp. $24.95
Type of work: Biography
Time: 1889-1964
Locale: India

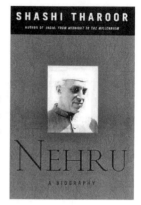

A biography of Jawaharlal Nehru, one of the founders of modern India, its first prime minister, and a major mid-twentieth century figure because of his nonalignment foreign policy in the Cold War era

Principal personages:
JAWAHARLAL NEHRU, India's first prime
    minister
MOTILAL NEHRU, his father, a lawyer
MAHATMA GANDHI, Indian leader who practiced nonviolent civil disobe-
    dience
INDIRA NEHRU GANDHI, Nehru's daughter, Indian prime minister
RAJIV GANDHI, Nehru's grandson, Indian prime minister
MOHAMMED ALI JINNAH, head of Muslim League, founder of Pakistan
LORD MOUNTBATTEN, last viceroy of India
EDWINA MOUNTBATTEN, Lord Mountbatten's wife
KAMALA KAUL NEHRU, Nehru's wife

Jawaharlal Nehru is among the most important personages of modern Indian history, second perhaps only to Mahatma Gandhi. When India gained its independence in August, 1947, Nehru became its first prime minister, a position he held until his death in 1964. During the 1950's Nehru bestrode the world stage as the spokesman of neutralism during the Cold War struggle between the United States and the Soviet Union. While Gandhi's fame continues to live, Nehru has largely vanished from public awareness outside India, with many of his policies having proved to be impractical failures. *Nehru: The Invention of India* is an attempt to assess Nehru's historical significance and his current relevance.

Shashi Tharoor, like Nehru, is an Indian with roots in the non-Indian world. Born in London, he was educated in India and the United States. He has served as the executive assistant to United Nations Secretary General Kofi Annan, who, as a young man, was an admirer of Nehru. *Nehru*, dedicated to Annan, is a popular rather than a scholarly work, and though Tharoor is an admirer of Nehru and finds his contributions to modern India immense, *Nehru* is not an uncritical account of the Indian statesman.

Nehru, as a Brahmin—the highest caste in India's traditional caste system—was born in 1889 and bred in the upper reaches of Indian society. India was, at that time, ruled by Great Britain. Nehru's father, Motilal, was a successful lawyer, and young Nehru, as his only surviving son, was spoiled as a child. Motilal was a strong presence in his son's life, and Tharoor claims that Nehru was always in need of a father figure, both for approval and for someone against whom to rebel. Nehru's mother was a strict Hindu, but Motilal was more cosmopolitan and secular, given to London suits and requiring English to be spoken in their home.

Shashi Tharoor was born in London and educated in India and the United States. The author of eight books including Reasons of State *(1982),* India: From Midnight to the Millennium *(1997), and* The Great Indian Novel *(1989), Tharoor is the United Nations' undersecretary general for communications and public information. He was the recipient of the Commonwealth Writers' Prize in 1991.*

At the age of fifteen Nehru enrolled at England's Harrow, the prestigious "public" school attended a decade earlier by Winston Churchill, a later nemesis of Nehru. The latter was only an average student at Trinity College, Cambridge, and studied law at the London School of Economics, mainly to please his father. After seven years in England, he returned to India in 1912.

In 1916 Nehru was married, and as was traditional, his father chose the bride, Kamala Kaul, the daughter of a flour-mill owner. At about this same time Nehru became involved in the Indian National Congress. Initially he believed that Britain could be petitioned into giving India home rule within the British empire, but by 1918 Nehru became convinced that peaceful resolutions would not achieve this goal. His belief was confirmed by the British massacre of 379 civilians at Amritsar in 1919.

With his political activism, Nehru had little time for his neglected wife. His daughter, Indira, was born in 1917, but Nehru was mostly an absentee father. Taking up the cause of India's landless peasants, he had found his public role. In 1921 he commented to his father, "Greatness is being thrust upon me." In that same year, both were arrested for their opposition to the British raj. It would not be their last arrest. In the following two decades, Nehru spent 3,262 days in prison for his anti-British activities.

Indian nationalists were deeply divided between radicals and conservatives and between Hindus and Muslims. Sectarian or communal violence was widespread. Mohammed Ali Jinnah, a British-trained lawyer like Nehru and Gandhi, claimed that the Muslim League was the sole entity speaking for Muslims. The Indian National Congress (INC) had always included representatives from all of India's religious groups, but Hindus were in the distinct majority. Nehru, the secular rationalist, consistently deplored Indian sectarianism. He held numerous positions in the INC, also known as the Congress Party, during those years, and political challenges were compounded by family concerns. Kamala suffered from tuberculosis, necessitating the family's relocation to Switzerland. It was during his European sojourn that Nehru became a convert to socialism. When he returned to India in 1927 he was convinced that dominion home rule was not enough: Only complete independence would satisfy him. Nehru's nationalism was an evolving process.

He became an icon in 1928, after being badly beaten by the police while protesting a visiting British commission. Gandhi instigated nonviolent civil disobedience against the British, famously in 1930 when he embarked on a 241-mile march against the British tax on salt. At its conclusion Gandhi, and then Nehru, were imprisoned, and shortly afterward so was Motilal, but the latter's health failed, and he died in early 1931. Tharoor stresses the impact that Nehru's father had on him, both in his secular rationalism and in his ability to compromise.

The 1930's was a difficult decade for Nehru. With his father dead and Kamala ill (she died in 1936), he was occasionally estranged from Gandhi over political tactics, but never permanently. Nehru was a practical politician and, psychologically, he needed the approval of Gandhi, as his surrogate father. When the British instituted elections for provincial assemblies for 1937, Nehru proved to be an excellent campaigner—handsome, energetic, inspiring. The Congress Party did well in the elections, but the ranks of Indian nationalists remained divided between the Congress Party and the Muslim League.

At the onset of World War II, Nehru would have been willing to join the Allies, including Britain, against Nazi Germany and the Axis Powers, but the politically obtuse British viceroy unilaterally declared war on India's behalf without consulting any Indians. Refusing to deal with the Congress Party, Britain flirted instead with Jinnah's Muslim League. Tharoor claims that the major mistake of Nehru and Gandhi was to not take seriously the concerns of India's minority Muslim population, which feared being submerged in an independent India with a Hindu majority. Nehru remained supportive of the Allies but not the British, demanding that the British should quit India. The result, not surprisingly, was that Nehru was again jailed, from August, 1942, until June, 1945. Before his longest imprisonment, his daughter, Indira, married Faroze Gandhi, no relation to Mahatma Gandhi. Nehru was not enthusiastic. Faroze was a Parsi with few economic prospects, but Nehru's relationship with Indira had been that of an absentee father, and he felt he could not object.

In July, 1945, Britain's Labour Party, traditionally more supportive of Indian aspirations than were the Conservatives, came to power. Its economic position weakened after years of war, Britain found it impossible to maintain its vast empire. There remained no serious barrier to Indian independence; at issue was whether India should become a single nation or should be partitioned into a majority-Hindu India and a Muslim "Pakistan" (meaning "land of the pure"). Gandhi and Nehru opposed partition, but both were Hindus.

With Gandhi's support, Nehru had been elected president of the Congress Party, but in subsequent discussions he had alienated Jinnah and the Muslim League. Tharoor considers whether Nehru should be held responsible for the rupture that ultimately led to an independent Pakistan but argues that there were deeper issues dividing the Muslim League from the Congress Party than mere personalities. In early 1947 Britain announced that it would withdraw from India no later than June, 1948. To implement the disengagement, Lord Louis Mountbatten, a war hero with ties to the monarchy, was named viceroy. He arrived in India in March, 1947, with his wife, Edwina.

Any biography of Nehru must deal with Edwina Mountbatten. It is possible that Edwina and Nehru, who became close friends, had a sexual affair. When Edwina died in 1960, Nehru's letters lay scattered on her bed. Tharoor claims that, whatever their relationship, Nehru's focus remained on gaining independence for India. He opposed a federalized India—a Balkanized India—with a weak central government, and partition seemed the only alternative. Independence came quickly. At midnight on August 15, 1947, India became independent, and Pakistan came into being. Independence, however, found many on the wrong side of the new borders. More than one million people died, and seventeen million relocated to Muslim Pakistan or Hindu India.

Nehru accepted dominion status within the British Commonwealth for India rather than that of an independent republic, a surprise to many. In 1950 India became a republic but remained in the Commonwealth. In January, 1948, Gandhi, who, as Nehru noted, embodied "the old spirit" of India, was assassinated by a fellow Hindu. In a national address, Nehru said, "the light has gone out of our lives." On a personal level, Nehru had lost another father. As India's first prime minister, his burden was overwhelming, including the travails caused by partition, the disputes with Pakistan in establishing the two nations, the incorporation of the princely states into the body politic, and numerous other matters. One of the controversial decisions was over Kashmir, which, with its majority Muslim population, was nonetheless ruled by a Hindu maharajah. It was incorporated into India, but Kashmir has remained the site of bloody conflict ever since.

Nehru was not a communist, as his opponents frequently claimed; he was a socialist. By 1948 there were several state monopolies and government involvement in numerous economic enterprises. A series of Five-Year Plans were implemented, and India formally adopted the goal of "a socialistic pattern of society." In reality, this policy might better be described as "state capitalism," and it retarded India's economic development until it was abandoned by Nehru's grandson, Prime Minister Rajiv Gandhi, decades later.

In foreign affairs, Nehru stood for nonalignment or neutralism between the United States and the Soviet Union, a controversial position during the Cold War years among those who believed he was too sympathetic to the Soviets. Tharoor is highly critical of Nehru's foreign policy, a policy based on morality rather than on India's national security needs. Nehru's ability to elucidate his neutralism, however, made him a major political force during the 1950's. In 1958 he expressed a desire to resign, and Tharoor believes he should have, but his supporters urged him to remain, as did such foreign leaders as Dwight Eisenhower in the United States and Nikita Khrushchev in the Soviet Union. Nehru's daughter Indira had become his official hostess. It has been claimed that Nehru groomed Indira to succeed him, but Tharoor argues that was not Nehru's intent, that his democratic philosophy was opposed to establishing a political dynasty, although that occurred.

Tharoor describes Nehru's compulsive energy—he worked sixteen-hour days—and his obsessiveness over the smallest details, his tendency to talk too much and too long, his reluctance to make decisions, and his mercurial temper. He had no peers among his colleagues, and the author claims that by his last years Nehru had lost touch with numerous matters. For many, Nehru had become a demigod. Corruption had seeped into the government, and bureaucratic regulations overwhelmed the system. Nehru bungled relations with China, resulting in a Chinese invasion in 1962 which led to an Indian defeat because of the military's lack of preparedness. His health declined and on May 27, 1964, a date foretold by one of his astrologers, he died. Power was peacefully transferred to Lal Bahadur Shastri, India's second prime minister.

The author states that when Nehru died, his influence was paramount in four areas, which included democratic nation-building, secularism, socialist economics, and a neutralist foreign policy. Although India remains the world's largest democracy, Nehru's daughter Indira Gandhi, as prime minister, established a quasi-dictatorship for a time. She and her son, and Nehru's grandson, Rajiv, were both assassinated. By the early twenty-first century, Hindu sectarianism had increased, and communal violence continued. State capitalism or socialism failed and it was not until that system was abandoned that India began to prosper economically. The end of the Cold War made moralistic nonalignment meaningless in a multipolar world. Nevertheless, Nehru was one of the greatest Indians: Tharoor claims in the subtitle of his biography that Nehru invented India even though present-day India is not necessarily the India he envisioned. *Nehru* is an excellent introduction to one of the central figures of the twentieth century.

Eugene Larson

Review Sources

Booklist 100, no. 4 (October 15, 2003): 382.
Kirkus Reviews 71, no. 18 (September 15, 2003): 1167-1168.
Library Journal 128, no. 17 (October 15, 2003): 76-77.
Publishers Weekly 250, no. 42 (October 20, 2003): 45-46.

THE NEW FINANCIAL ORDER
Risk in the Twenty-first Century

Author: Robert J. Shiller (1946-   )
Published: Princeton University Press (Princeton, N.J.). 366 pp. $29.95.
Type of work: Economics
Time: The twentieth and early twenty-first centuries
Locale: The United States and a broad array of countries throughout Europe, Asia, and Africa

Shiller calls for democratizing worldwide economic systems in order to eliminate economic inequalities and improve the lives of human beings around the globe

> *Principal personages:*
> ROBERT J. SHILLER, professor of economics at Yale University
> ALAN GREENSPAN, chairman of the Federal Reserve System
> OTTO VON BISMARCK, German chancellor from 1871 to 1898
> GEORGE C. MARSHALL, U.S. secretary of state from 1947 to 1949

When Otto von Bismarck, Germany's so-called iron chancellor, implemented the world's first national health program in 1883 and first national accident insurance in 1884, many world leaders thought he had taken leave of his senses and was surely leading Germany into the dark abyss of economic disaster. Bismarck's utopian ideas were so revolutionary when they first emerged that they were widely regarded as hopelessly impractical and doomed to unabashed failure.

Ironically, during the next ten years, Austria, Italy, Sweden, and the Netherlands adopted versions of the socioeconomic reforms Bismarck pioneered. By the beginning of the twentieth century, most developed countries had implemented them in one form or another. Robert J. Shiller's vision of a global society whose inequalities are minimized seems as radical to many people today as Bismarck's reforms initially seemed to a majority of people both within and outside Germany. Workers today almost universally take for granted most of Bismarck's reforms, regarded as shockingly radical when they first surfaced.

These policies included limiting child labor, providing old age insurance (essentially, Social Security), establishing maximum working hours, providing broad health insurance coverage to all citizens, and offering worker's compensation for job-related injuries. These ideas, astoundingly radical in the 1880's, gained widespread acceptance during the first half of the twentieth century.

Shiller, a profound and thoughtful economist, demonstrates an impressive historical and ideological grasp of his field. He confronts head-on salient problems associated with finance and risk management, applying to his thinking many of the ethical concepts of philosopher John Rawls. Management of risk, according to Shiller, is the quintessential subject matter of finance. Finance regards as risks the many forms

Robert J. Shiller, whose earlier book Irrational Exuberance *(2000) foresaw and predicted that the speculative stock market bubble of the late 1990's would burst, is the Stanley B. Resor Professor of Economics at Yale University. A major concern in his writing is risk analysis.*

of human calamity and economic upheaval that people face. In Shiller's view, global economics cannot be considered without also considering the ethical implications of economic actions and protocols.

Shiller's brave new financial world envisions global societies that cope effectively with changes occurring so quickly and universally that hordes of people trained to work at various tasks may suddenly discover that their skills are no longer valued, their services no longer required. Unsettling socioeconomic disruptions have occurred throughout the world as large corporations, employing advanced technologies, have downsized labor without reducing productivity.

The human costs of such downsizing are often catastrophic. Dependent children poised to enter college cancel their plans, mortgage payments that were once manageable cannot be met, once-confident and optimistic self-images are quickly shattered. Human relationships in such circumstances gradually crumble as many affected families disintegrate and the environment of the workplace becomes cutthroat.

Downsizing is not the greatest problem in developing nations. Socioeconomic stratification results in closing the door to majorities in populations that have no opportunity to prove and improve themselves. Human potential is quashed as people desperately struggle to survive at a basic subsistence level. Life expectancy is low. Diseases like acquired immunodeficiency syndrome (AIDS) and tuberculosis in developing countries wipe out thousands. Infant mortality skyrockets. The world at large is the loser when this happens, because each death heralds a loss of human potential.

What Shiller postulates is the global elimination of economic inequalities. He refers to this process as a democratization of the world's financial systems, accompanied by the emergence of a new financial order. Currently, health insurance is funded by payments from all participants, some of whom may never need to avail themselves of it in any major way. This makes it feasible for participants who legitimately require medical care to receive assistance in meeting their medical expenses. Every citizen worldwide in Shiller's projected new order would contribute to funds earmarked for the protection of everyone from the economic ruin that often threatens people in rapidly evolving societies.

Shiller, in a conversation with Alan Greenspan, chairman of the Federal Reserve System, associated the heady rise of stock markets in the 1990's with "irrational exuberance," a term Greenspan borrowed from Shiller and used in a 1996 speech. In Shiller's book *Irrational Exuberance* (2000), the author attempted to explain the runaway stock markets of the 1990's, examining the forces that fueled the unrestrained speculation of that decade and led to wild market gyrations. He noted that the erosion of capital when the bubble burst would be, in dollar terms, equivalent to destroying every house in the United States, although corporate income flows associated with the stock markets were not huge. Shiller's prediction that the bubble would burst proved valid.

The current book is more broadly conceived than *Irrational Exuberance*. Shiller complains that risk management was not sufficiently inclusive during the twentieth century. Risk management focuses on tangible risks like devastating fires or hurricanes, against which insurance can be obtained. Risk management in the investment world involves tactics such as diversifying stock and bond portfolios or hedging commodity risks.

Such tactics, however, largely serve the interests of affluent members of developed societies. They lack meaning for those who live at subsistence levels in many developing nations. Shiller's theories of economics extend into the lives of people at all levels of social and economic development. In essence, his democratization of the financial order is more socialistic or communistic than it is democratic. Its major premise is that, ideally, economic inequalities must be expunged from all world economies.

Shiller cites what has happened since Nigeria, an oil-rich country, gained independence in 1960, when its per capita gross domestic product (GDP) was $1,054. By 1998 this figure had slipped to $1,025, a shocking plunge in a country endowed with substantial natural resources. Shiller thinks that if the country had possessed the sort of insurance he envisions, it would have become prosperous. He grants that cash-strapped Nigeria could not have paid for such insurance in 1960 but suggests that it could have promised payment if its economy rebounded reasonably well. Unfortunately, he does not suggest how such insurance would be administered globally, and he appears to depend upon the inherent goodness of human beings to run his proposed program day to day.

In the new financial order, citizens would be insured against losing their sources of income through downsizing. Retraining would become an accepted element in a system of economic security that extends to everyone. The poor would not suffer the uncertainties and inequalities that, throughout history, have been their lot. Indeed, if Shiller's scheme works optimally, the poor will vanish, although some of the former wealthy might consider themselves poor.

It is perhaps naïve to assume that inequalities can be eliminated globally. Presumably, in any society there are those who prefer indolence over productivity. People who have worked with the homeless in the United States can verify that although many of them genuinely wish to be helped and are willing to participate productively in their rehabilitations, others cling to and cherish the freedom of joblessness.

Of particular interest in the development of Shiller's visionary theories is his discussion of the Marshall Plan implemented after World War II. Between 1948 and 1951, the United States poured thirteen billion dollars into European nations that had suffered the effects of the war. At least seventeen nations, ranging from Iceland and Switzerland to Germany, France, and Great Britain, benefited from this program, which, on the surface, seemed generous.

Shiller reminds his readers that the amount expended on the Marshall Plan repre-

Magill's Literary Annual 2004

sented 1.3 percent of the gross national product (GNP) of the United States during the four years when it flourished. He also recounts how the United States Congress had to be prepared psychologically before it would vote to support such an expenditure. General George C. Marshall, the United States' secretary of state, told Congress that the funding requested was a mere 5 percent of what it had cost the United States to participate in World War II, and that without assistance through the Marshall Plan, fascism and communism might again disturb the world's precarious equilibrium. Marshall, realizing that humans have a psychological urge to finish tasks, also emphasized that the United States, having achieved victory, now owed it to the world to complete the job it had begun.

In Shiller's view, however, the United States might have done more for the countries of Europe and, by doing so, might have achieved more impressive results than it did. Under his utopian scheme, those involved in the war would have entered into risk management contracts before the war to protect their livelihoods. Had such contracts been signed prior to the conflict, considerably more money would have gone to Europe at war's end. The United States, according to Shiller, might have given 10 percent or more of its GNP to countries damaged by the war. Such an expenditure would have had little long-term impact upon the United States, whereas its positive impact upon the damaged nations would have been immense.

Later in *The New Financial Order*, Shiller cites John Rawls's theory of distributive justice, focusing on the proposal of the Jubilee Debt Campaign of 2000 that supported the execution of an international agreement to cancel the foreign debt of financially strained developing nations. There is little hope that such countries can become sufficiently productive to offer their citizens better lives if they are forced to carry the heavy burdens of debt. It is hoped that if such debt is forgiven, these countries might become fuller participants in the world economy.

One must question, however, the validity of such a suggestion because many developing nations have been ruled by greedy, unscrupulous dictators who suppress their people while enhancing their personal wealth, often salting away billions in their foreign bank accounts and investments. Any new financial order will have to be played out on a global stage that must necessarily take into account the governance and political philosophy of each nation, which will have profound influences upon how any encompassing financial plan will be carried out.

Some readers will quibble with Shiller's ideas as he presents them in *The New Financial Order*. Despite the global outreach that he postulates and supports, he writes largely from an American and broadly Western viewpoint. He also neglects to present a consistent, concrete plan for administering the complex programs his new financial order requires. His controversial book will generate discussion among economists and politicians and may influence global economic theory. Shiller forces readers to step back and view the past critically, with an eye toward altering the future in positive ways, although perhaps less drastically than the author desires.

R. Baird Shuman

Review Sources

Business Week, April 14, 2003, p. 14.
The Economist 367, no. 8320 (April 19, 2003): 69.
Library Journal 128, no. 5 (March 15, 2003): 92.
The New Yorker 79, no. 9 (April 21-28, 2003): 185.
Publishers Weekly 250, no. 9 (March 3, 2003): 66.
The Wall Street Journal, April 24, 2003, p. D10.

NEW WORLDS OF DVOŘÁK
Searching in America for the Composer's Inner Life

Author: Michael B. Beckerman (1951-   )
Publisher: W. W. Norton (New York). 295 pp. $29.95
Type of work: Biography and music
Time: 1892-1904
Locale: New York; Spillville, Iowa; Prague

An examination of aspects of Antonin Dvořák's sojourn in America reveals new insights about the composer's life and his music

Principal personages:
ANTONIN DVOŘÁK, a Czech composer
JOSEF KOVÁŘIK, an American musician of
    Czech ancestry
JEANNETTE THURBER, an American patron
    of the arts

Antonin Dvořák (1841-1904) was a Czech composer in the Romantic mode of the later nineteenth century. Although he is not as highly ranked in the classical music pantheon as composers such as Ludwig van Beethoven or Johannes Brahms, his musical talents were great and diverse. He was a prolific master of composition in many forms including symphonies, concertos, operas, chamber music, choral music, songs, and music for solo instruments, especially the piano. His music is renowned for its lyrical and melodious qualities. Despite the accomplished and often complex character of his compositions, Dvořák and his music are not well understood.

Dvořák cultivated a nationalistic Czech musical idiom by incorporating elements of traditional Czech folk songs and dances into many of his works. Thus, his music seems to be particular in character. In addition, Dvořák, who preferred family life in the country, was a somewhat modest and reticent man, without the Romantic flair that many of his contemporaries displayed.

Michael Beckerman sees Dvořák, both the man and his music, in a different light. In his view, the composer's personality and psyche had depths and secrets which his music both reveals and camouflages. His book, *New Worlds of Dvořák*, probes one key episode in Dvořák's life, the approximately three years between 1892 and 1895 that Dvořák spent in the United States, to bring new insights that help elucidate that ephemeral interaction between a composer's outer as well as inner life, on one hand, and the compositions that listeners hear, on the other hand.

In the introduction, "A Composer Goes to America," the author briefly explains the circumstances that took Dvořák to the United States, examines possible reasons the composer went, and presents his case for the importance of this American visit in understanding Dvořák and his music. Dvořák went to New York be-

cause Jeannette Thurber, an important patron of
the arts, invited him to become director of the
National Conservatory of Music. She wanted a
composer of European stature to help inspire
the creation of great and distinctive American
music.

Beckerman offers several plausible motives
for Dvořák's acceptance of this position, including financial considerations, the intrigue of the
United States, and the freedom for artistic exploration that the venture offered. For anyone
trying to come to terms with Dvořák's music,
this American interlude provides a rich range of
resources. During Dvořák's stay, his almost con-
stant companion and amanuensis was Josef Kovářik, an American musician of Czech
ancestry, whose memoirs and letters have been published. Dvořák himself wrote letters, especially to family and friends at home. In addition, the press chronicled many
of Dvořák's activities.

~

*Michael Beckerman is a professor
of music at the University of
California, Santa Barbara. A
specialist in Czech and Eastern
European music, he has written
books and articles on Leos Janacek
and Dvořák, among others. He
received the Janáček Medal from
the Czech Republic and is a
laureate of the Czech Music
Council.*

~

The author uses all this documentation to bring new insights to the music that
Dvořák composed during his American sojourn. Much of Beckerman's study focuses
on two key issues. First, he examines the resources on which Dvořák drew to create
compositions that could be considered especially American. Second, he inquires into
Dvořák's state of mind and considers the ways that Dvořák's emotional state may be
related to his music. A compact disk that accompanies the book enables the reader to
hear musical examples that the author discusses.

The two primary musical influences which appear in Dvořák's American compositions come from American Indian lore and African American spirituals, and both
contribute to Dvořák's best-known symphony, the Ninth Symphony "From the New
World," which was his first major composition in the United States. Beckerman begins with a section on Dvořák and Henry Wadsworth Longfellow's poem *The Song of
Hiawatha* (1855). Dvořák had already read a Czech translation of this poem, and
Beckerman discusses the abortive plans that Dvořák and Jeanette Thurber pursued to
compose an opera based on the Hiawatha material. On the day of the symphony's premiere, December 15, 1893, articles and interviews in the *New York Herald* and the
New York Daily Tribune established Dvořák's claim that he had based the second and
third movements on Longfellow's poem. Starting from this point, Beckerman analyzes this work to show how musical images inspired by the poem are woven into the
symphony, including its finale.

If the American Indian influence came primarily from romanticized literary imagery, the role of African American music is more concrete. In the late spring of 1893,
about six months before the premiere of "From the New World," a series of newspaper articles argued the pros and cons of statements made by Dvořák about the potential of "Negro melodies" to form a basis for the future development of American music. Beckerman shows from many perspectives, including journalistic discussions,

articles about "Negro melodies" to which Dvořák was introduced, and Dvořák's close acquaintance with Harry Burleigh, an African American singer who was at the time a student at the National Conservatory of Music, that Dvořák had direct knowledge of these spirituals. Beckerman also analyzes the music to demonstrate where and how Dvořák incorporated ideas from these spirituals in his symphony. Particularly in his thorough discussion of Dvořák's relationship with three prominent journalists, the author contributes new information that provides a more complete picture of Dvořák's use of spirituals to create music that could be identified as American.

The second major topic that Beckerman examines is Dvořák's mental state. He foreshadows aspects of this topic in part 4, "American Influences, American Landscapes," but he discusses it more fully in part 5, "The Hidden Dvořák." Anecdotal evidence for Dvořák's mental condition comes from various remarks by his son, some of the journalists who interviewed and wrote about Dvořák, and Kovářik's memoirs, among other sources. When put together, these reports reveal a man who suffered from some kind of anxiety disorder. Dvořák was prone to "nerve storms." He was terrified of thunderstorms and was anxious in crowded situations. He frequently needed someone to accompany him, a role that Kovářik, for example, served, because Dvořák was fearful of being out on his own. Beckerman argues that these symptoms closely match the modern psychiatric profile for agoraphobia, a disorder that involves a number of characteristics including "anxiety about being in places or situations from which escape might be difficult (or embarrassing)." In addition, Beckerman discusses Dvořák's use of alcohol, and he concludes only that Dvořák used drinking as "self-medication for anxiety." However, the evidence that he presents, including the need for a drink in the morning, consumption of substantial amounts of alcohol to a point of passing out, and becoming unreasonable when unable to obtain a drink on a train ride through the "dry" area of Pennsylvania, points to alcoholism. Because Beckerman is willing to press for identification of Dvořák's agoraphobia using modern psychiatric diagnostic criteria, the same standards should be applied with reference to the ample available literature about alcoholism to the problem of Dvořák's drinking.

The main question that arises for Dvořák, as it does for many other composers such as Wolfgang Amadeus Mozart or Beethoven, concerns the relationship of his inner psychological world to his music. Does exposing a composer's mental and emotional states make a difference in how listeners hear and understand the music? For Dvořák, Beckerman offers the general view that "the morbidity, depression, and pain" that Dvořák experienced as a result of his anxiety and agoraphobia "became part of the emotional palette out of which he composed."

However, Beckerman only hints at ways that this "emotional palette" is heard in Dvořák's music. For example, in part 4, preceding the discussion of Dvořák's anxiety disorder in part 5, Beckerman analyzes the "Quartet in F," one of the works that Dvořák composed during his first summer in the United States when he vacationed in the Czech American community of Spillville, Iowa. The quartet's outer movements present a feeling of musical joy, as if "clouds have lifted, darkness is gone." In contrast, the second movement, a "D-minor lament," has a quality "that goes beyond the merely sad and laps at the shore of tragedy." The *Biblical Songs*, also composed while Dvořák was in the United States, seem to express deeply personal inner feelings. Song 3, a setting of Psalm 55, expresses in eloquent musical language the "terrors of death," the "escape to perfect calm" as on wings of a dove, and the fearful conclusion in "an octave-and-a-half chromatic descent" to words about escape from storm and tempest.

Beckerman implies that musical passages such as these in the quartet and the *Biblical Songs* can be seen as the alternation between the tempests of Dvořák's "nerve storms" and interludes of calm and peace. For the most part, in the book these connections between Dvořák's psychological situation and his music remain fleeting glimpses, and Beckerman does not fully address the extent to which Dvořák's exposure to American culture affected his emotional states.

This book comprises essays loosely connected by the subject of Dvořák and his experiences in the United States. While the author makes a number of interesting points and introduces new information about this episode in Dvořák's life, the book lacks full analysis and integration of these findings into a complete whole. More could be done with the historical context. The reader would benefit from additional background about Dvořák himself, and the American musical scene needs to be developed. Beckerman alludes to controversies between two major musical centers in New York and Boston, and he mentions some American composers, such as Amy Beach. However, it would be helpful to know more about the musical situation that Dvořák encountered, including the history of the National Conservatory of Music, of which Dvořák assumed the position of director.

Much attention is devoted to one of Dvořák's major American works, the Ninth Symphony "From the New World," but the book's organization with distinct sections on the American Indian and African American musical material leaves the symphony itself fragmented. Beckerman does pull these musical threads together to demonstrate how these disparate musical influences are woven in artistic terms to create the complete composition that the listener experiences in hearing the symphony.

The book raises two major questions about the impact of Dvořák's American sojourn; first, on music in the United States and second, on the composer and his music. Beckerman says little about Dvořák's departure, except to state that he "returned home to Bohemia in April of 1895" and that some discussions with Jeannette Thurber about his possible return took place. The first issue concerning the impact of Dvořák on American music is not taken up in this book, but it is a relevant question that deserves consideration. On the impact of the United States on Dvořák and his music, the author suggests that this experience freed Dvořák to follow his musical ambition, inspired by Richard Wagner, to compose operas.

Many questions remain, however. Did Dvořák continue to use musical influences that he encountered in the United States? Did the exposure to African American spirituals further enhance spiritual qualities in his music? Did his encounter with American culture exacerbate his anxiety disorder, and if so, did this impact reverberate in his later musical compositions? In sum, this book does, indeed, open "new worlds of Dvořák," that merit further exploration, analysis, and synthesis into the study of Dvořák and of the history of American music.

Karen Gould

Review Sources

Commentary 115, no. 3 (March, 2003): 70-74.
The New York Times, November 17, 2002, section 2, p. 30.
The New York Times, January 10, 2003, p. E50.
Notes 60, no. 1 (September, 2003): 167-169.

NOTES FROM THE DIVIDED COUNTRY

Author: Suji Kwock Kim (1968-   )
Publisher: Louisiana State University Press (Baton Rouge). 74 pp. $15.95
Type of work: Poetry
Time: 1929-2000
Locale: Korea, the United States, and Scotland

These poems range from the deeply personal to those reflecting on the horror, violence, and suffering brought on the people of Korea in the twentieth century

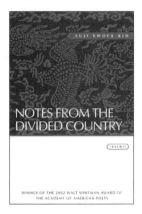

Principal characters:
THE PERSONA, the first-person speaker of most poems, a young woman who reflects on human life and Korean history
THE MOTHER, who has suffered through the Korean War before immigrating to the United States
THE FATHER, who fled from the Korean Communists and lost his parents
THE BROTHER, whom lack of prenatal care has left mentally handicapped
THE BOYFRIEND, who comes from a non-Korean, abusive family

With *Notes from the Divided Country*, Suji Kwock Kim offers her readers a powerful first book of poems. Her poetry, deeply personal, combines Western and Eastern poetic traditions with Asian themes and intensely reflects on crucial aspects of the Asian American experience. The poet's voice is detailed and observant. The poems focus on concrete objects as well as abstract emotions and offer a view of the terrifying swings of recent Korean history. In reading Kim's poetry, the reader is as likely to encounter a Korean American mother chopping food for her children in New Jersey as to learn of Korean nationalists being skinned alive by Japanese soldiers in World War II.

Ironically, the title can reflect Korea, a country still divided into a Communist North and a democratic South in 2003. However, it can also reflect the divided souls of recent immigrants, who are split by the memories of their native lands and their daily encounters with American culture. On a third level, the title can also be read as a subtle allusion to the author's view of American society as being divided among different ethnic and economic groups of people.

The opening poem, "Generation," expressively deals with the subject of human birth. It successfully introduces the scope, style, and focus of the poet's vision and launches the first of the book's four parts. "Generation" envisions a mystic world of unborn souls. The act of human sexual intercourse summons one unwilling soul to earth. To enter a newly created body in "the labyrinth of mother's body," the unborn soul must run "through benzene rain." Immediately, this image evokes a time of war, when inflammable chemicals are used to kill people. The idea of war is taken up fur-

~

Suji (Sue) Kwock Kim studied at Yale College, the Iowa Writer's Workshop, Seoul National University, and Stanford University. In Spring, 2003, she joined the English department of Drew University. Kim has won grants and scholarships from the National Endowment for the Arts and many other philanthropic institutions and received The Nation/Discovery Award.

~

ther when the poet reveals that the new soul will inhabit a body created by two "refugees running from mortar shells, immigrants driving to power plants in Jersey." Typical for Kim's poetry, the universal act of a violent birth is tied to a concrete, personal situation.

The titles of the next two poems, "The Tree of Unknowing" and "The Tree of Knowing," allude to Kim's rich grounding in the Western poetic tradition. Just as in William Blake's groundbreaking *Songs of Innocence and of Experience* (1839), in which a little boy learns the hazardous work of a child chimney sweep, Kim creates an effective juxtaposition. Her two poems portray a child's unhappy, forced confrontation with harsh knowledge. As a baby joyfully resting in her mother's arms, the persona does not yet know what misery the circumstances of her birth would cause her family. As an adolescent, she learns that her mother suffered from post-birth internal bleeding. Immediately she feels guilty, telling the reader that "I ripped her womb being born."

The persona reveals that the attending physician did not take her mother's bleeding seriously. Unchecked and untreated, the lacerations formed scar tissue, damaging the mother's uterus. Because his body and brain could not grow properly, the brother of the persona was born with mental and physical handicaps. Her sister was born prematurely and died, and her mother could never have any more children. The reader may begin to question whether American society is a divided country, too. The amount of medical care and attention, the poem suggests, clearly is different for the affluent, whose economic power has made them assertive. On the other hand, the immigrant poor are too shy to demand exhaustive examinations.

"Middle Kingdom" is an exquisitely crafted poem about the further tribulations of the persona's Korean American family. The title alludes to both the medieval term for China and, by extension, most of East Asia in the eyes of the West, signifying the immigrants' homeland. The title also points to the position of the immigrant family. They are trying to make a living in the middle between Korea and the United States.

It is the family, and particularly the figure of the mother, who provide the persona with a melancholy grounding. Sitting at the kitchen table with her mentally handicapped brother while her father is working an undesirable night shift, she feels that "Mother chopped pieces/ of her heart into the skillet." The mother sacrifices everything for her two children, and the persona feels it is an ongoing process, for "each morning her heart grew back." The melancholy of their situation threatens to overwhelm the young persona, and she pretends to pray so as not to worry her parents.

The persona's spiritual closeness to her mother is revealed again by "Translations from the Mother Tongue," the poem that concludes the first part of the book. Typical issues affecting immigrants are nicely presented with culturally specific and imaginative imagery. While the mother prepares jars of kimchee in the United States, her daughter reflects on what it must mean to leave one's native land, one's family, one's familiar social circle and culture, and one's first language. Among Korean American authors, Chang-Rae Lee's earlier masterpiece *Native Speaker* (1995) and Suki Kim's *The Interpreter* (2003) have looked at these issues within the context of their fiction. On the Asian American experience in general, Amy Tan's *The Joy Luck Club* (1989) remains perhaps the most widely read novel in the United States. Suji Kwock Kim's poetry adds another important layer here. She combines specific questions of Korean American heritage with the universal question as to "what's handed down/ from mother to daughter" in every new generation.

The poems of the second part of *Notes from the Divided Country* all take place in Korea. From 1910 to 1945, Korea was a colony of Japan. Koreans like the persona's grandparents and parents, who resisted the colonizers, experienced much suffering. "Occupation" likens the country of that time to a house made of human bones, its walls painted with blood. "Resistance," written to honor Kim's maternal great-grand-parents, tells of the plight of the Korean "guerillas who starved during the '29 uprisings" against the Japanese. In precise, terrifying language the poet recollects the images of murder, rape, and brutality experienced by Koreans living in these times.

Again, against the backdrop of a concrete historical situation, the poet raises universal issues. "What won't we do to each other?" is a question that is applicable to much of human history and answered too often with horrific examples of human brutality toward humans. "After liberation I saw a frenzy of reprisals against former collaborators," is the sad answer given. It reveals some disillusionment about the true nature of humanity.

When Japan was defeated in World War II, Korea was divided, and the suffering of the people continued. The North became Communist, and the South struggled to remain free. As Sergei Goncharov has shown in *Uncertain Partners: Stalin, Mao, and the Korean War* (1993), the North Korean Communist dictator Kim Il Sung launched an invasion of the South on June 25, 1950, in the hope of a quick victory. Under a mandate from the United Nations, the United States intervened, and an armistice became effective in July, 1953. In 2003, Korea was still a divided country.

Beginning with "The Chasm," Kim's poems describe the horror of the Korean War from the perspective of the persona's parents and their families. As civilians, they suffered great losses. Indeed, historically, three million Koreans, one million Chinese Communist soldiers, and fifty-four thousand American soldiers died in the war. From the persona's family's point of view, caught in the crossfire, there does not seem to be a distinction between Communist aggressor and the defenders of the South. The persona's uncle dies, "by Soviet T-34 tanks or U.S. rocket-launchers."

Something seems to be lost when the line between attacker and attacked is blurred so much. The poems never identify Communist aggression as the primary cause of the war. Kim's poetry shows that civilian suffering is related to the war. It does not trace suffering back to those who started the war and did so with inhuman and reckless contempt for their own people.

"Montage with Neon, Bok Choi, Gasoline, Lovers & Strangers" reflects the persona's visit to postwar, still-divided Korea celebrating Buddha's birthday in the democratic South. For her, the old male survivors symbolize the achievement of postwar southern society to start again. They also seem to express the warning to the next generation that "may you never do what we've done,/ may you never remember & may you never forget." The paradox in the last line can be read as a moral command not to dwell on the past horrors with morbid fascination or even to refight old battles. At the same time, it must never be forgotten that war smashes society and destroys lives.

In the third part, *Notes from the Divided Country* returns to the present of the persona's life. She observes the details of her life in the United States and of a trip to Scotland with her boyfriend. The food the boyfriend's mother cooks for him is lovingly described in "Leaving Chinatown," and its ingredients indicate that he has a Latin American, Caribbean, or Mexican American heritage. His father beat both him and his mother, creating "a nightmare of childhood" still haunting him as he relaxes with the persona. With their ultraprecise focus on the exact nature of an apparently everyday object that comes to reveal a larger truth about the Asian American immigrant experience, poems like "Nocturne" or "Monologue for an Onion" may remind readers of the poetry of Li-Young Lee, especially his masterpiece "Persimmons," in *Rose* (1986).

The fourth part contains poems that experiment with a wide range of styles and subjects. "On Sparrows" is clearly an ironic revision of Wallace Stevens's "Thirteen Ways of Looking at a Blackbird" (1917) and shows Kim's play with American poetic classics. "Transit Cars" is dedicated to the author's friend Keiko Yamada. The poem tells of a young Japanese or Japanese American woman whom the persona envisions fifty years ago. Then, she rode in a train to the American detention centers where people like the young woman were incarcerated after the Japanese attack on Pearl Harbor in 1941. After reading of the atrocities the Japanese committed in Korea, the reader is struck by the poet's even-handed focus on suffering everywhere.

"The Korean Community Garden in Queens" closes the book. It offers a tranquil, pastoral setting juxtaposed to the many poems focusing on human suffering. Thematically, it is linked to "The Couple Next Door" in part three. That poem features a sympathetic gay couple who find happiness by tending their garden. The book's last poem closes with the persona's heartfelt wish that she may "see life and paradise as one."

Notes from the Divided Country is Suji Kwock Kim's first book of poems, and it won for her the 2002 Walt Whitman Award of the Academy of American Poets. It is both intensely personal and grounded in the author's Korean American heritage. Kim's poems have moving, relevant content and are stylistically sophisticated, reflecting many experimental directions. The poems' juxtaposition of the horrors of war with the challenges, the disappointments, and the comforts of family life, and the persona's intense observations about natural and human life around her, make it a valuable work.

R. C. Lutz

Review Source

Booklist 99, no. 13 (March 1, 2003): 1141.

OF PARADISE AND POWER
America and Europe in the New World Order

Author: Robert Kagan (1959-   )
Publisher: Alfred A. Knopf (New York). 103 pp. $18.00
Type of work: Current affairs

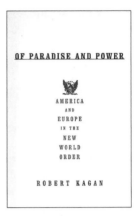

A distinguished student of international affairs exam-ines the roots of a growing rift between the United States and certain European countries, finding a primary cause in disparity of power between the United States and Europe

In the summer of 2002, a stunning analysis of the grow-ing conflict between Europe and the United States began circulating among a trans-Atlantic audience of government officials, scholars, and other interested parties. Written by Robert Kagan, senior associate at the Carnegie Endow-ment for International Peace, the analysis—in the form of an article in *Policy Re-view*—posited to readers a compelling answer to a timely question that grew more ur-gent as summer turned into autumn. Kagan's piece attracted the attention of Europe-ans as much as their erstwhile American allies. Indicative of the article's attractive power was that, thanks to electronically circulated copies, many participants at a con-ference of German and American political scientists and educators held in California early in October were well familiar with Kagan's thesis.

Early in the new year, the article, now grown to more than one hundred pages, was published as *Of Paradise and Power: America and Europe in the New World Order*. This slim volume did not so much open Pandora's box as observe the progress and consequences of a festering sore. In the lurid light Kagan shed on trans-Atlantic rela-tions (excluding the United States' fellow Anglo-Saxon ally) the roots of woes al-ready loosed upon the post-Cold War world by a growing fissure between various members of the North Atlantic Treaty Organization (NATO)—in particular, France and Germany, along with their "valet" state, Belgium—were plain for all who wished to see them.

Consequences of the rift were already fully transparent in early 2003, as the United States and Britain battled France and Germany (among others) at the United Nations Security Council over policy toward Iraq. Soon, U.S. defense secretary Donald Rumsfeld named the United States' adversaries "Old Europe," and the name stuck. The American position on Iraq was supported by most governments of the new de-mocracies ("New Europe") of Central and Eastern Europe, though not necessarily by their populations.

What were the roots of the tensions between Old Europe and those who were once their allies in the New World? The main thrust of Kagan's answer was that by the close of the Cold War period at the end of 1991, Europe and the United States had be-

~

Robert Kagan, senior associate at the Carnegie Endowment for International Peace, was educated at Yale and Harvard Universities and served at the U.S. State Department from 1984 to 1988. He was living in Brussels when Of Paradise and Power was written. Kagan contributes regularly to The Washington Post, The New Republic, *and* The Weekly Standard.

~

gun to think in qualitatively different ways, resulting in their living in two proverbial "different worlds."

Old Europe proceeded with its long-standing program of integration by approving the Maastricht Treaty in 1991, creating the European Union. Former ways of power politics, Bismarckian "Blood and Iron" policies, bitter national rivalries (especially between France and Germany), and, above all, war as a means of conflict resolution, were relics of the past. Soon, the newly emancipated peoples once held in thrall as Soviet satellites were clamoring for membership. (Even Muslim Turkey wanted in, though Europe was not so sure it wished to accept what it might have conceived as an Islamic Trojan horse.) This newly formed tide of peaceful relations among European states Kagan summarizes as "paradise." The realm of "perpetual peace," summoned to view in Immanuel Kant's essay of the same name (*Zum ewigen Frieden: Ein philosophischer Entwurf*, 1795; *Perpetual Peace*, 1957), had been reached at last. This was an event that called for more than celebration; it called forth as well a set of rules and institutions—the political and legal infrastructure of peace—as well as appropriate modes of conducting international relations, modes such as diplomacy and persuasion, emphasis on carrots rather than on sticks, as befits a world striding purposively toward a condition of universal amity as well as comity. In such a world, the "software" (or "soft power") of logical argument and patient cajoling would eclipse the "hardware" of military might.

Across the Atlantic, a behemoth had arisen that in European eyes challenged its arcadian vision of things by periodically flexing its military muscle on battlefields around the world. When the smoke cleared from the Cold War, the Soviet Union was no more and the United States alone remained. Now it was the world's only superpower, a fact of which it was only too well aware, in Old Europe's view. Indeed, it was more than a superpower; it was, according to French former foreign minister Hubert Vedriné, a *hyperpuissance*, a "hyperpower," which is to say, a holder of too much power. It needed to be controlled by the acolytes of peace in Paris and Berlin—balanced or blocked, persuaded or redirected—whatever tactic might deflect the American will to bend the world to American interests and values, and, like a mortal god, remake the world in its own image.

In the 1990's, the United States had fought three wars, two of them (to Europe's shame) on European soil, each time taking the lead and calling the shots, literally and figuratively. The shocking reality was that Europe was incapable of autonomously taking effective action in the absence of American will and might. That was the lesson of Bosnia, leaving Europe unsettled. The United States took the lead in defeating Iraq's Saddam Hussein in the Gulf War, then the Bosnian Serbs, followed by Serbia itself in the struggle over Kosovo. Finally, after the terrorist attacks in New York and

Washington D.C., on September 11, 2001, the Americans invaded and conquered Afghanistan, using ultramodern "smart weapons" to clean out the massive cave complex at Tora Bora—the same complex that had successfully held out for years against the Soviets in the 1980's—in a single weekend. Once the Americans were victorious, Europeans were asked to help out with mopping up and peacekeeping.

By late 2002 and early 2003, this scenario seemed once again set to recur. The United States appeared prepared to sweep aside European diplomatic know-how and finesse, making war where Old Europe sought to cope with the dangers of international life through peaceful means. That is to say, American power was poised to trump the European vision of "paradise," of peace on earth. In the event, the Americans followed Thomas Hobbes's dictum that when all else fails in politics, "clubs are trumps," and an almighty row was on. Hobbes, the seventeenth century English philosopher who wrote *Leviathan* (1651), was famed for his vision of international anarchy in which states struggle in a world of red-tooth and claw, where law is obligatory only if it can be enforced. To Old Europe and its adherents, the American policies perpetuated the Hobbesian world just at the time Kant's "sweet dream" of peace was at hand. All it took was good will, European skill, and the United States' forbearance of the military option, of which they were undisputed world champions.

Was Old Europe's view of the matter the last word on the subject? Robert Kagan does not think so. Instead, Kagan sees the underlying cause of current disputes and tensions over issues of war, peace, and diplomacy lying in great measure in the vast disparity of power between those on either side of the Atlantic. By comparison with the United States, Europe is weak indeed, incapable of stopping the slaughter of Bosnians on its doorstep without American intervention, unable to contribute more than token muscle during the joint NATO assault on Serbia.

To illuminate the situation, Kagan draws an analogy between two hunters in a forest menaced by a bear. One is armed with a gun, the other with a knife. It would be natural for the heavily armed hunter to search out and shoot the bear to eliminate the danger, while it would be equally natural for the other to hide or otherwise avoid direct confrontation. Thus, the deep differences that surfaced during the Iraq confrontation were not based on French or German anti-Americanism but on European weakness and American strength.

Why is there such a disparity? With 400,000,000 people, a ten-trillion-dollar economy, and considerable technological prowess, Europe could surely arm itself to American standards and play a role in the enforcement of international decency as well as in self-defense. At the close of the Cold War, the United States looked to Europe to become a strategic partner, but the European Union nations consistently choose low defense expenditure in favor of expansive (and expensive) welfare state programs. Europeans enjoyed U.S. protection throughout the Cold War; Americans view them as free riders on the U.S. defense budget. One result, Kagan explains, is a European "psychology of weakness." Europe tended to regard geopolitical concerns as a thing of the past; it was on "a holiday from strategy."

If disparity of power is the most salient underlying cause of trans-Atlantic tensions, it is not the only one. A disparity in outlook was evident throughout the 1990's.

Europeans had a markedly low level of perceived threat from non-European sources, compared with that of Americans. This was not just a matter of perception, however; the United States was the primary target of hostile forces, while Europe was not targeted or was only a secondary target. Moreover, European interests lay in a world where American strengths were irrelevant, and "those who cannot act unilaterally want to have a mechanism for controlling those who can."

On the other hand, Americans tend to believe that the idea that the world is, or through patient diplomacy can be made into, the European "paradise," is at best fanciful and in any case potentially suicidal. That is the lesson learned by the events of September 11, 2001, crimes planned in peaceful, postmodern, law-abiding Europe. They argue that governments responsible for the protection of their populations cannot afford to dwell in the arcadian heights of naïveté but rather on the messier, far more dangerous, lowland plains inhabited by the nonindustrialized world. They believe, with Niccolò Machiavelli, that those who live among wolves and behave as sheep will soon come to grief. In this view, the world has now entered an era of weapons of mass destruction (WMDs) held or potentially held by insane regimes such as North Korea or movements such as the Islamic fanatics, al-Qaeda. Because the United States is a principal target for WMD-armed rogue states and terrorists, Americans cannot mistake the world at large for peaceful, quasi-united Europe, however much they may admire Europe's post-World War II achievements.

To these Americans, Old Europe tends to see international politics as a form of social work, guiding regimes such as Iraq under Hussein or Afghanistan under the Taliban into the mores of civilization through diplomacy—the *mission civilisatrice*. American realists, however, believe that such regimes may have to be subdued militarily before they attack their neighbors or, especially, the United States. Human nature in this view is constant, and at crucial points international life is palpably Hobbesian. Moreover, international law is useless without enforcement. Kagan sees the United States not as the "cowboy" of European caricature but as the sheriff who attacks only "bad guys" and only to enforce the law. The accusation that Americans see the world as divided into good and evil is not accurate; rather, they see evil in the world that on some occasions must be opposed by force. Thus they consider the European view—especially German attempts to apply its pacifism universally—as hopelessly naïve and utopian as well as viscerally anti-American.

Kagan devises no escape from the conundrum he so compellingly describes. Instead, he offers the palliative of mutual understanding, with the implicit admonition that both sides accept the present disparity of power, cease useless mutual recrimination, and, in a word, get used to it. Long-term implications of American world hegemony, Kagan argues, are that "the United States must sometimes play by the rules of a Hobbesian world" and "refuse to abide by certain international conventions that may constrain its ability to fight effectively," as (idle dreams aside) this is the nature of international reality, not because the United States makes it so. Indeed, Kagan openly states that it is essential for the United States to operate according to a double standard, supporting arms control for others, for example, but not for itself. Moreover, the United States must sometimes act unilaterally—not because it relishes unilateralism but because "given a weak Europe that has moved beyond power, the United States has no choice *but* to act unilaterally." Accordingly, although Kagan exonerates the United States from Old Europe's charges, his prescription of reciprocal acceptance among those of disparate power and divergent outlooks is unlikely to be followed.

Charles F. Bahmueller

Review Sources

Booklist 99, no. 11 (February 1, 2003): 960.
Business Week, April 21, 2003, p. 24.
Commentary 115, no. 6 (June, 2003): 62-64.
Kirkus Reviews 71, no. 2 (January 15, 2003): 127.
Library Journal 128, no. 4 (March 1, 2003): 105-106.
National Review 55, no. 6 (April 7, 2003): 50-51.
The New York Times, March 5, 2003, p. E1.
The New York Times Book Review, March 30, 2003, p. 7.
Political Science Quarterly 118, no. 3 (Fall, 2003): 518-519.
The Wall Street Journal, March 11, 2003, p. D8.
The Washington Post Book Week, February 23, 2003, p. 6.

OLD SCHOOL

Author: Tobias Wolff (1945-   )
Publisher: Alfred A. Knopf (New York). 195 pp. $22.00
Type of work: Novel
Time: 1960-2003
Locale: A New England prep school

An unnamed narrator brings humiliations upon himself and other students at a New England prep school as he yearns to win a literary contest judged by Ernest Hemingway

Principal characters:
  NARRATOR, a senior student at a New England private school who becomes a writer
  ARCH MAKEPEACE, an English teacher, dean of the school
  HEADMASTER, the principal of the school, former student of Robert Frost
  MR. RAMSEY, an English teacher, later headmaster
  JEFF PURCELL,
  GEORGE KELLOG, and
  BILL WHITE, the narrator's friends and rivals at the school

Old School, Tobias Wolff's first novel, concerns tradition. Tradition, it shows, is personal, self-made. Accordingly, even the most intellectual of traditions, such as that of a nation's great literature, comes as much from native illusions and bamboozle as from the succession of native genius as one generation of writers supplants another. Hilarious, tender, discomfiting, and harshly candid, the novel depicts this succession intimately.

Old School takes place in a New England preparatory school for boys. The institution is old, most of the students come from wealth and privilege, and tradition suffuses the atmosphere. Among these traditions is the faculty's cultivation of literature. The English teachers are the leading intellects of the school, and some have personal connections to literary luminaries of the day. Furthermore, each year the school invites three famous writers to read from their own work and to judge a student literary contest. The winner gets a private interview. The novel's central character, who is unnamed, yearns with all his heart to win the contest and so receive the blessing of one of these great writers. Most keenly, he hopes Ernest Hemingway, scheduled to visit, will be the one to anoint him as a successor.

Early on, readers are likely to forget that they are reading fiction. Wolff's prose is so transparent, the point of view of an ambitious teenager so persuasively presented, and the story seemingly so effortless that the novel reads like a memoir. It fosters a sense of displacement, both intellectual and social, to 1960 and particularly the high school literary club milieu of the aspiring writer.

It is a novel nonetheless, carefully structured
toward a disturbing climax that forces readers to
consider what it takes to become a first-rate
writer and what is meant by literary tradition. At
the heart of the story are two characters, Arch
Makepeace, the school's dean and a literature
teacher, and the young narrator. A much-be-
loved fixture of the school, Makepeace is in late
middle age and carries with him a literary aura
because, first of all, he speaks of literary works
as communicating to him directly, not simply as
objects of analysis and, second, because he was
an ambulance driver during World War I, where

*A celebrated short-story writer,
Tobias Wolff has received the PEN/
Faulkner Award and the O. Henry
Award (three times), among other
honors. He also wrote two critically
acclaimed memoirs,* This Boy's Life
(1989) and In Pharaoh's Army
*(1994), and has edited short-story
collections. Wolff teaches at
Stanford University.*

he became friends with Hemingway. School legend has it that Makepeace was
the model for the leading character in Hemingway's *The Sun Also Rises* (1926).
Makepeace's origins are humble, but he has walked with the great and made himself
part of tradition thereby.

The narrator appears to be Makepeace's parallel, except that he is just starting on
his career, whereas Makepeace is finishing his. A senior, the boy comes from a sad,
dissembling home in Seattle. His father is a widower, and his background is commonplace. He is a scholarship student, but he longs to appear to be from the class of wealth
and heritage. He bends all of his wit to create the impression that he is. He is, in other
words, an strikingly adolescent mixture of ambition and pretense.

Spaced throughout the academic year, the visitations of the three writers show development in the narrator's character even as they intensify the suspense. They also
expose the underpinnings of literary reputation. The first to come is Robert Frost, an
august figure in American letters who recently has read at President John F. Kennedy's inauguration, a unique honor. Wolff's portrait of Frost is witty, venerating.
First the headmaster, Frost's former student, introduces him at the reading, and all the
trappings of tradition seem in place. Frost, though, is roguish. He plays upon his reputation as the wise old American poet to charm the students, making a show of fum-
bling and talking to himself, and picks on earnest Mr. Ramsey, a British-born English
teacher, to rib.

For his part, the narrator watches it all in a funk. He has lost in the poetry contest
that Frost judged. Instead, Frost chose a poem by the editor of the school's literary
magazine, George Kellog. A humorless grind, Kellog wrote a poem in imitation of
Frost's style, but Frost believes it to be a parody and is delighted because of it. Aghast,
Kellog barely can bring himself to meet Frost for the winner's interview, much to the
narrator's disgust.

If Frost represents the grand American literary tradition, then Ayn Rand personi-
fies the assault on it by modernism—or, again, so it seems. The author of *The Fountainhead* (1943) is the second literary visitor. The narrator reads Rand's novel and
falls under its spell, swallowing its thesis that tradition is a conspiracy to prevent originality and self-expression; the passage is a keenly written depiction of callow enthu-

siasm. The narrator, however, also loses the second literary contest, this time to a dull classmate whose winning entry is a rambling, fantastical science-fiction story. That comes as a shock, but Rand herself shocks even more. She arrives for her reading with great hauteur and a train of fawning groupies. In a wickedly comic episode, Wolff presents Rand as almost too grotesque to believe, a callous, prickly, ranting self-promoter—so much so that she is unable to answer questions and cannot tell when she is being mocked. Where Frost's performance was playful, hers is earnest; but she also plays her audience, and she also misinterprets the winning contest entry to fit her preconceptions.

The narrator now pins all his hopes on Hemingway, the final literary visitor. Although he has already won a scholarship to Columbia University, where he is to study with the eminent definer of literary tradition Lionel Trilling, the narrator is desperate to win Hemingway's blessing. Writer's block, however, stymies him. He takes to typing out Hemingway's short stories just to get the feel of the style. Still, nothing of his own comes. Meanwhile, he watches the competition poison his best friends and literary rivals: Jeff Purcell, Kellog, and his roommate, Bill White. Partly because of it, their friendships are injured, and the sense of class community, a source of tradition, suffers.

Finally, the night before the deadline for contest entries, the narrator discovers a moving short story in an old copy of a girls' school literary magazine. Although about a girl, the story speaks directly to his own experience. Like the narrator, she is a scholarship student from a poor background and half-Jewish in a population of rich Anglo Protestants. The story describes how she cynically postures, twists her personal history, and subordinates herself to friends with fewer talents, all in order to gain social acceptance.

The narrator types out this story, too, changing details and names to reflect his own experience. He does not think of it as a plagiarism; he thinks of it as his story. He submits it and wins not only the contest but also the enthusiastic praise of his teachers and fellow students. In a telephone interview with Mr. Ramsey, the contest coordinator, a drunk, sick, maundering Hemingway heaps encouragement on the narrator and compares him, nebulously, to F. Scott Fitzgerald. It is just what the narrator hoped for; still, like Frost and Rand, Hemingway is self-focused and deceived in his choice of winner. (Hemingway, however, never comes to the school; he commits suicide.)

The narrator's plagiarism is soon exposed. Mr. Ramsey, unexpectedly acting in place of Dean Makepeace, convenes a panel of inquiry, which forces the narrator to admit, numbly, his borrowing from another writer. He is summarily expelled, and a strangely solicitous Ramsey drives him straight to the train station. His college scholarship is lost, his future as a writer thrown into doubt. For a while he drifts, working in New York City and then joining the Army, but he never gives up his ambition.

Then the story leaps to 2003. The narrator has succeeded; he is a leading American writer. Because of it, his old school invites him to be a literary visitor, just like Frost, Rand, and Hemingway before him. The narrator is reluctant to visit because of the painful memory of his expulsion. Then, by chance, he meets Ramsey in a hotel bar in Seattle. Ramsey is now headmaster, on a fund-raising tour. As they reminisce about the plagiarism incident, he tells the narrator a surprising story. Dean Makepeace quit his job and abruptly left the school the same day the narrator was expelled in 1961, for something of the same reason. Makepeace had never met Hemingway. The school legend that had him connected with Hemingway was not his doing and based on a misunderstanding, and he thought it too silly ever to speak about in any way—until the day of the narrator's plagiarism. A scrupulously honest man, he could not bring himself to judge the narrator given his own specious reputation, or even stay in the school. Like the narrator, Makepeace drifted for a while. He ended up teaching in another school, far away, stung with shame and regrets. Eventually, the old prep school had an opening for an English teacher, and the headmaster invited him back. Like a wayward son, he returned and was received back into the academic family where he belonged.

The final sentence of the novel, alluding to the biblical parable of the prodigal son, is a beautifully moving, devastating recognition of what tradition is, if it is anything: acceptance, home. The ending implies that the narrator, too, will accept the invitation to visit and become part of the old school. So tradition is extended.

That the novel's narrator has no name may tempt readers to identify him with Wolff himself. Moreover, readers familiar with Wolff's actual memoirs, especially *This Boy's Life* (1989), will recognize how closely the story's background follows Wolff's adolescence. However, it is unnecessary and a disservice to the novel's coherence if Wolff's life is used to justify the narrative details. There are some other, lesser perplexities. The narrator, for instance, alternates between bald callowness and sophisticated perceptivity. Moreover, during the two occasions that he stands before school authorities, accused of serious infractions, he behaves with peculiar passivity.

Old School tells an especially American story about Americans and their culture. It is a culture "on the make." Looked at as it unfolds, an aspect of American culture such as literature might well seem to be a mixture of green ambition, ingenuous fraud, willful misapprehension, and talent for self-exposure. Looked back upon, as it is taught in schools and canonized by literary critics, it turns into "the past that most influenced the present," or tradition. Wolff shows readers how a somewhat shifty, somewhat foolish character like the narrator can realize his intellectual ambition, not by copying and posturing but by telling a story about his misbegotten youthful attempts to copy and posture, and by telling it frankly. That is a heartening view of American literature.

Roger Smith

Review Sources

Booklist 100, no. 1 (September 1, 2003): 9.
Kirkus Reviews 71, no. 17 (September 1, 2003): 1100.
Library Journal 128, no. 18 (November 1, 2003): 126-127.
The New York Times Book Review, November 23, 2003, p. 12.
Publishers Weekly 250, no. 41 (October 13, 2003): 57.
Time 162, no. 22 (December 1, 2003): 98.

ON THE NATURAL HISTORY OF DESTRUCTION

Author: W. G. Sebald (1944-2001)
First published: Luftkrieg und Literatur, 1999, in Germany
Translated from the German by Anthea Bell
Publisher: Random House (New York). 202 pp. $23.95
Type of work: Current affairs and history
Locale: Europe

Assessing the destruction visited on Germany during World War II, German liter-
ary scholar and novelist Sebald probes the silence, repression, evasion, and forget-
ting that he finds characteristic of German responses to the nation's largely self-
inflicted Nazi wounds

W. G. Sebald loved photography, but he was deeply troubled by the contrasting
pictures he reproduced in "Air War and Literature," the chapter that is both the opening and the centerpiece of his notable book *On the Natural History of Destruction.*
One postcard pairing shows the German city of Frankfurt am Main *Gestern* (yesterday) and *Heute* (today). Although the same cityscape is depicted, the scenes are utterly different. Dated 1947, one photograph shows a bombed and ruined city; the
other, dated 1997, portrays glistening skyscrapers that seemingly bear no witness to
the wasteland that existed fifty years earlier.

Sebald understands that Frankfurt's ruins in 1947 required the kind of rebuilding
that directed attention toward the future. He acknowledges that the contrasting photographs reveal an impressive postwar reconstruction. His concern, however, is that the
reconstruction also produced what he calls "a second liquidation in successive phases
of the nation's own past history." Rebuilding, which was not confined to bricks and
mortar but included personal and national identities, went hand in hand with evasion
of the past.

That burial included more than the removal of physical debris; it involved repress-
ing, if not forgetting, what Germans had experienced and done during the Third
Reich. Thus, there is irony in the title that Sebald gave this book. Destruction may
have a "natural history," for there is a logic in its unfolding. In Sebald's view, however, the postwar reinvention of German life, necessary though it has been, brought
with it silence, problematic rationalization, and dishonesty that remain as harmful as
they were understandable. Although German reluctance to confront—or, in some
cases, to keep confronting—the Nazi past may be "natural," Sebald writes to resist
that tendency. More pathologist than therapist, he offers no easy cure for the afflic-
tions he studies, but his book thoughtfully identifies the conditions—geographical,
psychological, spiritual—in which they are embedded.

While acknowledging that he cannot deal with all the subject's complexities,
Sebald ensures that his mapping is not a one-way indictment that simply faults Germany for failing to come to terms with its Nazi past. On the contrary, Sebald concentrates specifically on a topic that has received less attention than many other aspects

of World War II: the massive Allied bombing attacks on German cities and the immense death and suffering that those raids inflicted on German civilians and families. Sebald begins by observing that it is scarcely possible to visualize the destruction of German cities in the war's last years, nor can imagination fathom the hideous maiming and death that firestorm bombing produced in Cologne, Hamburg, Dresden, and many other large population centers.

During the bombing, temperatures soared to a thousand degrees as flames rose two thousand meters into the sky. Asphalt melted; even canals blazed. Air raid shelters became ovens that roasted people to death. Filled with rats, flies, and the rotting flesh on which they feasted, metropolis became necropolis. Sebald's statistics may not produce sympathy, let alone forgiveness, for citizens of Nazi Germany, who for the most part were willing followers of Adolf Hitler, but his data compel attention, and his concise, matter-of-fact descriptions merit heartache for the wasting of human life that they encompass. According to Sebald, for example, a million tons of British bombs alone fell on Germany. Air raids leveled scores of cities, destroyed more than three million homes, and left 7.5 million people homeless. The attacks took the lives of 600,000 German civilians. The destruction's scale, writes Sebald, was "without historical precedent."

W. G. Sebald is best known for novels, narratives, and reflections—including, in translation, The Rings of Saturn *(1998),* The Emigrants *(1996),* Vertigo *(1999), and* Austerlitz *(2001)—that focus on the twentieth century's destructiveness. Sebald was killed in a car crash at the age of fifty-seven.*

Sebald's account of the bombing of Germany took shape originally as a series of lectures that he delivered in Zurich, Switzerland, in the autumn of 1997. His commitment to write on the topic grew from links between his life and the air war. Although those links, he indicates, have been "entirely insignificant in themselves, they have nonetheless haunted my mind." Born "on the northern outskirts of the Alps" in rural Germany, Sebald was only a year old when the war ended. As time passed, he became increasingly gripped by the fact that "at the time, when I was lying in my bassinet on the balcony . . . and looking up at the pale blue sky, there was a pall of smoke in the air all over Europe, over the rearguard actions in the east and west, over the ruins of the German cities, over the camps where untold numbers of people were burnt."

He also realized that he had grown up with the absence of reflection by German writers about "the monstrous events in the background of my own life." Furthermore, as he spent his scholarly life in eastern England, Sebald knew that his British home stood near one of the seventy airfields that had been departure points for the bombing runs on his native Germany. The silence of those places—"most were abandoned after the war"—added to his puzzlement.

Such experiences, the author explains, "impelled me to go at least a little way into the question of why German writers would not or could not describe the destruction of the German cities as millions experienced it." His analysis focuses primarily on four factors, the first pointing back to the bombing descriptions with which his book begins. The bombing raids were catastrophic. Nazi Germany's governmental agencies were completely untrustworthy sources for truth about the devastation, and eyewitness accounts from reliable sources were not easily available at the time.

Stunned and traumatized, most survivors—many of them fleeing refugees "vacillating between a hysterical will to survive and leaden apathy"—were in no condition to write, although some diarists, Friedrich Reck and Victor Klemperer prominent among them, tried their best to describe as much as the limitations of information and language permitted. Noting that "the need to know was at odds with a desire to close down the senses," Sebald sums ups the situation by adding that "on the one hand, large quantities of disinformation were circulating; on the other, there were true stories that exceeded anyone's capacity to grasp them."

Sebald's analysis helps to show why immediately written eyewitness accounts about this chapter of German history are scarce. These gaps, moreover, do not strike him as the most decisive, because he believes that the bombing attacks must have paralyzed clear thinking among those who narrowly escaped them. Even when eyewitness accounts exist, Sebald thinks they have "only qualified value," which needs to be supplemented by careful historical study and what he calls synoptic perspectives. The gaps in these latter areas are what trouble him most. While Sebald continues to understand how natural it is that Germans have not accurately written the full story of their own destruction, his voice becomes more critical as he explores three more reasons for that outcome.

To grasp the significance of these three factors—humiliation, moral discrediting, and redefinition of identity—it is helpful to see more of what Sebald means by the natural history of destruction. Where, he asks, should such a history begin? Part of the answer is found in the abandoned British airfields. At first the bombing of German cities took place because the Western Allies needed to bring the war home to Germany. The strategy was to shatter German home-front morale, particularly among industrial workers. It remains arguable whether that strategy worked as well as expected, but as the bombing campaign ramped up, it took on a life of its own. The destruction of German cities, as Sebald sees it, became both the means to end the war and an end in itself. In that sense, the bombing was less strategic than total. The devastation escalated accordingly. If the immediate impact for Germans caught in the catastrophic raids was traumatizing horror, the aftermath brought humiliation, which is the second factor that Sebald identifies in his account of German inability or unwillingness to write about the devastation.

On February 18, 1943, with the tides of war already turned decisively against the Third Reich, Joseph Goebbels, Hitler's propaganda minister, urged the German people to devote themselves to "total war." Nazi Germany fought on for more than two years, but when unconditional surrender came in early May, 1945, the German price paid for Nazism was evident. Sebald underscores "the sense of unparalleled national humiliation felt by millions." Nazi ideology had proclaimed the German people to be superior in every way. There was some German dissent from those views, but it was insufficient to displace the welcome that Germans gave them. Crushing military defeat turned those claims to rubble. The ruins were uninhabitable, psychologically and spiritually, if not physically. Even when there were retrospective literary glances that focused upon them, the looking, says Sebald, was often an evasive "looking away at the same time."

The silence and evasion caused by humiliating defeat might have been more easily broken if the majority of Germans—many writers among them—had been less loyal to the Third Reich, "a society," says Sebald, "that was morally almost entirely discredited." Loyalty to a morally discredited regime could not be defended. One result, Sebald believes, is that for many Germans the horror of the Nazi period, including the bombing raids, became "taboo like a shameful family secret." Germans did not even debate openly whether the fire bombings were justified ethically, although in light of the fact that the nation "had murdered and worked to death millions of people in its camps," there were some Germans who "regarded the great firestorms as a just punishment, even an act of retribution on the part of a higher power with which there could be no dispute."

A sense of shame, however, was by no means the only explanation for the lack of a full and honest reckoning with the past. Sebald is most searing when he deals with writers who found that "the redefinition of their idea of themselves after 1945 was a more urgent business than depiction of the real conditions surrounding them." Sebald's essay on the German novelist Alfred Andersch epitomizes what he takes to be a widespread phenomenon. Andersch's fiction and self-estimate highlighted the concept of *innere Emigration* (inner emigration). Accepting an ambiguous identity, "inner emigrants" were those Germans who rejected National Socialism or claimed they did but chose not to leave Nazi Germany. Sebald measures Andersch's autobiographical fiction and postwar self-characterization against his actual life during the Third Reich. At best, Sebald concludes, Andersch turned out to be a compromised "inner emigrant," for he benefited from National Socialism more than he resisted it. What Sebald ironically calls "tactful omissions and other revisions" in Andersch's writing reflected postwar German tendencies for self-reinvention that did little to encourage openness and honesty about Germany's Nazi past.

In contrast to Andersch and those like him, Sebald ends his book with two essays that pay tribute to writers who are his soul mates. In German writings and radio talks, Jean Améry, an Austrian Jewish survivor of Auschwitz, spoke profoundly and honestly about the resentment he felt because Germans under Hitler had destroyed what Améry called trust in the world. In the German Jewish author and artist Peter Weiss, Sebald finds a voice insistent on remembering the past with passion, and persistence, which can make possible the recovery that only remorse can bring. At the end of this courageous book, Sebald's call for German honesty about the Nazi past comes full circle. He wants modern Germans to be able to know about and grieve openly over the destruction brought by the Allied bombing raids, but Sebald concludes that the price for release from silence and repression must include remorseful awareness that Germans themselves "provoked the annihilation of the cities in which we once lived."

John K. Roth

Review Sources

Christian Century 120, no. 22 (November 1, 2003): 38-41.
Kirkus Reviews 70, no. 21 (November 1, 2002): 1599.
Library Journal 128, no. 1 (January 1, 2003): 134.
Los Angeles Times, March 23, 2003, p. R9.
Maclean's 116, no. 19 (May 12, 2003): 59.
New Statesman 132, no. 4626 (February 24, 2003): 48-49.
The New York Review of Books 50, no. 3 (February 27, 2003): 8-10.
The New York Times, February 5, 2003, p. E8.
The New York Times Book Review, April 6, 2003, pp. 13-14.
Publishers Weekly 249, no. 50 (December 16, 2002): 58.
The Washington Post, March 23, 2003, p. T3.

ORIGINAL FIRE
Selected and New Poems

Author: Louise Erdrich (1954-   )
Publisher: HarperCollins (New York). 158 pp. $23.95
Type of work: Poetry

*Selected poems from Erdrich's previous books of poetry
plus new poems showcase her ability as a poet comparable
to her acclaimed work as a novelist*

Louise Erdrich opens *Original Fire* with the title poem
from the book *Jacklight* (1984), a depiction of difference
and similarity drawn as a confrontation between inhabitants and invaders of the wilderness. Erdrich locates the poetic perspective in the consciousness of deer spirits, whose
home ground has been disrupted by the incursion of human beings, for whom the forest is alien but inviting terrain. The meeting of disparate populations is one of
Erdrich's primary themes, exemplified in her novels by the interaction of Catholic
missionaries and American Indian tribal communities and by the intermingling of
German American pioneers, her father's family background, and the native Ojibway
people of her mother's family.

Erdrich is primarily known as a novelist. She published seven novels following the
continuing popularity and critical success of *Love Medicine*, which won the National
Book Critics Circle Award in 1984. Erdrich says that she "started out as a poet," inspired by her father's recital of poems by Robert Frost and George Gordon, Lord Byron, and that her writing method is to "curl up in a chair and just write it like I'm writing a poem."

The poems in *Jacklight* are designed to speak as, and for, a native community
whose processes of perception might seem implausible and unfathomable to those unfamiliar with American Indian ways of knowing and being. The poem "The Strange
People" carries an epigraph from *Pretty-Shield: Medicine Woman of the Crows*
(1932), noting that "The antelope are strange people." The poem "Captivity," an
imaginative entrance into the mind of Mrs. Mary Rowlandson, "who was taken prisoner by the Wapanoag" in 1676, recounts the dislocation Rowlandson experiences as
the strange ways of her captors gradually meld into the modes of her previous life.
Shifts in perspective to the consciousness of a nonhuman species are presented as natural to the degree that Erdrich does not attempt to explain or justify the opening lines
of "The Strange People": "All night I am the doe, breathing/ his name in a frozen
field" or the beginning of "Jacklight," which does not choose to identify the creature
speaking: "We have come to the edge of the woods,/ out of brown grass, where we
slept unseen,/ out of knotted twigs, out of leaves creaked shut,/ out of hiding."

Erdrich describes herself as a writer who functions "as an emissary of the between-
world, that increasingly common margin where cultures mix and collide." In these

Louise Erdrich is the author of novels, books for children, poetry, short stories, and a memoir of early motherhood. She won the National Book Critics Circle Award for Love Medicine *(1984) and the National Magazine Award for her short fiction.*

poems, the collision is not only between Indians and Anglos but also between humans and other species, with the humaness of animals functioning as a commentary on human ways, the animalistic instincts of humans linking them to a wider sphere of creation in the traditions of American Indian cultures. The hunters jacklighting the wilderness, in an attempt to penetrate an alluring and alien dark realm, are described as taking "the first steps, now knowing/ how deep the woods are and lightless/ How deep the woods are." Their entry into the woods is presented as a return to a place of origins, where there is a possibility of regaining powers of vision neglected for centuries.

However, the Indians themselves have lost something of their ease in the woods through interaction with the invaders of their lands, so that in "I Was Sleeping Where the Black Oaks Move" there is a longing in the recollection, "Sometimes now, we dream our way back to the heron dance" and an ethos of sorrow in the concluding question: "How long must we live in the broken figures/ their necks make, narrowing the sky." In many of the poems, a sense of unease bespeaks a loss that the poet is trying to understand, and by understanding, achieve some measure of rectification.

The difficulties inherent in this task are implied by the best known of the poems in the first section, which seizes the aura surrounding a major American cultural icon. "Dear John Wayne" begins, somewhat deceptively, with a description of a fundamental mid-twentieth century activity, summer nights spent lounging "on the hood of the Pontiac" at a packed drive-in movie theater. In a typical film, the "death-cloud" of arrows "swarming down on the settlers" calls forth a screen-filling face, "acres of blue squint and eye" that promises a "thick cloud of vengeance." John Wayne is implacable and irresistible, the representation of a grasping ethic that says *"Everything we see belongs to us."* Erdrich acknowledges the futility of resistance, but her chilling final image, declaring "Even his disease was the idea of taking everything./ Those cells, burning, doubling, splitting out of their skins," is a warning of the effect that this toxic blight has brought to the entire continent.

Following the poems from *Jacklight*, Erdrich sets a sequence recounting the life and afterlife of a questing trickster she calls Potchikoo, a figure akin to the legendary Coyote present in various incarnations in many Indian stories, who is also an echo of Nanapush, who appears in several of Erdrich's novels, most recently in *The Last Report on the Miracles at Little No Horse* (2001). These "stories"—whose appearance in a book of poems is an indication of an indifference to the formalist academic distinction among genres—are a kind of template for Indian existence.

Purporting to cover Potchikoo's life, the first four stories follow the familiar pattern of birth, marriage, old age, and death but then surge beyond the customary to detail "Potchikoo's Life After Death," further exploits in spirit form, followed by restoration to human form, additional reversals, and finally an apotheosis of sorts, "Saint Potchikoo," which merges Christian and Indian beliefs in a final vision of contentment. The narrative that Erdrich develops has a degree of distance that permits the astonishing antics of Potchikoo to assume a semblance of verity. The storyteller cautions, "You don't have to believe this," but this mock admonition pulls the tales into the imaginative space of a folkloric frame, where comments like "You know what. I don't have to say it" include speaker and audience in a reciprocal exchange that draws on an oral tradition spanning many generations.

Each of the five sections of the book depend on the establishment of a distinct *voice* which orders and controls the poems. The third section, "The Butcher's Wife," contains what might be called the seed of Erdrich's most recent novel, *The Master Butchers Singing Club* (2003). The eponymous butcher's wife introduces herself in the title poem with the declaration "Once, my braids hung heavy as ropes" and recalls the meeting with and marriage to the butcher, Otto Kröger, as an intense interlude ended by his death. The poems are like entries in a diary of her days with him, in "the dark of the shop" and in their home. She has married him, a widower, and adopted his children, responding to his proposal—"Otto asked me on the westbound bus/ to marry him,"—by acting on the ethic of the community: "I could not tell him no—/ We help our neighbors out. I loved him though/ It took me several years to know I did/ from that first time he walked in to deliver/ winter food."

The couple's lives are intertwined with those of their friends and neighbors, distinctive characters, often irritating, like "Step-and-a-Half Waleski" whose "headlong occurrence unnerved even Otto" but for whom "mine is a good word, and even that hurts./ A rhyme-and-a-half for a woman of parts," or unsettling, like Otto's sister Hilda, whose words "cut/ me serious—her questioning my life" but who touches the butcher's wife, who says "I think I loved her too/ in ways that I am not sure how to tell."

The sheer physicality of life is evident in the frequent references to the body's responses, which are paralleled by the requirements of the profession, constantly involved with animals, graphically and indelibly present "blood smeared on the lintel./ Mallet or bullet they lunge toward their darkness." One of the butcher's wife's most endearing thoughts about Otto is her fond recollection that "there was no one so deft/ as my Otto. So true, there is great tact involved/ in parting the flesh from the bones it loves."

After ten years of life with Otto's family and the idiosyncratic people of the town, the butcher's wife undergoes a transition and reformation. The last poem, "New Vows," implies a return to an earlier aspect of existence, something like a resurrection of primal values from native life that have been temporarily displaced by Euro-American ones. "Widowed by men, I married the dark firs," she declares. Although she "can't tell you yet/ how truly I belong," she has rediscovered an ancient language "through which, at certain times, I speak in tongues."

The section that follows, "The Seven Sleepers," has been described by the publishers as "a passionate search for the divine in all its forms." The poems are not as systematically organized as those in previous sections, but they constitute a journey of exploration that includes a review of a life cast in terms of "The Sacraments," starting with "Baptism" and continuing on to "Extreme Unction." The title section is a meditation on "Seven Christian youths of Ephesus" who hid in a cave to escape persecution in 250 C.E. and emerged, still young, two hundred years later. Erdrich notes that the seven sleepers are the patron saints of insomniacs, and the poems are replete with dream images, visions, and suggestive symbols. Other poems touch on well-known personages like Mary Magdalene and Jesus Christ in various guises. In an abrupt, even seismic shift, the last two poems in this section radically alter tone and stance as Erdrich, acting as "emissary of the between-world," adopts the structure of Christian prayer to fashion two sardonic supplications from an American Indian place. "The Buffalo Prayer" is addressed to versions of debased or destroyed Indian relics, setting a downward progression from "Our Lady of the Buffalo Bones" to "Our Lady of Destruction Everywhere" to "Our Lady of the Testicle Tobacco Pouch," ending with a request: "pray for us whose bones have nourished/ the ordered cornfields that have replaced/ the random grass which fed and nurtured and gave us life."

The dark humor of this poem is considerably exceeded by the bitterly hilarious catalog of plagues infecting Indian culture in "Rez Litany," an example of the comic counterattack employed by some American Indian writers. This stinging, satiric song of anger functions as a purgative agent, permitting a gentle final section, "Original Fire," with some poems on personal subjects, a retelling of another tribal story from the saga "Wampum Hair" by Nawaquay-geezhik (Charles Kawbawgam), a triad about a "New Mother," a note of "Advice to Myself," and the six-poem cycle "Asiniig," which is based on the Ojibway word for stone, *asin*. "Stones are alive," a prefatory note explains, and the poems in the cycle are cast as an abbreviated creation myth. "When the original fire which formed us/ subsided," the poet explains, the human species was created by the spirits of the stones, who "are still deciding whether that was/ wise." In these poems, the diction is direct, the rhythms straight and simple, the stanzaic structure basic.

These works lead toward the last poem in the volume. "Infinite Thought" is a kind of summation (although not a conclusion, as the poem is open-ended), expanding outward toward the entire cosmos. The stones are an emblem of a primal substance, and the poem suggests that human life on earth has deteriorated in terms of the separation of the human from the eternal. The poem is like a message. "Listen," it begins, "there is no consciousness/ before birth or/ after death/ except the one you share/ with us," and concludes with the reminder of how the world was viewed before the time when cultures mix and collide: "Your consciousness/ is the itch, the ghost of consciousness,/ remembered/ from how it felt/ to be one of us."

Leon Lewis

Review Source

Booklist 100, no. 2 (September 15, 2003): 195.

ORYX AND CRAKE

Author: Margaret Atwood (1939-   )
Publisher: Nan A. Talese/Doubleday (New York).
   374 pp. $26.00
Type of work: Novel
Time: The mid-twenty-first century
Locale: New York State

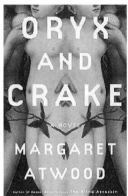

Atwood's disturbing novel reveals a storm-wracked Earth, where corporate greed and arrogant science have run amok, leaving the world in ruins

Principal characters:
> SNOWMAN (formerly known as JIMMY), a survivor of a global catastrophe
> CRAKE, a scientist, his lifelong friend
> ORYX, a young Asian woman, lover of both men
> JIMMY'S MOTHER, a microbiologist
> JIMMY'S FATHER, a genetic scientist
> THE CHILDREN OF CRAKE, green-eyed, genetically engineered humanoids

Oryx and Crake, Margaret Atwood's second view of dystopia, reveals a bug-ridden creature near a newly formed American seashore after the icecaps have melted. He calls himself Snowman, after the Abominable Snowman, "a white illusion of a man . . . existing and not existing." His name used to be Jimmy, he used to love words, and he is trying to stay alive. Scraps of sentences, random phrases, surface in his brain. He savors rare old words that are disappearing inside his head. When he forgets them, they will vanish forever from the world.

In his "authentic-replica" Red Sox baseball cap and a filthy sheet that protects him from the ultraviolet rays, Snowman watches the Children of Crake on the beach, naked innocents in a perverse Eden, as they bring him their broken treasures washed in by the waves. They speak simply and cannot read. Snowman is their mythmaker, inventing stories for the adult Children in exchange for their weekly tribute of fish. They remain in awe of him because he alone has seen their creator, Crake, a brilliant scientist and Snowman's best friend, with whom he still pretends to communicate by means of a broken wristwatch. They are fearless; he is terrified.

These humanoid Children are the product of Crake's creative gene-splicing at RejoovenEsense, a highly competitive corporate Compound. They possess luminous green eyes (courtesy of a deep-sea jellyfish gene) and citrus-scented skin which discourages the mosquitoes that plague Snowman. Their innocence is ingrained, too; their brains have been altered to exclude thoughts of hierarchy, racism, and religion. They have been programmed to survive.

Margaret Atwood has published more than thirty volumes of fiction, nonfiction, and poetry. Her novel The Blind Assassin *(2000) was awarded Britain's prestigious Booker Prize, and* Alias Grace *(1996) won both Canada's Giller Prize and Italy's Premio Mondello.*

The novel alternates between present and past action, viewed through the memories of Snowman-Jimmy. His father is a genographer, first at OrganInc Farms and later at the HelthWyzer Compound. These walled, fortresslike Compounds employ scouts to recruit the best scientific minds and security forces to protect their people. Competition between the biotechnological Compounds is fierce and deadly; the truly talented are automatically at risk of kidnapping or worse. Jimmy's father has been selected as an architect of the Pigoon Project, creating bigger, fatter pig hosts designed to grow multiple human-tissue organs and replace human skin.

Unlike Jimmy's pragmatic father, Jimmy's mother is a scientific idealist. As a microbiologist, she has modified living organisms to protect the pigoons against infection, but she is disillusioned by the increasing commercialization of science, "a moral cesspool." Depressed, she eventually flees the Compound, leaving Jimmy with a farewell note and a few cryptic postcards. She becomes an antitechnology activist, hunted by the relentless Corporation Security Corps (CorpSeCorps); occasionally Jimmy glimpses her on the television news.

The adolescent Jimmy is a confused dreamer. Green-eyed Crake, intelligent and relatively unemotional, is his new high school lab partner. When the teenagers play the Web game Extinctathon (identifying creatures that have become extinct within the past fifty years), he adopts the code name "Crake" (after an Australian marsh bird), which quickly replaces his real one. The boys also enjoy violent computer games like Blood and Roses, in which human atrocities are pitted against human achievements. While Jimmy prefers to focus on achievements, the more detached Crake favors the atrocities. These opposites seem to identify them, yet Jimmy's mother once told him that Crake is "intellectually honourable" and "doesn't lie to himself." Jimmy remains suspicious.

The boys also roam the Internet to view live beheadings (hedsoff.com), assisted suicides (nitee-nite.com), and continuous pornography. For them, the line between simulation and reality blurs; they fail to recognize reality when they see it. Crake, amused, argues that what they are watching is staged, not real. However, they accidentally discover a real little girl, Oryx, on a child pornography Web site (HottTotts), and Jimmy is stunned by her accusing gaze.

Although both of Crake's parents die mysteriously before his high school graduation, he remains at the top of his class, while Jimmy places in the middle even though his word scores are high. Crake is accepted as a transgenics student at the top-rated Watson-Crick Institute, but Jimmy goes to the seedy Martha Graham Academy, named for "some gory old dance goddess." This shabby school is poorly regarded, still possessing old-fashioned books in an antiquated library, and here Jimmy acquires his love of words. Culturally, study in the humanities is seen as a waste of time, an idea with which Crake appears to agree, but Jimmy prophetically does not: "When any civilization is dust and ashes, . . . art is all that's left over."

The discovery of ChickieNobs—a new food product developed at Watson-Crick, an "animal-protein tuber" that grows only chicken breasts, with no apparent brain, legs, or beak—horrifies Jimmy, who likens it to "eating a large wart." Believing that an ethical line has finally been crossed, he anticipates further problems, but Crake dismisses them. Still, Crake screams in his sleep every night.

Eventually Crake is hired at RejoovenEsense, which panders to the human desire for perfection and immortality, to create babies on order with preselected characteristics. Meanwhile Jimmy, now an advertising copywriter, is penning promotions for pills and workout equipment. He is skilled enough to convince himself with his own slogans. After seven years of increasing power and influence, Crake wants Jimmy on his team and ultimately convinces him to join the project he has spearheaded—the perfected Children of Crake. He is also working on immortality through the BlyssPluss Pill, which will increase human sexual energy, protect against sexually transmitted diseases, and prolong youth. It is also a birth control pill which is secretly intended to sterilize people. Jimmy will be in charge of the advertising campaign.

Crake brings Jimmy to the sealed bubble dome called Paradice, where Crake's creations, the Children, live. Here an adult Oryx reenters Jimmy's life as the Children's teacher. Delicate, fragile Oryx is from Southeast Asia, sold by her mother to various men who exploited her until she reached the United States and Crake ordered her from student (sexual) services at Watson-Crick. In flashbacks, she relates her life story to Jimmy, who idealizes her. Even though a prostitute, Oryx represents to him what is beautiful and good. He is outraged by her history, but she refuses to be angry or place blame; like Crake, she is practical. She always deflects the hard questions—nothing is unpleasant, nothing is painful. Jimmy, jealous and unsure of himself, is absolutely smitten with her. Then hemorrhagic fever abruptly breaks out in Brazil, and it is up to him to lead the Children out of Paradice.

Atwood's earlier dystopian novel, *The Handmaid's Tale* (1985), assumes a patriarchal United States in the grip of Christian fundamentalists who have relegated women to their biblical roles as wives, breeders, and servants. *Oryx and Crake* is written more in the spirit of the disintegrating societies envisioned by two English authors, Aldous Huxley and George Orwell. Huxley's *Brave New World* (1932) posits an England some six hundred years in the future, where a joyless bureaucracy drugs its citizens with soma (just as Atwood's characters ingest libido-enhancing BlyssPluss), while human reproduction and development are relegated to laboratory control (as are the Children of Crake and the many genetically altered animals like the huge, glowing green rabbits and sinister pigoons).

Orwell's landmark *Nineteen Eighty-Four* (1949), saturated with political slogans in a language (Newspeak) specifically designed to prevent thought, examines the repressive government of Oceania (England) under the watchful eye of the infamous Big Brother. Likewise, in the tightly regulated Compounds under the control of giant corporations, Atwood has created her own brand of Newspeak with ChickieNobs, pleeblands (cities), and CorpSeCorps.

Something has gone dreadfully wrong in Atwood's brave new world. Human selfishness and greed are unrestrained, demanding ever more wealth and power. People are undone by their fascination with sensation and mindless pleasure (Crack Cocaine perfume, high energy Joltbars for that extra surge, debasing pornography). Far more than corporate science is out of control. There is an abuse of nature, an absence of ethics, and a lack of concern for the consequences. A civilization, largely indifferent to people who mysteriously fall off overpasses or become fatally ill without explanation, has lost its humanity. Oddly enough, the cold-eyed Crake sees all this, but his proposed solution seems doubtful. His hope is to start all over again, believing that "all it takes is the elimination of one generation. . . . Break the link in time between one generation and the next, and it's game over forever." By eradicating all human weaknesses in the laboratory, he will make the world a better place.

Atwood is noted for her acerbic wit, and her dark humor is especially evident in her description of the so-called improvements made to the Children of Crake. For example, Crake has accelerated their childhood so that they are adolescents by four (not wasting time on infancy) and will drop dead at thirty, thus eliminating the problems of old age. A lusty rutting season controls their population, is designed to eliminate jealousy and infidelity, and includes a hilarious mating dance of blue-tinged, ecstatic males. Other animal behaviors have also been programmed into them; thus twice daily the males solemnly mark their territory with their urine to warn off predators. As always when reading Atwood, one learns things one may not want to know—in this case, all about cecotrophs.

Oryx and Crake is speculative fiction, offering an unnerving glimpse of a possible future much too close to present reality, but the book is not without hope. Some characters do exhibit empathy, and the Children are not as rigidly programmed as it first seems. Perhaps Alex the parrot, the actual subject of an animal behavior study, may serve as a final symbol. Alex becomes bored with the tests given him, invents some new words, and then simply flies off to take charge of his own life. Maybe Snowman will follow.

Joanne McCarthy

Review Sources

America 189, no. 4 (August 18, 2003): 24-25.
Booklist 99, no. 14 (March 15, 2003): 1252.

The Economist 367, no. 8322 (May 3, 2003): 76.
Kirkus Reviews 71, no. 6 (March 15, 2003): 408.
Library Journal 128, no. 8 (May 1, 2003): 152.
Maclean's 116, no. 17 (April 28, 2003): 44-49.
The New Republic 229, no. 12 (September 22, 2003): 31-36.
The New York Times, May 13, 2003, p. E9.
The New York Times Book Review, May 18, 2003, p. 12.
The New Yorker 79 (May 19, 2003): 88.
Publishers Weekly 250, no. 14 (April 7, 2003): 44.
Time 161, no. 20 (May 19, 2003): 72.

THE OTHER SIDE OF SILENCE

Author: André Brink (1935-   )
Publisher: Harcourt (New York). 311 pp. $25.00
Type of work: Novel
Time: The early 1900's
Locale: Bremen, Germany, and South-West Africa

Through the story of one woman's wretched life, the violence and violation that African natives and women suffered in the German-ruled colony of South-West Africa are revealed

> *Principal characters:*
> HANNA X, first a young girl in a German orphanage, then an abused and mutilated woman in Africa
> FRÄULEIN BRAUNSCHWEIG, Hanna's teacher and only friend
> FRAU AGATHE, the head of the orphanage where Hanna lives
> PASTOR ULRICH, the orphanage's spiritual adviser
> LOTTE, Hanna's friend and lover during the voyage to Africa
> KATJA, a young woman alone in Africa whom Hanna befriends
> THE REV. GOTTLIEB MAIER, a Christian missionary in Africa

André Brink frames *The Other Side of Silence* with an author's commentary to explain that much of the novel draws from the history of the German colony formerly known as South-West Africa. Brink establishes how the German government, during the early twentieth century, sent to Africa destitute German women—of childbearing age—to become the male colonists' wives and to produce a new generation of Germans who would rule and exploit the region for years to come. He also reveals how the men rejected some of the women whom they considered unattractive or disobedient or barren. These castoffs ended up in a remote settlement called the *Frauenstein*, where they lived isolated lives and occasionally served as sex partners for the German soldiers who were patrolling the countryside. Historical documents support all of these lurid details.

What intrigues Brink, though, are the actual women who made the trip to Africa in search of a better life. Their names and vital statistics appear in archives, but the reality of their womanhood and their individuality has been lost. Here the fiction writer sets out to re-create one of these desperate travelers, a person actually named Hanna X. She evolves into a kind of "everywoman" as she is cast into the colonial wilderness and left to the mercy of the dominant male population. Brink explains going through the records and discovering the woman to whom he gives life: "The name was what first intrigued me. Hanna X. . . . Town of origin, Bremen. That much was known, but no more."

In telling Hanna X's story, Brink recounts as well the brief but brutal history of Germany's colonial project. With the sanction of other European powers, South-West Africa—bordered by the Atlantic Ocean, South Africa, Botswana, and Angola—

became an official German colony in 1890, even though German traders had already established outposts there. During World War I, South Africa occupied the territory, then annexed it after World War II. Following years of revolts led by native Marxist organizations, independence finally came in 1990 under a United Nations peace plan. Now known as Namibia, the country is rich in diamonds and minerals—which is what attracted the Germans at the outset.

A versatile South African writer, André Brink has published fiction, drama, criticism, and essays in English and Afrikaans. Nominated twice for the Booker Prize, Brink has received the South African CNA Award three times. The French government has recognized his work by naming him a chevalier of the Legion of Honor.

Hanna's sad tale unfolds in a series of disconnected fragments that follow no chronological pattern, which is a typical narrative device used by Brink. Her experiences in Germany and Africa interweave with one another to reveal a life beset by cruelty, disappointment, and loss. An orphan, Hanna grows up in Bremen, a gloomy German port city near the North Sea. She spends her early years in a church-operated institution called the Little Children of Jesus, where she regularly receives beatings, goes hungry, and endures the presiding minister's sexual abuse. Turning old enough to go into service, Hanna is dispatched to a series of homes. There the mistresses of the various houses mistreat her, and the masters molest her.

Hanna, an ugly but intelligent girl, finds her only solace with a teacher who introduces her to literature and history—in particular Joan of Arc's story, which plays an important role later in Hanna's African experience. As a woman without means but with an adventurous spirit, she signs up to immigrate to South-West Africa. On the way out she shares a cabin with a young woman named Lotte. They engage in a sexual relationship, which ends when one of the ship's officers rapes Lotte. Suffering from his continued sexual brutality, Lotte dies and is buried at sea.

Once Hanna arrives in the colony's main settlement, she faces disillusionment when paired with a coarse farmer whom she refuses to marry. As a consequence, she finds herself on a train heading to *Frauenstein*. An officer attempts to rape her during the journey, but she bites his penis when he inserts it into her mouth. After he recovers, he orders his subalterns to punish Hanna. They cut out her tongue, trim off her nipples, and mutilate her genitals, then throw her off the train into the desert. Natives rescue Hanna, and after healing her wounds they deliver the woman to *Frauenstein*.

Enduring a lengthy period of resignation in the confines of this secular nunnery, Hanna finally takes action when a soldier during a drunken orgy attempts to rape Katja, a young girl whom she has befriended and for whom she has developed a sexual longing. She murders the intruder and buries his body. Soon after this act she and Katja leave *Frauenstein* and venture into the desert. As events unfold in a surreal fashion, Hanna forms a ragtag army consisting of outcast natives and the bitter wife of a German missionary. Like Joan of Arc in her mission to free France, Hanna leads the avengers into attacks on the German Reich to rid the land of this menace. Hanna's ultimate goal is to find the officer who ordered her mutilation and to exact her revenge. The tightly constructed passages that recount the military exploits of Hanna and her army provide high adventure. Brink excels at forceful yet economic narrative that lends immediacy and vitality to the action.

Throughout the novel a denunciation of the colonial experiment emerges in an effective and original way. In fact, Brink's indictment of the Germans' savagery toward those they considered savages is one of the strongest literary records of imperialism's dark side. Brink calls once more on the historical record to bring events into focus. In 1904 the Germans' appropriation of land and resources, their racist attitudes toward the natives, and their mistreatment of them, along with the catastrophic cattle plague, led the Herero and Nama tribes to rise up against these unwelcome occupiers. The revolt was a hopeless one, for the Germans, with their superior army, quickly and ruthlessly quelled the uprising. One historian has called the retaliation, led by a general named von Trotha, the first genocide of the twentieth century. Tens of thousands of the native people were slaughtered or were forced into starvation when driven into the wilderness of the Kalahari desert. This well-documented scourge hovers in the background throughout *The Other Side of Silence*.

Brink's prose style resembles the rhythmic sound of a stormy sea crashing against rocks. The breathless and choppy sentence structure manages to lend clarity to a multitude of characters and exactness to complex events, either personal or historical. Even when the uneven constructions appear overwrought or repetitious or self-conscious—as they sometimes do—the prose redeems itself in its rare mixture of suggestiveness and frankness. Here is a typical passage, which records Hanna's thoughts as her army is disintegrating and her mission of revenge is turning futile:

> Is this what she has become—an avenging demon? Nothing but this? In the dark silence, long after Katja has gone to sleep, Hanna remains looking up at the night. Words cannot reach where she wants to go. Only sounds and images remain. The sound of a piano broken apart, all its strings exploding, releasing the pent-up sound of years, lifetimes, darknesses. And behind the sound, the shadow of a woman she will never know and has never met, yet who will haunt her for ever, the shadow of whatever has remained unrealised in herself. *The second part is for you.*

Another of Brink's stylistic hallmarks is his graphic depiction of violence. In this novel, like much of his earlier work, such as *An Instant in the Wind* (1976) and *A Chain of Voices* (1982), blood flows freely, castrations and sexual mutilation multiply, bodies suffer dismemberment—all delineated in explicit detail.

This account of South-West Africa's bloody history under German rule evolves into dual and closely related thematic statements: one the stuff of violence, the other of violation. The European conquest of Africa in the nineteenth century grew out of violence, even as the interlopers declared that they were bearing "the white man's burden" to civilize and lift up the savages. While the destruction of the native peoples in South-West Africa may be the most barbaric exercise in the history of colonial power, the Germans were not alone in enforcing the white man's will once it was threatened. The Belgians in the Congo, along with the British in South Africa and the

French in other regions, share the guilt, which Brink makes universal in his recollection of the massacre in the German colony.

It has been said that Africa was conquered by Bibles as well as guns. The German missionary depicted in the novel does not carry out violent actions against the Africans. In a way, he practices something worse: that is, the act of violation. By trying to convert the so-called heathen to Christianity, the missionary violates the core of a people's culture—their customs, traditions, and beliefs. Holding nothing but contempt for his converts, he acts as though he is dealing with a total blankness on which he can inscribe a superior set of values. Ironically, in German his first name, Gottlieb, means Godlove.

While colonial Africa turned into a dangerous place for its native peoples, women in their own way also fared badly in this masculine world. The practice of sending out hapless women as breeders for the empire was not limited to Germany. England, for example, supplied Australia with woman convicts. According to one account, the day a ship carrying this human resource arrived in Sydney Harbor, the governor remarked: "There's another boatload of those damned whores." Brink's vivid description of the women's arrival in South-West Africa carries the same implication: that women are second-class creatures intended to serve and to be subservient to men.

How much Brink exaggerates the violence these hapless women experienced is difficult to determine. The rapes and multiple attacks likely did take place in a community of men who had been living in an uncivil environment without female companionship. While the extent of the violence might remain in question, the personal and physical violation the women suffered cannot be disputed.

Robert L. Ross

Review Sources

Booklist 99, no. 18 (May 15, 2003): 1637.
Kirkus Reviews 71, no. 8 (April 15, 2003): 550.
Library Journal 128, no. 4 (March 1, 2003): 116-117.
The New York Times Book Review, August 3, 2003, p. 6.
The New Yorker 79, no. 14 (June 2, 2003): 94.
Publishers Weekly 250, no. 14 (April 7, 2003): 42.
The Times Literary Supplement, September 13, 2002, p. 23.

OUR LADY OF THE FOREST

Author: David Guterson (1956-   )
Publisher: Alfred A. Knopf (New York). 323 pp. $25.95
Type of work: Novel
Time: 1999
Locale: North Fork, Washington

A sickly homeless girl in the depressed Pacific Northwest sees visions of the Virgin Mary; her claims draw multitudes, while various locals reckon with personal issues

Principal characters:
ANN HOLMES, a fifteen-year-old homeless
    mushroom picker
FATHER DONALD COLLINS, a small-town
    Catholic priest
CAROLYN GREER, a homeless woman in her twenties and Ann's guardian
    friend
TOM CROSS, a surly, unemployed logger with a volatile temper
ELEANOR CROSS, Tom's estranged wife and mother of Tom Junior
FATHER BUTLER, Father Collins's superior
TAMMY, a waitress at the Big Bottom tavern and Tom Cross's occasional
    lover
SHERIFF RANDOLPH NELSON, the local sheriff and Tom Cross's former
    classmate

Set against the landscape of an economically ravaged logging town in Washington near a privately owned rain forest, David Guterson's *Our Lady of the Forest* continues to demonstrate the author's intimate connection with the American wilderness. The town of North Fork has "sawn down its adjoining forests with purposeful enthusiasm," and now the only work unemployed loggers can get is at the local prison or the Punjabi-owned motel. Father Donald Collins, who runs the church, even has second thoughts about living and working here. The faithful remain few, and the jaded ex-loggers knock back beers and spout expletives during halftime.

Where *East of the Mountains* (1998), set in Eastern Washington, examines the personal crisis of a suicidal physician dying of cancer and *Snow Falling on Cedars* (1994) concerns tensions between people living on an island in Puget Sound, *Our Lady of the Forest* explores issues of faith, salvation, and redemption.

Henry David Thoreau writes in *Walden: Or, Life in the Woods* (1854) that he went to the woods "because [he] wanted to live deliberately, to front only the essential facts of life." In Guterson's novel, those who live near his Washington State forest appear merely to exist. They are social dropouts, miscreants, and directionless itinerants with questionable motives. Nevertheless, there is something ethereal and compelling about Ann Holmes, frequently referred to as "the visionary." Holmes ran away from home after suffering sexual abuse at the hands of her mother's drug-addicted boyfriend. She fights a persistent flu, appearing even more withdrawn as she alone witnesses visions of the Virgin Mary, who urges the girl to build a forest church. Carolyn Greer, Ann's friend and a sarcastic atheist, interprets her friend's visitations as being like those of "the sleepwalker engaged in a conversation with nobody in the room. Like the dreamer who falls from bed at night in lieu of a dream-world death." While Greer remains unconvinced, Ann's visions initiate a charismatic movement, the likes of which no one in North Fork has seen before.

In a morally bankrupt town, the priest's role is especially challenging. Husbands and wives keep secrets from each other, as each resident of this perpetually damp and forlorn place does from himself or herself. Father Collins lives in a trailer park, grappling with his corporeal desires like any man. When the visionary speaks with him about her first sighting, the priest notices that "she was slim, wet, and plainly ill, and she evoked in him both professional pity and a burst of sexual desire."

Guterson provides for all his characters detailed backgrounds. In such skilled hands, these backgrounds become like skeletons, through and around which all the connective tissues, muscles, and skin of the characters grow. Father Collins's domineering father whipped him "ten times on his bare backside, the number ten emblematic of order." He smoked marijuana and made out with a girl on a boat cruise. Father Collins is not the quintessentially forebearing priest, nor does he readily embrace Holmes's assertion about her visions, even though he secretly finds the waif attractive. When he is called upon to minister to Tom Cross, Junior, paralyzed and in a wheelchair, Collins can hardly bear to be in the boy's company. Tom Cross, his cruel father, readily admits to Father Collins his responsibility for Junior's paralysis. In a confessional scene, without quotation marks, Cross and Father Collins dialogue: "I caused it. But why would you do that? Cuz I hated his guts. You hated your son. I have a lot of hate . . . I'm evil, said Tom Cross. There's a hole in me."

With Holmes the angelic presence in the novel, Cross evolves into the lurching demoniac presence. Ironically, however, both characters search for salvation. Holmes has a burning desire for salvation under the belief she must cleanse herself of the molestation she suffered, while Cross stumbles through meaningless sex, petty thievery, and eventually an explosive confrontation in search of his salvation.

As the visionary's health worsens, she goes a second time into the woods to receive Mary, now with a dozen "pilgrims" and Father Collins in tow. When her vision appears, the priest is struck by Holmes's transformation: "In the throes of rapture, Ann appeared more diminutive than ever, her hood close like a monk's cowl . . . her hands clasped in desperate supplication, and he tried to commit her image to memory . . . It was going to have an effect on him, an impact on his ministry." Rather than making a value judgment on the genuineness of Holmes's visions, Guterson simply

∼

David Guterson taught high school English, later writing for Sports Illustrated *and working as contributing editor for* Harper's Magazine. *His works include* The Country Ahead of Us, The Country Behind *(1989),* Snow Falling on Cedars *(1994), and* East of the Mountains *(1998), and he has cofounded Field's End, a writing workshop.*

∼

allows his characters the experience. The first time Father Collins witnesses her going into ecstasy, "no one did a thing, not even the priest, who had to admit that he too felt spellbound and in the presence of something holy. The moment passed. His wavering skepticism righted itself."

Tom Cross once owned a successful timber business; that is, until circumstances forced him to sell his equipment for 10 percent of what he had paid. The bank took his house, while the Stinson Lumber Company, which seems to own the whole forest, continued its ruthless practices. What threatens to unglue Cross, beyond his redundancy as wage earner, is his eminent divorce from his wife, Eleanor, who surrounds herself with her zealous girlfriends and has her lawyer at the ready every time Cross ignores his restraining order.

Cross lives in a motel now. Working as the occasional handyman for the Punjabi couple who own the motel and as a night guard at the jail, Cross's dark resentment steadily rises. In addition to the conflict with his wife, Cross must live each day with the knowledge of having permanently paralyzed his son. Junior is the antithesis of his macho father, a scared computer nerd with zero interest in sports or logging. In a frenzied attempt to make a man out of him, Cross forced his son out into the forest to cut down a tree. The tree fell in the wrong direction, crushing the boy and snapping his neck. There is nowhere Cross can go and nothing he can do to redeem himself—except perhaps to the visionary.

Cross prowls about the periphery of action as pilgrims amass. Once-barren hotels fill with the faithful. Convenience stores and restaurants swell, too, as an Internet site reports on the sightings. Americans have a particular propensity toward a circuslike atmosphere when it comes to certain events: alien sightings, religious sightings, a celebrity's arrest. All draw the curious and the media in equal proportions. "Motor homes were docked like ships but staggered for access to their doors and here and there in the incidental places were arrangements of aluminum lawn chairs . . . A banner read KAY'S RELIGIOUS GIFTS; under it were plastic crucifixes, books, cassettes, and videotapes." Further along, Cross overhears a conversation between two men in a restroom as they exchange boasts about their religious photographs. The pilgrims eventually number in the thousands, threatening the forest's fragile ecosystem. Their compulsion toward a religious epiphany does not assume a sensitivity or compassion for the suffering of others. "A man doused a hard-boiled egg with salt . . . while a hungry man watched with concealed longing. This same juxtaposition of food and desire played itself out through the forest. It was the same with drinking water." Guterson acknowledges both the need for the extraordinary and the callousness inherent in human beings.

When Stinson Lumber finally steps in and refuses passage to the clearing where Holmes has her visions, Greer, bullhorn in hand, acts as Holmes's self-appointed spokeswoman. Greer is an insincere, sharp-tongued itinerant, as self-serving as any of the other hucksters making a buck off of the faithful; however, there are moments when the visionary almost moves Greer out of her sarcastic atheism. Still, she passes buckets around for donations, fantasizing about how she will spend the money: "The ramshackle campground made Greer yearn impatiently for Cabo San Lucas. She would sleep naked there and eat fruit and rice, drink margaritas, get high at 9 A.M., take pick-me-up tokes as needed. Shop for limes and tonic water; read travel books beneath the palm trees." Father Butler, appointed by the bishop to verify the visitations, remains deeply skeptical, particularly after he learns that Holmes has ingested hallucinogenic mushrooms.

Meanwhile, Cross has been kicked out of his lousy motel room, lost his prison guard gig, and caused a ruckus at his wife's house. Despite the economic downturn, loss of his business, and his son's paralysis, Cross appears to need little reason for going over the edge. Described as a woebegone Marlboro Man, Cross keeps an arsenal of guns in his car, and his emotions coil like a viper inside him. He finds himself compelled toward Holmes, from whom he catches "the barest hint of her eyes assessing him. Tom had once shot a raccoon in a culvert, the animal invisible except for luminous pupils that unsettled him . . . a penetrating moment of introspection before he'd squeezed the trigger." He also recognizes, though, that Holmes is just a child. As Cross grabs hold of her shoulder, he feels a force he hopes "might induce some kind of redemption," but instead Ann begins to cough uncontrollably. Greer steps in to protect her, assaulting Cross with pepper spray. The visionary dies from an asthmatic attack in the struggle.

Years later, Greer returns to find that Stinson Lumber had donated the land for a church, and the city had prospered enough from the pilgrimage to help pay for a beautiful edifice in the forest. Without taking sides, Guterson's exquisitely rendered novel avows the purifying effects of forgiveness while commenting wryly upon the United States' bizarre relationship with religious faith.

Nika Hoffman

Review Sources

Booklist 99, no. 22 (August 1, 2003): 1925.
Kirkus Reviews 71, no. 14 (July 15, 2003): 927.
Library Journal 128, no. 10 (June 1, 2003): 166.
Los Angeles Times, October 20, 2003, p. E1.
Los Angeles Times Book Review, September 28, 2003, p. R7.
The New York Times Book Review, November 2, 2003, p. 8.
Publishers Weekly 250, no. 30 (July 28, 2003): 75.
Time 162, no. 19 (November 3, 2003): 93.
The Times Literary Supplement, November 21, 2003, p. 21-22.

OWLS AND OTHER FANTASIES
Poems and Essays

Author: Mary Oliver (1935-   )
Publisher: Beacon Press (Boston). 67 pp. $22.00
Type of work: Poetry and essays

The newest collection of the renowned nature poet considers life, death, redemption, and reconciliation with the natural world through close and careful observation of birds

Mary Oliver, winner of the 1992 National Book Award, the 1984 Pulitzer Prize, and the 1998 Lannon Literary Award for poetry, offers in her newest collection twenty-six poems and two essays. *Owls and Other Fantasies* is beautifully illustrated with line drawings of bird feathers. While the poems and essays take a variety of birds as their subjects, they are also about the great cycle of life. For Oliver, closer to the end of her life than its beginning, the contemplation of birds brings meaning, reconciliation, and redemption.

Fittingly, "Wild Geese," Oliver's much-loved poem, opens the volume. Perhaps more than any other poem in the book, "Wild Geese" signals Oliver's purpose in this new collection: to welcome the reader home to the natural world. "You do not have to be good," she tells the reader. "You do not have to walk on your knees/ for a hundred miles through the desert, repenting." Like the wild geese overhead, the reader, too, is "heading home again." In lovely language and clear image, Oliver offers hope:

> Whoever you are, no matter how lonely,
> the world offers itself to your imagination,
> calls to you like the wild geese, harsh and exciting—
> over and over announcing your place
> in the family of things.

While the sentiment is reminiscent of "Desiderata," the invocation of the natural world removes the poem from sentimentality. Instead, Oliver leaves the reader with not only the sense of the passage of time but also with the sense of timelessness. Human beings are not the only children of the universe; rather, they are a part of the great family that includes geese, and owls, and hummingbirds.

Many of the poems take on a Zen-like quality through the precise and razor-sharp use of image. This is nowhere clearer than in the poem "Some Herons." One heron becomes "a blue preacher," while another is "an old Chinese poet,/ hunched in the white gown of his wings." The water is "dark silk/ that has silver lines/ shot through it/ when it is touched by the wind." While there is movement in this poem created by the arrival of additional herons, this movement does nothing to alter the impression of a still life, of a moment captured in words as surely as by a photograph.

Other poems in *Owls and Other Fantasies*, however, circle like hawks around questions of life and death. In "The Dipper," Oliver's poem about a small bird she observed more than fifty years before, the poet signals her understanding that her life is nearing its inevitable close: She muses that her sighting of the dipper happened "more than half a century ago— / more, certainly, than half my lifetime ago." This thought leads her to the conclusion that the dipper must have died many years earlier, "his crumble of white bones, his curl of flesh/ comfortable even so." For Oliver, the encounter with the dipper initiates her into the "ponderous book of riddles," the tome of nature. Through the dipper, she learns that "the world is full of leaves and feathers,/ and comfort, and instruction." In the book of nature, Oliver seems to assert, the reader can learn all that is worth learning.

~

Mary Oliver has published many volumes of poetry and essays, beginning with her 1963 No Voyage, and Other Poems, *and including her Pulitzer Prize-winning* American Primitive *(1984) and* New and Selected Poems *(1992), which won the National Book Award for poetry.*

~

Of all the birds observed in the book, Oliver seems to impart special significance to owls. Indeed, she devotes one full essay and two important poems to this bird. Spaced strategically across the collection, her references to owls serve to mark her growing understanding of and familiarity with death.

She begins this exploration in "Owls," a five-page essay selected by editor Robert Atwan for inclusion in *Best American Essays* (1996). "Owls" is a remarkable essay in terms of its language, its structure, and its growth. The essay opens with Oliver's narration of her hikes "upon the dunes and in the shaggy woodlands of the Provincelands" looking for the nest of the great horned owl. Her journey takes her past Pasture Pond, where more than a century earlier a Provincetown town crier reported his sighting of a six-headed sea serpent. Oliver does not ridicule this sighting; she merely reports it as she stares into the depths of the pond. This brief diversion signals the reader that this essay may be about far more than a hike in the woods looking for owls' nests.

Oliver marks a clear distinction between the screech owl and the great horned owl. She imagines that Athena's owl of wisdom, as well as Merlin's owl, were screech owls, and she says she can picture a screech owl "on my wrist." The great horned owl is another matter altogether. Perched in a tree above her, the great horned has "nothing but blood on its mind." She writes that "if one of those should touch me, it would touch to the center of my life, and I must fall. . . . I know this bird. If it could, it would eat the whole world."

Oliver's fear is not relieved by the screams of the owl's victims or by her discovery of headless rabbits and blue jays, evidence of the great horned owl's work in the world. There, however, is something even more terrifying:

> the scream of the owl, which is not of pain and hopelessness and the fear of being plucked out of the world, but of the sheer rollicking glory of the death-bringer, is more terrible still. When I hear it resounding through the woods, and then the five black pellets of its song dropping like stones into the air, I know I am standing at the edge of the mystery, in which terror is naturally and abundantly part of life.

At this most frightening of moments, the essay turns away from the owl and toward summer fields of roses. Oliver recalls that the sweetness of these flowers conquers her, that she is "filled to the last edges with an immobilizing happiness." She continues, "And is this not also terrible? Is this not also frightening?" It is here, at this moment of turning, that Oliver also begins a turn away from the fear of death and toward an embrace of the full cycle of life.

The second poem to explore the nature of owls is just past the mid-section of the book. "Little Owl Who Lives in the Orchard" contemplates a small owl, not the great horned type. Oliver here clearly identifies this owl with more than itself; she alludes to both William Blake and the Book of Revelation. The small owl is, like its larger cousin, a death-bringer. "Never mind," she writes, "that he is only a memo/ from the offices of fear." Whereas Oliver minimized the danger of the smaller owls in her essay, in this poem she recognizes the little owl for what he is. Her imagery here becomes sharp, precise, devastating: "I hear him in the orchard/ fluttering/ down the aluminum/ ladder of his scream." The scream causes a "flurry of palpitations/ as cold as sleet" that "racket[s] across the marshlands/ of my heart."

By the final stanza, Oliver recognizes the owl's role as one of the "important things" of the universe. The owl has been sent by "that mysterious conglomerate: *Oblivion and Co.*" Not only that, Oliver tells the reader, "the hooked head . . . could be a valentine." How does Oliver move from owl as object of fear to owl as symbol of love? The transition in this poem is swift, clearly one that needs further examination. Oliver provides this in her final owl poem, located late in the book.

In "White Owl Flies into and out of the Field," Oliver also examines death and the owl as the bringer of death. The owl, a skilled hunter and dangerous predator of the natural world, takes its place in the cycle of life. For Oliver, the owl is both "beautiful/ and accurate." The moment she captures is an owl's attack on some unnamed creature below:

> Coming down
> out of the freezing sky
> with its depths of light,
> like an angel,
> or a buddha with wings, . . .

The owl, then, is the angel of death: beautiful, luminous, swift. Tellingly, the owl's victim has no specificity. The reader does not know if it is some rabbit, or a vole, or a mouse snatched without warning. The victim becomes merely "whatever was there," and "what had been running." This contrast between the terrible and swift angel of death and the nameless, faceless, formerly living creature suggests to Oliver what happens to humans, too; perhaps death "isn't darkness, after all/ but so much light/ wrapping itself around us—/ as soft as feathers."

In the end, it is through death that all creatures escape the bonds of their bodies, "washed and washed/ out of our bones." The invocation of buddha in the fifth line of the poem suggests that, for Oliver, the owl (and by extension, death) offers the individual an escape from individuality, returning the individual to the grand community of nature, where all, ultimately, is one. In addition, the shape of the poem on the page seems to allude to metaphysical poet George Herbert's "Easter Wings." Oliver thus appeals not only to Christian notions of victory over death but also to an Eastern understanding of cycles.

"Long Afternoon at the Edge of Little Sister Pond," one of two closing poems, reinforces the Eastern notions of death and rebirth hinted at in the earlier poems. The first stanza opens with the words, "As for life . . . " Oliver seems to reflect back on her entire life, "how it has been hard as flint/ and soft as a spring pond." The fear and struggle sometimes evident in the earlier poems is gone; all that remains is the longing to lie down "at last/ to the long afterlife." The final stanza mirrors the opening: "As for death . . ." It seems as if Oliver here wants to close the poem and close her collection with hope: "I can't wait to be the hummingbird,/ can you?" These lines state openly her belief that all matter is returned to life. However, there is something strangely unsatisfying in these final two lines. After all the contemplation, the reflection, the struggle, these lines seem too sure, too pat.

Perhaps they seemed so to Oliver as well. She adds one additional poem, in an afterword. In the poem "Backyard," Oliver tells the reader that "I had no time to haul out all/ the dead stuff so it hung, limp/ or dry, wherever the wind swung it." She looks to the summer when the garden grows thick and untrimmed, around and over all the "dead stuff." Here, Oliver points toward the reclamation of Eden, the garden that eradicates all sign of human intervention. "The birds loved it," she closes. And with this, this slender volume of luminous prose and shimmering poetry comes rightly to a close, in the grand mystery of life.

Diane Andrews Henningfeld

Review Sources

Library Journal 128, no. 20 (December 15, 2003): 125.
Publishers Weekly 250, no. 29 (July 21, 2003): 188.

THE PALESTINIAN PEOPLE
A History

Authors: Baruch Kimmerling (1939-   ) and Joel S.
   Migdal (1945-   )
Publisher: Harvard University Press (Cambridge, Mass.).
   568 pp. $45.00
Type of work: History
Time: 1834-2002
Locale: Palestine

This new history updates the authors' 1993 book, Palestinians: The Making of a People, *with two new analyses,
one judging the effects of the Oslo peace talks and another
focusing on the difficult situation of Palestinians in Israel*

Principal personages:
> HAJ AMIN AL-HUSSEINI, the mufti of Jerusalem and president of the
>   Supreme Islamic Council, created in January, 1922
> YASSER ARAFAT, a long-time Palestinian activist who achieved world
>   prominence when in 1968, as its chairman, he reinvigorated the Pales-
>   tinian Liberation Organization (PLO)

In their preface, the authors immediately reject both the common claim by Palestinians that their history as a "singular people" reaches back to ancient times and the
Israeli denial of any such entity before it was created by Zionist successes. Instead, a
"self-identified Palestinian people" evolved only in the last two centuries, as a result
of European economic and political pressures and of Jewish settlement.

The authors stress, first, grass-roots changes in population distribution; second, the
relations between town and country, hill and plain, secular and religious, Christian
and Muslim, diaspora and Palestine-based, while ignoring claims of an essential Palestinian character; third, "capitalism's insidious penetration of the Ottoman Empire"
long before the rise of Zionism; and fourth, the central importance of the Palestinians,
with the Jews given a supporting role. The concept of a Palestinian society owes much
to the pressure exerted on it by Zionism, a fact recognized by Palestinians. Zionists,
however, have not acknowledged the effects on them of their engagement with the
Palestinians, for "perhaps doing so would involve too painful an encounter with Zionism's political counterpart—what we might call 'Palestinism': the belief that the Arab
population originating in the area of the Palestine mandate is distinct from other Arab
groups, with a right to its own nation-state in that territory."

Palestine is made up of the West Bank, the desert of the southern Negev, the narrow coastal strip that includes Gaza, Jaffa, Haifa, and Acre, and the beautiful valleys
and hills of the north. The story of Palestine's people is the history of the peasants,
who, with the large landowners, have enabled the emergence of a self-conscious society over the last two centuries. At the center of this history are three revolts: the unsuc-

cessful attempt in 1834 to thwart the Egyptian rulers' move to transform peasant society; the uprising in 1936-1939 against imperial Britain's dominance; and the *Intifada* ("shaking off") beginning in 1987 that sought fruitlessly to achieve political independence.

∾

Baruch Kimmerling is an associate professor of sociology at the Hebrew University of Jerusalem. Joel S. Migdal is chairman and professor of International Studies at the University of Washington.

∾

The 1834 outbreak began in May, ended in August with a brutal Egyptian victory, and was followed by broad changes in the peasants' lives. Subsistence farming succumbed to the high prices landowners enjoyed in selling their oranges, cotton, and other crops to European markets. The Egyptians had ruled Palestine only by Ottoman consent, and when the Ottomans returned in 1840 they instituted reforms that demanded titles of ownership for land, a policy that inevitably benefited the notables who quickly took over large tracts and left the peasants powerless. The initial wave of Jewish immigration into Palestine occurred in 1882, and as more Jewish immigrants arrived they changed the peasants' lives by buying the best land from absentee landlords. The influx of Russian Jews just before World War I included the core of the future Israeli leadership.

In the nineteenth century, inland towns such as Nablus, with their important families, declined in importance, while Haifa and Jaffa, bustling port cities, grew with innovations and vigorous trade. By the late 1920's, however, the economy had slowed, and Zionist labor policies forced Arab laborers into low-skilled jobs. Although family-oriented urban migrants retained their devotion to a myth of an idyllic rural life, their clumping together in cities encouraged social organizations and a growing intelligentsia that fostered a nascent Palestinian identity. Following the Great War, material culture bloomed under the British mandate, but the hill country peasants remained on the margins of this prosperity, forcing restless and unemployed young men and the urban poor into a revolutionary coalition that harassed Jewish settlers until the British quelled the rebels in 1935.

When the Jerusalem elite assumed more power after the 1834 revolt, Christians and Jews benefited, but the number of Muslims in administrative offices grew. Although the Ottomans prevented any one family from gaining dominance, the powerful clans of the Khalidis, the Alamis, and the Nashashibis earned experience that would help them later as advocates of Palestinian Arab nationalism. By the nineteenth century's end, the Jerusalem notables felt themselves at the center of events, began calling themselves Palestinians, and in 1891 sought to prevent Jews from buying land in Palestine. They were stunned, however, by Britain's facilitation of Jewish land acquisitions and by the 1917 Balfour Declaration, in which the British government announced its support for a Jewish homeland.

At the Third Arab Congress in 1920, the notables stressed Palestinian unity and independence as well as a rejection of any Jewish rights over Palestine. The collapse of Ottoman rule left Palestinian Muslims without a religious center, and the British tried to exert influence through a "compliant" Kamil al-Husseini, whom they appointed the first grand mufti of Jerusalem and the judge of the main Islamic law court. Upon

Kamil al-Husseini's death he was replaced by Haj Amin al-Husseini, whose positioning of Palestine at the center of Arab concerns made him the most significant figure in Palestine's history before Yasser Arafat. The convergence of Islam with swelling national feeling encouraged a sense of peril "to the moral state of Muslim society, through the corrupting practices brought to the country by the Jews, by the socialism and communism that many of the Zionists espoused, and by Western culture." Despite internal squabbles, by the mid-1930's a distinct Palestinian popular movement had evolved, largely thanks to the Jerusalem notables.

The rebellion of 1936-1939 reflected growing Palestinian nationalism and worries about Zionism, understood as an aspect of Western imperialism. A violent anti-British demonstration in Jaffa in 1933 foreshadowed the revolt that began there in April, 1936, and was supported by the leaders in Nablus. When Arabs in Nazareth assassinated the British commissioner, Lewis A. Andrews, in September, 1937, the British sought to arrest Amin al-Husseini, who went into exile but continued to influence events in Palestine. By this time peasant bands were mounting daily sabotage attacks against the British.

The collapse of the urban leadership coincided with a movement back to the hinterland by many new city dwellers, a reverse migration that produced, in effect, a class struggle by the peasants against the British, the Jews, and also the Arab notables. The bitter enmity between urban and rural Palestinians sent numerous well-to-do city Arabs into exile in Beirut. The general chaos often transformed rebels into rural bandits, and revulsion against their tactics led to civil war and the help of the antirebels in crushing the revolt in 1939. Despite the upheaval, the authors feel that "the revolt helped to create a nation—even while crippling its social and political basis."

Part 2, "Dispersal," reviews the disastrous Palestinian setbacks in 1947-1948. Widespread violence in Jerusalem followed the United Nations General Assembly's Resolution 181, passed on November 29, 1947, calling for the partition of the British-ruled Palestine Mandate into a Jewish state and an Arab state. The Palestinians' initial successes were followed by defeat and by Israel's declaration of independence on May 14, 1948. The war was marked by the Israelis' atrocities in the village of Dayr Yasin on April 9, a massacre that demonized the Israelis and helped elevate the war into a "cosmic injustice" in Palestinians' eyes. Israel's so-called Plan Dalet systematically banished potential enemies from the new state of Israel, resulting in a massive eviction of villagers and the destruction of their homes. Estimates of the number of refugees vary, but more than a half million must have been exiled, with no right to return. Around 400,000 migrated into that region of eastern Palestine, then part of Jordan and now officially the West Bank.

The disinherited Arabs living in Israel after 1948 became a powerless minority with curtailed rights, and the period after the 1967 war saw the collapse of agrarian life and the emergence of new political structures. The frustration of Israel's landless Arabs led on March 30, 1976, to Land Day, a strike that was suppressed by the police and reminded many Arabs of the Kfar Qassem massacre of 1956, when Israeli soldiers murdered forty-seven men, women, and children for breaking curfew in the fields. The outbreak of the first *Intifada* in 1987, combined with the broad Muslim revival in the Arab world and the shift toward negotiation in the Tunis-based Palestine Liberation Organization (PLO) policy, prompted political realignments. The riots of October, 2000, in Jerusalem expressed the anger of Israeli Arabs over their lack of civil liberties, despite their greater prosperity and political organization. Israeli Arabs in 2002 numbered more than one million, about 20 percent of the population, and the authors predict, "As the odd man out, the Palestinian citizens of Israel hold the promise of a new bridge to the future."

The dispersal of the Palestinians after 1948 was followed in 1967 by a reuniting of sorts when Israel took the Golan Heights from Syria, the Sinai and the Gaza Strip from Egypt, and the West Bank from Jordan. Face to face again with Jews, Palestinians identified with the *feday* ("one who sacrifices himself"), whose *kafiya* (traditional headcloth) and Kalishnokov rifle helped forge a Palestinian national consciousness; the passive hero of *sumud*, or steadfastness; and "the child of the stone," the rock throwing, tire burning rebel. The *Assifa* ("the storm"), the violent wing of the *Fatah* (Palestine National Liberation Movement), harassed the Israelis constantly with sabotage, and after the 1967 war the Fatah became the dominant group in Yasser Arafat's PLO. PLO power in Lebanon excited a civil war from 1975 to 1990 that claimed more than 100,000 lives and led to Arafat's move to Tunis. His helplessness was revealed by the Phalangists' 1982 slaughter of hundreds of Arab refugees in two camps near Beirut. The authors conclude that, despite its problems, the Fatah-dominated PLO "had nurtured a national mythology of heroism and sacrifice, the portrait of the downtrodden refugee giving way to that of the feday—which, in turn became the catalyst for the reconstruction of the national movement."

Economic discontent, as much as anything, sparked the 1987 *Intifada*, the uprising of the "children of the stone," with their *kafiyahs* and masks. The movement's effect on the Palestinian economy, however, was brutal, and the internal disagreements appear in the fact that in the occupied territories half as many Palestinians were killed as collaborators as died from Israeli military actions. The Iranian Revolution of 1978 abetted the rise of Hamas and Islamic Jihad, and the Islamic militant Sheikh Ahmad Ismail Yasin of Gaza agitated against the secular PLO until his arrest by Israel in 1989. The *Intifada* wrought significant change in that it "validated the replacement of the old landed elite with a new leadership based in the schools and universities of the West Bank and Gaza.

The Oslo talks in 1993 surprised everybody, and the Interim Agreement (Oslo II) of 1995 occasioned great optimism and revealed a large majority on both sides supporting it and accepting the other side's legitimacy. The accord replaced violence by negotiation, elicited a widespread acceptance of partition, and created the first Palestinian government. The Oslo process collapsed largely because Israel got what it wanted, a legitimate state secure in its boundaries, right up front, whereas the Palestinians' goals were scheduled to be met only gradually. The election of Benjamin Netanyahu in 1996 slowed negotiations, as did the Israelis' completion of a tunnel underneath Muslim holy sites in Jerusalem. Arafat's inability to control the Hamas militants revealed the Palestinians' internal political conflicts, and he was weakened by his failure to muster popular support for his concessions. The election of the right-wing candidate Ariel Sharon spelled the end for Oslo hopes. An excellent chronology and full notes enhance a book that deserves the widest possible readership.

Frank Day

Review Sources

Foreign Affairs 82, no. 5 (September/October, 2003): 187.
Library Journal 128, no. 4 (March 1, 2003): 106.
New Republic 228, nos. 15/16 (April 21, 2003): 31-42.
The Times Literary Supplement, August 1, 2003, p. 9.

PARTING THE DESERT
The Creation of the Suez Canal

Author: Zachary Karabell (1963-　)
Publisher: Alfred A. Knopf (New York). 310 pp. $27.50
Type of work: History
Time: The nineteenth century, especially 1854-1869
Locale: Primarily Egypt, with numerous events in Paris, London, and Istanbul

The story of how Ferdinand de Lesseps and his associates accomplished one of the great engineering feats of the nineteenth century, allowing large ships and Western influence to pass through the Muslim heartland

Principal personages:
> FERDINAND DE LESSEPS, an ex-diplomat who organized and supervised the ambitious Suez Canal project
> MUHAMMAD ALI, the founder of modern Egypt and its absolutist ruler from 1805 to 1848
> MUHAMMAD SAID PASHA, the ruler of Egypt (titled viceroy), 1854-1863
> ISMAIL PASHA, the ruler of Egypt (titled khedive), 1863-1879
> LORD PALMERSTON, the prime minister of Great Britain, 1855-1858 and 1859-1865
> NAPOLEON III, the emperor of France, 1851-1870
> EMPRESS EUGÉNIE, the wife of Napoleon III and Lesseps's cousin
> BARTHÉLEMY-PROSPER ENFANTIN, a mystical reformer who earlier promoted a canal
> BOGHOS NUBAR NUBARIAN, an Egyptian diplomat who led the effort to end forced labor

Zachary Karabell's *Parting the Desert* is a well-written and scholarly account of how one of the most important waterways in human history was conceived and constructed. Karabell concentrates on the ideas and activities of Ferdinand de Lesseps and the other prominent persons involved in the project, but his narration also provides abundant information about geography, cultural factors, political intrigue, and engineering problems. Throughout the book, Karabell demonstrates the extent to which the project was closely intertwined with the rivalries of the European powers within the region of the decaying Ottoman Empire, an imperial conflict known as the Eastern question.

The book is based on a prodigious amount of research in both primary and secondary sources. Karabell makes frequent references to the archives of the Suez Canal Company and the papers of Prosper Enfantin, both housed in France. In addition to using earlier works on the canal by J. E. Nourse and Lord Kinross, Karabell was able to study the published correspondence of Lesseps and other participants. He was also able to meet Ferdinand's descendent Alexander de Lesseps, who provided him with significant information about the history of his family. Karabell reports that there are very few Arabic sources on the subject, either in archives or publications.

~

Zachary Karabell, who holds a Ph.D. from Harvard University, has taught at his alma mater as well as at other major universities. He has published several books about American history and sociology, including Architects of Intervention *(1999),* The Last Campaign: How Harry Truman Won the 1948 Election *(2000), and* A Visionary Nation *(2001).*

~

The author observes that the idea of a canal to connect the Mediterranean Sea to the Red Sea goes back to ancient times. At least as early as the sixth century B.C.E., the Egyptians had constructed a canal that allowed small boats to travel from the Nile River to the Red Sea. Following several cycles of disrepair and redigging, this canal was entirely abandoned after the discovery of the trade route around the southern coast of Africa. Late in the eighteenth century, French emperor Napoleon's engineers investigated the possibility of digging a new maritime canal across the Egyptian isthmus. They concluded that such a project was probably impossible, in large part because they incorrectly calculated that the elevation levels of the two seas differed by about thirty feet, which would have meant a major problem of flooding.

Napoleon's expedition had the effect of instilling in France a passion for Egypt. Soon thereafter, Prosper Enfantin, a religious disciple of Henri de Saint-Simon, did even more than Napoleon's engineers to popularize the dream of linking the two seas. With his mystical perspective, Enfantin looked upon a canal as a means for achieving a spiritual connection between the East and the West. He and several followers traveled to Egypt with hopes of constructing a canal, but the rather strange delegation was unable to convince any political or financial leaders that such an ambitious project was possible. The reigning pasha of Egypt, Muhammad Ali, known as the founder of modern Egypt, agreed to meet with Enfantin in 1834, but the pasha had no interest in digging a canal, in large part because of his strong distrust of European imperialism.

Enfantin was a stubborn man who refused to abandon his dream. Returning to France, he organized the Suez Canal Study Group, which employed a number of outstanding engineers to do serious research into the feasibility of digging a canal. In 1847 the study group sent Robert Stephenson and other engineers to Egypt to conduct a land survey of the isthmus. The engineers concluded that there was little difference in the elevations of the two seas, which made the proposed canal seem more feasible than had been previously thought.

When Enfantin had visited Egypt, his ideas apparently had a profound impact on the thinking of Ferdinand de Lesseps, who was then in Egypt as a diplomatic representative of the French government. By a strange coincidence, the diplomat developed an extremely close relationship with Muhammad Ali, who decided in 1835 to give Lesseps the supervision his thirteen-year-old son, Muhammad Said. The pasha was especially desirous that the corpulent boy should lose weight. Lesseps, however, disregarded Ali's instructions and allowed the teenager to indulge in his craving for food, especially pasta. Lesseps took Said horseback riding almost daily, and Said came to consider him a mentor and a close friend. This friendship continued when Said later lived and studied in France.

Karabell describes Lesseps as "a potent combination of vision, pragmatism, and will." Without his vision, Lesseps could never have supported such a diverse group of people to invest so many resources into digging a canal across a hundred miles of almost uninhabited desert. Without his pragmatism, he could never have organized a venture that required so many technological innovations, including huge machines to dredge the soil and the largest jetty ever constructed. Without his stubborn will, he would never have been able to succeed when confronted with so many political rivalries, economic challenges, contradictory agendas, and engineering disagreements. Karabell writes: "A canal might have been built without Ferdinand de Lesseps, but not then, and not for many decades."

Following the revolutions of 1848 in Europe, Lesseps had the bad luck to be sent to Rome at a time that several rival armies confronted one another. As he struggled to bring order into an anarchistic situation, Lesseps lacked clear instructions about how to proceed, and the truce he negotiated displeased French officials in Paris. After being censored by the parliament, Lesseps was forced to submit his resignation. A few years thereafter, his wife and one of his sons died of scarlet fever. Karabell believes that Lesseps's sadness was of historical significance: "Lesseps himself would never have devoted himself so single-mindedly to implementing the project had he not suffered loss. . . . His pain became the source of his inspiration, and his ambition a way to heal himself." Whether or not this is true, in July, 1854, Lesseps learned that the Egyptian ruler, the older brother of Muhammad Said, had been assassinated, which meant that his friend and admirer now held the reins of power in Egypt.

Karabell finds abundant evidence that Lesseps had already digested and accepted the conclusions of Enfantin's study group. By November, 1854, Lesseps was in Egypt selling the idea of a canal to the new viceroy. It so happened that Said, who did everything in excess, was quite open to such suggestions. Optimistic about the prospects for his country, he was willing to borrow large sums of money in order to pursue a policy of modernization based on the models of Western Europe. Lesseps was a man with great persuasive skills who "had developed the silken tongue of a diplomat," and he "showered the new potentate with compliments." As soon as Lesseps explained how the canal would supply Egypt with power and wealth, Said immediately replied: "I am convinced. I accept your plan. . . . The matter is settled. You have my word." Karabell observes that this 1854 conversation in the desert "marked the transformation of the Suez Canal from an idea shared by many to a project led by one."

Within a few days Lesseps had a written concession, drawn up mostly by himself, giving him "the exclusive power" to organize an international company to establish a canal between the two seas. The concession further authorized the company to decide on the route and to choose the engineers. The company was responsible for the costs, but the agreement granted the company control of the then-uncultivated lands of the canal region for ninety-nine years. In later contracts, Said agreed to provide labor and financial assistance. Although these terms are often described as "misguided generosity on the part of Said," Karabell finds that they were common for the age, as well as necessary to entice investors to risk money on such a vast undertaking.

Strong political leaders disagreed about whether the canal was desirable. The British prime minister, Lord Palmerston, was convinced that the canal would enable a challenge to Britain's dominance in world trade and became Lesseps's most influential and determined opponent. The sultan of the Ottoman Empire was also against the project, and as Egypt was a part of the empire, he possessed the legal power to veto the canal. Ultimately, he decided not to use the veto, for he feared it might result in greater Egyptian independence. Enfantin continued to attack Lesseps from the sidelines but with little effect. Fortunately for Lesseps, the French emperor, Napoleon III, became a firm defender of the project and provided support at several critical points of the operation. Karabell was not able to determine the extent to which Napoleon's wife influenced his thinking.

On April 25, 1859, the actual work on the canal began at the coast of the Mediterranean when Lesseps gave the signal to approximately 150 Egyptian laborers to commence digging with their pickaxes. In his customary rhetoric, Lesseps declared: "In the name of the Universal Company of the Maritime Suez Canal, we are about to commence this work, which will open up the East to the commerce and civilization of the West." The excavations of soil and construction of the mammoth jetties would continue for the following ten years.

Karabell has much to say about the use of Egyptian peasant laborers, called fellahin, who were obtained through the traditional corvée, a governmental system of slave-like labor. In order to have twenty thousand fellahin actually working, the corvée had to raise sixty thousand fellahin. After Said's death in 1863, the new Egyptian ruler, Ismail Pasha, and his energetic deputy, Boghos Nubar Nubarian, tried to end the use of forced labor. Lesseps insisted that such a change would violate the terms of his contract with Said, unless the Egyptians paid for the additional labor costs. Following a long dispute, the issue was finally settled in Lesseps's favor by an arbitration commission appointed by Napoleon III.

When finished, the 101-mile-long canal was 26 feet deep, 72 feet wide at the bottom, and 230 feet wide at the surface. It required the dredging of more than 127 million cubic meters of material. The work was accomplished in two stages. During the first seven years, the fellahin used simple tools to do most of the work. For the last three years, the company relied primarily on huge, steam-powered engines, and it was in this second phase that the majority of the project was really completed. Karabell observes that the mechanization of the project was a revealing example of how the industrial age was transforming the nature of work and allowing the West "to alter the shape of the earth more quickly and dramatically than any humans ever had."

For the official inauguration of the canal on November 17, 1869, Lesseps's company and the Egyptian government held a huge extravaganza. The company paid the expenses for a thousand of the visitors and commissioned Giuseppe Verdi to write an opera, which was completed only later. Two days after the canal opened, Lesseps celebrated his sixty-fourth birthday. The following week, he married a twenty-one-year-old Creole woman from Mauritius, with whom he would have twelve children. During most of the following two decades, he was considered a larger-than-life hero. Then, at the age of seventy-eight, following the failure of his canal project in Panama, he and his son were found guilty of fraud and sentenced to five years in prison. The father evaded serving his prison term because of bad health.

After telling the story of the canal's construction, Karabell gives an interesting summary of its later history. He emphasizes that the canal did not provide many of the promised benefits for Egypt. As Egyptian debts increased, the British government, under Prime Minister Benjamin Disraeli, purchased 44 percent of the Canal Company in 1875. Soon thereafter, the British supervised Egypt's finances and gained control of the canal. During the Suez crisis of 1956, when Gamal Abdel Nasser nationalized the canal, an angry Egyptian mob destroyed the thirty-five-foot-high statue of Lesseps. Although the canal continues to function and to generate about two billion dollars a year for Egypt, its usage decreases as ships become larger. Karabell writes that the canal "is still a testament to nineteenth-century will and ingenuity. But its legacy for Egypt is a different, and sadder, story."

Thomas Tandy Lewis

Review Sources

Booklist 99, nos. 19/20 (June 1, 2003): 1736.
Contemporary Review 283, no. 1655 (December, 2003): 381.
The Economist 367, no. 8382 (July 20, 2003): 82.
Kirkus Reviews 71, no. 6 (March 15, 2003): 443.
Library Journal 128, no. 10 (June 1, 2003): 141.
Los Angeles Times, May 30, 2003, p. E22.
The New York Times Book Review, July 20, 2003, p. 9.
The Times Literary Supplement, September 26, 2003, p. 29.
The Washington Post, June 29, 2003, p. BW04.

PATTERN RECOGNITION

Author: William Gibson (1948-   )
Publisher: G. P. Putnam's Sons (New York). 356 pp.
  $25.95
Type of work: Novel
Time: 2002
Locale: London, New York, Tokyo, Moscow, and else-
  where in Russia

*Science-fiction writer Gibson sets a novel in the pres-
ent, which seems to have caught up with the future*

Principal characters:
  CAYCE POLLARD, a "coolhunter"
  WIN POLLARD, her father, a security consultant, presumed dead after the
    terrorist attacks on September 11, 2001
  HUBERTUS BIGEND, the Belgian founder of an innovative international
    advertising agency
  DOROTEA BENEDETTI, a graphics design executive engaged in industrial
    espionage
  STELLA and NORA VOLKOVA, twin sisters in Russia; Nora is the anony-
    mous creator of the mysterious video clips, known as "the footage,"
    which have attracted a cult following on the World Wide Web
  PARKABOY, a friend of Cayce via online chat and a fellow enthusiast of
    the footage

Pattern Recognition is William Gibson's first novel since *All Tomorrow's Parties*
(1999), which concluded the trilogy that began with *Virtual Light* (1993) and continued with *Idoru* (1996). In that most obvious sense, this book marks a point of departure. In other ways as well, while clearly in continuity with Gibson's earlier work all
the way back to his first novel, *Neuromancer* (1984), *Pattern Recognition* is different
from anything the author has done before. It is his first novel set in the present—a
bold departure for a writer of science fiction, even though his recent novels have been
set in the very near future. It is different in style, being far less fragmented and having
a narrative point of view that hews closely to the present-tense experience of the protagonist, Cayce Pollard. Its emotional texture is strikingly different from that in Gibson's characteristic works, allowing for deep sentiment (especially Cayce's love for
her father, Win) that is not undercut by reflexive irony.

Cayce Pollard is a "coolhunter." As she explains, "I hunt 'cool,' though I don't like
to describe it that way. Manufacturers use me to keep track of street fashion. . . . What
I do is pattern recognition. I try to recognize a pattern before anyone else does." (In
this she resembles earlier Gibson creations, especially Colin Laney of *Idoru*, "an intuitive fisher of patterns of information.")

Like much else in the book that might appear to be purely fictitious, Cayce's profession is a real one. (See, for example, Malcolm Gladwell's March 17, 1997, article

in *The New Yorker*, "The Coolhunt": "Who decides what's cool? Certain kids in certain places—and only the coolhunters know who they are.") Cayce, however, is a coolhunter the way Sherlock Holmes is a detective: mundane reality cubed, endowed with a quirky genius and a cluster of endearing peculiarities and vulnerabilities.

Like Holmes, she's well-nigh infallible when exercising her gift. ("She's met the very Mexican who first wore his baseball cap backward.") Holmes, too, was in the business of pattern recognition, finding the coherent explanation that makes sense of a bewildering array of "evidence." Whereas Holmes prides himself on deduction, Cayce works by instinct: Given a proposed design for a new logo, for example, she knows instantly, without conscious thought, whether it will work or not. So sensitive is her reaction to style and fashion that she is violently allergic to certain trademarks and brands: The Michelin Man makes her ill, and any-

Born in Virginia, William Gibson emigrated to Canada in 1968. His first novel, the best-selling Neuromancer *(1984), swept the major science-fiction prizes and introduced the world to "cyberspace," a term he had coined in a 1981 short story. His subsequent works include nine more books, a play, a screenplay, and two television scripts for the series* The X-Files.

thing by designer Tommy Hilfiger sets her off. *Pattern Recognition* is Gibson's funniest book and is all the funnier for never seeming to try too hard.

While Holmes sought solace in the violin—and, now and then, in cocaine—Cayce's refuge is "the footage," a series of enigmatic video frames released anonymously on the World Wide Web, one at a time and at unpredictable intervals, 135 in all so far. Each segment is like a tiny bit of a motion picture. How do the segments connect? Who is responsible for their creation? (Some devotees nominate this or that famous film director, others posit an unknown genius, a "Garage Kubrick.") Cayce and her fellow footageheads—including her friend Parkaboy, as he is styled in his e-mails, whom she has never met in person—debate such questions endlessly at an online chat forum devoted to the subject.

As the novel begins in the summer of 2002, Cayce has come from New York (where she lives) to London to do a quick consulting job for Blue Ant, an avant-garde international advertising agency founded by Hubertus Bigend, a formidable and wealthy Belgian. The real reason Bigend has brought Cayce to London is to see her coolhunting intuition at work. He is trying to discover the source of the footage—he sees its dissemination as a brilliant exercise in marketing, and he want to exploit it. Cayce, he suspects, might be capable of finding the maker, given sufficient resources. The consulting job is thereby a pretext for an audition of sorts—and Cayce passes the test with flying colors. Although she does not like Bigend, she accepts the assignment; the fascination of the footage is too strong to resist.

Meanwhile, for reasons not yet clear, other forces—represented most notably by the malign Dorotea Benedetti, a graphics design executive and industrial spy—are seeking to frighten and discourage Cayce sufficiently to send her home. They follow her to Tokyo and bedevil her there even as, with the help of Parkaboy, she is beginning to hone in on the source of footage. Ultimately the quest leads to Moscow, where Cayce meets Stella Volkova, a young Russian woman whose twin sister, Nora, is the maker; Stella is the disseminator. Both, as it turns out, have a great deal of help.

Stella explains that their parents were killed by enemies of their uncle, who has become one of the richest men in Russia in the post-Soviet era and for whom the twins' father worked. The method was remote detonation of a U.S.-issue claymore mine that somehow found its way into the hands of the Russian mafia. In the explosion, Stella suffered only minor injuries, but Nora was terribly wounded, rendered near-catatonic, and a fragment of the mine is still lodged in her brain, impossible to remove because of its location. A numerical coding embedded in each segment of the footage has led Parkaboy and a fellow Web savant to construct a "map" that turns out to correspond to this fragment. When, at last, Cayce is able to see Nora at work in a darkened studio, she knows that she is:

> in the presence of the splendid source, the headwaters of the digital Nile she and her friends had sought. It is here, in the languid yet precise moves of a woman's pale hand. In the faint click of image-capture. In the eyes only truly present when focused on this screen.

> Only the wound, speaking wordlessly in the dark.

This is the climactic moment of pattern recognition in a novel that explores this theme on many levels. Perhaps Gibson is suggesting metaphorically—as many have before him—that art typically grows from pain and loss. In a short autobiographical essay that was part of the press kit for *Pattern Recognition*, Gibson begins with science-fiction novelist Gene Wolfe's observation that "being an only child whose parents are dead is like being the sole survivor of drowned Atlantis. There was a whole civilization there, an entire continent, but it's gone. And you alone remember." So it is with him, Gibson says—his father died when Gibson was six years old, his mother when he was eighteen—and he approvingly cites another science-fiction master, Brian Aldiss, who "believes that if you look at the life of any novelist, you'll find an early traumatic break."

Perhaps so—or perhaps this is an example of what Win Pollard, Cayce's father, warned her against: "apophenia," the "perception of connections and meaningfulness in unrelated things." Certainly Gibson himself is keenly aware that apophenia is a persistent human temptation. "What if the sense of nascent meaning they all perceive in the footage is simply that," Cayce wonders: "an illusion of meaningfulness, faulty pattern recognition." There is a strain of modern thought—some would say the dominant strain in contemporary art, whatever the medium—which argues that all human attempts to see meaningfulness in the world is illusory in just this way.

Gibson's novel argues otherwise. While the unfolding action shows how easy it is to fall prey to "faulty pattern recognition," and while the footage remains enigmatic even when its maker is found and that "sense of nascent meaning" is magnificently vindicated—the connections, in other words, are far from neat, the meaning vibrant but elusive—*Pattern Recognition* shows that it is in the act of finding meaning, in the act of pattern recognition, that humans are most themselves, and what they are finding, at their best, is real. Hence the shadow of the Twin Towers of the World Trade Center, whose collapse on September 11, 2001—remembered by Cayce—haunts the entire book, the quintessentially, inescapably real, "an experience outside of culture," Gibson writes.

Indeed, Gibson builds into the novel an awareness not only of the dangers of apophenia but also of its opposite: a refusal—because of preconceptions—to acknowledge connections, patterns, even if they are virtually hitting one in the face. While Cayce greatly respects her father, a security consultant who was in the vicinity of the towers on September 11 and is presumed dead, though his body has never been found, she has little patience for the obsessions of her mother, who is part of "an intentional community of sorts" in Hawaii, dedicated to "Electronic Voice Phenomena" (EVP): "They scrutinize miles of audiotape, some of it fresh from its factory wrap, listening for voices of the dead."

Strange things happen in the course of the story. On several occasions when she is in peril, Cayce seems to sense her father's presence or even hear his voice, telling her what to do. This sense saves her life. (On the last such occasion, she has the certainty that he is now departing for good and will not "visit" her again.) Stranger still, at one point Cayce's mother passes on several EVP "messages" that she is sure are from Win to Cayce. At the time, Cayce is struck by the "banal, inchoate, utterly baffling nature of the supposed messages" in which her poor, nutty mother fervently believes. Subsequent events, however, invest these fragments with meaning—for instance, "Cayce, the bone . . . In the head, Cayce." Is it apophenia, with a vengeance, a little authorial joke, or something more—a warning against foreclosing possibilities? Gibson, as one might expect, leaves it for the reader to decide.

John Wilson

Review Sources

Booklist 99, no. 6 (November 15, 2002): 548.
Kirkus Reviews 70, no. 22 (November 15, 2002): 1641-1642.
Library Journal 128, no. 2 (February 1, 2003): 116.
New Scientist 178, no. 2397 (May 31, 2003): 50-51.
The New York Times Book Review, January 19, 2003, p. 7.
The New Yorker 78, no. 45 (February 3, 2003): 87.
Publishers Weekly 250, no. 3 (January 20, 2003): 57-58.
Time 161, no. 6 (February 10, 2003): 80.
The Times Literary Supplement, May 2, 2003, p. 24.

THE PELOPONNESIAN WAR

Author: Donald Kagan (1932-   )
Publisher: Viking (New York). 511 pp. $29.95
Type of work: History

An eminent classical historian's authoritative account of the Peloponnesian War, a long and disastrous conflict that marked the end of the golden age of ancient Greek civilization

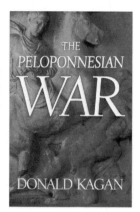

Principal personages:
PERICLES, an Athenian statesman
DEMOSTHENES, an Athenian general
CLEON, an Athenian politician
BRASIDAS, a Spartan general and diplomat
NICIAS, an Athenian statesman
ALCIBIADES, an Athenian politician and soldier
LYSANDER, a Spartan commander who successfully ended the war

Donald Kagan's *The Peloponnesian War* is a fitting capstone to a lifetime of research and writing on one of the most tragic and destructive conflicts in human history. Kagan is a distinguished historian. His exhaustive four-volume work on the great war between Athens and Sparta, published between 1969 and 1987, is widely regarded as a landmark of recent scholarship. In addition to his magnum opus, Kagan has written a number of other books, including a biography of the great Athenian statesman Pericles and a comparative history exploring the origins of wars. With his latest book, Kagan has distilled his years of study of ancient Greece and the Peloponnesian War into a highly readable narrative history designed for the general reader. The result is a book that both informs and enlightens.

The story that Kagan tells is classic in more than one sense. He addresses himself to a war that came to an end almost twenty-four hundred years ago, in a Greece where the Parthenon was still a relatively new building. This war lasted for twenty-seven years and brought an end to the most dynamic period of classical Greek civilization. The combatants were so badly wounded during this long struggle that the political destiny of Greece would come to be shaped by outsiders, first the Persian Empire and then by the kingdom of Macedon, led by Philip II, followed by his son Alexander the Great.

The memory of the Peloponnesian War has been preserved by one of the greatest books written in ancient times. Thucydides, a failed Athenian general, recognized early the significance of the conflict. He set out to produce a history that would be "a possession for all time." He succeeded brilliantly. Few books can compare with Thucydides' history for narrative force and analytical penetration. Beginning in ancient times, readers have turned to Thucydides for a somber commentary on the frightening limits of statemanship and human nature.

Kagan has spent his career working in the shadow of Thucydides, whose book remains the chief primary source on the Peloponnesian War. He readily acknowledges the greatness of his illustrious predecessor. He does not let himself be intimidated by Thucydides' authority, however. Thucydides famously strove for objectivity in his history. He was notably successful in this. Nevertheless, Kagan observes that Thucydides could not remove all traces of bias from his account; his judgment of men and events inevitably shaped his narrative and subsequent traditions about the war. Drawing upon sometimes fragmentary sources from antiquity, Kagan demonstrates that alternate interpretations of the war existed. Thus he is able to supplement the Thucydidean record, at times challenging Thucydides at crucial points. Also, because he died before he could complete his project, Thucydides' work breaks off nearly seven years before the end of the war. Kagan makes use of lesser-known historians to bring the story to a satisfactory close. Comparing Kagan to Thucydides would be a thankless and unfair proposition and something that Kagan himself would reject. He contents himself with modestly asserting that he has produced a lucid history for twenty-first century readers.

> *Donald Kagan is the Sterling Professor of Classics and History at Yale University. The recipient of a 2002 National Humanities Medal, Professor Kagan is the author of many books on ancient and modern history.*

The roots of the Peloponnesian War go back to the epic defense of Greece against a Persian invasion almost a half-century earlier. Athens and Sparta took the lead in the coalition of Greek city-states that took up arms against the Persians. At Salamis in 480 B.C.E., the Greeks routed the Persian navy before the eyes of Xerxes the Great. A year later they destroyed the army that the retreating Xerxes had left in Greece. Victory highlighted the differences between Athens and Sparta. Athens was a vibrant mercantile state. Athenians prized their hard-won democracy, which they continued to extend and perfect for the body of male citizens during the course of the fifth century. Athens became the home of artists, writers, and thinkers such as Phidias, Sophocles, and Socrates, creating a brilliant humanistic culture seldom equaled and never surpassed.

Sparta, on the other hand, was a garrison state. Here a small landowning elite ruled over a great mass of powerless helots, whom they treated little better than slaves. In order to maintain their position, the Spartans devoted themselves to war. Through a rigorous regime of military training, the Spartans made themselves the supreme soldiers of Greece. The price they paid was that they fitted themselves for little else. Their outlook remained narrow and provincial. Thus, when the Persians had been repulsed, the Spartans went home to keep an eye on their helots. The Athenians instead continued the war against the Persians. During the Persian invasion, the Athenians had sheltered on ships, their famous walls of wood, while the enemy ravaged their city and its environs. Now the Athenians used this fleet to lead a Greek counterattack on the Persian position in the Aegean Sea, liberating Greek cities in the islands and on the Ionian coast, what is now the Turkish mainland.

Tensions soon arose between the erstwhile allies. Sparta and its allies in the

Peloponnesus and in Boeotia could field formidable forces on land. They grew suspicious and increasingly anxious about the growing sea-power of Athens. These concerns were intensified when the Athenians built a wall enclosing their city and its harbor at Piraeus, effectively making Athens an island and invulnerable to a land assault. The Spartans became actively hostile when the Athenians converted the naval alliance against the Persians into an empire that they used to aggrandize themselves. Former Greek allies now became Athenian subjects, and the tribute collected from them was used to build the great architectural masterpieces that beautified Athens. In 460 Athenian ambitions in the heart of Greece collided with Spartan fears. The result was a war that lasted fifteen years.

In the Thirty Years' Peace that concluded hostilities, the Athenians gave up lands that they had taken on the Peloponnesus, and the Spartans effectively recognized the Athenian empire. Future grievances would be settled by binding arbitration. Peace thus ushered in what was essentially a cold-war situation, with Greece divided into two great alliance systems. Despite mutual mistrust, both the Athenians and the Spartans attempted to make the peace work. For a dozen years it held. Then, ironically, as a result of events on the periphery of the Greek world, the Athenians and Spartans were once again drawn into conflict.

The first crisis concerned the island of Cocyra, located in what for most Greeks was a remote location off the Adriatic coast of the mainland. Cocyra had been founded by the city of Corinth, a Spartan ally. The Cocyraeans and Corinthians did not get along, and in 433 they went to war. Athens intervened on the side of the Cocyraeans, hoping to prevent the Corinthians' winning control of the large Cocyraean navy. Conflict with Corinth led the Athenians to demand guarantees from their ally Potidaea, another Corinthian colony located in the north, in Chalcidice, along the shipping lanes crucial to Athenian survival. Egged on by the Corinthians, the Spartans promised support to the Potidaeans.

Thucydides, in recounting these events, argued that the real reason that the Spartans moved toward war against the Athenians was their fear of their power. Kagan supplements this insight with an economic argument. Thucydides pays little attention to a trade embargo that the Athenians imposed upon the Peloponnesian city of Megara. Contemporaries saw this as a major cause of the war. By acting against the interests of Corinth and Megara, the Athenians were hurting two major Spartan allies. If the Spartans did nothing, they risked the unraveling of their alliance. Thus, though not immediately threatened, the Spartans felt compelled to make ready for war. They sent a series of ultimatums to Athens, demanding concessions. The Athenians, for their part, believed that they had behaved with restraint, not violating the letter of the Thirty Years' Peace. The great Athenian statesman Pericles, who dominated Athenian politics at this time, refused any concessions to the Spartans without referral to arbitration as per the terms of the Peace. He believed that he could fight a limited war that would hurt the Spartans enough to bring them to their senses. When hostilities broke out in 431, he put his strategy into effect.

Pericles recognized the asymmetry between Spartan and Athenian power. The Spartans could field a great army but were short of the cash needed to sustain a long

war. The Athenians possessed an incomparable fleet and were rich. Pericles calculated that if he brought all the Athenians into the shelter of the city walls, abandoning
their farms and country estates to the depredations of the enemy, he could wear down
the resistance of the Spartans by using his navy to launch raids all along the Peloponnesian coast. As Kagan points out, this was an eminently reasonable plan, but it neglected the irrational element that always figures in human affairs, and it also failed to
take into account the vagaries of chance. Pericles' strategy was paradigmatic of the
tragedy of the Peloponnesian War. Time and again, well-intentioned policies would
lead to unexpected consequences and disaster.

The Athenians took Pericles' advice and crowded into the city. They soon
grew unhappy with Pericles' policy, however, as they watched Spartan forces raz-
ing their farms and burning their fields. Worse, the overcrowded conditions in the
city made the Athenians vulnerable to a plague, which, by the time it had run
its course, had killed between one-fourth and one-third of the population. Pericles
himself was among the victims. While this was going on, the military situation
remained at a stalemate. The Spartans and their allies could devastate the hinter-
lands of Athens every campaigning season but otherwise cause no serious harm to
the Athenian maritime empire. This was as Pericles had predicted. The Athenians
struck no major blows against the Spartans, who remained obstinately committed to
the war.

Thus during the 420's new leaders with new strategies came to the fore: The
general Demosthenes and the demagogue Cleon for Athens and the heroic commander Brasidas for Sparta infused new energy into the war. By 422 both sides
had won great victories but also suffered grievous losses. The people were ready
for peace. Nicias, an Athenian statesman devoted to the vision of Pericles, negotiated a peace. To get his peace, Nicias left a number of practical issues unresolved,
and the peace did not address the fundamental differences between Athens and
Sparta. As a result, the peace proved stillborn, and within a few years the war was raging again.

In 416 a brilliant but unscrupulous Athenian politician named Alcibiades proposed a campaign in Sicily. The chief city of Sicily, Syracuse, was friendly with
the Spartans. Control of Syracuse and Sicily held the promise of great military
and economic benefits. Nicias thought such a campaign was too dangerous while
the Spartans were still hostile closer to home. He tried to dissuade the Athenians by
emphasizing the difficulties of such an expedition. Ironically, the result of his arguments was an Athenian decision to send an even larger force than originally proposed,
with Nicias as one of the commanders. These decisions proved disastrous. The campaign did indeed prove to be more challenging than expected, and Nicias's half-
hearted and vacillating generalship resulted in the entire Athenian army being destroyed in 414.

Despite this crushing loss, the Athenians managed to fight on for another decade.
In the end, the Spartans were able to defeat the Athenians only by making a Faustian
bargain with the Persians. The Spartans took Persian money to buy ships and crews at
the price of Greek liberties in Ionia. When Athens surrendered in 404, Sparta was left,

briefly, as the dominant power in Greece. However, this was a Greece economically exhausted, with a population noticeably reduced by battles, civil strife, and the atrocities committed by both sides. Kagan, like Thucydides before him, has written a sobering indictment of human folly and the capacity of even the most brilliant of civilizations to self-destruct.

Daniel P. Murphy

Review Sources

Booklist 99, no. 16 (April 15, 2003): 1445.
Foreign Affairs 82, no. 5 (September/October, 2003): 174.
Kirkus Reviews 71, no. 6 (March 15, 2003): 442-443.
Library Journal 128, no. 9 (May 15, 2003): 102.
The New York Times Book Review, August 10, 2003, p. 9.
Publishers Weekly 250, no. 12 (March 24, 2003): 65-66.

POSITIVELY FIFTH STREET
Murderers, Cheetahs, and Binion's World Series of Poker

Author: James McManus (1951-   )
Publisher: Farrar, Straus and Giroux (New York). 422
  pp. $26.00
Type of work: Memoir
Time: 2000
Locale: Las Vegas

When Harper's Magazine *sent McManus to Las Vegas
to write about women competing in the World Series of
Poker and, incidentally, to cover a high-profile murder
trial taking place down the street, he used his advance to
enter the tournament and finished fifth against some of the
world's best players*

Principal personages:
  JAMES MCMANUS, the author, finished fifth in the 2000 World Series of
    Poker
  JENNIFER ANN ARRA, his wife
  TED BINION, the former owner of the Horseshoe Hotel and Casino
  BENNY BINION, Ted Binion's father, founder of the Horseshoe Hotel and
    Casino
  SANDRA MURPHY, convicted in 2000 of killing Ted Binion
  RICK TABISH, Murphy's boyfriend, convicted with Murphy of killing
    Ted Binion
  BECKY BEHNEN, Ted Binion's sister, owner of the Horseshoe Hotel and
    Casino
  T. J. CLOUTIER, who finished second in the 2000 World Series of Poker
  CHRIS "JESUS" FERGUSON, who finished first in the 2000 World Series of
    Poker

Largely a hand-by-hand account of the final four days of the 2000 annual World
Series of Poker (WSOP), *Positively Fifth Street* arrives in a moment of resurgent interest in Las Vegas as both a brightly lit tourist mecca and shadowy home to seedy
strip clubs and dangerous high-stakes gambling. Author James McManus combines
the moment-to-moment excitement of the poker tournament with true crime, covering the murder of Ted Binion, one-time owner of the Horseshoe Hotel and Casino,
where the WSOP originated.

Harper's Magazine sent McManus, a novelist and poet, to Las Vegas in May,
2000, ostensibly to write an article about women participating in the WSOP. The
world of professional and high-stakes poker had opened up to women with the legal-
ization of poker in the 1980's, and women have since won major tournaments, although not the World Series of Poker to date. McManus notes the increasing diversity of players in major tournaments; since its inception the WSOP has welcomed

∼

James McManus is a novelist, journalist, and poet whose honors include the Peter Lisagor Award for Sports Journalism and the Carl Sandburg Prize. McManus is a professor of writing at the School of the Arts Institute of Chicago, where he teaches a course on the literature and science of poker.

∼

competitors from every imaginable background and ethnicity, ballooning from seven players in 1970 to more than four hundred in 2000. In fact, in 2000 five thousand total players competed in several events.

McManus also planned to examine the effect on professional poker of two new developments in how players learn the game: computer games that simulate champion-level play and how-to manuals that reveal the strategies of high-stakes players. Although McManus had been playing poker for forty years and had participated in a few high-stakes games, he spent months preparing for the WSOP by practicing with computer games and studying books written by poker champs including T. J. Cloutier, Tom McEvoy, David Sklansky, and Doyle Brunson. McManus then used his four-thousand-dollar advance from *Harper's* to play in satellite games that offered a chance to win a seat in the tournament without putting up the otherwise requisite ten thousand dollars in cash.

A professor at the School of the Arts Institute of Chicago with a wife and four children, McManus could not afford to be cavalier with his *Harper's* advance and expended no little effort convincing his wife, Jennifer Arra, that playing in the tournament was his wisest course. McManus refers to himself throughout the book as "Good Jim" and "Bad Jim." Good Jim buys his wife an expensive diamond ring at a Las Vegas boutique; Bad Jim buys a lap dance at a strip club. Good Jim carries a small photo album containing pictures of his wife and children to each game and imagines his youngest daughter praising his more prudent moves at the table; Bad Jim raises his bets when he should fold.

The particular variation of poker played at the WSOP is No-Limit Texas Hold'em, a version of seven-card stud (for the poker-challenged, McManus explains Texas Hold'em—advising one to read *slowly*—and provides a bibliography, a rundown of hands, and a glossary of poker terms). Each player is dealt two cards facedown; the dealer then places three cards (the "flop") faceup on the table. Flop cards are communal, and each player considers how his or her facedown cards might combine with the flop and two subsequently dealt cards to make the best poker hand. Players determine how to bet after the flop, then as a fourth card ("fourth street") and fifth ("fifth street" or "the river") are dealt faceup. Players may continue raising bets (adding more money to the pot on the assumption that theirs will be the winning hand) or fold (abandoning the hand and losing their money already in the pot).

Although computer games allow players to practice playing a large number of hands in short time, McManus notes that playing against a computer game with the manuals open on his lap is a different experience from playing against human opponents. Even though a solid knowledge of the champions' statistical and tactical advice is useful in real games, McManus is often overtaken, if not overwhelmed, by the emotions and excitement of tournament play. Nonetheless, he is able to place an exhilarating fifth, winning $250,000 against top players with decades of high-stakes experience.

McManus's article for *Harper's* quickly eschewed coverage of women players and the Binion trial for an account of his own fifth-place win in the tournament. *Positively Fifth Street* provides an avenue for material McManus collected on women of the WSOP and on Ted Binion's murder.

Binion's father, Benny, founded the Horseshoe Hotel and Casino in 1951, a hard-gambling downtown saloon in contrast with the glittery, upscale casinos that have since come to typify Las Vegas. McManus provides a history of the Binion family, beginning with Benny's early days running illegal craps games in Texas. Binion's Horseshoe developed a worldwide reputation, largely as a result of the popularity of its annual championship poker tournament. After Benny's death, his three children fought for control of the Horseshoe casino and the right to use the Binion name. In the midst of the battle Ted Binion was arrested for trafficking in heroin, lost his gaming license, and was barred by the Nevada Gaming Control Board from entering any casino in the state, including his own family's beloved Horseshoe.

The murderers of *Positively Fifth Street* are Sandra Murphy, a strip-club dancer who lived with Ted Binion, and her boyfriend Rick Tabish. McManus's original assignment required him to provide coverage of their sensational murder trial, rife with gambling, kinky sex, and big money, as it occurred just down the street from the WSOP. Accordingly, *Positively Fifth Street* opens with a lurid, fictionalized account of the 1998 murder of Ted Binion. A known heroin addict, Binion appeared to have died from an overdose of heroin and prescription drugs; his death was initially considered either a suicide or an accidental overdose. Forensic investigators later determined that Sandra Murphy and Rick Tabish had forced Binion to ingest a fatal dose of heroin and Xanax and then burked (suffocated) him.

McManus's re-creation of the murder is based on interviews with friends and acquaintances of Murphy and Tabish. McManus had planned to base his report on coverage from Court TV and newspaper Web sites. A chance meeting with Ted's sister Becky Behnen led him to attend the verdict reading, but his reporting on the Binion-Murphy-Tabish triangle and the murder investigation vacillates between distant and fanciful. McManus struggles at times to make Murphy relevant to the story he really wants to tell—about his own progress at the World Series. At one point he even explains at length why Murphy is like the ten of clubs.

McManus's style is generally digressive, displaying the eclecticism of a poet, scholar, and teacher; in fact, he believes his literary skills and background allowed him to quickly learn the subtleties of competition among professional card players. McManus's account of the WSOP may not be unique in its references to Fyodor Dostoevski's *Igrok* (1866; *The Gambler*, 1887), but it may be in recalling or quoting writers Leo Tolstoy, James Joyce, Dante Alighieri, Herman Melville, and David Mamet. Tracing Sandra Murphy's progress from a strip club to the Binion mansion and from there to prison, McManus compares her to a character in Samuel Beckett's early novel *Murphy* (1938). In discussing A. Alvarez, author of *The Biggest Game in Town* (1983), McManus veers into Alvarez's friendship with the poet Sylvia Plath, examining Plath's poetic genius and her 1963 suicide. The chapter "Chicks with Decks" covers not only top women poker players but also Cheetahs Topless Club, Ted Binion's fall from grace, gambler Bob Stupak, the history of poker, playing cards as metaphors for a variety of cultural phenomena, and the new ethnic diversity characterizing the WSOP.

Although featured in the book's subtitle, Cheetahs Topless Club actually receives little coverage. McManus visited the club, where Sandra Murphy worked as a dancer and where she first met Ted Binion, only once. McManus notes the ambiance and Murphy's brief sojourn there (amid references to Beckett and Joyce), and locals assure him that Cheetahs is passé in comparison to the newer Spearmint Rhino, where McManus bought his own lap dance.

The prose can be dense and is heavily weighted with technicalities. In discussing mental illness and creative genius, McManus writes:

> In the back of their forehead, more specifically in the anterior cingulate of their frontal cortex, some humans have more vulnerable dopamine systems, "psyches" (as we used to call them) more easily hijacked by rewards like sex, dope, money, or laurels. Mastering the inherent unpredictability of any game or art form can trigger overpowering "pleasure," and this dopamine rush gets deeply embedded in the memory of some of the most talented practitioners.

Many scenes involve play-by-play at the poker table:

> We all watch the flop come 10-9-Q. After the guy in the small blind bets $1,000, Johnny Hale from the big blind tosses an orange $5,000 chip toward the pot. With top set, I decide to reraise all-in. With ten other pocket cards in action, I have to assume that somebody's holding a jack: J-K, J-Q, J-J . . . I've put Johnny Hale on—guessed he has—a straight draw, but even if he makes a straight, I'll have fourteen "outs." That is, any one of the remaining three tens or three nines would give me a full house, and the remaining queen would give me four-of-a-kind; and so, with the same seven outs (10,10,10,9,9,9,Q) on both fourth street and fifth street, I have fourteen chances to beat any straight, any flush.

McManus further provides several lists and diagrams indicating who sat where, the cards they held, and how many chips they had at given points in the tournament.

Nonetheless, McManus's emotional highs at the poker table are exhilarating, and *Positively Fifth Street* was well received as the story of an average guy using skill and luck to compete successfully against the pros. In fact, three years after McManus's surprise fifth-place finish, the 2003 WSOP would be won by an accountant who practiced online but had never before played high-stakes poker. A chronicle of just such an American adventure, *Positively Fifth Street* is a passionate and literate inside look at the World Series of Poker.

Maureen J. Puffer-Rothenberg

Review Sources

Booklist 99, no. 12 (February 15, 2003): 1018.
Commentary 116, no. 2 (September, 2003): 74-76.
Kirkus Reviews 71, no. 3 (February 1, 2003): 212.
Library Journal 128, no. 4 (March 1, 2003): 97.
The New York Times, April 8, 2003, p. E6.
The New York Times Book Review, June 1, 2003, p. 23.
Publishers Weekly 250, no. 9 (March 3, 2003): 62-63.
Time 161, no. 15 (April 14, 2003): 83.
The Wall Street Journal, April 16, 2003, p. D10.

RAISING AMERICA
Experts, Parents, and a Century of Advice About Children

Author: Ann Hulbert (1956-   )
Publisher: Alfred A. Knopf (New York). Illustrated. 450 pp. $27.50
Type of work: History
Time: The late nineteenth century through the twentieth century

Throughout the twentieth century, experts on child raising came and went in the United States, offering advice that is contradictory and often unsupported by science

> *Principal personages:*
> G. STANLEY HALL, the first American to earn a doctorate in psychology and author of *Adolescence* (1904)
> LUTHER EMMETT HOLT, the author of *The Care and Feeding of Children* (1894) and president of the American Pediatric Society in the early twentieth century
> ARNOLD GESELL, a student of Hall, who wrote *The Mental Growth of the Pre-school Child* (1925) and *Infancy and Human Growth* (1928)
> JOHN B. WATSON, the founder of behaviorism and the author of *Psychological Care of Infant and Child* (1928)
> BENJAMIN SPOCK, the most influential of the experts, author of the bestselling *The Common Sense Book of Baby and Child Care* (1946, and six further editions)
> BRUNO BETTELHEIM, the director of a treatment center for emotionally disturbed children and author of *The Uses of Enchantment: The Meaning and Importance of Fairy Tales* (1976)
> T. BERRY BRAZELTON, a pediatrician whose research focused on cognitive development and author of *Infants and Mothers: Differences in Development* (1969)
> JAMES DOBSON, the founder of nonprofit organization Focus on the Family and author of *Dare to Discipline* (1971)

The United States at the end of the nineteenth century seemed to many people to be a world spinning out of control. New technologies like doorbells, telephones, and mechanical toys were making people nervous. People were moving from the farms to the cities, women were going to college and to jobs outside the home, neighbors were strangers to each other. Children were isolated, overstimulated, growing up too fast. Without extended families to help them raise their children, parents became anxious. They found advice, much of it conflicting, in the books of a new branch of social science, the study of child development. In *Raising America: Experts, Parents, and a Century of Advice About Children*, Ann Hulbert traces the history of the new experts and their manuals from the end of the nineteenth century to the turn of the twenty-first.

Raising America is divided into four sections, each covering about one-quarter of the century. In each period, Hulbert finds that the experts divide neatly into two schools. The "hard" theorists advocate a parent-centered approach, with schedules, regimens, and firm discipline. The "soft" advocates of child-centered parenting believe in flexibility, feeding on demand, and treating children as equals.

Ann Hulbert is a former senior editor of The New Republic *and the author of* The Interior Castle: The Art and Life of Jean Stafford *(1992). She has published articles and reviews in* The New York Review of Books *and* The New York Times Book Review.

The first section, "The Birth of a Science," introduces pediatrician Luther Emmett Holt and psychologist G. Stanley Hall. Holt's *The Care and Feeding of Children* turned mothers into technicians, raising children according to strict schedules. The book advised that children should eat precise amounts of precisely measured formulas (rather than breast milk) at precise times; they should be put into bed according to schedule and left there until the schedule called for them to get up; they should be toilet trained by three months. Mothers should not play with their babies, or pick them up when they cried.

Hall took a "softer" view, encouraging mothers to be flexible and affectionate with their children and to turn a fond but blind eye to the youthful "immoderation, irregularity, irresponsibility" of adolescence. Masturbation should be ignored, if not encouraged, and children's questions about sex should be answered thoroughly. Holt and Hall were both confident, both scientific, and both concerned about children being forced to grow up too quickly. They began a pattern that would continue through the century: raising new reasons for anxiety in mothers and offering conflicting ways to relieve it.

The paired experts in Hulbert's second section, "Psychological Leaps," are Arnold Gesell and John B. Watson. For some twenty years, psychologist Gesell and his staff at Yale University filmed children at play in a gentle, softly lit environment and gathered data from their observations. The "soft" Gesell believed that children should be treated as equals and as individuals. He introduced the term "personality" and the theory of children developing through predictable stages, which mothers kept track of with daily color-coded charts. As Hulbert records in humorous detail, Gesell's daughter-in-law tried to keep up with the charts, and repeatedly complained to Gesell about the daunting nature of the task.

During the same period, behaviorist John B. Watson was making his famous claim that he could raise any twelve healthy infants and turn them into doctors, lawyers, butchers—anything he wanted—"regardless of his talents, penchants, tendencies, abilities, vocations and race of his ancestors." His idea was that personality was purely a product of one's reactions to various stimuli. Watson's research was based far more frequently on laboratory mice than on children, but Hulbert describes one unfortunate infant named Little Albert, who was exposed to loud noises, barking dogs, even rats, and who emerged from his "conditioning" fearing loud noises, barking dogs, and rats. In *Psychological Care of Infant and Child*, Watson ordered mothers not to cuddle their babies, and he even surpassed Holt, suggesting that toilet training could begin as early as three weeks.

The chapter "Identity Crisis" introduces pediatrician Benjamin Spock, whose seven editions of *The Common Sense Book of Baby and Child Care* have sold more than fifty million copies worldwide, and Bruno Bettelheim. Spock's opening lines, "Trust yourself, you know more than you think you do," encouraged generations of parents to draw on their own instincts. He advocated feeding on demand, plenty of affection, and toilet training on a child's own schedule. He did not approve of spanking but understood how a frustrated parent might be driven to it. Nevertheless, he is considered here the "hard" expert, in contrast with Bettelheim, who argued that mothers should step aside and let children develop on their own. Rather than being trained to calm their anger and fears, children should be permitted to express and explore them in order to become fully integrated selves and to "accept themselves as imperfect beings." Ironically, Spock, who was initially heralded for giving women confidence in their own judgment, was later criticized by Gloria Steinem for keeping women oppressed. It was the harsher Bettelheim who argued that for most women, being a full-time wife and mother could not be satisfying or fulfilling. Spock and Bettelheim later took their antagonism into new realms, as Spock became an activist against the Vietnam War and Bettelheim an outspoken defender of President Richard Nixon.

In the last section, "Psychological Limits," Hulbert analyzes the last quarter of the twentieth century. Because her readers can be expected to be somewhat familiar with T. Berry Brazelton, Penelope Leach, James Dobson, and John Rosemond, she can cover more ground in less detail. Significantly, the experts in this period have moved beyond traditional books and magazines, with Brazelton's cable television show *What Every Baby Knows*, radio programs by Dobson's Focus on the Family organization, and Covey's planners. The debates, however, seem largely unchanged: Children should have more or less cuddling, more or less discipline, more or less stimulation. They have too much access to technology. They are growing up too fast. After a century of data collecting and theorizing, science seems to have little to contribute to the discussion about what children need from their parents.

Substantial portions of *Raising America* are devoted to biographical information about the experts, demonstrating that academic knowledge about human relationships is not necessarily concordant with what is today called "emotional intelligence." To put it simply, many of the experts were themselves brought up by unloving parents, and they became unhappy adults. Hall's father was an unforgiving and unyielding evangelist; Hall's wife and daughter died in an accident, and Hall himself had severe doubts about the value of his work. Watson was fired from The Johns Hopkins University for committing adultery, and he spent the second half of his professional life as an advertising executive; his son committed suicide. Spock's mother was stern and never gave him approval; his first wife was unhappy for decades with his treatment of her and her alcoholism, and he became estranged from his children. Bettelheim survived a concentration camp but later exaggerated his heroism there, dealt violently with some of the children under his care, plagiarized in some of his most important writings, and committed suicide.

Hulbert is perhaps too insistent on her hard-soft dichotomy and its importance as she traces it through the decades. Logically, it could be argued that any description of the parent-child relationship must lean toward either the parent or the child, but Hulbert seems too eager to find one leading expert of each type for each period. Her examination of Spock shows most clearly the problem with assigning each expert into one camp or the other, for Spock's advice represents a thoughtful—and realistic—blending of the two. More compelling is the pattern Hulbert uncovers across the periods: a doubling—and even tripling—back in subsequent generations to ideas that were embraced and rejected previously. The forms and grids required for the Covey methods of organizing a family sound a lot like the charts that Holt's and Gesell's mothers valiantly fill out in the early part of the century. The grandmothers that Holt told mothers to ignore are held up by John Rosemond as a source of wisdom.

It is not fair to blame an author for writing the book she wrote instead of another book. Hulbert's research, however, raises questions she is not prepared or moved to address: How did black women and poor women embrace or reject the advice that wealthy white men offered for raising middle-class, white children? What are the implications of the experts' being men, their readers being women? How might more actively involved fathers have changed things? How do movements in child rearing echo other movements in American history? Why do Americans seem especially prone to seek the advice of strangers as they raise their children?

Raising America is analytical and richly detailed, and its prose reflects Hulbert's interest in thorough research more than her own opinions or responses. Some readers will prefer another book, Peter N. Stearns's *Anxious Parents: A History of Modern Childrearing in America* (2003), a shorter but livelier treatment of similar material. Together, these books provide an interesting look at the changing advice and the human failings of the so-called experts and lend encouragement to those parents who would raise their children by heart and instinct, rather than by the book.

As Hulbert makes clear in her final chapters, parents throughout the twentieth century read the books and even believed them, but on a day-to-day basis, with real temper tantrums and fussy eaters, parents ignored the advice and made their own rules. They learned through experience that "no fine-tuned scheme for shaping futures lies in the experts' manuals, much less in their own homes—or even, most of the time, in their dreams."

Cynthia A. Bily

Review Sources

The Atlantic Monthly 291, no. 4 (May 3, 2003): 118-122.
Booklist 99, no. 14 (March 15, 2003): 1263.
Kirkus Reviews 71, no. 3 (February 1, 2003): 207.

Library Journal 128, no. 4 (March 1, 2003): 107.
The New York Times, June 27, 2003, p. E32.
The New York Times Book Review, April 27, 2003, p. 9.
The New Yorker 79, no. 10 (May 5, 2003): 95-99.
Publishers Weekly 250, no. 10 (March 10, 2003): 67.
The Wall Street Journal, May 2, 2003, p. W8.
The Wilson Quarterly 27, no. 2 (Spring, 2003): 109-112.
The Women's Review of Books 20, no. 9 (June, 2003): 5-6.

RANDALL JARRELL AND HIS AGE

Author: Stephen Burt (1971-   )
Publisher: Columbia University Press (New York).
   320 pp. $29.50
Type of work: Literary biography, literary criticism, liter-
   ary history, and literary theory
Time: The twentieth century
Locale: The United States

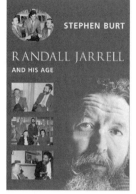

*This illuminating examination of Jarrell's contributions
to American letters situates the poet-critic's work within a
dynamically interactive frame, embracing social and cultural as well as aesthetic and psychological concerns*

Among those who care about reading and poetry and the
life of the mind, the reputation of writer Randall Jarrell still
looms large. Although his life was cut short when, at age fifty-one, he was struck by a
car under still-mysterious circumstances, Jarrell's wide-ranging body of work continues to resonate. There were poems, sensitive and tragic, some five hundred pages
worth, including the collection *The Woman at the Washington Zoo* (1960), which won
a National Book Award. There were incisive essays on and reviews of poetry and literature, some of which were published under the title *Poetry and the Age* in 1953.
There was a satiric novel set in a progressive women's college, *Pictures from an Institution* (1954), and a collection of essays and fables, *A Sad Heart at the Supermarket*
(1962). There were also children's books, notably *The Bat-Poet* (1964), *The Animal
Family* (1965), and *The Gingerbread Rabbit* (1964), all illustrated by Maurice
Sendak.

Since his tragic death in 1965—the result, depending on the source, of either an accident or a suicide—Jarrell's contributions have been commemorated in various
forms. There is a memorial volume, *Randall Jarrell 1914-1965* (1967), with contributions by fellow literary lions and friends Robert Lowell, Peter Taylor, Robert Penn
Warren, Elizabeth Bishop, Hannah Arendt, Marianne Moore, Robert Fitzgerald, John
Crowe Ransom, Adrienne Rich, Allen Tate, and Jarrell's second wife, Mary. Jarrell's
published verse was issued in 1969 under the title *Complete Poems*, while Jarrell's
translation of Johann Wolfgang von Goethe's work *Faust, Part I*, appeared posthumously in 1976. On a more personal note is a collection of private correspondence,
Letters (1985; revised 2002), annotated by Mary Jarrell, as well as her autobiographic
Remembering Randall (1999). Another selection of Jarrell's essays, *No Other Book*
(1999), was organized by Brad Leithauser.

Although he helped elucidate and consequently popularize the poetry of others—
most famously in his fine-grained analyses of the work of Robert Frost, Robert Lowell, Walt Whitman, and William Carlos Williams—Jarrell's initially well-received
poetry has become increasingly shrouded by lack of a critical consensus about its

∽

Stephen Burt is an assistant professor of English at Macalester College in Saint Paul, Minnesota. His critical commentaries on poets and poetry have been published in the Boston Review, *the* London Review of Books, *and* The New York Times. *His highly regarded collection of poems,* Popular Music, *won the Colorado Prize for 1999.*

∽

quality and the inexorable passing of time. *Randall Jarrell and His Age* aims to correct what author Stephen Burt believes to be a serious slight by arguing that Jarrell's poetry deserves to be taken seriously again and brought to the fore. In his introduction, Burt summarizes his project by noting that while Jarrell showed readers how to read his contemporaries, readers do not yet know how to read him.

Burt, whose own literary profile resembles that of Jarrell, is an English professor who is a well-regarded poet and cultural commentator. This remarkably similar background gives Burt a decided edge in critically rereading Jarrell against the cultural and social period in which he wrote and ultimately allows Burt to persuasively argue for the rehabilitation of Jarrell as an artist with which to reckon. Significantly, Burt reminds readers that Jarrell, although best known to the public for his cultural commentaries, considered himself first and last a poet. For Burt, the overarching principle that most effectively illuminates Jarrell's diverse and expansive oeuvre concerns the self:

> Poetry—or lyrical poetry, or poetry since the Romantic era—is frequently said to have as its province the inner life, or the psyche, or the self. That general vocation for poetry became Jarrell's special project. His poems and prose describe the distances between the self and the world, the self and history, the self and the social givens within which it is asked to behave. They show how the self seeks fantasy, and how it turns to memory, as refuges from the demands the world makes on it, or from (worse yet), the world's neglect. And they examine how the self seeks confirmation of its continuing existence, a confirmation it can finally have only through other people.

Along the way, Burt notes other themes essential to a better understanding of Jarrell. In particular, he notes the poet's trust in the good sense of the average reader, whom Jarrell believed was quite capable of negotiating even the most challenging poetry without benefit of the jargon-laden guides produced by many of his overly abstract literary friends. For Jarrell, the real challenge to developing a sure sense of self came from mid-twentieth century mass culture, from television and films, and the local variants of those mass-mediated argots as found in prosaic locales such as supermarkets, army barracks, and classrooms. Much of Jarrell's poetry also reveals preoccupation with the seasons of life, from childhood and adolescence to adulthood and old age. Epochal events from the era in which he wrote, such as World War II, echo as well. Along with children, as Burt makes clear in his discussion of "The Woman at the Washington Zoo," women also count.

Burt calls his first section "Antechapter: Randall Jarrell's Life." Here one learns about Jarrell's early fascination with films, an interest made manifest in an early poem titled "The Ballad of the Sheik Who Lost His Shine." One gets a glimpse of his college days at Vanderbilt, his early encounters with the poet-critics Robert Penn

Warren and John Crowe Ransom, and his infatuations with Gestalt psychology and Marxism. There are snapshots of his teaching career at Kenyon College, Sarah Lawrence College, and the University of North Carolina, Greensboro. Burt also surveys Jarrell's rise to national prominence through his contributions to *The Nation* and *The New Republic*. In the process, one gets a good sense of Jarrell's personal life, his two marriages, his growing dismay with American education and mass culture and eventually with life itself, an increasingly pessimistic frame of mind reflected in the anthology *A Sad Heart at the Supermarket*.

In "Chapter 1: Jarrell's Interpersonal Style," Burt takes up the notion of self as it depends on other aspects of self, showing how Jarrell's poetic style mediates that interdependence. Here, noting Jarrell's rejection of his teachers' conceptualization of poems as self-contained artifacts, Burt shows how Jarrell incorporated Wordsworthian views of poetry as troped speech. These views, Burt argues, gave Jarrell's verse its distinctive approach, a supple and yet poignant style incorporating devices such as irregular listeners, webs of quotation, multiple speakers, hesitations, self-interruptions, and subtle models of poetic listeners.

"Chapter 2: Institutions, Professions, Criticism" examines the self within and against societal organizations ranging from the army to the academy. Burt vivifies the subject by pointing out how Jarrell's work reflected and responded to such postwar phenomena as the rapid expansion of higher education, concerns about conformity, and anxieties over the impact of mass culture. These were among the benchmarks, Burt explains, against which Jarrell honed his understanding of literature in general and his own work in particular, as well as his attempt to distinguish individuals from their roles in society. The consequence of this roiling social-cultural *Zeitgeist* was a concern underpinning many of Jarrell's essays. It also provided a standard by which Jarrell gauged his critical assessments. Burt further stresses that the focus on self and society gave Jarrell a means of discriminating between aesthetic experience and professional activity. While expressed in his poetry, Burt finds the self-versus-society struggle of particular importance to understanding Jarrell's comic novel, *Pictures from an Institution*.

"Chapter 3: Psychology and Psychoanalysis" draws a bead on Jarrell's fascination with scientific approaches to the mind. Here Burt points to Jarrell's debt to 1930's Gestalt theory and to Sigmund Freud and Freud's heirs. Reworking notions of the unconscious, dream work, the death wish, and the persistence of infantile desires, Jarrell identified with psychoanalysts to the point that his work often explored, as Burt puts it, the intersubjective components of psychoanalysis and of emotion itself.

In contrast, "Chapter 4: Time and Memory" probes the role of the self traveling through and against time, with an emphasis on how the "I" who speaks a poem or lives a life may come to grips with and understand its past. Here Burt begins with philosophical issues pertinent to personal identity and a discussion of Jarrell's use of the works of Marcel Proust as a means of showing how certain poems dealing with old age, middle age, and childhood use verbal repetition to express the persistence of self over time.

"Chapter 5: Childhood and Youth" and "Chapter 6: Men, Women, Children, Families" address relationships among a multiplicity of selves. Here Burt parses out Jarrell's assumptions and intuitions about men, women, youth, parents, and children. While underscoring Jarrell's often-noted interest in childhood, Burt draws special attention to the poet's less discussed concern with adolescence, just emerging as an important social phenomenon in the postwar period. Typifying his method, in chapter 5 Burt calls on an array of authorities from fields ranging from psychology and sociology to literary criticism in order to establish his intertextual critical ground. In this case, the chapter concludes with powerful analyses of Jarrell's "The Night Before the Night Before Christmas" (1948) and "A Girl in a Library" (1951), in which one finds poignant insights into the world of youth and the literary means by which Jarrell achieved his telling effects. In chapter 6 Burt considers several short poems and a children's book before interrogating "The Lost World," Jarrell's most revered long poem drawing on the poet's youth and a mature work incorporating his most important themes and techniques.

An epilogue, "Conclusion: What We See and Feel and Are," ties up the case for resurrecting Jarrell through a final meditation on self which expands to Burt's disturbing consideration of the ultimate role of art:

> I have spent most of this book showing how Jarrell depicted interpersonal, interdependent, imagining selves, who speak and listen and play. Theories of such selves are now in demand, in some of the social sciences as well as in literary and cultural thought. Jarrell's poems manifest such selves; those manifestations show us what he accomplished. Poems such as "The Bronze David" and "The End of the Rainbow" also allow for a bleaker view: perhaps our senses of ourselves are not only interdependent but unsustainable. Perhaps, no matter how hard we look, we cannot find lasting recognition at all: we are so made as to seek what we cannot have, and art is our way of pretending to have it.

This is a somber coda. Nonetheless, it could be that Jarrell's most lasting lesson lies with his valiant effort to save private life and individual experience from mass culture through literary reading, a process requiring readers to distance themselves from institutions, professions, and disciplines.

If one's life is essentially constructed, as many contemporary cultural critics contend, then the issue of whether or not "art is our way of pretending" perhaps dissolves to other more immediate and tangible considerations, such as cognitive consonance. In spite of Burt's seemingly pessimistic summation, one might best read him as meaning that if a Jarrell poem helps one make a little more sense of the world or gives one a moment of pleasure, then that should be taken as a good day's work, psychologically and aesthetically. *Randall Jarrell and His Age* is a sophisticated and scholarly treatment of an artist and his metier that will be best appreciated by serious and broadly read specialists.

Chuck Berg

Review Sources

American Scholar 72, no. 2 (Spring, 2003): 144-147.
The Boston Globe, April 13, 2003, p. E3.
Library Journal 127, no. 20 (December 15, 2002): 125.
Los Angeles Times, April 13, 2003, p. R16.
Poetry 183, no. 3 (December, 2003): 169-175.
Publishers Weekly 249, no. 49 (December 9, 2002): 73.
The Times Literary Supplement, May 23, 2003, p. 11.

READING *LOLITA* IN TEHRAN
A Memoir in Books

Author: Azar Nafisi
Publisher: Random House (New York). 347 pp. $23.95
Type of work: Literary criticism and memoir
Time: 1979-1997
Locale: Tehran, Iran

In a work that is part memoir, part literary criticism, and part social history, Nafisi celebrates the powers of literature and the imagination as she recounts the story of a group of women meeting to discuss books in the repressive atmosphere of the Islamic Republic of Iran

> *Principal personages:*
> AZAR NAFISI, the author
> THE STUDENTS, her literature students (all identified by pseudonyms)
> BIJAN NADERI, her husband

In 1995, literature professor Azar Nafisi gathered together seven of the best woman students from her years in various universities in Tehran and started a special class she had been pondering for some time. For the next two years, until Nafisi's departure for the United States, the group would meet every Thursday morning in her home and discuss books. These books—Jane Austen's *Pride and Prejudice* (1813), Henry James's *The Ambassadors* (1903), F. Scott Fitzgerald's *The Great Gatsby* (1925), and Vladimir Nabokov's *Lolita* (1955), among others—are generally considered classics of English and American literature. Under the repressive regime of the Islamic Republic of Iran, they were considered dangerous examples of Western decadence, and for respectable young Iranian women to read and discuss them was a suspect activity at best, a punishable offense at worst. *Reading "Lolita" in Tehran* is a memoir of these years and a powerful commentary on how repression and fear can damage people's lives—and how literature and the imagination can help them to survive. During the course of the book, readers come to know a good deal about Nafisi, her students, her family and friends, and the culture of postrevolutionary Tehran.

Nafisi was born into a prominent Iranian family. Her father was the youngest mayor Tehran had ever had, though he was eventually to fall out of favor and even serve a jail term for insubordination to the national authorities. Her mother was among the first small group of women elected to the Iranian parliament in 1963. Among the privileges afforded by Nafisi's background was the chance to receive her secondary education in Europe and to attend college and graduate school in the United States. In the late 1970's, recently married and full of hope for her future and that of her homeland, she returned to Iran and took up a post teaching literature at the University of Tehran.

Before long, though, revolutionary forces under the leadership of Ayatollah Khomeini began to solidify their power and establish the Islamic Republic of Iran. Soon the freedoms Nafisi had long taken for granted—including the freedom to dress as she pleased, to conduct her classes as she saw fit, and to speak in public to men—began to be restricted. Though the new standards of behavior imposed by the Islamic Republic affected all Iranians, women were particularly burdened, and Nafisi describes the sensation of having her most cherished notions of self challenged: "I felt light and fictional, as if I were walking on air, as if I had been written into being and then erased in one quick swipe."

∾

Azar Nafisi was born in Tehran and educated primarily in Europe and the United States. Her previous writings include numerous newspaper, magazine, and academic journal articles. She lives in Washington, D.C., and teaches at The Johns Hopkins University in Baltimore, Maryland.

∾

Nafisi's students have had a rather different experience. By the time the group began meeting in 1995, the Islamic Republic was sixteen years old. The youngest of her students have only distant childhood memories of Iran before the revolution. As adults, they have never walked outdoors without wearing veils and heavy robes, nor have they experienced free mingling of the sexes outside of their families. Few of them ever had the opportunity to travel abroad and experience different ways of living. Their lives and identities, much more than Nafisi's, are restricted by the notions of women's propriety imposed by the government. For them, the literature class is much more than an opportunity to discuss great books. It is a rare chance to mingle with friends (unveiled, if they choose), to laugh out loud, to share stories, and to have their opinions taken seriously.

"The girls," as Nafisi calls them (rather jarringly, given her self-proclaimed feminism) range in age from their early twenties to their early thirties and are surprisingly diverse in their attitudes and backgrounds. Some are religious, others secular; some are married, others single; some are outspoken, others quiet. One was molested by her uncle when she was an adolescent. One is beaten and threatened by her husband. More than one has spent time in jail for political or moral offenses. Nafisi comments on how such individual differences among women tend to vanish under the required veil, emerging only when the women are alone together and at their ease. Thus, the portraits of Manna, Mashid, Nassrin, Yassi, Azin, Mitra, and Sanaz (all pseudonyms used to protect the women and their families still living in Iran) emerge slowly in the memoir, building in increments as their stories mingle with those of characters in the novels they read. Drawing a connection with Nabokov's young Lolita, Nafisi writes that "not only her life but also her life story is taken from her. We told ourselves we were in that class to prevent ourselves from falling victim to this second crime."

The men in this memoir never quite get the chance that the women do to become individuals for readers, though several play important parts in the story. Nafisi's husband, Bijan, is a somewhat shadowy presence, appearing occasionally in the background, often when the author needs to demonstrate how even the most sympathetic of men can fail to grasp the difficulties faced by women. The men who take her official classes tend to be more outspoken than the women (one of the reasons Nafisi excludes even the best of them from her private class) and often dominate the university scenes.

The most important male character, though, is the man Nafisi refers to only as "my magician," a former professor of film and drama who chose to leave his post rather than compromise with the powers restricting his academic freedoms. In leaving his job, the "magician" also retired from all public life and now lives a quiet existence, surrounding himself with artists and intellectuals, whom he supplies with contraband Western books and videos, European chocolates, and philosophical talk. Readers, however, must accept Nafisi's assessment of this man's remarkable charisma, as the source of his magic never quite becomes clear in the book.

Reading "Lolita" in Tehran is more, though, than a character study of the various women (and, to a lesser extent, men) who shaped Nafisi's life and thinking during her years in Iran. Indeed, it is remarkably hard to classify the book by genre. It is in part literary criticism, making clear and frequently compelling assertions about the interpretation of Humbert's character in *Lolita* or Austen's intent in *Pride and Prejudice*. In fact, Nafisi assumes her readers will have a certain familiarity with this literature, though she explains enough to remind them of key events and characters and often sparks a desire to reread certain books in the light of their own evolving lives. Woven seamlessly with literary observations are recalled lectures and conversations with university students, re-created scenes in classrooms and coffee shops, and, of course, the moving stories of her special literature class and her "girls."

The subtitle *A Memoir in Books* seems especially appropriate, as the memories and the books are irrevocably intertwined. The volume is divided into four sections, each named for a character or author featured prominently in that section—Lolita, Gatsby, James, and Austen. For instance, the "Lolita" section, the first in the book, introduces the young women in Nafisi's private class and the theme of stolen female lives and identities under the Islamic Republic of Iran. The "Gatsby" section deals with Nafisi's return to Tehran after seventeen years abroad and her reassimilation into Iranian culture in the early days of the revolution. It shows readers what happens when people attempt to make real the abstract dreams that should be left within the realms of fantasy. For Fitzgerald's Gatsby, the dream is romantic union with his beloved Daisy. For the Iranian revolutionaries, it is a society organized around their own strict interpretation of Islamic law. In both cases, the result is disastrous.

For Nafisi, one of the greatest disappointments is how repressively conservative values grow from what was once a radical vision of her country's future. While in graduate school in the United States, she had joined with leftist Iranian students in a quest to create an Iran more self-determined and less dependent on the values and influence of Europe and the United States. Back in Tehran, she is disturbed to see how the leftists collaborate with the Islamists, believing that restrictions in personal freedoms, particularly for women, are a small price to pay in order to eliminate the greater evil of Western dominance. Nafisi's unwavering critique of the Islamic Republic, in which she goes so far as to suggest that Islam is fundamentally incompatible with feminism, will no doubt lead some readers to accuse her of anti-Muslim proselytizing.

She does, however, attempt to preempt such criticism by describing with respect the faith of her devout grandmother and several of her students and by insisting that it is only the political dimension of Islam to which she objects, not the spiritual.

Against the background of her favorite books, then, Nafisi recounts her personal struggles in an Islamist Tehran very different from the city of her youth. One struggle that receives prominent attention is whether she will be allowed to teach these "decadent" books to her literature students or whether this academic freedom will be shut down by the objections of the university administration and the more conservative students themselves. At one point, she actually puts *The Great Gatsby* on trial in her class, with students acting as attorneys for the prosecution and defense. Equally critical is the personal decision she must make about whether to wear the veil in the classroom in accordance with new university regulations or to assert her personal freedom and values at the expense of her job. She chooses to leave her teaching post, but her moral victory is short-lived. Within a matter of months, a woman appearing anywhere in public showing a few strands of hair or a patch of skin on her throat will be subject to harassment by government morality squads, a jail sentence, and in some cases sanctioned beatings.

Nafisi's final struggle in Tehran was with the ultimate decision of whether to stay and try to make a difference in the homeland she has loved and for which she still feels nostalgic or to leave again, this time possibly forever. After eighteen years back in Tehran, she and her family returned to live in the United States, leaving behind her beloved city and country, her magician, and her girls. Had she chosen to stay, she would not have been able to publish this remarkable memoir about how a collection of American and English books intertwined with the minds and lives of an unexpected group of readers. Ultimately, while the book touches on many subjects—from freedom to fanaticism, from politics to parenting—it is first and foremost a book about the power of language and literature—power to teach, to transform, and to save.

Janet E. Gardner

Review Sources

The Atlantic Monthly 291, no. 5 (June, 2003): 103-104.
Commentary 116, no. 2 (September, 2003): 72-74.
The Nation 276, no. 23 (June 16, 2003): 11-12.
New Republic 229, no. 3 (July 21, 2003): 27-32.
New Statesman 132, no. 4645 (July 7, 2003): 53.
The New York Times, April 15, 2003, p. E6.
Washington Monthly 35, no. 6 (June, 2003): 58-59.
Wilson Quarterly 27, no. 3 (Summer, 2003): 126-127.

THE RED AND THE BLACKLIST
The Intimate Memoir of a Hollywood Expatriate

Author: Norma Barzman (1920-   )
Publisher: Thunder's Mouth Press (New York). 464 pp. $27.50
Type of work: Memoir
Time: 1942-1999
Locale: The United States, England, and France

The compelling true story of a film industry couple driven into exile by unscru-pulous politicians and their administration and corporate lackeys during an age of anxiety

Principal personages:
NORMA and BEN BARZMAN, screenwriters married forty-seven years
ADRIAN SCOTT, a writer and producer, jailed for contempt
EDWARD DMYTRYK, a film director who belatedly "named names"
SOPHIA LOREN, an Italian actress who starred in *El Cid*
HAROLD ROBBINS, a writer of trashy, best-selling novels

Norma Barzman's memoir describes the first wave of the 1947 anti-Red investiga-tion, which bore striking parallels to the Salem, Massachusetts, witch-hunt three cen-turies earlier. The House Committee on Un-American Activities (HUAC) issued nineteen subpoenas to prominent writers and directors. Most were friends of Norma and Ben Barzman and either "fellow travelers" or Communist Party members. Eleven of the nineteen were ordered to testify before Congress, including Dalton Trumbo (author of *Johnny Got His Gun*, 1939), Albert Maltz, Ring Lardner, Jr., and John Howard Lawson, first president of the Screen Writers Guild and head of Hollywood's CP branch. Fleeing the country was German-born Bertolt Brecht, whose play *Leben des Galilei* (pr. 1943; *The Life of Galileo*, 1947) excoriated cowardice in the face of evil inquisitors.

The others vehemently defied HUAC and were subsequently cited for contempt. After unsuccessful appeals, each of the "Hollywood Ten" spent up to a year in prison. Industry spokesmen initially defended the action of the Ten as a free-speech issue. Gradually but unequivocally, however, studio executives distanced themselves from those under suspicion. According to Victor S. Navasky's *Naming Names* (1980), timid turncoats became "friendly witnesses," confessing past associations with mem-bers of supposedly subversive organizations.

Once in demand as scriptwriters, the Barzmans found themselves becoming pari-ahs. Rather than wait for the proverbial axe to fall, they transplanted themselves to friendlier climes abroad. Like Norma Barzman's screenplay *Luxury Girls* (1953), *The Red and the Blacklist* contains frequent flashbacks and plentiful dialogue (sometimes annoying contrivances). Chapter 1, "Boy Meets Girl," opens at a 1942 Russian war relief benefit hosted by Beverly Hills writer and director Robert Rosser. Charmed upon meeting Ben Barzman, her charismatic future husband, but repelled by his chauvinistic manners, Norma throws a piece of lemon meringue pie in his face, emulating a silent-screen routine. Later Ben pours out his political passions while two restaurant eavesdroppers listen in shocked silence. According to the author's melodramatic recreation, Ben says:

∽

Norma Barzman is a screenwriter, novelist, and former journalist who lives in Beverly Hills, California. She lectures frequently on the blacklist era.

∽

> The American Communist Party is not revolutionary. Nobody wants to overthrow the government with force or violence. It's just the best, most organized way I know to fight Fascism and imperialist war and to aid the colonial peoples in their struggle for freedom.

Ben prods Norma into taking Marxism classes. A Communist Party meeting opens with a male-dominated discussion of Joseph Stalin's pamphlet *Nationalism*. Three months later, in a scene worthy of a 1940's screwball comedy, a defrocked rabbi in penny loafers performs Norma and Ben's nuptials.

The bride had sought marriage and motherhood but rebelled against attempts on Ben's part to domesticate her. Through sheer grit she landed a job with the Los Angeles *(Herald) Examiner*. The lone woman in its newsroom, she endured farting, belching, spitting, lewd gestures, and other crude behavior. Publisher William Randolph Hearst's private detective unearthed evidence of her politics and wanted her fired. An outspoken anticommunist, Hearst nonetheless would not hear of it. He and his wife Marion Davies admired her work. Norma even got invited to their San Simeon mansion on an errand to buy and deliver barrettes to Marion. Upon learning of President Franklin D. Roosevelt's death, the *Examiner* newsroom erupted in celebration. Norma fought back tears; her comrades rued the end of an era.

Thrilled at having been part of a grand crusade, she put up with Ben's bullying until he got an offer on their script *Never Say Goodbye* (1946). The catch was that a third collaborator would be brought in, and Norma's name would be dropped from the credits. Ben accepted the offer. "I felt betrayed, but I didn't fight for myself either. I gave in," Norma recalls. "In bed, for the first time, I pulled away." Believing it time to become less emotionally dependent on a single man, she commenced an affair with her husband's malleable best friend, Adrian Scott.

Featured in this spicy stew are memorable cameo appearances, such as that of her older cousin Henry Myers, the author's "first love" and a Screenwriters Guild founder, escorting thirteen-year-old Norma to Sardi's, where they were seated under his caricature. On the set of *Back to Bataan* (1945), she encountered John Wayne. The Duke's politics were loathsome to her, but his rugged sex appeal was undeniable. To test the former stuntman's mettle, director Eddie Dmytryk approved a risky special effect in which Wayne would be hoisted high in the air a split second before an explosion and then be dropped to within inches of the ground. The macho leading man insisted on doing both takes himself. Next Dmytryk devised a scene where Wayne's character eluded a Japanese patrol by jumping into freezing water and breathing from hollowed-out reeds. Told he deserved a Purple Heart after multiple takes, Wayne flashed his trademark crooked smile and drawled, "I've already got purple lips. That's good enough for me." Norma was dazzled.

The Barzmans were sipping drinks on their lawn one evening when an attractive blonde stopped in front of them on her way to a party hosted by Vincente Minnelli and Judy Garland. Sheriff's deputies, she informed them, were halting cars and inquiring about an address that corresponded to theirs. Ben had recently cancelled a meeting of the Committee for the First Amendment, a Hollywood Ten support group. Before parting, the blonde allegedly said, "I'm real glad there's people like you trying to figure out ways of not getting pushed around." Their visitor, Norma later realized, had been Marilyn Monroe.

To avoid subpoena servers, their friend Bernie Vorhaus, renowned for making "eight-day wonder" B-movies, suggested a swap of houses. When the Vorhauses and the Barzmans traded back, Norma kept a sex manual she had found. Shortly afterward, a functionary showed up at the Barzmans' home with a subpoena for Bernie. In February, 1949, the Barzmans set sail for England aboard the *Queen Mary*. Torn from creature comforts, a bitter Norma had an epiphany:

> In the filthy, moldy Hotel De Vere I'd realized that our fantastically beautiful life together had disappeared. At this moment with Ben I felt we'd never get it back again, that I'd never feel the glorious glow that all was right with the world and that we would help make it so.

Overcoming many obstacles, Ben shepherded his adaptation of Pietro di Donato's proletarian novel *Christ in Concrete* (1937) into an internationally acclaimed film titled *Give Us This Day* (1949). It was not distributed in the United States. The Barzmans joined a burgeoning expatriate community in Paris, soon counting among their friends *Herald-Tribune* nightlife columnist Art Buchwald and artist Pablo Picasso. Their "Herring Barrel Set" (a play on Secretary of State Dean Acheson having labeled the Alger Hiss case a "red herring") wrote television and film scripts under fictitious names, pooling resources like good communists. Ben, the most successful of the bunch, terminated the arrangement. Norma's *Finishing School*, directed by her then lover Bernard Vorhaus, did well in Europe under the title *Luxury Girls*. American distribution was limited to a two-week New York run in a pornographic theater. Pictures of nubile teens not in the film appeared on lobby billboards.

American officials hounded Communists in France. Following a triumphant Czechoslovakian film festival that featured *Give Us This Day*, Norma had her passport revoked, limiting her travel. With her resident permit expiring, sympathetic French officials extended it a full ten years. In 1958 the Supreme Court ordered the U.S. State Department to cease interfering with citizens traveling abroad. New York attorney Leonard Boudin advised Norma to reclaim her passport. A black embassy official hugged her and exclaimed, "I'm so happy it's *me* who's going to give it back to you!" The climate of fear had abated. The status of Canadian-born Ben was more complex. The same day his naturalized citizenship was restored, a government missive demanded nine years' back taxes. He ignored it, and nothing came of the matter.

In 1960 Norma "exchanged all kinds of giggly silliness" about men and their sexual prowess with Sophia Loren during the filming of *El Cid* (1961). Visiting the Spanish set were gossip columnist Hedda Hopper (perhaps checking to see if a certain blacklisted writer was around) and Great Britain's dapper Prince Philip. At a 1965 *Heroes of Telemark* premier, the husband of Queen Elizabeth told Ben, "I'm glad to see your name on this one." Customs officials gave him a hard time, however, upon his return to the United States. Norma and Ben rented the house of B-movie actor Rory Calhoun while Ben worked on *The Blue Max* (1966). Their arrival in Los Angeles coincided with the bloody Watts riot. In 1966 Norma attended her twenty-fifth anniversary reunion at Radcliffe College and visited Moscow. The former piqued her interest in feminism. She found the Soviet Union depressing. The French Communist Party's refusal in May of 1968 to support students and workers during the Paris uprising completed her disillusionment with international communism under its male leadership.

While at their villa near Cannes, France, the Barzmans befriended novelist Harold Robbins, author of *The Carpetbaggers* (1961). After she and Ben published *Rich Dreams* (1982), satirizing Robbins's lecherous persona, the novelist prohibited their daughters from socializing together. As a result of Ben's declining health, Norma augmented her research and writing assignments, including a pioneering column on aging, which appeared first in the *Examiner* and then in the *Los Angeles Times*. Obscenely soon (her assessment) after Ben's death in 1989, she hooked up with a virile "Old Lefty" in Cuba. Relishing her freedom, she limited the relationship to frequent excursions all over the world.

Like the protagonist in Stendhal's *The Red and the Black* (1830), which takes place in Paris and its provinces, Norma modeled her behavior after one who appealed to her idealism and sensuality. Unlike Julien, a reckless seducer who idolized Napoleon, she came to trust her instincts and emerged as a winsome and resilient mature adult. Surviving society's hypocrisies, she fully realized her dreams for herself, if not for society.

In 1999 Norma protested the presentation of a lifetime achievement Oscar to "stoolie" Elia Kazan, best known for directing *On the Waterfront* (1954). That same year, Abe Polonsky, who directed the 1948 film noir classic *Force of Evil*, admonished her to write her memoirs honestly. Is true self-definition possible, she wondered? Within boundaries, evidently, the answer is yes. Her effort deserves high praise despite surprising reticence about her father and her first husband (brilliant mathematician Claude Shannon, who once introduced her to Albert Einstein). On matters political, one wonders why such an independent-minded woman stayed in the Communist Party so long; refreshingly, she makes no apologies for her radicalism. Is the book truly intimate, or raunchy, as one reviewer asserted? One never learns under-the-covers details of her many trysts or whether her husband was equally experimental. On the surface, he indulged her affairs but never forgave her refusal to allow the great Picasso use of their house to cut lithographs. Her reason was that it would have inhibited the children.

The Red and the Blacklist deserves to rank alongside Lillian Hellman's *Scoundrel*

Time (1976) and Ring Lardner, Jr.'s *I'd Hate Myself in the Morning* (2000) as a mesmerizing, firsthand account of the chilling impact of the postwar Red Scare and one person's triumph over fear.

James B. Lane

Review Sources

Booklist 99, no. 16 (April 15, 2003): 1438.
Kirkus Reviews 71, no. 3 (February 1, 2003): 196-197.
Library Journal 128, no. 5 (March 15, 2003): 85-86.
The New York Times Book Review, June 22, 2003, p. 30.
Publishers Weekly 250, no. 6 (February 10, 2003): 170.

REEFER MADNESS
Sex, Drugs, and Cheap Labor in the American Black Market

Author: Eric Schlosser (1950-   )
Publisher: Houghton Mifflin (Boston). 310 pp. $23.00
Type of work: Current affairs and economics

Schlosser investigates the influence of the black market in the United States, particularly pornography, marijuana, and illegal immigration

Almost before his readers—the fans, converts, activists, company executives, and conservative critics—have "digested" the muckraking tour de force *Fast Food Nation* (2001), Eric Schlosser has given them a whole new subject to consider: the United States' thriving black-market economy. *Reefer Madness* awakens readers to the massive profits available to pornography magnates, the rising demand for domestic marijuana, the relationship between marijuana possession laws and national incarceration rates, and the American addiction to foods grown and processed by illegal migrant workers. Moreover, this volume matches—or even exceeds—its predecessor in the areas that made the latter such a huge success: an exquisite sense of the dramatic, reliance on academic social science as well as solid documents from governmental and nongovernmental organizations, gonzo daring in capturing original material, and vivid writing. Schlosser persuades by overwhelming and enticing his readers. One is taken to places one fears to go (labor camps, prisons, high-tech indoor marijuana nurseries), and yet this is a moral journey, aimed at high-minded social reform.

In his brief introduction, "The Underground," Schlosser claims that while the U.S. economy has always known different kinds of black-market activities (especially during Prohibition), the post-1960's era has seen their growth to undreamed-of proportions. Relying on the work of both the Internal Revenue Service and Austrian economist Friedrich Schneider, Schlosser asserts that about 10 percent of the United States' gross domestic product comes from shadow labor and illegal production. This means that in 1997, "Americans had failed to pay about $200 billion of federal taxes that were owed, an amount larger than the government's annual spending on Medicare." Moreover, the kind of underground economy that has evolved does far more damage than what preceded it.

In the sectors Schlosser examines—marijuana production, immigrant labor, and pornography—human costs are enormous. They come in the forms of bulging prisons, where merely disreputable "criminals" are mixed with the truly depraved; of widespread contempt for law enforcement authorities (who, in the case of marijuana investigations, often seem motivated by the desire to confiscate the property of the accused); of poverty, helplessness, and poisoning for Mexican "guest workers"; and of the multiple degradations associated with the pornography "industry."

Schlosser wants to accomplish more in this volume than simply arouse public consciousness of these three areas of economic deceit. He believes that "the underground is inextricably linked to the mainstream," and so the shape it takes indicates some-

A correspondent for The Atlantic Monthly, *Eric Schlosser achieved celebrity status with the publication of* Fast Food Nation: The Dark Side of the All-American Meal *(2001), which combined prodigious research and dramatic writing to expose abuses in the meat industry, fast-food chains, and government regulatory systems. Schlosser's reporting has earned both a National Magazine Award and a Sidney Hillman Foundation Award.*

thing less than desirable about the national soul. Thus, if many small operators thrive in a cash-based, tax-free secret economy that is "beneath contempt," a strong light is shed on the big operators—at companies such as Enron, Anderson, and Tyco—who evade taxes, or federal scrutiny, or responsibility for employee welfare.

In the essay "Reefer Madness," Schlosser brilliantly refines earlier writings for *The Atlantic Monthly* and *Rolling Stone.* He places his research within a narrative about Mark Young, a thirty-eight-year-old fisherman, marijuana lover, and Harley Davidson mechanic from Indianapolis. Young played a minor role in a large marijuana-growing venture and in 1992 received a life prison sentence without possibility of parole. Schlosser introduces Young's logic-defying case and then teases readers with bits of the story as he unfolds a much larger account. By the end, readers will have learned a great deal about the botany, history, and pharmacology of *Cannabis sativa;* its criminalization, decriminalization, and recriminalization; its association with anti-Mexican feeling in the Southwest; mandatory minimum sentence legislation; Leavenworth Penitentiary; and the ineffectiveness of antimarijuana policing.

Schlosser's writing is brisk, clear, and impassioned. "A society that can punish a marijuana offender more severely than a murderer is caught in the grip of a deep psychosis," he proclaims: "It has a bad case of reefer madness." The causes of the boom in domestic marijuana are mainly the result of bad public policy, he says. By spraying Mexican and Colombian fields with the herbicide paraquat, ignoring the suffering of small farmers, and persistently overstating the damaging effects of the drug, the government prepared the way for its clandestine domestic production, he argues. Midwestern farmers have been especially tempted—during World War II, the "Hemp for Victory" program encouraged them to plant the crop—and corn has fallen to record low prices. When a bushel of high quality marijuana can fetch seventy thousand dollars, corn becomes prized for its ability to hide the so-called ditchweed.

Schlosser is aware of the dangers of pot usage and favors informational campaigns to warn young people of its incompatibility with academic and athletic achievement. He recommends Portugal and Spain as models for decriminalizing the possession of all drugs, "placing emphasis instead on prosecuting drug dealers and providing treatment for drug abusers." On the whole, the more benign approaches found in Europe seem to be working, for rates of drug use there are lower than those in the United

States. The overwhelming problem, however, is the impossible cost of the anti-marijuana campaign. When police are preoccupied (and corrupted by) reefer madness, when courts and lawyers deplete public coffers, and when whole new gulags of prisons are established to handle people who offer no real threat to society—something decisive and of national scope must be done.

"In the Strawberry Fields," a relatively short piece, describes immigrant labor abuses in the central California towns of Guadalupe and Watsonville. For those who thought that César Chávez and the United Farm Workers had mostly eliminated the exploitation of "invisible workers," present realities will seem both shocking and complicated. To his credit, Schlosser appreciates that big growers confront harsh economic circumstances. The demand for fresh strawberries has risen sharply in recent decades, so real money can be made from this crop. Strawberries, however, are a farmer's nightmare. Highly perishable, subject to myriad pests and the wrong amounts of rain, heat, wind, and cold, strawberries require that growers have large reserves of capital to survive frequent poor harvests. Meanwhile, competition is so fierce that production costs can be held down in only one area—labor. The laborers are there, for despite the fact that strawberry picking leads inevitably to serious lower back problems and other health problems, illegal immigrants are happy to get the work.

How do growers avoid paying overtime, Social Security and Medicare taxes, and workers' compensation premiums? Schlosser reports that while "many strawberry growers play by the rules and treat their workers well," the temptation to keep workers off the books is too great for some to resist. Using savvy lawyers, growers have evolved modern sharecropping contracts that relieve them of large responsibilities. Mature workers are invited to manage portions of the fields in exchange for receiving 50 percent of the profits realized. The grower, legally described now as a "commission merchant," supplies the expensive ingredients to launch a particular crop, thus immediately putting the "independent operator" in debt. If the crop fails, this debt is rolled over into the next cycle's finances.

Meanwhile, the operators (often called *mexicanos*) take over the task of supplying labor. Under these novel arrangements, "the sharecropper became the employer of record, responsible for hiring strawberry pickers, paying their wages, withholding their taxes, and checking their green cards." While some succeed at this, the majority find themselves becoming "debt peons."

Throughout the book, Schlosser invites the reader to reflect on what level of dedication he or she is prepared to yield to the ideal of a free market. While the North American Free Trade Agreement (NAFTA) and the World Trade Organization seem to the majority to be generally beneficial, when applied to labor markets their essentially libertarian principles may mean that prosperity will flow to the ownership classes. What is happening in the strawberry fields of California is the result of the fifty-cents-an-hour wages in "the fields of Baja California and the mountain villages of Oaxaca." Left unchecked, current labor trends may mean that every American city will witness the growth of shantytowns, for the inherent tendency of a purely free market is to seek "a work force that is hungry, desperate, and cheap—a work force that is anything but free."

"An Empire of the Obscene" is Schlosser's final essay in the book. Expanded, it could have been a book in its own right. Exposés of the pornography industry are easy to find, for example, Susan Faludi's *Stiffed* (1999) and Gary W. Potter's *The Porn Merchants* (1986). What Schlosser offers is a relentless examination of the economic side of the business, as personified in the career of Reuben Sturman, who, before his death in 1997, "dominated the production and distribution of pornography not only in the United States but also throughout the world." The son of Russian Jewish immigrants, Sturman returned from military service in World War II determined to make it big by starting out small. He developed a business in selling unpurchased comic books to mom-and-pop stores in the Cleveland area. Occasionally, he acquired copies of "sex-pulp" novels and cheap imitations of *Playboy*. According to Schlosser, Sturman noticed that "there was a great demand for such publications and that a sex magazine produced at least twenty times the revenue per copy of a remaindered comic book."

Besides being able to segment his life almost totally (he was a respectable benefactor of the Cleveland Symphony), Sturman exhibited another unusual trait: He despised the Internal Revenue Service (IRS). Schlosser brilliantly develops the multileveled story: Sturman's efforts to keep his business ventures out of view, the use of Swiss bank accounts and dummy offshore corporations, his practice of "creaming" the profits from his peep-show franchises, his relations with the Cosa Nostra, and his penchant for suing the government when threatened by its representatives. Opposed to Sturman is Richard N. Rosfelder, a Cleveland-based IRS investigator, who requires twenty years to put Sturman in prison. Schlosser finally takes the reader directly to Sturman, having interviewed him in a Kentucky prison a year before his death. When the session is over, Schlosser watches Sturman walking in the courtyard:

> I pictured him as a young man, selling comic books from the trunk of his old car, getting to know the owners of Cleveland candy stores—and the power he later wielded, the wealth he made and lost, the businesses around the world, the houses, the Rolls-Royce, the millions of dollars in coins flowing through his peep machines, the millions spent to lay him low, all because of sex.

In signature fashion, Schlosser backgrounds this tale with exquisitely researched material on key aspects of the rise of pornography in American society. One learns about stag films; *Deep Throat* (1972); the 1970 report of the Commission on Pornography and Obscenity; the importance of the videocassette recorder (VCR), cable television, and the Internet; and how the San Fernando Valley became the world's foremost place for the production of "adult entertainment."

In moral terms, Schlosser is most concerned to press the case for national honesty. Pornography has emerged from the underground. Its use by major hotel and motel chains, "family friendly" cable companies, and other "respectable" businesses testifies to a normalization that is not publicly acknowledged. "In 2001, Americans spent about $465 million ordering adult films on pay-per-view," he reports. "Most of the money was earned by well-known companies that don't boast about their links with the sex trade, such as EchoStar, DirecTV, AT&T Broadband, and AOL Time Warner." Like inexpensive food in grocery stores, pornography testifies to a dedication to a free market whose full consequences in human suffering is not examined closely.

What is most impressive about pornography's ubiquity is the lack of any real resistance to it. A revolution in national values has taken place, but few are willing to confront that fact openly. "Sometimes the price of freedom is what freedom brings," says Schlosser. Black markets will always exist, he avers, but they will diminish in importance "when our public morality is consistent with our private one." The underground is, he concludes, a good measure of the health of nations, for "when much is wrong, much needs to be hidden."

Schlosser can be faulted on many points. Ever the moralist, he often cloaks his larger purposes by claiming that he is just following the money. On many issues he sounds like a libertarian, but the burden of his economic "reportage" is an appeal for strong government intervention. His clear, effective prose is not simply descriptive; rather, it arises out of moral outrage and a desire to see wrongs reformed—for example, the decriminalization of marijuana. Often he operates in the guise of the unbiased reporter. One is never sure if he works from a consistent political philosophy.

These shortcomings are forgivable, for Schlosser is a kind of national treasure. He has so embarrassed the fast-food industry that changes have already taken place. One awaits with great interest his next book, on the prison system. In a profession that can easily engender cynicism, Schlosser exhibits a confidence in the power of an informed public to deal with apparently insoluble problems. This is a great gift to a morally confused nation which presents itself as the world's foremost democracy.

Leslie E. Gerber

Review Sources

Booklist 99, no. 17 (May 1, 2003): 1506-1507.
Business Week, May 19, 2003, p. 22.
The Economist 367, no. 8323 (May 10, 2003): 72.
Kirkus Reviews 71, no. 6 (March 15, 2003): 448.
Library Journal 128, no. 7 (April 15, 2003): 110.
The New York Times, May 23, 2003, p. E38.
The New York Times Book Review, May 11, 2003, p. 17.
Publishers Weekly 250, no. 13 (March 31, 2003): 49.
Time 161, no. 17 (April 28, 2003): 71.

REGARDING THE PAIN OF OTHERS

Author: Susan Sontag (1933-   )
Publisher: Farrar, Straus and Giroux (New York). 144
  pp. $20.00
Type of work: Essays
Time: The nineteenth and twentieth centuries
Locale: Europe, Africa, Asia, North America, and South
  America

Sontag explores the world's reaction to human suffering in war from the time that images of human pain began to be captured in photographs

Principal personages:

VIRGINIA WOOLF (1882-1941), the English novelist who explored how photographs determine readers' reactions to the cruelty of war
FRANCISCO DE GOYA (1746-1828), the renowned Spanish artist who created one of the most striking series of pictures on the suffering wrought by war
ROBERT CAPA (1913-1954), the most famous wartime photojournalist of the twentieth century
MATTHEW BRADY (1823-1896), the celebrated Civil War photographer
WILLIAM WORDSWORTH (1770-1850), the Romantic poet who saw urban life as creating a profusion of images that dulled the human response to the pain of others

In *On Photography* (1977), Susan Sontag presented what is arguably the most important discussion of the meaning of photography in the English language. Her work has been cited—attacked and acclaimed—ever since it began appearing as a series of essays in *The New York Review of Books* in the early 1970's. In scattered essays and introductions to the work of others, she has extended her arguments about photography, but in *Regarding the Pain of Others* she has provided not only a major restatement of views but also a challenge to some of her earlier opinions. Although this book concentrates on reaction to photography, it is also, like *On Photography*, a deeply probing meditation on modern life.

Sontag begins her study of wartime photographs with a discussion of Virginia Woolf's *Three Guineas* (1938), a book which explores the origins of war by looking at a set of photographs depicting the Spanish Civil War (1936-1939). In it, Woolf examines the different ways women and men react to war, especially as war has been a male enterprise. Would a man revolted by war have the same feelings as a woman like Woolf, who has neither the power nor the desire to make war? The man who writes to her about his antiwar feelings assumes that his reactions are the same as those of Woolf's, but she does not believe that he can take his "we" (himself and Woolf) for granted.

Sontag does not so much challenge Woolf's feminist position as suggest it is not comprehensive enough, for she notes that Woolf herself later lapses into the same use of "we." "No 'we' should be taken for granted when the subject is looking at other people's pain," Sontag concludes. The distinction to be made, in other words, is not just between men's and women's reactions to the portrayal of war but also between the reality of war as others experience it and the perception of everyone else who only observes and responds to the images of war.

~

Susan Sontag, a critic of contemporary culture, established her authority with her first collection of articles, Against Interpretation *(1966), and with penetrating studies such as* Illness as Metaphor *(1978). Her novel* In America *(2000) won the National Book Award. In 2001 she was awarded the Jerusalem Prize for the body of her work.*

~

In fact, Woolf's generalizations about what photographs of war mean are questionable, Sontag suggests: "To read in the pictures . . . only what confirms a general abhorrence of war is to stand back from an engagement with Spain as a country with a history. It is to dismiss politics." The viewer who regards war as inevitable or a particular war as just will not regard the gruesome photographs as an antiwar argument at all. Indeed, the violence shown in photographs can be taken by some viewers as the consequence of heroic action, a fight for certain ideals, and an affirmation of human courage.

Sontag points out that many important antiwar collections of photographs were published between World War I and World War II, and although pacifists viewed the visual record as proving the horror of war and were spurred on to create agreements between countries to outlaw war, horrified responses to these images could not ultimately overcome the forces of history that Woolf ignored in *Three Guineas*. As the politics of an era change, so do the meaning of photographs. Thus Sontag concludes that in the "current political mood, the friendliest to the military in decades, the pictures of wretched hollow-eyed GIs that once seemed subversive of militarism and imperialism may seem inspirational. Their revised subject: ordinary American young men doing their unpleasant, ennobling duty."

Photographs not only change meaning in terms of the historical context in which they are viewed but they also share a problematic status because of their form of publication. Thus Robert Capa's famous photograph of a Spanish Republican soldier at the moment of death appeared in *Life* magazine across from a full-page advertisement for Vitalis, a hair cream, illustrated with photographs of men with shimmering hair. Two worlds collide in these side-by-side photographs, with one image no more important than the other. How can Capa's photograph—in spite of its shocking power—retain a hold on viewers in a world that is bombarded with the reproduction and diffusion of images?

There is a further, disturbing ambiguity in the Capa photograph that Sontag cannot ignore. It has been alleged that the photograph is, in fact, just a shot taken during a training exercise. In other words, like many other photographs Sontag discusses—such as the great work of Civil War photographer Matthew Brady and his assistants—this one may have been staged or rehearsed. When the image is thus called into doubt, it loses some of its power, because a photograph is taken to be a trace of an actual event, an undeniable representation of the real. Photographs, Sontag argues, cannot ever be as authentic as, say, Francisco de Goya's magnificent series of eighty-three etchings that protested Napoleon's invasion of France, because Goya's art is undeniably the work of his own hand, accompanied by captions that express his outrage at the inhumanity of war.

On one hand, Goya's work can never have quite the same immediacy as a photograph—which proclaims that the photographer was there, and the viewer can see what the photographer saw. On the other hand, the immediacy—even when the photograph has not been staged—necessarily has a degree of bias or subjectivity. The photograph has to be taken from an angle, and what the angle frames is also a testament to what is left out of the picture. As Sontag notes, viewers want to believe that photographs are literally true, but an examination of the medium shows this cannot be so.

Even though Sontag seems to discount heavily the reliability of photographs and their ultimate power to persuade and move people to antiwar actions, she nevertheless takes issue with her earlier book's pessimism that photographs have actually dominated the public's sense of reality and that war is only what they see in photographs or on television. She reexamines her earlier concern about the way photography and the mass media infiltrate human consciousness and sensationalize events in terms of images.

She notes that, beginning with the poetry of William Wordsworth, this distrust of modern life, of an urbanization that leads people to crave greater and greater visual stimulation that degrades their ability to reason, has evolved into the alarming writings of certain French philosophers who believe that people only see the world—including the pain of others in war—as a spectacle. Their senses have been so captivated by the mass media that they cannot think for themselves. History changes, in other words, only in so far as the media does. An outraged Sontag exclaims: "To speak of reality becoming a spectacle is a breathtaking provincialism." How can a group of intellectuals suppose that their jaded view of the media has any relevance to millions of people in the less priviledged world, whose suffering is real and not mediated by photographs or television. Millions who watch television lead less comfortable lives that do not allow them the "luxury of patronizing reality."

Sontag is not merely attacking her fellow intellectuals; rather, she is affirming a sense of reality that exists apart from portrayals of it. As she puts it: "There is still a reality that exists independent of the attempts to weaken its authority." *On Photography* never denied this reality, but it did seem to suggest reality could be overwhelmed by the plethora of photographic images. Seeing the extremes to which her own former argument can be taken, she recoils. No quantity of images, she implies, can ever actually supplant reality.

What, then, should be the proper attitude toward photography? Sontag is aware that some viewers simply refuse to look—to be inundated by images of wartime atrocities. Even when viewers do look, their very sympathy for suffering may only express their sense of distance from the pain they see. The photographs simply make for more spectators. What else can most people do, though, but watch? Sontag asks. It is in the nature of vision itself and not photographs to create a sense of distance, of removal from the action. Photographs have not invented the way people regard the pain of others.

Sontag does not believe it is a problem that viewers switch channels or turn pages when confronted with images of suffering. She believes there is no reproach involved, because photographs are no different from anything else one sees; that is, photographs cannot be expected to transform one's vision of the world any more than one's sight of anything else would. Similarly, photographs cannot be expected to reform the world, to give it a sense of history. At best, photographs are a goad to curiosity and may spark inquiries into origins of human suffering.

Ultimately, it is not possible to experience fully another's pain, Sontag concludes. One asks too much of photographs in this regard. They provide only an approach to the pain of others, an approach that can be explored or evaded. Either way, there is nothing inherent in the photographic medium that excludes alternative responses.

At the end of her book, Sontag returns to her insistence that "we," in regard to the experience of war, the reality of war, can only be used by those who have been there. When a journalist, a soldier, an aid worker—anyone who has been under fire during war—claims that "we" (everyone who has not experienced war) cannot imagine how horrible it is, Sontag replies, in the last sentence of her book, "they are right."

In her acknowledgments, Sontag provides a brief but highly informative survey of the literature on photography she used while composing her book. It is a pity, however, that *Regarding the Pain of Others* has no index. It is extraordinary that a writer who makes so many references to other writers, artists, and thinkers and her publisher—the only publisher she has ever had—have never included an index in any of her books. For both beginning students and scholars, a fully indexed Sontag would aid in rereading and cross-referencing her arguments within and between her books.

Carl Rollyson

Review Sources

Booklist 99, no. 11 (February 1, 2003): 954.
The Christian Science Monitor, March 27, 2003, p. 19.
Kirkus Reviews 71, no. 3 (February 1, 2003): 218.
Library Journal 128, no. 4 (March 1, 2003): 108.
Los Angeles Times, March 16, 2003, p. 8.
New Republic 228, no. 15/16 (April 21, 2003): 28-31.
New Statesman 132, no. 4650 (August 11, 2003): 34-35.
The New York Review of Books 50, no. 7 (May 1, 2003): 8-10.
The New York Times, March 11, 2003, p. E10.
The New York Times Book Review, March 23, 2003, p. 11-12.
Publishers Weekly 250, no. 7 (February 17, 2003): 67.
The San Francisco Chronicle, April 13, 2003, p. M6.

RESPECT IN A WORLD OF INEQUALITY

Author: Richard Sennett (1943-   )
Publisher: W. W. Norton (New York). 288 pp. $24.95
Type of work: Autobiography and sociology
Time: 2003
Locale: The United States

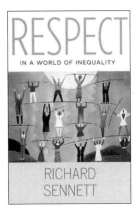

A literary experiment by one of the United States' premier sociologists and intellectuals in blending personal story with reflections about self-worth, talent, economic opportunity, and the welfare system

Part 1 of this volume is aptly titled "Scarcity of Respect." From most points on the political spectrum and from widely varying religious and cultural groups come complaints about a lack of respect. "Disrespecting" others seems to come naturally to today's youth, though they fight to keep from experiencing disrespect themselves. Lack of success in school engenders programs of "self-esteem" and "self-respect"— to many critics, an opiate that hides from youth the consequences of their indolence and failure to compete. This is not only a society which increasingly abjures titles; it is one in which it is easy to get along without knowing last names. Sociologist Robert Bly deplores the arrival of the "Sibling Society," in which too-quickly grown children and "half-adults" awkwardly negotiate situations of presumed equality, while the genuinely mature look on with bewilderment and pain. In short, respect is a problem.

Born in 1943 in Chicago, Richard Sennett was raised by a single mother from a well-placed family. Sennett's father (whose first name is never mentioned) was "a dreamy, irresponsible man, his thoughts gravitating to the problems of translating modern Spanish poetry." With his brother, he fought with the anti-Fascists in the Spanish Civil War. "My father fled when I was a few months old—I never met him— and my mother was financially down on her luck," reports Sennett. His uncle, William Sennett, had joined the Communist Party in 1931 and did not leave it until 1958, after which he became (while only moderately repentant) a wealthy capitalist. His oral history was published by the University of California in 1984 as *Communist Functionary and Corporate Executive.*

Thus, Sennett came by his radical credentials honesty. During his productive academic career he has been one of those rare intellectuals who could bridge the Old and the New Left, maintaining a steady interest in the lives of working-class people while appreciating the way capitalism has transformed itself in the last quarter-century into something Karl Marx could never have imagined. At the same time, paralleling a path created by the late Christopher Lasch, Sennett has integrated economics, psychology, urban planning, and nineteenth century social history in demonstrating how the "public sphere" has become both impoverished and curiously marginalized. In *The Fall of Public Man* (1976), he described the movement away from the res publica to a (con-

structed) zone of life defined as "private sphere,"
"realm of intimacy," and the realm of "narcissistic
self-exploration." Well before the Bill Clinton era,
he noticed how bored society had become with the
details of political programs (where "policy wonks"
operate) while at the same time being far too interested in the "integrity," "credibility," and personal
character of political leaders, especially as these are
revealed in their sexual behavior.

*Richard Sennett grew up in the
infamous Cabrini Green housing
project in Chicago. He now
teaches sociology at the London
School of Economics and at New
York University.*

These concerns form the background against which Sennett examines the idea of
respect, especially as it impacts welfare recipients and those whose private "failures"
have made them "public" persons by virtue of their "disgraceful" dependency on the
achievements and talents of others. Sennett has a good feel for such persons because
some of his childhood was spent in one of the United States' most notorious housing
projects, Cabrini Green in Chicago. While Sennett's ruminations on life in Cabrini
Green help structure *Respect in a World of Inequality*, of equal importance are reflections on how his musical and academic talents allowed him to exit this increasingly
dangerous environment.

Identified young as a gifted cellist, Sennett was sent to New York to become a per-
former, conductor, and composer. He and his mother left the project in 1950—though
she, as a professional social worker, continued to be a part of Chicago's legendary
struggle with poverty and racial animosity. Richard rose quickly in the elite world of
classical music performance and developed an abiding fascination for the pleasures
and disciplines of craftsmanship per se. While ambition is indispensable, "the development of any talent involves an element of craft, for doing something well for its
own sake, and it is this craft element which provides the individual with an inner sense
of self-respect," he writes. Further, "It's not so much a matter of getting ahead as of
becoming inside. The craft of music made that gift to me." Acute tendonitis in his left
hand led him to a surgeon suggested by the great pianist Rudolf Serkin. However, the
procedure to correct it failed, and at age twenty-one Sennett had to abandon his musical career. Still a cello player, he cherishes the memories of how his long training provided him with self-confidence, competence, and discipline.

While still a musician, Sennett had worked on an undergraduate degree in history
at the University of Chicago. After graduating he entered the renowned American
Civilization program at Harvard University, eager to pursue his interests in the history
of cities, sociology, and psychology. His mentors were David Riesman, Erik Erikson,
and Robert Merton. Deeply influenced by Marxism (as were so many in academe in
these years), vividly aware of "the ones left behind" in the ghettos of Chicago and the
trenches of Vietnam, Sennett disliked the pomposity of the Harvard atmosphere.
Also, he noticed that many of the most vitriolic critics of "the Establishment" came
from privileged backgrounds and were unaware of how their exquisite educations and
economic security were the "cultural capital" they drew upon to make themselves into
radicals. To be black and poor and ill-educated, he knew, made the task of achieving
self-certainty and self-respect an all-consuming business. Too, one could easily be-

come the target of "a compassion that wounds." Thus, even as the egalitarian student movement developed, harsh class realities were evolving in northern American cities—this, despite proclamations of equality and social renewal from the Civil Rights movement and Lyndon Johnson's Great Society. Unlike many leftists, Sennett remained steadfastly focused on these class phenomena.

By the age of thirty, Sennett had published five books and was a celebrated and controversial professor at New York University. His influential *The Hidden Injuries of Class* (1972), coauthored with Jonathan Cobb, was the result of extensive interviews with white working-class Bostonians. The study aimed at discovering "whether they had a distinctive consciousness of class and how it worked." In the process, Sennett came to understand how deep was his subjects' fear and suspicion of blacks, welfare recipients, and others "below them" on the social scale. Their verbal attacks revealed insecurities and self-doubts—and a desire to have these relieved by "attacking the integrity of others."

A child of poverty himself, Sennett assumed that he might be able to understand his research subjects, only to find that the barriers already thrown up by his education and social advancement were substantial. Subtler dynamics of the inequality-respect process began to emerge as the work progressed: "the need to hold back for the sake of respecting someone else, the divide between self-respect and group respect, the strength of self which diminishes others, the ill fit between self-confidence and the regard of others, the bond to others which results from the 'error' of imagining you are alike."

Respect in a World of Inequality proceeds through the explorations of a number of such memories, convictions, philosophic assessments, and historical reflections. Throughout, Sennett assigns great importance to the processes of deference, subordination, cooperation, and obedience among artists, artisans, and craftsmen. He is aware that abstract appeals to citizenship, moral and legal equality, and universal human dignity have little traction in the daily practices of a highly competitive society. This being the case, a new vocabulary for guiding behavior and perception is required. Such an effort, he thinks, might be helped by "trying to make society more resemble the concert; that is, by exploring ways to perform as equals, and so show mutual respect." Mutuality, in turn, "requires expressive work. It must be enacted or performed."

If this seems rather evanescent, one can take much from Sennett's analyses of a number of particular problems. Enlightenment societies are dedicated to the principal of "careers open to talent"—as opposed to careers open to inherited privilege. By promoting competition among people, the ideal of the key positions in society being occupied by the most capable is realized. What, however, of those who fall to their "natural" level of achievement? With reference to SAT testing and affirmative action, Sennett stands with Nicholas Lemann and Howard Gardner in pleading for a recognition of the limitations of intelligence testing and the need to provide honored places to those who too easily write themselves off as "losers." Here again, he offers the example of craftsmanship and the achievement of useful competencies. Implied is a society that extends prestige to those who work well—if not at the highest level of specialization or mastery. Sennett also pleads for an educational system that is less preoccupied with identifying potential (a very elusive concept) and more interested in honoring achievements based on small attainments linked together to form locally valued competencies.

Those who are dependant on others, especially welfare recipients, are often maligned or marginalized. Is there a culturewide agreement on what sorts of dependence are good? In chapter 4, "The Shame of Dependence," Sennett probes this topic at several levels. For example, he finds that Sigmund Freud provides a far more positive view of regression to childhood than does John Locke—the former picturing it as the recovery of earlier stages and, therefore, a "part of the psychodynamic of reasoning." In Japanese culture, Sennett notes, "people surrender to other adults, expecting to be cared for as by right." Shame and guilt can attend dependency, and the welfare system has indeed "infantalized" many adults in damaging ways. Sennett believes that this culture's constant intonation of the virtue of self-reliance has become nearly pathological. A steadfast insistence on toughing it out alone, never asking for help, produces "in the polity, as in the high tech company, a discussion of needs only after things have become a mess."

Autonomy is not exactly the opposite of dependency, in view of the fact that it requires the right social conditions (political freedom, for example) for its flourishing. In psychological terms, the autonomous self emerges in social interaction, in which subtle processes of identification, differentiation, giving and receiving operate. Autonomy becomes one of Sennett's key positive values, though he understands it in ways that are unfamiliar. It involves not only an acknowledgment of the other's difference but also his or her opacity. Realizing that people are not only unfathomable at some level but also uniquely aware of their own needs and capacities leads to humility and respect. "Conceived in this way, autonomy is a powerful recipe for equality," he writes. When, in a mutual way, one acknowledges in advance that he or she cannot understand important aspects of others, "you are treating the fact of their autonomy as equal to your own."

How can such an insight lead to welfare systems that lift up both the self-respect of recipients as well as their incomes? Sennett has no magic answers, but he is opposed to schemes that place "clients" in the role of passive spectators of inscrutable bureaucratic processes and the efforts of an ever-changing parade of social workers. As reviewer David Glenn puts it, Sennett wants to direct the emphasis of welfare away from ensuring equality of opportunity and the chance to "succeed": "He is much more concerned with the need to provide social respect to people who fail to climb the greasy pole defined by the professional classes." As a result, Sennett favors returning to the Richard Nixon-era discussions of guaranteed minimum incomes and the imagining of a "cleaner" system that protects recipients from condescension and humiliation.

How successful is Sennett's blend of analysis and memoir in this book? While his effort provides interesting and valuable pieces (the contrast between the welfare philosophies of Jane Addams and Mother Frances Xavier Cabrini is particularly insightful), Sennett fails to give the reader either completed narratives or rounded sociological conclusions. It is too easy to agree with him when he admits that "this essay has shifted, I know, between the extremes of concrete experience and social theory, leaving in the gap policies and plans." The sketchiness of the personal material is very irritating. He was a fatherless boy in the projects—how did he deal with this burden? What connections to the present crisis of fatherlessness might be drawn? What, indeed, became of his father? How did his extended family (barely mentioned) provide a platform for his own self-esteem and security? How did the Civil Rights movement and the New Left actually influence his outlooks? What of the urban riots of the late 1960's?

If Sennett disappoints by the thinness of the autobiography, he infuriates by his unwillingness to join the larger conversation on character, virtue, craftsmanship, and citizenship that has been going on for more than two decades among ethicists, social philosophers, and other sociologists. Despite the fact that he ploughs areas already scored by the likes of Robert Bellah, William Sullivan, Amitai Etzioni, Alasdair MacIntyre, Michael Sandel, Stephen Carter, and Stanley Hauerwas, Sennett blithely ignores this literature. He also makes insufficient use of Immanuel Kant, the dominant modern theorist of self-respect and human dignity.

The result of these omissions is to make the book seem disengaged, vaporous, and out of touch. This is particularly unfortunate because the companion volume, *The Corrosion of Character: The Personal Consequences of Work in the New Capitalism,* (1998), exhibited none of these flaws. Instead, it offered a detailed and disturbing picture of what it means to work in the "new capitalism," whose flexibility and decentralization seem to answer the left's historic critique of the corporation. At age sixty, Richard Sennett is at the pinnacle of his career. One hopes that better efforts will follow.

Leslie E. Gerber

Review Sources

Booklist 99, no. 7 (December 1, 2002): 633.
The Nation 276, no. 14 (April 14, 2003): 34.
New York 36, no. 2 (January 20, 2003): 68-69.
The New York Review of Books 50, no. 3 (February 27, 2003): 31-34.
The New York Times Book Review, March 9, 2003, p. 17.
Publishers Weekly 249, no. 43 (October 28, 2002): 59.
The Times Literary Supplement, March 21, 2003, p. 11.

RESURRECTION MEN

Author: Ian Rankin (1960-   )
Publisher: Little, Brown (Boston). 436 pp. $19.95
Type of work: Novel
Time: 2001
Locale: Scotland

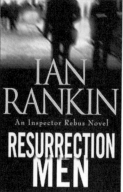

Scotland's best-known detective is back on the case and in trouble in the latest installment of Ian Rankin's Detective Inspector John Rebus series

Principal characters:
JOHN REBUS, a detective inspector in the
    Lothian and Borders Police
SIOBHAN CLARKE, his partner
MORRIS GERALD CAFFERTY, "BIG GER," a
    gangster who is Rebus's long-time nemesis
JAMES "JAZZ" MCCULLOUGH,
FRANCIS GRAY,
ALLAN WARD,
STU SUTHERLAND, and
TAM BARCLAY, police officers who are assigned to a refresher course
    and who, together with Rebus, make up "The Wild Bunch"

"Scots writers snubbed in UK book poll" ran the headline in the May 19, 2003, *Scotsman.* The BBC Big Read list of Britain's one hundred most popular books included works by fifty-nine English writers but those of just three Scots: J. K. Rowling (four books in her Harry Potter series), Kenneth Grahame (*The Wind in the Willows*, 1908), and Robert Louis Stevenson (*Treasure Island*, 1883). Sir Walter Scott did not make the list; neither did Muriel Spark, nor Irvine Welsh, author of *Trainspotting* (1993). It was the omission of Arthur Conan Doyle and Ian Rankin that especially irked Marc Lambert, head of the Scottish Book Trust: "It is just absurd that Ian Rankin isn't on the list. He is one of the top-selling crime writers of all time. Month to month, his Inspector Rebus novels are on the best seller lists. And where would crime fiction be without Conan Doyle, the inventor of Sherlock Holmes?" With a writer as popular and arguably as important as Rankin omitted from the BBC shortlist, some wondered what was becoming of literary Britain after devolution.

Born in 1960 in a small mining town in the Kingdom of Fife (just north of Edinburgh), Rankin may not have made the Big Read list, but he is already a Scottish institution (and virtually an industry). He published his first Inspector Rebus novel, *Knots and Crosses*, in 1987, a year after finishing postgraduate studies at the University of Edinburgh, and published thirteen more from 1991 to 2003, including two collections of short stories. (As prolific as he is popular, he published six other novels early in his career.) The Rebus novels, and therefore Rankin's career, did not take off until the

Since the publication of Ian Rankin's first Rebus novel, Knots and Crosses *(1987), the Rebus books have been translated into twenty-two languages, and three of them have been televised. The winner of many literary prizes, Rankin was awarded the Order of the British Empire in 2002 and is Great Britain's best-selling crime writer.*

1997 publication of *Black and Blue*, winner of the Crime Writers' Association's coveted Gold Dagger Award. Remarkably, even as they have become increasingly complex, the novels have become increasingly popular, and not just in Scotland.

Like all good detective fiction, the Rebus novels are entertaining (a good read) and stimulating (offering opportunities for mental gamesmanship), but they are something more as well. As English novelist John Lanchester has pointed out, Rankin's fiction occupies the middle ground between the high culture Rankin came to prize while a university student and the low or mass culture preferences of his working-class background. If his novels never quite rise literarily to the level of Louise Welsh's *The Cutting Room* (2002), they certainly rise beyond the formulaic nature of most detective fiction and have given rise to a distinctive variation on the police procedural genre: "tartan noir." As Rankin has pointed out, "The mechanics of the whodunit—its narrative conventions—do not really interest me. What interests me is the soul of the crime novel—what it tells us about humanity and what it is capable of."

The Rebus novels are long (four hundred-plus pages), well-plotted, crisply written, punctuated with mordant humor, filled with street-smart dialogue, and dead-smart about police work and the lives of police officers. Stylistically, Rankin rarely overreaches, though when he does, it shows: "Rebus sat down, one finger punching the desk as if trying to find the rewind on life's remote control" or "He imagined her: tousled hair, sun streaming in through her cream Hessian curtains." The novels are also topical, registering the impact that North Sea oil, Silicon Glen, the breakup of the Soviet Union, devolution, and other matters have had on Scottish life and the opportunities they offer for the greed, corruption, murder, and mayhem that are the stuff of which crime fiction is made.

Rebus's name may not be especially Scottish (as is William McIlvanney's Glaswegian inspector Jack Laidlaw's), but it is well suited to the genre in general and to the first Rebus novel in particular. A rebus, after all, is an enigmatic representation of a name or a place by figures, pictures, arrangement of letters, et cetera, which suggest the syllables of which it is made up. In *Knots and Crosses*, a serial killer sends Rebus a rebus made up of the first letters of the victims' names in order to announce his next victim: Rebus's daughter, Samantha.

Thanks to Rankin, "rebus" now refers to the detective he has created: a good cop with bad habits who believes in justice but who has trouble with authority and often breaks the rules, who is committed to his job but haunted by his many failures, personal and professional. His worst moments come not when he faces death (as he often does) but when, alone in his Arden Street flat, he has to face himself, with nothing to help him through the dark night of the soul but his cigarettes, his single-malts, his dated pop music collection, and occasionally his junior partner and confidante,

Siobhan Clarke. The self-destructiveness of Rankin's eponymous hero is at once idiosyncratic and representative of a type that dates back to the hard-boiled school of Raymond Chandler and James M. Cain. Rebus transcends type, however, the way Rankin's fiction does. In doing so, he has at least as much in common with the protagonists of novels by contemporary Scottish writers such as Irvine Welsh, Janice Galloway, A. L. Kennedy, James Kelman, and Alan Warner as with the protagonists of most crime novels.

Character is important to Rankin, who is not shy about introducing characters in his work, including ones from earlier novels and occasionally others, such as Detective Sergeant Liz Hetherington who, one suspects, may reappear in later novels. Whatever their roles, they tend to be introduced with a brief physical description. Andrea Thomson, for example, "was in her late thirties, short and large-hipped. Her hair was a thick mop of blonde with some darker streaks showing through. Her teeth were oversized. She was self-employed, didn't work for the police full-time." As for McCullough, "His real name was James, but those who know him seemed never to call him that. He was Jamesy, or more often Jazz. Tall, mid-forties, cropped black hair with just a few touches of grey at the temples. He was thin, patted his stomach now, just above the belt, as if to emphasize his lack of gut."

The physical is just the starting point for Rankin, who has a special admiration for crime writers—James Ellroy, Lawrence Block, and Ruth Rendel, for example—interested in "psychological depth" and "3-D characterization." Except for Rebus, however, this psychological depth is limned rather than plumbed, albeit in a way that is surprisingly suggestive and consistent with the books' open-endedness. In the Rebus novels, murders are solved, but not all mysteries are cleared up.

The real action is not in the characterizations but in the plot—or plots. In *Resurrection Men* there are anywhere from three to six, depending on who is counting and how. There is the murder of the art dealer Edward Marber outside his home in upscale Duddingston Village. Rebus works this case until he throws a cup of tea at his boss (and, in *Knots and Crosses*, his former lover), Detective Chief Superintendent Gill Templer. Too senior to be dismissed but too insubordinate to be let off with a reprimand, Rebus is assigned to a refresher course at the Scottish Police College in Tulliallan, midway between Edinburgh and Glasgow.

There, he and the other five like-minded police officers who make up "the Wild Bunch" are required to work as a team on an old, unsolved murder case. Although the exercise is standard, the case is not. The Eric Lomax case is one in which Rebus himself played a part, known only to himself and a small-time criminal named Richard Diamond. Rebus starts feeling a bit paranoid—as well he might, for Rebus's assignment to Tulliallan is not quite what it seems. He is there because Chief Constable David Strathern has asked him to investigate three members of the Wild Bunch. Strathern suspects these three may have stolen money from a Glasgow underworld figure, Bernie Johns, whom they helped put in prison.

Meanwhile, two Edinburgh officers, Claverhouse and Ormiston, also solicit Rebus's aid. Having caught the son of one of Edinburgh's biggest crime figures with a lorry full of drugs, they want Rebus to help them use the son to get to the father, known as the Weasel, who, they hope, will give up his boss—Rebus's long-time nemesis, Big Ger Cafferty. Curiously, Rebus suspects that Claverhouse and Ormiston may also be thinking of taking, and then selling, some of the drugs they have seized. He even wonders whether he, not McCullough, Gray, and Ward, may be Strathern's real target.

Meanwhile (everything in Rankin is meanwhile), Rebus's partner, Detective Sargeant Siobhan Clarke, with whom he stays in phone contact (even as he neglects his current lover, Jill Burchfield), is having problems of her own. Her investigation into Marber's murder results in the death of a prostitute and in Clarke's experiencing Rebus-size guilt. That the prostitute, Laura Stafford, was murdered by her former lover, Donnie Dow, who also happens to be on Big Ger's payroll, complicates, or clarifies, matters a bit more. That Rebus juggles the various cases as well as he does is a testament to the fictional detective's skills. That the reader keeps up with the proliferating plots, characters, and clues, the parallels, intersections, coincidences, connections, and cross-fertilizations, is a testament to Rankin's narrative talent in a novel made in the image of the city in which it is set.

Edinburgh is, as one character points out, "Knoxland," that is, the home of Calvinist preacher John Knox. As Rebus adds, Edinburgh is also the city of Dr. Robert Knox, the nineteenth century physician who advanced medical science by dissecting cadavers bought from two local and notorious "resurrection men" (grave robbers), William Burke and William Hare. Thus, the novel's title refers not only to the promise of future redemption (professional as well as spiritual) but to the city's (and Rebus's) inglorious past as well.

Edinburgh is a Jekyll-and-Hyde city, one that can be comprehended at a glance from its many hills but whose "bloody narrow streets, jinking this way and that" make it infamously difficult to navigate. It is a city literally cloven in two: Its eighteenth century New Town is a monument to Enlightenment ideals (and new wealth), while across the drained lake that had once been a cesspit rises the medieval old town, with its innumerable wynds and closes. Steps, literally, separate the touristy Royal Mile from the dark, narrow chasm of the Cowgate far below. In Edinburgh, the historical and prehistorical past is always visible in the looming castle to the east, Salisbury Crags to the west, the church steeples that attest the city's and the nation's Calvinist past, the spire of the Scott Memorial, Calton Hill, with the unfinished monument known as "Scotland's Disgrace."

The presence of the past, the way it shapes who and what one becomes, is the author's overall subject. Raised in a tiny mining town, Rankin arrived in Auld Reekie in 1978, appalled and fascinated by what he found. The Rebus novels are his attempt to understand Edinburgh and, through it, Scotland. It is a project he shares with other writers of his generation. As A. L. Kennedy wrote in 1996: "Having been drowned out by other cultures for so long, we now intend to be heard. . . . Death, brief joys, dark longings, hilarious despair: Scottish art is playing our song."

"So far, I'm not sure I've done more than scratch the surface of this bizarre, mixed-up country," Rankin added, " . . . but I'll keep trying." Rankin, who wrote *Resurrection Men* in just six to seven weeks, will have to hurry. Rebus lives in real time. Forty-one in *Knots and Crosses* and fifty-five in *Resurrection Men*, published exactly fourteen years and fourteen Rebus books later, he is just five years shy of the mandatory retirement age. (That is, if he makes it; Rebus could be killed by Big Ger or, given how out of shape and overweight he is, could go the way of Colin Dexter's Inspector Morse and suffer a fatal heart attack.) It is impossible to imagine Rebus retired: He would have too much time to mull over old failures. Readers need not worry, however, short or long term. A new Rebus novel, *A Question of Blood*, was published in Britain in 2003 and in the United States in 2004. Additionally, Rankin has been grooming Rebus's successor for several novels, most plainly in *Resurrection Men*. She is Siobhan Clarke, another guilt-ridden isolato, who at the end of this novel is exactly where Rebus was at the beginning: in counseling with "career analyst" Andrea Thomson.

Robert A. Morace

Review Sources

Booklist 99, no. 1 (September 1, 2002): 7.
Library Journal 128, no. 1 (January 1, 2003): 158.
London Review of Books, April 19, 2000, p. 18-20.
New Statesman 131, no. 4569 (January 7, 2002): 39.
The New York Times Book Review, February 9, 2003, p. 17.
People 59, no. 4 (February 3, 2003): 49.
Publishers Weekly 249, no. 49 (December 9, 2002): 64-65.
The Spectator 288 (January 12, 2002): 35-36.
The Times Literary Supplement, January 11, 2002, p. 20.

THE RIGHT MAN
The Surprise Presidency of George W. Bush

Author: David Frum (1960-   )
Publisher: Random House (New York). 303 pp. $25.95
Type of work: Current affairs
Time: 2000-2002
Locale: Washington, D.C.; Florida

The first inside account of the Bush White House, by his former special assistant and presidential speechwriter

Principal personages:
DAVID FRUM, a speechwriter
GEORGE W. BUSH, forty-third president of
the United States

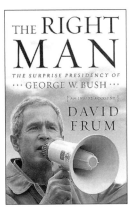

This is the first inside account of the first year of the presidency of George W. Bush, by the speechwriter who coined the memorable phrase "axis of evil." Author David Frum worked and traveled alongside the president during his one-year stay and was in a unique position to study Bush closely.

Early in his campaign for president, George W. Bush was the endless target of comments and jokes about his college and military record. People also questioned his overall intelligence and his ability to lead. As Frum observed, on television Bush did not look like a man ready to be president. Not since the days of Harry Truman did a man seem so unprepared for the rigors of being the chief executive. Starting his speechwriting job at the White House immediately after the inauguration, even Frum had serious doubts. Bush was aware of all of this and simply said that his critics misunderstood him.

Barely surviving the closest, most controversial, and most disputed presidential election in American history, Bush had little in the way of a political mandate, arriving in office politically crippled, Frum writes. In leaving under a cloud of moral miscues, President Bill Clinton had seriously weakened the credibility of the executive branch. Bush was determined to restore it.

It most certainly was a new day in the Oval Office when Bush arrived. Former President Clinton's laid-back and informal style was quickly replaced by an atmosphere of jackets and ties on weekends and prayers at the beginning of cabinet meetings. Bush surrounded himself with, as Frum describes them, "very able, solid, and reliable people" but almost none who could be characterized as being exceptionally brilliant. The staff members were hardworking and loyal, and they understood and endorsed the president's vision for the United States. Soon they would all be tested in ways no one could have imagined during the opening months of the new Bush administration.

The Bush presidency started with the threat of an economic recession. Frum's first speech had to address this issue. "A warning light is flashing on the dashboard of our economy," he wrote for Bush. It was the perfect sound bite and was quickly picked up and repeated by all the major news organizations. The president's speech was very well received and set the stage for his forthcoming tax cut proposal.

Frum offers what is perhaps the best inside account of the workings of the Bush White House during the first year of Bush's term. In addition, Frum provides a rare look at aspects of the president's personality few have seen. Many newspapers and political talk shows, for example, believed that Bush was naïve when it came to foreign policy. They charged that the president was relying mostly upon the instructions of his advisers and lacked a personal vision. Nothing could be further from the truth, Frum says. "Bush was not a lightweight," Frum states, but "rather, a very unfamiliar heavyweight." Words sometimes failed him, but his vision was clear. The president had the ability to make good decisions based on the advice of his staff. A president who consistently makes good decisions, Frum observes, is certainly smart enough to do the job.

David Frum worked in the George W. Bush White House from January, 2001, to February, 2002, as a special assistant for economic speechwriting. He has written regularly for the National Review, The Wall Street Journal, Forbes, *and the* Weekly Standard. *He is also the author of* Dead Right *(1994), an inside account of the American Conservative movement,* What's Right *(1996), a collection of political essays, and* How We Got Here *(2000), a widely acclaimed history of the 1970's.*

Frum also looks at the president's strong religious convictions. Although he was born into wealth and privilege, Bush in his early life was no stranger to failure and, eventually, alcohol abuse. His "intense Christianity," as Frum describes it, turned his life around. Bush is not afraid to acknowledge his checkered past; he uses the lessons learned from that time in his life to illustrate his amazing capacity for discipline, compassion, and growth.

Frum provides a fascinating look at the relationship between Bush and Vice President Dick Cheney. The press portrayed Cheney as a shadowy figure who told the president what to do and say, but this was not the case. The relationship between the two men was one of loyalty and trust, and although Cheney is one of the smartest and most powerful men ever to become vice president, it was Bush who made the final decisions. Although Cheney had strong views on many subjects, Bush had no problem overriding him.

By the summer of 2001, the Bush agenda was on track. Faith-based initiatives, a sweeping tax plan, a national energy policy, and education reform were put forward. Then the president's luck ran out. James Jeffords, a Republican senator from Vermont who often voted with the Democratic Party, became an Independent, thus upsetting the balance of power in the Senate. Bush had now lost his razor-thin Republican majority. Although the tax cut bill did clear the Senate, other presidential priorities were now in jeopardy. At the six-month mark of his term, the questions about Bush's leadership ability surfaced again. The faith-based initiative—an attempt to unite clergy and government in an effort to attack social problems—was voted down. Gone also were judicial appointments, a Social Security proposal, and a plan for oil exploration in Alaska. Employment began to sag, and gasoline prices rose. For the first time, the word "quagmire" was being used to portray the Bush White House. Frum summed up the first congressional session of the Bush presidency as "stalemate, stumbles, and defeats."

Then came the terrorist attacks on New York City and Washington, D.C., of September 11, 2001. In spite of the problems at home, Americans until this time had felt safe and remote from the troubles elsewhere in the world. The president was in Florida that fateful morning, but Frum was in his office in the White House when word of the first terrorist attack came. He vividly recalls those harrowing moments when the staff was forced to evacuate hurriedly and told to run away from the building and into the streets of Washington, D.C., as fast as possible. When Frum and a few White House staffers were allowed to return later in the day, there was nothing left to do but pray.

This would be the president's greatest test. The big question was whether the American people—stunned by the events of that incredibly tragic day, heading toward economic recession, and with a person in the White House who did not even win the popular vote—would rally to their leader in this time of crisis. Bush's hastily written speech, delivered from the Oval Office that night, was not particularly good, consoling, or inspiring. A speech three days later went better. His calm and self-restraint reassured the American people that he was solidly in command. It was during his visit to Ground Zero on September 13, 2001, amid the ruins of the collapsed Twin Towers of the World Trade Center in New York City, that the president's leadership emerged. Speaking spontaneously into a bullhorn to the crowd of rescue workers digging through the rubble, he promised a shocked and frightened nation, "The people who knocked down these buildings will hear all of us soon."

"We are at war," Bush told a grieving country. The nation's entire foreign policy, Frum writes, had been transformed. The president's approval rating soared. He would need the support of the American people during the difficult days ahead. The country was rocked by reports of anthrax being spread through the mail. Frantic efforts were being made to ensure "homeland security," as it came to be called. To make matters even worse, the events of September 11 sent the American economy into a rapid downward spiral. From September 11 to the end of 2001, more than one million Americans lost their jobs.

Toward the end of 2001, the administration's focus began to turn from the Taliban and al-Qaeda in Afghanistan to the dictatorial leader of Iraq, Saddam Hussein. Frum had sent a memo to Mike Gerson, Bush's head speechwriter, documenting the atrocities committed by Hussein. Frum notes that the suggestions in many such memos never materialize into anything; he was astonished when his words appeared, almost verbatim, in the draft of the president's upcoming State of the Union speech. This speech included that immortal phrase which Frum had penned: "axis of evil." When the speech was delivered, the phrase, Frum notes, was instantly controversial. It did, however, brilliantly sum up the president's vision and resolve to free the world from the enemies of democracy and human rights. Like former U.S. president Ronald Reagan, who characterized the Soviet Union as an "evil empire," Bush felt that he was merely telling the truth. He was, in effect, challenging American allies in Europe and elsewhere to join the United States in a crusade.

After finishing work on the State of the Union address in January, Frum handed in his resignation. On February 25, 2002, his job at the White House came to an end. His departure was tainted by a story written by the syndicated Washington columnist Robert Novak to the effect that Frum had been fired by Bush. The tale was not true, and Frum was not sure, even if he indeed was fired, why it would be front-page news. It turned out that the national press was feeling somewhat on the outside of the information loop and was eager for a scoop from a possibly disgruntled White House insider. Although the press hounded him relentlessly, Frum chose not to respond, and in a few weeks, the story faded away.

The last eleven pages of the book give Frum's personal insights into the man he served during that difficult time. His appraisal is balanced and fair and at times even harsh. He calls Bush "a good man who is not a weak man. He has many faults." Frum believes that before September 11, 2001, Bush's presidency was not on its way to being successful. His political vision was not clear, and his strategy was not working. He had received 538,000 fewer votes than his opponent and entered the office under a cloud of bitterness and suspicion. Frum says that the transformation which took place was Bush's move from being an uncertain peacetime president to a superb wartime leader.

The emergence of true leadership in times of great crisis remains one of the profound mysteries of politics. No one could have predicted that Abraham Lincoln would rise during the Civil War to become the greatest president the United States has ever seen. Critics dismissed Harry S. Truman as a political novice, utterly unprepared to deal with the passing of a great president, the ending of a world war raging on two continents, and a dangerous postwar world. Similarly, no one could have foreseen that George W. Bush would turn out to be "the right man," as Frum's title states, to lead the United States through and beyond one of the greatest turning points in its history.

Raymond Frey

Review Sources

Business Week, January 27, 2003, p. 18.
Commentary 115, no. 3 (March, 2003): 75-77.
National Review 55, no. 3 (February 24, 2003): 47-48.
The New York Times, January 9, 2003, p. E11.
The New York Times Book Review, January 26, 2003, p. 8.
USA Today Magazine 131, no. 2694 (March, 2003): 81.
The Wall Street Journal, January 8, 2003, p. D10.

RIVER OF SHADOWS
Eadweard Muybridge and the Technological Wild West

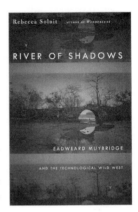

Author: Rebecca Solnit (1961-   )
Publisher: Viking (New York). 239 pp. $25.95
Type of work: History
Time: Primarily 1854-1892
Locale: Northern California (including San Francisco, Yosemite, and Palo Alto)

Muybridge provided a doorway between the nineteenth century's old world of time and space, a world already being transformed by the railroad and photography, and the modern world. Through his experiments with instantaneous photography he became one of the founders of the motion picture and the transformation of bodies and places into representations which followed

Principal personages:
EADWEARD MUYBRIDGE (1830-1904), a photographer
LELAND STANFORD (1824-1893), a railroad magnate

Eadweard Muybridge was born Edward James Muggeridge in Kingston-upon-Thames on April 9, 1830. He changed his name three times: from Muggeridge to Muygridge in the 1850's, from Muygridge to Muybridge in the 1860's, and finally from Edward to Eadweard in 1882. His family members were grain and coal merchants. After leaving the local grammar school, he also left his commercial family and their provincial town to sail for the United States. By the spring of 1856 he was established as a bookseller in San Francisco, where he would remain, on and off, until the 1880's. The later years of his life Muybridge spent working both in America and in Europe, exploiting the fame he had acquired as a pioneer of instantaneous photography. He died in Kingston-upon-Thames in 1904.

As Rebecca Solnit observes, time in the nineteenth century was transformed from a phenomenon which linked humans to the cosmos to one linking industrial activities to each other. This transformation changed the way humans imagined their world. Solnit sets up her study of Muybridge and his influence on photography and the understanding of the West by noting that four discoveries of the nineteenth century altered this sense of time and space, first in the United States and then in the rest of the world: the railroad, which transformed the experience of nature and the landscape; the founding of the science of geology, which expanded time by revealing the immense age of the earth; photography, which both froze time and, later, animated it; and the telegraph, which collapsed time by providing instantaneous communication over the expanse of space. These four discoveries reshaped previous ideas about time and space and transformed the Victorian age into the modern one.

Muybridge's good fortune was not only to have been born into a period of rapid technological and intellectual change but also to have spent his most productive years living and working in California, a place that offered opportunities to become a self-made man, to make money and to acquire fame, and to reinvent oneself in a place unburdened by the past.

Muybridge's life was marked by three major crises. First, a stagecoach accident nearly killed him and may have damaged his brain. Second,

~

Rebecca Solnit is a museum curator, art critic, and political activist. She writes on issues of environment, landscape, and a sense of place. Her other books include Secret Exhibition: Six California Artists of the Cold War Era *(1990). She lives in California.*

~

he murdered his wife's lover. Third, Muybridge ultimately broke off his relationship with Leland Stanford, who had for many years acted as his patron. After each of these crises Muybridge reconfigured his life. The brain damage resulting from the stagecoach accident may have sharpened his perception and helped to promote his career as a photographer. His trial and acquittal for the murder of his wife's lover propelled him out of the United States and marked the beginning of the transition period before he dedicated himself to his research with instantaneous photography. His break with Stanford forced him to pursue his fame and widen his experiments outside of California, at the University of Pennsylvania and in Europe.

The transition from bookseller to photographer developed over time. In 1860 Muybridge left San Francisco by stage, bound for New York. The accident which nearly cost him his life occurred in New Mexico. Although he intended to return to his business in California, he ended up wandering for some years, searching for a return to good health. He returned to England and later went to New York to pursue a suit against the Butterfield Stage Company. Solnit speculates that during this time he was exploring options for a new career. By the time he resurfaced in San Francisco in 1869, he had changed his name to Muybridge and was photographing landscapes under the name of Helios. Over the next few years he became one of the pioneer photographers of Yosemite, which was increasingly becoming a tourist destination. He took photos in and around San Francisco, documenting the earthquake damage in 1868. He also went to Alaska to photograph. His fame as one of the new breed of Western photographers introduced him to the painter Albert Bierstadt and the novelist, later of *Ramona* fame, Helen Hunt Jackson. Then, in 1872, Muybridge was hired by Stanford to do a series of photographs of his trotter, Occident. That commission changed Muybridge's life and brought him the recognition that he retains to this day.

The purpose of Stanford's study was to prove that a horse, when running, would at various stages have all four feet off the ground at the same time. Fulfilling this assignment required all of Muybridge's talents and eventually would release his true genius. With Stanford's considerable resources at his disposal, Muybridge set about inventing instantaneous photography, the capturing of motion on film, which by the spring of 1873 he accomplished with a cumbersome multicamera system. He would spend the rest of his life perfecting his discoveries, which eventually would lead to the technical development of the motion picture. The initial assignment for Stanford was short-lived, and afterward Muybridge returned to his landscape photography, particularly in the Yosemite Valley. In 1873 he won the Medal of Progress at the Vienna Exposition.

In 1874 the second of Muybridge's catastrophes occurred when he shot and killed his wife's lover. After his trial and subsequent acquittal, he went for a brief period to Central America, where he made a series of photographic studies in Guatemala. However, by 1877 he was back in San Francisco and was offering for sale his panoramic pictures of the city. At this time he was also back in Stanford's employ and was once again engaged in his motion studies, which occupied him as a photographer for the remainder of his working life. The breakthroughs in photochemistry and in the perfection of fast shutter speeds allowed him, over the next several years, to accomplish the three achievements for which he is remembered: a photographic process fast enough to capture bodies in motion, the creation of a succession of images that, when mounted together, constituted a cycle of motion, and their reanimation back into movement. His discoveries allowed him to capture motion photographically and earned him the sobriquet of father of the motion picture.

Muybridge's work in high-speed photography revolutionized the art and showed that what the eye saw conflicted with what the pictures revealed. Like the telescope and the microscope before him, it allowed humans to see the world differently.

By the early 1880's Muybridge formally severed his ties with Stanford and struck off once again on his own. In 1879 he had debuted his zoopraxiscope and later would go on to combine the technologies of the photograph, zootropes, and the magic lantern, the basis for the motion picture. He became a lecturer, demonstrating his various inventions to enthralled crowds. He ceaselessly worked to perfect the discoveries he had already made, and he began to travel to promote his various inventions. Muybridge had always been an experimentalist and a technophile; now he became a showman. In the process he became famous. Over the next few years he would work in Paris, London, Philadelphia, New Jersey, Chicago, and finally back in Kingston.

At the salon of the artist Étienne-Jules Marey, Muybridge met such eminent figures as the scientist Hermann von Helmholtz and the photographer Felix Nadar. From Marey, Muybridge learned more about dry-plate photography and Marey's gunlike camera. Both would have an influence on the developing technology of the cinema.

In London Muybridge was asked by the Royal Society, probably the most prestigious scientific body at the time, to present his findings on instantaneous photography. The experience was not to be a favorable one. In Muybridge's absence, under the auspices of Stanford, J. D. B. Stillman had taken over some of Muybridge's experiments and published a book on the horse in motion. Its appearance called into question Muybridge's prior claim to have discovered the techniques of his motion photography. Much to his disappointment, the Royal Society withdrew its invitation. The action forced Muybridge into an unwinnable suit against Stanford, who did everything he could to diminish Muybridge's accomplishments. However, as Solnit observes, with Stanford's support Muybridge had discovered not only the rudiments of the motion picture but also the marriage of art and commerce.

In 1885 Muybridge was conducting his experiments at the University of Pennsylvania, where he expanded his motion studies using the human body. In 1888 he visited Thomas Edison at his Orange, New Jersey, laboratory. The meeting was brief, but, according to Solnit, it was Muybridge who gave Edison the idea for combining images and sound and propelled Edison to increase the photographic research that eventually led to his version of the motion picture camera. Solnit further speculates that by the late 1880's the photographer had already envisioned the direction cinema would take, combining image and sound and theater and celebrity by suggesting the filming of such figures as Edwin Booth, the actor, and Lillian Russell, the entertainer. In 1893 Muybridge set up a booth, the Zoopraxigraphical Hall, at his own expense at the World's Colombian Exposition in Chicago to demonstrate his achievements. Little seems to have come of this, and by the 1890's Muybridge's researches had pretty much come to a halt.

By 1904 Muybridge was back where he started, in Kingston-upon-Thames, and he eventually settled in with an unmarried cousin, Kate Smith. He continued to lecture a bit and to edit some more books. The years of his achievement were now behind him. He died on May 8, 1904, of prostate cancer, and he was cremated. His remains were buried under a brown marble slab that wrongly listed his name as Maybridge.

Eadweard Muybridge had, through his work as a photographer, helped to invent the modern view of the West. Working as a photojournalist, he had covered many events of historical importance to the state of California. His experiments in motion photography transformed the way the nineteenth century observed time and space. His inventions in the field of instantaneous photography and the uses of it, which he envisioned rightfully, earned him the title of the father of the cinema and also transformed the way the twentieth century would see the world.

In *River of Shadows*, Solnit has written an engaging study of not only Eadweard Muybridge and his discoveries but also of the sweeping changes wrought by the industrial developments and the opening of the West during the years following the Civil War. Her book is also full of fascinating details about the early history of California. It provides compelling support for giving Muybridge the credit for the ultimate invention of the motion picture.

Charles L. P. Silet

Review Sources

American Scholar 72, no. 2 (Spring, 2003): 147-150.
Harper's Magazine 306, no. 1833 (February, 2003): 67-68.
Library Journal 128, no. 3 (February 15, 2003): 135-136.
The New Republic 228, no. 12 (March 31, 2003): 34-37.
New Scientist 177, no. 2378 (January 18, 2003): 46.
The New York Times Book Review, March 30, 2003, p. 6.

SAUL AND PATSY

Author: Charles Baxter (1947-   )
Publisher: Pantheon Books (New York). 317 pp. $24.00
Type of work: Novel
Time: The 1990's
Locale: Michigan

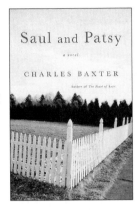

This novel of life in the Midwest tells the story of Saul and Patsy Bernstein, a young couple from the East Coast, living in the small fictional town of Five Oaks, Michigan, where they encounter both beauty and tragedy

Principal characters:
> SAUL BERNSTEIN, an urban Jew from Baltimore who gives up a high-paying job in Chicago to teach in Five Oaks
> PATSY BERNSTEIN, Saul's wife, and a bank loan officer who majored in dance at college
> HOWIE BERNSTEIN, Saul's handsome brother, an executive who lives in California
> DELIA BERNSTEIN, Saul's mother, who lives in Baltimore and is having an affair with a teenager

Charles Baxter, short-story writer and novelist, is one of the great treasures of the American Midwest. His previous novel, *Feast of Love* (2000), was not only a critical success, earning a National Book Award nomination, but was also a commercial success, bringing Baxter a much wider readership for his work. Likewise, *Saul and Patsy* has found favor with both critical and popular audiences.

For his main characters, Baxter returns to several of his earlier short stories, including "Saul and Patsy are Getting Comfortable in Michigan," from *Through the Safety Net* (1985); "Saul and Patsy are Pregnant" from *A Relative Stranger* (1990); and "Saul and Patsy are in Labor," from *Believers* (1997). In this novel, Saul and Patsy outgrow the boundaries of the short stories that contained them into fully developed characters in their own rights.

Baxter reports that he drew on his own experiences as a high school teacher in tiny Pinconning, Michigan, in the late 1960's to create Five Oaks and its inhabitants. In particular, he recalls a colleague, a Jewish teacher who felt himself in the middle of nowhere. A similar sense of isolation pervades the novel; both Saul and Patsy are outsiders in Five Oaks. The side stories of Saul's family also suggest the isolation of contemporary existence; yet all the characters of the novel struggle with the redemptive potential of love.

The book opens early in Saul and Patsy Bernstein's marriage. The two, both of whom are from the East Coast, met at Northwestern University. Saul, a Jew from Baltimore, has given up a good job in Chicago to become a high school teacher in the small backwater town of Five Oaks, Michigan, because he idealistically wants to make a statement against corporate America. Saul is a somewhat dark character, prone to melancholy and discontent. Patsy, a former Episcopalian, works as a bank loan officer. A dancer, Patsy seems to live more fully in her body and in the moment than does Saul.

The couple rent a farmhouse on Whitefeather Road. That Saul and Patsy are passionately in love with each other is patently clear; even a simple game of Scrabble ends up in lovemaking. That Saul and Patsy are out of their element in the rural Midwest is just as clear. Although Patsy superficially seems better adjusted to her life in Five Oaks, neither she nor Saul knows how to speak the language of the culture in which they find themselves, nor do the townspeople have any understanding of them. When their nearest neighbor, Mrs. O'Neill, invites them to her house, she asks Saul to examine her garage so that she can surreptitiously ask Patsy if Jews eat cookies.

Charles Baxter is the author of seven works of fiction, including The Feast of Love *(2000),* Harmony of the World *(1984),* Believers *(1997),* A Relative Stranger *(1990), and* First Light *(1987). He has also written or edited several volumes of nonfiction, including* Burning Down the House *(1997). Formerly the director of the MFA program at University of Michigan, he currently lives in Minneapolis and teaches at the University of Minnesota.*

Such instances rankle Saul. When, while driving, he sees an old man staring at him, Saul is convinced that the man harbors anti-Semitic sentiments, and he makes a rude gesture. This is evidence of Saul's inability to read his surroundings; only later does he discover that the man suffers from Alzheimer's disease and has no idea even of where he is. Although the incident seems to speak to Saul's paranoia, by the end of the book his suspicions have been largely confirmed.

Early in the book, a near-tragedy further reveals the gap between the Bernsteins and their neighbors. One night, driving home drunk from a party thrown by another high school teacher, the couple crash their car, rendering it undrivable. They walk to a nearby farmhouse for help and there find one of Saul's former students, Emory McPhee, and his young wife, Anne. Saul gave Emory a "D" in his class, and this grade, along with a general lack of ambition, leads Emory to leave school. In this encounter, Saul recognizes once again the gulf that separates him from the people of the town; he understands in himself "the lagoon of self-consciousness and irony." Seeing Emory and Anne in their home forces Saul to consider his own discontent with life: "This was like Schopenhauer arriving at the door with a big suitcase, settling down for a long stay in the brain."

Shortly thereafter, Saul has a dream in which he is pregnant. He awakens, takes Patsy's motorcycle for a drive, and sees an albino deer. This is his first sighting of the deer, which becomes a mystical sign throughout the rest of the book. Indeed, the moment is fraught with significance, although Saul cannot even identify what that significance is. After returning to his home, he makes love to Patsy, knowing that she will become pregnant.

As always happens, the introduction of children into a marriage irretrievably changes that marriage. Baxter writes:

Saul finished diapering Mary Esther and then walked into the upstairs hallway toward the bathroom. He brushed against Patsy, who was heading downstairs. Under the ceiling lights her eyes were shadowed with fatigue. They did not speak, and for ten seconds, she was a stranger to him. He could not remember why he had ever married her, and he could not remember having desire for her.

Is Saul jealous? Patsy's breast, formerly his property, has been commandeered by their tiny daughter. The malaise Saul and Patsy feel is pervasive in the middle section of the book without being overwhelming. Long-married couples will recognize in the Bernsteins the way people carefully work through the issues of a marriage.

Saul's professional life has also undergone profound change. He finds himself teaching remedial English to a group of seven students who have no interest in the language, nor in literature, nor in anything else. Most troubling are the pair he calls the "Child Cossacks," Bob Pawlak and Gordy Himmelman. Gordy is a young man with absolutely nothing going for him. Abandoned by his parents and living with an obscenely ugly aunt, he seems scarcely human to Saul:

> On his face were two rashes, one from acne, the other from blankness. Girls avoided him. His eyes, on those occasions when they met Saul's, were cold and lunar: If you were dying on the side of the road in a rainstorm, Saul thought, Gordy's eyes would pass over you and continue on, after you died, to the next interesting sight.

Saul is troubled on many levels by Gordy; his earlier idealistic notion of teaching the masses fades under Gordy's stony stare.

Likewise, the reader is troubled by Gordy. He is a cipher, an unknown, unknowable quantity. Every time Saul moves toward sympathy for Gordy, the latter does something hateful. Baxter challenges Saul, and the reader, to come to terms with Gordy as human; at times, however, it is almost impossible to see him this way.

Nevertheless, Saul persists. In response to his daughter's birth and his work with the remedial students, he begins a new hobby as a beekeeper. He takes pleasure in the work and finds new meaning in his life. About this time, however, Gordy shows up at Saul's house. The early, lighthearted passages of the novel become darker with the introduction of Gordy's obsession with Saul and Patsy. One night there is a terrible storm, and Gordy appears. He has destroyed all of Saul's beehives. Although Saul tells Gordy to go home and never return, he does return, and with a gun. Saul drives him home, where Gordy's custodial aunt slaps him.

Eventually and inevitably, with no fanfare, Gordy returns one more time to Saul and Patsy's house and blows out his own brains. This event, at the close of part 1, becomes the pivotal occurrence in the novel. In a strange twist of rural midwestern reasoning, Saul somehow becomes the focus of a cult of alienated teens, called the Himmels, who see the dead Gordy as their mascot. In another strange twist, the blame for Gordy's death falls on Saul's shoulders, as the anti-Semitism Saul feared groundlessly in the earlier chapters emerges in earnest here.

As Halloween approaches, the harassment by the Himmels increases. The youths egg the Bernsteins' house, and the couple worries about what will come next. The change is most evident in Patsy, now pregnant with their son Theo. Whereas earlier in the book, she has consistently been the trusting one, the one most likely to fit in, she now has one child and one on the way to protect, and she becomes increasingly bitter and isolated. She muses:

> Perhaps there would be escalation: rotten tomatoes, toilet paper, followed by firecrackers, then arson, the finally, gunshots. Or painted swastikas. Of the punishing of good deeds there would be no discernible end. All at once the idea of owning a handgun made perfect sense to her.

On Halloween night, the Himmels arrive to terrorize Saul, but he is ready for them. Saul confronts them, and, in a strangely appropriate scene, he manages to save his house and family, at least temporarily. Slowly, Saul and Patsy make peace with their neighbors, with Gordy's unquiet ghost and with themselves. As the book closes, Saul has taken a job as a columnist for the local newspaper. In this capacity, he seems to have found his niche: gadfly and instigator, making the conservative members of the community wild with rage. Ironically, it is here that Saul finds himself a fully functioning member of the community.

In addition to the main story line of Saul and Patsy's marriage, Baxter provides side stories of Saul's mother, Delia, and his brother Howie. Delia, a fashionable Baltimore doyen, has fallen deeply in love with the seventeen-year-old boy who takes care of her lawn. Howie, Saul's apparently successful brother, an Internet executive from California, shows up at the Bernsteins' door just before Halloween. He tells Saul that he has become engaged and that he has given Saul a gift of million dollars. Neither turns out to be true.

Saul and Patsy is both strange and wonderful, a careful narration of the internal workings of a marriage and a community. Most of all, *Saul and Patsy*, like the earlier *Feast of Love*, is an unsentimental, sometimes quirky, always on-target exploration of love in all its forms. From Delia's passion for the teenager, from Patsy's comparison of Saul to a jelly doughnut that "puts weight on," from handsome Howie's nonexistent fiancé, from Saul's unabashed and unabating love for Patsy, the reader comes to understand something about life, quietly. It is like standing in the dark, looking through the lighted windows of someone else's life: familiar and strange all at once.

Diane Andrews Henningfeld

Review Sources

The Atlantic Monthly 292, no. 2 (September 4, 2003): 152.
Book: The Magazine for the Reading Life, September/October, 2003, pp. 74-75.
Booklist 99, no. 22 (August, 2003): 1924.
Kirkus Reviews 71, no. 13 (July 1, 2003): 869.
Library Journal 128, no. 14 (September 1, 2003): 204.
The New York Times Book Review, September 14, 2003, p. 8.
Newsweek 142, no. 12 (September 22, 2003): 90.
Publishers Weekly 250, no. 30 (July 28, 2003): 76.
The Washington Post, September 9, 2003, p. C02.

SELECTED WRITINGS
Volume 4: 1938-1940

Author: Walter Benjamin (1892-1940)
Translated from the German by Edmund Jephcott and
  others
Edited by Howard Eiland and Michael W. Jennings
Publisher: The Belknap Press of Harvard University
  Press (Cambridge, Mass.). 477 pp. $39.95
Type of work: Essays, letters, and literary criticism
Time: 1892-1940

The final volume of four in what constitutes the first
comprehensive English translation and editing of the criti-
cal writings of the man many consider the last century's
definitive literary critic

Readers who want to get some sense of Walter Benjamin's formative years should
consult the essays in *Magill's Literary Annual* for books of 1996 and 1999. The chronological essays at the end of each of the earlier volumes of *Selected Writings* provide
an excellent biographical and intellectual history for the man and his ideas. Here, in
volume 4, the story of this remarkable man reaches its "heroic" and "tragic" conclusion. These adjectives are not used lightly. Benjamin's struggle to sharpen his ideas
about literature and culture under the shadow of the Nazi tyranny, which he had to try
to elude in the very act of challenging its stranglehold on the European mind, was heroic. The patience, fortitude, and resolution demanded of his weak heart would have
driven many a stronger man to despair.

Benjamin's decision to commit suicide, undertaken on the mistaken perception
that he would be turned over by Spanish authorities to the Vichy police or Gestapo in
occupied France, was not an act of weakness. He knew that his heart condition would
not tolerate the brutality of a concentration camp, and he took his life before the Nazis
could. The tragedy does not lie in the fact that he was mistaken, that on the following
day the Spanish guards would have let him pass. The tragedy is that modernity lost its
most prescient interpreter. The tragedy belongs to readers.

In the three years that span the period covered in this volume, Adolf Hitler annexed
Austria, invaded Poland, and crushed France. The persecution of the Jews gathered
momentum. Benjamin's brother was arrested in Berlin, and Benjamin himself was in-
volved in a ceaseless effort to obtain the necessary papers that would enable him to
get out of occupied Europe. His hope was to get an affidavit and visa to the United
States, where he could bring to completion a long-term project on the French poet
Charles Baudelaire. The working title was "Charles Baudelaire: A Lyric Poet in the
Age of High Capitalism."

For a decade Benjamin had toiled in Paris libraries over a massive effort that eventually earned the title of *Das Passagen-Werk* (1982; *The Arcades Project*, 1999). By pursuing Baudelaire's references to the sordid, commodified world, Benjamin amassed a great quantity of observations dealing with the streets, shops, fashions, and urban density of Paris. These observations, which provided the background he felt he needed in order to interpret Baudelaire's poetry, gradually took on a life of their own and seemed to overwhelm Baudelaire as a topic.

When Benjamin's patrons, Max Horkheimer and Theodor Adorno at the Institute of Social Research in New York, urged him in 1938 to prepare some part of his work on the Paris "Arcades" for publication in their journal, Benjamin decided to write an essay based on his research up to the moment, an essay that would justify the great pains he had taken to master the intricacies of Baudelaire's Paris. "The Paris of the Second Empire in Baudelaire" is the first major entry in volume 4. It was never published in Benjamin's lifetime. Adorno pounced on Benjamin's lack of sufficient structure. "This dialectic lacks mediation," wrote Adorno in a famous letter reproduced in this volume. What he meant was that Benjamin had merely juxtaposed Baudelaire's poetry to the urban and historical phenomena of "wine tax . . . barricades . . . arcades" (the galleried shops of nineteenth century Paris) but had not adequately analyzed the implications, political and cultural, of the connection.

In the chronology to volume 4, the editors explain that Adorno was unable to understand the "monad" driving Benjamin's work. What Adorno had dismissed as "wide-eyed presentation of facticity" was actually a "mode of construction" ahead of its time. Benjamin is quoted in defense of his method: "In the monad the textual detail which was frozen in a mythical rigidity comes alive." A strange combination of holistic and, at the same time, indeterminate discourse, a way of thinking and writing that has become prominent in intellectual circles in modern times—roughly, what is called postmodernism—is prefigured on Benjamin's essay, which, ironically, sees itself to be a critique of early modernism.

Adorno's criticism would have been hard to take under normal circumstances, but under the heel of Nazi persecution and with the hope of using the Institute of Social Research as his ticket to the United States, Benjamin could very easily have been reduced to despair. He did fall into deep depression. In early 1939 the Gestapo, aware of his anti-Nazi views, initiated a procedure which deprived him of his German citizenship. He was, for the time being, safe in Paris but stateless.

He was also absorbed in the "notes, reflections and excerpts" that constitute "Central Park," which he had been composing while writing "The Paris of the Sec-

Admired by a small coterie of prominent European intellectuals in the 1930's, Walter Benjamin, since the 1970's, has been regarded as one of the major thinkers of late modernism. His major works include Ursprung des deutschen Trauerspiels *(1928;* The Origins of German Tragic Drama, *1977), the essay "Über einiege Motive bei Baudelaire" (1939; "On Some Motifs in Baudelaire," 1968), and the posthumously published* Das Passagen-Werk *(1982;* The Arcades Project, *1999).*

ond Empire in Baudelaire." Although they were designed to bolster the book on Baudelaire, they seemed to gravitate toward the broader and wider ambitions of *The Arcades Project*. There are extensive ruminations over allegory and its affinity to modern materialism. He had called these reflections "Central Park" in a spirit of hope; he saw himself bringing this daunting bit of scholarship to resolution once he was safely settled in New York—somewhere close to what he imagined as the idyllic retreat of a great city park. Once the gloom caused by Adorno's attack had dissipated, Benjamin put aside "Central Park" and returned to the Baudelaire essay in earnest.

In revision, its title became "On Some Motifs in Baudelaire," and this time the institute would eventually publish it in 1940. Its central idea now turned on the distinction between two extremes of experience, momentary or immediate (*Erlebnis*) and deep or reflective (*Erfahrung*). *Erlebnis* had its most important incarnation in shock and *Erfahrung* in memory: "The greater the shock factor in particular impressions, the more vigilant consciousness has to be in screening stimuli; the more efficiently it does so, the less these impressions enter into long experience [*Erfahrung*] and the more they correspond to the concept of isolated experience [*Erlebnis*]." Baudelaire was tuned to the newly emerging modern world's taste for shock. As a poet, he reversed priorities and devoted his gift for creative memory to the expression of ephemera; he sacrificed *Erfahrung* to *Erlebnis:*

> Baudelaire battled the crowd—with the impotent rage of someone fighting the rain or the wind. This is the nature of the immediate experience [*Erlebnis*] to which Baudelaire has given the weight of long experience [*Erfahrung*]. He named the price for which the sensation of modernity could be had: the disintegration of the aura in immediate shock experience [*Chockerlebnis*].

Benjamin had explored this dialectic in two very important works earlier in the year. The first was a series of "commentaries" on the lyrics of the anti-Nazi communist German poet Bertolt Brecht, which was published partially in a Swiss newspaper. Brecht, who was both an admired poet and dramatist, enjoyed conversing with Benjamin and had invited him to share his exile in Denmark. While there, he had gathered the impressions that formed the heart of these fresh and spontaneous commentaries. For Benjamin, a commentary presumes the perfection or "classical" nature of a text and reserves the right to be "authoritarian" in judgment. Benjamin, who never joined the Communist Party, nevertheless saw in Brecht's simple and honest lyricism the embodiment of the true German culture which Hitler had parodied. In Brecht's theories of theatrical estrangement Benjamin found another critique of Nazi aesthetics: Hitler wanted Germany to lose itself in a mythic frenzy and admire him from afar; Brecht wanted his plays to close the gap between stage and audience, to shatter the illusion of theatrical awe and force self-conscious thought. Brecht encouraged *Erfahrung* and eschewed *Erlebnis.*

In 1936 Benjamin had already begun the first version of his most famous essay, "The Work of Art in the Age of Mechanical Reproduction." In 1939 he polished the final version, which, however, was not published until after the war, in 1955.

This last version, together with the Brecht Commentaries, labors the difference between shock effect, in this case photography and especially film, and the lost "aura" of specific works of art which encouraged *Erfahurung* instead of indulging *Erlebnis*.

Benjamin avoids nostalgia. He knows that modernity cannot reinvent the older contemplative experience of art, but he cautions the modern world to be as self-critical as possible of its penchant for the excitement of *Erlebnis*. He throws his support to the left and hopes that its political idealism will protect humanity from the demonic marriage between an art based on shock and narcissism and a politics of tyranny:

> Humankind, which once, in Homer, was an object of contemplation for the Olympian gods, has now become one for itself. Its self-alienation has reached the point where it can experience its own annihilation as a supreme aesthetic pleasure. *Such is the aestheticizing of politics, as practiced by fascism. Communism replies by politicizing art.*

Benjamin, however, was unable to settle exclusively for a political platform. The monad he was sure hovered over the particulars in his studies of nineteenth century Paris discouraged a rejection of history through a totalizing of revolution. As he put it in a fragment in 1940: "Marx says that revolutions are the locomotive of history. But perhaps it is quite otherwise. Perhaps revolutions are an attempt by the passengers on this train—namely, the human race—to activate the emergency brake."

In the last essay by him, "On the Concept of History," unpublished in his lifetime, he seems to blend *Erlebnis* and *Erfahrung* in one brilliant insight after another: "Articulating the past historically does not mean recognizing it 'the way it really was.' It means appropriating a memory as it flashes up in a moment of danger." Earlier he had praised Marcel Proust's aesthetic of involuntary memory, which enabled Proust to juxtapose the most immediate and intense experiences in life with great waves of memory that washed the mind in a sea where time lost became time regained. Benjamin's gift for reading texts with unusual brilliance had much to do with reverence for language and its eerie contract with metaphysical ideas. Well after Benjamin had become interested in Marxism, he wrote the following to his friend, the Swiss critic and poet Max Rychner: "I have never been able to do research and think in a way other than, if I may so put it, in a theological sense—namely in accordance with the Talmudic teaching of the forty-nine levels of meaning in every passage in the Torah."

Walter Benjamin was a semiotician fascinated by language, but he was also a humanist who, in the bitterness and anxieties of his last years, relied heavily on a deep trust in the contract between the legacies of the past and the hopes of the present. No matter how dark the times, humanity has a contract with its own best self. The true historian intuits the trajectory of human hopes. One of the last paragraphs of his last essay captures the visionary power of Benjamin's last days:

No state of affairs having causal significance is for that very reason historical. It became historical posthumously, as it were, through events that may be separated from it by thousands of years. . . . [The historian] grasps the constellation (sic., monad) into which his own era has entered, along with a very specific earlier one. Thus, he establishes a conception of the present as now-time shot through with splinters of messianic time.

Peter Brier

Review Sources

Publishers Weekly 250, no. 22 (June 2, 2003): 46.
The Times Literary Supplement, October 17, 2003, pp. 9-10.

SERIOUSLY FUNNY
The Rebel Comedians of the 1950's and 1960's

Author: Gerald Nachman (1938-   )
Publisher: Pantheon Books (New York). 659 pp. $29.95
Type of work: Media
Time: 1953-1965
Locale: San Francisco, Los Angeles, Chicago, and New York

This study of comedy in the twentieth century covers the lives and careers of twenty-five comedians, including Tom Lehrer, Steve Allen, Phyllis Diller, Mel Brooks, Woody Allen, and Joan Rivers

Appropriately, *Seriously Funny*, Gerald Nachman's study of the American comedy renaissance of the 1950's and 1960's, begins with Mort Sahl. Sahl was the first stand-up comic to comment on politics. He was an innovator of the first order, a hipster who wore slacks and sweaters in the style of the era's graduate students and who took the stage armed with a daily newspaper for a prop. "I'm for capital punishment. You've got to execute people—how else are they going to learn?"

In the early 1950's, nightclub comics wore tuxedos and did not discuss current events. Sahl was willing to mock presidents Dwight Eisenhower and Richard Nixon as well as Nikita Khrushchev, Fidel Castro, and Mao Zedong. Sahl's influence appears in following decades at stand-up microphones and the sketch comedy series *Saturday Night Live*'s news segment "Weekend Update."

Nachman organizes his chapters, each focusing on a different comedian, into a chronological, sociopolitical scheme to demonstrate how the comics influenced the mass culture of the United States and the world. First, however, they influenced one another. Sahl's conversations with the audience, for example, led to Shelley Berman's neurotic monologues. Berman spoke into an imaginary telephone as he sat sweating and twitching on a stool under the spotlight's glare. There, in front of the world, he asked the girlfriend who was jilting him if anything was wrong with him, and all the audience heard was, "'Uh-huh . . . uh-huh . . . uh-huh . . . uh-huh,' then 'Gosh, Shirley, a *lot* of guys breathe through their mouths. Hey, c'mon, I think yer reachin' now, Shirley.'"

Berman's angst-ridden act was adapted by Bob Newhart. Newhart spoke on the make-believe telephone, too, but to a historical personage such as a Visigoth or Abraham Lincoln (Newhart, playing the sixteenth president's public relations man, advises Lincoln not to shave off his beard), or in more recent times with a fantasy twist, as when playing a worried night watchman "at the Empire State Building who tries to report a giant gorilla atop the building swatting at airplanes." Newhart had never appeared before a crowd when Warner Brothers executives decided to buy his album. First they had to find a club in which to rerecord the routines with a live audience. It worked well. The audience had to imagine the recipients of Newhart's calls, and their participation made his halting delivery even funnier.

Journalist and musical revue writer Gerald Nachman has devoted his life to writing about theater, films, cabaret, and television for newspapers and magazines. His previous books include Raised on Radio *(1998),* Out on a Whim *(1983),* The Fragile Bachelor *(1989), and* Playing House *(1978).*

Mike Nichols, who became a highly successful film director, and Elaine May, who did not, were a hot comedy duo in the late 1950's.

May: "There is, always, another dimension to music. And it's apart from life. I can never believe that Bartók died on Central Park West."
Nichols: "Isn't that ugly?"
May: "Ugly, ugly, ugly . . . Oh, I love this part! Listen."
Nichols: "Almost hurts."
May: "Yes, beauty often does."

Their fans recognized themselves and laughed. May was a razor-tongued beauty, and Nichols was a Berlin-born New Yorker who synced with her perfectly in dialogues that satirized the pretensions of their sophisticated, college-educated audience.

So, too, did Dick Gregory, simply by being a clever black man playing to white audiences. Only a fraction of his material was about race. He wanted white people to see him not as a representative of black culture but as another human being who suffered from the same frustrations and irritations that they did. "I been readin' so much about cigarettes and cancer, I quit readin'." When he had sufficiently softened up his audience, Gregory let them have it with jokes about growing up poor: "Kids didn't eat off the floor. When I was a kid, you dropped something off the table—it never reached the floor." A man of deep convictions, Gregory abandoned stand-up comedy for the Civil Rights movement and other causes, including nutrition and fasting crusades that caused some to label him as a crank.

Godfrey Cambridge was another popular black comedian of the day; tragically, he died young of a heart attack. Cambridge, a man of extraordinary wit and charm, later acted in such films as *The President's Analyst* (1967), *Watermelon Man* (1970), and *Cotton Comes to Harlem* (1970). His satirical stand-up made his reputation and caught his audiences off-guard: "Do you realize the amount of havoc a Negro can cause just walking down the street on a Sunday morning with a copy of *The New York Times* real estate section under his arm?"

Bill Cosby came along in the 1960's and opted out of talking about race altogether. He and his manager decided to try for universality. Nachman discusses Cosby's wholesome image and enormous success in family comedy as well as occasional failures (and battles with the press) when he ventured into other types of entertainment. Despite his trademark childhood reminiscences, Cosby grew up with deprivation. His father abandoned him and his mother and brother; as a result, the family led an impoverished existence in the Philadelphia housing projects. Fat Albert, Old Weird Harold, and the rest of the beloved Cosby characters were based on real kids and were about playing ball, going to the movies, and listening to the radio late at night, as in the famous remembrance of the time Bill and his brother, Russell, were terrified by the *Lights Out* episode "Chicken Heart," one of the most famous radio plays ever aired.

Radio broadcast great comedy in the 1950's. Bob Elliott and Ray Goulding were a subtle team whose act was revived on National Public Radio (NPR) in the 1980's. Jean Shepherd told his darkly funny tales of growing up in Indiana on New York radio, attracting an audience of insomniacs, and later gained broader fame with humor articles in *Playboy* magazine and the 1983 holiday film classic *A Christmas Story*.

No comedian worth his or her salt failed to record an album after *Mort Sahl at Sunset*, cut in 1955, revolutionized the comedy industry. The monologue was not the only brand of humor blasting from college hi-fis in the 1950's. Tom Lehrer's acid-drenched show-tune parodies were played and sung on campuses across the nation. Stan Freberg convulsed listeners with his recording of "St. George and the Dragonet" and "Little Blue Riding Hood," featuring finely timed sound effects and brilliant character voices, all done by Freberg. He created what is probably the first comedy concept album, the highly satirical *Stan Freberg Presents the United States of America, Volume 1*. This record is "loaded with public-relations-speak. He let the audience in on the act itself. Freberg's songs and sketches, jammed with showbiz cant and PR jargon, foreshadowed Mort Sahl, Lenny Bruce, Bob Newhart, and Nichols & May."

Nachman's take on the infamous "dirty comic" Lenny Bruce is frank and incisive: "It is almost impossible any longer to get an accurate fix on Lenny Bruce—the comedian, not the martyr, or the myth, or the messiah, or even the man. Bruce's acolytes manufactured the Bruce we know best now, the Lenny of legend." Raised by his mother, stripper Sally Marr, Bruce grew up on the seamier side of show business, knew few inhibitions, and deferred to no institution. In perhaps his most famous monologue, he plays a PR man talking to the newly elected pope:

> "Hello, Johnny! [Pope John XXIII] What's shakin', baby? It's really been an election month, hasn't it, sweetie? Well, listen . . . yeah, the puff of white smoke knocked me out! We got an eight-page layout with Viceroy. 'The new Pope is a thinking man' . . . Billy [Graham] wants to know if you can get him one of those Dago sports cars? A Feraroo or some dumb thing. When you coming to the Coast? I'll get you the Sullivan show the nineteenth. Yeah, and send me some eight-by-ten glossies. It's good television. Wear the big ring. Don't worry, nobody knows you're Jewish."

The establishment's persecution of Bruce is a matter of common knowledge, as is his death by heroin overdose in 1966. In comparison, polymath Steve Allen, creator of *The Tonight Show*, ruled as comic, author, musician, and composer before dying in his sleep at age seventy-eight. Of the twenty-six comedians profiled here, three died young: Bruce, Cambridge, and Ernie Kovacs.

In a chapter titled "Televisionary," the Kovacs mystique is examined in some detail. On *The Ernie Kovacs Show* (1952-1956), he was an almost purely visual artist who used the fledgling medium as his palette. He pioneered the use of special effects, portraying inanimate objects coming to life, and once delivered an hour-long live show without any dialogue, pantomiming a benighted character named Eugene. Other memorably surreal bits included the Nairobi Trio (three musicians in gorilla suits) and the lisping poet Percy Dovetonsils. Like Cambridge, Kovacs had embarked on a film career when he died in an automobile crash in 1962.

The rest survived, but as Nachman details, they paid the high price of constantly being "on," of revealing their innermost fears to audiences for decades on end, of suffering hecklers and smoky clubs and life on the road. The brilliant Jonathan Winters famously had a breakdown at Fisherman's Wharf in San Francisco. Shelley Berman was caught on television bursting into rage during a documentary when a backstage telephone rang at crucial moments in his monologue. Sid Caesar, a comedy giant of early to mid-1950's television, was driven to alcoholism. Sahl read long excerpts from the Warren Report on the assassination of John F. Kennedy onstage, instead of making people laugh. Gregory pursued bizarre diets and health fads, including living for a time on nothing but air.

Only two women are profiled in *Seriously Funny*. One is Phyllis Diller, whose working-class, cackling housewife routine served her well for many years. The other is Joan Rivers, the daughter of a well-to-do family. Rivers modeled her early work on Woody Allen—a neurotic, self-effacing routine that never truly made her a star. Her act evolved as she got in tune with the raunch of the times and became what Nachman calls a "comic assassin." Her punch line-driven schtick focused on women's issues, and her humor grew grew increasingly cruel with the years: "Who picks Margaret Thatcher's clothes—Helen Keller?"

Nachman's prose is enthusiastic, and his research is thorough, relying on interviews with his subjects and their friends and spouses. His delightful study documents how the mid-century comedy renaissance shocked and provoked American audiences and affected future performers. It was one of the most important cultural developments of the era, Nachman argues—and he argues most persuasively, often through the words of the comedians themselves, generously quoting jokes and punch lines to situate them in their environment, support his assessments of their importance, and introduce them to a new audience.

Fiona Kelleghan

Review Sources

Booklist 99, no. 15 (April 1, 2003): 1364.
Kirkus Reviews 71, no. 4 (February 15, 2003): 288-289.
New York 36, no. 16 (May 12, 2003): 106-109.
The New York Times Book Review, June 8, 2003, p. 10.
The New Yorker 79, no. 11 (May 12, 2003): 106-09.
Publishers Weekly 250, no. 6 (February 10, 2003): 171-172.
Washington Monthly 35, no. 4 (April, 2003): 39-41.

A SHIP MADE OF PAPER

Author: Scott Spencer (1945-   )
Publisher: Ecco/HarperCollins (New York). 352 pp.
  $24.95
Type of work: Novel
Time: 1994-1995
Locale: The Hudson River Valley in upstate New York

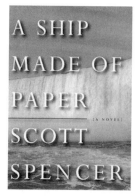

*Spencer's eighth novel tells the story of a love affair that
tests the boundaries of race, class, and family ties*

Principal characters:
  DANIEL EMERSON, a thirty-six-year-old
    lawyer
  KATE ELLIS, a novelist and journalist who
    lives with Daniel
  RUBY ELLIS, her four-year-old daughter from a former marriage
  IRIS DAVENPORT, a black graduate student
  HAMPTON WELLES, a successful black investment banker, married to Iris
  NELSON WELLES, their four-year-old son, Ruby's best friend

Like three of Spencer's previous novels, *A Ship Made of Paper* is set in the fictional town of Leyden, New York. Modeled on the historic town of Rhinebeck, where Spencer lives, Leyden has three distinct social classes: the old aristocracy of estate owners along the Hudson River, the old middle class of shop owners and professionals, and the affluent, cultured refugees from New York City, approximately one hundred miles downriver. On the surface, it seems the perfect place to live, scenic in all four seasons and needing only four policemen. However, it is a microcosm of the United States during the year of the O. J. Simpson murder trial, when racial prejudices and their consequences are painfully obvious to almost everyone. Even Leyden has its crime spree, when black youths break out of a juvenile home.

Daniel Emerson grew up in Leyden, the son of chiropractors who did everything for him short of showing any love: "they did not childproof their house, they houseproofed their child." After attending elite schools and earning a law degree from Columbia University, he worked as a civil rights lawyer in the South and did pro bono work for the poor in New York. He joins the white flight, however, when he is threatened and then attacked by friends of a drug dealer whom he has unsuccessfully defended. He returns to Leyden, bringing with him his girlfriend, Kate Ellis, and her preschool-age daughter, Ruby. They have a beautiful country house, which Kate has purchased with proceeds from her first novel and for which he contributes half the monthly payments. Daniel is a sensitive male who shops and cooks and takes Ruby to preschool. Kate is attractive and intelligent. They share witty repartee and a limited commitment: "a pledge to each other to be Swiss bankers of the heart." However, Daniel finds that he needs more.

~

Scott Spencer is best known for his third novel, Endless Love *(1979), named a Notable Book by the American Library Association and made into a notoriously bad film by Franco Zeffirelli in 1981. Spencer has taught at the Iowa Writing Project and serves on the executive board of PEN American Center.*

~

As the novel begins, Daniel is happiest driving Ruby to preschool. In her company he experiences "something tender at the center of creation, some meaning, some purpose and poetry." Unloved as a child, he begins to experience love as a surrogate father. He is fascinated with Iris Davenport, the mother of Ruby's schoolmate Nelson. In addition to being a loving mother, Iris is a beautiful African American. She keeps up a commuter marriage with Hampton Welles, a banker from a prominent African American family; he lives in New York during the week, and she lives in Leyden so she can pursue a graduate degree at nearby Marlowe College (closely modeled on Bard College).

Daniel's fascination becomes an obsession as he follows Iris's car, cruises past her house, and learns the details of her schedule. He takes every opportunity to mention Iris's name in conversation with Kate, because he likes to think about her but has no reason to think that she would reciprocate his desire. Kate gets suspicious and arranges an evening together for the two couples, an evening that proves disastrous when conversation turns to the Simpson trial, then in progress. Convinced of Simpson's guilt, Kate exposes the prejudices of her southern upbringing. Later that evening, after she collapses on her bed in a drunken stupor, Daniel drives past Iris's house. Little does he realize that she is standing at the window, watching his car while Hampton sleeps.

A few days later, an early ice storm hits the area, felling trees, downing power lines, and blocking roads. Daniel manages to drive as far as Iris's house, where he is to pick up Ruby, but the storm keeps them from leaving. As Daniel soaks in the details of Iris's life, she confesses that her husband pays no attention to her and that she finds Daniel's attention strangely flattering. Daniel confesses his love for her, and before the night is out they make love while their children sleep, passionate love such as neither has known before.

They see each other every day until Hampton returns for the weekend, and they come to regard these first days together as "the Rapture." They are in untenable positions: Iris fears that Hampton will harm her or take Nelson away, while Daniel hates the thought of hurting Kate or, worse still, Ruby. Somehow they continue their love affair, as well as their family affairs, through the Thanksgiving holiday. However, their families are stressed to the breaking point. When they two couples meet again, by chance, at a fund-raiser in late November, their lives are truly broken, changed forever by a freak accident.

The accident is provoked by another love triangle. Ferguson Richmond, the owner of a large and dilapidated estate, is having a satisfying affair with Marie Thorne, a young blind woman who grew up on the estate and returned to look after her dying father, the caretaker. Marie then stayed on to secure the estate's future as a historic site. Ferguson's wife, who is largely given over to New Age religion, has tolerated Marie's presence but will not be upstaged by her at the fund-raiser. Marie, "heart-sick and self-destructive," runs away on the sprawling grounds, leaving the others to set up a search party in the twilight. Daniel and Hampton team up, while Kate and Iris take their children home. Daniel is frightened of Hampton but realizes he that cares deeply for the man when he suddenly fears for their lives. Then tragedy strikes.

The fateful accident is recounted in chapter 14 but is anticipated in each preceding chapter, for each opens with a few lines about the search. The last four chapters skip to the following summer, when the characters meet again and reach a certain resignation. "Tragedy" seems the right word for the story. Daniel, especially, is a flawed character, still bearing the marks of his loveless childhood and yearning for a fulfillment that he cannot find in the white world, a fulfillment he identifies with Iris and her culture. Iris, meanwhile, has been hurt by a husband and a society that both take her for granted. On the night of the ice storm, she tells Daniel "the dirty little secret of the Africans in America. We really want y'all to like us."

Both want something more than the convenient color marker. Kate tells a marriage counselor that Daniel wants to be black; Hampton warns Daniel that Iris is as white as most stockbrokers. Daniel would like to think that love can win over "history," that is, over centuries of racial conflict. Iris would rather not think of her life "as part of the long and terrible story of Race in America—she thought she deserved both more and less than to be counted among the victims of racism." When danger threatens, though, they return automatically to the fears of the other race. They are proven wrong. What they learn from their suffering is that they cannot change their fate. Daniel gets the last word: "There's no turning back."

Spencer is also a good social satirist, so good that some readers may lose sympathy with the spurned spouses. Hampton is the model of success in the African American community, forever dropping the right names, acquiring the right products, and treating others with "colonial condescension." Kate is an attractive woman with no instinct for romance who has written a comic best-seller about the romantic trials of a plain woman. Unable to get started on her next novel, she writes nothing but commentaries on the Simpson trial, publicly denouncing the violence that she privately wishes on Iris. Hypocrisy is everywhere: in the town, on the campus, at the river estate. Even Daniel and Iris are full of contradictions in their self-conceptions and their images of each other. Daniel is a connoisseur of African American jazz and assumes that Iris will be too; imagine his distress when he looks through her CDs on the night of the ice storm and finds Fleetwood Mac.

Despite the tragic overtones and comic undertones, Spencer waxes lyrical when writing about love. In two experimental scenes, one before the accident and one after, he describes Daniel's nightly trance. Daniel's spirit flies over Leyden, lifted on the wings of love and dropping blessings on everyone, especially Iris. The first scene ends with a sudden recognition: "Happiness of this magnitude can only lead to sorrow. Joy lifts you up and joy casts you down." The second ends with the recognition that he and Iris will never find a life together, even though they can never return to their old lives. Rousing himself afterward, he thinks he has lost the sight in one eye, a loss that proves entirely psychosomatic.

The lyricism reaches deep into the culture. The novel takes its title from a verse in "Just to Be with You," a 1959 recording by a white doo-wop group called the Passions: "On a ship that's made of paper/ I would sail the seven seas/ just to be with you." That pretty well expresses Daniel's feelings for Iris, feelings that neither his girlfriend nor his male friends can understand. Kate's murderous thoughts about Daniel immediately after he admits he is having a passionate affair come straight out of Macbeth's vision of a floating dagger in the William Shakespeare tragedy: "The handle toward my hand, come let me clutch thee." The passions behind the Simpson murder case, on which she obsesses, lie deep in the human heart.

Told in the present tense, from several characters' points of view, this novel is gripping. Readers may find it addictive, much as Daniel finds his passion for Iris. However, they will have the advantage of getting through the year-long ordeal in a few memorable chapters, enjoying Daniel's "higher plane of devotion" without suffering his painful losses at home and at work. Some may feel that Spencer has manipulated the characters' stories to cast the best possible light on his lovers. Hampton and Kate are often too absurd and too self-absorbed to be likeable. To his credit, though, Spencer ends the novel before there is a decision in the Simpson case or about the characters' fates. He offers no closing argument. As noted in the Library of Congress classifications on the reverse title page, he has chosen to write about race relations as well as adultery and the Hudson River Valley, but he has worked hard to tell a good story that should offend no one. In Daniel Emerson he has created a middle-aged man experiencing the same obsessive love as the characters in his most compelling novels to date: the teenage David Axelrod in *Endless Love* (1979) and the widowed Fielding Pierce in *Waking the Dead* (1986). This is a story of sentiment which threatens to become sentimental but manages to keeps its edge.

Thomas Willard

Review Sources

The New York Times Book Review, March 23, 2003, p. 9.
The New Yorker 79, no. 2 (March 3, 2003): 90-91.
Newsweek 141, no. 10 (March 10, 2003): 64.
People 59, no. 13 (April 7, 2003): 50.
Publishers Weekly 250, no. 5 (February 3, 2003): 55.
Time 161, no. 11 (March 17, 2003): 72.
The Wall Street Journal, March 14, 2003, p. W8.
The Washington Post Book World, March 23, 2003, p. 5.

SHIPWRECK

Author: Louis Begley (1933-   )
Publisher: Alfred A. Knopf (New York). 244 pp. $23.00
Type of work: Novel
Time: 2000
Locale: Paris; New York City; Martha's Vineyard, Massachusetts; Long Island, New York; and the Greek island of Spetsai

A famous novelist tells a stranger in a café the story of his life and his tangled personal relationships

> *Principal characters:*
> JOHN NORTH, a successful American novelist
> LYDIA FRANK NORTH, his wife, a physician who specializes in kidney research
> THE NARRATOR, a man of about North's age who accidentally encounters North in a café
> LÉA MORONI, a young Parisian woman with whom North has an affair

Usually authors who start their writing careers later in life are telling only one story, even if they tell it in a series of books. It is difficult enough for a writer who follows a conventional career trajectory to be animated by fresh ideas, so much more the challenge for the writer who begins at a mature age. Louis Begley, whose first book, the well-received *Wartime Lies* (1991) was partially based on his boyhood experiences in Holocaust-era Poland, has confounded expectations by writing a totally new book each time out. Even *Schmidt Delivered* (2000), a sequel to the popular *About Schmidt* (1996), is so drastic a departure from its predecessor that it unnerved many who had admired the earlier volume. Of contemporary novelists who have begun late, only the British writer Anita Brookner has managed a similar originality.

Shipwreck is different from anything else Begley has written because it is more theoretical and more self-conscious than his other novels. Had a writer advertised as an experimentalist written it, one would not be surprised. Intricacies abound. John North, the book's main storyteller (though not its narrator), is himself a novelist, and the success of his book *The Anthill* plays a considerable role in *Shipwreck*. He tells his story to the narrator of the novel, an unnamed man whom North meets in a café called L'Entre Deux Mondes (between two worlds), denoting a kind of metaphysical bridge between fantasy and reality, salvation and damnation.

Self-reflexivity, once thought to be very avant-garde, has in the hands of younger American writers of the 1990's and 2000's become rather routine. No longer does it cause the frisson of aesthetic risk it did in the days of Jorge Luis Borges or Vladimir Nabokov a generation ago. Begley, however, brings a new sense of purpose to self-reflexivity. He persuades the reader that the figure of the novelist within a novel is not just a surrogate for Begley himself. It is a figure for a man prone to regard the contexts of his life as simply fictions from which he can distance himself as he wishes.

~

Louis Begley was born in Poland, survived the German occupation during World War II, and moved to New York in 1947. He has worked as a lawyer for many years and has been partner in the prestigious firm of Debevoise and Plimpton since 1968. He has received the PEN/Hemingway Prize and the Aer Lingus Irish Times *book prize, among many other awards.*

~

The narrator never seems to become bored with North's story, nor does he become frightened at North's frequent agitation and emotional outbursts. Occasionally, though, North does buy the narrator food or drink or make some other soothing social gesture. The reader, then, is conscious that, though in principle a monologue, the story is in form a dialogue. A fascinating moment occurs when North warns the narrator that the story is going to take on more sinister overtones. At that point, the two men cease drinks and hors d'oeuvres and shift to the main course.

The narrator gradually learns details of North's personal life. North is in his mid-forties and is married to the former Lydia Frank, a successful New York doctor who is five years older than he. The Franks are a wealthy family who have made their fortune in real estate. Their background is explicitly described as Jewish rather than white Anglo-Saxon Protestant (this fact has eluded many reviewers who see both the Franks and Norths as WASPs). North's own family is far less accomplished in immediate terms, although with far greater ancestral prestige. The usual scenario of the arriviste man of the newly wealthy family marrying the daughter of the aristocratic set is reversed. The Franks are not keen on North as a suitor. They see him as an improvident aesthete, whereas all their other in-laws are Wall Street millionaires.

Despite having no children (their only daughter is stillborn), North and Lydia have a happy marriage. North achieves success, unexpectedly, rather late with his novel *The Anthill.* Again, Begley shakes up customary expectations, as one might expect the success as a novelist (and the consequent laurels of prizes and lucrative film adaptation) to make North jovial and spirited. Alternating between biliousness and melancholy, though, he is no better off than before. He is working on a novel called *Loss.* This word not only has negative connotations but also specifically unbuilds the accumulation implied in *The Anthill,* as if both art and life were zero-sum games. He visits Paris, a city he knows and loves and where he has friends, to support his book's publicity. Even this does not seem to set off in him any zeal or spark. When North meets a young journalist from the French edition of *Vogue* magazine for an interview, he regards it as just another dreary exercise to which he has to submit. That the woman, Léa Moroni, becomes his lover is more of a surprise to North than it is to the reader.

The relationship with Léa, though full of sexual passion and gratification, is not without its tensions. For instance, in speaking French to North, Léa seeks to "demonstrate our intimacy by using the familiar *tu* in every sentence, although I pointedly used the neutral *vous.*" This is important in a novel whose story is being told to a "you." Léa, like the narrator, is an interlocutor, though a more reluctant one. There is also a doubling between Léa and Lydia; both have unusual names beginning with 'l' and ending with 'a'. North is always aware not only of the danger of being seen with Léa by those who know Lydia but also of the guilt he feels when he takes Lydia to a locale he has frequented with Léa. Even though he loves both women and does genuinely achieve happiness with them, both relationships are nonetheless strangely unsatisfactory, adding to the two women's subterranean kinship.

That kinship is also indicated by the way, for instance, that Lydia's medical work and Léa's painting—though she works as a journalist, the visual arts constitute the younger woman's core vocation—are mentioned within pages of each other. Adultery redeems North no more than does marriage or literary success. This is made gruesomely evident when he compares his preparations for adultery to those of a man plotting to commit murder, a comparison not without foreboding for the ultimate course of the plot. On one level, Léa is little more than a tramp, but on another she genuinely believes in the positive qualities of her liaison with the much older North. When it becomes clear that she is more invested in the affair than he is, the reader becomes steadily more sympathetic to Léa.

The denouement of the book begins with an odd episode of reminiscence in which North reveals that his mother had conducted a decades-long affair with a friend of her husband, the best man at their wedding. This man, a former secretary of the Navy, was, apparently without irony, designated by North's father as the chief eulogist at his funeral. The father's apparent tolerance of the liaison is evident either of an extreme social identification with his class (the senior North was a member of the then-ultra-elite diplomatic corps, and his friendship with the patrician Navy secretary may be an expression of caste solidarity), an utter indifference to his wife, or a latent homosexuality. North hints at this implication by his mention of the bisexual British aristocratic couple Harold Nicolson and Vita Sackville-West. Reflecting upon his father's strange instruction, North wonders if "honor rooted in dishonor" does not fundamentally inform the idea of a secret life. On the one hand, honor rooted in dishonor can be the best for which one can aim in a world of original sin. On the other hand, it can be a plausible cover to disguise an amoral and expedient stance.

The shocking ending, in which North (a character with whom the reader has come to empathize at least as much as the average person semi-willingly empathizes with a stranger who has monopolized two hours of their time) allows Léa to flail away at the waves before he snaps out of the trance he had fallen into and attempts to find her, jolts the reader's received expectations. (Its Martha's Vineyard locale, though not the precise nature of the event, recalls the Chappaquiddick incident involving Massachusetts Senator Edward Kennedy in 1969.) One does not know whether to be horrified or reassured that North then apparently returns to a serene life with a seemingly unsuspecting Lydia. It could be that he feels guilty about Léa's fate and that this guilt is being acted out in his disquisition to the narrator.

Begley may also be making a more general point about the nature of resolution in a novel. This speculation is given basis by Begley's lengthy passages on great novels of the past such as Leo Tolstoy's *Anna Karenina* (1875-1877; English translation, 1886) and George Eliot's *Daniel Deronda* (1876). When one reads, for instance, a Jane Austen novel, one sees the ending as a happy one, the unseemly threat to the social order dispelled forever. What if this is a mistake, not in interpretation but in emphasis? What if it is the threat to social norms that is the catalyzing force and the benign resolution simply the aftermath? The way Léa's fate overshadows the concord at the end makes the reader ask, not only about this novel but also many others, whether trusting entirely in a restored order at the end is to miss the forest for the trees. The fact that the novel is called *Shipwreck*, which is the term used by North to describe the final calamity of his adulterous relationship, is a further clue to the pertinence of this question.

The conclusion also reveals something about the "you" who tells the reader how he hears North's story told to him. At the end of the book, the reader realizes that the "you" is less a discrete personage than a figure for that reader, or perhaps for an externalized aspect of North's conscience acting as a monitor. This gives the book a certain resemblance to more overtly self-conscious books such as Italo Calvino's *Se una notte d'inverno un viaggiatore* (1979; *If on a Winter's Night a Traveler*, 1981) which use the "you" form of address at once to foreground the artificiality of the relationship between author and reader and make it more intimate. Begley's previous works have placed him largely in the realist camp. This delicate, subtle, and thought-provoking narrative asks pivotal questions about the nature of fiction itself.

Nicholas Birns

Review Sources

Booklist 100, no. 2 (September 15, 2003): 180.
The Boston Globe, September 21, 2003, p. D6.
Kirkus Reviews 71, no. 16 (August 15, 2003): 1030.
Library Journal 128, no. 15 (September 15, 2003): 89.
Los Angeles Times, September 29, 2003, p. E9.
The Nation 277, no. 16 (November 17, 2003): 36-38.
The New York Times, October 2, 2003, p. E9.
The New York Times Book Review, October 5, 2003, p. 7.
The New Yorker, September 22, 2003, p. 196.
Publishers Weekly 250, no. 32 (August 11, 2003): 257.
The Washington Post Book World, September 14, 2003, p. T15.

SHROUD

Author: John Banville (1945-   )
Publisher: Alfred A. Knopf (New York). 257 pp. $25.00
Type of work: Novel
Time: 2003
Locale: Turin, Italy

An elderly scholar who has relocated to the United States is suddenly forced to re-visit a past he strived an entire life to conceal

Principal characters:
> AXEL VANDER, an aging scholar who is secretive about his wartime past
> CASS CLEAVE, a young aspiring graduate student devoted to Vander's work
> FRANCO BARTOLI, an Italian colleague of Vander and a Romantic scholar
> KRISTINA KOVACS, another colleague and a former lover of Vander

Axel Vander is an elderly survivor of the Nazi purges. Having relocated to the United States, he teaches at a university in Arcady, California, and has a formidable reputation as one of literature's most controversial theorists. Vander heads off to Turin for a conference and to meet a woman who claims she has uncovered secrets from a past he prefers to keep hidden.

Cass Cleave, a character reprised from John Banville's previous novel, *Eclipse* (2000), appears as an emotionally ravaged graduate student who poses no deliberate threat to Vander. Her appearance, however, throws his life into unanticipated turmoil. In a long monologue addressed to Cleave, he reviews the details of his murky secrets. In short, Vander is not Vander; he assumed a boyhood friend's identity to keep himself out of the death camps. In so doing, however, he has inherited his friend's legacy of anti-Semitic articles written for a collaborationist Antwerp newspaper.

The irony in the whole arrangement is that the Vander character, born a Jew, agreed with Adolf Hitler's "final solution" and yearned to write articles himself which, he contends, would have been even more vituperative. Vander grows increasingly attached to Cleave, who eventually flees to parts unknown in the United States, leaving him once more a prisoner of his own self-involvement.

The book opens with a quote from Friedrich Nietzsche's *Der Wille zur Macht* (1901; *The Will to Power*, 1910), and the philosopher is a ghost haunting both Vander and the text itself. Nietzsche is quoted in various spots, and Vander refers to him frequently, using him as a North Star to guide the narrator on his dark journey. Not coincidentally, Turin, the novel's principal setting, was Nietzsche's last home before his mental collapse and death.

One of the novel's primary thematic concerns is the Nietzschean and existential notions of self and identity. Vander is a vain and cruel wretch who plunges into a vor-

∼

John Banville has authored thirteen novels, among them Kepler, *which was awarded the Guardian Prize for Fiction in 1981. In 1989 Banville's* The Book of Evidence, *was short-listed for the Booker Prize; it also won the Guinness Peat Aviation Award that year. He is the literary editor of* The Irish Times.

∼

tex of lacerating self-examination. Like Vladimir Nabokov's Humbert Humbert in *Lolita* (1955), Vander is a dissembler whose identity the reader can never quite discern. Indeed, the existential definition of identity is of something fluid and mutable, and Vander's rejection of a single self for the adoption of another would seem perfectly existential. However, he lives in bad faith, avoiding the responsibilities occasioned by such a choice. He refers to his adopted identity as burdensome, "a dead weight hung about my own neck," and suggests he is a collection of selves, "I am myself and also someone else."

Vander is at once his own creation, an original who is regarded by others as unique, yet he is also a borrowed thing, a self he both admires and despises. The reader is left in limbo, never able to disentangle the confused threads of being. Vander is at once all and none of the identities he puts on endless parade before his audience.

Although Vander practices some ventriloquistic impersonations of other voices, the narrative comes from his point of view, and, as with most subjective narrators, the issue of reliability becomes significant, even paramount. In this novel, as in so many of Banville's works, narrative reliability is foregrounded because the protagonist so persistently warns the reader not to accept him uncritically. For instance, during one of his monologues Vander is transported back into an idyllic memory of childhood, replete with the rustic splendors of a family farm, simple, hearty meals, and a spirit of community among siblings and seasonal laborers. As he builds to a crescendo of familial affection, ellipses suddenly intrude and are followed by the declaration, "All this I remembered, even though it had never happened."

The reader may be alarmed by such a confusing statement, except that Vander continually issues ominous warnings, such as "All my life I have lied. . . . It was a way of living; lies are life's almost-anagram." For Vander, existence is an endless act of subterfuge and prevarication. In fact, what he reveals of his most intimate relations with people are allegiances woven by a tissue of lies—friends, colleagues, lovers, and spouses are all deceived as he morphs from one self into another. The question for the reader, of course, is what to believe.

The answer may be found in the novel's title and dominant motif, the shroud. By locating the action in Turin, Banville inevitably provokes thoughts of one of the most controversial of religious icons: a miraculous article of faith to believers and a hoax to skeptics. Although Vander and Cleave plan to visit the alleged burial cloth of Jesus Christ, they never manage. Vander has no need to see it, for he has lived a life of shrouds, and, like the Shroud of Turin, he is both fraud and celebrity. His identity has been hidden behind the veils of other, increasingly disposable selves.

One night at a dinner party, near the novel's conclusion, Franco Bartoli, an Italian colleague cum Vander-admirer, notes that "Professor Vander . . . holds that every text conceals a shameful secret, the hidden understains left behind by the author in his necessarily bad faith, and which it is the critic's task to nose out." Indeed, Vander leaves "understains" for his readers to nose out in spite of all his dissembling and elusiveness. One can be sure that Vander is disturbed, even oppressed, by his past, and the prospect of pulling back his shroud and revealing his actual face is both terrifying and delightful.

In pouring forth a bizarre confessional, Vander joins company with a host of other Banville protagonists: the anonymous historian in *The Newton Letter* (1982), another anonymous authority on Flemish painting in *Athena* (1995), and Victor Maskell, art historian and Soviet spy in *The Untouchable* (1997). Each of these four men is self-admiring and intellectually presumptuous, and each is ripe for a fall. In composing presumably soul-searching narratives, each curiously manages to avoid an honest confrontation with himself, yet each is ultimately a self-betrayed character to the reader. The audience can never share in their delusions of grandiosity and instead regards them as weak, vulnerable outcasts from friendship and love. In the hopelessly addled Cass Cleave, Vander imagines he may have finally found genuine affection, only to realize that the love is entirely a product of his imaginings.

If the outlines of Vander's story sound familiar, they should, for Banville has cleverly created another understain, a portrait of Paul de Man (1919-1983), the leading exponent of deconstructive literary criticism in the United States. De Man was born in Antwerp, Belgium, and immigrated to the United States after World War II. Four years after his death, it was discovered that from 1940 to 1942 he had written 180 book reviews and articles for newspapers in Brussels that were sympathetic to the Nazi regime. In one article in particular, de Man issued an anti-Semitic broadside, and his disciples quickly scrambled to deconstruct the damage by arguing that the articles were not really what they seemed at all.

At the heart of the deconstuctionist critique is the belief that all writing is, first and foremost, rhetorical and cannot refer to anything outside of itself. Language, the deconstructionists argue, is ultimately self-referential, and therefore the idea that language can express or discover truth is unattainable. Truth vanishes into a complex network of endless signification, and, in the case of de Man, if there is no truth, then there can be no wrongdoing and no responsibility.

Such is Vander's position precisely. There is no self, and other people are simply impediments to the desires and appetites of the individual. He feels no compunction about using and abusing others as long as those actions advance his own interests. He candidly reveals this ethos when rejoicing:

> I was at last, I realised, a wholly free agent. Everything had been taken from me, therefore everything was to be permitted. I could do whatever I wished, follow my wildest whim. I could lie, cheat, steal, maim, murder, and justify it all. More: the necessity of justification would not arise, for the land I was entering now was a land without laws.

If literature can refer to nothing but itself, and if people are not human beings but so much raw material to be manipulated, then there is nothing to believe in, and Vander constructs his own nihilistic credo:

I would be pure existence [once relocated in America], an affectless point moving through time, nihilism's silver bullet, penetrating clean through every obstacle, shooting holes in the flanks of every moth-eaten monument of so-called civilisation. Negative faith! That was to be the foundation of my new religion. A passionate and all-consuming belief in nothing . . . my Church of the Singular Soul.

In presenting a character whose identity may be indeterminate, Banville manages to distance himself from Vander's self-absorption by revealing how thoroughly the man betrays his seeming invulnerability. Vander is oppressed by his past, and he may be far more responsible for his horrors than he realizes. He admits to killing his wife, though presumably as a form of euthanasia, when she is ravaged by disease, and he constantly recalls her with as much affection as he is capable. However, it is his relationship with the original Vander that proves most troubling. The narrator claims that he could never get to the bottom of his host's death because of a host of rumors: that he committed suicide over a failed love affair, that he was imprisoned as a communist, that he was killed in an obscure dispute with a military faction, or, the narrator's preferred explanation, that he was executed as a member of the Resistance.

At the novel's close, when Vander visits a dying colleague and former lover, Kristina Kovacs, he encounters a physician who once met the Vander parents as they tried to flee the Germans. The doctor tells the protagonist that his name is familiar, the same as that of the son of these frightened exiles: "Already they had lost a son, destroyed, so they told him, by the actions of a treacherous friend. 'Destroyed?' I said faintly. Or perhaps I only thought of saying it. I sat down slowly at my desk and leaned an arm on it. There are certain exhalations that sound like one's last breath." Banville has left Vander with no way out—he was not only envious of his friend, it appears he may have even abetted his death, which, until this unanticipated moment, he cannot admit to his audience or himself.

To say that Banville is a stylist understates the sheer brilliance of his achievement. As in each of his works, his extravagant prose is foregrounded, compelling the reader's attention as much as any of his characters or events, which again provokes comparison with another prodigious stylist, Nabokov. Banville's sentences are carefully crafted webs of lush, sensuous verbal apprehension. There is always the sense of a keenly observant eye scrutinizing the minutiae of experience and emotion. At the same time, he is one of the wittiest of writers, constantly modulating the narrative voice between extremes of mordant seriousness and ludicrous irony and understatement.

Shroud stands as further evidence that Banville is a major talent, and one not fully appreciated in the United States. His novels are urbane, erudite, and intellectually demanding. For some these works are daunting challenges, but they are as humane as they are demanding. *Shroud* is a harrowing, unforgettable book, a book to read and reread and a reminder of the dangers of uncritical self-regard.

David W. Madden

Review Sources

Booklist 99, no. 13 (March 1, 2003): 1145.
The Economist 365, no. 8297 (November 2, 2002): 83.
Kirkus Reviews 71, no. 2 (January 15, 2003): 101.
Library Journal 128, no. 5 (March 15, 2003): 113.
Los Angeles Times, June 8, 2003, p. 5.
New Statesman 131, no. 4614 (November 18, 2002): 55.
The New York Times Book Review, March 16, 2003, p. 9.
Publishers Weekly 250, no. 3 (January 27, 2003): 235.
Review of Contemporary Fiction 23, no. 2 (Summer, 2003): 129.
The Spectator, September 28, 2002, p. 69.
The Times Literary Supplement, September 20, 2002, p. 19.

THE SNACK THIEF

Author: Andrea Camilleri (1925-   )
First published: Il ladro di merendine, 1996, in Italy
Translated from the Italian by Stephen Sartarelli
Publisher: Viking (New York). 298 pp. $21.95
Type of work: Novel
Time: The 1990's
Locale: Fictional small towns along Sicily's southwest
coast

*Investigating two murders, enjoying the local cuisine,
and hosting a visit by his Genoese girlfriend, Inspector
Montalbano unravels a shadowy web of international plots
involving terrorists, the secret services, and high-level
governmental cover-ups*

Principal characters:
SALVO MONTALBANO, the chief inspector for the Vigàta police
LIVIA BURLANDO, his girlfriend from Genoa
"CAT" CATARELLA, the police department's telephone operator
MIMÌ AUGELLO, the department's second-in-command
FAZIO, GALLO, GALLUZZO, and GRASSO, other Vigàta policemen
JACOMUZZI, the head of the local police lab
BUSCAÌNO, a Mazàra policeman raised in Tunisia
VICE-COMMISSIONER VALENTE, the Mazàra police chief
THE COMMISSIONER, Montalbano's boss, nearing retirement
AURELIO LAPÈCORA, an elderly murder victim
ANTONIETTA PALMISANO LAPÈCORA, his wife
ANTONINO LAPÈCORA, their son, a doctor
AHMED "BEN DHAHAB" MOUSSA, a terrorist, the second murder victim
KARIMA MOUSSA, Ahmed's sister, a housecleaner and prostitute
FRANÇOIS MOUSSA, her five-year-old son
FAHRID, Ahmed's associate who betrays him
CLEMENTINA VASILE COZZA, a wheelchair-bound chief witness
AISHA, an old Tunisian woman, a witness
MASTER RAHMAN, an elementary-school teacher of Tunisian origin
ANGELO PRESTÌA, a fishing boat captain
ADELINA, Montalbano's housekeeper and cook

The Snack Thief is the third mystery novel in Andrea Camilleri's Inspector
Montalbano series to be translated into English. Translated in the order they were first
published, the two previous novels are *La forma dell'acqua* (1994; *The Shape of
Water,* 2002) and *Il cane di terracotta* (1996; *The Terra-Cotta Dog,* 2002). Presumably, several other novels and short-fiction collections in the series will be forthcoming in English. Besides the Inspector Montalbano series, Camilleri has published a

dozen or so other novels and for many years was a director and scriptwriter for television and the theater, where he first became known for dramatizing works by other famous mystery writers. Camilleri's Inspector Montalbano series has been immensely popular in Italy and other European countries as well as Japan.

Andrea Camilleri is a native of Sicily who now lives in Rome. Best known for his Inspector Montalbano mystery series, he is also the author of other novels and has been a director and scriptwriter for the theater and television.

The series's popularity is easy to understand. After a long apprenticeship, Camilleri has become a master of the mystery novel. In the nineteenth century, the mystery story was sometimes called a story of ratiocination. This quality of reasoning is preserved in Inspector Montalbano, who does not depend on car chases and guns for excitement but who reads books, considers human nature, conducts tricky cross-examinations, sets up his opponents, and ties clues together with the cleverness of famous fictional detective Sherlock Holmes.

While Montalbano carries on this rationalistic tradition, he is no pointy-headed intellectual, nor is he old-fashioned. Rather, he is a thoroughly postmodern man, almost antiheroic, with human failings and a liberal use of both four-letter words and the media. He has trouble with relationships, carrying on an affair with his girlfriend, Livia, mostly by long distance. In *The Snack Thief* Montalbano is forty-four years old, Livia is thirty-three, and their relationship has been going on for six years. When Livia comes to visit and talks about marriage, having children, and adoption, Montalbano is wracked by primal fears of family responsibility. He has the same trouble relating to his father, from whom he has become separated and who is now dying.

Instead, Montalbano is attached to his self-indulgence and to his career. When he is not on the job, he lives by himself in a little house by the sea, where he can enjoy the view and take a swim. His housekeeper, Adelina, prepares and leaves him food, he cruises the excellent restaurants in the area, and he can rustle up a dish or two on his own. While he consumes a good meal, he puts his work on hold, even making a secret service agent wait and watch him eat his dinner (without offering to share). He sometimes suffers indigestion, as when he eats three pounds of sardines *a beccafico*. Luckily, the cuisine in the area is based mostly on seafood, but still one wonders how much the inspector weighs.

Sometimes Montalbano appears downright comic, and not only in his gormandizing. He is prone to outbursts of expletives and emotions, such as the possessive jealousy he feels over his colleague Augello's attentions to Livia and even her attentions to the child François (the snack thief of the novel's title). He is far from heroic, expressing fright, taking clownish falls (in *The Terra-Cotta Dog*) and shooting out his mirror image (in *The Shape of Water*). An inveterate viewer of the nightly television news on both local channels, he has the thrill of watching himself be attacked by TeleVigàta editorialist Pippo Ragonese for investigating—in the midst of a crime wave worthy of Chicago in the Prohibition era—a snack thief.

If the only-too-human character of Inspector Montalbano is one of the attractions of this mystery series, another attraction is the local color of the setting, the southwest coast of Sicily, of which both the author and his inspector are representatives. Camilleri was born there in 1925 in Porto Empedocle, near Agrigento. Montalbano is actually from Catania, on Sicily's eastern coast, but he has grown so fond of the southwest coast that, in *The Snack Thief*, he resists promotion and transfer from the area. One reason he is averse to marriage is that he fears he might have to settle with Livia at Boccadesse, outside of Genoa. To some extent, the two characters represent the split between the north and south of Italy, and the southwest coast of Sicily is about as far as one can split without floating off to Africa.

In the popular imagination, Sicily is a backward place known for its poverty and the Mafia. Camilleri does not contradict this image, nor does he hesitate to depict other unsavory aspects of Sicily. For example, both its Fascist past and the Mafia are featured in *The Terra-Cotta Dog* (though the Mafia only receive mention in *The Snack Thief*). Camilleri also makes use of the popular image of Sicily for purposes of local color, satire, and social criticism. The Sicilians are vividly depicted as nosy, emotional, voluble, earthy, and interesting people overall. They speak in their own dialect, which those in some other parts of Italy have trouble understanding. The violent crimes that fill the local news satirize the media and mirror corruption on the national and international levels. As in Tony Hillerman's Navaho police series, the small-town Inspector Montalbano constantly shows up his clumsy counterparts from the national police forces.

Camilleri also suggests a depth to the Sicilian character that is lacking in the popular stereotype. If Sicily is now seen as a backward place, it has historically been at the crossroads of civilization, as waves of Greeks, Romans, Arabs, Normans, and others conquered and inhabited it. It is not surprising that, along with these cultural and linguistic infusions, Sicily has a rich literary tradition, going back to the Sicilian school of the thirteenth century that invented the canzone and sonnet forms. In the modern era, Sicily has produced many of the great figures of Italian literature, such as the novelist Giovanni Verga, the playwright Luigi Pirandello, and the poet Salvatore Quasimodo.

A prominent theme of Sicilian writers is the interplay of appearance and reality or multiple truths—perhaps a natural theme for a society that has had to adapt to different cultures and authorities (as in the simultaneous, side-by-side operation of the national police, the local police, and the Mafia). Camilleri adopts this theme and puts it to good use in his Inspector Montalbano series, as the inspector separates appearance from reality, truth from lies, and eventually puts together clues to solve the case. The case is never simple and obvious, despite its appearance of being so. It shifts and takes different forms as the evidence accumulates. As suggested by Camilleri's previous title, *The Shape of Water*, the truth takes the shape of its container.

In *The Snack Thief* two killings appear to be unrelated: the stabbing of an elderly man in the elevator of his apartment building and the shooting of an Italian fishing boat crewman by a Tunisian gunboat. Investigation of the second incident is even assigned to a different district, the Mazàra police—to Montalbano's great relief. His investigation of the first case, however, keeps coinciding with the second. The elderly man was carrying on an affair with a beautiful prostitute of Tunisian origin, who turns out to be the sister of the fishing boat crewman, who turns out to be a noted Tunisian terrorist who was lured to Sicily and a fatal meeting on the high seas by the undercover scheming of the Tunisian and Italian secret services.

The governments involved try to cover up the assassination as an unfortunate diplomatic incident, with protests and apologies duly rendered on each side. Unfortunately, the cover-up also requires that the prostitute and an old Tunisian woman who saw too much be killed. Others who might know something are endangered, including Montalbano, Livia, and the prostitute's young son. About this time, a secret service agent, Colonel Lohengrin Pera, pays Montalbano a visit to appeal to his patriotism. The dwarfish Colonel Pera, who quotes dictator Benito Mussolini and deplores "a useless massacre," comes across as the symbolic representative of a sinister shadow government no better than the Mafia. How Montalbano handles Pera and the secret services forms the climax of the novel.

Most of the novel is not as grim as these killings and the government cover-up. If anything, *The Snack Thief* has more of Montalbano's gormandizing, personal life, and comedy than the other two volumes of the series so far translated into English. The local color of Sicilian life in the novel never fails to entertain. For instance, the dynamics of neighborly life in the apartment building where the elderly man is killed become one object of satire as Montalbano goes around interviewing the tenants. The ability of Sicilians to assume the proper attitude and dress for the occasion is also satirized. So, also, is the tendency of older women to fall into a state of tragic expectancy: "There is no Sicilian woman alive, of any class, aristocrat or peasant, who, after her fiftieth birthday, isn't always expecting the worst. What kind of worst? Any, so long as it's the worst." One reason for their gloom is perhaps revealed when one reads about the uproarious sexual fetishes of most of the elderly men who were the prostitute's clients and whom Montalbano also has to interview.

The Snack Thief is so well written, well translated, and entertaining that one is immediately impelled to find the two earlier volumes of the Montalbano series and read them. The only trouble is that one might have to wait a while before additional volumes are translated. The Montalbano series therefore might be a good reason to take up the study of Italian. One could certainly find some vocabulary there not available in the standard handbooks.

Harold Branam

Review Sources

Booklist 99, no. 17 (May 1, 2003): 1536.
Kirkus Reviews 71, no. 6 (March 15, 2003): 428.
Library Journal 128, no. 7 (April 15, 2003): 130.
Publishers Weekly 250, no. 13 (March 31, 2003): 46.

SOMETHING FOR NOTHING
Luck in America

Author: Jackson Lears (1947-   )
Publisher: Viking (New York). 392 pp. $27.95
Type of work: History
Time: From the American colonial period to 2003
Locale: The United States

This history of conflicting attitudes toward chance contends that Americans have never relied solely upon perseverance or Providence in pursuit of the American Dream but have always hedged their bets through gambling and other appeals to fortune

Jackson Lears's subject in *Something for Nothing* is gambling, not merely the pastime or even the obsession, but gambling as a cultural stance from which to view and engage with the cosmos. Lears mines a four-hundred-year-long vein of lore about luck in America, extracting historical nuggets glittering with myriad colorful and quintessentially American characters, including American Indian shamans, African American fortune-tellers, Mississippi riverboat gamblers, and Wall Street day traders, all exhibiting a faith in the roll of the dice or its equivalent that rivals and sometimes trumps the power of prayer.

It is Lears's contention that these two competing strategies for influencing fate exemplify two competing cultures that have vied for dominance throughout American history: the "culture of chance" and the "culture of control." Representatives of the culture of chance include Charles Darwin, Fyodor Dostoevski, William James, Frank Norris, Damon Runyon, William S. Burroughs, Jack Kerouac, Roman Catholics, Gypsies, southern slave owners, and African Americans. A sampling from the culture of control includes Increase Mather, P. T. Barnum, Adam Smith, Ralph Waldo Emerson, Anthony Comstock, Jane Addams, John D. Rockefeller, Chinese Communists, Robert Kennedy, and German and Italian Fascists.

Although Lears admits that these contrasting cultures are not uniquely American, as the above lists of names indicate, he submits that nowhere else has their conflict been so protracted or divisive because nowhere else has the dominant creed been the Protestant ethic, the belief that hard work will lead to reward in this world. Inextricably linked with the technological innovations of the Industrial Revolution, this American can-do credo insists that man is not just the measure but the manipulator and sometimes master of at least some things, including fate. This self-reliant worldview reeks of hubris, according to Lears, who seems to favor the more humble citizens of the culture of chance, the supplicants of Lady Luck, or the goddess Fortuna. Lears's thesis thus establishes a familiar dichotomy: controlled, powerful, Protestant, white male versus impulsive, powerless, non-Protestant, nonwhite or female—one sober, industrious, rational, and dourly religious, and the other exuberant, playful, irrational, and charmingly superstitious.

While acknowledging that neither culture exists in a pure form, Lears claims that the culture of control seeks to minimize the disruptions of chance through belief in predestination, scientific rationality, and regulations outlawing gambling and other "victimless" crimes, while the culture of chance views the vagaries of luck as opportunity. Those who court luck by rejecting an all-knowing deity and cause and effect Lears approvingly imbues with what he calls "grace," a kind of spiritual insight gained through acceptance of one's ultimate powerlessness in a random universe, an opening of oneself to what the pragmatist William James describes as pure experience. Lears admires their engagement in "serious play" rather than in the mundane nose-to-grindstone world of sweat and toil and fiscal responsibility. In fact, the two cultures' contrasting attitudes toward finance are telling. Lears's culture of control values money: Its members may earn it, inherit it, hoard it, or invest it, but under no circumstances may they gamble with it. His culture of chance does not value money: To its happy-go-lucky folks, those pieces of paper are all just Monopoly money anyway, useful stuff for keeping score and a pleasure to give away but not worth worrying about. In fact, in the culture of chance, signs of attachment to filthy lucre are suspect.

Jackson Lears is Board of Governors Professor of History at Rutgers University and editor in chief of the Raritan Quarterly Review. *His previous books include* Fables of Abundance: A Cultural History of Advertising in America *(1994), winner of a* Los Angeles Times *Book Prize, and* No Place of Grace: Antimodernism and the Transformation of American Culture, 1880-1920 *(1981).*

There is a glint of a tantalizing truth to Lears's observations. Among amusing anecdotes of lady gamblers and confidence men are pointed criticisms of members of the culture of control who condemn gambling while claiming to have hoisted themselves up the ladder of success by their own bootstraps, forgetting to mention being lucky enough to be born to a higher rung than most or passing over the shady deal or lucky strike or two that gave them the stake they needed to get ahead. He makes the obvious comparisons: wheeling and dealing in the stock market, state lotteries, and church bingo versus playing the horses, numbers games, and keno. The point is true but trite: There is legal and illegal gambling, and for the state and moralists to claim that one is good and the other bad is hypocrisy.

However, because the culture of control is not really what concerns Lears, he dismisses its arguments against gambling while barely addressing them. His real focus is not on public policy but on the gallant gambler himself (and, as an afterthought and sop to feminists, herself), the free-spirited holy rambler, living in the present, generous to one and all, worshiping at the altar of Lady Luck, and careless of worldly concerns. Lears does remark almost casually that an addiction to gambling can be a bad thing, but he never takes a closer look because the gambler is his hero. His gambler is not compulsive, not a desperate loser. He is a man without a care or responsibility in the world. He is free. He is an individual, a risk-taker, a rebel, a James Dean, in short, a true American. He has taken Henry David Thoreau's exhortation to simplify one's life to heart and cast off all encumbrances for the sake of the game.

The fatal flaw in Lears's argument is that it refuses to ring true. First and foremost, American gamblers do not embrace chance, nor do any other gamblers the world over. On the contrary, they work hard to control luck; the only difference between them and the investment banker is that gamblers are more likely to use magical means rather than statistical data to influence their chances, and even that difference is debatable—think of gamblers poring over racing forms and batting averages while businessmen use quarterly sales figures to divine consumer confidence. Every craps shooter, card shark, and confidence man he mentions carries a lucky piece, mutters a charm, or performs a ritual to ensure that his luck is good because he, too, just like the pious churchgoer, stockbroker, or medical doctor, wants to control chance; like everyone else, he wants it to work in his favor.

Moreover, Lears offers no proof that gamblers do not value money. By definition, to gamble is to risk losing what is valuable. If the gambler does not value money, then losing money would entail no risk and mean nothing, but serious gamblers play only for real stakes. Indeed, to beat the odds, to win and win big, is the adrenaline rush all gamblers seek. If they did not value money, then gambling would truly be a game and not gaming, something one does for idle amusement on a rainy afternoon and not something so deadly serious that obsessive gamblers frequently ruin themselves and their families financially; lie, cheat, and steal to cover their losses; and sometimes commit suicide or are beaten or killed by mobsters when they cannot pay. Lears touches upon something important when he links this edgy culture with the "Other" America of the underclass, but that connection is surely sometimes not from choice but rather from necessity. Barred from less risky roads to success and security, desperate people take desperate measures.

Lears undercuts his own argument further by connecting belief in Providence to the culture of control and superstition to the culture of chance. There is superstition, and then there is gambling. Many, if not most, gamblers believe they have a system that works according to their own logic and which they constantly refine with as much diligence as white-coated scientists in laboratories do. They may pray, carry a rabbit's foot, and practice card-counting all at once in an effort to entice luck their way. Like the rest of humanity, they play the cards they are dealt by using whatever tools are at their disposal. Few gamblers are simply fatalists, stoically resigned to whatever fate dishes out; they try to rig the system, even if they draw the line at overt cheating. In fact, the gambler most Americans would rather emulate is likely to be more like a Bat Masterson than a slave to a slot machine. Skill at poker is admired, while blind obsession is not.

Perhaps Lears's most useful and certainly entertaining contribution to historical scholarship comes when he regales his readers with gambling Americana, including the invention of the slot machine and the American innovation of bluffing in poker. Most diverting are his descriptions of colorful characters like Diamond Jim Brady, the gambling gastronome who enjoyed playing faro for diamonds instead of cash; John Henry "Doc" Holliday, who pulled a knife or a gun on anyone who accused him, correctly or not, of cheating; John "Bet-a-Million" Gates, a barbed wire magnate, notorious for betting on any and everything—like which of two raindrops would hit the windowsill first; and Poker Alice, a female gambler who smoked a long black cigar and carried a Colt revolver.

As Lears strays farther afield, however, tossing together an indiscriminate mix of Caribbean voodoo, American Indian rituals, the social implications of Darwin's *On the Origin of Species by Means of Natural Selection* (1859), John Cage's aleatory art, and modern American philosophy and literature like Ralph Ellison's *Invisible Man* (1952), he begins to overplay his hand. His thesis becomes not just his obsession but everyone else's, best illustrated by his inexplicable conclusion that Ellison's Invisible Man's faith in the system is shattered by blind bad luck and not as a result of imperfect justice in the racist United States.

There may be an important theme here, and it is not the one Lears explores, though he may touch upon it. It is true that there are people more and less averse to risk in any society. Some people avoid risk altogether. Some enjoy the thrill of extreme sports; some explore hostile environments; some compete for glory on the battlefield; some sink all their savings into a business venture. Some play high stakes games in Las Vegas or wrestle with the "one-armed bandit." What is the difference among all these risk-takers, if indeed there is one? If one were to ask, they would all probably acknowledge luck as a factor in the success of their ventures. There is, however, one huge distinction: Only the gambler lacks any real means by which to affect the outcome, short of cheating. Practice, preparation, careful study, all can weigh the dice in favor of the skier, the astronaut, the mercenary, and the business tycoon. The gambler is powerless; the house always wins, whether that house is a mob-owned casino or a state-run lottery. Nobody is forced to gamble, so why do some people deliberately put themselves into such a vulnerable position?

Could it be that the culture of control and the culture of chance are just fancy names for something else, something as obvious as the practical versus the impractical or the prudent versus the imprudent or the easily amused versus the easily bored? Gamblers come from all social classes and all walks of life; whatever drives them to gamble is unclear. Lears correctly points out that many in the culture of control are insulated from the slings and arrows of fate by privilege, but many gamblers have money to burn or to gamble away. The opposite is also true. Many poor people play the numbers and dream of winning the lottery, but some of them save for a rainy day and invest their few extra dollars in savings bonds. Defining his terms and clarifying his arguments are not Lears's strong suits. Perhaps Lears is saying is that freedom is another word for "nothing left to lose."

Sue Tarjan

Review Sources

Booklist 99, nos. 9/10 (January 1-15, 2003): 817.
Commonweal 130, no. 9 (May 9, 2003): 36-37.

The Economist 366, no. 8315 (March 15, 2003): 78.
Kirkus Reviews 70, no. 23 (December 1, 2002): 1752.
Library Journal 128, no. 2 (February 1, 2003): 101.
The New York Times Book Review, March 9, 2003, p. 10.
The New Yorker 79, no. 9 (April 21-28, 2003): 185.
Publishers Weekly 249, no. 49 (December 9, 2002): 74.
The Times Literary Supplement, June 27, 2003, pp. 5-6.
The Virginia Quarterly Review 79, no. 3 (Summer, 2003): 103-104.
The Wall Street Journal, January 28, 2003, p. D6.
The Washington Post, February 25, 2003, p. C4.

THE SONGS OF THE KINGS

Author: Barry Unsworth (1930-   )
Publisher: Doubleday/Talese (New York). 352 pp. $26.00
Type of work: Novel
Time: 1260-1250 B.C.E.
Locale: Aulis, a port in ancient Greece; Mycenae

In this realistic reinterpretation of Homeric myth, the power-hungry Agamemnon is cleverly maneuvered into offering his daughter as a human sacrifice

Principal characters:
CALCHAS, a diviner and a priest of Apollo
THE SINGER, a blind bard
AGAMEMNON, king of Mycenae, a self-seeking, indecisive leader
IPHIGENEIA, his fourteen-year-old daughter, priestess of Artemis
SISIPYLA (AMANDRALETTES), Iphigeneia's devoted slave woman
CHASIMENOS, Agamemnon's right-hand man
ODYSSEUS, king of Ithaca, a cynical master of manipulation
ACHILLES, a famous warrior and a narcissist
NESTOR, king of Pylos, a senile elder statesman
CROTON, a priest of Zeus, Calchas's rival

In his many historical novels, Barry Unsworth has consistently focused on the theme of appearance versus reality. In *Morality Play* (1995), for example, a group of actors unashamedly converts a real incident into a theatrical fiction, while in both *Sugar and Rum* (1988) and *Losing Nelson* (1999), writer-historians search for the reality that underlies what they find are the fictions of recorded history. In *The Songs of the Kings*, Unsworth suggests that both history and art are false. The Greek leaders of Homeric legend are shown influencing the course of history by deceiving themselves and one another, then peddling their plausible falsehoods to a bard who is more interested in aesthetics than in truth. The end result is that the words of the bard violate the facts of history and celebrate the nobility of ignoble men.

The Songs of the Kings begins at Aulis, where the Greek ships have gathered prior to their departure for Troy. Ostensibly the mission of the Greeks is to retrieve or punish Helen, the wife of King Menelaus of Sparta, for running off with the young, handsome Trojan prince Paris and to wreak vengeance on Troy for granting refuge to the lovers. In actuality, however, almost everyone in the Greek camp, from the loftiest king to the lowliest foot soldier, can hardly wait to plunder what is known to be one of the wealthiest cities in the Mediterranean world.

The Greek flotilla has been ready to set sail for a week, but the ships have been held in port by adverse winds, and there is no sign of a coming shift in wind direction. The men are beginning to quarrel among themselves. It is only a matter of time before they turn on their leaders, and the man most at risk of losing his power is the one who has had himself made commander in chief of the expedition, King Agamemnon of My-

Barry Unsworth is best known for his historical novels. He was given the Heinemann Award for Literature for Mooncranker's Gift *(1973) and was a cowinner of the Booker Prize for* Sacred Hunger *(1992).*

cenae. On the morning of the seventh day, Agamemnon feels that he can wait no longer. He summons Calchas to him, hoping for an explanation of his ill fortune and a quick remedy for it.

The rest of the story is common knowledge: Agamemnon decides to placate the gods by sacrificing his daughter Iphigeneia. He sails to Troy, triumphs, and returns home, only to be slain by his wife Clytemnestra, who has nursed her anger over the long years of his absence. Unsworth does not make any major changes in this outline of events. Where he differs is in his portrayal of the people involved. While Homer's characters were heroic human beings with all-too-human flaws, almost all of Unsworth's are unheroic and despicable.

The Songs of the Kings is structured much like a five-act drama. The first section of the novel is called "The Eagles of Zeus" because while Agamemnon was still at Mycenae, it was reported to him that two male eagles had been seen hunting together. At the time, Calchas, a diviner, had been asked to comment on the unusual phenomenon. His interpretation was a simple one and one not likely to annoy his superiors, of whom Calchas had a healthy fear. The eagles, he said, represented Agamemnon and Menelaus, and the flight of the birds over Mycenae was meant to assure the kings that their cause was just. Now, however, three men have been brought to Agamemnon with additional information. They insist that they saw those eagles swoop down on a pregnant hare, kill her, and devour her along with her unborn young. Supposedly Agamemnon's next move will be governed by Calchas's interpretation of these details. However, in the next section of the novel, this honest if somewhat spineless priest is shown losing his influence over Agamemnon and being replaced by malevolent men.

In "The Heavy Burden of Command," the author traces the steps taken by Odysseus and Chasimenos as they maneuver Agamemnon into believing that his status as a great leader leaves him no choice but to sacrifice his daughter. Both men have selfish reasons for promoting the war. Chasimenos is motivated by his loyalty to Agamemnon; as a devoted civil servant, he is willing to do anything that will benefit his master. Odysseus, on the other hand, is interested only in what he can get out of the conquest of Troy; he is tired of being the ruler of a small, rocky, impoverished island, and he wants both wealth and power.

Despite the difference in their motivations, the two plotters are alike in that they are both intelligent, far more intelligent than anyone else in the novel. They are also amoral. That these two are meant to remind readers of present-day politicians is evident in their use of modern euphemisms for immoral acts. For example, after one of the witnesses they had coached adds details of his own to the story about the eagles, Odysseus suggests that the man needs to be "neutralized." Later Chasimenos, who is a master of casuistry, provides Odysseus with a word for what the two need to avoid: Agamemnon must not be set aside, or "marginalized." Their reasoning is impeccable. Chasimenos has long since hitched his wagon to Agamemnon's ascending star, and the wily Odysseus finds the easily influenced Agamemnon ideal for his own pursuit of power. All the two conspirators need is for the commander in chief to look like a decisive leader. He must maintain his image.

While Calchas is attempting to commune with the divine, Odysseus and Chasimenos recruit Croton, the priest of Zeus, to aid in their plan. As Odysseus points out, one does not have to like a man to use him. Calchas is too much of an intellectual to be decisive; moreover, he is much too religious. Odysseus and Chasimenos prefer to work with someone unprincipled, someone whose self-interest will keep him grafted to his superiors. Croton's goals are obvious. He wants the prestige and the power that come with being the high priest of the established religion, and he wants to spite his rival Calchas, who for so long has had the ear of Agamemnon. To Croton, it is the religious institution that is important; Zeus, if he exists at all, is just an accessory. Croton's agnosticism is evident in that he is not afraid of offending Artemis, the goddess whom both Calchas and Iphigeneia serve. He is quite willing to suggest that her worship involves witchcraft. The misogynist slanders Croton circulates are meant to discredit Calchas and to diminish the power of his cult. By appealing to the deep-seated prejudice against anything female that is pervasive among the men in the camp, he can also help Odysseus and Chasimenos propel Agamemnon into decreeing his daughter's death.

Odysseus has less success in enlisting the services of the Singer. Although he has been instructed to attribute the adverse winds to Zeus, the bard will not choose his subjects or tailor his material to please even a man as important as Odysseus. The Song is sacrosanct, says the Singer; it comes from the gods. Odysseus's philistine utterances about art have no effect on the bard. Of all the characters in *The Songs of the Kings*, he alone stands totally apart from the action. However, because he is more concerned with his art than with either truth or morality, the Singer will not use his considerable power to save Iphigeneia, and his account of the events that take place at Aulis turns out to be almost wholly the product of his imagination. Its connections to reality are very slight.

In the third section of *The Songs of the Kings*, which is called "At Mycenae," the setting changes. In these poignant chapters, the author focuses on the only two admirable characters in the novel. Iphigeneia is shown as an innocent fourteen-year-old girl who loves her father, takes her religious duties seriously, and has some hope of a happy marriage. When the delegation from Aulis arrives, bringing her word of her engagement to the great hero Achilles, she is overjoyed. It seems odd to her that when she goes to Aulis to meet her future husband, she is expected to leave her serving women behind. However, she persuades the men to let her take along just one of them, Sisipyla, the slave girl of her own age who is her only friend.

In the section that follows, appropriately called "Waiting for Iphigeneia," the Greek leaders treat their inferiors in ways that prove how brutal, how callous, and how cruel they are. However, the men are shown as being no better then their superiors; they can hardly wait for the sacrifice of the aristocratic virgin, which they see as a superb entertainment for their benefit. Agamemnon's standing among the men has never been higher. At this point, he could not call off the sacrifice even if he wanted to. In any case, Agamemnon is no longer thinking about his daughter. He has his mind on the knife that is being specially crafted for use in the sacrifice. He has to make sure that it is absolutely perfect.

Because there has always been speculation that Iphigeneia may have escaped, in "Dressing Up" the author suggests a scenario that would have saved her. Sisipyla offers to disguise herself and take her mistress's place on the altar while Iphigeneia flees to safety. However, at the last moment Odysseus hits on an argument that Iphigeneia cannot resist: By going willingly to her death, she can atone for the past sins of her family, thus ending the blood curse that has lasted for generations and saving her people.

Even a reader who is thoroughly steeped in the classics will find Unsworth's version of these events very persuasive. His use of contemporary slang and of the more familiar profanities contribute to the realism of this novel, and so, more subtly, does his insertion of political double-talk and gangsterish euphemisms into his characters' casual conversations.

The author's skill is nowhere more evident than in the way he handles characterization. Because much of the time the Greeks are busy deceiving one another, it is necessary for Unsworth to delineate clearly between what the characters say and what they think or feel. He solves this problem in two ways. At the first appearance of a character, he usually halts the action for an analysis of the character's strengths, weaknesses, habits, and preoccupations, much in the manner of the nineteenth century novelists. His second method is to move from mind to mind, revealing the thoughts and feelings of one character after another. So skillfully does Unsworth blend authorial comment and varying points of view that when one finishes *The Songs of the Kings*, it may be difficult to recall all the twists and turns of the plot, but the characters are so vividly imprinted on one's mind that they threaten to replace the Homeric originals. This is truly a memorable book.

Rosemary M. Canfield Reisman

Review Sources

Booklist 99, no. 12 (February 15, 2003): 1051.
Kirkus Reviews 71, no. 1 (January 1, 2003): 24-25.
The New York Review of Books, October 9, 2003, pp. 4-6.
The New York Times, March 19, 2003, p. E8.
The New York Times Book Review, March 30, 2003, p. 8.
The New Yorker 79, no. 15 (June 9, 2003): 103.
Publishers Weekly 250, no. 7 (February 17, 2003): 57.
The Spectator 290 (September 21, 2002): 47.
The Times Literary Supplement, August 30, 2002, p. 8.

SONS OF MISSISSIPPI
A Story of Race and Its Legacy

Author: Paul Hendrickson (1944-   )
Publisher: Alfred A. Knopf (New York). 368 pp. $26.00
Type of work: History
Time: 1962-2002
Locale: Mississippi

A photograph of seven Mississippi sheriffs taken in 1962, a few days before the riot accompanying James Meredith's registration at the University of Mississippi, frames an investigation of racism and redemption across three generations of Mississippians

> *Principal personages:*
> JAMES MEREDITH, the first African American student enrolled at the University of Mississippi
> CHARLES MOORE, a photographer whose photograph of seven Mississippi lawmen on the campus of the University of Mississippi appeared in *Life* magazine
> BILLY FERRELL, the sheriff of Natchez, Mississippi, 1960-1964, 1968-1988
> JOHN ED COTHRAN, the sheriff of Greenwood, Mississippi, 1960-1964
> JOHN HENRY SPENCER, the sheriff of Pittsboro, Mississippi, 1960-1964
> JAMES IRA GRIMSLEY, the sheriff of Pascagoula, Mississippi, 1960-1964
> BOB WALLER, the sheriff of Hattiesburg, Mississippi, 1960-1964
> JIMMY MIDDLETON, the sheriff of Port Gibson, Mississippi, 1950-1952, 1952-1956, 1960-1964
> JAMES WESLEY GARRISON, the deputy sheriff of Oxford, Mississippi, 1962

On Thursday afternoon, September 27, 1962, six sheriffs and one deputy from across the state of Mississippi gathered on the campus of the University of Mississippi in Oxford. Three days later, when James Meredith's arrival to register as the university's first African American student sparked a riot that left two dead and hundreds injured, most of these peace officers had departed. On the eve of that violence, though, these seven men met under spreading trees on the Oxford campus, there to support Mississippi governor Ross Barnett's stated insistence that Meredith would never be allowed to register as a student.

Because they arrived and departed from Oxford prior to one of the Civil Rights era's main events, history might not have noticed them but for the camera of Charles Moore. Moore photographed these sheriffs, circled around one of their number who gripped a billy club with pleasure, presumably in anticipation of using it to defend segregation in Mississippi. *Life* magazine originally published the photograph in 1962. Four decades later, former *Washington Post* journalist Paul Hendrickson discovered the photograph, and this discovery inspired *Sons of Mississippi*, the author's attempt to understand the persistence of racism and its possible redemption.

~

A former journalist for The Washington Post *who now teaches writing at the University of Pennsylvania, Paul Hendrickson is the author of three previous books:* Seminary: A Search *(1983),* Looking for the Light: The Hidden Life and Art of Marion Post Wolcott *(1992), and* the Living and the Dead: Robert McNamara and Five Lives of a Lost War *(1996).*

~

Sons of Mississippi is historical journalism after the pattern of James Agee's *Let Us Now Praise Famous Men* (1941), about Alabama sharecroppers. Hendrickson, in fact, carried a copy of Agee's book on at least one of his visits to Mississippi, and the author clearly seems to have attempted a work of investigative journalism marked by a similar lyricism, introspection, and marriage of word and image. Though history will not likely rank Hendrickson's effort alongside Agee's, *Sons of Mississippi* is nevertheless an important book, especially for those who seek to understand the wounds that racism continues to inflict upon some Americans and the scars that it has embedded in the American consciousness.

Sons of Mississippi examines first the seven sheriffs in Moore's photograph, "seven faces of Deep South apartheid." In asking how they became racists—the author is everywhere blunt with his moral judgments—Hendrickson emphasizes their representativeness of a racist southern culture. The violence they contemplated drew its energy from an elaborate web of social connections not visible in Moore's photograph, but "off the page, out of sight, past the borders." The Mississippi State Sovereignty Commission and the Ku Klux Klan thus feature prominently in the book, as the author investigates—and in some cases demonstrates—connections between these segregationist organizations and the men in the *Life* photograph.

In the years that followed the photographed moment, Hendrickson looks for some redemptive story in the lives of the seven sheriffs. Did remorse ever seize their consciences? Did regret ever make them wish to rewrite the history into which they had been so notoriously written by the lens on Moore's camera? No, the author concludes. Only two of the lawmen, Billy Ferrell and John Ed Cothran, were alive when Hendrickson began serious work on the book in 1997. Ferrell stands in the center of the photograph, with the billy club in his hands, and accounts of him and his children and grandchildren anchor the book. The author found no redemptive narrative in his interviews with the old sheriff, who was still impatient with talk about "civil rights crap," still convinced that American morals disintegrated as a result of desegregation, because "black people as a whole don't have the same morals as white people."

Cothran fares better in the book, but only by a little. His back is turned to the camera in the photograph, and Hendrickson takes this posture as a metaphor for the man's life as a segregationist who had never precisely been "a true hating seg." According to Hendrickson, Cothran had tried to look away while others had done the dirty business of Mississippi racism during the 1960's. Hendrickson thus brands him "inescapably tragic, unavoidably culpable, then as now."

Although *Sons of Mississippi* launches its inquiry through an investigation of the lives of seven Mississippi sheriffs, Hendrickson devotes even more energy to understanding the legacies left by these men in the lives of their children and grandchildren.

This is the book's second main narrative and, in fact, its predominant focus. "How did these seven white Southerners get to be this way, and how did it all end, or how is it still going on, and was there no eventual shame here, and what happened to their progeny, *especially* their progeny, and was it all just ineluctable?" Again, Ferrell's children and grandchildren find a central place in the book. Ferrell's son, Tom, is a sheriff like his father, recently elected president of the National Sheriffs' Association. Billy Ferrell's grandson, Ty, works for the federal border control; his granddaughter Christina, or "Crickett," recently graduated from the University of Mississippi Law School. Cothran's grandson works for Home Depot in Southaven, in north Mississippi near Memphis. Although Hendrickson tries to tease out of these lives some lesson about the history of racism across time, he is mostly unsuccessful. Ty Ferrell's work on the border of Texas, mainly stopping Latinos from illegally entering the United States, certainly involves issues of race, but one cannot readily see any connection between the racial issues Ty Ferrell must live with and those that defined his grandfather's life. Cothran's grandson has even less to offer an author bent on tracing the biological transmission of the racism gene. He has not ever been to a museum or a concert hall, readers learn, but this fact—and others assembled by the author—reveals little about the visiting of the racist sins of the father upon the son (or grandson).

The final strain of Hendrickson's narrative traces the life of James Meredith, whose proposed entry as a student at the University of Mississippi had generated such alarm in the seven sheriffs and others in Mississippi. No serious biography of Meredith has yet been attempted, and Hendrickson struggles, as other writers have, to fashion some narrative whole out of the disparate pieces of Meredith's life. Like others, he finds this extraordinarily difficult. How does one explain that a central figure in the Civil Rights movement eventually took a job working first for ultraconservative North Carolina senator Jesse Helms and then, as if to compound the enigma, with ex-Ku Klux Klan member David Duke? Hendrickson repeatedly interviewed Meredith, whose comments during these interviews mirrored the contradictions of his life. "He'd say something piercing," Hendrickson noted, "and then he'd say something cracked." Ultimately, Hendrickson surrendered to enigma, concluding that James Meredith was "an unfathomable man, unfathomably heroic, unfathomably messianic."

Just as *Sons of Mississippi* attempts to explore the effects of racism across time in the lives of the children and grandchildren of the seven sheriffs in Moore's photograph, Hendrickson investigated these effects in the lives of Meredith's children. One of his sons, Joseph, was a Ph.D. student in business at the University of Mississippi while Hendrickson was writing his book, and the author interviewed him there on more than one occasion. Shy and reclusive, struggling to cope with lupus, Joseph Meredith occupies himself with the work of finishing his dissertation and finding an academic position (at Elon University in North Carolina, ultimately). What connection is there between this young man and the experiences of his father, four decades before? Hendrickson suggests a kind of emotional equation: "What *they* did to his father, *he* had to carry."

In *Sons of Mississippi* Hendrickson couples historical and sociological investigation with a poetic imagination that often enlivens the reading but sometimes distracts the reader, such as when he likens the Mississippi sheriffs to a "strange-looking priest" and his "profane deacons" readying themselves for "their satanic rites." In his attempt to conduct an essentially moral investigation into the lives of these men, the author also has an annoying habit of describing physical appearances in a way that seems to suggest a crude correspondence between physical unsightliness and moral perversity. These minor blemishes do not ultimately undermine the book's narrative power.

The poet John Donne insisted that "every man is a peece of the *Continent*, a part of the *maine*," and the strength of *Sons of Mississippi* is its relentless commitment to demonstrate this human axiom. In the hands of Paul Hendrickson, life spills beyond the boundaries of the photograph taken in 1962 by Charles Moore, out into the lives of the children and grandchildren of seven sheriffs and the man they wished to bar from entering the University of Mississippi. These familial connections do not exhaust the associations forged out of a moment of crisis at the University of Mississippi four decades ago. Powerful men such as John F. Kennedy and Robert Kennedy found themselves plotting by telephone a scripted resolution of the crisis with Mississippi governor Ross Barnett. Subsequent administrators at the University of Mississippi have struggled to come to grips with Meredith's legacy. Even Hendrickson's readers— especially those who are white—are invited to imagine their connection to the photograph at the center of the book: "Aren't all of us who are white in America in Moore's frame too, unseen yet present, standing in the ring of batterers, maybe even trying on our own leer or sneer, just to see how it fits?"

Timothy L. Hall

Review Sources

American History 38, no. 3 (August, 2003): 82.
Booklist 99, no. 12 (February 15, 2003): 1038-1039.
The Boston Globe, June 8, 2003, p. H8.
Kirkus Reviews 71, no. 1 (January, 2003): 39.
Library Journal 128, no. 3 (February 15, 2003): 150.
Los Angeles Times, March 23, 2003, p. R7.
The New York Times, March 13, 2003, p. E10.
The New York Times Book Review, June 8, 2003, p. 18.
Publishers Weekly 250, no. 6 (February 10, 2003): 174-175.
Washington Monthly 35, no. 4 (April, 2003): 58-59.
The Washington Post, April 6, 2003, p. T09.

SPEAKING OF BEAUTY

Author: Denis Donoghue (1928-   )
Publisher: Yale University Press (New Haven, Conn.).
   209 pp. $24.95
Type of work: Literary criticism and philosophy
Time: From the time of ancient Athens to modern times
Locale: Worldwide

A dense and learned series of essays related to various theories concerning the nature and value of beauty in literature and the fine arts

Principal personages:
   IMMANUEL KANT (1724-1804), German
      philosopher
   FRIEDRICH VON SCHILLER (1759-1805),
      German dramatist, poet, and aesthetic critic
   JOHN RUSKIN (1819-1900), English art critic and social reformer

Denis Donoghue posits beauty as one of life's six indisputable virtues, along with life, love, truth, virtue, and justice. Other, more disputable values are power, belief, communication, and (surprisingly) money. Each of these values, he sighs, tends to seize the world in its favor and jostle its rivals aside. He gives five reasons for appreciating beauty, without necessarily agreeing with all of them: First, because its existence is related to goodness and truth; second, because the search for beauty encourages a "respect for intrinsic value, freedom, independence, selflessness"; third, because it encourages contemplation, appreciation, and patience; fourth, because, quoting novelist Iris Murdoch, "the appreciation of beauty is . . . a completely adequate entry into . . . the good life, since it *is* the checking of selfishness in the interest of seeing the real"; and fifth, because (Donoghue's preferred reason) "a beautiful thing holds its own and remains unintimidated by the analytic zeal that [Georg Wilhelm Friedrich] Hegel ascribes to the Understanding."

Donoghue wishes it were possible to establish an agreed-upon theory of beauty without ideological insistence but recognizes that the world has no common ground of values. He appreciates the ambitious attempt by I. A. Richards, in *The Foundations of Aesthetics* (1922), to establish sixteen theories of beauty but revises them into four main categories, adding a few notions of his own. The first postulate is beauty as a property of the object in question, which would offer symmetry, proportion, gradation, and harmony. The second is the genius of the artist. The third is beauty as an experience of the observer, producing in him or her an aesthetic impulse which cannot be defined. The last is beauty valued for some further reason, such as that it leads to desirable moral or social effects.

Donoghue is impressed by Friedrich Schiller's *Briefe über die ästhetische Erzie-*

Denis Donoghue is the Henry James Professor of English and American Letters at New York University. He is a distinguished critic of poetry and of critical and aesthetic theories. Among his thirty books are studies of Jonathan Swift, William Butler Yeats, Walter Pater, and T. S. Eliot as well as the influential Connoisseurs of Chaos: Ideas of Order in Modern American Poetry *(1965).*

hung des Menschen (1795; *On the Aesthetic Education of Man*, 1845). In it, Schiller declares that freedom is attained from passions and predilections through beauty, which is indifferent to knowledge and content, while its form is everything. Taking an opposing view are such deconstructionists as Paul de Man, who regards beauty and the aesthetic as distracting enemies of knowledge. Going even further is T. J. Clark, who, in *Farewell to an Idea* (1999), declares that "we all hate the beautiful so much," speaking for that small minority who resent the power of beauty as an escape from confronting the materialism that has overtaken the world.

On the other hand, some people have been ready to devote themselves to beauty as a supreme value, even if it entailed their being defeated by vulgar forces. Henry James, for instance, insists on having his favored protagonists worship beauty and the highest demands of the imagination, as when, in *The Princess Casamassima* (1885-1886), Hyacinth Robinson sends the princess a letter telling her that he has come to appreciate "the splendid accumulations of the happier few, to which doubtless the miserable many have also in their degree contributed."

Immanuel Kant, in *Kritik der Urteilskraft* (1790; *The Critique of Judgment*, 1892), was the first to regard the aesthetic as an independent value, subject only to taste, "disinterested, irresponsible, as free as play." Taste is contemplative, not cognitive. Aesthetic judgment is its own law. Donoghue points out that several cultural forces worked to establish the independent valuation of beauty. Most of them involved the secularization or domestication of religious values, so that William Hogarth could paint a travesty of the Last Supper and Alexander Pope, in *The Rape of the Lock* (1712), could use a Christian cross as a piece of jewelry on Belinda's bosom. In John Keats's famous poem "Ode on a Grecian Urn" (1819), the urn is pure form, removed from its first use, prophetic rather than descriptive, speaking of a time when beauty and truth will be alike as products of the imagination.

Modern aestheticians subject beauty and the aesthetic sense to more difficult contexts and relations. Theodor Adorno, in *Aesthetic Theory* (1949), declares that "the beautiful is no more to be defined than its concept can be dispensed with." Contemporary structuralists reject the notion of "genius" and submit every experience to concepts and codes. Donoghue demurs: "There is always an incalculable factor, whether we call it genius or something else." His culture hero is the writer Ray Limbert in Henry James's 1893 story "The Next Time." Limbert valiantly tries to turn out popular potboilers to support his family, but each of his works instead becomes an artistic success though a financial failure. Ill and dying, he nonetheless cannot bring himself to write trash. He dies "with a good conscience" though poverty-stricken, having used his literary gifts to their best possibilities.

Donoghue dwells on another little-known James story, "The Beldonald Holbein" (1896). Its narrator, an artist, is asked to paint an attractive American-born widow seeking to triumph in London society, Lady Beldonald, who is vapidly narcissistic. She employs, as a foil to her beauty, a widowed, poor, plain relative, Mrs. Brash. However, a visiting French painter ignores Lady Beldonald in favor of Mrs. Brash, saluting her as "the greatest of all the great Holbeins." The narrator comes to agree. Lady Beldonald is, however, offended at being thus passed over, while Mrs. Brash becomes a social success, fêted at parties as "the famous Holbein." After a few painful months the lady dismisses Mrs. Brash and sends her back to the United States to die. Lady Beldonald then informs the painter that she is willing to sit for her portrait, in the manner of a Titian. The story ends ambiguously. Will the painter pretend to show her as the Titian she is not, or as the empty, expressionless beauty she is? The presumption is the latter.

The topic of impressionism leads to a consideration of Walter Pater. Pater took care to separate his views from those of Matthew Arnold, whom he labeled a social and political critic. In his influential *Studies in the History of the Renaissance* (1873) he stressed the critic's acute susceptibility to beautiful objects. In his essay on Leonardo da Vinci's *Mona Lisa* (1504) he famously declared, "Hers is the head upon which all 'the ends of the world are come,' and the eyelids are a little weary." For him, the mind of the critic is all-important, while the formal properties of the work do not matter. French critic Roland Barthes parallels Pater's subjectivity in celebrating actor Greta Garbo's beauty in his *Mythologies* (1957; English translation, 1972). Her acting is immaterial; it is her face which is divine: "Garbo's face represents this fragile moment . . . when the clarity of the flesh as essence yields its place to a lyricism of Woman." Nothing that would make for expression is allowed to obtrude. Donoghue contrasts Garbo's mystery with the transparency of actor Julia Roberts, whose smile is indiscriminate and private life featured in fan magazines. She affords people democratic instead of mythical pleasures as her every move is globally chronicled.

Donoghue devotes a long chapter to the norms of artistic form, considering its relationship to both content and subject matter. While Archibald MacLeish seeks to associate poetry with politics as "public speech," William Butler Yeats, in a rejoining poem, opts for love or other equally compelling values. Donoghue agrees with Yeats: Form is what matters most in poetry, which is a composition rather than a designation. He likes the definition of poetry as a "well-wrought urn" whose primary achievement is that of form, and Richard Blackmur's insistence, in *The Lion and the Honeycomb: Essays in Solitude and Critique* (1955), that the poem is always at some remove from the behavior or feelings that incited it. Donoghue believes that many aesthetic theorists have discounted the importance of form, which he considers the distinguishing characteristic of art. Beauty is saved from political or moral polemics only by its articulation as particular forms.

He is disturbed that some critics are willing to deride a work's formal construction. He particularly opposes Jacques Derrida's deconstructionist view of form as having an invidious relation to force, but the theorist who most sets his teeth on edge is de Man, whom he regards as hostile to inventiveness, wit, memorable cadence, indeed form itself, as when he declares in *Allegories of Reading* (1979) that Rainer Maria Rilke's poems use forms as seductions from all truth claims.

While Donoghue seems sometimes evasive in stating his own views, he could not be firmer in affirming the primary importance of aesthetic form. "Recognition of artistic form, and of the values its achievement carries, is the ground upon which writers, readers, critics and intellectuals are constituted." He cites the ending of F. Scott Fitzgerald's *The Great Gatsby* (1925). By its last chapter Gatsby is dead, and the novel's narrator, Nick Carraway, has decided to return to the Midwest. Donoghue quotes the famous last page, which shows the author taking over the narrative from the limited Carraway to satisfy what he regards as Americans' desire for romance, beauty, wonder, and a transfigured world. Fitzgerald has Nick yield his individual thoughts, as the novel takes on the experience of an entire nation.

Donoghue honors in a climactic, long chapter the aesthetic theories of John Ruskin, a Victorian art critic whose moral and social criticism made him perhaps the most influential reformer in the England of his time. Ruskin sought to unite ethics with aesthetics, as in *The Stones of Venice* (1851-1853), wherein he saw the beauty of Gothic architecture as a product of the moral virtues of the society that produced it. On the other hand, he linked Venetian decay with Venice's sinister politics.

Donoghue appreciates Ruskin's delight in the intricacies of forms, multiplicity of tones, and the daring with which an individual voice emerges from a clutter of allusions. Ruskin's special love was the seascapes of J. M. W. Turner. In *Modern Painters* (vol. 1, 1843) he conveys his rapturous enthusiasm for works such as *The Slave-Ship*, "which burns like gold, and bathes like blood," as Ruskin's mind enters the horror of a scene where Turner shows the sky reflecting crimson and scarlet as slavers throw slaves into the waves to drown.

Ruskin's inclination is to blur any line of demarcation between beauty and morality, taste and judgment; all are acts of God. His notion of beauty is capacious enough to include the picturesque, the sublime, and the grotesque. For him, beauty includes every manifestation of the imagination. Ruskin, as an opponent of the Industrial Revolution and particular foe of railways, does have trouble with those of Turner's paintings that acknowledge the dynamics of industrial development by painting boilers, furnaces, fireboxes, and steam engines; he simply ignores or minimizes them.

Sadly, Donoghue concludes that Ruskin's anti-industrial influence has largely faded. He was "a major man," but essentially an advocate of lost causes. Many modern artists, such as Franz Kafka, T. S. Eliot, and Pablo Picasso, chose to subordinate the beautiful to the ugly and grotesque, as in Kafka's "In the Penal Colony" and Eliot's "Sweeney Erect." Kant's release of beauty from conceptual control has encouraged the liberation of art from representational, social, political, religious, and other demands. It has largely been alienated from considerations of truth and goodness. Donoghue concludes that beauty now is "wherever we allow ourselves to find it." Ruskin has convinced very few that works of art are the best indication of the health or disease of a particular society.

In *Speaking of Beauty*, Denis Donoghue has written a learned and deft essay on aesthetics. Not a theorist himself, he has provided interested readers with a valuable guidebook to the convictions of a large number of critics and philosophers.

Gerhard Brand

Review Sources

First Things: A Monthly Journal of Religion and Public Life, December, 2003, pp. 44-48.

Library Journal 128, no. 10 (June 1, 2003): 119.

The New York Review of Books 50, no. 18 (November 20, 2003): 46-48.

The New York Times Book Review, September 14, 2003, p. 12.

The Times Literary Supplement, July 25, 2003, p. 10.

STYLE AND FAITH

Author: Geoffrey Hill (1932-   )
Publisher: Counterpoint Press (New York). 219 pp.
$25.00
Type of work: Literary criticism

*A collection of essays exploring the intimate connec-
tions—and disconnections—between style and faith in the
work of a variety of canonical authors, ranging primarily
from the early sixteenth to the late seventeenth centuries*

Geoffrey Hill is generally recognized as one of the most accomplished poets and literary critics of the post-World War II period in English literature. He has published more than a dozen volumes of poetry since 1959, beginning with the much-acclaimed *For the Unfallen: Poems 1952-1958* (1959) and, most recently, *The Orchards of Syon* (2002). Although his poetry has gained much academic recognition, Hill's readership remains relatively small compared to that of many a lesser poet, due largely to the sheer difficulty of his work. His previous critical productions, *The Lords of Limit* (1984) and *The Enemy's Country* (1991), have also been quite formidable in their density and erudition, fully revealing their riches only to the most determined and vigilant reader. They, along with the present volume, display an impressive range of interest. Hill moves with astonishing ease from the literature of the Renaissance to the high modernism of T. S. Eliot and Ezra Pound.

Another feature of Hill's writing that distances it from the work of his contemporaries is its preoccupation with religious themes. In an increasingly secular age, Hill remains engaged with matters of belief and doubt and, above all, with the language of faith. This is, conspicuously, the case in *Style and Faith*, a gathering of seven essays focused largely, but not exclusively, upon literary figures of the Reformation era. All of these essays were previously published—all but one as lengthy book reviews—and appear to have been reprinted in this volume with little or no alteration. Nevertheless, the essays generally work together well, sharing a preoccupation with the convergence of style and faith. In the preface, Hill makes a claim that may pass as the work's thesis: "It is a characteristic of the best English writers of the early sixteenth to the late seventeenth centuries that authors were prepared and able to imitate the original authorship . . . of God, at least to the extent that forbade them to be idle spectators of their own writing." In these essays Hill seems mostly to explore the latter part of this claim. To be an idle spectator of one's own writing is to fail to understand that "style *is* faith," that style is no mere ornament but, rather, inseparable from the message it conveys.

The initial essay in the collection strikes one as an odd departure for a volume concerned with matters of style and faith. "Common Weal, Common Woe" was occasioned by the publication of the second edition of the *Oxford English Dictionary*

(1989). Hill demonstrates a detailed acquaintance with the publishing history of the dictionary since its late nineteenth century inception and does not fail to praise the editors for the breadth of their philological knowledge, their succinct and copious annotations, and "an initial vigilance of such scope that it can take up an out-of-the-way word, furnished with five instances of its usage . . . [then] does not grudge time and labour spent in adding a further five citations." He does find, however, much to fault in the editors' (past and present) reductive method, one which compiled exhaustive histories of usage and clearly demarcated significations of terms but which remained, on principle, indifferent to the "comparative elegance or inelegance of any given word," and thus to the signification inherent in style—a central preoccupation of Hill in all of his critical work. Thus, one can begin to see why this first essay was included, however awkwardly, in the present collection.

Geoffrey Hill is a professor of literature and religion and codirector of the Editorial Institute at Boston University. His other publications include The Lords of Limit: Essays on Literature and Ideas *(1984),* The Enemy's Country: Words, Contexture, and Other Circumstances of Language *(1991), and four recent volumes of poems. In 1996 Hill was elected to the American Academy of Arts and Sciences.*

The problem of style, of discerning the nuances of style and its subtle shaping of meaning, becomes especially apparent, Hill notes, in the dictionary's treatment of seventeenth century significations. There, under the pressures of civil war and religious rebellion, "distinct [and] even opposed senses of a word alternate in the work of a single author," as in Edward Clarendon's *History of the Rebellion* (1648; a work much cited throughout *Style and Faith*). In such cases, clear and distinct significations can be difficult to pin down. Moreover, new stylistic fields emerge out of the "compounding of language with political or religious commitment." Hill singles out Clarendon's brilliantly elusive use of the term "dexterity," which was what Hill calls one of the "rhetorical janus-words of seventeenth-century politics." His admiring reflection on Clarendon's rhetorical singularity serves not only as an indication of the weakness of the *Oxford English Dictionary* but also of the quality that Hill himself is most inclined to admire in a great writer: "When I say that Clarendon was a master of his style I mean that *dexterity* is a word embedded in the usage of the time . . . and that his partiality and animus are most notably successful when they are contriving their own exceptions in the midst of this common medium." It is precisely such exceptions that the dictionary frequently fails to capture.

Toward the end of the second essay in *Style and Faith*, Hill notes that "the English Bible and the English Dictionary [are] the two great recorders of our memory, conscience, travail and diligence." At the fountainhead of translations of the Bible into English is *Tyndale's New Testament*, usually recognized as a monument of the plain style. In "Of Diligence and Jeopardy," Hill reviews the Yale University Press 1989 edition of Tyndale's early sixteenth century religious and literary masterpiece, questioning the wisdom of the editor's decision to modernize the spelling. On the face of it, he concedes, the modernizers have a case: Modern spelling and orthography make a late medieval text more accessible to the common reader. Why, the modernizers might ask, should a religious and literary work of such significance remain the exclusive preserve of a handful of scholars and dilettantes? Those who oppose such tidying up of musty tomes are merely sentimentalists with an antiquarian passion for pristine artifacts. Hill's response to this view is anything but sentimental—though it may be, depending upon how one defines the term, elitist. He is concerned that the effort to make Tyndale's text more accessible to modern ears, to spare the reader unnecessary discomfort, is a betrayal of the spirit of Tyndale's work. The encounter with Tyndale should be uncomfortable, even jarring. Hill allows that Tyndale himself cultivated a plain style precisely for the purpose of reaching the lay reader, but he suggests that the "Yale editor writes in the apparent belief that there is little to distinguish 'today's reader' from Tyndale's 'laye people', . . . [that] ignorance at the end of the twentieth century is not to be distinguished from ignorance in the first quarter of the sixteenth." The difference is this: Ignorance in the present age derives from "methods of communication" (does he refer to mass media, the culture of the "sound bite"?) and a system of education that "have destroyed memory and dissipated attention." Tyndale, on the other hand, had no patience for common ignorance and presumed to make demands upon the "memory and attention" of his lay readers. To encourage the reader in his natural passivity—as the Yale editor seems to—would have been for Tyndale to yield to the lethargy inherent in humankind's fallen condition. It is all persuasive enough, but one wonders whether Hill disapproves of modern spelling editions of *all* literary works prior to the eighteenth century (when spellings began to be standardized in their present form). Should everyone be reading the works of William Shakespeare in the Elizabethan spelling?

The sixth essay in this volume, "The Weight of the World," dwells upon similar concerns. Originally a review of Isabel Rivers's *Reason, Grace, and Sentiment: A Study of the Language of Religion in England 1660-1780* (1991), it mercilessly dissects Rivers's authorial preoccupation with that "accessibility" which, Hill laments, has become little more "than a commodity cry." Hill's inaccessibility is so pronounced in this essay that one is hard-pressed to follow the thread of his argument. He claims, for example, that Rivers was mistaken in choosing to deal with matters of "reason" and "sentiment" in separate volumes of her book, on the grounds that "the quality of sentiment is itself a factor in the debate between 'grace' and 'reason.'" This sounds fair enough, as does the further claim that the influence of sentiment in the aforementioned debate "reveals itself mainly in grammar: vocabulary, syntactical order and affective device." Then Hill proceeds to illustrate his point with a series of quotations from the likes of Jeremy Taylor and Edward Stillingfleet, prominent seventeenth century preachers and writers. The examples turn on the usage of the term "nice," presumably—to judge by the quotes—a word loaded with sentiment, as in affective significance. Near the end of this string of examples, Hill remarks of the writers quoted, "In attempting to describe their several styles of rational persuasion, one is touching on a symptomatic elision of the deliberated and the unwitting." What is one to make of such an utterance? What light does it cast on the role of sentiment in the "debate between reason and grace"? Yes, the sentence makes a certain elusive sense, but even a specialist in the period under discussion would likely find it cryptic, to say the least. Unfortunately, such utterances turn up all too often in these essays, as if Hill were taking some perverse pleasure in his own obscurity.

The fourth essay in the collection, "A Pharisee to Pharisees," is the only one that did not originate as a review article but is, rather, a less discursive example of Hill's undeniable abilities as a literary critic. It is a well-organized and generally clear close reading of "The Night" by Henry Vaughan, a seventeenth century poet whose work is not often given the attention it deserves in contemporary literary studies. The poem, quoted at length in the essay and reprinted in the notes in its entirety, takes as its subject the New Testament story of Nicodemus, in which the Pharisee approaches Jesus by night to inquire the way to Heaven. The passage is, of course, the occasion for one of Jesus's best-known teachings: "Verily, verily, I say unto you, except a man be born again, he cannot see the Kingdom of God" (John 3:1-2). The "chop-logic" Nicodemus, genuinely perplexed, wishes to know how a man can enter a second time into his mother's womb. The spiritual paradox upon which Vaughan dwells is the matter of Nicodemus's "conversion" under cover of darkness, a movement from darkness to light: "There is in God (some say)/ A deep but dazling darkness. . . ./ O for that night! where I in him/ Might live invisible and dim." Hill performs upon the poem not so much an interpretation as a sharply nuanced explication of the mosaic of voices that are fused so effectively, and yet disturbingly, in Vaughan's poem. "The Night" is haunted by echoes not only of the Old and New Testaments but also by Vaughan's hermetic reading as well. In addition, Hill suggests that the poem's "several dark-nesses" may, to some extent, reflect the conditions of Vaughan's time, the period of the English Civil War. As a "Royalist and Anglican [he] was the adherent of twin causes, both defeated." Out of that defeat "The Night" can be read as "a positive em-bracing of abnegation, a transferring of potentiality from the darkness of a stricken soul, a stricken cause and a stricken church into a visionary intensity." A lesser critic might simply have claimed, in the jargon of psychoanalysis, that Vaughan "subli-mates" his sense of loss and defeat by channeling it into the private mysticism of his poetry, where loss is solipsistically transmuted into eternal bliss. Hill, however, re-minds one of the sense of contingency always just beneath the surface of Vaughan's lyricism, that "envisioning of perplexity" so evident in his use of conditional tenses, or the doubt that dogs his affirmations: "There is in God (some say)/ A deep, but dazling darkness."

Hill's affinity for the work and personality of Robert Burton, author of one of the finest works of seventeenth century prose, *The Anatomy of Melancholy* (1621-1651), is evident in every line of "Keeping to the Middle Way," the third essay in *Style and Faith*. First published as a review of the 1994 Clarendon Press edition of the *The Anatomy of Melancholy* (*Volume 3: Of Religious and Love Melancholy*), this essay situates Burton's masterpiece within the tradition of the great Elizabethan apologists, especially Richard Hooker, principal architect of the via media, the Anglican middle way between Roman Catholicism and the radical Calvinism of the English Puritans. In his *Ecclesiastical Polity* (1593-1597), Hooker was primarily concerned to point the way toward a reasonable theological compromise, but his work is also celebrated for its philosophical moderation, for its constant insistence upon the "need to free our mindes . . . from all distempered affections" so that a lasting communion of faith might be achieved. Hill locates the purpose of Burton's text in precisely that: "Burton anatomizes melancholy in its hydra-headed forms; he dissects its monstrous capacity to hinder communion and fellowship." Much of Hill's analysis is focused, as one would expect, upon stylistic traits shared by the Anglican apologists, including their mastery of "tonal indetermination" in the use of phrases such as "the common good." Hill is also alert to the striking stylistic differences between Burton and the Elizabethans. Where Hooker seeks to comprehend the obstacles to civil peace and theological accord by means of sober reason and law, Burton "is a parodist of 'loose regarde' and a hunter of vulgar folly," an approach that would not have met with much sympathy from Hooker. Hill is referring to Burton's well-known taste for exploring at great digressive length the realm of human folly and superstition. Like Thomas Nashe before him, Burton is inclined toward a "theatrical opportunism": His philosophical and moral purpose may be to "adjure us to keep our hearts with all diligence," but "[his words] catch the excitement of . . . voyages and romance." Hill comments, with some cogency, that the prose of Nashe and Burton reflects the frustrations inherent in attempting to translate philosophical wisdom into political praxis: "The energy has to go somewhere; since it cannot realize itself as legislative act, it turns back into the authority and eccentricity of style itself."

Hill's affinity for Burton may have something to do with the latter's brilliant and always fascinating "eccentricity of style." Certainly Hill's own work has of late veered more and more in that direction. Large tracts of the prose in these essays are seemingly designed with the purpose of frustrating the reader's need to extract from them some manageable generalization, but Hill's analyses are, for the most part, so stubbornly embedded in the vagaries of style that summary or paraphrase are rendered all but impossible. Add to that digressions within digressions, abrupt shifts of direction, and frequent lack of sufficient historical context, and even the most persistent readers may find themselves defeated by the effort to follow the labyrinthine movements of Hill's thought. *Style and Faith* seems to demand a reader who is as intimately acquainted as Hill is with the history and literature of the sixteenth and seventeenth centuries. Even that select few will find the adventure daunting.

Jack Trotter

Review Source

First Things: A Monthly Journal of Religion and Public Life, December, 2003, p. 58.

SYNC
The Emerging Science of Spontaneous Order

Author: Steven Strogatz (1959-   )
Publisher: Hyperion (New York). 338 pp. $24.95
Type of work: Science and history of science

In this significant and entertaining work, Strogatz explores the history of and the current state of synchrony, the emerging science of universal spontaneous order

Humans sense order in nature. Indeed, natural order is perhaps the single most pervasive theme of the history of human thought. The quality and construction of natural order, however, has not always been agreed on by people. The second law of thermodynamics, for instance, predicts that entropy, destructive disorder, will sooner or later overcome any system. Steven Strogatz rejects the universal application of this law in favor of an overarching natural order. Exactly what is the essence of natural order, however, remains a primary question of philosophers and scientists to this day. Storgatz is one of a long line of such philosophers and scientists to essay an answer to that question in his impressive book, *Sync*. Moreover, Strogatz has added to his difficulties by aiming his book at the lay reader. Although an applied mathematician by profession, Strogatz has eschewed relying on mathematics and turns instead to writing that is at once clear and lucid and to metaphors that are apt and charming. Consequently, not only is *Sync* a book dealing with complex and significant scientific theory, but it is also a true pleasure to read.

Strogatz begins with the rivers of Southeast Asia, along whose banks huge collections of fireflies blink in unison throughout the night. This endless synchronous display has delighted tourists and perplexed scientists for more than three hundred years. It is perhaps the most celebrated of nature's instances of spontaneous rhythmic unity but certainly not the most pervasive nor the most significant. For humans, as Strogatz observes, synchronous rhythm is the very essence of beauty, as in the performance of a fine symphony orchestra or in the choreography of a world-class ballet company.

The very synchronous order which informs most performing arts is deeply related to the rhythm which keeps people alive and aware of the world all around. One depends on the mysterious beating pattern of one's heart to keep one supplied with blood and breath. Indeed, once the underlying synchronization of heart muscles is better understood, people will be better able to prevent sudden heart failure that leads to unannounced attacks and death. More than vessels to contain a rhythmic heart muscle, people are able to arrange incoming sensory messages into thoughts and ideas, a process based upon the ability of the neurological system to fire in sync in patterns even more intricate than the beating of the heart.

As cardiac rhythms might suggest, synchrony—which may be defined as rhythmic patterns in time as opposed to the spatial patterns of classical physics—is a basic at-

~

Steven Strogatz is a professor of
applied mathematics at Cornell
University, having taught
previously at both Harvard and
the Massachusetts Institute of
Technology (MIT). Strogatz has
received numerous awards,
including MIT's highest teaching
award, and is the author of
Nonlinear Dynamics and Chaos:
With Applications to Physics,
Biology, Chemistry, and
Engineering *(1994).*

~

tribute of human beings. It has long been known that women who live together, as in sorority houses, tend to establish similar menstrual cycles. Some of this synchrony is based on certain senses, such as smell, but all humans, as well as other animals, share brain waves that tend toward the cyclic. Indeed, the cycles of a computer are a mechanical reproduction in many ways of the more subtle biological cycle of the brain wave. Hence it is no surprise that computers, like humans, tend to get involved in traffic jams or information "gliches" or in strange, riotous activities not unlike human mob violence. Both animate and inanimate phenomena are composed of oscillators. When and how these oscillators become spontaneously coupled and what results follow is the basis of the new science of synchrony.

Having laid out the fundamentals of his subject, Strogatz spends a chapter exploring one of the most fundamental rhythms of the human condition: the cycle of sleep versus waking. Called the circadian cycle (based on the Latin terms for "about a day"), the sleep-wake pattern is one engaged in by almost every human. Humans are not the only creatures who possess such a cycle, but they are among the most interesting to investigators. To be sure, most people are aware that they follow a regular pattern of sleep and wakefulness, but because sleep is such a personal and private experience, a thorough scientific study with closely controlled parameters of sleep cycles is difficult and elaborate. Strogatz presents interesting details from several such studies, such as the difficulty of keeping the study subjects from knowing the actual time of day so that the effect of sunlight or the imposition of prior habits can be eliminated. Indeed, in one such study where subjects were kept in a sealed environment, male researchers shaved every time they entered the study area so that the subjects could not be tipped off as to time of day by the growth of stubble. It is just such aspects of basic humanity that make Strogatz's work so interesting.

Of course, along with the human elements are the significant findings of the scientific experiments. Chief among these is that the circadian cycle is closely related to body temperature and also to the presence or absence of light. Even blind people tend to sleep more normally in the absence of light, which seems to imply that light preceptors go beyond normal vision. The vision of dreams, characterized by rapid eye movement (REM) during sleep, is also tied to personal circadian rhythms, as is the pattern of short-term memories and the secretion of the brain hormone melatonin. Body temperature, rhythm of sleep and wakefulness, and many other human body functions, in addition to heart rhythms, seem to be controlled by some sort of singular and extraordinary biological clock. Moreover, this clock may also be related in some manner to universal clocks found in both animate and inanimate matter.

In search of such a clock, Strogatz turns to the pendulum and its place in the history of physics. In 1665 Christiaan Huygens began his study of pairs of pendulums that achieve sympathetic motion. That study would ultimately lead to the solution of various navigational problems. Exactly three hundred years later, in 1965, a pair of modern mathematicians, D. E. McCumber and W. C. Stewart, discovered a bridge between certain electrical oscillations and the motion of the pendulum. The equation for the problem for their electrical oscillators was exactly the same as the classical one for the motion of the pendulum. Synchronicity had a long and unrealized history.

Strogatz goes on to describe several other bridges between classical physics and the new science of order in time, including the 1911 discovery of superconductivity and what he calls the "quantum chorus," or the tendency of quantum boson particles to "sing together" in unison. He completes his section on historical bridges with the problems surrounding a famous footbridge. The opening in June, 2000, of England's New Millennium Bridge across the river Thames created quite a news media storm because the bridge began to tremble violently as the first pedestrians began to cross it. The large and excited crowd had been held back until a precise moment, and, as they stepped onto the bridge, they involuntarily responded to the laws of synchronicity by entering into a lock step, causing the bridge to vibrate vigorously. From the swing of a pendulum to the inexplicable vibrations of a modern footbridge, the fundamental order of the universe had persisted.

Having established the validity of his subject, Strogatz devotes the latter third of his book to modern scientific issues and their relation to the new science of sync. The first is the mathematical concept of chaos, first proposed by Edward Lorenz in his now famous Lorenz equations, which captured the laws governing what had previously been considered random, unpredictable behavior. These nonlinear equations established a simple order at the basis of many seemingly disorganized phenomena which had previously been thought to be entirely linear. One example is the human nervous system, which is built entirely from nonlinear components, as is human psychology. For example, Strogatz points out that if one listens to two enjoyable songs at the same time, one will not necessarily experience double pleasure.

The establishment of chaos theory quickly led the way to complexity theory and thus inevitably to the science of sync. First, Strogatz relates how, in the early 1990's, mathematicians began to realize that chaos can synchronize. This realization made the understanding of synchronicity easier, and the two concepts are thenceforth tightly woven together. Strogatz explains this interweaving by returning to the fireflies of Southeast Asia, which not only flash in unison but also flash periodically at fixed intervals. Thus, the fireflies are organized in both time and space simultaneously. This rhythm, which joins phenomena in both space and time, does not have to be constant, merely persistent, in order to combine chaos and synchronicity. Strogatz's example is the violin section of a symphony orchestra, the members of which enter musically together and stay in sync throughout, though violins are not periodic in that they do not play the same passage over and over.

From chaos Strogatz moves to issues of three dimensions, especially in the organization of large systems. The study of nonlinear systems composed of enormous numbers of parts has come to be known as complexity theory. Such a complex system is the human body with its thousand of genes, hundreds of cells, and unimaginable numbers of chemical and electrical firings which occur every hour. Biological systems can best be conceived visually as a collection of various spiral waves, and Strogatz gives a clear and compelling discussion of this intricate and difficult phenomenon.

Strogatz also discusses sync as a means of combining with complexity theory to return to analyses of small world networks as well. He points out that modern society has become obsessed with networking, from the joining of computers and the use of the World Wide Web to the fear propagated by far-flung underground organizations such as al-Qaeda. These can now be studied through a subdivision of sync: network theory. Solutions to problems inherent in such systems will sooner or later be possible.

Finally, there is the human side of synchronicity, which is Strogatz's concluding presentation. He points out that it is now known that there are related areas, such as the emerging field of traffic physics, whose practitioners have firmly established that although there is little communication between drivers, traffic patterns are mathematically predictable. Complexity studies have clearly demonstrated that on large expressways, major traffic jams will develop, with a predictable rhythm, even without traffic accidents or other major obstructions. The ability to analyze such synchronous problems in traffic will lead to better use of the system of expressways and, consequently, to a better life.

Strogatz remarks that it is a thrilling time to be a scientist. Indeed, with quantum mechanics providing such extraordinary tools as the laser beam and with traffic physicists promising more insights into the increasing problems of commuting to work, as well as mathematical biologists now able to use sync and complexity theory to offer solutions to many medical ailments, it is an exciting time for all. This excitement is increased by Strogatz, who presents this brave new world in his book *Sync* with the insights of a gifted intellect and the storytelling talent of a major novelist.

August W. Staub

Review Sources

Booklist 99, no. 14 (March 15, 2003): 1255.
Discover 24, no. 4 (April, 2003): 80.
Kirkus Reviews 71, no. 1 (January, 2003): 48.
Nature 422, no. 6928 (March 13, 2003): 117-118.
New Scientist 177, no. 2381 (February 8, 2003): 54.
Publishers Weekly 250, no. 7 (February 17, 2003): 66-67.

THE TATTOOED GIRL

Author: Joyce Carol Oates (1938-   )
Publisher: HarperCollins (New York). 307 pp. $25.95
Type of work: Novel
Time: 2003
Locale: Carmel Heights, a suburb of Rochester, New York

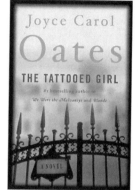

The unsettling tale of an unlikely relationship between a reserved intellectual and an abused, lower-class young woman

Principal characters:
> ALMA BUSCH, a young woman with strange tattoos on her face and body
> JOSHUA SEIGL, a writer and intellectual suffering from a degenerative nerve disorder
> DMITRI MEATTE, a waiter at a bistro frequented by Joshua
> SONDRA BLUMENTHAL, a longtime friend of Joshua's who becomes his lover
> JET, Joshua's older sister

The Tattooed Girl, Joyce Carol Oates's thirty-first novel, explores the uncomfortable connection between violence and love and the nature of hatred and bigotry. Joshua Seigl is an eccentric, wealthy, rather reclusive man in Carmel Heights, an upper-class suburb of Rochester, New York. He is the only son of a European Jew and an American Gentile. As a young man, Joshua achieved fame and adulation for *The Shadows,* a stream-of-consciousness novel about the Holocaust, loosely based on his father's stories of his grandparents' experiences in the concentration camp at Dachau. In the decade since the book's publication, Joshua has taught and lectured occasionally, started several writing projects, and dabbled at translating the classics.

Now thirty-eight years old, Joshua is becoming increasingly weak and unsteady. When he learns that his health problems are caused by an unusual degenerative condition, he reluctantly decides to hire an assistant. He expects the assistant to provide personal help and bring order to his disorganized files, help him catch up on years of unanswered mail, and catalog his work. He interviews several earnest, intellectual young men but finds a reason to reject each one.

Alma Busch is a blowsy, lower-class, inarticulate blonde, whose pale skin is marked by bizarre and sketchily drawn tattoos. She grew up in Akron County, Pennsylvania, in an emotionally and physically abusive family. Sexually promiscuous from her early teens, Alma tries to believe that the boys she has sex with like her, although they laugh at her and insult her. She also drinks heavily, uses drugs, and has been in trouble with the law.

Arriving in Carmel Heights with no money, Alma sits at an outdoor table at The Café, furtively eating food left by patrons who have gone. Dmitri, a waiter there, notices her and quickly realizes that she is a woman he can control. He seats her at a table

Joyce Carol Oates is the author of more than thirty novels, numerous collections of short stories, poems, and essays, and several plays. She has also written eight thrillers under the name Rosamond Smith. Oates has received the National Book Award and the PEN/Malamud Award for Excellence in Short Fiction.

in the back of the restaurant to wait until he can take her home with him. An abusive predator and a drug user, Dmitri is the type of man by whom Alma has been used in the past. She quickly becomes controlled by Dmitri, even agreeing to work as a prostitute to make money for him.

Although she is barely literate and cares nothing for books, she takes a job at a bookstore, angering Dmitri. There, Joshua, an avid reader and collector of rare books, meets Alma and, despite her obvious lack of education and breeding, offers her the job as his assistant and housekeeper. Although Joshua is sophisticated and urbane, he becomes enamored of and dependent on the slatternly Alma, ignoring his friends' and relatives' scorn. Against all evidence, Joshua ascribes to Alma attributes and aspirations that do not exist; he offers to pay for her education and seems oblivious to her complete disinterest in any intellectual pursuit.

Neither Joshua nor Dmitri is able to evoke from Alma the story of where and how she got the strange tattoos on her face, hands, and neck. Even Alma seems unsure of how she got them, who gave them to her, or why. The one on her face looks something like a butterfly but is so sketchy and vague that most people at first think it is a birthmark.

Joshua's older sister, Jet, is as dramatic as Joshua is reticent. Named Mary Beth by their parents, she adopted the Hebrew name Jetimah when she was a teenager and changed her name legally to Jetimah Steadman-Seigl when she was twenty-one years old. Although Joshua's book dealt with the Holocaust, and many people assumed he was Jewish, it is Jet who has appropriated their Jewish heritage. Having heard from another relative that Joshua is ill and must walk with a cane, Jet announces that she is coming from Florida to take care of him.

Joshua dreads his sister's staying with him, but the visit starts off well. When she first sees Alma, Jet assumes she is the cleaning woman and dismisses her as an earthy peasant. When she learns that Alma also assists Joshua with his papers, Jet is incensed that her brother allows this barely literate woman to take on a task he denies to Jet. She predicts that Alma will soon be stealing from him and accuses her of being his whore. That night Jet confronts Alma, then begins hitting her. To Joshua's amazement, Alma cowers and does not fight back, although she is larger and stronger than Jet. Jet then packs and leaves, not to be heard from again.

Joshua's dependence on Alma deepens, but as Jet predicted, Alma begins stealing from him. Born to wealth, Joshua has no head for business, often leaving checks uncashed. Alma brings Dmitri things that Joshua is unlikely to miss, such as gold cuff links and an unused leather briefcase. She also tells Dmitri embarrassing anecdotes about Joshua, reveling in his amusement at her employer's problems. Dmitri continues to abuse Alma emotionally, even expecting her to have sex with his friends.

Unknown to Joshua, Alma has a deep-seated hatred of Jews, which she acquired as a child and which is reinforced by Dmitri. In Akron County, the air and soil are polluted from fires that have burned in the coal mines for years. She has heard that the fires could have been put out long ago, but "Jew banker-owners" made billions of dollars by ignoring them, with the collusion of politicians. She believes that Joshua is Jewish, based on his name and appearance. Although she recognizes that he is kind, generous, and gentlemanly, her hatred for him escalates, fueled by Dmitri's hatred of Jews and his assertion that the Holocaust was probably a hoax.

Alma finds it impossible to appreciate Joshua's kindness and refined qualities. His politeness disgusts her—when he says he does not know how he would get along without her, she thinks with disdain, "Hire another assistant. It didn't take genius to figure that one out." She is aware that he wants to ask her about the marks on her face and body, but his polite reticence about prying into her life strikes her as rather stupid for a man who is accomplished enough to have written books. She sneers that he has all his clothes laundered and ironed, even his socks and underwear. Whenever he requests assistance from her, she rages inside that he should just tell her what do to, rather than ask her as if she had a choice. Nothing he does for her pleases her, but he remains oblivious to her contempt.

When Joshua first met Alma, she reminded him of Eastern European prostitutes he had seen but never hired. His female friends and relatives, in contrast, are refined, elegant, educated, and well traveled. His mother's great hope before she died was that he would marry and have a child, and he feels guilty that he failed her in this. Sondra Blumenthal, a university professor who has been a friend for many years, eventually becomes his lover, and he begins to think of marrying her and adopting her precocious son, Ethan. Still, his feelings for Alma do not diminish. As Joshua becomes less able to care for himself, he asks Alma to move into the guest room, and he becomes increasingly attached to her.

Four months into his illness, Joshua suddenly feels well. Although his disease is only in remission, he believes he is cured. Filled with a manic energy, he needs little sleep and is frenzied with passion. He begins writing a novel of bizarre polyphonic structure with a dithyrambic language pattern. His manic energy then dissipates, and he begins falling asleep suddenly, in his car or at his desk. Still he refuses to admit that he is not well. He gives Alma more time off, thinking he is doing her a favor, but she has little to do unless Dmitri is available to her. She feels unwelcome at the churches she has attended, and when she walks or shops in Carmel Heights, she is ignored, jeered at, or subject to crude propositions.

One night Joshua goes to The Café to play chess. He insists on playing two opponents at once, drinks heavily, and sneaks out the back door when the others try to convince him that he should not drive home. After picking up prostitutes in town, he staggers home, and Alma has to help him into the house. Within a few weeks, Joshua is sicker and weaker than he had been before the remission.

Alma begins plotting to kill Joshua and fantasizes that killing her Jewish employer will endear her to her father, who has disowned her. One night when Dmitri has taken her to a club to drink and dance, she announces loudly and repeatedly that she is going to "Kill the Jew!" In her first attempt, she laces a casserole with ground glass but drops it on the floor before she can serve it. As her cruelty and hatred intensify, she mixes up Joshua's pills, spits in his guests' drinks, contaminates his food with various bodily fluids, and tears up pages of his work.

Joshua continues to idealize Alma. Their only major confrontation comes when she challenges him about the reality of the Holocaust. When he shows her pictures of starving survivors of Buchenwald, she pouts that the pictures could have been faked. Still, after a brief bout of anger, Joshua feels sorry for her in her ignorance, never considering that she is an anti-Semite. When he tries again to explain to her about the Holocaust and to find out who told her that it was made up, he mentions that he is not Jewish and was baptized in the Presbyterian church. Alma is stunned that the man she has hated so deeply is not even Jewish. Later, however, she decides that his posing as a Jew is even worse than being Jewish.

Attempting to halt the progression of his disease, Joshua enters the hospital for a week of experimental treatment. Although he encourages Alma to use his time in the hospital for a vacation or a visit to her family, she insists on staying with him throughout his treatment. Before Joshua's hospitalization, Dmitri disappeared from town, and none of his friends will tell Alma where he has gone. One night when Alma comes home from the hospital, Dmitri is waiting for her at Seigl's house. When he demands that she give him money and let him in the house, the transformed Alma defies him for the first time.

Joshua returns from the hospital and begins regaining his strength. His appreciation for Alma increases, and he presents her with a beautiful necklace that had been his mother's. It seems that Alma is on the road to a new life. However, her luck quickly runs out, as tragedy befalls first Joshua and then Alma.

Many readers will find Alma's sudden transformation, apparently based on the fact that Joshua is not technically Jewish, jarring and hard to believe. The abrupt and melodramatic ending will also strike some as unsatisfying. Nevertheless, the book is engrossing and suspenseful. Although the relationship between Joshua and Alma is hard to believe, their characters are vividly drawn, and Oates's writing is as passionate and elegant as ever.

Irene Struthers Rush

Review Sources

Booklist 99, no. 13 (March 1, 2003): 1108.
Kirkus Reviews 71, no. 7 (April 1, 2003): 501.
Library Journal 128, no. 7 (April 15, 2003): 126.
The New York Times, August 29, 2003, p. E32.
The New York Times Book Review, July 13, 2003, p. 15.
Publishers Weekly 250, no. 16 (April 21, 2003): 36-37.

THE TEAMMATES
A Portrait of a Friendship

Author: David Halberstam (1934-   )
Publisher: Hyperion (New York). 217 pp. $22.95
Type of work: Memoir
Time: 2001, with flashbacks to the baseball days of four
teammates now in their eighties
Locale: Hernando, Florida; San Diego; San Francisco;
Portland; Junction City, Oregon; Boston; Marion, Mas-
sachusetts; the Bronx; Cooperstown, New York; and
Philadelphia

*Historian Halberstam frames his sixth book with an au-
tomobile trip by two teammates and a friend to visit a dying
Ted Williams in Florida in October, 2001. At the heart of
the memoir are the human stories not only of four intersect-
ing baseball lives—those of Williams, Bobby Doerr, Dom
DiMaggio, and Johnny Pesky—but also of their friendship*

Principal personages:

TED WILLIAMS, the Boston Red Sox superstar around whose life and
approaching death *The Teammates* pivots
BOBBY DOERR, a star second baseman; the only one of Williams's friends
who dared challenge the batting theories of the last man to hit .400
DOM DIMAGGIO, a center fielder like his more famous older brother Joe
JOHNNY PESKY, a onetime clubhouse attendant who played shortstop for
the Red Sox
BOO FERRIS, a pitcher for the Red Sox's pennant-winning 1946 team,
who suffered a career-ending sore arm in 1947
DICK FLAVIN, a Boston fan and television personality who drove with
DiMaggio and Pesky to visit their ailing friend and teammate
LOU KAUFMAN, Williams's longtime companion

"The memory of the heart is the longest." With these words, Robert Sylvester ends
"The Swede," a story about the after-death apotheosis of a discredited football coach,
modeled after Knute Rockne. *The Teammates* is a testament to the memory of the
heart. It provides a tonic for disenchanted fans for whom professional baseball has become a game whose key plays are enacted off the field by owners, agents, and the
moneymakers.

Although *The Teammates* qualifies as a baseball book and could be shelved with
Roger Angell's *The Summer Game* (1972) and David Halberstam's *Summer of '49*
(1989) as classics of that genre, its true place is with Roger Kahn's *The Boys of Summer* (1972) and Jane Leavy's *Koufax* (2002), books that are about baseball but transcend it.

~

David Halberstam, winner of the Pulitzer Prize for his reporting from Vietnam at the age of thirty, is one of the United States' best-known journalists and historians. Both Summer of '49 *(1989) and* The Best and the Brightest *(1969) went to number one on* The New York Times *best-seller list.*

~

Of all sports, baseball is tops in anecdotes and memorabilia. This book resonates with lovers of both. There were at least two—perhaps three—sides to Ted Williams, and in any guise he could be difficult but never dull. Growing up in angler-friendly Oregon, Bobby Doerr tells of seeing Williams at his best and worst while fishing with the master. Fish stories best display Williams's three-stage trademarks—pent-up displeasure, rage, and contrition.

The book is rich in baseball lore. Perhaps the worst moment in the history of the Red Sox was Enos Slaughter's mad dash to score from first on a pop fly for the St. Louis Cardinals to beat Boston in the 1946 World Series. Characteristically, Johnny Pesky has always accepted the blame for his hesitant throw, but, as revealed by expert witnesses including his three teammates, the real culprit was a journeyman center fielder subbing for Dom DiMaggio, who was slow recovering Harry "the Hat" Walker's hit.

The book is really about the enduring friendship of four friends over a half-century. Williams referred to Doerr, DiMaggio, and Pesky as "my guys," but each of them could have applied the same affectionate tag to the other three. All four were men of a certain generation, born right at the end of the World War I. They had played together on Boston Red Sox teams of the 1940's. Williams and Doerr went back even further: They were teenagers together in San Diego in the mid-1930's, when the Padres were in the Pacific Coast League.

"Ted was dying," Halberstam begins, "and the idea for the final trip, driving down to Florida to see him one last time, was Dominic's." The journey from DiMaggio's place in Marion, Massachusetts, to Williams's home in Hernando, Florida, would take three days. DiMaggio was accompanied by Pesky and a Boston admirer named Dick Flavin on the thirteen-hundred-mile journey. Sadly, Doerr's wife of sixty-three years, Monica, had suffered two strokes; Doerr would not be able to join his friends on the trip.

Halberstam is skilled in exploiting stops along the way for transitions. Thus, approaching Philadelphia, DiMaggio recalls how nervous he was meeting the difficult Lefty Grove, perhaps the Athletics' finest pitcher, in Boston in DiMaggio's rookie season, Grove's last, and catching the last out of Lefty's three-hundredth and last win. Pesky recalls being ridden as a "dumb Pollack" by the Polish slugger Al Simmons, although Pesky is Croatian.

When Flavin, who was driving, announced they were in Lancaster, Pennsylvania, Pesky said, "Oh my God, I used to manage here. Amish country." Then he ran down a long list of players and places—a unique map, Pesky's own United States of baseball. Halberstam devotes the next twenty pages to Pesky's career, which began in his home state, took him out of Oregon for the first time for stops in Rocky Mount, North Carolina, and Louisville, Kentucky, where he was the team's most valuable player before signing with Boston for four thousand dollars in 1942. He rarely missed a game for the next seven years until being traded, the only one of the four to play somewhere other than Boston.

Driving south, Flavin, a popular entertainer in Boston, recalls the annual Johnny Pesky dinner, which he often emceed. This forges still another vital transition. At the next dinner, Flavin decides they should play a home video featuring Williams and Doerr arguing about hitting in the middle of a fishing trip on the Rogue River.

"It was," writes Halberstam, "vintage Williams, Flavin thought, the man as he really was—so alive, argumentative, and dominating. . . . For sure, they would have to bleep out a number of words, but it would be perfect for the Pesky dinner, a way of showing [their] friendship." Reference to the fishing video also introduces perhaps the most fascinating of the friendships, that between Williams and Doerr, who were also antagonists. That this closest of friendships could endure for sixty-five years exemplifies the attraction of opposites. As a rookie, Mel Parnell, a rare left-hander who flourished in Boston's Fenway Park with its short fence in left field, thought Doerr the "nicest" of teammates and, later, "the nicest person I've ever met."

During their playing days, the handsome, pleasantly "square" Doerr served as a kind of translator of Williams to the world. As Halberstam explains, Doerr "understood better than anyone else his friend's passion to excel, his need to be the best, and how hollow his life was when he fell short of his expectations. Doing well, of course, meant hitting." On this single topic, Doerr never gave in to the master's constant nagging that he should alter his compact swing. It produced a .288 average and 223 homers, lifetime.

Doerr tried hard to keep Williams afloat during most of his nineteen stormy years in Boston with that city's confrontational writers and knowledgeable but frustrated fans. It was Dom DiMaggio, himself suffering from Paget's disease, who did the most for Williams's morale when his health broke. In mid-January of 2001, attended by fourteen doctors, nurses, and technicians, the eighty-two-year-old Williams underwent ten hours of open-heart surgery, which gave him one more agonizing year. DiMaggio recalled his own decline and what it was like dealing with his brother Joe in the Clipper's final days. As he told Williams, "Teddy, we're dealt a hand . . . we really don't understand. . . . We do the best we can for all of our lives. The whole world is proud of the way you played [yours] . . . and of what you've done with your life."

When phone conversation became impossible, DiMaggio thought of the final journey. Halberstam reconstructs the reunion in just five pages. Having seen Williams more recently than the others, DiMaggio was best prepared for what they saw: "a man once supremely powerful, shrunken now, down to perhaps 130 pounds, head down on his chest." Their two days together—four short visits—were enough to bring back the take-charge dynamo they had known. They relived some of Teddy Ballgame's finest hours. He died nine months later.

Halberstam learned of the visit over dinner at the DiMaggios' house in Palm Beach, Florida. When he told his old friend and fellow writer Russell Baker about this book, Baker's reply was, "That's not work—that's stealing." All memoirs are self-serving, but Halberstam's skill in being heard but not seen keeps the focus where it belongs. The journalist-historian on whom nothing is lost has brought a lyric touch to this story that brings to light the human vulnerability of a prince of play beneath the protective disguises.

Richard Hauer Costa

Review Sources

Booklist 99, no. 14 (March 15, 2003): 1250.
Kirkus Reviews 71, no. 6 (March 15, 2003): 440-441.
Library Journal 128, no. 2 (February 1, 2003): 89.
The New York Times Book Review, May 25, 2003, p. 9.
Publishers Weekly 250, no. 15 (April 14, 2003): 61-62.
Time 161, no. 20 (May 19, 2003): 64-66.
The Wall Street Journal, May 8, 2003, p. D8.

TEN LITTLE INDIANS

Author: Sherman Alexie (1966-   )
Publisher: Grove Press (New York). 243 pp. $24.00
Type of work: Short fiction

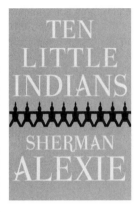

Alexie's characters call themselves Indians, but they embrace the pleasures of middle-class, urban American culture even while clinging to the best and most powerful qualities of their American Indian origins

In this work Sherman Alexie addresses Americans whose ideas about American Indians have been shaped by countless stereotypes, one-dimensional figures ranging from Iron Eyes Cody weeping in television spots to the sadly debased people who, sociologists note, are the poorest ethnic group in the United States to the poor but noble and spiritual people of Tony Hillerman's novels. Alexie has addressed these stereotypes in the past, but most of the Indians in this volume have left the reservation behind to enjoy the pleasures of middle-class American life. While these characters relish their high-tech jobs and all the indulgences that those jobs can provide, they affirm at the same time some of the traditional values of their people—their ironic humor, their modesty, their loyalty, and the joy with which they experience life.

Particularly notable is that these are very urban stories in which the reservation is always present but well in the background. The narrator of "Lawyer's League," for example, is the son of an "African American giant" who played football for the University of Washington and of a Spokane Indian ballet dancer. He himself is an honors graduate with a degree in political science from his father's university. Similarly William, the high-tech executive of "Flight Patterns," is "an Indian who didn't smoke or drink or eat processed sugar" and whose business forces him to leave his comfortable suburban house and loving family several times a month while he flies around the United States. "Sure, he was an enrolled member of the Spokane Indian tribe, but he was also a fully recognized member of the notebook-computer tribe and the security-checkpoint tribe and the rental-car tribe." In short, he could be recognized in any city's airport as a warrior for the great tribe of American business.

All of Alexie's characters are highly aware of their American Indian heritage, which is so much a part of them that one can scarcely say they honor it. In a sense, the themes of "Search Engine" are the themes of all these stories. In this story, Corliss is a college student, an English major with whom the works of poets such as Gerard Manley Hopkins resonate. Corliss has made it to the university by dint of enormous effort and personal drive. In Spokane she was the paradox of "a poor kid, and a middle-class Indian" whose intense motivation made her scavenge aluminum cans to finance an SAT prep course for herself and to contact local preparatory school teachers for help in meeting the university admissions requirements. She needed to be eli-

Sherman Alexie is the author of the novels Reservation Blues *(1995) and* Indian Killer *(1996). His short-story collection* The Lone Ranger and Tonto Fistfight in Heaven *(1993) was the source of his screenplay for the 1998 film* Smoke Signals. *He has received the PEN/Malamud Award for Excellence in Short Fiction as well as the Lila Wallace-Reader's Digest Award.*

gible for substantial scholarships. Alexie is careful to note that Corliss receives much-needed help from generous whites; his characters live in a world of institutional racism and personal integrity in people of all races. Corliss has received no money and little support from the men of her family.

> Indians were used to sharing and called it tribalism, but Corliss suspected it was yet another failed form of communism. Over the last two centuries, Indians had learned how to stand in lines for food, love, hope, sex, and dreams, but they didn't know how to step away. They were good at line-standing and didn't know if they'd be good at anything else.

Corliss's ironic but loving view of her people seems to be Alexie's own; it surfaces, with its sad humor, in most of the stories of this volume.

In the course of her story, Corliss discovers in the university library a long-forgotten volume of poetry by Harlan Atwater, a Spokane Indian. Although some of the poems are quite pedestrian, others have an element of freshness and insight, and Corliss is excited to find published poems by an Indian writer. When she tries to learn more about Atwater, however, she hits dead ends. Nothing has been written about him. Her mother, a repository of historical information about the Spokane reservation, has never heard of him. After a lengthy search (Corliss herself embodies the pun of "engine" and "injun" of the title) she manages to locate Atwater, an ordinary fellow who lives with his parents and has written no poetry for thirty years.

Under Corliss's questioning, he explains that although he is indeed a Spokane Indian, he was adopted as an infant by a loving white couple, the elderly parents for whom he now cares. He wrote the poems about life on the reservation he scarcely knew in an effort to feel more like an Indian, and he goes on to explain, comically, how he used his brief career as a poet to seduce women. His career ended when he had a reading and book signing at an Indian bar and, elated by the praise of his people, gave away all his self-published volumes to his drunken audience. Atwater confesses all this to Corliss to make her understand the depths of his deception, but she senses a level of truth in all his fictions. Atwater had asked her, in the light of this fakery, what kind of Indian she thought he was, and at the end Corliss knows that the question is unanswerable—about Atwater and about herself. Still, she replaces the book on the bookstore shelf face-outward, so that everyone can see it.

Throughout these stories, roots carry an ambiguous power, just as they did for Corliss. That the power cannot be analyzed makes it no less significant. In "Do Not Go Gentle," a young Indian couple's infant son is in a coma in a children's hospital. Like all the parents of dying children, they feel frantic in their powerlessness to do anything but watch their baby breathe through a medical network of tubes and monitors. At last the husband wanders out, to what he thinks is a toy store (its name is Toys in Babeland), only to discover that the store sells sex toys. Bemused, he buys a vibrator called "Chocolate Thunder" and takes it back to the hospital. After all, sex and love are the mysteries that have created all the babies in this ward; perhaps the vibrator can carry some sort of power. "Maybe some people can get by with quiet prayers, but I wanted to shout and scream and vibrate. So did plenty of other fathers and mothers in that sickroom," the narrator says. His wife uses the vibrator as a drumstick and beats on her hand drum while singing a song so powerful that all the children in the ward hear it and respond inwardly, and their own child opens his eyes to live again. The medicine that has returned him from the grave is a potent blend of creative forces, brought together in this case by his Indian heritage in his mother's song.

These stories are characterized by a ebullient humor which often involves sex. Corliss, the central character of "Search Engine," is started on her journey to find Atwater by watching a fellow student try to seduce a young woman in the student center. In "Flight Patterns," William's lovemaking with his wife is simultaneously funny and romantic. The title character of "The Life and Times of Estelle Walks About" is a sexually liberated woman who gives her son endless advice about women and sex. (Part of her advice is that women are aroused at the sight of a man running a vacuum cleaner.)

Much of the rest of the stories' humor rises from Alexie's ironic view of American Indians' place, both in the white world and on the reservation. Always, his characters are conscious of the endless chain formed by the racist ways of white institutions joined with a degree of American Indians' complicity in their own repression and, in turn, linked to stereotypes held by whites, even when those stereotypes are not negative.

One of the commonest of stereotypes concerns the drunken Indian, the subject of one of this volume's most appealing stories, "What You Pawn I Will Redeem." It is the only story to use characters based on this stereotype. Jackson, the narrator, is a homeless man whose life in the urban United States disintegrated when his mental health cracked. Now he is a moderately successful panhandler who manages to collect enough money to support his alcoholism. The story opens as he and his friends pass a pawnshop and he recognizes his grandmother's beaded dancing regalia, stolen from her some fifty years before (the narrator had seen it only in photographs). The pawnshop owner agrees to sell it to Jackson for nine hundred and ninety-nine dollars, an amount of money he has not seen for years but now must produce within twenty-four hours.

The rest of the story concerns his efforts to find the money. His first step is to use his last bit of money to buy liquor in the hope that it will inspire some ideas about finding more; instead it makes him and his friends dead drunk for an hour or so. He tries to borrow money from some Aleuts who have been sitting on the wharf for eleven years, waiting for their boat to take them back to Alaska. Jackson also tries selling newspapers. He wins a hundred dollars on the lottery but spends that money in a bar, buying drinks for other Indians (and himself). As he sobers up, he manages to talk a sympathetic cop into loaning him thirty dollars instead of forcing him to go to detox. He returns to the Aleuts and sings tribal songs with them for two hours; then he spends twenty-five dollars buying them breakfast. At last he returns to the pawnshop with the remaining five dollars, and the pawnbroker gives him the regalia. As the story ends, Jackson is wearing the regalia and dancing in a city intersection: "Pedestrians stopped. Cars stopped. The city stopped. They all watched me dance with my grandmother. I was my grandmother, dancing."

Several stories in the collection nod at the tradition of American Indians as passionate basketball players. In "What Ever Happened to Frank Snake Church?" the title character comes to a midlife crisis that leads him to try to regain his lost abilities on the basketball court. After a heart attack, intense training, and some time in a mental hospital, he enrolls in a community college in the hope that, at the age of forty-one, he can play for the school's team. That is impossible, as he learns, but not before he has made a heroic effort and has successfully shown the school's star players his amazing skills in a tribute to his dead parents.

Although some of the stories in this collection lose their narrative drive in a welter of satiric detail, they all offer insights into a world of people—white, brown, and red—whom Alexie clearly loves and whom he treats with dignity even as he laughs at them. He invites the reader to do the same.

Ann D. Garbett

Review Sources

Book: The Magazine for the Reading Life, July/August, 2003, p. 179.
Booklist 99, no. 16 (April 15, 2003): 1426-1427.
Kirkus Reviews 71, no. 8 (April 15, 2003): 548.
Library Journal 128, no. 9 (May 15, 2003): 129-130.
The New York Times, May 26, 2003, p. E10.
The New York Times Book Reviews, June 15, 2003, p. 13.
Publishers Weekly 250, no. 18 (May 5, 2003): 198.

TERROR AND LIBERALISM

Author: Paul Berman (1949-   )
Publisher: W. W. Norton (New York). 214 pp. $21.00
Type of work: Current affairs
Time: 2003

A sober, carefully argued essay in which Berman, long an eloquent spokesman for the American Left, endorses the United States' war on terrorism, including the conquest of Iraq, as part of a necessary struggle against the forces of Islamic totalitarianism

TERROR AND LIBERALISM

PAUL BERMAN

After the terrorist attacks in New York and Washington, D.C., on September 11, 2001, and the subsequent so-called war on terrorism, the American political Left was in an uncomfortable position. The United States had been attacked, and many people accepted that the nation had a right to strike back at its adversaries. The Left, however, long suspicious of what it saw as the imperialist tendencies of U.S. foreign policy, lined up with the small but vocal antiwar movement. It was a difficult and unpopular stance to take. One leading figure on the left, journalist Christopher Hitchens, publicly broke with his former colleagues and supported a war against what he called in the columns of *The Nation* "theocratic nihilists." Hitchens also, almost alone on the left, supported the American war against Iraq.

Now another venerable voice from the left, Paul Berman, comes out in favor of a vigorous, military response from the Western liberal democracies to what he describes as Islamic totalitarianism, an ideology that he argues poses a grave threat to Western values and way of life. *Terror and Liberalism* is not a journalistic polemic, however. It is a scholarly, deeply knowledgeable analysis of the roots of Islamic suicide terrorism and the failure of the West to recognize its dangerous, irrational nature.

One of Berman's main points is that many Islamic radicals—terrorists and suicide bombers included—live a kind of cultural double life. They are often as culturally Western, in terms of their education and day-to-day life, as they are Middle Eastern and Asian Islamic. Berman also explains at length that Islamic suicide terrorism, its worship of death and wholesale slaughter, has many roots in Western political and philosophical ideas and practices that began in the nineteenth century and flowered (if such a term may be permitted) in the totalitarian movements that dominated the twentieth century and produced so much misery for millions.

Using Albert Camus's *L'Homme révolté* (1951; *The Rebel*, 1956) for support, Berman argues that the origins of totalitarianism and its horrors lay in the perversion of the human need to reach for freedom through rebellion against conventional morality. This rebellion can be traced to, among other things, the morbid obsessions of Romantic poets such as Charles Baudelaire, which pointed toward a kind of nihilism in which senseless murder and suicide could be justified.

Through Russian nineteenth century terrorism, Western imperialist atrocities in

⌒

*Paul Berman is a political and
cultural critic whose writings
appear in* The New Republic, The
New York Times Magazine, The
New York Times Book Review,
Slate, *and other publications. He is
the author of* A Tale of Two
Utopias: The Political Journey of
the Generation of 1968 *(1996) and
the editor of* Debating PC *(1992).*

⌒

Africa, and the wholesale slaughter of World
War I, Berman traces this nihilistic impulse to its
ultimate expression in Soviet Communism, Italian Fascism, and German Nazism. All these
movements resembled one another and were
perversions of the impulse to rebel. The rebellion
was against the perceived inadequacies of liberal
democracy, and it was done in the name of sub-
mission to one quasi-divine authority. The mythical structure on which such movements were
based was always the same; they were variants
of the vision of Saint John the Divine in the Book
of Revelation: The people of God are being un-
dermined by an insidious enemy, aided by Satanic forces. The enemy would be defeated in a final war of Armageddon, followed by a reign of the pure society in a one-
party state under a superhuman leader. All these cults depended on mass death dealt
out indiscriminately to those it considered enemies.

Berman then argues persuasively that this cult of destruction was exported by the
West to other parts of the world, including the Islamic world. Baath Socialism, part of
the pan-Arab movement, was heavily influenced by racist Nazi philosophy. Other
founders of the Baath had communist leanings, and admired Joseph Stalin as an inspirational leader. Baath also embraced a myth that was similar in structure to Revelation's ur-myth: The Arabs were the nation of God and had to battle their enemies—
the Jews—who were corrupting them. In service of this holy war, Baath followers had
to be absolutely obedient to the party and cast conventional morality aside. The result
was the emergence in Iraq in the late 1960's of a nihilistic totalitarianism resembling
the totalitarian movements in the West in the 1930's.

Berman also traces the influence of Western totalitarianism on influential thinkers
in the Islamic world. For this he examines at length the writings of Sayyid Qutb of
Egypt, who is acknowledged as the most influential writer in the recent Islamic tradition, at least among the Sunni Arabs. Qutb was imprisoned and then hanged in 1966
by Egypt's military leader, Gamal Abdel Nasser, for his prominent role in the Muslim
Brotherhood. Much of Qutb's philosophy is contained in his thirty-volume commentary on the Qur'an, and Berman is one of few Western intellectuals to have taken the
trouble to study the three volumes of this work that have been translated into English.
Qutb puts the blame for modern humanity's alienated condition on the historical development of Christianity, which, having divorced itself from the Mosaic Code, gave
its followers little guidance in how to live their daily lives.

During the Renaissance and the seventeenth century, Christianity embodied a
steadily deepening "schizophrenic" attitude to the world, putting science on one side
and God on the other (which Islam does not) and also separating religion from the
state. For Qutb, the separation of church and state, on which the West prides itself, was
a disaster because it denied God's sovereignty on Earth. His domain was restricted to
the private morality of individuals. Western ideas of freedom, which rested at least in

part on freedom of worship and freedom from religious tyranny, were, in Qutb's view, just another form of schizophrenia. Under Islam, God cannot be shunted off into one corner of life, for this is little better than a denial of God altogether. Qutb was worried that such liberal notions would penetrate Muslim societies, and he raged about one historical event in particular: the abolition of the Islamic caliphate by Atatürk in Turkey in 1924 and his establishment of a secular society in which religion and state were separated. Qutb called for a jihad, or holy war, against the Muslims who compromised the faith in such ways and against Christians and Jews who were assaulting the faith from the outside. He envisioned a worldwide battle to save Islam. Berman points out that Qutb's revolutionary manifesto, although deeply Muslim, was also very European, because it utilized similar ideas that lay behind Western totalitarianism, complete with the myth of Armageddon based on the Revelation of Saint John.

After Qutb's death, the ideas he championed took root in countries as diverse as Saudi Arabia, Pakistan, Egypt, and especially Iran, where the Islamic revolution under Ayatollah Khomeini triumphed in 1979. As with totalitarianism in the West, the first fruit of revolution was war, in which Khomeini sent thousands of Iranian soldiers to their deaths in human wave assaults against Iraqi positions. Religious fervor and mass death were combined. It was a cult of slaughter. This pattern was repeated, according to Berman, everywhere that the Islamic movement made headway in the 1980's and 1990's, whether it was Saddam Hussein's Iraq, Algeria, Hezbollah terrorists in Lebanon, Kashmir, Afghanistan, Palestine, or the Sudan. Berman's conclusion is that Islamic radicalism was "as horrible as the fascism and Stalinism of Europe—fully as murderous, as destructive of societies and moralities, as devastating to civilization. The victims numbered in the multiple millions." It was out of this potent mix of ideology and war that al-Qaeda emerged. Osama bin Laden's world is similar to Qutb's: The warriors of Islam must fight against the pagans (the United States), the hypocrites (Muslims allied with the United States), and the Jews. For him, Islamic victory will be achieved by mass slaughter.

Berman goes on to accuse liberals and others in the West of continuing to indulge in denial about the true nature of this modern Islamic movement. In this, too, can be seen the history of the West in the twentieth century, in particular the refusal in many quarters in the 1930's to see the threat posed by Adolf Hitler or the murderous reality of Soviet Communism. Berman regards the current mindset of denial as like the "simple-minded optimism" that prevailed during the nineteenth century and lingered on in spite of the catastrophe that befell such ideas in World War I.

Berman argues that this denial rests on a refusal to admit that an irrational, pathological suicide-murder cult, drunk on killing, could ever get a grip on large numbers of people. It rests on a belief in the rationality of things. Such a belief has, however, indeed taken hold in parts of the Islamic world, as it did in twentieth century Europe. The Palestinian embrace of suicide terrorism, the cult of martyrdom and death, is an illustration. Berman criticizes the many attempts to explain it away as being a rational response to real-life conditions imposed (in the case of the Palestinians) by an occupying power. According to Berman, this has resulted in the demonization of Israel to a level that is out of proportion to the facts.

It is against this backdrop that Berman views the United States' current war on terrorism. Whether against the Taliban in Afghanistan or Saddam Hussein's supporters in Iraq, he regards it as a war against an Islamic fascist totalitarianism that is every bit as dangerous to the liberal democracies of the West as the Nazi or Soviet versions that preceded it. He hails the results of the war in Afghanistan: three million children enrolled in school for the first time; two million Afghan refugees returning to their homeland. He points out that although military force is necessary, this is also a war of ideas, of cultural persuasion. He calls for the establishment of a Third Force politics, neither right nor left but dedicated to human rights and women's rights in the Muslim world, as well as a host of other liberal tenets: religious tolerance, antiracism; secular education, pluralism and law; elimination of poverty and oppression. He sees in the response of the Afghan people to the overthrow of the Taliban some hope that a Third Force might take root in Islamic soil.

Berman has words of both praise and censure for U.S. president George W. Bush's handling of the war. It was Bush who spoke of a war against totalitarianism, cited the need for women's rights in Afghanistan, and held out hope for social progress in the Muslim world. Bush also failed to request sacrifices from the American people in terms of raising taxes or reducing the dependence on foreign oil. He also failed, however, according to Berman, to take up the larger war of ideas and was guilty of dishonest arguments in the buildup to the war against Iraq. He squandered the goodwill that the world extended to the United States in the wake of September 11.

This is not an optimistic book. Berman explains at length the many failures of the West that have led to the current situation as well as pointing to a failure of political courage and imagination in the Muslim world. He offers no confident recipe for success in the war against a formidable Islamic totalitarianism that may have much fuel yet to burn. The best he can hope for is that the West continues to stand fast for freedom and antinihilism.

Bryan Aubrey

Review Sources

America 189, no. 4 (August 18, 2003): 22-23.
Booklist 99, no. 17 (May 1, 2003): 1558.
Commonweal 130, no. 11 (June 6, 2003): 22-24.
The Economist 367, no. 8322 (May 3, 2003): 77-78.
Kirkus Reviews 71, no. 5 (March 1, 2003): 355.
The Nation 276, no. 16 (April 28, 2003): 31-34.
National Review 55, no. 9 (May 19, 2003): 56-58.
The New York Review of Books 50, no. 7 (May 1, 2003): 4-6.
The New York Times, April 5, 2003, p. D9.
The New York Times Book Review, June 1, 2003, p. 25.
Publishers Weekly 250, no. 12 (March 24, 2003): 70.
The Wall Street Journal, April 8, 2003, p. D4.

THE TERROR BEFORE TRAFALGAR
Nelson, Napoleon, and the Secret War

Author: Tom Pocock (1925-   )
Publisher: W. W. Norton (New York). 255 pp. $24.95
Type of work: History
Time: 1801-1805
Locale: Great Britain, France, and Spain

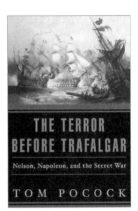

A stirring account of the period during the Napoleonic Wars, when England most feared an invasion by France

Principal personages:
> HORATIO, LORD NELSON, a vice admiral in the Royal Navy and Britain's greatest hero
> NAPOLEON, First Consul and later emperor of France, Britain's nemesis
> SIR SIDNEY SMITH, a rear admiral in the Royal Navy, a key figure in British espionage
> JOHN WESLEY WRIGHT, a captain in the Royal Navy and a British spy
> ROBERT FULTON, an American inventor
> SIR WILLIAM CONGREVE, a British inventor

To avid readers of Patrick O'Brian's superb novels of the period, the Napoleonic Wars are a triumphant succession of victories brought about by Captain Jack Aubrey of the British Royal Navy and master of political intrigue Dr. Stephen Maturin. The intrepid duo meet each other for the first time at a chamber music concert that takes place on April 1, 1800. From that initial novel in the series, *Master and Commander* (1969), to the twentieth and final volume, *Blue at the Mizzen* (1999), one can follow the exploits of these two companions as they survive numerous battles, shipwrecks, fortunes won and lost. Along the way, O'Brian allows readers to stand on the quarterdeck, to experience the carnage of war in a wooden ship, to smell the tarred rigging and black powder. O'Brian is justly celebrated for infusing life into events of the distant past. The fact that the series begins on April Fools' Day, however, is significant. O'Brian communicates to the reader that one should never equate the ordered appearance of a fictional reality with documented historical fact.

With this in mind, O'Brian's fictional view of this period proves to be an effective starting point for a discussion of *The Terror Before Trafalgar*, Tom Pocock's excellent nonfictional account of Britain at war with Napoleon Bonaparte (1769-1821). Pocock's work shocks the reader into the realization that, far from being merely Britain's isolated struggle with France, the Napoleonic period was perhaps the first true world war. It eventually involved all the major European military powers, including Russia, Prussia, and Spain, in addition to the two opponents glaring at each other across the English Channel.

A former reporter for two London newspapers, the Evening Standard *and* The Times, *Tom Pocock has written eight books about Lord Nelson.* Horatio Nelson *(1987) was runner-up for the Whitbread Book Award for biography. He has authored other biographies as well as books about his work as a war correspondent.*

While many readers recall that the naval battle at Trafalgar took place in 1805, the concluding land battle of the conflict, Waterloo, did not occur until ten years later. Given the massive scale of these wars, Pocock, a noted authority on Lord Nelson (1758-1805), focuses on the neglected period before the great naval battle. O'Brian paints a picture of a pugnacious Britain that stands on the threshold of becoming an economic, political, and military superpower; Pocock describes a reality that is nearly the exact opposite.

As *The Terror Before Trafalgar* opens, it is the year 1801, and England has been at war with revolutionary France for a full eight years. The prologue perfectly captures the mood of frustration that had taken hold of the nation and sets the tone for much of the book. Lord Nelson, after having annihilated the Danish fleet at Copenhagen as part of a plan to end the Armed Neutrality of the North, succeeded in forcing the crown prince to accept a truce. It was a costly battle all around: Casualties numbered in the thousands. What at first had seemed to be a great victory soon gave way to disenchantment when it was learned that the key figure in Denmark's alliance, Czar Paul I of Russia, had been killed prior to Nelson's attack. The battle had been in vain, and it effectively symbolized England's plight.

Years of war had produced what had come to be regarded as a virtual stalemate. Britain, with its large fleet and experienced seamen, could effectively oppose French naval actions, while France continued to accrue impressive victories in its land battles. The British army amounted to less than 130,000 men, and though more than 400,000 volunteers could defend the nation in some capacity, they were no match for Napoleon's battle-tested force of 500,000 men. It was for this reason that the English referred to this period as the "Great Terror"—the first time since 1066 that the island nation was faced with the threat of invasion.

This fearful prospect only loomed larger when Nelson's forces attempted to destroy the prime staging area for the French invasion at the port of Boulogne. When the British tried to sink or remove the French vessels in what was called a "cutting-out expedition," they were easily repulsed by the entrenched defenders. Pocock makes effective use of his source material by giving a human dimension to his descriptions of military actions. He provides a mesmerizing description of the Boulogne endeavor and enhances his narrative with vivid details from the participants. In one memorable scene, the ferocity of hand-to-hand combat is made clear when a French captain stabs a British tar attempting to board one of the French vessels.

Although the book is largely about a war and its effects, Pocock's narrative is also concerned with a treaty that was signed by Britain and France in October, 1801, the Peace of Amiens. Pocock's eye for the telling detail again comes to the fore, as he describes thousands of Britons rushing to France to see firsthand the enemy they had fought so long with so little success. Evoking the almost surrealistic nature of this period of relative calm, Pocock notes that English shipwrights swarmed across the channel to French ports soon after the peace began. Ironically, the absence of war had left them so little work that they accepted employment in French shipyards. The Admiralty, in a stunning lack of foresight, had suspended its own shipbuilding activities. Given the fact that the fear of invasion had only recently abated, it suggests how desperately the English wanted to believe that this would be a permanent peace. As incredible as it may seem, the English were constructing the very warships that would be used against them if war resumed. The fact that France's volatile dictator had continued to build such vessels in peacetime was perhaps the most significant clue to the real impact of the peace—a chance for the little Corsican to rebuild his forces.

If the war-weary English breathed a collective sigh of relief over the supposed cessation of hostilities, the conflict merely continued in a different form: espionage. Spying is an activity as old as civilization itself. It preceded and continued after the Peace of Amiens and was practiced by both sides. What the treaty changed was the nature of the espionage. In war, Britain and France officially sealed themselves off from each other as a means of protecting military intelligence. With the peace, Britain finally had the opportunity to penetrate what had been for them a relatively closed society since the beginning of the French Revolution. France had perhaps the most elaborate system of informers of any government prior to the Soviet Union. Pocock perfectly captures the tension in France when he quotes English visitor John Trotter as stating that "the system of espionage was carried to an incredible height, making suspicion of the slightest indisposition to government sufficient cause for individuals to be hurried away at night—many of them never to be heard of again."

Nevertheless, Britain was able to score a major victory over the French in the cloak-and-dagger world, the kind of success that eluded it on the battlefield. John Wesley Wright, a captain in the Royal Navy, managed to infiltrate France and spy for his government, despite the fact that he had previously been imprisoned by the French for his undercover activities. Just prior to the resumption of war on May 18, 1803, he was able to return to England with a mass of secret documents. One of the triumphs of Pocock's book is his recounting of Wright's exploits; Wright proved to be one of the great unsung heroes of British history. He continued this hazardous game of espionage, continually landing royalists on the French coast until he was captured once again by the authorities. He died in a French prison under suspicious circumstances.

Pocock also enriches his book with another little-known aspect of this period, the search for new weapons with which to break the military stalemate. This aspect of the book sheds light on the collective military culture of this period. Given the scale of the conflict and the dire consequences of defeat, one would think that both Britain and France would grasp at any development that would gain them an advantage in battle. However, these opponents proved to be ambivalent on the subject. Farsighted commanders such as Rear Admiral Sidney Smith seized upon the new technology as a means of undermining the French navy; the Admiralty as a whole found unconventional warfare to be distasteful, even dishonorable.

One such weapon was a type of rocket developed by Sir William Congreve, who envisioned it as a new kind of artillery. Although rockets by themselves were never considered to be the key to a decisive victory, Smith thought that they could effectively supplant conventional or unconventional weapons by creating a diversion. When the British were planning another assault upon Boulogne in 1805, five hundred of the Congreve rockets were ordered, to be launched from catamarans. In the actual battle, however, they proved to be of little use because the unsteady nature of the floating platforms made them difficult to aim. Only four were launched, and all exploded harmlessly in the water.

More creative, and marginally more effective, was the work of American Robert Fulton (1765-1815), who was later to gain fame as the inventor of the first successful steamboat. He developed an unconventional weapon that was perhaps the most practical of all—the torpedo. This was not the same self-propelled device that wrought such havoc in twentieth century wars. Rather, this was a sealed container filled with gunpowder that contained a clockwork fuse. The contraption was allowed to drift and snag itself on the mooring cable of an enemy vessel by means of a grappling hook. This device did sink a ship under ideal test conditions but proved to be little better than Congreve's rockets in battle. Undoubtedly, the most revolutionary of the unconventional weapons was Fulton's submarine, the *Nautilus*, which preceded Jules Verne's fictional vessel of the same name by half a century. Even though the craft proved itself in sea trials, both sides concluded that it too was impractical. Though one might fault Pocock for devoting too much space to such ineffective weapons, he correctly points out that Fulton and Congreve were anticipating the future of warfare. Nelson's triumph at Trafalgar, on the other hand, proved to be the last decisive victory at sea. Devotees of history and O'Brian will find *The Terror Before Trafalgar* enthralling.

Cliff Prewencki

Review Sources

Booklist 99, no. 16 (April 15, 2003): 1446.
The Economist 365, no. 8294 (October 12, 2002): 78-79.
Library Journal 128, no. 8 (May 1, 2003): 135.
The New York Times Book Review, June 22, 2003, p. 10.
The Spectator 290 (November 23, 2002): 60.

THREE NOVELLAS

Author: Thomas Bernhard (1931-1989)
Translated from the German by Peter Jansen and Kenneth
  J. Northcott
Foreword by Brian Evenson
Publisher: University of Chicago Press (Chicago). 186
  pp. $25.00
Type of work: Novellas
Time: Post-World War II
Locale: Innsbruck and Vienna, Austria

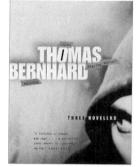

*Three novellas by Bernhard trace his development as a
writer with his idiosyncratic themes and characters: ranting suicides and madmen in a society hostile to all individual value*

Principal characters:
  Amras
  WALTER and K, brothers who survive a family suicide pact that kills
    their parents
  UNCLE, who takes over their property and lives

  Playing Watten
  DOCTOR, the narrator
  TRUCK DRIVER, who listens to narrator and "tells" about the traveler
  SILLER, a paper maker who hangs himself
  SCHAUSTELLER, a ruthless landlord
  THE TRAVELER, who finds Siller's body hanging in the forest

  Walking
  THE NARRATOR
  OEHLER, a friend of the narrator
  KARRER, a friend of the narrator, who has recently gone mad

   The first novella, *Amras*, is set in an ancient tower on the outskirts of Innsbruck,
capital of the Austrian Tyrol, an Alpine region which for author Thomas Bernhard is
the dark heart of the darkest beast in his tormented mythology, Austria itself. This novella, his second, shows that early in his career the writer was already grappling with
this beast with the same deadpan humor, as well as the deep spite, that carried him
throughout his entire career.
   Though *Amras* is dominated by the voice of a narrator, as in all of Bernhard's fiction, missing is the single uninterrupted monologue that becomes customary later on.
Amras is narrated by K, who, along with his brother, Walter, failed to die in a suicide
compact with their parents. The many sections and paragraphs of the novella contain
letters, a journal, and even the writings of Walter about a circus.

~

Thomas Bernhard grew up in Salzburg and Vienna but spent much of his life repudiating his native Austria. Nevertheless, Austria and Europe insisted on honoring him with many prizes for his plays and novels, including what many consider his masterpiece, Korrektur *(1975;* Correction, *1979).*

~

K gradually reveals that the family's wealth had been absorbed by their maternal uncle, who is a man of the world, unlike the other members of his family. Over the course of the story, the two brothers are whisked away by their uncle to ever more secure and isolated locations, with the narrator finally ending up in an insane asylum. It is never clear whether they are protected or imprisoned, or if, indeed, there is a distinction. Similarly, the contrast between the worldly and the incompetent is paralleled by the difference between the brothers. Walter is a musician (like Bernhard), and the narrator is a scientist. This distinction between the abstract and the concrete—which Bernhard believes to be completely fallacious—is examined throughout all three novellas in the book. Despite being false, it plagues and destroys many of the characters, in this case Walter. A year younger than the narrator and more delicate, he allows fear, or the so-called Tyrolean epilepsy, to destroy him.

Though Amras is a tower in the novella, the inspiration for this structure was the Hapsburg castle of Ambras, which serves Bernhard as a symbol of failure. Archduke Ferdinand II (1529-1595) gave it to his morganatic wife, Philippine Welser, whose knife figures in the novella. Her children could never inherit from the archduke, though his branch of the Hapsburg dynasty died out, just as in this novella the narrator's branch of the family dies out. Phallic in appearance, the tower forms a womb where the brothers are reborn as imperfect, needy halves of the other. Inside the womb there is fraternal incest that leads to fraternal fighting outside. The two halves cannot hold together, leaving the narrator a shadowy half-soul looking for his soul mate. When Walter commits suicide, the narrator, who no longer has any chance of being a full human character, breaks down completely. This is mirrored on the page, where the text breaks into fragments. This device results in the voice petering out, instead of becoming tighter—one reason this novella is not as compelling as the next two.

Watten, in the novella *Playing Watten*, is a card game with four players; in this game it is fair to give hints to one's partner, unlike, say, the game of bridge. Watten is played mostly in the Southern Tyrol, with local variations, and so represents both local society and the failure of local society when the narrator refuses to play. As nothing Bernhard writes has just one theme, this novella reads like a whirlpool of ideas on everything from death to religion to the stupidity of humankind.

A truck driver comes to the hut of the narrator, an aristocratic doctor who has abandoned his family castle, apparently giving it over to house eighty drug addicts, after having his medical license revoked for his own morphine use. The truck driver wants to lure the narrator back to the watten table after the fourth player, Siller, committed suicide—not by jumping into the convenient river, as everyone thought, but by hanging himself in a tree on the riverbank. The truck driver tells about the discovery of the body, but his account is embedded in the doctor's monologue, a device perfected in

Walking. Here it is a bit confusing as to who is recounting the events, but because the narrator's voice dominates, as intended, and the story line is never confusing, the final impact is not lessened.

The doctor will not return to the table, Siller's place having been taken by Schausteller, a ruthless landlord who represents everything that is repugnant to the doctor (and Bernhard) about commercial, bourgeois Austria. Bernhard mocks a society that appears to be collegial but can never be anything but a burlesque in which people take on false faces. On the other hand, Bernhard does not have any romantic notion of individualism. For him, the end is always insanity, because the individual mind is too weak to withstand reality. However, there are different kinds of insanity, and the "society" represented by the old group of players is one in which he is going mad "naturally," not in "the most humiliating and artificial way," which would be his lot in the other situation, playing with the ruthless landlord who wants to take Siller's place at the watten table.

In this satire, the more the narrator vents, the less rational he sounds, although all the more enticing and convincing. Few writers know how to use hyperbole as deftly as Bernhard. He believes it impossible to make any true statement because of the limitations of both human language and existence, and so he is forced to go to the extremes to get anything near the truth. "Nature does not need thought," he says. All logic falls afoul of paradox, and all consciousness is paralyzed by self-consciousness: "You cannot walk regularly either, as you know, if you think: walk regularly."

Of course, most people simply walk, or goose-step, on with their lives. One of the themes throughout Bernhard's work is his hatred of Austrians for their support of Adolf Hitler. That is one reason he likes people who resist the urge to conform to social norms. The paper maker Siller is seen as good because "of his frankness . . . his precision, lack of prejudice, modesty, his absolute incorruptibility." He comes as close as any character can to serve as a model of how to live in Bernhard's world—but kills himself because life is a punishment no one deserves.

Walking, the most powerful of these short works, is mostly the story of the enraged madness of Karrer, but suicide figures in it, as it does in the other two novellas. Karrer was influenced by a teacher, the chemist Hollensteiner, who killed himself because the government would no longer fund his program. This provides Bernhard with one of his finer and funnier anti-Austrian tirades: "If we strike a balance between the beauty of the country and the baseness of the state, says Oehler, we arrive at suicide."

The novella is divided into two parts, as Oehler and the nameless narrator circle the center of Vienna on foot. In this way, the story of Karrer's breakdown is told twice, the first time as an "objective" account of the fit Karrer has in Rustenschacher's store; then a second time, in a more abstract way, as the scene is replayed with an "explanation" (after the reader has have been told that there are no such things as explanations).

First, one hears the causes and aftermath of Hollensteiner's suicide. Only then is one told how Karrer storms into Rustenschacher's store. At first, he seems merely a lunatic who focuses on the "thin spots" in pants he insists are from Czechoslovakia, not England, as young Rustenschacher claims. It is while repeating that charge incessantly that Karrer's mind, torn between sensitivity and vulgarity, snaps for the second, and probably the last, time in eight years.

Rage permeates the whole constricted novella and builds up a tension that gives the ending a powerful punch. It unfolds and enfolds—"Rustenschacher told Karrer, I told Scherrer, says Oehler"—with increasing tension as Oehler and the narrator walk faster and faster around the heart of Vienna. Naturally, as the characters in both the past and present charge through the streets, Bernhard parallels the pace in his writing: "We had brought our walking and our thinking, the one out of the other, to an incredible, almost unbearable, state of nervous tension." Karrer and Oehler need to calm down and so go into Rustenschacher's store. In the past they have avoided this place, but this time they run into the store and then suddenly stop.

Now Karrer's rageful encounter is told for the second time, and one hears of the anti-Semitism in Vienna, especially of the way Jews were attacked on the street before World War II. Walking, one learns, was actually a futile response at the time, a form of flight and yet *"we walk from one hopelessness to another."* Karrer sees in the bad lot of pants more than anti-Semitism. He sees the whole history of Austria and the lies of Austria that made that country join with Hitler's Germany—a history there is no walking away from.

Bernhard does not expect the reader to sympathize too much with Karrer, who calls his own indifference to everything, including his sister, a "philosophical state,"—in Bernhard's world, already more than halfway to madness. Once again appears the division between philosophy and science, the conceptual and the actual. The paradox is that "we ourselves believe most of the time in the senselessness of thinking, because we know that thinking is total senselessness . . . on the other hand, we know that without the senselessness of thinking *we* do not exist or are nothing."

Supposedly, Bernhard's first novel, *Frost* (1963), was started as a series of poems that he turned into fiction. It shows that he knew his strengths. In reading these novellas, written between 1964 and 1971, one finds that his voice and power are unmistakable from the very start. What makes them most remarkable is the way that he takes what seems to be an intentionally boring and repetitive style and makes it engaging, even mesmerizing. He does this with confidence and self-assurance that enable him to hold the reader's attention for page after page of what are, by the second and third novellas, monologues with virtually no paragraph breaks. Bernhard shows himself to be a brilliant thinker, conversant with psychology and philosophy, especially that of another obsessive Austrian, Ludwig Wittgenstein (1889-1951), whose ideas of identity and language are reflected throughout his books. In *Walking*, for instance, when the narrator says, "Fundamentally, everything that is said is a quotation," he is drawing on Wittgenstein's ideas about the way people share the meaning of words.

In whatever story, the nameless narrator is always immersed in abstract thinking that becomes impossible because of imminent death or the collapse of identity under the weight of the oppressive point of view. Bernhard's ranting allows the reader no space to breathe, building up more and more tension in both the reader and the narrator. At the same time, the prose can almost intoxicate with its musical rhythms. It is

Bernhard's sense of humor that makes these books accessible to most readers, especially the way he refuses ever to commit to any position, while firmly grounding his characters in absurdity that keeps the reader off-guard and giddy.

This same style and these same themes—suicide, murder, madness—were getting a more strenuous workout in Bernhard's novels of this time, such as *Verstörung* (1967; *Gargoyles*, 1970) and *Das Kalkwerk* (1970; *The Lime Works*, 1973). As Brian Evenson makes clear in his foreword, these novellas form a perfect introduction to the works of Bernhard, one of the major European writers of the twentieth century, who influenced such writers as the German W. G. Sebald and the Englishman Tim Parks, among many others.

Philip McDermott

Review Sources

The Nation 277, no. 9 (September 29, 2003): 30-32.
The New Yorker 79, no. 18 (July 7, 2003): 77.
Review of Contemporary Fiction 23, no. 3 (Fall, 2003): 118.

THE THURBER LETTERS
The Wit, Wisdom, and Surprising Life of James Thurber

Author: James Thurber (1894-1961)
Edited by Harrison Kinney, with Rosemary A. Thurber
Publisher: Simon & Schuster (New York). Illustrated.
798 pp. $40.00
Type of work: Letters
Time: From June 28, 1918, to August 20, 1961
Locale: Washington, D.C.; Paris; Ohio; New York; Connecticut; and other places

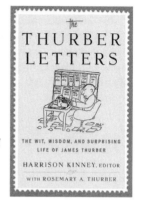

Letters written by Thurber to friends, family, editors, and others, from his early adulthood through the rest of his life

    Principal personages:
        JAMES THURBER, the popular author and
          cartoonist
        ELLIOTT NUGENT, an actor and his Ohio State University classmate
        MINETTE FRITTS, his Ohio State University classmate
        EVA PROUT, his grade-school classmate
        E. B. WHITE, a fellow writer and editor
        ANN HONEYCUTT, Thurber's friend
        ALTHEA ADAMS THURBER, Thurber's first wife
        HAROLD ROSS, Thurber's editor at *The New Yorker*
        HELEN WISMER THURBER, Thurber's second wife

James Thurber was one of the most popular humorists of the twentieth century. Many of his stories, essays, and drawings remain in print long after his death. This book, the second published volume of Thurber's letters, is almost three times the size of *Selected Letters of James Thurber* (1981). The challenge of editing Thurber's letters was "similar to trying to herd cats," editor Harrison Kinney writes in the book's introduction. While correcting mere typographical errors, he tried at the same time to preserve the "idiosyncratic mannerisms" that are essential to the character of Thurber's writings.

Kinney, a lifelong Thurber fan, is a former reporter for *The New Yorker*, and one of Thurber's biographers. He presents the letters chronologically, in five sections, as Thurber ambles into adulthood, wanders from place to place, has his greatest triumphs, and faces severe challenges.

In the first section, "The Emerging Years," the first letter has the twenty-three-year-old Thurber telling his friend Elliott Nugent about his new job. Thurber had dropped out of Ohio State University, started working as a code clerk for the United States Department of State in the aftermath of World War I, and was looking forward to a posting in Paris. He was also rather mixed up in affairs of the heart. His letters declare his adoration for Eva Prout, a grade-school classmate who became a singer and actress, along with a fondness for Minette Fritts, who had been his classmate at Ohio State University. According to Thurber's letters to each of the ladies and to Nugent, Fritts was quite attracted to him, but he was much more interested in Prout, who apparently was cordial but paid him little heed. Fritts eventually married another man and moved to Seattle. In 1922 Thurber married an Ohio State student, Althea Adams, whom he had met a year earlier. Although the marriage lasted thirteen years, it was rocky from the start.

≈

Author, cartoonist, and humorist James Thurber grew up in Columbus, Ohio. He became famous writing articles and cartoons that appeared in The New Yorker *magazine from 1927 until his death in 1961.*

≈

"When I was younger," he wrote to Fritts at age thirty-five, "a dedication to some woman seemed enough. It isn't. Women find out sooner than we do, that a dedication to one person will not serve. . . . Our feet of clay stick out from under the covers and get cold, or else our shoulders do. I spend a great deal of time sorting over my past. . . . Some of my emotions are . . . disturbing." He admitted that he harbored a "childish feeling" toward Fritts, that he had experienced similar feelings about Prout and also felt attracted to Ann Honeycutt, whom he met in 1927. None of this diminished his caring for his wife.

After leaving the foreign service, Thurber wrote some material for a college theater group, worked as a newspaper reporter, and tried unsuccessfully to make it as a freelance writer. He went back to France, tried to write a novel, then worked for the *Chicago Tribune*'s French editions. In 1926, broke, he returned to the United States.

The second section, "The Wandering Years," starts later that year, after Thurber had landed a job with *The New York Post*. He made his first freelance sale in 1927, to *The New Yorker* magazine. Thanks to E. B. White, who was then a staff writer, Thurber joined the magazine's staff and contributed numerous "casuals," the personal comic essays for which he and *The New Yorker* became known, along with some drawings. His first duties there were mostly editing and administrative chores. When he told editor Harold Ross that he wanted to write more, Ross grudgingly agreed but said it would be considered part of his editorial duties and thus for no additional pay. For five months Thurber worked seven days a week, until he demanded a day off. His half-dozen casuals drew enough attention that Ross eventually, and still grudgingly, made him a writer. Somehow, Thurber and Ross remained friends and correspondents until Ross's death in 1951.

Thurber's marriage suffered several separations during this time, but he and his wife moved to a country home in Connecticut and in 1931 had a daughter, Rosemary. By 1935, though, they had divorced, and Thurber promptly married magazine editor Helen Wismer and left the staff of *The New Yorker*. He continued to sell casuals and drawings to the magazine. He had never paid much heed to money, but after Helen began to handle his finances, she told him that *The New Yorker* had routinely underpaid him.

In "The Triumphant Years," the letters show the Thurbers becoming good friends of Ronald and Jane Williams, young publishers of *The Bermudian*, and giving some essays to their struggling little paper. In 1937 James and Helen headed for Europe, where they spent more than a year, including four months on the French Riviera.

Thurber kept in close touch with White, but other friends also received his letters from Europe.

Autumn of 1938 saw the Thurbers back in the United States, renting houses in several Connecticut communities before buying what Thurber called "The Great Good Place," in West Cornwall. He was exceptionally productive in 1939, writing *Fables for Our Time*, *The Last Flower*, and "The Secret Life of Walter Mitty." He also wrote the play *The Male Animal*, in collaboration with Nugent in Los Angeles. This show opened in New York in early 1940 and gave Thurber a substantial income for the first time in his life.

Along with this success, however, 1939 also brought various health problems, including the beginning of his blindness. He had lost his left eye at age seven, while playing with his brother. Now his right eye began to fail him. In June he wrote to Dr. Gordon Bruce, "Life is no good to me at all unless I can read, type, and draw. I would sell out for 13 cents." Despite five operations, the eye continued to deteriorate. When he could not see to type, he used pencil and yellow copy paper but eventually hired a secretary. He managed to continue producing drawings up to 1951.

"The Challenging Years" is by far the largest of the five sections, spanning 322 pages and fourteen years. When World War II ended their vacation trips to Bermuda, the Thurbers started vacationing in Virginia. With gasoline rationed, they took an apartment in Manhattan. Thurber met Peter De Vries, editor of *Poetry Magazine*, in 1944, and they became loyal friends and correspondents. He helped De Vries get hired as poetry editor for *The New Yorker*. In 1945 *The Thurber Carnival* was published, showcasing his best writings and drawings to date.

Samuel Goldwyn bought the film rights to "The Secret Life of Walter Mitty" and hired Thurber to work with scriptwriter Ken Englund. All of Thurber's suggestions were rejected, however, and he was scornful of the outcome. He told *Life* magazine of his fear of the motion picture being "spoiled by one or more of Mr. [Danny] Kaye's . . . famous, but to me, deplorable scat or git-gat-gittle songs." Indeed, he wrote, "Mr. Goldwyn . . . substituted what is to me an utterly horrifying, shockingly out-of-taste-and-mood piece of scat."

Thurber had long been a big fan of radio, and his blindness led to him to listen to it even more frequently. That, in turn, led him to research the world of soap operas for his *New Yorker* series "Soapland." In 1947, more than a year before the series started, he wrote that his letters and literature on the subject already ran to a half-million words. He even suggested to Ross that *The New Yorker* could sponsor a soap opera. By 1950, Thurber was a frequent guest on radio and television programs. More of his work was being adapted to stage shows and music.

From the late 1930's, his book reviews, essays, and letters had frequently condemned the politics of the literary Left. In the 1950's, though, he became concerned about the excesses of the House Un-American Activities Committee. He refused an honorary degree from Ohio State University, to protest its screening of campus lecturers for any hints of "unamerican" ideas. "I have always been a vehement anti-communist . . . " he wrote to James Pollard at the journalism department, "but I have no doubt that like almost all writers, I will one day be named as a Red." By such censorship, he said, "the university deprives itself of a wonderful chance to heckle and confound such speakers."

In 1951, he drew a self-portrait for *Time* magazine and announced that it would be his last drawing. The next spring, a hyperthyroid condition was wrongly diagnosed and treated. This lasted almost two years. Sometimes unable to tie his shoes or to tolerate alcohol, he grew irritable.

In the book's last section, "The Twilight Years," Thurber researched a book about his quarter-century of association with *New Yorker* editor Ross. Preparing "The Years with Ross" engendered much correspondence, as he and former contributors reminisced in lengthy letters. It began to run in *The Atlantic Monthly* magazine in late 1957. Some of Ross's associates disliked it as overly critical of *The New Yorker* and its founder, but it was a big success.

In 1959 a Peter Sellers film, *The Battle of the Sexes*, was produced, based on Thurber's story "The Catbird Seat." The Broadway musical review *A Thurber Carnival*, made from Thurber's prose and art, drew good reviews in 1960. At age sixty-six and blind, Thurber even joined the cast, playing himself. A year later, he and Helen tried and failed to promote a British production of it. The effort left them dejected and tired. In October, Thurber suffered a brain hemorrhage in his hotel room. He died a month later.

For serious Thurber devotees, *The Thurber Letters* is an excellent vehicle for getting into this creative man's mind. For more casual fans, a little of it can go a long way. It has an adequate index, although some names seem to be indexed at the merest mention while some important names and events, such as the House Un-American Activities Committee and Helen Thurber's detached retina, which imperiled her role as "seeing-eye wife," are not to be found. Numerous index entries with subentries also have undifferentiated page numbers following the main entries.

To its credit, the book includes numerous drawings sent by Thurber to accompany his letters. Included is an eight-page gallery of photographs of the writer, his friends, and his family members, from the 1920's through 1960.

J. Edmund Rush

Review Sources

Book: The Magazine for the Reading Life, July/August, 2003, p. 26.
Commonweal 130, no. 18 (October 24, 2003): 28-29.
The Economist 368, no. 8338 (August 23, 2003): 67.
Kirkus Reviews 71, no. 11 (June 1, 2003): 790.
Library Journal 128, no. 13 (August 15, 2003): 84.
Los Angeles Times, August 10, 2003, p. R3.
The New York Times, July 31, 2003, p. E8.
The New York Times Book Review, August 10, 2003, p. 7.
Publishers Weekly 250, no. 21 (May 26, 2003): 60.
The Wall Street Journal, August 1, 2003, p. W10.

THE TIME OF OUR SINGING

Author: Richard Powers (1957-   )
Publisher: Farrar, Straus and Giroux (New York). 631
    pp. $27.00
Type of work: Novel
Time: From the late 1930's to 2000
Locale: New York City; Philadelphia; and Washington,
    D.C.; Oakland, California; Brussels, Belgium; various
    other European venues

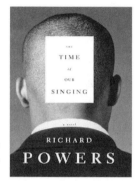

*The epic story of a German Jewish refugee and a musi-
cally talented American black woman and the family they
have together in a racially divided nation*

> *Principal characters:*
> DAVID "DA" STROM, a German Jewish refugee who teaches physics at
>   Columbia University
> DELIA DALEY, David's wife, a black American, musically talented
> JONAH STROM, their older son, an internationally successful professional
>   singer
> JOSEPH STROM, their younger son, a gifted pianist, Jonah's accompanist
> RUTH "ROOTIE" STROM, their youngest child, a racial activist
> DR. WILLIAM DALEY, Delia's father, a physician
> NETTIE ELLEN DALEY, Delia's mother
> TERESA WIERZBICKI, Joseph's lover
> ROBERT RIDER, Ruth's husband, a racial activist

On Easter morning, 1939, a crush of people have gathered on the Washington
Mall to hear a free concert by Marian Anderson, America's greatest contralto, who,
having gained an international reputation, has returned to the United States for a gru-
eling seventy-concert tour. When the Daughters of the American Revolution (DAR)
refuse Anderson the use of Constitution Hall because she is black, the concert,
through Eleanor Roosevelt's intervention, is moved to the Mall, where tens of thousands can attend. Delia, a voice student, has come to Washington, D.C., against the
admonitions of her father, Dr. William Daley, a physician in Philadelphia. He has
discouraged her musical pursuits in the hope that she will enter a profession, prefera-
bly law.

A mere pinpoint in the monumental crowd on the Mall, Delia, subvocalizing on the
train trip to Washington, D.C., continues to sing sotto voce as the concert proceeds.
Approaching the Mall to hear Anderson sing is David Strom, a Jewish refugee from
Nazi Germany. A scientist concerned with relativity and obsessed by such concepts
as curved time, Strom is a professor at Columbia University. A promising theoretical
physicist, David possesses scientific equipment consisting of his brain, a pencil, and a
notepad. His family in Europe has disappeared into the gaping maw of the Holocaust,

although, as is revealed late in the novel, his sister Hannah survives and returns to Germany. Delia's barely audible singing entices David.

Delia realizes more than David that a white Jewish refugee and a black American have no future because, in the eyes of most Americans, they are of different species. Despite their differences and the problems Delia knows will taint any relationship they might have, she and David are drawn irresistibly to each other and ultimately, against the counsel of Delia's family, they marry. *The Time of Our Singing* relates the story of their marriage and of their three offspring, all talented, all marked by the racial complexity that mixed marriages engendered at that time.

The two cannot go on a honeymoon because there is no public accommodation in the United States that will admit a mixed race couple. The story, of course, is about much more than a marriage and a family: It is a concise history of race relations in the United States from the late 1930's until the 1990's, including the days of the United States' greatest racial strife, the 1960's and 1970's. A controlling theme in the novel is alienation.

The Time of Our Singing is Richard Powers's eighth novel. Recipient of a MacArthur Fellowship, a Lannan Literary Award, and the James Fenimore Cooper Prize for Historical Fiction, Powers has been a finalist three times for the National Book Critics Award as well as a finalist for the National Book Award.

Powers has a commanding grasp of the sociopolitical forces that determined the course of American history during the torturous days when the murders of John F. and Robert Kennedy, Martin Luther King, Jr., Emmett Till, Malcolm X, and countless others filled headlines. He understands in considerable depth why the United States was burning in the 1960's and 1970's. He presents the details of these tensions through the eyes of the three Strom children, each of whom has a foot in two worlds, one black, the other white, but who belong in neither. The first-person narrator, Joseph Strom, lends to the story an immediacy and urgency that typifies first-person narration.

Initially, the Strom children are protected from much of the racial unrest in the Hamilton Heights section of New York City, where they live. As children, they have slight brushes with racial bullies, but Da, as David is called, and Delia decide to homeschool them, shielding them from the hazard of attending regular schools, public or private. The boys also protect their parents, not telling them about racial bullies who assault them in their neighborhood.

At the urging of Albert Einstein, one of Da's professional friends and associates, Da and Delia decide that Jonah must expand his musical education. He enters Boston's Boyleston Conservatory, where he is somewhat protected, although one student there proclaims that he is not supposed to eat a meal with a black person. The following year, when Joseph follows Jonah to Boyleston, the two are subjected to subtle racism but nothing like what they would have encountered in a typical New York City school.

The Time of Our Singing is essentially a *Bildungsroman* that traces intricately the development of three children from birth to maturity and, in Jonah's case, death. The Strom family begins as a happy and cohesive, if somewhat isolated, entity. Each child's life is family centered. The children all study with David and Delia. The family gathers for musical evenings in which the range of selections is daunting. By the time the children are eight or nine, each is moving irresistibly toward becoming a proficient musician.

Powers's comprehensive knowledge of music—such technical aspects of it as harmony and counterpoint as well as the vast areas of musical appreciation and musical history from Bach through bebop—is impressive, as is his mastery of the various dialects associated with his broad panoply of characters. He has a remarkable ear both for their music and for their talk. Added to these abilities is his solid grounding in physics that enables him to deal on a level of impressive professional expertise with the physics of time and space, both major concerns of David Strom.

The characters in this novel are vibrant, convincing, and beguiling. One identifies with them easily and genuinely cares about them and the outcomes of their lives as the novel proceeds. Joseph, the narrator, is particularly memorable. He is the middle child, the care giver, the one who sacrifices his own professional career, leaving Juilliard before graduation to be Jonah's accompanist. He considers Jonah's talent greater than his and generously sidetracks any personal ambitions he might harbor in order to further Jonah's career.

Jonah's career is intriguing. Blessed with a remarkable voice, Jonah is particularly sensitive about his race. He takes umbrage when a noted music critic reviews his Town Hall concert enthusiastically but predicts that he will be tops among black performers. When Jonah finally has an opportunity to sing at the Metropolitan Opera, he rejects the proffered contract because he is to be cast in a minor role. So substantial is his talent that the Met, remarkably, makes him another offer, this time to sing the lead role in *The Visitation* (1966), a Gunter Schuller opera that was taking Europe by storm. This time, however, Jonah refuses because the lead is identified throughout the score only as "The Negro." He cannot accept being cast in a role because of his color more than because of his abilities.

Jonah's racial stands veer toward the radical, although he struggles to remain apolitical, making music rather than racial politics the center of his life. He is, nevertheless, in Los Angeles when the Watts riot occurs, and he plunges into the middle of it, receiving injuries in the process. At the end of his life, when he has returned for an American concert tour from a long, self-imposed exile abroad, he again becomes involved in a race riot, this time being struck hard in the face by a policeman's baton. The next morning, he is found dead in his hotel room, not the victim of the clubbing but dead merely from having stopped breathing, seemingly from having given up.

The equilibrium of the Strom family's detached and somewhat idyllic existence ends when the boys are in their mid-teens and Rootie is ten. Jonah and Joseph, studying in Boston, are informed by their distraught father that Delia died when the furnace in their building exploded, causing a devastating fire. The boys return to New York, where they enroll at the Juilliard School of Music. Soon they take their own apartment in Greenwich Village and move toward establishing their careers.

Rootie remains at home with her father and Mrs. Samuels, his housekeeper. In time, however, Rootie, who has developed radical views, completely abandons her father, resenting him and questioning whether her mother's death was accidental. She marries Robert Rider, a member of the Black Panthers. Later, when an Oakland, California, policeman fires a rubber bullet into his knee, necessitating surgery, Robert dies as a result of the anesthesia. He and Rootie have two sons, Kwame and Robert, whose African name, Ode, is the name of a lost child Delia and David encountered during their first meeting on the Mall.

David Strom is diagnosed with pancreatic cancer and declines rapidly. Joseph, alone of the three children, sees his father through his final illness. In a death scene that rivals that of Ben Gant in Thomas Wolfe's *Look Homeward, Angel* (1929), Joseph is his father's greatest comfort. Jonah, living in Brussels and singing all over Europe, calls too late to come to his father's bedside. Rootie's whereabouts are unknown.

Joseph, no longer playing accompaniment for Jonah, who has moved to Europe, goes to Atlantic City, where he plays piano in a bar. There he meets Teresa Wierzbicki and develops a relationship with her, which alienates her from her racist father. The two continue their relationship until Jonah needs Joseph to sing bass in a group he is forming. Joseph leaves Teresa and flies to Brussels, where he spends several years touring with Jonah's group. Finally, however, learning of the death of Rootie's husband, he flies home and meets Rootie at their grandparents' home in Philadelphia, to which Rootie has retreated in her grief.

Finally, Joseph returns to Oakland with Rootie and her sons to become a music teacher in a primary school that Rootie establishes to honor her husband. Presumably, Joseph will spend what life remains to him teaching at the school. His nephew Robert, awesomely bright and musically gifted, seems destined to carry on the family tradition. Jonah visits Joseph when his group appears in Berkeley, then continues to Los Angeles, where he becomes involved in the 1992 riots following Rodney King's beating by the local police.

Seemingly, what remains of the Strom family will be associated more with the black world than with the white, although its future generations may do much to change the status of blacks in the United States. A major theme in this novel is recurrence but not the eternal recurrence described by Friedrich Nietzsche so much as that suggested by Arnold Toynbee, in which many elements of history are repeated but at increasingly higher levels of achievement.

The Time of Our Singing is clearly Powers's most accessible novel to date, yet no intellectual compromise has occurred to make it accessible. It has an intricate plot whose structure involves a multilevel time line, a criss-crossing of dates that provides a strong inner cohesion for the complex story Powers constructs. Speaking analogically, one might say that *The Time of Our Singing* is to Powers's *The Gold Bug Variations* (1991) as James Joyce's *A Portrait of the Artist as a Young Man* (1916) is to *Ulysses* (1924).

R. Baird Shuman

Review Sources

The Atlantic Monthly 241 (January/February, 2003): 190-193.
Booklist 99, no. 4 (October 15, 2002): 390.
The Economist 366, no. 8309 (February 1, 2003): 71.
Harper's Magazine 103, no. 1832 (January, 2003): 69-70.
Kirkus Reviews 70, no. 20 (November 15, 2002): 1500-1501.
Library Journal 127, no. 18 (November 1, 2002): 130.
New York 35, no. 2 (January 20-27, 2003): 68-69, 99.
The New York Times Book Review, January 26, 2003, p. 12-13.
The New York Times Book Review, February 23, 2003, p. 31.
The New Yorker 79 (January 11, 2003): 85-86.
Publishers Weekly 249, no. 40 (October 7, 2002): 50.

TO BEGIN THE WORLD ANEW
The Genius and Ambiguities of the American Founders

Author: Bernard Bailyn (1922-   )
Publisher: Alfred A. Knopf (New York). Illustrated. 185
pp. $26.00
Type of work: History
Time: The eighteenth and early nineteenth centuries
Locale: The original American colonies and Paris

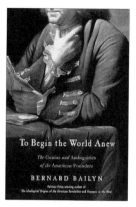

A *distinguished historian examines the ambiguities,*
complexities, and achievements of some of the most bril-
liant of the American Founding Fathers

Principal personages:
> JOHN ADAMS, an American representative at
> a peace conference in Paris in 1776-1777
> and second president of the United States
> BENJAMIN FRANKLIN, another peace conference representative, an inter-
> nationally recognized statesman
> THOMAS JEFFERSON, a diplomat, statesman, and third president of the
> United States
> ALEXANDER HAMILTON, an author of the *Federalist* papers and cabinet
> member
> JAMES MADISON, an author of the *Federalist* papers and fourth president
> of the United States

The five essays in this small book are based on various addresses to scholarly audiences—author Bernard Bailyn does not specify the occasions—which have been tai-
lored to suit the needs of a more general readership. Two of them seem particularly
suited to this wider audience. The first of these, "Jefferson and the Ambiguities of
Freedom," presents not just the ambiguities of freedom but also the ambiguities in the
complex being who was Thomas Jefferson. Of course, the record of Jefferson's life,
unusually detailed for his time, has given critics ample opportunities to discover his
inconsistencies. Jefferson furnished many of these opportunities himself by leaving
behind no fewer than nineteen thousand letters and by aspiring to a career of political
leadership.

Social background and personal inclination made this gentleman farmer a vigorous proponent of states' rights. The eight years of his presidency presented internal
and external threats to the young nation that forced him to accept a degree of federalism that he must have found alarming. The growth of northern industrial and banking
interests, which he hated and feared, drove him to abandon his former, and undoubtedly sincere, opposition to the expansion of slavery in the hope of maintaining the
precarious balance of power between North and South.

The actions of his presidency, often regarded as his best and worst, contributed to

Bernard Bailyn is Adams University Professsor Emeritus and director of the International Seminar on the Atlantic World at Harvard University. His previous books have been awarded two Pulitzer Prizes, a Bancroft Prize, and a National Book Award for History.

the image of hypocrite painted by his opponents, then and later. The Louisiana Purchase, which doubled the size of the nation, rendered a great increase in federal power inevitable. Jefferson's call for the Embargo Act of 1807 (devised, Bailyn argues, as an idealistic antidote to war with Great Britain) succeeded in benefiting the unscrupulous rich, injuring the poor whose plight Jefferson wished to ameliorate, and merely postponing the war that broke out five years later. His early role as articulator of American democratic ideals and his role a quarter-century later as president struggling with practical problems that forced compromise with those ideals left him perpetually exposed to hostile criticism. It is clear that the exigencies of eight years as chief executive forced Jefferson to trim his political sails.

Bailyn recognizes, however, that the evidence does not account for the "peculiarly venomous" judgments by his harsher critics, a number of whom he quotes. In defending Jefferson against what he clearly regards as the unfairness of many of the charges in such works as Leonard Levy's *Jefferson and Civil Liberties: The Darker Side* (1963), Michael Zuckerman's *Almost Chosen People* (1993), and Conor Cruise O'Brien's *The Long Affair: Thomas Jefferson and the French Revolution, 1785-1900* (1996), Bailyn argues that Jefferson's rare combination of political realism and radical idealism led him into "intractable dilemmas" that not even his brilliant mind could resolve.

These intellectual polarities appeared early. Having been elected to the Virginia House of Burgesses at age twenty-six and chosen to draft the Declaration of Independence at thirty-three, young Jefferson was forced into an awareness of the complexities of reconciling idealistic theory and the demands of practical politics. In the short compass of the Declaration of Independence, for instance, magnificent political idealism consorts with unsparing fixation on the harsh realities of British colonial rule.

In another essay Bailyn examines the illustrious collection of political arguments known as the *Federalist* papers, intended by its principal authors, James Madison and Alexander Hamilton, to allay a variety of fears regarding a potentially dangerous document—the proposed Constitution of the United States—and permit its passage. In the minds of thoughtful citizens of the new nation (a remarkably numerous group, according to Bailyn), the central power represented by a federal constitution contained the threat of reestablishment of the old European tyrannies and the evisceration of the sovereign states that had formed the federation.

Bailyn's essay helps the present-day citizen, who tends to take the benefits of that document for granted, understand those fears and the achievement of the *Federalist* authors in convincing those earlier citizens that the system of checks and balances devised by the Founding Fathers offered them adequate protection.

The *Federalist* papers are not just a historically significant document that assuaged the concerns of people who lived more than two hundred years ago but a work that scholars, lawyers, and judges have studied, analyzed, and venerated over the years.

Judges of the United States Supreme Court have cited the papers nearly 300 times, 194 times in the second half of the twentieth century alone. Judges on the left and right characteristically buttress their points by means of articles of the Constitution itself, the Court's prior decisions, and previous cases and laws. These same judges also opt, time after time, to cite a source that is not an integrated philosophical treatise but a collection of hastily contrived political arguments by men of sharply contrasting political views at a time when many of the issues facing the governments of today could not even be imagined.

In Bailyn's view, the makers of the *Federalist* papers succeeded so far beyond their own scope because they managed to remain true to the revolutionary spirit while encouraging the development of a constitution that formed the basis of an effective national government. Despite the intense pressures that the task imposed on them, Madison and Hamilton—and John Jay, who wrote five of the eighty-five papers—reached a level of profundity beyond that of the many other political essayists who engaged in the debate over the Constitution. Bailyn insists that "their political problems at the deepest level are ours; and we share their cautious optimism that personal freedom and national power—the preservation of private rights and the maintenance of public safety—can be compatible."

Two of Bailyn's essays come extensively illustrated. In "Politics and the Creative Imagination" he applies art critic Kenneth Clark's distinction between "metropolitan" and "provincial" art to the politics of the American Revolution. Metropolitan art is a product of long-established cultural centers and reflects a tradition of artistic assumptions and standards; provincial art emerges from a more peripheral or remote locality in which standards must, to a considerable extent, be created anew. Success is, of course, possible in both styles, but both are liable to weaknesses. Metropolitan art is subject to creative fatigue, repetition, overelaboration of past successes. Provincial art is subject to narrowness, insularity, and regressive primitivism. Bailyn offers visual contrasts of European metropolitan achievements in architecture and portraiture with their American provincial counterparts and suggests analogies with the political thought of the Revolutionary era. The Founding Fathers, though hardly ignorant of European political assumptions, nevertheless found it not only desirable but also necessary to reimagine the art of politics and reinvent political institutions.

Another lavishly illustrated essay, "Realism and Idealism in American Diplomacy," takes as its starting point Felix Gilbert's controversial *To the Farewell Address: Ideas of Early American Policy* (1961). The German-born Gilbert's background in Renaissance political history and his experience of Nazism and World War II give him an unusual perspective on the roots of American diplomacy. At critical points in American foreign policy, Gilbert argues, the achievements of its diplomats have resulted from a felicitous combination of two strains of thought that have tended to compete with each other over the decades: realism and idealism.

Gilbert exemplifies his thesis most thoroughly with the draft treaty produced by the Continental Congress of 1776 and taken to Europe by John Adams as a model of the new idealism that its authors hoped to introduce into the foreign policy of the new nation and perhaps inject into the larger world of European power politics. Bailyn concentrates his attention on Adams's colleague, the charismatic Benjamin Franklin, who charmed Europeans far more than did the dour and stodgy Adams. The second half of the essay incorporates some two dozen images (mostly by French artists in various media) of Franklin, the man who embodied American idealism in the minds of Europeans.

In the fifth and concluding essay, "Atlantic Dimensions," Bailyn examines the influence of the American federalist Constitution on other nations of Europe and of the Western Hemisphere, the most significant being Switzerland, Chile, and Argentina. The question of the extent to which the American political situation and experience can be applied in nations marked by differing values and beliefs is an interesting one at this time of discussion about the appropriateness and viability of applying American ideas of constitutional democracy to nations with long histories of repressive regimes.

The essay on Jefferson is the most provocative of the five—and the one most subject to serious criticism. Bailyn's explanation of the third president's tarnished image as a consequence of the conflicting claims of political idealism and realpolitik is certainly disputable. Abraham Lincoln, although not sharing with Jefferson the experience of participating in the establishment of American constitutional government, did contemplate it deeply. He shared a similar idealistic viewpoint even while faced with perilous presidential decisions during the nation's worst constitutional crisis. These decisions were at least as controversial as Jefferson's, and some of them probably made Lincoln even more despised in his own time.

If Jefferson's ambiguities with respect to slavery have raised the suspicions of critics, so have Lincoln's. Jefferson kept slaves, but Lincoln expressed willingness to maintain the peculiar institution, if necessary, to save the union. His doing so threatened an outcome not only more disastrous for African Americans but perilous to the integrity of the Constitution itself in the long run. Posterity, however, loves Lincoln in a way it does not love Jefferson. Just as the Jefferson Memorial's out-of-the-way site in Washington, D.C., does not adequately explain its relative obscurity compared to the revered Washington Monument and Lincoln Memorial, Jefferson's "double role" does not account for his more precarious reputation. Another possible explanation for Jefferson's sullied repute is the recognition by historians and students of history that this indisputably great man was also a deeply flawed one, although his critics may not agree on the nature of the flaws.

Bailyn may not have succeeded in saving Jefferson from his detractors, but in this and the other essays he has vividly recreated the efforts of the extraordinary men who managed the issues and conflicts that might otherwise have overwhelmed the infant republic. Unlike the writings that established Bailyn's towering reputation as American historiographer, *To Begin the World Anew* is not the work of fresh scholarship but a compact volume of seasoned reflections arising from his many years of study of the American Revolution and the achievements of the nation's great early leaders. As such, it is a most accessible and stimulating book for readers not previously acquainted with his work.

Robert P. Ellis

Review Sources

Booklist 99, no. 7 (December 1, 2002): 643.
Commentary 115, no. 2 (February, 2003): 68-70.
Journal of American History 90, no. 3 (December, 2003): 999-1000.
Kirkus Reviews 70, no. 21 (November 1, 2002): 1581.
New Leader 85, no. 6 (November/December, 2002): 32-34.
The New Republic 228, no. 22 (June 9, 2003): 33-37.
The New York Review of Books 50, no. 2 (February 13, 2003): 38-41.
The New York Times Book Review, February 16, 2003, p. 11.
Publishers Weekly 249, no. 46 (Novemer 18, 2002): 50.

TO CONQUER THE AIR
The Wright Brothers and the Great Race for Flight

Author: James Tobin (1956-   )
Publisher: Free Press (New York). 432 pp. $28.00
Type of work: Biography and history
Time: 1899-1948
Locale: Dayton, Ohio; Fort Myer, Virginia; Kitty Hawk, North Carolina; New York; Washington, D.C.; and Le Mans, France

A history of the birth of aviation and two of the men who made it possible, the Wright brothers

> *Principal personages:*
> WILBUR WRIGHT, an inventor and coowner of the Wright Cycle Company
> ORVILLE WRIGHT, his brother and business partner, also an inventor
> KATHARINE WRIGHT, their sister
> MILTON WRIGHT, their father
> SAMUEL PIERPONT LANGLEY, the secretary of the Smithsonian Institution and an aviation pioneer
> GLENN HAMMOND CURTISS, one of the Wright brothers' rival aviators

Perhaps the easiest question to answer in the history of technology concerns who invented the airplane. Virtually any schoolchild will state that it was Wilbur Wright (1867-1912) and his brother Orville (1871-1948). Most Americans also know that the brothers first flew their new machine in 1903 at Kitty Hawk, North Carolina. This is more than just an idle recitation of historical facts, for the Wright brothers have become synonymous with the great American myth of the self-made man: the belief that, through industry, an independent man can achieve fame and wealth. In short, they are American icons. While a century of powered flight undoubtedly invites a reexamination of its origins, this must have been a daunting task for author James Tobin. *To Conquer the Air* more than justifies revisiting this well-known territory, if only for the skill with which its author recounts the Wrights' inspiring story.

Nowadays it is difficult to conceive of a world without powered flight. People accept air travel as a necessity of the modern world, one that is vital to both commerce and international relations. Flight as an activity is so commonplace that airplanes have become little more than buses with wings. When Tobin's story begins, in the year 1899, the idea of practical powered flight was deemed by most people to be folly and its proponents to be little more than crackpots. Of course, flying by balloon had been known since the eighteenth century, and by the early twentieth century the first dirigibles had astonished the public with their graceful flights. These vessels, however, were lighter than air: Lift was created by means of heated air or gases such as hydrogen. The kind of travel envisioned by the Wrights was something resembling the flight of birds—a self-propelled craft that could be controlled by a pilot and that would be able to fly in a wide range of wind conditions. This may strike the modern reader as a modest, even elementary proposal, but Tobin's lucid text demonstrates that it was a bold idea and its attainment revolutionary.

James Tobin, who won the National Book Critics Circle Award for Ernie Pyle's War: America's Eyewitness to World War II *(1997) and is the author of* Great Projects: The Epic Story of the Building of America from the Taming of the Mississippi to the Invention of the Internet *(2001). He also won the J. Anthony Lukas Work-in-Progress Award in 2000 for* To Conquer the Air.

Aside from the Wrights, the leading American pioneer in aviation was Samuel Pierpont Langley (1834-1906), the secretary of the Smithsonian Institution. One of the joys of reading Tobin's work is encountering the striking contrasts and similarities between Langley and the Wrights. Curiously, both the Wrights and Langley lacked college diplomas at a time when serious scientific inquiry was increasingly relegated to academics in specialized fields. Langley found his way into the scientific establishment through his considerable research skills and his impressive social pedigree as a Boston Brahmin. The Wright clan was not entirely unlettered, though, for their sister Kate was a graduate of Oberlin College and a teacher of Latin. Unlike the well-born Langley, the Wrights were midwesterners of modest means; while the brothers lacked formal academic credentials, they compensated for this by an unlimited capacity for hard work and a disciplined curiosity.

Surprisingly, a fairly intense intellectual atmosphere pervaded the Wright home. Milton, the family patriarch, was a pugnacious bishop in the Church of the United Brethren in Christ. Pervasive factionalism within the church—mostly thanks to Bishop Wright himself—demanded well-constructed written and oral arguments. As the eldest son, Wilbur Wright was often called upon to defend his father in the aging patriarch's numerous church squabbles, and as such he proved himself to be a keen intellect with a quick wit. Tobin liberally quotes Wilbur from newspaper accounts to great effect, carefully underscoring the subtle irony that reporters failed to detect.

Even so, the Wrights' accomplishment is impressive when one considers their chief rival. Wilbur began serious investigations into the nature of flight in 1899. Langley had by that time been conducting his own research for some thirteen years and had the considerable resources of the Smithsonian Institution at his disposal. His experimental airplanes had evolved from small, handheld models to larger steam-driven, unmanned craft that could fly as far as a mile. By 1899 the War Department's Board of Ordnance and Fortification had allocated an initial fund of twenty-five thousand dollars for the construction of a piloted version of Langley's aircraft.

Unlike Langley, whose designs developed as a result of incessant experimentation, Wilbur Wright began his studies with a crucial insight gleaned from his observations of birds in flight. By warping or twisting wings, he discovered that one could exert control over a flying surface, something he proved through his experiments with kites. This was one of the fundamental discoveries of the Wright brothers, and it indicates a telling difference between Langley's approach and theirs. When Langley and his assistants developed a model that flew well in calm air, they essentially ceased further aerodynamic research in their quest for a gasoline engine that could power it. For the Wrights, engines were of less concern than steering and balance. Their goal from the beginning was to create a glider capable of controlled flight, and only when that was achieved would they add an engine. The resulting vehicle would be capable of flying, like a bird, under changing wind conditions—that is, a practical flying machine. In the driest of tones, Wilbur Wright disdained Langley's method of designing craft only for calm air: "Unfortunately, the wind usually blows."

An examination of the rivalry between these two schools of aeronautical research inevitably invites comparison with the biblical David and Goliath. The Wright brothers were limited both in the amount of financial resources available (they paid for it themselves) and in the time they could spend on the project (they conducted the research at Kitty Hawk during vacations). Langley's aerodrome—as he termed his flying machine—was a classic example of a government contract gone awry, complete with a final product that was twenty thousand dollars over budget and unable to perform as promised. While Langley's team labored four years to create a combustion engine capable of driving their ungainly craft, the Wrights' design for their Flyer was such that it only required a fairly ordinary engine. From design to fabrication, the power plant producing the Flyer required only some six weeks, a considerable tribute to their mechanical skills as well as the design of the aircraft itself. Incredibly, all of the Wrights' research up to and including the first powered flight of 1903 cost them just under one thousand dollars. To Tobin's credit, he interweaves these two narrative strands with great dexterity, providing a compelling account of a tale whose conclusion the reader already anticipates.

Aside from differences in method, the Wrights had other traits that served them well in their quest for mastery of the air. First and foremost was their ability to visualize something clearly even before they built it. A second element that made their success possible was just sheer mechanical genius, and this was especially true of Orville. In one of Tobin's most telling anecdotes, he describes how the younger brother once made a working printing press out of a headstone and some scrap materials. This was Yankee ingenuity raised to an entirely new level.

Perhaps the most significant contributing factor to the Wrights' success was what might be called their management style, something that Tobin adumbrates but does not address directly. Langley, with his patrician heritage, embodied an approach that has come to be known as top-down management: He and he alone conducted the preliminary research for his aerodrome, and he was solely responsible for the decision to develop a full-scale machine from a relatively modest model. No one within Langley's group would have dared to question, let alone challenge, the secretary on matters aeronautical.

As Tobin's text reveals, the situation with the Wrights could not have been more different. As the elder brother, Wilbur was undoubtedly the driving force within the duo, but his ideas alone did not prevail. The brothers would often argue heatedly over points of design and sometimes reverse their positions before coming to a consensus.

The result was a kind of dual testing process, between the two brothers as well as in actual experimentation. To the world, however, the Wright brothers always appeared to be of one mind on everything, often working together in near silence for hours.

Another reason for their success was the fact that they tried to understand all of the forces at play in flight. They excelled where others failed because, "They broke a job into its parts and proceeded one part at a time. They practiced each small task until they mastered it, then moved on. It didn't sound like much, but it avoided discouragement and led to success." This is essential to a full understanding of the Wrights' accomplishment, and it has to do with the enormity of their task. Like the other aviation pioneers, they understood that the wind was a significant force capable of sustaining heavier-than-air objects. The Wrights were attempting to control a flying machine in three axes, roll (rocking from side to side), pitch (the up-and-down movement of the nose and tail), and yaw (turning from side to side).

Other experimenters had accomplished much in showing how humans could glide in calm air, and the Wrights had, in fact, based their own research upon the work of German Otto Lilienthal (1848-1896). Even the so-called experts in aeronautics, however, failed initially to grasp what the Wrights were doing. This meant that few would accept the brothers' claims of having achieved powered flight until they had seen it for themselves, and as Tobin's text beautifully illustrates, the effect was both shocking and thrilling. People often stood slack-jawed and trembled as they watched man and machine become one with the birds. The result was a paradigm shift—a fundamental change in the way human beings perceived themselves in the world.

Tobin elucidates this idea in the high point of the book, Wilbur's demonstration flight over New York Harbor during the Hudson-Fulton Celebration in 1909. At the time, the Wrights were locked in a bitter controversy with fellow air pioneer Glenn Curtiss (1878-1930) over who was the first to achieve mastery of the air. When Curtiss bowed out of the exhibition due to high winds, Wilbur dispelled all doubts by flying his machine against the wind along Curtiss's projected route from Governor's Island to Grant's Tomb and back. Tobin views this as the Wrights' moment of triumph. For those who are technologically jaded, *To Conquer the Air* lets one feel what it was like at the birth of the airplane.

Cliff Prewencki

Review Sources

The Economist 367, no. 8327 (June 7, 2003): 75.
Forbes, May 26, 2003, FYI Supplement, p. 86-87.
Library Journal 128, no. 5 (March 15, 2003): 98-99.
Publishers Weekly 250, no. 7 (February 17, 2003): 65-66.

A TRAGIC HONESTY
The Life and Work of Richard Yates

Author: Blake Bailey
Publisher: Picador (New York). 656 pp. $35.00
Type of work: Literary biography
Time: 1926-1992
Locale: Westchester, New York; Greenwich Village, New York; Paris; and Iowa

A riveting account of a major figure in contemporary fiction, told with unblinking candor and compassion

> *Principal personages:*
> RICHARD YATES, an American novelist
> SHEILA BRYANT, his first wife
> MARTHA SPEER, his second wife
> GINA, MONICA, and SHARON YATES, his daughters
> RUTH YATES, his mother
> VINCENT YATES, his father
> GRACE SCHULMAN, a poet and friend of Yates
> JERRY SCHULMAN, Grace's husband, a friend of Yates
> R. V. CASSILL, a novelist and friend of Yates
> WILLIAM STYRON, a novelist and friend of Yates
> GEORGE GARRETT, a novelist, poet, and friend of Yates
> JOHN FRANKENHEIMER, the film director who wanted to film Yates's
> 1961 novel *Revolutionary Road*
> ROBERT KENNEDY, a politician who employed Yates as a speechwriter

Blake Bailey does not spare the reader Richard Yates's agonies—his lifelong alcoholism, psychotic episodes, failed marriages, and doubts about the value of his writing—any more than Yates spared his characters their indignities. April and Frank Wheeler, the principal figures in his greatest novel, *Revolutionary Road* (1961), begin their marriage in a 1950's Connecticut suburb—terrain familiar to readers of John Updike and John Cheever, to whom Yates has often been compared—with a sense of superiority, a dream of greatness that they manifestly will not be able to fulfill. It is an old story, the gap between aspiration and achievement, but Yates redeems the cliché by the vividness of his observations and his unrelenting, unsentimental revelation that this couple is not much different from their mediocre neighbors. This Fitzgerald/Gatsby fable of thwarted dreams would become Yates's signature tale, told again and again in exquisitely wrought stories and novels that critics praised for their art and condemned for their pessimism. As a result, Yates failed to capture the larger audience that gravitated toward Cheever and Updike. Yates might have been in the running for awards, but he was the kind of writer who always just missed the prize.

Perhaps Bailey will be the one finally to thrust Yates into the literary canon. Bailey has written not merely a splendid biography of Yates—one that makes a compelling case for his subject's greatness and explains why he has been neglected—but also one of the most moving and engrossing literary biographies of modern times. Bailey seductively interweaves the facts and fiction of Yates's life into a fine mesh of life and literature, which, the biographer candidly notes, cannot always be disentangled. First drafts of Yates's work used real names, and even the final drafts made only superficial changes, so that, for ex-

Blake Bailey has published extensively in newspapers, magazines, and literary journals, including The Gettysburg Review, The New England Review, *and* Night Train. *He lives in northern Florida with his wife, Mary Brinkmeyer.*

ample, his mother's nickname, Dookie, becomes Pookie. Mark Twain once said that history did not repeat itself, it rhymed. That is how Yates used fiction—as a kind of rhyme for his life.

Literary life is often portrayed as a competitive free-for-all; it may be that, but it can also be a heroic world in which writers like R. V. Cassill, Grace Schulman, and George Garrett treat Yates with an uplifting generosity and respect. Cassill, for example, made sure schools hired Yates for writing positions, and Schulman and her husband welcomed the bedraggled writer into their homes even when he was at his most paranoid. He did finally wear this couple out, but they retained and shared with Bailey their fond memories and their exasperation with a literary genius.

There is a good deal of humor in this book. The passage on Yates learning how to drive is priceless. There is also touching humor in the writer's effort to become a middle-class, dependable guy. His ex-wife told Bailey about an incident in which Yates set out to burn some trash in the back of his home. She heard him swearing but assumed he was just engaging in his usual bumbling attempt to prove he was competent to perform daily chores. Next she saw her husband dancing around a brushfire, which got out of control and resulted in a call to the local volunteer fire department. Afterward, in true Yatesian fashion, the writer signed up for duty and attended the fire department's weekly Saturday meetings.

Somehow, Bailey manages to make both the comic and the grim episodes of his subject's life absorbing. This may be because Yates put so much of his life into his fiction. Consequently, the biographer is spared the usual awkward shift from discussing the writer's work to narrating his life. It is as if Yates's whole life is material for his writing, and the biographer needs only to track the writer's import of fact into his fiction. Bailey's achievement is no accident, however, for it takes an exquisite sensibility to know just how much to tell of each part of Yates's life. This is a long account, but it is never too long because all of the details have an overwhelming cumulative effect.

An unexpected treat in this biography is a visit to the Kennedy White House. In a most improbable turn of events, Yates is invited to become a speechwriter for Robert F. Kennedy. Yates had no particular interest in politics, no affection for the Kennedys, or any desire—other than to earn money—to obtain such politically sensitive employment. He thrived working for Kennedy, though, writing speeches that made the master politician seem far more eloquent than Yates ever found him to be in person. Robert F. Kennedy speaking on civil rights became, in effect, Richard Yates on civil rights.

To give Kennedy his due, he treated Yates with great respect, even after he learned about the latter's mental problems stemming from alcohol and drug abuse. Although Yates remained a hired hand, Kennedy seemed to recognize and value great talent. So did fellow writer William Styron, who never tired of giving Yates a helping hand and who remained absolutely committed to his vision of Yates's genius. So did filmmaker John Frankenheimer, who tried again and again to bring a film version of *Revolutionary Road* to fruition. That he did not is one of those mystifying Hollywood stories that are all too familiar.

Although Yates was a genius recognized by his fellow writers, and though certain reviewers and critics hailed his achievements, somehow he never quite made it into the pantheon of contemporary fiction writers. In part, this is because his output was erratic, both in terms of the overall quality of his work and because he did not steadily produce a book every two or three years. A contributing factor to his failure (as he saw it) to win supreme critical favor can also be explained in terms of his dedication to realism. Although he was nearly always an exquisite stylist, he remained faithful to the tradition of F. Scott Fitzgerald, which meant that Yates wrote social fiction and eschewed the pyrotechnics of experimental novelists such as Robert Coover, whose vogue in the 1970's enraged Yates. Finally, there is the fact that Yates's first novel, *Revolutionary Road*, was considered his best by many critics, and so he had forever to confront the idea that he had not lived up to his promise.

Author Bailey seems untroubled by the idea that different writers attain their peak performances at different points in their careers—some even with their first books. Yates continued to write first-rate fiction throughout his career, which is what makes his personal struggle just to stay alive as his use of drink and drugs debilitates him a heroic story. Yates never stopped writing, even if it meant he was strapped to oxygen tanks and barely had enough money to eat and a place to sleep.

There is a curious, saintlike quality in Yates that emerges as he grows older. A man of limited culinary interests, he ate at the same tavern day after day. The staff, particularly his waitress and the establishment's owner, reserved a booth for the writer and became attuned to his moods and health crises. Even though these were not literary afficionados, even though Yates did not seem to share that much of his creative life with them, something in his deliberate manner and the way he conducted himself deeply impressed these people who had not read a word of his writing.

The responses of Yates's readers and his students were much the same. Yates never really wanted to teach, although he spent several years at the famous program at the University of Iowa, the Iowa Writers' Workshop. He needed the money, not the teaching experience. His students revered him, however, and he took their work seriously, including them in the world of literature, so to speak, that he lived in to the exclusion of all else—except for his daughters. While his relationship with them was ambivalent, his keen interest in their lives was always apparent, and he never got over the terrible feeling that he let them down because of his wayward life.

There is a fablelike quality to Yates's life—or it becomes fablelike because Bailey has seen better than anyone else how exemplary his subject's biography became. How fitting, if harrowing, to find Yates at the end of his life living in spartan fashion—in a room with almost no decoration or amenities and stripped bare of anything that might take his interest away from literature. In the end, that is all Yates had—his literature and his devotion to it. Nothing else finally mattered. Living in such austerity, he became a kind of sage of literature and one to be valued all the more because he had not "sold out."

Of course, Yates wanted success, and he even would have liked to be popular and earn a fortune. He spent some time in Hollywood, writing screenplays for his works and those of others. Nothing much came of this enterprise, although he seems to have turned himself into a good screenwriter. All this was sideshow. He could not stay in Hollywood for long, and he always knew that he belonged by himself in a room, writing a novel or one of his classic short stories.

Carl Rollyson

Review Sources

Booklist 99, nos. 19/20 (June 1, 2003): 1733.
The Boston Globe, July 13, 2003, p. B1.
Kirkus Reviews 71, no. 9 (May 1, 2003): 651.
Library Journal 128, no. 5 (March 15, 2003): 84.
The New York Times, June 26, 2003, p. E1.
The New York Times Book Review, August 3, 2003, p. 10.
The New Yorker 79, no. 29 (October 6, 2003): 118.
Publishers Weekly 250, no. 18 (May 5, 2003): 207.
San Francisco Chronicle, August 3, 2003, p. M2.
The Wall Street Journal, July 3, 2003, p. D8.
The Washington Post, June 29, 2003, p. T12.

THE TRIALS OF PHILLIS WHEATLEY
America's First Black Poet and Her Encounters with the Founding Fathers

Author: Henry Louis Gates, Jr. (1950-   )
Publisher: Basic *Civitas* Books (New York). 129 pp. $18.95
Type of work: Literary biography and literary criticism
Time: The late eighteenth century
Locale: Boston

The intellectual encounter between the admirers of Wheatley and President Thomas Jefferson sparked a controversy that would result in the founding of the African American literary tradition

Principal personages:
> PHILLIS WHEATLEY, a young slave born in Africa and brought to America as a child, a prodigy who learned to read and write English and Latin and created an impressive body of poetry
> THOMAS JEFFERSON, third president of the United States, who had read Wheatley's poetry but judged her and all Africans as intellectually inferior to white people
> THE COMMITTEE, composed of eighteen prominent Bostonians who met formally in 1772 to question Wheatley to determine whether she was the author of the poems she claimed to have written

This essay is an expanded version of the lecture Henry Louis Gates, Jr., presented at the Library of Congress in March, 2002, as one of a series of the prestigious Jefferson Lectures in the Humanities. In his analysis of the controversy surrounding Phillis Wheatley's poetry, Gates demonstrates that theoretical issues debated in the academy are indeed relevant to the everyday lives of Americans. Gates, chairman of the Department of African and African American Studies at Harvard University, is a prominent intellectual. In his preface he states that the National Endowment for the Humanities, in honoring him by inviting him to lecture, acknowledges the importance of African American studies in the intellectual life of the United States.

His extended argument is crafted to explain how Thomas Jefferson and Wheatley were instrumental in founding the tradition of African American literature. An exchange of letters between a French diplomat and Jefferson debated the question of the intellectual potential of African slaves. The controversy continued throughout the first half of the nineteenth century and was a central issue in the abolitionist movement.

Gates has demonstrated throughout a prolific publishing career his mastery of a variety of literary genres, from personal memoir to academic critical theory. In this essay he writes for a general audience, presenting his argument in forceful, eloquent prose. He tells a compelling story, with frequent witty references to topical issues. Although securely grounded in his identity as an African American, Gates argues that the reading and interpretation of literature must be free of racial bias. Despite the explosive growth in the past thirty years of publication of creative works and literary criticism in African American studies, many readers will not be familiar with Wheatley's life and work, so Gates provides the necessary biographical and historical background.

On October 8, 1772, Phillis Wheatley was called before a committee of eighteen prominent Bostonians who had gathered to judge whether the celebrated young poet was an imposter. The larger issue at stake was one widely debated in eighteenth century America and Europe: Did Africans have the intellectual capacity to create literature? At the heart of this question was the contemporary belief that Africans were a subspecies, existing somewhere between the apes and civilized humans. The confrontation between Wheatley and her interrogators was important. If she, an African, could create original literature, she must be recognized as fully human. Slavery, justified at that time by assuming the racial inferiority of Africans, would therefore be morally indefensible.

Henry Louis Gates, Jr., is chairman of the Department of African and African American Studies and the director of the W. E. B. Du Bois Institute for African and African American Research at Harvard University. He is the coeditor of Africana: The Encyclopedia of the African and African American Experience *(1999).*

Wheatley had arrived in Boston on a sailing ship from West Africa in 1761. She was estimated to be seven or eight years old at the time because she had lost her front baby teeth. Although her birthplace was unknown, Gates speculates that she spoke Wolof, a West African language. She was purchased as a house slave by John Wheatley, a successful merchant, for his wife Susanna, who named the child Phillis after the ship that had brought her to America.

The Wheatleys' daughter Mary taught Phillis to read and write both English and Latin. She was, without question, an immensely gifted child. In 1767 she began publishing her poetry in periodicals and broadsheets, poems printed on a single piece of paper and sold on the street. The public in both England and America gave her poetry an enthusiastic reception. She wrote primarily elegies and panegyrics, or praises for current events and well-known people. Her predominant form was the heroic couplet, pairs of rhymed lines in iambic pentameter, in the style of English poet Alexander Pope.

Placing Wheatley in the context of eighteenth century racial beliefs, Gates draws on the complex theories of such philosophers as Francis Bacon, Immanuel Kant, and David Hume to frame the public debate on the question of the humanity of Africans. He quotes extensively from contemporary texts to illustrate popular beliefs, many of which would appall twenty-first century readers.

In the light of this controversy, Wheatley was a disturbing force in a society that questioned her humanity. The outcome of this trial by eminent Bostonians would have important social and political implications and would, Gates argues, revolutionize American literature. Because no transcripts of the event exist, Gates imagines how the proceedings might have occurred. Present among the eighteen prominent citizens were Thomas Hutchinson, governor of Massachusetts; Andrew Oliver, a supporter of the Stamp Act of 1765; the Reverend Samuel Mather, son of Cotton Mather; Joseph Green, a satirical poet; and James Bowdoin, a friend of Benjamin Franklin. Many were Harvard graduates, representing the intellectual and political power elite of the eastern establishment, and most were slaveholders. They questioned Wheatley on the content of her poems, probably asking her to explain her allusions to the Bible and to classical Greek and Latin literature as proof that she was the author.

The committee's verdict was favorable; all signed a document agreeing that Wheatley was indeed the author of the poems. Gates notes this as an early example of the custom requiring well-known white people to testify to the authenticity of the slave narratives that were published to support the cause of the nineteenth century abolitionist movement.

Although Wheatley was freed by her masters and enjoyed a brief period of fame, her life was one of hardship. The Wheatleys, unable to find a publisher for Phillis's poetry in America, took her to England, where her book *Poems on Various Subjects, Religious and Moral* (1773) was the first volume of poetry published by an African American. As a popular figure in America before the Revolution, she met and spoke with many well-known people, including Benjamin Franklin, George Washington, and John Hancock, She married a black man, John Peters, and had three children who died in infancy. Abandoned by her husband and unable to find publishers for her later poems, she died in poverty at the age of thirty.

Gates focuses his argument on the theoretical encounter between Phillis Wheatley and Thomas Jefferson, concluding that the controversy about her work inspired the beginnings of African American literature. Jefferson, he says, had always fascinated African Americans because of the essential contradictions of his life. The author of the Declaration of Independence proclaiming the equality of all men, he owned slaves on his Virginia plantation. It was a popular belief among black people that Jefferson had fathered children with his slave mistress Sally Hemings, and some African Americans claimed Jefferson as an ancestor.

Jefferson's *Notes on the State of Virginia*, first printed privately in Paris in 1785, then in the United States in 1788, was inspired by his earlier correspondence with a French diplomat, the Marquis de Barbé-Marbois. Jefferson disagreed with Marbois's praise for Wheatley's poetry, stating that although black people were gifted in music, they were intellectually inferior to the white race and to American Indians. While he did not doubt that Wheatley, like all African slaves, had a human soul, her art was imitative, not original. He said: "Religion, indeed, has produced a Phillis Whatley [sic]; but it could not produce a poet." That is, Jefferson believed that while slaves had souls and were capable of having religious experiences, they lacked the qualities of originality and imagination that would make them the equal of white people.

Jefferson's views challenged black intellectuals to prove him wrong and generated a body of writing that demonstrated their creative abilities. Although Wheatley and Jefferson never met, Gates sees this public discussion of Jefferson's life and Wheatley's poetry as the foundation for the tradition of African American literature. He lists numerous examples of this literature. David Walker wrote *An Appeal in Four Articles; Together with a Preamble, to the Coloured Citizens of the World* (1829) in which he praised Jefferson's intellectual gifts and called upon black people to use the Declaration of Independence as a model for achieving their own freedom. Frederick Douglass, in a famous speech in 1852, said that he refused to celebrate the Fourth of July but at the same time praised Jefferson's genius in writing the Declaration of Independence. A popular novel by William Wells Brown, *Clotel: Or, The President's Daughter* (1853), furthered the rumor of Jefferson's liaison with Sally Hemings and included a scene in which he sold his own daughter.

Wheatley's poetry, originally praised by black intellectuals as evidence of the creative powers of African Americans, underwent a revision in the early twentieth century. At issue was an early poem, *On Being Brought from Africa to America* (1768), in which Wheatley appeared to support slavery by saying that she had been redeemed into her life as a Christian when she was brought to America. Ignoring other poems in which she attacked tyranny and praised freedom, critics began to denigrate her work on the evidence of this one short poem. James Weldon Johnson and Wallace Thurman, influential writers of the 1920's, saw her work as artistically inferior and timid in its failure to condemn slavery. Wheatley had been transformed from a symbol of black achievement to a representative of complicity with her white masters.

In Gates's view, the Black Arts movement of the 1960's was particularly vituperative in its criticism of Wheatley. Some critics of this period called her "an early Boston Aunt Jemima" and "a colonial handkerchief head." Gates strongly criticizes such influential black critics as Amiri Baraka, Addison Gayle, and Dudley Randall for their racist standards of political correctness in literature, determining who is "too white" or "not black enough."

Consistent with his philosophy in his other writings, Gates concludes with a plea for race-free criticism. "The challenge isn't to read white, or read black; it is to read. If Wheatley stood for anything, it was the creed that culture was, could be, the equal possession of all humanity." He cites the difficulties of Wheatley's life and her artistic achievement as the inspiration for other writers and urges that she be welcomed back into the history of American literature. A comprehensive bibliography includes references to the writings of and about Wheatley as well as references to racial issues in American history and biographies of the historical figures noted in the text.

Marjorie J. Podolsky

Review Sources

Booklist 99, no. 19/20 (June 1, 2003): 1728.
The New Yorker, January 20, 2003, pp. 82-87.
Washington Monthly 35, no. 6 (June, 2003): 54-55.
The Washington Post, March 26, 2002, p. C8.

TRIANGLE
The Fire That Changed America

Author: David Von Drehle (1961-   )
Publisher: Atlantic Monthly Press (New York). 339 pp.
$26.00
Type of work: History
Time: The early twentieth century
Locale: New York City

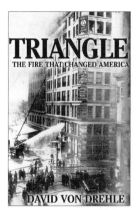

Von Drehle investigates the 1911 Triangle Shirtwaist Company factory fire that killed 146 garment workers and the fire's impact on subsequent labor and social policies

Principal personages:
CLARA LEMLICH, garment worker and leading figure in women garment workers' strikes
MAX BLANCK, part-owner of the Triangle factory
ISAAC HARRIS, part-owner of the Triangle factory
ALFRED E. SMITH, Tammany politician and New York governor, influential in labor law reform
FRANCES PERKINS, leading progressive reformer, later secretary of labor under President Franklin Roosevelt

Most of them young immigrant women, 146 workers perished when flames engulfed the Triangle Shirtwaist Company factory in New York's Greenwich Village in 1911. The factory, on the eighth, ninth, and tenth floors of the Asch building, was overcrowded with workers and highly flammable materials. Only one exit door was unlocked, and firefighting apparatus reached only to the sixth floor. In *Triangle*, David Von Drehle blends scholarly research and a lively narrative style, enabling him to report on the fire, the trial that followed it, and the contemporary social and political world with journalistic immediacy.

In Von Drehle's view, the fire at the Triangle factory in 1911 has been overlooked as a significant event in American history. Both the pre-fire labor movement and the Triangle fire itself, he argues, "helped to transform the political machinery of New York City—the most powerful machine in America, Tammany Hall."

To bring this tragedy to his readers, Von Drehle presents history with the immediacy of an investigative report. For example, the book's prologue echoes the melodrama of tabloid prose as it describes what New Yorkers called Misery Lane, the makeshift morgue crowded with people searching desperately for their missing daughters and wives among the burned human remains. The sense of immediacy in these opening paragraphs is maintained throughout the text, though for the most part the tabloid tone of the prose recedes. No scholar's footnotes interrupt the narrative flow. Rather, at the end of the book a notes section gives supporting details for textual data, and a selected bibliography follows.

The opening chapter illustrates Von Drehle's narrative style. "Spirit of the Age" begins with the arresting statement: "Burglary was the usual occupation of Lawrence Ferrone, also known as Charles Rose," who had been hired by Tammany Hall "to beat up a young woman" strike leader. His victim was Clara Lemlich, a heroic strike organizer for the International Garment Worker's Union local 25. Ferrone and his accomplices

David Von Drehle, a staff writer for The Washington Post, *is the author of* Among the Lowest of the Dead *(1995). He also collaborated with his colleagues at* The Washington Post *on* Deadlock: The Inside Story *of* America's Closest Election *(2001).*

were hired by the antilabor establishment, the rich and the powerful, to give "a quick and savage" beating to their enemy, this twenty-one-year-old seamstress. Von Drehle gives a full account of Lemlich's life and pro-labor activities because she represents the many women workers in New York's factories during this period who influenced "the drive for women's rights (and other civil rights), the rise of unions, and the use of activist government to address social problems."

Lemlich came from a family of many sisters working in an industry that employed women only in the lowest of positions and showered them with injustices. She was also one of many who fought back, again and again, in those years preceding the Triangle factory fire. Von Drehle's text is convincing: American history needs to recognize how this force of women "changed America."

Von Drehle highlights the attack on Lemlich as he begins his narrative, because the beating led "to the ravenous flames inside the Triangle Shirtwaist Company, which trapped and killed some of the hardiest strikers from the uprising Lemlich worked to inspire." This vicious beating represents the pre-fire battles between laborers and owners over those unjust working conditions that allowed the fire to take place. Similar attacks on individuals, the many police assaults on picket lines, the subsequent arrest and imprisonment of women strikers: All strengthened the workers' position and caught the attention of those among the rich and powerful who already leaned toward progressivism. New York in 1909 had a progressive governor, Charles Evans Hughes, while the United States had a progressive president, Theodore Roosevelt. New York City, however, still had Tammany Hall, which was anything but progressive in regard to labor conditions before the fire. First the strikers, then the fire (which killed so many that it stood as New York's greatest tragedy until the 2001 terrorist attacks on the World Trade Center) shocked that political machine, already weakened, into the changes for which the strikers and their allies had fought so hard.

Von Drehle looks at the many who were affected by the fire: workers, owners, politicians, lawyers. Surprisingly, all emerge from the immigrant and immigrant-descendant population in New York City, primarily of European stock, whether Eastern, Italian or Irish, Jewish or Catholic, who crowded into New York City tenements and factories at the end of the nineteenth century and the beginning of the twentieth century. Within this diverse population, two groups were affected by the fire: first, the garment workers and other labor movement pioneers; second, factory owners and their political allies. One side wanted progressive reform; the other side wanted no change from the laissez-faire status quo. Before the fire, the battle was in the streets; after the fire, the battle moved to the legal world. The fire and the trial that followed it were the bridge between these arenas. Von Drehle neatly structures his text to guide the reader through streets and factory, fire and trial, politics and legislation.

Throughout *Triangle*, Von Drehle brings to the pages of American history the lives of poverty-stricken workers and victims who walked through the period, documenting them as carefully as history books before his have documented the lives of the powerful. Without the former, the broader trends emerging from the era would not have taken hold.

One Triangle fire victim was Rosie Freedman. Von Drehle's research enables him to follow her from her birth in Poland in 1892 through the persecution of her Jewish people in pogroms in her village, her journey across the Atlantic Ocean and arrival at Ellis Island in 1907 to a relative's house in one of New York's Jewish neighborhoods, her life in a Bowery tenement, and a job in the Triangle factory. That factory, like so many others in that period, offered workers not only long hours, unsanitary working conditions, and low pay but also, for women workers like Rosie, blatant sexual harassment by male supervisors day after day. The reader sees Rosie during her long work days and in her scant free time, knows how she spent her small pay and what she sent back to relatives in her home village. She, like so many in the garment trade sweatshops, worked at the only jobs available and dreamed of a better life, if not for herself, at least for her children. Then she died in the Triangle fire. For the reader, Freedman is not a statistic; she is a real woman who was wronged.

Several other victims' stories emerge in the narrative, and all show vibrant young lives cut off by the tragedy. Von Drehle honors all who died by giving the names and available data for 140 victims in his List of Victims appendix. He lists the last six victims, analogous to the unknowns in military cemeteries, as "Unidentified." American history recognizes them at last.

Others who did not perish in the fire but who played a role in its importance are highlighted. These include union organizers who, before the fire, encouraged laborers to strike against factory owners (including the owners of the Triangle factory) to gain humane working conditions. They also include political leaders who, after the strike, worked to bring progressive labor reform laws into being. Robert Wagner and Alfred E. Smith are introduced as young members of the poor class in the immigrant neighborhoods of New York City. Through their hard work and political moves, they reached positions of local power in the Tammany Hall machine and the Democratic Party before labor reform was a goal; that is, before the Triangle fire. The postfire narrative brings these figures to powerful positions in the New York State Legislature and governor's mansion, where they became movers of labor reform legislation. Similarly, Frances Perkins is introduced as a union supporter in the pre-fire narrative and continues as a force for reform working with Smith and Wagner on the state level and later as secretary of labor under President Franklin Roosevelt.

When Von Drehle began his research, only one book-length source existed for the fire. He credits Leon Stein, author of *The Triangle Fire* (1962), with "put[ting] the story back on firm historical ground." This material Von Drehle supplements with an investigative reporter's diligent digging. One payoff stands out: The complete transcript of the trial against the factory's owners, *People of New York v. Isaac Harris and Max Blanck*, had long been missing. Like a detective, Von Drehle followed clue after clue until he located a well-preserved copy in the New York County Lawyers' Association Library, to which it had been willed by Max D. Steuer, the defense attorney in the case. This file became Von Drehle's best source, for in it, "the trial came to life. And not just the trial: the fire itself, and the survivors, and the Triangle factory."

The book's chapters which most grip the reader, "Inferno" and "Three Minutes," are based primarily on the details of the fire found in the recovered trial manuscript. These sections enable one to envision with great clarity the panic and the heroism of workers and managers. They diagram the placement of tables, cloth, personnel, exit doors, stairwells, and the roof. They show the fire beginning, spreading, and engulfing. Finally, they follow the struggle of those who escaped, the terror of those who died in the building, and the despair of those who leapt to their deaths.

There are villains in every good story, of course. In *Triangle*, ironically, the villains—the factory owners and the Tammany Hall politicians—like the strikers and the victims, come from the immigrant class. Isaac Harris and Max Blanck, owners of the Triangle factory, rose from poverty and their own experiences of unjust working conditions to positions of management and finally ownership. Before the fire, when Lemlich's oratory galvanized the workers of New York and their upper-class allies to strike, the "Shirtwaist Kings" Harris and Blanck galvanized factory owners throughout the city to hold out against the strikers, though they had once endured the same conditions that killed their workers. In the chapter "Trial," the story's villains, Harris and Blanck and Tammany Hall's lawyer for the defense, Steuer, prevailed over the fire's victims, despite the damning evidence presented by the prosecuting attorney. The owners were, it seemed, still winning the war.

In the end, however, despite the jury's decision, the politicians changed their ways. The story ends with Tammany Hall and the Democratic Party becoming the leaders in progressive reform legislation that indeed changed the United States by guaranteeing laborers better hours, greater safety, and more pay. Such liberal thinking did not surface miraculously; it rose up, in part, from the ashes of the Triangle fire and its 146 victims.

Francine Dempsey

Review Sources

America 189, no. 11 (October 13, 2003): 28-31.
Kirkus Reviews 71, no. 11 (June 1, 2003): 797.
Library Journal 128, no. 8 (May 1, 2003): 136.
The New Leader 86, no. 4 (July/August, 2003): 20-21.
The New York Times, August 31, 2003, p. 8.
The New York Times Book Review, September 7, 2003, p. 16.
Publishers Weekly 250, no. 20 (May 19, 2003): 59.

TYCHO AND KEPLER
The Unlikely Partnership That Forever Changed Our Understanding of the Heavens

Author: Kitty Ferguson (1941-   )
Publisher: Walker (New York). 402 pp. $28.00
Type of work: Biography and history of science
Time: 1546-1630
Locale: Denmark and central Europe

This dual biography intermeshes the lives of the six-teenth century's best naked-eye observer, Tycho Brahe, and the period's greatest theoretical scientist, Johannes Kepler, to show how they created modern astronomy

Principal personages:
TYCHO BRAHE (1546-1601), a Danish astronomer whose excellent instruments enabled him to track precise planetary positions
JOHANNES KEPLER (1571-1630), a German astronomer who discovered that the planets move around the Sun in elliptical orbits
NICOLAUS COPERNICUS (1473-1543), a Polish astronomer whose heliocentric system became a bone of contention between Brahe and Kepler
FREDERICK II (1534-1588), the king of Denmark, who financially supported the construction of Uraniborg, Brahe's observatory on Hven Island
RUDOLPH II (1552-1612), the Holy Roman emperor from 1576 to 1612, who supported both Brahe and Kepler as imperial mathematicians

God was never far from Johannes Kepler's thoughts, either in his life or in his science. It was therefore typical that he attributed his momentous meeting with Tycho Brahe in 1600 to Divine Providence. The ensuing interactions between these men of radically different temperaments and scientific visions were often tumultuous, permeated with dramatic misunderstandings, hurt feelings, and wounded pride. Nevertheless, as a Spanish proverb has it, God writes straight with crooked lines, and both men came to see the hand of God in their relationship. On Brahe's side, he came to appreciate Kepler's mathematical genius and illuminating astronomical imagination as the means to his own immortality. From Kepler's perspective, he was grateful for God's goodness in granting him access to Brahe's planetary data, which turned out to be the keys he needed to unlock the secrets of the solar system.

Though they were not collaborators in any conventional sense and though they did not see eye-to-eye on their fragile union, their interaction was synergistic in that they accomplished more for astronomy together than they did apart. Their interaction was also serendipitous, as both discovered what neither was, at first, seeking. Convinced that the heliocentric system violated basic physical laws and that the geocentric system needed revision, Brahe proposed a hybrid geoheliocentric system in which the Sun, with its orbiting planets, circled a stationary Earth. Kepler wanted to use Brahe's data to verify his modification of the Copernican system based on the interspersing of perfect three-dimensional forms among the planetary orbits. Neither of these models turned out to be true, but Kepler's search for a system that matched Brahe's data led to a model neither of them had initially imagined.

~

Kitty Ferguson became interested in science as a child but decided to pursue a career in music. For many years she was a professional musician, but in 1986 she returned to her early interest in astronomy, which resulted in five books and a new career as a science writer.

~

At first glance, Kitty Ferguson seems an unlikely person to tell the stories of these two astronomers. Her early training was in music, and for many years she was a professional singer, working under the direction of such composers as Igor Stravinsky, Zoltan Kodaly, and Leonard Bernstein. It was not until her mid-forties that she began researching and writing about science. Her eight-year-old daughter's science project on black holes was the precipitating event that led to Ferguson's first book, *Black Holes in Spacetime* (1991), written for young adults but praised by the world's expert on black holes, Stephen Hawking. Ferguson met Hawking, who agreed to cooperate with her on her next book, *Stephen Hawking: Quest for a Theory of Everything* (1992), the first Hawking biography (also written for the youth market). Her next three books, *Prisons of Light: Black Holes* (1996), *The Fire in the Equations: Science, Religion, and the Search for God* (1997), and *Measuring the Universe* (1999), were written for general audiences and manifested her evolving skills as a popularizer of science. *Tycho and Kepler* capitalizes on her interests in astronomy, biography, history, even music, as Kepler believed in the "music of the spheres."

Both Brahe and especially Kepler have been popular subjects for biographers. Ferguson's dual biography is not meant to supplant such definitive works as Victor Thoren's *The Lord of Uraniborg: A Biography of Tycho Brahe* (1990) and Max Casper's *Johannes Kepler* (1948). Instead, she hopes to communicate to nonscientists the complexities of the personalities, lives, achievements, and times of these two astronomers who helped revolutionize science. Her research has given her an insightful understanding of the political intrigues, religious conflicts, and cultural hypocrisies that defined post-Reformation Europe. Some scholars might question her theme that without Brahe, Kepler would never have discovered the laws of planetary motion. Historians of science will be unhappy that she fails to understand some of their discoveries; for example, she does not realize that Galileo, the Italian Copernican, did not have a correct understanding of inertia (his inertia was circular, not rectilinear). On the whole, though, her book is meticulously researched and clearly written.

After a prologue in which Ferguson describes how the two eccentrics, the fifty-three-year-old Brahe and the twenty-eight-year-old Kepler, first met, her approach is basically chronological. This allows her to make some instructive juxtapositions of these two lives, even when the men were living in different countries. For example,

Brahe's background was aristocratic and privileged, whereas Kepler's was plebeian and provincial. While the religious background of both men was Lutheran, each became unorthodox in his own way.

Ferguson admits that her account of Brahe's life depends heavily on Thoren's biography, but, unlike other authors, she strives to bring out the kindness as well as the cantankerousness of this famous eccentric. He was born in a Danish castle along with a twin brother who did not survive. He was raised not by his parents but by an aunt and uncle, whose castle was often visited by princes and kings. Brahe was educated at a cathedral school and the University of Copenhagen, where he learned and accepted the geocentric system of Aristotle and Ptolemy, ancient natural philosophers whose belief in uniform circular motion for all planets Brahe never abandoned.

To expand and deepen his provincial education, Brahe, at fifteen, traveled to central Europe where, during the following decade, he would study history, music, art, and astronomy at a variety of universities, including Leipzig, Basel, and Augsburg. During this time he managed to lose part of his nose in a duel and to have astronomical instruments built with which he made many observations of planetary positions. Astronomy, his new passion, was not a customary profession for an aristocrat, but when his father died in 1571, he realized that he would eventually become financially independent enough to pursue his fascination with the heavens.

Not only was his choice of profession unbecoming for a nobleman but also his choice of a life's companion. Kirsten Jorgensdatter, a clergyman's daughter, was far below his class and legally unable to become his wife. Brahe flouted convention and became her common-law husband, an arrangement that would later threaten his livelihood. In 1572, the year of his morganatic marriage, Brahe discovered a new star, which made his reputation as an astronomer. He proved that this star was neither a planet nor a comet but something genuinely new in the heavens, and his book on the subject was very successful.

As a nobleman, Brahe was barred from an academic career, and he spent years trying to find a place where he could pursue his passion for astronomy. Finally, King Frederick II offered Brahe an island, Hven, north of Copenhagen and south of Elsinore, where the astronomer used his inheritance and the king's largesse to construct Uraniborg, a combination of castle, observatory, and alchemical laboratory. In the days before the telescope, this astronomical palace, which Brahe equipped with such instruments as quadrants, armillary spheres, and a gigantic equatorial armillary, enabled him to solidify his status as the world's greatest naked-eye observer.

Meanwhile, in a town on the edge of the Black Forest in Germany, Johannes Kepler was born into a poor and dysfunctional family. His father, a mercenary soldier, was often away and eventually abandoned his family completely. Kepler was rescued from a life of ignorance and poverty by the Lutheran school system. He trained to become a Lutheran minister but abandoned this quest because of his growing heterodoxy and because he got a job teaching mathematics at a school in Graz, Austria. By this time Kepler's astronomical views were also heterodox, as, unlike Martin Luther and many Lutherans, he was a Copernican. However, Kepler became concerned with a question that never bothered Copernicus: Why did God create only six planets?

Kepler, who believed that God had fashioned a harmonious universe, was overjoyed when he discovered that God, the Great Geometer, had created six planets because he had modeled his solar system on the five perfect solids: the cube, tetrahedron, octahedron, dodecahedron, and icosahedron. Kepler did not believe that these solid polyhedra actually occupied the space between the planets, but he did believe that God had used them in determining the order and distances of the planetary orbits. In 1596 he published his discovery in *Mysteriium cosmographicum* (partially translated in *The Physicist's Conception of Nature*, 1958), a book that brought him a modicum of fame and a correspondence with Brahe.

By this time Brahe's situation in Denmark had become untenable. Despite his excellent astronomical work, he had alienated the tenants on Hven and his other estates. Autocratic and mercurial, Brahe would sometimes beat subordinates who displeased him. When King Frederick II died, the new king, Christian IV, was not as supportive of Brahe as his father had been. He also saw morganatic marriages such as Brahe's as evil, and he was unhappy that Brahe had diverted money which should have been used to keep a royal chapel in good repair to his observatory. This deteriorating financial and political situation forced Brahe to leave Hven, his home for twenty-one years. He was eventually able to use his European connections to obtain the post of imperial mathematician at Rudolph II's court in Prague.

During this period, Kepler suffered a similar decline in his fortunes because the Counter-Reformation in Graz forced the closing of Lutheran schools. Thus Kepler, like Brahe, was searching for a patron in 1598. In his new post, Brahe needed assistants and, impressed by Kepler's *Mysterium Cosmographicum*, he invited him to Prague. Their initial encounter was encouraging, but the relationship quickly deteriorated. Brahe treated Kepler as his underling instead of his colleague, and he wanted Kepler, a convinced Copernican, to use his observations of Mars to verify his geoheliocentric system. After Brahe's death in 1601, Rudolph II made Kepler his imperial mathematician, and Kepler became heir to Brahe's observations. As a Copernican, Kepler initially believed that the planets moved with uniform speed in perfectly circular orbits around the Sun, but he soon found that Brahe's precise data ruled out these assumptions of uniformity (the planets actually moved sometimes slower and sometimes faster) and circularity (Kepler was unable to fit Brahe's observed positions of Mars to a circular orbit). After many trials, he discovered, to his delight, that an elliptical orbit closely matched the data. Several years later, while studying the musical harmonies of the heavenly bodies, Kepler examined the ratios of the minimum and maximum speeds of each planet and discovered that these conformed to harmonious musical intervals. In the midst of this musical analysis, he stated the relationship between a planet's period (the time it takes to orbit the Sun) and its distance from the Sun. In modern terms, he found that the square of a planet's period is proportional to the cube of its average distance from the Sun.

To fulfil a promise made to the dying Brahe, Kepler worked for many years to finish a set of tables of planetary motions based on Brahe's observations. This work was interrupted when he had to help his mother fight a charge of witchcraft. (She was ultimately exonerated.) When Kepler completed his work on the tables, they were called

Tabulae Rudolphinae (Rudolfine Tables). Using these data, astronomers could calculate the position of any planet at any time of the past, present, or future.

Kepler's fame as an astronomer increased after his death, and his discoveries were appreciated more in the eighteenth and nineteenth centuries than they had been in his lifetime. The same can be said for the achievements of Brahe. Not long after Brahe left Uraniborg, his observatory began to be dismembered, and in time all his buildings were destroyed. However, in the twentieth century the Danes, finally realizing Brahe's greatness, erected a statue of the astronomer in the restored gardens of the Uraniborg site. Kepler died in Regensburg during a trip to try to get money that was owed him, but his grave site has been lost. However, poets, dramatists, novelists, and composers have kept his story and achievements alive. Historians of science regard Kepler as the founder of modern astronomy. Sir Isaac Newton once said that if he saw farther than other scientists, it was because he had stood on the shoulders of giants. Brahe and Kepler were two of these giants.

Robert J. Paradowski

Review Sources

Astronomy 31, no. 4 (April, 2003): 104-105.
Booklist 99, no. 7 (December 1, 2002): 636.
Kirkus Reviews 70, no. 21 (November 1, 2002): 1587.
Library Journal 127, no. 20 (December 1, 2002): 168-169.
Natural History 112, no. 3 (April, 2003): 70-72.
New Scientist 177, no. 2379 (January 25, 2003): 53.
Physics Today 56, no. 12 (December, 2003): 61-66.
Publishers Weekly 249, no. 48 (December 2, 2002): 46.

UNDER THE BANNER OF HEAVEN
A Story of Violent Faith

Author: Jon Krakauer (1954-   )
Publisher: Doubleday (New York). 372 pp. $26.00
Type of work: Religion and history
Time: 1805-2003
Locale: American Fork, Utah, and the "Arizona Strip" area including parts of Nevada, Arizona, and Utah

Murders committed by two former Mormons in 1984 are placed in context alongside violent incidents in the history of the Church of Jesus Christ of Latter-Day Saints

Principal personages:
> DAN LAFFERTY, convicted in 1985 for the murders of his sister-in-law Brenda Lafferty and her daughter; sentenced to two life terms
> RONALD WATSON LAFFERTY, also convicted for the murders of Brenda Lafferty and her daughter; sentenced to death
> BRENDA WRIGHT LAFFERTY, murdered in July, 1984, by her husband's older brothers Dan and Ronald
> ERICA LANE LAFFERTY, her fifteen-month-old daughter, murdered by Dan and Ronald Lafferty
> ALLEN LAFFERTY, the husband of Brenda Wright Lafferty and the father of Erica
> CHIP CARNES, an accomplice and witness to the murders of Brenda and Erica Lafferty
> DELOY BATEMAN, a former United Effort Plan (UEP) member
> DEBBIE PALMER, a former UEP member
> JOSEPH SMITH, JR., the founder of the Church of Jesus Christ of Latter-Day Saints (LDS)
> BRIGHAM YOUNG, an LDS leader after Smith's death

Jon Krakauer's three previous books, *Eiger Dreams* (1990), *Into the Wild* (1996), and *Into Thin Air* (1997), examined the struggle to survive in extreme climates. In *Under the Banner of Heaven: A Story of Violent Faith*, Krakauer deals with a different extreme, not of wilderness or high-altitude survival but of inner turmoil and delusion stemming from deeply held religious beliefs. *Under the Banner of Heaven* looks at religious fanaticism among fundamentalist offshoots of the Church of Jesus Christ of Latter-Day Saints (LDS), commonly known as the Mormons, and attempts to link the sometimes violent history of the LDS to a modern true-crime story involving two former members of the church.

In a prologue Krakauer outlines the 1984 murders of Brenda and Erica Lafferty, for which two of Brenda Lafferty's brothers-in-law were sent to prison (Ronald Lafferty to death row) in 1985. Ronald and Dan Lafferty believed that God had told them to kill their younger brother's wife and her baby daughter; Krakauer wants to understand how religious faith can become fanaticism and lead to murder. This pro-

Jonathan Krakauer has contributed articles to Outside, Rolling Stone, The New York Times, *and* National Geographic. *He was a finalist for the 1998 Pulitzer Prize in general nonfiction and has received a National Magazine Award, a Walter Sullivan Award for Excellence in Science Journalism, and an Academy Award in Literature.*

logue is followed by a description of Mormon fundamentalist communities that have removed themselves from the LDS, usually in disagreement with the mainstream LDS over the practice of polygamy (the taking of multiple wives, also called "spiritual" or "celestial" marriage). The LDS officially rejected polygamy as a sacred doctrine in the late 1800's.

Krakauer devotes a chapter each to polygamous communities in Colorado City, Utah (also known as Short Creek), and Bountiful, British Columbia. In Colorado City the elderly Rulon T. Jeffs presides over the Fundamentalist Church of Jesus Christ of Latter Day Saints (also called the United Effort Plan or UEP). Jeffs has seventy-five wives and nearly as many children. For an insider's view of Short Creek, Krakauer interviewed DeLoy Bateman, a former UEP member who lost his faith in Rulon Jeffs's authority and left the UEP. Polygamists in Colorado City and similar communities often marry girls in their early teens, who are told they face damnation unless they marry men chosen for them by community leaders. In Bountiful Krakauer interviewed Debbie Palmer, who grew up in the UEP. Palmer suffered through three arranged marriages and a variety of abuses from the men of Bountiful, becoming so depressed she set her own house on fire while her children were asleep.

Fourteen-year-old Elizabeth Smart, whose 2002 kidnapping and eventual rescue were described in a highly publicized book and television film the following year, was also a victim of Mormon fundamentalists and the doctrine of plural marriage. Brian David Mitchell, an independent Mormon fundamentalist, kidnapped Smart, believing that God had told him to take her as his second, spiritual wife. Mitchell and his wife held the girl captive for nine months. According to Krakauer, Smart made no attempt to escape, and she was returned to her family only after being apprehended by the police. Krakauer argues that Smart, whose parents are members of the mainstream LDS, was susceptible to Mitchell's fanatic indoctrination because of his extensive knowledge of Mormon sacred texts, which she had been taught to believe since childhood. Krakauer asserts that a young woman raised in a more skeptical or questioning environment might have defied her kidnappers' authority and escaped.

Krakauer makes it clear that the communities practicing plural marriage are separate from the LDS, which does not endorse polygamy. However, he points out that fundamentalist sects and the LDS believe in *The Book of Mormon* (1829) and are followers of church founder and prophet Joseph Smith, Jr. Fundamentalists believe that the LDS erred in ceasing its practice of spiritual marriage, a critically important tenet of Smith's original church.

Smith's revelations of the Mormon faith began in 1827, when an angel called Moroni led him to a set of golden tablets inscribed with a language that resembled Egyptian hieroglyphics. Smith received a pair of special glasses that enabled him to read the strange text. After translating and publishing the material—which he called

The Book of Mormon—Smith returned the golden pages to the angel, although several of Smith's friends and relatives claimed to have seen them. Krakauer notes that the foundations of other major religions are no less fantastic than Smith's story of the Angel Moroni and the golden plates; all religious belief ultimately depends on faith.

The Book of Mormon tells of a Christian religion based in the United States rather than distant Bethlehem or Jerusalem. According to it, a sixth century B.C.E. man named Lehi left Jerusalem and settled in North America, where his sons Nephi and Laman became rivals for leadership of his tribe. Jesus Christ appeared to followers of both brothers after his resurrection and instructed them to live together in peace, but eventually the Lamanites slaughtered the entire Nephite tribe.

Smith initially taught that all believers could receive divine revelations (although he later revised this so that only he, as president and revelator, could receive them). The second most important sacred text of the LDS is *The Doctrine and Covenants*, Smith's 133 core revelations, including doctrine number 132 commanding that Mormon men engage in polygamy.

Krakauer describes a church history fraught with persecution and bloody retaliation. Smith had begun gathering followers even before *The Book of Mormon* was published. His church grew rapidly but faced violent opposition from surrounding communities, and Smith moved his followers west. In Illinois in 1844 Smith was arrested and charged with violating the First Amendment; Mormons had destroyed a printing press on Smith's orders because its owners had published newspapers questioning his authority. Vigilantes shot and killed Smith in his jail cell before he could be tried.

Smith had at one time preached a doctrine of blood atonement. When the men who killed him were acquitted, his successor Brigham Young began preaching vengeance. Young moved the church farther west, into Utah, and under his leadership the Mormons became more committed to defending themselves, particularly against the federal government, as federal law threatened their communities and their practice of polygamy. Krakauer's account highlights the 1857 Mountain Meadows Massacre, wherein a group of Utah Mormons surrounded and slaughtered 120 men, women, and children traveling west through Mormon territory from Arkansas.

Brigham Young died in 1877 and was succeeded as Mormon president by John Taylor, who perpetuated Young's defiance of federal authorities. However, Taylor's successor Wilford Woodruff capitulated at last to the law and in 1890 announced that God had revealed he no longer sanctioned plural marriage.

The centerpiece of *Under the Banner of Heaven* is a chilling example of religious devotion taken too far: the 1984 murders of twenty-four-year-old Brenda Wright Lafferty and her fifteen-month-old daughter. Brenda Lafferty's husband, Allen, and his five brothers had formed their own small Mormon fundamentalist sect, separate from the LDS but loosely associated with a group called the School of the Prophets, led by self-styled prophet Robert Crossfield (the Prophet Onias). Dan Lafferty cancelled electrical and water service to his home, refused to carry a driver's license or pay taxes, and punished his wife with physical abuse if she disobeyed him. Ron Lafferty also became abusive toward his wife, Dianna, and discussed taking additional spiritual wives.

Brenda Lafferty resisted Allen's attempts to conform to his brothers' new beliefs. She encouraged the other Lafferty wives to stand up to their husbands and supported Dianna when she divorced Ron and moved to Florida with their six children. Ron subsequently received a revelation from God telling him four individuals, including Brenda Lafferty and her baby daughter, must be "removed" because they stood in the way of God's work. Everyone named in Ron's "removal revelation" had encouraged or assisted his wife as she planned to leave him.

Personal revelations from God are often discussed among groups of Mormon fundamentalist men, so that agreement can be reached as to whether a given revelation is truly divine. Ron and Dan presented their "removal revelation," to the general consternation of other fundamentalists. While no one confirmed its godly origin, neither did anyone step forward to warn their intended victims or report their plan.

Krakauer interviewed Dan Lafferty, who is serving two life terms in a Utah state prison and feels no discomfort or remorse over cutting the throats of his sister-in-law and tiny niece. Lafferty describes feeling "completely comfortable" while committing the murders and nineteen years later still believes God ordered him to kill. His account of the crime is truly horrifying and gives a lurid, true-crime cast to Krakauer's account, in contrast to his more traditional history of the LDS.

Krakauer intends to link the bloodshed surrounding nineteenth century Mormons with the Lafferty murders and with the abuses suffered by young spiritual wives in polygamous communities. However, the connections are not clear, in part because of the book's disjointed presentation of a wide variety of topics and a large number of personalities. Krakauer argues that Americans often ignore the negative aspects of religious faith and, especially since the terrorist attacks of September 11, 2001, are too quick to associate religious violence with Islamic fundamentalism. Krakauer believes any religious faith can lead to fanaticism and wants to show that, although the LDS is a uniquely American religious phenomenon, its past and present are littered with incidents of violence against people both inside and outside the faith.

Maureen J. Puffer-Rothenberg

Review Sources

The Economist 368, no. 8331 (July 5, 2003): 75.
The New York Times Book Review 152 (August 3, 2003): 7.
Newsweek 142, no. 3 (July 21, 2003): 56-57.
People 60, no. 3 (July 21, 2003): 47.
Publishers Weekly 250, no. 26 (June 20, 2003): 72.
Time 162, no. 3 (July 21, 2003): 62.
The Wall Street Journal, July 11, 2003, p. W14.

AN UNFINISHED LIFE
John F. Kennedy, 1917-1963

Author: Robert Dallek (1934-   )
Publisher: Little, Brown (Boston). 838 pp. $30.00
Type of work: Biography
Time: 1917-1963
Locale: Boston; Washington, D.C.; and Dallas

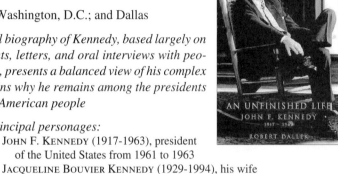

This thoughtful biography of Kennedy, based largely on original documents, letters, and oral interviews with people who knew him, presents a balanced view of his complex career and explains why he remains among the presidents most admired by American people

Principal personages:
JOHN F. KENNEDY (1917-1963), president
of the United States from 1961 to 1963
JACQUELINE BOUVIER KENNEDY (1929-1994), his wife
CAROLINE KENNEDY SCHLOSSBERG (1957-   ) and JOHN F. KENNEDY,
JR. (1960-1999), their children
LYNDON B. JOHNSON (1908-1973), vice president of the United States
from 1961 to 1963 and president from 1963 to 1969
JOSEPH P. KENNEDY, SR. (1888-1969) and ROSE KENNEDY (1890-1995),
President Kennedy's parents
JOSEPH P. KENNEDY, JR. (1915-1944), President Kennedy's older
brother, who died in action in World War II
BOBBY KENNEDY (1925-1968), President Kennedy's brother and his
attorney general
DWIGHT D. EISENHOWER (1890-1969), president of the United States
from 1953 to 1961 and supreme allied commander in Europe during
World War II
RICHARD M. NIXON (1913-1994), vice president of the United States
from 1953 to 1961 and unsuccessful presidential candidate in 1960

In the years since John F. Kennedy's death on November 22, 1963, at the relatively young age of forty-six, the American public has consistently held him in the highest esteem. Numerous public opinion polls have shown that Americans still rank John F. Kennedy among the two or three greatest American presidents. The only other presidents whom Americans consistently admire as much as John F. Kennedy are George Washington and Abraham Lincoln. Even revelations about Kennedy's personal weaknesses, such as his womanizing, have not had an adverse effect on public attitudes toward his life and political career. Author and historian Robert Dallek readily admits that this incredible admiration for a president whose service in the White House was under three years cannot be fully explained by Kennedy's assassination, because two other martyred presidents, James Garfield and William McKinley, are

*Robert Dallek is a professor of
history at Boston University and
an eminent presidential historian.
Among his major books are*
Franklin D. Roosevelt and
American Foreign Policy, 1932-
1945, *(1979),* Ronald Reagan:
The Politics of Symbolism
(1984), and Flawed Giant:
Lyndon Johnson and His Times,
1961-1973 *(1998).*

not greatly admired by either historians or the general public.

To research this book, Dallek consulted previously unavailable documents in the John F. Kennedy Library in Cambridge, Massachusetts, and relied on oral interviews with people who had known Kennedy. The Kennedy family granted Dallek access to the late president's medical records, also previously unavailable and now located in the Kennedy Library. Dalleck consulted a physician who enabled him to understand Kennedy's complex and various medical conditions. This is a very reliable and well-researched biography.

During his lifetime, Kennedy led the public to believe that his parents were loving and concerned parents who raised their children in a warm and religious family. The reality was quite different; his family was dysfunctional. His father, Joseph, was a womanizer and a shady businessman and financier who relied on inside information to make a considerable fortune in the stock market in the years before insider trading was a federal offense. President Kennedy's mother, Rose, was a distant mother who felt justly abandoned by her husband, whom she refused to divorce not only because her Catholic faith opposed divorce but also because she did not want to give up the elegant lifestyle her husband's vast fortune made possible.

Joseph and Rose set incredibly high standards for their children and especially for their four sons. They sent Jack, their second son, to Choate, even though the headmaster of this prestigious boarding school made no effort to hide his contempt for Catholics such as the Kennedys. Joseph and Rose ignored their son's dislike for this school because they wanted him to get to know the sons of influential Protestant businessmen. Dallek demonstrates that the teenage Jack Kennedy suffered from a severe case of Addison's disease (an adrenal illness) that required several hospitalizations at the Mayo Clinic in Minnesota. Letters to his friends make it clear that Jack would have preferred to live closer to home during and after his lengthy medical treatments, but his parents ignored his pleas.

Dallek argues persuasively that Jack Kennedy sought to separate himself from his parents in order to affirm his own identity. His father was an isolationist, even while he was serving as the American ambassador to Great Britain in the late 1930's. While he was an undergraduate at Harvard University, from which he graduated in 1940, Kennedy reacted against his father's isolationism; his senior thesis, which was also published in 1940, was titled *Why England Slept*. In this work, he analyzed the disastrous efforts by British prime ministers Stanley Baldwin and Neville Chamberlain to appease Adolf Hitler. Kennedy argued persuasively that the United States should support its British ally and oppose the absolute evil of the Nazis. Kennedy's opposition to the dangers of the Axis was not merely theoretical. He could have easily obtained a deferment from the draft because of his serious medical problems, but he asked his father to hide his medical records from Navy doctors so that he could be accepted as a candidate for officer training.

Dallek describes well Kennedy's real courage in the Solomon Islands when he swam through shark-infested waters to save the sailors serving under his command on the sunken PT-109. Although he later had to resign his commission as a naval officer for health reasons, Kennedy had both demonstrated his courage and convinced himself that he could accomplish a great deal despite his medical problems.

Dallek does an excellent job of placing Kennedy in the reality of American politics between his election to the House of Representatives in 1946 and his death in Dallas in 1963. Jack Kennedy had not planned to enter politics, but after the death of his older brother, Joe, in military action in 1944, he became the eldest surviving Kennedy son, and his father persuaded him in 1945 to run for Congress in a solidly Democratic district in Boston the following year. Joe, Sr. spent more than $300,000 in order to ensure his son's victories, first in a highly competitive Democratic primary and then in a relatively easy general election.

Jack Kennedy ran as a war hero who conveyed to his largely working-class constituents that he shared their concerns. This was quite an accomplishment because Kennedy had been raised in a very wealthy family and had lived away from Boston for most of his life, except for his early childhood and his four years at Harvard. The entire Kennedy family became involved in his 1946 campaigns and appealed very successfully to women and immigrant voters, who felt that Jack Kennedy would represent their wishes in Congress. He was viewed as a new type of politician. His opponents in both his primary and general elections in 1946 were not war heroes, and this contributed significantly to his success.

As a Congressman, Kennedy was very strongly anticommunist and a fiscally responsible conservative who provided excellent service both to his constituents and to others in Massachusetts. People considered him to be a sensible politician who understood both the real danger of expanding communist influence in Europe and the importance of balanced budgets. He appealed to liberal, moderate, and conservative voters who felt that he shared their values. He spoke regularly throughout Massachusetts and impressed people with his enthusiasm and apparent sincerity. He came across as an independent Democrat who disagreed with his own party, especially on matters related to national defense and the fight against communism.

Congressman Kennedy felt that President Harry S. Truman could have done more to fire communist sympathizers from government service. These anticommunist remarks went over very well with socially conservative voters in Massachusetts and persuaded them that Kennedy was a Democrat whom they could trust on matters of national defense and fiscal responsibility. His moderate policies and his extremely well-organized campaign contributed to his defeat of the incumbent Republican senator Henry Cabot Lodge in 1952, a year in which presidential candidate Dwight Eisenhower easily carried Massachusetts. Many voters in Kennedy's home state felt comfortable splitting their votes between the Republican Dwight Eisenhower and the Democrat Jack Kennedy.

Kennedy served in the U.S. Senate from 1953 to 1961. During these years, he married Jacqueline Bouvier and became nationally known. His politics continued to reflect his combination of fiscal conservatism, strong anticommunism, and a moderate approach to social change. At the 1956 Democratic Convention, he sought his party's nomination as Adlai Stevenson's running mate, but the convention delegates selected Senator Estes Kefauver of Tennessee to run with Stevenson against Eisenhower and Richard Nixon. In hindsight, it was probably a blessing that Kennedy had not been nominated in 1956, because some Democrats might have blamed Stevenson's defeat on the fact that Kennedy was a Catholic. In the 1928 presidential election, extreme anti-Catholic bias had contributed significantly to the defeat of the Democratic nominee Governor Alfred Smith of New York. Kennedy did not underestimate the depth of anti-Catholicism among certain American voters, but he refused to allow prejudice to continue dominating political life in the United States.

When he began his campaign in January, 1960, to win the Democratic presidential nomination, he was under no illusions about the difficulty of his undertaking. He had to persuade American voters that his policies would continue those of the extremely popular Dwight Eisenhower, who had given the United States eight years of relative prosperity, while at the same time getting people to believe that he could make the country even better. Kennedy had to overcome visceral distrust of Catholics and to persuade enough voters that he—and not Nixon—should be entrusted with maintaining economic growth and defending the United States.

At the 1960 Democratic Convention, Kennedy asked the Senate majority leader Lyndon B. Johnson to become his running mate, not because he liked Johnson but because he needed him on the ballot in order to carry key southern states in that year's election. Dallek argues persuasively that Kennedy could not have won in 1960 without Johnson as his running mate, but the author also discredits the oft-repeated claim that voting irregularities in Chicago contributed to Kennedy's victory. Dallek points out that Kennedy would have won in 1960, even if Nixon had carried Illinois.

Dallek does an excellent job in describing the many challenges faced by Kennedy during his less than three years in the White House. He helps readers to understand that the Soviet Union's decision to build the Berlin Wall in 1961 paradoxically put an end to a potential war between the United States and the Soviet Union over Berlin, because it made it possible for the Soviets to maintain their control over East Germany, while the United States kept its access to West Berlin.

The most significant portion in this excellent biography describes how Kennedy used the threat of nuclear weapons and exquisite diplomatic skills to resolve the Cuban Missile Crisis in 1962. Dallek explains well how very close the United States was to a nuclear war, which the Joint Chiefs of Staff wanted to begin against the Soviets. In his final chapter, Dallek imagines how life might have been had Kennedy not been assassinated in 1963. He suggests that the Vietnam War might not have expanded as quickly as it did under President Johnson. This is an excellent and very reliable biography of a greatly admired American president.

Edmund J. Campion

Review Sources

Library Journal 128, no. 12 (July 15, 2003): 102.
The New York Times, May 28, 2003, p. B1.
The New York Times Book Review, June 8, 2003, pp. 12-13.
The New Yorker 79, no. 19 (July 14, 2003): 99.
Newsweek 141, no. 20 (May 19, 2003): 76.
Publishers Weekly 250, no. 19 (May 12, 2003): 59.
Time 161, no. 20 (May 19, 2003): 67.
The Times Literary Supplement, August 22, 2003, pp. 3-4.
The Wall Street Journal, May 13, 2003, p. D5.

VANISHED ACT
The Life and Art of Weldon Kees

Author: James Reidel (1955-   )
Publisher: University of Nebraska Press (Lincoln). 398
   pp. $35.00
Type of work: Literary biography
Time: 1914-1955
Locale: Nebraska; Denver, Colorado; New York City;
   Provincetown, Massachusetts; and San Francisco

A thoughtful and heartbreaking biography of a mid-twentieth century American Renaissance man who, in a perfect world, would have earned more than mere cult figure status

Principal personages:
> WELDON KEES, a man of many talents who disappeared and is thought to
>   have committed suicide after failing to gain critical acclaim
> ANN SWAN KEES, his wife, who was supportive of her husband but
>   whose alcoholism and mental deterioration led to the couple's
>   breakup
> SARAH GREEN KEES, his caring and devoted mother
> JOHN KEES, his father, a successful business owner who worried about
>   his wayward son
> LOWRY WIMBERLY, an influential college professor and editor of the
>   *Prairie Schooner*

Weldon Kees can to be considered one of the forgotten men of American letters. When his abandoned car was discovered by authorities on July 18, 1955, near the Golden Gate Bridge, a thorough investigation into Kees's disappearance was begun. He had talked to friends about running off to Mexico and starting a new life. Kees also had talked about suicide and had done extensive research into the subject. Although his body was never found and no suicide note was discovered, authorities concluded that Kees had killed himself. After the police made their judgment in the matter, the case remained an unsolved mystery for others. Over the years, there have been whispers that Kees was sighted at various locations. These sightings could be no more than wishful thinking on the parts of friends and cult followers, but they do give one pause to think about what actually happened to this Renaissance man who was frustrated at almost every turn by bad luck or bad timing.

Since his disappearance, Kees has had a few stalwart supporters who believed in his talent and wished to set the record straight. James Reidel is one of these admirers and has made it his cause to put Kees back on the cultural radar screen. Born in Cincinnati, Ohio, Reidel was educated at Columbia and Rutgers Universities. He is a poet, a translator of such German authors as Thomas Bernhard, Franz Werfel, and

Ingeborg Bachmann, and an editor. *Vanished Act* has been a labor of love for Reidel and is his first published book. Previously, except for journal articles written by his friends and associates, there had been very little written about Kees. In 1985 *Weldon Kees: A Critical Introduction*, a collection of essays edited by Jim Elledge, was published. This collection reprints essays and reviews that had first appeared during the 1940's and 1950's. *Vanished Act* is the first book-length biography of the poet.

~

James Reidel is a respected independent scholar, a poet, an editor of Weldon Kees's works, and a translator of several German authors. Vanished Act *is his first published book.*

~

Reidel has been interested in Kees, the literary figure and the man, for more than twenty years. He was first introduced to the poet's work in the late 1970's, after being given a copy of *The Collected Poems of Weldon Kees* (1960) as a graduation gift. Reidel was fascinated by Kees's darkly ironic verse and felt compelled to find out who this strange and amazing poet was. He was surprised to find that very little had been written about Kees, whose work was not included in many poetry anthologies. Reidel took it upon himself to remedy the situation. He was determined to research the man and then write a biography. Reidel had previously edited two of Kees's works. He is the editor of the collection *Reviews and Essays, 1936-1955* (1988) and Kees's posthumously published novel *Fall Quarter* (1990).

Reidel begins his literary biography with a prologue dated July 18, 1955. This opening section covers what is known about Kees's ultimate vanishing act. In subsequent chapters the biography takes the reader from Kees's early days into the 1950's in an attempt to explain how Kees came to feel, by July 18, 1955, that "escaping" to Mexico or committing suicide were the only choices left to him. Born on February 24, 1914, Harry Weldon Kees grew up in Beatrice, Nebraska. In later years, Kees would describe having Beatrice as his hometown as like being born into an "existence of subnormal calm."

The only child of John Kees and Sarah Green Kees, young Weldon was encouraged to appreciate the arts. It is believed that his parents did not have any more children because giving birth again would have been extremely dangerous for Sarah Kees. John Kees ran the F. D. Kees Manufacturing Company, founded in 1874 by Weldon's grandfather Frederick Daniel Kees. Weldon's mother created a secure environment for her only son to experiment with many different artistic outlets. Kees was a very precocious child. His father did have hopes that his son would one day take over the family business, but he did not want to stand in the way of Weldon's other, more creative interests.

Weldon wrote stories and poems, learned to play the piano, and loved to draw. He also became fascinated with the films that came to the local movie theater. Young Weldon even went so far as to create his own fan magazines. His parents were devoted to him, and he learned to be a little adult at an early age. Although not a loner, Kees had a reputation for being rather bookish. One of his childhood friends was named Spangler Arlington Brugh. The two would remain friends for years and even go to the same college. Spangler Brugh would eventually go off to Hollywood to make a name for himself and would become the film star known to millions as Robert Taylor. During high school, Kees continued to follow his creative moods and to feel restless about where he was. Reidel makes it very clear that Kees had an insatiable appetite for learning and for believing that he was going to do great things.

In the fall of 1931, Kees enrolled in Doane College in Crete, Nebraska. Crete was not too far away from Beatrice and could not really be considered much of an escape from Beatrice High School. Hoping to study creative writing, Kees transferred to the University of Missouri. He was not satisfied by the literary community there, so he once again transferred, this time to the University of Nebraska, located in Lincoln. His father had graduated from the University of Nebraska, and Lowry Wimberly, the editor of the school's literary magazine, *Prairie Schooner*, was an English professor there. Kees would spend his senior year in Lincoln as a member of the literary group led by Wimberly.

Reidel emphasizes how important it was for Kees to be recognized as a literary talent. As did many young writers of the time, he had aspirations of becoming the next William Faulkner or Ernest Hemingway. While his efforts at writing novels proved frustrating, he had some success with placing his short stories in various small literary journals, including the *Prairie Schooner*. From the mid-1930's to the mid-1940's, more than forty of Kees's short stories were published. His short stories would not be collected until *Ceremony, and Other Stories* was published in 1984. This collection was edited by the acclaimed poet Dana Gioia. Gioia also would edit the 2002 *Selected Short Stories of Weldon Kees*.

During his senior year at the University of Nebraska, Kees met Ann Swan. She had transferred to Lincoln from Pomona College in California. Kees was quite taken with the petite young woman, and she became one of the few people whose opinions he trusted. In 1935 he graduated from the University of Nebraska with a B.A. in English. Kees was unsure at this point in time what he should do next. The United States was in the throes of the Depression, and there were few options available for anyone. After much conjecture, Kees found a job with the Federal Writers' Project in Lincoln. During his tenure there, he honed his skills as a poet.

While it was certainly not easy to find a job during the Depression, Kees found a position with the Denver Public Library in 1937. After he had settled in Denver, Weldon and Ann were married there. They were both heavy drinkers, prone to extreme mood swings. She was most helpful, though, as a sounding board for his creative projects. Ann got a job as a stenographer and typist at a law firm in Denver in order to help make ends meet. Although a frustrated librarian, Kees continued to write and dream of better days. Eventually, he would become the director of the Rocky Mountain Bibliographic Center for Research at the library. Despite holding this position, he still was of the opinion that he was living in a backwater of civilization.

The couple did their best to appear well-adjusted and happy, but bouts with alcohol abuse and depression began taking a toll on both Weldon and Ann. In 1943 Kees decided that it was time to escape Denver and his wife. The couple separated, and Kees moved to New York City. This was going to be his chance at making his literary mark in the Big Apple. While his novel *Fall Quarter* had been rejected by New York publisher Alfred A. Knopf in 1942, Kees believed that for his poetry and his ability to write critically on many subjects, he would finally receive the recognition he deserved. Being a poet himself, Reidel understands a poet's insecurity and how hard it can be to succeed at self-promotion.

Although he could be quite charming and a witty conversationalist, Kees tended to be aloof and fastidious. No matter his personal quirks, he became friends with such literary giants as Edmund Wilson, Allen Tate, Theodore Roethke, John Cheever, Malcolm Cowley, Mary McCarthy, and William Carlos Williams. For a short time, he wrote reviews for *Time* magazine. He was let go after falling "out of favor" with the editor Whittaker Chambers. Chambers bluntly told Kees, "Our readers don't want to hear you groan." Kees could never bring himself to pull his punches in anything he wrote.

Weldon and Ann finally ended their separation, and she joined him in New York. His first collection of poetry, *The Last Man*, was published in 1943. Although he worried about being drafted into the armed services during World War II, he need not have: He failed the Army's psychological fitness test. There was a dark side to Kees that was always there and always set him apart.

His years in New York were very productive and exhausting. He wrote for many leading periodicals, worked for a newsreel service, and championed the up-and-coming Abstract Expressionist movement. In 1947 his second book of poetry, *The Fall of Magicians*, was published. This collection received glowing reviews. By the late 1940's, he and Ann were spending their summers in Provincetown, Massachusetts. Kees immersed himself in the art colony there and took up painting. He became quite a good abstract painter and had a number of shows. Some of his paintings were included in group shows with the likes of Willem de Kooning and Hans Hofmann. Even with the summers in Provincetown, the strain of the New York environment finally became too much for him. In 1950 he and Ann drove across the United States, to San Francisco.

Their life on the West Coast, though, did not lead to the stable existence that both of them desperately needed. Kees became involved in myriad creative projects, including hosting a radio show, working on a documentary film, staging plays, and composing jazz songs. Money seemed always to be in short supply, and he was forced on many occasions to ask for funds from his parents. His parents, who had retired to Santa Barbara, became concerned with their son's seeming inability to make a living. Ann's alcoholism had taken a turn for the worse, and the couple finally divorced in 1954. Kees's third book of poetry, *Poems, 1947-1954*, was published that same year. He began abusing alcohol and amphetamines on a regular basis. By 1955 he was deeply depressed and had begun telling friends that he was seriously considering going to Mexico. It is unlikely that the question of what Kees did on July 18, 1955, after abandoning his car will ever be resolved to the satisfaction of all.

Reidel's thoughtful and clear-headed biography of Kees steers clear of psychological presumptions. Kees was an extremely complex person who may have been the victim of bad luck. It is more likely that, for all of his extraordinary talents, Kees was his own worst enemy at all the wrong times. *Vanished Act* is everything that he could have hoped for in a biography. It also includes a fascinating collection of black-and-white photographs.

Jeffry Jensen

Review Sources

The Chronicle of Higher Education, June 13, 2003, p. A14.
Kirkus Reviews 71, no. 8 (April 15, 2003): 593.
The New York Times Book Review, August 17, 2003, p. 12.
The Washington Post Book World, August 3, 2003, p. 3.
Weekly Standard 9 (September 22, 2003): 34.

THE VICTORIANS

Author: A. N. Wilson (1950-　　)
Publisher: W. W. Norton (New York). 544 pp. $35.00
Type of work: History
Time: 1832-1901
Locale: England

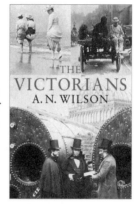

A comprehensive, one-volume survey of the decades that constitute the Victorian period in England, years of rapid, convulsive change that ushered in the modern industrialized world

Principal personages:
QUEEN VICTORIA (1819-1901), queen of
　Great Britain, 1837-1901
PRINCE ALBERT (1819-1861), her husband,
　the prince consort
CHARLES DARWIN (1809-1882), evolutionary biologist, author of *On the
　Origin of Species by Means of Natural Selection* (1859)
CHARLES DICKENS (1812-1870), popular novelist and social critic
BENJAMIN DISRAELI (1804-1881), Tory prime minister (1868, 1874-
　1880)
WILLIAM EWART GLADSTONE (1809-1898), Liberal prime minister
　(1868-1874, 1880-1885, 1886, 1892-1894)
CARDINAL MANNING (1807-1892), famous Roman Catholic convert and
　popular activist cleric

As a writer, A. N. Wilson is no stranger to monumental tasks. His magisterial biographies of Leo Tolstoy and C. S. Lewis, Jesus Christ and Saint Paul suggest he is undaunted by the challenge of traversing vast tracts of history and personality and undeterred by the fact that others may have been over his territory rather thoroughly before. To take on the better part of a century, to organize the tumultuous history of Victorian England—its sprawling events and richly complicated personalities—into a single coherent and readable volume requires a heroic grasp. Happily, in Wilson's rewarding text he shows himself to be fully up to the job. His steady, wide-ranging vision, confidence, and boldness of conviction might even be characterized as "Victorian."

The Victorians is an appropriately grand and lively affair, a triumphant collage of information on science and religion, economics and politics, popular culture and the arts. The narrative teems with piquant details but does not lack the broad shaping outlines which give the particulars real point. Wilson's book is, as he says, a "portrait of the age," a treatment reminiscent of earlier efforts to capture this protean era—the most famous of which is surely G. M. Young's *Victorian England: Portrait of an Age* (1936). Like Young's study—though on a much bigger scale—Wilson's is an attempt to give a personal reading which traces the defining features of these eventful

~

A. N. Wilson is literary editor of
The Evening Standard as well as
being the prolific author of
celebrated novels and numerous
well-received biographies,
including C. S. Lewis: A
Biography *(1990)*, Jesus *(1992)*,
Paul: The Mind of the Apostle
(1997), and Tolstoy *(1988)*.

~

years, identifying common characteristics while still honoring the period's insistent diversity, and to do this without nailing it all too tidily to a dominating thesis.

Wilson does have a thesis, of course, though it is not original and is largely unexceptionable: At the heart of the Victorian age there is a dichotomy, a fundamental two-mindedness. Look out at any point on the nineteenth century landscape and, he suggests, one will find coexistent oppositions: confidence and uncertainty, scientific clarity and moral bewilderment, smug optimism about progress and a paralyzing fear about its consequences, the headlong pull of the future and the nostalgic tug of the past. Whether it is the gothic excesses that drape new technologies (the first railway stations are vivid examples here) or the polarities that mark, say, John Ruskin as the father of socialism *and* the bluest of old Tories—the competing dualities (and the visible fissures they create) are there, putting a distinctive stamp on the period and its players.

As a result, Wilson proposes that a unique sort of doubt was *the* cultural experience from the 1840's onward, from the assault on orthodoxy launched by Charles Lyell's *Principles of Geology* (1830-1833) through the temblors caused by Charles Darwin's *On the Origin of Species by Means of Natural Selection* (1859) right up to the *fin de siècle* instabilities precipitated by aesthetic revolutions, Irish Home Rule debates, and Boer War skirmishes. The carefully assembled and artfully delivered details of Wilson's comprehensive chronicle amply support this claim of spiritual malaise going hand in hand with economic success and industrial progress. As the century unfolds, there is, in his view, a growing sense of something having gone alarmingly awry.

Wilson's history is a series of riveting stories, vignettes that place unlikely events and characters into revealing juxtapositions to convey this dizzying sense of the continuities and disruptions that were the very texture of Victorian life. He makes much, for example, of the death of Thomas Malthus, the fires in the Houses of Parliament, and the voyage of the *Beagle*, all occurring in 1834, to highlight the crisis of population and what government and science will be doing about it. In 1837, it is the erection of Euston Station and the enthusiastic reception of Charles Dickens's *The Pickwick Papers* (1836-1837) that he pulls together to suggest the passing of the stagecoach, the emergence of the steam engine, and the instant (and persistent) nostalgia these developments triggered in the Victorian public.

This interweaving of incident and character, the locating of abstract issues in the lives of real people, is one of Wilson's rhetorical signatures. The pathetic East End death of Ellen Green, age seven, in the first of the dreaded cholera epidemics launches his investigation of the links between poverty, trade, disease, and capital. The terrifying spread of cholera provides a memorable metaphor for the contagion of mammon. The Irish famine of 1845-1850, which resulted in more than 1.1 million deaths, is here a pathetic tale grounded in searing particulars. Wilson expertly layers in the contextual material—the lethal mix of anti-Irish prejudice, fear of state intervention, exclusive cultivation of potatoes, lack of educational opportunities—to spin tragedy from chilling historical facts. It is the novelist's sure sense of pace, character, scene setting, and dramatic action that is clearly evident, and it is this imaginative ability to render things in vividly concrete ways that makes this long book read like a much shorter one—that and his decision to break the text into brief topical chapters within sections devoted to each decade from the 1830's to the 1890's.

The format decisions—single-volume overview, thematic chapters, personal selections—raise questions about just who the audience is for this book. Wilson anticipates possible criticism from those who might suggest that it is too long and detailed for the nonspecialist and too quick-hitting and general for the professional. Can Chartism be handled properly in ten pages? Should the coverage of the scramble for Africa rate fewer pages than the debate over evolution or the proliferation of the railways? Does the space given to the Irish question seem too little, that to the Crimean War too much? Wilson understands that a book like his will provoke such questions, but he maintains that as he is not an academic historian, he has not felt compelled to be exhaustive in that particular way. He admits that he has deliberately given more time and space to incidents and figures who, in his opinion, have been misunderstood or underestimated. Far from detracting from the book's value, however, this personal dimension gives it real color and dramatic impact; nor is it anything less than thoroughly researched at all points. His preoccupations and judgments are not idiosyncratic even if they are individual.

Not surprisingly, then, Wilson has his heroes. Readers familiar with his earlier book on this period, *Eminent Victorians* (1989), will know to expect paeans to Prince Albert, measured but clear praise for Liberal prime minister William Gladstone, admiration for social activist Josephine Butler; and they will not be disappointed, for these figures reappear here and are given fitting treatment. Prince Albert's intelligence, his shrewd diplomacy, his invaluable stabilizing effect on the wilder, more capricious, and self-absorbed nature of his wife, the queen—all these Wilson examines, ending with the provocative observation that, in his opinion, had Albert not died at the early age of forty-two, his statesmanship, pan-German stature, and understanding of European tensions might have prevented the growth of competing nationalisms and made less likely World War I.

Beyond Albert, he praises Thomas Carlyle for his visionary social criticism and the way in which he embodied in his own dyspeptic being the conflicts of the age; Cardinal Manning for his insistence on taking religion to the dockworkers, the unionists, the invisible inhabitants of East End streets and for his sheer ability to get things done; Charles Dickens for his endlessly fertile imagination linked to a deeply responsive heart; Charles Darwin for his fearless mind and humble spirit; Thomas Hardy for his flinty refusal to sugarcoat the world as he saw it and his dignified call for intellectual honesty from the church; and Sir Robert Peel for his practicality and common-sense as prime minister, so unlike Lord Palmerston's blustering intransigence and supreme egotism when he held the office.

Perhaps the most unexpectedly positive portrait among these public figures is Wilson's depiction of Benjamin Disraeli, Gladstone's Tory counterpart during the century's middle decades. Disraeli predictably emerges as a figure of wit and charm, of conversational brilliance and novelistic savvy, the cagey mastermind who brokered the Suez Canal purchase and the addition of Empress of India to the Queen's official titles. He is also seen as a man who was, for all his lightness of touch, deadly earnest about his political initiatives and commitments and who brought a rare and desirable detachment to the job. Wilson finds him quite lovable, finally—not something he, nor anyone else, would say of Gladstone.

When Wilson knowingly poached his 1989 title from Lytton Strachey's brittle but brilliant 1918 indictment of these same "eminent Victorians," he pitted himself against the earlier Bloomsbury iconoclast. In so doing, he argued that these Victorian figures—for all of the excesses of piety, earnestness, and blind self-regard, which to Strachey seemed only signs of psychological disturbance and sources of derision—were, in fact, men and women of supreme accomplishment and worthy of admiration. Wilson can be seen as something of a champion, going as far as to admit that the most agreeable life he can imagine would be that of a rural parson born in the 1830's and living through the wonderfully eventful decades chronicled here.

Even so, Wilson is able to resist the lure of romanticizing the Victorians. He does not argue the position that, in spite of the doubts and fears, the perturbations of spirit that clearly plagued the better minds of the nineteenth century, these were fundamentally noble folk, industrious and energetic, endlessly optimistic and dutiful. They managed to tame the problems of their modern material world and create a stable, prosperous society. Wilson may be inclined to this view (his admiration is registered many times over), but he is not partisan, not sentimental. He is quite clear about the manifold failures, the blindness and misguided enthusiasms these Victorians made almost a defining feature of their time. In the end, *he* will not define them that way. While being candid about their obvious and unfortunate shortcomings—their signal failure to alleviate the suffering of the urban poor at home; their imperial brutality in Africa, India, and elsewhere abroad; their heartless neglect of conditions in Ireland; their fiercely asymmetrical gender order and staggeringly undemocratic system of government—he is open-minded enough to see the enormous range of accomplishments they, in fact, totted up.

Perhaps not surprisingly, one exits this richly packed survey feeling properly respectful of the Victorian achievement. There is something irresistible about these decades, the figures that dominated them, the legacy they clearly passed on. For better or worse, the "modern" age arrived in the nineteenth century, with its recognizable problems of industrialization, secularization, and urbanization. Wilson is at pains to show that "the Victorians are still with us," that, though changed, "the world they created is still here." Despite those changes, despite an intervening century or more, modern Westerners are still curiously connected to the remarkable individuals who confronted, shaped, and endured these Victorian years.

Thomas J. Campbell

Review Sources

The Atlantic Monthly 291, no. 2 (March, 2003): 113-119.
Booklist 99, no. 5 (November 1, 2002): 472-473.
History: Review of New Books 31, no. 3 (Spring, 2003): 99-100.
History Today 53, no. 3 (March, 2003): 56-58.
Kirkus Reviews 70, no. 20 (October 15, 2002): 1518.
The New Republic 228, no. 15/16 (April 21, 2003): 42-45.
Publishers Weekly 249, no. 45 (November 11, 2002): 50.
The Times Literary Supplement, September 20, 2002, p. 8.

THE VOICE AT 3:00 A.M.
Selected Late and New Poems

Author: Charles Simic (1938-   )
Publisher: Harcourt (New York). 177 pp. $25.00
Type of work: Poetry

A fine introduction to the work of one of the United States' major poets, these poems demonstrate Simic's fidelity to the poetic landscapes which have always informed his poems as well as his gradual development of longer lines and longer works

Charles Simic has been an important voice in American poetry for more than thirty years. His publications total more than sixty books, many of them volumes of poetry. It is significant that he has also published many translations of poetry from Central European countries, an interest which he surely owes to his birth and early life in Belgrade, Yugoslavia. In fact, although Simic has lived in the United States since 1953, his poetry has always displayed a sort of European sensibility that sets it apart from much other American writing. This volume, composed of poems from 1986 to 2003, will serve as a fine introduction to Simic's work for those who are unfamiliar with it.

Readers who already know Simic's poems will recognize many things here. His characteristic settings appear—the nameless city filled with great hotels and abandoned factories, inhabited by the anonymous poor or by philosophers, artists, or beautiful yet dangerous women. Here, too, is Simic's favorite weather: the dark night, the wintry storm. Many readers will also recognize folkloric qualities of much of his work. Cities and countries are nameless and unlocated. Rarely does the reader find the details of ordinary life which inform the work of many contemporary writers—no Chevrolets or Wonder Bread, no cell phones or computers, no Vietnams, only an occasional television set broadcasting news of atrocities. These poems demonstrate in Simic's work a familiar surrealism that defies paraphrasing into logical narrative.

"Toward Nightfall," a poem from *Unending Blues* (1986), demonstrates how these elements work together to create a world that seems fraught with ineffable significance. The opening lines assert that "tragic events" are weighing down everyone, even while some unnamed public assumes that the true age of tragedy—the classical world—is long past. In the present world, the omniscient viewer can see impotent figures on a scaffold and a dark autumn night that looks like what one would see if one were hunkered down in the "back of an open truck." If one had been walking, the bare trees would have seemed ready to cry out. Or one might have been in "One of these dying mill towns/ Inside a small dim grocery/ When the news broke." The air in that place smelled of blood or fear of approaching death. What has happened? What is about to happen? The landscape hints at portentous events which are never defined.

The poem's last stanza pictures a film poster on which monsters are displayed, "too," Simic adds, as if the world offers enough monsters without fictional ones. The poem concludes with an image of six factory girls, walking "Arm in arm, laughing/ As if they've been drinking." They seem oblivious of the dangers which surround them. "At the very least, one/ Could've been one of them," Simic remarks, suggesting that such obliviousness is not a bad thing.

∼

Charles Simic was born in Belgrade, Yugoslavia, and came to the United States in 1953. He began publishing the first of his more than sixty books in 1967. He received the Pulitzer Prize for The World Doesn't End: Prose Poems *in 1990. He is a professor of English at the University of New Hampshire.*

∼

Simic creates a similarly foreboding effect in "The Little Pins of Memory" from *The Book of Gods and Devils* (1990). The pins in this poem are the pins that hold a child's dress suit to a tailor's dummy in the window of a dusty shop which appears to have been closed for years. The speaker sees it one Sunday afternoon in the past while wandering lost through endless streets of "red-brick tenements." Remembering the "dark and heavy cloth" of the suit was like the pricking of pins as he walked those streets, and it continues to prick him even today as he recalls the sight. The tailor's closed shop seems to have much in common with the location of "Factory," from the same volume, where the speaker pictures himself camping like a fugitive in an abandoned factory, deprived of almost everything except the surreal vision of a naked woman who attempts to steal an apple which the speaker has stored in a dangling bird cage.

Simic's commentary is more specific in "The Big War," where he recalls that "We played war during the war." The rest of the poem describes his regiments of beautiful clay soldiers and his joy in playing with them. Humorously, he pictures his child-self from the soldiers' point of view—"a large, incomprehending creature/ With a moustache made of milk." Eventually the soldiers broke (some he broke intentionally), and he discovered the reality—that they were merely clay-covered wires with empty heads. The child general, rather like adult generals of "the big war," was left with only "an arm, now and then, an officer's arm,/ Wielding a saber from a crack/ In my deaf grandmother's kitchen floor."

Repeatedly, Simic reminds the reader that the world is a dangerous place for the weak and the powerful alike. In "Frightening Toys," the little girl will soon know that "everything comes out in the end/ Missing an arm or a leg"; all humanity is as fragile as the doll or the toy soldiers. Even "Folk Songs" (from *Hotel Insomnia*, 1992), record the work of the "Sausage-makers of History,/ the bloody kind." In their world, doomed heroes like Oedipus or Hamlet fall "like flies/ In the pot of cabbage soup."

To this vision Simic adds a dark humor as leavening. In the uncharacteristically long poem "Talking to the Ceiling" (from *Jackstraws*, 1999), he records the meditations of one who has been reading the evening papers with their usual bad news. He is led to "The big question, can we continue/ To keep the grim reaper laughing?"

"Mummy's Curse" makes playful use of the trappings of gothic fiction and the horror film, as can be seen when the Mummy himself appears—on a bicycle, making a pizza delivery. "Crazy About Her Shrimp" pictures a high-spirited speaker occupied alternately with lovemaking and food. "We keep our mouths full and busy/ Eating bread and cheese/ And smooching in between." The speaker chops hot peppers; the naked woman stirs shrimp on the stove. They both drink red wine. It is no wonder that the speaker can shout to the gods his wild devotion to her shrimp. In "Serving Time," Simic offers a wry picture of his life as an inmate in "time's invisible/ Penitentiary," where he makes license plates and studies law and philosophy—the only recourse against the impossible appeal board chaired by God. The description is bleak, but the description of "how time runs things around here" is unmistakably funny, even while, like much of Simic's humor, it unsettles.

These poems suggest that physical comforts—food, like the playfully cooked shrimp, and love—are what keep people going in a world where, as in "Sunday Dinner," Simic reminds one that "The butchery of the innocent/ Never stops. That's about all/ We can ever be sure of, love." Thus, the speaker will find his ironic respite in the lamb roast his wife offers for dinner. In "Unmade Beds," the speaker praises with rare hope "the moment of sweet indolence/ That follows lovemaking,/ When the meanest of hearts/ Comes to believe/ Happiness can last forever."

The volume's last section is made up of new poems. Read in the context of the late volumes, these seem to return to the shorter lines and freighted landscape of the earlier work. Once again, mortality prevails. In "Nearest Nameless," Simic addresses it:

> So damn familiar
> Most of the time,
> I don't even know you are here.
> My life,
> My portion of eternity . . .

What is the truth of this life that is so obvious that people mostly ignore it? In this poem, the answer lies in the bird's shriek that warns of the approaching cat, a shriek which makes the speaker shake in fear as he recognizes the common fate of humans and birds in the face of violence.

Empty barbershops, empty streets, the stranded driver who finds the Fates telling fortunes in a nursing home in Tennessee, the museum which opens at midnight—the furniture of this section seems to have come from Simic's endless stock of dream worlds, no two exactly the same, most of the newest including more sense of the writer as an actor—or observer, at least—than did his earlier poems, most of them reminding one that the world is full of bloodshed. One can cope with that knowledge only through the comforts of love, at the same time maintaining an ironic awareness that love is as transitory as a good meal, and terror is at the center of every bone.

Ann D. Garbett

Review Sources

Booklist 99, no. 15 (April 1, 2003): 1370.
Library Journal 128, no. 5 (March 15, 2003): 88.
The New York Review of Books, November 20, 2003, pp. 22-24.
The New York Times Book Review, April 6, 2003, p. 18.
Publishers Weekly 250, no. 7 (February 17, 2003): 71.
The Virginia Quarterly Review 79, no. 4 (Autumn, 2003): 136.

WAR AGAINST THE WEAK
Eugenics and America's Campaign to Create a Master Race

Author: Edwin Black
Publisher: Four Walls Eight Windows (New York). 559 pp. $27.00
Type of work: History
Time: From the mid-1800's to the late twentieth century

This history of the development of American eugenics activism argues that the movement was partly responsible for the Nazi mass murders during World War II

Principal personages:
FRANCIS J. GALTON, the pioneering British statistician who coined the term "eugenics."
CHARLES B. DAVENPORT, an American zoologist and eugenics activist who founded the Station for Experimental Evolution of the Carnegie Institution, the Eugenics Record Office, and the Eugenics Research Association
HARRY H. LAUGHLIN, a colleague of Davenport and eugenics activist
CARRIE BUCK, a young woman who was sentenced to be sterilized by Virginia law and who made a historic, unsuccessful appeal of her sentence to the U.S. Supreme Court
EDWIN KATZEN-ELLENBOGEN, a Polish-born American citizen and physician who was active in the American Eugenics Research Association and later became a prisoner at Buchenwald, where he allegedly collaborated with his Nazi captors
OTMAR FREIHERR VON VERSCHUER, a German physician and eugenicist who maintained connections with Davenport, Laughlin, and American eugenics organizations
JOSEF MENGELE, an assistant of Freiherr von Verschuer, whose eugenics research at Auschwitz made him a notorious war criminal

The word "eugenics," from Greek words for "well born," was coined by the English pioneer in statistics, Sir Francis Galton, a cousin of scientist Charles Darwin. Galton suggested that it might be possible to direct natural selection by encouraging marriages among people with desirable traits. Galton made some effort to obtain information on inherited traits, gathering data on family traits through questionnaires collected by his Anthropometric Laboratory at London's International Health Exposition. Galton's interest in eugenics remained largely theoretical, though; he confessed that it would be a long time before scientists had enough knowledge to direct evolution. He also maintained that eugenicists should stress "positive eugenics," matings between people with valued characteristics, and avoid "negative eugenics," the practice of preventing reproduction by people judged to be mentally or physically inferior.

In the United States, Galton's work inspired activists who put the British statistician's ideas into practice. Chief among these was Charles Benedict Davenport, who earned a doctorate in biology at Harvard University and taught zoology at Harvard and at the University of Chicago. Davenport managed to secure funds from the Carnegie Institute to set up a Station for Experimental Evolution at Cold Spring Harbor, New York, in 1904. The Institute would be devoted to finding ways to direct evolution.

In order to pursue this goal, Davenport obtained additional support from the widow of railroad magnate E. H. Harriman and created the Eugenics Record Office (ERO), which would register the genetic histories of American families, identifying desirable and undesirable hereditary strains. In 1913 the eugenicists, led by Davenport, created the Eugenics Research Association (ERA), which was dedicated to research and to promoting laws and policies. Two of the most prominent members of the ERA were Madison Grant and Lothrap Stoddard, best-selling authors who had published books arguing that the white race was threatened by the hereditary influences of inferior nonwhites.

~

Edwin Black is an investigative journalist whose writing has appeared in newspapers across the United States and Europe. Black's first book, The Transfer Agreement *(1984), won the Carl Sandburg Award for best nonfiction book. His book* IBM and the Holocaust *(2001) won the American Society of Journalists and Authors Award for best nonfiction book. Black is also author of the novel* Format C: *(1999).*

~

Many of the important figures in American social and intellectual history were involved in the eugenics movement. Margaret Sanger; the feminist campaigner for birth control and founder of Planned Parenthood, had ties to the movement. Henry Goddard, the pioneer of intelligence testing who coined the word "moron," was also connected to it.

Davenport's chief lieutenant in the crusade for eugenics was Harry Hamilton Laughlin. Laughlin was an ambitious teacher who met Davenport while attending a summer biology class at Cold Spring Harbor. When Davenport founded the ERO, he obtained permission from the generous Mrs. Harriman to make Laughlin the head of the office. Laughlin was a tireless promoter of the cause of eugenics. With the support of U.S. Secretary of Labor James J. Davis, in 1923 Laughlin set out on a six-month tour of Europe to encourage U.S. consular officials to obtain information on the supposedly hereditary characteristics of European nations that would be sending immigrants to the United States. Laughlin also acted as a consultant to Congressman Albert Johnson, chairman of the House Committee on Immigration and Naturalization. Although Laughlin's statistics on the intellectual superiority of northern Europeans sparked some scorn in the press, the eugenics activist played a part in the U.S. Immigration Act of 1924, which established a quota system for accepting immigrants which heavily favored people from northern and western Europe.

In this book, Edwin Black documents the impact of the eugenics movement on the treatment of the native-born population of the United States. The "weak" in the title of his book refers to people considered undesirable for a number of reasons. Members of racial minorities, the poor, and unemployed rural people living at the margins of an urbanizing society could all be seen as products of inferior family stock. Supporters of negative eugenics managed to have laws permitting sterilization of the supposedly unfit enacted in twenty-three states.

The most famous sterilization case was that of Carrie Buck in Virginia. With the advice and help of Harry Laughlin, eugenics activists in Virginia managed to get the state to pass a law allowing the sterilization of individuals in situations in which there had been three generations of mentally defective people in a family. On somewhat slender evidence, Buck, her mother, and her small child were all classified as feeble-minded. Buck was ordered to be sterilized. Objections to her having more children concentrated on her inability to support herself and on the illegitimacy of her child. These two facts were related, as she had lived with a family who had used her as a servant and then sent her away after she became pregnant, apparently as a result of being raped by a member of that family. Buck acquired supporters, and she appealed her case all the way to the U.S. Supreme Court. In words that became famous, Justice Oliver Wendell Holmes declared that "three generations of imbeciles are enough," and the Court accepted the legality of forced sterilization.

The influence of the American eugenics movement, according to Black, extended far beyond the United States' shores. Black argues that the United States became the center of worldwide eugenics activities and, ultimately, contributed to the Nazi Holocaust in Germany during World War II. The First International Congress of Eugenics, held in London in 1912, was dominated by ideas developed in the United States. German scientists and physicians promoting eugenics maintained close associations with the ERA, the ERO, and Harry Laughlin. American eugenics journals published and praised the work of the Germans, even when this work had heavy anti-Semitic overtones. Even more serious, American organizations such as the Rockefeller Foundation provided funding to German race biology, both before and after Adolf Hitler rose to power.

One of those who received Rockefeller money was Otmar Freiherr von Verschuer, a medical researcher interested in identifying hereditary traits through studies of twins. Verschuer maintained personal and professional ties with American eugenicists even after World War II, although these ties were strained by the accusations of involvement in war crimes that had been made against him. The notorious Josef Mengele, who conducted his own barbaric twin studies at the death camp at Auschwitz, was Verschuer's good friend and assistant. Black gives disturbing descriptions of Mengele's activities at Auschwitz, although he does not suggest that there was any American involvement in these activities.

In the story of Edwin Katzen-Ellenbogen, Black gives a fascinating case of an individual connection between the American eugenics movement and the German death camps. Katzen-Ellenbogen was a physician and psychologist who had been born in Poland and migrated to the United States in 1905. Although he maintained that his religious background was Catholic, he actually came from a Jewish family. He married in the United States, became an American citizen, and held a variety of prestigious positions, including that of lecturer on abnormal psychology at Harvard University. Katzen-Ellenbogen, also a charter member of the ERA, returned to Europe in 1915 and remained there for the rest of his life. During World War II he was identified as Jewish by the Germans, who placed him in the Buchenwald concentration camp. There he became a favored prisoner because of his medical skills and because he shared the racial and eugenics views of his captors. Inmates of Buchenwald later charged that Katzen-Ellenbogen had collaborated with Nazis in the cruelties of the camp. After the war, he was tried for war crimes and sentenced to life imprisonment, later reduced to twelve years on grounds of his poor health.

Black maintains that the science of genetics has roots in eugenics that are often unrecognized. After World War II, attempts to direct biological evolution were tainted by their association with racist ideology. Still, Cold Spring Harbor, where Davenport had established his headquarters, went on to be a center of genetic study. James Watson, one of the discoverers of the double helix structure of deoxyribonucleic acid (DNA), studied at Cold Spring Harbor, and it was there that he gave the first public presentation on DNA structure in 1953.

According to Black, many of the dangers to humanity posed by eugenics can also be found in genetic research. The possibility of discrimination against disfavored groups on the basis of DNA information is a major problem of scientific ethics. Further, Black claims, DNA identity banks being created by the Federal Bureau of Investigation and other police organizations around the world are beginning their work at the same point that the Eugenics Records Office began, with attempts to identify people with hereditary information.

Through the pages of this interesting and detailed volume, Black demonstrates that the American eugenicists had many professional and organizational ties with individuals in Germany who were active in the Holocaust. However, he may overestimate American responsibility. Some of the connections he makes between the American eugenics movement and the Nazis amount to charges of guilt by association. The fact that Freiherr von Verschuer communicated with the Americans and received support from them does not make American organizations responsible for the actions of Mengele. Moreover, it is misleading to characterize eugenics activities as "America's campaign." While the eugenicists were an energetic group, they were opposed by much of American popular opinion. In addition, the Holocaust probably had its most important roots in Germany itself. For example, the evolutionary biologist Ernst Haeckel (1834-1919) played an important part in the development of the concept of "race hygiene" in Germany, and Black does not even mention Haeckel. Ultimately, Black does not offer convincing evidence that American eugenics played much of a role in the Holocaust, but he does recount a shameful and important part of American social and scientific history.

Carl L. Bankston III

Review Sources

Booklist 99, no. 22 (August 1, 2003): 1932.
Discover 24, no. 9 (September, 2003): 77-78.
Kirkus Reviews 71, no. 14 (July 15, 2003): 945.
Library Journal 128, no. 12 (July 15, 2003): 118.
Mother Jones 28, no. 5 (September/October, 2003): 91-92.
National Review 55, no. 18 (September 29, 2003): 41-42.
The New York Times Book Review, October 5, 2003, p. 8.
Publishers Weekly 250, no. 34 (August 25, 2003): 52.

THE WAY TO PARADISE

Author: Mario Vargas Llosa (1936-   )
First published: El paraíso en la otra esquina, 2003, in
   Peru
Translated from the Spanish by Natasha Wimmer
Publisher: Farrar, Straus and Giroux (New York). 373
   pp. $25.00
Type of work: Novel
Time: 1844-1903
Locale: Various locations in France, including Paris and
   Arles; London; Arequipa and Lima, Peru; Tahiti; and
   Atuona in the Marquesas Islands

*A world-famous Peruvian writer pairs the life stories of
two unconventional historical figures, the reformer Flora
Tristán and her grandson, the painter Paul Gauguin*

   Principal personages:
   FLORA TRISTÁN, a socialist agitator, the daughter of a French mother and
      a Peruvian father
   PAUL GAUGUIN, her grandson, an artist, who deserted his family to live
      in the South Pacific
   ALINE CHAZAL GAUGUIN, Flora's neglected daughter and Paul's mother
   GUSTAVE AROSA, Aline's wealthy lover and Paul's guardian
   METTE GAD GAUGUIN, Paul's estranged wife
   VINCENT VAN GOGH, the fellow artist with whom Paul lived in Arles
   ANDRÉ CHAZAL, Flora's estranged husband and Aline's abusive father,
      an engraver
   DON PÍO TRISTÁN, Flora's uncle, a wealthy Peruvian
   OLYMPIA MALESZEWSKA CHODZKO, Flora's friend and lover, a Parisian
      society hostess

   During his childhood in Peru, Paul Gauguin may well have played a game called
"el paraiso en la otra esquina," or, translated literally, "paradise in the other corner."
Whether or not Gauguin later remembered the game, as Mario Vargas Llosa has his
Gauguin character do in the novel *El paraíso en la otra esquina,* the painter was indeed
obsessed by his search for an earthly Eden. What makes this book so fascinating is that
Vargas Llosa has paired the life story of the famous artist with that of Paul's grandmother, Flora Tristán, a social reformer, who was just as determined as her grandson
to find what the translator of Vargas Llosa's book called *The Way to Paradise.*
   On the surface, Flora Tristán and Paul Gauguin seem more different than similar.
Flora was at her best in public, haranguing crowds and organizing socialist cells; her
memoirs are now primarily of interest for their insights into social history. By contrast, the paintings that Paul produced in the quiet of his studio are in museums
throughout the world. Moreover, the two took very different directions in their quest

Among the awards given Mario Vargas Llosa for his writing are Peru's Congressional Medal of Honor, the Ritz Paris Hemingway Award for La guerra del fin del mundo *(1981;* The War of the End of the World, *1984) and the National Book Critics Circle Award for criticism for* Making Waves *(1996).*

for paradise. Paul sought it by fleeing from civilization toward a more primitive past. Thus he left Paris for the simpler life of Arles, then ventured to Tahiti, and finally, feeling Tahiti too civilized, settled in the even more remote Marquesas Islands. Flora, too, saw the defects of what was called civilization, but her focus was on the future, rather than on the past. Her goal was to eliminate poverty and exploitation by transforming the social institutions of her day; she was determined to awaken the working classes so that they would insist on the establishment of utopian socialistic states throughout the world.

As Vargas Llosa proceeds with his novel, relating the stories of his protagonists in alternate chapters, it becomes obvious why he chose to incorporate them into a single work. The grandmother and her grandson had more in common than one might think. In temperament, they were much alike. Both of them were rebels; both were hounded by the representatives of the status quo, especially by the Catholic Church; and if someone threatened them or those they cared about, both of them attacked, either verbally or physically, without any thought of consequences. When the villagers of Concarneau set upon his bohemian friends, Paul rushed into the fray; the result was a crushed ankle that tormented him throughout the rest of his life and eventually made it almost impossible for him to walk. As for Flora, it was no accident that she was widely known as Madame-la-Colère, for her tirades were directed at everyone she viewed as an oppressor and especially those who exploited workers or mistreated women.

One of the less likeable traits that Paul and Flora shared was their willingness to leave to others the care and responsibility for their children. Admittedly, in Flora's case there were some extenuating circumstances. After she fled from her tyrannical husband, André Chazal, Flora lived in fear of his taking vengeance on her by taking the children, as he had a legal right to do. On three occasions, he seized their daughter Adele, though when Flora discovered that he was routinely raping the young girl, she managed to get her daughter away from him. One can also understand why Flora did not take Adele with her on that arduous voyage to Peru, where with the help of her wealthy uncle, Don Pío Tristán, she expected to claim an inheritance that would enable her to support her family. On the other hand, when she felt impelled to make a lecture tour, Flora did not let motherhood stand in her way.

By contrast, Paul had no compunctions about abandoning his Danish wife, Mette Gad Gauguin, and the large family they had produced, nor did he make any attempt to support his children. He was just as casual about the illegitimate offspring he sired. Ironically, in his later years Paul felt more sympathy for his mother, Aline Chazal

Gauguin, than for the daughter he deserted, who was his mother's namesake. In the chapter titled "Portrait of Aline Gauguin," Paul recalled how beautiful his mother seemed to him and how intensely he loved her during that happy period in his childhood when they were living in Lima at the home of his great-great-uncle Don Pío Tristán. Only when they were back in Paris and Aline had agreed to become the mistress of a married man, the wealthy Gustave Arosa, did Paul come to hate her. When she died, he felt nothing. It was only after he landed in Tahiti twenty-eight years later that he was overcome by a sense of loss, made even more intense by his memory of his mother's prophecy, that he would alienate every friend he had and end up alone.

Paul's disapproval of his mother's relationship with Arosa is difficult to explain, for Paul always viewed sexual expression as a natural function. His own promiscuity resulted in his contracting syphilis, probably from a prostitute, long before he left for Tahiti. Interestingly, while he was in Arles with his friend, the artist Vincent van Gogh, the two men had discussed the effect of sexual activity on their work. Van Gogh insisted that he painted best when he abstained, but Paul believed that sexual expression inspired him. When he realized how casually the Tahitians engaged in sex, Paul was sure that he had found his paradise. Unfortunately, as his disease progressed, the sores and the stench associated with it repelled even the most willing native partners, and in the final months of his life, Paul found that syphilis had taken away his power to perform.

Flora, too, discovered that sexual relationships are not always as idyllic as one might believe. However, her disillusionment came early. When she was still very young and very poor, Flora was pushed by her mother into marriage, only to find that she was tied for life to an abusive husband. The experience turned her not only against sex but also against the institution of marriage and against the Catholic Church, which would not permit a woman to escape from what Flora saw as the cruelest kind of slavery. Although in later life Flora sometimes encountered a man she believed would be kind to her, she would not allow herself to take a chance. Her only experience of sexual fulfillment was with a woman, Olympia Maleszewska Chodzko, an important figure in Parisian society. Paul, too, was occasionally drawn to those of his own gender. The fact that in Tahiti there was no stigma attached to being a *mahu*, or man-woman, was to Paul one more sign that primitive peoples, who could live with ambiguity, were more perceptive than supposedly advanced societies.

After two happy years with Olympia, Flora ended their affair, not because she loved her any less, but because the shocking conditions she had seen in England had convinced her that she must devote all her energies to her cause. In fact, Flora had only five years left. Her health had long been fragile. For years she had suffered from abdominal distress, probably related to childbearing, and she also had a bullet in her chest, a final memento from her husband, who had been sent to prison as a result of that episode. During her last years, Flora was often ill, but she kept on with her public appearances until she was felled by what the doctors believed was typhoid fever. When the end came, she was just forty-one; her daughter Adele died at the same age. Paul lived to be fifty-five, and like his grandmother, he kept working almost to the end, despite physical weakness, despite pain, despite his dimming eyesight. When death approached, Paul still had one final moment of triumph, for he realized that by dying he would cheat the gendarme who had just succeeded in arranging to send him to prison.

The Way to Paradise is a brilliantly conceived book. Vargas Llosa chose for his subject two historical figures who never met, though they were blood relations, who lived fifty years apart, and who seem initially to have totally different attitudes as to the purpose of life. At first the reader may be convinced that Vargas Llosa has simply chosen to combine two historical novels. However, it is not long before the parallels between the characters and the variations on the themes become evident, and from that time on one is increasingly aware of the elaborate contrapuntal structure of the work.

Vargas Llosa's handling of time is just as subtle as his treatment of character and theme. On one hand, the chapters dealing with Paul are presented in chronological order, and each of them is headed with a date, sometimes even with a place. The chapters that tell Flora's story are ordered in the same way. However, because the author does not place any limits on his protagonists' thoughts, every chapter holds information about their past lives, which are then reinterpreted in the light of their more recent experiences.

Although Vargas Llosa has a well-deserved reputation as a master of his craft, it is difficult to explain one of his habits in *The Way to Paradise*. Most of the book is written in the third person voice, focusing either on Paul or on Flora. At times, however, Vargas Llosa suddenly switches into the second person, perhaps to suggest a character's debate with himself or herself, perhaps to insert the author's comments. Whatever the intention, the effect is annoying.

On balance, however, *The Way to Paradise* is one of the finest achievements of a writer whose insights and artistry have already brought him worldwide recognition. In these pages, he has brought Flora Tristán and Paul Gauguin to life as the complex, contradictory people they were. However, the book has a significance beyond its biographical and historical interest. It may remind twenty-first century idealists pursuing the idea of an earthly Eden that they may meet the same hostility as Vargas Llosa's protagonists. Like them, too, they may accomplish a good deal but die with their dream of paradise on earth still unfulfilled.

Rosemary M. Canfield Reisman

Review Sources

Booklist 100, no. 2 (September 15, 2003): 181.
The Economist 368, no. 8333 (July 19, 2003): 71.
Kirkus Reviews 71, no. 19 (October 1, 2003): 1200.
Library Journal 128, no. 17 (October 15, 2003): 100.
New Criterion 22 (October, 2003): 70-73.
New Statesman 132, no. 4665 (November 24, 2003): 55.
The New York Times Book Review, November 23, 2003, p. 11.
Publishers Weekly 250, no. 39 (September 29, 2003): 40.
Time 162, no. 22 (December 1, 2003): 93.
The Times Literary Supplement, December 19-26, 2003, p. 27.

WHAT I LOVED

Author: Siri Hustvedt (1956-   )
Publisher: Henry Holt (New York). 384 pp. $25.00
Type of work: Novel
Time: 1975-2000
Locale: Manhattan

Astute exploration of love, identity, art, evil and societal disintegration as played out within a circle of artists and intellectuals and their children living in Manhattan in the late twentieth century

> *Principal characters:*
> LEO HERTZBERG, an art historian and best friend of Bill Wechsler
> ERICA STEIN, his wife, an English professor
> MATT HERTZBERG, their son
> BILL WECHSLER, an experimental artist living and working in Soho
> LUCILLE ALCOTT, a neurotic poet, the ex-wife of Wechsler
> VIOLET BLOM, Bill's second wife, a warm-hearted cultural historian
> MARK WECHSLER, the troubled teenage son of Bill and Lucille
> TEDDY GILES, a flamboyant and sociopathic artist

What I Loved is divided into three parts, suggesting the fragmentation of relationships that is the novel's major topic. Presented as a memoir by the now-elderly art historian Leo Hertzberg, the narrative explores his twenty-five-year friendship with the brooding experimental artist Bill Wechsler as they cope with the inexplicable unraveling of their marriages and families. It is Leo whose consciousness holds together this novel, which otherwise might easily disperse into a series of confusing and contradictory fragments. It is he who represents the spirit of investigation and who is a source of stability for the reader, even when he struggles with the material about which he is writing.

Even with the presence of Leo's integrative consciousness, there are still unresolved strands, questions left over and unanswered, so that the narrative never allows the reader the flat satisfaction of a single, simple explanation. Instead, Leo's struggle with his writing creates a rich mix that includes an exploration of personal relations, the inner world of the artist, philosophical ideas, and social criticism.

One topic Leo explores is the increasingly consumer-oriented and deliberately shocking art world of the 1980's and 1990's, intertwined with a disturbing teenage subculture that developed coterminously in a number of Manhattan night clubs. Leo's narrative is also a study of marriage and child-rearing in that same period, especially the marriages of those whose identities were formed in the rebellious era of the 1960's and 1970's. In contradistinction to the youthful hopes and dreams of that decade, Leo depicts subsequent years of death, sickness, accident, and even murder, in which the dominant theme is not that of promise or fulfillment but loss, abandonment, estrangement, mourning.

Siri Hustvedt is the author of two previous novels, The Blindfold *(1992) and* The Enchantment of Lily Dahl *(1996), as well as a book of poems. She lives in Brooklyn with her husband, the novelist Paul Auster.*

Although the novel pulls itself in diverse directions, the heart of the narrative is the divorce in the 1970's of the introspective artist Bill Wechsler and his wife, Lucille, a poet, and its effect on their son, Mark. The influence of Lucille is suggested at the outset by one of Bill's early paintings, which depicts her as a disappearing figure who becomes increasingly unavailable, inscrutable, and cold. Lucille's mysterious emotional disappearance becomes one possible explanation for the personality disorder her son, Mark, develops as he grows into young adulthood. Additionally, Bill blames himself for abandoning Mark when he was a child, suggesting that his absence deprived Mark of the ability to construct a healthy identity.

While Leo and Bill maintain their friendship, their family lives become seriously strained by Bill's divorce and by fates of both their children. Things gets significantly worse when Leo's son, the artistic Matthew, drowns in a boating crash and, torn apart by the death of their child, the marriage between Erica and Leo dissolves. Leo's consciousness, however, is gradually raised so that he begins to see the big picture, namely a generation of lost or endangered children.

Leo's growing blindness as he ages, ironically, indicates his developing insight, his ability to see things to which he had previously been blind—particularly with regard to the antisocial personality developing in Bill's son, Mark. Mark does not literally die but begins to transform so dramatically as to seem a stranger to all who knew him when he was a child. This radical and unpredictable change is what leads Leo to ask himself deep questions about life and about human identity. Aided by Bill's sensitive and supportive second wife, Violet, Leo begins to explore a number of different explanations for the development of Mark's narcissistic personality.

A cultural historian, Violet suggests that there are intimate ties between individual personality and the influential wider culture that drives people, with or without their consent. Reinforced by her historical research, Violet posits the development of a mysteriously evil temper of the times that permeates, or even infects, each individual. She points to the corrupting influence of the young avant-garde artist Teddy Giles, who has become the leader of a group of Manhattan teenagers, introducing them to a subculture of theft, drug taking, cross-dressing, and violence.

The last half of this novel takes an unexpected turn with the new and insidious presence of Giles, whose influence had remained largely undetected by the adults. Mark, whose pleasant facade covers a deliberate pattern of deception, is, in reality, a member of Teddy's hedonistic and nihilistic inner circle. Amoral and devoid of empathy, this clique of "club kids," Violet suggests, can be said to be a product not simply of troubled marriages, but of a late-capitalistic society in which all codes and values are breaking down. Using the epidemic of hysteria that visited the late nineteenth century as a paradigm, Violet suggests that Mark is the victim of a cultural contagion working through carriers such as Teddy. Seen in this light, parents are helpless in the face of larger cultural and historical dynamic, represented by the criminal antics of

Teddy, from whom they cannot protect their children—he is somehow in the very air they breathe.

The second resonant meaning of the character of Teddy is in his identity as an artist. In addition to representing a contagious criminality, Teddy also represents developments in the art world in the 1990's that make Bill's work seem behind-the-times; in addition to stealing his son, Teddy is also replacing Bill as the new "hot" artist in New York. Teddy's art derives from the world of pop culture, especially horror movies, which he reconfigures as artistic and stylish. In addition, Teddy's protective, amoral irony allows him to deploy this pop art in the service of a commodified society, in which almost every cultural activity degenerates into a form of consumerism not dissimilar to drug addiction.

Teddy's own personality is also put into play as part of his work, so his life and his character become part of a larger theater of the self that requires a series of poses or invented identities. Teddy can switch genders and become something called the She-Monster; or Mark can pose as Teddy's pretty, blond wife or as his son. The two of them disport themselves in these disguises while traveling across the United States, ending up in the corny Opryland Hotel in Nashville with both a sense that nothing really "counts" or matters and a conviction that they are essentially invincible. The ironizing of their identities and lives has also allowed Teddy to implicate Mark as his accomplice in a murder that is soon stylized as an "art murder"; that is, as an extension of the series of performances and poses that have characterized Teddy's life as an artist and impresario in New York City.

Lionized as the next big thing, the flamboyant Teddy has been able to dominate Mark in such a way that Mark subsumes his identity into Teddy's, becoming his virtual twin and partner-in-crime. As Bill becomes increasingly exhausted by Mark, Leo begins to replace Bill as Mark's parent, just as Violet replaces Lucille as the material presence in Mark's life. As a result of his new responsibilities as Mark's surrogate father, Leo finds himself literally chasing Mark and Teddy around the Midwest before finding himself in a surreal Nashville hotel, personally threatened by the Teddy's absurdist violence.

As Leo is increasingly bedeviled by Mark and Teddy, he is at the same time exploring issues concerning the nature of identity and the nature of human perception, becoming less sure about the possibility of knowing for sure who anyone is or what anyone can know or predict about people or about the future. Dissatisfied with purely rational explanations, Leo finds he must also seek answers in the language of the traditional fairy tale, which evokes images of witches and other traditional symbols of wickedness. In the case of Mark, he is especially taken with the symbolic resonance of the familiar fairy-tale motif of goblins that will steal a baby and replace it with an identical copy, eventually exposed as a wicked substitute for the good child, who has disappeared. The idea of metaphysical evil suggested in the imagery of monsters, witches, and demons surfaces as well in Leo's historical memory of his grandmother, uncle and aunt, and their twin daughters, all of whom died at a concentration camp during the Holocaust. Along with the traditional images of evil deployed in fairy tales, the spiritual evil of Nazi Germany has, for Leo, some important connections to the emerging cultural atmosphere of New York at the end of the twentieth century.

Mark's involvement in Teddy's fantasy world and criminal activities ultimately overwhelms Bill, who is essentially driven to an early death by the stress of Mark's problems and by the interference of Teddy, who is obsessed with Bill as an artistic rival. One sees, however, that Bill's intriguing works of art suggest other ways of taking the situation in hand. It is in Bill's art that he seems to be able to cope with what is happening in his life and with his child. For instance, one of the late works involves the representation of a disappearing self, or a self that has become a empty, cryptic "zero." Here Bill seems to be able to render intuitively and come to terms with what has happened to Mark in a way that is impossible in his daily life. Similarly, the ideas of Leo and Violet also contribute to the understanding of what has happened to Mark and to other children like him. Leo's philosophical exploration of love, work, family, and friendships within the context of an unraveling society also becomes a celebration of the power of understanding and of the empathic imagination that does much to offset the demonic power of Teddy and his minions.

What I Loved is considered Hustvedt's breakthrough novel, exhibiting an intellectual range and depth of feeling that is an advance over her earlier work. Combining page-turning narrative suspense with intellectual and psychological insight, her narrative is both a dark and stylish psychological thriller and a fresh, fearless portrait of contemporary life as experienced and interpreted by its artists and intellectuals. Using both a risky fragmentation and narrative shifts that seem to break the novel into pieces, Hustvedt speaks to existential issues of strangeness and unknowability, social issues that suggest the presence of cultural epidemics, psychological issues concerning perception and the construction of identity, as well as issues that speak to the demonic and the tragic aspects of modern life. In *What I Loved*, Hustvedt has written both a novel about intimacy and a novel whose truth-seeking energy and grasp of important psychological, social, and artistic issues establishes it as a major work of fiction.

Margaret Boe Birns

Review Sources

Booklist 99, no. 11 (February 1, 2003): 971.
The Boston Globe, March 23, 2003, p. H7.
The Economist 366, no. 8315 (March 15, 2003): 77.
Kirkus Reviews 71, no. 1 (January, 2003): 12.
Library Journal 128, no. 1 (January 1, 2003): 154-155.
New Statesman 132, no. 4620 (January 13, 2003): 52-53.
The New York Times, March 28, 2003, p. E47.
The New York Times Book Review, March 9, 2003. p. 12.
Publishers Weekly 249, no. 50 (December 16, 2002): 43.
The Washington Post, March 30, 2003, p. 6.

WHEN HOLLYWOOD HAD A KING
The Reign of Lew Wasserman, Who Leveraged Talent into Power and Influence

Author: Connie Bruck (1946-   )
Publisher: Random House (New York). 512 pp. $29.95
Type of work: Biography
Time: 1896-2002
Locale: Chicago; Los Angeles; and Washington, D.C.

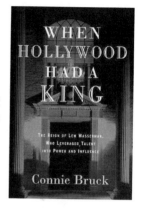

This detailed biography of Lew Wasserman, president of the Music Corporation of America, traces his impact on the film industry, politics, and American culture

Principal personages:
LYNDON B. JOHNSON, the president of the
    United States from 1963 to 1969
SIDNEY KORSHAK, a lawyer with ties to
    organized crime
JAMES C. PETRILLO, the president of the American Federation of
    Musicians
RONALD REAGAN, the president of the United States from 1981 to 1989
JULES STEIN, the founder of Music Corporation of America
LEW WASSERMAN, the president of Music Corporation of America

When Lew Wasserman, once the president of the Music Corporation of America (MCA), died in 2002, probably few Americans knew his name or his place in the cultural history of the United States during the twentieth century. For more than half of that century, Wasserman had been a key figure in deciding what films and television programs were aired, who the stars of such shows were, and how these entertainment offerings would be presented. As the president of MCA, he headed an organization that managed the professional services of many of the brightest stars in Hollywood's galaxy. Not content with being an agent, Wasserman expanded his company's operations into the development and production of films and television shows, to the point that he was probably the most powerful man in the world of entertainment. Connie Bruck's incisive biography of Wasserman and his business is a fascinating exploration of the realm of celebrity, politics, and art, plus a healthy dose of the influence of organized crime.

A staff writer on *The New Yorker* and the author of other well-reviewed books on business and politics, Bruck has done extensive research and interviewing in constructing her portrait of Wasserman and his world. She shows her expertise about the convoluted world of Hollywood, with its deals and schemes in both films and television. Her knowledge of how the major players in show business interact and relate to one another gives her account a lively immediacy that will interest even those not familiar with the milieu in which Wasserman functioned. Readers will learn much

Connie Bruck is a staff writer for
The New Yorker *who has
published several books about
modern business and financial
history, including* The Predators'
Ball *(1988) and* Master of the
Game *(1994).*

about the real way power is used and influence exerted in American entertainment in Bruck's lucid account of the temperamental, mercurial, and successful executive that Wasserman became.

In many respects, this book is more a history of MCA and the men who oversaw its development than it is a biography of Wasserman as such. As Wasserman's private life was not readily accessible to the author and because he spent most of his time on his business affairs, such an approach to the book makes sense. Wasserman does not appear in the first seventy pages of the book, which recount how Jules Stein founded MCA in the 1920's, then survived the rigors of a close association with organized crime in the early days of the business and finally moved his operations to California. In Hollywood, MCA achieved preeminence among the talent agencies of the burgeoning film industry. Stein's rise, facilitated by his connection with James C. Petrillo and the American Federation of Musicians, shows how entertainment agents evolved into power brokers within show business by their ability to control the careers of the people the public wanted to see. MCA's somewhat dubious origins, and the willingness of its leaders to reach back to their sordid origins in a crisis, were secrets of its enormous power in Hollywood.

When Wasserman came on the scene in 1939 at the age of twenty-three, his energy, skill, and ruthlessness quickly took him to a position of dominance within MCA. Stein understood that he had an unusually talented subordinate, and Wasserman emerged as first among equals in the growing MCA empire. He recognized that having good relations with the Hollywood stage unions was essential for stability within the motion picture industry. A violent strike by these ruthless labor leaders could result in a production shutdown that would interrupt the flow of films to a public eager for entertainment. Labor peace entailed dealing with the crime-ridden International Association of Theatrical Stage Employees (IATSE), then under the direction of such mob-linked leaders as George Brown and Willie Bioff. Wasserman proved to be a masterful negotiator with these union figures, thanks in part to the clandestine help that MCA received from Sidney Korshak, an influential Los Angeles attorney who had connections with the various national crime families on his own. One of the key contributions of the book is Bruck's ability to trace the interconnections between organized crime and the motion picture business. She also shows how the Mob's influence seeped into national politics in ways that historians have only just begun to explore in any depth.

Over the following two decades, Wasserman built himself into a dominant power in the film business. The picture that emerges from Bruck's lucid pages of Wasserman the man is not an attractive one. He could be a tyrant toward his employees and a hard-nosed negotiator with his business partners or rivals. He was subject to massive rages and abrupt departures from meetings to get his way. If an employee crossed him on even a small issue, immediate dismissal followed, coupled with a complete break in social relations of any kind. When he decided to injure someone's career, that person faced ruin. As one executive who dealt with Wasserman in a business deal put it, "MCA had what I call 'scare power.' It was as bad as [Joseph] McCarthy. Lew would put you through the ringer and ruin your career."

Whether these strong-arm tactics had grown out of emotional deprivation in Wasserman's past is not clear. His private life is not much discussed in Bruck's account. His difficult relations with his wife and daughter are hinted at, and he was probably a formidable man to have as a husband or father. Readers looking for clues in Wasserman's domestic life for insights into his business practices will not find them, probably because they did not exist. He concentrated all his energies on his work, to the exclusion of most other facets of his life. As a result, the treatment of his business adventures, for all Bruck's thoroughness in explaining them, can become a little wearing at times. A knowledge of the corporate structure of Hollywood deals is almost a prerequisite for understanding Wasserman the man.

Wasserman grasped that one intrinsic key to MCA's survival was political power. His mergers and insider deals often attracted the attention of the Department of Justice because of the anticompetitive practices that he regularly used. To ward off such unwelcome attention from government regulators and prosecutors, he saw to it that his business had strong ties with Washington power brokers. A Democrat, Wasserman forged a close friendship with Senator and later President Lyndon B. Johnson. According to Wasserman, Johnson offered him a Cabinet position in the 1960's. While that is unlikely, Bruck shows how much influence Wasserman had with the Johnson administration. A place was made for a former Johnson aide, Jack Valenti, as president of the Motion Picture Association of America, a link that helped MCA prosper even more in the years after Johnson left the White House.

An even more intriguing thread in Bruck's disclosures concerns Wasserman's relationship with the future president Ronald Reagan. The phase of Reagan's life during which he presided over the Screen Actors Guild is one of the more controversial of Reagan's political past. Reagan would often assert in later years that he learned about the menace of communism from dealing with organized labor in Hollywood. There is also the question of Reagan's willingness to inform on his former colleagues who had ties to the Communist Party. The extent to which Reagan revealed information about his colleagues to the Federal Bureau of Investigation is still not completely clear. Bruck shows that Reagan's involvement in these issues went into more depth than many of his biographers have shown. Intriguing hints of Reagan's closeness to certain Mob figures also emerges. This section of the book is very interesting as Bruck outlines these volatile issues.

In the case of one politician, Senator Estes Kefauver, the Tennessee Democrat who probed organized crime in televised hearings during the 1950's, Bruck recounts the story that mobsters, led by Sidney Korshak, supplied Kefauver with feminine companionship and then blackmailed the lawmaker. At least one biographer of Kefauver discounts the allegation, which is based on a single source who spoke long after the fact.

While a compelling case is made for Wasserman's powerful status in Hollywood, his impact on the product that the film and television industry presented to the world was less than inspiring. The films that did well under Wasserman's aegis at Universal Studios, such as *American Graffiti* (1973), *Jaws* (1975), and *The Sting* (1973), seem to have been made as much in spite of the studio's head as because of him. What excited Wasserman was not the artistic quality of the films but their money-making potential. As an associate recalled, "He could tell you what a particular gross was in any one of six hundred theaters, at any time." As Wasserman commented, "Numbers are what make the world go round."

Using that standard, Wasserman, like the rest of Hollywood, pursued the blockbuster film that would make huge amounts of money for the studio. In television programming, he achieved ratings success by appealing to the lowest common denominator of his prospective audience. Much of the tawdriness of modern entertainment can be traced to the ethos that Wasserman brought to the business in which he labored for more than half a century. So in the end, Bruck's admirable book becomes a tale of a man who created a world of power and influence and then saw it overtaken by the forces of commercialism and greed that he had both unleashed and embodied for so many years.

There is, at the end, a certain sadness about Wasserman's life. A master of business, he worked in an industry where what went up on the screen or on television mattered most. How the producers and executives behind the scenes put together the packages that made creativity possible is interesting for those fascinated with the inside games of Hollywood. Wasserman had the capacity to assemble the elements of art and, in some cases, to allow that elusive element to flourish. He was a big man in Tinseltown for a season, and he left his mark on the industry. In the history of films, he is an intriguing diversion from the real significance of the cinema. Bruck has thus done Wasserman's career full justice.

Lewis L. Gould

Review Sources

Booklist 99, no. 18 (May 15, 2003): 1618.
The Economist 367, no. 8325 (May 24, 2003): 84.
Kirkus Reviews 71, no. 9 (May 1, 2003): 651.
Library Journal 128, no. 9 (May 15, 2003): 91.
The Nation 276, no. 25 (June 30, 2003): 25-29.
The New Leader 86, no. 3 (May/June, 2003): 23-25.
The New York Times, June 2, 2003, p. E7.
The New York Times Book Review, June 22, 2003, pp. 13-14.
Publishers Weekly 250, no. 17 (April 28, 2003): 57.
The Wall Street Journal, June 6, 2003, p. W8.

WHEN THE MESSENGER IS HOT

Author: Elizabeth Crane (1961-   )
Publisher: Little, Brown (New York). 210 pp. $21.95
Type of work: Short fiction
Time: About 2002
Locale: New York and Chicago

Crane's debut collection of often humorous, experimental short stories chronicles urban women's struggles to maintain integrity and an identity in an increasingly fragmented society

Principal characters:

WENDY, a successful memoirist whose life is stolen by an actress who plays her in the film version

APPLE FOWLER, the actress who wins an Academy Award for her portrayal of Wendy

DAVE, one of a series of bad boyfriends, all named Dave

ALICE, a woman who joins Alcoholics Anonymous without having a drinking problem

Elizabeth Crane's debut collection of sixteen short stories is filled with agoraphobic, overly analytic women who detach themselves from the world because of bad childhoods, odd fetishes and phobias, and as a distrust of modern life in general. Mostly told from the first-person point of view, Crane's stories unfold from the mouths of various female Holden Caulfields whose internal monologues remark on popular culture topics as diverse as support group spirituality and tattoo artistry. Though most stories rely heavily on Crane's experimentation with form and style to create an edgy, postmodern ambiance, the characters within these stories also struggle with more old-fashioned concerns such as identity and its dissolution and the necessity for maintaining attachment to others within a worldview that privileges detachment. The combination of using new methods with an older sensibility for character development gives these stories their punch and readability, though when Crane pushes too far in either direction, the stories have difficulty sustaining their momentum.

The voices in Crane's stories are breathy ones, unrestricted by traditional form, content, style, or grammar. Narrators make lists and outlines. Words tumble over themselves in run-on sentences, weak parallelism, and fragments as characters discuss topics such as casual sex, tattoos, and the Dave Matthews Band. Though almost every story has a different first-person narrator, the voices begin to sound alike, as if Crane's universe contains multiple women who all live similar lives. For example, several of the stories feature a first-person narrator whose mother has died, though Crane makes no effort to show any additional interrelatedness between these stories. Furthermore, she relies very little on transitional devices or internal links within sto-

Elizabeth Crane has published stories in publications including The Sycamore Review, Washington Square, *and the* Sonora Review. *A former teacher, Crane grew up in Manhattan on the Upper West Side and now lives in Chicago.*

ries except in the most tangential of ways. Sometimes the associations seem as intuitive as the thought-process itself, a striving for a stream-of-consciousness logic that belies any writerly intrusion in the recording of the details.

To create further a sense of thought processes going by, Crane's narrators often divert the momentum of the stories with asides and digressions. This effect can best be seen in "The Super Fantastic New Zealand Triangle," which bears similarities to other novels such as Vladimir Nabokov's *Pale Fire* (1962) and David Foster Wallace's *Infinite Jest* (1996) in its use of footnotes that add a richly layered back story within a frame text masquerading as the main one. In this story, a woman recalls a fantasy—and its unlikelihood—about a love triangle including herself and a semi-famous New Zealander actor she once met. The footnote section serves as narrative comment on the action of the story, adding particulars to the retelling of the narrator's fantasy. Eventually, the specifics of the footnotes take precedence over the main text, revealing more interesting and telling detail than the sometimes ludicrous main story.

In this story and others, such as "The Intervention" and "The Archetype's Girlfriend," the digressive use of details attempts to show up the inherent inaccuracies of a master narrative, yet one of the dangers of such a method also frequently occurs: The story itself dissolves under the pressure of sustaining the digression. In "The Archetype's Girlfriend," for example, the listing of details about memorable girlfriends is so quirky and amusing that one forgets the basic premise of the story. "The Intervention" follows the whimsical actions of its main character, Alice, as she tries to figure out an approach to living which works for her. In the process, she details many anecdotes about various boyfriends who disappear from the narrative without comment. While the structure of all of these stories allows for, and remarks upon, the engagement of digression and detail, the story line is often sacrificed for the structural experiment.

A story that uses structural experimentation more effectively is "The Daves." It has the composition of a formal outline as the narrator attempts to discuss why men named Dave have been bad relationship choices. The outline breaks down, as outlines are wont to do, and that is part of the point—the senselessness of formal structure as a method for uncovering any sort of real "truth." In this case, the truth concerns the narrator's tendency to date the wrong kind of guy and why. By listing pluses and minuses in a relationship accounts ledger, the narrator hopes to arrive at some final word on the subject. Previously, she had been assuming that all men are really alike, all "Daves." The story then takes a surreal turn—as many of Crane's stories in this collection do—and suddenly all men are literally called Dave. However, the narrator gets her comeuppance when she is incorrectly called "Jennifer," thus showing her what happens when one spends too much time over-generalizing. "The Daves" has a metaliterary aspect in that the structure comments on the story itself. The author's distrust of formalizing structures becomes more apparent as the narrator reaches incorrect conclusions, then loses her own identity in the process. Crane communicates her writerly distrust of form while simultaneously using the same form she ridicules.

In "You Take Naps," Crane again shows how a story's structure can buttress its textual meaning. At first, this story seems rather conventional. A second-person narrator relates the differences between herself and her much younger boyfriend. The problems the couple faces are what one might expect, which she characterizes in dichotomies: "He has roommates. You have furniture," and "You have experience. He has hope." The narrator registers the clichéd nature of these comparisons, as well as the situation, yet she doesn't want the ending of the relationship to be predictable: "You want the ending to be neither cheesy or gloomy. You want the ending to be open." Just as the narrator does not want the relationship to end badly, neither does the author want the story of the relationship to end badly, either. As Crane reaches the conclusion of the story, she fights to maintain control over those two elements, particularly when the story itself is so banal. Like the narrator, Crane wants to keep the story open-ended and so, instead of happy or sad, she ends the story like this: "You want an ending of cautious hope. Better." Ending with a fragmented comment on the story structure allows Crane to dodge the hackneyed likelihoods of both the relationship and the story that details that relationship.

Crane's experimental tendencies do not stop at the structure and form level; she writes about unusual topics as well. One of her major themes concerns the loss of identity, but rather than submerging that theme within the story, Crane addresses these issues in a full-frontal, often surreal manner. For example, in "Something Shiny," the narrator, Wendy, writes a best-selling memoir which is to be made into a motion picture. Though her story details a pathetic, drunken, suicidal life, the memoir has suddenly made her famous. Apple Fowler, a celebrated actress, has been chosen to play her in the film version and wants to live with Wendy and study her pathetic life so she can better portray her. The scenes between the two women showcase the pathos of Wendy's life and the multidimensionality of the actress who has to assume the pathos. In a reversal of what one might expect when comparing actors to regular people, the actor has more integrity, more enthusiasm for the role than the person who has lived the life. As a result, Wendy's identity is symbolically but also literally stolen—she loses her boyfriend, her friends, even her pets because they all believe that Apple Fowler is Wendy. As Wendy says when Apple accepts the Academy Award for her starring role in the film:

> Apparently Apple Fowler is better at being me than me because not only does she show up on the red carpet wearing a tiara and my Prada dress, she actually . . . wins the Oscar for being me, and she bursts into tears and thanks her higher power and her agent and my sister and her *fiancé* my ex-boyfriend, who is naturally also weeping in the audience, and she's America's sweetheart and she's Apple Fowler again and there is something shiny with my name on it but there's still no me.

The story seems to suggest that telling one's story opens one to the risk of getting it stolen. Identity needs to retain its fluidity by not being put into writing, where it becomes static and rife for theft.

Despite the bizarre avenues that Crane explores in her work, she creates believable characters. Though the narrator of "Privacy and Coffee" chooses to build a house on the roof of rich friend's apartment building and live there out of a sense of agoraphobia, that character's ideas concerning the uninspired demands of modern life seem candid: "Looking down at all those tiny people moving around like that all the time, home, work, in, out, day after day, I dunno, it just seemed to me like it wasn't me who was acting strange." Though she eventually leaves her self-imposed isolation because of a lavender-shirt-wearing elevator boy who brings her prepared foods, these comments suggest the narrator's phobic reaction to humanity might be a reasonable response to an irrational condition.

Two of the stories deal realistically with death and the grief process. "Year-at-a-Glance" and "Return from the Depot!" both concern a narrator's reaction to her mother's death. Though it does not seem that the two women are quite the same, they do bear some similarities—the mother is an opera singer, and the mother's death was caused by lung cancer. In "Year-at-a-Glance," particularly, Crane's wise-cracking, ironic narrator becomes the victim of her own irony, as language and attitude turn in on themselves when the mother inexplicably dies. The form of the story, that of a mental diary recounting incidents from various points on her life calendar, also contributes to the journal effect as it forces the author to sketch the emotional response with detail, rather than abstraction. This shorthand favors understatement while allowing the reader glimpses into the details of grief, such as the sudden spasm of sorrow the narrator experiences when she finds the pink socks her mother wore in the hospital. In a similar but more fantastic manner, "Return from the Depot!" honors the details of a narrator's fantasy of her dead mother returning from the grave to star in her own sitcom. Though the narrator knows that many might find her to be delusional, she is comforted by this delusion's ability to give her hope where before she had none.

Crane's characters strive toward these moments of hope, largely in the ways they learn to respond to people as individuals rather than as groups. This necessity to connect with others also allows characters to learn more about themselves as a consequence. By experimenting with form and style, Crane suggests that the recognized methods for creating relationships might not be the best ones; certainly ironic disassociation does not allow her characters to become fully realized. Like the narrator of "You Take Naps," Crane allows for the possibility of connection between people by creating fictive worlds where cautious hope does not seem fraudulent. Although her characters are not always entirely successful in their endeavors, their effort is at least rewarded.

Rebecca Hendrick Flannagan

Review Sources

Booklist 99, nos. 9/10 (January 1-15, 2003): 846.
Kirkus Review 70, no. 21 (November 1, 2002): 1550.
Library Journal 128, no. 1 (January, 2003): 161-162.
The New York Times Book Review, February 23, 2003, p. 17.
Publishers Weekly 250, no. 1 (January 6, 2003): 40.

WHERE I WAS FROM

Author: Joan Didion (1934-   )
Publisher: Alfred A. Knopf (New York). 226 pp. $23.00
Type of work: Current affairs, history, and memoir
Time: 2003 and California's pioneer history
Locale: California

Part memoir, part history, part social criticism, Didion's book asks difficult questions about what it means to be from a particular place and time and about how people come to grips with their pasts

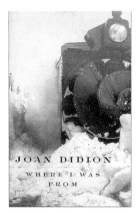

Principal personages:
　　LELAND STANFORD (1824-1893), the governor of California
　　JACK LONDON (1986-1916), a novelist
　　THOMAS KINKADE (1958-   ), a painter

Like much of Joan Didion's best work, *Where I Was From* performs a precarious balancing act: It manages to be simultaneously deeply intimate and broadly political. The book is both a personal memoir and an exploration of the big issues that define the author's home turf, the state of California. The opening paragraphs contain a capsule history of the eventful westward journey of Didion's pioneer family, focusing particularly on the women in the family and tracing back six generations the pedigree of her famous migraines. She tells the charmingly absurd tale of how her cousin donated to the Pacific University Museum the old potato masher that their ancestors carried across the plains. It is through her personal and family attachments to the place, Didion tells the reader, that she "began trying to find the 'point' of California, to locate some message in its history."

Personal and family history, however, quickly give way to other stories. Didion tells, for instance, of the immigrants who, as they draw near to the promised land, come across an abandoned adolescent girl and her sick brother, left by a previous group of pioneers to be found or to die. These two abandoned children, along with many other characters and incidents, are mentioned in passing, are then left, and then again returned to at various appropriate moments in the book. The old potato masher, likewise, returns several times as an ironic icon. By approaching California's myths from various angles and layering small snippets of stories upon one another, Didion allows the bigger picture to emerge. The technique is a familiar one to her fans, who will recognize it—along with some actual settings and incidents—from her best-known essays, including "Some Dreamers of the Golden Dream" and "Slouching Towards Bethlehem," both published in 1968.

Where I Was From is, in part, a series of verbal portraits of people with a real stake in the California dream: novelist Jack London, painter Thomas Kinkade, generations of ranchers and railroad men and developers, and the author's own family. In painting

Joan Didion has published several well-received novels, including Run River *(1963),* Play It as It Lays *(1970),* The Book of Common Prayer *(1977), and* Democracy *(1984). She is perhaps best known, however, for her essays, collected in such books as* Slouching Towards Bethlehem *(1968) and* The White Album *(1979).*

these portraits, Didion exposes what she believes to be the very heart of the California conundrum, the disconnect between the steadfast belief of the state's citizens in their individual freedom and self-determination and its nearly total reliance on government (mostly federal government) hand-outs in the form of tax relief, subsidies, and defense and building contracts. In describing many individual Californians, including earlier versions of herself, she allows the reader to perceive the warping of internal logic that allows these people to continue insisting they are free and self-determined, in spite of the pervasive evidence to the contrary.

Throughout this book, as in her earlier work, Didion uses the small, trenchant observation to lead her readers to the big picture. In discussing the aerospace industry, for instance, she focuses upon the Southern California community of Lakewood, planned and built by that industry. In the late 1990's this community faced a series of troubling reports of sexual harassment and rape perpetrated by a gang of youths who called themselves the Spur Posse. Didion contends, without quite making it seem a contention, that the collapse of the local industry is what has led to desperation among the local youth and their subsequent antisocial behavior. Her research for this portion of the book is wide-ranging enough to present her readers with the low SAT scores of students from Lakewood High School as well as quotations from the alleged criminals, their alleged victims, and the parents of both. All of this is aligned with statistics and interviews about the consistent decline in employment and salaries in Lakewood. Characteristically, she tracks not just the fact of the aerospace industry's collapse but also the language used to describe that fact—from "correctives" to "restructuring," further evidence of the citizens' unwillingness to face squarely the problems of their communities.

Where I Was From examines the persistent—and utterly untrue—notion that California is rich and that therefore poverty in any of its citizens must be either a temporary condition or a problem somehow less serious than it might be somewhere else. "Such was the power of the story on which I had grown up that this thought came to me as a kind of revelation: The settlement of the west, however inevitable, had not uniformly tended to the greater good, nor had it on every level benefited even those who reaped its most obvious rewards." Of course, the author is not as naïve as this statement might seem to indicate, and those who know Didion's work well will hear something slightly disingenuous in such a remark. She has, since the late 1960's, addressed the problems in California society and the flaws in the state's golden self-image. What has changed in this book is both the depth of her analysis and the candor with which she admits her own previous willingness to buy into at least selected portions of that image.

Thus the author peels away layer after layer of mythologies—personal, familial, local, regional, national. Didion is too hardheaded, too much an intellectual, to look away from the uncomfortable truth she slowly uncovers: that the glorious California, whose passing she (along with so many others) laments, never really existed at all. Still, hard-headed intellectual or not, she is clearly saddened by her own revelation. What she is (and readers are) left with, then, is not nostalgia for a lost golden age but rather nostalgia for nostalgia, a desire to return not to some past state of reality but to a past state of mind in which it was possible to believe that the dream had once, in some dim past, been real. In the end, though, she turns away (and takes her readers with her) from this once-removed nostalgia. For adults, she makes clear that it is counterproductive to believe in fairy tales. The consequences of such belief are too real and potentially too devastating to the environment and the society which, despite all, she still loves.

The "where" of the book's title may be California, but the book has significance far beyond this one state. (Indeed, Didion makes a point of reminding her readers frequently that she used to live in California but now makes her home in New York. Even the book's past-tense title reinforces this point.) "This is a country," the author says, "at some level not as big as we like to say it is." Didion asks difficult questions about California, and in the specific history and present of California she seeks answers. The same questions might well be asked about Nebraska or Georgia, or even New York: What are the myths of this place? What are the realities? Why does one continue to believe in the former despite all the visible evidence of the latter? What does it mean to be from a particular place? To what degree is one obligated to question and probe the myths of one's native places?

Didion sees how deeply political the myth of California really is. What might be surprising is what she identifies as the center of the politics. California, in Didion's analysis, is not "about" what one familiar with the California myth might expect. It is not about tourism, agriculture, motion pictures, and gold. Rather, it is about railroads, water, aerospace, prison building, and capital. It is, ultimately, about "a familiar California error: that of selling the future of the place we lived to the highest bidder."

Didion writes so compellingly, with such conviction and in such unerringly superb prose, that one is inclined simply to think her right. As with all things to do with the myth of California, the truth is not that simple. The author has a point to make, an ax which she grinds so subtly and with such verbal finesse that one almost cannot hear the whetstone. She is trying to press Californians (and others) into seeing that perhaps—just perhaps—California is not paying its fair share, not really carrying its own substantial weight, and that its success is not based on the fact that it is inherently special but on the fact that it has had unearned privilege. It is a tough case to make, given the pervasiveness of California's dream image of itself, aggressively marketed in everything from art to advertising to popular song.

All these various sources of the image come under the author's scrutiny at some point. The book's greatest strength, that it gives voice to Didion's academic bent, might be considered by some readers to be its greatest weakness as well. There is much quotation, much detailed analysis of data, and even a bit of literary criticism. Indeed, she might be considered an adherent of the school of criticism known as New Historicism, in that she compares a number of documents from widely varying sources to draw her portrait of the place. These documents are as diverse as Frank Norris's novel *The Octopus* (1901), contemporary newspaper stories, publications of the United States Bureau of Reclamation, her great-great-grandmother's letters, and her own eighth grade graduation speech made in 1948.

More than 200 pages into the 226-page book, the reader learns that Didion's mother recently died and that the author returned to California to help set her affairs in order and distribute various family mementos among the children and grandchildren. In a different sort of social history, this might seem a self-indulgent finale, but in the case of *Where I Was From*, the revelation comes to seem, like so much in Didion's work, not only necessary to the text but also an inevitable part of it. The author's convoluted but powerful speculations about family, history, and location make sudden sense when one sees her self-searching as brought on by both the death of a loved one and the return, under difficult circumstances, to a once-familiar place. When all one has loved about a place is gone, what is left but one's memories and illusions? Didion pushes the reader to ask the question: What is the use of such memories and illusions when they are built on a foundation of sand?

Janet E. Gardner

Review Sources

American Scholar 72, no. 4 (Autumn, 2003): 146-148.
Booklist 99, no. 21 (July 1, 2003): 1843.
Kirkus Review 71, no. 13 (July 1, 2003): 891-892.
Library Journal 128, no. 11 (June 15, 2003): 72.
National Review 55, no. 24 (December 22, 2003): 52-53.
The New York Review of Books, December 4, 2003, pp. 4-5.
The New York Times Book Review, September 28, 2003, p. 10.
Publishers Weekly 250, no. 26 (June 30, 2003): 68-69.
Time 162, no. 17 (October 27, 2003): 76.

WHO KILLED DANIEL PEARL?

Author: Bernard-Henri Lévy (1948-   )
First published: Qui a tué Daniel Pearl, 2003, in France
Translated from the French by James X. Mitchell
Publisher: Melville House (Hoboken, New Jersey).
    454 pp. $25.95
Type of work: Current affairs
Time: 2002-2003
Locale: Pakistan

Lévy claims that journalist Pearl was murdered because he was close to uncovering the full extent of Pakistani government officials' support for international Islamic terrorism

Principal personages:

BERNARD-HENRI LÉVY, the narrator of the investigation

DANIEL PEARL, a reporter for *The Wall Street Journal*, kidnapped and murdered in Karachi, Pakistan

OMAR SHEIKH, an organizer of the kidnapping plot who worked for both al-Qaeda and the Pakistani secret service

KHALID SHAIKH MOHAMMED, Pearl's Yemeni assassin, who was also involved in organizing the September 11, 2001, terrorist attacks

PIR MUBARAK ALI SHAH GILANI, the leader of a jihadist sect, Jamaat al-Fuqrah

OSAMA BIN LADEN, a leader of al-Qaeda, most likely hiding in Pakistan

GUL AGA SHERZAI, the governor of Kandahar in Afghanistan

BASHIRUDDIN MAHMOUD, a Pakistani nuclear scientist

ABDUL QADIR KAHN, the creator of Pakistan's atomic bomb

The very form of this book explains how its author, Bernard-Henri Lévy, could dare to visit the sites associated with the last days of Daniel Pearl and the lives of the men who murdered him. Lévy claimed to be writing a novel of the affair in order to explain his need to see the places and talk with the individuals associated with it.

The search began with the victim, Danny Pearl. Who was this Jewish reporter who was in Pakistan investigating the al-Qaeda leaders who had taken refuge in the country, some of them living quite openly and preaching hatred of "the crusaders"? Pearl's family was Israeli, and his politics were left of center. He spoke Hebrew and Arabic but had resisted being stranded in the pigeonhole of the Palestinian-Israeli conflict. After covering news around the world, he had become expert on the complexities of politics, religion, and social change in India and Pakistan; he was living in India with his pregnant wife, Mariane. He was a likeable person, knowledgeable and courageous. On January 23, 2002, he went to meet a potentially important source, Gilani, the teacher of Richard Reid, who had been arrested aboard a plane in December while trying to ignite a bomb in his shoe. Pearl was kidnapped.

~

Bernard-Henri Lévy is a philosopher, journalist, best-selling writer, director, and diplomat. He has published more than thirty books, including Le siècle de Sartre: Enquête philosophique *(2000;* Sartre: The Philosopher of the Twentieth Century, *2003) and* Le testament de Dieu *(1979;* Testament of God, *1980).*

~

The kidnappers first asked for a ransom which included the delivery of F-16 warplanes to Pakistan. Then they changed their minds and called in Yemeni killers who slit Pearl's throat and distributed a video of the grisly act. For unexplained reasons they cut the body into numerous pieces, then reassembled them for burial in the garden of the house where Pearl was slain.

As American investigators flooded the country, with implied threats of retaliation for noncooperation, Pakistani police arrested Omar Sheikh and three accomplices. He freely admitted his guilt. This was not his first kidnapping—in 1994 he had attempted to force India to release a terrorist captured in Kashmir. Sentenced to a long term in prison, he had been released five years later in return for freeing a skyjacked Indian airliner. Omar was very familiar with the West. He was born in England to immigrant Pakistani parents. Their successful export-import business subsidized an elite education that gave him the accent and manners of the upper class; his acquaintances considered him a perfect Englishman. He was a strong chess player and even more formidable in arm wrestling. His most notable oddity was a paralyzing shyness around girls—a true Muslim should not look upon the face of women. Another was his fixation on Muslim suffering in Bosnia.

It was Omar who promised to take Pearl to Gilani, who knew everyone in the terrorist movements. It was Omar, proud of his intelligence and knowledge of computers and other Western technologies, who left a trail of e-mail and phone messages that the Federal Bureau of Investigation (FBI) easily followed. Once arrested, he remained confident that either highly placed officials or his terrorist friends would soon procure his release. He admitted his guilt, gave details of the plot, described his military training in Afghanistan, and even wrote a prison diary describing not only this kidnapping but also the earlier one. He had begun to reshape his past, to make it more heroic, more Islamic. Lévy's research demolished the most important myths, but he discovered that behind Omar's many aliases and identities there was a consummate actor who knew how to please the men who held power.

Lévy was able to penetrate the labyrinthine world of Islamic terrorism, a feat that American and Pakistani police had not been able to achieve. Indian, Israeli, French, and occasionally Pakistani experts shared information that led him from one of Omar's past associates to another. With each interview, the terrorists' supporters became more suspicious. The closer he came to the story that Pearl had been following, the more dangerous the game became.

Lévy learned several things. First, few of the terrorists were deeply religious. They believed in the jihad, the obligation to make holy war, and, therefore, the pretexts (Israel, Kashmir, imperialism) were little more than opportunities to act. Second, the Pakistani secret service (ISI) was heavily infiltrated by sympathizers of the Taliban and al-Qaeda, who put their loyalty to international Islam above Pakistan. Third, many

Pakistanis shared those views. Pakistan was a failing nation, and somebody had to be blamed—India, the United States, the West, or, best of all, the Jews. The religious schools, the Madrasas, had made the mosques into temples of hate where warriors were recruited for Afghanistan and Kashmir now and for the ultimate war against Israel and the West later. Fourth, the skills of the West were being used against it. Osama bin Laden made great profits by selling airline stocks short the day before September 11, 2001. Fifth, radical Islam was a business that many joined in hope of acquiring power and wealth. Some became bankers and investors, or government officials and policemen—rising swiftly through important contacts. Others volunteered for jihad or offered their sons as suicide warriors, knowing that the honor of martyrdom would be crowned by monetary payments to the heroes' families.

This was all important, but none of it was new. Pearl had reported this himself, as had other well-informed reporters, both Pakistani and Western. Although reporters and intelligence services had been uncovering a fact here, a name there, and many connections, it was so confusing that it was difficult to see the connections among the many terrorist organizations and their supporters. The confusion was made worse by disinformation programs. This began to change when the FBI traced the September 11 hijackers' money back to the Near East and Karachi. In itself, this produced no surprises, but Lévy was stunned to learn that the man at the center was Omar, acting under one of his many aliases.

Western intelligence agencies had created the Taliban and other jihadist organizations, using the ISI. Now the ISI was operating on its own, still backing al-Qaeda. Omar worked for the ISI. The investigation began taking the author into very heart of holy war, and he was in Pakistan, stalking the killers in their own caves. What was it that the warriors wanted, other than the conquest of the entire world? The promised virgins, Lévy reasoned, though it was not quite clear what Omar would do with them. The martyr's right to name seventy-two persons to ascend into paradise with him would take care of even the largest extended family and circle of friends. Omar's immediate family, however, was small, and his friends were nonexistent.

Lévy heard the Taliban exiles explain their inverted values: that the Americans are the terrorists and the Jews give the orders. His visit to Kandahar had its bizarre aspects. Governor Gul had no interest in the subject until his visitor insinuated that he was a representative of the French government. It was a bluff, but it worked. The governor's subordinates quickly presented evidence that Omar had been to Afghanistan three times and that he was a favorite son of bin Laden. This was, for Lévy, the conclusive proof that the ISI and al-Qaeda were working together.

Omar was on the front lines in Afghanistan before American bombs began falling, but very quickly he was back in Pakistan, having had no difficulty reaching safety. Though now sentenced to hang, Omar remains confident that he will be released. He suggests that Bush's sons be kidnapped and exchanged for him. For an intelligent and educated man, this is remarkably stupid, but it demonstrates that he and his ilk have nothing but contempt for the West and its weaknesses.

Lévy's guise as an atheist was wearing thin. He had to use what time he had left, before he was exposed, to interview the elusive Gilani. He had to listen again to the harangues about the Holocaust never having happened and only being used to disguise the great sins of the Jews against Islam. What he learned, or sensed, is that Daniel Pearl died because he knew too much. He was a journalist, a Jew, and an American, three strikes to start with, and then he became what Pakistani president Pervez Musharraf called "overly intrusive."

The connection between factions of the ISI and al-Qaeda, however, was hardly a secret. What real secrets did Gilani possess? In January he had been arrested by the police during their sweep of suspects, but he had cooperated, giving up the names of people whom Pearl had contacted, sharing a few secrets, and reminding everyone of his past services. He was on the street again within days. Was it Richard Reid, Gilani's most famous disciple? That was not a secret, either. What few outsiders realized was that Gilani's little sect provided an intersection at which all the important terrorist groups could come together. Gilani coordinated their operations. He also already had a network of fundamentalist communes in place in the United States, perhaps as many as thirty secretive armed bases, the "Muslims of America." John Muhammad, one of the Washington, D.C., area snipers, may have been a convert to his cult. The real answer may be even more explosive—two men at the top of Pakistan's nuclear bomb program, Bashiruddin Mahmoud and Abdul Qadir Kahn, are associated with terrorist organizations, including bin Laden's. They intend to share their nation's nuclear secrets and even the "Islamic bomb" with the terrorists.

Lévy's startling conclusion is that Pakistan is the most dangerous country in the world. It pretends to be a friend of the West, but its leaders are merely biding time. It is a world of religious fanaticism, mad scientists, financiers, and secret police. Compared to Pakistan, Saddam Hussein's Iraq was not dangerous at all.

Lévy believes that the way out, short of war to the death between civilizations, is Islam. Muslims who believe in freedom and moderation, who espouse the gentle Islam held by the vast majority of believers, have to stand up against those who have stolen their religion and made it a vehicle of hatred. The contest inside Islam, Lévy believes, will be the central struggle of the future, not the terrorist war on the West.

William L. Urban

Review Sources

The Economist 367, no. 8325 (May 24, 2003): 83.
The New York Review of Books, December 4, 2003, pp. 53-56.
The New York Times Book Review, September 21, 2003, p. 18.
Publishers Weekly 250, no. 34 (August 25, 2003): 51-52.
The Times Literary Supplement, July 18, 2003, pp. 28-29.
The Wall Street Journal, September 18, 2003, p. D6.

THE WINTER QUEEN

Author: Boris Akunin (1956-   )
First published: Azazel, 1998, in Russia
Translated from the Russian by Andrew Bromfield
Publisher: Random House (New York). 244 pp. $19.95
Type of work: Novel
Time: May to September, 1876
Locale: Moscow, St. Petersburg, and London

The routine investigation of a suicide in a Moscow park gets young detective Erast Fandorin entangled with dissolute students, gamblers, a femme fatale, killers, members of high society, and an international organization plotting to take over the world

Principal characters:

ERAST PETROVICH FANDORIN, a talented, likable young detective
XAVIER FEOFILAKTOVICH GRUSHIN, his first superintendent
PYOTR ALEXANDROV KOKORIN, a young man who committed suicide in the park
ELIZAVETA "LIZANKA" ALEXANDROVNA VON EVERT-KOLOKOLTSEVA, a beautiful young witness
EMMA GOTTLIEBOVNA PFÜHL, Elizaveta's governess, another witness
NIKOLAI STEPANOVICH AKHTYRTSEV, the suicide's student friend
LADY MARGARET ASTAIR, a British philanthropist who inherits the suicide's estate
AMALIA "CLEOPATRA" KAZIMIROVNA BEZHETSKAYA, a femme fatale with whom the students were involved
COUNT HIPPOLYTE ALEXANDROVICH ZUROV, Amalia's lover, a gambler and duelist
IVAN FRANZEVICH BRILLING, Fandorin's second supervisor
GERALD CUNNINGHAM, Lady Astair's right-hand man
PORFIRII MARTYNOVICH PYZHOV, a double agent in the London embassy
JOHN MORBID, an English servant
NICHOLAS M. CROOG (NIKOLA MITROFANICH KRUG), a St. Petersburg courier
ADJUTANT GENERAL LAVRENTII ARKADIEVICH MIZINOV, Fandorin's third supervisor
FULL PRIVY COUNSELOR ALEXANDER APOLLODOROVICH VON EVERT-KOLOKOLTSEV, Elizaveta's father
PROFESSOR GEBHARDT BLANK, an experimenter with electricity

Boris Akunin's *The Winter Queen* is not great literature, but it is great entertainment. The first of ten novels (of a projected twelve) in the Erast Fandorin detective series, *The Winter Queen* is also the first of the series to be translated into English. *The Winter Queen* clearly shows why the immense popularity of the series in Russia has

Boris Akunin is the pen name of Grigory Chkhartishvili, scholar, critic, translator (of Japanese writers), and editor of the Moscow journal Inostrannaja Literatura *(Foreign Literature). Born in the Georgia Republic in 1956, he has lived most of his life in Moscow. He began publishing detective fiction in 1998.*

been dubbed "Erastomania": Introducing a young hero so straight and clean he could teach Sunday school, *The Winter Queen* offers traditional storytelling. Despite a few dialogue-heavy sections, for the most part the story moves swiftly, with so many twists and turns in the plot and so many narrow escapes for the hero that one wants to keep turning the pages. Like a fireworks display, the book begins with a bang and ends not with one but with two bangs. Even the settings, czarist Russia and Victorian England, and the style, with long chapter headings that comment wryly on the action, entertain in an old-fashioned way.

Part of the novel's appeal seems to be nostalgic, harking back for Russians to a simpler, albeit colorfully decadent time before communism, its sudden collapse, and the harsh reintroduction to capitalism. The setting provides some cultural and historical continuity and is a reminder that, even before communism, Russia was a great country. The novel's characters, with their long names, are also reminiscent of Russia's great nineteenth century literature: Akunin draws on such familiar types as the bored, dissolute student, the gambler and duelist, and the femme fatale. Place names, including numerous references to streets, also feed nostalgia, and Akunin furnishes such obligatory scenes as the rounds of Russian roulette (here called American roulette), the high-stakes gambling match, and the long train ride across Mother Russia.

Aside from references to some gruesome crimes and to orphans, Akunin does not dwell on the social ills, injustices, and suffering of the time, so prominent in nineteenth century Russian literature. Instead, from his mellowed historical perspective, he tends to depict the earlier time's social problems humorously. For example, there is the maddening Russian bureaucracy, as seen at the novel's beginning, in which young Fandorin's police duties consist only of writing and rewriting routine reports. There is also czarist Russia's obsession with rank, as seen in numerous references throughout the text and the need for an appendix, "The Table of Ranks," listing all fourteen levels in the civil and military hierarchies, with appropriate titles. Young Fandorin's success is marked by his rapid advancement in rank, from lowly "clerk and civil servant fourteenth class" to somewhere several rungs up.

Still another example of humor is Fandorin's homesickness as he travels from the familiar squalor of Mother Russia to the clean cities of Western Europe. England is particularly off-putting, sending a chill up Fandorin's spine, especially in the way people pass each other in the street without looking into each other's faces.

Historical perspective also gives Akunin a chance to play with references to science and pseudoscience. Among the more alarming characters, for instance, is Professor Gebhardt Blank, who has been experimenting with electric shock to erase memory in animals, creating a blank brain which can be written on at will: Erast Fandorin, forcibly restrained, is scheduled to become his first human subject. Fandorin is saved on this occasion, and others, because he practices the Chandra Johnson method of controlled breathing. Other marvelous inventions that come into play include the Lord Byron corset, the telegraph, disappearing ink, exploding bullets, time bombs, and the telephone, Alexander Graham Bell's unbelievable device for talking with someone at a distance.

Readers who are not Russians, of course, can also appreciate the rich patina of time and place in *The Winter Queen*, including the evocation of Victorian London in the Dickensian names of some characters and other references. The title *The Winter Queen* refers to a run-down London hotel. The novel's original title in Russian was *Azazel*, which raises another issue of perspective that Akunin plays with and that might be more of a challenge for English readers. During the Cold War, Russia headed an empire frequently construed as evil, which Western fictional heroes such as Ian Fleming's James Bond had to confront. In *The Winter Queen* (which might also be a slur on Britain's Queen Victoria), Akunin reverses the West's Cold War perspective: Here, England is the source of evil, from which emanates the sinister organization called Azazel. Under the guise of philanthropy, Azazel sends programmed orphans throughout the world to infiltrate and subvert foreign governments. Fandorin is Bond's Russian counterpart, who uncovers, sets back, and temporarily foils Azazel.

Young Fandorin is a far different person from the suave British agent 007, but perhaps that is the point. He is such a straight arrow, so eager, upbeat, and confident, that he could be the hero of an adventurous youth novel. He is attracted to pretty girls and is even vain enough to wear a Lord Byron whalebone corset (which coincidentally saves him from a stabbing), but does he ever think of sex? Having started out in life as a poor orphan, he lives in a grim room furnished only with a divan, a table, and a chair. His circumstances gain him sympathy, but his actions sometimes comically backfire, as when, after his stabbing, he sets his landlady's hemorrhoid medicine beside his sickbed to impress his new superior. His attempt in England to disguise himself with a false mustache is similarly comical, as are his disguises as a French artist and a Sherlock Holmes figure. Through this comic treatment of Fandorin (whose nickname in school was "Fanny"), Akunin seems to be poking fun at the detective genre, but he also creates a hero whose vulnerable humanity is Russian to the core.

Young Fandorin is not only vulnerable and comic but also incredibly lucky, like the proverbial cat with nine lives. His narrow escapes, and Akunin's repeated use of coincidence, defy belief. For example, Fandorin happens to be wearing his Lord Byron whalebone corset when he is stabbed, and he is twice saved by his Chandra Johnson training, which enables him to hold his breath for amazing periods, once when he is tossed into the Thames River tied up in a weighted sack and another time when he is smothered with chloroform. In the first instance, the villains do not find the stiletto sticking up his sleeve, and in the second instance, they do not find the gun sticking in his belt. Fandorin also escapes several bullets, a couple of bombs, and assorted other dangers. He is fantastically lucky in gambling and in love. However, if readers temporarily suspend their disbelief, they can move on and maybe even see Akunin as sharing more tongue-in-cheek fun.

Part of the fun also is that the novel is rich with familiar supporting characters, some from the police and spy genres. Fandorin's first superior, Grushin, is a satirical portrait of the lazy, clock-watching, old-school bureaucrat, while his second superior, Brilling, is a snappy, brilliant, technologically advanced man of the future who shakes up the department beyond recognition. The sleazy, grotesque English servants could be straight out of a Charles Dickens novel, while Professor Blank is the usual Dr. Frankenstein figure. The beautiful, seductive Amalia helps make up for the novel's lack of sex, even if she does have some dangerous kung fu moves. Young Elizaveta is again reminiscent of Dickens's sweet heroines, while her governess, Emma Pfühl, and Lady Margaret Astair recall the James Bond lineup from films, especially Lotte Lenya's portrayal of villain Rosa Klebb in *From Russia with Love* (1963).

The novel's action, enhanced by the changes of setting, rich characterization, and historical atmosphere, makes it a natural candidate for filming. Some scenes especially stand out for their visual and auditory effects, such as the opening scene of a young man blowing his brains out in the park, the soirée of suitors at Amalia's house, the stabbings outside the disreputable Crimea nightspot, the gambling match at Count Zurov's, Fandorin's climb up Amalia's drainpipe to spy on her, his near-fatal dunking in the river Thames, his near-fatal fight with Brilling, his near-fatal run-in with Professor Blank, and the explosions at the end.

Akunin, who is also a scholar, critic, and translator of Japanese writers, has done his research well. Not only does he evoke the rich atmosphere of place and time, but he also knows how to mix the ingredients of the detective and spy genres with just the right proportions of seriousness and parody. He is also prolific, publishing ten novels in the Erast Fandorin series in just five years, while turning out another series (about a nun sleuth, Pelageya) and producing scholarly work. Readers of English can expect to see further translations of Akunin and to follow the career of Erast Fandorin.

Harold Branam

Review Sources

Booklist 99, no. 18 (May 15, 2003): 1637.
Library Journal 128, no. 8 (May 1, 2003): 152.
The New York Times Book Review, July 13, 2003, p. 8.
People 59, no. 23 (June 16, 2003): 53.
Time 162, no. 6 (August 11, 2003): 58.
The Times Literary Supplement, May 16, 2003, p. 32.

WINTER WORLD
The Ingenuity of Animal Survival

Author: Bernd Heinrich (1940-   )
Publisher: HarperCollins (New York). 347 pp. $24.95
Type of work: Environment, natural history, nature, and
 science
Time: The twenty-first century

With poetical prose and personal anecdotes, Heinrich,
a Maine biologist and woodsman, examines how birds, in-
sects, amphibians, and mammals survive through the winter

Bernd Heinrich was born in Germany in 1940, the son
of an entomologist and collector for museums who taught
him how to observe and capture insects and animals. He
ran through the woods so often that his nickname was
Wiesel (weasel); in later life he became an award-winning ultramarathon runner. His
fascination with running led him to write the popular 2001 book *Racing the Antelope:*
What Animals Can Teach Us About Running and Life. His parents immigrated to the
United States when he was ten, and he grew up in Maine, where he loved the outdoors.
He earned his Ph.D. in biology in 1970 from the University of California, Los Angeles, and taught at Berkeley from 1971 until 1980, when he returned to New England
to teach at the University of Vermont. Though he began his scientific career as a cell
biologist studying protozoa, Heinrich is famous for his books on behavioral biology.
An admirer of insects, he has hunted scarab beetles in the Namib Desert and run from
dragonflies in Botswana. His first book was *Bumblebee Economics* (1979), now a
classic in its field.

Heinrich purchased a three-hundred-acre property in Maine in 1974 and hand-
built a cabin in which to live and study local wildlife. Many of his observations supply
the delightful stories for this book. The first thing the reader notices is his gorgeous,
autobiographical prose. The second is the beautiful, detailed illustrations, drawn by
Heinrich. In his introduction, he recalls the seminal Jack London short story "To
Build a Fire" (1902), about a newcomer to the frozen Yukon who needed to warm and
dry his chilled, wet body with a fire but who made amateur mistakes and died of the
cold. There are many small mammals and birds who cannot light fires; Heinrich asks,
how do they keep warm during the winter?

Heinrich describes the golden-crowned kinglet, a bird almost as tiny as the hummingbird, whose survival during the harsh Maine winters is wondrous. Watching
and wondering about these birds gave Heinrich the impetus to write this book. "The
kinglet is thus iconic not only of winter but also of adaptability under adverse
conditions. . . . It was the kinglet that led me further and further into the winter world
of the north woods, and into this book, spurring me on to find the miraculous." It is
the golden-crowned kinglet which provides a cohesive narrative thread to his anec-

~

Dr. Bernd Heinrich is a professor of biology at the University of Vermont. He has been a Guggenheim Fellow, a Harvard Fellow, and a recipient of an Alexander von Humboldt Foundation Senior Scientist Fellowship Award. Heinrich is the author of Mind of the Raven *(1999), which won the John Burroughs Medal for natural history writing and was a* New York Times *and* Los Angeles Times *Notable Book.*

~

dotal study, a mystery Heinrich has set out to solve.

Heinrich begins by defining and illustrating some terms for the layman which he will expand upon later, such as hibernation, supercooling, and antifreeze, and he provides a table for conversions between Celsius (or C), his preferred temperature scale, and Fahrenheit. His explanations are clear and accompanied by vivid examples; the reader who has always wondered what keeps an igloo dome from collapsing will find the pleasing answer here. Nonscientists will come away with a new appreciation for heat and cold, for water, ice, and snow and for the remarkable behaviors which have evolved in the animal kingdom to coexist comfortably with them.

Heinrich's remark that "biology is a sterile undertaking until one gets hands-on experience" seems to be his motto. Describing his own curiosity-driven forays into the wild, he leads his reader into the architectural marvel of a beaver lodge, into a cozy, warm bear den, and into the twiggy drey, or nest, of a northern flying squirrel. He explains why famous groundhog Punxatawney Phil can be relied upon to appear on the second day of each February in Pennsylvania.

He applauds the arctic ground squirrel, which, for eight months of the year, "curls up into a ball close to the ice of the permafrost, and maintains a body temperature at or below the freezing point of water." Heinrich has a merry sense of humor, recalling how one scientist wondered if the arctic ground squirrels' blood contained antifreeze. "The blood turned to ice at approximately $-0.6°$ C. It therefore did *not* contain antifreeze. These results deepen the mystery of winter survival: Why should the blood freeze in the lab but not in the animal? The riddle is not yet solved, but the best tentative explanation so far is that the squirrels supercool." Heinrich explains clearly the process of supercooling—falling below the freezing point without crystallizing into ice and damaging cell tissues—and how the squirrels avoid freezing to death. (To save a squirrel in captivity, one starts by making their toes colder; the torpid squirrels then wake up.) Heinrich's scientific agenda remains paramount; he loves the animals he describes, but he never sentimentalizes them. At times he explains why it may behoove humans to study them: "The hibernating arctic ground squirrels may hold keys to the riddle of why we need sleep, and also some medical problems, such as stroke."

Heinrich's tone is chatty and digressive, so that the experience is of accompanying him upon a nature walk while he points out various features of the landscape and its denizens. His narrative dives under blankets of snow to find rugged grouse and mice burrowing or nesting at the roots of trees, climbs up those trees to find woodpeckers and martens, inches out along branches to examine bird nests and cocoons, and swims under the surface of ponds to investigate turtles, muskrats, and the remarkable diving beetle, which carries bubbles of air under its wings to provide itself with oxygen.

Describing thermodynamics in a user-friendly way, Heinrich takes care to emphasize the crucial need for wintering birds and mammals to remain dry. "Ironically, in an insulated sock, mitten, or a squirrel's nest, a tiny bit of moisture is far more dangerous than deep cold; because wetness destroys insulation. Thus rain, at near 0° C, can be lethal, while snow at −30° C can ensure comfort because it won't wet and destroy insulation."

Frequently, while exploring the actions of other animals, he returns to the golden-crowned kinglet, pursuing the mystery of how it can survive nights when the weather drops forty degrees below freezing. "How do kinglets, who are out there day and night and who are no bigger than the end of my thumb, maintain their body temperature near 43 degrees to 44 degrees C?" Heinrich explains the physics of heating and cooling, so that his reader shares his puzzlement and awe. Having captured a kinglet and experimented with it at different temperatures, he shows that "a kinglet (with feathers) must expend at least 13 calories per minute to stay warm at −34° C," an impressive feat considering that a human weighing 150 pounds burns only 1.7 calories per minute while reading a book.

By way of discussing how feathers help to insulate kinglets from the cold, Heinrich detours into dinosaurs and boldly argues "that feathers for flight originated from insulation. The big question was and is: How can downy insulation evolve into *flight* feathers?" In one of the most exciting passages in *Winter World*, Heinrich wades into the old and ongoing debate over feather evolution and the famous winged dinosaur Archaeopteryx. He speculates that the original development of flat feathers was intended to reduce wetting, as wetness destroys insulation, yet that feathers might have evolved into tools for flight because, while developed as a parasol-like barrier to water, they will also become a barrier to air—that is, they will become aerodynamical. He is diffident about this intriguing hypothesis and concludes that "regardless of whether the parasol theory could resolve a long-standing evolutionary puzzle, it might at least help explain how kinglets survive a stormy night."

Some of the topics that recur are nesting, hibernation and torpor, eating and food-storing habits, and flocking habits. Heinrich's narrative method is to pose a question that he develops nto a mystery, to offer previous research and his observations about the phenomenon, and then to offer the solution. (Why do crows like to settle on trees in urban centers? Great horned owls are the greatest natural enemy of the crow, and owls do not live in the city.) This method provides a quasi-novelistic feel to the text, with its characterizations of animals, case histories, mini-dramas, comic asides, rich local color, and plot complications and resolutions. He even offers morals to his stories, demonstrating that human ignorance of animal behavior can be deadly, even though so many people are animal lovers and mean no harm. Heinrich keeps the reader gripped with one polished, witty chronicle after another. His prose is beautiful and often poetic, whether evoking honeybees harvesting nectar from August's blooming goldenrod in the fields, the brilliant crunching foliage of fall, or the deep snow, bare branches, and birdsong of the winter woodland.

Having set up the mystery of how the kinglet survives, Heinrich generates suspense and excitement when he reveals how he learned what it eats, surprising his fellow biologists. In the last chapter, he provides his conclusions about the many survival tactics the kinglets employ, finishing on an optimistic note.

The one weakness of this book is its lack of an index, which is sorely needed in a text that covers so many topics. It was also surprising to find Heinrich baldly assert that an asteroid killed off the dinosaurs, a hypothesis which pleases the public but does not satisfy most scientists. *Winter World* has many strengths, however, most particularly Heinrich's engaging tone, evident love for his subject, and revelations about the great variety of creatures that he follows and illustrates. The chapter on bears, for example, asks how the hibernating black bear can survive months without needing to drink water or urinate, then cuts to an orbiting space mission to dramatize the frightening effects of weightlessness on astronauts, who cannot laze the way a bear does without suffering bed sores, bone-density loss, and physical debilitation. Heinrich's allusions to literature, animal lore, and human culture ("In real estate, location is everything, especially in birds") guarantee that *Winter World* has something to offer everyone. The range and depth of his work place Heinrich among the most interesting science writers. *Winter World* belongs on the bookshelf of every animal lover as well as in every public and academic library.

Fiona Kelleghan

Review Sources

Booklist 99, nos. 9/10 (January 1-15, 2003): 820-821.
The Christian Science Monitor, March 13, 2003, p. 15.
Discover 24, no. 4 (April, 2003): 78.
Kirkus Reviews 70, no. 22 (November 15, 2002): 1674.
Library Journal 128, no. 1 (January 1, 2003): 150.
Los Angeles Times, February 23, 2003, p. R11.
New Scientist 177, no. 2376 (January 4, 2003): 46-47.
The New York Times Book Review, January 26, 2003, p. 15.
Publishers Weekly 249, no. 51 (December 23, 2002): 60.
Scientific American 288, no. 2 (February, 2003): 89.

THE WISDOM OF THE WORLD
The Human Experience of the Universe in Western Thought

Author: Rémi Brague (1947-   )
*First published: La Sagesse du monde: Histoire de
l'expérience humaine de l'univers*, 1999, in France
Translated from the French by Teresa Lavender Fagan
Publisher: University of Chicago Press (Chicago). 297
   pp. $35.00
Type of work: Philosophy

   A philosophical discourse on ancient and medieval visions of the world and their ethical and metaphysical relationship with humankind

   The title of this philosophical history is deceptive in its simplicity. Based upon a seminal passage from Plato's dialogue *Timaeos* (360-347 B.C.E.; *Timaeus*, 1793), the phrase actually suggests an essential and complex link between human perception (wisdom) and physical reality (the world). In *The Wisdom of the World* Rémi Brague combines astronomy, metaphyics, anthropology, ethics, and many other aspects of human experience as he takes his readers on a sweeping intellectual history of the Western world. He examines the ancient Babylonians, Egyptians, Greeks, and Romans, as well as medieval Arabs and modern Europeans, and describes the basic principles which informed the worldviews of these civilizations.

   The term Brague prefers to use for worldview is "cosmology," which he examines in the context of two other ancient Greek words of similar derivation: cosmography and cosmogony. Brague uses these two terms in their traditional sense: cosmography as a description of the world in a specific point in time and cosmogony as the story of the origin of the world. He does not, however, use cosmology according to its traditional definition as a combination of cosmography and cosmogony, that is, the study of the universe. Rather, Brague employs "cosmology" in a more specialized, philosophical sense, to refer to a discourse on the nature of the cosmos, or "that which makes the world a world." Human beings are essential points of reference, because they make the cosmological discourse possible. Humans focus an understanding of the nature of the world on its relationship with, and its meaning and implications for, humans themselves.

   In this context, the word "world" is as much a concept as a concrete place. It is anthropological as well as cosmographic. "World" means not just physical creation but also the environment in which humans function. *Le monde*, French for "the world," for example, means not only "world" but also "people." So, too, in English, the word "world" can be specialized and humanized in a phrase such as "the world of boxing."

   Essential to a cosmological discourse is a word for "world." Such vocabulary was apparently lacking in early human civilizations, especially those in Mesopotamia and

Rémi Brague is a professor of philosophy at the Sorbonne and at the University of Munich and has also taught in the United States and Switzerland. He has been a Humboldt Research Fellow at the University of Cologne and is the author of Eccentric Culture: A Theory of Western Civilization *(2002).*

Egypt. These civilizations had words for the earth as a place of habitation by humans and other living things and generally contrasted this place with the abode of the gods in heaven. Conspicuously absent, however, was a word which encompassed not only the human sphere but also the heavens and the realm of the gods. Instead, cultures of ancient Mesopotamia and Egypt used lists such as "the heavens and the earth" or collective words such as "everything" and "all," which, Brague argues, are not quite the same as "world." Lacking is the subjective element, the place of the human in this totality. The reference is objective rather than self-reflective. Also missing in these early societies was a view of this totality as an ordered cosmic structure. Rather, ancient civilizations tended to look at the physical and human worlds as interdependent. An imbalance in one sphere could result in an imbalance in the other.

The concept of world developed gradually in Greece. Homer did not have a word for "world." Instead, like the Egyptians and Mesopotamians, he listed the parts of the world, like "earth," "sky," and so on. The same is true for another early Greek poet, Hesiod (c. 700 B.C.E.), although Hesiod also uses the collective term "everything."

Important to Greek intellectual development, however, was the possibility of using a simple article with any word to create a noun. So the pre-Socratic philosopher Heraclitus of Ephesus (c. 540-c. 480 B.C.E.) referred to *ta panta* (the "all things"), which another pre-Socratic, Empedocles (c. 490-430 B.C.E.), transformed into the singular *to pan*, or "the all."

The Greeks' most innovative step, as Brague observes, was the formulation of a special word for the world. The word they chose, *kosmos*, was not a neologism but was found even in Homer, where it meant "order." The word *kosmos* never lost this original meaning in Greek, and the idea of order also survives in English derivatives like "cosmetics." Apparently the philosopher Pythagoras (c. 580-c. 500 B.C.E.) was the first to apply this word to the composite of "all things." The choice of vocabulary was intentional, specifically meant to identify the cosmos, or the world as Pythagoras conceived it, as an ordered totality.

Kosmos was definitively established by Plato in the *Timaeus* as a term for an ordered world, perceived as good and beautiful. In addition to this ethical dimension, Plato's *kosmos* also took on an important anthropological aspect, and "the wisdom of the world" was first viewed as the source of human intelligence. Brague emphasizes the significance of perception in this concept of the world: The presence of a perceiver (namely, the human) was critical.

The relationship between human and world was viewed in several different ways in antiquity. Brague examines four models in turn: the Timaean model, the Atomist or Epicurean model, the Abrahamic or Scripture model, and the Gnostic model.

The Timaean worldview described by Plato held intellectual sway for most of the ancient and medieval periods. Human observation of the cosmos provided a standard for human excellence, and the regularity of the celestial spheres should be imitated on the human plane. The "wisdom of the world," according to Plato, was imitation of the celestial order in human life. The moral good was achieved by imitating the beauty of the cosmos.

By contrast, for ancient atomists like the Greeks Democritus (c. 460-c. 370 B.C.E.) and Epicurus (341-270 B.C.E.) and the Roman Lucretius (c. 98-c. 55 B.C.E.), the world was not a source of order and beauty but of chaos and trouble. Humans sought happiness not by imitating the world but by escaping from it, by achieving *ataraxia*, or "lack of disturbance." The moral order for the atomists was not in the world but among human beings. Harmony among humans was more important than human harmony with the spheres.

Also different from the Timaean model was the worldview developed among the "peoples of the book," within the Judaic, Christian, and Islamic traditions. Here, the world was overseen by an infinitely good creator. In this view, humans should not rule their lives by a Timaean harmony of the spheres or an atomistic harmony among humans but by a divinely established harmony. God's law, expressed through Scripture in Judaism and Islam, or by an incarnation of God himself in Christianity, became the model for human excellence and morality. In the fourth ancient model, Gnosticism, the present world was a mere nightmare, a prison, which humans should not seek to imitate but rather to escape.

From the time of Plato through the emergence of the modern world, the Timaean model, tempered by Abrahamic elements, held sway. This view of the world was multi-leveled, both sublunary and superlunary. Everything below the moon was made of the four elements (earth, air, fire, and water), while everything above the moon consisted of a fifth, or quintessential, element. Superlunary things like the stars were considered eternal, while sublunary things were not. Humans were a microcosm of this cosmos. The human soul was superlunary in its immortality. The human body was sublunary in its ephemeral nature. The ability of humans to walk erect enabled them to view the superlunary regions and thus to imitate their orderliness. For humankind, the cosmos thus became an ethical affirmation, a model for the attainment of the good. Humankind was an essential observer; only under human eyes could the orderliness and goodness of the cosmos be objectified and affirmed. Philosophical contemplation of the cosmos was the human condition.

While this Timaean worldview remained dominant into medieval times, it was often modified and even challenged by certain aspects of the Abrahamic tradition. Here contemplation of the cosmos was less important than obedience to God's will. Proximity to God could be achieved by studying God's law rather than the superlunary world. The concept of divine providence further diminished the importance of the superlunary world; for the Christian, providence was felt not only in the superlunary world (to which it was limited in the Timaean worldview) but also in the sublunary world. The Christian worldview valued the human soul, made in the image of God and redeemed by an act of divine incarnation, more than all the rest of creation. Furthermore, while Timaeans viewed their cosmos in terms of nature and permanence, the Abrahamic tradition brought the world into a context of historical change via such events as the fall of Adam and the covenant of Abraham in Judaism, the life of Jesus in Christianity, and the life of Muhammad in Islam. For Christians, the eternal world of Plato was replaced by a world which faced the possibility of apocalypse.

Where the Timaean worldview emphasized contemplation of the superlunary world, the Christian worldview focused on the contemplation of God as an exercise in theology. Humans were to imitate Christ, not the superlunary world. Indeed, they could come to understand God as well through self-understanding as by understanding the world around them. In fact, some Christians like the sixth century Alexandrian philosopher John Philoponus and the fourteenth century English Franciscan philosopher William of Ockham even rejected the concept of superlunary vs. sublunary in favor of a single form of creative matter.

In the end, the Timaean worldview collapsed as modern science destroyed its cosmographic foundation through astronomical discoveries like Tycho Brahe's confirmation in 1577 that comets crossed the allegedly impenetrable boundary between superlunary and sublunary. Even the simple discovery of sunspots (by Christoph Scheiner in 1611) demonstrated that the impurity and corruptibility of matter existed in the superlunary as well as the sublunary world. In such circumstances the word cosmos yielded to universe as a way to distinguish "world" from "infinite universe."

Other developing disciplines spawned further change: Adam Smith's concept of an incomplete and unfinished world led to the nightmarish reflections of Gérard de Nerval (1808-1855) and the declaration of the death of God by Friedrich Nietzsche (1844-1900). The world also came to be perceived as indifferent to, or even destructive of, the human condition. For thinkers such as René Descartes (1596-1650), Isaac Newton (1642-1727), and Baruch Spinoza (1632-1677), only force mattered in the universe. Thus, in the modern view, humanity lost its special position and was governed by the same laws as the rest of the natural world. Even more critical was an inevitable separation of cosmology from morality. This concept of an autonomous morality is evident in the strongly subjective world of Blaise Pascal (1623-1662) and in the phenomenological concept of the world of Martin Heidegger (1889-1976).

Blague concludes by groping for a redefinition of the modern view of the world in terms of its relationship with humankind and by yearning for a recognition that even the modern world is incomplete without the human who contemplates it. Such a philosophical reformulation of "world" remains a work unfinished at the end of *The Wisdom of the World*.

Thomas J. Sienkewicz

Review Source

The Wall Street Journal, July 15, 2003, p. D8.

WORDS TO GOD'S MUSIC
A New Book of Psalms

Author: Laurance Wieder (1946-   )
Publisher: William B. Eerdmans (Grand Rapids, Mich.).
    150 pp. $25.00
Type of work: Poetry

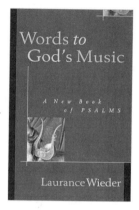

Over the centuries, many poets have translated the Old Testament psalms, but Wieder is only the third poet to produce an English interpretation all 150 of the Songs of David

Originally composed over a period of centuries by professional musicians who served in the sanctuaries and royal courts of ancient Israel and Judah, the Hebrew psalms have nurtured the faith of Jews and Christians for more than three thousand years. Believers have chanted and recited these sacred canticles during religious ceremonies and read them during private prayer. The psalms have also sparked the imaginations of well-known doubters such as Samuel Taylor Coleridge and George Gordon, Lord Byron.

Why have the psalms enjoyed such longevity and appeal? One answer could be because they are part of a sacred text, but their canonicity cannot fully explain such devotion or fascination. A second possible reason is that readers see themselves in the psalms' candid portrayal of the human condition, as well as in the representation of the sometimes contentious and often blessed relationship humanity shares with the divine. A third reason is that, because the psalms were composed over a period of a thousand years, they were often reworked or adapted to mirror later social, political, and religious realities. This fluidity of composition contributes to the timeless quality of the psalms, keeping the poems fresh and vital.

In *Words to God's Music,* Laurance Wieder follows the lead of previous psalmodists as he refashions the ancient songs into contemporary treatments of the biblical text. He is not the first poet to attempt to reinterpret these sacred texts. John Milton (1608-1674), George Herbert (1593-1633), and Ben Jonson (1573-1637), among others, all tried their hand at translating some of the psalms. Wieder claims, however, that in addition to Mary Sidney Herbert (1561-1621), her brother Philip (1554-1586), and Christopher Smart (1722-1771), he is the only other writer to produce a poetic rendering of the entire Psalter in English. Some of the poems included in this collection have been previously published, but many are appearing here for the first time.

Wieder arranges his collection of 150 poems in five sections, mirroring the traditional Hebrew division of the psalms into five books. A midrash, or rabbinical commentary, on the original biblical version of the first psalm records that the psalms were divided in this manner because David (c. 1030 - c. 962 B.C.E.) wished to have the five books of his songs correspond to the five books of the Pentateuch written by Mo-

〜

Laurance Wieder has taught at the Yale University School of Music and at Cornell University. His poems and essays have appeared in The New Yorker, Partisan Review, Commonweal, *and elsewhere. Among his compilations are the acclaimed* Chapters into Verse: Poetry in English Inspired by the Bible *(1993), with Robert Atwan, and* The Poets' Book of Psalms *(1995).*

〜

ses. The format of the biblical psalms leads readers on a spiritual journey from existential angst to a renewed relationship with God, just as the Pentateuch guides readers from creation in Genesis to the promised land of Deuteronomy.

Wieder follows the traditional scriptural framework, with each of his poems corresponding to a biblical psalm. Functioning in a way similar to the superscriptions of the originals, most of Wieder's titles consist of one or two words which concisely convey the themes of the individual pieces. Many of the titles are plays on words. For example, the title of Psalm 13 is "Unlucky," while the "Penult" and "Last" are the headings for Psalms 149 and 150, respectively. Wieder's renderings are not strict interpretations or translations. Some adhere fairly close to the biblical originals, others function as commentaries, while still others have little to do with the primary text.

The first section of *Words to God's Music* is titled "One Will Blossom" and covers psalms 1 through 41. The word "blossom" in the title suggests a correlation to the Genesis myth, and the first poem, "The Happy One," reinforces the allusion to Eden by using garden imagery. In it, the righteous man:

> . . . turns the Lord's laws over night and day,
> A gardener tilling the holy ground.
> And the happy one will blossom
> Like the fruit trees in a watered field
> Bearing plum peach walnut pear and apple
> Cupped by green leaves the long season,
> Harvest bushels crated by the orchard.

In contrast, the faithless are like "dead leaves,/ Clippings flattered by the wind." Foreshadowing the spiritual and psychological angst in many of the succeeding poems, "The Happy One" captures the tension between life and death, obedience and disobedience, faith and doubt, and sinfulness and redemption, emphasizing humanity's fallen condition, as well as humankind's longing for God.

Many of David's songs are familiar to modern readers who hail from a Judeo-Christian heritage, but perhaps the best known is Psalm 23. Underscoring the fact that his renderings are not literal translations of the biblical psalms, Wieder notes in his "Brief Explanation" that rather than trying to "improve what can't be improved," he has composed a "midrash" on the Twenty-third Psalm, which he calls "Solo." The serene opening of the traditional biblical piece—The Lord is my shepherd, I shall not want./ He makes me lie down in green pastures,/ he leads me beside still waters,/ he restores my soul—is replaced by: "I want no shepherd when I lie/ Down, don't need to be led to water, shade/ Or rest. One who restores/ Souls can't be lost forever." These unexpectedly jarring lines accentuate the speaker's spiritual isolation and rejection of God. Instead of being thankful that the Lord honors him by preparing a feast before his foes, the speaker asserts that it is "no trouble to sit/ Down with my enemy. He too must chew./ We dip our bread in oil." The speaker prefers the solidarity he experiences with his fellow humans, whether they be friends or not, to the dubious company of an unknown, unseen God. Wieder's poem is a commentary on the existentialism of a society that has lost touch with its spiritual moorings and has chosen to brave a hostile universe alone.

How will humanity escape from this self-imposed exile? The succeeding four sections take the reader on a spiritual journey in search of an answer. Likening the aimlessness of today's culture to the Hebrews' forty-year trek through the Sinai desert, several of the poems in the second section, titled "The Mountain Sound," portray humankind's longing to be delivered from a meaningless existence and to be reconciled to the divine. In "Bay," the first poem of the second section, the speaker cries: "O my rock,/ Can a rock be forgetting?/ In this night without starlight/ Death in my bones?/ 'Where is God?'." The agony of God's absence heightens the spiritual desolation that threads through this collection, but the sense of despair is balanced by the expectation that eventually "God will come."

This hope comes, in part, from the power of memory, which plays a key role in delivering a people from the spiritual desert, especially in tribal societies in which myth and story are central to cultural survival. Israelite ceremonies and festivals recalled and celebrated those instances when God intervened on behalf of his chosen people. For example, Psalm 66 celebrates the works of Yahweh by listing events from Israel's history and inviting readers to "come and see" God's greatness. The concluding two strophes are prayers of commitment and thanksgiving.

Wieder's corresponding psalm, "Worship," also deals with memory but lacks the jubilance of the original and is, instead, more reflective. The first stanza laments that "what made all the earth has been/ Forgotten even by the ones disposed to know" and goes on to offer a concise recounting of "what was done for Jacob's children" during the Exodus from Egypt. Although remembering the past can put the events of the present in perspective, the speaker cautions that there is danger in becoming trapped by remembrance. The Israelites rued the hardships of their nomadic life and longed "for Egypt's slave abundance" instead of appreciating God's deliverance. As a result, for "forty years as a generation looking backward/ disappeared." In Wieder's version of Psalm 66, memory is a double-edged sword and cuts two ways—it can either broaden or narrow a nation's vision of the past. "Worship" warns that if a society is to survive, it must first turn away from self-absorption and embrace a wider view of history that includes the God who governs time and events.

Because cultural survival is dependent upon not only memory but also a connection with the creator, separation from the God of history can lead to a profound breakdown of national identity. This psychological crisis is expressed in "Come," Psalm 80. This poem is a national prayer begging God to heal the people from their spiritual fragmentation: "Listen, reader of dreams/ Interpreted by Joseph, who led/ Israel into Egypt, brought them/ Up again: return us to ourselves./ However long it takes to mill/ To knead the sorry flour, our bread/ Crumbles and our neighbors jeer,/ Return us to ourselves." Paralleling the theme of societal dysfunction in its biblical counterpart, "Come" exposes the disordered state of modern society, acknowledging that "there is no going back" to the Eden that once was. Throughout the six-stanza poem, the refrain "return us to ourselves" appears four times, highlighting the people's splintered psyche and their longing for psychological and spiritual wholeness.

The idea of return is increasingly dominant in the fourth section, "Where We Have Always Lived," and is especially evident in "Gathering." Nearing the end of their journey, the Israelites take stock of where they have been and look ahead to where they are going. The original psalm, a hymn of thanksgiving, was written during the latter part of the exile in Babylon when the Hebrews were just beginning to re-form a national identity. The first lines of Wieder's poem echo the joy and anticipation of Psalm 106: "This people to the homes they left/ For foreign places, flavors rolled/ Upon the tongue, flat bread/ Broken at a stranger's table."

Memory and history are again foremost in this poem, but instead of conveying brokenness and sorrow, the terse recounting of the Exodus story and the Babylonian exile sparks a nascent national cohesion and points to an ordeal nearing its end. This sense of impending completeness is revealed in the last stanza: "Gather us together, Lord/ Captives scattered among strangers,/ Lead us back, for we remember/ Promises and praise."

The words of the last line of "Gathering" are reprised in the title of the fifth and final collection, "Return. Promise," which brings the journey full cycle. Although book 5 contains a few laments and vitriolic songs, the predominant theme is thanksgiving, just as it is in the last division of the Book of Psalms. God has brought the exiles home to the Promised Land, and the nation is whole again. Cultural and spiritual identity have been restored, but the continuance of the people depends on keeping alive the collective memory of the national saga. The last stanza of "Receipt" emphasizes the mythic dimension of history that stretches from generation to generation: "So the story keeps returning, of great armies/ Lost in deserts, of the small made splendid,/ Blessed with family and flocks, of the wicked/ Choking on their empty language, hands clapping/ Shut the mouth. Some parts return to mind./ A wise one sees things, and may understand them."

Laurance Wieder's richly imagined response to the Old Testament psalms gets to the core of these ancient works. Sometimes edgy, often lyrical, and always articulate, his renderings capture the deepest desires, loves, fears, sorrows, and joys of the human heart. One does not need any knowledge of the Bible to appreciate Wieder's Psalter because the message is timeless and universal. General readers will identify with this profound portrait of human existence, while those who view the Psalms as a sacred text may see their relationships with God and others in a new light.

Pegge Bochynski

Review Sources

Library Journal 128, no. 12 (July 15, 2003): 92.
The Weekly Standard 8 (June 16, 2003): 33.

THE X IN SEX
How the X Chromosome Controls Our Lives

Author: David Bainbridge (1948-   )
Publisher: Harvard University Press (Cambridge, Mass.).
205 pp. $22.95
Type of work: Science

A captivating biological and cultural tale which explores everything one ever wanted to know about the X chromosome, including its discovery, its function, and its influence on the course of history

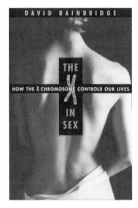

In his latest foray into science made sexy, David Bainbridge tells the story of "a little nugget of life called the X chromosome." He begins with a brief history of human speculation about the origins of sexuality and how this tiny bit of human programming is so essential to continuance of life. "Sexuality was a necessary obsession in the ancient world," notes the author. From the ancient Greeks to the scientists of the modern world, there has always been interest in the how and the why of the differences and origin of the sexes. Aristotle speculated on the opposition of the sexes but was not sure whether that distinction occurred at the moment of conception. Empedocles believed the early embryo to be sexless until its environment determined whether a boy or girl would result. For centuries the answers to questions sexual would continue to puzzle scientists. Many of the insights proffered by the ancients have turned out to have some grain of truth in them, as Bainbridge illustrates later in the discussion.

One of the most important breakthroughs in the field of genetics occurred in the late nineteenth century. Looking into his microscope in 1890, Herman Henking saw for the first time a collection of tiny flecks of purple (stained chromosomal material) which appeared to him to behave in an antisocial way relative to its confreres. What he had discovered as he observed the division of cells in the testicles of a fly, he would name the "wallflower chromosome." Because this particular bit of material did not join in the dance in which other chromosomes participated as they became germ cells (sperm or ova), Henking called it "X." Perhaps the name came from its perceived redundancy.

Henking's thoughts on the topic do not survive. Rather than redundant, this "X" chromosome would turn out to be very special, the basis of human life. While it has been determined that the Y chromosome has the power to dictate human maleness, it is the X chromosome that is the fallback design, or what might be termed the "natural" human state. The Y seems to have one primary function, but the X is much more. Rather than the woman being a "misbegotten male," as historical alliteration had suggested, it is the male animal that is nature's second thought.

Although Bainbridge's main "character" in the book is the X chromosome, carry-

∼

David Bainbridge is a reproductive
biologist and veterinarian who
lectures in comparative anatomy
and physiology at the Royal
Veterinary College in London. He
has been a fellow at St. Catherine's
College of Cambridge University.
He is the author of Making Babies:
The Science of Pregnancy *(2001).*

∼

ing its genetic repertoire with competence, it is the presence and influence of the bit player, the Y chromosome, whose one important spoken line determines the maleness of a particular offspring. This "standard mammal system" of Y's role holds, even in the aberrant situations in which offspring have additional X chromosomes. Y "wins," says the author, no matter how many extra X chromosomes nature includes in its genetic instruction manual. Spunk triumphs over numbers. It is a very specific gene, called *Sry* and carried on the Y, that will consistently determine that a male is produced and the "raw material" primed for femaleness will not become activated. It is Y's "macho power" which triggers a variety of male-producing chemical activity, sometimes from genes not located on the Y, that makes boys boys.

Having distinct sexes and specific chromosomes which determine them is a fairly recent adaptation in evolutionary history. The chromosomes which are known to function in this manner are likely the result of bits and pieces of other chromosomes being, as Bainbridge puts it, "cobbled together from non-sex chromosomes" over the eons of time. Many creatures still reproduce quite successfully without any sexual determination. There are those who bud, those who simply divide in two, and those who successfully endure and increase by any number of nonsexual processes. Even species with two distinct sexes do not always arrive in that state, as their mammalian cousins do. Many species' approach to making the male and female depends on external factors rather than the presence of specific X and Y determinants. Some factors which force sexual differences include the condition of the environment (for certain wormlike sea creatures), the temperature of the sand in which the females lay eggs (for crocodiles and turtles), and the death of an already existent dominant female (for bees).

The author includes a short chapter on the history of the discovery of deoxyribonucleic acid (DNA). He reprises the work of Gregor Mendel (tall and short peas resulting from genetic selection), Walther Flemming (the activity of dark-stained "chromosomes" in the nuclei of cells during cell division), and James Watson and Francis Crick (the "double helix" as the consistent basic structure of all genetic material). It was in 1953 that Watson and Crick published their work, so a complete understanding of how characteristics pass from one generation to another is a relatively recent advancement. In the last half century or so, much more has been learned about the workings of individual genes. Some of that information is detailed in Bainbridge's work.

Perhaps one of the most interesting sections of the book, particularly for those who are not fascinated with basic biological information, treats the history of the inherited trait for hemophilia, which afflicted a good number of the males of European royal families, from the time of Queen Victoria into the modern era. The gene for this disease is carried recessively on the X chromosome, so it would show up only in offspring (male) who inherited the blighted bit of genetic material from their mothers.

With two inherited X chromosomes, girls would have a "backup" X to make up what is lacking on the damaged X. The woman with this pair of X chromosomes (one with the damaged gene) would pass on only one X to each of her eggs. If the egg with the damaged X should rendezvous with a Y sperm, the characteristic which had remained unexpressed in the mother would reveal itself in a diseased son.

When Edward, duke of Kent, fathered Victoria, who was to reign over England with great fecundity for more than half a century, he had no idea that a mutation to his sperm would find its way through her into the royal families of England, Russia, and Spain. Bainbridge portrays Edward's mutation as a cosmic event, presumably the author's license with fact which may or may not be taken seriously. The dormant destroyer, the gene for a disease that prevented appropriate clotting of the blood in its victims, passed from Edward to his regal daughter. She shared it generously with many children, who either showed the disease (a son) or passed it unseen to male grandchildren. Because the gene that controls clotting is on the X chromosome, having only one affected chromosome—as do boys—can cause this serious illness. In the case of girls, the gene code on the second X—girls having two—makes up for the lack. It is extremely unlikely for girls to receive two damaged chromosomes, making them prone to the disease.

While hemophilia is perhaps the most exotic and best known of diseases carried recessively and unobserved on the X chromosome, there are others. The author details some of these as well. Included are muscular dystrophy and color blindness. Current and somewhat controversial speculation locates the cause of homosexuality on the X. A "gay gene" has yet to be isolated, however, and other factors which may coalesce to produce a homosexual individual are still under exploration.

Scientists have discovered that, although the X chromosome is certainly more important than the puny Y, women can do as well with one X as can men. Male offspring have only one X chromosome, inherited from the mother. While the female embryo inherits an X chromosome from each of her parents, this abundance is eschewed by the developing female. She "turns off" one of the X's in each of her cells. Interestingly, this turn-off mechanism is not consistent. One might think that all the X's from one parent would be inactivated. Rather, some of the female's cells retain the paternal-inherited X, while others retain that from the mother's genetic store. It is not yet known why this occurs nor if there is any pattern to it. The "mosaic" nature of the deactivation of half of the X chromosomes in female embryos is the source of such phenotypic variation as is seen in calico cats. Such felines inherit orange X from one parent, white X from the other. What appears to be random turning off of orange in some cells and white in the others results in the interesting coat-color pattern. In mammalian females the unused X chromosome retreats to the edge of the nucleus—much the way seeds in navel oranges move to the edge of the fruit—and remains there as inactive Barr bodies (named after their discoverer, Canadian neurobiologist Murray Barr).

The author has provided an extremely helpful glossary of terms that may be unfamiliar to some readers. In the "Further Reading" section he has broken the selections into not only chapter headings but also subchapter headings. This will allow the reader to pick and choose intelligently where to go to pursue the subject more thoroughly. Some of the sources are obscure and perhaps not readily available, but Bainbridge notes this as he gives a thorough commentary on the merits of what he proposed.

While it is written with clarity and style, the book is not an easy project. Even the reader who enjoys a strong background in biology and is familiar with the terms of the territory will be challenged. That is not to discourage anyone from reading this delightful, up-to-date, and clear picture of the life and history of the X chromosome and its fellow travelers. Bainbridge has written a wonderful exposé of sex. His use of anecdotes, clever illustrations, and solid historical and scientific information is skillful. It is hoped the title—if not the cover picture—will lure an audience into this treat for the intellect and the imagination.

Dolores L. Christie

Review Sources

Booklist 99, no. 11 (February 1, 2003): 962.
Kirkus Reviews 70, no. 23 (December 1, 2002): 1743.
Library Journal 128, no. 5 (March 15, 2003): 111.
New Scientist 178, no. 2401 (June 28, 2003): 50.
The New York Times Book Review, April 13, 2003, p. 22.
Psychology Today 36, no. 3 (May/June, 2003): 72.
The Times Literary Supplement, October 24, 2003, p. 35.

YELLOW DOG

Author: Martin Amis (1949-   )
Publisher: Miramax Books (New York). 340 pp. $24.95
Type of work: Novel
Time: 2003
Locale: London, Paris, the south of France, and Southern California

The beating of an actor and writer and a royal scandal lead to explorations of the worlds of crime, journalism, and pornography

Principal characters:
  XAN MEO, an actor and writer
  DR. RUSSIA TANNENBAUM, his wife, a history professor
  BILLIE and SOPHIE MEO, their young daughters
  HENRY IX, the king of England
  PRINCESS VICTORIA, Henry's daughter
  BRENDAN URQUHART-GORDON, Henry's private secretary
  CLINT SMOKER, writer for *The Morning Lark*
  JOSEPH ANDREWS, a retired criminal
  PEARL O'DANIEL, Xan's first wife
  CORA SUSAN/KARLA WHITE, Xan's niece, an actress in pornographic films
  MAL BALE, a criminal working for Andrews
  KATE, Clint's adoring fan
  HOMELESS JOHN, a beggar

As Martin Amis is generally considered one of the most brilliant British novelists of his generation, the publication of each of his books becomes a media event in Great Britain. Because novels such as *Money* (1984), *London Fields* (1989), and *The Information* (1995) are decidedly American in their styles and themes, with similarities to such writers as Saul Bellow and Don DeLillo, Amis also elicits considerable attention from the literary establishment in the United States. *Yellow Dog* is especially notable because of a controversy about its literary quality.

Xan Meo is a self-styled renaissance man: a well-known British actor; author of *Lucozade*, a collection of short stories; and occasional rhythm guitarist for a bar band. After an unhappy first marriage, he is married to Dr. Russia Tannenbaum, a history professor at King's College, London, and they have two young daughters. Though Xan has given up the bad habits of his past, every year on his birthday he celebrates his newfound sobriety by going to Hollywood, his onetime favorite pub, to drink and smoke. This year, shortly after his arrival, he is taken outside and beaten severely. Apparently, he has somewhere mentioned the name of someone who should not be mentioned.

The son of acclaimed novelist Kingsley Amis, Martin Amis has been a writer and editor for The Times Literary Supplement, New Statesman, *and* The Observer. *His honors include the Somerset Maugham Award for his first novel,* The Rachel Papers *(1973), the James Tait Black Memorial Prize for biography for* Experience *(2000), and the National Book Critics Circle Award for criticism for* The War Against Cliché: Essays and Reviews *(2001).*

Amis alternates between relating Xan's painful recovery from a head injury, (one that changes his perspective considerably, especially toward women) with events from the lives of three other sets of characters. One centers around Henry IX, king of Great Britain and Northern Ireland. Henry's life is also uneasy. He deplores "the condition of being royal: it was always on at you and it never let you be." Making matters worse, his queen, Pamela, lies in a coma following a fall from a horse, and his beloved only child, the fifteen-year-old Victoria, has been unwittingly photographed in the nude. Should Henry pull the plug on Pamela? Can he head off the unscrupulous media's exploitation of the video of his daughter?

Henry relies greatly upon his confidante and longtime best friend, Brendan Urquhart-Gordon. Brendan's situation is made more complex by his unrequited love for the princess, thirty years his junior.

Clint Smoker writes for the least scrupulous of London tabloids, *The Morning Lark.* Clint's employer ignores straight news at the expense of the sensational, promoting masturbatory fantasies and defending rapists. When not practicing his journalistic trade, Clint worries about his sexual inadequacies and corresponds with Kate, who sends him fan e-mails, assuring him that the size of a penis is irrelevant. Amis builds slowly to Clint's eventual meeting with his fan.

The other major protagonist does not appear until halfway through *Yellow Dog.* Joseph Andrews is an eighty-five-year-old, semi-retired London gangster living in Southern California but still controlling events back home. Andrews is an old antagonist of Xan's criminal father, Mick, and is also the source of Xan's recent misery, not realizing that the Joseph Andrews mentioned in Xan's fiction is named for the title character of Henry Fielding's 1742 novel. Andrews also tries to blackmail King Henry over the princess video.

Amis is commenting on the ways men and women misunderstand each other and the resulting suspicion and confusion. He is also observing the power and corruption of the media. As in much of his fiction, especially *London Fields,* Amis is concerned with the decline of Britain into mindless decadence, deploring "the obscenification of everyday life." He also pokes fun at politically correct views of the sexual battlefield.

Even though they realize they should not, men cannot avoid seeing women as sexual objects. The pre-injury Xan considers himself enlightened for going slightly beyond this view: "If you harbour an admiration for extreme womanly beauty, then feast your eyes on my wife—the mouth, the eyes, the aerodynamic cheekbones (and the light of high intelligence: he was very proud of her intelligence)." He thinks he is "the dream husband" because he shares the responsibilities of parenthood equally with Russia and is "a tender and punctual lover."

Women are more tenderhearted and more complicated. They enjoy prolonged departures from their loved ones, leaving men to stew in boredom: "Being kept waiting is a moderate reparation for their five million years in power." Women are less vengeful, more easily forgiving, though Pearl, Xan's first wife, has him arrested three times before they agree to divorce. Women are also unduly suspicious, quick to think the worst of their men, as with Russia's ungrounded fears that her husband may have sexual designs on their daughters. She also questions her role as wife: "Did I take two degrees and study history so I could get raped in a cave?"

At forty-seven, Xan experiences numerous signs of aging. Most upsetting is the fact that young women are beginning to look through him, unable to see his sexuality. The resulting insecurity makes Xan perceive his society as "A yellowworld of faith and fear, and paltry ingenuity. And all of us just flying blind." Xan's cousin Cora Susan, who works as the porn star Karla White, accuses him of subscribing in *Lucozade* "to various polite fictions about men and women. . . . As if all enmity is over and we both now drink the milk of concord." She adds that "good sex seems to be something that writing can't manage." Cora, who as a child was raped by her father, is used by Amis to speak for women as victims. Incest represents unimaginable crime and society's excesses at their worst.

Xan appears in one of Cora/Karla's films because that is the only work he can get after his injury. To try to give their films a touch of class, American pornographers like to hire British actors to play characters who watch others having sex. These pornographers' Anglophilia also leads them to name their stars Sir Dork Bogarde and Sir Phallic Guinness. Such humor does not detract from Amis's serious contemplation of this industry: "Is pornography just filmed prostitution or is it something more gladiatorial?" Amis the moralist sees it as demeaning to all involved. Nevertheless, he is sympathetic toward the performers themselves: "No one cared about pornographers and what porno people cared about." Xan wants to protect Cora/Karla "from all things—including things like himself."

Society's woes are cataloged throughout *Yellow Dog.* Even buildings are sick: Everyone at *The Morning Lark* is always sneezing, coughing, and retching. Homeless John, who lives at home with his mother, begs because homelessness is more lucrative than working for a living. Children carry mobile telephones for safety, only to be robbed of the phones. On their answering-machine messages, people leave "hate-crammed music inciting you to act like somebody crazy." The media offer little but "the Borgesian metropolis of electronic pornography." Andrews's henchman Mal Bale, protagonist of "State of England" in Amis's *Heavy Water* (1998), complains that there are "no *hard men* any more," only nutters and drug addicts. In this society has evolved "a new human type. . . . wised-up, affectless, and non-emphatic, high-IQ morons . . . were also supercontemporary in their acceptance of all technological and cultural change—an acceptance both unflinching and unsmiling." Amis's world is clearly headed for disaster, represented by the comet, called a Near Earth Object by the press, that many fear will destroy the planet. Xan's loss of memory is a metaphor for what seems to be a desired state of being.

The controversy in Great Britain over *Yellow Dog* began when novelist Tibor Fischer attacked Amis in London's *The Daily Telegraph*. After identifying himself as a longtime fan and defender of the novelist, Fischer objected that with *Yellow Dog*, Amis strains for profundity and creates a work "unworthy of his talent": "It's not-knowing-where-to-look bad. . . . It's like your favourite uncle being caught in a school playground, masturbating." In *The Independent*, Liz Jensen found it so "unfocused" that she "had to read it one and a half times in order to fathom what in the name of Crikey was going on. And even now I am not sure." Jensen also considered the targets of Amis's satire too easy.

Because there were many such negative reviews, observers were surprised when *Yellow Dog* appeared on the long list of twenty-three novels considered for the Booker Prize, the most highly regarded British literary award. It did not make the short list, however, and *The Sunday Times* reported that one of the judges labeled it dated and even ridiculous. Perhaps the most devastating American objection to *Yellow Dog* came from Michiko Kakutani of *The New York Times:* "Were Mr. Amis's name not emblazoned on this book, it seems unlikely to have found a publisher." Suzi Feay, Sunday literary editor of *The Independent*, likened the attacks on Amis to "watching someone clubbing a seal."

Amis's defenders included Robert Douglas-Fairhurst of *The Observer*, who called *Yellow Dog* "mind-tinglingly good," adding that Amis "seems to have guessed what you thought about the world, and then expressed it far better than you ever could." Douglas-Fairhurst surmised that Amis's highly literary style and complex narrative structure may be too daunting for some readers. Because Amis employs several types of vernacular, examines characters from all levels of society, and creates unexpected links between these characters, he becomes, in Douglas-Fairhurst's words, "Dickens with a snarl."

Regardless of any doubts about the overall quality of *Yellow Dog*, the novel's detractors must admit that Amis knows how to delineate characters and settings and express the tormented inner lives of the inhabitants of Amisland. He also writes extremely well: "If he turned right he would be heading for pram-torn Primrose Hill—itself pramlike, stately, Vicwardian, arching itself upwards in a posture of mild indignation." Xan's despair at the modern young woman's indifference to glamour displays Amis's attention to detail: "Typically she wore nine-inch bricks and wigwam flares; her midriff revealed a band of offwhite underpants and a navel traumatised by *bijouterie*; she had her car-keys in one cheek and her door-keys in the other, a plough in her nose and an anchor in her chin; and her earwax was all over her hair, as if via some inner conduit." Such consistently fine writing combined with insights into a society bent on destroying any traces of its innocence makes *Yellow Dog* a fitting addition to the Amis oeuvre.

Michael Adams

Review Sources

Booklist 100, no. 2 (September 15, 2003): 179-180.
Kirkus Reviews 71, no. 16 (August 15, 2003): 1029.
Library Journal 128, no. 17 (October 15, 2003): 95.
Los Angeles Times Book Review, November 2, 2003, p. 7.
The Nation 277, no. 19 (December 8, 2003): 50-54.
New Criterion 22, no. 3 (November, 2003): 59-66.
New Statesman 132, no. 4654 (September 8, 2003): 48-50.
The New York Times, October 28, 2003, p. E1.
The New York Times Book Review, November 9, 2003, p. 11.
Publishers Weekly 250, no. 41 (October 13, 2003): 55-56.
Time 162, no. 18 (November 3, 2003): 76.
The Times Literary Supplement, September 5, 2003, pp. 3-4.

YOGA FOR PEOPLE WHO CAN'T BE BOTHERED TO DO IT

Author: Geoff Dyer (1958-   )
Publisher: Pantheon Books (New York). 257 pp. $22.00
Type of work: Essays
Time: 1980-2000
Locale: Amsterdam; Cambodia; Rome; Indonesia; Libya; Detroit; Black Rock
City, Nevada; and Vietnam

> *In his collection of new and previously published essays, Dyer describes his travels across inner and outer landscapes, traversing the world in his quest for "the Zone"*

Principal personages:
GEOFF DYER, the narrator and author of the book
CIRCLE, his girlfriend, also known as Sarah
KATE,
MONICA, and
DAZED, some of his other girlfriends
MARIE, a woman whom Dyer meets in Paris

This is not, as one might suppose, a book for the sedentary bibliophile who would rather read about exercise than engage in physical activity. In fact, this is not a book about yoga at all, nor is this book truly "travel literature," the category to which it is most usually assigned. Indeed, *Yoga for People Who Can't Be Bothered to Do It* is an admittedly difficult book to categorize at all. Is it fiction, nonfiction, philosophy, or humor? Are the pieces essays or short stories? Even the author, Geoff Dyer, deliberately blurs generic categories in his introduction: "Everything in this book really happened," Dyer writes, "but some of the things that happened only happened in my head; by the same token, all things that didn't happen didn't happen there too."

The eleven essays that make up *Yoga for People Who Can't Be Bothered to Do It* trace Dyer's journeys from exotic location to exotic location as he attempts to find something, although just what that something is remains elusive. The travels span some twenty years of Dyer's life, but he seems no closer to finding this special something (or someone) at age forty-four than at age twenty-four. Indeed, if anything, Dyer seems to become more isolated, more detached, and more immobilized with the passage of time. As he writes in the essay "Leptis Magna," "I saw that I had spent the last fifteen years dragging the same burden of frustrated expectation from one corner of the world to the next. . . . I wished there were someone I could talk to, but as soon as this wish was realized I wished only to be alone."

In many ways, the title essay is emblematic of the collection as a whole. Dyer writes of his sojourn to the sanctuary on Ko Pha-ngan in Thailand, where he meets a woman named Kate and an assortment of other odd characters, including a handsome man named Troy. Troy tells Dyer that because he wanted to experience mortality, he once drank a bottle of poison. Ironically, although Troy survived the experience, he is unable to remember it. Dyer has a brief affair with Kate before the two go their separate ways. Like the rest of the book, the essay is very funny, particularly Troy's description of the blisters on his feet as a karmic exit for bad memories. Like the rest of the book, the essay is about drugs, drinking, and dissolution. Like the rest of the book, the essay is sometimes about nothing whatsoever, and it can be very sad. Dyer and Kate leave the island separately, their passionate connection reduced to the brief flickering of an e-mail message.

In addition to his three novels, Paris Trance *(1998),* The Search *(1993), and* The Colour of Memory *(1989), English writer Geoff Dyer has published a critical study of John Berger and three books of essays—* But Beautiful: A Book About Jazz *(1991),* The Missing of the Somme *(1994), and* Out of Sheer Rage *(1997). He lives in London.*

Dyer is at his best in the essay "Leptis Magna," the story of his trip to Libya to see Roman ruins on the Mediterranean coast. The opening of the essay is characteristically concerned with the details of his getting to Libya and negotiating the bureaucratic nightmare of the airport and hotel. "By their airports ye shall know them!" Dyer writes, noting the smokiness of the terminal and the surliness of the officials. Checking into the hotel requires filling out "hectares" of paper. In spite of his now-familiar rants and aggravations, however, it becomes clear that Dyer is becoming increasingly unglued. He catches a glimpse of himself in the hotel mirror, and through this clichéd device, he recognizes the part of himself that he had thought to hide: "You will become one . . . of the hundreds of people to whom you paid the bare minimum of attention simply because you did not like the way they looked," he tells himself. It is as if, in coming to see the ruins at Leptis Magna, he begins to confront the ruin that is his life.

Nevertheless, when Dyer finally, excruciatingly, gets himself to the ruins, the pettiness and minutia of life seem to fall away. "Ruins—antique ruins at least—are what is left when history has moved on. They are no longer at the mercy of history, only of time," he muses as he tries to make sense of the experience. Even time, however, falls away as Dyer observes the sharp edge between a ruined column and the sky, the "absolute separation between the timeless man-made and the eternal." Dyer realizes in the closing lines of the essay that from the "point of view of sea and sky—Leptis was still in the early stages of a career of ruination which would end ultimately as desert, when the horizon would be undisturbed by any vestige of the vertical: the final triumph of space over time."

The author further chronicles his descent into depression and breakdown in the essay "The Rain Inside." He decides that he wants to live in Detroit in order to write a book about classical Roman ruins. There, he instead finds himself unable to focus or concentrate. He suddenly realizes that he is the one in ruins. His description of this moment is both powerful and true: "I realized that . . . I had been in the midst of an ongoing nervous breakdown without even being aware of it, that I had, in fact, gone to pieces. I mean that as literally as possible. Everything had become scattered, fragmented." Characteristically, however, he moves from a compelling two-page description of what it feels like to be in the midst of such a breakdown to a multi-page description of his reaction to losing his sunglasses.

Although a much more hip and edgy essay than those mentioned previously, "Skunk" seems overall to be one of the less successful articles in the book. Dyer is in Paris in April of 1999, working on a book about walks to take in that city. Through mutual friends, he meets an attractive woman, Marie, who agrees to accompany him on a walk the next day. Over coffee, Dyer tells Marie that it would help his walk if he were stoned, and he invites her to share a pipe with him. The next pages describe their attempts to find a place to get high on "skunk," very strong marijuana. Although Marie tells Dyer that marijuana has never had any effect on her, the skunk affects her negatively. For the rest of the essay, she is in the grips of a drug-induced paranoia; she is particularly afraid that Dyer is writing about her, not the walk. "Skunk is like that," Dyer tells the reader, "it takes the normal dope smoker's paranoia and raises it to a level of reeling expressionist insight." At one point, Marie attempts to cross out her name and phone number from Dyer's book: "Unfortunately the pen had run out of ink . . . and so she began using it as a chisel, gashing out parts of that page and the three or four underneath."

Marie's dread is palpable throughout the essay. After she leaves, Dyer begins making notes to himself about what Marie said and did "in case one day I wanted to use what happened in a novel or a story." The essay in front of the reader is the clear proof that he has done just that—and that Marie's paranoia was therefore justified. While the essay has some very funny moments, readers might feel some discomfort in Dyer's lack of sympathy for his subject.

Set in Amsterdam, "Hotel Oblivion" is another article that depends on drug use for its most comical moments. After tromping around in a rainstorm under the influence of psychedelic mushrooms with his friends Dazed and Dave, Dyer decides to change into dry pants in the washroom of a restaurant. He has a difficult time with this simple task, first putting back on the wet pair he had just taken off, and then putting on the dry pair inside out. Later, the friends are unable to recognize their hotel and wander around the city looking for it. They still think they are in the wrong hotel when Dave tries his key in a door, only to discover that they are, indeed, in the right hotel (or at least, that the key works).

Certainly, there is a long history of humor connected to alcohol and drug use; many comedians have built whole careers on their depictions of drunk or stoned individuals. Readers who enjoy this kind of humor will find "Skunk" and "Hotel Oblivion" shatteringly funny. What ultimately renders these essays less than satisfying, however, is Dyer's lack of connection to the city he is in, the people he is with, and the writer he has become.

The last essay in the collection, "The Zone," is the story of Dyer's trip to Black Rock City, Nevada, to participate in the Burning Man celebration. The trip pushes

Dyer to consider his life and his travels and to find himself once more in what he calls "the Zone." He writes that watching the Burning Man was "one of those moments that make your whole like seem worthwhile because it has led to this, to this moment." Nevertheless, nearly by definition, the Zone is not something one can stay in for any length of time; as soon as one is aware of being in such a state, it immediately evaporates. Consequently, the closing lines of this essay seem to offer both hope and despair for the quester looking for transcendence: "Just before the Man was completely engulfed in flame, one of his knees gave way. He lurched forward and it looked, for a moment, as if he were to step clear of the fire that defined and claimed him."

Dyer's books, including this one, have been consistently well reviewed and have won the writer several prestigious awards. He has also attracted the praise and support of a number of influential readers and critics, including actor, writer, and comedian Steve Martin, who called *Yoga for People Who Can't Be Bothered to Do It* a "funny . . . readable . . . clear and wonderful" book. Certainly, Dyer offers moments of brilliance in these essays, moments of rare insight and beautiful language. However, the reader who finds drug humor offensive, and self-absorption tiring, might do well to avoid this particular example of Dyer's work.

Diane Andrews Henningfeld

Review Sources

Booklist 99, nos. 9/10 (January 1-15, 2003): 837.
Kirkus Reviews 70, no. 22 (November 15, 2002): 1670-1671.
Library Journal 128, no. 3 (February 15, 2003): 160.
New Statesman 132, no. 4634 (April 21, 2003): 53.
The New York Times, January 24, 2003, p. E46.
The New York Times Book Review, January 12, 2003, p. 7.
The New Yorker 78, no. 45 (February 3, 2003): 87.
Publishers Weekly 249, no. 45 (November 11, 2002): 49.
San Francisco Chronicle, February 15, 2003, p. D1.
The Times Literary Supplement, May 2, 2003, p. 31.

ZELDA FITZGERALD
Her Voice in Paradise

Author: Sally Cline (1938-   )
First published: 2002, in Great Britain
Publisher: Arcade (New York). 492 pp. $27.95
Type of work: Biography
Time: 1900-1948
Locale: The United States and Europe

Fitzgerald, the wife of a famed author, struggled throughout her life for the freedom to develop her many talents

Principal personages:
ZELDA SAYRE FITZGERALD, southern belle, wife of F. Scott Fitzgerald
FRANCIS SCOTT KEY FITZGERALD, famous author of *The Great Gatsby* (1925), an alcoholic
ERNEST HEMINGWAY, famous author, Zelda's enemy
GERALD MURPHY, wealthy and cultured friend of the Fitzgeralds
SARA MURPHY, Gerald's wife
LUBOV EGOROVA, Zelda's ballet teacher

Zelda Fitzgerald attained notoriety but little fame in her lifetime. She was known mainly as the southern belle who became a beautiful, zany, and mad wife, a character in F. Scott Fitzgerald's life story. In 1970 Nancy Milford published *Zelda: A Biography*, and much of that was changed. Milford's Zelda was a woman for the 1970's. As feminists grew in number, biographers began to focus on literary women. Sisters and wives of noted authors were seen to rival their brothers and husbands. Long, and often unfairly, neglected women poets and novelists were rediscovered and reprinted. The literary talent of Milford's Zelda had been resented by her husband and obscured by him. Her subsequent mental illness made her story a melancholy case in point.

Since then, so much more attention has been paid to Zelda that she stands as a figure in her own right. Most biographers encountered reticence by the living relatives of both F. Scott and Zelda to display some important material. By the 1990's, Sally Cline, an established British writer, was given full access to all relevant papers. Cline also tracked down all of Zelda's surviving paintings. As a result, this somewhat biased book benefits from more biographical evidence.

The story is a good one. Zelda Sayre was born in 1900 in Montgomery, Alabama, to Minerva ("Minnie") Machen Sayre and Judge Anthony Dickinson Sayre. Because Minnie loved romantic novels, Zelda's name was prophetically borrowed from several flamboyantly beautiful gypsy heroines. Moreover, on her mother's side Zelda came from a long line of what she called "the most audacious, impetuous, picturesque and irrepressible" ancestors. There was talk of a strain of mental illness.

As a girl, Zelda lived up to her name and ancestry. Although her friends were from old, established
families, Zelda was rebellious. She was a tomboy
and did not conform to the ideal of the southern lady. She did well enough in school but only
liked her art class. Her talk was wonderful—full of
wild metaphors, yet oddly disconnected. The word
around Montgomery was that Zelda had no shyness
and no morals. She lost her virginity when she was
fifteen. She may have been raped.

∼

*Sally Cline teaches part time at
Cambridge University in
England and holds a Royal
Literary Fund Writer's
Fellowship at the Anglia
Polytechnic University. Her
other books include the
biography* Radclyffe Hall: A
Woman Called John *(1996). She
lives in Cambridge.*

∼

In April, 1917, the United States entered World
War I. Montgomery was near two army bases, and
soldiers came to town. Zelda was the most popular
belle. Officers swarmed about, and her evenings were filled with dancing and parties.
At one of these she met a young officer, F. Scott Fitzgerald. He was intelligent, sensitive, and gentle. Even though Zelda loved him, she would not become engaged. Cline
disputes the usual implication that she hesitated because Scott had no money; rather,
Zelda was afraid of leaving her comfortable southern world. She also worried that
Scott had little self-confidence. With the publication of his novel *This Side of Paradise* in 1920, Scott gained both confidence and money. They married that year.

The story of the Fitzgeralds' married life has been told many times, and Cline fills
in the familiar outline well. They first lived in New York. Scott wrote articles which
inspired the popular press to acclaim the Fitzgeralds the representatives of the flamboyant postwar era, which Scott named "The Jazz Age." They danced, drank, and behaved outrageously. They rode on the hoods of taxis and splashed in the fountain in
front of The Plaza hotel. They were kicked out of hotels and restaurants for their behavior. They had money and spent more than they had.

When Zelda became pregnant, they returned to Scott's hometown of St. Paul.
Even though Scott worked on his second novel and Zelda gave birth to their daughter,
Scottie, the extravagant parties and excessive drinking continued. These activities did
not stop when they went East and rented a house in Great Neck, Long Island. A list of
their friends and acquaintances reads like a who's who of the literary and theatrical
worlds: Edmund Wilson, John Dos Passos, Maxwell Perkins, Ring Lardner, Anita
Loos, Rebecca West, Basil Rathbone, Leslie Howard. When they returned from Europe a few years later, that list would expand to include Edna Ferber, Sherwood Anderson, H. L. Mencken, Robert Benchley, George S. Kaufman, Dorothy Parker, Alexander Wollcott, Helen Hayes, Lillian Gish, Djuna Barnes, and Lillian Hellman.

The Fitzgeralds went to Europe in 1924, and for the following six years they
moved among Paris, Rome, and the French Riviera, returning to the United States
several times to live in New York again and in Hollywood. In Paris, they became
close friends of Gerald and Sara Murphy, a wealthy and artistic couple whose hospitality became legendary. Through the Murphys, they met songwriter Cole Porter,
painters Pablo Picasso and Fernand Léger, and writer Ernest Hemingway.

All through these years, Scott managed to turn out many fine short stories and two novels, the second of which, *The Great Gatsby*, would become a classic of American literature. During this time he also drank to excess. Cline records many terrible stories of his offensive and embarrassing behavior. At the same time, he was an authoritarian and even abusive husband—she portrays him as almost a monster. Zelda, whose natural exuberance blended into the wild life when they were the toast of New York, suffered from not having any role besides being Scott's flapper wife and suffered also from being a thousand miles away from home. She felt especially alienated in St. Paul. As the 1920's went on, her health worsened, and her behavior sometimes became odd and even self-destructive. She could be nasty or excessively sullen. On Easter in 1930, Zelda suffered her first nervous collapse: She heard flowers talking and other voices.

Zelda's life through the 1940's was terrible to live through but easy to summarize. She was in and out of clinics in Switzerland and the United States, ending up at Highland Hospital in Ashville, North Carolina, in 1936. Cline draws on newly available evidence to describe in excruciating detail the horrible treatments Zelda underwent. Some of the therapies may have been unnecessary, for Cline makes out a case that Zelda, probably because of her unique way of talking, was misdiagnosed as a schizophrenic. Cline cites other reasons for Zelda's mistreatment. Zelda had lesbian tendencies; contemporary doctors considered such behavior unnatural and tried to cure patients of it. Doctors also considered a women to be deviant if she was not a devoted mother or if she did not want a career.

Cline is also critical of what she sees as a flaw in Zelda's character: her "outrageous dependency" on Scott. (Zelda's loving letters to Scott during this decade, however, are very moving.) Zelda's mental problems were partly real, partly exacerbated by her treatment, and partly a myth built up by Scott's biographers and by the remarks made by people who knew her, especially Ernest Hemingway. Hemingway sensed that Zelda did not like him or his work and retaliated by calling her crazy.

Cline's revision of the usual accounts of Zelda's mental problems is important; so is her emphasis on Zelda's real talent, hard work, and artistic achievement. At every turn, Cline emphasizes that Zelda was not the shallow flapper and obsessive amateur that myth has made her. She was an independent and adventurous young woman. Even in Montgomery, she wrote, painted, and danced. As soon as she discovered that her wild life with Scott did not give her scope for personal and professional achievement, she attempted to establish herself as an artist in her own right. She began taking painting lessons and studied ballet in Paris under (and also fell in love with) Lubov Egorova, once a leading dancer in the Russian Imperial ballet. Zelda continued to paint until the end of her life. She threw herself into these activities with an energy that some thought obsessive. She wrote articles and stories that were published under Scott's name or both of their names. In her letters and articles, Zelda is truly witty and incisive; the reader hears an original and winning voice. In her fiction, she shows a wonderful ability to describe sights and smells sensuously.

What clinches Cline's argument that one should take Zelda seriously is what she did achieve. She was an accomplished enough dancer to be offered a position as a prima ballerina with the Teatro di San Carlo opera and ballet company in Naples, Italy, which she declined. Egorova thought she could dance with Léonide Massine's ballet company in New York. Cline especially emphasizes Zelda's success as a painter (though only one illustration of her work is given). Zelda had many exhibitions of her paintings, one in a prominent New York gallery and she sold many pictures. Reproductions of her paintings can be found in *Zelda: An Illustrated Life* (1996), edited by Eleanor Lanahan. As a writer, Zelda's success is measured by volume. She published a number of articles and stories in important magazines and in 1932 produced a well-received novel, *Save Me the Waltz*. Her accomplishments in all three fields were considerable.

Zelda Fitzgerald: Her Voice in Paradise may be too detailed for some readers. The account of Zelda's hospital stays becomes boring. Cline's partisanship may offend other readers, and her narrative is sometimes hard to follow. Her segues from topic to topic are awkward, perhaps because she tries to contribute to all of her arguments at all times. Over and over, Cline documents one of her most important themes: that both Fitzgeralds felt entitled to use the material of their joint experiences for their fiction. This was a major bone of contention in their marriage. Zelda draws upon their experience in her stories. Scott uses details of his courtship and Zelda's letters and diaries in *This Side of Paradise* and *The Beautiful and Damned* (1922), the plot of which mirrors the Fitzgeralds' life together. Zelda's remark after giving birth turns up in Daisy's mouth in *The Great Gatsby*.

Matters came to a head when, in the early 1930's, Scott was struggling with *Tender Is the Night* (1934). He wanted to draw upon their experiences with Zelda's hospitalization and was furious to learn that Zelda was using this material in a second novel of her own. During a long session with a doctor as referee, Scott argued that, as a professional novelist who supported his family, the material was his and that, as an amateur and wife, Zelda should defer to him. Zelda argued that she was entitled to write about her own life. Cline quotes much of the transcript of this session. One critic points out, however, that she inserts stage directions that tilt the scales in Zelda's favor.

Some readers may argue that, talented as she was, Zelda did not accomplish enough in her life to warrant all the attention that she has received. Most readers still regard Scott as the major talent. Certainly this biography is skewed in Zelda's favor. Nevertheless, she was a major player in the culture of her time, and Cline's biography gives the interested reader many new details of Zelda's life and many new and persuasive interpretations of them.

George Soule

Review Sources

Booklist 99, no. 17 (May 1, 2003): 1565.
London Review of Books 25, no. 12 (June 19, 2003): 31-32.
Publishers Weekly 250, no. 13 (March 31, 2003): 51.
The Times Literary Supplement, March 7, 2003, pp. 7-8.
The Women's Review of Books 21, no. 1 (October, 2003): 1-3.

ZITHER AND AUTOBIOGRAPHY

Author: Leslie Scalapino (1953-   )
Publisher: Wesleyan University Press (Middletown,
   Conn.). 110 pp. $30.00
Type of work: Poetry and autobiography
Time: From the late 1950's to the early twenty-first cen-
   tury
Locale: Largely the West Coast of the United States

*A leading experimental poet tells her life story along-
side an experimental poem that questions the nature of perception and reality*

   Principal personages:
      LESLIE SCALAPINO, an experimental poet
         and narrator of the prose autobiography
      ROBERT SCALAPINO, her father, a University of California political sci-
         ence professor and specialist on Asia
      TOM WHITE, her husband

   It is rather typical for critics hyperbolically to describe books as being unlike any
other. Leslie Scalapino's poetic and prose meditation deserves this description if anything does. The first part of the book, "Autobiography," is a narrative, if hardly expos-
itory, account of the first fifty years of Scalapino's life. The second, "Zither," is an experimental poem which expands on hints dropped in the autobiography but cannot
really be said to be derived from it.

   There is a prefatory—but crucial—quote from Paul de Man on how the genre of
autobiography often determines the content, rather than vice versa, as is traditionally
assumed. Then "Autobiography" begins with letters from Scalapino to Norman
Fischer, a poet who has been associated with Zen Buddhist monasteries and presses.
Scalapino has been interested in Buddhism throughout her career. She is interested in
the instability of language and the puzzling nature of the human apprehension of reality. These concepts have analogues in Zen thought, although there are Western philosophical sources on them as well.

   Scalapino's involvement with Eastern thought is not merely an intellectual one.
Her father, Robert Scalapino, is an influential American political scientist who taught
at the University of California at Berkeley and, as a specialist on East Asia, advised Republican and Democratic presidential administrations. Leslie Scalapino
had firsthand exposure to Asia as a child. She saw Noh and Kabuki theater in Japan
and watched the film *Mother India* in India. These early encounters with other cultures presage an interest in the otherness of experience throughout her work. This
is not just an anthropological interest in otherness. It is an interest in the otherness of
experience itself, even that experience which one usually takes to be nearest at hand.
It would be a mistake, however, to see Scalapino's early contact with Asian cultures

as the sole source for these affinities. She couches her memories in letters to Fischer, rather than relating them as a straightforward developmental narrative. Scalapino's later conscious study of Zen guides the contents of her memories as much as the memories foreshadow the interests.

A subtle sense of the vagaries of specific states of experiences pervades the early portions of "Autobiography." Scalapino quotes the poet Lyn Hejinian: "Travel is sentimentality." In other words, to think one can gain any knowledge by going some other place— knowledge of oneself or of that place— may be chimerical. Scalapino, while concurring that the illusion of travel can serve as a substitute for

Leslie Scalapino grew up in California and graduated from Reed College. She is the author of many acclaimed books, including Way *(1988) and* Goya's L.A. *(1994). She has been a well-known figure in avant-garde and Language Poetry circles, and her work has received much academic attention.*

real experience, also asks if experience itself is necessarily real. What she calls "occurrence" may be something one can never know. Experience blocks as much as it reveals. Occurrence itself may be another avatar of impermanence. (This is similar to Scalapino's insight that objectivity is allusion. In other words, there is no "zero point" of objectivity, no place in which objectivity simply exists. It always alludes, even in its objectivity, to another state of being.)

The apparent influence of Buddhist thought here is presented in the writer's own register. It is revealed inductively, by watching one's own actions closely. Scalapino recalls standing on the edge of a school baseball field, after the teacher had excused her from participating in the game because of her obvious physical pain. Scalapino suddenly felt as if she could see the mentalities of other people. This is not something preternatural but a worldly act of concentration.

At times, bracketed annotations describing what the author is doing in 1997, as the essay is being written, appear among the reminiscences. They provide a kind of palimpsest that acknowledges the composed and layered nature of memory. Scalapino also includes photographs of herself and her family, which allow the reader to see the faces of the people described in the text. More subtly, by tracing the changes in clothes, looks, and personal idiom through the decades, the images serve as a visual narrative channel to complement the verbal one that is the reader's main focus. The photographs of Scalapino's bright, lively visage also render the voice of the words on the page as less oracular and more individual.

A preoccupation of "Autobiography" is Scalapino's relationships with men, including her father, her uncle, and her first two boyfriends at Reed College. Scalapino critically examines these men, fascinated by their occasional penchant for control. This control, less sadistic than epistemic, has more to do with knowledge than with power. "One is in reference only to a man," Scalapino comments. Even when men do not particularly have any views, they manufacture the illusion of a coherent policy in order to determine, as a mode of cognitive surveillance, where the woman stands in relation to that policy. This is seen in a shocking way when an older man, a convinced Stalinist, seems totally undisturbed by the attempted extirpation of Buddhism in then-

Soviet-dominated Mongolia, which Scalapino had lamented. This imperviousness is less a political stance than one of automatic gender assumptions. This mode of gender cognition, of women being rendered extrinsic to men even in their own perception, is a major preoccupation of the poem "Zither" (occasional previews of which are given in the essay).

Toward the end of the essay, Scalapino gives a sense of her poetics, particularly her interest in syntax and morphology. She tacitly likens her poetics to the scientific work of Tom White, her husband. White helped work out a method to determine the level of human immunodeficiency virus (HIV) in AIDS patients. His work was kept in mothballs by bureaucratic stupidity, only to prove worthwhile and be accepted years later. The similarity between Scalapino's procedures and the scientific process of trial and error to see if a result is achieved and if it is of any utility is notable. As experimental poetry, Scalapino's linguistic processes, like scientific experiments, do not necessarily yield discernible results immediately. They are aspects of a long-term process, from which meaning emerges comprehensively.

After acknowledging a comprehensive list of fellow practitioners of Language Poetry, Scalapino reveals that the essay was originally commissioned by a reference book publisher. Scalapino was supposed to write a conventional essay on her life, but instead she produced this wild mixture of poem and fact, reality and subjectivity. It is not surprising that the reference firm rejected it. Scalapino shows that she can shake up accepted givens in prose as well as in poetry.

"Zither" starts out by revealing that the action is based on William Shakespeare's *King Lear* (pr. c. 1605-1606), as complemented by the Japanese director Akira Kurosawa's version of the play in his 1985 film *Ran*. There is no direct connection in character, plot, or setting, nor is the mood cognate. Rather than dark and atavistic, "Zither" is probing and curious, interested in the "early" (a word used often) and not the sufficient ripeness of *King Lear*. In *King Lear*, women are forced to fend for themselves, yet they are dependent on male-monitored networks as civilization enters a new, savage phase. Scalapino likens the viewer to the character of Lear. Like Lear, the viewer may be disoriented, mad, or the viewer may, in assuming the position of centrality Lear tries to retain, even after abdication, be pretending to a place of transparent comprehension the poem disallows. A character named Mayfly struggles to come to maturity, while avoiding the normative definitions of what a woman should be. Scalapino uses the word "his" not to denote the male possessive but to denote external reality as such. External reality, if not literally named by men, is anchored by stereotypical "male" assumptions of existential solidity, symbolized by the evil "brownshirts" in the poem, who make the Mayfly their minion. The analogue to the content of "Autobiography" is just sufficiently removed to be unenforceable.

As in Scalapino's earlier poetry, coherence is achieved through certain key words that are repeated, like motifs in a musical composition. "Base," for instance, is used frequently. A base is something upon which things stand. It is a presupposition to experience, but it also claims its own identity and solidity. A base is the promise of what is constructed on it and yet has claims equal to that construct. The forbidding of these claims in a thought-world dominated by the achieved constructions render the idea of "base" provisional. They tear it, in other words, from the "brownshirt" vocabulary, though Scalapino is never this moralistic. Another key word is "fan." Fans are separated from their source. They fan out. As a simple machine, they cool the air by disturbing it. As a motion, fanning extends and dissipates meaning. Fans increase action, yet the motion of fanning is a plural one. There is no mere accretion. This is reminiscent of the titular idea of a zither. Zithers, instruments with strings stretching over empty chambers, similarly interplay surface and echo.

The key words create an aura of a natural tableau that is yet constructed by language. There is a contest to wake into meaning, to claim the dawn of the morning of meaning for one's own. There is also an awareness of how ramified and enmeshed these acts of perception must be with language. Words are, inherently, no more liberating than oppressive. They are no more exhilarating than banal. One cannot know, for example, trees directly. One can analyze their constituents. One can stack up their by-products. The tree, however, will always be behind a scrim of images, experiences, occurrences. It can never be there for once and for all. The glimmer of light through its leaves, however, is ineradicable.

Although much harder to read, "Zither" is a more complete experience than is "Autobiography." Perhaps this is why it is listed first in the book's title. Scalapino knows the constraining nature of autobiographical convention. She quotes de Man on the way "the autobiographical project itself may produce and determine the 'life.'" In both prose and poem, Scalapino is alert to cognitive experience—the reading of books, the response to nature, the acknowledgment of a spiritual dimension. She looks to cognitive experience to take the focus off subjectivity. Given how tired the standard autobiographical approach can be, this is most welcome. There may be an unmet need not just to outflank autobiographical norms but also to recast them. For all its verbal unconventionality, Scalapino's life trajectory is typical of that of her baby-boom generation. There is the cultured upbringing, the prestigious college, the political involvement which fragments after the Vietnam War, the interest in Eastern spiritualities. A more substantive incorporation of these historical issues might well have added to the book. Reservations such as these are the inevitable consequence of Scalapino's venture in revealing the connections between her life and her poetics. *Zither and Autobiography* is a challenging and illuminating book.

Nicholas Birns

Review Sources

Library Journal 128, no. 8 (May 15, 2003): 94.
Publishers Weekly 250, no. 29 (July 21, 2003): 189.

MAGILL'S
LITERARY ANNUAL
2004

BIOGRAPHICAL WORKS BY SUBJECT

1977-2004

ABEL, LIONEL
    Intellectual Follies (Abel) (85) 451
ABERNATHY, RALPH DAVID
    And the Walls Came Tumbling Down (Abernathy) (90) 39
ACHEBE, CHINUA
    Home and Exile (Achebe) (01) 408
ACHESON, DEAN
    Dean Acheson (McLellan) (77) 197
ADAMS, ABIGAIL
    Descent from Glory (Nagel) (H-84) 121
ADAMS, CHARLES FRANCIS
    Descent from Glory (Nagel) (H-84) 121
ADAMS, HENRY
    Descent from Glory (Nagel) (H-84) 121
    Five of Hearts, The (O'Toole) (91) 295
    Letters of Henry Adams, 1858-1892, The (Adams) (84) 441
    Letters of Henry Adams, 1892-1918, The (Adams) (90) 516
ADAMS, JOHN
    Descent from Glory (Nagel) (H-84) 121
    Faces of Revolution (Bailyn) (91) 279
    John Adams (Ferling) (93) 413
    John Adams (McCullough) (02) 444
ADAMS, JOHN G.
    Without Precedent (Adams) (H-84) 497
ADAMS, JOHN QUINCY
    Descent from Glory (Nagel) (H-84) 121
    John Quincy Adams (Nagel) (98) 472
ADAMS, MIRIAM "CLOVER"
    Five of Hearts, The (O'Toole) (91) 295
ADLER, MORTIMER J.
    Philosopher at Large (Adler) (78) 654
AGEE, JAMES
    James Agee (Bergreen) (85) 473
AGEE, JOEL
    Twelve Years (Agee) (82) 854
AIKEN, CONRAD
    Conrad Aiken (Butscher) (89) 207
    Selected Letters of Conrad Aiken (Aiken) (79) 652
AKHMATOVA, ANNA
    Akhmatova Journals, 1938-41, The (Chukovskaya) (95) 19
    Anna Akhmatova (Reeder) (95) 38
    Nightingale Fever (Hingley) (82) 555
ALABI, PANTO
    Alabi's World (Price) (91) 10
ALBEE, EDWARD
    Edward Albee (Gussow) (00) 199
ALEXANDER
    Search for Alexander, The (Lane Fox) (81) 712
ALI, MUHAMMAD
    King of the World (Remnick) (99) 453
ALLEN, FRED
    Province of Reason (Warner) (H-85) 368
ALLEN, PAULA GUNN
    I Tell You Now (Swann and Krupat, eds.) (88) 413

ALLENDE, SALVADOR
    Overthrow of Allende and the Politics of Chile, 1964-1976, The (Sigmund) (78) 630
ALS, HILTON
    Women, The (Als) (98) 874
ALSOP, JOSEPH "JOE"
    Taking on the World (Merry) (97) 802
ALSOP, STEWART
    Taking on the World (Merry) (97) 802
AMIS, KINGSLEY
    Kingsley Amis (Jacobs) (99) 457
AMIS, MARTIN
    Experience (Amis) (01) 290
ANDERSON, SHERWOOD
    Sherwood Anderson (Anderson) (85) 820
    Sherwood Anderson (Townsend) (88) 817
ANGELOU, MAYA
    All God's Children Need Traveling Shoes (Angelou) (87) 25
    Singin' and Swingin' and Gettin' Merry Like Christmas (Angelou) (77) 738
ANGERMEYER, JOHANNA
    My Father's Island (Angermeyer) (91) 614
ANTHONY, SUSAN B.
    Elizabeth Cady Stanton, Susan B. Anthony, Correspondence, Writings, Speeches (Stanton and Anthony) (82) 214
    Not for Ourselves Alone (Ward and Burns) (00) 580
ANTIN, MARY
    Province of Reason (Warner) (H-85) 368
ARBUS, DIANE NEMEROV
    Diane Arbus (Bosworth) (96) 174
ARENDT, HANNAH
    Between Friends (Arendt and McCarthy) (96) 73
    Hannah Arendt (Hill, ed.) (80) 395
    Hannah Arendt (Young-Bruehl) (83) 322
    Passionate Minds (Pierpont) (01) 694
ARLETTY
    Six Exceptional Women (Lord) (95) 724
ARNOLD, MATTHEW
    Life of Matthew Arnold, A (Murray) (98) 500
    Matthew Arnold (Honan) (82) 518
ARTAUD, ANTONIN
    Antonin Artaud (Artaud) (77) 52
    Antonin Artaud (Esslin) (78) 68
ARVIN, NEWTON
    Scarlet Professor, The (Werth) (02) 727
ASHE, ARTHUR
    Days of Grace (Ashe and Rampersad) (94) 213
ATHENS, LONNIE
    Why They Kill (Rhodes) (00) 843
ATTLEE, CLEMENT
    Attlee (Harris) (H-84) 33
ATWOOD, MARGARET
    Negotiating with the Dead (Atwood) (03) 568

AUDEN, W. H.
 Auden (Davenport-Hines) (97) 79
 Later Auden (Mendelson) (00) 475
 W. H. Auden (Carpenter) (82) 923
 W. H. Auden (Osborne) (80) 860
AUGUSTINE, SAINT
 Saint Augustine (Wills) (00) 665
AUSTEN, JANE
 Jane Austen (Honan) (89) 409
 Jane Austen (Nokes) (98) 468
 Jane Austen (Tanner) (87) 435
 Life of Jane Austen, The (Halperin) (85) 564
AUSTER, PAUL
 Hand to Mouth (Auster) (98) 374

BACON, SIR FRANCIS
 Francis Bacon (Zagorin) (99) 303
BACH, JOHANN SEBASTIAN
 Johann Sebastian Bach (Wolff) (01) 494
BAGWELL, ORLANDO
 I've Known Rivers (Lawrence-Lightfoot) (95) 384
BAKER, CHET
 Deep in a Dream (Gavin) (03) 192
BAKER, RUSSELL
 Good Times, The (Baker) (90) 309
 Growing Up (Baker) (83) 317
BAKHTIN, MIKHAIL
 Mikhail Bakhtin (Clark and Holquist) (86) 608
 Mikhail Bakhtin (Morson and Emerson) (92) 500
BALCH, EMILY GREENE
 Province of Reason (Warner) (H-85) 368
BALDWIN, JAMES
 James Baldwin (Leeming) (95) 388
 Talking at the Gates (Campbell) (92) 795
BALL, LUCILLE
 Ball of Fire (Kanfer) (04) 49
BALLARD, MARTHA
 Midwife's Tale, A (Ulrich) (91) 596
BALZAC, HONORÉ DE
 Balzac (Robb) (95) 60
BANCROFT, GEORGE
 George Bancroft (Handlin) (H-85) 162
BARNARD, MARY
 Assault on Mount Helicon (Barnard) (85) 27
BARNES, DJUNA
 Djuna (Field) (84) 234
 Djuna (Herring) (96) 194
BARNES, JIM
 I Tell You Now (Swann and Krupat, eds.) (88) 413
BARNES, KIM
 Hungry for the World (Barnes) (01) 432
BARTHES, ROLAND
 Roland Barthes (Barthes) (78) 730
 Roland Barthes (Calvet) (96) 664
BARUCH, BERNARD M.
 Speculator (Schwarz) (82) 800
BARUK, HENRI
 Patients Are People Like Us (Baruk) (79) 532
BARZMAN, BEN
 Red and the Blacklist, The (Barzman) (04) 638
BARZMAN, NORMA
 Red and the Blacklist, The (Barzman) (04) 638
BATES, H. E.
 Great Friends (Garnett) (81) 386
BATESON, GREGORY
 With a Daughter's Eye (Bateson) (H-85) 507

BAUDELAIRE, CHARLES-PIERRE
 Baudelaire (Pichois) (91) 70
 Baudelaire (Richardson) (96) 65
 Baudelaire the Damned (Hemmings) (83) 49
BAYLEY, JOHN
 Elegy for Iris (Bayley) (00) 213
 Iris and Her Friends (Bayley) (00) 439
BEACH, SYLVIA
 Sylvia Beach and the Lost Generation (Fitch)
  (84) 854
BEAL, FRED ERWIN
 Province of Reason (Warner) (H-85) 368
BEARDEN, ROMARE
 Romare Bearden (Schwartzman) (92) 684
BEAUCHAMP, KATHERINE MANSFIELD. See
 MANSFIELD, KATHERINE
BEAUVOIR, SIMONE DE
 Hearts and Minds (Madsen) (78) 379
 Letters to Sartre (Beauvoir) (93) 449
 Simone de Beauvoir (Bair) (91) 740
BEAVERBROOK, LORD
 Lord Beaverbrook (Chisholm and Davie) (94) 488
BECKETT, SAMUEL
 Damned to Fame (Knowlson) (97) 191
 Samuel Beckett (Bair) (79) 636
 Samuel Beckett (Cronin) (98) 688
BELL, CLIVE
 Bloomsbury (Edel) (80) 88
BELL, MARY
 Cries Unheard (Sereny) (00) 151
BELL, VANESSA
 Art and Affection (Reid) (97) 66
 Bloomsbury (Edel) (80) 88
 Vanessa Bell (Spalding) (84) 900
BELLOC, HILAIRE
 Hilaire Belloc (Wilson) (85) 385
BELLOW, SAUL
 Bellow (Atlas) (01) 84
 Saul Bellow (Miller) (92) 707
 Saul Bellow, Vision and Revision (Fuchs)
  (85) 776
 To Jerusalem and Back (Bellow) (77) 828
BEN-GURION, DAVID
 Ben-Gurion, 1886-1948 (Teveth) (88) 90
BENJAMIN, WALTER
 Correspondence of Walter Benjamin, 1910-1940,
  The (Benjamin) (95) 149
 Reflections (Benjamin) (79) 575
 Selected Writings, 1927-1934 (Benjamin) (00) 693
 Selected Writings, 1938-1940 (Benjamin) (04) 674
BENZER, SEYMOUR
 Time, Love, Memory (Weiner) (00) 754
BERENSON, BERNARD
 Bernard Berenson (Samuels) (80) 73
BERG, MOE
 Catcher Was a Spy, The (Dawidoff) (95) 104
BERGMAN, INGMAR
 Magic Lantern, The (Bergman) (89) 525
BERLIN, IRVING
 As Thousands Cheer (Bergreen) (91) 61
BERLIN, ISAIAH
 Isaiah Berlin (Gray) (97) 466
 Personal Impressions (Berlin) (82) 632
BERNHARD, THOMAS
 Gathering Evidence (Bernhard) (87) 317
 Wittgenstein's Nephew (Bernhard) (90) 908

BERNHARDT, SARAH
Sarah Bernhardt and Her World (Richardson)
(78) 740

BERNSTEIN, CARL
Loyalties (Bernstein) (90) 543

BERNSTEIN, JEREMY
Life It Brings, The (Bernstein) (88) 477

BERRY, WENDELL
Art of the Commonplace, The (Berry) (03) 33

BERRYMAN, JOHN
Dream Song (Mariani) (91) 235
Life of John Berryman, The (Haffenden) (83) 410
Poets in Their Youth (Simpson) (83) 608

BÉRUBÉ, JAMES LYON "JAMIE"
Life As We Know It (Bérubé) (97) 498

BÉRUBÉ, MICHAEL
Life As We Know It (Bérubé) (97) 498

BÉRUBÉ, NICHOLAS "NICK"
Life As We Know It (Bérubé) (97) 498

BESANT, ANNIE
Annie Besant (Taylor) (93) 23

BESS OF HARDWICK
Eminent Elizabethans (Rowse) (H-84) 147

BHUTTO, BENAZIR
Daughter of Destiny (Bhutto) (90) 152

BIDEN, JOSEPH
What It Takes (Cramer) (93) 874

BIRKIRTS, SVEN
My Sky Blue Trades (Birkerts) (03) 549

BISHOP, ELIZABETH
Collected Prose, The (Bishop) (85) 121
Elizabeth Bishop (Goldensohn) (92) 179
Elizabeth Bishop (Millier) (94) 264
Life Sentences (Epstein) (98) 504
One Art (Bishop) (95) 572

BISMARCK, OTTO VON
Bismarck (Crankshaw) (82) 50
Gold and Iron (Stern) (78) 354

BLACK, HUGO
Hugo Black and the Judicial Revolution (Dunne)
(78) 418
Hugo L. Black (Ball) (97) 415

BLACKMUR, R. P.
Poets in Their Youth (Simpson) (83) 608

BLACKWOOD, ALGERNON
Algernon Blackwood (Ashley) (03) 10

BLAKE, WILLIAM
Blake (Ackroyd) (97) 123

BLEICHRÖDER, GERSON VON
Gold and Iron (Stern) (78) 354

BLOOM, CLAIRE
Leaving a Doll's House (Bloom) (97) 494

BLUM, LÉON
Léon Blum (Lacouture) (H-83) 253

BLUMENFELD, LAURA
Revenge (Blumenfeld) (03) 658

BOGAN, LOUISE
Louise Bogan (Frank) (86) 542

BOGART, HUMPHREY
Bogart (Sperber and Lax) (98) 125

BOHR, NIELS
Niels Bohr's Times (Pais) (92) 569

BOLEYN, ANNE
Mistress Anne (Erickson) (H-85) 319

BÖLL, HEINRICH
What's to Become of the Boy (Böll) (85) 1018

BOMBERG, DAVID
David Bomberg (Cork) (88) 238

BONAPARTE, NAPOLEON
Reign of Napoleon Bonaparte, The (Asprey)
(02) 688

BONTEMPS, ARNA
Arna Bontemps-Langston Hughes Letters,
1925-1967 (Bontemps and Hughes) (81) 57

BOOTH, WAYNE
For the Love of It (Booth) (00) 273

BORGES, JORGE LUIS
Borges (Borges) (82) 63
Borges (Woodall) (98) 130
Jorge Luis Borges (Monegal) (80) 444

BORMANN, MARTIN
Secretary, Martin Bormann, The (Lang) (80) 746

BOSWELL, JAMES
Boswell (Boswell) (78) 140
James Boswell (Brady) (85) 479

BOSWELL, JOHN
Boswell's Presumptuous Task (Sisman) (02) 120

BOSWORTH, SHEILA
World Unsuspected, A (Harris, ed.) (88) 984

BOURKE, JOHN GREGORY
Paper Medicine Man (Porter) (87) 636

BOWEN, ELIZABETH
Elizabeth Bowen (Glendinning) (79) 179

BOWLES, JANE
Little Original Sin, A (Dillon) (82) 470
Out in the World (Bowles) (86) 723

BOWLES, PAUL
In Touch (Bowles) (95) 372
Invisible Spectator, An (Sawyer-Laucanno)
(90) 424

BOYLE, KAY
Kay Boyle (Mellen) (95) 417

BRADLEE, BEN
Good Life, A (Bradlee) (96) 316

BRADLEY, OMAR N.
Eisenhower's Lieutenants (Weigley) (82) 210
General's Life, A (Bradley and Blair) (H-84) 171

BRAHE, TYCHO
Tycho and Kepler (Ferguson) (04) 782

BRALY, MALCOLM
False Starts (Braly) (77) 269

BRANDEIS, LOUIS D.
Brandeis (Paper) (H-84) 73
Louis D. Brandeis and the Progressive Tradition
(Urofsky) (82) 488

BRANDYS, KAZIMIERZ
Warsaw Diary, A (Brandys) (84) 926

BRASILLACH, ROBERT
Collaborator, The (Kaplan) (01) 199

BRECHT, BERTOLT
Brecht (Hayman) (84) 118

BRENAN, GERALD
Gerald Brenan (Gathorne-Hardy) (94) 350

BRETON, ANDRÉ
Revolution of the Mind (Polizzotti) (96) 633

BREYTENBACH, BREYTEN
True Confessions of an Albino Terrorist, The
(Breytenbach) (86) 913

BRIDGMAN, LAURA
Education of Laura Bridgman, The (Freeberg)
(02) 230

BRITTEN, BENJAMIN
   Benjamin Britten (Carpenter) (94) 75
BROCK, DAVID
   Blinded by the Right (Brock) (03) 83
BRODKEY, HAROLD
   This Wild Darkness (Brodkey) (97) 816
BRODSKY, JOSEPH
   Joseph Brodsky and the Creation of Exile (Bethea)
      (95) 404
   Less Than One (Brodsky) (87) 471
BROMBERT, VICTOR
   Trains of Thought (Brombert) (03) 843
BRONTË, ANNE
   Brontës, The (Barker) (96) 81
BRONTË, CHARLOTTE
   Brontës, The (Barker) (96) 81
   Charlotte Brontë (Gordon) (96) 94
BRONTË, EMILY
   Brontës, The (Barker) (96) 81
   Chainless Soul, A (Frank) (91) 127
BRONTË, PATRICK BRANWELL
   Brontës, The (Barker) (96) 81
BRONTË, THE REVEREND PATRICK
   Brontës, The (Barker) (96) 81
BROOKE, ALAN FRANCIS
   Alanbrooke (Fraser) (H-83) 14
BROOKS, CLEANTH, JR.
   Cleanth Brooks and the Rise of Modern Criticism
      (Winchell) (97) 156
BROOKS, GWENDOLYN
   Life of Gwendolyn Brooks, A (Kent) (90) 526
BROOKS, VAN WYCK
   Van Wyck Brooks (Nelson) (82) 874
BROWN, JOHN
   Black Hearts of Men, The (Stauffer) (03) 74
BROWNING, ELIZABETH BARRETT
   Elizabeth Barrett Browning (Forster) (90) 203
BROWNING, ROBERT
   Elizabeth Barrett Browning (Forster) (90) 203
   Robert Browning (Thomas) (84) 741
BRUCHAC, JOSEPH
   I Tell You Now (Swann and Krupat, eds.)
      (88) 413
BRZEZINSKI, ZBIGNIEW
   Power and Principle (Brzezinski) (H-84) 351
BUBER, MARTIN
   Martin Buber's Life and Work (Friedman)
      (H-84) 293
BUCHANAN, PATRICK J.
   Right from the Beginning (Buchanan) (89) 730
BUCK, PEARL SYDENSTRICKER
   Pearl S. Buck (Conn) (97) 661
BUCKLEY, GAIL LUMET
   Hornes, The (Buckley) (87) 410
BUCKLEY, WILLIAM F., Jr.
   Atlantic High (Buckley) (83) 29
   Nearer, My God (Buckley) (98) 575
   William F. Buckley, Jr. (Judis) (89) 908
BUECHNER, FREDERICK
   Now and Then (Buechner) (84) 624
   Sacred Journey, The (Buechner) (83) 670
BUKHARIN, NIKOLAI
   Nikolai Bukharin (Medvedev) (81) 614
BULGAKOV, MIKHAIL
   Bulgakov (Proffer) (85) 62

BUNTING, BASIL
   Bunting (Makin) (93) 115
BUNYAN, JOHN
   Tinker and a Poor Man, A (Hill) (90) 814
BURGESS, ANTHONY
   Little Wilson and Big God (Burgess) (88) 497
   You've Had Your Time (Burgess) (92) 933
BURKE, EDMUND
   Edmund Burke (Ayling) (90) 198
   Great Melody, The (O'Brien) (93) 316
   Rage of Edmund Burke, The (Kramnick) (78) 686
BURNEY, FANNY
   Fanny Burney (Harman) (02) 275
BURNS, ROBERT
   Burns (Mackay) (94) 113
BURR, AARON
   Aaron Burr, 1756-1805 (Lomask) (80) 6
   Aaron Burr, 1805-1836 (Lomask) (H-83) 1
   Burr, Hamilton, and Jefferson (Kennedy) (00) 112
BURROUGHS, AUGUSTEN
   Running with Scissors (Burroughs) (03) 695
BURTON, CAPTAIN SIR RICHARD FRANCIS
   Captain Sir Richard Francis Burton (Rice)
      (91) 123
BUSH, BARNEY
   I Tell You Now (Swann and Krupat, eds.)
      (88) 413
BUSH, GEORGE
   What It Takes (Cramer) (93) 874
BUSH, GEORGE W.
   Ambling into History (03) 14
BUSH, VANNEVAR
   Province of Reason (Warner) (H-85) 368
BYRON, GEORGE GORDON, LORD
   Byron (Grosskurth) (98) 142
   Byron's Letters and Journals (Byron) (81) 108
   Claire Clairmont and the Shelleys, 1798-1897
      (Gittings and Manton) (93) 157
   Lord Byron (Byron) (83) 418

CALAMITY JANE
   Figures in a Western Landscape (Stevenson)
      (95) 231
CALHOUN, JOHN C.
   Great Triumvirate, The (Peterson) (88) 363
CALVIN, JOHN
   Calvin Against Himself (Selinger) (H-85) 59
   John Calvin (Bouwsma) (88) 433
CALVINO, ITALO
   Hermit in Paris (Calvino) (04) 339
   Road to San Giovanni, The (Calvino) (94) 705
CAMUS, ALBERT
   Albert Camus (Lottman) (80) 15
   Albert Camus (Todd) (98) 18
   Camus (McCarthy) (83) 96
CANARIS, WILHELM
   Canaris (Höhne) (80) 124
CANETTI, ELIAS
   Torch in My Ear, The (Canetti) (83) 827
CANNON, KATIE
   I've Known Rivers (Lawrence-Lightfoot) (95) 384
CAPOTE, TRUMAN GARCIA
   Capote (Clarke) (89) 135
CAPRA, FRANK
   Frank Capra (McBride) (93) 298

CARLYLE, THOMAS
    Correspondence of Thomas Carlyle and John
      Ruskin, The (Carlyle and Ruskin) (83) 153
    Parallel Lives (Rose) (84) 662
    Thomas Carlyle (Kaplan) (84) 869
CARRINGTON, DORA
    Love in Bloomsbury (Partridge) (82) 504
CARROLL, JAMES
    American Requiem, An (Carroll) (97) 38
CARROLL, GENERAL JOSEPH
    American Requiem, An (Carroll) (97) 38
CARROLL, LEWIS
    Letters of Lewis Carroll, ca. 1837-1885, The
      (Carroll) (80) 474
    Lewis Carroll (Cohen) (96) 422
CARSON, RACHEL
    Province of Reason (Warner) (H-85) 368
    Rachel Carson (Lear) (98) 656
CARTER, JIMMY
    Crisis (Jordan) (H-83) 93
    Keeping Faith (Carter) (H-83) 239
    Unfinished Presidency, The (Brinkley) (99) 822
    Why Not the Best? (Carter) (77) 906
CARTER, ROSALYNN
    First Lady from Plains (Carter) (H-85) 146
CARVER, GEORGE WASHINGTON
    George Washington Carver (McMurry) (82) 310
CASTRO, FIDEL
    Fidel (Szulc) (87) 282
    Fidel Castro (Quirk) (94) 287
CATHER, WILLA
    Willa (Robinson) (84) 945
    Willa Cather (Lee) (91) 896
    Willa Cather (O'Brien) (87) 994
CATHERINE THE GREAT
    Catherine, Empress of All the Russias (Cronin)
      (79) 80
    Catherine the Great (Haslip) (78) 155
    Catherine the Great (Troyat) (81) 117
CAVAFY, CONSTANTINE P.
    Life Sentences (Epstein) (98) 504
CAVOUR
    Cavour (Mack Smith) (86) 104
CAXTON, WILLIAM
    William Caxton (Painter) (78) 909
CELAN, PAUL
    Paul Celan (Colin) (92) 619
    Paul Celan (Felstiner) (96) 577
CÉLINE, LOUIS-FERDINAND
    Louis-Ferdinand Céline (Thomas) (81) 529
CERVANTES
    Cervantes (Byron) (79) 84
CHAMBERLAIN, HOUSTON STEWART
    Evangelist of Race (Field) (82) 256
CHAMBERLAIN, NEVILLE
    Neville Chamberlain and Appeasement (Fuchser)
      (H-83) 314
CHAMBERS, WHITTAKER
    Whittaker Chambers (Tanenhaus) (98) 841
CHAMFORT, SÉBASTIEN ROCH NICOLAS DE
    Chamfort (Arnaud) (93) 143
CHANDLER, OTIS
    Privileged Son (McDougal) (02) 669

CHANDLER, RAYMOND
    Life of Raymond Chandler, The (MacShane)
      (77) 427
    Raymond Chandler (Hiney) (98) 665
    Selected Letters of Raymond Chandler (Chandler)
      (82) 757
CHANG, JUNG
    Wild Swans (Chang) (92) 894
CHAPLIN, CHARLES
    Chaplin (Robinson) (86) 116
CHAPLIN, THOMAS B.
    Tombee (Rosengarten, ed.) (87) 875
CHARLES STUART II
    Charles the Second (Hutton) (91) 132
    Royal Charles (Fraser) (80) 732
CHATEAUBRIAND
    Chateaubriand (1768-93) (Painter) (79) 95
CHATWIN, BRUCE
    Bruce Chatwin (Shakespeare) (01) 148
    With Chatwin (Clapp) (98) 862
CHAUCER, GEOFFREY
    Chaucer (Howard) (88) 141
    Life of Geoffrey Chaucer, The (Pearsall) (93) 459
CHAUDHURI, AMIT
    Real Time (Chaudhuri) (03) 643
CHAUDHURI, NIRAD C.
    Portraits (Shils) (98) 639
CHEEVER, JOHN
    Home Before Dark (Cheever) (85) 405
    John Cheever (Donaldson) (89) 422
    Journals of John Cheever, The (Cheever) (92) 393
    Letters of John Cheever, The (Cheever) (89) 480
CHEKHOV, ANTON
    Anton Chekhov (Rayfield) (99) 57
    Chekhov (Pritchett) (89) 155
    Chekhov (Troyat) (87) 105
    New Life of Anton Chekhov, A (Hingley) (77) 543
CHESTERTON, GILBERT KEITH
    Outline of Sanity, The (Dale) (83) 582
CHILD, LYDIA MARIA FRANCIS
    First Woman in the Republic, The (Karcher)
      (96) 273
CHING, FRANK
    Ancestors (Ching) (89) 19
CHOMKY, NOAM
    Noam Chomsky (Barsky) (98) 598
CHOPIN, FRÉDÉRIC
    Chopin in Paris (Szulc) (99) 168
    Chopin's Funeral (Eisler) (04) 118
CHOPIN, KATE
    Kate Chopin (Toth) (91) 475
CHRISTINE DE PIZAN
    Christine de Pizan (Willard) (86) 126
CHURCHILL, JOHN
    First Churchill, The (Thomson) (81) 344
CHURCHILL, WINSTON SPENCER
    Churchill (Morgan) (H-83) 65
    Churchill and de Gaulle (Kersaudy) (H-83) 70
    Last Lion, 1874-1932, The (Manchester) (H-84) 278
    Last Lion, 1932-1940, The (Manchester) (89) 455
    Roosevelt and Churchill, 1939-1941 (Lash) (77) 685
    Winston Churchill's World View (Thompson)
      (H-84) 493
    Winston S. Churchill, 1922-1939 (Gilbert) (78) 917
    Winston S. Churchill, 1939-1941 (Gilbert)
      (H-85) 500
    Winston S. Churchill, 1941-1945 (Gilbert) (87) 1001
    Winston S. Churchill, 1945-1965 (Gilbert) (89) 913

CID, EL. *See* DÍAZ, RODRIGO

CLAIRMONT, CLAIRE
Claire Clairmont and the Shelleys, 1798-1879 (Gittings and Manton) (93) 157

CLARE, JOHN
John Clare (Bate) (04) 377

CLARK, JIM
The New New Thing (Lewis) (00) 571

CLARK, WILLIAM
Lewis and Clark Journals, The (Lewis and Clark) (04) 442
Undaunted Courage (Ambrose) (97) 853

CLAY, HENRY
Great Triumvirate, The (Peterson) (88) 363

CLAY, LUCIUS DUBIGNON
Winds of History (Backer) (H-84) 488

CLEMENS, SAMUEL LANGHORNE. *See* TWAIN, MARK

CLIFFORD, CLARK
Counsel to the President (Clifford, with Holbrooke) (92) 123

CLIFT, MONTGOMERY
Montgomery Clift (Bosworth) (79) 457

CLIFTON, LUCILLE
Generations (Clifton) (77) 318

CLINTON, HILLARY RODHAM
First in His Class (Maraniss) (96) 263
Living History (Clinton) (04) 455

CLINTON, WILLIAM JEFFERSON "BILL"
First in His Class (Maraniss) (96) 263
Natural, The (Klein) (03) 554

COETZEE, J. M.
Boyhood (Coetzee) (98) 134

COHN, HARRY
Empire of Their Own, An (Gabler) (89) 278

COHN, ROY MARCUS
Citizen Cohn (von Hoffman) (89) 164

COLEBROOK, JOAN HEALE
House of Trees, A (Colebrook) (88) 403

COLERIDGE, SAMUEL TAYLOR
Coleridge, Darker Reflections (Holmes) (00) 138
Coleridge, Early Visions (Holmes) (91) 147
Gang, The (Worthen) (02) 321
Life of Samuel Taylor Coleridge, The (Ashton) (97) 516

COLERIDGE, SARAH
Gang, The (Worthen) (02) 321

COLETTE
Colette (Lottman) (92) 99
Colette (Sarde) (81) 161
Secrets of the Flesh (Thurman) (00) 679

COLLINS, WILKIE
King of Inventors, The (Peters) (94) 440

COLUMBUS, CHRISTOPHER
Imaginative Landscape of Christopher Columbus, The (Flint) (93) 365
Mysterious History of Columbus, The (Wilford) (92) 540

COLVILLE, JOHN
Fringes of Power, The (Colville) (86) 320

COMMINS, SAXE
What Is an Editor? (Commins) (79) 839

COMPTON-BURNETT, IVY
Ivy (Spurling) (85) 461

CONANT, JAMES BRYANT
Province of Reason (Warner) (H-85) 368

CONE, DAVID
Pitcher's Story, A (Angell) (02) 641

CONRAD, JOSEPH
Collected Letters of Joseph Conrad, 1861-1897, The (Conrad) (84) 178
Collected Letters of Joseph Conrad, 1898-1902, The (Conrad) (87) 138
Collected Letters of Joseph Conrad, 1903-1907, The (Conrad) (89) 175
Conrad (Watt) (81) 193
Great Friends (Garnett) (81) 386
Group Portrait (Delbanco) (83) 312
Joseph Conrad (Karl) (80) 449
Joseph Conrad (Najder) (84) 395
Joseph Conrad (Tennant) (82) 412

CONWAY, JILL KER
Road from Coorain, The (Conway) (90) 699
True North (Conway) (95) 801

COOK-LYNN, ELIZABETH
I Tell You Now (Swann and Krupat, eds.) (88) 413

COOKE, HOPE
Time Change (Cooke) (82) 839

CORNELL, JOSEPH
Joseph Cornell's Theater of the Mind (Cornell) (95) 408
Utopia Parkway (Solomon) (98) 801

CORNWALLIS, CHARLES
Cornwallis (Wickwire and Wickwire) (81) 203

CORTÁZAR, JULIO
Around the Day in Eighty Worlds (Cortázar) (87) 45

COUGHLIN, CHARLES
Voices of Protest (Brinkley) (H-83) 449

COVICI, PASCAL, SR.
Steinbeck and Covici (Fensch) (80) 780

COWARD, NOËL
Noël Coward (Hoare) (97) 630
Noël Coward Diaries, The (Coward) (83) 549

COWLEY, MALCOLM
Dream of the Golden Mountains, The (Cowley) (81) 249
Malcolm Cowley (Bak) (94) 492

COZZENS, JAMES GOULD
James Gould Cozzens (Bruccoli) (84) 384
Just Representations (Cozzens) (79) 343

CRANE, HART
Broken Tower, The (Mariani) (00) 108
Lives of the Modern Poets (Pritchard) (81) 520

CRANE, STEPHEN
Badge of Courage (Davis) (99) 78
Double Life of Stephen Crane, The (Benfey) (93) 239
Group Portrait (Delbanco) (83) 312

CRANMER, THOMAS
Thomas Cranmer (MacCulloch) (97) 821

CRAYENCOUR, MARGUERITE DE. *See* YOURCENAR, MARGUERITE

CRITCHFIELD, RICHARD
Those Days (Critchfield) (87) 858

CROMWELL, OLIVER
Cromwell (Howell) (78) 219

CROSBY, BING
Bing Crosby (Giddins) (02) 88

CROSSMAN, RICHARD
Diaries of a Cabinet Minister, The (Crossman) (77) 211

BIOGRAPHICAL WORKS BY SUBJECT

CRUM, BARTLEY
Anything Your Little Heart Desires (Bosworth) (98) 68
CRUM, PATRICIA BOSWORTH
Anything Your Little Heart Desires (Bosworth) (98) 68
CRUZ, SOR JUANA INÉS DE LA
Sor Juana (Paz) (89) 808
CUSTER, GEORGE ARMSTRONG
Custer and the Little Big Horn (Hofling) (82) 161
Son of the Morning Star (Connell) (H-85) 420

DAHL, ROALD
Roald Dahl (Treglown) (95) 660
DALEY, RICHARD J.
American Pharaoh (Cohen and Taylor) (01) 34
Himself! (Kennedy) (79) 273
DANIELS, PAMELA
Working It Out (Ruddick and Daniels, eds.) (78) 937
DARROW, CLARENCE
Clarence Darrow (Weinberg and Weinberg) (81) 152
Darrow (Tierney) (80) 188
DARWIN, CHARLES
Charles Darwin (Bowlby) (92) 83
Charles Darwin (Brent) (82) 87
Charles Darwin, Power of Place, The (Browne) (03) 142
Charles Darwin, Voyaging (Browne) (96) 90
Charles Darwin's Letters (Darwin) (97) 148
Darwin (Desmond and Moore) (93) 196
DAVIE, DONALD
These the Companions (Davie) (83) 787
DAVIES, ROBERTSON
Robertson Davies (Grant) (96) 660
DAVIS, JEFFERSON
Jefferson Davis (Eaton) (78) 464
DAY, DOROTHY
Dorothy Day (Coles) (88) 252
DAYAN, MOSHE
Decisions in Crisis (Brecher and Geist) (81) 228
Moshe Dayan (Dayan) (77) 513
DAZAI, OSAMU
Saga of Dazai Osamu, The (Lyons) (86) 783
DEAN, JOHN W., III
Blind Ambition (Dean) (77) 96
DE BEAUVOIR, SIMONE. See BEAUVOIR, SIMONE DE
DEBS, EUGENE V.
Harp Song for a Radical (Young) (00) 358
DEFOE, DANIEL
Daniel Defoe (Backscheider) (90) 143
DE GAULLE, CHARLES
Churchill and de Gaulle (Kersaudy) (H-83) 70
De Gaulle, 1890-1944 (Lacouture) (91) 192
De Gaulle, 1945-1970 (Lacouture) (93) 219
DE MAN, PAUL
Signs of the Times (Lehman) (92) 752
DE QUINCEY, THOMAS
Infection of Thomas De Quincey, The (Barrell) (92) 354
DERRIDA, JACQUES
Memoirs of the Blind (Derrida) (95) 473
DESCARTES, RENÉ
Descartes (Gaukroger) (96) 170

DE SMET, PIERRE JEAN
Figures in a Western Landscape (Stevenson) (95) 231
DEUTSCH, HELENE
Helene Deutsch (Roazen) (86) 402
DE VERE, EDWARD
Eminent Elizabethans (Rowse) (H-84) 147
DEVERS, JACOB M.
Eisenhower's Lieutenants (Weigley) (82) 210
DEW, ROBB FORMAN
World Unsuspected, A (Harris, ed.) (88) 984
DEWEY, JOHN
John Dewey and American Democracy (Westbrook) (92) 388
John Dewey and the High Tide of American Liberalism (Ryan) (96) 393
DEWEY, THOMAS E.
Thomas E. Dewey and His Times (Smith) (H-83) 421
DÍAZ, RODRIGO
Quest for El Cid, The (Fletcher) (91) 684
DICKENS, CATHERINE HOGARTH
Parallel Lives (Rose) (84) 662
DICKENS, CHARLES
Dickens (Ackroyd) (92) 170
Dickens (Kaplan) (89) 241
Parallel Lives (Rose) (84) 662
DICKEY, JAMES
James Dickey (Hart) (01) 475
DICKINSON, EMILY
Emily Dickinson (Wolff) (87) 233
Passion of Emily Dickinson, The (Farr) (93) 610
My Wars Are Laid Away in Books (Habegger) (02) 562
DICKINSON, JOHN
John Dickinson (Flower) (H-84) 248
DIDEROT, DENIS
Diderot (Furbank) (93) 229
DIDION, JOAN
Where I Was From (Didion) (04) 831
DILLARD, ANNIE
American Childhood, An (Dillard) (88) 25
DiMAGGIO, DOM
Teammates, The (Halberstam) (04) 731
DiMAGGIO, JOSEPH
Joe DiMaggio (Cramer) (01) 489
DINESEN, ISAK
Isak Dinesen (Thurman) (83) 358
DISRAELI, BENJAMIN
Disraeli (Bradford) (H-84) 135
Disraeli (Weintraub) (94) 239
DJILAS, MILOVAN
Wartime (Djilas) (78) 894
DODGSON, CHARLES LUTWIDGE. See CARROLL, LEWIS
DODSON, OWEN
Sorrow Is the Only Faithful One (Hatch) (94) 755
DOERR, BOBBY
Teammates, The (Halberstam) (04) 731
DOLE, ROBERT
What It Takes (Cramer) (93) 874
DOLOT, MIRON
Execution by Hunger (Dolot) (86) 254
DÖNITZ, KARL
Dönitz, the Last Führer (Padfield) (H-85) 115

DONOGHUE, DENIS
  Warrenpoint (Donoghue) (91) 871
DONOVAN, WILLIAM J.
  Donovan (Dunlop) (H-83) 99
DOOLITTLE, HILDA. *See* H. D.
DORR, HARBOTTLE, Jr.
  Faces of Revolution (Bailyn) (91) 279
DORRIS, MICHAEL
  Broken Cord, The (Dorris) (90) 76
DOS PASSOS, JOHN
  Dos Passos (Carr) (85) 194
  John Dos Passos (Ludington) (81) 464
  Life Sentences (Epstein) (98) 504
DOSTOEVSKY, FYODOR
  Dostoevsky (Dostoevsky) (77) 230
  Dostoevsky, 1821-1849 (Frank) (77) 236
  Dostoevsky, 1850-1859 (Frank) (84) 244
  Dostoevsky, 1860-1865 (Frank) (87) 212
  Dostoevsky, 1865-1871 (Frank) (96) 202
  Dostoevsky, 1871-1881 (Frank) (03) 219
  Selected Letters of Fyodor Dostoevsky
    (Dostoevsky) (88) 806
DOTY, MARK
  Heaven's Coast (Doty) (97) 368
DOUGLAS, KIRK
  Ragman's Son, The (Douglas) (89) 692
DOUGLASS, FREDERICK
  Frederick Douglass (McFeely) (92) 232
  Black Hearts of Men, The (Stauffer) (03) 74
DOYLE, ARTHUR CONAN
  Teller of Tales (Stashower) (00) 741
DRAKE, SIR FRANCIS
  Sir Francis Drake (Sugden) (92) 757
DREISER, THEODORE
  Theodore Dreiser, 1871-1907 (Lingeman)
    (87) 847
  Theodore Dreiser, 1908-1945 (Lingeman)
    (91) 798
DRUCKER, PETER
  World According to Peter Drucker, The (Beatty)
    (99) 872
DRYDEN, JOHN
  John Dryden and His World (Winn) (88) 438
DU BOIS, W. E. B.
  W. E. B. Du Bois, 1868-1919 (Lewis) (94) 847
  W. E. B. Du Bois, 1919-1963 (Lewis) (01) 882
DUKAKIS, MICHAEL
  What It Takes (Cramer) (93) 874
DULLES, ALLEN
  Dulles (Mosley) (79) 170
DULLES, ELEANOR
  Dulles (Mosley) (79) 170
DULLES, JOHN FOSTER
  Dulles (Mosley) (79) 170
  John Foster Dulles (Pruessen) (H-83) 229
DU MAURIER, DAPHNE
  Daphne du Maurier (Forster) (94) 204
DUNBAR-NELSON, ALICE
  Give Us This Day (Dunbar-Nelson) (86) 349
DUNNE, JOHN GREGORY
  Harp (Dunne) (90) 364
DU PONTS, THE
  Blood Relations (Mosley) (81) 93
  du Pont Family, The (Gates) (80) 240

DURANT, ARIEL
  Dual Autobiography, A (Durant and Durant)
    (78) 280
DURANT, WILL
  Dual Autobiography, A (Durant and Durant)
    (78) 280
DURHAM, JIMMIE
  I Tell You Now (Swann and Krupat, eds.)
    (88) 413
DVOŘÁK, ANTONIN
  New Worlds of Dvořák (Beckerman) (04) 556
DYLAN, BOB
  Down the Highway (Sounes) (02) 208

EARLS, FELTON
  I've Known Rivers (Lawrence-Lightfoot) (95) 384
EATON, EDITH MAUDE. *See* SUI SIN FAR
EBAN, ABBA
  Abba Eban (Eban) (78) 1
  Decisions in Crisis (Brecher and Geist) (81) 228
EDEN, ANTHONY
  Another World, 1897-1917 (Eden) (78) 59
EDISON, THOMAS ALVA
  Edison (Clark) (78) 284
  Streak of Luck, A (Conot) (80) 790
EDWARD VII
  Edward VII (St. Aubyn) (80) 264
  Uncle of Europe (Brook-Shepherd) (77) 861
EDWARD VIII
  King Edward VIII (Ziegler) (92) 403
EDWARDS, JONATHAN
  Jonathan Edwards (Marsden) (04) 391
EGGERS, DAVID
  A Heartbreaking Work of Staggering Genius
    (Eggers) (01) 389
EHRLICH, GRETEL
  Solace of Open Space, The (Ehrlich) (86) 840
EHRLICHMAN, JOHN
  Witness to Power (Ehrlichman) (H-83) 473
EINSTEIN, ALBERT
  Albert Einstein (Einstein) (80) 19
  Driving Mr. Albert (Paterniti) (01) 258
  Einstein, Picasso (Miller) (02) 235
EISENHOWER, DWIGHT DAVID
  Diary of James C. Hagerty, The (Hagerty)
    (H-84) 125
  Eisenhower, Vol. I (Ambrose) (H-84) 141
  Eisenhower, Vol. II (Ambrose) (H-85) 120
  Eisenhower and the Cold War (Divine) (82) 195
  Eisenhower Diaries, The (Eisenhower) (82) 199
  Eisenhower the President (Ewald) (82) 205
  Eisenhower's Lieutenants (Weigley) (82) 210
  Hidden-Hand Presidency, The (Greenstein)
    (H-83) 190
ELEANOR OF AQUITAINE
  Eleanor of Aquitaine (Seward) (80) 277
ELIADE, MIRCEA
  Ordeal by Labyrinth (Eliade) (83) 572
ELIOT, ANDREW
  Faces of Revolution (Bailyn) (91) 279
  Parallel Lives (Rose) (84) 662
ELIOT, GEORGE
  George Eliot (Ashton) (98) 335
  Woman of Contradictions, A (Taylor) (91) 909

BIOGRAPHICAL WORKS BY SUBJECT

ELIOT, T. S.
  Eliot's New Life (Gordon) (89) 262
  Letters of T. S. Eliot, The (Eliot) (89) 488
  Lives of the Modern Poets (Pritchard) (81) 520
  Pound/Williams (Pound and Williams) (97) 675
  T. S. Eliot (Ackroyd) (85) 932
  T. S. Eliot (Bush) (85) 937
  T. S. Eliot (Gordon) (00) 737
ELIZABETH I
  Elizabeth Regina (Plowden) (81) 272
  Elizabethan Deliverance, The (Bryant) (H-83) 114
  First Elizabeth, The (Erickson) (H-84) 164
ELLIS, HAVELOCK
  Havelock Ellis (Grosskurth) (81) 412
ELLISON, RALPH
  Collected Essays of Ralph Ellison, The (Ellison)
    (96) 128
  Ralph Ellison (Jackson) (03) 638
ELLSBERG, DANIEL
  Secrets (Ellsberg) (03) 718
EMERSON, RALPH WALDO
  Emerson (Barish) (91) 249
  Emerson (Richardson) (96) 222
  Emerson Among the Eccentrics (Baker) (97) 239
  Emerson in His Journals (Emerson) (83) 224
  Ralph Waldo Emerson (McAleer) (85) 717
  Waldo Emerson (Allen) (82) 902
ENGELS, FRIEDRICH
  Selected Letters (Marx and Engels) (83) 722
EPSTEIN, JOSEPH
  With My Trousers Rolled (Epstein) (96) 818
ERDÓS, PAUL
  Man Who Loved Only Numbers, The (Hoffman)
    (99) 515
ESHKOL, LEVI
  Decisions in Crisis (Brecher and Geist) (81) 228
ESKIN, BLAKE
  Life in Pieces, A (Eskin) (03) 480
EUGÉNIE
  Napoleon III and Eugénie (Ridley) (81) 587
EVANS, MARIAN. See ELIOT, GEORGE
EVANS, MARY ANN. See ELIOT, GEORGE
EVANS, WALKER
  Walker Evans (Mellow) (00) 805

FABIANS, THE
  Fabians, The (MacKenzie and MacKenzie)
    (78) 300
FAIRBANK, JOHN KING
  Chinabound (Fairbank) (H-83) 61
FANTE, JOHN
  Full of Life (Cooper) (01) 319
FAULKNER, WILLIAM
  Faulkner, a Comprehensive Guide to the Brodsky
    Collection (Faulkner) (85) 266
  William Faulkner (Karl) (90) 899
  William Faulkner (Minter) (81) 932
  William Faulkner (Singal) (98) 850
FERDINAND, FRANZ
  Archduke of Sarajevo (Brook-Shepherd)
    (H-85) 33
FEYNMAN, RICHARD P.
  Genius (Gleick) (93) 308
  "Surely You're Joking, Mr. Feynman!" (Feynman,
    with Leighton) (86) 868
FIELDING, HENRY
  Henry Fielding (Battestin, with Battestin) (91) 395

FISHER, M. F. K.
  M. F. K. Fisher (Barr, Moran, and Moran, eds.)
    (99) 501
FitzGERALD, EDWARD
  With Friends Possessed (Martin) (86) 954
FITZGERALD, F. SCOTT
  F. Scott Fitzgerald (Le Vot) (84) 318
  Life Sentences (Epstein) (98) 504
  Scott Fitzgerald (Meyers) (95) 696
  Some Sort of Epic Grandeur (Bruccoli) (82) 782
FITZGERALD, JOHN FRANCIS
  Fitzgeralds and the Kennedys, The (Goodwin)
    (88) 323
FITZGERALD, ZELDA
  Zelda Fitzgerald (Cline) (04) 868
FLANNER, JANET
  Darlinghissima (Flanner) (86) 213
FLAUBERT, GUSTAVE
  Flaubert (Lottman) (90) 268
  Flaubert-Sand (Flaubert and Sand) (94) 300
  Letters of Gustave Flaubert, 1830-1857, The
    (Flaubert) (81) 494
  Letters of Gustave Flaubert, 1857-1880, The
    (Flaubert) (83) 395
FONG DUN SHUNG
  On Gold Mountain (See) (96) 523
FORBES, JACK D.
  I Tell You Now (Swann and Krupat, eds.)
    (88) 413
FORD, EDSEL
  Ford (Lacey) (87) 297
FORD, FORD MADOX
  Ford Madox Ford (Judd) (92) 218
  Great Friends (Garnett) (81) 386
  Group Portrait (Delbanco) (83) 312
  Pound/Ford (Pound and Ford) (83) 621
  Presence of Ford Madox Ford, The (Stang, ed.)
    (82) 652
FORD, HENRY
  Ford (Lacey) (87) 297
FORD, HENRY, II
  Ford (Lacey) (87) 297
FORSTER, E. M.
  E. M. Forster (Beauman) (95) 195
  E. M. Forster (Furbank) (79) 183
  Great Friends (Garnett) (81) 386
  Selected Letters of E. M. Forster, 1879-1920
    (Forster) (84) 773
  Selected Letters of E. M. Forster, 1921-1970
    (Forster) (86) 793
FOUCAULT, MICHEL
  Michel Foucault (Eribon) (92) 495
  Passion of Michel Foucault, The (Miller) (93) 614
FOUCQUET, JEAN FRANÇOIS
  Question of Hu, The (Spence) (89) 679
FOURIER, CHARLES
  Charles Fourier (Beecher) (88) 138
FOWLER, HENRY WATSON
  Warden of English, The (McMorris) (02) 838
FOWLIE, WALLACE
  Sites (Fowlie) (88) 823
FRANCIS OF ASSISI
  God's Fool (Green) (86) 354
FRANCO, FRANCISCO
  Franco (Preston) (95) 257

FRANKFURTER, FELIX
Felix Frankfurter and His Times (Parrish)
(H-83) 140
FRANKLIN, BENJAMIN
Benjamin Franklin (Clark) (H-84) 54
Benjamin Franklin (Isaacson) (04) 70
Benjamin Franklin (Morgan) (03) 61
Franklin of Philadelphia (Wright) (87) 303
FRAZER, JAMES GEORGE
J. G. Frazer (Ackerman) (89) 418
FRAZIER, IAN
Family (Frazier) (95) 222
FREIDENBERG, OLGA
Correspondence of Boris Pasternak and Olga
Freidenberg, 1910-1954, The (Pasternak and
Freidenberg) (83) 147
FREUD, ANNA
Anna Freud (Young-Bruehl) (89) 23
FREUD, SIGMUND
Anna Freud (Young-Bruehl) (89) 23
Complete Letters of Sigmund Freud to Wilhelm
Fliess (Freud) (86) 187
Freud (Clark) (81) 357
Freud (Gay) (89) 311
Freud (Roth, ed.) (99) 311
Secret Symmetry, A (Carotenuto) (83) 709
FRIEDAN, BETTY
Betty Friedan (Hennessee) (00) 53
Life So Far (Friedan) (01) 532
FROST, ROBERT
Frost (Pritchard) (85) 312
Into My Own (Walsh) (89) 390
Lives of the Modern Poets (Pritchard) (81) 520
Robert Frost (Meyers) (97) 705
Robert Frost (Parini) (00) 651
Robert Frost (Poirier) (78) 722
FRY, ROGER
Roger Fry (Spalding) (81) 699
FUGARD, ATHOL
Notebooks (Fugard) (85) 653
FULBRIGHT, J. WILLIAM
Fulbright (Woods) (96) 294
FULLER, MARGARET
Letters of Margaret Fuller, 1817-1841, The (Fuller)
(84) 449
Letters of Margaret Fuller, 1842-1844, The (Fuller)
(85) 559
Margaret Fuller (Blanchard) (79) 422
FULTON, ROBERT
Robert Fulton (Morgan) (78) 726

GALBRAITH, JOHN KENNETH
Life in Our Times, A (Galbraith) (82) 458
GALILEO
Galileo's Daughter (Sobel) (00) 295
GALSWORTHY, JOHN
Great Friends (Garnett) (81) 386
GANDHI, MOHANDAS "MAHATMA"
Gandhi (Brown) (91) 321
Tolstoy and Gandhi, Men of Peace (Green)
(H-84) 447
GARCÍA LORCA, FEDERICO
Federico García Lorca (Gibson) (90) 245
Selected Letters (García Lorca) (84) 768
GARCÍA MÁRQUEZ, GABRIEL
García Márquez (Bell-Villada) (91) 325
Living to Tell the Tale (García Márquez) (04) 460

GARNETT, DAVID
Great Friends (Garnett) (81) 386
GARVEY, MARCUS
Marcus Garvey and Universal Negro Improvement
Association Papers, The (Hill, ed.) (H-85) 283
GATES, HENRY LOUIS, Jr.
Colored People (Gates) (95) 141
GATES, WILLIAM H., III
Gates (Manes and Andrews) (94) 335
GAUDIER-BRZESKA, HENRI
Gaudier-Brzeska (Silber) (98) 331
GELLHORN, MARTHA
Nothing Ever Happens to the Brave (Rollyson)
(91) 639
GENET, JEAN
Genet (White) (94) 339
GEPHARDT, RICHARD
What It Takes (Cramer) (93) 874
GIACOMETTI, ALBERTO
Giacometti (Lord) (86) 343
GILBERT, CELIA
Working It Out (Ruddick and Daniels, eds.)
(78) 937
GILMAN, CHARLOTTE PERKINS
To Herland and Beyond (Lane) (91) 820
GILMAN, RICHARD
Faith, Sex, Mystery (Gilman) (88) 303
GINSBERG, ALLEN
Journals (Ginsberg) (78) 483
GINZBURG, EUGENIA SEMENOVA
Within the Whirlwind (Ginzburg) (82) 963
GINZBURG, NATALIA
Family Sayings (Ginzburg) (85) 255
GISSING, GEORGE
Gissing (Halperin) (83) 283
GLADSTONE, WILLIAM EWART
Gladstone (Jenkins) (98) 344
GLANCY, DIANE
I Tell You Now (Swann and Krupat, eds.)
(88) 413
GLENN, JOHN
John Glenn (Glenn and Taylor) (00) 443
GODDEN, RUMER
House with Four Rooms, A (Godden) (90) 396
Time to Dance, No Time to Weep, A (Godden)
(89) 835
GÖDEL, KURT
Gödel (Casti and DePauli) (01) 346
Logical Dilemmas (Dawson) (98) 517
GODWIN, WILLIAM
William Godwin (Marshall) (85) 1028
GOEBBELS, JOSEPH
Final Entries, 1945 (Goebbels) (79) 212
Goebbels Diaries, The (Goebbels) (H-84) 176
GOETHE, JOHANN WOLFGANG
Goethe, 1749-1790 (Boyle) (92) 247
Goethe, 1790-1803 (Boyle) (01) 356
GOLDBERG, MICHEL
Namesake (Goldberg) (83) 518
GOLDMAN, EMMA
Emma Goldman (Wexler) (H-85) 125
GOLDWATER, BARRY M.
Barry Goldwater (Goldberg) (96) 60
Goldwater (Goldwater) (89) 321
GOLDWYN, SAMUEL
Goldwyn (Berg) (90) 303

GOLLOB, HERMAN
Me and Shakespeare (Gollob) (03) 518
GOMBROWICZ, WITOLD
Diary, 1953-1956 (Gombrowicz) (89) 236
Diary, 1957-1961 (Gombrowicz) (90) 177
Diary, 1961-1966 (Gombrowicz) (94) 225
GOMPERS, SAMUEL
Samuel Gompers and Organized Labor in America
(Livesay) (79) 641
GONNE, MAUD
Gonne-Yeats Letters 1893-1938, The (Gonne and
Yeats) (94) 368
Lucky Eyes and a High Heart (Cardozo) (79) 409
GONZAGAS, THE
Renaissance Tapestry, A (Simon) (89) 708
GOODALL, JANE
Reason for Hope (Goodall with Berman) (00) 643
GOODWIN, RICHARD N.
Remembering America (Goodwin) (89) 703
GORDIMER, NADINE
Writing and Being (Gordimer) (96) 839
GORDON, CAROLINE
Poets in Their Youth (Simpson) (83) 608
GORDON, DAVID
Shadow Man, The (Gordon) (97) 749
GORDON, MARY
Shadow Man, The (Gordon) (97) 749
GORKY, ARSHILE
From a High Place (Spender) (00) 290
GOYA, FRANCISCO DE
Goya (Hughes) (04) 303
GRAHAM, KATHARINE MEYER
Personal History (Graham) (98) 629
GRAHAM, MARTHA
Martha (de Mille) (92) 485
GRANT, ROBERT
Province of Reason (Warner) (H-85) 368
GRANT, ULYSSES S.
Grant (McFeeley) (82) 338
GRAVES, ROBERT VON RANKE
Robert Graves (Seymour) (96) 650
Robert Graves (Seymour-Smith) (84) 746
Robert Graves, 1895-1926 (Graves) (88) 770
Robert Graves, 1926-1940 (Graves) (91) 706
GREALY, LUCY
Autobiography of a Face (Grealy) (95) 56
GREEN, HENRY
Romancing (Treglown) (02) 708
GREEN, JOANN
Working It Out (Ruddick and Daniels, eds.)
(78) 937
GREENBERG, CLEMENT
Clement Greenberg (Rubenfeld) (99) 181
GREENE, GRAHAM
Getting to Know the General (Greene) (H-85) 168
Life of Graham Greene, The, 1904-1939 (Sherry)
(90) 521
Life of Graham Greene, The, 1939-1955 (Sherry)
(96) 430
Other Man, The (Greene and Allain) (84) 651
Ways of Escape (Greene) (82) 918
World of My Own, A (Greene) (95) 890
GREENSPAN, ALAN
Greenspan (Martin) (01) 365
GROPIUS, WALTER
Art and Act (Gay) (77) 67

GUGGENHEIMS, THE
Guggenheims, The (Davis) (79) 260
GUINNESS, ALEC
Blessings in Disguise (Guinness) (87) 71
GUSTON, PHILIP
Guston in Time (Feld) (04) 320

HAILEY, KENDALL
Day I Became an Autodidact, The (Hailey)
(89) 222
HALL, RADCLYFFE
Our Three Selves (Baker) (86) 719
HAMILTON, ALEXANDER
Alexander Hamilton (McDonald) (80) 23
Alexander Hamilton, American (Brookhiser)
(00) 1
Burr, Hamilton, and Jefferson (Kennedy) (00) 112
Rise and Fall of Alexander Hamilton, The
(Hendrickson) (82) 687
Witnesses at the Creation (Morris) (86) 959
Young Hamilton, The (Flexner) (79) 922
HAMILTON, ALICE
Alice Hamilton (Sicherman) (H-85) 6
HAMMETT, DASHIELL
Dashiell Hammett (Johnson) (84) 212
Shadow Man (Layman) (82) 761
HAMOD, KAY KEESHAN
Working It Out (Ruddick and Daniels, eds.)
(78) 937
HAMSUN, KNUT
Enigma (Ferguson) (88) 279
HANCOCK, JOHN
Baron of Beacon Hill, The (Fowler) (81) 66
HANDKE, PETER
Weight of the World, The (Handke) (85) 1013
HANNAH, BARRY
World Unsuspected, A (Harris, ed.) (88) 984
HANSEN, ROGER
Remembering Denny (Trillin) (94) 692
HARDING, WARREN G.
Ohio Gang, The (Mee) (82) 575
HARDY, THOMAS
Hardy (Seymour-Smith) (95) 291
Hardy the Creator (Gatrell) (90) 348
Lives of the Modern Poets (Pritchard) (81) 520
Thomas Hardy (Millgate) (83) 806
HARINGTON, JOHN
Eminent Elizabethans (Rowse) (H-84) 147
HARJO, JOY
I Tell You Now (Swann and Krupat, eds.)
(88) 413
HARRINGTON, MICHAEL
Other American, The (Isserman) (01) 689
HARRIS, MARY. See MOTHER JONES
HARRISON, BARBARA GRIZZUTI
Accidental Autobiography, An (Harrison) (97) 1
HART, GARY
What It Takes (Cramer) (93) 874
HAVEL, VÁCLAV
Disturbing the Peace (Havel) (91) 216
Letters to Olga (Havel) (89) 492
Vaclav Havel (Keane) (01) 863
HAWKING, STEPHEN
Stephen Hawking (White and Gribbin) (93) 758

HAWTHORNE, NATHANIEL
Hawthorne's Secret (Young) (85) 358
Nathaniel Hawthorne in His Times (Mellow)
(81) 593
Salem Is My Dwelling Place (Miller) (93) 702
HAY, CLARA
Five of Hearts, The (O'Toole) (91) 295
HAY, JOHN
Five of Hearts, The (O'Toole) (91) 295
HAYSLIP, LE LY
When Heaven and Earth Changed Places (Hayslip,
with Wurts) (90) 879
HAZLITT, WILLIAM
Hazlitt (Bromwich) (85) 363
Hazlitt (Jones) (91) 381
H. D.
End to Torment (H. D.) (80) 290
Gift, The (H. D.) (83) 278
H. D. (Robinson) (83) 331
Herself Defined (Guest) (85) 374
HEARN, LAFCADIO
Wandering Ghost (Cott) (92) 863
HEARST, WILLIAM RANDOLPH
Chief, The (Nasaw) (01) 185
HEAT-MOON, WILLIAM LEAST
Blue Highways (Heat-Moon) (84) 95
HEGEL, GEORG WILHELM FRIEDRICH
Hegel (Pinkard) (01) 393
HEIDEGGER, MARTIN
Martin Heidegger (Ott) (94) 512
Martin Heidegger (Safranski) (99) 529
HEINLEIN, ROBERT A.
Grumbles from the Grave (Heinlein) (91) 372
HEISENBERG, WERNER
Heisenberg's War (Powers) (94) 380
Uncertainty (Cassidy) (93) 824
HELLMAN, LILLIAN
Lillian Hellman (Rollyson) (89) 511
Scoundrel Time (Hellman) (77) 702
HEMINGWAY, ERNEST
Along with Youth (Griffin) (86) 16
Ernest Hemingway, 1917-1961 (Hemingway)
(82) 245
Ernest Hemingway and His World (Burgess)
(79) 196
Hemingway (Lynn) (88) 372
Hemingway (Meyers) (86) 406
Hemingway, The American Homecoming
(Reynolds) (93) 325
Hemingway, The Final Years (Reynolds) (00) 377
Hemingway, The 1930's (Reynolds) (98) 379
Hemingway, The Paris Years (Reynolds) (90) 369
Hemingway Women, The (Kert) (84) 337
True at First Light (Hemingway) (00) 768
Young Hemingway, The (Reynolds) (87) 1021
HEMINGWAY, MARY WELSH
How It Was (Hemingway) (77) 362
HENRY, PATRICK
Son of Thunder, A (Mayer) (87) 789
HENRY VIII
Great Harry (Erickson) (81) 391
Thomas Cranmer (MacCulloch) (97) 821
HENTOFF, NAT
Boston Boy (Hentoff) (87) 84
Speaking Freely (Hentoff) (98) 717
HEPBURN, KATHARINE
Kate Remembered (Berg) (04) 400

HERBST, JOSEPHINE
Josephine Herbst (Langer) (85) 499
HERR, MICHAEL
Dispatches (Herr) (78) 272
HERRERA, OMAR TORRIJOS. See TORRIJOS,
OMAR
HERRIOT, JAMES
Lord God Made Them All, The (Herriot) (82) 480
HERZL, THEODOR
Labyrinth of Exile, The (Pawel) (90) 495
HEYDRICH, REINHARD
Reinhard Heydrich (Deschner) (82) 666
HIGGINS, AIDAN
Flotsam and Jetsam (Higgins) (03) 307
HIGHSMITH, PATRICIA
Beautiful Shadow (Wilson) (04) 62
HILLESUM, ETTY
Interrupted Life, An (Hillesum) (85) 456
HIMES, CHESTER
Chester Himes (Sallis) (02) 149
HIPPOCRATES
Hippocrates (Jouanna) (00) 381
HISS, ALGER
Alger Hiss (Smith) (77) 38
HITLER, ADOLF
Hitler (Stone) (81) 434
Hitler Among the Germans (Binion) (77) 357
Hitler and Stalin (Bullock) (93) 349
Hitler and the Final Solution (Fleming) (H-85) 213
Hitler, 1889-1936 (Kershaw) (00) 386
Hitler of History, The (Lukacs) (98) 396
Hitler's War (Irving) (78) 398
Meaning of Hitler, The (Haffner) (80) 528
Munich 1923 (Dornberg) (H-83) 298
Psychopathic God, The (Waite) (78) 677
Secret Diaries of Hitler's Doctor, The (Irving and
Morell) (H-84) 398
War Path, The (Irving) (79) 819
HO CHI MINH
Ho Chi Minh (Duiker) (01) 403
HOBBES, THOMAS
Hobbes (Martinich) (00) 400
HODGES, COURTNEY H.
Eisenhower's Lieutenants (Weigley) (82) 210
HOFFMAN, EVA
Lost in Translation (Hoffman) (90) 539
HOFMANNSTHAL, HUGO VON
Hugo von Hofmannsthal and His Time (Broch)
(85) 410
HOGAN, LINDA
I Tell You Now (Swann and Krupat, eds.)
(88) 413
HÖLDERLIN, FRIEDRICH
Hölderlin (Constantine) (89) 354
HOLMES, OLIVER WENDELL
Improper Bostonian, The (Hoyt) (80) 414
Justice Oliver Wendell Holmes (White) (94) 431
HOLMES, RICHARD
Footsteps (Holmes) (86) 297
HOLROYD, MICHAEL
Basil Street Blues (Holroyd) (01) 64
HONG XIUQUAN
God's Chinese Son (Spence) (97) 339
HONGO, GARRETT
Volcano (Hongo) (96) 802

HOOK, SIDNEY
  Out of Step (Hook) (88) 646
  Portraits (Shils) (98) 639
HOOVER, HERBERT
  Herbert Hoover (Burner) (80) 400
  Life of Herbert Hoover, The (Nash) (H-84) 288
HOOVER, JOHN EDGAR
  J. Edgar Hoover (Gentry) (92) 369
  Secrecy and Power (Powers) (88) 801
HOPKINS, GERARD MANLEY
  Gerard Manley Hopkins (Hopkins) (91) 343
  Hopkins (White) (93) 353
HOPKINS, HARRY
  Harry Hopkins (Adams) (78) 375
HOPPER, EDWARD
  Edward Hopper (Levin) (96) 214
HORNE, LENA
  Hornes, The (Buckley) (87) 410
HORNEY, KAREN
  Mind of Her Own, A (Quinn) (88) 558
HOROWITZ, DAVID
  Radical Son (Horowitz) (98) 661
HORWITZ, ROGER
  Borrowed Time (Monette) (89) 112
HOWE, IRVING
  Irving Howe (Sorin) (04) 364
  Margin of Hope, A (Howe) (83) 451
HOWE, SAMUEL GRIDLEY
  Education of Laura Bridgman, The (Freeberg)
    (02) 230
HU, JOHN
  Question of Hu, The (Spence) (89) 679
HUDSON, W. H.
  Great Friends (Garnett) (81) 386
  W. H. Hudson (Tomalin) (84) 935
HUGENBERG, ALFRED
  Alfred Hugenberg (Leopold) (78) 28
HUGHES, LANGSTON
  Arna Bontemps-Langston Hughes Letters
    (Bontemps and Hughes) (81) 57
  Langston Hughes (Berry) (84) 422
  Life of Langston Hughes, 1902-1941, The
    (Rampersad) (87) 489
  Life of Langston Hughes, 1941-1967, The
    (Rampersad) (89) 501
HUGHES, TED
  Her Husband (Middlebrook) (04) 335
  Silent Woman, The (Malcolm) (95) 719
HUGO, VICTOR
  Victor Hugo (Robb) (99) 838
  Victor Hugo and the Visionary Novel (Brombert)
    (85) 969
HUMBOLDT, WILHELM VON
  Wilhelm von Humboldt, 1767-1808 (Sweet)
    (79) 868
HUMPHREYS, JOSEPHINE
  World Unsuspected, A (Harris, ed.) (88) 984
HUMPHRIES, ROLFE
  Poets, Poetics, and Politics (Humphries) (93) 642
HUNSDON, HENRY
  Eminent Elizabethans (Rowse) (H-84) 147
HURSTON, ZORA NEALE
  Passionate Minds (Pierpont) (01) 694
  Zora Neale Hurston, Vol. II (Hurston) (96) 852
HUTCHINS, ROBERT MAYNARD
  Portraits (Shils) (98) 639

HUTCHINSON, MARY
  Gang, The (Worthen) (02) 321
HUTCHINSON, SARA
  Gang, The (Worthen) (02) 321
HUTCHINSON, THOMAS
  Faces of Revolution (Bailyn) (91) 279
HUXLEY, ALDOUS
  Aldous Huxley (Murray) (04) 13
  Moksha (Huxley) (79) 451
HUXLEY, THOMAS HENRY
  Charles Darwin's Letters (Darwin) (97) 148
  Huxley (Desmond) (98) 411
HYNES, SAMUEL
  Growing Seasons, The (Hynes) (04) 312

IONE, CAROLE
  Pride of Family (Ione) (92) 641
IRVING, JOHN
  Trying to Save Piggy Sneed (Irving) (97) 838
IRVING, WASHINGTON
  Sojourners (McFarland) (80) 771
ISABELLA
  Isabel the Queen (Liss) (93) 399
ISHERWOOD, CHRISTOPHER
  Christopher and His Kind (Isherwood) (77) 158
  Christopher Isherwood (Finney) (80) 145
  Diaries (Isherwood) (98) 249

JACKSON, ANDREW
  Andrew Jackson and His Indian Wars (Remini)
    (02) 43
  Andrew Jackson and the Course of American
    Democracy, 1833-1845 (Remini) (H-85) 28
  Andrew Jackson and the Course of American
    Empire, 1767-1821 (Remini) (78) 50
  Andrew Jackson and the Course of American
    Freedom, 1822-1832 (Remini) (82) 11
JACKSON, DAVID
  Familiar Spirits (Lurie) (02) 271
JACKSON, HELEN HUNT
  Helen Hunt Jackson (Phillips) (04) 330
JACKSON, JESSE
  Jesse (Frady) (97) 474
JACKSON, SHIRLEY
  Private Demons (Oppenheimer) (89) 668
JACKSON, THOMAS "STONEWALL"
  Stonewall Jackson (Robertson) (98) 736
JACOB, FRANÇOIS
  Statue Within, The (Jacob) (89) 813
JACOBSON, DAN
  Time and Time Again (Jacobson) (86) 883
JAMES, ALICE
  Alice James (Strouse) (81) 21
  Jameses, The (Lewis) (92) 374
JAMES, CLIVE
  Unreliable Memoirs (James) (82) 870
JAMES, HENRY
  Complete Notebooks of Henry James, The (James)
    (88) 179
  Group Portrait (Delbanco) (83) 312
  Henry James (Kaplan) (93) 330
  Henry James Letters, 1883-1895 (James) (81) 421
  Henry James Letters, 1895-1916 (James) (85) 368
  Jameses, The (Lewis) (92) 374
  Return Passages (Ziff) (02) 698

JAMES, HENRY, SR.
Jameses, The (Lewis) (92) 374

JAMES, P. D.
Time to be in Earnest (James) (01) 830

JAMES, WILLIAM
Genuine Reality (Simon) (99) 329
Jameses, The (Lewis) (92) 374
William James (Myers) (87) 997

JAMES, WILLIAM, SR.
Jameses, The (Lewis) (92) 374

JARRELL, RANDALL
Poets in Their Youth (Simpson) (83) 608
Randall Jarrell (Pritchard) (91) 696
Randall Jarrell and His Age (Burt) (04) 629
Randall Jarrell's Letters (Jarrell) (86) 757

JAY, JOHN
Witnesses at the Creation (Morris) (86) 959

JEFFERSON, THOMAS
American Sphinx (Ellis) (98) 55
Burr, Hamilton, and Jefferson (Kennedy) (00) 112
Faces of Revolution (Bailyn) (91) 279
Jefferson and the Presidency (Johnstone) (79) 331
Sage of Monticello, Vol. VI, The (Malone) (82) 722
Thomas Jefferson (Bedini) (91) 809
Thomas Jefferson (Randall) (94) 797
Undaunted Courage (Ambrose) (97) 853
What Kind of Nation (Simon) (03) 877
Wolf by the Ears, The (Miller) (78) 928

JIANG QING
White Boned Demon, The (Terrill) (H-85) 495

JOAN OF ARC
Joan of Arc (Gordon) (01) 485
Joan of Arc (Lucie-Smith) (78) 472

JOHN PAUL II, POPE
His Holiness (Bernstein and Politi) (97) 388
Man of the Century (Kwitny) (98) 538
Witness to Hope (Weigel) (00) 847

JOHNSON, LYNDON BAINES
Counsel to the President (Clifford, with Holbrooke) (92) 123
Flawed Giant (Dallek) (99) 286
Lone Star Rising (Dallek) (92) 450
Lyndon (Miller) (81) 540
Lyndon Johnson and the American Dream (Kearns) (77) 465
Politician, The (Dugger) (H-83) 348
Presidency of Lyndon B. Johnson, The (Bornet) (H-84) 355
Progressive Presidents, The (Blum) (81) 665
Years of Lyndon Johnson, Master of the Senate, The (Caro) (03) 907
Years of Lyndon Johnson, Means of Ascent, The (Caro) (91) 919
Years of Lyndon Johnson, The Path to Power, The (Caro) (H-83) 478

JOHNSON, SAMUEL
Dr. Johnson and Mr. Savage (Holmes) (95) 176
Letters of Samuel Johnson, 1731-1781, The (Johnson) (93) 444
Life of Samuel Johnson, The (DeMaria) (94) 471
Samuel Johnson (Bate) (78) 735
Samuel Johnson (Lipking) (99) 683

JOHNSON, STEPHEN
Faces of Revolution (Bailyn) (91) 279

JOHNSTONE-WILSON, ANGUS FRANK. See
WILSON, ANGUS

JONES, JAMES
Into Eternity (MacShane) (86) 471
James Jones (Garrett) (85) 484

JONES, JOHN PAUL
John Paul Jones (Thomas) (04) 381

JONES, R. V.
Wizard War, The (Jones) (79) 888

JONSON, BEN
Ben Jonson (Riggs) (90) 58
Ben Jonson, Dramatist (Barton) (85) 37

JOPLIN, JANIS
Scars of Sweet Paradise (Echols) (00) 670

JOPLIN, SCOTT
King of Ragtime (Berlin) (95) 422

JORDAN, DOROTHY "DORA" BLAND
Mrs. Jordan's Profession (Tomalin) (96) 465

JORDAN, HAMILTON
Crisis (Jordan) (H-83) 93

JORDAN, MICHAEL
Playing for Keeps (Halberstam) (00) 618

JOSEPH I, EMPEROR
In Quest and Crisis (Ingrao) (80) 426

JOYCE, JAMES
James Joyce (Costello) (94) 418
Nora (Maddox) (89) 605
Portraits of the Artist in Exile (Potts, ed.) (80) 675

JOYCE, NORA
Nora (Maddox) (89) 605

JUNG, CARL G.
Jung (Bair) (04) 396
Secret Symmetry, A (Carotenuto) (83) 709

KAFKA, FRANZ
Franz Kafka (Karl) (92) 227
Hesitation Before Birth, A (Mailloux) (90) 378
Kafka (Hayman) (83) 372
Letters to Friends, Family, and Editors (Kafka) (78) 526
Letters to Ottla and the Family (Kafka) (83) 401
Nightmare of Reason, The (Pawel) (85) 645

KAGANOVICH, LAZAR MOISEYEVICH
All Stalin's Men (Medvedev) (H-85) 12

KAHLO, FRIDA
Diary of Frida Kahlo, The (Kahlo) (96) 182

KANT, IMMANUEL
Kant (Kuehn) (02) 458

KAPLAN, JONATHAN
Dressing Station, The (Kaplan) (03) 238

KARR, MARY
Cherry (Karr) (01) 181
Liar's Club, The (Karr) (96) 426

KAYSEN, SUSANNA
Girl, Interrupted (Kaysen) (94) 360

KAZAN, ELIA
Elia Kazan (Kazan) (89) 257

KAZIN, ALFRED
New York Jew (Kazin) (79) 475
Writing Was Everything (Kazin) (96) 843

KEATS, JOHN
Keats (Motion) (99) 449

KEES, WELDON
Vanished Act (Reidel) (04) 796

KELLER, EVELYN FOX
Working It Out (Ruddick and Daniels, eds.) (78) 937

KENNAN, GEORGE F.
Sketches from a Life (Kennan) (90) 742

KENNEDY, JOHN F.
Counsel to the President (Clifford, with Holbrooke) (92) 123
Fitzgeralds and the Kennedys, The (Goodwin) (88) 323
Jack (Parmet) (81) 454
JFK (Hamilton) (93) 408
Kennedy Imprisonment, The (Wills) (H-83) 244
Of Kennedys and Kings (Wofford) (81) 633
President Kennedy (Reeves) (94) 662
Question of Character, A (Reeves) (92) 660
Robert Kennedy in His Own Words (Kennedy) (89) 744
Unfinished Life, An (Dallek) (04) 791

KENNEDY, JOSEPH P.
Fitzgeralds and the Kennedys, The (Goodwin) (88) 323
Kennedy and Roosevelt (Beschloss) (81) 467

KENNEDY, JOSEPH P., Jr.
Fitzgeralds and the Kennedys, The (Goodwin) (88) 323

KENNEDY, KATHLEEN
Fitzgeralds and the Kennedys, The (Goodwin) (88) 323

KENNEDY, ROBERT
Of Kennedys and Kings (Wofford) (81) 633
Robert Kennedy in His Own Words (Kennedy) (89) 744

KENNEDY, ROSE FITZGERALD
Fitzgeralds and the Kennedys, The (Goodwin) (88) 323

KENNY, MAURICE
I Tell You Now (Swann and Krupat, eds.) (88) 413

KENT, LOUISE ANDREWS
Province of Reason (Warner) (H-85) 368

KEPLER, JOHANNES
Tycho and Kepler (Ferguson) (04) 782

KEROUAC, JACK
Portable Jack Kerouac, The (Kerouac) (96) 597

KEYNES, JOHN MAYNARD
Bloomsbury (Edel) (80) 88
Great Friends (Garnett) (81) 386
John Maynard Keynes (Hession) (H-85) 250
John Maynard Keynes, 1920-1937 (Skidelsky) (95) 400
John Maynard Keynes, 1937-1946 (Skidelsky) (02) 453

KHAN, KHUBILAI
Khubilai Khan (Rossabi) (89) 432

KHODASEVICH, VLADISLAV
Khodasevich (Bethea) (84) 408

KHRUSHCHEV, NIKITA
Khrushchev (Medvedev) (H-84) 266
Khrushchev (Taubman) (04) 404

KIDD, WILLIAM
Captain Kidd and the War Against the Pirates (Ritchie) (87) 99

KIM IL SUNG
Uncertain Partners (Goncharov, Lewis, and Xue) (95) 809

KING, CLARENCE
Five of Hearts, The (O'Toole) (91) 295

KING, MARTIN LUTHER, Jr.
And the Walls Came Tumbling Down (Abernathy) (90) 39
Bearing the Cross (Garrow) (87) 55
I May Not Get There With You (Dyson) (01) 442
Let the Trumpet Sound (Oates) (H-83) 259
Of Kennedys and Kings (Wofford) (81) 633
Papers of Martin Luther King, Jr., January 1929-June 1951, The (King) (93) 601
Papers of Martin Luther King, Jr., July 1951-November 1955, The (King) (95) 590
Papers of Martin Luther King, Jr., December 1955-December 1956, The (King) (98) 625
Preacher King, The (Lischer) (96) 601

KING, STEPHEN
Danse Macabre (King) (82) 171
On Writing (King) (01) 675

KINGSOLVER, BARBARA
Small Wonder (Kingsolver) (03) 779

KINGSTON, MAXINE HONG
China Men (Kingston) (81) 137
Woman Warrior, The (Kingston) (77) 932

KIPLING, RUDYARD
Letters of Rudyard Kipling, 1872-89 and 1890-99, The (Kipling) (92) 421
Rudyard Kipling (Ricketts) (01) 750
Strange Ride of Rudyard Kipling (Wilson) (79) 717

KISSINGER, HENRY
Arabs, Israelis, and Kissinger, The (Sheehan) (77) 57
Kissinger (Isaacson) (93) 426
Price of Power, The (Hersh) (H-84) 361
Secret Conversations of Henry Kissinger, The (Golan) (77) 709
Uncertain Greatness (Morris) (78) 869
White House Years (Kissinger) (80) 866
Years of Renewal (Kissinger) (00) 867

KLEE, PAUL
Paul Klee (Lanchner, ed.) (88) 668

KLEIST, HEINRICH VON
Kleist (Maass) (84) 418

KLEMPERER, VICTOR
I Will Bear Witness (Klepmerer) (01) 447

KONNER, MELVIN
Becoming a Doctor (Konner) (88) 77

KONWICKI, TADEUSZ
Moonrise, Moonset (Konwicki) (88) 579

KOPELEV, LEV
Ease My Sorrows (Kopelev) (84) 263

KORCZAK, JANUSZ
King of Children, The (Lifton) (89) 436

KORDA, ALEXANDER
Charmed Lives (Korda) (80) 141

KORDA, MICHAEL
Charmed Lives (Korda) (80) 141

KORDA, VINCENT
Charmed Lives (Korda) (80) 141

KORDA, ZOLTÁN
Charmed Lives (Korda) (80) 141

KOSINSKI, JERZY
Jerzy Kosinski (Sloan) (97) 470

KOUFAX, SANDY
Sandy Koufax (Leavy) (03) 713

KOVIC, RON
Born on the Fourth of July (Kovic) (77) 115

KUHN, THOMAS
Thomas Kuhn (Fuller) (01) 820

LACAN, JACQUES
Jacques Lacan (Roudinesco) (98) 463
LAEMMLE, CARL
Empire of Their Own, An (Gabler) (89) 278
LAFAYETTE, MARQUISE DE
Lafayette (Buckman) (78) 495
LAING, R. D.
Wing of Madness, The (Burston) (97) 885
LAMOTT, ANNE
Traveling Mercies (Lamott) (00) 764
LAMPEDUSA, GIUSEPPE DI
Last Leopard, The (Gilmour) (92) 413
LANCASTER, BURT
Burt Lancaster (Buford) (01) 158
LARDNER, RING, JR. (AND FAMILY)
Lardners, The (Lardner) (77) 404
LARKIN, PHILIP
Life Sentences (Epstein) (98) 504
Philip Larkin (Motion) (94) 626
Selected Letters of Philip Larkin (Larkin) (94) 724
LASKI, HAROLD
Portraits (Shils) (98) 639
LASOFF, ANNE
Working It Out (Ruddick and Daniels, eds.)
(78) 937
LAWRENCE, D. H.
D. H. Lawrence (Ellis) (98) 244
D. H. Lawrence (Kinkead-Weekes) (97) 214
D. H. Lawrence (Maddox) (95) 167
D. H. Lawrence (Meyers) (91) 206
D. H. Lawrence (Worthen) (92) 166
D. H. Lawrence's Nightmare (Delany) (80) 223
Great Friends (Garnett) (81) 386
Letters of D. H. Lawrence, September 1901-May
1913, The (Lawrence) (80) 469
Letters of D. H. Lawrence, October 1916-June
1921, The (Lawrence) (86) 520
Letters of D. H. Lawrence, June 1921-March 1924,
The (Lawrence) (88) 466
Letters of D. H. Lawrence, March 1924-March
1927, The (Lawrence) (90) 512
Letters of D. H. Lawrence, March 1927- November
1928, The (Lawrence) (92) 417
Letters of D. H. Lawrence, November
1928-February 1930, The (Lawrence) (94) 467
LAWRENCE, FRIEDA VON RICHTHOFEN
WEEKLEY
D. H. Lawrence (Kinkead-Weekes) (97) 214
LAWRENCE, T. E.
Lawrence of Arabia (Wilson) (91) 512
Prince of Our Disorder, A (Mack) (77) 637
T. E. Lawrence (Lawrence) (90) 782
T. E. Lawrence (Stewart) (78) 813
LAWS, CAROLYN
On Gold Mountain (See) (96) 523
LEDYARD, JOHN
Return Passages (Ziff) (02) 698
LEE, ANDREA
Russian Journal (Lee) (82) 713
LEE, LI-YOUNG
Winged Seed, The (Lee) (96) 814
LEE, ROBERT EDWARD
Robert E. Lee (Thomas) (96) 645
LEIB, GLIKL BAS JUDAH
Women on the Margins (Davis) (96) 826
LEM, STANISŁAW
Microworlds (Lem) (86) 595

LENNON, JOHN
Nowhere Man (Rosen) (01) 661
LEONARDO DA VINCI
Leonardo da Vinci (Kemp and Roberts, with
Steadman) (90) 505
LEOPOLD I
Leopold I of Austria (Spielman) (78) 518
LERMONTOV, MIKHAIL
Lermontov (Kelly) (79) 373
LESSER, WENDY
The Amateur (Lesser) (00) 10
LESSING, DORIS
Passionate Minds (Pierpont) (01) 694
Under My Skin (Lessing) (95) 814
Walking in the Shade (Lessing) (98) 823
LEVERTOV, DENISE
Tesserae (Levertov) (96) 740
LEVI, PRIMO
Double Bond, The (Angier) (03) 224
Drowned and the Saved, The (Levi) (89) 250
Periodic Table, The (Levi) (85) 682
LEWES, GEORGE HENRY
Parallel Lives (Rose) (84) 662
LEWIS, C. S.
C. S. Lewis (Wilson) (91) 175
LEWIS, JOHN L.
John L. Lewis (Dubofsky and Van Tine) (78) 478
LEWIS, MERIWETHER
Figures in a Western Landscape (Stevenson)
(95) 231
Lewis and Clark Journals, The (Lewis and Clark)
(04) 442
Undaunted Courage (Ambrose) (97) 853
LEWIS, SINCLAIR
Sinclair Lewis (Lingeman) (03) 755
LEWIS, WYNDHAM
Pound/Lewis (Pound and Lewis) (86) 747
Rude Assignment (Lewis) (86) 778
LIDDY, G. GORDON
Will (Liddy) (81) 928
LIEBKNECHT, WILHELM
Wilhelm Liebknecht and the Founding of the
German Social Democratic Party (Dominick)
(H-83) 467
LINCOLN, ABRAHAM
Abraham Lincoln (Anderson) (H-83) 5
Honor's Voice (Wilson) (99) 379
Last Best Hope of Earth, The (Neely) (94) 449
Lincoln (Donald) (96) 436
Lincoln's Virtues (Miller) (03) 490
LINCOLN, TREBITSCH
Secret Lives of Trebitsch Lincoln, The
(Wasserstein) (89) 762
LINDBERGH, ANNE MORROW
Flower and the Nettle, The (Lindbergh) (77) 294
War Within and Without (Lindbergh) (81) 890
LINDBERGH, CHARLES AUGUSTUS
Autobiography of Values (Lindbergh) (79) 43
Flower and the Nettle, The (Lindbergh) (77) 294
Lindbergh (Berg) (99) 478
Lindbergh (Mosley) (77) 433
LINDSAY, NICHOLAS VACHEL
Letters of Vachel Lindsay (Lindsay) (80) 479
LIPPMANN, WALTER
Walter Lippmann (Blum) (H-85) 470
Walter Lippmann and the American Century
(Steel) (81) 886

LISTON, SONNY
Devil and Sonny Liston, The (Tosches) (01) 237
LLERENA, MARIO
Unsuspected Revolution, The (Llerena) (79) 799
LODGE, HENRY CABOT
Henry Cabot Lodge and the Search for an
American Foreign Policy (Widenor) (81) 416
LONDON, JACK
Jack (Sinclair) (78) 454
LONG, HUEY
Voices of Protest (Brinkley) (H-83) 449
LOOMIS, ALFRED LEE
Tuxedo Park (Conant) (03) 848
LOPATE, PHILLIP
Bachelorhood (Lopate) (82) 40
LORD, JAMES
Six Exceptional Women (Lord) (95) 724
LORD, LOUISE BENNETT
Six Exceptional Women (Lord) (95) 724
LOVE, DAVID
Rising from the Plains (McPhee) (87) 722
LOWELL, ROBERT
Collected Prose (Lowell) (88) 173
Lost Puritan (Mariani) (95) 455
Poets in Their Youth (Simpson) (83) 608
Robert Lowell (Hamilton) (83) 654
LOWRY, MALCOLM
Pursued by Furies (Bowker) (96) 610
LOYD, ANTHONY
My War Gone By, I Miss It So (Loyd) (01) 604
LUDENDORFF, ERICH
Tormented Warrior (Parkinson) (80) 827
LUKÁCS, GEORG
Young Lukács, The (Congdon) (84) 992
LUTHER, MARTIN
Luther (Haile) (81) 535
Luther (Oberman) (91) 553
Martin Luther (Marius) (00) 515
LYELL, CHARLES
Charles Darwin's Letters (Darwin) (97) 148
LYNDON, ALICE ATKINSON
Working It Out (Ruddick and Daniels, eds.)
(78) 937
LYON, JANET
Life As We Know It (Bérubé) (97) 498

MacARTHUR, DOUGLAS
American Caesar (Manchester) (79) 20
Years of MacArthur (James) (86) 980
MACAULAY, ROSE
Rose Macaulay (Emery) (93) 693
McCARTHY, DESMOND
Bloomsbury (Edel) (80) 88
McCARTHY, JOSEPH R.
Conspiracy So Immense, A (Oshinsky) (H-84) 100
Life and Times of Joe McCarthy, The (Reeves)
(H-83) 270
Without Precedent (Adams) (H-84) 497
McCARTHY, MARY
Between Friends (Arendt and McCarthy) (96) 73
How I Grew (McCarthy) (88) 407
Mary McCarthy (Gelderman) (89) 539
Seeing Mary Plain (Kiernan) (01) 764
Writing Dangerously (Brightman) (93) 887
McCLOSKEY, DEIRDRE N.
Crossing (McCloskey) (00) 155

McCLOY, JOHN J.
Chairman, The (Bird) (93) 138
McCORMICK, ROBERT R.
Colonel, The (Smith) (98) 202
McCOURT, FRANK
Angela's Ashes (McCourt) (97) 43
'Tis (McCourt) (00) 759
McCULLERS, CARSON
Great Friends (Garnett) (81) 386
MacDONALD, DWIGHT
Rebel in Defense of Tradition, A (Wreszin)
(95) 630
MACDONALD, ROSS
Ross Macdonald (Bruccoli) (85) 766
Ross Macdonald (Nolan) (00) 660
MACHIAVELLI, NICCOLO
Niccolo's Smile (Viroli) (01) 641
MacLEISH, ARCHIBALD
Archibald MacLeish (Donaldson) (93) 28
Letters of Archibald MacLeish (MacLeish)
(84) 436
McLUHAN, MARSHALL
Letters of Marshall McLuhan (McLuhan) (89) 484
Marshall McLuhan (Gordon) (98) 542
Marshall McLuhan (Marchand) (90) 562
McMANUS, JAMES
Positively Fifth Street (McManus) (04) 619
MACMILLAN, HAROLD
Harold Macmillan (Fisher) (H-83) 185
Harold Macmillan, 1894-1956 (Horne) (90) 352
Harold Macmillan, 1957-1986 (Horne) (90) 358
Past Masters, The (Macmillan) (77) 610
War Diaries (Macmillan) (H-85) 474
McMURTRY, LARRY
Walter Benjamin at the Dairy Queen (McMurtry)
(00) 817
MacNEICE, LOUIS
Louis MacNeice (Stallworthy) (96) 444
McPHERSON, JAMES ALAN
World Unsuspected, A (Harris, ed.) (88) 984
MADISON, JAMES
Mr. Madison's War (Stagg) (H-84) 303
Witnesses at the Creation (Morris) (86) 959
MAHLER, ALMA SCHINDLER
Gustav Mahler, 1892-1904 (La Grange) (96) 321
MAHLER, GUSTAV
Gustav Mahler, 1892-1904 (La Grange) (96) 321
MAILER, NORMAN
Lives of Norman Mailer, The (Rollyson) (92) 445
Mailer (Mills) (83) 428
MAIRS, NANCY
Ordinary Time (Mairs) (94) 594
Voice Lessons (Mairs) (95) 835
Waist High in the World (Mairs) (98) 814
MALAN, RIAN
My Traitor's Heart (Malan) (91) 624
MALCOLM X
Malcolm (Perry) (92) 474
MALENKOV, GEORGY MAKSIMILIANOVICH
All Stalin's Men (Medvedev) (H-85) 12
MALLARMÉ, STÉPHANE
Throw of the Dice, A (Millan) (95) 782
MALRAUX, ANDRÉ
Lazarus (Malraux) (78) 515

MANDELA, NELSON
Mandela (Sampson) (00) 506
Nelson Mandela (Meredith) (99) 552

MANDELSTAM, OSIP
Nightingale Fever (Hingley) (82) 555

MANET, ÉDOUARD
Art and Act (Gay) (77) 67

MANN, HEINRICH
Brothers Mann, The (Hamilton) (80) 119

MANN, THOMAS
Brothers Mann, The (Hamilton) (80) 119

MANSFIELD, KATHERINE
Collected Letters of Katherine Mansfield,
1903-1917, The (Mansfield) (85) 106
Collected Letters of Katherine Mansfield,
1918-1919, The (Mansfield) (88) 165
Katherine Mansfield (Tomalin) (89) 427

MAO, MADAME. See JIANG QING

MAO ZEDONG
Mao (Short) (01) 554
Mao (Terrill) (81) 549
Mao Zedong (Spence) (00) 511
People's Emperor (Wilson) (81) 645
Uncertain Partners (Goncharov, Lewis, and Xue)
(95) 809

MARIE DE L'INCARNATION
Women on the Margins (Davis) (96) 826

MARKHAM, BERYL
Straight on till Morning (Lovell) (88) 865

MARLBOROUGH, DUKE OF. See CHURCHILL,
JOHN

MARLOWE, CHRISTOPHER
Reckoning, The (Nicholl) (95) 639

MARQUAND, JOHN PHILLIP
Marquand (Bell) (80) 517

MÁRQUEZ, GABRIEL GARCÍA. See GARCÍA
MÁRQUEZ, GABRIEL

MARSHALL, GEORGE C.
General of the Army (Cray) (91) 333
George C. Marshall, 1945-1959 (Pogue) (88) 346
Marshall (Mosley) (H-83) 283

MARSHALL, JOHN
John Marshall and the Heroic Age of the Supreme
Court (Newmyer) (03) 432
What Kind of Nation (Simon) (03) 877

MARSHALL, LAURENCE K.
Province of Reason (Warner) (H-85) 368

MARSHALL, THURGOOD
Dream Makers, Dream Breakers (Rowan) (94) 252

MARVELL, ANDREW
World Enough and Time (Murray) (01) 930

MARX, JULIUS HENRY
Groucho (Kanfer) (01) 370

MARX, KARL
Karl Marx (Padover) (79) 349
Karl Marx (Wheen) (01) 504
Selected Letters (Marx and Engels) (83) 722

MARY TUDOR
Bloody Mary (Erickson) (79) 64

MASON, BOBBIE ANN
World Unsuspected, A (Harris, ed.) (88) 984

MASTERS, EDGAR LEE
Edgar Lee Masters (Russell) (02) 226

MASTERS, HILARY
Last Stands (Masters) (83) 386

MATHER, COTTON
Life and Times of Cotton Mather, The (Silverman)
(H-85) 256

MATISSE, HENRI
Matisse (Schneider) (H-85) 303
Unknown Matisse, The (Spurling) (99) 826

MATTHIESSEN, PETER
Indian Country (Matthiessen) (H-85) 241
Snow Leopard, The (Matthiessen) (79) 685

MAUGHAM, W. SOMERSET
Maugham (Morgan) (81) 559

MAYER, LOUIS B.
Empire of Their Own, An (Gabler) (89) 278

MAYHEW, JONATHAN
Faces of Revolution (Bailyn) (91) 279

MEAD, MARGARET
With a Daughter's Eye (Bateson) (H-85) 507

MEDAWAR, PETER
Memoir of a Thinking Radish (Medawar) (87) 541

MEHTA, VED
Ledge Between the Streams, The (Mehta) (85) 539
Remembering Mr. Shawn's "New Yorker" (Mehta)
(99) 649
Sound-Shadows of the New World (Mehta)
(87) 802
Stolen Light, The (Mehta) (90) 758
Up at Oxford (Mehta) (94) 823

MEIJI
Emperor of Japan (Keene) (03) 255

MEITNER, LISE
Lise Meitner (Sime) (97) 526

MEIR, GOLDA
Decisions in Crisis (Brecher and Geist) (81) 228

MEITNER, LISE
Lise Meitner (Sime) (97) 526

MELLONS, THE
Mellons, The (Koskoff) (79) 434

MELVILLE, HERMAN
Herman Melville (Parker) (97) 373
Melville (Robertson-Lorant) (97) 568

MENCKEN, H. L.
Diary of H. L. Mencken, The (Mencken) (91) 211
Mencken (Hobson) (95) 477
New Mencken Letters, The (Mencken) (78) 603
Skeptic, The (Teachout) (03) 770

MENDEL, GREGOR
Monk in the Garden, The (Henig) (01) 588

MENGEL, NANETTE VONNEGUT
Working It Out (Ruddick and Daniels, eds.)
(78) 937

MERIAN, MARIA SIBYLLA
Women on the Margins (Davis) (96) 826

MERILLAT, HERBERT CHRISTIAN
Guadalcanal Remembered (Merillat) (H-83) 181

MERISI, MICHELANGELO
M (Robb) (01) 549

MERRILL, JAMES
Different Person, A (Merrill) (94) 234
Familiar Spirits (Lurie) (02) 271

MERTON, THOMAS
Seven Mountains of Thomas Merton, The (Mott)
(85) 815

MERWIN, W. S.
Regions of Memory (Merwin) (88) 742

METCALF, PAUL
Collected Works (Metcalf) (98) 199

MEW, CHARLOTTE
Charlotte Mew and Her Friends (Fitzgerald)
(89) 145
MICHENER, DIANA
Working It Out (Ruddick and Daniels, eds.)
(78) 937
MIKOYAN, ANASTAS IVANOVICH
All Stalin's Men (Medvedev) (H-85) 12
MILL, HARRIET TAYLOR
Parallel Lives (Rose) (84) 662
MILL, JOHN STUART
Parallel Lives (Rose) (84) 662
MILLAY, EDNA ST. VINCENT
Savage Beauty (Milford) (02) 722
MILLER, ARTHUR
Timebends (Miller) (88) 897
MILLER, HENRY
Happiest Man Alive, The (Dearborn) (92) 266
MIŁOSZ, CZESŁAW
Conversations with Czesław Miłosz (Miłosz)
(88) 194
Land of Ulro, The (Miłosz) (85) 520
Native Realm (Miłosz) (81) 597
Year of the Hunter, A (Miłosz) (95) 900
MILTON, JOHN
Milton and the English Revolution (Hill) (79) 444
MIN, ANCHEE
Red Azalea (Min) (95) 643
MITCHELL, DWIKE
Willie and Dwike (Zinsser) (85) 1036
MITCHELL, MARGARET
Passionate Minds (Pierpont) (01) 694
Southern Daughter (Pyron) (92) 775
MITFORD, DEBORAH
Sisters, The (Lovell) (03) 760
MITFORD, DIANA
Sisters, The (Lovell) (03) 760
MITFORD, JESSICA
Sisters, The (Lovell) (03) 760
MITFORD, NANCY
Sisters, The (Lovell) (03) 760
MITFORD, PAMELA
Sisters, The (Lovell) (03) 760
MITFORD, UNITY
Sisters, The (Lovell) (03) 760
MOBUTU, JOSEPH
In the Footsteps of Mr. Kurtz (Wrong) (02) 413
MOHAMMAD REZA PAHLAVI
Answer to History (Pahlavi) (81) 47
Shah of Shahs (Kapuciski) (86) 811
Shah's Last Ride, The (Shawcross) (89) 784
MOLOTOV, VYACHESLAV MIKAILOVICH
All Stalin's Men (Medvedev) (H-85) 12
MOMADAY, N. SCOTT
Names, The (Momaday) (78) 594
MOMIGLIANO, ARNALDO DANTE
Portraits (Shils) (98) 639
MONDRIAN, PIET
Art and Act (Gay) (77) 67
MONET, CLAUDE
Claude Monet (Tucker) (96) 120
MONETTE, PAUL
Becoming a Man (Monette) (93) 62
Borrowed Time (Monette) (89) 112
MONTAIGNE, MICHEL DE
Life Sentences (Epstein) (98) 504

MONTGOMERY, BERNARD L.
Eisenhower's Lieutenants (Weigley) (82) 210
Monty (Hamilton) (82) 531
MOORE, GEORGE
Great Friends (Garnett) (81) 386
MOORE, MARIANNE
Marianne Moore (Molesworth) (91) 562
Selected Letters of Marianne Moore, The (Moore)
(98) 702
MORE, THOMAS
Statesman and Saint (Ridley) (H-84) 420
Thomas More (Marius) (H-85) 435
MORELL, THEODOR GILBERT
Secret Diaries of Hitler's Doctor, The (Irving and
Morell) (H-84) 398
MORGAN, JOHN PIERPONT, SR.
J. P. Morgan (Jackson) (H-84) 257
Morgan (Strouse) (00) 524
MORGENTHAU, HENRY
Mostly Morgenthaus (Morgenthau) (92) 529
MORGENTHAU, HENRY, Jr.
Mostly Morgenthaus (Morgenthau) (92) 529
MORGENTHAU, HENRY, III
Mostly Morgenthaus (Morgenthau) (92) 529
MORGENTHAU, LAZARUS
Mostly Morgenthaus (Morgenthau) (92) 529
MORRIS, WILLIAM
Redesigning the World (Stansky) (86) 761
William Morris (Thompson) (78) 913
MORRIS, WRIGHT
Cloak of Light, A (Morris) (86) 140
Solo (Morris) (84) 803
Will's Boy (Morris) (82) 950
MORROW, LANCE
Chief, The (Morrow) (86) 121
MORTIMER, JOHN
Clinging to the Wreckage (Mortimer) (83) 127
MOTHER JONES
Mother Jones (Gorn) (02) 546
MOUNTBATTEN, LORD LOUIS
Mountbatten (Hough) (82) 542
Mountbatten (Ziegler) (86) 629
MOZART, WOLFGANG AMADÉ
Mozart (Solomon) (96) 490
Mozart in Vienna, 1781-1791 (Braunbehrens)
(91) 606
MUNRO, HECTOR HUGH
Saki (Langguth) (82) 726
MURDOCH, IRIS
Elegy for Iris (Bayley) (00) 213
Iris and Her Friends (Bayley) (00) 439
Iris Murdoch (Conradi) (02) 428
MURRAY, BRUCE
Journey into Space (Murray) (90) 464
MURRAY, JAMES A. H.
Caught in the Web of Words (Murray) (78) 160
MURRAY, NATALIA DANESI
Darlinghissima (Flanner) (86) 213
MURRAY, PAULI
Songs in a Weary Throat (Murray) (88) 835
MURROW, EDWARD
Murrow (Sperber) (87) 582
MUSA AL-SADR
Vanished Imam, The (Ajami) (87) 901
MUSIL, ROBERT
Life Sentences (Epstein) (98) 504

MUSSOLINI, BENITO
Mussolini (Mack Smith) (H-83) 308
Mussolini's Roman Empire (Mack Smith)
(77) 520
MUTSOHITO
Emperor of Japan (Keene) (03) 255

NABOKOV, VLADIMIR VLADIMIROVICH
Nabokov (Field) (78) 590
Nabokov-Wilson Letters, The (Nabokov and
Wilson) (80) 564
Nabokov's Fifth Arc (Rivers and Nicol, eds.)
(83) 511
Strong Opinions (Nabokov) (77) 789
Véra (Mrs. Vladimir Nabokov) (Schiff) (00) 789
Vladimir Nabokov, Selected Letters (Nabokov)
(90) 849
Vladimir Nabokov, The American Years (Boyd)
(92) 854
Vladimir Nabokov, The Russian Years (Boyd)
(91) 856
VN (Field) (87) 912
NAFISI, AZAR
Reading Lolita in Tehran (Nafisi) (04) 634
NA GOPALEEN, MYLES. See O'BRIEN, FLANN
NAIPAUL, SHIVA
Beyond the Dragon's Mouth (Naipaul) (86) 56
NAIPAUL, V. S.
Finding the Center (Naipaul) (85) 281
Sir Vidia's Shadow (Theroux) (99) 711
NAPOLEON BONAPARTE
Escape from Elba, The (MacKenzie) (H-83) 134
NAPOLEON III
Napoleon and Eugénie (Ridley) (81) 587
NASH, JOHN
Beautiful Mind, A (Nasar) (99) 87
NASHE, THOMAS
Cup of News, A (Nicholl) (85) 147
NEHRU, JAWAHARLAL
Nehru (Tharoor) (04) 546
NERO
Nero (Griffin) (86) 650
NERVAL, GÉRARD DE
Footsteps (Holmes) (86) 297
NESBIT, EVELYN
Evelyn Nesbit and Stanford White (Mooney)
(77) 260
NEUMAN, ALMA
Always Straight Ahead (Neuman) (94) 11
NEWMAN, JOHN HENRY
John Henry Newman (Ker) (90) 459
NEWTON, ISAAC
In the Presence of the Creator (Christianson)
(H-85) 236
Isaac Newton (Gleick) (04) 369
Newton's Gift (Berlinski) (01) 637
NGOR, HAING
Haing Ngor (Ngor, with Warner) (89) 335
NIATUM, DUANE
I Tell You Now (Swann and Krupat, eds.) (88) 413
NICHOLAS I
Nicholas I (Lincoln) (79) 479
NICHOLSON, NANCY
Robert Graves (Seymour) (96) 650
NICOLSON, SIR HAROLD
Harold Nicolson (Nicolson) (81) 406

NIEBUHR, REINHOLD
Reinhold Niebuhr (Fox) (86) 766
NIEMÖLLER, MARTIN
Martin Niemöller, 1892-1984 (Bentley)
(H-85) 298
NIETZSCHE, FRIEDRICH W.
Conversations with Nietzsche (Gilman, ed.)
(88) 199
Nietzsche (Safranski) (02) 584
Young Nietzsche (Pletsch) (92) 928
NIN, ANAÏS
Anaïs (Fitch) (94) 20
Anaïs Nin (Bair) (96) 34
Diary of Anaïs Nin, 1955-1966, The (Nin)
(77) 217
Diary of Anaïs Nin, 1966-1974, The (Nin)
(81) 234
Early Diary of Anaïs Nin, 1920-1923, The (Nin)
(83) 220
Early Diary of Anaïs Nin, 1923-1927, The (Nin)
(84) 257
Passionate Minds (Pierpont) (01) 694
NISA
Nisa (Shostak) (82) 559
NITZE, PAUL
Master of the Game, The (Talbott) (89) 544
NIXON, RICHARD M.
In the Arena (Nixon) (91) 441
Nixon, 1913-1962 (Ambrose) (88) 594
Nixon, 1962-1972 (Ambrose) (90) 608
Nixon, 1973-1990 (Ambrose) (92) 577
Nixon Off the Record (Crowley) (97) 622
No More Vietnams (Nixon) (86) 659
One of Us (Wicker) (92) 597
Price of Power, The (Hersh) (H-84) 361
Richard Milhous Nixon (Morris) (90) 694
RN (Nixon) (79) 605
Time of Illusion, The (Schell) (77) 822
NOAILLES, MARIE-LAURE DE
Six Exceptional Women (Lord) (95) 724
NOGUCHI, ISAMU
Noguchi East and West (Ashton) (93) 570
NOLAN, CHRISTOPHER
Under the Eye of the Clock (Nolan) (89) 868
NOONAN, PEGGY
What I Saw at the Revolution (Noonan) (91) 881
NORRIS, KATHLEEN
Cloister Walk, The (Norris) (97) 160
Dakota (Norris) (94) 200
NOWAK, JAN
Courier from Warsaw (Nowak) (H-83) 85
NULAND, SHERWIN B.
Lost in America (Nuland) (04) 469

O'BRIAN, PATRICK
Patrick O'Brian (King) (01) 707
O'BRIEN, FLANN
No Laughing Matter (Cronin) (91) 629
O'BRIEN, GEORGE
Village of Longing, The, and Dancehall Days
(O'Brien) (91) 851
O'CASEY, SEAN
Sean O'Casey (O'Connor) (89) 757
O'CONNOR, FLANNERY
Flannery O'Connor's South (Coles) (81) 350
Habit of Being, The (O'Connor) (80) 391
O'CONNOR, FRANK
Voices (Matthews) (84) 921

O'CONNOR, SANDRA DAY
Lazy B (O'Connor and Day) (03) 460
O'FAOLAIN, NUALA
Almost There (O'Faolain) (04) 22
OFFUTT, CHRIS
Same River Twice, The (Offutt) (94) 717
OGLETREE, CHARLES
I've Known Rivers (Lawrence-Lightfoot) (95) 384
O'HARA, FRANK
City Poet (Gooch) (94) 128
O'HARA, JOHN
Art of Burning Bridges, The (Wolff) (04) 45
Selected Letters of John O'Hara (O'Hara) (79) 656
O'KEEFFE, GEORGIA
Georgia O'Keeffe (Robinson) (90) 289
Georgia O'Keeffe (Turner) (00) 300
OLMSTED, FREDERICK LAW
Clearing in the Distance, A (Rybczynski) (00) 126
OLSEN, TILLIE
Working It Out (Ruddick and Daniels, eds.) (78) 937
OLSON, CHARLES
Charles Olson (Clark) (92) 88
O'NEILL, EUGENE
Selected Letters of Eugene O'Neill (O'Neill) (89) 771
O'NEILL, THOMAS P., Jr.
Man of the House (Novak, with Novak) (88) 524
Tip O'Neill and the Democratic Century (Farrell) (02) 791
O'NOLAN, BRIAN. See O'BRIEN, FLANN
OPPEN, GEORGE
Selected Letters of George Oppen, The (Oppen) (91) 726
ORTEGA Y GASSET, JOSÉ
Imperative of Modernity, The (Gray) (90) 410
ORTIZ, SIMON J.
I Tell You Now (Swann and Krupat, eds.) (88) 413
ORWELL, GEORGE
Orwell (Orwell) (86) 715
Orwell (Shelden) (92) 602
OSBORNE, JOHN
Better Class of Person, A (Osborne) (82) 45
OSWALD, LEE HARVEY
Oswald's Tale (Mailer) (96) 549
O'TOOLE, PETER
Loitering with Intent (O'Toole) (98) 522

PAGE, WALTER HINES
Walter Hines Page (Cooper) (78) 888
PAHLAVI, MOHAMMAD REZA. See MOHAMMAD REZA PAHLAVI
PAINE, THOMAS
Faces of Revolution (Bailyn) (91) 279
Tom Paine (Keane) (96) 760
PALMERSTON, HENRY JOHN TEMPLE, 3rd VISCOUNT
Palmerston (Bourne) (H-83) 329
PAPP, JOE
Joe Papp (Epstein) (95) 396
PARK, MUNGO
Mungo Park the African Traveler (Lupton) (80) 550

PARKS, GORDON
Voices in the Mirror (Parks) (91) 861
PARNELL, CHARLES STEWART
Charles Stewart Parnell (Lyons) (78) 169
PARSONS, ROBERT
Eminent Elizabethans (Rowse) (H-84) 147
PARTRIDGE, FRANCES
Love in Bloomsbury (Partridge) (82) 504
PARTRIDGE, RALPH
Love in Bloomsbury (Partridge) (82) 504
PASTERNAK, BORIS
Boris Pasternak, 1890-1928 (Barnes) (91) 96
Correspondence of Boris Pasternak and Olga Freidenberg, 1910-1954, The (Pasternak and Freidenberg) (83) 147
Letters (Pasternak, Tsvetayeva, and Rilke) (86) 514
Nightingale Fever (Hingley) (82) 555
Pasternak (Hingley) (84) 673
PASTERNAK, LEONID
Memoirs of Leonid Pasternak, The (Pasternak) (84) 528
PATER, WALTER
Walter Pater (Donoghue) (96) 810
PATON, ALAN
Alan Paton (Alexander) (95) 23
PATTON, GEORGE SMITH
Eisenhower's Lieutenants (Weigley) (82) 210
Last Days of Patton, The (Farago) (82) 428
PAULING, LINUS CARL
Force of Nature (Hager) (96) 286
PAZ, OCTAVIO
Itinerary (Paz) (01) 471
PEARSON, T. R.
World Unsuspected, A (Harris, ed.) (88) 984
PERCY, LEROY
Percys of Mississippi, The (Baker) (84) 682
PERCY, WALKER
Percys of Mississippi, The (Baker) (84) 682
Pilgrim in the Ruins (Tolson) (93) 633
Walker Percy (Samway) (98) 818
PERCY, WILLIAM ALEXANDER
Percys of Mississippi, The (Baker) (84) 682
PERDIKIDI, ERRIETA
Six Exceptional Women (Lord) (95) 724
PEREC, GEORGES
Georges Perec (Bellos) (95) 262
PERELMAN, S. J.
Last Laugh, The (Perelman) (82) 443
PERKINS, MAX
Max Perkins (Berg) (79) 428
PERÓN, EVA
Eva Perón (Fraser and Navarro) (82) 249
PERÓN, JUAN DOMINGO
Perón (Page) (H-84) 336
PERSHING, JOHN J.
Black Jack, Vol. I and Vol. II (Vandiver) (78) 96
Pershing (Smythe) (87) 660
PERSONS, TRUMAN STRECKFUS. See CAPOTE, TRUMAN GARCIA
PESKY, JOHNNY
Teammates, The (Halberstam) (04) 731
PETER THE GREAT
Fire and Water (de Jonge) (81) 335
Peter the Great (Massie) (81) 651
PHILBY, H. ST. JOHN
Treason in the Blood (Cave Brown) (95) 796

PHILBY, KIM
    Treason in the Blood (Cave Brown) (95) 796
PHILIP II OF SPAIN
    The Grand Strategy of Philip II (Parker) (00) 326
PHILLIPS, WILLIAM
    Partisan View, A (Phillips) (85) 677
PICASSO, PABLO
    Einstein, Picasso (Miller) (02) 235
    Life of Picasso, 1881-1906 (Richardson) (92) 431
    Life of Picasso, 1907-1917 (Richardson) (97) 511
PITT, WILLIAM
    William Pitt the Younger (Reilly) (80) 873
PIUS XII, POPE
    Hitler's Pope (Cornwell) (00) 396
PLATH, SYLVIA
    Bitter Fame (Stevenson) (90) 71
    Her Husband (Middlebrook) (04) 335
    Journals of Sylvia Plath, The (Plath) (83) 367
    Rough Magic (Alexander) (92) 689
    Silent Woman, The (Malcolm) (95) 719
    Sylvia Plath (Butscher, ed.) (78) 809
    Sylvia Plath (Wagner-Martin) (88) 874
PODHORETZ, NORMAN
    Breaking Ranks (Podhoretz) (80) 101
POE, EDGAR ALLAN
    Edgar A. Poe (Silverman) (92) 174
    Poe Log, 1809-1849 (Thomas and Jackson) (88) 701
POLLOCK, JACKSON
    Jackson Pollock (Naifeh and Smith) (91) 466
POPE, ALEXANDER
    Alexander Pope (Mack) (87) 20
POPPER, KARL
    Wittgenstein's Poker (Edmonds and Eidinow) (02) 875
PORTER, KATHERINE ANNE
    Katherine Anne Porter (Givner) (83) 376
    Letters of Katherine Anne Porter (Porter) (91) 517
POUND, EZRA
    End to Torment (H. D.) (80) 290
    Ezra Pound (Heymann) (77) 264
    Ezra Pound and Dorothy Shakespear, Their Letters, 1909-1914 (Pound and Shakespear) (85) 243
    Lives of the Modern Poets (Pritchard) (81) 520
    Pound/Ford (Pound and Ford) (83) 621
    Pound/Lewis (Pound and Lewis) (86) 747
    Pound/Williams (Pound and Williams) (97) 675
    Roots of Treason (Torrey) (84) 751
    Serious Character, A (Carpenter) (89) 779
POWELL, ANTHONY
    Infants of the Spring (Powell) (78) 447
    Strangers All Are Gone, The (Powell) (84) 833
POWELL, COLIN L.
    My American Journey (Powell, with Persico) (96) 494
POWELL, DAWN
    Diaries of Dawn Powell, 1931-1965, The (Powell) (96) 178
POWELL, PADGETT
    World Unsuspected, A (Harris, ed.) (88) 984
PRICE, REYNOLDS
    Clear Pictures (Price) (90) 104
    Learning a Trade (Price) (99) 470
    Whole New Life, A (Price) (95) 871
PRITCHETT, V. S.
    Life Sentences (Epstein) (98) 504

PROUST, MARCEL
    Marcel Proust (Carter) (01) 559
    Marcel Proust, Selected Letters, 1880-1903 (Proust) (84) 504
    Marcel Proust, Selected Letters, 1904-1909 (Proust) (90) 557
PUSHKIN, ALEKSANDR
    Pushkin (Feinstein) (00) 634
    Strolls with Pushkin (Tertz) (95) 773
PYM, BARBARA
    Life and Work of Barbara Pym, The (Salwak, ed.) (88) 471
    Very Private Eye, A (Pym) (85) 964

RAND, AYN
    Passionate Minds (Pierpont) (01) 694
RANKE, LEOPOLD VON
    Ranke (Krieger) (78) 690
RASPUTIN, GRIGORII
    Life and Times of Grigorii Rasputin, The (de Jonge) (H-83) 264
RATUSHINSKAYA, IRINA
    Grey Is the Color of Hope (Ratushinskaya) (89) 330
RAY, JAMES EARL
    Making of an Assassin, The (McMillan) (77) 470
REAGAN, RONALD
    American Life, An (Reagan) (91) 24
    Dutch (Morris) (00) 185
    Reagan (Cannon) (H-83) 362
    Reagan's America (Wills) (88) 725
    Triumph of Politics, The (Stockman) (87) 886
    What I Saw at the Revolution (Noonan) (91) 881
REEVE, CHRISTOPHER
    Still Me (Reeve) (99) 733
REID, JAN
    Bullet Meant for Me, The (Reid) (03) 119
REMBRANDT
    Rembrandt's House (Bailey) (79) 580
REMIET, PIERRE
    Master of Death (Camille) (97) 555
RENAULT, MARY
    Mary Renault (Sweetman) (94) 521
REVARD, CARTER
    I Tell You Now (Swann and Krupat, eds.) (88) 413
REXROTH, KENNETH
    Life of Kenneth Rexroth, A (Hamalian) (92) 426
RHODES, RICHARD
    Hole in the World, A (Rhodes) (91) 418
RHYS, JEAN
    Jean Rhys (Angier) (92) 379
    Letters of Jean Rhys, The (Rhys) (85) 554
RICCI, MATTEO
    Memory Palace of Matteo Ricci, The (Spence) (H-85) 309
RICH, ADRIENNE
    Working It Out (Ruddick and Daniels, eds.) (78) 937
RICHARDS, I. A.
    I. A. Richards (Russo) (90) 401
RICHARDS, LAURA ELIZABETH
    Province of Reason (Warner) (H-85) 368
RIDING, LAURA
    Robert Graves, 1926-1940 (Graves) (91) 706
    Robert Graves (Seymour) (96) 650

BIOGRAPHICAL WORKS BY SUBJECT

RILKE, RAINER MARIA
Letters (Pasternak, Tsvetayeva, and Rilke) (86) 514
Life of a Poet (Freedman) (97) 502
Rilke (Leppmann) (85) 757
RIMBAUD, ARTHUR
Rimbaud (Pettifils) (88) 765
Rimbaud (Robb) (01) 736
RIVERA, DIEGO
Diary of Frida Kahlo, The (Kahlo) (96) 182
RIVERA, EDWARD
Family Installments (Rivera) (83) 240
ROBESON, PAUL
Paul Robeson (Duberman) (90) 652
ROBINSON, EDWIN ARLINGTON
Lives of the Modern Poets (Pritchard) (81) 520
ROBINSON, JACKIE
Jackie Robinson (Rampersad) (98) 458
ROCKEFELLER, ABBY ALDRICH
Life of Nelson A. Rockefeller, 1908-1958, The
(Reich) (97) 506
ROCKEFELLER, JOHN D.
John D. (Hawke) (81) 459
Life of Nelson A. Rockefeller, 1908-1958, The
(Reich) (97) 506
Titan (Chernow) (99) 768
ROCKEFELLER, MARY TODHUNTER CLARK
Life of Nelson A. Rockefeller, 1908-1958, The
(Reich) (97) 506
ROCKEFELLER, NELSON A.
Imperial Rockefeller, The (Persico) (H-83) 206
Life of Nelson A. Rockefeller, 1908-1958, The
(Reich) (97) 506
RODGERS, RICHARD
Richard Rodgers (Hyland) (99) 658
RODIN, AUGUSTE
Rodin (Grunfeld) (88) 780
RODRIGUEZ, RICHARD
Hunger of Memory (Rodriguez) (82) 377
ROLLIN, BETTY
First, You Cry (Rollin) (77) 291
ROMMEL, ERWIN
Rommel's War in Africa (Heckmann) (82) 700
Trail of the Fox, The (Irving) (78) 856
ROOSEVELT, ELEANOR
Eleanor Roosevelt, 1884-1933 (Cook) (93) 253
Eleanor Roosevelt, 1933-1938 (Cook) (00) 204
No Ordinary Time (Goodwin) (95) 554
World of Love, A (Lash, ed.) (H-85) 521
World Made New, A (Glendon) (02) 884
ROOSEVELT, FRANKLIN D.
Eleanor Roosevelt, 1884-1933 (Cook) (93) 253
FDR, 1933-1937 (Davis) (87) 276
FDR, 1937-1940 (Davis) (94) 278
FDR, 1940-1943 (Davis) (01) 300
FDR (Miller) (H-84) 158
FDR (Morgan) (86) 269
First-Class Temperament, A (Ward) (90) 258
Franklin D. Roosevelt and American Foreign
Policy, 1932-1945 (Dallek) (80) 328
Kennedy and Roosevelt (Beschloss) (81) 467
No Ordinary Time (Goodwin) (95) 554
Progressive Presidents, The (Blum) (81) 665
Roosevelt and Churchill, 1939-1941 (Lash)
(77) 685

ROOSEVELT, THEODORE
Mornings on Horseback (McCullough) (82) 537
Progressive Presidents, The (Blum) (81) 665
Rise of Theodore Roosevelt, The (Morris) (80) 717
Theodore Rex (Morris) (02) 777
Theodore Roosevelt (Miller) (93) 783
Warrior and the Priest, The (Cooper) (H-84) 476
ROOSEVELTS, THE
Roosevelt Chronicles, The (Miller) (80) 726
Roosevelts, The (Collier, with Horowitz) (95) 664
ROREM, NED
Knowing When to Stop (Rorem) (95) 427
RORTY, AMELIE OKSENBERG
Working It Out (Ruddick and Daniels, eds.)
(78) 937
ROSE, WENDY
I Tell You Now (Swann and Krupat, eds.) (88) 413
ROSENKRANTZ, LINDA
My Life as a List (Rosenkrantz) (00) 554
ROSS, HAROLD
Genius in Disguise (Kunkel) (96) 303
ROSS, LILLIAN
Here but Not Here (Ross) (99) 360
ROSSETTI, CHRISTINA GEORGINA
Christina Rossetti (Marsh) (96) 107
ROTH, PHILIP
Facts, The (Roth) (89) 288
Leaving a Doll's House (Bloom) (97) 494
Patrimony (Roth) (92) 615
ROTHKO, MARK
Mark Rothko (Breslin) (94) 504
ROUSSEAU, JEAN-JACQUES
Jean-Jacques (Cranston) (H-84) 237
Noble Savage, The (Cranston) (92) 583
Rousseau (Miller) (H-85) 395
ROUVROY, LOUIS DE. See SAINT-SIMON,
DUC DE
ROVERE, RICHARD
Arrivals and Departures (Rovere) (77) 62
Final Reports (Rovere) (H-85) 141
RUBENS, PETER PAUL
Peter Paul Rubens (White) (88) 690
RUDDICK, SARAH
Working It Out (Ruddick and Daniels, eds.) (78) 937
RUFF, WILLIE
Willie and Dwike (Zinsser) (85) 1036
RUSK, DEAN
As I Saw It (Rusk) (91) 56
RUSKIN, EFFIE GRAY
Parallel Lives (Rose) (84) 662
RUSKIN, JOHN
Correspondence of Thomas Carlyle and John
Ruskin, The (Carlyle and Ruskin) (83) 153
John Ruskin, The Early Years (Hilton) (86) 487
John Ruskin, The Later Years (Hilton) (01) 499
Parallel Lives (Rose) (84) 662
Wider Sea, The (Hunt) (83) 908
RUSSELL, BERTRAND
Life of Bertrand Russell, The (Clark) (77) 423
Bertrand Russell, 1872-1921 (Monk) (97) 105
Bertrand Russell, 1921-1970 (Monk) (02) 78
Bertrand Russell (Moorehead) (94) 85
RUSSELL, CHARLES M.
Figures in a Western Landscape (Stevenson)
(95) 231

RYBCZYNSKI, WITOLD
  Most Beautiful House in the World, The
    (Rybczynski) (90) 582
RYCROFT, CHARLES
  Wing of Madness, The (Burston) (97) 885

SACCO, NICOLA
  Justice Crucified (Feuerlicht) (78) 487
SACKVILLE-WEST, VITA
  Art and Affection (Reid) (97) 66
  Vita (Glendinning) (84) 916
SAGAN, CARL
  Carl Sagan (Davidson) (00) 121
SAGE, LORNA
  Bad Blood (Sage) (03) 51
SAID, EDWARD W.
  Out of Place (Said) (00) 597
SAINT-EXUPÉRY, ANTOINE DE
  Saint-Exupéry (Schiff) (95) 683
ST. JUST, MARIA
  Five O'Clock Angel (Williams) (91) 291
SAINT-SIMON, DUC DE
  Saint-Simon and the Court of Louis XIV (Ladurie
    and Fitou) (02) 717
SAKHAROV, ANDREI
  Memoirs (Sakharov) (91) 582
  Sakharov (Lourie) (03) 703
SAKI. See MUNRO, HECTOR HUGH
SALINGER, J. D.
  In Search of J. D. Salinger (Hamilton) (89) 373
SALISBURY, HARRISON E.
  Journey for Our Times, A (Salisbury) (H-84) 252
SALISBURY, RALPH
  I Tell You Now (Swann and Krupat, eds.)
    (88) 413
SALTER, JAMES
  Burning the Days (Salter) (98) 138
SAND, GEORGE
  Flaubert-Sand (Flaubert and Sand) (94) 300
SANFORD, JOHN
  Color of the Air, The (Sanford) (86) 178
SAPIR, EDWARD
  Edward Sapir (Darnell) (91) 245
SAPOLSKY, ROBERT M.
  Primate's Memoir, A (Sapolsky) (02) 659
SAROYAN, WILLIAM
  Chance Meetings (Saroyan) (79) 92
SARRAUTE, NATHALIE
  Childhood (Sarraute) (85) 89
SARTON, MAY
  May Sarton (Peters) (98) 551
  World of Light, A (Sarton) (77) 941
SARTRE, JEAN-PAUL
  Adieux (Beauvoir) (85) 1
  Hearts and Minds (Madsen) (78) 379
  Letters to Sartre (Beauvoir) (93) 449
  Life/Situations (Sartre) (78) 529
  Sartre (Cohen-Solal) (88) 795
  War Diaries (Sartre) (86) 932
SAUD FAMILY
  House of Saud, The (Holden and Johns) (H-83) 195
SAVAGE, RICHARD
  Dr. Johnson and Mr. Savage (Holmes) (95) 176
SCALAPINO, LESLIE
  Zither and Autobiography (Scalapino) (04) 872

SCHAPIRO, MIRIAM
  Working It Out (Ruddick and Daniels, eds.)
    (78) 937
SCHIESLER, M. ANTOINETTE
  I've Known Rivers (Lawrence-Lightfoot) (95) 384
SCHLESINGER, ARTHUR, JR.
  Life in the Twentieth Century, A (Schlesinger)
    (01) 527
SCHOENBRUN, DAVID
  America Inside Out (Schoenbrun) (H-85) 22
SCHOLEM, GERSHOM
  Life in Letters, 1914-1982, A (Scholem) (03) 475
SCHOPENHAUER, ARTHUR
  Schopenhauer and the Wild Years of Philosophy
    (Safranski) (91) 711
SCHORER, MARK
  Pieces of Life (Schorer) (78) 657
SCHREINER, OLIVE
  Passionate Minds (Pierpont) (01) 694
SCHULZ, BRUNO
  Regions of the Great Heresy (Ficowski) (03) 648
SCHWARTZ, DELMORE
  Delmore Schwartz (Atlas) (78) 249
  Letters of Delmore Schwartz (Schwartz) (85) 548
  Poets in Their Youth (Simpson) (83) 608
SCOTT, WALTER
  Walter Scott (Millgate) (85) 989
SEABROOK, JOHN
  Deeper (98) 235
SEARS, CYNTHIA LOVELACE
  Working It Out (Ruddick and Daniels, eds.)
    (78) 937
SEE, CAROLYN LAWS
  On Gold Mountain (See) (96) 523
SEE, EDDY (MING QUAN)
  On Gold Mountain (See) (96) 523
SEE, FONG
  On Gold Mountain (See) (96) 523
SEE, LETTICIE (TICIE) PRUETT
  On Gold Mountain (See) (96) 523
SEE, LISA
  On Gold Mountain (See) (96) 523
SEE, RICHARD
  On Gold Mountain (See) (96) 523
SELZER, RICHARD
  Down from Troy (Selzer) (93) 244
SENGHOR, LÉOPOLD SÉDAR
  Black, French, and African (Vaillant) (91) 80
SENNETT, RICHARD
  Respect in a World of Inequality (04) 652
SÉVIGNÉ, MADAME DE
  Madame de Sévigné (Mossiker) (85) 595
SEXTON, ANNE
  Anne Sexton (Middlebrook) (92) 21
  Anne Sexton (Sexton) (78) 54
SHACKLETON, ERNEST
  Shackleton (Huntford) (87) 765
SHAKESPEAR, DOROTHY
  Ezra Pound and Dorothy Shakespear, Their Letters,
    1909-1914 (Pound and Shakespear) (85) 243
  Pound/Williams (Pound and Williams) (97) 675

BIOGRAPHICAL WORKS BY SUBJECT

SHAKESPEARE, WILLIAM
Real Shakespeare, The (Sams) (96) 619
Shakespeare (Fraser) (93) 723
Shakespeare (Honan) (00) 702
Shakespeare (Wells) (96) 704
Shakespeare's Professional Career (Thomson)
(93) 728
Young Shakespeare (Fraser) (89) 933

SHAW, GEORGE BERNARD
Bernard Shaw, 1856-1898 (Holroyd) (89) 89
Bernard Shaw, 1898-1918 (Holroyd) (90) 63
Bernard Shaw, 1918-1950 (Holroyd) (92) 34
Bernard Shaw, 1950-1991 (Holroyd) (94) 80
Bernard Shaw (Shaw) (89) 84
Collected Letters, 1911-1925 (Shaw) (86) 145

SHAW, ROBERT GOULD
Blue-Eyed Child of Fortune (Shaw) (93) 91

SHAWN, WILLIAM
Here but Not Here (Ross) (99) 360
Remembering Mr. Shawn's "New Yorker" (Mehta)
(99) 649

SHEED, WILFRID
Frank and Maisie (Sheed) (86) 313

SHELLEY, MARY WOLLSTONECRAFT
Claire Clairmont and the Shelleys, 1798-1879
(Gittings and Manton) (93) 157
Footsteps (Holmes) (86) 297
Letters of Mary Wollstonecraft Shelley, Vol. I, The
(Shelley) (81) 501

SHELLEY, PERCY BYSSHE
Claire Clairmont and the Shelleys, 1798-1879
(Gittings and Manton) (93) 157
Footsteps (Holmes) (86) 297

SHERIDAN, RICHARD
Traitor's Kiss, A (O'Toole) (99) 773

SHEVCHENKO, ARKADY N.
Breaking with Moscow (Shevchenko) (86) 81

SHILS, EDWARD
Portraits (Shils) (98) 639

SHIRER, WILLIAM L.
Twentieth Century Journey, Vol. II (Shirer)
(H-85) 451

SHOSTAKOVICH, DMITRI
Testimony (Shostakovich) (80) 808

SICKLES, DANIEL EDGAR
American Scoundrel (Keneally) (03) 28

SIDNEY, SIR PHILIP
Sir Philip Sidney (Duncan-Jones) (92) 761

SIMENON, GEORGES
Simenon (Assouline) (98) 712

SIMON, HERBERT
Models of My Life (Simon) (92) 519

SIMON, KATE
Bronx Primitive (Simon) (83) 80
Wider World, The (Simon) (87) 985

SIMON, NEIL
Rewrites (Simon) (97) 692

SIMPSON, EILEEN
Poets in Their Youth (Simpson) (83) 608

SINGER, ISAAC BASHEVIS
Isaac Bashevis Singer (Hadda) (98) 449
Lost in America (Singer) (82) 485

SIRICA, JOHN J.
To Set the Record Straight (Sirica) (80) 822

SITWELL, EDITH
Edith Sitwell (Glendinning) (82) 190

SITWELLS, THE
Sitwells, The (Pearson) (80) 763

SLATER, LAUREN
Lying (Slater) (01) 545

SMITH, AL
Empire Statesman (Slayton) (02) 248

SMITH, DAVID
World Unsuspected, A (Harris, ed.) (88) 984

SMITH, FLORENCE MARGARET "STEVIE"
Stevie (Barbera and McBrien) (88) 860

SMITH, GERRITT
Black Hearts of Men, The (Stauffer) (03) 74

SMITH, JAMES McCUNE
Black Hearts of Men, The (Stauffer) (03) 74

SMITH, WILLIAM
Map That Changed the World, The (Winchester)
(02) 503

SOCRATES
Socrates (Vlastos) (92) 766

SOLZHENITSYN, ALEXANDER
Alexander Solzhenitsyn (Thomas) (99) 24
Solzhenitsyn (Scammell) (85) 839
Solzhenitsyn and the Modern World (Ericson)
(94) 751
Solzhenitsyn in Exile (Dunlop, Haugh, and
Nicholson, eds.) (86) 843

SONDHEIM, STEPHEN
Stephen Sondheim (Secrest) (99) 728

SONTAG, SUSAN
Susan Sontag (Rollyson and Paddock) (01) 805

SOONG, CHARLIE
Soong Dynasty, The (Seagrave) (86) 852

SOREL, GEORGES
Cult of Violence, The (Roth) (81) 215

SOROS, GEORGE
Soros (Kaufman) (03) 794

SOTO, GARY
Summer Life, A (Soto) (91) 782

SOUTHERLAND, ELLEASE
World Unsuspected, A (Harris, ed.) (88) 984

SOYINKA, WOLE
Aké (Soyinka) (83) 10
Open Sore of a Continent, The (Soyinka) (97) 648

SPARK, MURIEL
Curriculum Vitae (Spark) (94) 196

SPEER, ALBERT
Albert Speer (Sereny) (96) 5
Spandau (Speer) (77) 764

SPENDER, STEPHEN
Journals, 1939-1983 (Spender) (87) 446

SPIELBERG, STEVEN
Steven Spielberg (McBride) (98) 731

SPIELREIN, SABINA
Secret Symmetry (Carotenuto) (83) 709

SPINOZA, BARUCH
Spinoza (Nadler) (00) 725
Spinoza and Other Heretics, Vol. I and Vol. II
(Yovel) (91) 768

STAFFORD, JEAN
Interior Castle, The (Hulbert) (93) 386
Jean Stafford (Goodman) (91) 471
Jean Stafford (Roberts) (89) 414
Poets in Their Youth (Simpson) (83) 608

STALIN, JOSEPH
Hitler and Stalin (Bullock) (93) 349
Koba the Dread (Amis) (03) 446
Stalin (Conquest) (92) 780
Time of Stalin, The (Antonov-Ovseyenko) (82) 845
Uncertain Partners (Goncharov, Lewis, and Xue)
(95) 809
STANTON, ELIZABETH CADY
Elizabeth Cady Stanton, Susan B. Anthony,
Correspondence, Writings, Speeches (Stanton
and Anthony) (82) 214
In Her Own Right (Griffith) (H-85) 230
Not for Ourselves Alone (Ward and Burns)
(00) 580
STAPLES, BRENT
Parallel Time (Staples) (95) 594
STEGNER, WALLACE
Wallace Stegner (Benson) (97) 871
STEIGER, ROD
Leaving a Doll's House (Bloom) (97) 494
STEIN, GERTRUDE
Passionate Minds (Pierpont) (01) 694
Six Exceptional Women (Lord) (95) 724
STEINBECK, JOHN
John Steinbeck (Parini) (96) 398
Steinbeck and Covici (Fensch) (80) 780
True Adventures of John Steinbeck, Writer, The
(Benson) (85) 927
STEINER, GEORGE
Errata (Steiner) (99) 261
STENDHAL
Lion for Love, A (Alter) (80) 497
Stendhal (Keates) (98) 726
STEPHEN, THOBY
Bloomsbury (Edel) (80) 88
STEPHENS, JOHN LLOYD
Return Passages (Ziff) (02) 698
STERN, RICHARD
Sistermony, A (Stern) (96) 716
STEVENS, MAY
Working It Out (Ruddick and Daniels, eds.)
(78) 937
STEVENS, WALLACE
Lives of the Modern Poets (Pritchard) (81) 520
Parts of a World (Brazeau) (84) 668
Wallace Stevens (Doggett and Buttel, eds.) (81) 879
Wallace Stevens (Longenbach) (92) 859
Wallace Stevens, 1879-1923 (Richardson) (87) 927
Wallace Stevens, 1923-1955 (Richardson) (89) 882
STEVENSON, ADLAI
Adlai Stevenson and the World (Martin) (78) 6
STEVENSON, ROBERT LOUIS
Footsteps (Holmes) (86) 297
Robert Louis Stevenson (Calder) (81) 694
Robert Louis Stevenson (McLynn) (96) 655
STEVENSON, WILLIAM S.
Man Called Intrepid, A (Stevenson) (77) 475
STIEGLITZ, ALFRED
Georgia O'Keeffe (Robinson) (90) 289
Stieglitz (Lowe) (H-84) 426
STIMPSON, CATHARINE R.
Working It Out (Ruddick and Daniels, eds.)
(78) 937
STONE, CHARLES A.
Province of Reason (Warner) (H-85) 368
STOWE, HARRIET BEECHER
Harriet Beecher Stowe (Hedrick) (95) 296

STRACHEY, LYTTON
Bloomsbury (Edel) (80) 88
Great Friends (Garnett) (81) 386
Love in Bloomsbury (Partridge) (82) 504
STREICHER, JULIUS
Julius Streicher (Bytwerk) (H-83) 234
STRINDBERG, AUGUST
August Strindberg (Lagercrantz) (85) 32
STUART, JESSE HILTON
Jesse (Richardson) (85) 494
STYRON, WILLIAM
Darkness Visible (Styron) (91) 184
William Styron (West) (99) 864
SUI SIN FAR
Sui Sin Far/Edith Maude Eaton (White-Parks)
(96) 732
SULLIVAN, LOUIS
Louis Sullivan (Twombly) (87) 499
SUN YAT-SEN
Sun Yat-sen (Schiffrin) (81) 777
SUSLOV, MIKHAIL ANDREYEVICH
All Stalin's Men (Medvedev) (H-85) 12
SWIFT, JONATHAN
Jonathan Swift (Glendinning) (00) 448
Swift, the Man, His Works, and the Age
(Ehrenpreis) (84) 849
SWOFFORD, ANTHONY
Jarhead (Swofford) (04) 373
SZILARD, LEO
Portraits (Shils) (98) 639

TALESE, GAY
Unto the Sons (Talese) (93) 842
TALLMOUNTAIN, MARY
I Tell You Now (Swann and Krupat, eds.) (88) 413
TATE, ALLEN
Poets in Their Youth (Simpson) (83) 608
TAYLOR, BAYARD
Return Passages (Ziff) (02) 698
TAYLOR, FREDERICK WINSLOW
One Best Way, The (Kanigel) (98) 607
TEASDALE, SARA
Sara Teasdale (Drake) (80) 741
TECUMSEH
Tecumseh (Sugden) (99) 746
TENNYSON, ALFRED, LORD
Poetry of Tennyson, The (Culler) (78) 665
TENSKWATAWA
Shawnee Prophet, The (Edmunds) (H-84) 409
TERTZ, ABRAM
Voice from the Chorus, A (Tertz) (77) 892
THANT, U
View from the UN (Thant) (79) 809
THATCHER, MARGARET
Downing Street Years, The (Thatcher) (94) 248
Iron Lady, The (Young) (90) 429
Path to Power, The (Thatcher) (96) 573
THEREMIN, LEON
Theremin (Glinsky) (01) 815
THEROUX, PAUL
Old Patagonian Express, The (Theroux) (80) 619
Riding the Iron Rooster (Theroux) (89) 726
Sir Vidia's Shadow (Theroux) (99) 711
THOMAS, DYLAN
Collected Letters of Dylan Thomas, The (Thomas)
(87) 132

THOMAS, EDWARD
  Great Friends (Garnett) (81) 386
THOMAS, NORMAN
  Norman Thomas (Swanberg) (77) 570
THOREAU, HENRY DAVID
  Henry Thoreau (Richardson) (87) 387
  Thoreau's Seasons (Lebeaux) (85) 895
THORNTON, NAOMI
  Working It Out (Ruddick and Daniels, eds.)
    (78) 937
THURBER, JAMES
  James Thurber (Kinney) (96) 389
  Thurber Letters, The (Thurber) (04) 752
TOKLAS, ALICE B.
  Six Exceptional Women (Lord) (95) 724
TOLKIEN, J. R. R.
  Letters of J. R. R. Tolkien, The (Tolkien)
    (82) 448
  Tolkien (Carpenter) (78) 851
TOLSTOY, LEV
  Tolstoi in the Sixties (Eikenbaum) (83) 816
  Tolstoi in the Seventies (Eikenbaum) (83) 821
  Tolstoy (Wilson) (89) 845
  Tolstoy and Gandhi, Men of Peace (Green)
    (H-84) 447
  Tolstoy's Letters, Vol. I and Vol. II (Tolstoy)
    (79) 754
TOOMER, JEAN
  Jean Toomer, Artist (McKay) (85) 489
  Wayward and the Seeking, The (Toomer)
    (81) 904
TORRIJOS, OMAR
  Getting to Know the General (Greene)
    (H-85) 168
TOTH, SUSAN ALLEN
  Blooming (Toth) (82) 55
  Ivy Days (Toth) (85) 466
TREVOR, WILLIAM
  Excursions in the Real World (Trevor) (95) 214
TRILLIN, ABE
  Messages from My Father (Trillin) (97) 573
TRILLIN, CALVIN
  Messages from My Father (Trillin) (97) 573
  Remembering Denny (Trillin) (94) 692
TRISTAN, FLORA
  Flora Tristan's London Journal, 1840 (Tristan)
    (82) 288
TROGDON, WILLIAM. See HEAT-MOON,
  WILLIAM LEAST
TROLLOPE, ANTHONY
  Anthony Trollope (Glendinning) (94) 29
  Trollope (Hall) (92) 825
TROTSKY, LEON
  Leon Trotsky (Howe) (79) 368
TRUFFAUT, FRANÇOIS
  Truffaut (de Baecque and Toubiana) (00) 772
TRUMAN, BESS
  Dear Bess (Truman) (H-84) 117
TRUMAN, HARRY S.
  Conflict and Crisis (Donovan) (78) 210
  Counsel to the President (Clifford, with Holbrooke)
    (92) 123
  Dear Bess (Truman) (H-84) 117
  Harry S. Truman and the Modern American
    Presidency (Ferrell) (H-84) 185
  Truman (McCullough) (93) 810
  Truman's Crises (Gosnell) (81) 836
  Tumultuous Years (Donovan) (H-83) 435

TRUTH, SOJOURNER
  Sojourner Truth (Painter) (97) 772
TSVETAYEVA, MARINA
  Letters (Pasternak, Tsvetayeva, and Rilke)
    (86) 514
  Marina Tsvetaeva (Feiler) (95) 464
  Marina Tsvetaeva (Karlinsky) (87) 520
  Passionate Minds (Pierpont) (01) 694
TURGENEV, IVAN
  Gentle Barbarian, The (Pritchett) (78) 340
  Turgenev (Schapiro) (80) 832
  Turgenev Letters (Turgenev) (84) 879
TURIN, LUCA
  Emperor of Scent, The (Burr) (04) 224
TWAIN, MARK
  Making of Mark Twain, The (Lauber) (86) 561
  Mark Twain A to Z (Rasmussen) (96) 452
  Mark Twain's Letters (Twain) (89) 535
  Return Passages (Ziff) (02) 698
TYNAN, KENNETH
  Letters (Tynan) (99) 474
  Life of Kenneth Tynan, The (Tynan) (88) 482

UNAMUNO, MIGUEL DE
  Private World, The (Unamuno) (85) 701
UPDIKE, JOHN
  Self-Consciousness (Updike) (90) 725

VALIAN, VIRGINIA
  Working It Out (Ruddick and Daniels, eds.)
    (78) 937
VAN BUREN, MARTIN
  Martin Van Buren (Niven) (H-84) 298
VANCE, CYRUS
  Hard Choices (Vance) (H-84) 180
VAN GOGH, VINCENT
  Van Gogh (Sweetman) (91) 843
VANN, JOHN PAUL
  Bright, Shining Lie, A (Sheehan) (89) 125
VANZETTI, BARTOLOMEO
  Justice Crucified (Feuerlicht) (78) 487
VARGAS LLOSA, MARIO
  Fish in the Water, A (Vargas Llosa) (95) 239
VASSILTCHIKOV, MARIE
  Berlin Diaries, 1940-1945 (Vassiltchikov) (88) 95
VELÁZQUEZ, DIEGO RODRÍGUEZ DE SILVA Y
  Velázquez (Brown) (87) 907
VERGHESE, ABRAHAM
  My Own Country (Verghese) (95) 515
VIDAL, GORE
  Gore Vidal (Kaplan) (00) 321
  Palimpsest (Vidal) (96) 561
  Screening History (Vidal) (93) 707
VIZENOR, GERALD
  I Tell You Now (Swann and Krupat, eds.)
    (88) 413
VOLTAIRE
  Voltaire (Mason) (82) 885
  Voltaire (Orieux) (80) 850
VONNEGUT, KURT
  Palm Sunday (Vonnegut) (82) 609
  Timequake (Vonnegut) (98) 760
VOROSHILOV, KLIMENT YEFREMOVICH
  All Stalin's Men (Medvedev) (H-85) 12

WALEY, ARTHUR
    Great Friends (Garnett) (81) 386
WALKER, ALICE
    Working It Out (Ruddick and Daniels, eds.)
    (78) 937
WALLACE, ALFRED RUSSEL
    Alfred Russel Wallace (Raby) (02) 30
    In Darwin's Shadow (Shermer) (03) 400
WALLACE, HENRY A.
    American Dreamer (Culver) (01) 24
WARNER, HARRY
    Empire of Their Own, An (Gabler) (89) 278
WARNER, JACK
    Empire of Their Own, An (Gabler) (89) 278
WARNER, SYLVIA TOWNSEND
    Letters (Warner) (84) 432
    Scenes of Childhood and Other Stories (Warner)
    (83) 679
WARREN, EARL
    Earl Warren (Pollack) (80) 255
    Earl Warren (White) (H-83) 109
    Memoirs of Earl Warren, The (Warren) (78) 567
    Super Chief (Schwartz) (H-84) 435
WARREN, ROBERT PENN
    Robert Penn Warren (Blotner) (98) 678
WASHINGTON, GEORGE
    Cincinnatus (Wills) (H-85) 78
    David Humphreys' "Life of General Washington"
    (Humphreys and Washington) (92) 147
WASSERMAN, LEW
    When Hollywood Had a King (Bruck) (04) 823
WAT, ALEKSANDER
    Aleksander Wat (Venclova) (97) 18
    My Century (Wat) (89) 571
WATKINS, PAUL
    Stand Before Your God (Watkins) (95) 752
WATSON, JAMES D.
    DNA (Watson and Berry) (04) 179
WATSON, RICHARD
    Philosopher's Demise, The (Watson) (96) 581
WATSON, THOMAS, SR.
    Maverick and His Machine, The (Maney) (04) 501
WAUGH, EVELYN
    Diaries of Evelyn Waugh, The (Waugh) (78) 258
    Evelyn Waugh (Hastings) (96) 237
    Evelyn Waugh, 1903-1939 (Stannard) (88) 293
    Evelyn Waugh, 1939-1966 (Stannard) (93) 275
    Letters of Evelyn Waugh, The (Waugh) (81) 489
WAYNE, JOHN
    John Wayne's America (Wills) (98) 477
WEBB, BEATRICE
    Letters of Sidney and Beatrice Webb, The (Webb
    and Webb) (79) 378
WEBB, SIDNEY
    Letters of Sidney and Beatrice Webb, The (Webb
    and Webb) (79) 378
WEBER, MAX
    Max Weber (Diggins) (97) 559
WEBSTER, DANIEL
    Daniel Webster (Bartlett) (79) 143
    Daniel Webster (Remini) (98) 221
    Great Triumvirate, The (Peterson) (88) 363
    One and Inseparable (Baxter) (H-85) 339
    Province of Reason (Warner) (H-85) 368
WEEKS, EDWARD
    Writers and Friends (Weeks) (83) 928

WEIGL, BRUCE
    Circle of Hanh, The (Weigl) (01) 190
WEIL, SIMONE
    Simone Weil (Fiori) (90) 738
    Simone Weil (Nevin) (93) 736
    Utopian Pessimist (McLellan) (91) 838
WEISSTEIN, NAOMI
    Working It Out (Ruddick and Daniels, eds.)
    (78) 937
WEIZMANN, CHAIM
    Chaim Weizmann (Reinharz) (86) 111
WELCH, DENTON
    Journals of Denton Welch, The (Welch)
    (85) 504
WELCHMAN, GORDON
    Hut Six Story, The (Welchman) (H-83) 201
WELLER, SHEILA
    Dancing at Ciro's (Weller) (04) 151
WELLES, ORSON
    Orson Welles (Leaming) (86) 709
WELLS, H. G.
    Great Friends (Garnett) (81) 386
    Group Portrait (Delbanco) (83) 312
    H. G. Wells (West) (85) 380
    Invisible Man, The (Coren) (94) 410
    Rebecca West (Rollyson) (97) 684
WELTY, EUDORA
    Conversations with Eudora Welty (Prenshaw)
    (85) 137
    Eudora (Waldron) (00) 240
    Eudora Welty's Achievement of Order (Kreyling)
    (81) 288
    One Writer's Beginnings (Welty) (85) 663
    Passionate Minds (Pierpont) (01) 694
WERFEL, FRANZ
    Franz Werfel (Jungk) (91) 313
WEST, DOROTHY
    Richer, the Poorer, The (West) (96) 641
WEST, JESSAMYN
    Woman Said Yes, The (West) (77) 928
WEST, MAE
    Passionate Minds (Pierpont) (01) 694
WEST, REBECCA
    Rebecca West (Glendinning) (88) 732
    Rebecca West (Rollyson) (97) 684
    Young Rebecca, The (West) (83) 932
WHARTON, EDITH
    Feast of Words, A (Wolff) (78) 314
    Letters of Edith Wharton, The (Wharton)
    (89) 475
    No Gifts from Chance (Benstock) (95) 544
WHEATLEY, PHILLIS
    Trials of Phillis Wheatley, The (Gates) (04) 774
WHITE, E. B.
    E. B. White (Elledge) (85) 209
    Letters of E. B. White (White) (77) 413
WHITE, KATHARINE S.
    Onward and Upward (Davis) (88) 630
WHITE, PATRICK
    Flaws in the Glass (White) (83) 257
    Patrick White (Marr) (93) 619
    Patrick White (White) (97) 656
WHITE, STANFORD
    Evelyn Nesbit and Stanford White (Mooney)
    (77) 260
WHITE, T. H.
    Great Friends (Garnett) (81) 386

BIOGRAPHICAL WORKS BY SUBJECT

WHITE, THEODORE H.
In Search of History (White) (79) 314
WHITEHEAD, ALFRED NORTH
Alfred North Whitehead, 1861-1910 (Lowe)
(86) 5
Alfred North Whitehead, 1910-1947 (Lowe)
(91) 20
WHITMAN, WALT
Walt Whitman (Kaplan) (81) 883
Walt Whitman (Zweig) (85) 984
Walt Whitman's America (Reynolds)
(96) 806
WHITNEY, DOROTHY PAYNE
Whitney Father, Whitney Heiress (Swanberg)
(81) 921
WHITNEY, WILLIAM COLLINS
Whitney Father, Whitney Heiress (Swanberg)
(81) 921
WIDEMAN, JOHN EDGAR
Brothers and Keepers (Wideman) (85) 57
Fatheralong (Wideman) (95) 227
WIDEMAN, ROBBY
Brothers and Keepers (Wideman) (85) 57
WIESEL, ELIE
All Rivers Run to the Sea (Wiesel) (96) 18
And the Sea Is Never Full (Wiesel) (00) 22
WILBERFORCE, WILLIAM
Wilberforce (Pollock) (79) 862
WILDE, OSCAR
Oscar Wilde (Ellmann) (89) 630
WILDE-MENOZZI, WALLIS
Mother Tongue (Wilde-Menozzi) (98) 567
WILDER, THORNTON
Enthusiast, The (Harrison) (84) 272
Journals of Thornton Wilder, 1939-1961, The
(Wilder) (86) 491
Thornton Wilder (Simon) (80) 815
WILHELM II
Last Kaiser, The (Tyler-Whittle) (78) 509
WILKOMIRSKI, BINJAMIN
Life in Pieces, A (Eskin) (03) 480
WILLIAM, DUKE OF CLARENCE
Mrs. Jordan's Profession (Tomalin) (96) 465
WILLIAMS, CHARLES
Charles Williams (Hadfield) (84) 153
WILLIAMS, GEORGE WASHINGTON
George Washington Williams (Franklin)
(86) 332
WILLIAMS, TED
Teammates, The (Halberstam) (04) 731
WILLIAMS, TENNESSEE
Five O'Clock Angel (Williams) (91) 291
Memoirs (Williams) (77) 494
Tom (Leverich) (96) 756
WILLIAMS, TERRY TEMPEST
Leap (Williams) (01) 513
WILLIAMS, WILLIAM CARLOS
Lives of the Modern Poets (Pritchard)
(81) 520
Pound/Williams (Pound and Williams)
(97) 675
William Carlos Williams (Mariani)
(82) 946
WILLS, CHERYLE
I've Known Rivers (Lawrence-Lightfoot)
(95) 384

WILSON, ANGUS
Angus Wilson (Drabble) (97) 48
WILSON, EDMUND
Edmund Wilson (Meyers) (96) 210
Forties, The (Wilson) (84) 309
Letters on Literature and Politics, 1912-1972
(Wilson) (78) 522
Nabokov-Wilson Letters, The (Nabokov and
Wilson) (80) 564
Thirties, The (Wilson) (81) 795
Writing Dangerously (Brightman) (93) 887
WILSON, EDWARD O.
Naturalist (Wilson) (95) 528
WILSON, SLOAN
What Shall We Wear to This Party? (Wilson)
(77) 901
WILSON, WOODROW
Progressive Presidents, The (Blum) (81) 665
Warrior and the Priest, The (Cooper)
(H-84) 476
Woodrow Wilson (Heckscher) (92) 914
Woodrow Wilson (Mulder) (79) 892
WINNER, LAUREN F.
Girl Meets God (Winner) (03) 330
WINTHROP, JOHN
John Winthrop (Bremer) (04) 386
WITTGENSTEIN, LUDWIG
Wittgenstein, A Life (McGuinness) (89) 918
Wittgenstein's Poker (Edmonds and Eidinow)
(02) 875
WITTGENSTEIN, PAUL
Wittgenstein's Nephew (Bernhard) (90) 908
WODEHOUSE, P. G.
P. G. Wodehouse (Donaldson) (83) 587
WOIWODE, LARRY
What I Think I Did (Woiwode) (01) 896
WOJTYŁA, KAROL. See JOHN PAUL II, POPE
WOLF, CHRISTA
Cassandra (Wolf) (85) 74
WOLFE, THOMAS
Look Homeward (Donald) (88) 502
WOLFF, GEOFFREY
Duke of Deception, The (Wolff) (80) 236
WOLFF, TOBIAS
In Pharaoh's Army (Wolff) (95) 347
This Boy's Life (Wolff) (90) 796
WOLLSTONECRAFT, MARY
Mary Wollstonecraft (Todd) (01) 569
WOLSEY, THOMAS CARDINAL
Statesman and Saint (Ridley) (H-84) 420
Thomas Cardinal Wolsey (Harvey)
(81) 800
WOOD, WILLIAM MADISON
Province of Reason (Warner) (H-85) 368
WOODHULL, VICTORIA
Other Powers (Goldsmith) (99) 601
WOODS, DONALD
Asking for Trouble (Woods) (82) 28
WOOLF, LEONARD
Art and Affection (Reid) (97) 66
Bloomsbury (Edel) (80) 88
WOOLF, VIRGINIA
Art and Affection (Reid) (97) 66
Bloomsbury (Edel) (80) 88
Diary of Virginia Woolf, 1915-1919, The (Woolf)
(78) 264

Diary of Virginia Woolf, 1920-1924, The (Woolf) (79) 147
Diary of Virginia Woolf, 1925-1930, The (Woolf) (81) 240
Diary of Virginia Woolf, 1931-1935, The (Woolf) (83) 185
Diary of Virginia Woolf, 1936-1941, The (Woolf) (85) 178
Great Friends (Garnett) (81) 386
Letters of Virginia Woolf, 1912-1922, The (Woolf) (77) 418
Letters of Virginia Woolf, 1923-1928, The (Woolf) (79) 382
Letters of Virginia Woolf, 1929-1931, The (Woolf) (80) 483
Letters of Virginia Woolf, 1932-1935, The (Woolf) (80) 487
Letters of Virginia Woolf, 1936-1941, The (Woolf) (81) 506
Passionate Apprentice, A (Woolf) (92) 607
Virginia Woolf (Gordon) (86) 927
Virginia Woolf (King) (96) 794
Virginia Woolf (Lee) (98) 805
WORDSWORTH, DOROTHY
Gang, The (Worthen) (02) 321
WORDSWORTH, WILLIAM
Gang, The (Worthen) (02) 321
Hidden Wordsworth, The (Johnston) (99) 364
William Wordsworth (Gill) (90) 904
WRIGHT, FRANK LLOYD
Frank Lloyd Wright (Secrest) (93) 303
Many Masks (Gill) (88) 534
WRIGHT, ORVILLE
To Conquer the Air (Tobin) (04) 766
Wilbur and Orville (Howard) (88) 959
WRIGHT, RICHARD
Richard Wright (Rowley) (02) 703
Richard Wright, Daemonic Genius (Walker) (89) 722
Richard Wright Reader (Wright) (79) 597
WRIGHT, WILBUR
To Conquer the Air (Tobin) (04) 766
Wilbur and Orville (Howard) (88) 959
YATES, RICHARD
Tragic Honesty, A (Bailey) (04) 770
YEAGER, CHUCK
Yeager (Yeager and Janos) (86) 974

YEATS, ELIZABETH CORBET (LOLLIE)
Family Secrets (Murphy) (96) 253
YEATS, JOHN BUTLER
Family Secrets (Murphy) (96) 253
YEATS, JOHN BUTLER (JACK), JR.
Family Secrets (Murphy) (96) 253
YEATS, SUSAN MARY (LILY)
Family Secrets (Murphy) (96) 253
YEATS, SUSAN POLLEXFEN
Family Secrets (Murphy) (96) 253
YEATS, WILLIAM BUTLER
Collected Letters of W. B. Yeats, 1865-1895, The (Yeats) (87) 142
Family Secrets (Murphy) (96) 253
Gonne-Yeats Letters 1893-1938, The (Gonne and Yeats) (94) 368
Lives of the Modern Poets (Pritchard) (81) 520
Pound/Williams (Pound and Williams) (97) 675
W. B. Yeats (Jeffares) (91) 876
W. B. Yeats, 1865-1914 (Foster) (98) 809
YELTSIN, BORIS
Yeltsin (Aron) (01) 940
YORKE, HENRY VINCENT. See GREEN, HENRY
YOUNG, AL
World Unsuspected, A (Harris, ed.) (88) 984
YOUNG, LESTER
Lester Leaps In (Daniels) (03) 470
YOUNG, MARILYN
Working It Out (Ruddick and Daniels, eds.) (78) 937
YOUNGBLOOD, JOHNNY RAY
Upon this Rock (Freedman) (94) 827
YOURCENAR, MARGUERITE
Marguerite Yourcenar (Savigneau) (94) 500
YU, CONNIE YOUNG
Working It Out (Ruddick and Daniels, eds.) (78) 937

ZHOU ENLAI
Zhou Enlai (Wilson) (H-85) 526
ZOLA, ÉMILE
Zola (Brown) (96) 847
ZUKOR, ADOLPH
Empire of Their Own, An (Gabler) (89) 278

CATEGORY INDEX

1977-2004

AUTOBIOGRAPHY, MEMOIRS,
DIARIES, and LETTERS 909
BIOGRAPHY 914
CURRENT AFFAIRS 918
ECONOMICS 921
EDUCATION 921
ESSAYS 921
ETHICS and LAW. 924
FICTION. 924
FINE ARTS, FILM, and
MUSIC 938
HISTORY 938
LANGUAGE. 946
LITERARY BIOGRAPHY 946

LITERARY CRITICISM, HISTORY,
and THEORY. 950
MEDIA. 953
NATURE, NATURAL HISTORY,
and the ENVIRONMENT 953
PHILOSOPHY and RELIGION 953
POETRY and DRAMA 955
PSYCHOLOGY 958
SCIENCE, HISTORY OF SCIENCE,
TECHNOLOGY, and MEDICINE. . . . 959
SOCIOLOGY, ARCHAEOLOGY,
and ANTHROPOLOGY 961
TRAVEL. 961
WOMEN'S ISSUES 962

ANTHROPOLOGY. *See* SOCIOLOGY,
ARCHAEOLOGY, and ANTHROPOLOGY

ARCHAEOLOGY. *See* SOCIOLOGY,
ARCHAEOLOGY, and ANTHROPOLOGY

AUTOBIOGRAPHY, MEMOIRS, DIARIES, and
LETTERS
Abba Eban (Eban) (78) 1
Accidental Autobiography, An (Harrison) (97) 1
Adieux (Beauvoir) (85) 1
Aké (Soyinka) (83) 10
Akhmatova Journals, 1938-41, The (Chukovskaya)
(95) 19
Albert Einstein (Einstein) (80) 19
All God's Children Need Traveling Shoes (Angelou)
(87) 25
All Rivers Run to the Sea (Wiesel) (96) 18
Almost There (O'Faolain) (04) 22
Always Straight Ahead (Neuman) (94) 11
Amateur, The (Lesser) (00) 10
Amazing Grace (Norris) (99) 40
America Inside Out (Schoenbrun) (H-85) 22
American Chica (Arana) (02) 35
American Childhood, An (Dillard) (88) 25
American Life, An (Reagan) (91) 24
American Requiem, An (Carroll) (97) 38
And the Sea Is Never Full (Wiesel) (00) 22
And the Walls Came Tumbling Down (Abernathy)
(90) 39
Angela's Ashes (McCourt) (97) 43
Anne Sexton (Sexton) (78) 54
Another World, 1897-1917 (Eden) (78) 59
Answer to History (Mohammad Reza Pahlavi) (81) 47
Antonin Artaud (Artaud) (77) 52
Anything Your Little Heart Desires (Bosworth) (98) 68
Arna Bontemps-Langston Hughes Letters, 1925-1927
(Bontemps and Hughes) (81) 57
Around the Day in Eighty Worlds (Cortázar) (87) 45
Arrivals and Departures (Rovere) (77) 62
As I Saw It (Rusk) (91) 56
Asking for Trouble (Woods) (82) 28
Assault on Mount Helicon (Barnard) (85) 27

Atlantic High (Buckley) (83) 29
Autobiography of a Face (Grealy) (95) 56
Autobiography of Values (Lindbergh) (79) 43
Bad Blood (Sage) (03) 51
Basil Street Blues (Holroyd) (01) 64
Becoming a Doctor (Konner) (88) 77
Becoming a Man (Monette) (93) 62
Berlin Diaries, 1940-1945 (Vassiltchikov) (88) 95
Bernard Shaw, 1856-1898 (Holroyd) (89) 89
Bernard Shaw, Collected Letters, 1926-1950 (Shaw)
(89) 84
Better Class of Person, A (Osborne) (82) 45
Between Friends (Arendt and McCarthy) (96) 73
Beyond the Dragon's Mouth (Naipaul) (86) 56
Blessings in Disguise (Guinness) (87) 71
Blind Ambition (Dean) (77) 96
Blinded by the Right (Brock) (03) 83
Bloods (Terry) (H-85) 48
Blooming (Toth) (82) 55
Blue-Eyed Child of Fortune (Duncan, ed.) (93) 91
Body Toxic (Antonetta) (02) 97
Born on the Fourth of July (Kovic) (77) 115
Borrowed Time (Monette) (89) 112
Boston Boy (Hentoff) (87) 84
Boswell (Boswell) (78) 140
Boyhood (Coetzee) (98) 134
Breaking Ranks (Podhoretz) (80) 101
Breaking with Moscow (Shevchenko) (86) 81
Broken Cord, The (Dorris) (90) 76
Bronx Primitive (Simon) (83) 80
Brothers and Keepers (Wideman) (85) 57
Bullet Meant for Me, The (Reid) (03) 119
Burning the Days (Salter) (98) 138
Byron's Letters and Journals, 1822-1823 (Byron)
(81) 108
Cassandra (Wolf) (85) 74
Chance Meetings (Saroyan) (79) 92
Charles Darwin's Letters (Darwin) (97) 148
Cherry (Karr) (01) 181
Chief, The (Morrow) (86) 121
Childhood (Sarraute) (85) 89
China Men (Kingston) (81) 137
Chinabound (Fairbank) (H-83) 61

Christopher and His Kind (Isherwood) (77) 158
Circle of Hanh, The (Weigl) (01) 190
Clear Pictures (Price) (90) 104
Clinging to the Wreckage (Mortimer) (83) 127
Cloak of Light, A (Morris) (86) 140
Cloister Walk, The (Norris) (97) 160
Collected Letters, 1911-1925 (Shaw) (86) 145
Collected Letters of Dylan Thomas, The (Thomas) (87) 132
Collected Letters of Joseph Conrad, 1861-1897, The (Conrad) (84) 178
Collected Letters of Joseph Conrad, 1898-1902, The (Conrad) (87) 138
Collected Letters of Joseph Conrad, 1903-1907, The (Conrad) (89) 175
Collected Letters of Katherine Mansfield, 1903-1917, The (Mansfield) (85) 106
Collected Letters of Katherine Mansfield, 1918-1919, The (Mansfield) (88) 165
Collected Letters of W. B. Yeats, 1865-1895, The (Yeats) (87) 142
Collected Prose, The (Bishop) (85) 121
Collected Prose (Celan) (91) 157
Collected Prose (Lowell) (88) 173
Collected Works (Metcalf) (98) 199
Color of the Air, The (Sanford) (86) 178
Colored People (Gates) (95) 141
Complete Letters of Sigmund Freud to Wilhelm Fliess, The (Freud) (86) 187
Complete Notebooks of Henry James, The (James) (88) 179
Complete Works of Isaac Babel, The (Babel) (02) 158
Confederates in the Attic (Horwitz) (99) 208
Congregation (Rosenberg, ed.) (88) 189
Conversations with Czesław Miłosz (Miłosz) (88) 194
Conversations with Eudora Welty (Prenshaw, ed.) (85) 137
Correspondence of Boris Pasternak and Olga Freidenberg, 1910-1954, The (Pasternak and Freidenberg) (83) 147
Correspondence of Thomas Carlyle and John Ruskin, The (Carlyle and Ruskin) (83) 153
Correspondence of Walter Benjamin, 1910-1940, The (Benjamin) (95) 149
Counsel to the President (Clifford, with Holbrooke) (92) 123
Courier from Warsaw (Nowak) (H-83) 85
Crisis (Jordan) (H-83) 93
Crossing (McCloskey) (00) 155
Curriculum Vitae (Spark) (94) 196
Dakota (Norris) (94) 200
Dancehall Days and The Village of Longing (O'Brien) (91) 851
Dancing at Ciro's (Weller) (04) 151
Danse Macabre (King) (82) 171
Darkness Visible (Styron) (91) 184
Darlinghissima (Flanner) (86) 213
Daughter of Destiny (Bhutto) (90) 152
Day I Became an Autodidact, The (Hailey) (89) 222
Days of Grace (Ashe and Rampersad) (94) 213
Days of Obligation (Rodriguez) (93) 204
Dear Bess (Truman) (H-84) 117
Deeper (Seabrook) (98) 235
Diaries (Isherwood) (98) 249
Diaries of a Cabinet Minister, The (Crossman) (77) 211
Diaries of Dawn Powell, 1931-1965, The (Powell) (96) 178
Diaries of Evelyn Waugh, The (Waugh) (78) 258
Diary, 1953-1956 (Gombrowicz) (89) 236
Diary, 1957-1961 (Gombrowicz) (90) 177
Diary, 1961-1966 (Gombrowicz) (94) 225
Diary of Anaïs Nin, 1955-1966, The (Nin) (77) 217
Diary of Anaïs Nin, 1966-1974, The (Nin) (81) 234

Diary of Frida Kahlo, The (Kahlo) (96) 182
Diary of H. L. Mencken, The (Mencken) (91) 211
Diary of James C. Hagerty, The (Hagerty) (H-84) 125
Diary of Virginia Woolf, 1915-1919, The (Woolf) (78) 264
Diary of Virginia Woolf, 1920-1924, The (Woolf) (79) 147
Diary of Virginia Woolf, 1925-1930, The (Woolf) (81) 240
Diary of Virginia Woolf, 1931-1935, The (Woolf) (83) 185
Diary of Virginia Woolf, 1936-1941, The (Woolf) (85) 178
Different Person, A (Merrill) (94) 234
Dispatches (Herr) (78) 272
Disturbing the Peace (Havel) (91) 216
DNA (Watson and Berry) (04) 179
Dostoevsky (Dostoevsky) (77) 230
Down from Troy (Selzer) (93) 244
Downing Street Years, The (Thatcher) (94) 248
Dream of the Golden Mountains, The (Cowley) (81) 249
Dreaming Me (Willis) (02) 212
Dressing Station, The (Kaplan) (03) 238
Drowned and the Saved, The (Levi) (89) 250
Dual Autobiography, A (Durant and Durant) (78) 280
Duke of Deception, The (Wolff) (80) 236
Early Diary of Anaïs Nin, 1920-1923, The (Nin) (83) 220
Early Diary of Anaïs Nin, 1923-1927, The (Nin) (84) 257
Ease My Sorrows (Kopelev) (84) 263
Eisenhower Diaries, The (Eisenhower) (82) 199
Elegy for Iris (Bayley) (00) 213
Elia Kazan (Kazan) (89) 257
Elizabeth Cady Stanton, Susan B. Anthony (Stanton and Anthony) (82) 214
Elsewhere Community, The (Kenner) (01) 272
Emerson in His Journals (Emerson) (83) 224
End to Torment (H. D.) (80) 290
Ernest Hemingway, Selected Letters, 1917-1961 (Hemingway) (82) 245
Errata (Steiner) (99) 261
Excursions in the Real World (Trevor) (95) 214
Execution by Hunger (Dolot) (86) 254
Experience (Amis) (01) 290
Ezra Pound and Dorothy Shakespear, Their Letters, 1909-1914 (Pound and Shakespear) (85) 243
Factory of Facts, The (Sante) (99) 278
Facts, The (Roth) (89) 288
Faith, Sex, Mystery (Gilman) (88) 303
False Starts (Braly) (77) 269
Familiar Spirits (Lurie) (02) 271
Family Installments (Rivera) (83) 240
Family Sayings (Ginzburg) (85) 255
Fatheralong (Wideman) (95) 227
Faulkner, a Comprehensive Guide to the Brodsky Collection, Vol. II (Faulkner) (85) 266
Final Entries, 1945 (Goebbels) (79) 212
Final Reports (Rovere) (H-85) 14
Finding the Center (Naipaul) (85) 281
First Lady from Plains (Carter) (H-85) 146
First, You Cry (Rollin) (77) 291
Fish in the Water, A (Vargas Llosa) (95) 239
Five O'Clock Angel (Williams) (91) 291
Flaubert-Sand (Flaubert and Sand) (94) 300
Flaws in the Glass (White) (83) 257
Flora Tristan's London Journal, 1840 (Tristan) (82) 288
Flotsam and Jetsam (Higgins) (03) 307
Flower and the Nettle, The (Lindbergh) (77) 294
Footsteps (Holmes) (86) 297
For the Love of It (Booth) (00) 273
Forties, The (Wilson) (84) 309

CATEGORY INDEX

Frank and Maisie (Sheed) (86) 313
Fringes of Power, The (Colville) (86) 320
Gathering Evidence (Bernhard) (87) 317
General's Life, A (Bradley and Blair) (H-84) 171
Gerard Manley Hopkins, Selected Letters (Hopkins) (91) 343
Getting to Know the General (Greene) (H-85) 168
Gift, The (H. D.) (83) 278
Girl, Interrupted (Kaysen) (94) 360
Girl Meets God (Winner) (03) 330
Give Us Each Day (Dunbar-Nelson) (86) 349
Goebbels Diaries, The (Goebbels) (H-84) 176
Goldwater (Goldwater and Casserly) (89) 321
Gonne-Yeats Letters 1893-1938, The (Gonne and Yeats) (94) 368
Good Life, A (Bradlee) (96) 316
Good Times, The (Baker) (90) 309
Great Books (Denby) (97) 360
Great Friends (Garnett) (81) 386
Grey Is the Color of Hope (Ratushinskaya) (89) 330
Growing Seasons, The (Hynes) (04) 312
Growing Up (Baker) (83) 317
Grumbles from the Grave (Heinlein) (91) 372
Guadalcanal Remembered (Merillat) (H-83) 181
Gulag Archipelago, The (Solzhenitsyn) (78) 370
Guston in Time (Feld) (04) 320
Habit of Being, The (O'Connor) (80) 391
Haing Ngor (Ngor, with Warner) () (89) 335
Hand to Mouth (Auster) (98) 374
Hard Choices (Vance) (H-84) 180
Harold Nicolson (Nicolson) (81) 406
Harp (Dunne) (90) 364
Heartbreaking Work of Staggering Genius, A (Eggers) (01) 389
Heaven's Coast (Doty) (97) 368
Henry James Letters, 1883-1895 (James) (81) 421
Henry James Letters, 1895-1916 (James) (85) 368
Here but Not Here (Ross) (99) 360
Hermit in Paris (Calvino) (04) 339
Hole in the World, A (Rhodes) (91) 418
Home and Exile (Achebe) (01) 408
Hornes, The (Buckley) (87) 410
House of Trees, A (Colebrook) (88) 403
House with Four Rooms, A (Godden) (90) 396
How I Grew (McCarthy) (88) 407
How It Was (Hemingway) (77) 362
Hunger of Memory (Rodriguez) (82) 377
Hungry for the World (Barnes) (01) 432
Hut Six Story, The (Welchman) (H-83) 201
I Tell You Now (Swann and Krupat, eds.) (88) 413
In Pharaoh's Army (Wolff) (95) 347
In Search of History (White) (79) 314
In the Arena (Nixon) (91) 441
In Touch (Bowles) (95) 372
Indian Country (Matthiessen) (H-85) 241
Infants of the Spring (Powell) (78) 447
Intellectual Follies, The (Abel) (85) 451
Interrupted Life, An (Hillesum) (85) 456
Iris and Her Friends (Bayley) (00) 439
Ìsarà (Soyinka) (90) 435
Itinerary (Paz) (01) 471
Ivy Days (Toth) (85) 466
Jarhead (Swofford) (04) 373
John Glenn (Glenn and Taylor) (00) 443
Joseph Cornell's Theater of the Mind (Cornell) (95) 408
Journals (Ginsberg) (78) 483
Journals, 1939-1983 (Spender) (87) 446
Journals of Denton Welch, The (Welch) (85) 504
Journals of John Cheever, The (Cheever) (92) 393
Journals of Sylvia Plath, The (Plath) (83) 367
Journals of Thornton Wilder, 1939-1961, The (Wilder) (86) 491

Journey for Our Times, A (Salisbury) (H-84) 252
Journey into Space (Murray) (90) 464
Keeping Faith (Carter) (H-83) 239
Knowing When to Stop (Rorem) (95) 427
Land of Ulro, The (Miłosz) (85) 520
Last Laugh, The (Perelman) (82) 433
Last Stands (Masters) (83) 386
Lazarus (Malraux) (78) 515
Lazy B (O'Connor and Day) (03) 460
Leap (Williams) (01) 513
Leaving a Doll's House (Bloom) (97) 494
Ledge Between the Streams, The (Mehta) (85) 539
Less Than One (Brodsky) (87) 471
Letters (Pasternak, Tsvetayeva, and Rilke) (86) 514
Letters (Tynan) (99) 474
Letters (Warner) (84) 432
Letters and Drawings of Bruno Schulz (Schulz) (89) 470
Letters of Archibald MacLeish (MacLeish) (84) 436
Letters of Delmore Schwartz (Schwartz) (85) 548
Letters of D. H. Lawrence, September 1901-May 1913, The (Lawrence) (80) 469
Letters of D. H. Lawrence, October 1916-June 1921, The (Lawrence) (86) 520
Letters of D. H. Lawrence, June 1921-March 1924, The (Lawrence) (88) 466
Letters of D. H. Lawrence, March 1924-March 1927, The (Lawrence) (90) 512
Letters of D. H. Lawrence, March 1927-November 1928, The (Lawrence) (92) 417
Letters of D. H. Lawrence, November 1928-February 1930, The (Lawrence) (94) 467
Letters of E. B. White (White) (77) 413
Letters of Edith Wharton, The (Wharton) (89) 475
Letters of Evelyn Waugh, The (Waugh) (81) 489
Letters of Gustave Flaubert, 1830-1857, The (Flaubert) (81) 494
Letters of Gustave Flaubert, 1857-1880, The (Flaubert) (83) 395
Letters of Henry Adams, 1858-1892, The (Adams) (84) 441
Letters of Henry Adams, 1892-1918, The (Adams) (90) 516
Letters of Jean Rhys, The (Rhys) (85) 554
Letters of John Cheever, The (Cheever) (89) 480
Letters of J. R. R. Tolkien, The (Tolkien) (82) 448
Letters of Katherine Anne Porter (Porter) (91) 517
Letters of Lewis Carroll, ca. 1837-1885, The (Carroll) (80) 474
Letters of Margaret Fuller, 1817-1841, The (Fuller) (84) 449
Letters of Margaret Fuller, 1842-1844, The (Fuller) (85) 559
Letters of Marshall McLuhan (McLuhan) (89) 484
Letters of Mary Wollstonecraft Shelley, Vol. I, The (Shelley) (81) 501
Letters of Rudyard Kipling, 1872-89, The (Kipling) (92) 421
Letters of Rudyard Kipling, 1890-99, The (Kipling) (92) 421
Letters of Samuel Johnson, The (Johnson) (93) 444
Letters of Sidney and Beatrice Webb, The (Webb and Webb) (79) 378
Letters of T. S. Eliot, The (Eliot) (89) 488
Letters of Vachel Lindsay (Lindsay) (80) 479
Letters of Virginia Woolf, 1912-1922, The (Woolf) (77) 418
Letters of Virginia Woolf, 1923-1928, The (Woolf) (79) 382
Letters of Virginia Woolf, 1929-1931, The (Woolf) (80) 483
Letters of Virginia Woolf, 1932-1935, The (Woolf) (80) 487

Letters of Virginia Woolf, 1936-1941, The (Woolf)
  (81) 506
Letters on Literature and Politics, 1912-1972 (Wilson)
  (78) 522
Letters to Friends, Family, and Editors (Kafka)
  (78) 526
Letters to Olga (Havel) (89) 492
Letters to Ottla and the Family (Kafka) (83) 401
Letters to Sartre (Beauvoir) (93) 449
Lewis and Clark Journals, The (Lewis and Clark)
  (04) 442
Liar's Club, The (Karr) (96) 426
Life As We Know It (Bérubé) (97) 498
Life in Letters, 1914-1982, A (Scholem) (03) 475
Life in Our Times, A (Galbraith) (82) 458
Life in Pieces, A (Eskin) (03) 480
Life in the Twentieth Century, A (Schlesinger) (01) 527
Life It Brings, The (Bernstein) (88) 477
Life So Far (Friedan) (01) 532
Little Wilson and Big God (Burgess) (88) 497
Living History (Clinton) (04) 455
Living to Tell the Tale (García Márquez) (04) 460
Loitering with Intent (O'Toole) (98) 522
Lord Byron, Selected Letters and Journals (Byron)
  (83) 418
Lord God Made Them All, The (Herriot) (82) 480
Lost in America (Nuland) (04) 469
Lost in America (Singer) (82) 485
Lost in Translation (Hoffman) (90) 539
Love in Bloomsbury (Partridge) (82) 504
Loyalties (Bernstein) (90) 543
Lying (Slater) (01) 545
M. F. K. Fisher (Barr, Moran, and Moran, eds.) (99)
  501
Magdalena and Balthasar (Ozment) (87) 508
Magic Lantern, The (Bergman) (89) 525
Man of the House (O'Neill, with Novak) (88) 524
Marcel Proust, Selected Letters, 1880-1903 (Proust)
  (84) 504
Marcel Proust, Selected Letters, 1904-1909 (Proust)
  (90) 557
Marcus Garvey and Universal Negro Improvement
  Association Papers, The (Hill, ed.) (H-85) 283
Margin of Hope, A (Howe) (83) 451
Mark Twain's Letters (Twain) (89) 535
Me and Shakespeare (Gollob) (03) 518
Memoir of a Thinking Radish (Medawar) (87) 541
Memoir of Misfortune, A (Su) (02) 515
Memoirs (Sakharov) (91) 582
Memoirs (Williams) (77) 494
Memoirs of Earl Warren, The (Warren) (78) 567
Memoirs of Leonid Pasternak, The (Pasternak) (84) 528
Messages from My Father (Trillin) (97) 573
Microworlds (Lem) (86) 595
Midwife's Tale, A (Ulrich) (91) 596
Models of My Life (Simon) (92) 519
Moksha (Huxley) (79) 451
Moonrise, Moonset (Konwicki) (88) 579
Moshe Dayan (Dayan) (77) 513
Most Beautiful House in the World, The (Rybczynski)
  (90) 582
Mother Tongue (Wilde-Menozzi) (98) 567
My American Journey (Powell, with Persico) (96) 494
My Century (Wat) (89) 571
My Father's Island (Angermeyer) (91) 614
My Life as a List (Rosenkrantz) (00) 554
My Own Country (Verghese) (95) 515
My Sky Blue Trades (Birkerts) (03) 549
My Traitor's Heart (Malan) (91) 624
My War Gone By, I Miss It So (Loyd) (01) 604
Nabokov-Wilson Letters, The (Nabokov and Wilson)
  (80) 564
Names, The (Momaday) (78) 594

Namesake (Goldberg) (83) 518
Native Realm (Miłosz) (81) 597
Naturalist (Wilson) (95) 528
Nearer, My God (Buckley) (98) 575
Negotiating with the Dead (Atwood) (03) 568
New Mencken Letters, The (Mencken) (78) 603
New York Jew (Kazin) (79) 475
Nisa (Shostak) (82) 559
Nixon Off the Record (Crowley) (97) 622
No More Vietnams (Nixon) (86) 659
Noël Coward Diaries, The (Coward) (83) 549
Noonday Demon, The (Solomon) (02) 596
Notebooks (Fugard) (85) 653
Now and Then (Buechner) (84) 624
Of America East and West (Horgan) (H-85) 334
Old Glory (Raban) (82) 580
Old Patagonian Express, The (Theroux) (80) 619
On Borrowed Words (Stavans) (02) 600
On Writing (King) (01) 675
Once Again for Thucydides (Handke) (99) 589
One Art (Bishop) (95) 572
One Writer's Beginnings (Welty) (85) 663
Open Sore of a Continent, The (Soyinka) (97) 648
Ordeal by Labyrinth (Eliade) (83) 572
Ordinary Time (Mairs) (94) 594
Orwell, the Lost Writings (Orwell) (86) 715
Out in the World (Bowles) (86) 723
Out of Place (Said) (00) 597
Out of Step (Hook) (88) 646
Palimpsest (Vidal) (96) 561
Palm Sunday (Vonnegut) (82) 609
Papers of Martin Luther King, Jr., January 1929-June
  1951, The (King) (93) 601
Papers of Martin Luther King, Jr., July 1951-November
  1955, The (King) (95) 590
Papers of Martin Luther King, Jr., December
  1955-December 1956, The (King) (98) 625
Parallel Time (Staples) (95) 594
Partisan View, A (Phillips) (85) 677
Passionate Apprentice, A (Woolf) (92) 607
Path to Power, The (Thatcher) (96) 573
Patients Are People Like Us (Baruk) (79) 532
Patrick White (White) (97) 656
Patrimony (Roth) (92) 615
Periodic Table, The (Levi) (85) 682
Personal History (Graham) (98) 629
Philosopher at Large (Adler) (78) 654
Philosopher's Demise, The (Watson) (96) 581
Pieces of Life (Schorer) (78) 657
Poets in Their Youth (Simpson) (83) 608
Poets, Poetics, and Politics (Humphries) (93) 642
Positively Fifth Street (McManus) (04) 619
Pound/Ford, the Story of a Literary Friendship (Pound
  and Ford) (83) 621
Pound/Lewis (Pound and Lewis) (86) 747
Pound/Williams (Pound and Williams) (97) 675
Power and Principle (Brzezinski) (H-84) 351
Pride of Family (Ione) (92) 641
Primate's Memoir, A (Sapolsky) (02) 659
Private World, The (Unamuno) (85) 701
Radical Son (Horowitz) (98) 661
Ragman's Son, The (Douglas) (89) 692
Randall Jarrell's Letters (Jarrell) (86) 757
Reading Lolita in Tehran (Nafisi) (04) 634
Real Time (Chaudhuri) (03) 643
Reason for Hope (Goodall with Berman) (00) 643
Red and the Blacklist, The (Barzman) (04) 638
Red Azalea (Min) (95) 643
Reflections (Benjamin) (79) 575
Regions of Memory (Merwin) (88) 742
Remembering America (Goodwin) (89) 703
Remembering Denny (Trillin) (94) 692
Remembering Heaven's Face (Balaban) (92) 674

Remembering Mr. Shawn's "New Yorker" (Mehta) (99) 649
Respect in a World of Inequality (Sennett) (04) 652
Revenge (Blumenfeld) (03) 658
Rewrites (Simon) (97) 692
Richard Wright Reader (Wright) (79) 597
Riding the Iron Rooster (Theroux) (89) 726
Right from the Beginning (Buchanan) (89) 730
RN (Nixon) (79) 605
Road from Coorain, The (Conway) (90) 699
Road to San Giovanni, The (Calvino) (94) 705
Robert Kennedy in His Own Words (Kennedy) (89) 744
Roland Barthes (Barthes) (78) 730
Rude Assignment (Lewis) (86) 778
Ruined by Reading (Schwartz) (97) 710
Running with Scissors (Burroughs) (03) 695
Russian Journal (Lee) (82) 713
Sacred Journey, The (Buechner) (83) 670
Saga of Dazai Osamu, The (Lyons) (86) 783
Same River Twice, The (Offutt) (94) 717
Scenes of Childhood and Other Stories (Warner) (83) 679
Scoundrel Time (Hellman) (77) 702
Screening History (Vidal) (93) 707
Secret Diaries of Hitler's Doctor, The (Irving and Morell) (H-84) 398
Secret Symmetry, A (Carotenuto) (83) 709
Secrets (Ellsberg) (03) 718
Selected Letters (García Lorca) (84) 768
Selected Letters (Marx and Engels) (83) 722
Selected Letters of Conrad Aiken (Aiken) (79) 652
Selected Letters of E. M. Forster, 1879-1920 (Forster) (84) 773
Selected Letters of E. M. Forster, 1921-1970 (Forster) (86) 793
Selected Letters of Eugene O'Neill (O'Neill) (89) 771
Selected Letters of Fyodor Dostoyevsky (Dostoyevsky) (88) 806
Selected Letters of George Oppen, The (Oppen) (91) 726
Selected Letters of John O'Hara (O'Hara) (79) 656
Selected Letters of Marianne Moore, The (Moore) (98) 702
Selected Letters of Philip Larkin, 1940-1985 (Larkin) (94) 724
Selected Letters of Raymond Chandler (Chandler) (82) 757
Selected Writings, 1927-1934 (Benjamin) (00) 693
Selected Writings, 1938-1940 (Benjamin) (04) 674
Self-Consciousness (Updike) (90) 725
Shadow Man, The (Gordon) (97) 749
Sherwood Anderson, Selected Letters (Anderson) (85) 820
Singin' and Swingin' and Gettin' Merry Like Christmas (Angelou) (77) 738
Sir Vidia's Shadow (Theroux) (99) 711
Sistermony, A (Stern) (96) 716
Sites (Fowlie) (88) 823
Situation and the Story, The (Gornick) (02) 752
Six Exceptional Women (Lord) (95) 724
Sketches from a Life (Kennan) (90) 742
Small Wonder (Kingsolver) (03) 779
Snow Leopard, The (Matthiessen) (79) 685
Solo (Morris) (84) 803
Song in a Weary Throat (Murray) (88) 835
Sound-Shadows of the New World (Mehta) (87) 802
Spandau (Speer) (77) 764
Speaking Freely (Hentoff) (98) 717
Stand Before Your God (Watkins) (95) 752
Statue Within, The (Jacob) (89) 813
Steinbeck and Covici (Fensch) (80) 780
Still Me (Reeve) (99) 733
Stolen Light, The (Mehta) (90) 758

Storyteller (Silko) (82) 812
Strangers All Are Gone, The (Powell) (84) 833
Strong Opinions (Nabokov) (77) 789
Summer Life, A (Soto) (91) 782
"Surely You're Joking, Mr. Feynman!" (Feynman, with Leighton) (86) 868
T. E. Lawrence, The Selected Letters (Lawrence) (90) 782
Tale of Two Utopias, A (Berman) (97) 807
Teammates, The (Halberstam) (04) 731
Tesserae (Levertov) (96) 740
Testimony (Shostakovich) (80) 808
These the Companions (Davie) (83) 787
Thirties, The (Wilson) (81) 795
Thirties and After, The (Spender) (79) 745
This Boy's Life (Wolff) (90) 796
This Wild Darkness (Brodkey) (97) 816
Thurber Letters, The (Thurber) (04) 752
Time and Time Again (Jacobson) (86) 883
Time Change (Cooke) (82) 839
Time of Our Time, The (Mailer) (99) 764
Time to Be in Earnest (James) (01) 830
Time to Dance, No Time to Weep, A (Godden) (89) 835
Timebends (Miller) (88) 897
Timequake (Vonnegut) (98) 760
'Tis (McCourt) (00) 759
To Set the Record Straight (Sirica) (80) 822
Tolstoy's Letters, Vol. I and Vol. II (Tolstoy) (79) 754
Tombee (Rosengarten, ed.) (87) 875
Torch in My Ear, The (Canetti) (83) 827
Trains of Thought (Brombert) (03) 843
Traveling Mercies (Lamott) (00) 764
Triumph of Politics, The (Stockman) (87) 886
Truants, The (Barrett) (83) 833
True at First Light (Hemingway) (00) 768
True Confessions of an Albino Terrorist, The (Breytenbach) (86) 913
True North (Conway) (95) 801
Truth About Chernobyl, The (Medvedev) (92) 835
Trying to Save Piggy Sneed (Irving) (97) 838
Turbulent Souls (Dubner) (99) 803
Turgenev Letters (Turgenev) (84) 879
Twelve Years (Agee) (82) 854
Twentieth Century Journey, Vol. II (Shirer) (H-85) 451
U and I (Baker) (92) 844
Ultimate Journey (Bernstein) (02) 808
Unafraid of the Dark (Bray) (99) 812
Under My Skin (Lessing) (95) 814
Under the Eye of the Clock (Nolan) (89) 868
Unreliable Memoirs (James) (82) 870
Unsuspected Revolution, The (Llerena) (79) 799
Unto the Sons (Talese) (93) 842
Up at Oxford (Mehta) (94) 823
Very Private Eye, A (Pym) (85) 964
View from the UN (Thant) (79) 809
Village of Longing, The, and Dancehall Days (O'Brien) (91) 851
Vladimir Nabokov, Selected Letters (Nabokov) (90) 849
Voice from the Chorus, A (Tertz) (77) 892
Voices in the Mirror (Parks) (91) 861
Volcano (Hongo) (96) 802
Waist High in the World (Mairs) (98) 814
Walking in the Shade (Lessing) (98) 823
Walter Benjamin at the Dairy Queen (McMurtry) (00) 817
Wanderlust (Solnit) (01) 887
War Diaries (MacMillan) (H-85) 474
War Diaries of Jean-Paul Sartre, The (Sartre) (86) 932
War Within and Without (Lindbergh) (81) 890
Warrenpoint (Donoghue) (91) 871
Warsaw Diary, A (Brandys) (84) 926

Wartime (Djilas) (78) 894
Ways of Escape (Greene) (82) 918
Wayward and the Seeking, The (Toomer) (81) 904
Weight of the World, The (Handke) (85) 1013
What I Saw at the Revolution (Noonan) (91) 881
What I Think I Did (Woiwode) (01) 896
What Shall We Wear to This Party? (Wilson) (77) 901
What's to Become of the Boy? (Böll) (85) 1018
When Heaven and Earth Changed Places (Hayslip, with
  Wurts) (90) 879
Where I Was From (Didion) (04) 831
White House Years (Kissinger) (80) 866
Whole New Life, A (Price) (95) 871
Why Not the Best? (Carter) (77) 906
Wider World, A (Simon) (87) 985
Will (Liddy) (81) 928
Will's Boy (Morris) (82) 950
Winged Seed, The (Lee) (96) 814
Winner Names the Age, The (Smith) (79) 879
With a Daughter's Eye (Bateson) (H-85) 507
Within the Whirlwind (Ginzburg) (82) 963
Without Precedent (Adams) (H-84) 497
Witness to Power (Ehrlichman) (H-83) 473
Wittgenstein's Nephew (Bernhard) (90) 908
Wizard War, The (Jones) (79) 888
Woman Said Yes, The (West) (77) 928
Woman Warrior, The (Kingston) (77) 932
Women, The (Als) (98) 874
Working It Out (Ruddick and Daniels, eds.) (78) 937
World of Light, A (Sarton) (77) 941
World of Love, A (Lash, ed.) (H-85) 521
World of My Own, A (Greene) (95) 890
World Unsuspected, A (Harris, ed.) (88) 984
Writers and Friends (Weeks) (83) 928
Writing Was Everything (Kazin) (96) 843
Writings (Du Bois) (88) 993
Yeager (Yeager and Janos) (86) 974
Year of the Hunter, A (Miłosz) (95) 900
Years of Renewal (Kissinger) (00) 867
Young Rebecca, The (West) (83) 932
You've Had Your Time (Burgess) (92) 933
Zither and Autobiography (Scalapino) (04) 872
Zora Neale Hurston, Vol. I and Vol. II (Hurston)
  (96) 852

BIOGRAPHY. See also LITERARY BIOGRAPHY
Aaron Burr, 1756-1805 (Lomask) (80) 6
Aaron Burr, 1805-1836 (Lomask) (H-83) 1
Abraham Lincoln (Anderson) (H-83) 5
Adlai Stevenson and the World (Martin) (78) 6
Adlai Stevenson of Illinois (Martin) (77) 12
Adolf Hitler (Toland) (77) 17
Alanbrooke (Fraser) (H-83) 14
Albert Speer (Sereny) (96) 5
Alexander Hamilton (McDonald) (80) 23
Alexander Hamilton, American (Brookhiser) (00) 1
Alexander Solzhenitsyn (Thomas) (99) 24
Alfred Hugenberg (Leopold) (78) 28
Alfred North Whitehead, 1861-1910 (Lowe) (86) 5
Alfred North Whitehead, 1910-1947 (Lowe) (91) 20
Alfred Russel Wallace (Raby) (02) 30
Alice Hamilton (Sicherman) (H-85) 6
All Stalin's Men (Medvedev) (H-85) 12
American Caesar (Manchester) (79) 20
American Dreamer (Culver and Hyde) (01) 24
American Pharaoh (Cohen and Taylor) (01) 34
American Scoundrel (Keneally) (03) 28
American Sphinx (Ellis) (98) 55
Ancestors (Ching) (89) 19
Andrew Jackson and His Indian Wars (Remini) (02) 43
Andrew Jackson and the Course of American
  Democracy, 1833-1845 (Remini) (H-85) 28

Andrew Jackson and the Course of American Empire,
  1767-1821 (Remini) (78) 50
Andrew Jackson and the Course of American Freedom,
  1822-1832 (Remini) (82) 11
Anna Freud (Young-Bruehl) (89) 23
Annie Besant (Taylor) (93) 23
Archduke of Sarajevo (Brook-Shepherd) (H-85) 33
As Thousands Cheer (Bergreen) (91) 61
Attlee (Harris) (H-84) 33
Ball of Fire (Kanfer) (04) 49
Baron of Beacon Hill, The (Fowler) (81) 66
Barry Goldwater (Goldberg) (96) 60
Bearing the Cross (Garrow) (87) 55
Beautiful Mind, A (Nasar) (99) 87
Beautiful Shadow (Wilson) (04) 62
Ben-Gurion, 1886-1948 (Teveth) (88) 90
Benjamin Britten (Carpenter) (94) 75
Benjamin Franklin (Clark) (H-84) 54
Benjamin Franklin (Isaacson) (04) 70
Benjamin Franklin (Morgan) (03) 61
Bernard Berenson (Samuels) (80) 73
Bertrand Russell, 1872-1921 (Monk) (97) 105
Bertrand Russell, 1921-1970 (Monk) (02) 78
Bertrand Russell (Moorehead) (94) 85
Betty Friedan (Hennessee) (00) 53
Bing Crosby (Giddins) (02) 88
Bismarck (Crankshaw) (82) 50
Black, French, and African (Vaillant) (91) 80
Black Hearts of Men, The (Stauffer) (03) 74
Black Jack, Vol. I and Vol. II (Vandiver) (78) 96
Black Sun (Wolff) (77) 91
Blood Relations (Mosley) (81) 93
Bloody Mary (Erickson) (79) 64
Bogart (Sperber and Lax) (98) 125
Brandeis (Paper) (H-84) 73
Bright Shining Lie, A (Sheehan) (89) 125
Brothers Reuther, The (Reuther) (77) 124
Brothers Singer, The (Sinclair) (84) 127
Burr, Hamilton, and Jefferson (Kennedy) (00) 112
Burt Lancaster (Buford) (01) 158
Calamities of Exile (Weschler) (99) 136
Calvin Against Himself (Selinger) (H-85) 59
Canaris (Höhne) (80) 125
Captain Kidd and the War Against the Pirates (Ritchie)
  (87) 99
Captain Sir Richard Francis Burton (Rice) (91) 123
Carl Sagan (Davidson) (00) 121
Catcher Was a Spy, The (Dawidoff) (95) 104
Catherine, Empress of All the Russias (Cronin) (79) 80
Catherine the Great (Haslip) (78) 155
Catherine the Great (Troyat) (81) 117
Caught in the Web of Words (Murray) (78) 160
Cavour (Mack Smith) (86) 105
Chaim Weizmann (Reinharz) (86) 111
Chairman, The (Bird) (93) 138
Chaplin (Robinson) (86) 116
Charles Darwin (Bowlby) (92) 83
Charles Darwin (Brent) (82) 87
Charles Darwin, Power of Place, The (Browne)
  (03) 142
Charles Darwin, Voyaging (Browne) (96) 90
Charles Fourier (Beecher) (88) 138
Charles Stewart Parnell (Lyons) (78) 169
Charles the Second (Hutton) (91) 132
Charmed Lives (Korda) (80) 141
Chief, The (Nasaw) (01) 185
Chopin in Paris (Szulc) (99) 168
Chopin's Funeral (Eisler) (04) 118
Churchill (Morgan) (H-83) 65
Citizen Cohn (von Hoffman) (89) 164
Clarence Darrow (Weinberg and Weinberg) (81) 152
Claude Monet (Tucker) (96) 120
Clearing in the Distance, A (Rybczynski) (00) 126

CATEGORY INDEX

Clement Greenberg (Rubenfeld) (99) 181
Collaborator, The (Kaplan) (01) 199
Colonel, The (Smith) (98) 202
Conspiracy So Immense, A (Oshinsky) (H-84) 100
Conversations with Nietzsche (Gilman, ed.) (88) 199
Cornwallis (Wickwire and Wickwire) (81) 203
Cries Unheard (Sereny) (00) 151
Cromwell (Howell) (78) 219
Custer and the Little Big Horn (Hofling) (82) 161
Daniel Defoe (Backscheider) (90) 143
Daniel Webster (Bartlett) (79) 143
Daniel Webster (Remini) (98) 221
Darrow (Tierney) (80) 188
Darwin (Desmond and Moore) (93) 196
David Bomberg (Cork) (88) 238
David Humphreys' "Life of General Washington"
    (Humphreys and Washington) (92) 147
Dean Acheson (McLellan) (77) 197
De Gaulle, 1890-1944 (Lacouture) (91) 192
De Gaulle, 1945-1970 (Lacouture) (93) 219
Deep in a Dream (Gavin) (03) 192
Descartes (Gaukroger) (96) 170
Devil and Sonny Liston, The (Tosches) (01) 237
Diane Arbus (Bosworth) (96) 174
Disraeli (Bradford) (H-84) 135
Disraeli (Weintraub) (94) 239
Dönitz, the Last Führer (Padfield) (H-85) 115
Donovan (Dunlop) (H-83) 99
Dorothy Day (Coles) (88) 252
Double Bond, The (Angier) (03) 224
Down the Highway (Sounes) (02) 208
Dream Makers, Dream Breakers (Rowan) (94) 252
Driving Mr. Albert (Paterniti) (01) 258
Dulles (Mosley) (79) 170
Du Pont Family, The (Gates) (80) 240
Dutch (Morris) (00) 185
Earl Warren (Pollack) (80) 255
Earl Warren (White) (H-83) 109
Edison (Clark) (78) 284
Edmund Burke (Ayling) (90) 198
Education of Laura Bridgman, The (Freeberg) (02) 230
Edward Hopper (Levin) (96) 214
Edward Sapir (Darnell) (91) 245
Edward VII (St. Aubyn) (80) 264
Einstein, Picasso (Miller) (02) 235
Eisenhower, Vol. I (Ambrose) (H-84) 141
Eisenhower, Vol. II (Ambrose) (H-85) 120
Eisenhower the President (Ewald) (82) 205
Eleanor of Aquitaine (Seward) (80) 277
Eleanor Roosevelt, 1884-1933 (Cook) (93) 253
Eleanor Roosevelt, 1933-1938 (Cook) (00) 204
Elizabeth Regina (Plowden) (81) 272
Eminent Elizabethans (Rowse) (H-84) 147
Emma Goldman (Wexler) (H-85) 125
Emperor of Japan (Keene) (03) 255
Emperor of Scent, The (Burr) (04) 224
Empire of Their Own, An (Gabler) (89) 278
Empire Statesman (Slayton) (02) 248
Eva Perón (Fraser and Navarro) (82) 249
Evangelist of Race (Field) (82) 256
Evelyn Nesbit and Stanford White (Mooney) (77) 260
Faces of Revolution (Bailyn) (91) 279
Family (Frazier) (95) 222
FDR, 1933-1937 (Davis) (87) 276
FDR, 1937-1940 (Davis) (94) 278
FDR, 1940-1943 (Davis) (01) 300
FDR (Miller) (H-84) 158
FDR (Morgan) (86) 269
Felix Frankfurter and His Times (Parrish) (H-83) 140
Fidel (Szulc) (87) 282
Fidel Castro (Quirk) (94) 287
Figures in a Western Landscape (Stevenson) (95) 231
Fire and Water (de Jonge) (81) 335

First Churchill, The (Thomson) (81) 344
First-Class Temperament, A (Ward) (90) 258
First Elizabeth, The (Erickson) (H-84) 164
First in His Class (Maraniss) (96) 263
Fitzgeralds and the Kennedys, The (Goodwin) (88) 323
Five of Hearts, The (O'Toole) (91) 295
Flawed Giant (Dallek) (99) 286
Force of Nature (Hager) (96) 286
Ford (Lacey) (87) 297
Francis Bacon (Zagorin) (99) 303
Franco (Preston) (95) 257
Frank Capra (McBride) (93) 298
Frank Lloyd Wright (Secrest) (93) 303
Franklin of Philadelphia (Wright) (87) 303
Frederick Douglass (McFeely) (92) 232
Freud (Clark) (81) 357
Freud (Gay) (89) 311
Freud (Roth, ed.) (99) 311
From a High Place (Spender) (00) 290
Fulbright (Woods) (96) 294
Galileo's Daughter (Sobel) (00) 295
Gandhi (Brown) (91) 321
Gates (Manes and Andrews) (94) 335
Gaudier-Brzeska (Silber) (98) 331
General of the Army (Cray) (91) 333
Generations (Clifton) (77) 318
Genius (Gleick) (93) 308
Genius in Disguise (Kunkel) (96) 303
Genuine Reality (Simon) (99) 329
George Bancroft (Handlin) (H-85) 162
George C. Marshall (Pogue) (88) 346
George Washington Carver (McMurry) (82) 310
George Washington Williams (Franklin) (86) 332
Georgia O'Keeffe (Robinson) (90) 289
Georgia O'Keeffe (Turner) (00) 300
Giacometti (Lord) (86) 343
Gladstone (Jenkins) (98) 344
Gödel (Casti and DePauli) (01) 346
God's Chinese Son (Spence) (97) 339
God's Fool (Green) (86) 354
Gold and Iron (Stern) (78) 354
Goldwyn (Berg) (90) 303
Goya (Hughes) (04) 303
Grand Strategy of Philip II, The (Parker) (00) 326
Grant (McFeely) (82) 338
Great Harry (Erickson) (81) 391
Great Melody, The (O'Brien) (93) 316
Great Triumvirate, The (Peterson) (88) 363
Greenspan (Martin) (01) 365
Groucho (Kanfer) (01) 370
Guggenheims (Davis) (79) 260
Gustav Mahler, 1892-1904 (La Grange) (96) 321
Guston in Time (Feld) (04) 320
Harold Macmillan (Fisher) (H-83) 185
Harold Macmillan, 1894-1956 (Horne) (90) 352
Harold Macmillan, 1957-1986 (Horne) (90) 358
Harp Song for a Radical (Young) (00) 358
Harriet Beecher Stowe (Hedrick) (95) 296
Harry Hopkins (Adams) (78) 375
Harry S. Truman and the Modern American Presidency
    (Ferrell) (H-84) 185
Havelock Ellis (Grosskurth) (81) 412
Hegel (Pinkard) (01) 393
Helene Deutsch (Roazen) (86) 402
Henry Cabot Lodge and the Search for an American
    Foreign Policy (Widenor) (81) 416
Herbert Hoover (Burner) (80) 400
Himself! (Kennedy) (79) 273
Hippocrates (Jouanna) (00) 381
His Holiness (Bernstein and Politi) (97) 388
Hitler (Stone) (81) 434
Hitler and Stalin (Bullock) (93) 349
Hitler, 1889-1936 (Kershaw) (00) 386

Hitler of History, The (Lukacs) (98) 396
Hitler's Pope (Cornwell) (00) 396
Hobbes (Martinich) (00) 400
Ho Chi Minh (Duiker) (01) 403
Honor's Voice (Wilson) (99) 379
Hornes, The (Buckley) (87) 410
House of Morgan, The (Chernow) (91) 432
Hugo Black and the Judicial Revolution (Dunne) (78) 418
Hugo L. Black (Ball) (97) 415
Huxley (Desmond) (98) 411
I May Not Get There with You (Dyson) (01) 442
Imaginative Landscape of Christopher Columbus, The (Flint) (93) 365
Imperative of Modernity, The (Gray) (90) 410
Imperial Rockefeller, The (Persico) (H-83) 206
Improper Bostonian, The (Hoyt) (80) 414
In Darwin's Shadow (Shermer) (03) 400
In Her Own Right (Griffith) (H-85) 230
In the Footsteps of Mr. Kurtz (Wrong) (02) 413
In the Presence of the Creator (Christianson) (H-85) 236
Iron Lady, The (Young) (90) 429
Isaac Newton (Gleick) (04) 369
Isabel the Queen (Liss) (93) 399
Isaiah Berlin (Gray) (97) 466
I've Known Rivers (Lawrence-Lightfoot) (95) 384
J. Edgar Hoover (Gentry) (92) 369
J. G. Frazer (Ackerman) (89) 418
J. P. Morgan (Jackson) (H-84) 257
Jack (Parmet) (81) 454
Jackie Robinson (Rampersad) (98) 458
Jackson Pollock (Naifeh and Smith) (91) 466
Jacques Lacan (Roudinesco) (98) 463
Jameses (Lewis) (92) 374
Jean-Jacques (Cranston) (H-84) 237
Jefferson Davis (Eaton) (78) 464
Jesse (Frady) (97) 474
JFK (Hamilton) (93) 408
Joan of Arc (Gordon) (01) 485
Joan of Arc (Lucie-Smith) (78) 472
Joe Dimaggio (Cramer) (01) 489
Joe Papp (Epstein) (95) 396
Johann Sebastian Bach (Wolff) (01) 494
John Adams (Ferling) (93) 413
John Adams (McCullough) (02) 444
John Calvin (Bouwsma) (88) 433
John D. (Hawke) (81) 459
John Dewey and American Democracy (Westbrook) (92) 388
John Dewey and the High Tide of American Liberalism (Ryan) (96) 393
John Dickinson (Flower) (H-84) 248
John Foster Dulles (Pruessen) (H-83) 229
John Henry Newman (Ker) (90) 459
John L. Lewis (Dubofsky and Van Tine) (78) 478
John Marshall and the Heroic Age of the Supreme Court (Newmyer) (03) 432
John Maynard Keynes (Hession) (H-85) 250
John Maynard Keynes, 1920-1937 (Skidelsky) (95) 400
John Maynard Keynes, 1937-1946 (Skidelsky) (02) 453
John Paul Jones (Thomas) (04) 381
John Quincy Adams (Nagel) (98) 472
John Ruskin, The Early Years (Hilton) (86) 487
John Ruskin, The Later Years (Hilton) (01) 499
John Wayne's America (Wills) (98) 477
John Winthrop (Bremer) (04) 386
Jonathan Edwards (Marsden) (04) 391
Julius Streicher (Bytwerk) (H-83) 234
Jung (Bair) (04) 396
Justice Crucified (Feuerlicht) (78) 487
Justice Oliver Wendell Holmes (White) (94) 431
Kant (Kuehn) (02) 458

Karl Marx (Padover) (79) 349
Karl Marx (Wheen) (01) 504
Kate Remembered (Berg) (04) 400
Kennedy and Roosevelt (Beschloss) (81) 467
Kennedy Imprisonment, The (Wills) (H-83) 244
Khrushchev (Medvedev) (H-84) 266
Khrushchev (Taubman) (04) 404
Khubilai Khan (Rossabi) (89) 432
King Edward VIII (Ziegler) (92) 403
King of Children, The (Lifton) (89) 436
King of Ragtime (Berlin) (95) 422
King of the World (Remnick) (99) 453
Kissinger (Isaacson) (93) 426
Koba the Dread (Amis) (03) 446
Labyrinth of Exile, The (Pawel) (90) 495
Lafayette (Buckman) (78) 495
Lardners, The (Lardner) (77) 404
Last Days of Patton, The (Farago) (82) 428
Last Kaiser, The (Tyler-Whittle) (78) 509
Last Lion, 1874-1932, The (Manchester) (H-84) 278
Last Lion, 1932-1940, The (Manchester) (89) 455
Lawrence of Arabia (Wilson) (91) 512
Léon Blum (Lacouture) (H-83) 253
Leon Trotsky (Howe) (79) 368
Leopold I of Austria (Spielman) (78) 518
Lester Leaps In (Daniels) (03) 470
Let the Trumpet Sound (Oates) (H-83) 259
Life and Times of Cotton Mather, The (Silverman) (H-85) 256
Life and Times of Grigorii Rasputin, The (de Jonge) (H-83) 264
Life and Times of Joe McCarthy, The (Reeves) (H-83) 270
Life in Pieces, A (Eskin) (03) 480
Life of Bertrand Russell, The (Clark) (77) 423
Life of Herbert Hoover, The (Nash) (H-84) 288
Life of Nelson A. Rockefeller, 1908-1958, The (Reich) (97) 506
Life of Picasso, 1881-1906 (Richardson) (92) 431
Life of Picasso, 1907-1917 (Richardson) (97) 511
Lincoln (Donald) (96) 436
Lincoln's Virtues (Miller) (03) 490
Lindbergh (Berg) (99) 478
Lindbergh (Mosley) (77) 433
Lise Meitner (Sime) (97) 526
Lives of Norman Mailer, The (Rollyson) (92) 445
Logical Dilemmas (Dawson) (98) 517
Lone Star Rising (Dallek) (92) 450
Lord Beaverbrook (Chisholm and Davie) (94) 488
Louis D. Brandeis and the Progressive Tradition (Urofsky) (82) 488
Louis Sullivan (Twombly) (87) 499
Lucky Eyes and a High Heart (Cardozo) (79) 409
Luther (Haile) (81) 535
Luther (Oberman) (91) 553
Lyndon (Miller) (81) 540
Lyndon Johnson and the American Dream (Kearns) (77) 465
M (Robb) (01) 549
Making of an Assassin, The (McMillan) (77) 470
Malcolm (Perry) (92) 474
Man Called Intrepid, A (Stevenson) (77) 475
Man of the Century (Kwitny) (98) 538
Man Who Loved Only Numbers, The (Hoffman) (99) 515
Mandela (Sampson) (00) 506
Many Masks (Gill) (88) 534
Mao (Short) (01) 554
Mao (Terrill) (81) 549
Mao Zedong (Spence) (00) 511
Map That Changed the World, The (Winchester) (02) 503
Margaret Fuller (Blanchard) (79) 422

CATEGORY INDEX

Mark Rothko (Breslin) (94) 504
Marshall (Mosley) (H-83) 283
Marshall McLuhan (Gordon) (98) 542
Marshall McLuhan (Marchand) (90) 562
Martha (De Mille) (92) 485
Martin Buber's Life and Work (Friedman) (H-84) 293
Martin Heidegger (Ott) (94) 512
Martin Heidegger (Safranski) (99) 529
Martin Luther (Marius) (00) 515
Martin Niemöller, 1892-1984 (Bentley) (H-85) 298
Martin Van Buren (Niven) (H-84) 298
Master of Death (Camille) (97) 555
Master of the Game, The (Talbott) (89) 544
Matisse (Schneider) (H-85) 303
Maverick and His Machine, The (Maney) (04) 501
Max Perkins (Berg) (79) 428
Max Weber (Diggins) (97) 559
Meaning of Hitler, The (Haffner) (80) 528
Mellons, The (Koskoff) (79) 434
Memory Palace of Matteo Ricci, The (Spence) (H-85) 309
Mencken (Hobson) (95) 477
Michel Foucault (Eribon) (92) 495
Mind of Her Own, A (Quinn) (88) 558
Mistress Anne (Erickson) (H-85) 319
Monk in the Garden, The (Henig) (01) 588
Montgomery Clift (Bosworth) (79) 457
Monty (Hamilton) (82) 531
Morgan (Strouse) (00) 524
Mornings on Horseback (McCullough) (82) 537
Mostly Morgenthaus (Morgenthau) (92) 529
Mother Jones (Gorn) (02) 546
Mountbatten (Hough) (82) 542
Mountbatten (Ziegler) (86) 629
Mozart (Solomon) (96) 490
Mozart in Vienna, 1781-1791 (Braunbehrens) (91) 606
Mrs. Jordan's Profession (Tomalin) (96) 465
Mungo Park the African Traveler (Lupton) (80) 550
Murrow (Sperber) (87) 582
Mussolini (Mack Smith) (H-83) 308
Mysterious History of Columbus, The (Wilford) (92) 540
Napoleon III and Eugénie (Ridley) (81) 587
Nelson Mandela (Meredith) (99) 552
Nehru (Tharoor) (04) 546
Nero (Griffin) (86) 650
New New Thing, The (Lewis) (00) 571
New Worlds of Dvořák (Beckerman) (04) 556
Newer World, A (Roberts) (01) 627
Newton's Gift (Berlinski) (01) 637
Niccolò's Smile (Viroli) (01) 641
Nicholas I (Lincoln) (79) 479
Niels Bohr's Times (Pais) (92) 569
Nietzsche (Safranski) (02) 584
Nikolai Bukharin (Medvedev) (81) 614
Nixon, 1913-1962 (Ambrose) (88) 594
Nixon, 1962-1972 (Ambrose) (90) 608
Nixon, 1973-1990 (Ambrose) (92) 577
No Ordinary Time (Goodwin) (95) 554
Noam Chomsky (Barsky) (98) 598
Noble Savage, The (Cranston) (92) 583
Noël Coward (Hoare) (97) 630
Noguchi East and West (Ashton) (93) 570
Norman Thomas (Swanberg) (77) 570
Not for Ourselves Alone (Ward and Burns) (00) 580
Nowhere Man (Rosen) (01) 661
Old and on Their Own (Coles) (99) 576
On Gold Mountain (See) (96) 523
One and Inseparable (Baxter) (H-85) 339
One Best Way, The (Kanigel) (98) 607
One of Us (Wicker) (92) 597
Orson Welles (Leaming) (86) 709
Oswald's Tale (Mailer) (96) 549

Other American, The (Isserman) (01) 689
Other Powers (Goldsmith) (99) 601
Palmerston (Bourne) (H-83) 329
Paper Medicine Man (Porter) (87) 636
Passion of Michel Foucault, The (Miller) (93) 614
Paul Robeson (Duberman) (90) 652
People's Emperor, The (Wilson) (81) 645
Perón (Page) (H-84) 336
Pershing (Smythe) (87) 660
Peter Paul Rubens (White) (88) 690
Peter the Great (Massie) (81) 651
Pitcher's Story, A (Angell) (02) 641
Playing for Keeps (Halberstam) (00) 618
Politician, The (Dugger) (H-83) 348
Portraits (Shils) (98) 639
Preacher King, The (Lischer) (96) 601
President Kennedy (Reeves) (94) 662
Prince of Our Disorder, A (Mack) (77) 637
Privileged Son (McDougal) (02) 669
Province of Reason (Warner) (H-85) 368
Quest for El Cid, The (Fletcher) (91) 684
Question of Character, A (Reeves) (92) 660
Question of Hu, The (Spence) (89) 679
Rachel Carson (Lear) (98) 656
Rage of Edmund Burke, The (Kramnick) (78) 686
Ranke (Krieger) (78) 690
Reagan (Cannon) (H-83) 362
Reagan's America (Wills) (88) 725
Rebel in Defense of Tradition, A (Wreszin) (95) 630
Red and the Blacklist, The (Barzman) (04) 638
Refugee Scholars in America (Coser) (85) 738
Regions of the Great Heresy (Ficowski) (03) 648
Reign of Napoleon Bonaparte, The (Asprey) (02) 688
Reinhard Heydrich (Deschner) (82) 666
Reinhold Niebuhr (Fox) (86) 766
Rembrandt's House (Bailey) (79) 580
Renaissance Tapestry, A (Simon) (89) 708
Return Passages (Ziff) (02) 698
Richard Milhous Nixon (Morris) (90) 694
Richard Rodgers (Hyland) (99) 658
Rise and Fall of Alexander Hamilton, The (Hendrickson) (82) 687
Rise of Theodore Roosevelt, The (Morris) (80) 717
Rising from the Plains (McPhee) (87) 722
Robert E. Lee (Thomas) (96) 645
Robert Fulton (Morgan) (78) 726
Rodin (Grunfeld) (88) 780
Roger Fry (Spalding) (81) 699
Romare Bearden (Schwartzman) (92) 684
Roosevelt and Churchill, 1939-1941 (Lash) (77) 685
Roosevelt Chronicles, The (Miller) (80) 726
Roosevelts, The (Horowitz) (95) 664
Rousseau (Miller) (H-85) 395
Royal Charles (Fraser) (80) 732
Sage of Monticello, Vol. VI, The (Malone) (82) 722
Saint Augustine (Wills) (00) 665
Saint-Simon and the Court of Louis XIV (Ladurie and Fitou) (02) 717
Sakharov (Lourie) (03) 703
Samuel Gompers and Organized Labor in America (Livesay) (79) 641
Sandy Koufax (Leavy) (03) 713
Sarah Bernhardt and Her World (Richardson) (78) 740
Scars of Sweet Paradise (Echols) (00) 670
Schopenhauer and the Wild Years of Philosophy (Safranski) (91) 711
Seabiscuit (Hillenbrand) (02) 737
Search for Alexander, The (Lane Fox) (81) 712
Secrecy and Power (Powers) (88) 801
Secret Lives of Trebitsch Lincoln, The (Wasserstein) (89) 762
Secret Symmetry, A (Carotenuto) (83) 709
Secretary, Martin Bormann, The (Lang) (80) 746

917

Shackleton (Huntford) (87) 765
Shah's Last Ride, The (Shawcross) (89) 784
Shawnee Prophet, The (Edmunds) (H-84) 409
Simone de Beauvoir (Bair) (91) 740
Simone Weil (Fiori) (90) 738
Simone Weil (Nevin) (93) 736
Sir Francis Drake (Sugden) (92) 757
Sisters, The (Lovell) (03) 760
Sitwells, The (Pearson) (80) 763
Slaves in the Family (Ball) (99) 716
Sojourner Truth (Painter) (97) 772
Somewhere a Master (Wiesel) (83) 756
Son of the Morning Star (Connell) (H-85) 420
Son of Thunder, A (Mayer) (87) 789
Soong Dynasty, The (Seagrave) (86) 852
Soros (Kaufman) (03) 794
Southern Daughter (Pyron) (92) 775
Speculator, The (Schwarz) (82) 800
Spinoza (Nadler) (00) 725
Stalin (Conquest) (92) 780
Statesman and Saint (Ridley) (H-84) 420
Stephen Hawking (White and Gribbin) (93) 758
Stephen Sondheim (Secrest) (99) 728
Steven Spielberg (McBride) (98) 731
Stieglitz (Lowe) (H-84) 426
Stonewall Jackson (Robertson) (98) 736
Streak of Luck, A (Conot) (80) 790
Sun Yat-sen (Schiffrin) (81) 777
Super Chief (Schwartz) (H-84) 435
T. E. Lawrence (Stewart) (78) 813
Taking on the World (Merry) (97) 802
Theodore Rex (Morris) (02) 777
Theodore Roosevelt (Miller) (93) 783
Theremin (Glinsky) (01) 815
Thomas Cardinal Wolsey (Harvey) (81) 800
Thomas Cranmer (MacCulloch) (97) 821
Thomas E. Dewey and His Times (Smith) (H-83) 421
Thomas Jefferson (Bedini) (91) 809
Thomas Jefferson (Randall) (94) 797
Thomas More (Marius) (H-85) 435
Those Days (Critchfield) (87) 858
Time, Love, Memory (Weiner) (00) 754
Time of Stalin, The (Antonov-Ovseyenko) (82) 845
Tinker and a Poor Man, A (Hill) (90) 814
Tip O'Neill and the Democratic Century (Farrell) (02) 791
Titan (Chernow) (99) 768
To Conquer the Air (Tobin) (04) 766
Tolstoy and Gandhi, Men of Peace (Green) (H-84) 447
Tom Paine (Keane) (96) 760
Tormented Warrior (Parkinson) (80) 827
Trail of the Fox, The (Irving) (78) 856
Traitor's Kiss, A (O'Toole) (99) 773
Treason in the Blood (Brown) (95) 796
Trollope (Hall) (92) 825
Truffaut (de Baecque and Toubiana) (00) 772
Truman (McCullough) (93) 810
Truman's Crises (Gosnell) (81) 836
Tuxedo Park (Conant) (03) 848
Tycho and Kepler (Ferguson) (04) 782
Uncertainty (Cassidy) (93) 824
Uncle of Europe (Brook-Shepherd) (77) 861
Undaunted Courage (Ambrose) (97) 853
Unfinished Life, An (Dallek) (04) 791
Unfinished Presidency, The (Brinkley) (99) 822
Unknown Matisse, The (Spurling) (99) 826
Upon This Rock (Freedman) (94) 827
Utopia Parkway (Solomon) (98) 801
Utopian Pessimist (McLellan) (91) 838
Vaclav Havel (Keane) (01) 863
Van Gogh (Sweetman) (91) 843
Vanished Imam, The (Ajami) (87) 901
Velázquez (Brown) (87) 907

Victor Hugo (Robb) (99) 838
W. E. B. Du Bois, 1868-1919 (Lewis) (94) 847
W. E. B. Du Bois, 1919-1963 (Lewis) (01) 882
Walker Evans (Mellow) (00) 805
Walter Hines Page (Cooper) (78) 888
Walter Lippmann and the American Century (Steel) (81) 886
Wandering Ghost (Cott) (92) 863
Warden of English, The (McMorris) (02) 838
Warrior and the Priest, The (Cooper) (H-84) 476
What Is an Editor? (Commins) (79) 839
What Kind of Nation (Simon) (03) 877
When Hollywood Had a King (Bruck) (04) 823
White Boned Demon, The (Terrill) (H-85) 495
Whitney Father, Whitney Heiress (Swanberg) (81) 921
Whittaker Chambers (Tanenhaus) (98) 841
Why They Kill (Rhodes) (00) 843
Wilberforce (Pollock) (79) 862
Wilbur and Orville (Howard) (88) 959
Wild Swans (Chang) (92) 894
Wilhelm Liebknecht and the Founding of the German Social Democratic Party (Dominick) (H-83) 467
Wilhelm von Humboldt, 1767-1808 (Sweet) (79) 868
William Caxton (Painter) (78) 909
William F. Buckley, Jr. (Judis) (89) 908
William James (Myers) (87) 997
William Morris (Thompson) (78) 913
William Pitt the Younger (Reilly) (80) 873
Winds of History (Backer) (H-84) 488
Wing of Madness, The (Burston) (97) 885
Winston S. Churchill, 1922-1939 (Gilbert) (78) 917
Winston S. Churchill, 1939-1941 (Gilbert) (H-85) 500
Winston S. Churchill, 1941-1945 (Gilbert) (87) 1001
Winston S. Churchill, 1945-1965 (Gilbert) (89) 913
Witness to Hope (Weigel) (00) 847
Witnesses at the Creation (Morris) (86) 959
Wittgenstein, A Life (McGuinness) (89) 918
Wittgenstein's Poker (Edmonds and Eidinow) (02) 875
Wolf by the Ears, The (Miller) (78) 928
Women on the Margins (Davis) (96) 826
Woodrow Wilson (Heckscher) (92) 914
Woodrow Wilson (Mulder) (79) 892
World According to Peter Drucker, The (Beatty) (99) 872
Years of Lyndon Johnson, Master of the Senate, The (Caro) (03) 907
Years of Lyndon Johnson, Means of Ascent, The (Caro) (91) 919
Years of Lyndon Johnson, The Path to Power, The (Caro) (H-83) 478
Years of MacArthur, 1945-64 (James) (86) 980
Yeltsin (Aron) (01) 940
Young Hamilton, The (Flexner) (79) 922
Young Lukács, The (Congdon) (84) 992
Young Nietzsche (Pletsch) (92) 928
Zelda Fitzgerald (Cline) (04) 868
Zhou Enlai (Wilson) (H-85) 526

CURRENT AFFAIRS
Active Faith (Reed) (97) 9
Adversary, The (Carrère) (02) 14
Age of Uncertainty, The (Galbraith) (78) 23
AIDS and Its Metaphors (Sontag) (90) 19
Alien Nation (Brimelow) (96) 9
All-American Skin Game, The (Crouch) (96) 14
All Fall Down (Sick) (86) 10
All That Is Solid Melts into Air (Berman) (83) 15
Amazing Grace (Kozol) (96) 30
Ambling into History (Bruni) (03) 14
American Dream Global Nightmare (Vogelgesang) (81) 31
American Exceptionalism (Lipset) (97) 33
American Jihad (Emerson) (03) 23

CATEGORY INDEX

American Journey (Reeves) (H-83) 46
American Kaleidoscope, The (Fuchs) (92) 17
American Way of Death Revisited, The (Mitford) (99) 44
America's Quest for the Ideal Self (Clecak) (H-84) 16
Among Schoolchildren (Kidder) (90) 34
Among the Believers (Naipaul) (82) 6
Anatomy of Power, The (Galbraith) (H-84) 21
And the Band Played On (Shilts) (88) 36
Arab and Jew (Shipler) (87) 35
Arabists, The (Kaplan) (94) 42
Around the Cragged Hill (Kennan) (94) 52
At a Century's Ending (Kennan) (97) 71
At the Highest Levels (Beschloss and Talbott) (94) 62
Balkan Ghosts (Kaplan) (94) 66
Balkan Odyssey (Owen) (97) 95
Bell Curve, The (Herrnstein and Murray) (95) 70
Betrayal (*The Boston Globe* Investigative Staff) (03) 65
Beyond Belief (Naipaul) (99) 96
Blood and Belonging (Ignatieff) (95) 89
Bloods (Terry) (H-85) 48
Bowling Alone (Putnam) (01) 139
Breaking the Deadlock (Posner) (02) 130
Breaking the News (Fallows) (97) 132
Bright Shining Lie, A (Sheehan) (89) 125
Broken Cord, The (Dorris) (90) 76
Brown (Rodriguez) (03) 114
Business of Books, The (Schiffrin) (01) 163
Capitol Games (Phelps and Winternitz) (93) 128
Case Against Immigration, The (Beck) (97) 136
Certain Trumpets (Wills) (95) 114
China Without Mao (Hsü) (H-84) 87
Civil Action, A (Harr) (96) 116
Civility (Carter) (99) 177
Clock of the Long Now, The (Brand) (00) 130
Closing of the American Mind, The (Bloom) (88) 159
Cloud of Danger, The (Kennan) (78) 183
Coal (Freese) (04) 126
Cohesion and Dissension in Eastern Europe (Simon) (H-84) 91
Coming Anarchy, The (Kaplan) (01) 208
Command of the Seas (Lehman) (90) 132
Commanding Heights (Yergin and Stanislaw) (99) 204
Confederates in the Attic (Horwitz) (99) 208
Conspiracy Theories (Fenster) (00) 142
Content of Our Character, The (Steele) (91) 170
Convenient Spy, A (Stober and Hoffman) (03) 164
Cool Fire, The (Shanks) (77) 180
Crisis of Islam, The (Lewis) (04) 142
Crowded Earth, The (Gupte) (H-85) 94
Cruelty and Silence (Makiya) (94) 177
Cuban Threat, The (Robbins) (H-84) 106
Cultural Literacy (Hirsch) (88) 223
Culture of Complaint (Hughes) (94) 186
Culture of Disbelief, The (Carter) (94) 191
Danger and Survival (Bundy) (89) 217
Dead Elvis (Marcus) (92) 157
Deadly Gambits (Talbott) (H-85) 110
Decade of Decisions (Quandt) (78) 243
Deep Politics and the Death of JFK (Scott) (94) 221
Democracy's Discontents (Sandel) (97) 205
Den of Thieves (Stewart) (92) 162
Destructive Generation (Collier and Horowitz) (90) 168
Diaspora (Sachar) (86) 226
Distant Neighbors (Riding) (86) 234
Divorce Culture, The (Whitehead) (98) 254
Double Fold (Baker) (02) 204
Dressing Station, The (Kaplan) (03) 238
Empire Wilderness, An (Kaplan) (99) 247
End of Equality, The (Kaus) (93) 258
End of History and the Last Man, The (Fukuyama) (93) 262

End of Nature, The (McKibben) (90) 211
End of Racism, The (D'Souza) (96) 227
End Papers (Breytenbach) (87) 242
Ends of the Earth, The (Kaplan) (97) 252
Europe, Europe (Enzensberger) (90) 227
Every Spy a Prince (Raviv and Melman) (91) 271
Everything for Sale (Kuttner) (98) 294
Face of the Nation, The (Fitzgerald) (97) 265
Facing Up (Weinberg) (02) 263
Family and Nation (Moynihan) (87) 259
Far from Home (Powers) (92) 193
Farm (Rhodes) (90) 240
Fast Food Nation (Schlosser) (02) 280
Faster (Gleick) (00) 252
Fatherless America (Blankenhorn) (96) 258
Feminism Without Illusions (Fox-Genovese) (92) 205
Final Reports (Rovere) (H-85) 141
Food Politics (Nestle) (03) 311
Fourth and Richest Reich, The (Hartrich) (81) 353
Freaks (Fiedler) (79) 235
Freedom Spent (Harris) (77) 304
Friendly Fire (Bryan) (77) 309
From Beirut to Jerusalem (Friedman) (90) 283
From the Congo to Soweto (Jackson) (H-83) 155
Frozen Desire (Buchan) (98) 327
Future of China After Mao, The (Terrill) (79) 240
Future of Freedom, The (Zakaria) (04) 279
Germany and the United States (Gatzke) (81) 368
Germany East and West (Whetten) (81) 373
Globalization and Its Discontents (Stiglitz) (03) 334
Good Life and Its Discontents, The (Samuelson) (97) 345
Grand Failure, The (Brzezinski) (90) 329
Gratitude (Buckley) (91) 359
Habits of the Heart (Bellah, et al.) (86) 380
Harvest of Empire (González) (01) 384
Haunted Land, The (Rosenberg) (96) 330
. . . Heavens and the Earth, The (McDougall) (86) 396
Heaven's Door (Borjas) (00) 367
Henry Cabot Lodge and the Search for an American Foreign Policy (Widenor) (81) 416
Higher Superstition (Gross and Levitt) (95) 301
How We Die (Nuland) (95) 324
In My Father's House (Appiah) (93) 370
In the Age of the Smart Machine (Zuboff) (89) 377
In the Shadow of the Epidemic (Odets) (96) 368
India (Naipaul) (92) 346
Indian Country (Matthiessen) (H-85) 241
Inequality Reexamined (Sen) (93) 382
Inheritance, The (Freedman) (97) 451
Inner Reaches of Outer Space, The (Campbell) (87) 429
Intifada (Schiff and Ya'ari) (91) 461
Islam and the West (Lewis) (94) 414
Japanese, The (Reischauer) (78) 459
Jefferson and the Presidency (Johnstone) (79) 331
Jew vs. Jew (Freedman) (01) 480
Jihad (Kepel) (03) 428
Jihad (Rashid) (03) 423
Kindly Inquisitors (Rauch) (94) 436
Kings of Cocaine (Gugliotta and Leen) (90) 490
Knocking on the Door (Paton) (77) 396
Law Unto Itself, A (Burnham) (91) 507
Lenin's Tomb (Remnick) (94) 458
Letters from the Country (Bly) (82) 444
Liberalism and Republicanism in the Historical Imagination (Appleby) (93) 454
Liftoff (Collins) (89) 506
Lonely in America (Gordon) (77) 445
Looking at the Sun (Fallows) (95) 451
Loose Canons (Gates) (93) 483
Losing Ground (Eckholm) (77) 450
Losing Ground (Murray) (H-85) 268

Love Thy Neighbor (Maass) (97) 543
Madness in the Streets (Isaac and Armat) (91) 558
Manufacturing Matters (Cohen and Zysman) (88) 529
Martyrs' Day (Kelly) (94) 516
Master of the Game, The (Talbott) (89) 544
Medical Nemesis (Illich) (77) 489
Miami (Didion) (88) 553
Microcosm (Gilder) (90) 568
Miles to Go (Moynihan) (97) 581
Money (Hacker) (98) 562
Moneyball (Lewis) (04) 514
Moral Freedom (Wolfe) (02) 541
Moral Life of Children, The (Coles) (87) 573
Moral Politics (Lakoff) (97) 600
Moral Sense, The (Wilson) (94) 539
Mormon America (Ostling and Ostling) (00) 529
Mother Country (Robinson) (90) 586
Move Your Shadow (Lelyveld) (86) 635
Mullahs on the Mainframe (Blank) (02) 550
My Own Country (Verghese) (95) 515
My Traitor's Heart (Malan) (91) 624
Mystic Chords of Memory (Kammen) (92) 545
Naked Public Square, The (Neuhaus) (H-85) 324
Necessary Evil, A (Wills) (00) 567
New Birth of Freedom, A (Black) (98) 579
New Diplomacy, The (Eban) (H-84) 317
New High Ground, The (Karas) (H-84) 323
New Rules (Yankelovich) (82) 548
New White Nationalism in America, The (Swain) (03) 572
New World Disorder (Jowitt) (93) 559
Next (Lewis) (02) 576
Next Christendom, The (Jenkins) (03) 581
Next 200 Years, The (Kahn, Brown, and Martel) (77) 559
Nicaragua (Christian) (86) 655
Nickel and Dimed (Ehrenreich) (02) 580
Nigger (Kennedy) (03) 586
Nightmare (Lukas) (77) 565
1999 (Nixon) (89) 595
Nixon Off the Record (Crowley) (97) 622
North Atlantic Alliance and the Soviet Union in the 1980's, The (Critchley) (H-83) 320
Not Out of Africa (Lefkowitz) (97) 635
Notes of a Hanging Judge (Crouch) (91) 634
Notes of a White Black Woman (Scales-Trent) (96) 514
Nuclear Fear (Weart) (89) 610
Nuclear Strategy in a Dynamic World (Snow) (82) 565
Of Paradise and Power (Kagan) (04) 565
Official Negligence (Cannon) (99) 571
Old World's New World, The (Woodward) (92) 592
On the Natural History of Destruction (Sebald) (04) 574
On the Rez (Frazier) (01) 670
On the Road with Charles Kuralt (Kuralt) (86) 691
One by One from the Inside Out (Loury) (96) 532
One World, Ready or Not (Greider) (98) 612
Open Sore of a Continent, The (Soyinka) (97) 648
Overspent American, The (Schor) (99) 610
Overworked American, The (Schor) (93) 597
Pacific War, The (Ienaga) (79) 520
Palestinian State, A (Heller) (H-84) 326
Parting the Waters (Branch) (89) 649
People Shapers, The (Packard) (78) 649
Perestroika (Gorbachev) (88) 677
Political Liberalism (Rawls) (94) 649
Political Life of Children, The (Coles) (87) 665
Politics in Black and White (Sonenshein) (94) 654
Politics of Energy, The (Commoner) (80) 671
Politics of Rich and Poor, The (Phillips) (91) 674
Pop Internationalism (Krugman) (97) 666
Postville (Bloom) (01) 716
Power Game, The (Smith) (89) 658

Power to Lead, The (Burns) (H-85) 363
Praying for Sheetrock (Greene) (92) 636
Preparing for the Twenty-first Century (Kennedy) (94) 658
Price of Citizenship, The (Katz) (02) 655
Price of Power, The (Hersh) (H-84) 361
Primacy or World Order (Hoffmann) (79) 551
Prize, The (Yergin) (92) 645
"Problem from Hell, A" (Power) (03) 629
Progressive Presidents, The (Blum) (81) 665
Promised Land, The (Lemann) (92) 650
Proximity to Death (McFeely) (00) 630
Quality of Mercy, The (Shawcross) (H-85) 373
Rachel and Her Children (Kozol) (89) 687
Reason and Realpolitik (Beres) (H-85) 385
Reckoning, The (Halberstam) (87) 695
Reefer Madness (Schlosser) (04) 643
Reflections of an Affirmative Action Baby (Carter) (92) 669
Rethinking Social Policy (Jencks) (93) 682
Reversal of Fortune (Dershowitz) (87) 716
Revolt of the Elites, The (Lasch) (96) 628
Right Man, The (Frum) (04) 662
Right Stuff, The (Wolfe) (80) 713
Russians, The (Smith) (77) 694
Savage Inequalities (Kozol) (92) 712
Second Stage, The (Friedan) (82) 752
Secret Conversations of Henry Kissinger, The (Golan) (77) 709
Seeing Voices (Sacks) (90) 720
Sex and Destiny (Greer) (H-85) 406
Shah of Shahs (Kapuściński) (86) 811
Shah's Last Ride, The (Shawcross) (89) 784
Sikhs, The (Singh) (01) 774
Sleeping with Extra-Terrestrials (Kaminer) (00) 712
Small Wonder (Kingsolver) (03) 779
Smoke Ring, The (Taylor) (H-85) 415
Solzhenitsyn and the Modern World (Ericson) (94) 751
Soros (Kaufman) (03) 794
Soviet Triangle, The (Shanor) (81) 759
Spirit Catches You and You Fall Down, The (Fadiman) (98) 722
Strange Justice (Mayer and Abramson) (95) 765
Struggle for Afghanistan, The (Newell and Newell) (82) 817
Subliminal Politics (Nimmo and Combs) (81) 773
Tale of Two Utopias, A (Berman) (97) 807
"Target Is Destroyed, The" (Hersh) (87) 841
Technical Difficulties (Jordan) (93) 779
Tempting of America, The (Bork) (90) 787
Terror and Liberalism (Berman) (04) 739
Them (Ronson) (03) 829
There Are No Children Here (Kotlowitz) (92) 813
Thinking About National Security (Brown) (H-84) 439
Three Degrees Above Zero (Bernstein) (H-85) 441
Thunder on the Right (Crawford) (81) 804
To Be an American (Hing) (98) 765
Tragedy of Cambodian History, The (Chandler) (93) 800
Transformation of Southern Politics, The (Bass and De Vries) (77) 832
Trapped in the Net (Rochlin) (98) 773
Trouble with Computers, The (Landauer) (96) 773
Truly Disadvantaged, The (Wilson) (88) 910
Trust (Fukuyama) (96) 777
Turning Right (Savage) (93) 815
Tyranny of the Majority, The (Guinier) (95) 805
Uncertain Greatness (Morris) (78) 869
Underground (Murakami) (02) 813
Underground Empire, The (Mills) (87) 896
Understanding Inflation (Case) (82) 866
Unfinished War, The (Capps) (H-83) 440

CATEGORY INDEX

United States in the Middle East, The (Tillman) (H-83) 445
Unseen Revolution, The (Drucker) (77) 872
Unwelcome Strangers (Reimers) (99) 830
Upon This Rock (Freedman) (94) 827
Veil (Woodward) (88) 923
Vermont Papers, The (Bryan and McClaughry) (90) 839
Wages of Guilt, The (Buruma) (95) 840
Waltzing with a Dictator (Bonner) (88) 949
Watches of the Night, The (Caudill) (77) 896
Way Out There in the Blue (FitzGerald) (01) 891
Western Alliance, The (Grosser) (81) 911
What It Takes (Cramer) (93) 874
What Kind of Life (Callahan) (91) 886
When Work Disappears (Wilson) (97) 880
Where I Was From (Didion) (04) 831
Which Side Are You On? (Geoghegan) (92) 885
White Tribe of Africa, The (Harrison) (H-83) 459
Who Killed Daniel Pearl? (Lévy) (04) 835
Who Voted for Hitler? (Hamilton) (H-83) 462
Whole Woman, The (Greer) (00) 834
Why They Kill (Rhodes) (00) 843
With the Stroke of a Pen (Mayer) (02) 870
Within the Context of No Context (Trow) (98) 866
Work of Nations, The (Reich) (92) 919
World After Oil, The (Nussbaum) (H-84) 502
Wrath of Nations, The (Pfaff) (94) 864
Yellow Wind, The (Grossman) (89) 928

DIARIES. *See* AUTOBIOGRAPHY, MEMOIRS, DIARIES, and LETTERS

DRAMA. *See* POETRY and DRAMA

ECONOMICS
Accidental Theorist, The (Krugman) (99) 10
Cash Nexus, The (Ferguson) (02) 145
Commanding Heights (Yergin and Stanislaw) (99) 204
Disposable People (Bales) (00) 181
Food Politics (Nestle) (03) 311
Frozen Desire (Buchan) (98) 327
Globalization and Its Discontents (Stiglitz) (03) 334
Going Up the River (Hallinan) (02) 352
Good Life and Its Discontents, The (Samuelson) (97) 345
Greenspan (Martin) (01) 365
Heaven's Door (Borjas) (00) 367
John Maynard Keynes, 1920-1937 (Skidelsky) (95) 400
John Maynard Keynes, 1937-1946 (Skidelsky) (02) 453
Lexus and the Olive Tree, The (Friedman) (00) 483
Money (Hacker) (98) 562
Nature of Economies, The (Jacobs) (01) 613
New Financial Order, The (Shiller) (04) 551
New New Thing, The (Lewis) (00) 571
One World, Ready or Not (Greider) (98) 612
Overspent American, The (Schor) (99) 610
Pop Internationalism (Krugman) (97) 666
Price of Citizenship, The (Katz) (02) 655
Reefer Madness (Schlosser) (04) 643
Soros (Kaufman) (03) 794
Wealth and Democracy (Phillips) (03) 872
When Work Disappears (Wilson) (97) 880

EDUCATION
Among Schoolchildren (Kidder) (90) 34
Big Test, The (Lemann) (00) 57
Call of Stories, The (Coles) (90) 81
Content of Our Character, The (Steele) (91) 170
Cultural Literacy (Hirsch) (88) 223
Higher Superstition (Gross and Levitt) (95) 301

Howard Mumford Jones and the Dynamics of Liberal Humanism (Brier) (95) 329
Innumeracy (Paulos) (90) 420
John Dewey and American Democracy (Westbrook) (92) 388
Literature Lost (Ellis) (98) 512
Number Sense, The (Dehaene) (98) 603
Recalcitrance, Faulkner, and the Professors (Wright) (91) 701
Savage Inequalities (Kozol) (92) 712
Seeing Voices (Sacks) (90) 720
Small Victories (Freedman) (91) 750
Soul of the American University, The (Marsden) (95) 744
There Are No Children Here (Kotlowitz) (92) 813
Vocation of a Teacher, The (Booth) (90) 854

ENVIRONMENT. *See* NATURE, NATURAL HISTORY, and the ENVIRONMENT

ESSAYS
a long the riverrun (Ellmann) (90) 1
Accidental Asian, The (Liu) (99) 5
Actual Minds, Possible Worlds (Bruner) (87) 11
Aesthetics, Method, and Epistemology (Foucault) (99) 15
After Henry (Didion) (93) 1
Afterlife, The (Fitzgerald) (04) 1
Against the Current (Berlin) (81) 9
Agon (Bloom) (83) 1
AIDS and Its Metaphors (Sontag) (90) 19
Always in Pursuit (Crouch) (99) 36
Amazing Grace (Norris) (99) 40
Americans at War (Ambrose) (98) 64
—And I Worked at the Writer's Trade (Cowley) (79) 24
Anthropologist on Mars, An (Sacks) (96) 47
Argufying (Empson) (89) 46
Around the Day in Eighty Worlds (Cortázar) (87) 45
Art & Ardor (Ozick) (84) 44
Art in the Light of Conscience (Tsvetaeva) (93) 36
Art of Telling, The (Kermode) (84) 49
Art of the Commonplace, The (Berry) (03) 33
Art of the Novel, The (Kundera) (89) 54
Art of the Personal Essay, The (Lopate, ed.) (95) 47
Artificial Wilderness, An (Birkerts) (88) 68
Arts of the Possible (Rich) (02) 53
Aspects of the Present (Mead and Metraux) (81) 62
At Home (Vidal) (89) 59
Avoidance of Literature, The (Sisson) (80) 40
Bachelorhood (Lopate) (82) 40
Bad Mouth (Adams) (78) 81
Balancing Acts (Hoagland) (93) 45
Barthes Reader, A (Barthes) (83) 44
Bartleby in Manhattan (Hardwick) (84) 82
Beyond Geography (Turner) (81) 82
Beyond the Dragon's Mouth (Naipaul) (86) 56
Black Athena Revisited (Lefkowitz and Rogers, eds.) (97) 114
Black Holes and Baby Universes and Other Essays (Hawking) (94) 94
Bodies in Motion and at Rest (Lynch) (01) 122
Borges, a Reader (Borges) (82) 63
Bottom Translation, The (Kott) (88) 116
Boy Scout Handbook and Other Observations, The (Fussell) (83) 70
Brainchildren (Dennett) (99) 122
Breathing Under Water and Other East European Essays (Barańczak) (91) 105
Bully for Brontosaurus (Gould) (92) 69
Burning Forest, The (Leys) (86) 86
But Do Blondes Prefer Gentlemen? (Burgess) (87) 94
Camera Age, The (Arlen) (82) 73
Camera Lucida (Barthes) (82) 78

Catbird's Song, The (Wilbur) (98) 156
Celebrations and Attacks (Howe) (80) 136
Choice of Days, A (Mencken) (81) 142
City of Bits (Mitchell) (96) 112
Collected Essays of Ralph Ellison, The (Ellison) (96) 128
Collected Essays of Robert Creeley, The (Creeley) (90) 108
Collected Prose (Lowell) (88) 173
Collected Works (Metcalf) (98) 199
Complete Collected Essays (Pritchett) (93) 179
Complete Prefaces, 1889-1913, The (Shaw) (95) 145
Complete Prose of Marianne Moore, The (Moore) (87) 165
Congregation (Rosenberg, ed.) (88) 189
Correspondent Breeze, The (Abrams) (85) 142
Cosmic Code, The (Pagels) (83) 156
Crooked Timber of Humanity, The (Berlin) (92) 133
Cutting Edges (Krauthammer) (86) 208
Cycles of American History, The (Schlesinger) (87) 183
Daguerreotypes and Other Essays (Dinesen) (80) 180
Dark Brain of Piranesi and Other Essays, The (Yourcenar) (85) 152
Days of Obligation (Rodriguez) (93) 204
Dead Elvis (Marcus) (92) 157
Death of Adam, The (Robinson) (99) 226
Devil Problem, The (Remnick) (97) 210
Desire in Language (Kristeva) (81) 231
Destructive Generation (Collier and Horowitz) (90) 168
Dirt Under My Nails (Foster) (03) 207
Doing What Comes Naturally (Fish) (90) 190
Don't Tell the Grown-ups (Lurie) (91) 231
Down the River (Abbey) (83) 205
Dream Palace of the Arab World, The (Ajami) (99) 238
Earthly Delights, Unearthly Adornments (Morris) (79) 175
Echoes Down the Corridor (Miller) (01) 263
Economists, The (Silk) (77) 251
Edward Hoagland Reader, The (Hoagland) (80) 260
Eiffel Tower and Other Mythologies, The (Barthes) (80) 269
Empire of Signs, The (Barthes) (83) 230
Encounters with Chinese Writers (Dillard) (85) 223
End Papers (Breytenbach) (87) 242
Enigma of Anger, The (Keizer) (03) 265
Essays (Knox) (90) 219
Essays, Articles and Reviews of Evelyn Waugh, The (Waugh) (85) 238
Essays in Appreciation (Ricks) (97) 256
Essays in Feminism (Gornick) (80) 302
Essays of E. B. White (White) (78) 295
Essays of Virginia Woolf, 1904-1912, The (Woolf) (88) 288
Essays of Virginia Woolf, 1912-1918, The (Woolf) (89) 283
Essays of Virginia Woolf, 1919-1924, The (Woolf) (90) 222
Ethics (Foucault) (98) 289
Eudora Welty (Prenshaw, ed.) (81) 283
Europe, Europe (Enzensberger) (90) 227
Every Force Evolves a Form (Davenport) (88) 298
Ex Libris (Fadiman) (99) 269
Examined Life, The (Nozick) (90) 231
Experience of Place, The (Hiss) (91) 275
Eye of the Story, The (Welty) (79) 200
Faith in a Seed (Thoreau) (94) 274
Faith of a Writer, The (Oates) (04) 240
Fame and Folly (Ozick) (97) 269
Familiar Territory (Epstein) (80) 310
Fate of the Earth, The (Schell) (83) 244
Fatheralong (Wideman) (95) 227
Figures of Thought (Nemerov) (79) 209

Flower and the Leaf, The (Cowley) (86) 288
Forever Young (Cott) (79) 231
Founding Fish, The (McPhee) (03) 316
Friday Book, The (Barth) (85) 307
Genes, Peoples, and Languages (Cavalli-Sforza) (01) 327
Giving Good Weight (McPhee) (80) 358
Giving Offense (Coetzee) (97) 335
Gödel, Escher, Bach (Hofstadter) (80) 367
Going to the Territory (Ellison) (87) 331
Good Boys and Dead Girls (Gordon) (92) 256
Good Word & Other Words, The (Sheed) (80) 375
Government of the Tongue, The (Heaney) (90) 319
Great Movies, The (Ebert) (03) 348
Gutenberg Elegies, The (Birkerts) (96) 326
Habitations of the Word (Gass) (86) 376
Hannah Arendt (Hill, ed.) (80) 395
Happy Alchemy (Davies) (99) 346
Hermit in Paris (Calvino) (04) 339
Historical Fictions (Kenner) (91) 400
History of Private Life, Riddles of Identity in Modern Times, A (Prost and Vincent, eds.) (92) 294
History of Private Life, From Pagan Rome to Byzantium, A (Veyne) (88) 386
History of the World in 10½ Chapters, A (Barnes) (90) 390
How to Be Alone (Franzen) (03) 374
Hugging the Shore (Updike) (84) 358
Human Situation, The (Huxley) (78) 422
Hunter Gracchus, The (Davenport) (97) 419
I Tell You Now (Swann and Krupat, eds.) (88) 413
Illness as Metaphor (Sontag) (79) 295
Imaginary Homelands (Rushdie) (92) 324
In Search of Our Mothers' Gardens (Walker) (84) 368
In the Age of Prose (Heller) (85) 431
Innocent Eye, The (Shattuck) (85) 445
Invisible Republic (Marcus) (98) 441
Irons in the Fire (McPhee) (98) 445
Islam and the West (Lewis) (94) 414
Island of the Colorblind and Cycad Island, The (Sacks) (98) 454
Islands, the Universe, Home (Ehrlich) (92) 364
It All Adds Up (Bellow) (95) 381
Janus (Koestler) (79) 326
Japan in War and Peace (Dower) (95) 392
Joyce's Dislocations (Senn) (85) 509
Just as I Thought (Paley) (99) 441
Just Representations (Cozzens) (79) 343
Language, Counter-Memory, Practice (Foucault) (78) 504
Language in Literature (Jakobson) (89) 450
Last Decade, The (Trilling) (81) 480
Last Empire, The (Vidal) (02) 472
Less Than One (Brodsky) (87) 471
Letters from Prison (Michnik) (87) 477
Letters from the Country (Bly) (82) 444
Life and Work of Barbara Pym, The (Salwak, ed.) (88) 471
Life of the Mind, The (Arendt) (79) 393
Life Sentences (Epstein) (98) 504
Life/Situations (Sartre) (78) 529
Little Order, A (Waugh) (81) 517
Look, Listen, Read (Lévi-Strauss) (98) 526
Loose Canons (Gates) (93) 483
Love Undetectable (Sullivan) (99) 492
Man Made of Words, The (Momaday) (98) 534
Man Who Mistook His Wife for a Hat, The (Sacks) (87) 516
Marriage and Morals Among the Victorians (Himmelfarb) (87) 525
Me Again (Smith) (83) 458
Meditations from a Movable Chair (Dubus) (99) 538
Medusa and the Snail, The (Thomas) (80) 533

CATEGORY INDEX

Men in the Off Hours (Carson) (01) 583
Metropol (Aksyonov, et al., eds.) (84) 533
Microworlds (Lem) (86) 595
Middle of My Tether, The (Epstein) (84) 539
Migrations to Solitude (Halpern) (93) 513
Milosz's ABC's (Miłosz) (02) 533
Missing Persons and Other Essays (Böll) (78) 577
Modernist Quartet (Lentricchia) (95) 499
Moksha (Huxley) (79) 451
Most Beautiful House in the World, The (Rybczynski) (90) 582
Moving Target, A (Golding) (83) 506
Music of What Happens, The (Vendler) (89) 566
Myself with Others (Fuentes) (89) 577
Myth Makers, The (Pritchett) (80) 560
Nabokov's Fifth Arc (Rivers and Nicol, eds.) (83) 511
Nearer, My God (Buckley) (98) 575
New Critical Essays (Barthes) (81) 609
New Lives (Rabinowitz) (77) 549
No Other Book (Jarrell) (00) 576
Nobody Better, Better Than Nobody (Frazier) (88) 605
Northrop Frye on Culture and Literature (Frye) (79) 496
Notes of a Hanging Judge (Crouch) (91) 634
Odd Jobs (Updike) (92) 588
Of Poetry and Poets (Eberhart) (80) 610
On Grief and Reason (Brodsky) (97) 644
On Lies, Secrets, and Silence (Rich) (80) 622
On Writing and Politics (Grass) (86) 695
Once Again for Thucydides (Handke) (99) 589
One by One from the Inside Out (Loury) (96) 532
One Earth, Four or Five Worlds (Paz) (86) 701
One Good Turn (Rybczynski) (01) 679
One Way to Spell Man (Stegner) (83) 563
Operette Morali (Leopardi) (84) 643
Ordeal by Labyrinth (Eliade) (83) 572
Orwell, the Lost Writings (Orwell) (86) 715
Owls and Other Fantasies (Oliver) (04) 596
Panda's Thumb, The (Gould) (81) 640
Paul Klee (Lanchner, ed.) (88) 668
Personal Impressions (Berlin) (82) 632
Philosophical Explanations (Nozick) (82) 638
Phoenicians, The (Moscati, ed.) (90) 665
Pieces and Pontifications (Mailer) (83) 597
Pieces of Soap (Elkin) (93) 629
Place in Space, A (Snyder) (96) 585
Plausible Prejudices (Epstein) (86) 737
Poet as Journalist, The (Whittemore) (77) 623
Poet's Work (Gibbons, ed.) (80) 668
Politics and Ideology in the Age of the Civil War (Foner) (81) 661
Portable Jack Kerouac, The (Kerouac) (96) 597
Pound/Ford, the Story of a Literary Friendship (Pound and Ford) (83) 621
Practicing History (Tuchman) (82) 647
Presence of Ford Madox Ford, The (Stang, ed.) (82) 652
Primary Colors, The (Theroux) (95) 613
Profane Art, The (Oates) (84) 716
Professing Poetry (Wain) (79) 561
Proper Study of Mankind, The (Berlin) (99) 640
Purple Decades, The (Wolfe) (83) 626
Pushcart Prize, III, The (Henderson, ed.) (79) 565
Quarrel and Quandary (Ozick) (01) 721
Questioning the Millennium (Gould) (98) 652
Reasonable Creatures (Pollitt) (95) 626
Rebellions, Perversities, and Main Events (Kempton) (95) 635
Red Smith Reader, The (Smith) (83) 645
Red Wolves and Black Bears (Hoagland) (77) 658
Reflections (Benjamin) (79) 575
Reflections on Exile and Other Essays (Said) (02) 684
Regarding the Pain of Others (Sontag) (04) 648

Regions of Memory (Merwin) (88) 742
Representations (Marcus) (77) 673
Required Writing (Larkin) (85) 747
Rethinking Social Policy (Jencks) (93) 682
Return of Eva Perón, The (Naipaul) (81) 686
Richer, the Poorer, The (West) (96) 641
Riders on the Earth (MacLeish) (79) 601
Risk and Blame (Douglas) (93) 687
Road-Side Dog (Miłosz) (99) 666
Russian Thinkers (Berlin) (79) 627
Science Observed (Bernstein) (83) 689
Second American Revolution, The (Vidal) (83) 700
Second Life of Art, The (Montale) (83) 705
Second Words (Atwood) (85) 785
Selected Essays (Berger) (03) 732
Selected Essays of Cyril Connolly, The (Connolly) (85) 793
Selected Essays of John Crowe Ransom (Ransom) (85) 797
Selected Non-Fictions (Borges) (00) 683
Selected Prose, A (Duncan) (96) 690
Selected Writings, 1913-1926 (Benjamin) (97) 746
Selected Writings, 1927-1934 (Benjamin) (00) 693
Selected Writings, 1938-1940 (Benjamin) (04) 674
Selected Writings of James Weldon Johnson, Vol. I and Vol. II, The (Johnson) (96) 694
Sense of Sight, The (Berger) (87) 754
Shrovetide in Old New Orleans (Reed) (79) 681
Signposts in a Strange Land (Percy) (92) 747
Singularities (Simon) (77) 742
Six Memos for the Next Millennium (Calvino) (89) 799
Size of Thoughts, The (Baker) (97) 757
Small Wonder (Kingsolver) (03) 779
Solace of Open Spaces, The (Ehrlich) (86) 840
Solzhenitsyn in Exile (Dunlop, Haugh, and Nicholson, eds.) (86) 843
Something Said (Sorrentino) (86) 847
Something to Declare (Alvarez) (99) 720
Speaking of Literature and Society (Trilling) (81) 764
Standing by Words (Berry) (84) 813
State of the Language, The (Ricks and Michaels, eds.) (91) 773
Step Across This Line (Rushdie) (03) 799
Still Life with a Bridle (Herbert) (92) 785
Stuff of Sleep and Dreams (Edel) (83) 765
Summer Life, A (Soto) (91) 782
Supposedly Fun Thing I'll Never Do Again, A (Wallace) (98) 750
Susan Sontag Reader, A (Sontag) (83) 769
Sylvia Plath (Butscher, ed.) (78) 809
Table of Contents (McPhee) (86) 873
Taking the World in for Repairs (Selzer) (87) 836
Tale Bearers, The (Pritchett) (81) 786
Teaching a Stone to Talk (Dillard) (83) 773
Technical Difficulties (Jordan) (93) 779
Terrorists and Novelists (Johnson) (83) 783
Testaments Betrayed (Kundera) (96) 744
Tests of Time (Gass) (03) 825
Theater Essays of Arthur Miller, The (Miller) (79) 742
Theater of Essence, The (Kott) (85) 890
Thirties and After, The (Spender) (79) 745
This Quiet Dust and Other Writings (Styron) (83) 796
Time of Our Time, The (Mailer) (99) 764
Time Pieces (Morris) (90) 805
Time to Hear and Answer, A (Littleton, ed.) (78) 841
Tolstoy's Dictaphone (Birkerts, ed.) (97) 834
Traveling Light (Barich) (85) 923
Traveling Mercies (Lamott) (00) 764
Trying to Save Piggy Sneed (Irving) (97) 838
Tugman's Passage, The (Hoagland) (83) 836
Twentieth Century Pleasures (Hass) (85) 941
Uncivil Liberties (Trillin) (83) 849
Under Review (Powell) (95) 819

Under the Sign of Saturn (Sontag) (81) 848
Undertaking, The (Lynch) (98) 786
United States (Vidal) (94) 819
Unlocking the English Language (Burchfield) (92) 849
Vectors and Smoothable Curves (Bronk) (84) 905
Ved Mehta Reader, A (Mehta) (99) 834
View from 80, The (Cowley) (81) 867
View from Highway 1, The (Arlen) (77) 884
Visions from San Francisco Bay (Miłosz) (83) 860
Voice Lessons (Mairs) (95) 835
Voices and Visions (Vendler, ed.) (88) 943
Wallace Stevens (Doggett and Buttel, eds.) (81) 879
Watergate and the Constitution (Kurland) (79) 830
What Am I Doing Here (Chatwin) (90) 874
What the Twilight Says (Walcott) (99) 851
Where Do You Put the Horse? (Metcalf) (87) 963
Where the Stress Falls (Sontag) (02) 842
White Album, The (Didion) (80) 862
White Lantern, The (Connell) (81) 916
Why Big Fierce Animals Are Rare (Colinvaux) (79) 857
Winner Names the Age, The (Smith) (79) 879
With All Disrespect (Trillin) (86) 950
With My Trousers Rolled (Epstein) (96) 818
Within the Context of No Context (Trow) (98) 866
Women and the Common Life (Lasch) (98) 878
Women on Love (Sullerot) (81) 947
Words That Must Somehow Be Said (Boyle) (86) 966
Working It Out (Ruddick and Daniels, eds.) (78) 937
World, the Text, and the Critic, The (Said) (84) 971
World Unsuspected, A (Harris, ed.) (88) 984
World Within the Word, The (Gass) (79) 913
Worm of Consciousness and Other Essays, The (Chiaromonte) (77) 956
Wormholes (Fowles) (99) 877
Writer and the World, The (Naipaul) (03) 902
Writing and Being (Gordimer) (96) 839
Writing in a State of Siege (Brink) (84) 983
Writings (Du Bois) (88) 993
Yoga for People Who Can't Be Bothered to Do It (Dyer) (04) 864
Young Rebecca, The (West) (83) 932
Zora Neale Hurston, Vol. I and Vol. II (Hurston) (96) 852

God's Secretaries (Nicolson) (04) 295
Going Up the River (Hallinan) (02) 352
Good Natured (De Waal) (97) 350
How We Die (Nuland) (95) 324
Hugo L. Black (Ball) (97) 415
Inequality Reexamined (Sen) (93) 382
Integrity (Carter) (97) 456
Justice Oliver Wendell Holmes (White) (94) 431
Kindly Inquisitors (Rauch) (94) 436
Law Unto Itself, A (Burnham) (91) 507
Laws Harsh as Tigers (Salyer) (96) 418
Lincoln's Virtues (Miller) (03) 490
Making Stories (Bruner) (03) 509
Mayhem (Bok) (99) 534
Metaphysics as a Guide to Morals (Murdoch) (94) 526
Moral Sense, The (Wilson) (94) 539
Neither Friend nor Foe (Packard) (93) 545
New Birth of Freedom, A (Black) (98) 579
New White Nationalism in America, The (Swain) (03) 572
Nigger (Kennedy) (03) 586
Our Posthuman Future (Fukuyama) (03) 615
Perpetrators, Victims, Bystanders (Hilberg) (93) 624
Place in Space, A (Snyder) (96) 585
"Probable Cause" and "Beyond Reasonable Doubt" (Shapiro) (93) 75
Proximity to Death (McFeely) (00) 630
Rethinking Social Policy (Jencks) (93) 682
Reversal of Fortune (Dershowitz) (87) 716
Risk and Blame (Douglas) (93) 687
Saving the Heart (Klaidman) (01) 754
Sex and Social Justice (Nussbaum) (00) 697
Strange Justice (Mayer and Abramson) (95) 765
Tempting of America, The (Bork) (90) 787
Transformation of American Law, 1870-1960, The (Horwitz) (93) 805
Trust (Fukuyama) (96) 777
Turning Right (Savage) (93) 815
Tyranny of the Majority, The (Guinier) (95) 805
What Kind of Life (Callahan) (91) 886
What Kind of Nation (Simon) (03) 877
Whose Justice? Which Rationality? (MacIntyre) (89) 902
Wisdom of the Body, The (Nuland) (98) 854
World Made New, A (Glendon) (02) 884

ETHICS and LAW
Alien Nation (Brimelow) (96) 9
Amending America (Bernstein and Agel) (94) 15
Bakke Case, The (Dreyfuss and Lawrence) (80) 45
"Beyond Reasonable Doubt" and "Probable Cause" (Shapiro) (93) 75
Better than Well (Elliott) (04) 79
Biotech Century, The (Rifkin) (99) 100
Capitol Games (Phelps and Winternitz) (93) 128
Civil Action, A (Harr) (96) 116
Civility (Carter) (99) 177
Clone (Kolata) (99) 186
Court and the Constitution, The (Cox) (88) 213
Crime and Punishment in American History (Friedman) (94) 173
Democracy on Trial (Smith) (96) 165
Diversity in America (Schuck) (04) 174
Doing What Comes Naturally (Fish) (90) 190
Dream Makers, Dream Breakers (Rowan) (94) 252
Elephant Destiny (Meredith) (04) 215
End of Equality, The (Kaus) (93) 258
Enough (McKibben) (04) 236
Ethics (Foucault) (98) 289
From Brown to Bakke, The Supreme Court and School Integration (Wilkinson) (80) 334
Genocidal Mentality, The (Lifton and Markusen) (91) 338
Genome (Ridley) (01) 332

FICTION
Aberration of Starlight (Sorrentino) (81) 1
About a Boy (Hornby) (99) 1
About My Table (Delbanco) (84) 1
Absolute Truths (Howatch) (96) 1
Abyss, The (Yourcenar) (77) 1
Academic Question, An (Pym) (87) 1
Accident, The (Plante) (92) 5
Accident (Wolf) (90) 6
Accidental Tourist, The (Tyler) (86) 1
According to Queeney (Bainbridge) (02) 1
Accordion Crimes (Proulx) (97) 5
Achilles (Cook) (03) 1
Across (Handke) (87) 6
Across the Bridge (Gallant) (94) 1
Acts of King Arthur and His Noble Knights, The (Steinbeck) (77) 7
Acts of Worship (Mishima) (90) 10
Actual, The (Bellow) (98) 1
Adventures of Huckleberry Finn (Twain) (02) 9
After Hannibal (Unsworth) (98) 9
After Rain (Trevor) (97) 14
After the Plague (Boyle) (02) 18
After the Quake (Murakami) (03) 5
After the War (Adams) (01) 6
Afterlife and Other Stories, The (Updike) (95) 6
Afternoon of a Writer, The (Handke) (90) 14

CATEGORY INDEX

Age of Grief, The (Smiley) (88) 6
Age of Iron (Coetzee) (91) 5
Age of Wonders, The (Appelfeld) (82) 1
Agüero Sisters, The (García) (98) 14
Ah, But Your Land Is Beautiful (Paton) (83) 6
Aiding and Abetting (Spark) (02) 26
Air and Fire (Thomson) (95) 15
Airships (Hannah) (79) 5
Aladdin's Problem (Jünger) (93) 6
Alias Grace (Atwood) (97) 23
Alice in Bed (Schine) (84) 12
All-Bright Court (Porter) (92) 9
All Souls' Rising (Bell) (96) 22
All the Days and Nights (Maxwell) (96) 26
All the Names (Saramago) (01) 15
All the Pretty Horses (McCarthy) (93) 10
All Tomorrow's Parties (Gibson) (00) 6
All-True Travels and Adventures of Lidie Newton, The
   (Smiley) (99) 32
Alma (Burn) (93) 15
Almanac of the Dead (Silko) (92) 13
Almost Innocent (Bosworth) (85) 7
Alnilam (Dickey) (88) 15
Already Dead (Johnson) (98) 23
Altered States (Brookner) (98) 27
Always Coming Home (Le Guin) (86) 21
Amateurs (Barthelme) (78) 37
Amateur's Guide to the Night, An (Robison) (84) 16
Amazing Adventures of Kavalier and Clay, The
   (Chabon) (01) 19
American Ambassador, The (Just) (88) 20
American Appetites (Oates) (90) 29
American Falls (Batchelor) (98) 27
American Owned Love (Boswell) (98) 41
American Pastoral (Roth) (98) 45
Amongst Women (McGahern) (91) 33
Amsterdam (McEwan) (00) 14
Amy and Isabelle (Strout) (00) 18
Anarchists' Convention, The (Sayles) (80) 28
Anatomy Lesson, The (Roth) (84) 26
Ancient Evenings (Mailer) (84) 31
And Never Said a Word (Böll) (79) 29
Angel of Light (Oates) (82) 17
Angels and Insects (Byatt) (94) 25
Anil's Ghost (Ondaatje) (01) 44
Animal Dreams (Kingsolver) (91) 38
Annie John (Kincaid) (86) 33
Anniversary and Other Stories, The (Auchincloss)
   (00) 31
Annunciation (Plante) (95) 42
Another I, Another You (Schickel) (79) 34
Another World (Barker) (00) 40
Another You (Beattie) (96) 39
Anpao (Highwater) (78) 63
Antarctic Navigation (Arthur) (96) 43
Antarctica (Robinson) (99) 48
Antelope Wife, The (Erdrich) (99) 53
Anthills of the Savannah (Achebe) (89) 28
Anthology of Chinese Literature, An (Owen, ed.)
   (97) 53
Any Human Heart (Boyd) (04) 40
Any Old Iron (Burgess) (90) 44
Anything for Billy (McMurtry) (89) 33
Anywhere but Here (Simpson) (88) 42
Arabesques (Shammas) (89) 37
Arabian Jazz (Abu-Jaber) (94) 38
Ararat (Thomas) (84) 36
Arc d'X (Erickson) (94) 47
Ark Baby (Jensen) (99) 64
Arrest Sitting Bull (Jones) (78) 72
As Max Saw It (Begley) (95) 51
As She Climbed Across the Table (Lethem) (98) 85

Assassination of Jesse James by the Coward Robert
   Ford, The (Hansen) (84) 54
Asylum (McGrath) (98) 90
At the Bottom of the River (Kincaid) (84) 59
At Weddings and Wakes (McDermott) (93) 40
Athena (Banville) (96) 51
Atlas, The (Vollmann) (97) 76
Atonement (McEwan) (03) 42
Attachments (Rossner) (78) 77
Aunt Julia and the Scriptwriter (Vargas Llosa) (83) 34
Austerlitz (Sebald) (02) 62
Autobiography of My Mother, The (Brown) (77) 72
Autobiography of My Mother, The (Kincaid) (97) 83
Autograph Man, The (Smith) (03) 46
Autumn (Mojtabai) (83) 39
Autumn of the Patriarch, The (García Márquez) (77) 77
Ax, The (Westlake) (98) 95
Babel Tower (Byatt) (97) 87
Bachelorhood (Lopate) (82) 40
Back Room, The (Martín Gaite) (84) 71
Back When We Were Grownups (Tyler) (02) 66
Bad Lands, The (Hall) (79) 47
Bag of Bones (King) (99) 83
Bandits (Leonard) (88) 71
Banker (Francis) (84) 76
Barracks Thief, The (Wolff) (86) 48
Bass Saxophone, The (Škvorecký) (80) 54
Bastard Out of Carolina (Allison) (93) 58
Baudolino (Eco) (03) 56
Bay of Angels, The (Brookner) (02) 70
Bay of Souls (Stone) (04) 54
Beach Music (Conroy) (96) 69
Beachmasters (Astley) (87) 51
Bean Trees, The (Kingsolver) (89) 72
Bear and His Daughter (Stone) (98) 99
Beard's Roman Women (Burgess) (77) 81
Beautiful Room Is Empty, The (White) (89) 76
Beauty of Men, The (Holleran) (97) 100
Because It Is Bitter, and Because It Is My Heart (Oates)
   (91) 75
Because They Wanted To (Gaitskill) (98) 104
Bech at Bay (Updike) (99) 92
Bech Is Back (Updike) (83) 53
Becoming Madame Mao (Min) (01) 69
Bee Season (Goldberg) (01) 74
Beet Queen, The (Erdrich) (87) 61
Before and After (Brown) (93) 67
Before the Dawn (Shimazaki) (88) 81
Being Dead (Crace) (01) 79
Believers (Baxter) (98) 113
Bellarosa Connection, The (Bellow) (90) 53
Bellefleur (Oates) (81) 78
Beloved (Morrison) (88) 85
Bend in the River, A (Naipaul) (80) 69
Bertolt Brecht Short Stories, 1921-1946 (Brecht)
   (84) 86
Best Friends (Berger) (04) 75
Best of Sholom Aleichem, The (Aleichem) (80) 77
Bet They'll Miss Us When We're Gone (Wiggins)
   (92) 39
Betsey Brown (Shange) (86) 52
Beyond the Dragon's Mouth (Naipaul) (86) 56
Beyond the Pale and Other Stories (Trevor) (83) 57
Big as Life (Howard) (02) 83
Big If (Costello) (03) 69
Billy Bathgate (Doctorow) (90) 67
Bingo Palace, The (Erdrich) (95) 76
Binstead's Safari (Ingalls) (89) 94
Biography (Gitelson) (92) 48
Birds of America (Moore) (99) 105
Birdsong (Faulks) (97) 110
Birdy (Wharton) (80) 79

Birth of the People's Republic of Antarctica, The (Batchelor) (84) 91
Black Betty (Mosley) (95) 80
Black Dogs (McEwan) (93) 79
Black Orchid (Meyer and Kaplan) (78) 100
Black Robe (Moore) (86) 61
Black Ulysses (Geeraerts) (79) 55
Black Water (Oates) (93) 83
Blacker than a Thousand Midnights (Straight) (95) 85
Blackwater (Ekman) (97) 119
Blanco (Wier) (80) 83
Blind Assassin, The (Atwood) (01) 94
Blind Date (Kosinski) (78) 104
Blindness (Saramago) (99) 114
Blonde (Oates) (01) 99
Blood Meridian (McCarthy) (86) 67
Bloodshed and Three Novellas (Ozick) (77) 101
Bloodsmoor Romance, A (Oates) (83) 61
Blow Fly (Cornwell) (04) 87
Blow Your House Down (Barker) (85) 47
Blue Angel (Prose) (01) 104
Blue at the Mizzen (O'Brian) (00) 78
Blue Bedspread, The (Jha) (01) 108
Blue Calhoun (Price) (93) 87
Blue Flower, The (Fitzgerald) (98) 121
Blue Hammer, The (Macdonald) (77) 105
Blue Pastoral (Sorrentino) (84) 99
Blue Shoe (Lamott) (03) 87
Bluebeard (Frisch) (84) 105
Bluebeard (Vonnegut) (88) 107
Bodega Dreams (Quiñonez) (01) 117
Bodily Harm (Atwood) (83) 65
Body and Soul (Conroy) (94) 100
Body Artist, The (DeLillo) (02) 93
Body Farm, The (Cornwell) (95) 94
Bohin Manor (Konwicki) (91) 86
Bondwoman's Narrative, The (Crafts) (03) 92
Bone (Ng) (94) 105
Bone by Bone (Matthiessen) (00) 82
Bone People, The (Hulme) (86) 72
Bonesetter's Daughter, The (Tan) (02) 102
Bonfire of the Vanities, The (Wolfe) (88) 112
Book Against God, The (Wood) (04) 96
Book and the Brotherhood, The (Murdoch) (89) 103
Book Class, The (Auchincloss) (85) 52
Book of Common Prayer, A (Didion) (78) 121
Book of Ebenezer Le Page, The (Edwards) (82) 59
Book of Evidence, The (Banville) (91) 91
Book of Happiness, The (Berberova) (00) 86
Book of Illusions, The (Auster) (03) 97
Book of Kings, The (Thackara) (00) 90
Book of Laughter and Forgetting, The (Kundera) (81) 99
Book of Merlyn, The (White) (78) 126
Book of Salt, The (Truong) (04) 100
Book of Sand, The (Borges) (78) 131
Book of Sorrows, The (Wangerin) (86) 77
Boone's Lick (McMurtry) (01) 131
Border Crossing (Barker) (02) 115
Borges, a Reader (Borges) (82) 63
Born Brothers (Woiwode) (89) 107
Bottle in the Smoke, A (Wilson) (91) 100
Box of Matches, A (Baker) (04) 105
Boy Without a Flag, The (Rodriguez) (93) 96
Braided Lives (Piercy) (83) 75
Brain Storm (Dooling) (99) 118
Brazil (Updike) (95) 99
Bread of Those Early Years, The (Böll) (77) 119
Bread Upon the Waters (Shaw) (82) 67
Breaks, The (Price) (84) 112
Breathing Lessons (Tyler) (89) 116
Brendan (Buechner) (88) 121
Bridegroom, The (Ha Jin) (01) 144

Bridget Jones's Diary (Fielding) (99) 132
Brief Interviews with Hideous Men (Wallace) (00) 95
Brief Lives (Brookner) (92) 60
Broke Heart Blues (Oates) (00) 99
Brotherly Love (Dexter) (92) 64
Buddha's Little Finger (Pelevin) (01) 153
Buenos Aires Affair, The (Puig) (77) 129
Buffalo Girls (McMurtry) (91) 110
Building, The (Glynn) (87) 90
Burden of Proof, The (Turow) (91) 115
Burger's Daughter (Gordimer) (80) 123
Burn, The (Aksyonov) (85) 68
Burning House, The (Beattie) (83) 86
Burnt Water (Fuentes) (81) 103
Business of Fancydancing, The (Alexie) (93) 124
Butcher Boy, The (McCabe) (94) 118
Buzzing, The (Knipfel) (04) 109
By the Lake (McGahern) (03) 123
Cabal and Other Stories, The (Gilchrist) (01) 168
Cadence of Grass, The (McGuane) (03) 128
Cadillac Jack (McMurtry) (83) 90
Cal (MacLaverty) (84) 132
California's Over (Jones) (98) 147
Call, The (Hersey) (86) 91
Campaign, The (Fuentes) (92) 79
Candido (Sciascia) (80) 129
Cannibal Galaxy, The (Ozick) (84) 137
Cannibals and Missionaries (McCarthy) (80) 133
Captain and the Enemy, The (Greene) (89) 140
Captain Pantoja and the Special Service (Vargas Llosa) (79) 75
Caramelo (Cisneros) (03) 132
Careless Widow and Other Stories, A (Pritchett) (90) 86
Carnival (Dinesen) (78) 150
Carpenter's Gothic (Gaddis) (86) 96
Carter Beats the Devil (Gold) (02) 140
Case of Curiosities, A (Kurzweil) (93) 133
Cassandra (Wolf) (85) 74
Cat Who Walks Through Walls, The (Heinlein) (86) 100
Cathedral (Carver) (84) 143
Cat's Eye (Atwood) (90) 91
Cattle Killing, The (Wideman) (97) 142
Cavedweller (Allison) (99) 145
Caveman's Valentine, The (Green) (95) 109
Century's Son (Boswell) (03) 137
Ceremony and Other Stories, The (Kees) (85) 79
Certain Justice, A (James) (98) 160
Certain Lucas, A (Cortázar) (85) 84
Chain of Voices, A (Brink) (83) 101
Chaneysville Incident, The (Bradley) (82) 82
Change of Gravity, A (Higgins) (98) 164
Change of Light, A (Cortázar) (81) 122
Charles Ryder's Schooldays and Other Stories (Waugh) (83) 105
Charming Billy (McDermott) (99) 154
Chatterton (Ackroyd) (89) 150
Chesapeake (Michener) (79) 99
Chess Garden, The (Hansen) (96) 98
Child in Time, The (McEwan) (88) 146
Child of My Heart (McDermott) (03) 147
Children of Dune (Herbert) (77) 139
Children of Light (Stone) (87) 112
Children of Men, The (James) (94) 123
Childwold (Oates) (77) 149
Chilly Scenes of Winter (Beattie) (77) 154
China Men (Kingston) (81) 137
Christopher Unborn (Fuentes) (90) 95
Chronicle of a Death Foretold (García Márquez) (84) 163
Cider House Rules, The (Irving) (86) 131
Circles (McCarthy) (78) 179

CATEGORY INDEX

Cities of Salt (Munif) (89) 160
Cities of the Plain (McCarthy) (99) 173
City of Your Final Destination, The (Cameron) (03) 151
Civil Wars (Brown) (85) 101
Clara (Galloway) (04) 122
Clear Light of Day (Desai) (81) 156
!Click Song (Williams) (83) 124
Cliff, The (Slavitt) (95) 123
Clockers (Price) (93) 161
Close Quarters (Golding) (88) 155
Close Range (Proulx) (00) 134
Closed Eye, A (Brookner) (93) 166
Closing Arguments (Busch) (92) 94
Closing Time (Heller) (95) 128
Cloud Chamber (Dorris) (98) 168
Cloudsplitter (Banks) (99) 190
Coast of Chicago, The (Dybek) (91) 142
Coffin Tree, The (Law-Yone) (84) 168
Cold Mountain (Frazier) (98) 172
Cold Snap (Jones) (96) 124
Collaborators (Kauffman) (87) 127
Collected Prose, The (Bishop) (85) 121
Collected Short Fiction of Bruce Jay Friedman, The (Friedman) (96) 132
Collected Stories, 1939-1976 (Bowles) (80) 151
Collected Stories (Morris) (87) 160
Collected Stories (O'Connor) (82) 100
Collected Stories (Paley) (95) 133
Collected Stories, The (Price) (94) 150
Collected Stories (Pritchett) (83) 131
Collected Stories, The (Theroux) (98) 194
Collected Stories, The (Tuohy) (85) 126
Collected Stories (Williams) (86) 170
Collected Stories of Caroline Gordon, The (Gordon) (82) 106
Collected Stories of Colette, The (Colette) (84) 194
Collected Stories of Elizabeth Bowen, The (Bowen) (81) 173
Collected Stories of Eudora Welty, The (Welty) (81) 178
Collected Stories of Evan S. Connell, The (Connell) (96) 136
Collected Stories of Isaac Bashevis Singer, The (Singer) (83) 135
Collected Stories of Louis Auchincloss, The (Auchincloss) (95) 137
Collected Stories of Mavis Gallant, The (Gallant) (97) 171
Collected Stories of Sean O'Faolain, The (O'Faolain) (84) 198
Collected Stories of Wallace Stegner (Stegner) (91) 161
Collected Stories of William Humphrey, The (Humphrey) (86) 175
Collected Works, 1956-1976 (Metcalf) (97) 175
Color Purple, The (Walker) (83) 139
Come to Me (Bloom) (94) 154
Company (Beckett) (81) 184
Company, The (Littell) (03) 159
Company Man (Wade) (93) 176
Company of Women, The (Gordon) (82) 115
Complete Collected Stories (Pritchett) (92) 109
Complete Prose of Marianne Moore, The (Moore) (87) 165
Complete Stories of Bernard Malamud, The (Malamud) (98) 207
Complete Works of Isaac Babel, The (Babel) (02) 158
Concrete (Bernhard) (85) 131
Confederacy of Dunces, A (Toole) (81) 188
Consenting Adults (De Vries) (81) 198
Consider This, Señora (Doerr) (94) 163
Conspiracy of Paper, A (Liss) (01) 213
Consul's File, The (Theroux) (78) 215

Corrections, The (Franzen) (02) 176
Counterlife, The (Roth) (88) 204
Country, The (Plante) (82) 140
Coup, The (Updike) (79) 133
Covenant, The (Michener) (81) 210
Crabwalk (Grass) (04) 138
Crampton Hodnet (Pym) (86) 194
Crazed, The (Jin) (03) 168
Creation (Vidal) (82) 151
Crooked Little Heart (Lamott) (98) 211
Cross Channel (Barnes) (97) 183
Crossing to Safety (Stegner) (88) 218
Crossing, Volume Two, The (McCarthy) (95) 157
Crusoe's Daughter (Gardam) (87) 175
Cryptonomicon (Stephenson) (00) 159
Cubs and Other Stories, The (Vargas Llosa) (80) 165
Cunning Little Vixen, The (Tesnohlidek) (86) 204
Cunning Man, The (Davies) (96) 144
Curranne Trueheart (Newlove) (87) 179
Dad (Wharton) (82) 166
Dalva (Harrison) (89) 212
Damascus Gate (Stone) (99) 221
Dancing After Hours (Dubus) (97) 196
Dancing at the Rascal Fair (Doig) (88) 228
Dancing Girls and Other Stories (Atwood) (83) 169
Dangerous Woman, A (Morris) (92) 138
Daniel Martin (Fowles) (78) 225
Dante Club, The (Pearl) (04) 156
Dark Back of Time (Marías) (02) 181
Dark Half, The (King) (90) 147
Dark Lady, The (Auchincloss) (78) 229
Darkness (Mukherjee) (87) 194
Darkness Visible (Golding) (80) 184
Darts of Cupid, and Other Stories, The (Templeton) (03) 182
Daughter of Fortune (Allende) (00) 168
Daughters (Marshall) (92) 142
Daughters of Albion (Wilson) (93) 200
Da Vinci Code, The (Brown) (04) 147
Da Vinci's Bicycle (Davenport) (80) 195
Davita's Harp (Potok) (86) 217
Day Lasts More than a Hundred Years, The (Aitmatov) (84) 219
Day of Creation, The (Ballard) (89) 226
Day of Judgment, The (Satta) (88) 242
Dead Languages (Shields) (90) 163
Dead Man in Deptford, A (Burgess) (96) 153
Dead Zone, The (King) (80) 205
Deadeye Dick (Vonnegut) (83) 174
Dean's December, The (Bellow) (83) 179
Death in Holy Orders (James) (02) 185
Death in the Andes (Vargas Llosa) (97) 200
Death Is a Lonely Business (Bradbury) (86) 222
Death of Bernadette Lefthand, The (Querry) (94) 217
Death of Methuselah and Other Stories, The (Singer) (89) 231
Death of the Detective, The (Smith) (77) 202
Death of the King's Canary, The (Thomas and Davenport) (78) 238
Death of Vishnu, The (Suri) (02) 190
December 6 (Smith) (03) 187
Deception (Roth) (91) 188
Deep River (Endō) (96) 160
Defending Billy Ryan (Higgins) (93) 214
Delirium Eclipse and Other Stories (Lasdun) (87) 204
Delusions of Grandma (Fisher) (95) 162
Democracy (Didion) (85) 172
Demonology (Moody) (02) 195
Desert Rose, The (McMurtry) (84) 225
Desirable Daughters (Mukherjee) (03) 202
Desires (L'Heureux) (82) 181
Dessa Rose (Williams) (87) 207

Destinies of Darcy Dancer, Gentleman, The (Donleavy) (78) 254
Destiny (Parks) (01) 232
Details of a Sunset and Other Stories (Nabokov) (77) 206
Devices and Desires (James) (91) 202
Devil Wears Prada, The (Weisberger) (04) 169
Devil's Stocking, The (Algren) (84) 230
Dewey Defeats Truman (Mallon) (98) 239
Dictionary of the Khazars (Pavić) (89) 245
Different Seasons (King) (83) 189
Difficult Loves (Calvino) (85) 184
Difficulties with Girls (Amis) (90) 181
Dinner at the Homesick Restaurant (Tyler) (83) 194
Discovery of Heaven, The (Mulisch) (97) 225
Discovery of Slowness, The (Nadolny) (88) 247
Disgrace (Coetzee) (00) 177
Disobedience (Hamilton) (01) 242
Distant Relations (Fuentes) (83) 200
Distinguished Guest, The (Miller) (96) 186
Dive from Clausen's Pier, The (Packer) (03) 211
Diving Rock on the Hudson, A (Roth) (96) 190. *See also* From Bondage *and* Mercy of a Rude Stream
Do the Windows Open? (Hecht) (98) 259
Doctor Fischer of Geneva or the Bomb Party (Greene) (81) 244
Doctor's House, The (Beattie) (03) 215
Doctor's Wife, The (Moore) (77) 226
Documents Relating to the Sentimental Agents in the Volyen Empire (Lessing) (84) 239
Dogeaters (Hagedorn) (91) 221
Dolly (Brookner) (95) 180
Don't Tell Anyone (Busch) (01) 246
Double Honeymoon (Connell) (77) 242
Double Tongue, The (Golding) (96) 206
Down by the River (O'Brien) (98) 263
Dream Children (Wilson) (99) 234
Dream of Scipio, The (Pears) (03) 229
Dream Stuff (Malouf) (01) 250
Dreamer (Johnson) (99) 242
Dreaming in Cuban (Garcia) (93) 249
Dreams of Sleep (Humphreys) (85) 199
Dressing Up for the Carnival (Shields) (01) 254
Drift, The (Ridley) (03) 242
Drinking Coffee Elsewhere (Packer) (04) 189
Drop City (Boyle) (04) 193
Dubin's Lives (Malamud) (80) 231
Duncan's Colony (Petesch) (83) 210
During the Reign of the Queen of Persia (Chase) (84) 252
Dusk and Other Stories (Salter) (89) 254
Dutch Shea, Jr. (Dunne) (83) 216
Dying Animal, The (Roth) (02) 217
Early Stories, The (Updike) (04) 203
Earthly Powers (Burgess) (81) 260
East Is East (Boyle) (91) 240
East of the Mountains (Guterson) (00) 190
Easter Parade, The (Yates) (77) 247
Easy in the Islands (Shacochis) (86) 240
Echo House (Just) (98) 277
Eclipse (Banville) (02) 222
Eclogues (Davenport) (82) 185
Edisto (Powell) (85) 213
1876 (Vidal) (77) 256
Einstein's Dreams (Lightman) (94) 256
Elementary Particles, The (Houellebecq) (01) 267
Elephant Vanishes, The (Murakami) (94) 260
Elizabeth Costello (Coetzee) (04) 219
Elizabeth Stories, The (Huggan) (88) 256
Ellen Foster (Gibbons) (88) 261
Ellis Island and Other Stories (Helprin) (82) 219
Emigrants, The (Sebald) (98) 282
Emperor of Ocean Park, The (Carter) (03) 260

Emperor of the Air (Canin) (89) 268
Empire (Vidal) (88) 275
Empire Falls (Russo) (02) 244
Empire of the Sun (Ballard) (85) 218
Empress of the Splendid Season (Hijuelos) (00) 221
Enchantment (Merkin) (87) 238
End of the Hunt, The (Flanagan) (95) 200
End of the World News, The (Burgess) (84) 267
End of Vandalism, The (Drury) (95) 204
Ender's Shadow (Card) (00) 226
Endless Love (Spencer) (80) 294
Enduring Love (McEwan) (99) 257
Engineer of Human Souls, The (Škvorecký) (85) 227
England, England (Barnes) (00) 231
English Creek (Doig) (85) 232
English Disease, The (Skibell) (04) 232
English Music (Ackroyd) (93) 266
English Patient, The (Ondaatje) (93) 271
Enigma of Arrival, The (Naipaul) (88) 283
Entered from the Sun (Garrett) (91) 257
Equal Affections (Leavitt) (90) 215
Equal Love (Davies) (01) 286
Equal Music, An (Seth) (00) 236
Escapes (Williams) (91) 262
Eternal Curse on the Reader of These Pages (Puig) (83) 235
Evening Performance, An (Garrett) (86) 250
Evensong (Godwin) (00) 244
Everything Is Illuminated (Foer) (03) 274
Everything You Need (Kennedy) (02) 253
Everything's Eventual (King) (03) 279
Eve's Apple (Rosen) (98) 299
Evolution of Jane, The (Schine) (99) 265
Executioner's Song, The (Mailer) (80) 306
Extinction (Bernhard) (96) 242
Eye for Dark Places, An (Marder) (94) 269
Eye in the Door, The (Barker) (95) 218
Eye of the Heron, The (Le Guin) (84) 291
Eyre Affair, The (Fforde) (03) 283
Faithless (Oates) (02) 267
Falconer (Cheever) (78) 309
Falling in Place (Beattie) (81) 304
Falling Slowly (Brookner) (00) 248
Family (Gold) (82) 267
Family Album, A (Galloway) (79) 204
Family Arsenal, The (Theroux) (77) 274
Family Dancing (Leavitt) (85) 250
Family Feeling (Yglesias) (77) 277
Family Madness, A (Keneally) (87) 265
Family Matters (Mistry) (03) 292
Family Orchard, The (Eve) (01) 295
Family Pictures (Miller) (91) 283
Famished Road, The (Okri) (93) 279
Fanatic Heart, A (O'Brien) (85) 260
Fanny (Jong) (81) 309
Far Cry from Kensington, A (Spark) (89) 293
Farewell Party, The (Kundera) (77) 283
Farewell Symphony, The (White) (98) 303
Father and Son (Brown) (97) 274
Father Melancholy's Daughter (Godwin) (92) 201
Fathers and Crows (Vollmann) (93) 288
Father's Words, A (Stern) (87) 271
Feast of the Goat, The (Vargas Llosa) (02) 290
Feather Crowns (Mason) (94) 283
Female Ruins (Nicholson) (01) 305
Fetishist, The (Tournier) (85) 272
Feud, The (Berger) (84) 295
Fever (Wideman) (90) 249
Few Short Notes on Tropical Butterflies, A (Murray) (04) 253
Few Things I Know About Glafkos Thrassakis, The (Vassilikos) (04) 257
Fiasco (Lem) (88) 318

CATEGORY INDEX

Fifth Child, The (Lessing) (89) 298
Fifty Stories (Boyle) (81) 325
Figure on the Boundary Line, The (Meckel) (85) 276
Fima (Oz) (94) 296
Final Martyrs, The (Endō) (95) 235
Final Payments (Gordon) (79) 218
Finishing School, The (Godwin) (86) 274
Fire Down Below (Golding) (90) 253
Fires (Yourcenar) (82) 275
First Man, The (Camus) (96) 268
First Man on the Sun, The (Dillard) (84) 304
First Polka, The (Bienek) (85) 286
Fisher King, The (Powell) (87) 287
Fiskadoro (Johnson) (86) 279
Five for Sorrow, Ten for Joy (Godden) (80) 325
Five Seasons (Yehoshua) (90) 263
Flag for Sunrise, A (Stone) (82) 284
Flaming Corsage, The (Kennedy) (97) 282
Flanders (Anthony) (99) 282
Flashman and the Dragon (Fraser) (87) 292
Flaubert's Parrot (Barnes) (86) 284
Floating World, The (Kadohata) (90) 273
Flotsam and Jetsam (Higgins) (03) 307
Flounder, The (Grass) (79) 226
Flutie (Glancy) (99) 291
Flying Home and Other Stories (Ellison) (97) 287
Flying to Nowhere (Fuller) (85) 292
Foe (Coetzee) (88) 334
Folding Star, The (Hollinghurst) (95) 244
Following Story, The (Nooteboom) (95) 249
Footprints (Hearon) (97) 292
For Kings and Planets (Canin) (99) 299
For Love (Miller) (94) 305
For the Relief of Unbearable Urges (Englander) (00) 277
Foreign Affairs (Lurie) (85) 297
Foreign Land (Raban) (86) 302
Foreseeable Future, The (Price) (92) 222
Fork River Space Project, The (Morris) (78) 319
Fortress of Solitude, The (Lethem) (04) 266
Foucault's Pendulum (Eco) (90) 277
Foul Matter (Grimes) (04) 271
Found, Lost, Found (Priestley) (78) 325
Four Wise Men, The (Tournier) (83) 267
Fourteen Sisters of Emilio Montez O'Brien, The (Hijuelos) (94) 308
Fourth Hand, The (Irving) (02) 305
Foxfire (Oates) (94) 313
Foxybaby (Jolley) (86) 306
Fragments (Fuller) (85) 301
Fraud (Brookner) (94) 317
Fredy Neptune (Murray) (00) 286
Freedomland (Price) (99) 307
Frequency of Souls, The (Zuravleff) (97) 315
Friend of My Youth (Munro) (91) 317
Friend of the Earth, A (Boyle) (01) 310
From Bondage (Roth) (97) 319. See also Diving Rock on the Hudson, A, and Mercy of a Rude Stream
Fup (Dodge) (85) 318
Furies, The (Hobhouse) (94) 321
Fury (Rushdie) (02) 317
Gain (Powers) (99) 324
Galápagos (Vonnegut) (86) 326
Galatea 2.2 (Powers) (96) 299
Game Men Play, A (Bourjaily) (81) 364
Garden of Eden, The (Hemingway) (87) 313
Gardens of Kyoto, The (Walbert) (02) 326
Gathering of Old Men, A (Gaines) (84) 323
General in His Labyrinth, The (García Márquez) (91) 329
General of the Dead Army, The (Kadare) (92) 242
Genesis (Crace) (04) 283
Gentlemen in England (Wilson) (87) 322

George Mills (Elkin) (83) 273
Gertrude and Claudius (Updike) (01) 337
Gesture Life, A (Lee) (00) 305
Get Shorty (Leonard) (91) 351
Getting a Life (Simpson) (02) 334
Getting Mother's Body (Parks) (04) 291
Ghost Dance (Maso) (87) 326
Ghost Road, The (Barker) (96) 307
Ghost Story (Straub) (80) 349
Ghost Writer, The (Roth) (80) 354
Ghosts (Banville) (94) 355
Ghosts of Manila (Hamilton-Paterson) (95) 267
Giant's House, The (McCracken) (97) 331
Gift of Asher Lev, The (Potok) (91) 355
Gift of Stones, The (Crace) (90) 294
Ginger Tree, The (Wynd) (78) 349
Girl from the Coast, The (Toer) (03) 326
Girl in a Swing, The (Adams) (81) 377
Girl in Landscape (Lethem) (99) 337
Girl with a Monkey, A (Michaels) (01) 342
Girl with Curious Hair (Wallace) (90) 299
Girls (Busch) (98) 340
Girls' Guide to Hunting and Fishing, The (Bank) (00) 309
Glamorama (Ellis) (00) 313
Glass Palace, The (Ghosh) (02) 342
Glimmering (Hand) (98) 348
Glitter Dome, The (Wambaugh) (82) 325
Glue (Welsh) (02) 347
God Against the Gods, A (Drury) (77) 332
God Emperor of Dune (Herbert) (82) 329
God of Small Things, The (Roy) (98) 357
Godric (Buechner) (81) 382
God's Grace (Malamud) (83) 291
Going Native (Wright) (95) 271
Gold Bug Variations, The (Powers) (92) 252
Gold Coast, The (Robinson) (89) 316
Golden Age, The (Vidal) (01) 361
Golden Days (See) (87) 335
Golden Gate, The (Seth) (87) 340
Gone to Soldiers (Piercy) (88) 358
Good Apprentice, The (Murdoch) (87) 345
Good as Gold (Heller) (80) 372
Good Faith (Smiley) (04) 299
Good Husband, The (Godwin) (95) 275
Good Mother, The (Miller) (87) 352
Good Terrorist, The (Lessing) (86) 358
Good Will and Ordinary Love (Smiley) (90) 642
Goodnight! (Tertz) (90) 314
Gorky Park (Smith) (82) 333
Gospel According to the Son, The (Mailer) (98) 366
Gossip from the Forest (Keneally) (77) 336
Gould's Book of Fish (Flanagan) (03) 338
Grace Abounding (Howard) (83) 296
Grand Complication, The (Kurzweil) (02) 362
Greasy Lake and Other Stories (Boyle) (86) 372
Great Days (Barthelme) (80) 385
Great Fire, The (Hazzard) (04) 308
Green Knight, The (Murdoch) (95) 279
Green River Rising (Willocks) (95) 283
Greenlanders, The (Smiley) (89) 326
Gringos (Portis) (92) 262
Ground Beneath Her Feet, The (Rushdie) (00) 341
Guardian of the Word, The (Laye) (85) 334
Had I a Hundred Mouths (Goyen) (86) 386
Half a Heart (Brown) (01) 375
Half a Life (Naipul) (02) 372
Half Asleep in Frog Pajamas (Robbins) (95) 287
Half Moon Street (Theroux) (85) 338
Handbook for Visitors from Outer Space, A (Kramer) (85) 344
Handling Sin (Malone) (87) 366
Handmaid's Tale, The (Atwood) (87) 371

Happy to Be Here (Keillor) (83) 326
Hard Time (Paretsky) (00) 350
Harland's Half Acre (Malouf) (85) 348
Harlot's Ghost (Mailer) (92) 276
Harm Done (Rendell) (00) 354
Haroun and the Sea of Stories (Rushdie) (91) 376
Harry Gold (Dillon) (01) 379
Harry Potter and the Order of the Phoenix (Rowling) (04) 324
Harvesting Ballads (Kimball) (85) 352
Haunting of L., The (Norman) (03) 352
Hawksmoor (Ackroyd) (87) 382
He/She (Gold) (81) 426
Headbirths (Grass) (83) 336
Healing, The (Jones) (99) 355
Hearing Secret Harmonies (Powell) (77) 347
Hearing Voices (Wilson) (97) 364
Hearts in Atlantis (King) (00) 362
Heat and Dust (Jhabvala) (77) 352
Heat and Other Stories (Oates) (92) 281
Heather Blazing, The (Tóibín) (94) 376
Heavy Water and Other Stories (Amis) (00) 372
Hell to Pay (Pelecanos) (03) 361
Hemingway's Suitcase (Harris) (91) 390
Hence (Leithauser) (90) 373
Her First American (Segal) (86) 416
Her Own Place (Sanders) (94) 385
Her Own Terms (Grossman) (89) 345
Her Victory (Sillitoe) (83) 340
Here's to You, Jesusa! (Poniatowska) (02) 381
HERmione (H. D.) (82) 349
Herself in Love and Other Stories (Wiggins) (88) 377
Hey Jack! (Hannah) (88) 382
Hide, The (Unsworth) (97) 378
High Cotton (Pinckney) (93) 335
High Jinx (Buckley) (87) 392
High Latitudes (Buchan) (97) 383
Him with His Foot in His Mouth and Other Stories (Bellow) (85) 390
His Master's Voice (Lem) (84) 342
Hitler's Niece (Hansen) (00) 391
Hocus Pocus (Vonnegut) (91) 413
Holder of the World, The (Mukherjee) (94) 401
Hollywood (Vidal) (91) 423
Holy Pictures (Boylan) (84) 347
Home Truths (Gallant) (86) 431
Honeymoon (Gerber) (86) 440
Hood (Donoghue) (97) 410
Horse Heaven (Smiley) (01) 412
Hospital of the Transfiguration (Lem) (89) 357
Hotel du Lac (Brookner) (86) 445
Hotel New Hampshire, The (Irving) (82) 368
Hothouse, The (Koeppen) (02) 396
Hourglass (Kiš) (91) 427
Hourmaster (Bataille) (99) 383
House Gun, The (Gordimer) (99) 387
House of Leaves (Danielewski) (01) 417
House of the Spirits, The (Allende) (86) 455
Household Saints (Prose) (82) 373
How It All Began (Bukharin) (99) 391
How the Dead Live (Self) (01) 422
How to Make an American Quilt (Otto) (92) 309
How to Read an Unwritten Language (Graham) (96) 347
How to Save Your Own Life (Jong) (78) 413
Hula (Shea) (95) 334
Hullabaloo in the Guava Orchard (Desai) (99) 396
Human Factor, The (Greene) (79) 286
Human Stain, The (Roth) (01) 427
Hundred Secret Senses, The (Tan) (96) 351
Hunts in Dreams (Drury) (01) 437
I Hear America Swinging (De Vries) (77) 372
I Heard My Sister Speak My Name (Savage) (78) 427

I Know This Much Is True (Lamb) (99) 401
I Married a Communist (Roth) (99) 406
I Should Be Extremely Happy in Your Company (Hall) (04) 352
I the Supreme (Roa Bastos) (87) 419
I Wish This War Were Over (O'Hehir) (85) 415
Ice Age, The (Drabble) (78) 431
Ice-Cream War, An (Boyd) (84) 363
Identity (Kundera) (99) 410
If on a winter's night a traveler (Calvino) (82) 380
If the River Was Whiskey (Boyle) (90) 406
Ignorance (Kundera) (03) 392
I'm Losing You (Wagner) (97) 423
Image and Other Stories, The (Singer) (86) 461
Imaginary Crimes (Ballantyne) (83) 353
Imaginary Magnitude (Lem) (85) 421
Imaginative Experience, An (Wesley) (96) 359
Immortal Bartfuss, The (Appelfeld) (89) 362
Immortality (Kundera) (92) 329
In a Father's Place (Tilghman) (91) 437
In a Shallow Grave (Purdy) (77) 380
In America (Sontag) (01) 452
In Another Country (Kenney) (85) 427
In Between the Sheets and Other Stories (McEwan) (80) 417
In Evil Hour (García Márquez) (80) 421
In My Father's House (Gaines) (79) 311
In Sunlight, in a Beautiful Garden (Cambor) (02) 404
In the Beauty of the Lilies (Updike) (97) 433
In the City (Silber) (88) 418
In the Country of Last Things (Auster) (88) 423
In the Eye of the Sun (Soueif) (94) 406
In the Forest (O'Brien) (03) 410
In the Garden of the North American Martyrs (Wolff) (82) 392
In the Heart of the Valley of Love (Kadohata) (93) 374
In the Image (Horn) (03) 415
In the Lake of the Woods (O'Brien) (95) 355
In the Palace of the Movie King (Calisher) (95) 359
In the Penny Arcade (Millhauser) (87) 424
In the Shadow of the Wind (Hébert) (85) 436
In the Skin of a Lion (Ondaatje) (88) 428
In the Tennessee Country (Taylor) (95) 363
In the Time of the Butterflies (Alvarez) (95) 367
Incidents in the Rue Laugier (Brookner) (97) 437
Incline Our Hearts (Wilson) (90) 415
Incubus (Arensberg) (00) 418
Independence Day (Ford) (96) 372
Indian Affairs (Woiwode) (93) 378
Indian Killer (Alexie) (97) 442
Infinite Jest (Wallace) (97) 446
Information, The (Amis) (96) 381
Ingenious Pain (Miller) (98) 428
Innocent, The (McEwan) (91) 456
Innocent Eréndira and Other Stories (García Márquez) (79) 318
Inquisitors' Manual, The (Antunes) (04) 356
Inside, Outside (Wouk) (86) 466
Instance of the Fingerpost, An (Pears) (99) 418
Interpreter, The (Kim) (04) 360
Interpreter of Maladies (Lahiri) (00) 430
Interview with the Vampire (Rice) (77) 384
Intuitionist, The (Whitehead) (00) 435
Iron Tracks, The (Appelfeld) (99) 422
Ironweed (Kennedy) (84) 379
Irrawaddy Tango (Law-Yone) (95) 376
Isaac and His Devils (Eberstadt) (92) 359
Ìsarà (Soyinka) (90) 435
Island (MacLeod) (02) 432
Island of the Day Before, The (Eco) (96) 385
Issa Valley, The (Miłosz) (82) 403
Italian Folktales (Calvino) (81) 450
Italian Stories (Papaleo) (03) 419

CATEGORY INDEX

Jack Gance (Just) (90) 445
Jack Maggs (Carey) (99) 432
Jack of Diamonds (Spencer) (89) 405
Jailbird (Vonnegut) (80) 436
Jasmine (Mukherjee) (90) 450
Jazz (Morrison) (93) 403
Jesus' Son (Johnson) (94) 427
Joe (Brown) (92) 384
John Dollar (Wiggins) (90) 454
John Henry Days (Whitehead) (02) 449
Joke, The (Kundera) (83) 363
Journey to the End of the Millennium, A (Yehoshua) (00) 453
Journey to the Sky (Highwater) (79) 335
Journey to the West, Vol. IV, The (Wu Ch'êng-ên) (84) 401
Joy Luck Club, The (Tan) (90) 468
Jubal Sackett (L'Amour) (86) 496
Julip (Harrison) (95) 413
July, July (O'Brien) (03) 437
July's People (Gordimer) (82) 417
Jump (Gordimer) (92) 398
Juneteenth (Ellison) (00) 457
Just Above My Head (Baldwin) (80) 456
Just Representations (Cozzens) (79) 343
Kate Vaiden (Price) (87) 451
Katerina (Appelfeld) (93) 418
Keep the Change (McGuane) (90) 473
Kentucky Straight (Offutt) (93) 422
Killing Ground, The (Settle) (83) 381
Killing Mister Watson (Matthiessen) (91) 480
Killshot (Leonard) (90) 482
Kiln People (Brin) (03) 442
Kinflicks (Alther) (77) 391
King, The (Barthelme) (91) 485
King in the Tree, The (Millhauser) (04) 409
King Is Dead, The (Lewis) (04) 413
King of the Fields, The (Singer) (89) 441
King of the Jews (Epstein) (80) 458
King of the World (Gerber) (91) 489
King of Torts, The (Grisham) (04) 417
Kingdom of Shadows (Furst) (02) 463
King's Way, The (Chandernagor) (85) 515
Kitchen (Yoshimoto) (94) 445
Kitchen God's Wife, The (Tan) (92) 408
Kite Runner, The (Hosseini) (04) 421
Kith (Newby) (78) 491
Knight, Death, and the Devil, The (Leffland) (91) 493
Known World, The (Jones) (04) 426
Krazy Kat (Cantor) (89) 445
Krik? Krak! (Danticat) (96) 406
Krippendorf's Tribe (Parkin) (87) 456
Labors of Love (Cassill) (81) 471
Ladder of Years (Tyler) (96) 410
Lady of Situations, The (Auchincloss) (91) 498
Lady Oracle (Atwood) (77) 400
L'Affaire (Johnson) (04) 434
Lake Wobegon Days (Keillor) (86) 500
Lake Wobegon Summer 1956 (Keillor) (02) 468
Lambs of God (Day) (99) 462
Lancelot (Percy) (78) 501
Landing on the Sun, A (Frayn) (93) 431
Lands of Memory (Hernández) (03) 451
Larry's Party (Shields) (98) 486
Last Convertible, The (Myrer) (79) 359
Last Days (Oates) (85) 524
Last Girls, The (Smith) (03) 456
Last Life, The (Messud) (00) 471
Last of the Savages, The (McInerney) (97) 478
Last Orders (Swift) (97) 482
Last Report on the Miracles at Little No Horse, The (Erdrich) (02) 477
Last Resort, The (Lurie) (99) 466

Last Thing He Wanted, The (Didion) (97) 486
Last Things (Jones) (91) 503
Late Divorce, A (Yehoshua) (85) 530
Latecomers (Brookner) (90) 500
Later the Same Day (Paley) (86) 509
Latin Deli, The (Cofer) (94) 454
Laws of Our Fathers, The (Turow) (97) 490
Lazar Malkin Enters Heaven (Stern) (88) 457
Le Divorce (Johnson) (98) 490
Le Mariage (Johnson) (01) 509
Leaving Home (Keillor) (88) 461
Leaving the Land (Unger) (85) 535
Left-Handed Woman, The (Handke) (79) 363
Legends of the Fall (Harrison) (80) 462
Lemprière's Dictionary (Norfolk) (93) 435
Leper's Companions, The (Blackburn) (00) 479
Lesson Before Dying, A (Gaines) (94) 463
Let the Dead Bury Their Dead (Kenan) (93) 439
Letourneau's Used Auto Parts (Chute) (89) 460
Letter Left to Me, The (McElroy) (89) 465
Letters (Barth) (80) 466
Levitation (Ozick) (83) 405
Lewis Percy (Brookner) (91) 521
Liars in Love (Yates) (82) 453
Libra (DeLillo) (89) 496
Licks of Love (Updike) (01) 522
Lies of Silence (Moore) (91) 527
Life and Fate (Grossman) (87) 483
Life & Times of Michael K (Coetzee) (84) 455
Life Before Man (Atwood) (81) 512
Life I Really Lived, The (West) (80) 491
Life of Pi (Martel) (03) 485
Life with a Star (Weil) (90) 531
Light (Figes) (84) 459
Light of Day, The (Swift) (04) 446
Lila (Pirsig) (92) 440
Lincoln (Vidal) (85) 570
Lincoln's Dreams (Willis) (88) 487
Linden Hills (Naylor) (86) 525
Little Drummer Girl, The (le Carré) (84) 468
Little Friend, The (Tartt) (03) 495
Little Green Men (Buckley) (00) 488
Little Infamies (Karnezis) (04) 451
Little Jinx (Tertz) (93) 473
Little Yellow Dog, A (Mosley) (97) 535
Lives of the Poets (Doctorow) (85) 574
Lives of the Saints (Slavitt) (91) 530
Living, The (Dillard) (93) 478
Living in the Maniototo (Frame) (80) 502
Local Girls (Hoffman) (00) 497
Loitering with Intent (Spark) (82) 475
London Embassy, The (Theroux) (84) 472
London Fields (Amis) (91) 534
Lone Ranger and Tonto Fistfight in Heaven, The (Alexie) (94) 475
Lonesome Dove (McMurtry) (86) 533
Long Way from Home (Busch) (94) 479
Longings of Women, The (Piercy) (95) 446
Look at Me (Brookner) (84) 476
Loon Lake (Doctorow) (81) 524
Loser, The (Bernhard) (92) 455
Loser, The (Konrád) (83) 423
Lost Father, The (Simpson) (93) 487
Lost Flying Boat, The (Sillitoe) (85) 579
Lost in the City (Jones) (93) 491
Lost Language of Cranes, The (Leavitt) (87) 494
Lost Light (Connelly) (04) 474
Lost Man's River (Matthiessen) (98) 530
Love (Morrison) (04) 479
Love, Again (Lessing) (97) 539
Love, etc. (Barnes) (02) 495
Love Hunter, The (Hassler) (82) 499

931

Love in the Time of Cholera (García Márquez) (89) 521
Love Letter, The (Schine) (96) 448
Love Me (Keillor) (04) 483
Love Medicine (Erdrich) (85) 584
Love of a Good Woman, The (Munro) (99) 488
Love Unknown (Wilson) (88) 507
Lovely Bones, The (Sebold) (03) 499
Lover, The (Duras) (86) 547
Lovers and Tyrants (Gray) (77) 455
Lover's Discourse, A (Barthes) (79) 404
Loving Monsters (Hamilton-Paterson) (03) 504
Loving Pedro Infante (Chávez) (02) 499
Low Tide (Eberstadt) (86) 551
Lucifer Unemployed (Wat) (91) 545
Lucinella (Segal) (77) 460
Lucky Bastard (McCarry) (99) 497
Lucy (Kincaid) (91) 549
Luisa Domic (Dennison) (86) 556
Lyre of Orpheus, The (Davies) (90) 548
MacGuffin, The (Elkin) (92) 465
Machine Dreams (Phillips) (85) 589
Madder Music (De Vries) (78) 546
Magician's Wife, The (Moore) (99) 506
Magnetic Field(s) (Loewinsohn) (84) 487
Mailman (Lennon) (04) 487
Major André (Bailey) (88) 512
Making of the Representative for Planet 8, The (Lessing) (83) 432
Making Things Better (Brookner) (04) 491
Malgudi Days (Narayan) (83) 436
Mama Day (Naylor) (89) 530
Mambo Kings Play Songs of Love, The (Hijuelos) (90) 553
Mammoth Hunters, The (Auel) (86) 566
Man in Full, A (Wolfe) (99) 511
Man in the Holocene (Frisch) (81) 545
Man in the Tower, The (Krüger) (94) 496
Man of the House, The (McCauley) (97) 546
Manly-Hearted Woman, The (Manfred) (77) 480
Mantissa (Fowles) (83) 443
Manual for Manuel, A (Cortázar) (79) 418
Mao II (DeLillo) (92) 479
Map of the World, A (Hamilton) (95) 460
Marbot (Hildesheimer) (84) 498
Marco Polo, If You Can (Buckley) (83) 447
Marcovaldo (Calvino) (84) 509
Marriages Between Zones Three, Four, and Five, The (Lessing) (81) 555
Married Man, A (Read) (80) 522
Married Man, The (White) (01) 564
Marry Me (Updike) (77) 485
Mary Reilly (Martin) (91) 572
Masks (Enchi) (84) 514
Mason and Dixon (Pynchon) (98) 546
Mason's Retreat (Tilghman) (97) 550
Master Butchers Singing Club, The (Erdrich) (04) 496
Master of Petersburg, The (Coetzee) (95) 469
Masters of Atlantis (Portis) (86) 579
Mating (Rush) (92) 490
Matisse Stories, The (Byatt) (96) 457
Meditation, A (Benet) (83) 464
Meditations in Green (Wright) (84) 523
Meeting at Telgte, The (Grass) (82) 523
Meeting Evil (Berger) (93) 505
Memoirs of a Space Traveler (Lem) (83) 469
Memoirs of a Geisha (Golden) (98) 558
Memories of the Ford Administration (Updike) (93) 509
Men and Angels (Gordon) (86) 589
Mercy of a Rude Stream, A Star Shines over Mt. Morris Park (Roth) (95) 482. See also Diving Rock on the Hudson, A, and From Bondage

Meridian (Walker) (77) 501
Message to the Planet, The (Murdoch) (91) 587
Messiah of Stockholm, The (Ozick) (88) 549
Metropol (Aksyonov, et al., eds.) (84) 533
Mickelsson's Ghosts (Gardner) (83) 475
Midair (Conroy) (86) 603
Middle Ground, The (Drabble) (81) 564
Middle Passage (Johnson) (91) 591
Middleman and Other Stories, The (Mukherjee) (89) 553
Middlesex (Eugenides) (03) 527
Midnight Clear, A (Wharton) (83) 480
Midnight Water (Norman) (84) 543
Millroy the Magician (Theroux) (95) 491
Minor Apocalypse, A (Konwicki) (84) 547
Miracle at St. Anna (McBride) (03) 540
Miracle Game, The (Škvorecký) (92) 509
Misalliance, The (Brookner) (88) 564
Misery (King) (88) 569
Miss Herbert (Stead) (77) 509
Missed Connections (Ford) (84) 552
Mists of Avalon, The (Bradley) (84) 561
Model World, A (Chabon) (92) 514
Moksha (Huxley) (79) 451
Mom Kills Kids and Self (Saperstein) (80) 541
Moment of True Feeling, A (Handke) (78) 585
Momo (Ajar) (79) 454
Mona in the Promised Land (Jen) (97) 595
Money (Amis) (86) 624
Mongoose, R.I.P. (Buckley) (88) 574
Monkeys (Minot) (87) 557
Monkey's Wrench, The (Levi) (87) 564
Monsignor Quixote (Greene) (83) 489
Monstruary (Ríos) (02) 537
Montgomery's Children (Perry) (85) 629
Moo (Smiley) (96) 473
Moon Deluxe (Barthelme) (84) 576
Moon Pinnace, The (Williams) (87) 568
Moon Tiger (Lively) (89) 558
Moonrise, Moonset (Konwicki) (88) 579
Moons of Jupiter, The (Munro) (84) 580
Moor's Last Sigh, The (Rushdie) (96) 478
More Collected Stories (Pritchett) (84) 584
More Die of Heartbreak (Bellow) (88) 583
Morgan's Passing (Tyler) (81) 573
Mortal Friends (Carroll) (79) 462
Mosquito Coast, The (Theroux) (83) 496
Mother and Two Daughters, A (Godwin) (83) 501
Motherless Brooklyn (Lethem) (00) 542
Mountain Time (Doig) (00) 546
Mr. Bedford and the Muses (Godwin) (84) 556
Mr. Ives' Christmas (Hijuelos) (96) 461
Mr. Mani (Yehoshua) (93) 527
Mr Noon (Lawrence) (85) 619
Mr. Palomar (Calvino) (86) 620
Mr. Phillips (Lanchester) (01) 594
Mr. Summer's Story (Süskind) (94) 535
Mrs. Ted Bliss (Elkin) (96) 469
M31 (Wright) (89) 562
Mulligan Stew (Sorrentino) (80) 544
Multitude of Sins, A (Ford) (03) 545
Murder Room, The (James) (04) 524
Murther and Walking Spirits (Davies) (92) 535
Music and Silence (Tremain) (01) 599
Music Room, The (McFarland) (91) 610
My Dream of You (O'Faolain) (02) 554
My Father, Dancing (Broyard) (00) 550
My Heart Laid Bare (Oates) (99) 542
My Life as a Fake (Carey) (04) 528
My Life, Starring Dara Falcon (Beattie) (98) 571
My Name Is Red (Pamuk) (02) 558
My Name Is Saroyan (Saroyan) (84) 588
My Son's Story (Gordimer) (91) 619

Mysteries of Motion (Calisher) (84) 593
Mysteries of Pittsburgh, The (Chabon) (89) 581
Mysteries of Winterthurn (Oates) (85) 640
Name of the Rose, The (Eco) (84) 598
Names, The (DeLillo) (83) 515
Names of the Dead, The (O'Nan) (97) 615
Namesake, The (Lahiri) (04) 532
Naomi (Tanizaki) (86) 640
Napoleon Symphony (Burgess) (77) 525
Narcissa and Other Fables (Auchincloss) (84) 603
Native Speaker (Lee) (96) 499
Natives and Strangers (Dawkins) (86) 644
Natural History (Howard) (93) 540
Natural Man, The (McClanahan) (84) 608
Needful Things (King) (92) 564
Neighbors (Berger) (81) 606
Neon Bible, The (Toole) (90) 596
Neumiller Stories, The (Woiwode) (90) 600
New Islands and Other Stories (Bombal) (83) 523
New Life, The (Pamuk) (98) 583
New World, A (Chaudhuri) (01) 623
Nice Work (Lodge) (90) 603
Night in Question, The (Wolfe) (97) 618
Night Manager, The (le Carré) (94) 559
Night-Side (Oates) (78) 608
Night Thoughts of a Classical Physicist (McCormmach) (83) 532
Night Train (Amis) (99) 557
Night Travellers, The (Spencer) (92) 573
1934 (Moravia) (84) 613
1985 (Burgess) (79) 484
No Country for Young Men (O'Faolain) (88) 601
No Fond Return of Love (Pym) (83) 536
No Man's Land (Walser) (90) 619
No Other Life (Moore) (94) 563
No Other Tale to Tell (Perry) (95) 559
No Place on Earth (Wolf) (83) 540
Noble Rot (Stern) (90) 624
Nobody's Angel (McGuane) (83) 544
None to Accompany Me (Gordimer) (95) 564
North Gladiola (Wilcox) (86) 664
Norwegian Wood (Murakami) (01) 651
Not the End of the World (Stowe) (93) 575
Notebooks of Don Rigoberto, The (Vargas Llosa) (99) 562
Nothing but Blue Skies (McGuane) (93) 580
Nothing Happens in Carmincross (Kiely) (86) 668
November 1916 (Solzhenitsyn) (00) 589
Now Playing at Canterbury (Bourjaily) (77) 575
Nowhere Man (Hemon) (03) 598
Nuns and Soldiers (Murdoch) (81) 628
O, How the Wheel Becomes It! (Powell) (84) 628
Obasan (Kogawa) (83) 554
October Light (Gardner) (77) 580
Odd Sea, The (Reiken) (99) 566
Of Love and Other Demons (García Márquez) (96) 518
Of Such Small Differences (Greenberg) (89) 616
Off for the Sweet Hereafter (Pearson) (87) 611
Officers' Wives, The (Fleming) (82) 570
Oh What a Paradise It Seems (Cheever) (83) 558
Old Devils, The (Amis) (88) 610
Old Forest and Other Stories, The (Taylor) (86) 673
Old Gringo, The (Fuentes) (86) 680
Old Left, The (Menaker) (88) 616
Old Love (Singer) (80) 614
Old Masters (Bernhard) (93) 584
Old School (Wolff) (04) 570
Oldest Living Confederate Widow Tells All (Gurganus) (90) 633
On a Dark Night I Left My Silent House (Handke) (01) 665
On Distant Ground (Butler) (86) 685
On Heroes and Tombs (Sábato) (82) 585

On Keeping Women (Calisher) (78) 613
On the Black Hill (Chatwin) (84) 638
On the Edge of the Cliff (Pritchett) (80) 627
On the Golden Porch (Tolstaya) (90) 637
On the Occasion of My Last Afternoon (Gibbons) (99) 584
On the Stroll (Shulman) (82) 590
Once in Europa (Berger) (88) 625
Once Upon a Time (Barth) (95) 568
One Human Minute (Lem) (87) 615
One Man's Bible (Gao) (03) 602
One Thing Leading to Another (Warner) (85) 658
Only Problem, The (Spark) (85) 668
Open Doors and Three Novellas (Sciascia) (93) 589
Open Secrets (Munro) (95) 578
Operation Shylock (Roth) (94) 581
Operation Wandering Soul (Powers) (94) 586
Oracle at Stoneleigh Court, The (Taylor) (94) 590
Oral History (Smith) (84) 647
Ordinary Love and Good Will (Smiley) (90) 642
Ordinary Money (Jones) (91) 647
Ordinary People (Guest) (77) 597
Oriental Tales (Yourcenar) (86) 706
Original Bliss (Kennedy) (00) 593
Original Sin (James) (96) 545
Orsinian Tales (Le Guin) (77) 601
Oryx and Crake (Atwood) (04) 583
Oscar and Lucinda (Carey) (89) 626
Other Side, The (Gordon) (90) 647
Other Side of Silence, The (Brink) (04) 588
Our Game (le Carré) (96) 553
Our Lady of the Forest (Guterson) (04) 592
Out of India (Jhabvala) (87) 626
Out of the Woods (Offutt) (00) 601
Out to Canaan (Karon) (98) 620
Outerbridge Reach (Stone) (93) 593
O-Zone (Theroux) (87) 631
Pacific Tremors (Stern) (02) 614
Packages (Stern) (81) 636
Paco's Story (Heinemann) (88) 651
Paddy Clarke Ha Ha Ha (Doyle) (94) 603
Painted House, A (Grisham) (02) 618
Painter of Signs, The (Narayan) (77) 605
Palace Thief, The (Canin) (95) 586
Palm Latitudes (Braverman) (89) 639
Paper Men, The (Golding) (85) 672
Paperboy, The (Dexter) (96) 565
Paradise (Morrison) (99) 615
Paradise News (Lodge) (93) 606
Paradise of the Blind (Duong) (94) 607
Paradise Park (Goodman) (02) 622
Paradise Postponed (Mortimer) (87) 640
Pardoner's Tale, The (Wain) (80) 640
Paris Trout (Dexter) (89) 644
Park City (Beattie) (99) 620
Particles and Luck (Jones) (94) 611
Passing On (Lively) (91) 651
Passion, The (Winterson) (89) 654
Passion Artist, The (Hawkes) (80) 644
Passion Play (Kosinski) (80) 649
Pastoralia (Saunders) (01) 703
Patchwork Planet, A (Tyler) (99) 624
Pattern Recognition (Gibson) (04) 610
Peace Breaks Out (Knowles) (82) 621
Peace Like a River (Enger) (02) 626
Peacock Spring, The (Godden) (77) 614
Peckham's Marbles (De Vries) (87) 650
Peerless Flats (Freud) (94) 618
Penitent, The (Singer) (84) 678
People and Uncollected Stories, The (Malamud) (90) 661
Perfect Recall (Beattie) (02) 631
Perfect Spy, A (le Carré) (87) 654

Persian Nights (Johnson) (88) 683
Personal Injuries (Turow) (00) 605
Philadelphia Fire (Wideman) (91) 661
Philosopher's Pupil, The (Murdoch) (84) 690
Pickup, The (Gordimer) (02) 636
Picturing Will (Beattie) (91) 665
Pieces of Life (Schorer) (78) 657
Pigs in Heaven (Kingsolver) (94) 631
Pitch Dark (Adler) (84) 699
Place I've Never Been, A (Leavitt) (91) 670
Places in the World a Woman Could Walk (Kauffman) (85) 688
Plague Dogs, The (Adams) (79) 546
Plain and Normal (Wilcox) (99) 632
Plains Song (Morris) (81) 655
Plainsong (Haruf) (00) 614
Platte River (Bass) (95) 609
Players (DeLillo) (78) 661
Pleading Guilty (Turow) (94) 636
Pleasure-Dome (Madden) (80) 659
Plowing the Dark (Powers) (01) 711
Poet and Dancer (Jhabvala) (94) 645
Point, The (D'Ambrosio) (96) 589
Polish Complex, The (Konwicki) (83) 611
Polish Officer, The (Furst) (96) 593
Polonaise (Read) (77) 632
Pope's Rhinoceros, The (Norfolk) (97) 671
Porcupine, The (Barnes) (93) 646
Portable Jack Kerouac, The (Kerouac) (96) 597
Portage to San Cristóbal of A. H., The (Steiner) (83) 616
Portrait in Sepia (Allende) (02) 650
Possessing the Secret of Joy (Walker) (93) 651
Possession (Byatt) (91) 679
Prague (Phillips) (03) 624
Prayer for Owen Meany, A (Irving) (90) 677
Prayer for the Dying, A (O'Nan) (00) 622
Price Was High, The (Fitzgerald) (80) 693
Prick of Noon, The (De Vries) (86) 752
Primary Colors (Klein) (97) 679
Prisoner's Dilemma (Powers) (89) 663
Prize Stories 1978 (Abrahams, ed.) (79) 556
Problems and Other Stories (Updike) (80) 697
Prodigal Child, A (Storey) (84) 711
Professor of Desire, The (Roth) (78) 669
Progress of Love, The (Munro) (87) 677
Promise of Light, The (Watkins) (94) 667
Promise of Rest, The (Price) (96) 606
Providence (Brookner) (85) 712
Puffball (Weldon) (81) 670
Pugilist at Rest, The (Jones) (94) 676
Purple America (Moody) (98) 643
Purple Decades, The (Wolfe) (83) 626
Pushcart Prize, III, The (Henderson, ed.) (79) 565
Puttermesser Papers, The (Ozick) (98) 648
Quantity Theory of Insanity, The (Self) (96) 615
Quarantine (Crace) (99) 645
Question of Bruno, The (Hemon) (01) 725
Quinn's Book (Kennedy) (89) 683
Rabbi of Lud, The (Elkin) (88) 715
Rabbis and Wives (Grade) (83) 630
Rabbit at Rest (Updike) (91) 688
Rabbit Is Rich (Updike) (82) 656
Radiant Way, The (Drabble) (88) 720
Raider, The (Ford) (77) 662
Rameau's Niece (Schine) (94) 680
Rape of the Rose, The (Hughes) (94) 684
Rat Man of Paris (West) (87) 681
Rates of Exchange (Bradbury) (84) 721
Ratner's Star (DeLillo) (77) 647
Ravelstein (Bellow) (01) 731
Ray (Hannah) (81) 674

Real Life of Alejandro Mayta, The (Vargas Llosa) (87) 685
Real Losses, Imaginary Gains (Morris) (77) 652
Real Time (Chaudhuri) (03) 643
Reality and Dreams (Spark) (98) 670
Rebel Angels, The (Davies) (83) 641
Recapitulation (Stegner) (80) 702
Reckless Eyeballing (Reed) (87) 690
Red Mars (Robinson) (94) 688
Red Men, The (McGinley) (88) 737
Regeneration (Barker) (93) 677
Regina (Epstein) (83) 650
Regions of Memory (Merwin) (88) 742
Regular Guy, A (Simpson) (97) 688
Reindeer Moon (Thomas) (88) 748
Reinhart's Women (Berger) (82) 671
Remains of the Day, The (Ishiguro) (90) 690
Repetition (Handke) (89) 713
Requiem for a Dream (Selby) (79) 589
Requiem for Harlem (Roth) (99) 654
Rest of Life, The (Gordon) (94) 701
Resurrection Men (Rankin) (04) 657
Resuscitation of a Hanged Man (Johnson) (92) 679
Retreat, The (Appelfeld) (85) 752
Return of Little Big Man, The (Berger) (00) 647
Return of the Caravels, The (Antunes) (03) 653
Return to Región (Benet) (86) 771
Return to Thebes (Drury) (78) 708
Reversible Errors (Turow) (03) 663
Rhine Maidens (See) (82) 684
Rich in Love (Humphreys) (88) 759
Richard Wright Reader (Wright) (79) 597
Richer, the Poorer, The (West) (96) 641
Rifles, The (Vollmann) (95) 647
Rings of Saturn, The (Sebald) (99) 662
Rites of Passage (Golding) (81) 690
River Beyond the World, The (Peery) (97) 701
River Sorrow, The (Holden) (95) 652
Road to Wellville, The (Boyle) (94) 709
Roadwalkers (Grau) (95) 656
Robber Bride, The (Atwood) (94) 713
Rock Cried Out, The (Douglas) (80) 722
Rock Springs (Ford) (88) 776
Roger's Version (Updike) (87) 727
Rogue's March (Tyler) (83) 659
Romantics, The (Mishra) (01) 741
Roots (Haley) (77) 690
Roscoe (Kennedy) (03) 681
Rotters' Club, The (Coe) (03) 685
Rouse Up O Young Men of the New Age! (Ōe) (03) 690
Roxanna Slade (Price) (99) 675
Royal Family, The (Vollmann) (01) 745
Rubicon Beach (Erickson) (87) 736
Ruby (Hood) (99) 679
Ruin of Kasch, The (Calasso) (95) 669
Rule of the Bone (Banks) (96) 668
Rumor Has It (Dickinson) (92) 694
Run to the Waterfall (Vivante) (80) 736
Runaway Soul, The (Brodkey) (92) 698
Running Dog (DeLillo) (79) 617
Russia House, The (le Carré) (90) 707
Russian Girl, The (Amis) (95) 674
S. (Updike) (89) 748
Sabbath's Theater (Roth) (96) 672
Sabbatical (Barth) (83) 665
Sacrament of Lies (Dewberry) (03) 699
Sacred Hunger (Unsworth) (93) 698
Saga of Dazai Osamu, The (Lyons) (86) 783
Saint Augustine's Pigeon (Connell) (81) 703
Saint Maybe (Tyler) (92) 703
Samurai, The (Endō) (83) 674

CATEGORY INDEX

Sanatorium Under the Sign of the Hourglass (Schulz) (79) 645
Sandro of Chegem (Iskander) (84) 756
Sarah Phillips (Lee) (85) 771
Saskiad, The (Hall) (98) 698
Satanic Verses, The (Rushdie) (90) 711
Sauce for the Goose (De Vries) (82) 742
Saul and Patsy (Baxter) (04) 670
Scandal (Endō) (89) 752
Scandalmonger (Safire) (01) 759
Scapegoat, The (Settle) (81) 707
Schindler's List (Keneally) (83) 684
Sea Came in at Midnight, The (Erickson) (00) 675
Searoad (Le Guin) (92) 722
Second Chance and Other Stories, The (Sillitoe) (82) 747
Second Coming, The (Percy) (81) 717
Second Generation (Fast) (79) 648
Second Marriage (Barthelme) (85) 780
Second Nature (Hoffman) (95) 701
Second Sight (McCarry) (92) 727
Secret History, The (Tartt) (93) 711
Secret Pilgrim, The (le Carré) (92) 732
Secrets (Farah) (99) 693
Secrets and Other Stories (MacLaverty) (85) 790
Seeing Calvin Coolidge in a Dream (Derbyshire) (97) 732
Seek My Face (Updike) (03) 727
Seizure of Power, The (Miłosz) (83) 713
Selected Short Stories of Padraic Colum (Colum) (86) 803
Selected Stories (Gordimer) (77) 725
Selected Stories (Munro) (97) 742
Selected Stories (Pritchett) (79) 669
Selected Stories (Walser) (83) 734
Selected Stories of Philip K. Dick (Dick) (03) 737
Selected Writings of James Weldon Johnson, Vol. I and Vol. II, The (Johnson) (96) 694
Sent for You Yesterday (Wideman) (84) 779
Sergeant Getúlio (Ubaldo Ribeiro) (79) 672
Setting the World on Fire (Wilson) (81) 727
Seven Rivers West (Hoagland) (84) 760
Sexing the Cherry (Winterson) (91) 735
Shadows *and* Stillness (Gardner) (87) 822
Shakespeare's Dog (Rooke) (84) 784
Shame (Rushdie) (84) 788
Sharpest Sight, The (Owens) (93) 732
Shawl, The (Ozick) (90) 734
Shelley's Heart (McCarry) (96) 708
Shelter (Phillips) (95) 709
Shikasta (Lessing) (80) 753
Shiloh and Other Stories (Mason) (83) 739
Ship Fever and Other Stories (Barrett) (97) 753
Ship Made of Paper, A (Spencer) (04) 683
Shipping News, The (Proulx) (94) 733
Shipwreck (Begley) (04) 687
Shoeless Joe (Kinsella) (83) 742
Short History of a Prince, The (Hamilton) (99) 706
Shosha (Singer) (79) 677
Shroud (Banville) (04) 691
Sights Unseen (Gibbons) (96) 712
Sigismund (Gustafsson) (86) 816
Signs and Wonders (Bukiet) (00) 707
Silent Passengers (Woiwode) (94) 738
Silken Eyes (Sagan) (78) 776
Silmarillion, The (Tolkien) (78) 780
Simple Habana Melody, A (Hijuelos) (03) 746
Simple Story, A (Agnon) (86) 826
Sin Killer (McMurtry) (03) 750
Siren, The (Buzzati) (85) 825
Sirian Experiments, The (Lessing) (81) 737
Sister Age (Fisher) (84) 792

Six Problems for Don Isidro Parodi (Borges and Bioy-Casares) (82) 771
Sixty Stories (Barthelme) (82) 776
Skinned Alive (White) (96) 720
Slapstick (Vonnegut) (77) 749
Slaves of New York (Janowitz) (87) 784
Sleepless Nights (Hardwick) (80) 768
Sleepwalker in a Fog (Tolstaya) (93) 740
Slouching Towards Kalamazoo (De Vries) (84) 796
Slow Homecoming (Handke) (86) 830
Slow Learner (Pynchon) (85) 830
Slowness (Kundera) (97) 761
Small World (Lodge) (86) 835
Smilla's Sense of Snow (Hoeg) (94) 747
Snack Thief, The (Camilleri) (04) 696
Snooty Baronet (Lewis) (85) 835
Snow Falling on Cedars (Guterson) (95) 729
So I Am Glad (Kennedy) (01) 778
So Long, See You Tomorrow (Maxwell) (81) 741
Soldier of the Great War, A (Helprin) (92) 770
Soldier's Embrace, A (Gordimer) (81) 745
Solomon Gursky Was Here (Richler) (91) 755
Sombrero Fallout (Brautigan) (78) 785
Some Tame Gazelle (Pym) (84) 809
Somebody's Darling (McMurtry) (79) 689
Something Out There (Gordimer) (85) 844
Something to Be Desired (McGuane) (85) 849
Son of the Circus, A (Irving) (95) 739
Son of the Morning (Oates) (79) 693
Song of Solomon (Morrison) (78) 789
Song of the Earth, The (Nissenson) (02) 756
Songlines, The (Chatwin) (88) 840
Songs of the Kings, The (Unsworth) (04) 705
Sonny Liston Was a Friend of Mine (Jones) (00) 717
Sophie's Choice (Styron) (80) 774
Sorcerer's Apprentice, The (Johnson) (87) 795
Souls and Bodies (Lodge) (83) 761
Sound of One Hand Clapping, The (Flanagan) (01) 791
Source of Light, The (Price) (82) 790
South of the Border, West of the Sun (Murakami) (00) 721
Southern Family, A (Godwin) (88) 845
Southern Woman, The (Spencer) (02) 760
Spartina (Casey) (90) 748
Spectator Bird, The (Stegner) (77) 769
Speedboat (Adler) (77) 776
Spencer Holst Stories (Holst) (77) 780
Spidertown (Rodriguez) (94) 760
Sport of Nature, A (Gordimer) (88) 850
Sportswriter, The (Ford) (87) 813
Spring Moon (Lord) (82) 806
Stained Glass Elegies (Endō) (86) 856
Stained White Radiance, A (Burke) (93) 753
Stanley and the Women (Amis) (86) 859
Star Called Henry, A (Doyle) (00) 729
Star Shines over Mt. Morris Park, A. *See* Mercy of a Rude Stream
Staring at the Sun (Barnes) (88) 855
Stars in My Pockets like Grains of Sand (Delany) (85) 860
Stars of the New Curfew (Okri) (90) 753
State of Ireland, The (Kiely) (81) 766
Statement, The (Moore) (97) 782
Staying On (Scott) (78) 795
Stern Men (Gilbert) (01) 801
Still Life with a Bridle (Herbert) (92) 785
Stillness *and* Shadows (Gardner) (87) 822
Stone Carvers, The (Urquhart) (03) 803
Stone Diaries, The (Shields) (95) 756
Stone Junction (Dodge) (91) 777
Stone Kiss (Kellerman) (03) 807
Stones for Ibarra (Doerr) (85) 869
Stopping Place, A (Mojtabai) (80) 785

Stories (Lessing) (79) 708
Stories in an Almost Classical Mode (Brodkey) (89) 822
Stories of Bernard Malamud, The (Malamud) (84) 819
Stories of Breece D'J Pancake, The (Pancake) (84) 824
Stories of Heinrich Böll, The (Böll) (87) 827
Stories of John Cheever, The (Cheever) (79) 713
Stories of John Edgar Wideman, The (Wideman) (93) 762
Stories of Muriel Spark (Spark) (86) 864
Stories of Ray Bradbury, The (Bradbury) (81) 769
Stories of Stephen Dixon, The (Dixon) (95) 761
Stories of Vladimir Nabokov, The (Nabokov) (96) 724
Stories of William Trevor, The (Trevor) (84) 829
Story of Henri Tod, The (Buckley) (85) 874
Story of Lucy Gault, The (Trevor) (03) 811
Storyteller (Silko) (82) 812
Storyteller, The (Vargas Llosa) (90) 763
Straight Man (Russo) (98) 745
Straight Through the Night (Allen) (90) 767
Stranger in This World, A (Canty) (95) 769
Street of Crocodiles, The (Schulz) (78) 804
Streets of Laredo (McMurtry) (94) 769
Strong Motion (Franzen) (93) 766
Succession, The (Garrett) (84) 842
Suicide's Wife, The (Madden) (79) 727
Suitable Boy, A (Seth) (94) 774
Summons to Memphis, A (Taylor) (87) 832
Superior Women (Adams) (85) 879
Susan Sontag Reader, A (Sontag) (83) 769
Sweet Hereafter, The (Banks) (92) 790
Sweet Talk (Vaughn) (91) 786
Sweetest Dream, The (Lessing) (03) 820
Swimming in the Volcano (Shacochis) (94) 779
Symposium (Spark) (91) 790
T. C. Boyle Stories (Boyle) (99) 742
Table of Green Fields, A (Davenport) (94) 783
Tabloid Dreams (Butler) (97) 792
Tailor of Panama, The (le Carré) (97) 797
Take the A Train (Blankfort) (79) 737
Takeover, The (Spark) (77) 802
Taking the World in for Repairs (Selzer) (87) 836
Tale of Genji, The (Murasaki) (02) 769
Tales of Burning Love (Erdrich) (97) 812
Talking It Over (Barnes) (92) 799
Taps (Morris) (02) 773
Tar Baby (Morrison) (82) 828
Tattered Cloak and Other Novels, The (Berberova) (92) 804
Tattooed Girl, The (Oates) (04) 727
Tax Inspector, The (Carey) (93) 775
Tehanu (Le Guin) (91) 794
Ten Little Indians (Alexie) (04) 735
Tenants of Time, The (Flanagan) (89) 826
Tengu Child (Itaya) (84) 863
Tennis Players, The (Gustafsson) (84) 866
Terra Nostra (Fuentes) (77) 807
Terrible Twos, The (Reed) (83) 778
Territorial Rights (Spark) (80) 804
Testament, The (Grisham) (00) 749
Testimony and Demeanor (Casey) (80) 811
Testing the Current (McPherson) (85) 884
Texas (Michener) (86) 878
Texaco (Chamoiseau) (98) 755
Texasville (McMurtry) (88) 878
Thanatos Syndrome, The (Percy) (88) 883
That Night (McDermott) (88) 888
Theft, A (Bellow) (90) 792
Therapy (Lodge) (96) 748
They Burn the Thistles (Kemal) (78) 817
Thief of Time, A (Hillerman) (89) 830
Thin Mountain Air, The (Horgan) (78) 821
Things They Carried, The (O'Brien) (91) 803

Thinks . . . (Lodge) (02) 782
13th Valley, The (Del Vecchio) (83) 791
This Is Not a Novel (Markson) (02) 786
Thorn Birds, The (McCullough) (78) 831
Thousand Acres, A (Smiley) (92) 817
Three Evenings (Lasdun) (93) 788
Three Thousand Dollars (Lipsky) (90) 801
Three Novellas (Bernhard) (04) 747
Through the Ivory Gate (Dove) (93) 792
Tidewater Tales, The (Barth) (88) 892
Tiger's Tail (Lee) (97) 830
Time (Pickover) (99) 760
Time and Place (Woolley) (78) 836
Time and Tide (O'Brien) (93) 796
Time of Desecration (Moravia) (81) 809
Time of Our Singing, The (Powers) (04) 756
Time of Our Time, The (Mailer) (99) 764
Timequake (Vonnegut) (98) 760
Times Are Never So Bad, The (Dubus) (84) 873
Time's Arrow (Amis) (92) 821
Tirant lo Blanc (Martorell and de Galba) (85) 907
Tishomingo Blues (Leonard) (03) 834
To Asmara (Keneally) (90) 819
To Keep Our Honor Clean (McDowell) (81) 813
To See You Again (Adams) (83) 811
To Skin a Cat (McGuane) (87) 863
To the Hermitage (Bradbury) (02) 796
To the Land of the Cattails (Appelfeld) (87) 871
To the Wedding (Berger) (96) 752
To the White Sea (Dickey) (94) 802
Torn Skirt, The (Godfrey) (03) 839
Tortilla Curtain, The (Boyle) (96) 764
Tough Guys Don't Dance (Mailer) (85) 912
Toward the End of Time (Updike) (98) 769
Track to Bralgu, The (Wongar) (79) 768
Tracks (Erdrich) (89) 850
Transactions in a Foreign Currency (Eisenberg) (87) 881
Transatlantic Blues (Sheed) (79) 772
Trans-Atlantyk (Gombrowicz) (95) 791
Transit of Venus, The (Hazzard) (81) 822
Transports and Disgraces (Henson) (81) 827
Traveling on One Leg (Mueller) (99) 778
Travesty (Hawkes) (77) 837
Treason by the Book (Spence) (02) 800
Treatment, The (Menaker) (99) 783
Tree of Life, The (Nissenson) (86) 896
Trial of Elizabeth Cree, The (Ackroyd) (96) 768
Trick of the Ga Bolga, The (McGinley) (86) 903
Trinity (Uris) (77) 842
Triphammer (McCall) (91) 829
True History of the Kelly Gang (Carey) (02) 804
Trust Me (Updike) (88) 915
Truth About Lorin Jones, The (Lurie) (89) 860
Trying to Save Piggy Sneed (Irving) (97) 838
Tumble Home (Hempel) (98) 778
Tunnel, The (Gass) (96) 782
Turtle Beach (d'Alpuget) (84) 886
Turtle Diary (Hoban) (77) 852
Turtle Moon (Hoffman) (93) 820
Twenty-seventh Kingdom, The (Ellis) (00) 776
Twice Shy (Francis) (83) 841
Two Cities (Wideman) (99) 808
2010 (Clarke) (83) 844
Two Wings to Veil My Face (Forrest) (85) 946
Twyborn Affair, The (White) (81) 840
Typical American (Jen) (92) 840
Tzili (Appelfeld) (84) 890
Ulverton (Thorpe) (94) 814
Unbearable Lightness of Being, The (Kundera) (85) 958
Uncle (Markus) (79) 783

Uncollected Stories of William Faulkner (Faulkner) (80) 838
Unconsoled, The (Ishiguro) (96) 786
Under the Banyan Tree (Narayan) (86) 918
Under the 82nd Airborne (Eisenberg) (93) 829
Under the Fifth Sun (Shorris) (81) 844
Under the Jaguar Sun (Calvino) (89) 872
Underpainter, The (Urquhart) (98) 782
Understand This (Tervalon) (95) 823
Underworld (DeLillo) (98) 791
Undue Influence (Brookner) (01) 855
Undying Grass, The (Kemal) (79) 787
Unfortunate Woman, An (Brautigan) (01) 859
Union Street (Barker) (84) 895
Unless (Shields) (03) 858
Unlocking the Air (Le Guin) (97) 858
Unmade Bed, The (Sagan) (79) 791
Unsuitable Attachment, An (Pym) (83) 855
Unto the Soul (Appelfeld) (95) 827
Untouchable, The (Banville) (98) 796
Utz (Chatwin) (90) 835
Van Gogh's Room at Arles (Elkin) (94) 831
Vanished (Morris) (89) 877
Various Antidotes (Scott) (95) 831
Vertigo (Sebald) (01) 868
Very Old Bones (Kennedy) (93) 846
Viaduct, The (Wheldon) (84) 910
Victory over Japan (Gilchrist) (85) 973
Vindication (Sherwood) (94) 835
Vineland (Pynchon) (90) 844
Virtual Light (Gibson) (94) 839
Vision of Emma Blau, The (Hegi) (01) 877
Visitors (Brookner) (99) 842
Void, A (Perec) (96) 799
Volcano Lover, The (Sontag) (93) 856
Wait for November (Nossack) (83) 864
Waiting (Jin) (00) 801
Waiting to Exhale (McMillan) (93) 860
Waking (Figes) (83) 869
Waking the Dead (Spencer) (87) 922
Walkin' the Dog (Mosley) (00) 809
Wall Jumper, The (Schneider) (85) 978
Walnut Door, The (Hersey) (78) 883
War, The (Duras) (87) 941
War of the End of the World, The (Vargas Llosa) (85) 995
Wartime Lies (Begley) (92) 868
Watch, The (Bass) (90) 869
Watch in the Night, A (Wilson) (97) 876
Watchfires (Auchincloss) (83) 878
Watching TV with the Red Chinese (Whisnant) (93) 864
Waterland (Swift) (85) 1000
Waterworks, The (Doctorow) (95) 849
Way in the World, A (Naipaul) (95) 853
Way to Paradise, The (Vargas Llosa) (04) 815
Wayward and the Seeking, The (Toomer) (81) 904
We Love Glenda So Much and Other Tales (Cortázar) (84) 931
Well, The (Jolley) (87) 958
Wet Work (Buckley) (92) 872
What I Lived For (Oates) (95) 858
What I Loved (Hustvedt) (04) 819
What Was Mine (Beattie) (92) 876
What We Talk About When We Talk About Love (Carver) (82) 926
What's Bred in the Bone (Davies) (86) 939
Wheat That Springeth Green (Powers) (89) 892
When the Messenger Is Hot (Crane) (04) 827
When the Sons of Heaven Meet the Daughters of the Earth (Eberstadt) (98) 836
When Things of the Spirit Come First (Beauvoir) (83) 890

When We Were Orphans (Ishiguro) (01) 900
Where I'm Calling From (Carver) (89) 897
Where You Find It (Galloway) (03) 882
Where You'll Find Me (Beattie) (87) 967
While England Sleeps (Leavitt) (94) 851
While I Was Gone (Miller) (00) 826
Whistle (Jones) (79) 843
White Castle, The (Pamuk) (92) 890
White Hotel, The (Thomas) (82) 932
White Man's Grave (Dooling) (95) 862
White Noise (DeLillo) (86) 945
White Plague, The (Herbert) (83) 900
White Teeth (Smith) (01) 910
Whiteness of Bones, The (Moore) (90) 884
Who Do You Love (Thompson) (00) 830
Who Is Teddy Villanova? (Berger) (78) 899
Whore's Child, and Other Stories, The (Russo) (03) 886
Who's Irish? (Jen) (00) 839
Why Can't We Live Together Like Civilized Human Beings? (Kumin) (83) 903
Why Did I Ever (Robison) (02) 847
Widow for One Year, A (Irving) (99) 859
Widower's Son, The (Sillitoe) (78) 904
Wild Birds, The (Berry) (87) 989
Wild Decembers (O'Brien) (01) 915
Wild Life (Gloss) (01) 920
Wilderness Tips (Atwood) (92) 900
Wildlife (Ford) (91) 891
Will You Please Be Quiet, Please? (Carver) (77) 914
Wind Done Gone, The (Randall) (02) 865
Wine-Dark Sea, The (O'Brian) (94) 856
Winning the City (Weesner) (91) 905
Winter Garden (Bainbridge) (82) 958
Winter Queen, The (Akunin) (04) 839
Winter's Tale (Helprin) (84) 954
Winterspelt (Andersch) (79) 883
Winthrop Covenant, The (Auchincloss) (77) 923
Wise Children (Carter) (93) 879
Witch of Exmoor, The (Drabble) (98) 858
Witches of Eastwick, The (Updike) (85) 1041
Without a Hero (Boyle) (95) 880
Wobegon Boy (Keillor) (98) 870
Woman and the Ape, The (Høeg) (97) 890
Woman Hollering Creek (Cisneros) (92) 909
Woman Named Drown, A (Powell) (88) 968
Woman of Singular Occupation, A (Gilliatt) (90) 912
Woman of the Aeroplanes (Laing) (91) 914
Woman of the Inner Sea (Keneally) (94) 860
Woman Who Cut Off Her Leg at the Maidstone Club and Other Stories, The (Slavin) (00) 855
Woman Who Gave Birth to Rabbits, The (Donoghue) (03) 894
Woman Who Lived in a Prologue, The (Schneider) (81) 941
Woman Who Walked into Doors, The (Doyle) (97) 895
Women and Men (McElroy) (88) 973
Women in Their Beds (Berriault) (97) 900
Women of Brewster Place, The (Naylor) (83) 918
Women with Men (Ford) (98) 882
Wonder Boys (Chabon) (96) 831
Wonderful Fool (Endō) (84) 967
Wonders of the Invisible World, The (Gates) (00) 859
Woods, The (Plante) (83) 923
World According to Garp, The (Irving) (79) 908
World Below, The (Miller) (02) 880
World of Wonders (Davies) (77) 952
World's End (Boyle) (88) 988
World's Fair (Doctorow) (86) 970
Wrinkles (Simmons) (79) 918
Written on the Body (Winterson) (94) 873
Year of the French, The (Flanagan) (80) 880
Years of Rice and Salt, The (Robinson) (03) 912

Years with Laura Díaz, The (Fuentes) (01) 935
Yellow (Lee) (02) 889
Yellow Admiral, The (O'Brian) (97) 904
Yellow Dog (Amis) (04) 859
Yellow Raft in Blue Water, A (Dorris) (88) 1004
¡Yo! (Alvarez) (98) 886
Yonder Stands Your Orphan (Hannah) (02) 894
You Can't Keep a Good Woman Down (Walker) (82) 976
You Must Remember This (Oates) (88) 1009
Young Rebecca, The (West) (83) 932
Your Blues Ain't Like Mine (Campbell) (93) 896
Yukiko (Harris) (78) 942
Zone, The (Dovlatov) (86) 985
Zora Neale Hurston, Vol. I and Vol. II (Hurston) (96) 852
Zuckerman Unbound (Roth) (82) 981

FILM. See FINE ARTS, FILM, and MUSIC

FINE ARTS, FILM, and MUSIC
American Visions (Hughes) (98) 59
Art of Arts, The (Albus) (01) 54
As Thousands Cheer (Bergreen) (91) 61
Benjamin Britten (Carpenter) (94) 75
Bing Crosby (Giddins) (02) 88
Blood of Kings, The (Schele and Miller) (87) 75
Bright Earth (Ball) (03) 110
Buried Mirror, The (Fuentes) (93) 119
Catholic Imagination, The (Greeley) (01) 176
Chuck Jones (Kenner) (95) 119
Claude Monet (Tucker) (96) 120
Clement Greenberg (Rubenfeld) (99) 181
David Bomberg (Cork) (88) 238
Demon and the Angel, The (Hirsch) (03) 197
Diane Arbus (Bosworth) (96) 174
Diary of Frida Kahlo, The (Kahlo) (96) 182
Down the Highway (Sounes) (02) 208
Dreamland (Lesy) (98) 272
Edward Hopper (Levin) (96) 214
Einstein, Picasso (Miller) (02) 235
Essays on Music (Adorno) (03) 269
Fast-Talking Dames (DiBattista) (02) 285
Frank Capra (McBride) (93) 298
Frank Lloyd Wright (Secrest) (93) 303
Gaudier-Brzeska (Silber) (98) 331
Geometry of Love, The (Visser) (02) 330
Georgia O'Keeffe (Robinson) (90) 289
Georgia O'Keeffe (Turner) (00) 300
Giacometti (Lord) (86) 343
Goldwyn (Berg) (90) 303
Great Directors at Work (Jones) (87) 362
Great Movies, The (Ebert) (03) 348
Gustav Mahler, 1892-1904 (La Grange) (96) 321
Happy Alchemy (Davies) (99) 346
His Other Half (Lesser) (92) 285
History of the Surrealist Movement (Durozoi) (03) 370
Hole in Our Soul (Bayles) (95) 314
Hunter Gracchus, The (Davenport) (97) 419
In the Country of Country (Dawidoff) (98) 419
Invisible Republic (Marcus) (98) 441
Jackson Pollock (Naifeh and Smith) (91) 466
Johann Sebastian Bach (Wolff) (01) 494
Joseph Cornell's Theater of the Mind (Cornell) (95) 408
King of Ragtime (Berlin) (95) 422
Knowing When to Stop (Rorem) (95) 427
Leap (Williams) (01) 513
Leaving a Doll's House (Bloom) (97) 494
Leonardo da Vinci (Kemp and Roberts, with Steadman) (90) 505
Lester Leaps In (Daniels) (03) 470
Life of Picasso, 1881-1906 (Richardson) (92) 431

Life of Picasso, 1907-1917 (Richardson) (97) 511
Loitering with Intent (O'Toole) (98) 522
London Yankees, The (Weintraub) (80) 508
Look, Listen, Read (Lévi-Strauss) (98) 526
M (Robb) (01) 549
Mark Rothko (Breslin) (94) 504
Mark Rothko (Weiss) (99) 524
Martha (De Mille) (92) 485
Master of Death (Camille) (97) 555
Memoirs of the Blind (Derrida) (95) 473
Mozart (Solomon) (96) 490
Mozart in Vienna, 1781-1791 (Braunbehrens) (91) 606
Mrs. Jordan's Profession (Tomalin) (96) 465
Nature of Order, The (Alexander) (04) 537
New Worlds of Dvořák (Beckerman) (04) 556
Noël Coward (Hoare) (97) 630
Noguchi East and West (Ashton) (93) 570
Obstacle Race, The (Greer) (80) 600
On Photography (Sontag) (78) 618
One Nation Under a Groove (Early) (96) 537
Paul Klee (Lanchner, ed.) (88) 668
Peter Paul Rubens (White) (88) 690
Phantom Empire, The (O'Brien) (94) 622
Phoenicians, The (Moscati, ed.) (90) 665
Pleasures of the Imagination, The (Brewer) (98) 634
Ransom of Russian Art, The (McPhee) (95) 622
Red and Hot (Starr) (84) 726
Reeling (Kael) (77) 662
Rewrites (Simon) (97) 692
Richard Rodgers (Hyland) (99) 658
Rodin (Grunfeld) (88) 780
Romare Bearden (Schwartzman) (92) 684
Screening History (Vidal) (93) 707
Selected Essays (Berger) (03) 732
Sound, Speech, and Music (Burrows) (91) 759
Still Life with a Bridle (Herbert) (92) 785
Testaments Betrayed (Kundera) (96) 744
Theremin (Glinsky) (01) 815
Tiepolo's Hound (Walcott) (01) 825
Truffaut (de Baecque and Toubiana) (00) 772
Van Gogh (Sweetman) (91) 843
Velázquez (Brown) (87) 907
Vladimir's Carrot (Peter) (88) 937
Walker Evans (Mellow) (00) 805
Watermelon Wine (Gaillard) (79) 835

HISTORY
Abandonment of the Jews, The (Wyman) (H-85) 1
Above the Battle (Leonard) (79) 1
Abraham Lincoln and the Second American Revolution (McPherson) (92) 1
Accounting for Genocide (Fein) (80) 10
Adam, Eve, and the Serpent (Pagels) (89) 4
Advisors, The (York) (77) 27
Affair, The (Bredin) (87) 15
Afghanistan and the Soviet Union (Bradsher) (H-84) 1
Africa (Reader) (99) 19
Africa Explored (Hibbert) (H-84) 6
After the Fact (Davidson and Lytle) (H-83) 10
Age of Empire, The (Hobsbawm) (89) 14
Age of Federalism, The (Elkins and McKitrick) (94) 5
Age of Homespun, The (Ulrich) (02) 22
Age of Napoleon, The (Durant and Durant) (77) 33
Age of Surveillance, The (Donner) (81) 16
Alabi's World (Price) (91) 10
Albion (Ackroyd) (04) 9
Albion's Seed (Fischer) (90) 24
Alexander to Actium (Green) (91) 15
Alger Hiss (Smith) (77) 38
All the Years of American Popular Music (Ewen) (78) 33
Allies (Eisenhower) (H-83) 20
Allies of a Kind (Thorne) (79) 9

CATEGORY INDEX

Ambiguous Iroquois Empire, The (Jennings) (H-85) 18
Amending America (Bernstein and Agel) (94) 15
Amerasia Spy Case, The (Klehr and Radosh) (97) 28
America and the Survivors of the Holocaust (Dinnerstein) (H-83) 25
America in Black and White (Thernstrom and Thernstrom) (98) 31
America in Search of Itself (White) (H-83) 29
America in the Twenties (Perrett) (H-83) 33
America in Vietnam (Lewy) (79) 14
American Assassins (Clarke) (H-83) 37
American Catholic (Morris) (98) 36
American Dream, The (Cullen) (04) 26
American Establishment, The (Silk and Silk) (81) 36
American Inquisition, The (Kutler) (H-83) 41
American Jihad (Emerson) (03) 23
American Kaleidoscope, The (Fuchs) (92) 17
American Magic, The (Lewin) (H-83) 52
American Myth, American Reality (Robertson) (81) 39
American Pharaoh (Cohen and Taylor) (01) 34
American Presidency, The (McDonald) (95) 28
American Scoundrel (Keneally) (03) 28
American Scripture (Maier) (98) 50
American Style of Foreign Policy, The (Dallek) (H-84) 11
American Tragedy (Kaiser) (01) 39
American Visions (Hughes) (98) 59
Americans at War (Ambrose) (98) 64
Anahulu (Kirch and Sahlins) (93) 20
Ancestors (Ching) (89) 19
Ancient Slavery and Modern Ideology (Finley) (81) 43
And the Walls Came Tumbling Down (Abernathy) (90) 39
Anglomania (Buruma) (00) 27
Another Part of the Fifties (Carter) (H-84) 24
Anti-Semitic Moment, The (Birnbaum) (04) 30
Anxious Parents (Stearns) (04) 35
Apocalypses (Weber) (00) 44
Approaching Fury, The (Oates) (98) 72
Arab and Jew (Shipler) (87) 35
Arab Reach (Levins) (H-84) 28
Arabists, The (Kaplan) (94) 42
Arabs, Israelis, and Kissinger, The (Sheehan) (77) 57
Archaeology and Language (Renfrew) (89) 41
Armada (Padfield) (89) 50
Armed Truce (Thomas) (88) 57
Arming America (Bellesiles) (01) 49
Arrogance and Anxiety (Farrar) (82) 22
Art and Act (Gay) (77) 67
Art of Arts, The (Albus) (01) 54
Art of Warfare in the Age of Napoleon, The (Rothenberg) (79) 38
At a Century's Ending (Kennan) (97) 71
At Dawn We Slept (Prange) (82) 33
At the End of an Age (Lukacs) (03) 37
Atom (Krauss) (02) 57
Attack and Die (McWhiney and Jamieson) (H-83) 57
Awash in a Sea of Faith (Butler) (91) 65
Aztecs (Clendinnen) (92) 30
Bad Land (Raban) (97) 91
Bakke Case, The (Dreyfuss and Lawrence) (80) 45
Balkans, The (Glenny) (01) 59
Barbarians and Romans (Randers-Pehrson) (H-84) 39
Barbary Coast, The (Wolf) (80) 49
Barcelona (Hughes) (93) 49
Bargaining for Supremacy (Leutze) (78) 85
Battle Cry of Freedom (McPherson) (89) 67
Battle for the Falklands, The (Hastings and Jenkins) (H-84) 43
Bay of Pigs (Wyden) (80) 59
Bearing the Cross (Garrow) (87) 55
Becoming American (Archdeacon) (H-84) 48
Been in the Storm So Long (Litwack) (80) 65

Beggar and the Professor, The (Le Roy Ladurie) (98) 108
Beginnings of Western Science, The (Lindberg) (93) 71
Beyond Our Means (Malabre) (88) 101
"Beyond Reasonable Doubt" and "Probable Cause" (Shapiro) (93) 75
Big Test, The (Lemann) (00) 57
Birth of a New Europe, The (Hamerow) (H-84) 61
Birth of Purgatory, The (Le Goff) (H-85) 43
Birth of the Modern, The (Johnson) (92) 52
Black Book of Communism, The (Courtois et al., eds) (00) 66
Black Death, The (Gottfried) (H-84) 68
Black Family in Slavery and Freedom, 1750-1925, The (Gutman) (77) 87
Black Hawk Down (Bowden) (00) 70
Black Hearts of Men, The (Stauffer) (03) 74
Blitzkrieg (Deighton) (81) 88
Blockade Busters (Barker) (78) 108
Blood of Kings, The (Schele and Miller) (87) 75
Boer War, The (Pakenham) (80) 97
Bolsheviks Come to Power, The (Rabinowitch) (77) 109
Bourgeois Experience, Victoria to Freud, Vol. I, The (Gay) (H-85) 53
Box, The (Kisseloff) (96) 77
Breaking the Deadlock (Posner) (02) 130
Breaking the Slump (Alexander) (03) 106
Brethren, The (Woodward and Armstrong) (80) 104
Brink, The (Detzer) (80) 110
Britain, Europe and the World, 1850-1982 (Porter) (H-84) 78
British Revolution, 1880-1939, The (James) (78) 145
Britons (Colley) (93) 105
Broken Staff, The (Manuel) (93) 110
Brown (Rodriguez) (03) 114
Buried Mirror, The (Fuentes) (93) 119
Burr, Hamilton, and Jefferson (Kennedy) (00) 112
Byzantine Journey, A (Ash) (96) 86
Cairo (Raymond) (02) 135
Cairo (Rodenbeck) (00) 117
Campaign for North Africa, The (Coggins) (81) 113
Captain Kidd and the War Against the Pirates (Ritchie) (87) 99
Cash Nexus, The (Ferguson) (02) 145
Celts, The (Herm) (78) 164
Century of the Scottish People, 1830-1950, A (Smout) (88) 127
Certain Trumpets (Wills) (95) 114
Chairman, The (Bird) (93) 138
Chance and Circumstance (Baskir and Strauss) (79) 88
Changes in the Land (Cronon) (H-84) 82
Changing of the Guard (Broder) (81) 127
Chan's Great Continent, The (Spence) (99) 149
Charles the Second (Hutton) (91) 132
Chechnya (Lieven) (99) 158
Children, The (Halberstam) (99) 163
Chile (Timerman) (88) 150
Chinese Communist Party in Power, 1949-1976, The (Guillermaz) (79) 174
Chinese Foreign Policy After the Cultural Revolution, 1966-1977 (Sutter) (79) 108
Chinese in America, The (Chang) (04) 113
Chivalry (Keen) (H-85) 63
Christianizing the Roman Empire (a.d. 100-400) (MacMullen) (H-85) 68
Chronicle of the Łódź Ghetto, 1941-1944, The (Dobroszycki, ed.) (H-85) 73
Churchill and de Gaulle (Kersaudy) (H-83) 70
Churchill Coalition, The (Lee) (81) 147
Cincinnatus (Wills) (H-85) 78
Circus Fire, The (O'Nan) (01) 194
Cities and the Wealth of Nations (Jacobs) (H-85) 83

Cities on a Hill (FitzGerald) (87) 121
Citizens (Schama) (90) 99
City of Joy, The (Lapierre) (86) 136
Civil War, The (Ward, et al.) (91) 137
Civil War Command and Strategy (Jones) (93) 153
Closing the Circle (Hoyt) (H-83) 75
Coal (Freese) (04) 126
Coasts of Bohemia, The (Sayer) (99) 195
Collaborator, The (Kaplan) (01) 199
Collected Works, 1956-1976 (Metcalf) (97) 175
Collected Works, 1976-1997 (Metcalf) (98) 199
Coming Alive (Garside) (82) 111
Coming Anarchy, The (Kaplan) (01) 208
Command of the Seas (Lehman) (90) 132
Commanding Heights (Yergin and Stanislaw) (99) 204
Common Ground (Lukas) (86) 182
Conduct Unbecoming (Shilts) (94) 158
Confederate Nation, The (Thomas) (80) 156
Confederates in the Attic (Horwitz) (99) 208
Conflict and Crisis (Donovan) (78) 210
Conflict of Duty (Dowart) (H-84) 96
Conflict of Visions, A (Sowell) (88) 184
Congo Cables, The (Kalb) (H-83) 80
Conquest of America, The (Todorov) (H-85) 89
Conquests and Cultures (Sowell) (99) 212
Constantine's Sword (Carroll) (02) 167
Cooper's Wife Is Missing, The (Hoff and Yeates)
    (01) 218
Courier from Warsaw (Nowak) (H-83) 85
Court and the Constitution, The (Cox) (88) 213
Cousins' Wars, The (Phillips) (00) 146
Crabgrass Frontier (Jackson) (87) 170
Crazy Years, The (Wiser) (84) 207
Creating the Entangling Alliance (Ireland) (82) 145
Creation of Feminist Consciousness, The (Lerner)
    (94) 168
Crime and Punishment in American History (Friedman)
    (94) 173
Crime of the Century (Kurtz) (H-83) 90
Crisis (Jordan) (H-83) 93
Crisis of Islam, The (Lewis) (04) 142
Crisis on the Left (McAuliffe) (79) 138
Crisis Years, The (Beschloss) (92) 128
Cromwell (Howell) (78) 219
Crooked Timber of Humanity, The (Berlin) (92) 133
Crossroads of Death (Weingartner) (80) 162
Crucible of Race, The (Williamson) (H-85) 99
Cultural Cold War, The (Saunders) (01) 227
Culture and Imperialism (Said) (94) 181
Cycles of American History, The (Schlesinger)
    (87) 183
Damnable Question, The (Dangerfield) (77) 188
Danger and Survival (Bundy) (89) 217
Dangerous Relations (Ulam) (H-84) 111
Dark Continent (Mazower) (00) 164
Dark Side of Camelot, The (Hersh) (98) 225
Dawn of Modern Science (Goldstein) (81) 219
Day America Crashed, The (Shachtman) (80) 200
Day One (Wyden) (H-85) 104
Days of the French Revolution, The (Hibbert) (81) 222
Dead Certainties (Schama) (92) 152
Deadly Medicine (Mancall) (96) 157
Death Valley and the Amargosa (Lingenfelter) (87) 198
Debacle (Ledeen and Lewis) (82) 175
Decline of Bismarck's European Order, The (Kennan)
    (80) 215
Deep Politics and the Death of JFK (Scott) (94) 221
De Gaulle, 1890-1944 (Lacouture) (91) 192
De Gaulle, 1945-1970 (Lacouture) (93) 219
Deliberate Speed (Lhamon) (91) 197
Democracy on Trial (Smith) (96) 165
Descent from Glory (Nagel) (H-84) 121
Devices and Desires (Tone) (02) 199

Devil in the White City, The (Larson) (04) 165
Devil's Horsemen, The (Chambers) (80) 220
Different Mirror, A (Takaki) (94) 230
Diplomacy (Kissinger) (95) 171
Discoverers, The (Boorstin) (H-84) 130
Distant Mirror, A (Tuchman) (79) 151
Divided Left, The (Cantor) (79) 157
Double Lives (Koch) (95) 185
Drawing the Line (Blum) (H-83) 104
Drawn with the Sword (McPherson) (97) 229
Dream Endures, The (Starr) (98) 268
Dream of Greatness, A (Perrett) (80) 226
Dream of Reason, The (Bush) (79) 165
Dreamland (Sachar) (03) 233
Driving Mr. Albert (Paterniti) (01) 258
Dust Bowl, The (Bonnifield) (80) 251
Dust Bowl (Worster) (80) 244
Dust of Empire, The (Meyer) (04) 198
Dynamics of Nazism, The (Weinstein) (81) 254
Eisenhower and the Cold War (Divine) (82) 195
Eisenhower, at War (Eisenhower) (87) 226
Eisenhower's Lieutenants (Weigley) (82) 210
Elites in American History (Burch) (81) 268
Elizabethan Deliverance, The (Bryant) (H-83) 114
Embarrassment of Riches, The (Schama) (88) 266
Embattled Courage (Linderman) (88) 271
Embattled Dreams (Starr) (03) 250
Emergence of Modern India, The (Lall) (82) 223
Émigré New York (Mehlman) (01) 277
Emperor of Japan (Keene) (03) 255
Empire (Ferguson) (04) 228
Empire of Fortune (Jennings) (89) 273
Empire of Liberty (Tucker and Hendrickson) (91) 253
Empire of Reason, The (Commager) (78) 290
Empire of Their Own, An (Gabler) (89) 278
Empire Wilderness, An (Kaplan) (99) 247
Empires in the Balance (Willmott) (H-83) 119
Enchanted Loom, The (Corsi, ed.) (92) 183
End of Order, The (Mee) (81) 277
End of the Old Order in Rural Europe, The (Blum)
    (79) 188
End of the War in Asia, The (Allen) (80) 285
End of the World, The (Friedrich) (H-83) 125
Endangered Dreams (Starr) (97) 247
English Civil War, The (Ashton) (80) 297
English Culture and the Decline of the Industrial Spirit,
    1850-1980 (Wiener) (82) 234
Entertaining Satan (Demos) (H-83) 130
Entrepreneurs of Ideology (Stark) (82) 240
Escape from Elba, The (MacKenzie) (H-83) 134
Essays (Knox) (90) 219
Essays on Music (Adorno) (03) 269
Europe (Davies) (97) 260
Europe, Europe (Enzensberger) (90) 227
Europeans, The (Barzini) (H-84) 153
Eve (Phillips) (H-85) 130
Evolution's Workshop (Larson) (02) 258
Execution by Hunger (Dolot) (86) 254
Exiled in Paradise (Heilbut) (84) 284
Explaining America (Wills) (82) 261
Explaining Hitler (Rosenbaum) (99) 273
Fabians, The (Mackenzie and Mackenzie) (78) 300
Face of Battle, The (Keegan) (78) 305
Face of the Nation, The (Fitzgerald) (97) 265
Faces of Revolution (Bailyn) (91) 279
Fall of Berlin, 1945, The (Beevor) (03) 288
Fall of France, The (Jackson) (04) 244
Fall of the House of Labor, The (Montgomery)
    (88) 308
Fall of the Peacock Throne (Forbis) (81) 297
Family and Nation (Moynihan) (87) 259
Farm (Rhodes) (90) 240
Farther Shore, The (Gifford) (91) 287

CATEGORY INDEX

Fascism (Payne) (81) 314
Fatal Environment, The (Slotkin) (86) 264
Fatal Shore, The (Hughes) (88) 312
Fateful Alliance, The (Kennan) (H-85) 135
Feminism Without Illusions (Fox-Genovese) (92) 205
Fierce Discontent, A (McGerr) (04) 261
Fifties, The (Halberstam) (94) 292
Fifty Years of Europe (Morris) (98) 308
Figures in a Western Landscape (Stevenson) (95) 231
Fin-de-siècle Vienna (Schorske) (81) 330
Fire in the Minds of Men (Billington) (81) 340
First Great Triumph (Zimmermann) (03) 297
First Moderns, The (Everdell) (98) 312
First Salute, The (Tuchman) (89) 302
First World War, The (Keegan) (00) 264
Flu (Kolata) (00) 268
Footnote, The (Grafton) (98) 317
For the Time Being (Dillard) (00) 282
Forces of Production (Noble) (H-85) 152
Ford (Lacey) (87) 297
Forest of Kings, A (Schele and Freidel) (91) 308
Forged in Fire (Copp) (H-83) 145
Forgotten War, The (Blair) (89) 307
Fortress Without a Roof (Morrison) (H-83) 150
Founding Father (Brookhiser) (97) 306
Founding the Far West (Johnson) (93) 293
Fourth and Richest Reich, The (Hartrich) (81) 353
France Under Napoleon (Bergeron) (82) 296
Franklin D. Roosevelt and American Foreign Policy, 1932-1945 (Dallek) (80) 328
Frederick Douglass (McFeely) (92) 232
Freedom (Patterson) (92) 237
From Beirut to Jerusalem (Friedman) (90) 283
From *Brown* to *Bakke*, The Supreme Court and School Integration (Wilkinson) (80) 334
From Dawn to Decadence (Barzun) (01) 314
From Prejudice to Destruction (Katz) (81) 362
From Time Immemorial (Peters) (H-85) 156
From Wealth to Power (Zakaria) (99) 315
From West to East (Schwartz) (99) 319
Frontiers of Change (Cochran) (82) 301
Future of Freedom, The (Zakaria) (04) 279
Gabriel's Rebellion (Egerton) (94) 325
Gate of Heavenly Peace, The (Spence) (82) 305
Generation of 1914, The (Wohl) (80) 337
Genius for War, A (Dupuy) (78) 332
Genocidal Mentality, The (Lifton and Markusen) (91) 338
German Army, 1933-1945, The (Cooper) (79) 245
German Army, 1933-45, The (Seaton) (H-83) 161
German Big Business and the Rise of Hitler (Turner) (86) 338
German Rearmament and the West, 1932-1933 (Bennett) (80) 344
German Socialism and Weimar Democracy (Breitman) (82) 315
Germans, The (Craig) (H-83) 166
Germany and the Two World Wars (Hillgruber) (82) 321
Germany and the United States (Gatzke) (81) 368
Germany East and West (Whetten) (81) 373
Germany 1866-1945 (Craig) (79) 249
Giants, The (Barnet) (78) 345
Gifts of the Jews, The (Cahill) (99) 333
Gilligan Unbound (Cantor) (02) 338
Glorious Cause, The (Middlekauff) (H-83) 171
Gnostic Gospels, The (Pagels) (80) 363
God's Chinese Son (Spence) (97) 339
God's Funeral (Wilson) (00) 317
God's Long Summer (Marsh) (98) 362
God's Name in Vain (Carter) (01) 351
God's Secretaries (Nicolson) (04) 295
Gold and Iron (Stern) (78) 354

Good Life and Its Discontents, The (Samuelson) (97) 345
Good War, The (Terkel) (H-85) 173
Gospel of Gentility, The (Hunter) (H-85) 179
Gracefully Insane (Beam) (03) 343
Grammatical Man (Campbell) (83) 301
Grand Delusion, A (Mann) (02) 367
Grand Expectations (Patterson) (97) 355
Grand Failure, The (Brzezinski) (90) 329
Grand Strategy of Philip II, The (Parker) (00) 326
Great Cat Massacre and Other Episodes in French Cultural History, The (Darnton) (H-85) 183
Great Fear, The (Caute) (79) 255
Great Map of Mankind, The (Marshall and Williams) (H-83) 176
Great Melody, The (O'Brien) (93) 316
Great Plains (Frazier) (90) 334
Great Rebellion, The (Ruíz) (81) 396
Great Republic, The (Bailyn, et al.) (78) 360
Great Shame, The (Keneally) (00) 336
Great Triumvirate, The (Peterson) (88) 363
Great Wall of China, The (Waldron) (91) 368
Greatest Benefit to Mankind, The (Porter) (99) 341
Greatest Power on Earth, The (Clark) (82) 343
Guadalcanal Remembered (Merillat) (H-83) 181
Gulag (Applebaum) (04) 316
Gulag Archipelago, The (Solzhenitsyn) (78) 370
Gunfighters, Highwaymen, and Vigilantes (McGrath) (H-85) 190
Guns, Germs, and Steel (Diamond) (98) 370
Gypsies, The (Fraser) (93) 321
Hamlet in Purgatory (Greenblatt) (02) 376
Hands and Hearts (Rothman) (H-85) 195
Harvest of Empire (González) (01) 384
Harvest of Sorrow, The (Conquest) (87) 376
Haunted Land, The (Rosenberg) (96) 330
Haunts of the Black Masseur (Sprawson) (94) 372
Haymarket Tragedy, The (Avrich) (H-85) 201
Heaven on Earth (Muravchik) (03) 356
. . . Heavens and the Earth, The (McDougall) (86) 396
Heisenberg's War (Powers) (94) 380
Heyday of American Communism, The (Klehr) (H-85) 206
Hidden-Hand Presidency, The (Greenstein) (H-83) 190
High Walls of Jerusalem, The (Sanders) (H-84) 197
Hiroshima (Takaki) (96) 334
History of American Wars, The (Williams) (82) 354
History of Architecture, A (Kostof) (86) 421
History of Black Americans (Foner) (H-84) 202
History of Britain, A (Schama) (01) 398
History of Europe, A (Roberts) (98) 383
History of Heaven, A (Russell) (98) 387
History of Philosophy in America, 1720-2000, A (Kuklick) (03) 366
History of Private Life, Passions of the Renaissance, A (Chartier, ed.) (90) 386
History of Private Life, Revelations of the Medieval World, A (Duby, ed.) (89) 349
History of Private Life, From the Fires of Revolution to the Great War, A (Perrot, ed.) (91) 404
History of Private Life, Riddles of Identity in Modern Times, A (Prost and Vincent, eds.) (92) 294
History of Private Life, From Pagan Rome to Byzantium, A (Veyne) (88) 386
History of Reading, A (Manguel) (97) 395
History of South Africa, A (Thompson) (91) 408
History of Southern Literature, The (Rubin, ed.) (86) 426
History of the American People, A (Johnson) (99) 374
History of the Arab Peoples, A (Hourani) (92) 299
History of the Breast, A (Yalom) (98) 391
History of the German Resistance, 1933-1945, The (Hoffmann) (78) 388

History of the Idea of Progress (Nisbet) (81) 430
History of the Jews, A (Johnson) (88) 392
History of the Jews in America, A (Sachar) (93) 340
History of the Ottoman Empire and Modern Turkey,
    The (Shaw and Shaw) (78) 393
History of the Surrealist Movement (Durozoi) (03) 370
History of the Westward Movement (Merk) (79) 277
History of Wales, A (Davies) (95) 309
History of Women in the West, From Ancient
    Goddesses to Christian Saints, A (Pantel, ed.)
    (93) 345
History Wars (Linenthal and Engelhardt, eds.) (97) 400
Hitler Among the Germans (Binion) (77) 357
Hitler and Stalin (Bullock) (93) 349
Hitler and the Final Solution (Fleming) (H-85) 213
Hitler and the Forgotten Nazis (Pauley) (82) 360
Hitler in Vienna, 1907-1913 (Jones) (H-84) 207
Hitler of History, The (Lukacs) (98) 396
Hitler over Germany (Mitchell) (H-84) 213
Hitler State, The (Broszat) (82) 363
Hitler vs. Roosevelt (Bailey and Ryan) (80) 404
Hitler's Pope (Cornwell) (00) 396
Hitler's Spies (Kahn) (79) 281
Hitler's War (Irving) (78) 398
Hitler's Willing Executioners (Goldhagen) (97) 405
Hobbes (Martinich) (00) 400
Hole in Our Soul (Bayles) (95) 314
Holocaust and the Crisis of Human Behavior, The (Kren
    and Rappoport) (81) 439
Holocaust in American Life, The (Novick) (00) 404
Holocaust Testimonies (Langer) (92) 304
Home (Rybczynski) (87) 402
Home to War (Nicosia) (02) 386
Honorable Defeat, An (Davis) (02) 391
Hopkins, the Self, and God (Ong) (87) 406
Hornes, The (Buckley) (87) 410
House (Kidder) (86) 450
House of Morgan, The (Chernow) (91) 432
House of Saud, The (Holden and Johns) (H-83) 195
How "Natives" Think (Sahlins) (96) 338
How the Irish Saved Civilization (Cahill) (96) 343
Hundred Years War, The (Seward) (79) 291
Hungry Ghosts (Becker) (98) 406
Hut Six Story, The (Welchman) (H-83) 201
I Will Bear Witness (Klemperer) (01) 447
Idea of Decline in Western History, The (Herman)
    (98) 415
Idea of Poverty, The (Himmelfarb) (H-85) 219
Ideology and Revolution in Modern Europe (Tholfsen)
    (H-85) 225
Illusion of Peace (Szulc) (79) 300
I'm Radcliffe! Fly Me! (Baker) (77) 376
Imaginative Landscape of Christopher Columbus, The
    (Flint) (93) 365
Immaculate Invasion, The (Shacochis) (00) 413
Impatient Armies of the Poor (Folsom) (92) 334
Imperfect Garden (Todorov) (03) 396
Imperial Experience in Sub-Saharan Africa Since 1870,
    The (Wilson) (78) 436
Imperialism at Bay (Louis) (79) 305
In Harm's Way (Stanton) (02) 400
In Quest and Crisis (Ingrao) (80) 426
In Retrospect (McNamara, with VanDeMark) (96) 363
In Search of Equality (McClain) (95) 351
In the Beginning (McGrath) (02) 408
In the Country of Country (Dawidoff) (98) 419
In the Devil's Snare (Norton) (03) 405
In the Footsteps of Mr. Kurtz (Wrong) (02) 413
In the Heart of the Sea (Philbrick) (01) 457
In the Name of the People (Ulam) (78) 442
In the Shadow of FDR (Leuchtenburg) (H-84) 223
In War's Dark Shadow (Lincoln) (H-84) 227
India (Wolpert) (92) 350

Inevitable Revolutions (LaFeber) (H-84) 232
Infamy (Toland) (H-83) 210
Infiltration (Speer) (82) 398
Inheritance, The (Freedman) (97) 451
Inheriting the Revolution (Appleby) (01) 462
Intellectual Life of the British Working Classes, The
    (Rose) (02) 418
International Norms and National Policy (Bonkovsky)
    (81) 445
Intifada (Schiff and Ya'ari) (91) 461
Intruders in Paradise (Sanford) (98) 432
Inventing America (Wills) (79) 322
Inventing Herself (Showalter) (02) 423
Inventing the Dream (Starr) (86) 477
Inventing the Middle Ages (Cantor) (93) 394
Invention of the Restaurant, The (Spang) (01) 467
Iraq and Iran (Ismael) (H-83) 216
Isabel the Queen (Liss) (93) 399
Islam and the West (Lewis) (94) 414
Israel (Gilbert) (99) 427
Itinerary (Paz) (01) 471
It Seemed Like Nothing Happened (Carroll) (H-83) 220
Italian Fascism (De Grand) (H-83) 224
Jack Tars and Commodores (Fowler) (H-85) 246
Japan Before Perry (Totman) (82) 408
Japan in War and Peace (Dower) (95) 392
Jefferson and the Presidency (Johnstone) (79) 331
Jefferson's Pillow (Wilkins) (02) 440
Jesus Through the Centuries (Pelikan) (86) 482
Jewish Self-Hatred (Gilman) (87) 440
Jews (Hertzberg and Hirt-Manheimer) (99) 436
Jews in the Eyes of the Germans (Low) (80) 439
Jews of East Central Europe Between the World Wars,
    The (Mendelsohn) (H-84) 243
Jihad (Kepel) (03) 428
Jihad (Rashid) (03) 423
John Adams (McCullough) (02) 444
John Marshall and the Heroic Age of the Supreme Court
    (Newmyer) (03) 432
John Maynard Keynes, 1920-1937 (Skidelsky) (95) 400
John Maynard Keynes, 1937-1946 (Skidelsky) (02) 453
John Wayne's America (Wills) (98) 477
Journey into Space (Murray) (90) 464
Justice at Nuremberg (Conot) (H-84) 261
Kaddish (Wieseltier) (99) 445
Karl Marx (Wheen) (01) 504
Khrushchev (Taubman) (04) 404
Khubilai Khan (Rossabi) (89) 432
Kindness of Strangers, The (Boswell) (90) 486
Kissinger Transcripts, The (Burr, ed.) (00) 466
Koba the Dread (Amis) (03) 446
Kolyma (Conquest) (79) 354
Korean War, The (Hastings) (88) 447
Krakatoa (Winchester) (04) 430
Kronstadt, 1917-1921 (Getzler) (H-84) 271
Land of Savagery/Land of Promise (Billington) (82) 421
Landscape and Memory (Schama) (96) 414
Last Best Hope of Earth, The (Neely) (94) 449
Law Unto Itself, A (Burnham) (91) 507
Lawrence of Arabia (Wilson) (91) 512
Laws Harsh as Tigers (Salyer) (96) 418
Leaders (Nixon) (H-83) 248
Left Bank, The (Lottman) (83) 390
Leonardo da Vinci (Kemp and Roberts, with Steadman)
    (90) 506
Lester Leaps In (Daniels) (03) 470
Lewis and Clark Journals, The (Lewis and Clark)
    (04) 442
Liberalism and Republicanism in the Historical
    Imagination (Appleby) (93) 454
Liberty and Slavery (Cooper) (H-84) 283
Life in Pieces, A (Eskin) (03) 480
Life with the Enemy (Rings) (H-83) 274

Lincoln at Gettysburg (Wills) (93) 464
Lincoln in American Memory (Peterson) (95) 435
Little Saint (Green) (01) 540
Lloyd's of London (Hodgson) (H-85) 262
Local People (Dittmer) (95) 440
Lonely Vigil (Lord) (78) 534
Long March, The (Salisbury) (86) 537
Lords of the Horizons (Goodwin) (00) 501
Lost Tribes and Promised Lands (Sanders) (79) 398
Low Life (Sante) (92) 460
Lucifer (Russell) (H-85) 272
Luther (Oberman) (91) 553
Machine That Would Go of Itself, A (Kammen) (87) 503
Magdalena and Balthasar (Ozment) (87) 508
Maginot Line, The (Kemp) (H-83) 278
Making of Adolf Hitler, The (Davidson) (78) 552
Making of the Atomic Bomb, The (Rhodes) (88) 517
Man Called Intrepid, A (Stevenson) (77) 475
Mandela (Sampson) (00) 506
Many Thousands Gone (Berlin) (99) 519
Mao (Short) (01) 554
Mao Zedong (Spence) (00) 511
Mao's China (Meisner) (78) 557
Marathon (Witcover) (78) 562
March of Folly, The (Tuchman) (H-85) 277
Marcus Garvey and Universal Negro Improvement Association Papers, The (Hill, ed.) (H-85) 283
Marshall Plan, The (Mee) (H-85) 292
Marxism (Sowell) (86) 572
Masters of Death (Rhodes) (03) 513
Material Dreams (Starr) (91) 577
Matisse (Schneider) (H-85) 303
Maverick and His Machine, The (Maney) (04) 501
Mayday (Beschloss) (87) 530
Meaning of Hitler, The (Haffner) (80) 528
Memory of Fire, Century of the Wind (Galeano) (89) 548
Memory of Fire, Faces and Masks (Galeano) (88) 544
Memory of Fire, Genesis (Galeano) (86) 584
Men's Lives (Matthiessen) (87) 547
Mephistopheles (Russell) (87) 553
Metamorphosis of Greece Since World War II, The (McNeill) (79) 438
Metaphysical Club, The (Menand) (02) 524
Mexican Phoenix (Brading) (02) 528
Midwife's Tale, A (Ulrich) (91) 596
Migrations and Cultures (Sowell) (97) 577
Mind of Egypt, The (Assmann) (03) 531
Miracle at Midway (Prange, Goldstein, and Dillon) (H-83) 288
Miracle of Dunkirk, The (Lord) (H-83) 293
Mirror Makers, The (Fox) (H-85) 313
Mistress Anne (Erickson) (H-85) 319
Modern American Religion, 1919-1941 (Marty) (92) 524
Modern European Thought (Baumer) (78) 581
Modern Ireland (Foster) (90) 573
Modern Times (Johnson) (H-84) 306
Money (Hacker) (98) 562
Morality, Reason, and Power (Smith) (87) 577
More Perfect Union, A (Peters) (88) 589
Mormon America (Ostling and Ostling) (00) 529
Mosquitoes, Malaria and Man (Harrison) (79) 466
Mother Country (Robinson) (90) 586
Mountain of Fame (Wills) (95) 509
Mr. Madison's War (Stagg) (H-84) 303
Munich (Taylor) (80) 555
Munich 1923 (Dornberg) (H-83) 298
Muslim Discovery of Europe, The (Lewis) (H-83) 303
Mussolini's Roman Empire (Mack Smith) (77) 520
My Traitor's Heart (Malan) (91) 624

Mysterious History of Columbus, The (Wilford) (92) 540
Mystic Chords of Memory (Kammen) (92) 545
Natural, The (Klein) (03) 554
Nature of the Book, The (Johns) (99) 547
Nature's Metropolis (Cronon) (92) 554
Nazi Party, The (Kater) (H-84) 313
Nazi Prisoners of War in America (Krammer) (80) 573
Nazi Terror (Johnson) (01) 618
Nazi War Against Soviet Partisans, 1941-1944, The (Cooper) (80) 577
Nazi War on Cancer, The (Proctor) (00) 562
Near a Thousand Tables (Fernández-Armesto) (03) 564
Neither Friend nor Foe (Packard) (93) 545
Neville Chamberlain and Appeasement (Fuchser) (H-83) 314
New Age Now Begins, A (Smith) (77) 529
New Dealers, The (Schwarz) (94) 555
New Emperors, The (Salisbury) (93) 554
New Golden Land, The (Honour) (77) 538
New History of India, A (Wolpert) (78) 598
New Lives (Rabinowitz) (77) 549
New World Disorder (Jowitt) (93) 559
Newer World, A (Roberts) (01) 627
News About the News, The (Downie and Kaiser) (03) 577
News of a Kidnapping (García Márquez) (98) 588
Next American Nation, The (Lind) (96) 509
Next Christendom, The (Jenkins) (03) 581
Nicaragua (Christian) (86) 655
Night of Stone (Merridale) (02) 588
1929 (Sloat) (80) 591
1943 (Grigg) (81) 619
1945 (Lukacs) (79) 490
No Man's Land (Toland) (81) 624
Nomonhan (Coox) (87) 594
Nonzero (Wright) (01) 646
Not for Ourselves Alone (Ward and Burns) (00) 580
Not Out of Africa (Lefkowitz) (97) 635
Nothing Like It in the World (Ambrose) (01) 656
Nothing That Is, The (Kaplan) (00) 585
Novus Ordo Seclorum (McDonald) (87) 604
Nuclear Delusion, The (Kennan) (H-83) 324
Obstacle Race, The (Greer) (80) 600
October Revolution, The (Medvedev) (80) 605
Of America East and West (Horgan) (H-85) 334
Of Kennedys and Kings (Wofford) (81) 633
Ohio Gang, The (Mee) (82) 575
Oil Power (Solberg) (77) 588
Old World's New World, The (Woodward) (92) 592
On the Origins of War and the Preservation of Peace (Kagan) (96) 528
On the Natural History of Destruction (Sebald) (04) 574
One Kind of Freedom (Ransom and Sutch) (78) 622
One Nation Under a Groove (Early) (96) 537
Only Land They Knew, The (Wright) (82) 594
Opening of American Society, The (Wiebe) (H-85) 344
Operation Sunrise (Smith and Agarossi) (80) 631
Original Intent and the Framers' Constitution (Levy) (89) 621
Origins of History, The (Butterfield) (82) 604
Origins of the Second World War, The (Baumont) (79) 516
Ornament of the World, The (Menocal) (03) 610
Ornamentalism (Cannadine) (02) 609
Oswald's Tale (Mailer) (96) 549
Other American, The (Isserman) (01) 689
Our Tempestuous Day (Erickson) (87) 620
Out of Chaos (Halle) (78) 627
Overlord (Hastings) (H-85) 349
Overthrow of Allende and the Politics of Chile, 1964-1976, The (Sigmund) (78) 630

Pacific War, The (Ienaga) (79) 520
Pagans and Christians (Lane Fox) (88) 655
Palestinian People, The (Kimmerling and Migdal) (04) 600
Palestine Triangle, The (Bethell) (80) 634
Papers of Martin Luther King, Jr., January 1929-June 1951, The (King) (93) 601
Papers of Martin Luther King, Jr., July 1951-November 1955, The (King) (95) 590
Papers of Martin Luther King, Jr., December 1955-December 1956, The (King) (98) 625
Paramilitary Politics in Weimar Germany (Diehl) (79) 526
Paris in the Third Reich (Pryce-Jones) (82) 615
Parting the Desert (Karabell) (04) 605
Parting the Waters (Branch) (89) 649
Partners in Command (Glatthaar) (95) 599
Passionate War, The (Wyden) (H-84) 330
Past Is a Foreign Country, The (Lowenthal) (87) 645
Past Masters, The (MacMillan) (77) 610
Path Between the Seas, The (McCullough) (78) 636
Patriots and Liberators (Schama) (78) 642
Paul Revere's Ride (Fischer) (95) 604
Peace Brokers, The (Touval) (H-83) 335
Peace to End All Peace, A (Fromkin) (90) 657
Pearl Harbor (Prange, Goldstein, and Dillon) (86) 732
Peloponnesian War, The (Kagan) (04) 614
Pencil, The (Petroski) (91) 656
Perjury (Weinstein) (79) 540
Perpetrators, Victims, Bystanders (Hilberg) (93) 624
Persistence of the Old Regime, The (Mayer) (82) 626
Personal Politics (Evans) (80) 655
Perspective of the World, Vol. III, The (Braudel) (H-85) 353
Phoenicians, The (Moscati, ed.) (90) 665
Phony War, 1939-1940, The (Shachtman) (H-83) 338
Pilgrims in Their Own Land (Marty) (H-85) 358
Pillar of Fire (Branch) (99) 628
Pioneer Women (Stratton) (82) 642
Pity of War, The (Ferguson) (00) 609
Plagues and Peoples (McNeill) (77) 618
Planning a Tragedy (Berman) (H-83) 343
Playing for Keeps (Halberstam) (00) 618
Pleasures of the Imagination, The (Brewer) (98) 634
Political Repression in Nineteenth Century Europe (Goldstein) (H-84) 342
Politics in Black and White (Sonenshein) (94) 654
Politics of Recovery, The (Romasco) (H-84) 347
Poverty and Compassion (Himmelfarb) (92) 627
Power on the Left (Lader) (80) 680
Power to Lead, The (Burns) (H-85) 363
Powers That Be, The (Halberstam) (80) 684
Practicing History (Tuchman) (82) 647
PrairyErth (Heat-Moon) (92) 632
Praying for Sheetrock (Greene) (92) 636
Presidency of Lyndon B. Johnson, The (Bornet) (H-84) 355
Price of Citizenship, The (Katz) (02) 655
Privileged Son (McDougal) (02) 669
Prize, The (Yergin) (92) 645
"Probable Cause" and "Beyond Reasonable Doubt" (Shapiro) (93) 75
"Problem from Hell, A" (Power) (03) 629
Progress and Privilege (Tucker) (H-83) 352
Progressive Presidents, The (Blum) (81) 665
Promise of Pragmatism, The (Diggins) (95) 617
Promised Land, The (Lemann) (92) 650
Property and Freedom (Pipes) (00) 626
Protecting Soldiers and Mothers (Skocpol) (94) 671
Province of Reason (Warner) (H-85) 368
Psychopathic God, The (Waite) (78) 677
Puritan Way of Death, The (Stannard) (78) 682
Pursuit of Power, The (McNeill) (H-83) 357

Queens, Concubines, and Dowagers (Stafford) (H-84) 371
Quest for El Cid, The (Fletcher) (91) 684
Race and Slavery in the Middle East (Lewis) (91) 692
Radical Enlightenment (Israel) (02) 679
Radicalism of the American Revolution, The (Wood) (93) 665
Raising America (Hulbert) (04) 624
Reaching Judgment at Nuremberg (Smith) (78) 695
Reckoning, The (Halberstam) (87) 695
Reconstruction (Foner) (89) 697
Red and Hot (Starr) (84) 726
Redesigning the World (Stansky) (86) 761
Regions of the Great Heresy (Ficowski) (03) 648
Reich and Nation (Gagliardo) (81) 678
Renaissance Tapestry, A (Simon) (89) 708
Reshaping the German Right (Eley) (81) 682
Resistance (Foot) (78) 704
Restless People, A (Handlin and Handlin) (H-83) 366
Resurrection (Remnick) (98) 673
Rethinking the Holocaust (Bauer) (02) 693
Return Passages (Ziff) (02) 698
Reversal of Fortune (Dershowitz) (87) 716
Revolt of the Elites, The (Lasch) (96) 628
Revolution and Regeneration (Hoffer) (H-84) 376
Revolutionary Empire (Calder) (82) 675
Revolutionary Mexico (Hart) (89) 717
Revolutionary Russia, 1917 (Thompson) (82) 679
Rhineland Crisis, The (Emmerson) (78) 712
Richard Milhous Nixon (Morris) (90) 694
Rise and Fall of the British Empire, The (James) (97) 696
Rise and Fall of the Great Powers, The (Kennedy) (89) 735
Rise of Industrial America, The (Smith) (H-85) 391
River Congo, The (Forbath) (78) 717
River of Shadows (Solnit) (04) 666
Road to Confrontation, The (Stueck) (82) 690
Road to Nuremberg, The (Smith) (82) 695
Road to Verdun, The (Ousby) (03) 676
Rome '44 (Trevelyan) (H-83) 372
Rommel's War in Africa (Heckmann) (82) 700
Roosevelt and Churchill, 1939-1941 (Lash) (77) 685
Roosevelt and the Isolationists (Cole) (H-84) 382
Roots of Conflict (Leach) (87) 732
Roots of Confrontation in South Asia (Wolpert) (H-83) 376
Rosenberg File, The (Radosh and Milton) (H-84) 388
Rousseau (Miller) (H-85) 395
Ruling Race, The (Oakes) (H-83) 384
Russia in Revolution, 1900-1930 (Salisbury) (79) 622
Russia in the Age of Catherine the Great (de Madariaga) (82) 708
Russia's Failed Revolutions (Ulam) (82) 717
Sacred Chain, The (Cantor) (95) 678
Safe for Democracy (Gardner) (H-85) 400
St. Clair (Wallace) (88) 790
Saint-Simon and the Court of Louis XIV (Ladurie and Fitou) (02) 717
Saints and Sinners (Duffy) (98) 683
Salt (Kurlansky) (03) 708
Same-Sex Unions in Premodern Europe (Boswell) (95) 687
Scandinavia During the Second World War (Nissen, ed.) (H-84) 393
Schindler's List (Keneally) (83) 684
Schnitzler's Century (Gay) (02) 732
Scholastic Humanism and the Unification of Europe, Vol. I (Southern) (97) 718
Scramble for Africa, The (Pakenham) (92) 717
Seabiscuit (Hillenbrand) (02) 737
Search for Alexander, The (Lane Fox) (81) 712
Search for Modern China, The (Spence) (91) 716

Second World War, The (Gilbert) (90) 716
Second World War, The (Keegan) (91) 721
Secrecy (Moynihan) (99) 688
Secret World of American Communism, The (Klehr, Haynes, and Firsov, eds.) (96) 685
Secrets of the Temple (Greider) (89) 766
Seeing Voices (Sacks) (90) 720
Seekers, The (Boorstin) (99) 697
Self-Rule (Wiebe) (96) 699
Seven Days to Disaster (Hickey and Smith) (H-83) 387
1777 (Pancake) (78) 757
Shadow of the Winter Palace, The (Crankshaw) (77) 730
Shadow Warriors, The (Smith) (H-84) 403
Shaping of America, 1492-1800, The (Meinig) (87) 771
Shaping of America, 1800-1867, The (Meinig) (94) 729
"Shattered Nerves" (Oppenheim) (92) 742
Shattered Peace (Yergin) (78) 766
Shays' Rebellion (Szatmary) (81) 732
Sheba (Clapp) (02) 747
Sideshow (Shawcross) (80) 758
Siege, The (O'Brien) (87) 776
Sikhs, The (Singh) (01) 774
Simple Justice (Kluger) (77) 735
Simple Life, The (Shi) (86) 820
Six Armies in Normandy (Keegan) (H-83) 390
Six Days of War (Oren) (03) 765
Slavery and Human Progress (Davis) (H-85) 411
Slaves in the Family (Ball) (99) 716
Soldiers (Ziegler) (03) 789
Soldiers in a Narrow Land (Spooner) (95) 733
Soldiers of the Night (Schoenbrun) (81) 750
Solzhenitsyn and the Modern World (Ericson) (94) 751
Something for Nothing (Lears) (04) 700
Sons of Mississippi (Hendrickson) (04) 709
Soul By Soul (Johnson) (01) 787
Soul of the American University, The (Marsden) (95) 744
Southern Honor (Wyatt-Brown) (H-83) 396
Southern Tradition, The (Genovese) (95) 748
Soviet Dissent in Historical Perspective (Shatz) (82) 795
Soviet Paradox, The (Bialer) (87) 807
Soviet Union and the Arms Race, The (Holloway) (H-84) 414
Spanish Frontier in North America, The (Weber) (93) 749
Spanish War, The (O'Toole) (H-85) 425
Spinoza (Nadler) (00) 725
Spinoza and Other Heretics, Vol. I and Vol. II (Yovel) (91) 768
Stalin Embattled, 1943-1948 (McCagg) (79) 702
Stalin's American Policy (Taubman) (H-83) 400
Stiffed (Faludi) (00) 733
Story of American Freedom, The (Foner) (99) 737
Strangers from a Different Shore (Takaki) (90) 772
Strategies of Containment (Gaddis) (H-83) 405
Struggle for Black Equality, 1954-1980, The (Sitkoff) (82) 822
Struggle for Power, A (Draper) (97) 787
Submarines at War (Hoyt) (H-84) 430
Such a Peace (Sulzberger) (H-83) 411
Sudden Glory (Sanders) (96) 728
Summer of '49 (Halberstam) (90) 777
Summons of the Trumpet (Palmer) (79) 732
Sunday Between Wars, A (Maddow) (80) 798
Superhistorians, The (Barker) (H-83) 416
Target Tokyo (Prange) (H-85) 430
Tecumseh (Sugden) (99) 746
Tempting of America, The (Bork) (90) 787
Terrible Honesty (Douglas) (96) 736
Terrible Secret, The (Laqueur) (82) 834
Terror Before Trafalgar, The (Pocock) (04) 743

Theodore Rex (Morris) (02) 777
Theremin (Glinsky) (01) 815
Thinking in Time (Neustadt and May) (87) 853
Thirteenth Tribe, The (Koestler) (77) 817
This Was Harlem (Anderson) (83) 800
Thomas Jefferson (Bedini) (91) 809
Through the Looking Glass (Verrier) (H-84) 444
Time of Illusion, The (Schell) (77) 822
Tinker and a Poor Man, A (Hill) (90) 814
Tip O'Neill and the Democratic Century (Farrell) (02) 791
To Begin the World Anew (Bailyn) (04) 761
To Conquer the Air (Tobin) (04) 766
To Keep and Bear Arms (Malcolm) (95) 787
To the Halls of the Montezumas (Johannsen) (86) 887
To the Marianas (Hoyt) (81) 817
To Win a War (Terraine) (82) 850
Tombee (Rosengarten, ed.) (87) 875
Toward the Brink, 1785-1787 (Manceron) (H-84) 452
Toward the Final Solution (Mosse) (79) 761
Trading with the Enemy (Higham) (H-84) 457
Tragedy of Cambodian History, The (Chandler) (93) 800
Transfer Agreement, The (Black) (H-85) 445
Transformation of American Law, 1870-1960, The (Horwitz) (93) 805
Transforming Russia and China (Rosenberg and Young) (H-83) 426
Trial by Fire (Smith) (H-83) 431
Trial of Socrates, The (Stone) (89) 855
Triangle (Von Drehle) (04) 778
Trouble in Mind (Litwack) (99) 795
True and Only Heaven, The (Lasch) (92) 830
True Confessions of an Albino Terrorist, The (Breytenbach) (86) 913
Truly Disadvantaged, The (Wilson) (88) 910
Trust (Fukuyama) (96) 777
Truth About Chernobyl, The (Medvedev) (92) 835
Tumultuous Years (Donovan) (H-83) 435
Twilight of Capitalism, The (Harrington) (77) 857
Twilight of the Old Order, 1774-1778 (Manceron) (78) 864
Two Faces of Islam, The (Schwartz) (03) 853
Ultimate Journey (Bernstein) (02) 808
Uncertain Partners (Goncharov, Lewis, and Xue) (95) 809
Under the Banner of Heaven (Krakauer) (04) 787
Under Western Skies (Worster) (93) 833
Underground Empire, The (Mills) (87) 896
Unequal Justice (Auerbach) (77) 866
Unfinished Presidency, The (Brinkley) (99) 822
United States and the Berlin Blockade, 1948-1949, The (Shlaim) (H-84) 469
United States and the Caribbean, 1900-1970, The (Langley) (81) 853
Unraveling of America, The (Matusow) (H-85) 460
Unto the Sons (Talese) (93) 842
Unwanted, The (Marrus) (86) 923
Unwelcome Strangers (Reimers) (99) 830
U.S.S.R. in Crisis (Goldman) (H-84) 472
V Was for Victory (Blum) (77) 880
Valley of Darkness (Havens) (79) 804
Vanished Imam, The (Ajami) (87) 901
Vatican Diplomacy and the Jews During the Holocaust, 1939-1943 (Morley) (81) 861
Venona (Haynes and Klehr) (00) 784
Victorian Anthropology (Stocking) (88) 928
Victorian Feminists (Caine) (93) 851
Victorian Sensation (Secord) (02) 822
Victorians, The (Wilson) (04) 801
Vietnam 1945 (Marr) (97) 867
Viking World, The (Graham-Campbell) (81) 873
Vindication of Tradition, The (Pelikan) (H-85) 467

Virtual Tibet (Schell) (01) 873
Visions of Harmony (Taylor) (88) 932
Voices of Protest (Brinkley) (H-83) 449
Voyage of the Armada, The (Howarth) (82) 891
Voyagers to the West (Bailyn, with DeWolfe) (87) 917
Wages of Guilt, The (Buruma) (95) 840
Walking on Water (Kenan) (00) 813
Walking the Bible (Feiler) (02) 826
Walt Whitman's America (Reynolds) (96) 806
Walter Lippmann (Blum) (H-85) 470
Waltzing with a Dictator (Bonner) (88) 949
Wanderlust (Solnit) (01) 887
War Against the Weak (Black) (04) 810
War in a Time of Peace (Halberstam) (02) 834
War of 1812, The (Hickey) (90) 859
War Path, The (Irving) (79) 819
War That Hitler Won, The (Herzstein) (79) 823
War with Spain in 1898, The (Trask) (82) 908
War Within (Singal) (83) 873
War Within, The (Wells) (95) 844
War Without a Name, The (Talbott) (81) 896
War Without Mercy (Dower) (87) 947
Wartime (Fussell) (90) 864
Washington Goes to War (Brinkley) (89) 887
Waterloo (Chandler) (82) 912
Way of the World, The (Fromkin) (00) 821
Way Out There in the Blue (FitzGerald) (01) 891
We Men Who Feel Most German (Chickering)
    (H-85) 479
We Were Soldiers Once . . . and Young (Moore and
    Galloway) (93) 868
Weaker Vessel, The (Fraser) (H-85) 483
Wealth and Democracy (Phillips) (03) 872
Wealth and Poverty of Nations, The (Landes) (99) 846
What Kind of Nation (Simon) (03) 877
When Heaven and Earth Changed Places (Hayslip, with
    Wurts) (90) 879
When the Mind Hears (Lane) (H-85) 488
When Tigers Fight (Wilson) (H-83) 454
Where I Was From (Didion) (04) 831
White Man's Indian, The (Berkhofer) (79) 847
White Supremacy (Fredrickson) (82) 937
White Tribe of Africa, The (Harrison) (H-83) 459
Who Voted for Hitler? (Hamilton) (H-83) 462
Why Did the Heavens Not Darken? (Mayer) (90) 893
Why the Jews? (Prager and Telushkin) (H-84) 481
Why the South Lost the Civil War (Beringer, Hattaway,
    Jones, and Still) (87) 980
Wild Blue, The (Ambrose) (02) 856
Wilderness of Mirrors (Martin) (81) 924
Wilkomirski Affair, The (Maechler) (02) 861
Wind Will Not Subside, The (Milton and Milton)
    (77) 918
Winston Churchill's World View (Thompson)
    (H-84) 493
With the Stroke of a Pen (Mayer) (02) 870
Witness to Hope (Weigel) (00) 847
Witnesses at the Creation (Morris) (86) 959
Women and the American Experience (Woloch)
    (H-85) 511
Women and the Common Life (Lasch) (98) 878
Women on the Margins (Davis) (96) 826
Women Volunteering (Kaminer) (H-85) 516
Work Ethic in Industrial America, 1850-1920, The
    (Rodgers) (79) 904
World at Arms, A (Weinberg) (95) 885
World Made New, A (Glendon) (02) 884
World of Our Fathers (Howe) (77) 947
Worlds of Reference (McArthur) (87) 1015
Worlds of Wonder, Days of Judgment (Hall) (90) 925
Wrath of Nations, The (Pfaff) (94) 864
Writing in the New Nation (Ziff) (92) 924
XYZ Affair, The (Stinchcombe) (82) 972

Years of Renewal (Kissinger) (00) 867
Years of Upheaval (Kissinger) (H-83) 483
Yeltsin (Aron) (01) 940
Young Men and Fire (Maclean) (93) 892
Zuñi and the American Imagination (McFeely)
    (02) 898

HISTORY OF SCIENCE. *See* SCIENCE, HISTORY
    OF SCIENCE, TECHNOLOGY, and MEDICINE

LANGUAGE
Archaeology and Language (Renfrew) (89) 41
Decadence (Gilman) (80) 210
Desire in Language (Kristeva) (81) 231
Dictionary of American Regional English, Vol. I
    (Cassidy, ed.) (86) 230
Edward Sapir (Darnell) (91) 245
Genes, Peoples, and Languages (Cavalli-Sforza)
    (01) 327
Geography of Thought, The (Nisbett) (04) 287
Grammatical Man (Campbell) (83) 301
Keywords (Williams) (77) 388
Le Ton Beau de Marot (Hofstadter) (98) 495
Meaning of Everything, The (Winchester) (04) 506
Nigger (Kennedy) (03) 586
Orality and Literacy (Ong) (83) 568
Philosopher's Demise, The (Watson) (96) 581
Power of Babel, The (McWhorter) (03) 619
Reflections on Language (Chomsky) (77) 668
Search for the Perfect Language, The (Eco) (96) 680
Semiotics and the Philosophy of Language (Eco)
    (85) 807
Sound, Speech, and Music (Burrows) (91) 759
Standing by Words (Berry) (84) 813
State of the Language, The (Ricks and Michaels, eds.)
    (91) 773
Unlocking the English Language (Burchfield) (92) 849
Warden of English, The (McMorris) (02) 838
Women, Fire, and Dangerous Things (Lakoff) (88) 979
Words and Rules (Pinker) (00) 863

LAW. *See* ETHICS and LAW

LETTERS. *See* AUTOBIOGRAPHY, MEMOIRS,
    DIARIES, and LETTERS

LITERARY BIOGRAPHY
Adventures of Conan Doyle, The (Higham) (77) 22
Alan Paton (Alexander) (95) 23
Albert Camus (Lottman) (80) 15
Albert Camus (Todd) (98) 18
Aldous Huxley (Murray) (04) 13
Aleksander Wat (Venclova) (97) 18
Alexander Pope (Mack) (87) 20
Algernon Blackwood (Ashley) (03) 10
Alice James (Strouse) (81) 21
Along with Youth (Griffin) (86) 16
Anaïs (Fitch) (94) 20
Anaïs Nin (Bair) (96) 34
André Malraux (Lacouture) (77) 43
Angus Wilson (Drabble) (97) 48
Anna Akhmatova (Reeder) (95) 38
Anne Sexton (Middlebrook) (92) 21
Anthony Trollope (Glendinning) (94) 29
Anton Chekhov (Rayfield) (99) 57
Archibald MacLeish (Donaldson) (93) 28
Art and Affection (Reid) (97) 66
Art of Burning Bridges, The (Wolff) (04) 45
Art of the Commonplace, The (Berry) (03) 33
Auden (Davenport-Hines) (97) 79
August Strindberg (Lagercrantz) (85) 32
Badge of Courage (Davis) (99) 78

CATEGORY INDEX

Balzac (Robb) (95) 60
Baudelaire (Pichois) (91) 70
Baudelaire (Richardson) (96) 65
Baudelaire the Damned (Hemmings) (83) 49
Beautiful Shadow (Wilson) (04) 62
Bellow (Atlas) (01) 84
Ben Jonson (Riggs) (90) 58
Bernard Shaw, 1856-1898 (Holroyd) (89) 89
Bernard Shaw, 1898-1918 (Holroyd) (90) 63
Bernard Shaw, 1918-1950 (Holroyd) (92) 34
Bernard Shaw, 1950-1991 (Holroyd) (94) 80
Bitter Fame (Stevenson) (90) 71
Black, French, and African (Vaillant) (91) 80
Blake (Ackroyd) (97) 123
Bloomsbury (Edel) (80) 88
Borges (Woodall) (98) 130
Boris Pasternak, 1890-1928 (Barnes) (91) 96
Boswell's Presumptuous Task (Sisman) (02) 120
Brecht (Hayman) (84) 118
Broken Tower, The (Mariani) (00) 108
Brontës, The (Barker) (96) 81
Brothers Mann, The (Hamilton) (80) 119
Bruce Chatwin (Shakespeare) (01) 148
Bulgakov (Proffer) (85) 62
Bunting (Makin) (93) 115
Burns (Mackay) (94) 113
Byron (Grosskurth) (98) 142
C. S. Lewis (Wilson) (91) 175
Camus (McCarthy) (83) 96
Capote (Clarke) (89) 135
Céline (McCarthy) (77) 134
Cervantes (Byron) (79) 84
Chainless Soul, A (Frank) (91) 127
Chamfort (Arnaud) (93) 143
Charles Olson (Clark) (92) 88
Charles Williams (Hadfield) (84) 153
Charlotte Brontë (Gordon) (96) 94
Charlotte Mew and Her Friends (Fitzgerald) (89) 145
Chateaubriand (1768-93) (Painter) (79) 95
Chaucer (Howard) (88) 141
Chekhov (Pritchett) (89) 155
Chekhov (Troyat) (87) 105
Chester Himes (Sallis) (02) 149
Christina Rossetti (Marsh) (96) 107
Christine de Pizan (Willard) (86) 126
Christopher Isherwood (Finney) (80) 145
City Poet (Gooch) (94) 128
Claire Clairmont and the Shelleys, 1798-1879 (Gittings and Manton) (93) 157
Cleanth Brooks and the Rise of Modern Criticism (Winchell) (97) 156
Coleridge, Darker Reflections (Holmes) (00) 138
Coleridge, Early Visions (Holmes) (91) 147
Colette (Lottman) (92) 99
Colette (Sarde) (81) 161
Conrad Aiken (Butscher, ed.) (89) 207
Cup of News, A (Nicholl) (85) 147
D. H. Lawrence (Ellis) (98) 244
D. H. Lawrence (Kinkead-Weekes) (97) 214
D. H. Lawrence (Maddox) (95) 167
D. H. Lawrence (Meyers) (91) 206
D. H. Lawrence (Worthen) (92) 166
D. H. Lawrence's Nightmare (Delany) (80) 223
Damned to Fame (Knowlson) (97) 191
Daphne du Maurier (Forster) (94) 204
Dashiell Hammett (Johnson) (84) 212
Delmore Schwartz (Atlas) (78) 249
Dickens (Ackroyd) (92) 170
Dickens (Kaplan) (89) 241
Diderot (Furbank) (93) 229
Djuna (Field) (84) 234
Djuna (Herring) (96) 194
Dr. Johnson and Mr. Savage (Holmes) (95) 176

Dos Passos (Carr) (85) 194
Dostoevsky, 1821-1849 (Frank) (77) 236
Dostoevsky, 1850-1859 (Frank) (84) 244
Dostoevsky, 1860-1865 (Frank) (87) 212
Dostoevsky, 1865-1871 (Frank) (96) 202
Dostoevsky, 1871-1881 (Frank) (03) 219
Double Bond, The (Angier) (03) 224
Double Life of Stephen Crane, The (Benfey) (93) 239
Dream Song (Mariani) (91) 235
E. B. White (Elledge) (85) 209
E. M. Forster (Beauman) (95) 195
E. M. Forster (Furbank) (79) 183
Edgar A. Poe (Silverman) (92) 174
Edgar Lee Masters (Russell) (02) 226
Edith Sitwell (Glendinning) (82) 190
Edmund Wilson (Meyers) (96) 210
Edward Albee (Gussow) (00) 199
Eliot's New Life (Gordon) (89) 262
Elizabeth Barrett Browning (Forster) (90) 203
Elizabeth Bishop (Goldensohn) (92) 179
Elizabeth Bishop (Millier) (94) 264
Elizabeth Bowen (Glendinning) (79) 179
Emerson (Barish) (91) 249
Emerson (Richardson) (96) 222
Emerson Among the Eccentrics (Baker) (97) 239
Emily Dickinson (Wolff) (87) 233
Enigma (Ferguson) (88) 279
Enthusiast, The (Harrison) (84) 272
Ernest Hemingway and His World (Burgess) (79) 196
Eudora (Waldron) (00) 240
Evelyn Waugh (Hastings) (96) 237
Evelyn Waugh, 1903-1939 (Stannard) (88) 293
Evelyn Waugh, 1939-1966 (Stannard) (93) 275
Ezra Pound (Heymann) (77) 264
F. Scott Fitzgerald (Le Vot) (84) 318
Family Secrets (Murphy) (96) 253
Familiar Spirits (Lurie) (02) 271
Fanny Burney (Harman) (02) 275
Federico García Lorca (Gibson) (90) 245
First Woman in the Republic, The (Karcher) (96) 273
Flaubert (Lottman) (90) 268
Ford Madox Ford (Judd) (92) 218
Frank and Maisie (Sheed) (86) 313
Franz Kafka (Karl) (92) 227
Franz Werfel (Jungk) (91) 313
Frost (Pritchard) (85) 312
Full of Life (Cooper) (01) 319
Gang, The (Worthen) (02) 321
García Márquez (Bell-Villada) (91) 325
Genet (White) (94) 339
Genius in Disguise (Kunkel) (96) 303
Gentle Barbarian, The (Pritchett) (78) 340
George Eliot (Ashton) (98) 335
Georges Perec (Bellos) (95) 262
Gerald Brenan (Gathorne-Hardy) (94) 350
Gissing (Halperin) (83) 283
Goethe, 1749-1790 (Boyle) (92) 247
Goethe, 1790-1803 (Boyle) (01) 356
Gore Vidal (Kaplan) (00) 321
Group Portrait (Delbanco) (83) 312
H. D. (Robinson) (83) 331
H. G. Wells (West) (85) 380
Hand to Mouth (Auster) (98) 374
Hannah Arendt (Young-Bruehl) (83) 322
Happiest Man Alive, The (Dearborn) (92) 266
Hardy (Seymour-Smith) (95) 291
Harriet Beecher Stowe (Hedrick) (95) 296
Hazlitt (Bromwich) (85) 363
Hazlitt (Jones) (91) 381
Hearts and Minds (Madsen) (78) 379
Helen Hunt Jackson (Phillips) (04) 330
Hemingway (Lynn) (88) 372
Hemingway (Meyers) (86) 406

Hemingway, The American Homecoming (Reynolds) (93) 325
Hemingway, The Final Years (Reynolds) (00) 377
Hemingway, The 1930's (Reynolds) (98) 379
Hemingway, The Paris Years (Reynolds) (90) 369
Hemingway Women, The (Kert) (84) 337
Henry Fielding (Battestin and Battestin) (91) 395
Henry James (Kaplan) (93) 330
Henry Thoreau (Richardson) (87) 387
Her Husband (Middlebrook) (04) 335
Herman Melville (Parker) (97) 373
Herself Defined (Guest) (85) 374
Hesitation Before Birth, A (Mailloux) (90) 378
Hidden Wordsworth, The (Johnston) (99) 364
Hilaire Belloc (Wilson) (85) 385
Hölderlin (Constantine) (89) 354
Home Before Dark (Cheever) (85) 405
Hopkins (White) (93) 353
I. A. Richards (Russo) (90) 401
In Search of J. D. Salinger (Hamilton) (89) 373
Interior Castle, The (Hulbert) (93) 386
Into Eternity (MacShane) (86) 471
Into My Own (Walsh) (89) 390
Invisible Man, The (Coren) (94) 410
Invisible Spectator, An (Sawyer-Laucanno) (90) 424
Iris Murdoch (Conradi) (02) 428
Irving Howe (Sorin) (04) 364
Isaac Bashevis Singer (Hadda) (98) 449
Isak Dinesen (Thurman) (83) 358
Ivy (Spurling) (85) 461
J. R. R. Tolkien (Shippey) (02) 436
Jack (Sinclair) (78) 454
James Agee (Bergreen) (85) 473
James Baldwin (Leeming) (95) 388
James Boswell (Brady) (85) 479
James Dickey (Hart) (01) 475
James Gould Cozzens (Bruccoli) (84) 384
James Jones (Garrett) (85) 484
James Joyce (Costello) (94) 418
James Thurber (Kinney) (96) 389
Jameses (Lewis) (92) 374
Jane Austen (Honan) (89) 409
Jane Austen (Nokes) (98) 468
Jean Rhys (Angier) (92) 379
Jean Stafford (Goodman) (91) 471
Jean Stafford (Roberts) (89) 414
Jean Toomer, Artist (McKay) (85) 489
Jerzy Kosinski (Sloan) (97) 470
Jesse (Richardson) (85) 494
John Cheever (Donaldson) (89) 422
John Clare (Bate) (04) 377
John Dos Passos (Ludington) (81) 464
John Dryden and His World (Winn) (88) 438
John Ruskin, The Early Years (Hilton) (86) 487
John Ruskin, The Later Years (Hilton) (01) 499
John Steinbeck (Parini) (96) 398
Jonathan Swift (Glendinning) (00) 448
Jorge Luis Borges (Monegal) (80) 444
Joseph Conrad (Karl) (80) 449
Joseph Conrad (Najder) (84) 395
Joseph Conrad (Tennant) (82) 412
Josephine Herbst (Langer) (85) 499
Kafka (Hayman) (83) 372
Kate Chopin (Toth) (91) 475
Katherine Anne Porter (Givner) (83) 376
Katherine Mansfield (Tomalin) (89) 427
Kay Boyle (Mellen) (95) 417
Keats (Motion) (99) 449
Khodasevich (Bethea) (84) 408
King of Inventors, The (Peters) (94) 440
Kingsley Amis (Jacobs) (99) 457
Kleist (Maass) (84) 418
Langston Hughes (Berry) (84) 422

Last Leopard, The (Gilmour) (92) 413
Later Auden (Mendelson) (00) 475
Learning a Trade (Price) (99) 470
Left Bank, The (Lottman) (83) 390
Lermontov (Kelly) (79) 373
Lewis Carroll (Cohen) (96) 422
Life of a Poet (Freedman) (97) 502
Life of Geoffrey Chaucer, The (Pearsall) (93) 459
Life of Graham Greene, The, 1904-1939 (Sherry) (90) 521
Life of Graham Greene, The, 1939-1955 (Sherry) (96) 430
Life of Gwendolyn Brooks, A (Kent) (90) 526
Life of Jane Austen, The (Halperin) (85) 564
Life of John Berryman, The (Haffenden) (83) 410
Life of Kenneth Rexroth, A (Hamalian) (92) 426
Life of Kenneth Tynan, The (Tynan) (88) 482
Life of Langston Hughes, 1902-1941, The (Rampersad) (87) 489
Life of Langston Hughes, 1941-1967, The (Rampersad) (89) 501
Life of Matthew Arnold, A (Murray) (98) 500
Life of Raymond Chandler, The (MacShane) (77) 427
Life of Samuel Johnson, The (DeMaria) (94) 471
Life of Samuel Taylor Coleridge, The (Ashton) (97) 516
Life Sentences (Epstein) (98) 504
Lillian Hellman (Rollyson) (89) 511
Lion for Love, A (Alter) (80) 497
Little Original Sin, A (Dillon) (82) 470
Lives of Norman Mailer, The (Rollyson) (92) 445
Look Homeward (Donald) (88) 502
Lost Puritan (Mariani) (95) 455
Louis-Ferdinand Céline (Thomas) (81) 529
Louis MacNeice (Stallworthy) (96) 444
Louise Bogan (Frank) (86) 542
Madame de Sévigné (Mossiker) (85) 595
Mailer (Mills) (83) 428
Making of Mark Twain, The (Lauber) (86) 561
Malcolm Cowley (Bak) (94) 492
Marguerite Yourcenar (Savigneau) (94) 500
Marcel Proust (Carter) (01) 559
Marianne Moore (Molesworth) (91) 562
Marina Tsvetaeva (Feiler) (95) 464
Marina Tsvetaeva (Karlinsky) (87) 520
Mark Twain A to Z (Rasmussen) (96) 452
Marquand (Bell) (80) 517
Mary McCarthy (Gelderman) (89) 539
Mary Renault (Sweetman) (84) 521
Mary Wollstonecraft (Todd) (01) 569
Matthew Arnold (Honan) (82) 518
Maugham (Morgan) (81) 559
May Sarton (Peters) (98) 551
Melville (Robertson-Lorant) (97) 568
Mencken (Hobson) (95) 477
Mikhail Bakhtin (Clark and Holquist) (86) 608
Milton and the English Revolution (Hill) (79) 444
My Wars Are Laid Away in Books (Habegger) (02) 562
Nabokov (Field) (78) 590
Nabokov's Fifth Arc (Rivers and Nicol, eds.) (83) 511
Nathaniel Hawthorne in His Times (Mellow) (81) 593
New Life of Anton Chekhov, A (Hingley) (77) 543
Nightingale Fever (Hingley) (82) 555
Nightmare of Reason, The (Pawel) (85) 645
No Gifts from Chance (Benstock) (95) 544
No Laughing Matter (Cronin) (91) 629
Nora (Maddox) (89) 605
Nothing Ever Happens to the Brave (Rollyson) (91) 639
Onward and Upward (Davis) (88) 630
Orwell (Shelden) (92) 602
Oscar Wilde (Ellmann) (89) 630

Other Man, The (Greene and Allain) (84) 651
Our Three Selves (Baker) (86) 719
Outline of Sanity (Dale) (83) 582
P. G. Wodehouse (Donaldson) (83) 587
Parallel Lives (Rose) (84) 662
Parts of a World (Brazeau) (84) 668
Passion of Emily Dickinson, The (Farr) (93) 610
Passionate Minds (Pierpont) (01) 694
Pasternak (Hingley) (84) 673
Patrick O'Brian (King) (01) 707
Patrick White (Marr) (93) 619
Paul Celan (Felstiner) (96) 577
Pearl S. Buck (Conn) (97) 661
Percys of Mississippi, The (Baker) (84) 682
Philip Larkin (Motion) (94) 626
Pilgrim in the Ruins (Tolson) (93) 633
Poe Log, The (Thomas and Jackson) (88) 701
Poets in Their Youth (Simpson) (83) 608
Portraits of the Artist in Exile (Potts, ed.) (80) 675
Private Demons (Oppenheimer) (89) 668
Pursued by Furies (Bowker) (96) 610
Pushkin (Feinstein) (00) 634
Ralph Ellison (Jackson) (03) 638
Ralph Waldo Emerson (McAleer) (85) 717
Randall Jarrell (Pritchard) (91) 696
Randall Jarrell and His Age (Burt) (04) 629
Raymond Chandler (Hiney) (98) 665
Real Shakespeare, The (Sams) (96) 619
Rebecca West (Glendinning) (88) 732
Rebecca West (Rollyson) (97) 684
Reckoning, The (Nicholl) (95) 639
Regions of the Great Heresy (Ficowski) (03) 648
Revolution of the Mind (Polizzotti) (96) 633
Richard Wright (Rowley) (02) 703
Richard Wright, Daemonic Genius (Walker) (89) 722
Rilke (Leppmann) (85) 757
Rimbaud (Petitfils) (88) 765
Rimbaud (Robb) (01) 736
Roald Dahl (Treglown) (95) 660
Robert Browning (Thomas) (84) 741
Robert Frost (Meyers) (97) 705
Robert Frost (Parini) (00) 651
Robert Graves (Seymour) (96) 650
Robert Graves (Seymour-Smith) (84) 746
Robert Graves, 1895-1926 (Graves) (88) 770
Robert Graves, 1926-1940 (Graves) (91) 706
Robert Louis Stevenson (Calder) (81) 694
Robert Louis Stevenson (McLynn) (96) 655
Robert Lowell (Hamilton) (83) 654
Robert Penn Warren (Blotner) (98) 678
Robertson Davies (Grant) (96) 660
Roland Barthes (Calvet) (96) 664
Romancing (Treglown) (02) 708
Roots of Treason, The (Torrey) (84) 751
Rose Macaulay (Emery) (93) 693
Ross Macdonald (Bruccoli) (85) 766
Ross Macdonald (Nolan) (00) 660
Rough Magic (Alexander) (92) 689
Rudyard Kipling (Ricketts) (01) 750
Saga of Dazai Osamu, The (Lyons) (86) 783
Saint-Exupéry (Schiff) (95) 683
Saki (Langguth) (82) 726
Salem Is My Dwelling Place (Miller) (93) 702
Samuel Beckett (Bair) (79) 636
Samuel Beckett (Cronin) (98) 688
Samuel Johnson (Bate) (78) 735
Samuel Johnson (Lipking) (99) 683
Sara Teasdale (Drake) (80) 741
Sartre (Cohen-Solal) (88) 795
Saul Bellow (Miller) (92) 707
Savage Beauty (Milford) (02) 722
Scarlet Professor, The (Werth) (02) 727
Scott Fitzgerald (Meyers) (95) 696

Sean O'Casey (O'Connor) (89) 757
Secrets of the Flesh (Thurman) (00) 679
Seeing Mary Plain (Kiernan) (01) 764
Serious Character, A (Carpenter) (89) 779
Seven Mountains of Thomas Merton, The (Mott)
  (85) 815
Shadow Man (Layman) (82) 761
Shakespeare (Fraser) (93) 723
Shakespeare (Honan) (00) 702
Sherwood Anderson (Townsend) (88) 817
Simenon (Assouline) (98) 712
Simone de Beauvoir (Bair) (91) 740
Sinclair Lewis (Lingeman) (03) 755
Sir Philip Sidney (Duncan-Jones) (92) 761
Skeptic, The (Teachout) (03) 770
Sojourners (McFarland) (80) 771
Solzhenitsyn (Scammell) (85) 839
Solzhenitsyn and the Modern World (Ericson) (94) 751
Some Sort of Epic Grandeur (Bruccoli) (82) 782
Sor Juana (Paz) (89) 808
Sorrow Is the Only Faithful One (Hatch) (94) 755
Southern Daughter (Pyron) (92) 775
Stendhal (Keates) (98) 726
Stevie (Barbera and McBrien) (88) 860
Straight on till Morning (Lovell) (88) 865
Strange Ride of Rudyard Kipling, The (Wilson)
  (79) 717
Sui Sin Far/Edith Maude Eaton (White-Parks) (96) 732
Susan Sontag (Rollyson and Paddock) (01) 805
Swift, the Man, His Works, and the Age, Vol. III
  (Ehrenpreis) (84) 849
Sylvia Beach and the Lost Generation (Fitch) (84) 854
Sylvia Plath (Wagner-Martin) (88) 874
T. S. Eliot (Ackroyd) (85) 932
T. S. Eliot (Bush) (85) 937
T. S. Eliot (Gordon) (00) 737
Talking at the Gates (Campbell) (92) 795
Teller of Tales (Stashower) (00) 741
Theodore Dreiser, 1871-1907 (Lingeman) (87) 847
Theodore Dreiser, 1908-1945 (Lingeman) (91) 798
Thomas Carlyle (Kaplan) (84) 869
Thomas Hardy (Millgate) (83) 806
Thoreau's Seasons (Lebeaux) (85) 895
Thornton Wilder (Simon) (80) 815
Throw of the Dice, A (Millan) (95) 782
To Herland and Beyond (Lane) (91) 820
Tolkien (Carpenter) (78) 851
Tolstoi in the Seventies (Eikenbaum) (83) 821
Tolstoi in the Sixties (Eikenbaum) (83) 816
Tolstoy (Wilson) (89) 845
Tom (Leverich) (96) 756
Tragic Honesty, A (Bailey) (04) 770
Trials of Phillis Wheatley, The (Gates) (04) 774
Trollope (Hall) (92) 825
True Adventures of John Steinbeck, Writer, The
  (Benson) (85) 927
Turgenev (Schapiro) (80) 832
Vanessa Bell (Spalding) (84) 900
Vanished Act (Reidel) (04) 796
Van Wyck Brooks (Nelson) (82) 874
Véra (Mrs. Vladimir Nabokov) (Schiff) (00) 789
Virginia Woolf (Gordon) (86) 927
Virginia Woolf (King) (96) 794
Virginia Woolf (Lee) (98) 805
Vita (Glendinning) (84) 916
Vladimir Nabokov, The American Years (Boyd)
  (92) 854
Vladimir Nabokov, The Russian Years (Boyd) (91) 856
VN (Field) (87) 912
Voices (Matthews) (84) 921
Voltaire (Mason) (82) 885
Voltaire (Orieux) (80) 850
W. B. Yeats (Jeffares) (91) 876

W. B. Yeats, 1865-1914 (Foster) (98) 809
W. H. Auden (Carpenter) (82) 923
W. H. Auden (Osborne) (80) 860
W. H. Hudson (Tomalin) (84) 935
Waldo Emerson (Allen) (82) 902
Walker Percy (Samway) (98) 818
Wallace Stegner (Benson) (97) 871
Wallace Stevens, 1879-1923 (Richardson) (87) 927
Wallace Stevens, 1923-1955 (Richardson) (89) 882
Walt Whitman (Kaplan) (81) 883
Walt Whitman (Zweig) (85) 984
Walt Whitman's America (Reynolds) (96) 806
Walter Pater (Donoghue) (96) 810
Wandering Ghost (Cott) (92) 863
Wider Sea, The (Hunt) (83) 908
Willa (Robinson) (84) 945
Willa Cather (Lee) (91) 896
Willa Cather (O'Brien) (87) 994
William Carlos Williams (Mariani) (82) 946
William Faulkner (Karl) (90) 899
William Faulkner (Minter) (81) 932
William Faulkner (Singal) (98) 850
William Godwin (Marshall) (85) 1028
William Styron (West) (99) 864
William Wordsworth (Gill) (90) 904
Willie and Dwike (Zinsser) (85) 1036
With Chatwin (Clapp) (98) 862
With Friends Possessed (Martin) (86) 954
Woman of Contradictions, A (Taylor) (91) 909
Women of the Left Bank (Benstock) (87) 1009
World Enough and Time (Murray) (01) 930
Writing Dangerously (Brightman) (93) 887
Young Hemingway, The (Reynolds) (87) 1021
Young Shakespeare (Fraser) (89) 933
Zola (Brown) (96) 847

LITERARY CRITICISM, HISTORY, and THEORY
a long the riverrun (Ellmann) (90) 1
About Town (Yagoda) (01) 1
Abroad (Fussell) (81) 5
Achievement of Cormac McCarthy, The (Bell) (89) 1
Adam's Curse (Donoghue) (02) 5
Advantage of Lyric, The (Hardy) (78) 11
Aeschylus' Oresteia (Conacher) (88) 1
Agon (Bloom) (83) 1
Alluring Problem, The (Enright) (88) 11
American Babel (Shell, ed.) (03) 19
American Fictions, 1940-1980 (Karl) (84) 21
American Historical Romance, The (Dekker) (88) 31
American Moderns (Stansell) (01) 29
American Poetry (Bly) (91) 29
American Procession, An (Kazin) (85) 12
Anthology of Chinese Literature, An (Owen, ed.) (97) 53
Antigones (Steiner) (85) 17
Antonin Artaud (Esslin) (78) 68
Appropriating Shakespeare (Vickers) (94) 33
Arches & Light (Cowart) (84) 40
Argufying (Empson) (89) 46
Ariadne's Thread (Miller) (93) 32
Art in the Light of Conscience (Tsvetaeva) (93) 36
Art of Biblical Poetry, The (Alter) (86) 38
Art of Excess, The (LeClair) (90) 49
Art of Fiction, The (Gardner) (85) 22
Art of Shakespeare's Sonnets, The (Vendler) (98) 80
Art of the Novel, The (Kundera) (89) 54
Artificial Wilderness, An (Birkerts) (88) 68
Atrocity and Amnesia (Boyers) (86) 43
Bashō and His Interpreters (Ueda) (93) 53
Beckett's Dying Words (Ricks) (94) 71
Being and Race (Johnson) (89) 80
Ben Jonson, Dramatist (Barton) (85) 37
Berryman's Shakespeare (Berryman) (00) 49

Birth-mark, The (Howe) (94) 90
Bloomers on the Liffey (van Caspel) (87) 80
Bloomsbury (Edel) (80) 88
Blue Devils of Nada, The (Murray) (97) 127
Book Business (Epstein) (02) 106
Book of Prefaces, The (Gray) (01) 126
Book of Questions, The (Jabès) (84) 108
Book of the Fourth World (Brotherston) (94) 109
Borges, a Reader (Borges) (82) 63
Bottom Translation, The (Kott) (88) 116
Breathing Under Water and Other East European Essays (Barańczak) (91) 105
Brecht and Method (Jameson) (99) 127
British Writers of the Thirties (Cunningham) (89) 130
Broken Estate, The (Wood) (00) 103
Brothers Singer, The (Sinclair) (84) 127
Canon and Creativity (Alter) (01) 172
Cassandra (Wolf) (85) 74
Catbird's Song, The (Wilbur) (98) 156
Charles Williams (Cavaliero) (84) 158
Chekhov (Pritchett) (89) 155
Children of the Sun (Green) (77) 144
Coherent Splendor, A (Gelpi) (89) 169
Colder Eye, A (Kenner) (84) 173
Collected Essays of Robert Creeley, The (Creeley) (90) 108
Collected Prose (Celan) (91) 157
Collected Prose (Lowell) (88) 173
Company We Keep, The (Booth) (89) 202
Complete Collected Essays (Pritchett) (93) 179
Composition of Four Quartets, The (Gardner) (79) 128
Compulsory Figures (Taylor) (93) 192
Congregation (Rosenberg, ed.) (88) 189
Conrad (Watt) (81) 193
Consoling Intelligence, The (Kubal) (83) 144
Critical Observations (Symons) (82) 156
Critical Times (May) (03) 177
Cultural Selection (Taylor) (97) 187
Culture and Imperialism (Said) (94) 181
Czesław Miłosz and the Insufficiency of Lyric (Davie) (87) 189
Danse Macabre (King) (82) 171
Dawn to the West (Keene) (85) 157
Day of the Leopards (Wimsatt) (77) 194
Decadence (Gilman) (80) 210
Demon and the Angel, The (Hirsch) (03) 197
Devolving English Literature (Crawford) (93) 224
Dialogic Novels of Malcolm Bradbury and David Lodge, The (Morace) (90) 173
Diversity and Depth in Fiction (Wilson) (85) 190
Doing What Comes Naturally (Fish) (90) 190
Don Juan and Regency England (Graham) (91) 227
Don't Tell the Grown-ups (Lurie) (91) 231
Elizabeth Bishop (Goldensohn) (92) 179
Émigré New York (Mehlman) (01) 277
Enemy's Country (Hill) (92) 188
Enlarging the Change (Fitzgerald) (86) 244
Eros the Bittersweet (Carson) (87) 248
Essays (Knox) (90) 219
Essays in Appreciation (Ricks) (97) 256
Essays of Virginia Woolf, 1904-1912, The (Woolf) (88) 288
Essays of Virginia Woolf, 1912-1918, The (Woolf) (89) 283
Essays of Virginia Woolf, 1919-1924, The (Woolf) (90) 222
Eternal Moment, The (Fiut) (91) 266
Eudora Welty's Achievement of Order (Kreyling) (81) 288
Every Force Evolves a Form (Davenport) (88) 298
Fabricating Lives (Leibowitz) (90) 236
Faith of a Writer, The (Oates) (04) 240
Fall into Eden, The (Wyatt) (87) 253

CATEGORY INDEX

Feast of Words, A (Wolff) (78) 314
Ferocious Alphabets (Donoghue) (82) 271
Fiction and Repetition (Miller) (83) 253
Flannery O'Connor's South (Coles) (81) 350
Flight from Eden (Cassedy) (92) 210
Flower and the Leaf, The (Cowley) (86) 288
Flutes of Dionysus, The (Stock) (91) 304
Forbidden Knowledge (Shattuck) (97) 296
Foregone Conclusions (Bernstein) (95) 253
Fortunes of the Courtier, The (Burke) (97) 301
Freedom of the Poet, The (Berryman) (77) 299
Friendship and Literature (Sharp) (87) 309
From the Beast to the Blonde (Warner) (96) 290
Fugitive from Utopia, A ((Barańczak) (88) 340
Gang, The (Worthen) (02) 321
García Márquez (Bell-Villada) (91) 325
Gates of Eden (Dickstein) (78) 328
Genesis (Alter) (97) 327
Genius and Lust (Mailer) (77) 322
George Eliot (Ashton) (98) 335
German Romanticism and Its Institutions (Ziolkowski)
   (91) 347
Gift, The (Hyde) (84) 330
God and the American Writer (Kazin) (98) 352
God's Secretaries (Nicolson) (04) 295
Going to the Territory (Ellison) (87) 331
Government of the Tongue, The (Heaney) (90) 319
Grammars of Creation (Steiner) (02) 357
Great Books (Denby) (97) 360
Great Code, The (Frye) (83) 306
Great Directors at Work (Jones) (87) 362
Hamlet in Purgatory (Greenblatt) (02) 376
Hardy the Creator (Gatrell) (90) 348
Haunts of the Black Masseur (Sprawson) (94) 372
Hawthorne's Secret (Young) (85) 358
Hemingway's Art of Non-Fiction (Weber) (91) 386
Hermit in Paris (Calvino) (04) 339
Hidden Law, The (Hecht) (94) 389
His Other Half (Lesser) (92) 285
Historian of the Strange (Zeitlin) (94) 393
Historical Fictions (Kenner) (91) 400
History of Afro-American Literature, A (Jackson)
   (90) 382
History of Gay Literature, A (Woods) (99) 369
History of Modern Criticism, 1750-1950, A (Wellek)
   (92) 290
History of Reading, A (Manguel) (97) 395
History of Russian Symbolism, A (Pyman) (95) 305
History of Southern Literature, The (Rubin, ed.)
   (86) 426
History of the Bible as Literature, A (Norton) (94) 397
History of the Surrealist Movement (Durozoi) (03) 370
Home and Exile (Achebe) (01) 408
Homer (Edwards) (88) 398
Homer to Joyce (Gray) (86) 435
Hopkins, the Self, and God (Ong) (87) 406
Housman's Poems (Bayley) (93) 361
How to Suppress Women's Writing (Russ) (84) 353
Howard Mumford Jones and the Dynamics of Liberal
   Humanism (Brier) (95) 329
Hugo von Hofmannsthal and His Time (Broch)
   (85) 410
Hunter Gracchus, The (Davenport) (97) 419
Imaginary Homelands (Rushdie) (92) 324
In the Beginning (McGrath) (02) 408
Infection of Thomas De Quincey, The (Barrell)
   (92) 354
Ink of Melancholy, The (Bleikasten) (91) 452
Inside Picture Books (Spitz) (00) 422
Instigations (Sieburth) (80) 431
Interpretation and Overinterpretation (Eco) (93) 390
Inventing Ireland (Kiberd) (97) 461
Invention of Hebrew Prose, The (Alter) (89) 395

Irving Howe (Sorin) (04) 364
J. R. R. Tolkien (Shippey) (02) 436
James Jones (Garrett) (85) 484
Jane Austen (Tanner) (87) 435
John Cheever (Hunt) (84) 389
Joseph Brodsky and the Creation of Exile (Bethea)
   (95) 404
Joyce's Book of the Dark (Bishop) (88) 443
Joyce's Voices (Kenner) (79) 340
Kenneth Burke (Henderson) (90) 478
Language in Literature (Jakobson) (89) 450
Le Ton Beau de Marot (Hofstadter) (98) 495
Lectures on Don Quixote (Nabokov) (84) 427
Lectures on Literature (Nabokov) (81) 485
Lectures on Russian Literature (Nabokov) (82) 437
Lectures on Shakespeare (Auden) (02) 481
Left Bank, The (Lottman) (83) 390
Leopards in the Temple (Dickstein) (03) 465
Life and Work of Barbara Pym, The (Salwak, ed.)
   (88) 471
Life Sentences (Epstein) (98) 504
Lighting Out for the Territory (Fishkin) (97) 521
Literary Guide to the Bible, The (Alter and Kermode,
   eds.) (88) 492
Literary Mind, The (Turner) (97) 530
Literary Theory (Eagleton) (84) 464
Literary Women (Moers) (77) 439
Literature and Its Theorists (Todorov) (89) 515
Literature and the Gods (Calasso) (02) 486
Literature Lost (Ellis) (98) 512
Lives of Animals, The (Coetzee) (00) 492
Lives of the Modern Poets (Pritchard) (81) 520
Living by Fiction (Dillard) (83) 413
London Yankees, The (Weintraub) (80) 508
Look, Listen, Read (Lévi-Strauss) (98) 526
Looking at Shakespeare (Kennedy) (94) 483
Loose Canons (Gates) (93) 483
Madwoman in the Attic, The (Gilbert and Gubar)
   (80) 512
Making Stories (Bruner) (03) 509
Man of Letters, A (Pritchett) (87) 512
Marginalia (Jackson) (02) 507
Marina Tsvetaeva (Karlinsky) (87) 520
Mark Twain A to Z (Rasmussen) (96) 452
Marriage of Cadmus and Harmony, The (Calasso)
   (94) 508
Me Again (Smith) (83) 458
Mechanic Muse, The (Kenner) (87) 536
Mikhail Bakhtin (Clark and Holquist) (86) 608
Mikhail Bakhtin (Morson and Emerson) (92) 500
Mikhail Bakhtin (Todorov) (85) 614
Minotaur (Paulin) (93) 518
Miscellaneous Verdicts (Powell) (93) 522
Missing Measures (Steele) (91) 601
Modern Greek Poetry (Keeley) (85) 624
Modern Irish Literature (Mercier) (95) 495
Modern Japanese Poets and the Nature of Literature
   (Ueda) (84) 566
Modern Poetic Sequence, The (Rosenthal and Gall)
   (84) 570
Modernist Quartet (Lentricchia) (95) 499
More than Cool Reason (Lakoff and Turner) (90) 578
Mortal Hero, The (Schein) (85) 635
Muse Learns to Write, The (Havelock) (87) 590
Music of What Happens, The (Vendler) (89) 566
Mystery to a Solution, The (Irwin) (95) 519
Myth Makers, The (Pritchett) (80) 560
Myths of Modern Individualism (Watt) (97) 610
Nabokov's Early Fiction (Connolly) (93) 536
Nabokov's Fifth Arc (Rivers and Nicol, eds.) (83) 511
Nabokov's Otherworld (Alexandrov) (92) 550
Narrative and Freedom (Morson) (95) 523
Nature of the Book, The (Johns) (99) 547

Necessary Angels (Alter) (92) 559
Negotiating with the Dead (Atwood) (03) 568
Nightingale Fever (Hingley) (82) 555
Nightmare on Main Street (Edmundson) (98) 593
1985 (Burgess) (79) 484
No Man's Land, Letters from the Front (Gilbert and Gubar) (95) 549
No Man's Land, Sexchanges (Gilbert and Gubar) (90) 614
No Man's Land, The War of the Words (Gilbert and Gubar) (89) 600
No Passion Spent (Steiner) (97) 626
Noah's Curse (Haynes) (03) 594
Northrop Frye on Shakespeare (Frye) (87) 599
Novel in Antiquity, The (Hägg) (84) 618
Odd Jobs (Updike) (92) 588
On Becoming a Novelist (Gardner) (84) 633
On Being Blue (Gass) (77) 594
On Grief and Reason (Brodsky) (97) 644
On Histories and Stories (Byatt) (02) 605
On Moral Fiction (Gardner) (79) 511
On Reading Ruskin (Proust) (88) 621
On Writing (King) (01) 675
Orality and Literacy (Ong) (83) 568
Order of Books, The (Chartier) (95) 582
Origins of the English Novel, 1600-1740, The (McKeon) (88) 641
Other Pushkin, The (Debreczeny) (84) 657
Our Vampires, Ourselves (Auerbach) (96) 557
Passionate Minds (Pierpont) (01) 694
Paul Celan (Colin) (92) 619
Pause and Effect (Parkes) (94) 615
Playgoing in Shakespeare's London (Gurr) (88) 696
Poetics of Aristotle, The (Halliwell) (88) 706
Poetry and Repression (Bloom) (77) 627
Poetry into Drama (Herington) (86) 742
Poetry of Tennyson, The (Culler) (78) 665
Poet's Work, The (Nathan and Quinn) (92) 623
Postscript to *The Name of the Rose* (Eco) (85) 697
Practice of Reading, The (Donoghue) (99) 636
Presence of Ford Madox Ford, The (Stang, ed.) (82) 652
Printing Technology, Letters, and Samuel Johnson (Kernan) (88) 710
Prisoners of Hope (Hughes) (84) 705
Problems of Dostoevsky's Poetics (Bakhtin) (85) 706
Profession of the Playwright, The (Stephens) (93) 655
Prophets of Past Time (Dawson) (89) 674
Publics and Counterpublics (Warner) (03) 634
Randall Jarrell and His Age (Burt) (04) 629
Reading *Billy Budd* (Parker) (92) 665
Reading for the Plot (Brooks) (85) 723
Reading *Lolita* in Tehran (Nafisi) (04) 634
Reading Raymond Carver (Runyon) (93) 669
Real Presences (Steiner) (90) 681
Realistic Imagination, The (Levine) (83) 635
Recalcitrance, Faulkner, and the Professors (Wright) (91) 701
Redress of Poetry, The (Heaney) (96) 624
Reflections on Exile and Other Essays (Said) (02) 684
Regions of the Great Heresy (Ficowski) (03) 648
Reich and Nation (Gagliardo) (81) 678
Reinventing Shakespeare (Taylor) (90) 685
Remembering Poets (Hall) (79) 584
Remembrances (Owen) (87) 708
Renaissance *Hamlet*, The (Frye) (85) 742
Republic of Letters, The (Webster) (80) 705
Responses (Wilbur) (77) 679
Return Passages (Ziff) (02) 698
Revolution in Taste, A (Simpson) (80) 709
Road to Middle-Earth, The (Shippey) (84) 736
Robert Frost (Poirier) (78) 722
Roland Barthes (Calvet) (96) 664

Ruin the Sacred Truths (Bloom) (90) 703
Sailing into the Unknown (Rosenthal) (79) 632
Samuel Johnson and the Life of Reading (DeMaria) (98) 693
Saul Bellow (Miller) (92) 707
Saul Bellow, Vision and Revision (Fuchs) (85) 776
Seeds in the Heart (Keene) (94) 721
Selected Essays of R. P. Blackmur (Blackmur) (87) 749
Selected Non-Fictions (Borges) (00) 683
Selected Writings, 1913-1926 (Benjamin) (97) 746
Selected Writings, 1938-1940 (Benjamin) (04) 674
Semiotics and the Philosophy of Language (Eco) (85) 807
Shakespeare (Bloom) (99) 701
Shakespeare (Wells) (96) 704
Shakespeare's Division of Experience (French) (82) 767
Shakespeare's Language (Kermode) (01) 769
Shakespeare's Professional Career (Thomson) (93) 728
Shape of Apocalypse in Modern Russian Fiction, The (Bethea) (90) 729
Short Stories of Thomas Hardy, The (Brady) (83) 747
Short Story, The (Bayley) (89) 788
Signs of the Times (Lehman) (92) 752
Silent Woman, The (Malcolm) (95) 719
Sinking Island, A (Kenner) (89) 793
Situation and the Story, The (Gornick) (02) 752
Six Memos for the Next Millennium (Calvino) (89) 799
Skepticism and Modern Enmity (Perl) (91) 746
Sounds of Poetry, The (Pinsky) (99) 724
Southern Renaissance, A (King) (81) 753
Speaking in Beauty (Donoghue) (04) 713
Stone Cottage (Longenbach) (89) 818
Stranger Shores (Coetzee) (02) 764
Strolls with Pushkin (Tertz) (95) 773
Stuff of Sleep and Dreams (Edel) (83) 765
Style and Faith (Hill) (04) 718
Sudden Glory (Sanders) (96) 728
Sylvia Beach and the Lost Generation (Fitch) (84) 854
T. S. Eliot (Bush) (85) 937
Testaments Betrayed (Kundera) (96) 744
Theater of Envy, A (Girard) (92) 809
Theater of Essence, The (Kott) (85) 890
Thomas Hardy and the Proper Study of Mankind (Gatrell) (94) 793
Three Gospels (Price) (97) 826
Time and Narrative, Vol. I (Ricoeur) (85) 902
To Tell a Free Story (Andrews) (87) 867
To Wake the Nations (Sundquist) (94) 806
Tradition of Return, The (Perl) (85) 917
Transatlantic Patterns (Green) (78) 860
Translingual Imagination, The (Kellman) (01) 840
Travelers of a Hundred Years (Keene) (90) 823
Traveling in Mark Twain (Bridgman) (88) 907
Trials of Phillis Wheatley, The (Gates) (04) 774
Trickster Makes This World (Hyde) (99) 787
Triumph of the Novel, The (Guerard) (77) 847
Trollope (Wall) (90) 827
Truants, The (Barrett) (83) 833
Two-Bit Culture (Davis) (85) 952
U and I (Baker) (92) 844
Unbeliever, The (Parker) (89) 864
Under Briggflatts (Davie) (91) 833
Under Review (Powell) (95) 819
Untying the Knot (Hasan-Rokem and Shulman, eds.) (97) 862
Victor Hugo and the Visionary Novel (Brombert) (85) 969
View of Victorian Literature, A (Tillotson) (79) 814
Vigour of Prophecy, The (Henry) (91) 847
Vladimir's Carrot (Peter) (88) 937
Voices and Visions (Vendler, ed.) (88) 943
Vortex (Materer) (80) 855

CATEGORY INDEX

Walking the Bible (Feiler) (02) 826
Wallace Stevens (Longenbach) (92) 859
Walter Scott (Millgate) (85) 989
War Against Cliché, The (Amis) (02) 830
War Within (Singal) (83) 873
Was Huck Black? (Fishkin) (94) 843
We Irish (Donoghue) (87) 953
What Was Literature? (Fiedler) (83) 884
When Memory Speaks (Conway) (99) 855
Where the Stress Falls (Sontag) (02) 842
Wide as the Waters (Bobrick) (02) 851
Willa Cather (Lee) (91) 896
William Faulkner, First Encounters (Brooks) (84) 950
William Faulkner, Toward Yoknapatawpha and Beyond
  (Brooks) (79) 874
William Faulkner (Singal) (98) 850
Witches and Jesuits (Wills) (95) 876
With My Trousers Rolled (Epstein) (96) 818
Witness of Poetry, The (Miłosz) (84) 959
Woman and the Demon (Auerbach) (83) 913
Words Alone (Donoghue) (01) 925
World of Biblical Literature, The (Alter) (93) 883
Writers in Russia (Hayward) (84) 977
Writing in the New Nation (Ziff) (92) 924
Writing Life, The (Dillard) (90) 930
Writing Women in Jacobean England (Lewalski)
  (94) 869
Yeats (Archibald) (84) 988

LITERARY HISTORY. *See* LITERARY CRITICISM,
  HISTORY, and THEORY

LITERARY THEORY. *See* LITERARY CRITICISM,
  HISTORY, and THEORY

MEDIA
About Town (Yagoda) (01) 1
Breaking the News (Fallows) (97) 132
Conspiracy Theories (Fenster) (00) 142
Essays on Music (Adorno) (03) 269
Gilligan Unbound (Cantor) (02) 338
History of Reading, A (Manguel) (97) 395
Media Unlimited (Gitlin) (03) 523
News About the News, The (Downie and Kaiser)
  (03) 577
Primetime Blues (Bogle) (02) 664
Privileged Son (McDougal) (02) 669
Publics and Counterpublics (Warner) (03) 634
Seriously Funny (Nachman) (04) 679
Small Wonder (Kingsolver) (03) 779
Tolstoy's Dictaphone (Birkerts, ed.) (97) 834

MEDICINE. *See* SCIENCE, HISTORY OF SCIENCE,
  TECHNOLOGY, and MEDICINE

MEMOIRS. *See* AUTOBIOGRAPHY, MEMOIRS,
  DIARIES, and LETTERS

MUSIC. *See* FINE ARTS, FILM, and MUSIC

NATURAL HISTORY. *See* NATURE, NATURAL
  HISTORY, and the ENVIRONMENT

NATURE, NATURAL HISTORY, and the
  ENVIRONMENT
Alfred Russel Wallace (Raby) (02) 30
Anatomy of a Rose (Russell) (02) 39
Ape and the Sushi Master, The (de Waal) (02) 48
Arctic Dreams (Lopez) (87) 69
Art of the Commonplace, The (Berry) (03) 33
At the Water's Edge (Zimmer) (99) 69

Bayou Farewell (Tidwell) (04) 58
Beak of the Finch, The (Weiner) (95) 65
Biological Exuberance (Bagemihl) (00) 62
Body Toxic (Antonetta) (02) 97
Botany of Desire, The (Pollan) (02) 125
Brain for All Seasons, A (Calvin) (03) 102
Bully for Brontosaurus (Gould) (92) 69
Charles Darwin (Browne) (96) 90
Chimpanzees of Gombe (Goodall) (87) 116
Coal (Freese) (04) 126
Control of Nature, The (McPhee) (90) 137
Dinosaur in a Haystack (Gould) (97) 219
Dirt Under My Nails (Foster) (03) 207
DNA (Watson and Berry) (04) 179
Elephant Destiny (Meredith) (04) 215
Encompassing Nature (Torrance) (99) 252
Enough (McKibben) (04) 236
Farm (Rhodes) (90) 240
Founding Fish, The (McPhee) (03) 316
Future of Life, The (Wilson) (03) 321
In Search of Nature (Wilson) (97) 428
Inside the Animal Mind (Page) (00) 426
Islands, the Universe, Home (Ehrlich) (92) 364
Landscape and Memory (Schama) (96) 414
Leap (Williams) (01) 513
Man and the Natural World (Thomas) (84) 492
Mars (Sheehan and O'Meara) (02) 511
Monk in the Garden, The (Henig) (01) 588
Monster of God (Quammen) (04) 519
Naturalist (Wilson) (95) 528
Nature of Order, The (Alexander) (04) 537
Nature's Metropolis (Cronon) (92) 554
Nonzero (Wright) (01) 646
Place in Space, A (Snyder) (96) 585
PrairyErth (Heat-Moon) (92) 632
Primate's Memoir, A (Sapolsky) (02) 659
Purified by Fire (Prothero) (02) 674
Sand Rivers (Matthiessen) (82) 737
Small Wonder (Kingsolver) (03) 779
Structure of Evolutionary Theory, The (Gould) (03) 815
Truth About Chernobyl, The (Medvedev) (92) 835
Under Western Skies (Worster) (93) 833
Unsettling of America, The (Berry) (79) 795
Volcano (Hongo) (96) 802
Why Big Fierce Animals Are Rare (Colinvaux) (79) 857
Winter World (Heinrich) (04) 843
Women on the Margins (Davis) (96) 826

PHILOSOPHY and RELIGION
Active Faith (Reed) (97) 9
Adam, Eve, and the Serpent (Pagels) (89) 4
Adam's Curse (Donoghue) (02) 5
Alfred North Whitehead, 1910-1947 (Lowe) (91) 20
Amazing Grace (Norris) (99) 40
American Catholic (Morris) (98) 36
Among the Believers (Naipaul) (82) 6
Art of the Commonplace, The (Berry) (03) 33
At the End of an Age (Lukacs) (03) 37
Atom (Krauss) (02) 57
Beginning of Wisdom, The (Kass) (04) 66
Bertrand Russell (Monk) (97) 105
Betrayal (*The Boston Globe* Investigative Staff) (03) 65
Beyond Belief (Naipaul) (99) 96
Broken Staff, The (Manuel) (93) 110
Catholic Imagination, The (Greeley) (01) 176
Cloister Walk, The (Norris) (97) 160
Congregation (Rosenberg, ed.) (88) 189
Conscious Mind, The (Chalmers) (97) 179
Consciousness Explained (Dennett) (92) 119
Crisis of Islam, The (Lewis) (04) 142
Crooked Timber of Humanity, The (Berlin) (92) 133
Cult of Violence, The (Roth) (81) 215
Culture of Disbelief, The (Carter) (94) 191

Darwin's Dangerous Idea (Dennett) (96) 148
Democracy's Discontents (Sandel) (97) 205
Descartes (Gaukroger) (96) 170
Dreaming Me (Willis) (02) 212
Driving Mr. Albert (Paterniti) (01) 258
Emerson (Richardson) (96) 222
End of History and the Last Man, The (Fukuyama) (93) 262
End of Time, The (Barbour) (01) 281
Engine of Reason, the Seat of the Soul, The (Churchland) (96) 232
Enigma of Anger, The (Keizer) (03) 265
Essays on Music (Adorno) (03) 269
Ethics (Foucault) (98) 289
Examined Life, The (Nozick) (90) 231
Feeling of What Happens, The (Damasio) (00) 256
For the Time Being (Dillard) (00) 282
Francis Bacon (Zagorin) (99) 303
Freedom (Patterson) (92) 237
Freedom Evolves (Dennett) (04) 275
Genesis (Alter) (97) 327
Geography of Thought, The (Nisbett) (04) 287
Geometry of Love, The (Visser) (02) 330
Gifts of the Jews, The (Cahill) (99) 333
Girl Meets God (Winner) (03) 330
Gnostic Gospels, The (Pagels) (80) 363
God (Miles) (96) 311
God and the American Writer (Kazin) (98) 352
Gödel (Casti and DePauli) (01) 346
God's Funeral (Wilson) (00) 317
God's Long Summer (Marsh) (98) 362
God's Name in Vain (Carter) (01) 351
God's Secretaries (Nicolson) (04) 295
Grammars of Creation (Steiner) (02) 357
Grammatical Man (Campbell) (83) 301
Guide for the Perplexed, A (Schumacher) (78) 364
His Holiness (Bernstein and Politi) (97) 388
History of Heaven, A (Russell) (98) 387
History of Philosophy in America, 1720-2000, A (Kuklick) (03) 366
History of the Idea of Progress (Nisbet) (81) 430
History of the Jews in America, A (Sachar) (93) 340
Hitler's Pope (Cornwell) (00) 396
Hobbes (Martinich) (00) 400
Holy the Firm (Dillard) (78) 404
Hopkins, the Self, and God (Ong) (87) 406
Illusion of Technique, The (Barrett) (80) 409
Imperfect Garden (Todorov) (03) 396
In My Father's House (Appiah) (93) 370
In the Beginning . . . (Asimov) (82) 386
In the Beginning (McGrath) (02) 408
Inner Reaches of Outer Space, The (Campbell) (87) 429
Integrity (Carter) (97) 456
Isaiah Berlin (Gray) (97) 466
Jameses (Lewis) (92) 374
Jew vs. Jew (Freedman) (01) 480
Jews (Hertzberg and Hirt-Manheimer) (99) 436
Jihad (Kepel) (03) 428
Jihad (Rashid) (03) 423
John Calvin (Bouwsma) (88) 433
John Dewey and American Democracy (Westbrook) (92) 388
John Dewey and the High Tide of American Liberalism (Ryan) (96) 393
Kaddish (Wieseltier) (99) 445
Kant (Kuehn) (02) 458
King of the Ants, The (Herbert) (00) 462
Life of the Mind, The (Arendt) (79) 393
Lifelines (Rose) (98) 508
Lila (Pirsig) (92) 440
Literature and the Gods (Calasso) (02) 486
Lives of Animals, The (Coetzee) (00) 492

Lost in the Cosmos (Percy) (84) 482
Love and Responsibility (Wojtyla) (82) 494
Luther (Oberman) (91) 553
Martin Heidegger (Ott) (94) 512
Martin Heidegger (Safranski) (99) 529
Martin Luther (Marius) (00) 515
Mephistopheles (Russell) (87) 553
Metaphysics as a Guide to Morals (Murdoch) (94) 526
Mexican Phoenix (Brading) (02) 528
Michel Foucault (Eribon) (92) 495
Mind and Nature (Bateson) (80) 536
Mind of Egypt, The (Assmann) (03) 531
Minds, Brains and Science (Searle) (86) 614
Modern American Religion, 1919-1941 (Marty) (92) 524
Moral Freedom (Wolfe) (02) 541
Moral Sense, The (Wilson) (94) 539
Mormon America (Ostling and Ostling) (00) 529
Mullahs on the Mainframe (Blank) (02) 550
Mysterious Flame, The (McGinn) (00) 558
Nature of Economies, The (Jacobs) (01) 613
Nature of Love, The (Singer) (89) 585
Nature of Order, The (Alexander) (04) 537
Nearer, My God (Buckley) (98) 575
Necessary Evil, A (Wills) (00) 567
Next Christendom, The (Jenkins) (03) 581
New Buddhism, The (Coleman) (02) 571
Nietzsche (Safranski) (02) 584
Noah's Curse (Haynes) (03) 594
Noble Savage, The (Cranston) (92) 583
Nonzero (Wright) (01) 646
Nothing That Is, The (Kaplan) (00) 585
Ordinary Time (Mairs) (94) 594
Origin of Satan, The (Pagels) (96) 541
Our Posthuman Future (Fukuyama) (03) 615
Passion of Michel Foucault, The (Miller) (93) 614
Philosopher's Demise, The (Watson) (96) 581
Philosophical Explanations (Nozick) (82) 638
Philosophy in the Twentieth Century (Ayer) (83) 592
Political Liberalism (Rawls) (94) 649
Preacher King, The (Lischer) (96) 601
Principle of Hope, The (Bloch) (87) 670
Promise of Pragmatism, The (Diggins) (95) 617
Purified by Fire (Prothero) (02) 674
Quantum Philosophy (Omnès) (00) 638
Radical Enlightenment (Israel) (02) 679
Reason for Hope (Goodall with Berman) (00) 643
Reasons and Persons (Parfit) (85) 729
Rediscovery of the Mind, The (Searle) (93) 673
Renewing Philosophy (Putnam) (94) 696
Robot (Moravec) (99) 670
Rocks of Ages (Gould) (00) 656
Sacred Chain, The (Cantor) (95) 678
Saints and Sinners (Duffy) (98) 683
Schopenhauer and the Wild Years of Philosophy (Safranski) (91) 711
Search for the Perfect Language, The (Eco) (96) 680
Selected Non-Fictions (Borges) (00) 683
Selected Writings, 1913-1926 (Benjamin) (97) 746
Semiotics and the Philosophy of Language (Eco) (85) 807
Sex and Social Justice (Nussbaum) (00) 697
Simone Weil (Nevin) (93) 736
Socrates (Vlastos) (92) 766
Somewhere a Master (Wiesel) (83) 756
Soul of the American University, The (Marsden) (95) 744
Sources of the Self (Taylor) (91) 763
Speaking of Beauty (Donoghue) (04) 713
Spinoza (Nadler) (00) 725
Spinoza and Other Heretics, Vol. I and Vol. II (Yovel) (91) 768
Stroll with William James, A (Barzun) (84) 837

CATEGORY INDEX

Testaments Betrayed (Kundera) (96) 744
Thomas Kuhn (Fuller) (01) 820
Three Gospels (Price) (97) 826
Three Rival Versions of Moral Enquiry (MacIntyre) (91) 815
Time and Narrative, Vol. I (Ricoeur) (85) 902
Traveling Mercies (Lamott) (00) 764
Triple Helix, The (Lewontin) (01) 845
Truth and Progress (Rorty) (99) 799
Two Faces of Islam, The (Schwartz) (03) 853
Under the Banner of Heaven (Krakauer) (04) 787
Underground (Murakami) (02) 813
Upon This Rock (Freedman) (94) 827
Utopian Pessimist (McLellan) (91) 838
Walking the Bible (Feiler) (02) 826
Wanderlust (Solnit) (01) 887
War Within (Singal) (83) 873
Wide as the Waters (Bobrick) (02) 851
Wisdom of the World, The (Brague) (04) 847
Witness to Hope (Weigel) (00) 847
Wittgenstein's Poker (Edmonds and Eidinow) (02) 875
Women, Reason and Nature (McMillan) (84) 964
Works and Lives (Geertz) (89) 923
World of Biblical Literature, The (Alter) (93) 883
Worlds of Wonder, Days of Judgment (Hall) (90) 925
Young Nietzsche (Pletsch) (92) 928

POETRY and DRAMA
"A" (Zukofsky) (80) 1
Adventures in Ancient Egypt (Goldbarth) (98) 5
After the Lost War (Hudgins) (89) 9
Afterlife, The (Levis) (78) 17
Against the Evidence (Ignatow) (95) 10
Aimé Césaire, the Collected Poetry (Césaire) (84) 5
Alabanza (Espada) (04) 5
All Day Permanent Red (Logue) (04) 17
All of Us (Carver) (99) 28
All of Us Here (Feldman) (87) 29
Amadeus (Shaffer) (81) 27
Amen (Amichai) (78) 42
American Buffalo (Mamet) (78) 46
Angel of History, The (Forché) (95) 33
Angle of Ascent (Hayden) (77) 48
Annunciations (Tomlinson) (91) 43
Antarctic Traveller (Pollitt) (83) 20
Anthology of Chinese Literature, An (Owen, ed.) (97) 53
Ants on the Melon (Adair) (97) 57
Any Body's Song (Langland) (81) 53
Appalachia (Wright) (99) 61
Ararat (Glück) (91) 51
Archer in the Marrow (Viereck) (88) 46
Argot Merchant Disaster, The (Starbuck) (83) 25
Ark (Johnson) (97) 62
Arkansas Testament, The (Walcott) (88) 52
Articulation of Sound Forms in Time (Howe) (88) 63
As We Know (Ashbery) (80) 31
Ashes (Levine) (80) 35
Atlantis (Doty) (96) 55
Atlas of the Difficult World, Poems 1988-1991, An (Rich) (92) 25
Autobiography of Red (Carson) (99) 74
Available Light (Piercy) (89) 63
Axe Handles (Snyder) (84) 65
Bashō and His Interpreters (Ueda) (93) 53
Before Sleep (Booth) (81) 71
Before Time Could Change Them (Cavafy) (02) 74
Beginning with O (Broumas) (78) 91
Being Here (Warren) (81) 76
Bells in Winter (Miłosz) (79) 51
Beowulf (Anonymous) (01) 89
Best Hour of the Night, The (Simpson) (85) 42
Between the Chains (Cassity) (92) 44

Beyond Silence (Hoffman) (04) 83
Birthday Letters (Hughes) (99) 109
Black Zodiac (Wright) (98) 117
Blood, Hook & Eye (Wier) (78) 112
Blood Mountain (Engels) (78) 117
Blood, Tin, Straw (Olds) (00) 74
Bloodfire (Chappell) (79) 60
Blue Hour (Forché) (04) 91
Blue Wine and Other Poems (Hollander) (80) 94
Body Blows (Bagg) (89) 98
Boleros (Wright) (92) 56
Book of My Nights (Lee) (02) 110
Book of the Body, The (Bidart) (78) 136
Boss Cupid (Gunn) (01) 135
Bread Without Sugar (Stern) (93) 101
Burnt Pages, The (Ash) (92) 75
Cage for Loulou, A (von Abele) (79) 70
Canaan (Hill) (98) 152
Carnival Evening (Pastan) (99) 141
Changing Light at Sandover, The (Merrill) (84) 148
Cheer, The (Meredith) (81) 133
Chickamauga (Wright) (96) 103
Chieko's Sky (Takamura) (79) 105
Children in Exile (Fenton) (85) 96
Chinese Insomniacs, The (Jacobsen) (83) 110
Chosen Poems, Old and New (Lorde) (83) 113
Circles on the Water (Piercy) (83) 119
Cities of Memory (Hinsey) (97) 152
Cleared for Landing (Darr) (79) 113
Climbing into the Roots (Saner) (77) 164
Coast of Trees, A (Ammons) (82) 92
Collected Early Poems, 1950-1970 (Rich) (94) 133
Collected Poems, 1948-1976 (Abse) (78) 192
Collected Poems, 1957-1982 (Berry) (86) 159
Collected Poems (Berryman) (90) 117
Collected Poems (Bowers) (98) 177
Collected Poems (Bunting) (79) 119
Collected Poems, 1970-1983 (Davie) (84) 183
Collected Poems, 1947-1980 (Ginsberg) (85) 110
Collected Poems (Hayden) (86) 152
Collected Poems (Hill) (87) 146
Collected Poems, 1956-1994 (Kinsella) (97) 165
Collected Poems, The (Kunitz) (01) 204
Collected Poems (Larkin) (90) 112
Collected Poems (Lowell) (04) 130
Collected Poems, The (Miłosz) (89) 185
Collected Poems, The (Plath) (82) 96
Collected Poems, The (Price) (98) 181
Collected Poems, 1935-1992 (Prince) (94) 142
Collected Poems, The (Rukeyser) (80) 148
Collected Poems (Sarton) (94) 137
Collected Poems, 1940-1978 (Shapiro) (79) 124
Collected Poems (Simpson) (89) 180
Collected Poems, 1919-1976 (Tate) (78) 188
Collected Poems (Tomlinson) (87) 151
Collected Poems, 1953-1993 (Updike) (94) 146
Collected Poems, 1956-1976 (Wagoner) (78) 197
Collected Poems, The (Yevtushenko) (92) 104
Collected Poems of Amy Clampitt, The (Clampitt) (98) 185
Collected Poems of George Garrett, The (Garrett) (85) 116
Collected Poems of Henri Coulette, The (Coulette) (91) 152
Collected Poems of Howard Nemerov, The (Nemerov) (78) 200
Collected Poems of John Ciardi, The (Ciardi) (98) 190
Collected Poems of Octavio Paz, The (Paz) (88) 169
Collected Poems of Paul Blackburn, The (Blackburn) (86) 164
Collected Poems of Robert Creeley, The (Creeley) (84) 189

Collected Poems of Sterling A. Brown, The (Brown) (81) 168
Collected Poems of Stevie Smith, The (Smith) (77) 168
Collected Poems of William Carlos Williams, 1909-1939, The (Williams) (87) 155
Collected Poems of William Carlos Williams, 1939-1962, The (Williams) (89) 190
Collected Poetry of Robinson Jeffers, 1920-1928, The (Jeffers) (89) 195
Collected Poetry of Robinson Jeffers, 1928-1938, The (Jeffers) (90) 122
Collected Shorter Poems, 1946-1991 (Carruth) (93) 171
Color Wheel, The (Steele) (96) 140
Combinations of the Universe (Goldbarth) (04) 134
Comedians (Griffiths) (77) 174
Coming to Jakarta (Scott) (90) 127
Commons (Kim) (03) 155
Compass Flower, The (Merwin) (78) 205
Complete Poems, The (Sexton) (82) 120
Complete Poems of Anna Akhmatova, The (Akhmatova) (91) 165
Complete Poems of C. Day Lewis, The (Day Lewis) (93) 184
Complete Poems of Marianne Moore, The (Moore) (82) 126
Complete Poems of William Empson, The (Empson) (02) 153
Complete Short Poetry (Zukofsky) (92) 114
Conscious and Verbal (Murray) (02) 163
Constant Defender (Tate) (84) 202
Cool, Calm, and Collected (Kizer) (02) 172
Cosmopolitan Greetings (Ginsberg) (95) 152
Country Between Us, The (Forché) (83) 161
Cradle of the Real Life, The (Valentine) (01) 223
Crimes of the Heart (Henley) (83) 165
Cross Ties (Kennedy) (86) 199
Crown of Weeds (Gerstler) (98) 216
Cuba Night (Smith) (91) 179
Dark Harbor (Strand) (94) 209
Day by Day (Lowell) (78) 233
Daylight Moon and Other Poems, The (Murray) (90) 157
Dead and the Living, The (Olds) (85) 162
Dead Kingdom, The (Montague) (85) 167
Destructive Element, The (Cassity) (99) 230
Dirty Linen and New-Found-Land (Stoppard) (78) 268
Divine Comedies (Merrill) (77) 222
Door in the Hive, A (Levertov) (90) 194
Door in the Wall, The (Tomlinson) (94) 244
Double Witness, The (Belitt) (78) 276
Dread (Ai) (04) 185
Dream of a Common Language, The (Rich) (79) 160
Dream Work (Oliver) (87) 219
Each in a Place Apart (McMichael) (95) 190
Each Leaf Shines Separate (Warren) (85) 204
Earthsleep (Chappell) (81) 264
Eclogues of Virgil, The (Vergil) (00) 194
Ecstatic in the Poison (Hudgins) (04) 207
Edge Effect (McPherson) (97) 234
Edwin Denby, the Complete Poems (Denby) (87) 223
Electric Light (Heaney) (02) 240
Elegy for the Departure and Other Poems (Herbert) (00) 217
Elephant Man, The (Pomerance) (80) 280
Emerald City of Las Vegas, The (Wakoski) (96) 218
Endless Life (Ferlinghetti) (82) 229
English Auden, The (Auden) (79) 193
Entries (Berry) (95) 209
Erosion (Graham) (84) 279
Errancy, The (Graham) (98) 286
Explanation of America, An (Pinsky) (81) 293
Facing the River (Miłosz) (96) 247
False Prophet (Rice) (04) 249

Fate (Ai) (92) 197
Father, The (Olds) (93) 284
Feel of Rock, The (Whittemore) (83) 250
Felt (Fulton) (02) 295
Field Work (Heaney) (80) 315
5th of July (Wilson) (80) 320
Figured Wheel, The (Pinsky) (97) 278
First Light (Wagoner) (84) 299
Five Stages of Grief, The (Pastan) (79) 222
Flesh and Blood (Williams) (88) 330
Flood (Matthews) (83) 262
Flow Chart (Ashbery) (92) 214
Flying Change, The (Taylor) (86) 293
Folding Cliffs, The (Merwin) (99) 295
For the Living and the Dead (Tranströmer) (96) 283
Fortunate Traveller, The (Walcott) (82) 293
Fox (Rich) (02) 309
Fraction of Darkness, A (Pastan) (86) 310
Frame Structures (Howe) (97) 311
Fredy Neptune (Murray) (00) 286
From a Three-Cornered World (Mitsui) (98) 322
From the First Nine (Merrill) (84) 314
From the Mountain, from the Valley (Still) (02) 313
Garbage (Ammons) (94) 331
Gathering the Tribes (Forché) (77) 314
Geography III (Bishop) (77) 326
Gilgamesh (Sîn-leqi-unninnì) (85) 324
Glass Face in the Rain, A (Stafford) (83) 288
God of Indeterminacy, The (McPherson) (94) 364
Gold Cell, The (Olds) (88) 353
Good Trembling (Wormser) (86) 364
Goshawk, Antelope (Smith) (80) 380
Grace Notes (Dove) (90) 324
Granite Pail, The (Niedecker) (86) 368
Great Blue (Galvin) (91) 364
Great Tranquillity (Amichai) (84) 334
Greeting, The (Dillard) (83) 309
Groom Falconer (Dubie) (90) 338
Ground Work (Duncan) (85) 329
Groundwork (Morgan) (80) 390
Handwriting (Ondaatje) (00) 346
Hang-Gliding from Helicon (Hoffman) (89) 340
Happy Alchemy (Davies) (99) 346
Happy as a Dog's Tail (Swir) (86) 391
Happy Hour (Shapiro) (88) 368
Hard Evidence (Miller) (92) 271
Hay (Muldoon) (99) 350
Hello, Darkness (Sissman) (79) 264
Henry Purcell in Japan (Salter) (86) 411
Henry's Fate & Other Poems, 1967-1972 (Berryman) (78) 384
History of My Heart (Pinsky) (85) 399
Hotel Lautréamont (Ashbery) (93) 358
Houseboat Days (Ashbery) (78) 408
How We Became Human (Harjo) (03) 379
Hundreds of Fireflies (Leithauser) (83) 348
Hurricane Lamp (Cassity) (87) 415
Husbands, The (Logue) (96) 355
"I Am" (Clare) (04) 347
If I Had Wheels or Love (Miller) (92) 319
If Not, Winter (Sappho) (03) 388
Imperfect Paradise, The (Pastan) (89) 367
Imperfect Thirst (Kinnell) (95) 339
In a Time of Violence (Boland) (95) 343
In Mediterranean Air (Stanford) (78) 439
In the House of the Judge (Smith) (84) 374
In the Western Night (Bidart) (91) 447
Inferno of Dante, The (Dante) (96) 376
Inner Room, The (Merrill) (89) 386
Inventions of the March Hare (Eliot) (98) 436
Jason the Sailor (Wakoski) (94) 422
Jubilation (Tomlinson) (96) 403
Kingfisher, The (Clampitt) (84) 413

CATEGORY INDEX

Lady from Dubuque, The (Albee) (81) 475
Lamplit Answer, The (Schnackenberg) (86) 505
Land of Superior Mirages (Stoutenburg) (87) 461
Last Poems (Celan) (87) 466
Latin Deli, The (Cofer) (94) 454
Lay Back the Darkness (Hirsch) (04) 438
Leaping Clear (Feldman) (77) 408
Learning Human (Murray) (01) 518
Letters from the Floating World (Cedering) (85) 544
Life in the Forest (Levertov) (79) 386
Life Supports (Bronk) (82) 466
Light the Dead See, The (Stanford) (92) 436
Listening to the Candle (Scott) (93) 469
Little Girls in Church (Norris) (96) 440
Little Voices of the Pears, The (Morris) (90) 535
Local Visitations (Dunn) (04) 465
Luck's Shining Child (Garrett) (82) 509
Lucky Life (Stern) (78) 540
Madoc (Muldoon) (92) 469
Making Certain It Goes On (Hugo) (85) 603
Man in the Black Coat Turns, The (Bly) (83) 439
Man Who Shook Hands, The (Wakoski) (79) 414
Man with Night Sweats, The (Gunn) (93) 495
Maximus Poems, The (Olson) (84) 519
Mayan Astronomer in Hell's Kitchen, A (Espada) (01) 574
Mayflies (Wilbur) (01) 579
Me Again (Smith) (83) 458
Meadowlands (Glück) (97) 564
Men in the Off Hours (Carson) (01) 583
Mercurochrome (Coleman) (02) 519
Mercy, The (Levine) (00) 547
Metropol (Aksyonov, et al., eds.) (84) 533
Middle Earth (Cole) (04) 510
MiddlePassages (Brathwaite) (95) 486
Midsummer (Walcott) (85) 609
Millennium Hotel, The (Rudman) (97) 586
Millions of Strange Shadows (Hecht) (78) 572
Mind-Reader, The (Wilbur) (77) 505
Miniatures, and Other Poems (Guest) (03) 536
Mirabell (Merrill) (79) 448
Mixed Company (Shapiro) (97) 590
Monolithos (Gilbert) (83) 484
Moon Crossing Bridge (Gallagher) (93) 532
Moortown (Hughes) (81) 569
Morning of the Poem, The (Schuyler) (81) 578
Mornings Like This (Dillard) (96) 482
Mortal Acts, Mortal Words (Kinnell) (81) 582
Mother Love (Dove) (96) 486
Mount Eagle (Montague) (90) 591
Mountains and Rivers Without End (Snyder) (97) 605
Mousetrap and Other Plays, The (Christie) (79) 470
Mr. Cogito (Herbert) (94) 530
Mr. Happiness *and* The Water Engine (Mamet) (79) 828
Museum of Clear Ideas, The (Hall) (94) 543
My Alexandria (Doty) (94) 547
My Name Is Saroyan (Saroyan) (84) 588
Natural Histories (Ullman) (80) 569
Need to Hold Still, The (Mueller) (81) 603
Neon Vernacular (Komunyakaa) (94) 551
Nerve Storm (Gerstler) (95) 535
New and Collected Poems, 1952-1992 (Hill) (95) 540
New & Collected Poems, 1917-1976 (MacLeish) (77) 534
New and Collected Poems, 1931-2001 (Miłosz) (02) 567
New and Collected Poems (Wilbur) (89) 590
New and Selected Poems (Feldman) (80) 580
New and Selected Poems (Oliver) (93) 549
New and Selected Poems (Soto) (96) 504
New & Selected Things Taking Place (Swenson) (79) 472

New-Found-Land *and* Dirty Linen (Stoppard) (78) 268
New Poems (Montale) (77) 553
News from the Glacier (Haines) (83) 527
Night and Day (Stoppard) (80) 586
Night Picnic (Simic) (02) 592
Nine Horses (Collins) (03) 590
No Nature (Snyder) (93) 565
Nonconformist's Memorial, The (Howe) (94) 568
Notes from the Castle (Moss) (80) 597
Notes from the Divided Country (Kim) (04) 561
Now and Then (Warren) (79) 501
Odyssey, The (Homer) (97) 640
Old Men and Comets (Enright) (94) 577
Omeros (Walcott) (91) 643
On Love (Hirsch) (99) 580
Only the Dreamer Can Change the Dream (Logan) (82) 599
Open Closed Open (Amichai) (01) 684
Opened Ground (Heaney) (99) 597
Orchards of Syon, The (Hill) (03) 606
Oregon Message, An (Stafford) (88) 636
Original Fire (Erdrich) (04) 579
Otherwise (Kenyon) (97) 651
Our Ground Time Here Will Be Brief (Kumin) (83) 577
Outskirts of Troy, The (Dennis) (89) 635
Owl in the Mask of the Dreamer, The (Haines) (94) 598
Owls and Other Fantasies (Oliver) (04) 596
Partial Accounts (Meredith) (88) 663
Passing Through (Kunitz) (96) 569
Passwords (Stafford) (92) 612
Past, The (Kinnell) (86) 727
Pastoral (Phillips) (01) 699
Phenomena (Hankla) (84) 686
Picture Bride (Song) (84) 695
PM/AM (Pastan) (83) 603
Poems (Knott) (90) 669
Poems, 1968-1998 (Muldoon) (02) 645
Poems, The (Yeats) (85) 692
Poems New and Selected, 1962-1992 (Van Brunt) (94) 641
Poems of Paul Celan (Celan) (90) 673
Poems of Stanley Kunitz, 1928-1978, The (Kunitz) (80) 665
Poetical Works of Federico García Lorca (García Lorca) (93) 637
Portable Jack Kerouac, The (Kerouac) (96) 597
Proust Screenplay, The (Pinter) (78) 673
Provinces (Miłosz) (92) 656
Pushcart Prize, III, The (Henderson, ed.) (79) 565
Rabbiter's Bounty, The (Murray) (93) 660
Rainbow Grocery, The (Dickey) (79) 570
Red Coal, The (Stern) (82) 661
Relations (Booth) (87) 703
Relativity (Cherry) (78) 700
Resuming Green (Flint) (84) 731
Retrieval System, The (Kumin) (79) 593
Return, The (Tomlinson) (88) 753
Rhapsody in Plain Yellow (Chin) (03) 668
Richard Wright Reader (Wright) (79) 597
Rimbaud Complete (Rimbaud) (03) 672
River (Hughes) (85) 762
River of Heaven, The (Hongo) (89) 741
Road-Side Dog (Miłosz) (99) 666
Roundhouse Voices, The (Smith) (86) 775
Rounding the Horn (Slavitt) (79) 608
Rumor Verified (Warren) (82) 704
Runner, The (Gildner) (79) 613
Sabbaths (Berry) (88) 785
Sailing Alone Around the Room (Collins) (02) 713
Saints and Strangers (Hudgins) (86) 788
Sam Shepard, Seven Plays (Shepard) (82) 731
Sands of the Well (Levertov) (97) 714

Sapphics Against Anger (Steele) (87) 741
Scattering of Salts, A (Merrill) (96) 676
School Figures (Song) (95) 691
Science of Goodbyes, The (Sklarew) (83) 694
Scrambled Eggs and Whiskey (Carruth) (97) 722
Searching for the Ox (Simpson) (77) 706
Seeing Things (Heaney) (92) 737
Selected and Collected Poems (Knott) (78) 748
Selected and New Poems (Dubie) (84) 761
Selected & New Poems (Harrison) (83) 718
Selected Poems (Ashbery) (86) 798
Selected Poems (Atwood) (79) 661
Selected Poems (Borges) (00) 688
Selected Poems (Clarke) (77) 715
Selected Poems (Garrigue) (93) 715
Selected Poems, 1947-1995 (Ginsberg) (97) 737
Selected Poems, 1950-1975 (Gunn) (80) 750
Selected Poems (Harrison) (88) 812
Selected Poems (Kinnell) (83) 726
Selected Poems, 1960-1990 (Kumin) (98) 707
Selected Poems (Lowell) (77) 720
Selected Poems (McGrath) (89) 775
Selected Poems (Masefield) (79) 666
Selected Poems, 1946-1985 (Merrill) (93) 719
Selected Poems (Nims) (83) 730
Selected Poems (Paz) (85) 802
Selected Poems (Strand) (81) 723
Selected Poems, 1923-1975 (Warren) (78) 753
Selected Writings of James Weldon Johnson, Vol. I and
    Vol. II, The (Johnson) (96) 694
Selves (Booth) (91) 731
Sense of Sight, The (Berger) (87) 754
Separate Notebooks, The (Miłosz) (85) 811
Seven Ages, The (Glück) (02) 742
Shadow Box, The (Cristofer) (78) 762
Short History of the Shadow, A (Wright) (03) 741
Silence Opens, A (Clampitt) (95) 713
Sleeping with the Dictionary (Mullen) (03) 775
Small Congregations (Moss) (94) 743
So Forth (Brodsky) (97) 766
Soldier's Play, A (Fuller) (83) 751
Somewhere Is Such a Kingdom (Hill) (77) 758
Song of Napalm (Weigl) (89) 803
Songlines in Michaeltree (Harper) (01) 782
Sorrow of Architecture, The (Rector) (85) 855
Spectral Emanations (Hollander) (79) 699
Spirit Level, The (Heaney) (97) 777
Springhouse, The (Dubie) (87) 818
Squares and Courtyards (Hacker) (01) 796
Star-Apple Kingdom, The (Walcott) (80) 777
Station Island (Heaney) (85) 865
Stops (Sloman) (98) 741
Stories That Could Be True (Stafford) (78) 799
Stranger Music (Cohen) (94) 764
Strength of Fields, The (Dickey) (80) 794
Striking the Earth (Woods) (77) 784
Study for the World's Body (St. John) (95) 777
Sumerian Vistas (Ammons) (88) 869
Summer Celestial (Plumly) (84) 846
Sunflower Splendor (Liu and Lo) (77) 792
Sure Signs (Kooser) (81) 782
Taking Light from Each Other (Burden) (93) 771
Talley's Folly (Wilson) (81) 790
Talking Dirty to the Gods (Komunyakaa) (01) 811
Tar (Williams) (84) 859
Ten Commandments, The (McClatchy) (99) 751
Texas Trilogy, A (Jones) (77) 812
Theater of Essence, The (Kott) (85) 890
These Are My Rivers (Ferlinghetti) (94) 788
Things That I Do in the Dark (Jordan) (78) 826
This Blessèd Earth (Wheelock) (79) 749
This Time (Stern) (99) 756
Tiepolo's Hound (Walcott) (01) 825

Time's Power (Rich) (90) 809
To a Blossoming Pear Tree (Wright) (78) 847
To Urania (Brodsky) (89) 840
Transparent Man, The (Hecht) (91) 825
Traveler's Tree, The (Smith) (81) 831
Travels (Merwin) (94) 811
Tread the Dark (Ignatow) (79) 777
Triumph of Achilles, The (Glück) (86) 908
Triumph of Love, The (Hill) (99) 791
Ultima Thule (McCombs) (01) 850
Unattainable Earth (Miłosz) (87) 892
Unbearable Heart, The (Hahn) (97) 843
Uncollected Poems (Rilke) (97) 848
Under the Vulture-Tree (Bottoms) (88) 919
Undersong (Lorde) (93) 838
Venetian Vespers, The (Hecht) (80) 841
Ventriloquist, The (Huff) (78) 873
Vice (Ai) (00) 793
View with a Grain of Sand (Szymborska) (96) 790
Views & Spectacles (Weiss) (80) 846
Viper Jazz (Tate) (77) 888
Visions of Kerouac (Duberman) (78) 878
Visit to Civilization, A (McPherson) (03) 863
Vita Nova (Glück) (00) 797
Voice at 3:00 A.M., The (Simic) (04) 806
Waiting for My Life (Pastan) (82) 897
Walls of Thebes, The (Slavitt) (87) 936
Want Bone, The (Pinsky) (91) 866
War Music (Logue) (88) 954
Water Engine and Mr. Happiness, The (Mamet)
    (79) 828
Waterborne (Gregerson) (03) 867
Wave, A (Ashbery) (85) 1008
West Wind (Oliver) (98) 828
What the Living Do (Howe) (98) 832
What Work Is (Levine) (92) 880
Whisper to the Earth (Ignatow) (83) 894
White Pine (Oliver) (95) 867
White Shroud (Ginsberg) (87) 974
White Wave, The (Daniels) (85) 1023
White Words, The (Wormser) (84) 940
Who Shall Be the Sun? (Wagoner) (79) 852
Who Whispered Near Me (Clary) (90) 889
Wild Patience Has Taken Me This Far, A (Rich)
    (82) 942
Wind Mountain (Chappell) (80) 877
Windows (Creeley) (91) 901
Windrose (Ghiselin) (81) 935
With Ignorance (Williams) (78) 923
Without End (Zagajewski) (03) 890
Wolfwatching (Hughes) (92) 905
Woman Who Fell from the Sky, The (Harjo) (96) 822
Words for Dr. Y (Sexton) (79) 897
Words to God's Music (Wieder) (04) 851
Words Under the Words (Nye) (96) 835
Work, for the Night Is Coming (Carter) (82) 968
Working Girl Can't Win, A (Garrison) (99) 868
World, The Flesh, and Angels, The (Campbell)
    (90) 921
Worshipful Company of Fletchers (Tate) (95) 895
X/Self (Brathwaite) (88) 999
Zither and Autobiography (Scalapino) (04) 872

PSYCHOLOGY
Achilles in Vietnam (Shay) (95) 1
Acts of Meaning (Bruner) (91) 1
Anna Freud (Young-Bruehl) (89) 23
Another Country (Pipher) (00) 36
Anthropologist on Mars, An (Sacks) (96) 47
Autobiography of a Face (Grealy) (95) 56
Bell Curve, The (Herrnstein and Murray) (95) 70
Blank Slate, The (Pinker) (03) 79
Bobos in Paradise (Brooks) (01) 112

CATEGORY INDEX

Consciousness Explained (Dennett) (92) 119
Custer and the Little Big Horn (Hofling) (82) 161
Darkness Visible (Styron) (91) 184
Deadly Medicine (Mancall) (96) 157
Destroying the World to Save It (Lifton) (00) 172
Engine of Reason, the Seat of the Soul, The (Churchland) (96) 232
Enigma of Anger, The (Keizer) (03) 265
Farther Shore, The (Gifford) (91) 287
Feeling of What Happens, The (Damasio) (00) 256
Flow (Csikszentmihalyi) (91) 299
Fluid Concepts and Creative Analogies (Hofstadter) (96) 277
Freud (Roth, ed.) (99) 311
Genie (Rymer) (94) 345
Genocidal Mentality, The (Lifton and Markusen) (91) 338
Geography of Thought, The (Nisbett) (04) 287
Girl, Interrupted (Kaysen) (94) 360
Gracefully Insane (Beam) (03) 343
Grasp of Consciousness, The (Piaget) (77) 341
Guided Tour of the Collected Works of C. G. Jung, A (Hopcke) (90) 343
Helene Deutsch (Roazen) (86) 402
How the Mind Works (Pinker) (98) 401
How We Die (Nuland) (95) 324
In the Palaces of Memory (Johnson) (92) 342
In the Shadow of the Epidemic (Odets) (96) 368
In the Theater of Consciousness (Baars) (98) 424
Inside Picture Books (Spitz) (00) 422
Inside the Animal Mind (Page) (00) 426
Jacques Lacan (Roudinesco) (98) 463
Living with Our Genes (Hamer and Copeland) (99) 483
Madness in the Streets (Isaac and Armat) (91) 558
Making Stories (Bruner) (03) 509
Meeting at the Crossroads (Brown and Gilligan) (93) 500
Mind of Her Own, A (Quinn) (88) 558
Models of My Life (Simon) (92) 519
Moral Animal, The (Wright) (95) 504
Moral Life of Children, The (Coles) (87) 573
Moral Politics (Lakoff) (97) 600
Nature of Order, The (Alexander) (04) 537
Nazi Psychoanalysis (Rickels) (03) 559
Noonday Demon, The (Solomon) (02) 596
Old and on Their Own (Coles) (99) 576
Psychopathic God, The (Waite) (78) 677
Publics and Counterpublics (Warner) (03) 634
Rewriting the Soul (Hacking) (96) 637
Running with Scissors (Burroughs) (03) 695
Searching for Memory (Schacter) (97) 727
Shadows of the Mind (Penrose) (95) 705
"Shattered Nerves" (Oppenheim) (92) 742
Stiffed (Faludi) (00) 733
Survivor, The (Des Pres) (77) 797
Tipping Point, The (Gladwell) (01) 835
Unauthorized Freud (Crews, ed.) (99) 817
Underground (Murakami) (02) 813
Uses of Enchantment, The (Bettelheim) (77) 876
Wild Boy of Aveyron, The (Lane) (77) 910
Wing of Madness, The (Burston) (97) 885
Woman's Inhumanity to Woman (Chesler) (03) 898
World of My Own, A (Greene) (95) 890

RELIGION. See PHILOSOPHY and RELIGION

SCIENCE, HISTORY OF SCIENCE, TECHNOLOGY, and MEDICINE

Acts of Meaning (Bruner) (91) 1
Alfred Russel Wallace (Raby) (02) 30
Anthropologist on Mars, An (Sacks) (96) 47
Ants, The (Hölldobler and Wilson) (91) 47
Ape and the Sushi Master, The (de Waal) (02) 48

Are We Unique? (Trefil) (98) 76
Assembling California (McPhee) (94) 57
At the End of an Age (Lukacs) (03) 37
At the Water's Edge (Zimmer) (99) 69
Atom (Krauss) (02) 57
Atoms of Silence (Reeves) (H-85) 39
Beak of the Finch, The (Weiner) (95) 65
Beginnings of Western Science, The (Lindberg) (93) 71
Better than Well (Elliott) (04) 79
Biotech Century, The (Rifkin) (99) 100
Black Holes and Baby Universes and Other Essays (Hawking) (94) 94
Blank Slate, The (Pinker) (03) 79
Botany of Desire, The (Pollan) (02) 125
Brain for All Seasons, A (Calvin) (03) 102
Brief History of Time, A (Hawking) (89) 121
Bright Earth (Ball) (03) 110
Broca's Brain (Sagan) (80) 116
Bully for Brontosaurus (Gould) (92) 69
Camping with the Prince and Other Tales of Science in Africa (Bass) (91) 119
Carl Sagan (Davidson) (00) 121
Chaos (Gleick) (88) 132
Charles Darwin (Bowlby) (92) 83
Charles Darwin, Power of Place, The (Browne) (03) 142
Charles Darwin, Voyaging (Browne) (96) 90
Chimpanzees of Gombe (Goodall) (87) 116
City of Bits (Mitchell) (96) 112
Clone (Kolata) (99) 186
Coal (Freese) (04) 126
Coming of Age in the Milky Way (Ferris) (89) 199
Complexity (Lewin) (93) 188
Consciousness Explained (Dennett) (92) 119
Consilience (Wilson) (99) 216
Control of Nature, The (McPhee) (90) 137
Cosmic Dawn (Chaisson) (82) 130
Cosmic Discovery (Harwit) (82) 135
Creation of Psychopharmacology, The (Healy) (03) 172
Darkness at Night (Harrison) (88) 233
Darwin (Desmond and Moore) (93) 196
Darwin's Dangerous Idea (Dennett) (96) 148
Deadly Feasts (Rhodes) (98) 230
Deeper (Seabrook) (98) 235
Devices and Desires (Tone) (02) 199
Dinosaur in a Haystack (Gould) (97) 219
Discovering (Root-Bernstein) (90) 186
Diversity of Life, The (Wilson) (93) 235
Dominion (Eldredge) (96) 198
DNA (Watson and Berry) (04) 179
Driving Mr. Albert (Paterniti) (01) 258
Eighth Day of Creation, The (Judson) (80) 273
Einstein, Picasso (Miller) (02) 235
Einstein's Clocks, Poincaré's Maps (Galison) (04) 211
Elegant Universe, The (Greene) (00) 208
Elephant Destiny (Meredith) (04) 215
Emperor of Scent, The (Burr) (04) 224
Emperor's New Mind, The (Penrose) (90) 207
Enchanted Loom, The (Corsi, ed.) (92) 183
End of Nature, The (McKibben) (90) 211
End of Science, The (Horgan) (97) 243
End of Time, The (Barbour) (01) 281
Engine of Reason, the Seat of the Soul, The (Churchland) (96) 232
Enough (McKibben) (04) 236
Evolution's Workshop (Larson) (02) 258
Facing Up (Weinberg) (02) 263
Faith in a Seed (Thoreau) (94) 274
Faster (Gleick) (00) 252
Feeling of What Happens, The (Damasio) (00) 256
Fifth Miracle, The (Davies) (00) 260
First Moderns, The (Everdell) (98) 312
First Stargazers, The (Cornell) (82) 280

Flesh and Machines (Brooks) (03) 302
Flow (Csikszentmihalyi) (91) 299
Flu (Kolata) (00) 268
Fluid Concepts and Creative Analogies (Hofstadter) (96) 277
Food Politics (Nestle) (03) 311
For the Time Being (Dillard) (00) 282
Force of Nature (Hager) (96) 286
Forgetting, The (Shenk) (02) 300
Founding Fish, The (McPhee) (03) 316
Full House (Gould) (97) 323
Geeks (Katz) (01) 323
Genes, Peoples, and Languages (Cavalli-Sforza) (01) 327
Genius (Gleick) (93) 308
Genome (Ridley) (01) 332
Gödel (Casti and DePauli) (01) 346
Good Natured (De Waal) (97) 350
Gracefully Insane (Beam) (03) 343
Great and Desperate Cures (Valenstein) (87) 357
Great Deep, The (Hamilton-Paterson) (93) 312
Greatest Power on Earth, The (Clark) (82) 343
Heisenberg's War (Powers) (94) 380
Hen's Teeth and Horse's Toes (Gould) (H-84) 190
Higher Superstition (Gross and Levitt) (95) 301
Hippocrates (Jouanna) (00) 381
History of Statistics, The (Stigler) (87) 397
Hot Zone, The (Preston) (95) 319
How the Cows Turned Mad (Schwartz) (04) 343
How We Die (Nuland) (95) 324
I Have Landed (Gould) (03) 384
Illusion of Technique, The (Barrett) (80) 409
In Darwin's Shadow (Shermer) (03) 400
In Search of Human Nature (Degler) (92) 338
In Search of Nature (Wilson) (97) 428
In Suspect Terrain (McPhee) (H-84) 218
In the Age of the Smart Machine (Zuboff) (89) 377
In the Beginning . . . (Asimov) (82) 386
In the Palaces of Memory (Johnson) (92) 342
Infinite in All Directions (Dyson) (89) 381
Information Ages (Hobart and Schiffman) (99) 414
Innumeracy (Paulos) (90) 420
Invention of Memory, The (Rosenfield) (89) 400
Isaac Newton (Gleick) (04) 369
Island of the Colorblind and Cycad Island, The (Sacks) (98) 454
Journey into Space (Murray) (90) 464
Kasparov Versus Deep Blue (Newborn) (98) 482
Krakatoa (Winchester) (04) 430
Language Instinct, The (Pinker) (95) 431
Launching of Modern American Science, The (Bruce) (88) 452
Le Ton Beau de Marot (Hofstadter) (98) 495
Leonardo da Vinci (Kemp and Roberts, with Steadman) (90) 505
Life It Brings, The (Bernstein) (88) 477
Life Itself (Crick) (82) 462
Lifelines (Rose) (98) 508
Life's Matrix (Ball) (01) 536
Lise Meitner (Sime) (97) 526
Living with Our Genes (Hamer and Copeland) (99) 483
Lucy (Johanson and Edey) (82) 514
Making of the Atomic Bomb, The (Rhodes) (88) 517
Map That Changed the World, The (Winchester) (02) 503
Mars (Sheehan and O'Meara) (02) 511
Mars Beckons (Wilford) (91) 568
Maverick and His Machine, The (Maney) (04) 501
Measure of Reality, The (Crosby) (98) 555
Medicine, Mind, and the Double Brain (Harrington) (88) 539
Microcosm (Gilder) (90) 568

Mind and Nature (Bateson) (80) 536
Mismeasure of Man, The (Gould) (82) 527
Models of My Life (Simon) (92) 519
Monk in the Garden, The (Henig) (01) 588
Moral Animal, The (Wright) (95) 504
My Own Country (Verghese) (95) 515
Mysteries Within, The (Nuland) (01) 609
Naturalist (Wilson) (95) 528
Nature of Order, The (Alexander) (04) 537
Nature of the Book, The (Johns) (99) 547
Nature via Nurture (Ridley) (04) 541
Nazi War on Cancer, The (Proctor) (00) 562
New New Thing, The (Lewis) (00) 571
Newton's Gift (Berlinski) (01) 637
Next (Lewis) (02) 576
Niels Bohr's Times (Pais) (92) 569
Noonday Demon, The (Solomon) (02) 596
Not in Our Genes (Lewontin, Rose, and Kamin) (H-85) 329
Nothing That Is, The (Kaplan) (00) 585
Number Sense, The (Dehaene) (98) 603
Old Man's Toy, An (Zee) (90) 628
Origins of Virtue, The (Ridley) (98) 616
Pencil, The (Petroski) (91) 656
Promethean Fire (Lumsden and Wilson) (H-84) 366
Quantum Philosophy (Omnès) (00) 638
Questioning the Millennium (Gould) (98) 652
Rainbows, Snowflakes, and Quarks (von Baeyer) (H-85) 379
Reason for Hope (Goodall with Berman) (00) 643
Rediscovery of the Mind, The (Searle) (93) 673
Rewriting the Soul (Hacking) (96) 637
Robot (Moravec) (99) 670
Rocks of Ages (Gould) (00) 656
Saving the Heart (Klaidman) (01) 754
Scientists Under Hitler (Beyerchen) (78) 743
Searching for Memory (Schacter) (97) 727
Seeing in the Dark (Ferris) (03) 723
Shadows of the Mind (Penrose) (95) 705
Small Wonder (Kingsolver) (03) 779
Society of Mind, The (Minsky) (88) 828
Soul of a New Machine, The (Kidder) (82) 787
Spirit Catches You and You Fall Down, The (Fadiman) (98) 722
Statue Within, The (Jacob) (89) 813
Stephen Hawking (White and Gribbin) (93) 758
Structure of Evolutionary Theory, The (Gould) (03) 815
Sync (Strogatz) (04) 723
Theremin (Glinsky) (01) 815
Thomas Jefferson (Bedini) (91) 809
Thomas Kuhn (Fuller) (01) 820
Time, Love, Memory (Weiner) (00) 754
Time's Arrow, Time's Cycle (Gould) (88) 902
Toward a More Natural Science (Kass) (86) 892
Trapped in the Net (Rochlin) (98) 773
Triple Helix, The (Lewontin) (01) 845
Trouble with Computers, The (Landauer) (96) 773
Tuxedo Park (Conant) (03) 848
2081 (O'Neill) (82) 860
Tycho and Kepler (Ferguson) (04) 782
Uncertainty (Cassidy) (93) 824
Undiscovered Mind, The (Horgan) (00) 780
Unexpected Vista, The (Trefil) (H-84) 462
Universe in a Nutshell, The (Hawking) (02) 818
Unsettling of America, The (Berry) (79) 795
Victorian Sensation (Secord) (02) 822
White Death, The (Dormandy) (01) 905
Whole Shebang, The (Ferris) (98) 846
Winston Churchill's Afternoon Nap (Campbell) (88) 964
Winter World (Heinrich) (04) 843
Wisdom of the Body, The (Nuland) (98) 854

CATEGORY INDEX

Women, Fire, and Dangerous Things (Lakoff) (88) 979
Wonderful Life (Gould) (90) 916
X in Sex, The (Bainbridge) (04) 855

SOCIOLOGY, ARCHAEOLOGY, and
 ANTHROPOLOGY
Against Race (Gilroy) (01) 10
Anahulu (Kirch and Sahlins) (93) 20
Another Country (Pipher) (00) 36
Anxious Parents (Stearns) (04) 35
At the Water's Edge (Zimmer) (99) 69
Aztecs (Clendinnen) (92) 30
Blank Slate, The (Pinker) (03) 79
Bobos in Paradise (Brooks) (01) 112
Bowling Alone (Putnam) (01) 139
Brain for All Seasons, A (Calvin) (03) 102
Broken Cord, The (Dorris) (90) 76
Brown (Rodriguez) (03) 114
Catholic Imagination, The (Greeley) (01) 176
Cold New World (Finnegan) (99) 200
Counterpoints (Needham) (88) 209
Cries Unheard (Sereny) (00) 151
Crime and Punishment in American History (Friedman)
 (94) 173
Cultural Contradictions of Capitalism, The (Bell)
 (77) 184
Cultural Materialism (Harris) (80) 170
Culture of Narcissism, The (Lasch) (80) 175
Death Without Weeping (Scheper-Hughes) (93) 209
Decisions in Crisis (Brecher and Geist) (81) 228
Destroying the World to Save It (Lifton) (00) 172
Divorce Culture, The (Whitehead) (98) 254
Dream Endures, The (Starr) (98) 268
Enough (McKibben) (04) 236
Essays on Music (Adorno) (03) 269
Exemplars (Needham) (86) 259
Fast Food Nation (Schlosser) (02) 280
Faster (Gleick) (00) 252
Fatherless America (Blankenhorn) (96) 258
FBI (Ungar) (77) 287
Forest of Kings, A (Schele and Freidel) (91) 308
From Dawn to Decadence (Barzun) (01) 314
Geeks (Katz) (01) 323
Geography of Thought, The (Nisbett) (04) 287
Geometry of Love, The (Visser) (02) 330
Gift, The (Hyde) (84) 330
Gilligan Unbound (Cantor) (02) 338
Going Up the River (Hallinan) (02) 352
Great Disruption, The (Fukuyama) (00) 331
Home Town (Kidder) (00) 409
Hometown (Davis) (83) 344
How "Natives" Think (Sahlins) (96) 338
Hunting Hypothesis, The (Ardrey) (77) 367
Intellectual Life of the British Working Classes, The
 (Rose) (02) 418
Lost Children of Wilder, The (Bernstein) (02) 491
Miles to Go (Moynihan) (97) 581
Mind of Egypt, The (Assmann) (03) 531
Moral Freedom (Wolfe) (02) 541
Mother Nature (Hrdy) (00) 538
Mullahs on the Mainframe (Blank) (02) 550
Nazi Psychoanalysis (Rickels) (03) 559
New Buddhism, The (Coleman) (02) 571
New White Nationalism in America, The (Swain)
 (03) 572
Newjack (Conover) (01) 632
Nisa (Shostak) (82) 559
Nonzero (Wright) (01) 646
Of Woman Born (Rich) (77) 584
Old Friends (Kidder) (94) 572
On Human Nature (Wilson) (79) 506
One Nation, After All (Wolfe) (99) 593
Other Side of the River, The (Kotlowitz) (99) 606

Overspent American, The (Schor) (99) 610
People of the Lake (Leakey and Lewin) (79) 535
Prehistoric Avebury (Burl) (80) 688
Price of Citizenship, The (Katz) (02) 655
Primetime Blues (Bogle) (02) 664
Publics and Counterpublics (Warner) (03) 634
Purified by Fire (Prothero) (02) 674
Respect in a World of Inequality (Sennett) (04) 652
Risk and Blame (Douglas) (93) 687
St. Clair (Wallace) (88) 790
Scapegoat, The (Girard) (87) 744
Seven Day Circle, The (Zerubavel) (86) 807
Sex and Social Justice (Nussbaum) (00) 697
Slim's Table (Duneier) (93) 744
Snobbery (Epstein) (03) 784
Sociology as an Art Form (Nisbet) (77) 753
Spirit Catches You and You Fall Down, The (Fadiman)
 (98) 722
Them (Ronson) (03) 829
There Are No Children Here (Kotlowitz) (92) 813
Thomas Kuhn (Fuller) (01) 820
Tipping Point, The (Gladwell) (01) 835
Trickster Makes This World (Hyde) (99) 787
Truly Disadvantaged, The (Wilson) (88) 910
Victorian Anthropology (Stocking) (88) 928
Viking World, The (Graham-Campbell) (81) 873
Villages (Critchfield) (82) 879
Walking on Water (Kenan) (00) 813
Walking the Bible (Feiler) (02) 826
Watermelon Wine (Gaillard) (79) 835
When Work Disappears (Wilson) (97) 880
Why They Kill (Rhodes) (00) 843
Woman (Angier) (00) 851
Woman's Inhumanity to Woman (Chesler) (03) 898
Women of the Shadows (Cornelisen) (77) 937
Zora Neale Hurston, Vol. I and Vol. II (Hurston)
 (96) 852
Zuñi and the American Imagination (McFeely)
 (02) 898

TECHNOLOGY. See SCIENCE, HISTORY OF
 SCIENCE, TECHNOLOGY, and MEDICINE

TRAVEL
Atlantic High (Buckley) (83) 29
Bad Land (Raban) (97) 91
Barcelona (Hughes) (93) 49
Beyond Belief (Naipaul) (99) 96
Bird of Life, Bird of Death (Maslow) (87) 66
Blue Highways (Heat-Moon) (84) 95
Byzantine Journey, A (Ash) (96) 86
Cairo (Raymond) (02) 135
Cairo (Rodenbeck) (00) 117
Dark Star Safari (Theroux) (04) 160
Driving Mr. Albert (Paterniti) (01) 258
Eight Men and a Duck (Thorpe) (03) 246
Elsewhere Community, The (Kenner) (01) 272
Empire Wilderness, An (Kaplan) (99) 247
Ends of the Earth, The (Kaplan) (97) 252
Europe, Europe (Enzensberger) (00) 227
Finding the Center (Naipaul) (85) 281
Flotsam and Jetsam (Higgins) (03) 307
Great Deep, The (Hamilton-Paterson) (93) 312
Great Plains (Frazier) (90) 334
Hunting Mister Heartbreak (Raban) (92) 314
India (Naipaul) (92) 346
Italian Days (Harrison) (90) 441
Little Saint (Green) (01) 540
Looking for a Ship (McPhee) (91) 540
Mind of the Traveler, The (Leed) (92) 505
My Father's Island (Angermeyer) (91) 614
Old Glory (Raban) (82) 580
Old Patagonian Express, The (Theroux) (80) 619

PrairyErth (Heat-Moon) (92) 632
Russian Journal (Lee) (82) 713
Sheba (Clapp) (02) 747
Sicilian Carousel (Durrell) (78) 771
Songlines, The (Chatwin) (88) 840
To Jerusalem and Back (Bellow) (77) 828
Turn in the South, A (Naipaul) (90) 831
Ultimate Journey (Bernstein) (02) 808
Walking the Bible (Feiler) (02) 826

WOMEN'S ISSUES
Accidental Autobiography, An (Harrison) (97) 1
Annie Besant (Taylor) (93) 23
Art and Affection (Reid) (97) 66
Autobiography of a Face (Grealy) (95) 56
Birth-mark, The (Howe) (94) 90
Change, The (Greer) (93) 148
Creation of Feminist Consciousness, The (Lerner)
    (94) 168
Eleanor Roosevelt, 1884-1933 (Cook) (93) 253
Essays in Feminism (Gornick) (80) 302
Feminism Without Illusions (Fox-Genovese) (92) 205
First Woman in the Republic, The (Karcher) (96) 273
From the Beast to the Blonde (Warner) (96) 290
Good Boys and Dead Girls (Gordon) (92) 256
His Other Half (Lesser) (92) 285
History of the Breast, A (Yalom) (98) 391
History of Women in the West, From Ancient
    Goddesses to Christian Saints, A (Pantel, ed.)
    (93) 345
How to Suppress Women's Writing (Russ) (84) 353
Inventing Herself (Showalter) (02) 423
Life So Far (Friedan) (01) 532
Lise Meitner (Sime) (97) 526
Meeting at the Crossroads (Brown and Gilligan)
    (93) 500
Mosquito and Ant (Hahn) (00) 533

No Man's Land, Letters from the Front (Gilbert and
    Gubar) (95) 549
No Man's Land, Sexchanges (Gilbert and Gubar)
    (90) 614
No Man's Land, The War of the Words (Gilbert and
    Gubar) (89) 600
Not for Ourselves Alone (Ward and Burns) (00) 580
Notes of a White Black Woman (Scales-Trent) (96) 514
Obstacle Race, The (Greer) (80) 600
Of Woman Born (Rich) (77) 584
On Gold Mountain (See) (96) 523
Ordinary Time (Mairs) (94) 594
Other Powers (Goldsmith) (99) 601
Passion of Emily Dickinson, The (Farr) (93) 610
Pearl S. Buck (Conn) (97) 661
Possessing the Secret of Joy (Walker) (93) 651
Protecting Soldiers and Mothers (Skocpol) (94) 671
Publics and Counterpublics (Warner) (03) 634
Reasonable Creatures (Pollitt) (95) 626
Rebecca West (Rollyson) (97) 684
Sex and Destiny (Greer) (H-85) 406
Sex and Social Justice (Nussbaum) (00) 697
Small Wonder (Kingsolver) (03) 779
Sojourner Truth (Painter) (97) 772
'Tis (McCourt) (00) 759
Unafraid of the Dark (Bray) (99) 812
Victorian Feminists (Caine) (93) 851
Voice Lessons (Mairs) (95) 835
Whole Woman, The (Greer) (00) 834
Woman (Angier) (00) 851
Woman's Inhumanity to Woman (Chesler) (03) 898
Women and the Common Life (Lasch) (98) 878
Women on Love (Sullerot) (81) 947
Women on the Margins (Davis) (96) 826
Women, Reason and Nature (McMillan) (84) 964
Writing Women in Jacobean England (Lewalski)
    (94) 869

TITLE INDEX

1977-2004

"A" (Zukofsky) (80) 1
a long the riverrun (Ellmann) (90) 1
Aaron Burr, 1756-1805 (Lomask) (80) 6
Aaron Burr, 1805-1836 (Lomask) (H-83) 1
Abandonment of the Jews, The (Wyman) (H-85) 1
Abba Eban (Eban) (78) 1
Aberration of Starlight (Sorrentino) (81) 1
About a Boy (Hornby) (99) 1
About My Table (Delbanco) (84) 1
About Town (Yagoda) (01) 1
Above the Battle (Leonard) (79) 1
Abraham Lincoln (Anderson) (H-83) 5
Abraham Lincoln and the Second American Revolution
  (McPherson) (92) 1
Abroad (Fussell) (81) 5
Absolute Truths (Howatch) (96) 1
Abyss, The (Yourcenar) (77) 1
Academic Question, An (Pym) (87) 1
Accident, The (Plante) (92) 5
Accident (Wolf) (90) 6
Accidental Asian, The (Liu) (99) 5
Accidental Autobiography, An (Harrison) (97) 1
Accidental Theorist, The (Krugman) (99) 10
Accidental Tourist, The (Tyler) (86) 1
According to Queeney (Bainbridge) (02) 1
Accordion Crimes (Proulx) (97) 5
Accounting for Genocide (Fein) (80) 10
Achievement of Cormac McCarthy, The (Bell) (89) 1
Achilles (Cook) (03) 1
Achilles in Vietnam (Shay) (95) 1
Across (Handke) (87) 6
Across the Bridge (Gallant) (94) 1
Active Faith (Reed) (97) 9
Acts of King Arthur and His Noble Knights, The
  (Steinbeck) (77) 7
Acts of Meaning (Bruner) (91) 1
Acts of Worship (Mishima) (90) 10
Actual, The (Bellow) (98) 1
Actual Minds, Possible Worlds (Bruner) (87) 11
Adam, Eve, and the Serpent (Pagels) (89) 4
Adam's Curse (Donoghue) (02) 5
Adieux (de Beauvoir) (85) 1
Adlai Stevenson and the World (Martin) (78) 6
Adlai Stevenson of Illinois (Martin) (77) 12
Adolf Hitler (Toland) (77) 17
Advantage of Lyric, The (Hardy) (78) 11
Adventures in Ancient Egypt (Goldbarth) (98) 5
Adventures of Conan Doyle, The (Higham) (77) 22
Adventures of Huckleberry Finn (Twain) (02) 9
Adversary, The (Carrère) (02) 14
Advisors, The (York) (77) 27
Aeschylus' Oresteia (Conacher) (88) 1
Aesthetics, Method, and Epistemology (Foucault)
  (99) 15
Affair, The (Bredin) (87) 15
Afghanistan and the Soviet Union (Bradsher) (H-84) 1
Africa (Reader) (99) 19
Africa Explored (Hibbert) (H-84) 6
After Hannibal (Unsworth) (98) 9
After Henry (Didion) (93) 1
After Rain (Trevor) (97) 14
After the Fact (Davidson and Lytle) (H-83) 10
After the Lost War (Hudgins) (89) 9
After the Plague (Boyle) (02) 18
After the Quake (Murakami) (03) 5

After the War (Adams) (01) 6
Afterlife, The (Fitzgerald) (04) 1
Afterlife, The (Levis) (78) 17
Afterlife and Other Stories, The (Updike) (95) 6
Afternoon of a Writer, The (Handke) (90) 14
Against Race (Gilroy) (01) 10
Against the Current (Berlin) (81) 9
Against the Evidence (Ignatow) (95) 10
Age of Empire, The (Hobsbawm) (89) 14
Age of Federalism, The (Elkins and McKitrick) (94) 5
Age of Grief, The (Smiley) (88) 6
Age of Homespun, The (Ulrich) (02) 22
Age of Iron (Coetzee) (91) 5
Age of Napoleon, The (Durant and Durant) (77) 33
Age of Surveillance, The (Donner) (81) 16
Age of Uncertainty, The (Galbraith) (78) 23
Age of Wonders, The (Appelfeld) (82) 1
Agon (Bloom) (83) 1
Agüero Sisters, The (García) (98) 14
Ah, But Your Land Is Beautiful (Paton) (83) 6
Aiding and Abetting (Spark) (02) 26
AIDS and Its Metaphors (Sontag) (90) 19
Aimé Césaire, the Collected Poetry (Césaire) (84) 5
Air and Fire (Thomson) (95) 15
Airships (Hannah) (79) 5
Aké (Soyinka) (83) 10
Akhmatova Journals, 1938-41, The (Chukovskaya)
  (95) 19
Alabanza (Espada) (04) 5
Alabi's World (Price) (91) 10
Aladdin's Problem (Jünger) (93) 6
Alan Paton (Alexander) (95) 23
Alanbrooke (Fraser) (H-83) 14
Albert Camus (Lottman) (80) 15
Albert Camus (Todd) (98) 18
Albert Einstein (Einstein) (80) 19
Albert Speer (Sereny) (96) 5
Albion (Ackroyd) (04) 9
Albion's Seed (Fischer) (90) 24
Aldous Huxley (Murray) (04) 13
Aleksander Wat (Venclova) (97) 18
Alexander Hamilton (McDonald) (80) 23
Alexander Hamilton, American (Brookhiser) (00) 1
Alexander Pope (Mack) (87) 20
Alexander Solzhenitsyn (Thomas) (99) 24
Alexander to Actium (Green) (91) 15
Alfred Hugenberg (Leopold) (78) 28
Alfred North Whitehead, 1861-1910 (Lowe) (86) 5
Alfred North Whitehead, 1910-1947 (Lowe) (91) 20
Alfred Russel Wallace (Raby) (02) 30
Alger Hiss (Smith) (77) 38
Algernon Blackwood (Ashley) (03) 10
Alias Grace (Atwood) (97) 23
Alice Hamilton (Sicherman) (H-85) 6
Alice in Bed (Schine) (84) 12
Alice James (Strouse) (81) 21
Alien Nation (Brimelow) (96) 9
All-American Skin Game, The (Crouch) (96) 14
All-Bright Court (Porter) (92) 9
All Day Permanent Red (Logue) (04) 17
All Fall Down (Sick) (86) 10
All God's Children Need Traveling Shoes (Angelou)
  (87) 25
All of Us (Carver) (99) 28
All of Us Here (Feldman) (87) 29

All Rivers Run to the Sea (Wiesel) (96) 18
All Souls' Rising (Bell) (96) 22
All Stalin's Men (Medvedev) (H-85) 12
All That Is Solid Melts into Air (Berman) (83) 15
All the Days and Nights (Maxwell) (96) 26
All the Names (Saramago) (01) 15
All the Pretty Horses (McCarthy) (93) 10
All the Years of American Popular Music (Ewen) (78) 33
All Tomorrow's Parties (Gibson) (00) 6
All-True Travels and Adventures of Lidie Newton, The (Smiley) (99) 32
Allies (Eisenhower) (H-83) 20
Allies of a Kind (Thorne) (79) 9
Alluring Problem, The (Enright) (88) 11
Alma (Burn) (93) 15
Almanac of the Dead (Silko) (92) 13
Almost Innocent (Bosworth) (85) 7
Almost There (O'Faolain) (04) 22
Alnilam (Dickey) (88) 15
Along with Youth (Griffin) (86) 16
Already Dead (Johnson) (98) 23
Altered States (Brookner) (98) 27
Always Coming Home (Le Guin) (86) 21
Always in Pursuit (Crouch) (99) 36
Always Straight Ahead (Neuman) (94) 11
Amadeus (Shaffer) (81) 27
Amateur, The (Lesser) (00) 10
Amateurs (Barthelme) (78) 37
Amateur's Guide to the Night, An (Robison) (84) 16
Amazing Adventures of Kavalier and Clay, The (Chabon) (01) 19
Amazing Grace (Kozol) (96) 30
Amazing Grace (Norris) (99) 40
Ambiguous Iroquois Empire, The (Jennings) (H-85) 18
Ambling into History (Bruni) (03) 14
Amen (Amichai) (78) 42
Amending America (Bernstein and Agel) (94) 15
Amerasia Spy Case, The (Klehr and Radosh) (97) 28
America and the Survivors of the Holocaust (Dinnerstein) (H-83) 25
America in Black and White (Thernstrom and Thernstrom) (98) 31
America in Search of Itself (White) (H-83) 29
America in the Twenties (Perrett) (H-83) 33
America in Vietnam (Lewy) (79) 14
America Inside Out (Schoenbrun) (H-85) 22
American Ambassador, The (Just) (88) 20
American Appetites (Oates) (90) 29
American Assassins (Clarke) (H-83) 37
American Babel (Shell, ed.) (03) 19
American Buffalo (Mamet) (78) 46
American Caesar (Manchester) (79) 20
American Catholic (Morris) (98) 36
American Chica (Arana) (02) 35
American Childhood, An (Dillard) (88) 25
American Dream, The (Cullen) (04) 26
American Dream Global Nightmare (Vogelgesang) (81) 31
American Dreamer (Culver and Hyde) (01) 24
American Establishment, The (Silk and Silk) (81) 36
American Exceptionalism (Lipset) (97) 33
American Falls (Batchelor) (86) 27
American Fictions, 1940-1980 (Karl) (84) 21
American Historical Romance, The (Dekker) (88) 31
American Inquisition, The (Kutler) (H-83) 41
American Jihad (Emerson) (03) 23
American Journey (Reeves) (H-83) 46
American Kaleidoscope, The (Fuchs) (92) 17
American Life, An (Reagan) (91) 24
American Magic, The (Lewin) (H-83) 52
American Moderns (Stansell) (01) 29
American Myth, American Reality (Robertson) (81) 39
American Owned Love (Boswell) (98) 41

American Pastoral (Roth) (98) 45
American Pharaoh (Cohen and Taylor) (01) 34
American Poetry (Bly) (91) 29
American Presidency, The (McDonald) (95) 28
American Procession, An (Kazin) (85) 12
American Requiem, An (Carroll) (97) 38
American Scoundrel (Keneally) (03) 28
American Scripture (Maier) (98) 50
American Sphinx (Ellis) (98) 55
American Style of Foreign Policy, The (Dallek) (H-84) 11
American Tragedy (Kaiser) (01) 39
American Visions (Hughes) (98) 59
American Way of Death Revisited, The (Mitford) (99) 44
Americans at War (Ambrose) (98) 64
America's Quest for the Ideal Self (Clecak) (H-84) 16
Among Schoolchildren (Kidder) (90) 34
Among the Believers (Naipaul) (82) 6
Amongst Women (McGahern) (91) 33
Amsterdam (McEwan) (00) 14
Amy and Isabelle (Strout) (00) 18
Anahulu (Kirch and Sahlins) (93) 20
Anaïs (Fitch) (94) 20
Anaïs Nin (Bair) (96) 34
Anarchists' Convention, The (Sayles) (80) 28
Anatomy Lesson, The (Roth) (84) 26
Anatomy of a Rose (Russell) (02) 39
Anatomy of Power, The (Galbraith) (H-84) 21
Ancestors (Ching) (89) 19
Ancient Evenings (Mailer) (84) 31
Ancient Slavery and Modern Ideology (Finley) (81) 43
—And I Worked at the Writer's Trade (Cowley) (79) 24
And Never Said a Word (Böll) (79) 29
And the Band Played On (Shilts) (88) 36
And the Sea Is Never Full (Wiesel) (00) 22
And the Walls Came Tumbling Down (Abernathy) (90) 39
André Malraux (Lacouture) (77) 43
Andrew Jackson and His Indian Wars (Remini) (02) 43
Andrew Jackson and the Course of American Democracy, 1833-1845 (Remini) (H-85) 28
Andrew Jackson and the Course of American Empire, 1767-1821 (Remini) (78) 50
Andrew Jackson and the Course of American Freedom, 1822-1832 (Remini) (82) 11
Angel of History, The (Forché) (95) 33
Angel of Light (Oates) (82) 17
Angela's Ashes (McCourt) (97) 43
Angels and Insects (Byatt) (94) 25
Angle of Ascent (Hayden) (77) 48
Anglomania (Buruma) (00) 27
Angus Wilson (Drabble) (97) 48
Anil's Ghost (Ondaatje) (01) 44
Animal Dreams (Kingsolver) (91) 38
Anna Akhmatova (Reeder) (95) 38
Anna Freud (Young-Bruehl) (89) 23
Anne Sexton (Middlebrook) (92) 21
Anne Sexton (Sexton) (78) 54
Annie Besant (Taylor) (93) 23
Annie John (Kincaid) (86) 33
Anniversary and Other Stories, The (Auchincloss) (00) 31
Annunciation (Plante) (95) 42
Annunciations (Tomlinson) (91) 43
Another Country (Pipher) (00) 36
Another I, Another You (Schickel) (79) 34
Another Part of the Fifties (Carter) (H-84) 24
Another World (Barker) (00) 40
Another World, 1897-1917 (Eden) (78) 59
Another You (Beattie) (96) 39
Anpao (Highwater) (78) 63

TITLE INDEX

Answer to History (Mohammad Reza Pahlavi) (81) 47
Antarctic Navigation (Arthur) (96) 43
Antarctic Traveller (Pollitt) (83) 20
Antarctica (Robinson) (99) 48
Antelope Wife, The (Erdrich) (99) 53
Anthills of the Savannah (Achebe) (89) 28
Anthology of Chinese Literature, An (Owen, ed.) (97) 53
Anthony Trollope (Glendinning) (94) 29
Anthropologist on Mars, An (Sacks) (96) 47
Antigones (Steiner) (85) 17
Anti-Semitic Moment, The (Birnbaum) (04) 30
Anton Chekhov (Rayfield) (99) 57
Antonin Artaud (Artaud) (77) 52
Antonin Artaud (Esslin) (78) 68
Ants, The (Hölldobler and Wilson) (91) 47
Ants on the Melon (Adair) (97) 57
Anxious Parents (Stearns) (04) 35
Any Body's Song (Langland) (81) 53
Any Human Heart (Boyd) (04) 40
Any Old Iron (Burgess) (90) 44
Anything for Billy (McMurtry) (89) 33
Anything Your Little Heart Desires (Bosworth) (98) 68
Anywhere but Here (Simpson) (88) 42
Ape and the Sushi Master, The (de Waal) (02) 48
Apocalypses (Weber) (00) 44
Appalachia (Wright) (99) 61
Approaching Fury, The (Oates) (98) 72
Appropriating Shakespeare (Vickers) (94) 33
Arab and Jew (Shipler) (87) 35
Arab Reach (Levins) (H-84) 28
Arabesques (Shammas) (89) 37
Arabian Jazz (Abu-Jaber) (94) 38
Arabists, The (Kaplan) (94) 42
Arabs, Israelis, and Kissinger, The (Sheehan) (77) 57
Ararat (Glück) (91) 51
Ararat (Thomas) (84) 36
Arc d'X (Erickson) (94) 47
Archaeology and Language (Renfrew) (89) 41
Archduke of Sarajevo (Brook-Shepherd) (H-85) 33
Archer in the Marrow (Viereck) (88) 46
Arches & Light (Cowart) (84) 40
Archibald MacLeish (Donaldson) (93) 28
Arctic Dreams (Lopez) (87) 40
Are We Unique? (Trefil) (98) 76
Argot Merchant Disaster, The (Starbuck) (83) 25
Argufying (Empson) (89) 46
Ariadne's Thread (Miller) (93) 32
Ark (Johnson) (97) 62
Ark Baby (Jensen) (99) 64
Arkansas Testament, The (Walcott) (88) 52
Armada (Padfield) (89) 50
Armed Truce (Thomas) (88) 57
Arming America (Bellesiles) (01) 49
Arna Bontemps-Langston Hughes Letters, 1925-1927 (Bontemps and Hughes) (81) 57
Around the Cragged Hill (Kennan) (94) 52
Around the Day in Eighty Worlds (Cortázar) (87) 45
Arrest Sitting Bull (Jones) (78) 72
Arrivals and Departures (Rovere) (77) 62
Arrogance and Anxiety (Farrar) (82) 22
Art and Act (Gay) (77) 67
Art and Affection (Reid) (97) 66
Art & Ardor (Ozick) (84) 44
Art in the Light of Conscience (Tsvetaeva) (93) 36
Art of Arts, The (Albus) (01) 54
Art of Biblical Poetry, The (Alter) (86) 38
Art of Burning Bridges, The (Wolff) (04) 45
Art of Excess, The (LeClair) (90) 49
Art of Fiction, The (Gardner) (85) 22
Art of Shakespeare's Sonnets, The (Vendler) (98) 80
Art of Telling, The (Kermode) (84) 49
Art of the Commonplace, The (Berry) (03) 33

Art of the Novel, The (Kundera) (89) 54
Art of the Personal Essay, The (Lopate, ed.) (95) 47
Art of Warfare in the Age of Napoleon, The (Rothenberg) (79) 38
Articulation of Sound Forms in Time (Howe) (88) 63
Artificial Wilderness, An (Birkerts) (88) 68
Arts of the Possible (Rich) (02) 53
As I Saw It (Rusk) (91) 56
As Max Saw It (Begley) (95) 51
As She Climbed Across the Table (Lethem) (98) 85
As Thousands Cheer (Bergreen) (91) 61
As We Know (Ashbery) (80) 31
Ashes (Levine) (80) 35
Asking for Trouble (Woods) (82) 28
Aspects of the Present (Mead and Metraux) (81) 62
Assassination of Jesse James by the Coward Robert Ford, The (Hansen) (84) 54
Assault on Mount Helicon (Barnard) (85) 27
Assembling California (McPhee) (94) 57
Asylum (McGrath) (98) 90
At a Century's Ending (Kennan) (97) 71
At Dawn We Slept (Prange) (82) 33
At Home (Vidal) (89) 59
At the Bottom of the River (Kincaid) (84) 59
At the End of an Age (Lukacs) (03) 37
At the Highest Levels (Beschloss and Talbott) (94) 62
At the Water's Edge (Zimmer) (99) 69
At Weddings and Wakes (McDermott) (93) 40
Athena (Banville) (96) 51
Atlantic High (Buckley) (83) 29
Atlantis (Doty) (96) 55
Atlas, The (Vollmann) (97) 76
Atlas of the Difficult World, Poems 1988-1991, An (Rich) (92) 25
Atom (Krauss) (02) 57
Atoms of Silence (Reeves) (H-85) 39
Atonement (McEwan) (03) 42
Atrocity and Amnesia (Boyers) (86) 43
Attachments (Rossner) (78) 77
Attack and Die (McWhiney and Jamieson) (H-83) 57
Attlee (Harris) (H-84) 33
Auden (Davenport-Hines) (97) 79
August Strindberg (Lagercrantz) (85) 32
Aunt Julia and the Scriptwriter (Vargas Llosa) (83) 34
Austerlitz (Sebald) (02) 62
Autobiography of a Face (Grealy) (95) 56
Autobiography of My Mother, The (Brown) (77) 72
Autobiography of My Mother, The (Kincaid) (97) 83
Autobiography of Red (Carson) (99) 74
Autobiography of Values (Lindbergh) (79) 43
Autograph Man, The (Smith) (03) 46
Autumn (Mojtabai) (83) 39
Autumn of the Patriarch, The (García Márquez) (77) 77
Available Light (Piercy) (89) 63
Avoidance of Literature, The (Sisson) (80) 40
Awash in a Sea of Faith (Butler) (91) 65
Ax, The (Westlake) (98) 95
Axe Handles (Snyder) (84) 65
Aztecs (Clendinnen) (92) 30

Babel Tower (Byatt) (97) 87
Bachelorhood (Lopate) (82) 40
Back Room, The (Martín Gaite) (84) 71
Back When We Were Grownups (Tyler) (02) 66
Bad Blood (Sage) (03) 51
Bad Land (Raban) (97) 91
Bad Lands, The (Hall) (79) 47
Bad Mouth (Adams) (78) 81
Badge of Courage (Davis) (99) 78
Bag of Bones (King) (99) 83
Bakke Case, The (Dreyfuss and Lawrence) (80) 45
Balancing Acts (Hoagland) (93) 45
Balkan Ghosts (Kaplan) (94) 66

Balkan Odyssey (Owen) (97) 95
Balkans, The (Glenny) (01) 59
Ball of Fire (Kanfer) (04) 49
Balzac (Robb) (95) 60
Bandits (Leonard) (88) 71
Banker (Francis) (84) 76
Barbarians and Romans (Randers-Pehrson) (H-84) 39
Barbary Coast, The (Wolf) (80) 49
Barcelona (Hughes) (93) 49
Bargaining for Supremacy (Leutze) (78) 85
Baron of Beacon Hill, The (Fowler) (81) 66
Barracks Thief, The (Wolff) (86) 48
Barry Goldwater (Goldberg) (96) 60
Barthes Reader, A (Barthes) (83) 44
Bartleby in Manhattan (Hardwick) (84) 82
Bashō and His Interpreters (Ueda) (93) 53
Basil Street Blues (Holroyd) (01) 64
Bass Saxophone, The (Škvorecký) (80) 54
Bastard Out of Carolina (Allison) (93) 58
Battle Cry of Freedom (McPherson) (89) 67
Battle for the Falklands, The (Hastings and Jenkins) (H-84) 43
Baudelaire (Pichois) (91) 70
Baudelaire (Richardson) (96) 65
Baudelaire the Damned (Hemmings) (83) 49
Baudolino (Eco) (03) 56
Bay of Angels, The (Brookner) (02) 70
Bay of Pigs (Wyden) (80) 59
Bay of Souls (Stone) (04) 54
Bayou Farewell (Tidwell) (04) 58
Beach Music (Conroy) (96) 69
Beachmasters (Astley) (87) 51
Beak of the Finch, The (Weiner) (95) 65
Bean Trees, The (Kingsolver) (89) 72
Bear and His Daughter (Stone) (98) 99
Beard's Roman Women (Burgess) (77) 81
Bearing the Cross (Garrow) (87) 55
Beautiful Mind, A (Nasar) (99) 87
Beautiful Room Is Empty, The (White) (89) 76
Beautiful Shadow (Wilson) (04) 62
Beauty of Men, The (Holleran) (97) 100
Because It Is Bitter, and Because It Is My Heart (Oates) (91) 75
Because They Wanted To (Gaitskill) (98) 104
Bech at Bay (Updike) (99) 92
Bech Is Back (Updike) (83) 53
Beckett's Dying Words (Ricks) (94) 71
Becoming a Doctor (Konner) (88) 77
Becoming a Man (Monette) (93) 62
Becoming American (Archdeacon) (H-84) 48
Becoming Madame Mao (Min) (01) 69
Bee Season (Goldberg) (01) 74
Been in the Storm So Long (Litwack) (80) 65
Beet Queen, The (Erdrich) (87) 61
Before and After (Brown) (93) 67
Before Sleep (Booth) (81) 71
Before the Dawn (Shimazaki) (88) 81
Before Time Could Change Them (Cavafy) (02) 74
Beggar and the Professor, The (Le Roy Ladurie) (98) 108
Beginning of Wisdom, The (Kass) (04) 66
Beginning with O (Broumas) (78) 91
Beginnings of Western Science, The (Lindberg) (93) 71
Being and Race (Johnson) (89) 80
Being Dead (Crace) (01) 79
Being Here (Warren) (81) 76
Believers (Baxter) (98) 113
Bell Curve, The (Herrnstein and Murray) (95) 70
Bellarosa Connection, The (Bellow) (90) 53
Bellefleur (Oates) (81) 78
Bellow (Atlas) (01) 84
Bells in Winter (Miłosz) (79) 51
Beloved (Morrison) (88) 85

Ben-Gurion, 1886-1948 (Teveth) (88) 90
Ben Jonson (Riggs) (90) 58
Ben Jonson, Dramatist (Barton) (85) 37
Bend in the River, A (Naipaul) (80) 69
Benjamin Britten (Carpenter) (94) 75
Benjamin Franklin (Clark) (H-84) 54
Benjamin Franklin (Isaacson) (04) 70
Benjamin Franklin (Morgan) (03) 61
Beowulf (Anonymous) (01) 89
Berlin Diaries, 1940-1945 (Vassiltchikov) (88) 95
Bernard Berenson (Samuels) (80) 73
Bernard Shaw, 1856-1898 (Holroyd) (89) 89
Bernard Shaw, 1898-1918 (Holroyd) (90) 63
Bernard Shaw, 1918-1950 (Holroyd) (92) 34
Bernard Shaw, 1950-1991 (Holroyd) (94) 80
Bernard Shaw, Collected Letters, 1926-1950 (Shaw) (89) 84
Berryman's Shakespeare (Berryman) (00) 49
Bertolt Brecht Short Stories, 1921-1946 (Brecht) (84) 86
Bertrand Russell, 1872-1921 (Monk) (97) 105
Bertrand Russell, 1921-1970 (Monk) (02) 78
Bertrand Russell (Moorehead) (94) 85
Best Friends (Berger) (04) 75
Best Hour of the Night, The (Simpson) (85) 42
Best of Sholom Aleichem, The (Aleichem) (80) 77
Bet They'll Miss Us When We're Gone (Wiggins) (92) 39
Betrayal (The Boston Globe Investigative Staff) (03) 65
Betsey Brown (Shange) (86) 52
Better Class of Person, A (Osborne) (82) 45
Better than Well (Elliott) (04) 79
Betty Friedan (Hennessee) (00) 53
Between Friends (Arendt and McCarthy) (96) 73
Between the Chains (Cassity) (92) 44
Beyond Belief (Naipaul) (99) 96
Beyond Geography (Turner) (81) 82
Beyond Our Means (Malabre) (88) 101
"Beyond Reasonable Doubt" and "Probable Cause" (Shapiro) (93) 75
Beyond Silence (Hoffman) (04) 83
Beyond the Dragon's Mouth (Naipaul) (86) 56
Beyond the Pale and Other Stories (Trevor) (83) 57
Big as Life (Howard) (02) 83
Big If (Costello) (03) 69
Big Test, The (Lemann) (00) 57
Billy Bathgate (Doctorow) (90) 67
Bing Crosby (Giddins) (02) 88
Bingo Palace, The (Erdrich) (95) 76
Binstead's Safari (Ingalls) (89) 94
Biography (Gitelson) (92) 48
Biological Exuberance (Bagemihl) (00) 62
Biotech Century, The (Rifkin) (99) 100
Bird of Life, Bird of Death (Maslow) (87) 66
Birds of America (Moore) (99) 105
Birdsong (Faulks) (97) 110
Birdy (Wharton) (80) 79
Birth-mark, The (Howe) (94) 90
Birth of a New Europe, The (Hamerow) (H-84) 61
Birth of Purgatory, The (Le Goff) (H-85) 43
Birth of the Modern, The (Johnson) (92) 52
Birth of the People's Republic of Antarctica, The (Batchelor) (84) 91
Birthday Letters (Hughes) (99) 109
Bismarck (Crankshaw) (82) 50
Bitter Fame (Stevenson) (90) 71
Black Athena Revisited (Lefkowitz and Rogers, eds.) (97) 114
Black Betty (Mosley) (95) 80
Black Book of Communism, The (Courtois et al., eds.) (00) 66
Black Death, The (Gottfried) (H-84) 68
Black Dogs (McEwan) (93) 79

TITLE INDEX

Black Family in Slavery and Freedom, 1750-1925, The (Gutman) (77) 87
Black, French, and African (Vaillant) (91) 80
Black Hawk Down (Bowden) (00) 70
Black Hearts of Men, The (Stauffer) (03) 74
Black Holes and Baby Universes and Other Essays (Hawking) (94) 94
Black Jack, Vol. I and Vol. II (Vandiver) (78) 96
Black Orchid (Meyer and Kaplan) (78) 100
Black Robe (Moore) (86) 61
Black Sun (Wolff) (77) 91
Black Ulysses (Geeraerts) (79) 55
Black Water (Oates) (93) 83
Black Zodiac (Wright) (98) 117
Blacker than a Thousand Midnights (Straight) (95) 85
Blackwater (Ekman) (97) 119
Blake (Ackroyd) (97) 123
Blanco (Wier) (80) 83
Blank Slate, The (Pinker) (03) 79
Blessings in Disguise (Guinness) (87) 71
Blind Ambition (Dean) (77) 96
Blind Assassin, The (Atwood) (01) 94
Blind Date (Kosinski) (78) 104
Blinded by the Right (Brock) (03) 83
Blindness (Saramago) (99) 114
Blitzkrieg (Deighton) (81) 88
Blockade Busters (Barker) (78) 108
Blonde (Oates) (01) 99
Blood and Belonging (Ignatieff) (95) 89
Blood, Hook & Eye (Wier) (78) 112
Blood Meridian (McCarthy) (86) 67
Blood Mountain (Engels) (78) 117
Blood of Kings, The (Schele and Miller) (87) 75
Blood Relations (Mosley) (81) 93
Blood, Tin, Straw (Olds) (00) 74
Bloodfire (Chappell) (79) 60
Bloods (Terry) (H-85) 48
Bloodshed and Three Novellas (Ozick) (77) 101
Bloodsmoor Romance, A (Oates) (83) 61
Bloody Mary (Erickson) (79) 64
Bloomers on the Liffey (van Caspel) (87) 80
Blooming (Toth) (82) 55
Bloomsbury (Edel) (80) 88
Blow Fly (Cornwell) (04) 87
Blow Your House Down (Barker) (85) 47
Blue Angel (Prose) (01) 104
Blue at the Mizzen (O'Brian) (00) 78
Blue Bedspread, The (Jha) (01) 108
Blue Calhoun (Price) (93) 87
Blue Devils of Nada, The (Murray) (97) 127
Blue-Eyed Child of Fortune (Duncan, ed.) (93) 91
Blue Flower, The (Fitzgerald) (98) 121
Blue Hammer, The (Macdonald) (77) 105
Blue Highways (Heat-Moon) (84) 95
Blue Hour (Forché) (04) 91
Blue Pastoral (Sorrentino) (84) 99
Blue Shoe (Lamott) (03) 87
Blue Wine and Other Poems (Hollander) (80) 94
Bluebeard (Frisch) (84) 105
Bluebeard (Vonnegut) (88) 107
Bobos in Paradise (Brooks) (01) 112
Bodega Dreams (Quiñonez) (01) 117
Bodies in Motion and at Rest (Lynch) (01) 122
Bodily Harm (Atwood) (83) 65
Body and Soul (Conroy) (94) 100
Body Artist, The (DeLillo) (02) 93
Body Blows (Bagg) (89) 98
Body Farm, The (Cornwell) (95) 94
Body Toxic (Antonetta) (02) 97
Boer War, The (Pakenham) (80) 97
Bogart (Sperber and Lax) (98) 125
Bohin Manor (Konwicki) (91) 86
Boleros (Wright) (92) 56

Bolsheviks Come to Power, The (Rabinowitch) (77) 109
Bondwoman's Narrative, The (Crafts) (03) 92
Bone (Ng) (94) 105
Bone by Bone (Matthiessen) (00) 82
Bone People, The (Hulme) (86) 72
Bonesetter's Daughter, The (Tan) (02) 102
Bonfire of the Vanities, The (Wolfe) (88) 112
Book Against God, The (Wood) (04) 96
Book and the Brotherhood, The (Murdoch) (89) 103
Book Business (Epstein) (02) 106
Book Class, The (Auchincloss) (85) 52
Book of Common Prayer, A (Didion) (78) 121
Book of Ebenezer Le Page, The (Edwards) (82) 59
Book of Evidence, The (Banville) (91) 91
Book of Happiness, The (Berberova) (00) 86
Book of Illusions, The (Auster) (03) 97
Book of Kings, The (Thackara) (00) 90
Book of Laughter and Forgetting, The (Kundera) (81) 99
Book of Merlyn, The (White) (78) 126
Book of My Nights (Lee) (02) 110
Book of Prefaces, The (Gray) (01) 126
Book of Questions, The (Jabès) (84) 108
Book of Salt, The (Truong) (04) 100
Book of Sand, The (Borges) (78) 131
Book of Sorrows, The (Wangerin) (86) 77
Book of the Body, The (Bidart) (78) 136
Book of the Fourth World (Brotherston) (94) 109
Boone's Lick (McMurtry) (01) 131
Border Crossing (Barker) (02) 115
Borges (Woodall) (98) 130
Borges, a Reader (Borges) (82) 63
Boris Pasternak, 1890-1928 (Barnes) (91) 96
Born Brothers (Woiwode) (89) 107
Born on the Fourth of July (Kovic) (77) 115
Borrowed Time (Monette) (89) 112
Boss Cupid (Gunn) (01) 135
Boston Boy (Hentoff) (87) 84
Boswell (Boswell) (78) 140
Boswell's Presumptuous Task (Sisman) (02) 120
Botany of Desire, The (Pollan) (02) 125
Bottle in the Smoke, A (Wilson) (91) 100
Bottom Translation, The (Kott) (88) 116
Bourgeois Experience, Victoria to Freud, Vol. I, The (Gay) (H-85) 53
Bowling Alone (Putnam) (01) 139
Box, The (Kisseloff) (96) 77
Box of Matches, A (Baker) (04) 105
Boy Scout Handbook and Other Observations, The (Fussell) (83) 70
Boy Without a Flag, The (Rodriguez) (93) 96
Boyhood (Coetzee) (98) 134
Braided Lives (Piercy) (83) 75
Brain for All Seasons, A (Calvin) (03) 102
Brain Storm (Dooling) (99) 118
Brainchildren (Dennett) (99) 122
Brandeis (Paper) (H-84) 73
Brazil (Updike) (95) 99
Bread of Those Early Years, The (Böll) (77) 119
Bread Upon the Waters (Shaw) (82) 67
Bread Without Sugar (Stern) (93) 101
Breaking Ranks (Podhoretz) (80) 101
Breaking the Deadlock (Posner) (02) 130
Breaking the News (Fallows) (97) 132
Breaking the Slump (Alexander) (03) 106
Breaking with Moscow (Shevchenko) (86) 81
Breaks, The (Price) (84) 112
Breathing Lessons (Tyler) (89) 116
Breathing Under Water and Other East European Essays (Barańczak) (91) 105
Brecht (Hayman) (84) 118
Brecht and Method (Jameson) (99) 127

Brendan (Buechner) (88) 121
Brethren, The (Woodward and Armstrong) (80) 104
Bridegroom, The (Ha Jin) (01) 144
Bridget Jones's Diary (Fielding) (99) 132
Brief History of Time, A (Hawking) (89) 121
Brief Interviews with Hideous Men (Wallace) (00) 95
Brief Lives (Brookner) (92) 60
Bright Earth (Ball) (03) 110
Bright Shining Lie, A (Sheehan) (89) 125
Brink, The (Detzer) (80) 110
Britain, Europe and the World, 1850-1982 (Porter)
  (H-84) 78
British Revolution, 1880-1939, The (James) (78) 145
British Writers of the Thirties (Cunningham) (89) 130
Britons (Colley) (93) 105
Broca's Brain (Sagan) (80) 116
Broke Heart Blues (Oates) (00) 99
Broken Cord, The (Dorris) (90) 76
Broken Estate, The (Wood) (00) 103
Broken Staff, The (Manuel) (93) 110
Broken Tower, The (Mariani) (00) 108
Brontës, The (Barker) (96) 81
Bronx Primitive (Simon) (83) 80
Brotherly Love (Dexter) (92) 64
Brothers and Keepers (Wideman) (85) 57
Brothers Mann, The (Hamilton) (80) 119
Brothers Reuther, The (Reuther) (77) 124
Brothers Singer, The (Sinclair) (84) 127
Brown (Rodriguez) (03) 114
Bruce Chatwin (Shakespeare) (01) 148
Buddha's Little Finger (Pelevin) (01) 153
Buenos Aires Affair, The (Puig) (77) 129
Buffalo Girls (McMurtry) (91) 110
Building, The (Glynn) (87) 90
Bulgakov (Proffer) (85) 62
Bullet Meant for Me, The (Reid) (03) 119
Bully for Brontosaurus (Gould) (92) 69
Bunting (Makin) (93) 115
Burden of Proof, The (Turow) (91) 115
Burger's Daughter (Gordimer) (80) 123
Buried Mirror, The (Fuentes) (93) 119
Burn, The (Aksyonov) (85) 68
Burning Forest, The (Leys) (86) 86
Burning House, The (Beattie) (83) 86
Burning the Days (Salter) (98) 138
Burns (Mackay) (94) 113
Burnt Pages, The (Ash) (92) 75
Burnt Water (Fuentes) (81) 103
Burr, Hamilton, and Jefferson (Kennedy) (00) 112
Burt Lancaster (Buford) (01) 158
Business of Books, The (Schiffrin) (01) 163
Business of Fancydancing, The (Alexie) (93) 124
But Do Blondes Prefer Gentlemen? (Burgess) (87) 94
Butcher Boy, The (McCabe) (94) 118
Buzzing, The (Knipfel) (04) 109
By the Lake (McGahern) (03) 123
Byron (Grosskurth) (98) 142
Byron's Letters and Journals, 1822-1823 (Byron)
  (81) 108
Byzantine Journey, A (Ash) (96) 86

C. S. Lewis (Wilson) (91) 175
Cabal and Other Stories, The (Gilchrist) (01) 168
Cadence of Grass, The (McGuane) (03) 128
Cadillac Jack (McMurtry) (83) 90
Cage for Loulou, A (von Abele) (79) 70
Cairo (Raymond) (02) 135
Cairo (Rodenbeck) (00) 117
Cal (MacLaverty) (84) 132
Calamities of Exile (Weschler) (99) 136
California's Over (Jones) (98) 147
Call, The (Hersey) (86) 91
Call of Stories, The (Coles) (90) 81

Calvin Against Himself (Selinger) (H-85) 59
Camera Age, The (Arlen) (82) 73
Camera Lucida (Barthes) (82) 78
Campaign, The (Fuentes) (92) 79
Campaign for North Africa, The (Coggins) (81) 113
Camping with the Prince and Other Tales of Science in
  Africa (Bass) (91) 119
Camus (McCarthy) (83) 96
Canaan (Hill) (98) 152
Canaris (Höhne) (80) 125
Candido (Sciascia) (80) 129
Cannibal Galaxy, The (Ozick) (84) 137
Cannibals and Missionaries (McCarthy) (80) 133
Canon and Creativity (Alter) (01) 172
Capitol Games (Phelps and Winternitz) (93) 128
Capote (Clarke) (89) 135
Captain and the Enemy, The (Greene) (89) 140
Captain Kidd and the War Against the Pirates (Ritchie)
  (87) 99
Captain Pantoja and the Special Service (Vargas Llosa)
  (79) 75
Captain Sir Richard Francis Burton (Rice) (91) 123
Caramelo (Cisneros) (03) 132
Careless Widow and Other Stories, A (Pritchett)
  (90) 86
Carl Sagan (Davidson) (00) 121
Carnival (Dinesen) (78) 150
Carnival Evening (Pastan) (99) 141
Carpenter's Gothic (Gaddis) (86) 96
Carter Beats the Devil (Gold) (02) 140
Case Against Immigration, The (Beck) (97) 136
Case of Curiosities, A (Kurzweil) (93) 133
Cash Nexus, The (Ferguson) (02) 145
Cassandra (Wolf) (85) 74
Cat Who Walks Through Walls, The (Heinlein)
  (86) 100
Catbird's Song, The (Wilbur) (98) 156
Catcher Was a Spy, The (Dawidoff) (95) 104
Cathedral (Carver) (84) 143
Catherine, Empress of All the Russias (Cronin) (79) 80
Catherine the Great (Haslip) (78) 155
Catherine the Great (Troyat) (81) 117
Catholic Imagination, The (Greeley) (01) 176
Cat's Eye (Atwood) (90) 91
Cattle Killing, The (Wideman) (97) 142
Caught in the Web of Words (Murray) (78) 160
Cavedweller (Allison) (99) 145
Caveman's Valentine, The (Green) (95) 109
Cavour (Mack Smith) (86) 105
Celebrations and Attacks (Howe) (80) 136
Céline (McCarthy) (77) 134
Celts, The (Herm) (78) 164
Century of the Scottish People, 1830-1950, A (Smout)
  (88) 127
Century's Son (Boswell) (03) 137
Ceremony and Other Stories, The (Kees) (85) 79
Certain Justice, A (James) (98) 160
Certain Lucas, A (Cortázar) (85) 84
Certain Trumpets (Wills) (95) 114
Cervantes (Byron) (79) 84
Chaim Weizmann (Reinharz) (86) 111
Chain of Voices, A (Brink) (83) 101
Chainless Soul, A (Frank) (91) 127
Chairman, The (Bird) (93) 138
Chamfort (Arnaud) (93) 143
Chance and Circumstance (Baskir and Strauss) (79) 88
Chance Meetings (Saroyan) (79) 92
Chaneysville Incident, The (Bradley) (82) 82
Change, The (Greer) (93) 148
Change of Gravity, A (Higgins) (98) 164
Change of Light, A (Cortázar) (81) 122
Changes in the Land (Cronon) (H-84) 82
Changing Light at Sandover, The (Merrill) (84) 148

TITLE INDEX

Changing of the Guard (Broder) (81) 127
Chan's Great Continent, The (Spence) (99) 149
Chaos (Gleick) (88) 132
Chaplin (Robinson) (86) 116
Charles Darwin (Bowlby) (92) 83
Charles Darwin (Brent) (82) 87
Charles Darwin, Power of Place, The (Browne) (03) 142
Charles Darwin, Voyaging (Browne) (96) 90
Charles Darwin's Letters (Darwin) (97) 148
Charles Fourier (Beecher) (88) 138
Charles Olson (Clark) (92) 88
Charles Ryder's Schooldays and Other Stories (Waugh) (83) 105
Charles Stewart Parnell (Lyons) (78) 169
Charles the Second (Hutton) (91) 132
Charles Williams (Cavaliero) (84) 158
Charles Williams (Hadfield) (84) 153
Charlotte Brontë (Gordon) (96) 94
Charlotte Mew and Her Friends (Fitzgerald) (89) 145
Charmed Lives (Korda) (80) 141
Charming Billy (McDermott) (99) 154
Chateaubriand (1768-93) (Painter) (79) 95
Chatterton (Ackroyd) (89) 150
Chaucer (Howard) (88) 141
Chechnya (Lieven) (99) 158
Cheer, The (Meredith) (81) 133
Chekhov (Pritchett) (89) 155
Chekhov (Troyat) (87) 105
Cherry (Karr) (01) 181
Chesapeake (Michener) (79) 99
Chess Garden, The (Hansen) (96) 98
Chester Himes (Sallis) (02) 149
Chickamauga (Wright) (96) 103
Chief, The (Morrow) (86) 121
Chief, The (Nasaw) (01) 185
Chieko's Sky (Takamura) (79) 105
Child in Time, The (McEwan) (88) 146
Child of My Heart (McDermott) (03) 147
Childhood (Sarraute) (85) 89
Children, The (Halberstam) (99) 163
Children in Exile (Fenton) (85) 96
Children of Dune (Herbert) (77) 139
Children of Light (Stone) (87) 112
Children of Men, The (James) (94) 123
Children of the Sun (Green) (77) 144
Childwold (Oates) (77) 149
Chile (Timerman) (88) 150
Chilly Scenes of Winter (Beattie) (77) 154
Chimpanzees of Gombe (Goodall) (87) 116
China Men (Kingston) (81) 137
China Without Mao (Hsü) (H-84) 87
Chinabound (Fairbank) (H-83) 61
Chinese Communist Party in Power, 1949-1976, The (Guillermaz) (78) 174
Chinese Foreign Policy After the Cultural Revolution, 1966-1977 (Sutter) (79) 108
Chinese in America, The (Chang) (04) 113
Chinese Insomniacs, The (Jacobsen) (83) 110
Chivalry (Keen) (H-85) 63
Choice of Days, A (Mencken) (81) 142
Chopin in Paris (Szulc) (99) 168
Chopin's Funeral (Eisler) (04) 118
Chosen Poems, Old and New (Lorde) (83) 113
Christianizing the Roman Empire (A.D. 100-400) (MacMullen) (H-85) 68
Christina Rossetti (Marsh) (96) 107
Christine de Pizan (Willard) (86) 126
Christopher and His Kind (Isherwood) (77) 158
Christopher Isherwood (Finney) (80) 145
Christopher Unborn (Fuentes) (90) 95
Chronicle of a Death Foretold (García Márquez) (84) 163

Chronicle of the Łódź Ghetto, 1941-1944, The (Dobroszycki, ed.) (H-85) 73
Chuck Jones (Kenner) (95) 119
Churchill (Morgan) (H-83) 65
Churchill and de Gaulle (Kersaudy) (H-83) 70
Churchill Coalition, The (Lee) (81) 147
Cider House Rules, The (Irving) (86) 131
Cincinnatus (Wills) (H-85) 78
Circle of Hanh, The (Weigl) (01) 190
Circles (McCarthy) (78) 179
Circles on the Water (Piercy) (83) 119
Circus Fire, The (O'Nan) (01) 194
Cities and the Wealth of Nations (Jacobs) (H-85) 83
Cities of Memory (Hinsey) (97) 152
Cities of the Plain (McCarthy) (99) 173
Cities of Salt (Munif) (89) 160
Cities on a Hill (FitzGerald) (87) 121
Citizen Cohn (von Hoffman) (89) 164
Citizens (Schama) (90) 99
City of Bits (Mitchell) (96) 112
City of Joy, The (Lapierre) (86) 136
City of Your Final Destination, The (Cameron) (03) 151
City Poet (Gooch) (94) 128
Civil Action, A (Harr) (96) 116
Civil War, The (Ward et al.) (91) 137
Civil War Command and Strategy (Jones) (93) 153
Civil Wars (Brown) (85) 101
Civility (Carter) (99) 177
Claire Clairmont and the Shelleys, 1798-1879 (Gittings and Manton) (93) 157
Clara (Galloway) (04) 122
Clarence Darrow (Weinberg and Weinberg) (81) 152
Claude Monet (Tucker) (96) 120
Cleanth Brooks and the Rise of Modern Criticism (Winchell) (97) 156
Clear Light of Day (Desai) (81) 156
Clear Pictures (Price) (90) 104
Cleared for Landing (Darr) (79) 113
Clearing in the Distance, A (Rybczynski) (00) 126
Clement Greenberg (Rubenfeld) (99) 181
!Click Song (Williams) (83) 124
Cliff, The (Slavitt) (95) 123
Climbing into the Roots (Saner) (77) 164
Clinging to the Wreckage (Mortimer) (83) 127
Cloak of Light, A (Morris) (86) 140
Clock of the Long Now, The (Brand) (00) 130
Clockers (Price) (93) 161
Cloister Walk, The (Norris) (97) 160
Clone (Kolata) (99) 186
Close Quarters (Golding) (88) 155
Close Range (Proulx) (00) 134
Closed Eye, A (Brookner) (93) 166
Closing Arguments (Busch) (92) 94
Closing of the American Mind, The (Bloom) (88) 159
Closing the Circle (Hoyt) (H-83) 75
Closing Time (Heller) (95) 128
Cloud Chamber (Dorris) (98) 168
Cloud of Danger, The (Kennan) (78) 183
Cloudsplitter (Banks) (99) 190
Coal (Freese) (04) 126
Coast of Chicago, The (Dybek) (91) 142
Coast of Trees, A (Ammons) (82) 92
Coasts of Bohemia, The (Sayer) (99) 195
Coffin Tree, The (Law-Yone) (84) 168
Coherent Splendor, A (Gelpi) (89) 169
Cohesion and Dissension in Eastern Europe (Simon) (H-84) 91
Cold Mountain (Frazier) (98) 172
Cold New World (Finnegan) (99) 200
Cold Snap (Jones) (96) 124
Colder Eye, A (Kenner) (84) 173
Coleridge, Darker Reflections (Holmes) (00) 138

Coleridge, Early Visions (Holmes) (91) 147
Colette (Lottman) (92) 99
Colette (Sarde) (81) 161
Collaborator, The (Kaplan) (01) 199
Collaborators (Kauffman) (87) 127
Collected Early Poems, 1950-1970 (Rich) (94) 133
Collected Essays of Ralph Ellison, The (Ellison)
  (96) 128
Collected Essays of Robert Creeley, The (Creeley)
  (90) 108
Collected Letters, 1911-1925 (Shaw) (86) 145
Collected Letters of Dylan Thomas, The (Thomas)
  (87) 132
Collected Letters of Joseph Conrad, 1861-1897, The
  (Conrad) (84) 178
Collected Letters of Joseph Conrad, 1898-1902, The
  (Conrad) (87) 138
Collected Letters of Joseph Conrad, 1903-1907, The
  (Conrad) (89) 175
Collected Letters of Katherine Mansfield, 1903-1917,
  The (Mansfield) (85) 106
Collected Letters of Katherine Mansfield, 1918-1919,
  The (Mansfield) (88) 165
Collected Letters of W. B. Yeats, 1865-1895, The
  (Yeats) (87) 142
Collected Poems, 1948-1976 (Abse) (78) 192
Collected Poems, 1957-1982 (Berry) (86) 159
Collected Poems (Berryman) (90) 117
Collected Poems (Bowers) (98) 177
Collected Poems (Bunting) (79) 119
Collected Poems, 1970-1983 (Davie) (84) 183
Collected Poems, 1947-1980 (Ginsberg) (85) 110
Collected Poems (Hayden) (86) 152
Collected Poems (Hill) (87) 146
Collected Poems, 1956-1994 (Kinsella) (97) 165
Collected Poems, The (Kunitz) (01) 204
Collected Poems (Larkin) (90) 112
Collected Poems (Lowell) (04) 130
Collected Poems, The (Miłosz) (89) 185
Collected Poems, The (Plath) (82) 96
Collected Poems, The (Price) (98) 181
Collected Poems, 1935-1992 (Prince) (94) 142
Collected Poems, The (Rukeyser) (80) 148
Collected Poems (Sarton) (94) 137
Collected Poems, 1940-1978 (Shapiro) (79) 124
Collected Poems (Simpson) (89) 180
Collected Poems, 1919-1976 (Tate) (78) 188
Collected Poems (Tomlinson) (87) 151
Collected Poems, 1953-1993 (Updike) (94) 146
Collected Poems, 1956-1976 (Wagoner) (78) 197
Collected Poems, The (Yevtushenko) (92) 104
Collected Poems of Amy Clampitt, The (Clampitt)
  (98) 185
Collected Poems of George Garrett, The (Garrett)
  (85) 116
Collected Poems of Henri Coulette, The (Coulette)
  (91) 152
Collected Poems of Howard Nemerov, The (Nemerov)
  (78) 200
Collected Poems of John Ciardi, The (Ciardi) (98) 190
Collected Poems of Octavio Paz, The (Paz) (88) 169
Collected Poems of Paul Blackburn, The (Blackburn)
  (86) 164
Collected Poems of Robert Creeley, The (Creeley)
  (84) 189
Collected Poems of Sterling A. Brown, The (Brown)
  (81) 168
Collected Poems of Stevie Smith, The (Smith) (77) 168
Collected Poems of William Carlos Williams,
  1909-1939, The (Williams) (87) 155
Collected Poems of William Carlos Williams,
  1939-1962, The (Williams) (89) 190

Collected Poetry of Robinson Jeffers, 1920-1928, The
  (Jeffers) (89) 195
Collected Poetry of Robinson Jeffers, 1928-1938, The
  (Jeffers) (90) 122
Collected Prose, The (Bishop) (85) 121
Collected Prose (Celan) (91) 157
Collected Prose (Lowell) (88) 173
Collected Short Fiction of Bruce Jay Friedman, The
  (Friedman) (96) 132
Collected Shorter Poems, 1946-1991 (Carruth) (93) 171
Collected Stories, 1939-1976 (Bowles) (80) 151
Collected Stories (Morris) (87) 160
Collected Stories (O'Connor) (82) 100
Collected Stories, The (Paley) (95) 133
Collected Stories, The (Price) (94) 150
Collected Stories (Pritchett) (83) 131
Collected Stories, The (Theroux) (98) 194
Collected Stories, The (Tuohy) (85) 126
Collected Stories (Williams) (86) 170
Collected Stories of Caroline Gordon, The (Gordon)
  (82) 106
Collected Stories of Colette, The (Colette) (84) 194
Collected Stories of Elizabeth Bowen, The (Bowen)
  (81) 173
Collected Stories of Eudora Welty, The (Welty)
  (81) 178
Collected Stories of Evan S. Connell, The (Connell)
  (96) 136
Collected Stories of Isaac Bashevis Singer, The (Singer)
  (83) 135
Collected Stories of Louis Auchincloss, The
  (Auchincloss) (95) 137
Collected Stories of Mavis Gallant, The (Gallant)
  (97) 171
Collected Stories of Sean O'Faolain, The (O'Faolain)
  (84) 198
Collected Stories of Wallace Stegner (Stegner) (91) 161
Collected Stories of William Humphrey, The
  (Humphrey) (86) 175
Collected Works, 1956-1976 (Metcalf) (97) 175
Collected Works, 1976-1997 (Metcalf) (98) 199
Colonel, The (Smith) (98) 202
Color of the Air, The (Sanford) (86) 178
Color Purple, The (Walker) (83) 139
Color Wheel, The (Steele) (96) 140
Colored People (Gates) (95) 141
Combinations of the Universe (Goldbarth) (04) 134
Come to Me (Bloom) (94) 154
Comedians (Griffiths) (77) 174
Coming Alive (Garside) (82) 111
Coming Anarchy, The (Kaplan) (01) 208
Coming of Age in the Milky Way (Ferris) (89) 199
Coming to Jakarta (Scott) (90) 127
Command of the Seas (Lehman) (90) 132
Commanding Heights (Yergin and Stanislaw) (99) 204
Common Ground (Lukas) (86) 182
Commons (Kim) (03) 155
Company (Beckett) (81) 184
Company, The (Littell) (03) 159
Company Man (Wade) (93) 176
Company of Women, The (Gordon) (82) 115
Company We Keep, The (Booth) (89) 202
Compass Flower, The (Merwin) (78) 205
Complete Collected Essays (Pritchett) (93) 179
Complete Collected Stories (Pritchett) (92) 109
Complete Letters of Sigmund Freud to Wilhelm Fliess,
  The (Freud) (86) 187
Complete Notebooks of Henry James, The (James)
  (88) 179
Complete Poems, The (Sexton) (82) 120
Complete Poems of Anna Akhmatova, The
  (Akhmatova) (91) 165

Complete Poems of C. Day Lewis, The (Day Lewis) (93) 184
Complete Poems of Marianne Moore, The (Moore) (82) 126
Complete Poems of William Empson, The (Empson) (02) 153
Complete Prefaces, 1889-1913, The (Shaw) (95) 145
Complete Prose of Marianne Moore, The (Moore) (87) 165
Complete Short Poetry (Zukofsky) (92) 114
Complete Stories of Bernard Malamud, The (Malamud) (98) 207
Complete Works of Isaac Babel, The (Babel) (02) 158
Complexity (Lewin) (93) 188
Composition of *Four Quartets*, The (Gardner) (79) 128
Compulsory Figures (Taylor) (93) 192
Concrete (Bernhard) (85) 131
Conduct Unbecoming (Shilts) (94) 158
Confederacy of Dunces, A (Toole) (81) 188
Confederate Nation, The (Thomas) (80) 156
Confederates in the Attic (Horwitz) (99) 208
Conflict and Crisis (Donovan) (78) 210
Conflict of Duty (Dowart) (H-84) 96
Conflict of Visions, A (Sowell) (88) 184
Congo Cables, The (Kalb) (H-83) 80
Congregation (Rosenberg, ed.) (88) 189
Conquest of America, The (Todorov) (H-85) 89
Conquests and Cultures (Sowell) (99) 212
Conrad (Watt) (81) 193
Conrad Aiken (Butscher, ed.) (89) 207
Conscious and Verbal (Murray) (02) 163
Conscious Mind, The (Chalmers) (97) 179
Consciousness Explained (Dennett) (92) 119
Consenting Adults (De Vries) (81) 198
Consider This, Señora (Doerr) (94) 163
Consilience (Wilson) (99) 216
Consoling Intelligence, The (Kubal) (83) 144
Conspiracy of Paper, A (Liss) (01) 213
Conspiracy So Immense, A (Oshinsky) (H-84) 100
Conspiracy Theories (Fenster) (00) 142
Constant Defender (Tate) (84) 202
Constantine's Sword (Carroll) (02) 167
Consul's File, The (Theroux) (78) 215
Content of Our Character, The (Steele) (91) 170
Control of Nature, The (McPhee) (90) 137
Convenient Spy, A (Stober and Hoffman) (03) 164
Conversations with Czesław Miłosz (88) 194
Conversations with Eudora Welty (Prenshaw, ed.) (85) 137
Conversations with Nietzsche (Gilman, ed.) (88) 199
Cool, Calm, and Collected (Kizer) (02) 172
Cool Fire, The (Shanks) (77) 180
Cooper's Wife Is Missing, The (Hoff and Yeates) (01) 218
Cornwallis (Wickwire and Wickwire) (81) 203
Corrections, The (Franzen) (02) 176
Correspondence of Boris Pasternak and Olga Freidenberg, 1910-1954, The (Pasternak and Freidenberg) (83) 147
Correspondence of Thomas Carlyle and John Ruskin, The (Carlyle and Ruskin) (83) 153
Correspondence of Walter Benjamin, 1910-1940, The (Benjamin) (95) 149
Correspondent Breeze, The (Abrams) (85) 142
Cosmic Code, The (Pagels) (83) 156
Cosmic Dawn (Chaisson) (82) 130
Cosmic Discovery (Harwit) (82) 135
Cosmopolitan Greetings (Ginsberg) (95) 152
Counsel to the President (Clifford, with Holbrooke) (92) 123
Counterlife, The (Roth) (88) 204
Counterpoints (Needham) (88) 209
Country, The (Plante) (82) 140

Country Between Us, The (Forché) (83) 161
Coup, The (Updike) (79) 133
Courier from Warsaw (Nowak) (H-83) 85
Court and the Constitution, The (Cox) (88) 213
Cousins' Wars, The (Phillips) (00) 146
Covenant, The (Michener) (81) 210
Crabgrass Frontier (Jackson) (87) 170
Crabwalk (Grass) (04) 138
Cradle of the Real Life, The (Valentine) (01) 223
Crampton Hodnet (Pym) (86) 194
Crazed, The (Jin) (03) 168
Crazy Years, The (Wiser) (84) 207
Creating the Entangling Alliance (Ireland) (82) 145
Creation (Vidal) (82) 151
Creation of Feminist Consciousness, The (Lerner) (94) 168
Creation of Psychopharmacology, The (Healy) (03) 172
Cries Unheard (Sereny) (00) 151
Crime and Punishment in American History (Friedman) (94) 173
Crime of the Century (Kurtz) (H-83) 90
Crimes of the Heart (Henley) (83) 165
Crisis (Jordan) (H-83) 93
Crisis of Islam, The (Lewis) (04) 142
Crisis on the Left (McAuliffe) (79) 138
Crisis Years, The (Beschloss) (92) 128
Critical Observations (Symons) (82) 156
Critical Times (May) (03) 177
Cromwell (Howell) (78) 219
Crooked Little Heart (Lamott) (98) 211
Crooked Timber of Humanity, The (Berlin) (92) 133
Cross Channel (Barnes) (97) 183
Cross Ties (Kennedy) (86) 199
Crossing (McCloskey) (00) 155
Crossing to Safety (Stegner) (88) 218
Crossing, Volume Two, The (McCarthy) (95) 157
Crossroads of Death (Weingartner) (80) 162
Crowded Earth, The (Gupte) (H-85) 94
Crown of Weeds (Gerstler) (98) 216
Crucible of Race, The (Williamson) (H-85) 99
Cruelty and Silence (Makiya) (94) 177
Crusoe's Daughter (Gardam) (87) 175
Cryptonomicon (Stephenson) (00) 159
Cuba Night (Smith) (91) 179
Cuban Threat, The (Robbins) (H-84) 106
Cubs and Other Stories, The (Vargas Llosa) (80) 165
Cult of Violence, The (Roth) (81) 215
Cultural Cold War, The (Saunders) (01) 227
Cultural Contradictions of Capitalism, The (Bell) (77) 184
Cultural Literacy (Hirsch) (88) 223
Cultural Materialism (Harris) (80) 170
Cultural Selection (Taylor) (97) 187
Culture and Imperialism (Said) (94) 181
Culture of Complaint (Hughes) (94) 186
Culture of Disbelief, The (Carter) (94) 191
Culture of Narcissism, The (Lasch) (80) 175
Cunning Little Vixen, The (Tesnohlidek) (86) 204
Cunning Man, The (Davies) (96) 144
Cup of News, A (Nicholl) (85) 147
Curranne Trueheart (Newlove) (87) 179
Curriculum Vitae (Spark) (94) 196
Custer and the Little Big Horn (Hofling) (82) 161
Cutting Edges (Krauthammer) (86) 208
Cycles of American History, The (Schlesinger) (87) 183
Czesław Miłosz and the Insufficiency of Lyric (Davie) (87) 189

D. H. Lawrence (Ellis) (98) 244
D. H. Lawrence (Kinkead-Weekes) (97) 214
D. H. Lawrence (Maddox) (95) 167
D. H. Lawrence (Meyers) (91) 206

D. H. Lawrence (Worthen) (92) 166
D. H. Lawrence's Nightmare (Delany) (80) 223
Da Vinci Code, The (Brown) (04) 147
Da Vinci's Bicycle (Davenport) (80) 195
Dad (Wharton) (82) 166
Daguerreotypes and Other Essays (Dinesen) (80) 180
Dakota (Norris) (94) 200
Dalva (Harrison) (89) 212
Damascus Gate (Stone) (99) 221
Damnable Question, The (Dangerfield) (77) 188
Damned to Fame (Knowlson) (97) 191
Dancehall Days *and* The Village of Longing (O'Brien)
   (91) 851
Dancing After Hours (Dubus) (97) 196
Dancing at Ciro's (Weller) (04) 151
Dancing at the Rascal Fair (Doig) (88) 228
Dancing Girls and Other Stories (Atwood) (83) 169
Danger and Survival (Bundy) (89) 217
Dangerous Relations (Ulam) (H-84) 111
Dangerous Woman, A (Morris) (92) 138
Daniel Defoe (Backscheider) (90) 143
Daniel Martin (Fowles) (78) 225
Daniel Webster (Bartlett) (79) 143
Daniel Webster (Remini) (98) 221
Danse Macabre (King) (82) 171
Dante Club, The (Pearl) (04) 156
Daphne du Maurier (Forster) (94) 204
Dark Back of Time (Marías) (02) 181
Dark Brain of Piranesi and Other Essays, The
   (Yourcenar) (85) 152
Dark Continent (Mazower) (00) 164
Dark Half, The (King) (90) 147
Dark Harbor (Strand) (94) 209
Dark Lady, The (Auchincloss) (78) 229
Dark Side of Camelot, The (Hersh) (98) 225
Dark Star Safari (Theroux) (04) 160
Darkness (Mukherjee) (87) 194
Darkness at Night (Harrison) (88) 233
Darkness Visible (Golding) (80) 184
Darkness Visible (Styron) (91) 184
Darlinghissima (Flanner) (86) 213
Darrow (Tierney) (80) 188
Darts of Cupid, and Other Stories, The (Templeton)
   (03) 182
Darwin (Desmond and Moore) (93) 196
Darwin's Dangerous Idea (Dennett) (96) 148
Dashiell Hammett (Johnson) (84) 212
Daughter of Destiny (Bhutto) (90) 152
Daughter of Fortune (Allende) (00) 168
Daughters (Marshall) (92) 142
Daughters of Albion (Wilson) (93) 200
David Bomberg (Cork) (88) 238
David Humphreys' "Life of General Washington"
   (Humphreys and Washington) (92) 147
Davita's Harp (Potok) (86) 217
Dawn of Modern Science (Goldstein) (81) 219
Dawn to the West (Keene) (85) 157
Day America Crashed, The (Shachtman) (80) 200
Day by Day (Lowell) (78) 233
Day I Became an Autodidact, The (Hailey) (89) 222
Day Lasts More than a Hundred Years, The (Aitmatov)
   (84) 219
Day of Creation, The (Ballard) (89) 226
Day of Judgment, The (Satta) (88) 242
Day of the Leopards (Wimsatt) (77) 194
Day One (Wyden) (H-85) 104
Daylight Moon and Other Poems, The (Murray)
   (90) 157
Days of Grace (Ashe and Rampersad) (94) 213
Days of Obligation (Rodriguez) (93) 204
Days of the French Revolution, The (Hibbert) (81) 222
Dead and the Living, The (Olds) (85) 162
Dead Certainties (Schama) (92) 152

Dead Elvis (Marcus) (92) 157
Dead Kingdom, The (Montague) (85) 167
Dead Languages (Shields) (90) 163
Dead Man in Deptford, A (Burgess) (96) 153
Dead Zone, The (King) (80) 205
Deadeye Dick (Vonnegut) (83) 174
Deadly Feasts (Rhodes) (98) 230
Deadly Gambits (Talbott) (H-85) 110
Deadly Medicine (Mancall) (96) 157
Dean Acheson (McLellan) (77) 197
Dean's December, The (Bellow) (83) 179
Dear Bess (Truman) (H-84) 117
Death in Holy Orders (James) (02) 185
Death in the Andes (Vargas Llosa) (97) 200
Death Is a Lonely Business (Bradbury) (86) 222
Death of Adam, The (Robinson) (99) 226
Death of Bernadette Lefthand, The (Querry) (94) 217
Death of Methuselah and Other Stories, The (Singer)
   (89) 231
Death of the Detective, The (Smith) (77) 202
Death of the King's Canary, The (Thomas and
   Davenport) (78) 238
Death of Vishnu, The (Suri) (02) 190
Death Valley and the Amargosa (Lingenfelter) (87) 198
Death Without Weeping (Scheper-Hughes) (93) 209
Debacle (Ledeen and Lewis) (82) 175
Decade of Decisions (Quandt) (78) 243
Decadence (Gilman) (80) 210
December 6 (Smith) (03) 187
Deception (Roth) (91) 188
Decisions in Crisis (Brecher and Geist) (81) 228
Decline of Bismarck's European Order, The (Kennan)
   (80) 215
Deep in a Dream (Gavin) (03) 192
Deep Politics and the Death of JFK (Scott) (94) 221
Deep River (Endō) (96) 160
Deeper (Seabrook) (98) 235
Defending Billy Ryan (Higgins) (93) 214
De Gaulle, 1890-1944 (Lacouture) (91) 192
De Gaulle, 1945-1970 (Lacouture) (93) 219
Deliberate Speed (Lhamon) (91) 197
Delirium Eclipse and Other Stories (Lasdun) (87) 204
Delmore Schwartz (Atlas) (78) 249
Delusions of Grandma (Fisher) (95) 162
Democracy (Didion) (85) 172
Democracy on Trial (Smith) (96) 165
Democracy's Discontents (Sandel) (97) 205
Demon and the Angel, The (Hirsch) (03) 197
Demonology (Moody) (02) 195
Den of Thieves (Stewart) (92) 162
Descartes (Gaukroger) (96) 170
Descent from Glory (Nagel) (H-84) 121
Desert Rose, The (McMurtry) (84) 225
Desirable Daughters (Mukherjee) (03) 202
Desire in Language (Kristeva) (81) 231
Desires (L'Heureux) (82) 181
Dessa Rose (Williams) (87) 207
Destinies of Darcy Dancer, Gentleman, The (Donleavy)
   (78) 254
Destiny (Parks) (01) 232
Destroying the World to Save It (Lifton) (00) 172
Destructive Element, The (Cassity) (99) 230
Destructive Generation (Collier and Horowitz) (90) 168
Details of a Sunset and Other Stories (Nabokov)
   (77) 206
Devices and Desires (James) (91) 202
Devices and Desires (Tone) (02) 199
Devil and Sonny Liston, The (Tosches) (01) 237
Devil in the White City, The (Larson) (04) 165
Devil Problem, The (Remnick) (97) 210
Devil Wears Prada, The (Weisberger) (04) 169
Devil's Horsemen, The (Chambers) (80) 220
Devil's Stocking, The (Algren) (84) 230

Devolving English Literature (Crawford) (93) 224
Dewey Defeats Truman (Mallon) (98) 239
Dialogic Novels of Malcolm Bradbury and David Lodge, The (Morace) (90) 173
Diane Arbus (Bosworth) (96) 174
Diaries (Isherwood) (98) 249
Diaries of a Cabinet Minister, The (Crossman) (77) 211
Diaries of Dawn Powell, 1931-1965, The (Powell) (96) 178
Diaries of Evelyn Waugh, The (Waugh) (78) 258
Diary, 1953-1956 (Gombrowicz) (89) 236
Diary, 1957-1961 (Gombrowicz) (90) 177
Diary, 1961-1966 (Gombrowicz) (94) 225
Diary of Anaïs Nin, 1955-1966, The (Nin) (77) 217
Diary of Anaïs Nin, 1966-1974, The (Nin) (81) 234
Diary of Frida Kahlo, The (Kahlo) (96) 182
Diary of H. L. Mencken, The (Mencken) (91) 211
Diary of James C. Hagerty, The (Hagerty) (H-84) 125
Diary of Virginia Woolf, 1915-1919, The (Woolf) (78) 264
Diary of Virginia Woolf, 1920-1924, The (Woolf) (79) 147
Diary of Virginia Woolf, 1925-1930, The (Woolf) (81) 240
Diary of Virginia Woolf, 1931-1935, The (Woolf) (83) 185
Diary of Virginia Woolf, 1936-1941, The (Woolf) (85) 178
Diaspora (Sachar) (86) 226
Dickens (Ackroyd) (92) 170
Dickens (Kaplan) (89) 241
Dictionary of American Regional English, Vol. I (Cassidy, ed.) (86) 230
Dictionary of the Khazars (Pavić) (89) 245
Diderot (Furbank) (93) 229
Different Mirror, A (Takaki) (94) 230
Different Person, A (Merrill) (94) 234
Different Seasons (King) (83) 189
Difficult Loves (Calvino) (85) 184
Difficulties with Girls (Amis) (90) 181
Dinner at the Homesick Restaurant (Tyler) (83) 194
Dinosaur in a Haystack (Gould) (97) 219
Diplomacy (Kissinger) (95) 171
Dirt Under My Nails (Foster) (03) 207
Dirty Linen and New-Found-Land (Stoppard) (78) 268
Discoverers, The (Boorstin) (H-84) 130
Discovering (Root-Bernstein) (90) 186
Discovery of Heaven, The (Mulisch) (97) 225
Discovery of Slowness, The (Nadolny) (88) 247
Disgrace (Coetzee) (00) 177
Disobedience (Hamilton) (01) 242
Dispatches (Herr) (78) 272
Disposable People (Bales) (00) 181
Disraeli (Bradford) (H-84) 135
Disraeli (Weintraub) (94) 239
Distant Mirror, A (Tuchman) (79) 151
Distant Neighbors (Riding) (86) 234
Distant Relations (Fuentes) (83) 200
Distinguished Guest, The (Miller) (96) 186
Disturbing the Peace (Havel) (91) 216
Dive from Clausen's Pier, The (Packer) (03) 211
Diversity and Depth in Fiction (Wilson) (85) 190
Diversity in America (Schuck) (04) 174
Diversity of Life, The (Wilson) (93) 235
Divided Left, The (Cantor) (79) 157
Divine Comedies (Merrill) (77) 222
Diving Rock on the Hudson, A (Roth) (96) 190. See also From Bondage, Mercy of a Rude Street, and Requiem for Harlem
Divorce Culture, The (Whitehead) (98) 254
Djuna (Field) (84) 234
Djuna (Herring) (96) 194
DNA (Watson and Berry) (04) 179

Do the Windows Open? (Hecht) (98) 259
Doctor Fischer of Geneva or the Bomb Party (Greene) (81) 244
Dr. Johnson and Mr. Savage (Holmes) (95) 176
Doctor's House, The (Beattie) (03) 215
Doctor's Wife, The (Moore) (77) 226
Documents Relating to the Sentimental Agents in the Volyen Empire (Lessing) (84) 239
Dogeaters (Hagedorn) (91) 221
Doing What Comes Naturally (Fish) (90) 190
Dolly (Brookner) (95) 180
Dominion (Eldredge) (96) 198
Don Juan and Regency England (Graham) (91) 227
Dönitz, the Last Führer (Padfield) (H-85) 115
Don't Tell Anyone (Busch) (01) 246
Don't Tell the Grown-ups (Lurie) (91) 231
Door in the Hive, A (Levertov) (90) 194
Door in the Wall, The (Tomlinson) (94) 244
Dorothy Day (Coles) (88) 252
Dos Passos (Carr) (85) 194
Dostoevsky (Dostoevsky) (77) 230
Dostoevsky, 1821-1849 (Frank) (77) 236
Dostoevsky, 1850-1859 (Frank) (84) 244
Dostoevsky, 1860-1865 (Frank) (87) 212
Dostoevsky, 1865-1871 (Frank) (96) 202
Dostoevsky, 1871-1881 (Frank) (03) 209
Double Bond, The (Angier) (03) 224
Double Fold (Baker) (02) 204
Double Honeymoon (Connell) (77) 242
Double Life of Stephen Crane, The (Benfey) (93) 239
Double Lives (Koch) (95) 185
Double Tongue, The (Golding) (96) 206
Double Witness, The (Belitt) (78) 276
Down by the River (O'Brien) (98) 263
Down from Troy (Selzer) (93) 244
Down the Highway (Sounes) (02) 208
Down the River (Abbey) (83) 205
Downing Street Years, The (Thatcher) (94) 248
Drawing the Line (Blum) (H-83) 104
Drawn with the Sword (McPherson) (97) 229
Dread (Ai) (04) 185
Dream Children (Wilson) (99) 234
Dream Endures, The (Starr) (98) 268
Dream Makers, Dream Breakers (Rowan) (94) 252
Dream of a Common Language, The (Rich) (79) 160
Dream of Greatness, A (Perrett) (80) 226
Dream of Reason, The (Bush) (79) 165
Dream of Scipio, The (Pears) (03) 229
Dream of the Golden Mountains, The (Cowley) (81) 249
Dream Palace of the Arab World, The (Ajami) (99) 238
Dream Song (Mariani) (91) 235
Dream Stuff (Malouf) (01) 250
Dream Work (Oliver) (87) 219
Dreamer (Johnson) (99) 242
Dreaming in Cuban (Garcia) (93) 249
Dreaming Me (Willis) (02) 212
Dreamland (Lesy) (98) 272
Dreamland (Sachar) (03) 233
Dreams of Sleep (Humphreys) (85) 199
Dressing Station, The (Kaplan) (03) 238
Dressing Up for the Carnival (Shields) (01) 254
Drift, The (Ridley) (03) 242
Drinking Coffee Elsewhere (Packer) (04) 189
Driving Mr. Albert (Paterniti) (01) 258
Drop City (Boyle) (04) 193
Drowned and the Saved, The (Levi) (89) 250
Dual Autobiography, A (Durant and Durant) (78) 280
Dubin's Lives (Malamud) (80) 231
Duke of Deception, The (Wolff) (80) 236
Dulles (Mosley) (79) 170
Duncan's Colony (Petesch) (83) 210

Du Pont Family, The (Gates) (80) 240
During the Reign of the Queen of Persia (Chase) (84) 252
Dusk and Other Stories (Salter) (89) 254
Dust Bowl, The (Bonnifield) (80) 251
Dust Bowl (Worster) (80) 244
Dust of Empire, The (Meyer) (04) 198
Dutch (Morris) (00) 185
Dutch Shea, Jr. (Dunne) (83) 216
Dying Animal, The (Roth) (02) 217
Dynamics of Nazism, The (Weinstein) (81) 254

E. B. White (Elledge) (85) 209
E. M. Forster (Beauman) (95) 195
E. M. Forster (Furbank) (79) 183
Each in a Place Apart (McMichael) (95) 190
Each Leaf Shines Separate (Warren) (85) 204
Earl Warren (Pollack) (80) 255
Earl Warren (White) (H-83) 109
Early Diary of Anaïs Nin, 1920-1923, The (Nin) (83) 220
Early Diary of Anaïs Nin, 1923-1927, The (Nin) (84) 257
Early Stories, The (Updike) (04) 203
Earthly Delights, Unearthly Adornments (Morris) (79) 175
Earthly Powers (Burgess) (81) 260
Earthsleep (Chappell) (81) 264
Ease My Sorrows (Kopelev) (84) 263
East Is East (Boyle) (91) 240
East of the Mountains (Guterson) (00) 190
Easter Parade, The (Yates) (77) 247
Easy in the Islands (Shacochis) (86) 240
Echo House (Just) (98) 277
Echoes Down the Corridor (Miller) (01) 263
Eclipse (Banville) (02) 222
Eclogues (Davenport) (82) 185
Eclogues of Virgil, The (Vergil) (00) 194
Economists, The (Silk) (77) 251
Ecstatic in the Poison (Hudgins) (04) 207
Edgar A. Poe (Siverman) (92) 174
Edgar Lee Masters (Russell) (02) 226
Edge Effect (McPherson) (97) 234
Edison (Clark) (78) 284
Edisto (Powell) (85) 213
Edith Sitwell (Glendinning) (82) 190
Edmund Burke (Ayling) (90) 198
Edmund Wilson (Meyers) (96) 210
Education of Laura Bridgman, The (Freeberg) (02) 230
Edward Albee (Gussow) (00) 199
Edward Hoagland Reader, The (Hoagland) (80) 260
Edward Hopper (Levin) (96) 214
Edward Sapir (Darnell) (91) 245
Edward VII (St. Aubyn) (80) 264
Edwin Denby, the Complete Poems (Denby) (87) 223
Eiffel Tower and Other Mythologies, The (Barthes) (80) 269
Eight Men and a Duck (Thorpe) (03) 246
1876 (Vidal) (77) 256
Eighth Day of Creation, The (Judson) (80) 273
Einstein, Picasso (Miller) (02) 235
Einstein's Clocks, Poincaré's Maps (Galison) (04) 211
Einstein's Dreams (Lightman) (94) 256
Eisenhower, Vol. I (Ambrose) (H-84) 141
Eisenhower, Vol. II (Ambrose) (H-85) 120
Eisenhower and the Cold War (Divine) (82) 195
Eisenhower, at War (Eisenhower) (87) 226
Eisenhower Diaries, The (Eisenhower) (82) 199
Eisenhower the President (Ewald) (82) 205
Eisenhower's Lieutenants (Weigley) (82) 210
Eleanor of Aquitaine (Seward) (80) 277
Eleanor Roosevelt, 1884-1933 (Cook) (93) 253
Eleanor Roosevelt, 1933-1938 (Cook) (00) 204

Electric Light (Heaney) (02) 240
Elegant Universe, The (Greene) (00) 208
Elegy for Iris (Bayley) (00) 213
Elegy for the Departure and Other Poems (Herbert) (00) 217
Elementary Particles, The (Houellebecq) (01) 267
Elephant Destiny (Meredith) (04) 215
Elephant Man, The (Pomerance) (80) 280
Elephant Vanishes, The (Murakami) (94) 260
Elia Kazan (Kazan) (89) 257
Eliot's New Life (Gordon) (89) 262
Elites in American History (Burch) (81) 268
Elizabeth Barrett Browning (Forster) (90) 203
Elizabeth Bishop (Goldensohn) (92) 179
Elizabeth Bishop (Millier) (94) 264
Elizabeth Bowen (Glendinning) (79) 179
Elizabeth Cady Stanton, Susan B. Anthony (Stanton and Anthony) (82) 214
Elizabeth Costello (Coetzee) (04) 219
Elizabeth Regina (Plowden) (81) 272
Elizabeth Stories, The (Huggan) (88) 256
Elizabethan Deliverance, The (Bryant) (H-83) 114
Ellen Foster (Gibbons) (88) 261
Ellis Island and Other Stories (Helprin) (82) 219
Elsewhere Community, The (Kenner) (01) 272
Embarrassment of Riches, The (Schama) (88) 266
Embattled Courage (Linderman) (88) 271
Embattled Dreams (Starr) (03) 250
Emerald City of Las Vegas, The (Wakoski) (96) 218
Emergence of Modern India, The (Lall) (82) 223
Emerson (Barish) (91) 249
Emerson (Richardson) (96) 222
Emerson Among the Eccentrics (Baker) (97) 239
Emerson in His Journals (Emerson) (83) 224
Emigrants, The (Sebald) (98) 282
Émigré New York (Mehlman) (01) 277
Emily Dickinson (Wolff) (87) 233
Eminent Elizabethans (Rowse) (H-84) 147
Emma Goldman (Wexler) (H-85) 125
Emperor of Japan (Keene) (03) 255
Emperor of Ocean Park, The (Carter) (03) 260
Emperor of Scent, The (Burr) (04) 224
Emperor of the Air (Canin) (89) 268
Emperor's New Mind, The (Penrose) (90) 207
Empire (Ferguson) (04) 228
Empire (Vidal) (88) 275
Empire Falls (Russo) (02) 244
Empire of Fortune (Jennings) (89) 273
Empire of Liberty (Tucker and Hendrickson) (91) 253
Empire of Reason, The (Commager) (78) 290
Empire of Signs, The (Barthes) (83) 230
Empire of the Sun (Ballard) (85) 218
Empire of Their Own, An (Gabler) (89) 278
Empire Statesman (Slayton) (02) 248
Empire Wilderness, An (Kaplan) (99) 247
Empires in the Balance (Willmott) (H-83) 119
Empress of the Splendid Season (Hijuelos) (00) 221
Enchanted Loom, The (Corsi, ed.) (92) 183
Enchantment (Merkin) (87) 238
Encompassing Nature (Torrance) (99) 252
Encounters with Chinese Writers (Dillard) (85) 223
End of Equality, The (Kaus) (93) 258
End of History and the Last Man, The (Fukuyama) (93) 262
End of Nature, The (McKibben) (90) 211
End of Order, The (Mee) (81) 277
End of Racism, The (D'Souza) (96) 227
End of Science, The (Horgan) (97) 243
End of the Hunt, The (Flanagan) (95) 200
End of the Old Order in Rural Europe, The (Blum) (79) 188
End of the War in Asia, The (Allen) (80) 285
End of the World, The (Friedrich) (H-83) 125

TITLE INDEX

End of the World News, The (Burgess) (84) 267
End of Time, The (Barbour) (01) 281
End of Vandalism, The (Drury) (95) 204
End Papers (Breytenbach) (87) 242
End to Torment (H. D.) (80) 290
Endangered Dreams (Starr) (97) 247
Ender's Shadow (Card) (00) 226
Endless Life (Ferlinghetti) (82) 229
Endless Love (Spencer) (80) 294
Ends of the Earth, The (Kaplan) (97) 252
Enduring Love (McEwan) (99) 257
Enemy's Country (Hill) (92) 188
Engine of Reason, the Seat of the Soul, The (Churchland) (96) 232
Engineer of Human Souls, The (Škvorecký) (85) 227
England, England (Barnes) (00) 231
English Auden, The (Auden) (79) 193
English Civil War, The (Ashton) (80) 297
English Creek (Doig) (85) 232
English Culture and the Decline of the Industrial Spirit, 1850-1980 (Wiener) (82) 234
English Disease, The (Skibell) (04) 232
English Music (Ackroyd) (93) 266
English Patient, The (Ondaatje) (93) 271
Enigma (Ferguson) (88) 279
Enigma of Anger, The (Keizer) (03) 265
Enigma of Arrival, The (Naipaul) (88) 283
Enlarging the Change (Fitzgerald) (86) 244
Enough (McKibben) (04) 236
Entered from the Sun (Garrett) (91) 257
Entertaining Satan (Demos) (H-83) 130
Enthusiast, The (Harrison) (84) 272
Entrepreneurs of Ideology (Stark) (82) 240
Entries (Berry) (95) 209
Equal Affections (Leavitt) (90) 215
Equal Love (Davies) (01) 286
Equal Music, An (Seth) (00) 236
Ernest Hemingway, Selected Letters, 1917-1961 (Hemingway) (82) 245
Ernest Hemingway and His World (Burgess) (79) 196
Eros the Bittersweet (Carson) (87) 248
Erosion (Graham) (84) 279
Errancy, The (Graham) (98) 286
Errata (Steiner) (99) 261
Escape from Elba, The (MacKenzie) (H-83) 134
Escapes (Williams) (91) 262
Essays (Knox) (90) 219
Essays, Articles and Reviews of Evelyn Waugh, The (Waugh) (85) 238
Essays in Appreciation (Ricks) (97) 256
Essays in Feminism (Gornick) (80) 302
Essays of E. B. White (White) (78) 295
Essays of Virginia Woolf, 1904-1912, The (Woolf) (88) 288
Essays of Virginia Woolf, 1912-1918, The (Woolf) (89) 283
Essays of Virginia Woolf, 1919-1924, The (Woolf) (90) 222
Essays on Music (Adorno) (03) 269
Eternal Curse on the Reader of These Pages (Puig) (83) 235
Eternal Moment, The (Fiut) (91) 266
Ethics (Foucault) (98) 289
Eudora (Waldron) (00) 240
Eudora Welty (Prenshaw, ed.) (81) 283
Eudora Welty's Achievement of Order (Kreyling) (81) 288
Europe (Davies) (97) 260
Europe, Europe (Enzensberger) (90) 227
Europeans, The (Barzini) (H-84) 153
Eva Perón (Fraser and Navarro) (82) 249
Evangelist of Race (Field) (82) 256
Eve (Phillips) (H-85) 130

Evelyn Nesbit and Stanford White (Mooney) (77) 260
Evelyn Waugh (Hastings) (96) 237
Evelyn Waugh, 1903-1939 (Stannard) (88) 293
Evelyn Waugh, 1939-1966 (Stannard) (93) 275
Evening Performance, An (Garrett) (86) 250
Evensong (Godwin) (00) 244
Every Force Evolves a Form (Davenport) (88) 298
Every Spy a Prince (Raviv and Melman) (91) 271
Everything for Sale (Kuttner) (98) 294
Everything Is Illuminated (Foer) (03) 274
Everything You Need (Kennedy) (02) 253
Everything's Eventual (King) (03) 279
Eve's Apple (Rosen) (98) 299
Evolution of Jane, The (Schine) (99) 265
Evolution's Workshop (Larson) (02) 258
Ex Libris (Fadiman) (99) 269
Examined Life, The (Nozick) (90) 231
Excursions in the Real World (Trevor) (95) 214
Execution by Hunger (Dolot) (86) 254
Executioner's Song, The (Mailer) (80) 306
Exemplars (Needham) (86) 259
Exiled in Paradise (Heilbut) (84) 284
Experience (Amis) (01) 290
Experience of Place, The (Hiss) (91) 275
Explaining America (Wills) (82) 261
Explaining Hitler (Rosenbaum) (99) 273
Explanation of America, An (Pinsky) (81) 293
Extinction (Bernhard) (96) 242
Eye for Dark Places, An (Marder) (94) 269
Eye in the Door, The (Barker) (95) 218
Eye of the Heron, The (Le Guin) (84) 291
Eye of the Story, The (Welty) (79) 200
Eyre Affair, The (Fforde) (03) 283
Ezra Pound (Heymann) (77) 264
Ezra Pound and Dorothy Shakespear, Their Letters, 1909-1914 (Pound and Shakespear) (85) 243

F. Scott Fitzgerald (Le Vot) (84) 318
Fabians, The (Mackenzie and Mackenzie) (78) 300
Fabricating Lives (Leibowitz) (90) 236
Face of Battle, The (Keegan) (78) 305
Face of the Nation, The (Fitzgerald) (97) 265
Faces of Revolution (Bailyn) (91) 279
Facing the River (Miłosz) (96) 247
Facing Up (Weinberg) (02) 263
Factory of Facts, The (Sante) (99) 278
Facts, The (Roth) (89) 288
Faith in a Seed (Thoreau) (94) 274
Faith of a Writer, The (Oates) (04) 240
Faith, Sex, Mystery (Gilman) (88) 303
Faithless (Oates) (02) 267
Falconer (Cheever) (78) 309
Fall into Eden, The (Wyatt) (87) 253
Fall of Berlin, 1945, The (Beevor) (03) 288
Fall of France, The (Jackson) (04) 244
Fall of the House of Labor, The (Montgomery) (88) 308
Fall of the Peacock Throne (Forbis) (81) 297
Falling in Place (Beattie) (81) 304
Falling Slowly (Brookner) (00) 248
False Prophet (Rice) (04) 249
False Starts (Braly) (77) 269
Fame and Folly (Ozick) (97) 269
Familiar Spirits (Lurie) (02) 271
Familiar Territory (Epstein) (80) 310
Family (Frazier) (95) 222
Family (Gold) (82) 267
Family Album, A (Galloway) (79) 204
Family and Nation (Moynihan) (87) 259
Family Arsenal, The (Theroux) (77) 274
Family Dancing (Leavitt) (85) 250
Family Feeling (Yglesias) (77) 277
Family Installments (Rivera) (83) 240

Family Madness, A (Keneally) (87) 265
Family Matters (Mistry) (03) 292
Family Orchard, The (Eve) (01) 295
Family Pictures (Miller) (91) 283
Family Sayings (Ginzburg) (85) 255
Family Secrets (Murphy) (96) 253
Famished Road, The (Okri) (93) 279
Fanatic Heart, A (O'Brien) (85) 260
Fanny (Jong) (81) 309
Fanny Burney (Harman) (02) 275
Far Cry from Kensington, A (Spark) (89) 293
Far from Home (Powers) (92) 193
Farewell Party, The (Kundera) (77) 283
Farewell Symphony, The (White) (98) 303
Farm (Rhodes) (90) 240
Farther Shore, The (Gifford) (91) 287
Fascism (Payne) (81) 314
Fast Food Nation (Schlosser) (02) 280
Fast-Talking Dames (DiBattista) (02) 285
Faster (Gleick) (00) 252
Fatal Environment, The (Slotkin) (86) 264
Fatal Shore, The (Hughes) (88) 312
Fate (Ai) (92) 197
Fate of the Earth, The (Schell) (83) 244
Fateful Alliance, The (Kennan) (H-85) 135
Father, The (Olds) (93) 284
Father and Son (Brown) (97) 274
Father Melancholy's Daughter (Godwin) (92) 201
Fatheralong (Wideman) (95) 227
Fatherless America (Blankenhorn) (96) 258
Fathers and Crows (Vollmann) (93) 288
Father's Words, A (Stern) (87) 271
Faulkner, a Comprehensive Guide to the Brodsky
    Collection, Vol. II (Faulkner) (85) 266
FBI (Ungar) (77) 287
FDR (Miller) (H-84) 158
FDR (Morgan) (86) 269
FDR, 1933-1937 (Davis) (87) 276
FDR, 1937-1940 (Davis) (94) 278
FDR, 1940-1943 (Davis) (01) 300
Feast of the Goat, The (Vargas Llosa) (02) 290
Feast of Words, A (Wolff) (78) 314
Feather Crowns (Mason) (94) 283
Federico García Lorca (Gibson) (90) 245
Feel of Rock, The (Whittemore) (83) 250
Feeling of What Happens, The (Damasio) (00) 256
Felix Frankfurter and His Times (Parrish) (H-83) 140
Felt (Fulton) (02) 295
Female Ruins (Nicholson) (01) 305
Feminism Without Illusions (Fox-Genovese)
    (92) 205
Ferocious Alphabets (Donoghue) (82) 271
Fetishist, The (Tournier) (85) 272
Feud, The (Berger) (84) 295
Fever (Wideman) (90) 249
Few Short Notes on Tropical Butterflies, A (Murray)
    (04) 253
Few Things I Know About Glafkos Thrassakis, The
    (Vassilikos) (04) 257
Fiasco (Lem) (88) 318
Fiction and Repetition (Miller) (83) 253
Fidel (Szulc) (87) 282
Fidel Castro (Quirk) (94) 287
Field Work (Heaney) (80) 315
Fierce Discontent, A (McGerr) (04) 261
Fifth Child, The (Lessing) (89) 298
Fifth Miracle, The (Davies) (00) 260
5th of July (Wilson) (80) 320
Fifties, The (Halberstam) (94) 292
Fifty Stories (Boyle) (81) 325
Fifty Years of Europe (Morris) (98) 308
Figure on the Boundary Line, The (Meckel) (85) 276
Figured Wheel, The (Pinsky) (97) 278

Figures in a Western Landscape (Stevenson) (95) 231
Figures of Thought (Nemerov) (79) 209
Fima (Oz) (94) 296
Fin-de-siècle Vienna (Schorske) (81) 330
Final Entries, 1945 (Goebbels) (79) 212
Final Martyrs, The (Endō) (95) 235
Final Payments (Gordon) (79) 218
Final Reports (Rovere) (H-85) 141
Finding the Center (Naipaul) (85) 281
Finishing School, The (Godwin) (86) 274
Fire and Water (de Jonge) (81) 335
Fire Down Below (Golding) (90) 253
Fire in the Minds of Men (Billington) (81) 340
Fires (Yourcenar) (82) 275
First Churchill, The (Thomson) (81) 344
First-Class Temperament, A (Ward) (90) 258
First Elizabeth, The (Erickson) (H-84) 164
First Great Triumph (Zimmermann) (03) 297
First in His Class (Maraniss) (96) 263
First Lady from Plains (Carter) (H-85) 146
First Light (Wagoner) (84) 299
First Man, The (Camus) (96) 268
First Man on the Sun, The (Dillard) (84) 304
First Moderns, The (Everdell) (98) 312
First Polka, The (Bienek) (85) 286
First Salute, The (Tuchman) (89) 302
First Stargazers, The (Cornell) (82) 280
First, You Cry (Rollin) (77) 291
First Woman in the Republic, The (Karcher) (96) 273
First World War, The (Keegan) (00) 264
Fish in the Water, A (Vargas Llosa) (95) 239
Fisher King, The (Powell) (87) 287
Fiskadoro (Johnson) (86) 279
Fitzgeralds and the Kennedys, The (Goodwin) (88) 323
Five for Sorrow, Ten for Joy (Godden) (80) 325
Five O'Clock Angel (Williams) (91) 291
Five of Hearts, The (O'Toole) (91) 295
Five Seasons (Yehoshua) (90) 263
Five Stages of Grief, The (Pastan) (79) 222
Flag for Sunrise, A (Stone) (82) 284
Flaming Corsage, The (Kennedy) (97) 282
Flanders (Anthony) (99) 282
Flannery O'Connor's South (Coles) (81) 350
Flashman and the Dragon (Fraser) (87) 292
Flaubert (Lottman) (90) 268
Flaubert-Sand (Flaubert and Sand) (94) 300
Flaubert's Parrot (Barnes) (86) 284
Flawed Giant (Dallek) (99) 286
Flaws in the Glass (White) (83) 257
Flesh and Blood (Williams) (88) 330
Flesh and Machines (Brooks) (03) 302
Flight from Eden (Cassedy) (92) 210
Floating World, The (Kadohata) (90) 273
Flood (Matthews) (83) 262
Flora Tristan's London Journal, 1840 (Tristan)
    (82) 288
Flotsam and Jetsam (Higgins) (03) 307
Flounder, The (Grass) (79) 226
Flow (Csikszentmihalyi) (91) 299
Flow Chart (Ashbery) (92) 214
Flower and the Leaf, The (Cowley) (86) 288
Flower and the Nettle, The (Lindbergh) (77) 294
Flu (Kolata) (00) 268
Fluid Concepts and Creative Analogies (Hofstadter)
    (96) 277
Flutes of Dionysus, The (Stock) (91) 304
Flutie (Glancy) (99) 291
Flying Change, The (Taylor) (86) 293
Flying Home and Other Stories (Ellison) (97) 287
Flying to Nowhere (Fuller) (85) 292
Foe (Coetzee) (88) 334
Folding Cliffs, The (Merwin) (99) 295
Folding Star, The (Hollinghurst) (95) 244

TITLE INDEX

Following Story, The (Nooteboom) (95) 249
Food Politics (Nestle) (03) 311
Footnote, The (Grafton) (98) 317
Footprints (Hearon) (97) 292
Footsteps (Holmes) (86) 297
For Kings and Planets (Canin) (99) 299
For Love (Miller) (94) 305
For the Living and the Dead (Tranströmer) (96) 283
For the Love of It (Booth) (00) 273
For the Relief of Unbearable Urges (Englander) (00) 277
For the Time Being (Dillard) (00) 282
Forbidden Knowledge (Shattuck) (97) 296
Force of Nature (Hager) (96) 286
Forces of Production (Noble) (H-85) 152
Ford (Lacey) (87) 297
Ford Madox Ford (Judd) (92) 218
Foregone Conclusions (Bernstein) (95) 253
Foreign Affairs (Lurie) (85) 297
Foreign Land (Raban) (86) 302
Foreseeable Future, The (Price) (92) 222
Forest of Kings, A (Schele and Freidel) (91) 308
Forever Young (Cott) (79) 231
Forged in Fire (Copp) (H-83) 145
Forgetting, The (Shenk) (02) 300
Forgotten War, The (Blair) (89) 307
Fork River Space Project, The (Morris) (78) 319
Forties, The (Wilson) (84) 309
Fortress of Solitude, The (Lethem) (04) 266
Fortress Without a Roof (Morrison) (H-83) 150
Fortunate Traveller, The (Walcott) (82) 293
Fortunes of the Courtier, The (Burke) (97) 301
Foucault's Pendulum (Eco) (90) 277
Foul Matter (Grimes) (04) 271
Found, Lost, Found (Priestley) (78) 325
Founding Father (Brookhiser) (97) 306
Founding Fish, The (McPhee) (03) 316
Founding the Far West (Johnson) (93) 293
Four Wise Men, The (Tournier) (83) 267
Fourteen Sisters of Emilio Montez O'Brien, The (Hijuelos) (94) 308
Fourth and Richest Reich, The (Hartrich) (81) 353
Fourth Hand, The (Irving) (02) 305
Fox (Rich) (02) 309
Foxfire (Oates) (94) 313
Foxybaby (Jolley) (86) 306
Fraction of Darkness, A (Pastan) (86) 310
Fragments (Fuller) (85) 301
Frame Structures (Howe) (97) 311
France Under Napoleon (Bergeron) (82) 296
Francis Bacon (Zagorin) (99) 303
Franco (Preston) (95) 257
Frank and Maisie (Sheed) (86) 313
Frank Capra (McBride) (93) 298
Frank Lloyd Wright (Secrest) (93) 303
Franklin D. Roosevelt and American Foreign Policy, 1932-1945 (Dallek) (80) 328
Franklin of Philadelphia (Wright) (87) 303
Franz Kafka (Karl) (92) 227
Franz Werfel (Jungk) (91) 313
Fraud (Brookner) (94) 317
Freaks (Fiedler) (79) 235
Frederick Douglass (McFeely) (92) 232
Fredy Neptune (Murray) (00) 286
Freedom (Patterson) (92) 237
Freedom Evolves (Dennett) (04) 275
Freedom of the Poet, The (Berryman) (77) 299
Freedom Spent (Harris) (77) 304
Freedomland (Price) (99) 307
Frequency of Souls, The (Zuravleff) (97) 315
Freud (Clark) (81) 357
Freud (Gay) (89) 311
Freud (Roth) (99) 311

Friday Book, The (Barth) (85) 307
Friend of My Youth (Munro) (91) 317
Friend of the Earth, A (Boyle) (01) 310
Friendly Fire (Bryan) (77) 309
Friendship and Literature (Sharp) (87) 309
Fringes of Power, The (Colville) (86) 320
From a High Place (Spender) (00) 290
From a Three-Cornered World (Mitsui) (98) 322
From Beirut to Jerusalem (Friedman) (90) 283
From Bondage (Roth) (97) 319. *See also* Diving Rock on the Hudson, A, Mercy of a Rude Stream, *and* Requiem for Harlem
From *Brown* to *Bakke*, The Supreme Court and School Integration (Wilkinson) (80) 334
From Dawn to Decadence (Barzun) (01) 314
From Prejudice to Destruction (Katz) (81) 362
From the Beast to the Blonde (Warner) (96) 290
From the Congo to Soweto (Jackson) (H-83) 155
From the First Nine (Merrill) (84) 314
From the Mountain, from the Valley (Still) (02) 313
From Time Immemorial (Peters) (H-85) 156
From Wealth to Power (Zakaria) (99) 315
From West to East (Schwartz) (99) 319
Frontiers of Change (Cochran) (82) 301
Frost (Pritchard) (85) 312
Frozen Desire (Buchan) (98) 327
Fugitive from Utopia, A (Barańczak) (88) 340
Fulbright (Woods) (96) 294
Full House (Gould) (97) 323
Full of Life (Cooper) (01) 319
Fup (Dodge) (85) 318
Furies, The (Hobhouse) (94) 321
Fury (Rushdie) (02) 317
Future of China After Mao, The (Terrill) (79) 240
Future of Freedom, The (Zakaria) (04) 279
Future of Life, The (Wilson) (03) 321

Gabriel's Rebellion (Egerton) (94) 325
Gain (Powers) (99) 324
Galápagos (Vonnegut) (86) 326
Galatea 2.2 (Powers) (96) 299
Galileo's Daughter (Sobel) (00) 295
Game Men Play, A (Bourjaily) (81) 364
Gandhi (Brown) (91) 321
Gang, The (Worthen) (02) 321
Garbage (Ammons) (94) 331
García Márquez (Bell-Villada) (91) 325
Garden of Eden, The (Hemingway) (87) 313
Gardens of Kyoto, The (Walbert) (02) 326
Gate of Heavenly Peace, The (Spence) (82) 305
Gates (Manes and Andrews) (44) 335
Gates of Eden (Dickstein) (78) 328
Gathering Evidence (Bernhard) (87) 317
Gathering of Old Men, A (Gaines) (84) 323
Gathering the Tribes (Forché) (77) 314
Gaudier-Brzeska (Silber) (98) 331
Geeks (Katz) (01) 323
General in His Labyrinth, The (García Márquez) (91) 329
General of the Army (Cray) (91) 333
General of the Dead Army, The (Kadare) (92) 242
General's Life, A (Bradley and Blair) (H-84) 171
Generation of 1914, The (Wohl) (80) 337
Generations (Clifton) (77) 318
Genes, Peoples, and Languages (Cavalli-Sforza) (01) 327
Genesis (Alter) (97) 327
Genesis (Crace) (04) 283
Genet (White) (94) 339
Genie (Rymer) (94) 345
Genius (Gleick) (93) 308
Genius and Lust (Mailer) (77) 322
Genius for War, A (Dupuy) (78) 332

Genius in Disguise (Kunkel) (96) 303
Genocidal Mentality, The (Lifton and Markusen) (91) 338
Genome (Ridley) (01) 332
Gentle Barbarian, The (Pritchett) (78) 340
Gentlemen in England (Wilson) (87) 322
Genuine Reality (Simon) (99) 329
Geography of Thought, The (Nisbett) (04) 287
Geography III (Bishop) (77) 326
Geometry of Love, The (Visser) (02) 330
George Bancroft (Handlin) (H-85) 162
George C. Marshall (Pogue) (88) 346
George Eliot (Ashton) (98) 335
George Mills (Elkin) (83) 273
George Washington Carver (McMurry) (82) 310
George Washington Williams (Franklin) (86) 332
Georges Perec (Bellos) (95) 262
Georgia O'Keeffe (Robinson) (90) 289
Georgia O'Keeffe (Turner) (00) 300
Gerald Brenan (Gathorne-Hardy) (94) 350
Gerard Manley Hopkins, Selected Letters (Hopkins) (91) 343
German Army, 1933-1945, The (Cooper) (79) 245
German Army, 1933-45, The (Seaton) (H-83) 161
German Big Business and the Rise of Hitler (Turner) (86) 338
German Rearmament and the West, 1932-1933 (Bennett) (80) 344
German Romanticism and Its Institutions (Ziolkowski) (91) 347
German Socialism and Weimar Democracy (Breitman) (82) 315
Germans, The (Craig) (H-83) 166
Germany and the Two World Wars (Hillgruber) (82) 321
Germany and the United States (Gatzke) (81) 368
Germany East and West (Whetten) (81) 373
Germany 1866-1945 (Craig) (79) 249
Gertrude and Claudius (Updike) (01) 337
Gesture Life, A (Lee) (00) 305
Get Shorty (Leonard) (91) 351
Getting a Life (Simpson) (02) 334
Getting Mother's Body (Parks) (04) 291
Getting to Know the General (Greene) (H-85) 168
Ghost Dance (Maso) (87) 326
Ghost Road, The (Barker) (96) 307
Ghost Story (Straub) (80) 349
Ghost Writer, The (Roth) (80) 354
Ghosts (Banville) (94) 355
Ghosts of Manila (Hamilton-Paterson) (95) 267
Giacometti (Lord) (86) 343
Giants, The (Barnet) (78) 345
Giant's House, The (McCracken) (97) 331
Gift, The (H. D.) (83) 278
Gift, The (Hyde) (84) 330
Gift of Asher Lev, The (Potok) (91) 355
Gift of Stones, The (Crace) (90) 294
Gifts of the Jews, The (Cahill) (99) 333
Gilgamesh (Sîn-leqi-unninni) (85) 324
Gilligan Unbound (Cantor) (02) 338
Ginger Tree, The (Wynd) (78) 349
Girl from the Coast, The (Toer) (03) 326
Girl in a Swing, The (Adams) (81) 377
Girl in Landscape (Lethem) (99) 337
Girl, Interrupted (Kaysen) (94) 360
Girl Meets God (Winner) (03) 334
Girl with a Monkey, A (Michaels) (01) 342
Girl with Curious Hair (Wallace) (90) 299
Girls (Busch) (98) 340
Girls' Guide to Hunting and Fishing, The (Bank) (00) 309
Gissing (Halperin) (83) 283
Give Us Each Day (Dunbar-Nelson) (86) 349

Giving Good Weight (McPhee) (80) 358
Giving Offense (Coetzee) (97) 335
Gladstone (Jenkins) (98) 344
Glamorama (Ellis) (00) 313
Glass Face in the Rain, A (Stafford) (83) 288
Glass Palace, The (Ghosh) (02) 342
Glimmering (Hand) (98) 348
Glitter Dome, The (Wambaugh) (82) 325
Globalization and Its Discontents (Stiglitz) (03) 334
Glorious Cause, The (Middlekauff) (H-83) 171
Glue (Welsh) (02) 347
Gnostic Gospels, The (Pagels) (80) 363
God (Miles) (96) 311
God Against the Gods, A (Drury) (77) 332
God and the American Writer (Kazin) (98) 352
God Emperor of Dune (Herbert) (82) 329
God of Indeterminacy, The (McPherson) (94) 364
God of Small Things, The (Roy) (98) 357
Gödel (Casti and DePauli) (01) 346
Gödel, Escher, Bach (Hofstadter) (80) 367
Godric (Buechner) (81) 382
God's Chinese Son (Spence) (97) 339
God's Fool (Green) (86) 354
God's Funeral (Wilson) (00) 317
God's Grace (Malamud) (83) 291
God's Long Summer (Marsh) (98) 362
God's Name in Vain (Carter) (01) 351
God's Secretaries (Nicolson) (04) 295
Goebbels Diaries, The (Goebbels) (H-84) 176
Goethe, 1749-1790 (Boyle) (01) 356
Goethe, 1790-1803 (Boyle) (92) 247
Going Native (Wright) (95) 271
Going to the Territory (Ellison) (87) 331
Going Up the River (Hallinan) (02) 352
Gold and Iron (Stern) (78) 354
Gold Bug Variations, The (Powers) (92) 252
Gold Cell, The (Olds) (88) 353
Gold Coast, The (Robinson) (89) 316
Golden Age, The (Vidal) (01) 361
Golden Days (See) (87) 335
Golden Gate, The (Seth) (87) 340
Goldwater (Goldwater and Casserly) (89) 321
Goldwyn (Berg) (90) 303
Gone to Soldiers (Piercy) (88) 358
Gonne-Yeats Letters 1893-1938, The (Gonne and Yeats) (94) 368
Good Apprentice, The (Murdoch) (87) 345
Good as Gold (Heller) (80) 372
Good Boys and Dead Girls (Gordon) (92) 256
Good Faith (Smiley) (04) 299
Good Husband, The (Godwin) (95) 275
Good Life, A (Bradlee) (96) 316
Good Life and Its Discontents, The (Samuelson) (97) 345
Good Mother, The (Miller) (87) 352
Good Natured (De Waal) (97) 350
Good Terrorist, The (Lessing) (86) 358
Good Times, The (Baker) (90) 309
Good Trembling (Wormser) (86) 364
Good War, The (Terkel) (H-85) 173
Good Will and Ordinary Love (Smiley) (90) 642
Good Word & Other Words, The (Sheed) (80) 375
Goodnight! (Tertz) (90) 314
Gore Vidal (Kaplan) (00) 321
Gorky Park (Smith) (82) 333
Goshawk, Antelope (Smith) (80) 380
Gospel According to the Son, The (Mailer) (98) 366
Gospel of Gentility, The (Hunter) (H-85) 179
Gossip from the Forest (Keneally) (77) 336
Gould's Book of Fish (Flanagan) (03) 338
Government of the Tongue, The (Heaney) (90) 319
Goya (Hughes) (04) 303
Grace Abounding (Howard) (83) 296

Grace Notes (Dove) (90) 324
Gracefully Insane (Beam) (03) 343
Grammars of Creation (Steiner) (02) 357
Grammatical Man (Campbell) (83) 301
Grand Complication, The (Kurzweil) (02) 362
Grand Delusion, A (Mann) (02) 367
Grand Expectations (Patterson) (97) 355
Grand Failure, The (Brzezinski) (90) 329
Grand Strategy of Philip II, The (Parker) (00) 326
Granite Pail, The (Niedecker) (86) 368
Grant (McFeely) (82) 338
Grasp of Consciousness, The (Piaget) (77) 341
Gratitude (Buckley) (91) 359
Greasy Lake and Other Stories (Boyle) (86) 372
Great and Desperate Cures (Valenstein) (87) 357
Great Blue (Galvin) (91) 364
Great Books (Denby) (97) 360
Great Cat Massacre and Other Episodes in French
    Cultural History, The (Darnton) (H-85) 183
Great Code, The (Frye) (83) 306
Great Days (Barthelme) (80) 385
Great Deep, The (Hamilton-Paterson) (93) 312
Great Directors at Work (Jones) (87) 362
Great Disruption, The (Fukuyama) (00) 331
Great Fear, The (Caute) (79) 255
Great Fire, The (Hazzard) (04) 308
Great Friends (Garnett) (81) 386
Great Harry (Erickson) (81) 391
Great Map of Mankind, The (Marshall and Williams)
    (H-83) 176
Great Melody, The (O'Brien) (93) 316
Great Movies, The (Ebert) (03) 348
Great Plains (Frazier) (90) 334
Great Rebellion, The (Ruíz) (81) 396
Great Republic, The (Bailyn et al.) (78) 360
Great Shame, The (Keneally) (00) 336
Great Tranquillity (Amichai) (84) 334
Great Triumvirate, The (Peterson) (88) 363
Great Wall of China, The (Waldron) (91) 368
Greatest Benefit to Mankind, The (Porter) (99) 341
Greatest Power on Earth, The (Clark) (82) 343
Green Knight, The (Murdoch) (95) 279
Green River Rising (Willocks) (95) 283
Greenlanders, The (Smiley) (89) 326
Greenspan (Martin) (01) 365
Greeting, The (Dillard) (83) 309
Grey Is the Color of Hope (Ratushinskaya) (89) 330
Gringos (Portis) (92) 262
Groom Falconer (Dubie) (90) 338
Groucho (Kanfer) (01) 370
Ground Beneath Her Feet, The (Rushdie) (00) 341
Ground Work (Duncan) (85) 329
Groundwork (Morgan) (80) 390
Group Portrait (Delbanco) (83) 312
Growing Seasons, The (Hynes) (04) 312
Growing Up (Baker) (83) 317
Grumbles from the Grave (Heinlein) (91) 372
Guadalcanal Remembered (Merillat) (H-83) 181
Guardian of the Word, The (Laye) (85) 334
Guggenheims (Davis) (79) 260
Guide for the Perplexed, A (Schumacher) (78) 364
Guided Tour of the Collected Works of C. G. Jung, A
    (Hopcke) (90) 343
Gulag (Applebaum) (04) 316
Gulag Archipelago, The (Solzhenitsyn) (78) 370
Gunfighters, Highwaymen, and Vigilantes (McGrath)
    (H-85) 190
Guns, Germs, and Steel (Diamond) (98) 370
Gustav Mahler, 1892-1904 (La Grange) (96) 321
Guston in Time (Feld) (04) 320
Gutenberg Elegies, The (Birkerts) (96) 326
Gypsies, The (Fraser) (93) 321

H. D. (Robinson) (83) 331
H. G. Wells (West) (85) 380
Habit of Being, The (O'Connor) (80) 391
Habitations of the Word (Gass) (86) 376
Habits of the Heart (Bellah et al.) (86) 380
Had I a Hundred Mouths (Goyen) (86) 386
Haing Ngor (Ngor, with Warner) (89) 335
Half a Heart (Brown) (01) 375
Half a Life (Naipaul) (02) 372
Half Asleep in Frog Pajamas (Robbins) (95) 287
Half Moon Street (Theroux) (85) 338
Hamlet in Purgatory (Greenblatt) (02) 376
Hand to Mouth (Auster) (98) 374
Handbook for Visitors from Outer Space, A (Kramer)
    (85) 344
Handling Sin (Malone) (87) 366
Handmaid's Tale, The (Atwood) (87) 371
Hands and Hearts (Rothman) (H-85) 195
Handwriting (Ondaatje) (00) 346
Hang-Gliding from Helicon (Hoffman) (89) 340
Hannah Arendt (Hill, ed.) (80) 395
Hannah Arendt (Young-Bruehl) (83) 322
Happiest Man Alive, The (Dearborn) (92) 266
Happy Alchemy (Davies) (99) 346
Happy as a Dog's Tail (Swir) (86) 391
Happy Hour (Shapiro) (88) 368
Happy to Be Here (Keillor) (83) 326
Hard Choices (Vance) (H-84) 180
Hard Evidence (Miller) (92) 271
Hard Time (Paretsky) (00) 350
Hardy (Seymour-Smith) (95) 291
Hardy the Creator (Gatrell) (90) 348
Harland's Half Acre (Malouf) (85) 348
Harlot's Ghost (Mailer) (92) 276
Harm Done (Rendell) (00) 354
Harold Macmillan (Fisher) (H-83) 185
Harold Macmillan, 1894-1956 (Horne) (90) 352
Harold Macmillan, 1957-1986 (Horne) (90) 358
Harold Nicolson (Nicolson) (81) 406
Haroun and the Sea of Stories (Rushdie) (91) 376
Harp (Dunne) (90) 364
Harp Song for a Radical (Young) (00) 358
Harriet Beecher Stowe (Hedrick) (95) 296
Harry Gold (Dillon) (01) 379
Harry Hopkins (Adams) (78) 375
Harry Potter and the Order of the Phoenix (Rowling)
    (04) 324
Harry S. Truman and the Modern American Presidency
    (Ferrell) (H-84) 185
Harvest of Empire (González) (01) 384
Harvest of Sorrow, The (Conquest) (87) 376
Harvesting Ballads (Kimball) (85) 352
Haunted Land, The (Rosenberg) (96) 330
Haunting of L., The (Norman) (03) 352
Haunts of the Black Masseur (Sprawson) (94) 372
Havelock Ellis (Grosskurth) (81) 412
Hawksmoor (Ackroyd) (87) 382
Hawthorne's Secret (Young) (85) 358
Hay (Muldoon) (99) 350
Haymarket Tragedy, The (Avrich) (H-85) 201
Hazlitt (Bromwich) (85) 363
Hazlitt (Jones) (91) 381
He/She (Gold) (81) 426
Headbirths (Grass) (83) 336
Healing, The (Jones) (99) 355
Hearing Secret Harmonies (Powell) (77) 347
Hearing Voices (Wilson) (97) 364
Heartbreaking Work of Staggering Genius, A (Eggers)
    (01) 389
Hearts and Minds (Madsen) (78) 379
Hearts in Atlantis (King) (00) 362
Heat and Dust (Jhabvala) (77) 352
Heat and Other Stories (Oates) (92) 281

Heather Blazing, The (Tóibín) (94) 376
Heaven on Earth (Muravchik) (03) 356
. . . Heavens and the Earth, The (McDougall) (86) 396
Heaven's Coast (Doty) (97) 368
Heaven's Door (Borjas) (00) 367
Heavy Water and Other Stories (Amis) (00) 372
Hegel (Pinkard) (01) 393
Heisenberg's War (Powers) (94) 380
Helen Hunt Jackson (Phillips) (04) 330
Helene Deutsch (Roazen) (86) 402
Hell to Pay (Pelecanos) (03) 361
Hello, Darkness (Sissman) (79) 264
Hemingway (Lynn) (88) 372
Hemingway (Meyers) (86) 406
Hemingway, The American Homecoming (Reynolds)
  (93) 325
Hemingway, The Final Years (Reynolds) (00) 377
Hemingway, The 1930's (Reynolds) (98) 379
Hemingway, The Paris Years (Reynolds) (90) 369
Hemingway Women, The (Kert) (84) 337
Hemingway's Art of Non-Fiction (Weber) (91) 386
Hemingway's Suitcase (Harris) (91) 390
Hence (Leithauser) (90) 373
Henry Cabot Lodge and the Search for an American
  Foreign Policy (Widenor) (81) 416
Henry Fielding (Battestin and Battestin) (91) 395
Henry James (Kaplan) (93) 330
Henry James Letters, 1883-1895 (James) (81) 421
Henry James Letters, 1895-1916 (James) (85) 368
Henry Purcell in Japan (Salter) (86) 411
Henry Thoreau (Richardson) (87) 387
Henry's Fate & Other Poems, 1967-1972 (Berryman)
  (78) 384
Hen's Teeth and Horse's Toes (Gould) (H-84) 190
Her First American (Segal) (86) 416
Her Husband (Middlebrook) (04) 335
Her Own Place (Sanders) (94) 385
Her Own Terms (Grossman) (89) 345
Her Victory (Sillitoe) (83) 340
Herbert Hoover (Burner) (80) 400
Here but Not Here (Ross) (99) 360
Here's to You, Jesusa! (Poniatowska) (02) 381
Herman Melville (Parker) (97) 373
HERmione (H. D.) (82) 349
Hermit in Paris (Calvino) (04) 339
Herself Defined (Guest) (85) 374
Herself in Love and Other Stories (Wiggins) (88) 377
Hesitation Before Birth, A (Mailloux) (90) 378
Hey Jack! (Hannah) (88) 382
Heyday of American Communism, The (Klehr)
  (H-85) 206
Hidden-Hand Presidency, The (Greenstein) (H-83) 190
Hidden Law, The (Hecht) (94) 389
Hidden Wordsworth, The (Johnston) (99) 364
Hide, The (Unsworth) (97) 378
High Cotton (Pinckney) (93) 335
High Jinx (Buckley) (87) 392
High Latitudes (Buchan) (97) 383
High Walls of Jerusalem, The (Sanders) (H-84) 197
Higher Superstition (Gross and Levitt) (95) 301
Hilaire Belloc (Wilson) (85) 385
Him with His Foot in His Mouth and Other Stories
  (Bellow) (85) 390
Himself! (Kennedy) (79) 273
Hippocrates (Jouanna) (00) 381
Hiroshima (Takaki) (96) 334
His Holiness (Bernstein and Politi) (97) 388
His Master's Voice (Lem) (84) 342
His Other Half (Lesser) (92) 285
Historian of the Strange (Zeitlin) (94) 393
Historical Fictions (Kenner) (91) 400
History of Afro-American Literature, A (Jackson)
  (90) 382

History of American Wars, The (Williams) (82) 354
History of Architecture, A (Kostof) (86) 421
History of Black Americans (Foner) (H-84) 202
History of Britain, A (Schama) (01) 398
History of Europe, A (Roberts) (98) 383
History of Gay Literature, A (Woods) (99) 369
History of Heaven, A (Russell) (98) 387
History of Modern Criticism, 1750-1950, A (Wellek)
  (92) 290
History of My Heart (Pinsky) (85) 399
History of Philosophy in America, 1720-2000, A
  (Kuklick) (03) 366
History of Private Life, Passions of the Renaissance, A
  (Chartier, ed.) (90) 386
History of Private Life, Revelations of the Medieval
  World, A (Duby, ed.) (89) 349
History of Private Life, From the Fires of Revolution to
  the Great War, A (Perrot, ed.) (91) 404
History of Private Life, Riddles of Identity in Modern
  Times, A (Prost and Vincent, eds.) (92) 294
History of Private Life, From Pagan Rome to
  Byzantium, A (Veyne) (88) 386
History of Reading, A (Manguel) (97) 395
History of Russian Symbolism, A (Pyman) (95) 305
History of South Africa, A (Thompson) (91) 408
History of Southern Literature, The (Rubin, ed.)
  (86) 426
History of Statistics, The (Stigler) (87) 397
History of the American People, A (Johnson) (99) 374
History of the Arab Peoples, A (Hourani) (92) 299
History of the Bible as Literature, A (Norton) (94) 397
History of the Breast, A (Yalom) (98) 391
History of the German Resistance, 1933-1945, The
  (Hoffmann) (78) 388
History of the Idea of Progress (Nisbet) (81) 430
History of the Jews, A (Johnson) (88) 392
History of the Jews in America, A (Sachar) (93) 340
History of the Ottoman Empire and Modern Turkey,
  The (Shaw and Shaw) (78) 393
History of the Surrealist Movement (Durozoi) (03) 370
History of the Westward Movement (Merk) (79) 277
History of the World in 10½ Chapters, A (Barnes)
  (90) 390
History of Wales, A (Davies) (95) 309
History of Women in the West, From Ancient
  Goddesses to Christian Saints, A (Pantel, ed.)
  (93) 345
History Wars (Linenthal and Engelhardt, eds.) (97) 400
Hitler (Stone) (81) 434
Hitler Among the Germans (Binion) (77) 357
Hitler and Stalin (Bullock) (93) 349
Hitler and the Final Solution (Fleming) (H-85) 213
Hitler and the Forgotten Nazis (Pauley) (82) 360
Hitler, 1889-1936 (Kershaw) (00) 386
Hitler in Vienna, 1907-1913 (Jones) (H-84) 207
Hitler of History, The (Lukacs) (98) 396
Hitler over Germany (Mitchell) (H-84) 213
Hitler State, The (Broszat) (82) 363
Hitler vs. Roosevelt (Bailey and Ryan) (80) 404
Hitler's Niece (Hansen) (00) 391
Hitler's Pope (Cornwell) (00) 396
Hitler's Spies (Kahn) (79) 281
Hitler's War (Irving) (78) 398
Hitler's Willing Executioners (Goldhagen) (97) 405
Ho Chi Minh (Duiker) (01) 403
Hobbes (Martinich) (00) 400
Hocus Pocus (Vonnegut) (91) 413
Holder of the World, The (Mukherjee) (94) 401
Hölderlin (Constantine) (89) 354
Hole in Our Soul (Bayles) (95) 314
Hole in the World, A (Rhodes) (91) 418
Hollywood (Vidal) (91) 423

Holocaust and the Crisis of Human Behavior, The (Kren and Rappoport) (81) 439
Holocaust in American Life, The (Novick) (00) 404
Holocaust Testimonies (Langer) (92) 304
Holy Pictures (Boylan) (84) 347
Holy the Firm (Dillard) (78) 404
Home (Rybczynski) (87) 402
Home and Exile (Achebe) (01) 408
Home Before Dark (Cheever) (85) 405
Home to War (Nicosia) (02) 386
Home Town (Kidder) (00) 409
Home Truths (Gallant) (86) 431
Homer (Edwards) (88) 398
Homer to Joyce (Gray) (86) 435
Hometown (Davis) (83) 344
Honeymoon (Gerber) (86) 440
Honorable Defeat, An (Davis) (02) 391
Honor's Voice (Wilson) (99) 379
Hood (Donoghue) (97) 410
Hopkins (White) (93) 353
Hopkins, the Self, and God (Ong) (87) 406
Hornes, The (Buckley) (87) 410
Horse Heaven (Smiley) (01) 412
Hospital of the Transfiguration (Lem) (89) 357
Hothouse, The (Koeppen) (02) 396
Hot Zone, The (Preston) (95) 319
Hotel du Lac (Brookner) (86) 445
Hotel Lautréamont (Ashbery) (93) 358
Hotel New Hampshire, The (Irving) (82) 368
Hourglass (Kiš) (91) 427
Hourmaster (Bataille) (99) 383
House (Kidder) (86) 450
House Gun, The (Gordimer) (99) 387
House of Leaves (Danielewski) (01) 417
House of Morgan, The (Chernow) (91) 432
House of Saud, The (Holden and Johns) (H-83) 195
House of the Spirits, The (Allende) (86) 455
House of Trees, A (Colebrook) (88) 403
House with Four Rooms, A (Godden) (90) 396
Houseboat Days (Ashbery) (78) 408
Household Saints (Prose) (82) 373
Housman's Poems (Bayley) (93) 361
How I Grew (McCarthy) (88) 407
How It All Began (Bukharin) (99) 391
How It Was (Hemingway) (77) 362
How "Natives" Think (Sahlins) (96) 338
How the Cows Turned Mad (Schwartz) (04) 343
How the Dead Live (Self) (01) 422
How the Irish Saved Civilization (Cahill) (96) 343
How the Mind Works (Pinker) (98) 401
How to Be Alone (Franzen) (03) 374
How to Make an American Quilt (Otto) (92) 309
How to Read an Unwritten Language (Graham) (96) 347
How to Save Your Own Life (Jong) (78) 413
How to Suppress Women's Writing (Russ) (84) 353
How We Became Human (Harjo) (03) 379
How We Die (Nuland) (95) 324
Howard Mumford Jones and the Dynamics of Liberal Humanism (Brier) (95) 329
Hugging the Shore (Updike) (84) 358
Hugo Black and the Judicial Revolution (Dunne) (78) 418
Hugo L. Black (Ball) (97) 415
Hugo von Hofmannsthal and His Time (Broch) (85) 410
Hula (Shea) (95) 334
Hullabaloo in the Guava Orchard (Desai) (99) 396
Human Factor, The (Greene) (79) 286
Human Situation, The (Huxley) (78) 422
Human Stain, The (Roth) (01) 452
Hundred Secret Senses, The (Tan) (96) 351
Hundred Years War, The (Seward) (79) 291

Hundreds of Fireflies (Leithauser) (83) 348
Hunger of Memory (Rodriguez) (82) 377
Hungry for the World (Barnes) (01) 432
Hungry Ghosts (Becker) (98) 406
Hunter Gracchus, The (Davenport) (97) 419
Hunting Hypothesis, The (Ardrey) (77) 367
Hunting Mister Heartbreak (Raban) (92) 314
Hunts in Dreams (Drury) (01) 437
Hurricane Lamp (Cassity) (87) 415
Husbands, The (Logue) (96) 355
Hut Six Story, The (Welchman) (H-83) 201
Huxley (Desmond) (98) 411

I. A. Richards (Russo) (90) 401
"I Am" (Clare) (04) 347
I Have Landed (Gould) (03) 384
I Hear America Swinging (De Vries) (77) 372
I Heard My Sister Speak My Name (Savage) (78) 427
I Know This Much Is True (Lamb) (99) 401
I Married a Communist (Roth) (99) 406
I May Not Get There with You (Dyson) (01) 442
I Should Be Extremely Happy in Your Company (Hall) (04) 352
I Tell You Now (Swann and Krupat, eds.) (88) 413
I the Supreme (Roa Bastos) (87) 419
I Will Bear Witness (Klemperer) (01) 447
I Wish This War Were Over (O'Hehir) (85) 415
Ice Age, The (Drabble) (78) 431
Ice-Cream War, An (Boyd) (84) 363
Idea of Poverty, The (Himmelfarb) (H-85) 219
Idea of Decline in Western History, The (Herman) (98) 415
Identity (Kundera) (99) 410
Ideology and Revolution in Modern Europe (Tholfsen) (H-85) 225
If I Had Wheels or Love (Miller) (92) 319
If Not, Winter (Sappho) (03) 388
If on a winter's night a traveler (Calvino) (82) 380
If the River Was Whiskey (Boyle) (90) 406
Ignorance (Kundera) (03) 392
Illness as Metaphor (Sontag) (79) 295
Illusion of Peace (Szulc) (79) 300
Illusion of Technique, The (Barrett) (80) 409
I'm Losing You (Wagner) (97) 423
I'm Radcliffe! Fly Me! (Baker) (77) 376
Image and Other Stories, The (Singer) (86) 461
Imaginary Crimes (Ballantyne) (83) 353
Imaginary Homelands (Rushdie) (92) 324
Imaginary Magnitude (Lem) (85) 421
Imaginative Experience, An (Wesley) (96) 359
Imaginative Landscape of Christopher Columbus, The (Flint) (93) 365
Immaculate Invasion, The (Shacochis) (00) 413
Immortal Bartfuss, The (Appelfeld) (89) 362
Immortality (Kundera) (92) 329
Impatient Armies of the Poor (Folsom) (92) 334
Imperative of Modernity, The (Gray) (90) 410
Imperfect Garden (Todorov) (03) 396
Imperfect Paradise, The (Pastan) (89) 367
Imperfect Thirst (Kinnell) (95) 339
Imperial Experience in Sub-Saharan Africa Since 1870, The (Wilson) (78) 436
Imperial Rockefeller, The (Persico) (H-83) 206
Imperialism at Bay (Louis) (79) 305
Improper Bostonian, The (Hoyt) (80) 414
In a Father's Place (Tilghman) (01) 437
In a Shallow Grave (Purdy) (77) 380
In a Time of Violence (Boland) (95) 343
In America (Sontag) (01) 452
In Another Country (Kenney) (85) 427
In Between the Sheets and Other Stories (McEwan) (80) 417
In Darwin's Shadow (Shermer) (03) 400

In Evil Hour (García Márquez) (80) 421
In Harm's Way (Stanton) (02) 400
In Her Own Right (Griffith) (H-85) 230
In Mediterranean Air (Stanford) (78) 439
In My Father's House (Appiah) (93) 370
In My Father's House (Gaines) (79) 311
In Pharaoh's Army (Wolff) (95) 347
In Quest and Crisis (Ingrao) (80) 426
In Retrospect (McNamara, with VanDeMark) (96) 363
In Search of Equality (McClain) (95) 351
In Search of History (White) (79) 314
In Search of Human Nature (Degler) (92) 338
In Search of J. D. Salinger (Hamilton) (89) 373
In Search of Nature (Wilson) (97) 428
In Search of Our Mothers' Gardens (Walker) (84) 368
In Sunlight, in a Beautiful Garden (Cambor) (02) 404
In Suspect Terrain (Mcphee) (H-84) 218
In the Age of Prose (Heller) (85) 431
In the Age of the Smart Machine (Zuboff) (89) 377
In the Arena (Nixon) (91) 441
In the Beauty of the Lilies (Updike) (97) 433
In the Beginning . . . (Asimov) (82) 386
In the Beginning (McGrath) (02) 408
In the City (Silber) (88) 418
In the Country of Country (Dawidoff) (98) 419
In the Country of Last Things (Auster) (88) 423
In the Devil's Snare (Norton) (03) 405
In the Eye of the Sun (Soueif) (94) 406
In the Footsteps of Mr. Kurtz (Wrong) (02) 413
In the Forest (O'Brien) (03) 410
In the Garden of the North American Martyrs (Wolff) (82) 392
In the Heart of the Sea (Philbrick) (01) 457
In the Heart of the Valley of Love (Kadohata) (93) 374
In the House of the Judge (Smith) (84) 374
In the Image (Horn) (03) 415
In the Lake of the Woods (O'Brien) (95) 355
In the Name of the People (Ulam) (78) 442
In the Palace of the Movie King (Calisher) (95) 359
In the Palaces of Memory (Johnson) (92) 342
In the Penny Arcade (Millhauser) (87) 424
In the Presence of the Creator (Christianson) (H-85) 236
In the Shadow of FDR (Leuchtenburg) (H-84) 223
In the Shadow of the Epidemic (Odets) (96) 368
In the Shadow of the Wind (Hébert) (85) 436
In the Skin of a Lion (Ondaatje) (88) 428
In the Tennessee Country (Taylor) (95) 363
In the Theater of Consciousness (Baars) (98) 424
In the Time of the Butterflies (Alvarez) (95) 367
In the Western Night (Bidart) (91) 447
In Touch (Bowles) (95) 372
In War's Dark Shadow (Lincoln) (H-84) 227
Incidents in the Rue Laugier (Brookner) (97) 437
Incline Our Hearts (Wilson) (90) 415
Incubus (Arensberg) (00) 418
Independence Day (Ford) (96) 372
India (Naipaul) (92) 346
India (Wolpert) (92) 350
Indian Affairs (Woiwode) (93) 378
Indian Country (Matthiessen) (H-85) 241
Indian Killer (Alexie) (97) 442
Inequality Reexamined (Sen) (93) 382
Inevitable Revolutions (LaFeber) (H-84) 232
Infamy (Toland) (H-83) 210
Infants of the Spring (Powell) (78) 447
Infection of Thomas De Quincey, The (Barrell) (92) 354
Inferno of Dante, The (Dante) (96) 376
Infiltration (Speer) (82) 398
Infinite in All Directions (Dyson) (89) 381
Infinite Jest (Wallace) (97) 446
Information, The (Amis) (96) 381

Information Ages (Hobart and Schiffman) (99) 414
Ingenious Pain (Miller) (98) 428
Inheritance, The (Freedman) (97) 451
Inheriting the Revolution (Appleby) (01) 462
Ink of Melancholy, The (Bleikasten) (91) 452
Inner Reaches of Outer Space, The (Campbell) (87) 429
Inner Room, The (Merrill) (89) 386
Innocent, The (McEwan) (91) 456
Innocent Eréndira and Other Stories (García Márquez) (79) 318
Innocent Eye, The (Shattuck) (85) 445
Innumeracy (Paulos) (90) 420
Inquisitors' Manual, The (Antunes) (04) 356
Inside, Outside (Wouk) (86) 466
Inside Picture Books (Spitz) (00) 422
Inside the Animal Mind (Page) (00) 426
Instance of the Fingerpost, An (Pears) (99) 418
Instigations (Sieburth) (80) 431
Integrity (Carter) (97) 456
Intellectual Follies, The (Abel) (85) 451
Intellectual Life of the British Working Classes, The (Rose) (02) 418
Interior Castle, The (Hulbert) (93) 386
International Norms and National Policy (Bonkovsky) (81) 445
Interpretation and Overinterpretation (Eco) (93) 390
Interpreter, The (Kim) (04) 360
Interpreter of Maladies (Lahiri) (00) 430
Interrupted Life, An (Hillesum) (85) 456
Interview with the Vampire (Rice) (77) 384
Intifada (Schiff and Ya'ari) (91) 461
Into Eternity (MacShane) (86) 471
Into My Own (Walsh) (89) 390
Intruders in Paradise (Sanford) (98) 432
Intuitionist, The (Whitehead) (00) 435
Inventing America (Wills) (79) 322
Inventing Herself (Showalter) (02) 423
Inventing Ireland (Kiberd) (97) 461
Inventing the Dream (Starr) (86) 477
Inventing the Middle Ages (Cantor) (93) 394
Invention of Hebrew Prose, The (Alter) (89) 395
Invention of Memory, The (Rosenfield) (89) 400
Invention of the Restaurant, The (Spang) (01) 467
Inventions of the March Hare (Eliot) (98) 436
Invisible Man, The (Coren) (94) 410
Invisible Republic (Marcus) (98) 441
Invisible Spectator, An (Sawyer-Laucanno) (90) 424
Iraq and Iran (Ismael) (H-83) 216
Iris and Her Friends (Bayley) (00) 439
Iris Murdoch (Conradi) (02) 428
Iron Lady, The (Young) (90) 429
Iron Tracks, The (Appelfeld) (99) 422
Irons in the Fire (McPhee) (98) 445
Ironweed (Kennedy) (84) 379
Irrawaddy Tango (Law-Yone) (95) 376
Irving Howe (Sorin) (04) 364
Isaac and His Devils (Eberstadt) (92) 359
Isaac Bashevis Singer (Hadda) (98) 449
Isaac Newton (Gleick) (04) 369
Isabel the Queen (Liss) (93) 399
Isaiah Berlin (Gray) (97) 466
Isak Dinesen (Thurman) (83) 358
Ìsarà (Soyinka) (90) 435
Islam and the West (Lewis) (94) 414
Island (MacLeod) (02) 432
Island of the Colorblind and Cycad Island, The (Sacks) (98) 454
Island of the Day Before, The (Eco) (96) 385
Islands, the Universe, Home (Ehrlich) (92) 364
Israel (Gilbert) (99) 427
Issa Valley, The (Miłosz) (82) 403
It All Adds Up (Bellow) (95) 381

It Seemed Like Nothing Happened (Carroll) (H-83) 220
Italian Days (Harrison) (90) 441
Italian Fascism (De Grand) (H-83) 224
Italian Folktales (Calvino) (81) 450
Italian Stories (Papaleo) (03) 419
Itinerary (Paz) (01) 471
I've Known Rivers (Lawrence-Lightfoot) (95) 384
Ivy (Spurling) (85) 461
Ivy Days (Toth) (85) 466

J. Edgar Hoover (Gentry) (92) 369
J. G. Frazer (Ackerman) (89) 418
J. P. Morgan (Jackson) (H-84) 257
J. R. R. Tolkien (Shippey) (02) 436
Jack (Parmet) (81) 454
Jack (Sinclair) (78) 454
Jack Gance (Just) (90) 445
Jack Maggs (Carey) (99) 432
Jack of Diamonds (Spencer) (89) 405
Jack Tars and Commodores (Fowler) (H-85) 246
Jackie Robinson (Rampersad) (98) 458
Jackson Pollock (Naifeh and Smith) (91) 466
Jacques Lacan (Roudinesco) (98) 463
Jailbird (Vonnegut) (80) 436
James Agee (Bergreen) (85) 473
James Baldwin (Leeming) (95) 388
James Boswell (Brady) (85) 479
James Dickey (Hart) (01) 475
James Gould Cozzens (Bruccoli) (84) 384
James Jones (Garrett) (85) 484
James Joyce (Costello) (94) 418
James Thurber (Kinney) (96) 389
Jameses (Lewis) (92) 374
Jane Austen (Honan) (89) 409
Jane Austen (Nokes) (98) 468
Jane Austen (Tanner) (87) 435
Janus (Koestler) (79) 326
Japan Before Perry (Totman) (82) 408
Japan in War and Peace (Dower) (95) 392
Japanese, The (Reischauer) (78) 459
Jarhead (Swofford) (04) 373
Jasmine (Mukherjee) (90) 450
Jason the Sailor (Wakoski) (94) 422
Jazz (Morrison) (93) 403
Jean-Jacques (Cranston) (H-84) 237
Jean Rhys (Angier) (92) 379
Jean Stafford (Goodman) (91) 471
Jean Stafford (Roberts) (89) 414
Jean Toomer, Artist (McKay) (85) 489
Jefferson and the Presidency (Johnstone) (79) 331
Jefferson Davis (Eaton) (78) 464
Jefferson's Pillow (Wilkins) (02) 440
Jerzy Kosinski (Sloan) (97) 470
Jesse (Frady) (97) 474
Jesse (Richardson) (85) 494
Jesus' Son (Johnson) (94) 427
Jesus Through the Centuries (Pelikan) (86) 482
Jew vs. Jew (Freedman) (01) 480
Jewish Self-Hatred (Gilman) (87) 440
Jews (Hertzberg and Hirt-Manheimer) (99) 436
Jews in the Eyes of the Germans (Low) (80) 439
Jews of East Central Europe Between the World Wars,
    The (Mendelsohn) (H-84) 243
Jihad (Kepel) (03) 428
Jihad (Rashid) (03) 423
JFK (Hamilton) (93) 408
Joan of Arc (Gordon) (01) 485
Joan of Arc (Lucie-Smith) (78) 472
Joe (Brown) (92) 384
Joe Dimaggio (Cramer) (01) 489
Joe Papp (Epstein) (95) 396
Johann Sebastian Bach (Wolff) (01) 494
John Adams (Ferling) (93) 413

John Adams (McCullough) (02) 444
John Calvin (Bouwsma) (88) 433
John Cheever (Donaldson) (89) 422
John Cheever (Hunt) (84) 389
John Clare (Bate) (04) 377
John D. (Hawke) (81) 459
John Dewey and American Democracy (Westbrook)
    (92) 388
John Dewey and the High Tide of American Liberalism
    (Ryan) (96) 393
John Dickinson (Flower) (H-84) 248
John Dollar (Wiggins) (90) 454
John Dos Passos (Ludington) (81) 464
John Dryden and His World (Winn) (88) 438
John Foster Dulles (Pruessen) (H-83) 229
John Glenn (Glenn and Taylor) (00) 443
John Henry Days (Whitehead) (02) 449
John Henry Newman (Ker) (90) 459
John L. Lewis (Dubofsky and Van Tine) (78) 478
John Marshall and the Heroic Age of the Supreme Court
    (Newmyer) (03) 432
John Maynard Keynes (Hession) (H-85) 250
John Maynard Keynes, 1920-1937 (Skidelsky) (95) 400
John Maynard Keynes, 1937-1946 (Skidelsky) (02) 453
John Paul Jones (Thomas) (04) 381
John Quincy Adams (Nagel) (98) 472
John Ruskin, The Early Years (Hilton) (86) 487
John Ruskin, The Later Years (Hilton) (01) 499
John Steinbeck (Parini) (96) 398
John Wayne's America (Wills) (98) 477
John Winthrop (Bremer) (04) 386
Joke, The (Kundera) (83) 363
Jonathan Edwards (Marsden) (04) 391
Jonathan Swift (Glendinning) (00) 448
Jorge Luis Borges (Monegal) (80) 444
Joseph Brodsky and the Creation of Exile (Bethea)
    (95) 404
Joseph Conrad (Karl) (80) 449
Joseph Conrad (Najder) (84) 395
Joseph Conrad (Tennant) (82) 412
Joseph Cornell's Theater of the Mind (Cornell)
    (95) 408
Josephine Herbst (Langer) (85) 499
Journals (Ginsberg) (78) 483
Journals, 1939-1983 (Spender) (87) 446
Journals of Denton Welch, The (Welch) (85) 504
Journals of John Cheever, The (Cheever) (92) 393
Journals of Sylvia Plath, The (Plath) (83) 367
Journals of Thornton Wilder, 1939-1961, The (Wilder)
    (86) 491
Journey for Our Times, A (Salisbury) (H-84) 252
Journey into Space (Murray) (90) 464
Journey to the End of the Millennium, A (Yehoshua)
    (00) 453
Journey to the Sky (Highwater) (79) 335
Journey to the West, Vol. IV, The (Wu Ch'êng-ên)
    (84) 401
Joy Luck Club, The (Tan) (90) 468
Joyce's Book of the Dark (Bishop) (88) 443
Joyce's Dislocutions (Senn) (85) 509
Joyce's Voices (Kenner) (79) 340
Jubal Sackett (L'Amour) (86) 496
Jubilation (Tomlinson) (96) 403
Jung (Bair) (04) 396
Julip (Harrison) (95) 413
Julius Streicher (Bytwerk) (H-83) 234
July, July (O'Brien) (03) 437
July's People (Gordimer) (82) 417
Jump (Gordimer) (92) 398
Juneteenth (Ellison) (00) 457
Just Above My Head (Baldwin) (80) 456
Just as I Thought (Paley) (99) 441
Just Representations (Cozzens) (79) 343

Justice at Nuremberg (Conot) (H-84) 261
Justice Crucified (Feuerlicht) (78) 487
Justice Oliver Wendell Holmes (White) (94) 431

Kaddish (Wieseltier) (99) 445
Kafka (Hayman) (83) 372
Kant (Kuehn) (02) 458
Karl Marx (Padover) (79) 349
Karl Marx (Wheen) (01) 504
Kasparov Versus Deep Blue (Newborn) (98) 482
Kate Chopin (Toth) (91) 475
Kate Remembered (Berg) (04) 400
Kate Vaiden (Price) (87) 451
Katerina (Appelfeld) (93) 418
Katherine Anne Porter (Givner) (83) 376
Katherine Mansfield (Tomalin) (89) 427
Kay Boyle (Mellen) (95) 417
Keats (Motion) (99) 449
Keep the Change (McGuane) (90) 473
Keeping Faith (Carter) (H-83) 239
Kennedy and Roosevelt (Beschloss) (81) 467
Kennedy Imprisonment, The (Wills) (H-83) 244
Kenneth Burke (Henderson) (90) 478
Kentucky Straight (Offutt) (93) 422
Keywords (Williams) (77) 388
Khodasevich (Bethea) (84) 408
Khrushchev (Medvedev) (H-84) 266
Khrushchev (Taubman) (04) 404
Khubilai Khan (Rossabi) (89) 432
Killing Ground, The (Settle) (83) 381
Killing Mister Watson (Matthiessen) (91) 480
Killshot (Leonard) (90) 482
Kiln People (Brin) (03) 442
Kindly Inquisitors (Rauch) (94) 436
Kindness of Strangers, The (Boswell) (90) 486
Kinflicks (Alther) (77) 391
King, The (Barthelme) (91) 485
King Edward VIII (Ziegler) (92) 403
King in the Tree, The (Millhauser) (04) 409
King Is Dead, The (Lewis) (04) 413
King of Children, The (Lifton) (89) 436
King of Inventors, The (Peters) (94) 440
King of Ragtime (Berlin) (95) 422
King of the Ants, The (Herbert) (00) 462
King of the Fields, The (Singer) (89) 441
King of the Jews (Epstein) (80) 458
King of the World (Gerber) (91) 489
King of the World (Remnick) (99) 453
King of Torts, The (Grisham) (04) 417
Kingdom of Shadows (Furst) (02) 463
Kingfisher, The (Clampitt) (84) 413
Kings of Cocaine (Gugliotta and Leen) (90) 490
King's Way, The (Chandernagor) (85) 515
Kingsley Amis (Jacobs) (99) 457
Kissinger (Isaacson) (93) 426
Kissinger Transcripts, The (Burr, ed.) (00) 466
Kitchen (Yoshimoto) (94) 445
Kitchen God's Wife, The (Tan) (92) 408
Kite Runner, The (Hosseini) (04) 421
Kith (Newby) (78) 491
Kleist (Maass) (84) 418
Knight, Death, and the Devil, The (Leffland) (91) 493
Knocking on the Door (Paton) (77) 396
Knowing When to Stop (Rorem) (95) 427
Known World, The (Jones) (04) 426
Koba the Dread (Amis) (03) 446
Kolyma (Conquest) (79) 354
Korean War, The (Hastings) (88) 447
Krakatoa (Winchester) (04) 430
Krazy Kat (Cantor) (89) 445
Krik? Krak! (Danticat) (96) 406
Krippendorf's Tribe (Parkin) (87) 456
Kronstadt, 1917-1921 (Getzler) (H-84) 271

Labors of Love (Cassill) (81) 471
Labyrinth of Exile, The (Pawel) (90) 495
Ladder of Years (Tyler) (96) 410
Lady from Dubuque, The (Albee) (81) 475
Lady of Situations, The (Auchincloss) (91) 498
Lady Oracle (Atwood) (77) 400
Lafayette (Buckman) (78) 495
L'Affaire (Johnson) (04) 434
Lake Wobegon Days (Keillor) (86) 500
Lake Wobegon Summer 1956 (Keillor) (02) 468
Lambs of God (Day) (99) 462
Lamplit Answer, The (Schnackenberg) (86) 505
Lancelot (Percy) (78) 501
Land of Savagery/Land of Promise (Billington) (82) 421
Land of Superior Mirages (Stoutenburg) (87) 461
Land of Ulro, The (Miłosz) (85) 520
Landing on the Sun, A (Frayn) (93) 431
Lands of Memory (Hernández) (03) 451
Landscape and Memory (Schama) (96) 414
Langston Hughes (Berry) (84) 422
Language, Counter-Memory, Practice (Foucault) (78) 504
Language in Literature (Jakobson) (89) 450
Language Instinct, The (Pinker) (95) 431
Lardners, The (Lardner) (77) 404
Larry's Party (Shields) (98) 486
Last Best Hope of Earth, The (Neely) (94) 449
Last Convertible, The (Myrer) (79) 359
Last Days (Oates) (85) 524
Last Days of Patton, The (Farago) (82) 428
Last Decade, The (Trilling) (81) 480
Last Empire, The (Vidal) (02) 472
Last Girls, The (Smith) (03) 456
Last Kaiser, The (Tyler-Whittle) (78) 509
Last Laugh, The (Perelman) (82) 433
Last Leopard, The (Gilmour) (92) 413
Last Life, The (Messud) (00) 471
Last Lion, 1874-1932, The (Manchester) (H-84) 278
Last Lion, 1932-1940, The (Manchester) (89) 455
Last of the Savages, The (McInerney) (97) 478
Last Orders (Swift) (97) 482
Last Poems (Celan) (87) 466
Last Report on the Miracles at Little No Horse, The (Erdrich) (02) 477
Last Resort, The (Lurie) (99) 466
Last Stands (Masters) (83) 386
Last Thing He Wanted, The (Didion) (97) 486
Last Things (Jones) (91) 503
Late Divorce, A (Yehoshua) (85) 530
Latecomers (Brookner) (90) 500
Later Auden (Mendelson) (00) 475
Later the Same Day (Paley) (86) 509
Latin Deli, The (Cofer) (94) 454
Launching of Modern American Science, The (Bruce) (88) 452
Law Unto Itself, A (Burnham) (91) 507
Lawrence of Arabia (Wilson) (91) 512
Laws Harsh as Tigers (Salyer) (96) 418
Laws of Our Fathers, The (Turow) (97) 490
Lay Back the Darkness (Hirsch) (04) 438
Lazar Malkin Enters Heaven (Stern) (88) 457
Lazarus (Malraux) (78) 515
Lazy B (O'Connor and Day) (03) 460
Le Divorce (Johnson) (98) 490
Le Mariage (Johnson) (01) 509
Le Ton Beau de Marot (Hofstadter) (98) 495
Leaders (Nixon) (H-83) 248
Leap (Williams) (01) 513
Leaping Clear (Feldman) (77) 408
Learning a Trade (Price) (99) 470
Learning Human (Murray) (01) 518
Leaving a Doll's House (Bloom) (97) 494

Leaving Home (Keillor) (88) 461
Leaving the Land (Unger) (85) 535
Lectures on Don Quixote (Nabokov) (84) 427
Lectures on Literature (Nabokov) (81) 485
Lectures on Russian Literature (Nabokov) (82) 437
Lectures on Shakespeare (Auden) (02) 481
Ledge Between the Streams, The (Mehta) (85) 539
Left Bank, The (Lottman) (83) 390
Left-Handed Woman, The (Handke) (79) 363
Legends of the Fall (Harrison) (80) 462
Lemprière's Dictionary (Norfolk) (93) 435
Lenin's Tomb (Remnick) (94) 458
Leon Trotsky (Howe) (79) 368
Léon Blum (Lacouture) (H-83) 253
Leonardo da Vinci (Kemp and Roberts, with Steadman) (90) 505
Leopards in the Temple (Dickstein) (03) 465
Leopold I of Austria (Spielman) (78) 518
Leper's Companions, The (Blackburn) (00) 479
Lermontov (Kelly) (79) 373
Less Than One (Brodsky) (87) 471
Lesson Before Dying, A (Gaines) (94) 463
Lester Leaps In (Daniels) (03) 470
Let the Dead Bury Their Dead (Kenan) (93) 439
Let the Trumpet Sound (Oates) (H-83) 259
Letourneau's Used Auto Parts (Chute) (89) 460
Letter Left to Me, The (McElroy) (89) 465
Letters (Barth) (80) 466
Letters (Pasternak, Tsvetayeva, and Rilke) (86) 514
Letters (Tynan) (99) 474
Letters (Warner) (84) 432
Letters and Drawings of Bruno Schulz (Schulz) (89) 470
Letters from Prison (Michnik) (87) 477
Letters from the Country (Bly) (82) 444
Letters from the Floating World (Cedering) (85) 544
Letters of Archibald MacLeish (MacLeish) (84) 436
Letters of Delmore Schwartz (Schwartz) (85) 548
Letters of D. H. Lawrence, September 1901-May 1913, The (Lawrence) (80) 469
Letters of D. H. Lawrence, October 1916-June 1921, The (Lawrence) (86) 520
Letters of D. H. Lawrence, June 1921-March 1924, The (Lawrence) (88) 466
Letters of D. H. Lawrence, March 1924-March 1927, The (Lawrence) (90) 512
Letters of D. H. Lawrence, March 1927-November 1928, The (Lawrence) (92) 417
Letters of D. H. Lawrence, November 1928-February 1930, The (Lawrence) (94) 467
Letters of E. B. White (White) (77) 413
Letters of Edith Wharton, The (Wharton) (89) 475
Letters of Evelyn Waugh, The (Waugh) (81) 489
Letters of Gustave Flaubert, 1830-1857, The (Flaubert) (81) 494
Letters of Gustave Flaubert, 1857-1880, The (Flaubert) (83) 395
Letters of Henry Adams, 1858-1892, The (Adams) (84) 441
Letters of Henry Adams, 1892-1918, The (Adams) (90) 516
Letters of Jean Rhys, The (Rhys) (85) 554
Letters of John Cheever, The (Cheever) (89) 480
Letters of J. R. R. Tolkien, The (Tolkien) (82) 448
Letters of Katherine Anne Porter (Porter) (91) 517
Letters of Lewis Carroll, ca. 1837-1885, The (Carroll) (80) 474
Letters of Margaret Fuller, 1817-1841, The (Fuller) (84) 449
Letters of Margaret Fuller, 1842-1844, The (Fuller) (85) 559
Letters of Marshall McLuhan (McLuhan) (89) 484

Letters of Mary Wollstonecraft Shelley, Vol. I, The (Shelley) (81) 501
Letters of Rudyard Kipling, 1872-89, The (Kipling) (92) 421
Letters of Rudyard Kipling, 1890-99, The (Kipling) (92) 421
Letters of Samuel Johnson, The (Johnson) (93) 444
Letters of Sidney and Beatrice Webb, The (Webb and Webb) (79) 378
Letters of T. S. Eliot, The (Eliot) (89) 488
Letters of Vachel Lindsay (Lindsay) (80) 479
Letters of Virginia Woolf, 1912-1922, The (Woolf) (77) 418
Letters of Virginia Woolf, 1923-1928, The (Woolf) (79) 382
Letters of Virginia Woolf, 1929-1931, The (Woolf) (80) 483
Letters of Virginia Woolf, 1932-1935, The (Woolf) (80) 487
Letters of Virginia Woolf, 1936-1941, The (Woolf) (81) 506
Letters on Literature and Politics, 1912-1972 (Wilson) (78) 522
Letters to Friends, Family, and Editors (Kafka) (78) 526
Letters to Olga (Havel) (89) 492
Letters to Ottla and the Family (Kafka) (83) 401
Letters to Sartre (Beauvoir) (93) 449
Levitation (Ozick) (83) 405
Lewis and Clark Journals, The (Lewis and Clark) (04) 442
Lewis Carroll (Cohen) (96) 422
Lewis Percy (Brookner) (91) 521
Lexus and the Olive Tree, The (Friedman) (00) 483
Liar's Club, The (Karr) (96) 426
Liars in Love (Yates) (82) 453
Liberalism and Republicanism in the Historical Imagination (Appleby) (93) 454
Liberty and Slavery (Cooper) (H-84) 283
Libra (DeLillo) (89) 496
Licks of Love (Updike) (01) 522
Lies of Silence (Moore) (91) 527
Life and Fate (Grossman) (87) 483
Life and Times of Cotton Mather, The (Silverman) (H-85) 256
Life and Times of Grigorii Rasputin, The (de Jonge) (H-83) 264
Life and Times of Joe McCarthy, The (Reeves) (H-83) 270
Life & Times of Michael K (Coetzee) (84) 455
Life and Work of Barbara Pym, The (Salwak, ed.) (88) 471
Life As We Know It (Bérubé) (97) 498
Life Before Man (Atwood) (81) 512
Life I Really Lived, The (West) (80) 491
Life in Letters, 1914-1982, A (Scholem) (03) 475
Life in Our Times, A (Galbraith) (82) 458
Life in Pieces, A (Eskin) (03) 480
Life in the Forest (Levertov) (79) 386
Life in the Twentieth Century, A (Schlesinger) (01) 527
Life It Brings, The (Bernstein) (88) 477
Life Itself (Crick) (82) 462
Life of a Poet (Freedman) (97) 502
Life of Bertrand Russell, The (Clark) (77) 423
Life of Geoffrey Chaucer, The (Pearsall) (93) 459
Life of Graham Greene, The, 1904-1939 (Sherry) (90) 521
Life of Graham Greene, The, 1939-1955 (Sherry) (96) 430
Life of Gwendolyn Brooks, A (Kent) (90) 526
Life of Herbert Hoover, The (Nash) (H-84) 288
Life of Jane Austen, The (Halperin) (85) 564
Life of John Berryman, The (Haffenden) (83) 410

Life of Kenneth Rexroth, A (Hamalian) (92) 426
Life of Kenneth Tynan, The (Tynan) (88) 482
Life of Langston Hughes, 1902-1941, The (Rampersad) (87) 489
Life of Langston Hughes, 1941-1967, The (Rampersad) (89) 501
Life of Matthew Arnold, A (Murray) (98) 500
Life of Nelson A. Rockefeller, 1908-1958, The (Reich) (97) 506
Life of Pi (Martel) (03) 485
Life of Picasso, 1881-1906 (Richardson) (92) 431
Life of Picasso, 1907-1917 (Richardson) (97) 511
Life of Raymond Chandler, The (MacShane) (77) 427
Life of Samuel Johnson, The (DeMaria) (94) 471
Life of Samuel Taylor Coleridge, The (Ashton) (97) 516
Life of the Mind, The (Arendt) (79) 393
Life Sentences (Epstein) (98) 504
Life/Situations (Sartre) (78) 529
Life So Far (Friedan) (01) 532
Life Supports (Bronk) (82) 466
Life with a Star (Weil) (90) 531
Life with the Enemy (Rings) (H-83) 274
Lifelines (Rose) (98) 508
Life's Matrix (Ball) (01) 536
Liftoff (Collins) (89) 506
Light (Figes) (84) 459
Light of Day, The (Swift) (04) 446
Light the Dead See, The (Stanford) (92) 436
Lighting Out for the Territory (Fishkin) (97) 521
Lila (Pirsig) (92) 440
Lillian Hellman (Rollyson) (89) 511
Lincoln (Donald) (96) 436
Lincoln (Vidal) (85) 570
Lincoln at Gettysburg (Wills) (93) 464
Lincoln in American Memory (Peterson) (95) 435
Lincoln's Dreams (Willis) (88) 487
Lincoln's Virtues (Miller) (03) 490
Lindbergh (Berg) (99) 478
Lindbergh (Mosley) (77) 433
Linden Hills (Naylor) (86) 525
Lion for Love, A (Alter) (80) 497
Lise Meitner (Sime) (97) 526
Listening to the Candle (Scott) (93) 469
Literary Guide to the Bible, The (Alter and Kermode, eds.) (88) 492
Literary Mind, The (Turner) (97) 530
Literary Theory (Eagleton) (84) 464
Literary Women (Moers) (77) 439
Literature and Its Theorists (Todorov) (89) 515
Literature and the Gods (Calasso) (02) 486
Literature Lost (Ellis) (98) 512
Little Drummer Girl, The (le Carré) (84) 468
Little Friend, The (Tartt) (03) 495
Little Girls in Church (Norris) (96) 440
Little Green Men (Buckley) (00) 488
Little Infamies (Karnezis) (04) 451
Little Jinx (Tertz) (93) 473
Little Order, A (Waugh) (81) 517
Little Original Sin, A (Dillon) (82) 470
Little Saint (Green) (01) 540
Little Voices of the Pears, The (Morris) (90) 535
Little Yellow Dog, A (Mosley) (97) 535
Little Wilson and Big God (Burgess) (88) 497
Lives of Animals, The (Coetzee) (00) 492
Lives of Norman Mailer, The (Rollyson) (92) 445
Lives of the Modern Poets (Pritchard) (81) 520
Lives of the Poets (Doctorow) (85) 574
Lives of the Saints (Slavitt) (91) 530
Living, The (Dillard) (93) 478
Living by Fiction (Dillard) (83) 413
Living History (Clinton) (04) 455
Living in the Maniototo (Frame) (80) 502

Living to Tell the Tale (García Márquez) (04) 460
Living with Our Genes (Hamer and Copeland) (99) 483
Lloyd's of London (Hodgson) (H-85) 262
Local Girls (Hoffman) (00) 497
Local People (Dittmer) (95) 440
Local Visitations (Dunn) (04) 465
Logical Dilemmas (Dawson) (98) 517
Loitering with Intent (O'Toole) (98) 522
Loitering with Intent (Spark) (82) 475
London Embassy, The (Theroux) (84) 472
London Fields (Amis) (91) 534
London Yankees, The (Weintraub) (80) 508
Lone Ranger and Tonto Fistfight in Heaven, The (Alexie) (94) 475
Lone Star Rising (Dallek) (92) 450
Lonely in America (Gordon) (77) 445
Lonely Vigil (Lord) (78) 534
Lonesome Dove (McMurtry) (86) 533
Long March, The (Salisbury) (86) 537
Long Way from Home (Busch) (94) 479
Longings of Women, The (Piercy) (95) 446
Look at Me (Brookner) (84) 476
Look Homeward (Donald) (88) 502
Look, Listen, Read (Lévi-Strauss) (98) 526
Looking at Shakespeare (Kennedy) (94) 483
Looking at the Sun (Fallows) (95) 451
Looking for a Ship (McPhee) (91) 540
Loon Lake (Doctorow) (81) 524
Loose Canons (Gates) (93) 483
Lord Beaverbrook (Chisholm and Davie) (94) 488
Lord Byron, Selected Letters and Journals (Byron) (83) 418
Lord God Made Them All, The (Herriot) (82) 480
Lords of the Horizons (Goodwin) (00) 501
Loser, The (Bernhard) (92) 455
Loser, The (Konrád) (83) 423
Losing Ground (Eckholm) (77) 450
Losing Ground (Murray) (H-85) 268
Lost Children of Wilder, The (Bernstein) (02) 491
Lost Father, The (Simpson) (93) 487
Lost Flying Boat, The (Sillitoe) (85) 579
Lost in America (Nuland) (04) 469
Lost in America (Singer) (82) 485
Lost in the City (Jones) (93) 491
Lost in the Cosmos (Percy) (84) 482
Lost in Translation (Hoffman) (90) 539
Lost Language of Cranes, The (Leavitt) (87) 494
Lost Light (Connelly) (04) 474
Lost Man's River (Matthiessen) (98) 530
Lost Puritan (Mariani) (95) 455
Lost Tribes and Promised Lands (Sanders) (79) 398
Louis D. Brandeis and the Progressive Tradition (Urofsky) (82) 488
Louis-Ferdinand Céline (Thomas) (81) 529
Louis MacNeice (Stallworthy) (96) 444
Louis Sullivan (Twombly) (87) 499
Louise Bogan (Frank) (86) 542
Love (Morrison) (04) 479
Love, Again (Lessing) (97) 539
Love and Responsibility (Wojtyla) (82) 494
Love, etc. (Barnes) (02) 495
Love Hunter, The (Hassler) (82) 499
Love in Bloomsbury (Partridge) (82) 504
Love in the Time of Cholera (García Márquez) (89) 521
Love Letter, The (Schine) (96) 448
Love Me (Keillor) (04) 483
Love Medicine (Erdrich) (85) 584
Love of a Good Woman, The (Munro) (99) 488
Love Thy Neighbor (Maass) (97) 543
Love Undetectable (Sullivan) (99) 492
Love Unknown (Wilson) (88) 507
Lovely Bones, The (Sebold) (03) 499

Lover, The (Duras) (86) 547
Lovers and Tyrants (Gray) (77) 455
Lover's Discourse, A (Barthes) (79) 404
Loving Monsters (Hamilton-Paterson) (03) 504
Loving Pedro Infante (Chávez) (02) 499
Low Life (Sante) (92) 460
Low Tide (Eberstadt) (86) 551
Loyalties (Bernstein) (90) 543
Lucifer (Russell) (H-85) 272
Lucifer Unemployed (Wat) (91) 545
Lucinella (Segal) (77) 460
Luck's Shining Child (Garrett) (82) 509
Lucky Bastard (McCarry) (99) 497
Lucky Eyes and a High Heart (Cardozo) (79) 409
Lucky Life (Stern) (78) 540
Lucy (Johanson and Edey) (82) 514
Lucy (Kincaid) (91) 549
Luisa Domic (Dennison) (86) 556
Luther (Haile) (81) 535
Luther (Oberman) (91) 553
Lying (Slater) (01) 545
Lyndon (Miller) (81) 540
Lyndon Johnson and the American Dream (Kearns) (77) 465
Lyre of Orpheus, The (Davies) (90) 548

M (Robb) (01) 549
M. F. K. Fisher (Barr, Moran, and Moran, eds.) (99) 501
MacGuffin, The (Elkin) (92) 465
Machine Dreams (Phillips) (85) 589
Machine That Would Go of Itself, A (Kammen) (87) 503
Madame de Sévigné (Mossiker) (85) 595
Madder Music (De Vries) (78) 546
Madness in the Streets (Isaac and Armat) (91) 558
Madoc (Muldoon) (92) 469
Madwoman in the Attic, The (Gilbert and Gubar) (80) 512
Magdalena and Balthasar (Ozment) (87) 508
Magic Lantern, The (Bergman) (89) 525
Magician's Wife, The (Moore) (99) 506
Maginot Line, The (Kemp) (H-83) 278
Magnetic Field(s) (Loewinsohn) (84) 487
Mailer (Mills) (83) 428
Mailman (Lennon) (04) 487
Major André (Bailey) (88) 512
Making Certain It Goes On (Hugo) (85) 603
Making of Adolf Hitler, The (Davidson) (78) 552
Making of an Assassin, The (McMillan) (77) 470
Making of Mark Twain, The (Lauber) (86) 561
Making of the Atomic Bomb, The (Rhodes) (88) 517
Making of the Representative for Planet 8, The (Lessing) (83) 432
Making Stories (Bruner) (03) 509
Making Things Better (Brookner) (04) 491
Malcolm (Perry) (92) 474
Malcolm Cowley (Bak) (94) 492
Malgudi Days (Narayan) (83) 436
Mama Day (Naylor) (89) 530
Mambo Kings Play Songs of Love, The (Hijuelos) (90) 553
Mammoth Hunters, The (Auel) (86) 566
Man and the Natural World (Thomas) (84) 492
Man Called Intrepid, A (Stevenson) (77) 475
Man in Full, A (Wolfe) (99) 511
Man in the Black Coat Turns, The (Bly) (83) 439
Man in the Holocene (Frisch) (81) 545
Man in the Tower, The (Krüger) (94) 496
Man Made of Words, The (Momaday) (98) 534
Man of Letters, A (Pritchett) (87) 512
Man of the Century (Kwitny) (98) 538
Man of the House, The (McCauley) (97) 546

Man of the House (O'Neill, with Novak) (88) 524
Man Who Loved Only Numbers, The (Hoffman) (99) 515
Man Who Mistook His Wife for a Hat, The (Sacks) (87) 516
Man Who Shook Hands, The (Wakoski) (79) 414
Man with Night Sweats, The (Gunn) (93) 495
Mandela (Sampson) (00) 506
Manly-Hearted Woman, The (Manfred) (77) 480
Mantissa (Fowles) (83) 443
Manual for Manuel, A (Cortázar) (79) 418
Manufacturing Matters (Cohen and Zysman) (88) 529
Many Masks (Gill) (88) 534
Many Thousands Gone (Berlin) (99) 519
Mao (Short) (01) 554
Mao (Terrill) (81) 549
Mao II (DeLillo) (92) 479
Mao Zedong (Spence) (00) 511
Mao's China (Meisner) (78) 557
Map of the World, A (Hamilton) (95) 460
Map That Changed the World, The (Winchester) (02) 503
Marathon (Witcover) (78) 562
Marbot (Hildesheimer) (84) 498
Marcel Proust (Carter) (01) 559
Marcel Proust, Selected Letters, 1880-1903 (Proust) (84) 504
Marcel Proust, Selected Letters, 1904-1909 (Proust) (90) 557
March of Folly, The (Tuchman) (H-85) 277
Marco Polo, If You Can (Buckley) (83) 447
Marcovaldo (Calvino) (84) 509
Marcus Garvey and Universal Negro Improvement Association Papers, The (Hill, ed.) (H-85) 283
Margaret Fuller (Blanchard) (79) 422
Margin of Hope, A (Howe) (83) 451
Marginalia (Jackson) (02) 507
Marguerite Yourcenar (Savigneau) (94) 500
Marianne Moore (Molesworth) (91) 562
Marina Tsvetaeva (Feiler) (95) 464
Marina Tsvetaeva (Karlinsky) (87) 520
Mark Rothko (Breslin) (94) 504
Mark Rothko (Weiss) (99) 524
Mark Twain A to Z (Rasmussen) (96) 452
Mark Twain's Letters (Twain) (89) 535
Marquand (Bell) (80) 517
Marriage and Morals Among the Victorians (Himmelfarb) (87) 525
Marriage of Cadmus and Harmony, The (Calasso) (94) 508
Marriages Between Zones Three, Four, and Five, The (Lessing) (81) 555
Married Man, A (Read) (80) 522
Married Man, The (White) (01) 564
Marry Me (Updike) (77) 485
Mars (Sheehan and O'Meara) (02) 511
Mars Beckons (Wilford) (91) 568
Marshall (Mosley) (H-83) 283
Marshall McLuhan (Gordon) (98) 542
Marshall McLuhan (Marchand) (90) 562
Marshall Plan, The (Mee) (H-85) 292
Martha (De Mille) (92) 485
Martin Buber's Life and Work (Friedman) (H-84) 293
Martin Heidegger (Ott) (94) 512
Martin Heidegger (Safranski) (99) 529
Martin Luther (Marius) (00) 515
Martin Niemöller, 1892-1984 (Bentley) (H-85) 298
Martin Van Buren (Niven) (H-84) 298
Martyrs' Day (Kelly) (94) 516
Marxism (Sowell) (86) 572
Mary McCarthy (Gelderman) (89) 539
Mary Reilly (Martin) (91) 572
Mary Renault (Sweetman) (94) 521

Mary Wollstonecraft (Todd) (01) 569
Masks (Enchi) (84) 514
Mason and Dixon (Pynchon) (98) 546
Mason's Retreat (Tilghman) (97) 550
Master Butchers Singing Club, The (Erdrich) (04) 496
Master of Death (Camille) (97) 555
Master of Petersburg, The (Coetzee) (95) 469
Master of the Game, The (Talbott) (89) 544
Masters of Atlantis (Portis) (86) 579
Masters of Death (Rhodes) (03) 513
Material Dreams (Starr) (91) 577
Mating (Rush) (92) 490
Matisse (Schneider) (H-85) 303
Matisse Stories, The (Byatt) (96) 457
Matthew Arnold (Honan) (82) 518
Maugham (Morgan) (81) 559
Maverick and His Machine, The (Maney) (04) 501
Max Perkins (Berg) (79) 428
Max Weber (Diggins) (97) 559
Maximus Poems, The (Olson) (84) 519
May Sarton (Peters) (98) 551
Mayan Astronomer in Hell's Kitchen, A (Espada) (01) 574
Mayday (Beschloss) (87) 530
Mayflies (Wilbur) (01) 579
Mayhem (Bok) (99) 534
Me Again (Smith) (83) 458
Me and Shakespeare (Gollob) (03) 518
Meadowlands (Glück) (97) 564
Meaning of Everything, The (Winchester) (04) 506
Meaning of Hitler, The (Haffner) (80) 528
Measure of Reality, The (Crosby) (98) 555
Mechanic Muse, The (Kenner) (87) 536
Media Unlimited (Gitlin) (03) 523
Medical Nemesis (Illich) (77) 489
Medicine, Mind, and the Double Brain (Harrington) (88) 539
Meditation, A (Benet) (83) 464
Meditations from a Movable Chair (Dubus) (99) 538
Meditations in Green (Wright) (84) 523
Medusa and the Snail, The (Thomas) (80) 533
Meeting at Telgte, The (Grass) (82) 523
Meeting at the Crossroads (Brown and Gilligan) (93) 500
Meeting Evil (Berger) (93) 505
Mellons, The (Koskoff) (79) 434
Melville (Robertson-Lorant) (97) 568
Memoir of a Thinking Radish (Medawar) (87) 541
Memoir of Misfortune, A (Su) (02) 515
Memoirs (Sakharov) (91) 582
Memoirs (Williams) (77) 494
Memoirs of a Geisha (Golden) (98) 558
Memoirs of a Space Traveler (Lem) (83) 469
Memoirs of Earl Warren, The (Warren) (78) 567
Memoirs of Leonid Pasternak, The (Pasternak) (84) 528
Memoirs of the Blind (Derrida) (95) 473
Memories of the Ford Administration (Updike) (93) 509
Memory of Fire, Century of the Wind (Galeano) (89) 548
Memory of Fire, Faces and Masks (Galeano) (88) 544
Memory of Fire, Genesis (Galeano) (86) 584
Memory Palace of Matteo Ricci, The (Spence) (H-85) 309
Men and Angels (Gordon) (86) 589
Men in the Off Hours (Carson) (01) 583
Mencken (Hobson) (95) 477
Men's Lives (Matthiessen) (87) 547
Mephistopheles (Russell) (87) 553
Mercurochrome (Coleman) (02) 519
Mercy, The (Levine) (00) 519

Mercy of a Rude Stream, A Star Shines over Mt. Morris Park (Roth) (95) 482. See also Diving Rock on the Hudson, A, From Bondage, and Requiem for Harlem
Meridian (Walker) (77) 501
Message to the Planet, The (Murdoch) (91) 587
Messages from My Father (Trillin) (97) 573
Messiah of Stockholm, The (Ozick) (88) 549
Metamorphosis of Greece Since World War II, The (McNeill) (79) 438
Metaphysical Club, The (Menand) (02) 524
Metaphysics as a Guide to Morals (Murdoch) (94) 526
Metropol (Aksyonov et al., eds.) (84) 533
Mexican Phoenix (Brading) (02) 528
Miami (Didion) (88) 553
Michel Foucault (Eribon) (92) 495
Mickelsson's Ghosts (Gardner) (83) 475
Microcosm (Gilder) (90) 568
Microworlds (Lem) (86) 595
Midair (Conroy) (86) 603
Middle Earth (Cole) (04) 510
Middle Ground, The (Drabble) (81) 564
Middle of My Tether, The (Epstein) (84) 539
Middle Passage (Johnson) (91) 591
Middleman and Other Stories, The (Mukherjee) (89) 553
MiddlePassages (Brathwaite) (95) 486
Middlesex (Eugenides) (03) 527
Midnight Clear, A (Wharton) (83) 480
Midnight Water (Norman) (84) 543
Midsummer (Walcott) (85) 609
Midwife's Tale, A (Ulrich) (91) 596
Migrations and Cultures (Sowell) (97) 577
Migrations to Solitude (Halpern) (93) 513
Mikhail Bakhtin (Clark and Holquist) (86) 608
Mikhail Bakhtin (Morson and Emerson) (92) 500
Mikhail Bakhtin (Todorov) (85) 614
Miles to Go (Moynihan) (77) 581
Millennium Hotel, The (Rudman) (97) 586
Millions of Strange Shadows (Hecht) (78) 572
Millroy the Magician (Theroux) (95) 491
Milosz's ABC's (Miłosz) (02) 533
Milton and the English Revolution (Hill) (79) 444
Mind and Nature (Bateson) (80) 536
Mind of Egypt, The (Assmann) (03) 531
Mind of Her Own, A (Quinn) (88) 558
Mind of the Traveler, The (Leed) (92) 505
Mind-Reader, The (Wilbur) (77) 505
Minds, Brains and Science (Searle) (86) 614
Miniatures, and Other Poems (Guest) (03) 536
Minor Apocalypse, A (Konwicki) (84) 547
Minotaur (Paulin) (93) 518
Mirabell (Merrill) (79) 448
Miracle at Midway (Prange, Goldstein, and Dillon) (H-83) 288
Miracle at St. Anna (McBride) (03) 540
Miracle Game, The (Škvorecký) (92) 509
Miracle of Dunkirk, The (Lord) (H-83) 293
Mirror Makers, The (Fox) (H-85) 313
Misalliance, The (Brookner) (88) 564
Miscellaneous Verdicts (Powell) (93) 522
Misery (King) (88) 569
Mismeasure of Man, The (Gould) (82) 527
Miss Herbert (Stead) (77) 509
Missed Connections (Ford) (84) 552
Missing Measures (Steele) (91) 601
Missing Persons and Other Essays (Böll) (78) 577
Mistress Anne (Erickson) (H-85) 319
Mists of Avalon, The (Bradley) (84) 561
Mixed Company (Shapiro) (97) 590
Model World, A (Chabon) (92) 514
Models of My Life (Simon) (92) 519
Modern American Religion, 1919-1941 (Marty) (92) 524
Modern European Thought (Baumer) (78) 581
Modern Greek Poetry (Keeley) (85) 624

Modern Ireland (Foster) (90) 573
Modern Irish Literature (Mercier) (95) 495
Modern Japanese Poets and the Nature of Literature (Ueda) (84) 566
Modern Poetic Sequence, The (Rosenthal and Gall) (84) 570
Modern Times (Johnson) (H-84) 306
Modernist Quartet (Lentricchia) (95) 499
Moksha (Huxley) (79) 451
Mom Kills Kids and Self (Saperstein) (80) 541
Moment of True Feeling, A (Handke) (78) 585
Momo (Ajar) (79) 454
Mona in the Promised Land (Jen) (97) 595
Money (Amis) (86) 624
Money (Hacker) (98) 562
Moneyball (Lewis) (04) 514
Mongoose, R.I.P. (Buckley) (88) 574
Monk in the Garden, The (Henig) (01) 588
Monkeys (Minot) (87) 557
Monkey's Wrench, The (Levi) (87) 564
Monolithos (Gilbert) (83) 484
Monsignor Quixote (Greene) (83) 489
Monster of God (Quammen) (04) 519
Monstruary (Ríos) (02) 537
Montgomery Clift (Bosworth) (79) 457
Montgomery's Children (Perry) (85) 629
Monty (Hamilton) (82) 531
Moo (Smiley) (96) 473
Moon Crossing Bridge (Gallagher) (93) 532
Moon Deluxe (Barthelme) (84) 576
Moon Pinnace, The (Williams) (87) 568
Moon Tiger (Lively) (89) 558
Moonrise, Moonset (Konwicki) (88) 579
Moons of Jupiter, The (Munro) (84) 580
Moor's Last Sigh, The (Rushdie) (96) 478
Moortown (Hughes) (81) 569
Moral Animal, The (Wright) (95) 504
Moral Freedom (Wolfe) (02) 541
Moral Life of Children, The (Coles) (87) 573
Moral Politics (Lakoff) (97) 600
Moral Sense, The (Wilson) (94) 539
Morality, Reason, and Power (Smith) (87) 577
More Collected Stories (Pritchett) (84) 584
More Die of Heartbreak (Bellow) (88) 583
More Perfect Union, A (Peters) (88) 589
More than Cool Reason (Lakoff and Turner) (90) 578
Morgan (Strouse) (00) 524
Morgan's Passing (Tyler) (81) 573
Mormon America (Ostling and Ostling) (00) 529
Morning of the Poem, The (Schuyler) (81) 578
Mornings Like This (Dillard) (96) 482
Mornings on Horseback (McCullough) (82) 537
Mortal Acts, Mortal Words (Kinnell) (81) 582
Mortal Friends (Carroll) (79) 462
Mortal Hero, The (Schein) (85) 635
Moshe Dayan (Dayan) (77) 513
Mosquito and Ant (Hahn) (00) 533
Mosquito Coast, The (Theroux) (83) 496
Mosquitoes, Malaria and Man (Harrison) (79) 466
Most Beautiful House in the World, The (Rybczynski) (90) 582
Mostly Morgenthaus (Morgenthau) (92) 529
Mother and Two Daughters, A (Godwin) (83) 501
Mother Country (Robinson) (90) 586
Mother Jones (Gorn) (02) 546
Mother Love (Dove) (96) 486
Mother Nature (Hrdy) (00) 538
Mother Tongue (Wilde-Menozzi) (98) 567
Motherless Brooklyn (Lethem) (00) 542
Mount Eagle (Montague) (90) 591
Mountain of Fame (Wills) (95) 509
Mountain Time (Doig) (00) 546
Mountains and Rivers Without End (Snyder) (97) 605

Mountbatten (Hough) (82) 542
Mountbatten (Ziegler) (86) 629
Mousetrap and Other Plays, The (Christie) (79) 470
Move Your Shadow (Lelyveld) (86) 635
Moving Target, A (Golding) (83) 506
Mozart (Solomon) (96) 490
Mozart in Vienna, 1781-1791 (Braunbehrens) (91) 606
Mr. Bedford and the Muses (Godwin) (84) 556
Mr. Cogito (Herbert) (94) 530
Mr. Happiness and The Water Engine (Mamet) (79) 828
Mr. Ives' Christmas (Hijuelos) (96) 461
Mr. Madison's War (Stagg) (H-84) 303
Mr. Mani (Yehoshua) (93) 527
Mr Noon (Lawrence) (85) 619
Mr. Palomar (Calvino) (86) 620
Mr. Phillips (Lanchester) (01) 594
Mr. Summer's Story (Süskind) (94) 535
Mrs. Jordan's Profession (Tomalin) (96) 465
Mrs. Ted Bliss (Elkin) (96) 469
M31 (Wright) (89) 562
Mullahs on the Mainframe (Blank) (02) 550
Mulligan Stew (Sorrentino) (80) 544
Multitude of Sins, A (Ford) (03) 545
Mungo Park the African Traveler (Lupton) (80) 550
Munich (Taylor) (80) 555
Munich 1923 (Dornberg) (H-83) 298
Murder Room, The (James) (04) 524
Murrow (Sperber) (87) 582
Murther and Walking Spirits (Davies) (92) 535
Muse Learns to Write, The (Havelock) (87) 590
Museum of Clear Ideas, The (Hall) (94) 543
Music and Silence (Tremain) (01) 599
Music of What Happens, The (Vendler) (89) 566
Music Room, The (McFarland) (91) 610
Muslim Discovery of Europe, The (Lewis) (H-83) 303
Mussolini (Mack Smith) (H-83) 308
Mussolini's Roman Empire (Mack Smith) (77) 520
My Alexandria (Doty) (94) 547
My American Journey (Powell, with Persico) (96) 494
My Century (Wat) (89) 571
My Dream of You (O'Faolain) (02) 554
My Father, Dancing (Broyard) (00) 550
My Father's Island (Angermeyer) (91) 614
My Heart Laid Bare (Oates) (99) 542
My Life as a Fake (Carey) (04) 528
My Life as a List (Rosenkrantz) (00) 554
My Life, Starring Dara Falcon (Beattie) (98) 571
My Name Is Red (Pamuk) (02) 558
My Name Is Saroyan (Saroyan) (84) 588
My Own Country (Verghese) (95) 515
My Sky Blue Trades (Birkerts) (03) 549
My Son's Story (Gordimer) (91) 619
My Traitor's Heart (Malan) (91) 624
My War Gone By, I Miss It So (Loyd) (01) 604
My Wars Are Laid Away in Books (Habegger) (02) 562
Myself with Others (Fuentes) (89) 577
Mysteries of Motion (Calisher) (84) 593
Mysteries of Pittsburgh, The (Chabon) (89) 581
Mysteries of Winterthurn (Oates) (85) 640
Mysteries Within, The (Nuland) (01) 609
Mysterious Flame, The (McGinn) (00) 558
Mysterious History of Columbus, The (Wilford) (92) 540
Mystery to a Solution, The (Irwin) (95) 519
Mystic Chords of Memory (Kammen) (92) 545
Myth Makers, The (Pritchett) (80) 560
Myths of Modern Individualism (Watt) (97) 610

Nabokov (Field) (78) 590
Nabokov-Wilson Letters, The (Nabokov and Wilson) (80) 564
Nabokov's Early Fiction (Connolly) (93) 536
Nabokov's Fifth Arc (Rivers and Nicol, eds.) (83) 511

Nabokov's Otherworld (Alexandrov) (92) 550
Naked Public Square, The (Neuhaus) (H-85) 324
Name of the Rose, The (Eco) (84) 598
Names, The (DeLillo) (83) 515
Names, The (Momaday) (78) 594
Names of the Dead, The (O'Nan) (97) 615
Namesake (Goldberg) (83) 518
Namesake, The (Lahiri) (04) 532
Naomi (Tanizaki) (86) 640
Napoleon Symphony (Burgess) (77) 525
Napoleon III and Eugénie (Ridley) (81) 587
Narcissa and Other Fables (Auchincloss) (84) 603
Narrative and Freedom (Morson) (95) 523
Nathaniel Hawthorne in His Times (Mellow) (81) 593
Native Realm (Miłosz) (81) 597
Native Speaker (Lee) (96) 499
Natives and Strangers (Dawkins) (86) 644
Natural, The (Klein) (03) 554
Natural Histories (Ullman) (80) 569
Natural History (Howard) (93) 540
Natural Man, The (McClanahan) (84) 608
Naturalist (Wilson) (95) 528
Nature of Economies, The (Jacobs) (01) 613
Nature of Love, The (Singer) (89) 585
Nature of Order, The (Alexander) (04) 537
Nature of the Book, The (Johns) (99) 547
Nature via Nurture (Ridley) (04) 541
Nature's Metropolis (Cronon) (92) 554
Nazi Party, The (Kater) (H-84) 313
Nazi Prisoners of War in America (Krammer) (80) 573
Nazi Psychoanalysis (Rickels) (03) 559
Nazi Terror (Johnson) (01) 618
Nazi War Against Soviet Partisans, 1941-1944, The (Cooper) (80) 577
Nazi War on Cancer, The (Proctor) (00) 562
Near a Thousand Tables (Fernández-Armesto) (03) 564
Nearer, My God (Buckley) (98) 575
Necessary Angels (Alter) (92) 559
Necessary Evil, A (Wills) (00) 567
Need to Hold Still, The (Mueller) (81) 603
Needful Things (King) (92) 564
Negotiating with the Dead (Atwood) (03) 568
Nehru (Tharoor) (04) 546
Neighbors (Berger) (81) 606
Neither Friend nor Foe (Packard) (93) 545
Nelson Mandela (Meredith) (99) 552
Neon Bible, The (Toole) (90) 596
Neon Vernacular (Komunyakaa) (94) 551
Nero (Griffin) (86) 650
Nerve Storm (Gerstler) (95) 535
Neumiller Stories, The (Woiwode) (90) 600
Neville Chamberlain and Appeasement (Fuchser) (H-83) 314
New Age Now Begins, A (Smith) (77) 529
New and Collected Poems, 1952-1992 (Hill) (95) 540
New & Collected Poems, 1917-1976 (MacLeish) (77) 534
New and Collected Poems, 1931-2001 (Miłosz) (02) 567
New and Collected Poems (Wilbur) (89) 590
New and Selected Poems (Feldman) (80) 580
New and Selected Poems (Oliver) (93) 549
New and Selected Poems (Soto) (96) 504
New & Selected Things Taking Place (Swenson) (79) 472
New Birth of Freedom, A (Black) (98) 579
New Buddhism, The (Coleman) (02) 571
New Critical Essays (Barthes) (81) 609
New Dealers, The (Schwarz) (94) 555
New Diplomacy, The (Eban) (H-84) 317
New Emperors, The (Salisbury) (93) 554
New Financial Order, The (Shiller) (04) 551
New-Found-Land *and* Dirty Linen (Stoppard) (78) 268

New Golden Land, The (Honour) (77) 538
New High Ground, The (Karas) (H-84) 323
New History of India, A (Wolpert) (78) 598
New Islands and Other Stories (Bombal) (83) 523
New Life, The (Pamuk) (98) 583
New Life of Anton Chekhov, A (Hingley) (77) 543
New Lives (Rabinowitz) (77) 549
New Mencken Letters, The (Mencken) (78) 603
New New Thing, The (Lewis) (00) 571
New Poems (Montale) (77) 553
New Rules (Yankelovich) (82) 548
New White Nationalism in America, The (Swain) (03) 572
New World, A (Chaudhuri) (01) 623
New World Disorder (Jowitt) (93) 559
New Worlds of Dvořák (Beckerman) (04) 556
New York Jew (Kazin) (79) 475
Newer World, A (Roberts) (01) 627
Newjack (Conover) (01) 632
News About the News, The (Downie and Kaiser) (03) 577
News from the Glacier (Haines) (83) 527
News of a Kidnapping (García Márquez) (98) 588
Newton's Gift (Berlinski) (01) 637
Next (Lewis) (02) 576
Next American Nation, The (Lind) (96) 509
Next Christendom, The (Jenkins) (03) 581
Next 200 Years, The (Kahn, Brown, and Martel) (77) 559
Nicaragua (Christian) (86) 655
Niccolò's Smile (Viroli) (01) 641
Nice Work (Lodge) (90) 603
Nicholas I (Lincoln) (79) 479
Nickel and Dimed (Ehrenreich) (02) 580
Niels Bohr's Times (Pais) (92) 569
Nietzsche (Safranski) (02) 584
Nigger (Kennedy) (03) 586
Night and Day (Stoppard) (80) 586
Night in Question, The (Wolfe) (97) 618
Night Manager, The (le Carré) (94) 559
Night of Stone (Merridale) (02) 588
Night Picnic (Simic) (02) 592
Night-Side (Oates) (78) 608
Night Thoughts of a Classical Physicist (McCormmach) (83) 532
Night Train (Amis) (99) 557
Night Travellers, The (Spencer) (92) 573
Nightingale Fever (Hingley) (82) 555
Nightmare (Lukas) (77) 565
Nightmare of Reason, The (Pawel) (85) 645
Nightmare on Main Street (Edmundson) (98) 593
Nikolai Bukharin (Medvedev) (81) 614
Nine Horses (Collins) (03) 590
1929 (Sloat) (80) 591
1934 (Moravia) (84) 613
1943 (Grigg) (81) 619
1945 (Lukacs) (79) 490
1985 (Burgess) (79) 484
1999 (Nixon) (89) 595
Nisa (Shostak) (82) 559
Nixon, 1913-1962 (Ambrose) (88) 594
Nixon, 1962-1972 (Ambrose) (90) 608
Nixon, 1973-1990 (Ambrose) (92) 577
Nixon Off the Record (Crowley) (97) 622
No Country for Young Men (O'Faolain) (88) 601
No Fond Return of Love (Pym) (83) 536
No Gifts from Chance (Benstock) (95) 544
No Laughing Matter (Cronin) (91) 629
No Man's Land (Toland) (81) 624
No Man's Land (Walser) (90) 619
No Man's Land, Letters from the Front (Gilbert and Gubar) (95) 549

No Man's Land, Sexchanges (Gilbert and Gubar) (90) 614
No Man's Land, The War of the Words (Gilbert and Gubar) (89) 600
No More Vietnams (Nixon) (86) 659
No Nature (Snyder) (93) 565
No Ordinary Time (Goodwin) (95) 554
No Other Book (Jarrell) (00) 576
No Other Life (Moore) (94) 563
No Other Tale to Tell (Perry) (95) 559
No Passion Spent (Steiner) (97) 626
No Place on Earth (Wolf) (83) 540
Noah's Curse (Haynes) (03) 594
Noam Chomsky (Barsky) (98) 598
Noble Rot (Stern) (90) 624
Noble Savage, The (Cranston) (92) 583
Nobody Better, Better Than Nobody (Frazier) (88) 605
Nobody's Angel (McGuane) (83) 544
Noël Coward (Hoare) (97) 630
Noël Coward Diaries, The (Coward) (83) 549
Noguchi East and West (Ashton) (93) 570
Nomonhan (Coox) (87) 594
Nonconformist's Memorial, The (Howe) (94) 568
None to Accompany Me (Gordimer) (95) 564
Nonzero (Wright) (01) 646
Noonday Demon, The (Solomon) (02) 596
Nora (Maddox) (89) 605
Norman Thomas (Swanberg) (77) 570
North Atlantic Alliance and the Soviet Union in the 1980's, The (Critchley) (H-83) 320
North Gladiola (Wilcox) (86) 664
Northrop Frye on Culture and Literature (Frye) (79) 496
Northrop Frye on Shakespeare (Frye) (87) 599
Norwegian Wood (Murakami) (01) 651
Not for Ourselves Alone (Ward and Burns) (00) 580
Not in Our Genes (Lewontin, Rose, and Kamin) (H-85) 329
Not Out of Africa (Lefkowitz) (97) 635
Not the End of the World (Stowe) (93) 575
Notebooks (Fugard) (85) 653
Notebooks of Don Rigoberto, The (Vargas Llosa) (99) 562
Notes from the Castle (Moss) (80) 597
Notes from the Divided Country (Kim) (04) 561
Notes of a Hanging Judge (Crouch) (91) 634
Notes of a White Black Woman (Scales-Trent) (96) 514
Nothing but Blue Skies (McGuane) (93) 580
Nothing Ever Happens to the Brave (Rollyson) (91) 639
Nothing Happens in Carmincross (Kiely) (86) 668
Nothing Like It in the World (Ambrose) (01) 656
Nothing That Is, The (Kaplan) (00) 585
Novel in Antiquity, The (Hägg) (84) 618
November 1916 (Solzhenitsyn) (00) 589
Novus Ordo Seclorum (McDonald) (87) 604
Now and Then (Buechner) (84) 624
Now and Then (Warren) (79) 501
Now Playing at Canterbury (Bourjaily) (77) 575
Nowhere Man (Hemon) (03) 598
Nowhere Man (Rosen) (01) 661
Nuclear Delusion, The (Kennan) (H-83) 324
Nuclear Fear (Weart) (89) 610
Nuclear Strategy in a Dynamic World (Snow) (82) 565
Number Sense, The (Dehaene) (98) 603
Nuns and Soldiers (Murdoch) (81) 628

O, How the Wheel Becomes It! (Powell) (84) 628
Obasan (Kogawa) (83) 554
Obstacle Race, The (Greer) (80) 600
October Light (Gardner) (77) 580
October Revolution, The (Medvedev) (80) 605
Odd Jobs (Updike) (92) 588

Odd Sea, The (Reiken) (99) 566
Odyssey, The (Homer) (97) 640
Of America East and West (Horgan) (H-85) 334
Of Kennedys and Kings (Wofford) (81) 633
Of Love and Other Demons (García Márquez) (96) 518
Of Paradise and Power (Kagan) (04) 565
Of Poetry and Poets (Eberhart) (80) 610
Of Such Small Differences (Greenberg) (89) 616
Of Woman Born (Rich) (77) 584
Off for the Sweet Hereafter (Pearson) (87) 611
Officers' Wives, The (Fleming) (82) 570
Official Negligence (Cannon) (99) 571
Oh What a Paradise It Seems (Cheever) (83) 558
Ohio Gang, The (Mee) (82) 575
Oil Power (Solberg) (77) 588
Old and on Their Own (Coles) (99) 576
Old Devils, The (Amis) (88) 610
Old Forest and Other Stories, The (Taylor) (86) 673
Old Friends (Kidder) (94) 572
Old Glory (Raban) (82) 580
Old Gringo, The (Fuentes) (86) 680
Old Left, The (Menaker) (88) 616
Old Love (Singer) (80) 614
Old Man's Toy, An (Zee) (90) 628
Old Masters (Bernhard) (93) 584
Old Men and Comets (Enright) (94) 577
Old Patagonian Express, The (Theroux) (80) 619
Old School (Wolff) (04) 570
Old World's New World, The (Woodward) (92) 592
Oldest Living Confederate Widow Tells All (Gurganus) (90) 633
Omeros (Walcott) (91) 643
On a Dark Night I Left My Silent House (Handke) (01) 665
On Becoming a Novelist (Gardner) (84) 633
On Being Blue (Gass) (77) 594
On Borrowed Words (Stavans) (02) 600
On Distant Ground (Butler) (86) 685
On Gold Mountain (See) (96) 523
On Grief and Reason (Brodsky) (97) 644
On Heroes and Tombs (Sábato) (82) 585
On Histories and Stories (Byatt) (02) 605
On Human Nature (Wilson) (79) 506
On Keeping Women (Calisher) (78) 613
On Lies, Secrets, and Silence (Rich) (80) 622
On Love (Hirsch) (99) 580
On Moral Fiction (Gardner) (79) 511
On Photography (Sontag) (78) 618
On Reading Ruskin (Proust) (88) 621
On the Black Hill (Chatwin) (84) 638
On the Edge of the Cliff (Pritchett) (80) 627
On the Golden Porch (Tolstaya) (90) 637
On the Natural History of Destruction (Sebald) (04) 574
On the Occasion of My Last Afternoon (Gibbons) (99) 584
On the Origins of War and the Preservation of Peace (Kagan) (96) 528
On the Rez (Frazier) (01) 670
On the Road with Charles Kuralt (Kuralt) (86) 691
On the Stroll (Shulman) (82) 590
On Writing (King) (01) 675
On Writing and Politics (Grass) (86) 695
Once Again for Thucydides (Handke) (99) 589
Once in Europa (Berger) (88) 625
Once Upon a Time (Barth) (95) 568
One and Inseparable (Baxter) (H-85) 339
One Art (Bishop) (95) 572
One Best Way, The (Kanigel) (98) 607
One by One from the Inside Out (Loury) (96) 532
One Earth, Four or Five Worlds (Paz) (86) 701
One Good Turn (Rybczynski) (01) 679
One Human Minute (Lem) (87) 615

One Kind of Freedom (Ransom and Sutch) (78) 622
One Man's Bible (Gao) (03) 602
One Nation, After All (Wolfe) (99) 593
One Nation Under a Groove (Early) (96) 537
One of Us (Wicker) (92) 597
One Thing Leading to Another (Warner) (85) 658
One Way to Spell Man (Stegner) (83) 563
One World, Ready or Not (Greider) (98) 612
One Writer's Beginnings (Welty) (85) 663
Only Land They Knew, The (Wright) (82) 594
Only Problem, The (Spark) (85) 668
Only the Dreamer Can Change the Dream (Logan) (82) 599
Onward and Upward (Davis) (88) 630
Open Closed Open (Amichai) (01) 684
Open Doors and Three Novellas (Sciascia) (93) 589
Open Secrets (Munro) (95) 578
Open Sore of a Continent, The (Soyinka) (97) 648
Opened Ground (Heaney) (99) 597
Opening of American Society, The (Wiebe) (H-85) 344
Operation Shylock (Roth) (94) 581
Operation Sunrise (Smith and Agarossi) (80) 631
Operation Wandering Soul (Powers) (94) 586
Operette Morali (Leopardi) (84) 643
Oracle at Stoneleigh Court, The (Taylor) (94) 590
Oral History (Smith) (84) 647
Orality and Literacy (Ong) (83) 568
Orchards of Syon, The (Hill) (03) 606
Ordeal by Labyrinth (Eliade) (83) 572
Order of Books, The (Chartier) (95) 582
Ordinary Love and Good Will (Smiley) (90) 642
Ordinary Money (Jones) (91) 647
Ordinary People (Guest) (77) 597
Ordinary Time (Mairs) (94) 594
Oregon Message, An (Stafford) (88) 636
Oriental Tales (Yourcenar) (86) 706
Origin of Satan, The (Pagels) (96) 541
Original Bliss (Kennedy) (00) 593
Original Fire (Erdrich) (04) 579
Original Intent and the Framers' Constitution (Levy) (89) 621
Original Sin (James) (96) 545
Origins of History, The (Butterfield) (82) 604
Origins of the English Novel, 1600-1740, The (McKeon) (88) 641
Origins of the Second World War, The (Baumont) (79) 516
Origins of Virtue, The (Ridley) (98) 616
Ornament of the World, The (Menocal) (03) 610
Ornamentalism (Cannadine) (02) 609
Orsinian Tales (Le Guin) (77) 601
Orson Welles (Leaming) (86) 709
Orwell (Shelden) (92) 602
Orwell, the Lost Writings (Orwell) (86) 715
Oryx and Crake (Atwood) (04) 583
Oscar and Lucinda (Carey) (89) 626
Oscar Wilde (Ellmann) (89) 630
Oswald's Tale (Mailer) (96) 549
Other American, The (Isserman) (01) 689
Other Man, The (Greene and Allain) (84) 651
Other Powers (Goldsmith) (99) 601
Other Pushkin, The (Debreczeny) (84) 657
Other Side, The (Gordon) (90) 647
Other Side of Silence, The (Brink) (04) 588
Other Side of the River, The (Kotlowitz) (99) 606
Otherwise (Kenyon) (97) 651
Our Game (le Carré) (96) 553
Our Ground Time Here Will Be Brief (Kumin) (83) 577
Our Lady of the Forest (Guterson) (04) 592
Our Posthuman Future (Fukuyama) (03) 615
Our Tempestuous Day (Erickson) (87) 620
Our Three Selves (Baker) (86) 719

Our Vampires, Ourselves (Auerbach) (96) 557
Out in the World (Bowles) (86) 723
Out of Chaos (Halle) (78) 627
Out of India (Jhabvala) (87) 626
Out of Place (Said) (00) 597
Out of Step (Hook) (88) 646
Out of the Woods (Offutt) (00) 601
Out to Canaan (Karon) (98) 620
Outerbridge Reach (Stone) (93) 593
Outline of Sanity (Dale) (83) 582
Outskirts of Troy, The (Dennis) (89) 635
Overlord (Hastings) (H-85) 349
Overspent American, The (Schor) (99) 610
Overthrow of Allende and the Politics of Chile, 1964-1976, The (Sigmund) (78) 630
Overworked American, The (Schor) (93) 597
Owl in the Mask of the Dreamer, The (Haines) (94) 598
Owls and Other Fantasies (Oliver) (04) 596
O-Zone (Theroux) (87) 631

P. G. Wodehouse (Donaldson) (83) 587
Pacific Tremors (Stern) (02) 614
Pacific War, The (Ienaga) (79) 520
Packages (Stern) (81) 636
Paco's Story (Heinemann) (88) 651
Paddy Clarke Ha Ha Ha (Doyle) (94) 603
Pagans and Christians (Lane Fox) (88) 655
Painted House, A (Grisham) (02) 618
Painter of Signs, The (Narayan) (77) 605
Palace Thief, The (Canin) (95) 586
Palestine Triangle, The (Bethell) (80) 634
Palestinian People, The (Kimmerling and Migdal) (04) 600
Palestinian State, A (Heller) (H-84) 326
Palimpsest (Vidal) (96) 561
Palm Latitudes (Braverman) (89) 639
Palm Sunday (Vonnegut) (82) 609
Palmerston (Bourne) (H-83) 329
Panda's Thumb, The (Gould) (81) 640
Paper Medicine Man (Porter) (87) 636
Paper Men, The (Golding) (85) 672
Paperboy, The (Dexter) (96) 565
Papers of Martin Luther King, Jr., January 1929-June 1951, The (King) (93) 601
Papers of Martin Luther King, Jr., July 1951-November 1955, The (King) (95) 590
Papers of Martin Luther King, Jr., December 1955-December 1956, The (King) (98) 625
Paradise (Morrison) (99) 615
Paradise News (Lodge) (93) 606
Paradise of the Blind (Duong) (94) 607
Paradise Park (Goodman) (02) 622
Paradise Postponed (Mortimer) (87) 640
Parallel Lives (Rose) (84) 662
Parallel Time (Staples) (95) 594
Paramilitary Politics in Weimar Germany (Diehl) (79) 526
Pardoner's Tale, The (Wain) (80) 640
Paris in the Third Reich (Pryce-Jones) (82) 615
Paris Trout (Dexter) (89) 644
Park City (Beattie) (99) 620
Partial Accounts (Meredith) (88) 663
Particles and Luck (Jones) (94) 611
Parting the Desert (Karabell) (04) 605
Parting the Waters (Branch) (89) 649
Partisan View, A (Phillips) (85) 677
Partners in Command (Glatthaar) (95) 599
Parts of a World (Brazeau) (84) 668
Passing On (Lively) (91) 651
Passing Through (Kunitz) (96) 569
Passion, The (Winterson) (89) 654
Passion Artist, The (Hawkes) (80) 644
Passion of Emily Dickinson, The (Farr) (93) 610

TITLE INDEX

Passion of Michel Foucault, The (Miller) (93) 614
Passion Play (Kosinski) (80) 649
Passionate Apprentice, A (Woolf) (92) 607
Passionate Minds (Pierpont) (01) 694
Passionate War, The (Wyden) (H-84) 330
Passwords (Stafford) (92) 612
Past, The (Kinnell) (86) 727
Past Is a Foreign Country, The (Lowenthal) (87) 645
Past Masters, The (MacMillan) (77) 610
Pasternak (Hingley) (84) 673
Pastoral (Phillips) (01) 699
Pastoralia (Saunders) (01) 703
Patchwork Planet, A (Tyler) (99) 624
Path Between the Seas, The (McCullough) (78) 636
Path to Power, The (Thatcher) (96) 573
Patients Are People Like Us (Baruk) (79) 532
Patrick O'Brian (King) (01) 707
Patrick White (Marr) (93) 619
Patrick White (White) (97) 656
Patrimony (Roth) (92) 615
Patriots and Liberators (Schama) (78) 642
Pattern Recognition (Gibson) (04) 610
Paul Celan (Colin) (92) 619
Paul Celan (Felstiner) (96) 577
Paul Klee (Lanchner, ed.) (88) 668
Paul Revere's Ride (Fischer) (95) 604
Paul Robeson (Duberman) (90) 652
Pause and Effect (Parkes) (94) 615
Peace Breaks Out (Knowles) (82) 621
Peace Brokers, The (Touval) (H-83) 335
Peace Like a River (Enger) (02) 626
Peace to End All Peace, A (Fromkin) (90) 657
Peacock Spring, The (Godden) (77) 614
Pearl Harbor (Prange, Goldstein, and Dillon) (86) 732
Pearl S. Buck (Conn) (97) 661
Peckham's Marbles (De Vries) (87) 650
Peerless Flats (Freud) (94) 618
Peloponnesian War, The (Kagan) (04) 614
Pencil, The (Petroski) (91) 656
Penitent, The (Singer) (84) 678
People and Uncollected Stories, The (Malamud)
    (90) 661
People of the Lake (Leakey and Lewin) (79) 535
People Shapers, The (Packard) (78) 649
People's Emperor, The (Wilson) (81) 645
Percys of Mississippi, The (Baker) (84) 682
Perestroika (Gorbachev) (88) 677
Perfect Recall (Beattie) (02) 631
Perfect Spy, A (le Carré) (87) 654
Periodic Table, The (Levi) (85) 682
Perjury (Weinstein) (79) 540
Perón (Page) (H-84) 336
Perpetrators, Victims, Bystanders (Hilberg) (93) 624
Pershing (Smythe) (87) 660
Persian Nights (Johnson) (88) 683
Persistence of the Old Regime, The (Mayer) (82) 626
Personal History (Graham) (98) 629
Personal Impressions (Berlin) (82) 632
Personal Injuries (Turow) (00) 605
Personal Politics (Evans) (80) 655
Perspective of the World, Vol. III, The (Braudel)
    (H-85) 353
Peter Paul Rubens (White) (88) 690
Peter the Great (Massie) (81) 651
Phantom Empire, The (O'Brien) (94) 622
Phenomena (Hankla) (84) 686
Philadelphia Fire (Wideman) (91) 661
Philip Larkin (Motion) (94) 626
Philosopher at Large (Adler) (78) 654
Philosopher's Demise, The (Watson) (96) 581
Philosopher's Pupil, The (Murdoch) (84) 690
Philosophical Explanations (Nozick) (82) 638
Philosophy in the Twentieth Century (Ayer) (83) 592

Phoenicians, The (Moscati, ed.) (90) 665
Phony War, 1939-1940, The (Shachtman) (H-83) 338
Pickup, The (Gordimer) (02) 636
Picture Bride (Song) (84) 695
Picturing Will (Beattie) (91) 665
Pieces and Pontifications (Mailer) (83) 597
Pieces of Life (Schorer) (78) 657
Pieces of Soap (Elkin) (93) 629
Pigs in Heaven (Kingsolver) (94) 631
Pilgrim in the Ruins (Tolson) (93) 633
Pilgrims in Their Own Land (Marty) (H-85) 358
Pillar of Fire (Branch) (99) 628
Pioneer Women (Stratton) (82) 642
Pitch Dark (Adler) (84) 699
Pitcher's Story, A (Angell) (02) 641
Pity of War, The (Ferguson) (00) 609
Place in Space, A (Snyder) (96) 585
Place I've Never Been, A (Leavitt) (91) 670
Places in the World a Woman Could Walk (Kauffman)
    (85) 688
Plague Dogs, The (Adams) (79) 546
Plagues and Peoples (McNeill) (77) 618
Plain and Normal (Wilcox) (99) 632
Plains Song (Morris) (81) 655
Plainsong (Haruf) (00) 614
Planning a Tragedy (Berman) (H-83) 343
Platte River (Bass) (95) 609
Plausible Prejudices (Epstein) (86) 737
Players (DeLillo) (78) 661
Playgoing in Shakespeare's London (Gurr) (88) 696
Playing for Keeps (Halberstam) (00) 618
Pleading Guilty (Turow) (94) 636
Pleasure-Dome (Madden) (80) 659
Pleasures of the Imagination, The (Brewer) (98) 634
Plowing the Dark (Powers) (01) 711
PM/AM (Pastan) (83) 603
Poe Log, The (Thomas and Jackson) (88) 701
Poems (Knott) (90) 669
Poems, 1968-1998 (Muldoon) (02) 645
Poems, The (Yeats) (85) 692
Poems New and Selected, 1962-1992 (Van Brunt)
    (94) 641
Poems of Paul Celan (Celan) (90) 673
Poems of Stanley Kunitz, 1928-1978, The (Kunitz)
    (80) 665
Poet and Dancer (Jhabvala) (94) 645
Poet as Journalist, The (Whittemore) (77) 623
Poetical Works of Federico García Lorca (García Lorca)
    (93) 637
Poetics of Aristotle, The (Halliwell) (88) 706
Poetry and Repression (Bloom) (77) 627
Poetry into Drama (Herington) (86) 742
Poetry of Tennyson, The (Culler) (78) 665
Poets in Their Youth (Simpson) (83) 608
Poets, Poetics, and Politics (Humphries) (93) 642
Poet's Work (Gibbons, ed.) (80) 668
Poet's Work, The (Nathan and Quinn) (92) 623
Point, The (D'Ambrosio) (96) 589
Polish Complex, The (Konwicki) (83) 611
Polish Officer, The (Furst) (96) 593
Political Liberalism (Rawls) (94) 649
Political Life of Children, The (Coles) (87) 665
Political Repression in Nineteenth Century Europe
    (Goldstein) (H-84) 342
Politician, The (Dugger) (H-83) 348
Politics and Ideology in the Age of the Civil War
    (Foner) (81) 661
Politics in Black and White (Sonenshein) (94) 654
Politics of Energy, The (Commoner) (80) 671
Politics of Recovery, The (Romasco) (H-84) 347
Politics of Rich and Poor, The (Phillips) (91) 674
Polonaise (Read) (77) 632
Pop Internationalism (Krugman) (97) 666

Pope's Rhinoceros, The (Norfolk) (97) 671
Porcupine, The (Barnes) (93) 646
Portable Jack Kerouac, The (Kerouac) (96) 597
Portage to San Cristóbal of A. H., The (Steiner)
    (83) 616
Portrait in Sepia (Allende) (02) 650
Portraits (Shils) (98) 639
Portraits of the Artist in Exile (Potts, ed.) (80) 675
Positively Fifth Street (McManus) (04) 619
Possessing the Secret of Joy (Walker) (93) 651
Possession (Byatt) (91) 679
Postscript to *The Name of the Rose* (Eco) (85) 697
Postville (Bloom) (01) 716
Pound/Ford, the Story of a Literary Friendship (Pound
    and Ford) (83) 621
Pound/Lewis (Pound and Lewis) (86) 747
Pound/Williams (Pound and Williams) (97) 675
Poverty and Compassion (Himmelfarb) (92) 627
Power and Principle (Brzezinski) (H-84) 351
Power Game, The (Smith) (89) 658
Power of Babel, The (McWhorter) (03) 619
Power on the Left (Lader) (80) 680
Power to Lead, The (Burns) (H-85) 363
Powers That Be, The (Halberstam) (80) 684
Practice of Reading, The (Donoghue) (99) 636
Practicing History (Tuchman) (82) 647
Prague (Phillips) (03) 624
PrairyErth (Heat-Moon) (92) 632
Prayer for Owen Meany, A (Irving) (90) 677
Prayer for the Dying, A (O'Nan) (00) 622
Praying for Sheetrock (Greene) (92) 636
Preacher King, The (Lischer) (96) 601
Prehistoric Avebury (Burl) (80) 688
Preparing for the Twenty-first Century (Kennedy)
    (94) 658
Presence of Ford Madox Ford, The (Stang, ed.)
    (82) 652
Presidency of Lyndon B. Johnson, The (Bornet)
    (H-84) 355
President Kennedy (Reeves) (94) 662
Price of Citizenship, The (Katz) (02) 655
Price of Power, The (Hersh) (H-84) 361
Price Was High, The (Fitzgerald) (80) 693
Prick of Noon, The (De Vries) (86) 752
Pride of Family (Ione) (92) 641
Primacy or World Order (Hoffmann) (79) 551
Primary Colors (Klein) (97) 679
Primary Colors, The (Theroux) (95) 613
Primate's Memoir, A (Sapolsky) (02) 659
Primetime Blues (Bogle) (02) 664
Prince of Our Disorder, A (Mack) (77) 637
Principle of Hope, The (Bloch) (87) 670
Printing Technology, Letters, and Samuel Johnson
    (Kernan) (88) 710
Prisoner's Dilemma (Powers) (89) 663
Prisoners of Hope (Hughes) (84) 705
Private Demons (Oppenheimer) (89) 668
Private World, The (Unamuno) (85) 701
Privileged Son (McDougal) (02) 669
Prize, The (Yergin) (92) 645
Prize Stories 1978 (Abrahams, ed.) (79) 556
"Probable Cause" *and* "Beyond Reasonable Doubt"
    (Shapiro) (93) 75
"Problem from Hell, A" (Power) (03) 629
Problems and Other Stories (Updike) (80) 697
Problems of Dostoevsky's Poetics (Bakhtin) (85) 706
Prodigal Child, A (Storey) (84) 711
Profane Art, The (Oates) (84) 716
Professing Poetry (Wain) (79) 561
Profession of the Playwright, The (Stephens) (93) 655
Professor of Desire, The (Roth) (78) 669
Progress and Privilege (Tucker) (H-83) 352
Progress of Love, The (Munro) (87) 677

Progressive Presidents, The (Blum) (81) 665
Promethean Fire (Lumsden and Wilson) (H-84) 366
Promise of Light, The (Watkins) (94) 667
Promise of Pragmatism, The (Diggins) (95) 617
Promise of Rest, The (Price) (90) 606
Promised Land, The (Lemann) (92) 650
Proper Study of Mankind, The (Berlin) (99) 640
Property and Freedom (Pipes) (00) 626
Prophets of Past Time (Dawson) (89) 674
Protecting Soldiers and Mothers (Skocpol) (94) 671
Proust Screenplay, The (Pinter) (78) 673
Providence (Brookner) (85) 712
Province of Reason (Warner) (H-85) 368
Provinces (Miłosz) (92) 656
Proximity to Death (McFeely) (00) 630
Psychopathic God, The (Waite) (78) 677
Publics and Counterpublics (Warner) (03) 634
Puffball (Weldon) (81) 670
Pugilist at Rest, The (Jones) (94) 676
Purified by Fire (Prothero) (02) 674
Puritan Way of Death, The (Stannard) (78) 682
Purple America (Moody) (98) 643
Purple Decades, The (Wolfe) (83) 626
Pursued by Furies (Bowker) (96) 610
Pursuit of Power, The (McNeill) (H-83) 357
Pushcart Prize, III, The (Henderson, ed.) (79) 565
Pushkin (Feinstein) (00) 634
Puttermesser Papers, The (Ozick) (98) 648

Quality of Mercy, The (Shawcross) (H-85) 373
Quantity Theory of Insanity, The (Self) (96) 615
Quantum Philosophy (Omnès) (00) 638
Quarantine (Crace) (99) 645
Quarrel and Quandary (Ozick) (01) 721
Queens, Concubines, and Dowagers (Stafford)
    (H-84) 371
Quest for El Cid, The (Fletcher) (91) 684
Question of Bruno, The (Hemon) (01) 725
Question of Character, A (Reeves) (92) 660
Question of Hu, The (Spence) (89) 679
Questioning the Millennium (Gould) (98) 652
Quinn's Book (Kennedy) (89) 683

Rabbi of Lud, The (Elkin) (88) 715
Rabbis and Wives (Grade) (83) 630
Rabbit at Rest (Updike) (91) 688
Rabbit Is Rich (Updike) (82) 656
Rabbiter's Bounty, The (Murray) (93) 660
Race and Slavery in the Middle East (Lewis) (91) 692
Rachel and Her Children (Kozol) (89) 687
Rachel Carson (Lear) (98) 656
Radiant Way, The (Drabble) (88) 720
Radical Enlightenment (Israel) (02) 679
Radical Son (Horowitz) (98) 661
Radicalism of the American Revolution, The (Wood)
    (93) 665
Rage of Edmund Burke, The (Kramnick) (78) 686
Ragman's Son, The (Douglas) (89) 692
Raider, The (Ford) (77) 642
Rainbow Grocery, The (Dickey) (79) 570
Rainbows, Snowflakes, and Quarks (von Baeyer)
    (H-85) 379
Raising America (Hulbert) (04) 624
Ralph Ellison (Jackson) (03) 638
Ralph Waldo Emerson (McAleer) (85) 717
Rameau's Niece (Schine) (94) 680
Randall Jarrell (Pritchard) (91) 696
Randall Jarrell and His Age (Burt) (04) 629
Randall Jarrell's Letters (Jarrell) (86) 757
Ranke (Krieger) (78) 690
Ransom of Russian Art, The (McPhee) (95) 622
Rape of the Rose, The (Hughes) (94) 684

TITLE INDEX

Rat Man of Paris (West) (87) 681
Rates of Exchange (Bradbury) (84) 721
Ratner's Star (DeLillo) (77) 647
Ravelstein (Bellow) (01) 731
Ray (Hannah) (81) 674
Raymond Chandler (Hiney) (98) 665
Reaching Judgment at Nuremberg (Smith) (78) 695
Reading *Billy Budd* (Parker) (92) 665
Reading for the Plot (Brooks) (85) 723
Reading *Lolita* in Tehran (Nafisi) (04) 634
Reading Raymond Carver (Runyon) (93) 669
Reagan (Cannon) (H-83) 362
Reagan's America (Wills) (88) 725
Real Life of Alejandro Mayta, The (Vargas Llosa) (87) 685
Real Losses, Imaginary Gains (Morris) (77) 652
Real Presences (Steiner) (90) 681
Real Shakespeare, The (Sams) (96) 619
Real Time (Chaudhuri) (03) 643
Realistic Imagination, The (Levine) (83) 635
Reality and Dreams (Spark) (98) 670
Reason and Realpolitik (Beres) (H-85) 385
Reason for Hope (Goodall with Berman) (00) 643
Reasonable Creatures (Pollitt) (95) 626
Reasons and Persons (Parfit) (85) 729
Rebecca West (Glendinning) (88) 732
Rebecca West (Rollyson) (97) 684
Rebel Angels, The (Davies) (83) 641
Rebel in Defense of Tradition, A (Wreszin) (95) 630
Rebellions, Perversities, and Main Events (Kempton) (95) 635
Recalcitrance, Faulkner, and the Professors (Wright) (91) 701
Recapitulation (Stegner) (80) 702
Reckless Eyeballing (Reed) (87) 690
Reckoning, The (Halberstam) (87) 695
Reckoning, The (Nicholl) (95) 639
Reconstruction (Foner) (89) 697
Red and Hot (Starr) (84) 726
Red and the Blacklist, The (Barzman) (04) 638
Red Azalea (Min) (95) 643
Red Coal, The (Stern) (82) 661
Red Mars (Robinson) (94) 688
Red Men, The (McGinley) (88) 737
Red Smith Reader, The (Smith) (83) 645
Red Wolves and Black Bears (Hoagland) (77) 658
Redesigning the World (Stansky) (86) 761
Rediscovery of the Mind, The (Searle) (93) 673
Redress of Poetry, The (Heaney) (96) 624
Reefer Madness (Schlosser) (04) 643
Reeling (Kael) (77) 662
Reflections (Benjamin) (79) 575
Reflections of an Affirmative Action Baby (Carter) (92) 669
Reflections on Exile and Other Essays (Said) (02) 684
Reflections on Language (Chomsky) (77) 668
Refugee Scholars in America (Coser) (85) 738
Regarding the Pain of Others (Sontag) (04) 648
Regeneration (Barker) (93) 677
Regina (Epstein) (83) 650
Regions of Memory (Merwin) (88) 742
Regions of the Great Heresy (Ficowski) (03) 648
Regular Guy, A (Simpson) (97) 688
Reich and Nation (Gagliardo) (81) 678
Reign of Napoleon Bonaparte, The (Asprey) (02) 688
Reindeer Moon (Thomas) (88) 748
Reinhard Heydrich (Deschner) (82) 666
Reinhart's Women (Berger) (82) 671
Reinhold Niebuhr (Fox) (86) 766
Reinventing Shakespeare (Taylor) (90) 685
Relations (Booth) (87) 703
Relativity (Cherry) (78) 700
Remains of the Day, The (Ishiguro) (90) 690

Rembrandt's House (Bailey) (79) 580
Remembering America (Goodwin) (89) 703
Remembering Denny (Trillin) (94) 692
Remembering Heaven's Face (Balaban) (92) 674
Remembering Mr. Shawn's "New Yorker" (Mehta) (99) 649
Remembering Poets (Hall) (79) 584
Remembrances (Owen) (87) 708
Renaissance *Hamlet*, The (Frye) (85) 742
Renaissance Tapestry, A (Simon) (89) 708
Renewing Philosophy (Putnam) (94) 696
Repetition (Handke) (89) 713
Representations (Marcus) (77) 673
Republic of Letters, The (Webster) (80) 705
Requiem for a Dream (Selby) (79) 589
Requiem for Harlem (Roth) (99) 654. *See also* From Bondage *and* Mercy of a Rude Stream
Required Writing (Larkin) (85) 747
Reshaping the German Right (Eley) (81) 682
Resistance (Foot) (78) 704
Respect in a World of Inequality (Sennett) (04) 652
Responses (Wilbur) (77) 679
Rest of Life, The (Gordon) (94) 701
Restless People, A (Handlin and Handlin) (H-83) 366
Resuming Green (Flint) (84) 731
Resurrection (Remnick) (98) 673
Resurrection Men (Rankin) (04) 657
Resuscitation of a Hanged Man (Johnson) (92) 679
Rethinking Social Policy (Jencks) (93) 682
Rethinking the Holocaust (Bauer) (02) 693
Retreat, The (Appelfeld) (85) 752
Retrieval System, The (Kumin) (79) 593
Return, The (Tomlinson) (88) 753
Return of Eva Perón, The (Naipaul) (81) 686
Return of Little Big Man, The (Berger) (00) 647
Return of the Caravels, The (Antunes) (03) 653
Return Passages (Ziff) (02) 698
Return to Región (Benet) (86) 771
Return to Thebes (Drury) (78) 708
Revenge (Blumenfeld) (03) 658
Reversal of Fortune (Dershowitz) (87) 716
Reversible Errors (Turow) (03) 663
Revolt of the Elites, The (Lasch) (96) 628
Revolution and Regeneration (Hoffer) (H-84) 376
Revolution in Taste, A (Simpson) (80) 709
Revolution of the Mind (Polizzotti) (96) 633
Revolutionary Empire (Calder) (82) 675
Revolutionary Mexico (Hart) (89) 717
Revolutionary Russia, 1917 (Thompson) (82) 679
Rewrites (Simon) (97) 692
Rewriting the Soul (Hacking) (96) 637
Rhapsody in Plain Yellow (Chin) (03) 668
Rhine Maidens (See) (82) 684
Rhineland Crisis, The (Emmerson) (78) 712
Rich in Love (Humphreys) (88) 759
Richard Milhous Nixon (Morris) (90) 694
Richard Rodgers (Hyland) (99) 658
Richard Wright (Rowley) (02) 703
Richard Wright, Daemonic Genius (Walker) (89) 722
Richard Wright Reader (Wright) (79) 597
Richer, the Poorer, The (West) (96) 641
Riders on the Earth (MacLeish) (79) 601
Riding the Iron Rooster (Theroux) (89) 726
Rifles, The (Vollmann) (95) 647
Right from the Beginning (Buchanan) (89) 730
Right Man, The (Frum) (04) 662
Right Stuff, The (Wolfe) (80) 713
Rilke (Leppmann) (85) 757
Rimbaud (Petitfils) (88) 765
Rimbaud (Robb) (01) 736
Rimbaud Complete (Rimbaud) (03) 672
Rings of Saturn, The (Sebald) (99) 662

Rise and Fall of Alexander Hamilton, The (Hendrickson) (82) 687
Rise and Fall of the British Empire, The (James) (97) 696
Rise and Fall of the Great Powers, The (Kennedy) (89) 735
Rise of Industrial America, The (Smith) (H-85) 391
Rise of Theodore Roosevelt, The (Morris) (80) 717
Rising from the Plains (McPhee) (87) 722
Risk and Blame (Douglas) (93) 687
Rites of Passage (Golding) (81) 690
River (Hughes) (85) 762
River Beyond the World, The (Peery) (97) 701
River Congo, The (Forbath) (78) 717
River of Heaven, The (Hongo) (89) 741
River of Shadows (Solnit) (04) 666
River Sorrow, The (Holden) (95) 652
RN (Nixon) (79) 605
Road from Coorain, The (Conway) (90) 699
Road-Side Dog (Miłosz) (99) 666
Road to Confrontation, The (Stueck) (82) 690
Road to Middle-Earth, The (Shippey) (84) 736
Road to Nuremberg, The (Smith) (82) 695
Road to San Giovanni, The (Calvino) (94) 705
Road to Verdun, The (Ousby) (03) 676
Road to Wellville, The (Boyle) (94) 709
Roadwalkers (Grau) (95) 656
Roald Dahl (Treglown) (95) 660
Robber Bride, The (Atwood) (94) 713
Robert Browning (Thomas) (84) 741
Robert E. Lee (Thomas) (96) 645
Robert Frost (Meyers) (97) 705
Robert Frost (Parini) (00) 651
Robert Frost (Poirier) (78) 722
Robert Fulton (Morgan) (78) 726
Robert Graves (Seymour) (96) 650
Robert Graves (Seymour-Smith) (84) 746
Robert Graves, 1895-1926 (Graves) (88) 770
Robert Graves, 1926-1940 (Graves) (91) 706
Robert Kennedy in His Own Words (Kennedy) (89) 744
Robert Louis Stevenson (Calder) (81) 694
Robert Louis Stevenson (McLynn) (96) 655
Robert Lowell (Hamilton) (83) 654
Robert Penn Warren (Blotner) (98) 678
Robertson Davies (Grant) (96) 660
Robot (Moravec) (99) 670
Rock Cried Out, The (Douglas) (80) 722
Rock Springs (Ford) (88) 776
Rocks of Ages (Gould) (00) 656
Rodin (Grunfeld) (88) 780
Roger Fry (Spalding) (81) 699
Roger's Version (Updike) (87) 727
Rogue's March (Tyler) (83) 659
Roland Barthes (Barthes) (78) 730
Roland Barthes (Calvet) (96) 664
Romancing (Treglown) (02) 708
Romantics, The (Mishra) (01) 741
Romare Bearden (Schwartzman) (92) 684
Rome '44 (Trevelyan) (H-83) 372
Rommel's War in Africa (Heckmann) (82) 700
Roosevelt and Churchill, 1939-1941 (Lash) (77) 685
Roosevelt and the Isolationists (Cole) (H-84) 382
Roosevelt Chronicles, The (Miller) (80) 726
Roosevelts, The (Horowitz) (95) 664
Roots (Haley) (77) 690
Roots of Conflict (Leach) (87) 732
Roots of Confrontation in South Asia (Wolpert) (H-83) 376
Roots of Treason, The (Torrey) (84) 751
Roscoe (Kennedy) (03) 681
Rose Macaulay (Emery) (93) 693
Rosenberg File, The (Radosh and Milton) (H-84) 388

Ross Macdonald (Bruccoli) (85) 766
Ross Macdonald (Nolan) (00) 660
Rotters' Club, The (Coe) (03) 685
Rough Magic (Alexander) (92) 689
Roundhouse Voices, The (Smith) (86) 775
Rounding the Horn (Slavitt) (79) 608
Rouse Up O Young Men of the New Age! (Ōe) (03) 690
Rousseau (Miller) (H-85) 395
Roxanna Slade (Price) (99) 675
Royal Charles (Fraser) (80) 732
Royal Family, The (Vollmann) (01) 745
Rubicon Beach (Erickson) (87) 736
Ruby (Hood) (99) 679
Rude Assignment (Lewis) (86) 778
Rudyard Kipling (Ricketts) (01) 750
Ruin of Kasch, The (Calasso) (95) 669
Ruin the Sacred Truths (Bloom) (90) 703
Ruined by Reading (Schwartz) (97) 710
Rule of the Bone (Banks) (96) 668
Ruling Race, The (Oakes) (H-83) 384
Rumor Has It (Dickinson) (92) 694
Rumor Verified (Warren) (82) 704
Run to the Waterfall (Vivante) (80) 736
Runaway Soul, The (Brodkey) (92) 698
Runner, The (Gildner) (79) 613
Running Dog (DeLillo) (79) 617
Running with Scissors (Burroughs) (03) 695
Russia House, The (le Carré) (90) 707
Russia in Revolution, 1900-1930 (Salisbury) (79) 622
Russia in the Age of Catherine the Great (de Madariaga) (82) 708
Russian Girl, The (Amis) (95) 674
Russian Journal (Lee) (82) 713
Russian Thinkers (Berlin) (79) 627
Russians, The (Smith) (77) 694
Russia's Failed Revolutions (Ulam) (82) 717

S. (Updike) (89) 748
Sabbaths (Berry) (88) 785
Sabbath's Theater (Roth) (96) 672
Sabbatical (Barth) (83) 665
Sacrament of Lies (Dewberry) (03) 699
Sacred Chain, The (Cantor) (95) 678
Sacred Hunger (Unsworth) (93) 698
Sacred Journey, The (Buechner) (83) 670
Safe for Democracy (Gardner) (H-85) 400
Saga of Dazai Osamu, The (Lyons) (86) 783
Sage of Monticello, Vol. VI, The (Malone) (82) 722
Sailing Alone Around the Room (Collins) (02) 713
Sailing into the Unknown (Rosenthal) (79) 632
Saint Augustine (Wills) (00) 665
Saint Augustine's Pigeon (Connell) (81) 703
St. Clair (Wallace) (88) 790
Saint-Exupéry (Schiff) (95) 683
Saint Maybe (Tyler) (92) 703
Saint-Simon and the Court of Louis XIV (Ladurie and Fitou) (02) 717
Saints and Sinners (Duffy) (98) 683
Saints and Strangers (Hudgins) (86) 788
Sakharov (Lourie) (03) 703
Saki (Langguth) (82) 726
Salem Is My Dwelling Place (Miller) (93) 702
Salt (Kurlansky) (03) 708
Sam Shepard, Seven Plays (Shepard) (82) 731
Same River Twice, The (Offutt) (94) 717
Same-Sex Unions in Premodern Europe (Boswell) (95) 687
Samuel Beckett (Bair) (79) 636
Samuel Beckett (Cronin) (98) 688
Samuel Gompers and Organized Labor in America (Livesay) (79) 641
Samuel Johnson (Bate) (78) 735

Samuel Johnson (Lipking) (99) 683
Samuel Johnson and the Life of Reading (DeMaria) (98) 693
Samurai, The (Endō) (83) 674
Sanatorium Under the Sign of the Hourglass (Schulz) (79) 645
Sand Rivers (Matthiessen) (82) 737
Sandro of Chegem (Iskander) (84) 756
Sands of the Well (Levertov) (97) 714
Sandy Koufax (Leavy) (03) 713
Sapphics Against Anger (Steele) (87) 741
Sara Teasdale (Drake) (80) 741
Sarah Bernhardt and Her World (Richardson) (78) 740
Sarah Phillips (Lee) (85) 771
Sartre (Cohen-Solal) (88) 795
Saskiad, The (Hall) (98) 698
Satanic Verses, The (Rushdie) (90) 711
Sauce for the Goose (De Vries) (82) 742
Saul and Patsy (Baxter) (04) 670
Saul Bellow (Miller) (92) 707
Saul Bellow, Vision and Revision (Fuchs) (85) 776
Savage Beauty (Milford) (02) 722
Savage Inequalities (Kozol) (92) 712
Saving the Heart (Klaidman) (01) 754
Scandal (Endō) (89) 752
Scandalmonger (Safire) (01) 759
Scandinavia During the Second World War (Nissen, ed.) (H-84) 393
Scapegoat, The (Girard) (87) 744
Scapegoat, The (Settle) (81) 707
Scarlet Professor, The (Werth) (02) 727
Scars of Sweet Paradise (Echols) (00) 670
Scattering of Salts, A (Merrill) (96) 676
Scenes of Childhood and Other Stories (Warner) (83) 679
Schindler's List (Keneally) (83) 684
Schnitzler's Century (Gay) (02) 732
Scholastic Humanism and the Unification of Europe, Vol. I (Southern) (97) 718
School Figures (Song) (95) 691
Schopenhauer and the Wild Years of Philosophy (Safranski) (91) 711
Science Observed (Bernstein) (83) 689
Science of Goodbyes, The (Sklarew) (83) 694
Scientists Under Hitler (Beyerchen) (78) 743
Scott Fitzgerald (Meyers) (95) 696
Scoundrel Time (Hellman) (77) 702
Scramble for Africa, The (Pakenham) (92) 717
Scrambled Eggs and Whiskey (Carruth) (97) 722
Screening History (Vidal) (93) 707
Sea Came in at Midnight, The (Erickson) (00) 675
Seabiscuit (Hillenbrand) (02) 737
Sean O'Casey (O'Connor) (89) 757
Search for Alexander, The (Lane Fox) (81) 712
Search for Modern China, The (Spence) (91) 716
Search for the Perfect Language, The (Eco) (96) 680
Searching for Memory (Schacter) (97) 727
Searching for the Ox (Simpson) (77) 706
Searoad (Le Guin) (92) 722
Second American Revolution, The (Vidal) (83) 700
Second Chance and Other Stories, The (Sillitoe) (82) 747
Second Coming, The (Percy) (81) 717
Second Generation (Fast) (79) 648
Second Life of Art, The (Montale) (83) 705
Second Marriage (Barthelme) (85) 780
Second Nature (Hoffman) (95) 701
Second Sight (McCarry) (92) 727
Second Stage, The (Friedan) (82) 752
Second Words (Atwood) (85) 785
Second World War, The (Gilbert) (90) 716
Second World War, The (Keegan) (91) 721
Secrecy (Moynihan) (99) 688

Secrecy and Power (Powers) (88) 801
Secret Conversations of Henry Kissinger, The (Golan) (77) 709
Secret Diaries of Hitler's Doctor, The (Irving and Morell) (H-84) 398
Secret History, The (Tartt) (93) 711
Secret Lives of Trebitsch Lincoln, The (Wasserstein) (89) 762
Secret Pilgrim, The (le Carré) (92) 732
Secret Symmetry, A (Carotenuto) (83) 709
Secret World of American Communism, The (Klehr, Haynes, and Firsov, eds.) (96) 685
Secretary, Martin Bormann, The (Lang) (80) 746
Secrets (Ellsberg) (03) 718
Secrets (Farah) (99) 693
Secrets and Other Stories (MacLaverty) (85) 790
Secrets of the Flesh (Thurman) (00) 679
Secrets of the Temple (Greider) (89) 766
Seeds in the Heart (Keene) (94) 721
Seeing Calvin Coolidge in a Dream (Derbyshire) (97) 732
Seeing in the Dark (Ferris) (03) 723
Seeing Mary Plain (Kiernan) (01) 764
Seeing Things (Heaney) (92) 737
Seeing Voices (Sacks) (90) 720
Seek My Face (Updike) (03) 727
Seekers, The (Boorstin) (99) 697
Seizure of Power, The (Miłosz) (83) 713
Selected and Collected Poems (Knott) (78) 748
Selected and New Poems (Dubie) (84) 761
Selected & New Poems (Harrison) (83) 718
Selected Essays (Berger) (03) 732
Selected Essays of Cyril Connolly, The (Connolly) (85) 793
Selected Essays of John Crowe Ransom (Ransom) (85) 797
Selected Essays of R. P. Blackmur (Blackmur) (87) 749
Selected Letters (García Lorca) (84) 768
Selected Letters (Marx and Engels) (83) 722
Selected Letters of Conrad Aiken (Aiken) (79) 652
Selected Letters of E. M. Forster, 1879-1920 (Forster) (84) 773
Selected Letters of E. M. Forster, 1921-1970 (Forster) (86) 793
Selected Letters of Eugene O'Neill (O'Neill) (89) 771
Selected Letters of Fyodor Dostoyevsky (Dostoyevsky) (88) 806
Selected Letters of George Oppen, The (Oppen) (91) 726
Selected Letters of John O'Hara (O'Hara) (79) 656
Selected Letters of Marianne Moore, The (Moore) (98) 702
Selected Letters of Philip Larkin, 1940-1985 (Larkin) (94) 724
Selected Letters of Raymond Chandler (Chandler) (82) 757
Selected Non-Fictions (Borges) (00) 683
Selected Poems (Ashbery) (86) 798
Selected Poems (Atwood) (79) 661
Selected Poems (Borges) (00) 688
Selected Poems (Clarke) (77) 715
Selected Poems (Garrigue) (93) 715
Selected Poems, 1947-1995 (Ginsberg) (97) 737
Selected Poems, 1950-1975 (Gunn) (80) 750
Selected Poems (Harrison) (88) 812
Selected Poems (Kinnell) (83) 726
Selected Poems, 1960-1990 (Kumin) (98) 707
Selected Poems (Lowell) (77) 720
Selected Poems (McGrath) (89) 775
Selected Poems (Masefield) (79) 666
Selected Poems, 1946-1985 (Merrill) (93) 719
Selected Poems (Nims) (83) 730
Selected Poems (Paz) (85) 802

Selected Poems (Strand) (81) 723
Selected Poems, 1923-1975 (Warren) (78) 753
Selected Prose, A (Duncan) (96) 690
Selected Short Stories of Padraic Colum (Colum) (86) 803
Selected Stories (Gordimer) (77) 725
Selected Stories (Munro) (97) 742
Selected Stories (Pritchett) (79) 669
Selected Stories (Walser) (83) 734
Selected Stories of Philip K. Dick (Dick) (03) 737
Selected Writings, 1913-1926 (Benjamin) (97) 746
Selected Writings, 1927-1934 (Benjamin) (00) 693
Selected Writings, 1938-1940 (Benjamin) (04) 674
Selected Writings of James Weldon Johnson, The (Johnson) (96) 694
Self-Consciousness (Updike) (90) 725
Self-Rule (Wiebe) (96) 699
Selves (Booth) (91) 731
Semiotics and the Philosophy of Language (Eco) (85) 807
Sense of Sight, The (Berger) (87) 754
Sent for You Yesterday (Wideman) (84) 779
Separate Notebooks, The (Miłosz) (85) 811
Sergeant Getúlio (Ubaldo Ribeiro) (79) 672
Serious Character, A (Carpenter) (89) 779
Seriously Funny (Nachman) (04) 679
Setting the World on Fire (Wilson) (81) 727
Seven Ages, The (Glück) (02) 742
Seven Day Circle, The (Zerubavel) (86) 807
Seven Days to Disaster (Hickey and Smith) (H-83) 387
Seven Mountains of Thomas Merton, The (Mott) (85) 815
Seven Rivers West (Hoagland) (87) 760
1777 (Pancake) (78) 757
Sex and Destiny (Greer) (H-85) 406
Sex and Social Justice (Nussbaum) (00) 697
Sexing the Cherry (Winterson) (91) 735
Shackleton (Huntford) (87) 765
Shadow Box, The (Cristofer) (78) 762
Shadow Man, The (Gordon) (97) 749
Shadow Man (Layman) (82) 761
Shadow of the Winter Palace, The (Crankshaw) (77) 730
Shadow Warriors, The (Smith) (H-84) 403
Shadows and Stillness (Gardner) (87) 822
Shadows of the Mind (Penrose) (95) 705
Shah of Shahs (Kapuściński) (86) 811
Shah's Last Ride, The (Shawcross) (89) 784
Shakespeare (Bloom) (99) 701
Shakespeare (Fraser) (93) 723
Shakespeare (Honan) (00) 702
Shakespeare (Wells) (96) 704
Shakespeare's Division of Experience (French) (82) 767
Shakespeare's Dog (Rooke) (84) 784
Shakespeare's Language (Kermode) (01) 769
Shakespeare's Professional Career (Thomson) (93) 728
Shame (Rushdie) (84) 788
Shape of Apocalypse in Modern Russian Fiction, The (Bethea) (90) 729
Shaping of America, 1492-1800, The (Meinig) (87) 771
Shaping of America, 1800-1867, The (Meinig) (94) 729
Sharpest Sight, The (Owens) (93) 732
"Shattered Nerves" (Oppenheim) (92) 742
Shattered Peace (Yergin) (78) 766
Shawl, The (Ozick) (90) 734
Shawnee Prophet, The (Edmunds) (H-84) 409
Shays' Rebellion (Szatmary) (81) 732
Sheba (Clapp) (02) 747
Shelley's Heart (McCarry) (96) 708
Shelter (Phillips) (95) 709
Sherwood Anderson (Townsend) (88) 817

Sherwood Anderson, Selected Letters (Anderson) (85) 820
Shikasta (Lessing) (80) 753
Shiloh and Other Stories (Mason) (83) 739
Ship Fever and Other Stories (Barrett) (97) 753
Ship Made of Paper, A (Spencer) (04) 683
Shipping News, The (Proulx) (94) 733
Shipwreck (Begley) (04) 687
Shoeless Joe (Kinsella) (83) 742
Short History of a Prince, The (Hamilton) (99) 706
Short History of the Shadow, A (Wright) (03) 741
Short Stories of Thomas Hardy, The (Brady) (83) 747
Short Story, The (Bayley) (89) 788
Shosha (Singer) (79) 677
Shroud (Banville) (04) 691
Shrovetide in Old New Orleans (Reed) (79) 681
Sicilian Carousel (Durrell) (78) 771
Sideshow (Shawcross) (80) 758
Siege, The (O'Brien) (87) 776
Sights Unseen (Gibbons) (96) 712
Sigismund (Gustafsson) (86) 816
Signposts in a Strange Land (Percy) (92) 747
Signs and Wonders (Bukiet) (00) 707
Signs of the Times (Lehman) (92) 752
Sikhs, The (Singh) (01) 774
Silence Opens, A (Clampitt) (95) 713
Silent Passengers (Woiwode) (94) 738
Silent Woman, The (Malcolm) (95) 719
Silken Eyes (Sagan) (78) 776
Silmarillion, The (Tolkien) (78) 780
Simenon (Assouline) (98) 712
Simone de Beauvoir (Bair) (91) 740
Simone Weil (Fiori) (90) 738
Simone Weil (Nevin) (93) 736
Simple Habana Melody, A (Hijuelos) (03) 746
Simple Justice (Kluger) (77) 735
Simple Life, The (Shi) (86) 820
Simple Story, A (Agnon) (86) 826
Sin Killer (McMurtry) (03) 750
Sinclair Lewis (Lingeman) (03) 755
Singin' and Swingin' and Gettin' Merry Like Christmas (Angelou) (77) 738
Singularities (Simon) (77) 742
Sinking Island, A (Kenner) (89) 793
Sir Francis Drake (Sugden) (92) 757
Sir Philip Sidney (Duncan-Jones) (92) 761
Sir Vidia's Shadow (Theroux) (99) 711
Siren, The (Buzzati) (85) 825
Sirian Experiments, The (Lessing) (81) 737
Sister Age (Fisher) (84) 792
Sistermony, A (Stern) (96) 716
Sisters, The (Lovell) (03) 760
Sites (Fowlie) (88) 823
Situation and the Story, The (Gornick) (02) 752
Sitwells, The (Pearson) (80) 763
Six Armies in Normandy (Keegan) (H-83) 390
Six Days of War (Oren) (03) 765
Six Exceptional Women (Lord) (95) 724
Six Memos for the Next Millennium (Calvino) (89) 799
Six Problems for Don Isidro Parodi (Borges and Bioy-Casares) (82) 771
Sixty Stories (Barthelme) (82) 776
Size of Thoughts, The (Baker) (97) 757
Skeptic, The (Teachout) (03) 770
Skepticism and Modern Enmity (Perl) (91) 746
Sketches from a Life (Kennan) (90) 742
Skinned Alive (White) (96) 720
Slapstick (Vonnegut) (77) 749
Slavery and Human Progress (Davis) (H-85) 411
Slaves in the Family (Ball) (99) 716
Slaves of New York (Janowitz) (87) 784
Sleeping with Extra-Terrestrials (Kaminer) (00) 712
Sleeping with the Dictionary (Mullen) (03) 775

Sleepless Nights (Hardwick) (80) 768
Sleepwalker in a Fog (Tolstaya) (93) 740
Slim's Table (Duneier) (93) 744
Slouching Towards Kalamazoo (De Vries) (84) 796
Slow Homecoming (Handke) (86) 830
Slow Learner (Pynchon) (85) 830
Slowness (Kundera) (97) 761
Small Congregations (Moss) (94) 743
Small Victories (Freedman) (91) 750
Small Wonder (Kingsolver) (03) 779
Small World (Lodge) (86) 835
Smilla's Sense of Snow (Hoeg) (94) 747
Smoke Ring, The (Taylor) (H-85) 415
Snack Thief, The (Camilleri) (04) 696
Snobbery (Epstein) (03) 784
Snooty Baronet (Lewis) (85) 835
Snow Falling on Cedars (Guterson) (95) 729
Snow Leopard, The (Matthiessen) (79) 685
So Forth (Brodsky) (97) 766
So I Am Glad (Kennedy) (01) 778
So Long, See You Tomorrow (Maxwell) (81) 741
Society of Mind, The (Minsky) (88) 828
Sociology as an Art Form (Nisbet) (77) 753
Socrates (Vlastos) (92) 766
Sojourner Truth (Painter) (97) 772
Sojourners (McFarland) (80) 771
Solace of Open Spaces, The (Ehrlich) (86) 840
Soldier of the Great War, A (Helprin) (92) 770
Soldiers (Ziegler) (03) 789
Soldier's Embrace, A (Gordimer) (81) 745
Soldiers in a Narrow Land (Spooner) (95) 733
Soldiers of the Night (Schoenbrun) (81) 750
Soldier's Play, A (Fuller) (83) 751
Solo (Morris) (84) 803
Solomon Gursky Was Here (Richler) (91) 755
Solzhenitsyn (Scammell) (85) 839
Solzhenitsyn and the Modern World (Ericson) (94) 751
Solzhenitsyn in Exile (Dunlop, Haugh, and Nicholson, eds.) (86) 843
Sombrero Fallout (Brautigan) (78) 785
Some Sort of Epic Grandeur (Bruccoli) (82) 782
Some Tame Gazelle (Pym) (84) 809
Somebody's Darling (McMurtry) (79) 689
Something for Nothing (Lears) (04) 700
Something Out There (Gordimer) (85) 844
Something Said (Sorrentino) (86) 847
Something to Be Desired (McGuane) (85) 849
Something to Declare (Alvarez) (99) 720
Somewhere a Master (Wiesel) (83) 756
Somewhere Is Such a Kingdom (Hill) (77) 758
Son of the Circus, A (Irving) (95) 739
Son of the Morning (Oates) (79) 693
Son of the Morning Star (Connell) (H-85) 420
Son of Thunder, A (Mayer) (87) 789
Song in a Weary Throat (Murray) (88) 835
Song of Napalm (Weigl) (89) 803
Song of Solomon (Morrison) (78) 789
Song of the Earth, The (Nissenson) (02) 756
Songlines, The (Chatwin) (88) 840
Songlines in Michaeltree (Harper) (01) 782
Songs of the Kings, The (Unsworth) (04) 705
Sonny Liston Was a Friend of Mine (Jones) (00) 717
Sons of Mississippi (Hendrickson) (04) 709
Soong Dynasty, The (Seagrave) (86) 852
Sophie's Choice (Styron) (80) 774
Sor Juana (Paz) (89) 808
Sorcerer's Apprentice, The (Johnson) (87) 795
Soros (Kaufman) (03) 794
Sorrow Is the Only Faithful One (Hatch) (94) 755
Sorrow of Architecture, The (Rector) (85) 855
Soul By Soul (Johnson) (01) 787
Soul of a New Machine, The (Kidder) (82) 787

Soul of the American University, The (Marsden) (95) 744
Souls and Bodies (Lodge) (83) 761
Sound of One Hand Clapping, The (Flanagan) (01) 791
Sound-Shadows of the New World (Mehta) (87) 802
Sound, Speech, and Music (Burrows) (91) 759
Sounds of Poetry, The (Pinsky) (99) 724
Source of Light, The (Price) (82) 790
Sources of the Self (Taylor) (91) 763
South of the Border, West of the Sun (Murakami) (00) 721
Southern Daughter (Pyron) (92) 775
Southern Family, A (Godwin) (88) 845
Southern Honor (Wyatt-Brown) (H-83) 396
Southern Renaissance, A (King) (81) 753
Southern Tradition, The (Genovese) (95) 748
Southern Woman, The (Spencer) (02) 760
Soviet Dissent in Historical Perspective (Shatz) (82) 795
Soviet Paradox, The (Bialer) (87) 807
Soviet Triangle, The (Shanor) (81) 759
Soviet Union and the Arms Race, The (Holloway) (H-84) 414
Spandau (Speer) (77) 764
Spanish Frontier in North America, The (Weber) (93) 749
Spanish War, The (O'Toole) (H-85) 425
Spartina (Casey) (90) 748
Speaking Freely (Hentoff) (98) 717
Speaking of Beauty (Donoghue) (04) 713
Speaking of Literature and Society (Trilling) (81) 764
Spectator Bird, The (Stegner) (77) 769
Spectral Emanations (Hollander) (79) 699
Speculator, The (Schwarz) (82) 800
Speedboat (Adler) (77) 776
Spencer Holst Stories (Holst) (77) 780
Spidertown (Rodriguez) (94) 760
Spinoza (Nadler) (00) 725
Spinoza and Other Heretics, Vol. I and Vol. II (Yovel) (91) 768
Spirit Catches You and You Fall Down, The (Fadiman) (98) 722
Spirit Level, The (Heaney) (97) 777
Sport of Nature, A (Gordimer) (88) 850
Sportswriter, The (Ford) (87) 813
Spring Moon (Lord) (82) 806
Springhouse, The (Dubie) (87) 818
Squares and Courtyards (Hacker) (01) 796
Stained Glass Elegies (Endō) (86) 856
Stained White Radiance, A (Burke) (93) 753
Stalin (Conquest) (92) 780
Stalin Embattled, 1943-1948 (McCagg) (79) 702
Stalin's American Policy (Taubman) (H-83) 400
Stand Before Your God (Watkins) (95) 752
Standing by Words (Berry) (84) 813
Stanley and the Women (Amis) (86) 859
Star-Apple Kingdom, The (Walcott) (80) 777
Star Called Henry, A (Doyle) (00) 729
Star Shines over Mt. Morris Park, A. See Mercy of a Rude Stream
Staring at the Sun (Barnes) (88) 855
Stars in My Pockets like Grains of Sand (Delany) (85) 860
Stars of the New Curfew (Okri) (90) 753
State of Ireland, The (Kiely) (81) 766
State of the Language, The (Ricks and Michaels, eds.) (91) 773
Statement, The (Moore) (97) 782
Statesman and Saint (Ridley) (H-84) 420
Station Island (Heaney) (85) 865
Statue Within, The (Jacob) (89) 813
Staying On (Scott) (78) 795
Steinbeck and Covici (Fensch) (80) 780

Stendhal (Keates) (98) 726
Step Across This Line (Rushdie) (03) 799
Stephen Hawking (White and Gribbin) (93) 758
Stephen Sondheim (Secrest) (99) 728
Stern Men (Gilbert) (01) 801
Steven Spielberg (McBride) (98) 731
Stevie (Barbera and McBrien) (88) 860
Stieglitz (Lowe) (H-84) 426
Stiffed (Faludi) (00) 733
Still Life with a Bridle (Herbert) (92) 785
Still Me (Reeve) (99) 733
Stillness and Shadows (Gardner) (87) 822
Stolen Light, The (Mehta) (90) 758
Stone Carvers, The (Urquhart) (03) 803
Stone Cottage (Longenbach) (89) 818
Stone Diaries, The (Shields) (95) 756
Stone Junction (Dodge) (91) 777
Stone Kiss (Kellerman) (03) 807
Stones for Ibarra (Doerr) (85) 869
Stonewall Jackson (Robertson) (98) 736
Stops (Sloman) (98) 741
Stopping Place, A (Mojtabai) (80) 785
Stories (Lessing) (79) 708
Stories in an Almost Classical Mode (Brodkey) (89) 822
Stories of Bernard Malamud, The (Malamud) (84) 819
Stories of Breece D'J Pancake, The (Pancake) (84) 824
Stories of Heinrich Böll, The (Böll) (87) 827
Stories of John Cheever, The (Cheever) (79) 713
Stories of John Edgar Wideman, The (Wideman) (93) 762
Stories of Muriel Spark (Spark) (86) 864
Stories of Ray Bradbury, The (Bradbury) (81) 769
Stories of Stephen Dixon, The (Dixon) (95) 761
Stories of Vladimir Nabokov, The (Nabokov) (96) 724
Stories of William Trevor, The (Trevor) (84) 829
Stories That Could Be True (Stafford) (78) 799
Story of American Freedom, The (Foner) (99) 737
Story of Henri Tod, The (Buckley) (85) 874
Story of Lucy Gault, The (Trevor) (03) 811
Storyteller (Silko) (82) 812
Storyteller, The (Vargas Llosa) (90) 763
Straight Man (Russo) (98) 745
Straight on till Morning (Lovell) (88) 865
Straight Through the Night (Allen) (90) 767
Strange Justice (Mayer and Abramson) (95) 765
Strange Ride of Rudyard Kipling, The (Wilson) (79) 717
Stranger in This World, A (Canty) (95) 769
Stranger Music (Cohen) (94) 764
Stranger Shores (Coetzee) (02) 764
Strangers All Are Gone, The (Powell) (84) 833
Strangers from a Different Shore (Takaki) (90) 772
Strategies of Containment (Gaddis) (H-83) 405
Streak of Luck, A (Conot) (80) 790
Street of Crocodiles, The (Schulz) (78) 804
Streets of Laredo (McMurtry) (94) 769
Strength of Fields, The (Dickey) (80) 794
Striking the Earth (Woods) (77) 784
Stroll with William James, A (Barzun) (84) 837
Strolls with Pushkin (Tertz) (95) 773
Strong Motion (Franzen) (93) 766
Strong Opinions (Nabokov) (77) 789
Structure of Evolutionary Theory, The (Gould) (03) 815
Struggle for Afghanistan, The (Newell and Newell) (82) 817
Struggle for Black Equality, 1954-1980, The (Sitkoff) (82) 822
Struggle for Power, A (Draper) (97) 787
Study for the World's Body (St. John) (95) 777
Stuff of Sleep and Dreams (Edel) (83) 765
Style and Faith (Hill) (04) 718

Subliminal Politics (Nimmo and Combs) (81) 773
Submarines at War (Hoyt) (H-84) 430
Succession, The (Garrett) (84) 842
Such a Peace (Sulzberger) (H-83) 411
Sudden Glory (Sanders) (96) 728
Sui Sin Far/Edith Maude Eaton (White-Parks) (96) 732
Suicide's Wife, The (Madden) (79) 727
Suitable Boy, A (Seth) (94) 774
Sumerian Vistas (Ammons) (88) 869
Summer Celestial (Plumly) (84) 846
Summer Life, A (Soto) (91) 782
Summer of '49 (Halberstam) (90) 777
Summons of the Trumpet (Palmer) (79) 732
Summons to Memphis, A (Taylor) (87) 832
Sun Yat-sen (Schiffrin) (81) 777
Sunday Between Wars, A (Maddow) (80) 798
Sunflower Splendor (Liu and Lo) (77) 792
Super Chief (Schwartz) (H-84) 435
Superhistorians, The (Barker) (H-83) 416
Superior Women (Adams) (85) 879
Supposedly Fun Thing I'll Never Do Again, A (Wallace) (98) 750
Sure Signs (Kooser) (81) 782
"Surely You're Joking, Mr. Feynman!" (Feynman, with Leighton) (86) 868
Survivor, The (Des Pres) (77) 797
Susan Sontag (Rollyson and Paddock) (01) 805
Susan Sontag Reader, A (Sontag) (83) 769
Sweet Hereafter, The (Banks) (92) 790
Sweet Talk (Vaughn) (91) 786
Sweetest Dream, The (Lessing) (03) 820
Swift, the Man, His Works, and the Age, Vol. III (Ehrenpreis) (84) 849
Swimming in the Volcano (Shacochis) (94) 779
Sylvia Beach and the Lost Generation (Fitch) (84) 854
Sylvia Plath (Butscher, ed.) (78) 809
Sylvia Plath (Wagner-Martin) (88) 874
Symposium (Spark) (91) 790
Sync (Strogatz) (04) 723

T. C. Boyle Stories (Boyle) (99) 742
T. E. Lawrence (Stewart) (78) 813
T. E. Lawrence, The Selected Letters (Lawrence) (90) 782
T. S. Eliot (Ackroyd) (85) 932
T. S. Eliot (Bush) (85) 937
T. S. Eliot (Gordon) (00) 737
Table of Contents (McPhee) (86) 873
Table of Green Fields, A (Davenport) (94) 783
Tabloid Dreams (Butler) (97) 792
Tailor of Panama, The (le Carré) (97) 797
Take the A Train (Blankfort) (79) 737
Takeover, The (Spark) (77) 802
Taking Light from Each Other (Burden) (93) 771
Taking on the World (Merry) (97) 802
Taking the World in for Repairs (Selzer) (87) 836
Tale Bearers, The (Pritchett) (81) 786
Tale of Genji, The (Murasaki) (02) 769
Tale of Two Utopias, A (Berman) (97) 807
Tales of Burning Love (Erdrich) (97) 812
Talking at the Gates (Campbell) (92) 795
Talking Dirty to the Gods (Komunyakaa) (01) 811
Talking It Over (Barnes) (92) 799
Talley's Folly (Wilson) (81) 790
Taps (Morris) (02) 773
Tar (Williams) (84) 859
Tar Baby (Morrison) (82) 828
"Target Is Destroyed, The" (Hersh) (87) 841
Target Tokyo (Prange) (H-85) 430
Tattered Cloak and Other Novels, The (Berberova) (92) 804
Tattooed Girl, The (Oates) (04) 727
Tax Inspector, The (Carey) (93) 775

Teaching a Stone to Talk (Dillard) (83) 773
Teammates, The (Halberstam) (04) 731
Technical Difficulties (Jordan) (93) 779
Tecumseh (Sugden) (99) 746
Tehanu (Le Guin) (91) 794
Teller of Tales (Stashower) (00) 741
Tempting of America, The (Bork) (90) 787
Ten Commandments, The (McClatchy) (99) 751
Ten Little Indians (Alexie) (04) 735
Tenants of Time, The (Flanagan) (89) 826
Tengu Child (Itaya) (84) 863
Tennis Players, The (Gustafsson) (84) 866
Terra Nostra (Fuentes) (77) 807
Terrible Honesty (Douglas) (96) 736
Terrible Secret, The (Laqueur) (82) 834
Terrible Twos, The (Reed) (83) 778
Territorial Rights (Spark) (80) 804
Terror and Liberalism (Berman) (04) 739
Terror Before Trafalgar, The (Pocock) (04) 743
Terrorists and Novelists (Johnson) (83) 783
Tesseract, The (Garland) (00) 745
Tesserae (Levertov) (96) 740
Testament, The (Grisham) (00) 749
Testaments Betrayed (Kundera) (96) 744
Testimony (Shostakovich) (80) 808
Testimony and Demeanor (Casey) (80) 811
Testing the Current (McPherson) (85) 884
Tests of Time (Gass) (03) 825
Texaco (Chamoiseau) (98) 755
Texas (Michener) (86) 878
Texas Trilogy, A (Jones) (77) 812
Texasville (McMurtry) (88) 878
Thanatos Syndrome, The (Percy) (88) 883
That Night (McDermott) (88) 888
Theater Essays of Arthur Miller, The (Miller) (79) 742
Theater of Envy, A (Girard) (92) 809
Theater of Essence, The (Kott) (85) 890
Theft, A (Bellow) (90) 792
Them (Ronson) (03) 829
Theodore Dreiser, 1871-1907 (Lingeman) (87) 847
Theodore Dreiser, 1908-1945 (Lingeman) (91) 798
Theodore Rex (Morris) (02) 777
Theodore Roosevelt (Miller) (93) 783
Therapy (Lodge) (96) 748
There Are No Children Here (Kotlowitz) (92) 813
Theremin (Glinsky) (01) 815
These Are My Rivers (Ferlinghetti) (94) 788
These the Companions (Davie) (83) 787
They Burn the Thistles (Kemal) (78) 817
Thief of Time, A (Hillerman) (89) 830
Thin Mountain Air, The (Horgan) (78) 821
Things That I Do in the Dark (Jordan) (78) 826
Things They Carried, The (O'Brien) (91) 803
Thinking About National Security (Brown) (H-84) 439
Thinking in Time (Neustadt and May) (87) 853
Thinks . . . (Lodge) (02) 782
Thirteenth Tribe, The (Koestler) (77) 817
13th Valley, The (Del Vecchio) (83) 791
Thirties, The (Wilson) (81) 795
Thirties and After, The (Spender) (79) 745
This Blessèd Earth (Wheelock) (79) 749
This Boy's Life (Wolff) (90) 796
This Is Not a Novel (Markson) (02) 786
This Quiet Dust and Other Writings (Styron) (83) 796
This Time (Stern) (99) 756
This Was Harlem (Anderson) (83) 800
This Wild Darkness (Brodkey) (97) 816
Thomas Cardinal Wolsey (Harvey) (81) 800
Thomas Carlyle (Kaplan) (84) 869
Thomas Cranmer (MacCulloch) (97) 821
Thomas E. Dewey and His Times (Smith) (H-83) 421
Thomas Hardy (Millgate) (83) 806

Thomas Hardy and the Proper Study of Mankind (Gatrell) (94) 793
Thomas Jefferson (Bedini) (91) 809
Thomas Jefferson (Randall) (94) 797
Thomas Kuhn (Fuller) (01) 820
Thomas More (Marius) (H-85) 435
Thoreau's Seasons (Lebeaux) (85) 895
Thorn Birds, The (McCullough) (78) 831
Thornton Wilder (Simon) (80) 815
Those Days (Critchfield) (87) 858
Thousand Acres, A (Smiley) (92) 817
Three Degrees Above Zero (Bernstein) (H-85) 441
Three Evenings (Lasdun) (93) 788
Three Gospels (Price) (97) 826
Three Novellas (Bernhard) (04) 747
Three Rival Versions of Moral Enquiry (MacIntyre) (91) 815
Three Thousand Dollars (Lipsky) (90) 801
Through the Ivory Gate (Dove) (93) 792
Through the Looking Glass (Verrier) (H-84) 444
Throw of the Dice, A (Millan) (95) 782
Thunder on the Right (Crawford) (81) 804
Thurber Letters, The (Thurber) (04) 752
Tidewater Tales, The (Barth) (88) 892
Tiepolo's Hound (Walcott) (01) 825
Tiger's Tail (Lee) (97) 830
Time (Pickover) (99) 760
Time and Narrative, Vol. I (Ricoeur) (85) 902
Time and Place (Woolley) (78) 836
Time and Tide (O'Brien) (93) 796
Time and Time Again (Jacobson) (86) 883
Time Change (Cooke) (82) 839
Time, Love, Memory (Weiner) (00) 754
Time of Desecration (Moravia) (81) 809
Time of Illusion, The (Schell) (77) 822
Time of Our Singing, The (Powers) (04) 756
Time of Our Time, The (Mailer) (99) 764
Time of Stalin, The (Antonov-Ovseyenko) (82) 845
Time Pieces (Morris) (90) 805
Time to Be in Earnest (James) (01) 830
Time to Dance, No Time to Weep, A (Godden) (89) 835
Time to Hear and Answer, A (Littleton, ed.) (78) 841
Timebends (Miller) (88) 897
Timequake (Vonnegut) (98) 760
Times Are Never So Bad, The (Dubus) (84) 873
Time's Arrow (Amis) (92) 821
Time's Arrow, Time's Cycle (Gould) (88) 902
Time's Power (Rich) (90) 809
Tinker and a Poor Man, A (Hill) (90) 814
Tip O'Neill and the Democratic Century (Farrell) (02) 791
Tipping Point, The (Gladwell) (01) 835
Tirant lo Blanc (Martorell and de Galba) (85) 907
Tishomingo Blues (Leonard) (03) 834
Titan (Chernow) (99) 768
To a Blossoming Pear Tree (Wright) (78) 847
To Asmara (Keneally) (90) 819
To Be an American (Hing) (98) 765
To Begin the World Anew (Bailyn) (04) 761
To Conquer the Air (Tobin) (04) 766
To Herland and Beyond (Lane) (91) 820
To Jerusalem and Back (Bellow) (77) 828
To Keep and Bear Arms (Malcolm) (95) 787
To Keep Our Honor Clean (McDowell) (81) 813
To See You Again (Adams) (83) 811
To Set the Record Straight (Sirica) (80) 822
To Skin a Cat (McGuane) (87) 863
To Tell a Free Story (Andrews) (87) 867
To the Halls of the Montezumas (Johannsen) (86) 887
To the Hermitage (Bradbury) (02) 796
To the Land of the Cattails (Appelfeld) (87) 871
To the Marianas (Hoyt) (81) 817

To the Wedding (Berger) (96) 752
To the White Sea (Dickey) (94) 802
To Urania (Brodsky) (89) 840
To Wake the Nations (Sundquist) (94) 806
To Win a War (Terraine) (82) 850
Tolkien (Carpenter) (78) 851
Tolstoi in the Seventies (Eikenbaum) (83) 821
Tolstoi in the Sixties (Eikenbaum) (83) 816
Tolstoy (Wilson) (89) 845
Tolstoy and Gandhi, Men of Peace (Green) (H-84) 447
Tolstoy's Dictaphone (Birkerts, ed.) (97) 834
Tolstoy's Letters, Vol. I and Vol. II (Tolstoy) (79) 754
Tom (Leverich) (96) 756
Tom Paine (Keane) (96) 760
Tombee (Rosengarten, ed.) (87) 875
Torch in My Ear, The (Canetti) (83) 827
Tormented Warrior (Parkinson) (80) 827
Torn Skirt, The (Godfrey) (03) 839
Tortilla Curtain, The (Boyle) (96) 764
Tough Guys Don't Dance (Mailer) (85) 912
Toward a More Natural Science (Kass) (86) 892
Toward the Brink, 1785-1787 (Manceron) (H-84) 452
Toward the End of Time (Updike) (98) 769
Toward the Final Solution (Mosse) (79) 761
Track to Bralgu, The (Wongar) (79) 768
Tracks (Erdrich) (89) 850
Trading with the Enemy (Higham) (H-84) 457
Tradition of Return, The (Perl) (85) 917
Tragedy of Cambodian History, The (Chandler) (93) 800
Tragic Honesty, A (Bailey) (04) 770
Trail of the Fox, The (Irving) (78) 856
Trains of Thought (Brombert) (03) 843
Traitor's Kiss, A (O'Toole) (99) 773
Transactions in a Foreign Currency (Eisenberg) (87) 881
Transatlantic Blues (Sheed) (79) 772
Transatlantic Patterns (Green) (78) 860
Trans-Atlantyk (Gombrowicz) (95) 791
Transfer Agreement, The (Black) (H-85) 445
Transformation of American Law, 1870-1960, The (Horwitz) (93) 805
Transformation of Southern Politics, The (Bass and De Vries) (77) 832
Transforming Russia and China (Rosenberg and Young) (H-83) 426
Transit of Venus, The (Hazzard) (81) 822
Translingual Imagination, The (Kellman) (01) 840
Transparent Man, The (Hecht) (91) 825
Transports and Disgraces (Henson) (81) 827
Trapped in the Net (Rochlin) (98) 773
Travelers of a Hundred Years (Keene) (90) 823
Traveler's Tree, The (Smith) (81) 831
Traveling in Mark Twain (Bridgman) (88) 907
Traveling Light (Barich) (85) 923
Traveling Mercies (Lamott) (00) 764
Traveling on One Leg (Mueller) (99) 778
Travels (Merwin) (94) 811
Travesty (Hawkes) (77) 837
Tread the Dark (Ignatow) (79) 777
Treason by the Book (Spence) (02) 800
Treason in the Blood (Brown) (95) 796
Treatment, The (Menaker) (99) 783
Tree of Life, The (Nissenson) (86) 896
Trial by Fire (Smith) (H-83) 431
Trial of Elizabeth Cree, The (Ackroyd) (96) 768
Trial of Socrates, The (Stone) (89) 855
Trials of Phillis Wheatley, The (Gates) (04) 774
Triangle (Von Drehle) (04) 778
Trick of the Ga Bolga, The (McGinley) (86) 903
Trickster Makes This World (Hyde) (99) 787
Trinity (Uris) (77) 842

Triphammer (McCall) (91) 829
Triple Helix, The (Lewontin) (01) 845
Triumph of Achilles, The (Glück) (86) 908
Triumph of Love, The (Hill) (99) 791
Triumph of Politics, The (Stockman) (87) 886
Triumph of the Novel, The (Guerard) (77) 847
Trollope (Hall) (92) 825
Trollope (Wall) (90) 827
Trouble in Mind (Litwack) (99) 795
Trouble with Computers, The (Landauer) (96) 773
Truants, The (Barrett) (83) 833
True Adventures of John Steinbeck, Writer, The (Benson) (85) 927
True and Only Heaven, The (Lasch) (92) 830
True at First Light (Hemingway) (00) 768
True Confessions of an Albino Terrorist, The (Breytenbach) (86) 913
True History of the Kelly Gang (Carey) (02) 804
True North (Conway) (95) 801
Truffaut (de Baecque and Toubiana) (00) 772
Truly Disadvantaged, The (Wilson) (88) 910
Truman (McCullough) (93) 810
Truman's Crises (Gosnell) (81) 836
Trust (Fukuyama) (96) 777
Trust Me (Updike) (88) 915
Truth About Chernobyl, The (Medvedev) (92) 835
Truth About Lorin Jones, The (Lurie) (89) 860
Truth and Progress (Rorty) (99) 799
Trying to Save Piggy Sneed (Irving) (97) 838
Tugman's Passage, The (Hoagland) (83) 836
Tumble Home (Hempel) (98) 778
Tumultuous Years (Donovan) (H-83) 435
Tunnel, The (Gass) (96) 782
Turbulent Souls (Dubner) (99) 803
Turgenev (Schapiro) (80) 832
Turgenev Letters (Turgenev) (84) 879
Turn in the South, A (Naipaul) (90) 831
Turning Right (Savage) (93) 815
Turtle Beach (d'Alpuget) (84) 886
Turtle Diary (Hoban) (77) 852
Turtle Moon (Hoffman) (93) 820
Tuxedo Park (Conant) (03) 848
Twelve Years (Agee) (82) 854
Twentieth Century Journey, Vol. II (Shirer) (H-85) 451
Twentieth Century Pleasures (Hass) (85) 941
Twenty-seventh Kingdom, The (Ellis) (00) 776
Twice Shy (Francis) (83) 841
Twilight of Capitalism, The (Harrington) (77) 857
Twilight of the Old Order, 1774-1778 (Manceron) (78) 864
Two-Bit Culture (Davis) (85) 952
Two Cities (Wideman) (99) 808
Two Faces of Islam, The (Schwartz) (03) 853
2010 (Clarke) (83) 844
2081 (O'Neill) (82) 860
Two Wings to Veil My Face (Forrest) (85) 946
Twyborn Affair, The (White) (81) 840
Tycho and Kepler (Ferguson) (04) 782
Typical American (Jen) (92) 840
Tyranny of the Majority, The (Guinier) (95) 805
Tzili (Appelfeld) (84) 890

U and I (Baker) (92) 844
Ultima Thule (McCombs) (01) 850
Ultimate Journey (Bernstein) (02) 808
Ulverton (Thorpe) (94) 814
Unafraid of the Dark (Bray) (99) 812
Unattainable Earth (Miłosz) (87) 892
Unauthorized Freud (Crews, ed.) (99) 817
Unbearable Heart, The (Hahn) (97) 843
Unbearable Lightness of Being, The (Kundera) (85) 958
Unbeliever, The (Parker) (89) 864

TITLE INDEX

Uncertain Greatness (Morris) (78) 869
Uncertain Partners (Goncharov, Lewis, and Xue) (95) 809
Uncertainty (Cassidy) (93) 824
Uncivil Liberties (Trillin) (83) 849
Uncle (Markus) (79) 783
Uncle of Europe (Brook-Shepherd) (77) 861
Uncollected Poems (Rilke) (97) 848
Uncollected Stories of William Faulkner (Faulkner) (80) 838
Unconsoled, The (Ishiguro) (96) 786
Undaunted Courage (Ambrose) (97) 853
Under Briggflatts (Davie) (91) 833
Under My Skin (Lessing) (95) 814
Under Review (Powell) (95) 819
Under the Banner of Heaven (Krakauer) (04) 787
Under the Banyan Tree (Narayan) (86) 918
Under the 82nd Airborne (Eisenberg) (93) 829
Under the Eye of the Clock (Nolan) (89) 868
Under the Fifth Sun (Shorris) (81) 844
Under the Jaguar Sun (Calvino) (89) 872
Under the Sign of Saturn (Sontag) (81) 848
Under the Vulture-Tree (Bottoms) (88) 919
Under Western Skies (Worster) (93) 833
Undersong (Lorde) (93) 838
Understand This (Tervalon) (95) 823
Understanding Inflation (Case) (82) 866
Undertaking, The (Lynch) (98) 786
Underworld (DeLillo) (98) 791
Undiscovered Mind, The (Horgan) (00) 780
Undue Influence (Brookner) (01) 855
Undying Grass, The (Kemal) (79) 787
Unequal Justice (Auerbach) (77) 866
Unexpected Vista, The (Trefil) (H-84) 462
Unfinished Life, An (Dallek) (04) 791
Unfinished Presidency, The (Brinkley) (99) 822
Unfinished War, The (Capps) (H-83) 440
Unfortunate Woman, An (Brautigan) (01) 859
Union Street (Barker) (84) 895
United States (Vidal) (94) 819
United States and the Berlin Blockade, 1948-1949, The (Shlaim) (H-84) 469
United States and the Caribbean, 1900-1970, The (Langley) (81) 853
United States in the Middle East, The (Tillman) (H-83) 445
Universe in a Nutshell, The (Hawking) (02) 818
Unknown Matisse, The (Spurling) (99) 826
Unless (Shields) (03) 858
Unlocking the Air (Le Guin) (97) 858
Unlocking the English Language (Burchfield) (92) 849
Unmade Bed, The (Sagan) (79) 791
Unraveling of America, The (Matusow) (H-85) 460
Unreliable Memoirs (James) (82) 870
Unseen Revolution, The (Drucker) (77) 872
Unsettling of America, The (Berry) (79) 795
Unsuitable Attachment, An (Pym) (83) 855
Unsuspected Revolution, The (Llerena) (79) 799
Unto the Sons (Talese) (93) 842
Unto the Soul (Appelfeld) (95) 827
Untouchable, The (Banville) (98) 796
Untying the Knot (Hasan-Rokem and Shulman, eds.) (97) 862
Unwanted, The (Marrus) (86) 923
Unwelcome Strangers (Reimers) (99) 830
Up at Oxford (Mehta) (94) 823
Upon This Rock (Freedman) (94) 827
Uses of Enchantment, The (Bettelheim) (77) 876
U.S.S.R. in Crisis (Goldman) (H-84) 472

Utopia Parkway (Solomon) (98) 801
Utopian Pessimist (McLellan) (91) 838
Utz (Chatwin) (90) 835

V Was for Victory (Blum) (77) 880
Vaclav Havel (Keane) (01) 863
Valley of Darkness (Havens) (79) 804
Vanessa Bell (Spalding) (84) 900
Van Gogh (Sweetman) (91) 843
Van Gogh's Room at Arles (Elkin) (94) 831
Vanished (Morris) (89) 877
Vanished Act (Reidel) (04) 796
Vanished Imam, The (Ajami) (87) 901
Van Wyck Brooks (Nelson) (82) 874
Various Antidotes (Scott) (95) 831
Vatican Diplomacy and the Jews During the Holocaust, 1939-1943 (Morley) (81) 861
Vectors and Smoothable Curves (Bronk) (84) 905
Ved Mehta Reader, A (Mehta) (99) 834
Veil (Woodward) (88) 923
Velázquez (Brown) (87) 907
Venetian Vespers, The (Hecht) (80) 841
Venona (Haynes and Klehr) (00) 784
Ventriloquist, The (Huff) (78) 873
Véra (Mrs. Vladimir Nabokov) (Schiff) (00) 789
Vermont Papers, The (Bryan and McClaughry) (90) 839
Vertigo (Sebald) (01) 868
Very Old Bones (Kennedy) (93) 846
Very Private Eye, A (Pym) (85) 964
Viaduct, The (Wheldon) (84) 910
Vice (Ai) (00) 793
Victor Hugo (Robb) (99) 838
Victor Hugo and the Visionary Novel (Brombert) (85) 969
Victorian Anthropology (Stocking) (88) 928
Victorian Feminists (Caine) (93) 851
Victorian Sensation (Secord) (02) 822
Victorians, The (Wilson) (04) 801
Victory over Japan (Gilchrist) (85) 973
Vietnam 1945 (Marr) (97) 867
View from 80, The (Cowley) (81) 867
View from Highway 1, The (Arlen) (77) 884
View from the UN (Thant) (79) 809
View of Victorian Literature, A (Tillotson) (79) 814
View with a Grain of Sand (Szymborska) (96) 790
Views & Spectacles (Weiss) (80) 846
Vigour of Prophecy, The (Henry) (91) 847
Viking World, The (Graham-Campbell) (81) 873
Village of Longing, The, and Dancehall Days (O'Brien) (91) 851
Villages (Critchfield) (82) 879
Vindication (Sherwood) (94) 835
Vindication of Tradition, The (Pelikan) (H-85) 467
Vineland (Pynchon) (90) 844
Viper Jazz (Tate) (77) 888
Virginia Woolf (Gordon) (86) 927
Virginia Woolf (King) (96) 794
Virginia Woolf (Lee) (98) 805
Virtual Light (Gibson) (94) 839
Virtual Tibet (Schell) (01) 873
Vision of Emma Blau, The (Hegi) (01) 877
Visions from San Francisco Bay (Miłosz) (83) 860
Visions of Harmony (Taylor) (88) 932
Visions of Kerouac (Duberman) (78) 878
Visit to Civilization, A (McPherson) (03) 863
Visitors (Brookner) (99) 842
Vita (Glendinning) (84) 916
Vita Nova (Glück) (00) 797
Vladimir Nabokov, The American Years (Boyd) (92) 854
Vladimir Nabokov, The Russian Years (Boyd) (91) 856

1003

Vladimir Nabokov, Selected Letters (Nabokov) (90) 849
Vladimir's Carrot (Peter) (88) 937
VN (Field) (87) 912
Vocation of a Teacher, The (Booth) (90) 854
Voice at 3:00 A.M., The (Simic) (04) 806
Voice from the Chorus, A (Tertz) (77) 892
Voice Lessons (Mairs) (95) 835
Voices (Matthews) (84) 921
Voices and Visions (Vendler, ed.) (88) 943
Voices in the Mirror (Parks) (91) 861
Voices of Protest (Brinkley) (H-83) 449
Void, A (Perec) (96) 799
Volcano (Hongo) (96) 802
Volcano Lover, The (Sontag) (93) 856
Voltaire (Mason) (82) 885
Voltaire (Orieux) (80) 850
Vortex (Materer) (80) 855
Voyage of the Armada, The (Howarth) (82) 891
Voyagers to the West (Bailyn, with DeWolfe) (87) 917

W. B. Yeats (Jeffares) (91) 876
W. B. Yeats, 1865-1914 (Foster) (98) 809
W. E. B. Du Bois, 1868-1919 (Lewis) (94) 847
W. E. B. Du Bois, 1919-1963 (Lewis) (01) 882
W. H. Auden (Carpenter) (82) 923
W. H. Auden (Osborne) (80) 860
W. H. Hudson (Tomalin) (84) 935
Wages of Guilt, The (Buruma) (95) 840
Waist High in the World (Mairs) (98) 814
Wait for November (Nossack) (83) 864
Waiting (Jin) (00) 801
Waiting for My Life (Pastan) (82) 897
Waiting to Exhale (McMillan) (93) 860
Waking (Figes) (83) 869
Waking the Dead (Spencer) (87) 922
Waldo Emerson (Allen) (82) 902
Walker Evans (Mellow) (00) 805
Walker Percy (Samway) (98) 818
Walkin' the Dog (Mosley) (00) 809
Walking in the Shade (Lessing) (98) 823
Walking on Water (Kenan) (00) 813
Walking the Bible (Feiler) (02) 826
Wall Jumper, The (Schneider) (85) 978
Wallace Stegner (Benson) (97) 871
Wallace Stevens (Doggett and Buttel, eds.) (81) 879
Wallace Stevens (Longenbach) (92) 859
Wallace Stevens, 1879-1923 (Richardson) (87) 927
Wallace Stevens, 1923-1955 (Richardson) (89) 882
Walls of Thebes, The (Slavitt) (87) 936
Walnut Door, The (Hersey) (78) 883
Walt Whitman (Kaplan) (81) 883
Walt Whitman (Zweig) (85) 984
Walt Whitman's America (Reynolds) (96) 806
Walter Benjamin at the Dairy Queen (McMurtry) (00) 817
Walter Hines Page (Cooper) (78) 888
Walter Lippmann (Blum) (H-85) 470
Walter Lippmann and the American Century (Steel) (81) 886
Walter Pater (Donoghue) (96) 810
Walter Scott (Millgate) (85) 989
Waltzing with a Dictator (Bonner) (88) 949
Wandering Ghost (Cott) (92) 863
Wanderlust (Solnit) (01) 887
Want Bone, The (Pinsky) (91) 866
War, The (Duras) (87) 941
War Against Cliché, The (Amis) (02) 830
War Against the Weak (Black) (04) 810
War Diaries (MacMillan) (H-85) 474
War Diaries of Jean-Paul Sartre, The (Sartre) (86) 932
War in a Time of Peace (Halberstam) (02) 834
War Music (Logue) (88) 954

War of 1812, The (Hickey) (90) 859
War of the End of the World, The (Vargas Llosa) (85) 995
War Path, The (Irving) (79) 819
War That Hitler Won, The (Herzstein) (79) 823
War with Spain in 1898, The (Trask) (82) 908
War Within (Singal) (83) 873
War Within, The (Wells) (95) 844
War Within and Without (Lindbergh) (81) 890
War Without a Name, The (Talbott) (81) 896
War Without Mercy (Dower) (87) 947
Warden of English, The (McMorris) (02) 838
Warrenpoint (Donoghue) (91) 871
Warrior and the Priest, The (Cooper) (H-84) 476
Warsaw Diary, A (Brandys) (84) 926
Wartime (Djilas) (78) 894
Wartime (Fussell) (90) 864
Wartime Lies (Begley) (92) 868
Was Huck Black? (Fishkin) (94) 843
Washington Goes to War (Brinkley) (89) 887
Watch, The (Bass) (90) 869
Watch in the Night, A (Wilson) (97) 876
Watches of the Night, The (Caudill) (77) 896
Watchfires (Auchincloss) (83) 878
Watching TV with the Red Chinese (Whisnant) (93) 864
Water Engine and Mr. Happiness, The (Mamet) (79) 828
Waterborne (Gregerson) (03) 867
Watergate and the Constitution (Kurland) (79) 830
Waterland (Swift) (85) 1000
Waterloo (Chandler) (82) 912
Watermelon Wine (Gaillard) (79) 835
Waterworks, The (Doctorow) (95) 849
Wave, A (Ashbery) (85) 1008
Way in the World, A (Naipaul) (95) 853
Way of the World, The (Fromkin) (00) 821
Way Out There in the Blue (FitzGerald) (01) 891
Way to Paradise, The (Vargas Llosa) (04) 815
Ways of Escape (Greene) (82) 918
Wayward and the Seeking, The (Toomer) (81) 904
We Irish (Donoghue) (87) 953
We Love Glenda So Much and Other Tales (Cortázar) (84) 931
We Men Who Feel Most German (Chickering) (H-85) 479
We Were Soldiers Once . . . and Young (Moore and Galloway) (93) 868
Weaker Vessel, The (Fraser) (H-85) 483
Wealth and Democracy (Phillips) (03) 872
Wealth and Poverty of Nations, The (Landes) (99) 846
Weight of the World, The (Handke) (85) 1013
Well, The (Jolley) (87) 958
West Wind (Oliver) (98) 828
Western Alliance, The (Grosser) (81) 911
Wet Work (Buckley) (92) 872
What Am I Doing Here (Chatwin) (90) 874
What I Lived For (Oates) (95) 858
What I Loved (Hustvedt) (04) 819
What I Saw at the Revolution (Noonan) (91) 881
What I Think I Did (Woiwode) (01) 896
What Is an Editor? (Commins) (79) 839
What It Takes (Cramer) (93) 874
What Kind of Life (Callahan) (91) 886
What Kind of Nation (Simon) (03) 877
What Shall We Wear to This Party? (Wilson) (77) 901
What the Living Do (Howe) (98) 832
What the Twilight Says (Walcott) (99) 851
What Was Literature? (Fiedler) (83) 884
What Was Mine (Beattie) (92) 876
What We Talk About When We Talk About Love (Carver) (82) 926
What Work Is (Levine) (92) 880

TITLE INDEX

What's Bred in the Bone (Davies) (86) 939
What's to Become of the Boy? (Böll) (85) 1018
Wheat That Springeth Green (Powers) (89) 892
When Heaven and Earth Changed Places (Hayslip, with Wurts) (90) 879
When Hollywood Had a King (Bruck) (04) 823
When Memory Speaks (Conway) (99) 855
When the Messenger Is Hot (Crane) (04) 827
When the Mind Hears (Lane) (H-85) 488
When the Sons of Heaven Meet the Daughters of the Earth (Eberstadt) (98) 836
When Things of the Spirit Come First (Beauvoir) (83) 890
When Tigers Fight (Wilson) (H-83) 454
When We Were Orphans (Ishiguro) (01) 900
When Work Disappears (Wilson) (97) 880
Where Do You Put the Horse? (Metcalf) (87) 963
Where I Was From (Didion) (04) 831
Where I'm Calling From (Carver) (89) 897
Where the Stress Falls (Sontag) (02) 842
Where You Find It (Galloway) (03) 882
Where You'll Find Me (Beattie) (87) 967
Which Side Are You On? (Geoghegan) (92) 885
While England Sleeps (Leavitt) (94) 851
While I Was Gone (Miller) (00) 826
Whisper to the Earth (Ignatow) (83) 894
Whistle (Jones) (79) 843
White Album, The (Didion) (80) 862
White Boned Demon, The (Terrill) (H-85) 495
White Castle, The (Pamuk) (92) 890
White Death, The (Dormandy) (01) 905
White Hotel, The (Thomas) (82) 932
White House Years (Kissinger) (80) 866
White Lantern, The (Connell) (81) 916
White Man's Grave (Dooling) (95) 862
White Man's Indian, The (Berkhofer) (79) 847
White Noise (DeLillo) (86) 945
White Pine (Oliver) (95) 867
White Plague, The (Herbert) (83) 900
White Shroud (Ginsberg) (87) 974
White Supremacy (Fredrickson) (82) 937
White Teeth (Smith) (01) 910
White Tribe of Africa, The (Harrison) (H-83) 459
White Wave, The (Daniels) (85) 1023
White Words, The (Wormser) (84) 940
Whiteness of Bones, The (Moore) (90) 884
Whitney Father, Whitney Heiress (Swanberg) (81) 921
Whittaker Chambers (Tanenhaus) (98) 841
Who Do You Love (Thompson) (00) 830
Who Is Teddy Villanova? (Berger) (78) 899
Who Killed Daniel Pearl? (Lévy) (04) 835
Who Shall Be the Sun? (Wagoner) (79) 852
Who Voted for Hitler? (Hamilton) (H-83) 462
Who Whispered Near Me (Clary) (90) 889
Whole New Life, A (Price) (95) 871
Whole Shebang, The (Ferris) (98) 846
Whole Woman, The (Greer) (00) 834
Whore's Child, and Other Stories, The (Russo) (03) 886
Who's Irish? (Jen) (00) 839
Whose Justice? Which Rationality? (MacIntyre) (89) 902
Why Big Fierce Animals Are Rare (Colinvaux) (79) 857
Why Can't We Live Together Like Civilized Human Beings? (Kumin) (83) 903
Why Did I Ever (Robison) (02) 847
Why Did the Heavens Not Darken? (Mayer) (90) 893
Why Not the Best? (Carter) (77) 906
Why the Jews? (Prager and Telushkin) (H-84) 481
Why the South Lost the Civil War (Beringer, Hattaway, Jones, and Still) (87) 980
Why They Kill (Rhodes) (00) 843

Wide as the Waters (Bobrick) (02) 851
Wider Sea, The (Hunt) (83) 908
Wider World, A (Simon) (87) 985
Widow for One Year, A (Irving) (99) 859
Widower's Son, The (Sillitoe) (78) 904
Wilberforce (Pollock) (79) 862
Wilbur and Orville (Howard) (88) 959
Wild Birds, The (Berry) (87) 989
Wild Blue, The (Ambrose) (02) 856
Wild Boy of Aveyron, The (Lane) (77) 910
Wild Decembers (O'Brien) (01) 915
Wild Life (Gloss) (01) 920
Wild Patience Has Taken Me This Far, A (Rich) (82) 942
Wild Swans (Chang) (92) 894
Wilderness of Mirrors (Martin) (81) 924
Wilderness Tips (Atwood) (92) 900
Wildlife (Ford) (91) 891
Wilhelm Liebknecht and the Founding of the German Social Democratic Party (Dominick) (H-83) 467
Wilhelm von Humboldt, 1767-1808 (Sweet) (79) 868
Wilkomirski Affair, The (Maechler) (02) 861
Will (Liddy) (81) 928
Will You Please Be Quiet, Please? (Carver) (77) 914
Willa (Robinson) (84) 945
Willa Cather (Lee) (91) 896
Willa Cather (O'Brien) (87) 994
William Carlos Williams (Mariani) (82) 946
William Caxton (Painter) (78) 909
William F. Buckley, Jr. (Judis) (89) 908
William Faulkner, First Encounters (Brooks) (84) 950
William Faulkner, Toward Yoknapatawpha and Beyond (Brooks) (79) 874
William Faulkner (Karl) (90) 899
William Faulkner (Minter) (81) 932
William Faulkner (Singal) (98) 850
William Godwin (Marshall) (85) 1028
William James (Myers) (87) 997
William Morris (Thompson) (78) 913
William Pitt the Younger (Reilly) (80) 873
William Styron (West) (99) 864
William Wordsworth (Gill) (90) 904
Willie and Dwike (Zinsser) (85) 1036
Will's Boy (Morris) (82) 950
Wind Done Gone, The (Randall) (02) 865
Wind Mountain (Chappell) (80) 877
Wind Will Not Subside, The (Milton and Milton) (77) 918
Windows (Creeley) (91) 901
Windrose (Ghiselin) (81) 935
Winds of History (Backer) (H-84) 488
Wine-Dark Sea, The (O'Brian) (94) 856
Wing of Madness, The (Burston) (97) 885
Winged Seed, The (Lee) (96) 814
Winner Names the Age, The (Smith) (79) 879
Winning the City (Weesner) (91) 905
Winston Churchill's Afternoon Nap (Campbell) (88) 964
Winston Churchill's World View (Thompson) (H-84) 493
Winston S. Churchill, 1922-1939 (Gilbert) (78) 917
Winston S. Churchill, 1939-1941 (Gilbert) (H-85) 500
Winston S. Churchill, 1941-1945 (Gilbert) (87) 1001
Winston S. Churchill, 1945-1965 (Gilbert) (89) 913
Winter Garden (Bainbridge) (82) 958
Winter Queen, The (Akunin) (04) 839
Winter World (Heinrich) (04) 843
Winter's Tale (Helprin) (84) 954
Winterspelt (Andersch) (79) 883
Winthrop Covenant, The (Auchincloss) (77) 923
Wisdom of the Body, The (Nuland) (98) 854
Wisdom of the World, The (Brague) (04) 847
Wise Children (Carter) (93) 879

Witch of Exmoor, The (Drabble) (98) 858
Witches and Jesuits (Wills) (95) 876
Witches of Eastwick, The (Updike) (85) 1041
With a Daughter's Eye (Bateson) (H-85) 507
With All Disrespect (Trillin) (86) 950
With Chatwin (Clapp) (98) 862
With Friends Possessed (Martin) (86) 954
With Ignorance (Williams) (78) 923
With My Trousers Rolled (Epstein) (96) 818
With the Stroke of a Pen (Mayer) (02) 870
Within the Context of No Context (Trow) (98) 866
Within the Whirlwind (Ginzburg) (82) 963
Without a Hero (Boyle) (95) 880
Without End (Zagajewski) (03) 890
Without Precedent (Adams) (H-84) 497
Witness of Poetry, The (Miłosz) (84) 959
Witness to Hope (Weigel) (00) 847
Witness to Power (Ehrlichman) (H-83) 473
Witnesses at the Creation (Morris) (86) 959
Wittgenstein, A Life (McGuinness) (89) 918
Wittgenstein's Nephew (Bernhard) (90) 908
Wittgenstein's Poker (Edmonds and Eidinow) (02) 875
Wizard War, The (Jones) (79) 888
Wobegon Boy (Keillor) (98) 870
Wolf by the Ears, The (Miller) (78) 928
Wolfwatching (Hughes) (92) 905
Woman (Angier) (00) 851
Woman and the Ape, The (Høeg) (97) 890
Woman and the Demon (Auerbach) (83) 913
Woman Hollering Creek (Cisneros) (92) 909
Woman Named Drown, A (Powell) (88) 968
Woman of Contradictions, A (Taylor) (91) 909
Woman of Singular Occupation, A (Gilliatt) (90) 912
Woman of the Aeroplanes (Laing) (91) 914
Woman of the Inner Sea (Keneally) (94) 860
Woman Said Yes, The (West) (77) 928
Woman Warrior, The (Kingston) (77) 932
Woman Who Cut Off Her Leg at the Maidstone Club
  and Other Stories, The (Slavin) (00) 855
Woman Who Fell from the Sky, The (Harjo) (96) 822
Woman Who Gave Birth to Rabbits, The (Donoghue)
  (03) 894
Woman Who Lived in a Prologue, The (Schneider)
  (81) 941
Woman Who Walked into Doors, The (Doyle) (97) 895
Woman's Inhumanity to Woman (Chesler) (03) 898
Women, The (Als) (98) 874
Women and Men (McElroy) (88) 973
Women and the American Experience (Woloch)
  (H-85) 511
Women and the Common Life (Lasch) (98) 878
Women, Fire, and Dangerous Things (Lakoff) (88) 979
Women in Their Beds (Berriault) (97) 900
Women of Brewster Place, The (Naylor) (83) 918
Women of the Left Bank (Benstock) (87) 1009
Women of the Shadows (Cornelisen) (77) 937
Women on Love (Sullerot) (81) 947
Women on the Margins (Davis) (96) 826
Women, Reason and Nature (McMillan) (84) 964
Women Volunteering (Kaminer) (H-85) 516
Women with Men (Ford) (98) 882
Wonder Boys (Chabon) (96) 831
Wonderful Fool (Endō) (84) 967
Wonderful Life (Gould) (90) 916
Wonders of the Invisible World, The (Gates) (00) 859
Woodrow Wilson (Heckscher) (92) 914
Woodrow Wilson (Mulder) (79) 892
Woods, The (Plante) (83) 923
Words Alone (Donoghue) (01) 925
Words and Rules (Pinker) (00) 863
Words for Dr. Y (Sexton) (79) 897
Words That Must Somehow Be Said (Boyle) (86) 966
Words to God's Music (Wieder) (04) 851

Words Under the Words (Nye) (96) 835
Work Ethic in Industrial America, 1850-1920, The
  (Rodgers) (79) 904
Work, for the Night Is Coming (Carter) (82) 968
Work of Nations, The (Reich) (92) 919
Working Girl Can't Win, A (Garrison) (99) 868
Working It Out (Ruddick and Daniels, eds.) (78) 937
Works and Lives (Geertz) (89) 923
World According to Garp, The (Irving) (79) 908
World According to Peter Drucker, The (Beatty) (99)
  872
World After Oil, The (Nussbaum) (H-84) 502
World at Arms, A (Weinberg) (95) 885
World Below, The (Miller) (02) 880
World Enough and Time (Murray) (01) 930
World Made New, A (Glendon) (02) 884
World of Biblical Literature, The (Alter) (93) 883
World of Light, A (Sarton) (77) 941
World of Love, A (Lash, ed.) (H-85) 521
World of My Own, A (Greene) (95) 890
World of Our Fathers (Howe) (77) 947
World of Wonders (Davies) (77) 952
World, The, Flesh, and Angels, The (Campbell)
  (90) 921
World, the Text, and the Critic, The (Said) (84) 971
World Unsuspected, A (Harris, ed.) (88) 984
World Within the Word, The (Gass) (79) 913
World's End (Boyle) (88) 988
World's Fair (Doctorow) (86) 970
Worlds of Reference (McArthur) (87) 1015
Worlds of Wonder, Days of Judgment (Hall) (90) 925
Worm of Consciousness and Other Essays, The
  (Chiaromonte) (77) 956
Wormholes (Fowles) (99) 877
Worshipful Company of Fletchers (Tate) (95) 895
Wrath of Nations, The (Pfaff) (94) 864
Wrinkles (Simmons) (79) 918
Writer and the World, The (Naipaul) (03) 902
Writers and Friends (Weeks) (83) 928
Writers in Russia (Hayward) (84) 977
Writing and Being (Gordimer) (96) 839
Writing Dangerously (Brightman) (93) 887
Writing in a State of Siege (Brink) (84) 983
Writing in the New Nation (Ziff) (92) 924
Writing Life, The (Dillard) (90) 930
Writing Was Everything (Kazin) (96) 843
Writing Women in Jacobean England (Lewalski)
  (94) 869
Writings (Du Bois) (88) 993
Written on the Body (Winterson) (94) 873

X in Sex, The (Bainbridge) (04) 855
X/Self (Brathwaite) (88) 999
XYZ Affair, The (Stinchcombe) (82) 972

Yeager (Yeager and Janos) (86) 974
Year of the French, The (Flanagan) (80) 880
Year of the Hunter, A (Miłosz) (95) 900
Years of Lyndon Johnson, Master of the Senate, The
  (Caro) (03) 907
Years of Lyndon Johnson, Means of Ascent, The (Caro)
  (91) 919
Years of Lyndon Johnson, The Path to Power, The
  (Caro) (H-83) 478
Years of MacArthur, 1945-64 (James) (86) 980
Years of Renewal (Kissinger) (00) 867
Years of Rice and Salt, The (Robinson) (03) 912
Years of Upheaval (Kissinger) (H-83) 483
Years with Laura Díaz, The (Fuentes) (01) 935
Yeats (Archibald) (84) 988
Yellow (Lee) (02) 889
Yellow Admiral, The (O'Brian) (97) 904

TITLE INDEX

Yellow Dog (Amis) (04) 859
Yellow Raft in Blue Water, A (Dorris) (88) 1004
Yellow Wind, The (Grossman) (89) 928
Yeltsin (Aron) (01) 940
¡Yo! (Alvarez) (98) 886
Yoga for People Who Can't Be Bothered to Do It (Dyer) (04) 864
Yonder Stands Your Orphan (Hannah) (02) 894
You Can't Keep a Good Woman Down (Walker) (82) 976
You Must Remember This (Oates) (88) 1009
You've Had Your Time (Burgess) (92) 933
Young Hamilton, The (Flexner) (79) 922
Young Hemingway, The (Reynolds) (87) 1021
Young Lukács, The (Congdon) (84) 992
Young Men and Fire (Maclean) (93) 892

Young Nietzsche (Pletsch) (92) 928
Young Rebecca, The (West) (83) 932
Young Shakespeare (Fraser) (89) 933
Your Blues Ain't Like Mine (Campbell) (93) 896
Yukiko (Harris) (78) 942

Zelda Fitzgerald (Cline) (04) 868
Zhou Enlai (Wilson) (H-85) 526
Zither and Autobiography (Scalapino) (04) 872
Zola (Brown) (96) 847
Zone, The (Dovlatov) (86) 985
Zora Neale Hurston (Hurston) (96) 852
Zuckerman Unbound (Roth) (82) 981
Zuñi and the American Imagination (McFeely) (02) 898

AUTHOR INDEX

1977-2004

ABBEY, EDWARD
Down the River (83) 205
ABEL, LIONEL
Intellectual Follies, The (85) 451
ABERNATHY, RALPH DAVID
And the Walls Came Tumbling Down (90) 39
ABRAHAMS, WILLIAM, editor
Prize Stories 1978 (79) 556
ABRAMS, M. H.
Correspondent Breeze, The (85) 142
ABRAMSON, JILL, and JANE MAYER
Strange Justice (95) 765
ABSE, DANNIE
Collected Poems, 1948-1976 (78) 192
ABU-JABER, DIANA
Arabian Jazz (94) 38
ACHEBE, CHINUA
Anthills of the Savannah (89) 28
Home and Exile (01) 408
ACKERMAN, ROBERT
J. G. Frazer (89) 418
ACKROYD, PETER
Albion (04) 9
Blake (97) 123
Chatterton (89) 150
Dickens (92) 170
English Music (93) 266
Hawksmoor (87) 382
T. S. Eliot (85) 932
Trial of Elizabeth Cree, The (96) 768
ADAIR, GILBERT, translator
Void, A (96) 799
ADAIR, VIRGINIA HAMILTON
Ants on the Melon (97) 57
ADAMS, ALICE
After the War (01) 6
Superior Women (85) 879
To See You Again (83) 811
ADAMS, HENRY
Letters of Henry Adams, 1858-1892, The (84) 441
Letters of Henry Adams, 1892-1918, The (90) 516
ADAMS, HENRY H.
Harry Hopkins (78) 375
ADAMS, JOHN G.
Without Precedent (H-84) 497
ADAMS, RICHARD
Girl in a Swing, The (81) 377
Plague Dogs, The (79) 546
ADAMS, ROBERT M.
Bad Mouth (78) 81
ADLER, MORTIMER J.
Philosopher at Large (78) 654
ADLER, RENATA
Pitch Dark (84) 699
Speedboat (77) 776
ADORNO, THEODOR W.
Essays on Music (03) 269
AGAROSSI, ELENA, and BRADLEY F. SMITH
Operation Sunrise (80) 631

AGEE, JOEL
Twelve Years (82) 854
AGEL, JEROME, and RICHARD B. BERNSTEIN
Amending America (94) 15
AGNON, S. Y.
Simple Story, A (86) 826
AI
Dread (04) 185
Fate (92) 197
Vice (00) 793
AIKEN, CONRAD
Selected Letters of Conrad Aiken (79) 652
AITMATOV, CHINGIZ
Day Lasts More than a Hundred Years, The (84) 219
AJAMI, FOUAD
Dream Palace of the Arab World, The (99) 238
Vanished Imam, The (87) 901
AJAR, ÉMILE
Momo (79) 454
AKHMATOVA, ANNA
Complete Poems of Anna Akhmatova, The (91) 165
AKSYONOV, VASILY
Burn, The (85) 68
AKSYONOV, VASILY, et al., editors
Metropol (84) 533
AKUNIN, BORIS
Winter Queen, The (04) 839
ALBEE, EDWARD
Lady from Dubuque, The (81) 475
ALBUS, ANITA
Art of Arts, The (01) 54
ALEICHEM, SHOLOM
Best of Sholom Aleichem, The (80) 77
ALEXANDER, CHARLES C.
Breaking the Slump (03) 106
ALEXANDER, CHRISTOPHER
Nature of Order, The (04) 537
ALEXANDER, PAUL
Rough Magic (92) 689
ALEXANDER, PETER F.
Alan Paton (95) 23
ALEXANDROV, VLADIMIR E.
Nabokov's Otherworld (92) 550
ALEXIE, SHERMAN
Business of Fancydancing, The (93) 124
Indian Killer (97) 442
Lone Ranger and Tonto Fistfight in Heaven, The (94) 475
Ten Little Indians (04) 735
ALGREN, NELSON
Devil's Stocking, The (84) 230
ALLAIN, MARIE-FRANÇOISE, and GRAHAM GREENE
Other Man, The (84) 651
ALLEN, EDWARD
Straight Through the Night (90) 767

1009

ALLEN, GAY WILSON
    Waldo Emerson (82) 902
ALLEN, LOUIS
    End of the War in Asia, The (80) 285
ALLENDE, ISABEL
    Daughter of Fortune (00) 168
    House of the Spirits, The (86) 455
    Portrait in Sepia (02) 650
ALLISON, DOROTHY
    Bastard Out of Carolina (93) 58
    Cavedweller (99) 145
ALS, HILTON
    Women, The (98) 874
ALTER, ROBERT
    Art of Biblical Poetry, The (86) 38
    Canon and Creativity (01) 172
    Genesis (97) 327
    Invention of Hebrew Prose, The (89) 395
    Lion for Love, A (80) 497
    Necessary Angels (92) 559
    World of Biblical Literature, The (93) 883
ALTER, ROBERT, and FRANK KERMODE, editors
    Literary Guide to the Bible, The (88) 492
ALTHER, LISA
    Kinflicks (77) 391
ALVAREZ, JULIA
    In the Time of the Butterflies (95) 367
    Something to Declare (99) 720
    ¡Yo! (98) 886
AMBROSE, STEPHEN E.
    Americans at War (98) 64
    Eisenhower, Vol. I (H-84) 141
    Eisenhower, Vol. II (H-85) 120
    Nixon, 1913-1962 (88) 594
    Nixon, 1962-1972 (90) 608
    Nixon, 1973-1990 (92) 577
    Nothing Like It in the World (01) 656
    Undaunted Courage (97) 853
    Wild Blue, The (02) 856
AMICHAI, YEHUDA
    Amen (78) 42
    Great Tranquillity (84) 334
    Open Closed Open (01) 684
AMIS, KINGSLEY
    Difficulties with Girls (90) 181
    Old Devils, The (88) 610
    Russian Girl, The (95) 674
    Stanley and the Women (86) 859
AMIS, MARTIN
    Experience (01) 290
    Heavy Water and Other Stories (00) 372
    Information, The (96) 381
    Koba the Dread (03) 446
    London Fields (91) 534
    Money (86) 624
    Night Train (99) 557
    Time's Arrow (92) 821
    War Against Cliché, The (02) 830
    Yellow Dog (04) 859
AMMONS, A. R.
    Coast of Trees, A (82) 92
    Garbage (94) 331
    Sumerian Vistas (88) 869
ANDERSCH, ALFRED
    Winterspelt (79) 883
ANDERSON, DWIGHT G.
    Abraham Lincoln (H-83) 5
ANDERSON, JERVIS
    This Was Harlem (83) 800

ANDERSON, SHERWOOD
    Sherwood Anderson, Selected Letters (85) 820
ANDREWS, PAUL, and STEPHEN MANES
    Gates (94) 335
ANDREWS, WILLIAM L.
    To Tell a Free Story (87) 867
ANGELL, ROGER
    Pitcher's Story, A (02) 641
ANGELOU, MAYA
    All God's Children Need Traveling Shoes
      (87) 25
    Singin' and Swingin' and Gettin' Merry Like
      Christmas (77) 738
ANGERMEYER, JOHANNA
    My Father's Island (91) 614
ANGIER, CAROLE
    Double Bond, The (03) 224
    Jean Rhys (92) 379
ANGIER, NATALIE
    Woman (00) 851
ANTHONY, PATRICIA
    Flanders (99) 282
ANTHONY, SUSAN B., and ELIZABETH CADY
STANTON
    Elizabeth Cady Stanton, Susan B. Anthony,
      Correspondence, Writings, Speeches (82) 214
ANTONETTA, SUSANNE
    Body Toxic (02) 97
ANTONOV-OVSEYENKO, ANTON
    Time of Stalin, The (82) 845
ANTUNES, ANTÓNIO LOBO
    Inquisitors' Manual, The (04) 356
    Return of the Caravels, The (03) 653
APPELFELD, AHARON
    Age of Wonders, The (82) 1
    Immortal Bartfuss, The (89) 362
    Iron Tracks, The (99) 422
    Katerina (93) 418
    Retreat, The (85) 752
    To the Land of the Cattails (87) 871
    Tzili (84) 890
    Unto the Soul (95) 827
APPIAH, KWAME ANTHONY
    In My Father's House (93) 370
APPLEBAUM, ANNE
    Gulag (04) 316
APPLEBY, JOYCE
    Inheriting the Revolution (01) 462
    Liberalism and Republicanism in the Historical
      Imagination (93) 454
ARANA, MARIE
    American Chica (02) 35
ARCHDEACON, THOMAS J.
    Becoming American (H-84) 48
ARCHIBALD, DOUGLAS
    Yeats (84) 988
ARDREY, ROBERT
    Hunting Hypothesis, The (77) 367
ARENDT, HANNAH
    Life of the Mind, The (79) 393
ARENDT, HANNAH, and MARY McCARTHY
    Between Friends (96) 73
ARENSBERG, ANN
    Incubus (00) 418

AUTHOR INDEX

ARLEN, MICHAEL J.
  Camera Age, The (82) 73
  View from Highway 1, The (77) 884
ARMAT, VIRGINIA C., and RAEL JEAN ISAAC
  Madness in the Streets (91) 558
ARMSTRONG, SCOTT, and BOB WOODWARD
  Brethren, The (80) 104
ARNAUD, CLAUDE
  Chamfort (93) 143
ARON, LEON
  Yeltsin (01) 940
ARTAUD, ANTONIN
  Antonin Artaud (77) 52
ARTHUR, ELIZABETH
  Antarctic Navigation (96) 43
ASH, JOHN
  Burnt Pages, The (92) 75
  Byzantine Journey, A (96) 86
ASHBERY, JOHN
  As We Know (80) 31
  Flow Chart (92) 214
  Hotel Lautréamont (93) 358
  Houseboat Days (78) 408
  Selected Poems (86) 798
  Wave, A (85) 1008
ASHE, ARTHUR, and ARNOLD RAMPERSAD
  Days of Grace (94) 213
ASHLEY, MIKE
  Algernon Blackwood (03) 10
ASHTON, DORE
  Noguchi East and West (93) 570
ASHTON, ROBERT
  English Civil War, The (80) 297
ASHTON, ROSEMARY
  George Eliot (98) 335
  Life of Samuel Taylor Coleridge, The (97) 516
ASIMOV, ISAAC
  In the Beginning . . . (82) 386
ASPREY, ROBERT B.
  Reign of Napoleon Bonaparte, The (02) 688
ASSMANN, JAN
  Mind of Egypt, The (03) 531
ASSOULINE, PIERRE
  Simenon (98) 712
ASTLEY, THEA
  Beachmasters (87) 51
ATLAS, JAMES
  Bellow (01) 84
  Delmore Schwartz (78) 249
ATWOOD, MARGARET
  Alias Grace (97) 23
  Blind Assassin, The (01) 94
  Bodily Harm (83) 65
  Cat's Eye (90) 91
  Dancing Girls and Other Stories (83) 169
  Handmaid's Tale, The (87) 371
  Lady Oracle (77) 400
  Life Before Man (81) 512
  Negotiating with the Dead (03) 568
  Oryx and Crake (04) 583
  Robber Bride, The (94) 713
  Second Words (85) 785
  Selected Poems (79) 661
  Wilderness Tips (92) 900

AUCHINCLOSS, LOUIS
  Anniversary and Other Stories, The (00) 31
  Book Class, The (85) 52
  Collected Stories of Louis Auchincloss, The (95) 137
  Dark Lady, The (78) 229
  Lady of Situations, The (91) 498
  Narcissa and Other Fables (84) 603
  Watchfires (83) 878
  Winthrop Covenant, The (77) 923
AUDEN, W. H.
  English Auden, The (79) 193
  Lectures on Shakespeare (02) 481
AUEL, JEAN M.
  Mammoth Hunters, The (86) 566
AUERBACH, JEROLD S.
  Unequal Justice (77) 866
AUERBACH, NINA
  Our Vampires, Ourselves (96) 557
  Woman and the Demon (83) 913
AUSTER, PAUL
  Book of Illusions, The (03) 97
  Hand to Mouth (98) 374
  In the Country of Last Things (88) 423
AVRICH, PAUL
  Haymarket Tragedy, The (H-85) 201
AYER, A. J.
  Philosophy in the Twentieth Century (83) 592
AYLING, STANLEY
  Edmund Burke (90) 198

BAARS, BERNARD J.
  In the Theater of Consciousness (98) 424
BABEL, ISAAC
  Complete Works of Isaac Babel, The (02) 158
BACKER, JOHN H.
  Winds of History (H-84) 488
BACKSCHEIDER, PAULA R.
  Daniel Defoe (90) 143
BAGEMIHL, BRUCE
  Biological Exuberance (00) 62
BAGG, ROBERT
  Body Blows (89) 98
BAILEY, ANTHONY
  Major André (88) 512
  Rembrandt's House (79) 580
BAILEY, BLAKE
  Tragic Honesty, A (04) 770
BAILEY, THOMAS A., and PAUL B. RYAN
  Hitler vs. Roosevelt (80) 404
BAILYN, BERNARD
  Faces of Revolution (91) 279
  To Begin the World Anew (04) 761
BAILYN, BERNARD, et al.
  Great Republic, The (78) 360
BAILYN, BERNARD, with BARBARA DE WOLFE
  Voyagers to the West (87) 917
BAINBRIDGE, BERYL
  According to Queeney (02) 1
  Winter Garden (82) 958
BAINBRIDGE, DAVID
  X in Sex, The (04) 855
BAIR, DEIRDRE
  Anaïs Nin (96) 34
  Jung (04) 396
  Samuel Beckett (79) 636
  Simone de Beauvoir (91) 740

BALL, PHILIP
    Bright Earth (03) 110

BAK, HANS
    Malcolm Cowley (94) 492

BAKER, CARLOS
    Emerson Among the Eccentrics (97) 239

BAKER, LEWIS
    Percys of Mississippi, The (84) 682

BAKER, LIVA
    I'm Radcliffe! Fly Me! (77) 376

BAKER, MICHAEL
    Our Three Selves (86) 719

BAKER, NICHOLSON
    Box of Matches, A (04) 105
    Double Fold (02) 204
    Size of Thoughts, The (97) 757
    U and I (92) 844

BAKER, RUSSELL
    Good Times, The (90) 309
    Growing Up (83) 317

BAKHTIN, MIKHAIL
    Problems of Dostoevsky's Poetics (85) 706

BALABAN, JOHN
    Remembering Heaven's Face (92) 674

BALDWIN, JAMES
    Just Above My Head (80) 456

BALES, KEVIN
    Disposable People (00) 181

BALL, EDWARD
    Slaves in the Family (99) 716

BALL, HOWARD
    Hugo L. Black (97) 415

BALL, PHILIP
    Life's Matrix (01) 536

BALLANTYNE, SHEILA
    Imaginary Crimes (83) 353

BALLARD, J. G.
    Day of Creation, The (89) 226
    Empire of the Sun (85) 218

BANK, MELISSA
    Girls' Guide to Hunting and Fishing, The (00) 309

BANKS, RUSSELL
    Cloudsplitter (99) 190
    Rule of the Bone (96) 668
    Sweet Hereafter, The (92) 790

BANVILLE, JOHN
    Athena (96) 51
    Book of Evidence, The (91) 91
    Eclipse (02) 222
    Ghosts (94) 355
    Shroud (04) 691
    Untouchable, The (98) 796

BARAŃCZAK, STANISŁAW
    Breathing Under Water and Other East European
        Essays (91) 105
    Fugitive from Utopia, A (88) 340

BARBERA, JACK, and WILLIAM McBRIEN
    Stevie (88) 860

BARBOUR, JULIAN B.
    End of Time, The (01) 281

BARICH, BILL
    Traveling Light (85) 923

BARISH, EVELYN
    Emerson (91) 249

BARKER, JOHN
    Superhistorians, The (H-83) 416

BARKER, JULIET
    Brontës, The (96) 81

BARKER, PAT
    Another World (00) 40
    Blow Your House Down (85) 47
    Border Crossing (02) 115
    Eye in the Door, The (95) 218
    Ghost Road, The (96) 307
    Regeneration (93) 677
    Union Street (84) 895

BARKER, RALPH
    Blockade Busters (78)108

BARNARD, MARY
    Assault on Mount Helicon (85) 27

BARNES, CHRISTOPHER
    Boris Pasternak, 1890-1928 (91) 96

BARNES, JULIAN
    Cross Channel (97) 183
    England, England (00) 231
    Flaubert's Parrot (86) 284
    History of the World in 10½ Chapters, A (90) 390
    Love, etc. (02) 495
    Porcupine, The (93) 646
    Staring at the Sun (88) 855
    Talking It Over (92) 799

BARNES, KIM
    Hungry for the World (01) 432

BARNET, RICHARD J.
    Giants, The (78) 345

BARR, NORAH K., MARSHA MORAN, and
    PATRICK MORAN, eds.
    M. F. K. Fisher (99) 501

BARRETT, ANDREA
    Ship Fever and Other Stories (97) 753

BARRELL, JOHN
    Infection of Thomas De Quincey, The (92) 354

BARRETT, WILLIAM
    Illusion of Technique, The (80) 409
    Truants, The (83) 833

BARSKY, ROBERT F.
    Noam Chomsky (98) 598

BARTH, JOHN
    Friday Book, The (85) 307
    Letters (80) 466
    Once Upon a Time (95) 568
    Sabbatical (83) 665
    Tidewater Tales, The (88) 892

BARTHELME, DONALD
    Amateurs (78) 37
    Great Days (80) 385
    King, The (91) 485
    Sixty Stories (82) 776

BARTHELME, FREDERICK
    Moon Deluxe (84) 576
    Second Marriage (85) 780

BARTHES, ROLAND
    Barthes Reader, A (83) 44
    Camera Lucida (82) 78
    Eiffel Tower and Other Mythologies, The (80) 269
    Empire of Signs, The (83) 230
    Lover's Discourse, A (79) 404
    New Critical Essays (81) 609
    Roland Barthes (78) 730

BARTLETT, IRVING H.
    Daniel Webster (79) 143

BARTON, ANNE
    Ben Jonson, Dramatist (85) 37

AUTHOR INDEX

BARUK, HENRI
Patients Are People Like Us (79) 532
BARZINI, LUIGI
Europeans, The (H-84) 153
BARZMAN, NORMA
Red and the Blacklist, The (04) 638
BARZUN, JACQUES
From Dawn to Decadence (01) 314
Stroll with William James, A (84) 837
BASKIR, LAWRENCE M., and WILLIAM A.
STRAUSS
Chance and Circumstance (79) 88
BASS, JACK, and WALTER DE VRIES
Transformation of Southern Politics, The (77) 832
BASS, RICK
Platte River (95) 609
Watch, The (90) 869
BASS, THOMAS A.
Camping with the Prince and Other Tales of
Science in Africa (91) 119
BATAILLE, CHRISTOPHE
Hourmaster (99) 383
BATCHELOR, JOHN CALVIN
American Falls (86) 27
Birth of the People's Republic of Antarctica, The
(84) 91
BATE, JONATHAN
John Clare (04) 377
BATE, W. JACKSON
Samuel Johnson (78) 735
BATESON, GREGORY
Mind and Nature (80) 536
BATESON, MARY CATHERINE
With a Daughter's Eye (H-85) 507
BATTESTIN, MARTIN C., with RUTHE R.
BATTESTIN
Henry Fielding (91) 395
BATTESTIN, RUTHE R., with MARTIN C.
BATTESTIN
Henry Fielding (91) 395
BAUER, YEHUDA
Rethinking the Holocaust (02) 693
BAUMER, FRANKLIN L.
Modern European Thought (78) 581
BAUMONT, MAURICE
Origins of the Second World War, The (79) 516
BAXTER, CHARLES
Believers (98) 113
Saul and Patsy (04) 670
BAXTER, MAURICE G.
One and Inseparable (H-85) 339
BAYLES, MARTHA
Hole in Our Soul (95) 314
BAYLEY, JOHN
Elegy for Iris (00) 213
Housman's Poems (93) 361
Iris and Her Friends (00) 439
Short Story, The (89) 788
BEAM, ALEX
Gracefully Insane (03) 343

BEATTIE, ANN
Another You (96) 39
Burning House, The (83) 86
Chilly Scenes of Winter (77) 154
Doctor's House, The (03) 215
Falling in Place (81) 304
My Life, Starring Dara Falcon (98) 571
Park City (99) 620
Perfect Recall (02) 631
Picturing Will (91) 665
What Was Mine (92) 876
Where You'll Find Me (87) 967
BEATTY, JACK
World According to Peter Drucker, The (99) 872
BEAUMAN, NICOLA
E. M. Forster (95) 195
BEAUVOIR, SIMONE DE
Adieux (85) 1
Letters to Sartre (93) 449
When Things of the Spirit Come First (83) 890
BECK, ROY
Case Against Immigration, The (97) 136
BECKER, JASPER
Hungry Ghosts (98) 406
BECKERMAN, MICHAEL B.
New Worlds of Dvořák (04) 556
BECKETT, SAMUEL
Company (81) 184
BEDINI, SILVIO A.
Thomas Jefferson (91) 809
BEECHER, JONATHAN
Charles Fourier (88) 138
BEEVOR, ANTHONY
Fall of Berlin 1945, The (03) 288
BEGLEY, LOUIS
As Max Saw It (95) 51
Shipwreck (04) 687
Wartime Lies (92) 868
BELITT, BEN
Double Witness, The (78) 276
BELL, DANIEL
Cultural Contradictions of Capitalism, The (77) 184
BELL, MADISON SMARTT
All Souls' Rising (96) 22
BELL, MILLICENT
Marquand (80) 517
BELL, VEREEN M.
Achievement of Cormac McCarthy, The (89) 1
BELL-VILLADA, GENE H.
García Márquez (91) 325
BELLAH, ROBERT, et al.
Habits of the Heart (86) 380
BELLESILES, MICHAEL A.
Arming America (01) 49
BELLOS, DAVID
Georges Perec (95) 262
BELLOW, SAUL
Actual, The (98) 1
Bellarosa Connection, The (90) 53
Dean's December, The (83) 215
Him with His Foot in His Mouth and Other Stories
(85) 390
It All Adds Up (95) 381
More Die of Heartbreak (88) 583
Ravelstein (01) 731
Theft, A (90) 792
To Jerusalem and Back (77) 828

BENET, JUAN
  Meditation, A (83) 464
  Return to Región (86) 771
BENFEY, CHRISTOPHER
  Double Life of Stephen Crane, The (93) 239
BENJAMIN, WALTER
  Correspondence of Walter Benjamin, 1910-1940,
    The (95)149
  Reflections (79) 575
  Selected Writings, 1913-1926 (97) 746
  Selected Writings, 1927-1934 (00) 693
  Selected Writings, 1938-1940 (04) 674
BENNETT, EDWARD W.
  German Rearmament and the West, 1932-1933
    (80) 344
BENSON, JACKSON J.
  True Adventures of John Steinbeck, Writer, The
    (85) 927
  Wallace Stegner (97) 871
BENSTOCK, SHARI
  No Gifts from Chance (95) 544
  Women of the Left Bank (87) 1009
BENTLEY, JAMES
  Martin Niemöller, 1892-1984 (H-85) 298
BERBEROVA, NINA
  Book of Happiness, The (00) 86
  Tattered Cloak and Other Novels, The (92) 804
BERES, LOUIS RENÉ
  Reason and Realpolitik (H-85) 385
BERG, A. SCOTT
  Goldwyn (90) 303
  Kate Remembered (04) 400
  Lindbergh (99) 478
  Max Perkins (79) 428
BERGER, JOHN
  Once in Europa (88) 625
  Selected Essays (03) 732
  Sense of Sight, The (87) 754
  To the Wedding (96) 752
BERGER, THOMAS
  Best Friends (04) 75
  Feud, The (84) 295
  Meeting Evil (93) 505
  Neighbors (81) 606
  Reinhart's Women (82) 671
  Return of Little Big Man, The (00) 647
  Who Is Teddy Villanova? (78) 899
BERGERON, LOUIS
  France Under Napoleon (82) 296
BERGMAN, INGMAR
  Magic Lantern, The (89) 525
BERGREEN, LAURENCE
  As Thousands Cheer (91) 61
  James Agee (85) 473
BERINGER, RICHARD E., HERMAN HATTAWAY,
  ARCHER JONES, and WILLIAM N. STILL, JR.
  Why the South Lost the Civil War (87) 980
BERKHOFER, ROBERT F., JR.
  White Man's Indian, The (79) 847
BERLIN, EDWARD A.
  King of Ragtime (95) 422
BERLIN, IRA
  Many Thousands Gone (99) 519

BERLIN, ISAIAH
  Against the Current (81) 9
  Crooked Timber of Humanity, The (92) 133
  Personal Impressions (82) 632
  Proper Study of Mankind, The (99) 640
  Russian Thinkers (79) 627
BERLINSKI, DAVID
  Newton's Gift (01) 637
BERMAN, LARRY
  Planning a Tragedy (H-83) 343
BERMAN, MARSHALL
  All That Is Solid Melts into Air (83) 15
BERMAN, PAUL
  Tale of Two Utopias, A (97) 807
  Terror and Liberalism (04) 739
BERMAN, PHILLIP, with JANE GOODALL
  Reason for Hope (00) 643
BERNHARD, THOMAS
  Concrete (85) 131
  Extinction (96) 242
  Gathering Evidence (87) 317
  Loser, The (92) 455
  Old Masters (93) 584
  Three Novellas (04) 747
  Wittgenstein's Nephew (90) 908
BERNSTEIN, CARL
  Loyalties (90) 543
BERNSTEIN, CARL, and MARCO POLITI
  His Holiness (97) 388
BERNSTEIN, JEREMY
  Life It Brings, The (88) 477
  Science Observed (83) 689
  Three Degrees Above Zero (H-85) 441
BERNSTEIN, MICHAEL ANDRÉ
  Foregone Conclusions (95) 253
BERNSTEIN, NINA
  Lost Children of Wilder, The (02) 491
BERNSTEIN, RICHARD
  Ultimate Journey (02) 808
BERNSTEIN, RICHARD B., with JEROME AGEL
  Amending America (94) 15
BERRIAULT, GINA
  Women in Their Beds (97) 900
BERRY, ANDREW, with JAMES D. WATSON
  DNA (04) 179
BERRY, FAITH
  Langston Hughes (84) 422
BERRY, WENDELL
  Art of the Commonplace, The (03) 33
  Collected Poems, 1957-1982 (86) 159
  Entries (95) 209
  Sabbaths (88) 785
  Standing by Words (84) 813
  Unsettling of America, The (79) 795
  Wild Birds, The (87) 989
BERRYMAN, JOHN
  Berryman's Shakespeare (00) 49
  Collected Poems (90) 117
  Freedom of the Poet, The (77) 299
  Henry's Fate & Other Poems, 1967-1972 (78) 384
BÉRUBÉ, MICHAEL
  Life As We Know It (97) 498
BESCHLOSS, MICHAEL R.
  Crisis Years, The (92) 128
  Kennedy and Roosevelt (81) 467
  Mayday (87) 530

AUTHOR INDEX

BESCHLOSS, MICHAEL R., and STROBE TALBOTT
At the Highest Levels (94) 62

BETHEA, DAVID M.
Khodasevich (84) 408
Joseph Brodsky and the Creation of Exile (95) 404
Shape of Apocalypse in Modern Russian Fiction, The (90) 729

BETHELL, NICHOLAS
Palestine Triangle, The (80) 634

BETTELHEIM, BRUNO
Uses of Enchantment, The (77) 876

BEYERCHEN, ALAN D.
Scientists Under Hitler (78) 743

BHUTTO, BENAZIR
Daughter of Destiny (90) 152

BIALER, SEWERYN
Soviet Paradox, The (87) 807

BIDART, FRANK
Book of the Body, The (78) 136
In the Western Night (91) 447

BIENEK, HORST
First Polka, The (85) 286

BILLINGTON, JAMES H.
Fire in the Minds of Men (81) 340

BILLINGTON, RAY ALLEN
Land of Savagery/Land of Promise (82) 421

BINION, RUDOLPH
Hitler Among the Germans (77) 357

BIOY-CASARES, ADOLFO, and JORGE LUIS BORGES
Six Problems for Don Isidro Parodi (82) 771

BIRD, KAI
Chairman, The (93) 138

BIRKERTS, SVEN
Artificial Wilderness, An (88) 68
Gutenberg Elegies, The (96) 326
My Sky Blue Trades (03) 549
Tolstoy's Dictaphone (97) 834

BIRNBAUM, PIERRE
Anti-Semitic Moment, The (04) 30

BISHOP, ELIZABETH
Collected Prose, The (85) 121
Geography III (77) 326
One Art (95) 572

BISHOP, JOHN
Joyce's Book of the Dark (88) 443

BITOV, ANDREI, et al., editors
Metropol (84) 533

BLACK, CHARLES L., JR.
New Birth of Freedom, A (98) 579

BLACK, EDWIN
Transfer Agreement, The (H-85) 445
War Against the Weak (04) 810

BLACKBURN, JULIA
Leper's Companions, The (00) 479

BLACKBURN, PAUL
Collected Poems of Paul Blackburn, The (86) 164

BLACKMUR, R. P.
Selected Essays of R. P. Blackmur (87) 749

BLAIR, CLAY
Forgotten War, The (89) 307

BLAIR, CLAY, and OMAR N. BRADLEY
General's Life, A (H-84) 171

BLANCHARD, PAULA
Margaret Fuller (79) 422

BLANK, JONAH
Mullahs on the Mainframe (02) 550

BLANKENHORN, DAVID
Fatherless America (96) 258

BLANKFORT, MICHAEL
Take the A Train (79) 737

BLEIKASTEN, ANDRÉ
Ink of Melancholy, The (91) 452

BLOCH, ERNST
Principle of Hope, The (87) 670

BLOOM, ALLAN
Closing of the American Mind, The (88) 159

BLOOM, AMY
Come to Me (94) 154

BLOOM, CLAIRE
Leaving a Doll's House (97) 494

BLOOM, HAROLD
Agon (83) 1
Poetry and Repression (77) 627
Ruin the Sacred Truths (90) 703
Shakespeare (99) 701

BLOOM, STEPHEN G.
Postville (01) 716

BLOTNER, JOSEPH
Robert Penn Warren (98) 678

BLUM, D. STEVEN
Walter Lippmann (H-85) 470

BLUM, JEROME
End of the Old Order in Rural Europe, The (79) 188

BLUM, JOHN MORTON
Progressive Presidents, The (81) 665
V Was for Victory (77) 880

BLUM, ROBERT M.
Drawing the Line (H-83) 104

BLUMENFELD, LAURA
Revenge (03) 658

BLY, CAROL
Letters from the Country (82) 444

BLY, ROBERT
American Poetry (91) 29
Man in the Black Coat Turns, The (83) 439

BOBRICK, BENSON
Wide as the Waters (02) 851

BODE, CARL, editor
New Mencken Letters, The (78) 603

BOGLE, DONALD
Primetime Blues (02) 664

BOK, SISSELA
Mayhem (99) 534

BOLAND, EAVAN
In a Time of Violence (95) 343

BÖLL, HEINRICH
And Never Said a Word (79) 29
Bread of Those Early Years, The (77) 119
Missing Persons and Other Essays (78) 577
Stories of Heinrich Böll, The (87) 827
What's to Become of the Boy? (85) 1018

BOMBAL, MARÍA LUISA
New Islands and Other Stories (83) 523

BONKOVSKY, FREDERICK O.
International Norms and National Policy (81) 445

BONNER, RAYMOND
Waltzing with a Dictator (88) 949

BONNIFIELD, PAUL
Dust Bowl, The (80) 251

BONTEMPS, ARNA, and LANGSTON HUGHES
Arna Bontemps-Langston Hughes Letters,
1925-1927 (81) 57

BOORSTIN, DANIEL J.
Discoverers, The (H-84) 130
Seekers, The (99) 697

BOOTH, PHILIP
Before Sleep (81) 71
Relations (87) 703
Selves (91) 731

BOOTH, WAYNE C.
Company We Keep, The (89) 202
For the Love of It (00) 273
Vocation of a Teacher, The (90) 854

BORGES, JORGE LUIS
Book of Sand, The (78) 131
Borges, a Reader (82) 63
Selected Non-Fictions (00) 683
Selected Poems (00) 688

BORGES, JORGE LUIS, and ADOLFO
BIOY-CASARES
Six Problems for Don Isidro Parodi (82) 771

BORJAS, GEORGE J.
Heaven's Door (00) 367

BORK, ROBERT H.
Tempting of America, The (90) 787

BORNET, VAUGHN DAVIS
Presidency of Lyndon B. Johnson, The (H-84) 355

BOSTON GLOBE INVESTIGATIVE STAFF
Betrayal (03) 65

BOSWELL, JAMES
Boswell (78) 140

BOSWELL, JOHN
Kindness of Strangers, The (90) 486
Same-Sex Unions in Premodern Europe (95) 687

BOSWELL, ROBERT
American Owned Love (98) 41
Century's Son (03) 137

BOSWORTH, PATRICIA
Anything Your Little Heart Desires (98) 68
Diane Arbus (96) 174
Montgomery Clift (79) 457

BOSWORTH, SHEILA
Almost Innocent (85) 7

BOTTOMS, DAVID
Under the Vulture-Tree (88) 919

BOURJAILY, VANCE
Game Men Play, A (81) 364
Now Playing at Canterbury (77) 575

BOURNE, KENNETH
Palmerston (H-83) 329

BOUWSMA, WILLIAM J.
John Calvin (88) 433

BOWDEN, MARK
Black Hawk Down (00) 70

BOWEN, ELIZABETH
Collected Stories of Elizabeth Bowen, The
(81) 173

BOWERS, EDGAR
Collected Poems (98) 177

BOWKER, GORDON
Pursued by Furies (96) 610

BOWLBY, JOHN
Charles Darwin (92) 83

BOWLES, JANE
Out in the World (86) 723

BOWLES, PAUL
In Touch (95) 372
Collected Stories, 1939-1976 (80) 151

BOYD, BRIAN
Vladimir Nabokov, The American Years (92) 854
Vladimir Nabokov, The Russian Years (91) 856

BOYD, WILLIAM
Any Human Heart (04) 40
Ice-Cream War, An (84) 363

BOYERS, ROBERT
Atrocity and Amnesia (86) 43

BOYLAN, CLARE
Holy Pictures (84) 347

BOYLE, KAY
Fifty Stories (81) 325
Words That Must Somehow Be Said (86) 966

BOYLE, NICHOLAS
Goethe, 1749-1790 (92) 247
Goethe, 1790-1803 (01) 356

BOYLE, T. CORAGHESSAN
After the Plague (02) 18
Drop City (04) 193
East Is East (91) 240
Friend of the Earth, A (01) 310
Greasy Lake and Other Stories (86) 372
If the River Was Whiskey (90) 406
Road to Wellville, The (94) 709
T. C. Boyle Stories (99) 742
Tortilla Curtain, The (96) 764
Without a Hero (95) 880
World's End (88) 988

BRADBURY, MALCOLM
Rates of Exchange (84) 721
To the Hermitage (02) 796

BRADBURY, RAY
Death Is a Lonely Business (86) 222
Stories of Ray Bradbury, The (81) 769

BRADFORD, SARAH
Disraeli (H-84) 135

BRADING, DAVID A.
Mexican Phoenix (02) 528

BRADLEE, BEN
Good Life, A (96) 316

BRADLEY, DAVID
Chaneysville Incident, The (82) 82

BRADLEY, MARION ZIMMER
Mists of Avalon, The (84) 561

BRADLEY, OMAR N., and CLAY BLAIR
General's Life, A (H-84) 171

BRADSHER, HENRY S.
Afghanistan and the Soviet Union (H-84) 1

BRADY, FRANK
James Boswell (85) 479

BRADY, KRISTIN
Short Stories of Thomas Hardy, The (83) 747

BRAGUE, RÉMI
Wisdom of the World, The (04) 847

BRALY, MALCOLM
False Starts (77) 269

BRANCH, TAYLOR
Parting the Waters (89) 649
Pillar of Fire (99) 628

BRAND, STEWART
Clock of the Long Now, The (00) 130

BRANDYS, KAZIMIERZ
Warsaw Diary, A (84) 926

AUTHOR INDEX

BRATHWAITE, EDWARD KAMAU
  MiddlePassages (95) 486
  X/Self (88) 999
BRAUDEL, FERNAND
  Perspective of the World, Vol. III, The (H-85) 353
BRAUNBEHRENS, VOLKMAR
  Mozart in Vienna, 1781-1791 (91) 606
BRAUTIGAN, RICHARD
  Sombrero Fallout (78) 785
  Unfortunate Woman, An (01) 859
BRAVERMAN, KATE
  Palm Latitudes (89) 639
BRAY, ROSEMARY L.
  Unafraid of the Dark (99) 812
BRAZEAU, PETER
  Parts of a World (84) 668
BRECHER, MICHAEL, and BENJAMIN GEIST
  Decisions in Crisis (81) 228
BRECHT, BERTOLT
  Bertolt Brecht Short Stories, 1921-1946 (84) 86
BREDIN, JEAN-DENIS
  Affair, The (87) 15
BREITMAN, RICHARD
  German Socialism and Weimar Democracy
    (82) 315
BREMER, FRANCIS J.
  John Winthrop (04) 386
BRENT, PETER
  Charles Darwin (82) 87
BRESLIN, JAMES E. B.
  Mark Rothko (94) 504
BREWER, JOHN
  Pleasures of the Imagination, The (98) 634
BREYTENBACH, BREYTEN
  End Papers (87) 242
  True Confessions of an Albino Terrorist, The
    (86) 913
BRIDGMAN, RICHARD
  Traveling in Mark Twain (88) 907
BRIER, PETER
  Howard Mumford Jones and the Dynamics of
    Liberal Humanism (95) 329
BRIGHTMAN, CAROL
  Writing Dangerously (93) 887
BRIMELOW, PETER
  Alien Nation (96) 9
BRIN, DAVID
  Kiln People (03) 442
BRINK, ANDRÉ
  Chain of Voices, A (83) 101
  Other Side of Silence, The (04) 588
  Writing in a State of Siege (84) 983
BRINKLEY, ALAN
  Voices of Protest (H-83) 449
BRINKLEY, DAVID
  Washington Goes to War (89) 887
BRINKLEY, DOUGLAS
  Unfinished Presidency, The (99) 822
BROCH, HERMANN
  Hugo von Hofmannsthal and His Time (85) 410
BROCK, DAVID
  Blinded by the Right (03) 83
BRODER, DAVID S.
  Changing of the Guard (81) 127

BRODKEY, HAROLD
  Runaway Soul, The (92) 698
  Stories in an Almost Classical Mode (89) 822
  This Wild Darkness (97) 816
BRODSKY, JOSEPH
  Less Than One (87) 471
  On Grief and Reason (97) 644
  So Forth (97) 766
  To Urania (89) 840
BROMBERT, VICTOR
  Trains of Thought (03) 843
  Victor Hugo and the Visionary Novel (85) 969
BROMWICH, DAVID
  Hazlitt (85) 363
BRONK, WILLIAM
  Life Supports (82) 466
  Vectors and Smoothable Curves (84) 905
BROOK-SHEPHERD, GORDON
  Archduke of Sarajevo (H-85) 33
  Uncle of Europe (77) 861
BROOKHISER, RICHARD
  Alexander Hamilton, American (00) 1
  Founding Father (97) 306
BROOKNER, ANITA
  Altered States (98) 27
  Bay of Angels, The (02) 70
  Brief Lives (92) 60
  Closed Eye, A (93) 166
  Dolly (95) 180
  Falling Slowly (00) 248
  Fraud (94) 317
  Hotel du Lac (86) 445
  Incidents in the Rue Laugier (97) 437
  Latecomers (90) 500
  Lewis Percy (91) 521
  Look at Me (84) 476
  Making Things Better (04) 491
  Misalliance, The (88) 564
  Providence (85) 712
  Undue Influence (01) 855
  Visitors (99) 842
BROOKS, CLEANTH
  William Faulkner, First Encounters (84) 950
  William Faulkner, Toward Yoknapatawpha and
    Beyond (79) 874
BROOKS, DAVID
  Bobos in Paradise (01) 112
BROOKS, PETER
  Reading for the Plot (85) 723
BROOKS, RODNEY A.
  Flesh and Machines (03) 302
BROSZAT, MARTIN
  Hitler State, The (82) 363
BROTHERSTON, GORDON
  Book of the Fourth World (94) 109
BROUMAS, OLGA
  Beginning with O (78) 91
BROWN, ANTHONY CAVE. See CAVE BROWN,
  ANTHONY
BROWN, DAN
  Da Vinci Code, The (04) 147
BROWN, FREDERICK
  Zola (96) 847
BROWN, HAROLD
  Thinking About National Security (H-84) 439
BROWN, JONATHAN
  Velázquez (87) 907

BROWN, JUDITH M.
  Gandhi (91) 321
BROWN, LARRY
  Father and Son (97) 274
  Joe (92) 384
BROWN, LYN MIKEL, and CAROL GILLIGAN
  Meeting at the Crossroads (93) 500
BROWN, ROSELLEN
  Autobiography of My Mother, The (77) 72
  Before and After (93) 67
  Civil Wars (85) 101
  Half a Heart (01) 375
BROWN, STERLING A.
  Collected Poems of Sterling A. Brown, The
    (81) 168
BROWN, WILLIAM, HERMAN KAHN, and LEON
  MARTEL
  Next 200 Years, The (77) 559
BROWNE, JANET
  Charles Darwin, Power of Place, The (03) 142
  Charles Darwin, Voyaging (96) 90
BROYARD, BLISS
  My Father, Dancing (00) 550
BRUCCOLI, MATTHEW J.
  James Gould Cozzens (84) 384
  Ross Macdonald (85) 766
  Some Sort of Epic Grandeur (82) 782
BRUCE, ROBERT V.
  Launching of Modern American Science, The
    (88) 452
BRUCK, CONNIE
  When Hollywood Had a King (04) 823
BRUNER, JEROME
  Acts of Meaning (91) 1
  Actual Minds, Possible Worlds (87) 11
  Making Stories (03) 509
BRUNI, FRANK
  Ambling into History (03) 14
BRUNT, LLOYD VAN. See VAN BRUNT, LLOYD
BRYAN, C. D. B.
  Friendly Fire (77) 309
BRYAN, FRANK, and JOHN McCLAUGHRY
  Vermont Papers, The (90) 839
BRYANT, ARTHUR
  Elizabethan Deliverance, The (H-83) 114
BRZEZINSKI, ZBIGNIEW
  Grand Failure, The (90) 329
  Power and Principle (H-84) 351
BUCHANAN, PATRICK J.
  Right from the Beginning (89) 730
BUCHAN, JAMES
  Frozen Desire (98) 327
  High Latitudes (97) 383
BUCKLEY, CHRISTOPHER
  Little Green Men (00) 488
  Wet Work (92) 872
BUCKLEY, GAIL LUMET
  Hornes, The (87) 410
BUCKLEY, WILLIAM F., JR.
  Atlantic High (83) 29
  Gratitude (91) 359
  High Jinx (87) 392
  Marco Polo, If You Can (83) 447
  Mongoose, R.I.P. (88) 574
  Nearer, My God (98) 575
  Story of Henri Tod, The (85) 874

BUCKMAN, PETER
  Lafayette (78) 495
BUECHNER, FREDERICK
  Brendan (88) 121
  Godric (81) 382
  Now and Then (84) 624
  Sacred Journey, The (83) 670
BUFORD, KATE
  Burt Lancaster (01) 158
BUKHARIN, NIKOLAI
  How It All Began (99) 391
BUKIET, MELVIN JULES
  Signs and Wonders (00) 707
BULLOCK, ALAN
  Hitler and Stalin (93) 349
BUNDY, McGEORGE
  Danger and Survival (89) 217
BUNTING, BASIL
  Collected Poems (79) 119
BURCH, PHILIP H., JR.
  Elites in American History (81) 268
BURCHFIELD, ROBERT
  Unlocking the English Language (92) 849
BURDEN, JEAN
  Taking Light from Each Other (93) 771
BURGESS, ANTHONY
  Any Old Iron (90) 44
  Beard's Roman Women (77) 81
  But Do Blondes Prefer Gentlemen? (87) 94
  Dead Man in Deptford, A (96) 153
  Earthly Powers (81) 260
  End of the World News, The (84) 267
  Ernest Hemingway and His World (79) 196
  Little Wilson and Big God (88) 497
  Napoleon Symphony (77) 525
  1985 (79) 484
  You've Had Your Time (92) 933
BURKE, JAMES LEE
  Stained White Radiance, A (93) 753
BURKE, PETER
  Fortunes of the Courtier, The (97) 301
BURL, AUBREY
  Prehistoric Avebury (80) 688
BURN, GORDON
  Alma (93) 15
BURNER, DAVID
  Herbert Hoover (80) 400
BURNHAM, DAVID
  Law Unto Itself, A (91) 507
BURNS, JAMES MacGREGOR
  Power to Lead, The (H-85) 363
BURNS, KEN, and GEOFFREY C. WARD
  Not for Ourselves Alone (00) 580
BURNS, KEN, et al.
  Civil War, The (91) 137
BURNS, RIC, et al.
  Civil War, The (91) 137
BURR, CHANDLER
  Emperor of Scent, The (04) 224
BURR, WILLIAM, editor
  Kissinger Transcripts, The (00) 466
BURROUGHS, AUGUSTEN
  Running with Scissors (03) 695
BURROWS, DAVID
  Sound, Speech, and Music (91) 759

AUTHOR INDEX

BURSTON, DANIEL
  Wing of Madness, The (97) 885
BURT, STEPHEN
  Randall Jarrell and His Age (04) 629
BURUMA, IAN
  Anglomania (00) 27
  Wages of Guilt, The (95) 840
BUSCH, FREDERICK
  Closing Arguments (92) 94
  Don't Tell Anyone (01) 246
  Girls (98) 340
  Long Way from Home (94) 479
BUSH, CLIVE
  Dream of Reason, The (79) 165
BUSH, RONALD
  T. S. Eliot (85) 937
BUTLER, JON
  Awash in a Sea of Faith (91) 65
BUTLER, ROBERT OLEN
  On Distant Ground (86) 685
  Tabloid Dreams (97) 792
BUTSCHER, EDWARD, editor
  Conrad Aiken (89) 207
  Sylvia Plath (78) 809
BUTTEL, ROBERT, and FRANK DOGGETT, editors
  Wallace Stevens (81) 879
BUTTERFIELD, HERBERT
  Origins of History, The (82) 604
BUZZATI, DINO
  Siren, The (85) 825
BYATT, A. S.
  Angels and Insects (94) 25
  Babel Tower (97) 87
  Matisse Stories, The (96) 457
  On Histories and Stories (02) 605
  Possession (91) 679
BYRON, GEORGE GORDON, LORD
  Byron's Letters and Journals, 1822-1823 (81) 108
  Lord Byron, Selected Letters and Journals
    (83) 418
BYRON, WILLIAM
  Cervantes (79) 84
BYTWERK, RANDALL L.
  Julius Streicher (H-83) 234

CAHILL, THOMAS
  Gifts of the Jews, The (99) 333
  How the Irish Saved Civilization (96) 343
CAINE, BARBARA
  Victorian Feminists (93) 851
CALASSO, ROBERTO
  Literature and the Gods (02) 486
  Marriage of Cadmus and Harmony, The (94) 508
  Ruin of Kasch, The (95) 669
CALDER, ANGUS
  Revolutionary Empire (82) 675
CALDER, JENNI
  Robert Louis Stevenson (81) 694
CALISHER, HORTENSE
  Mysteries of Motion (84) 593
  On Keeping Women (78) 613
CALISHER, HORTENSE
  In the Palace of the Movie King (95) 359
CALLAHAN, DANIEL
  What Kind of Life (91) 886

CALVET, LOUIS-JEAN
  Roland Barthes (96) 664
CALVIN, WILLIAM H.
  Brain for All Seasons, A (03) 102
CALVINO, ITALO
  Difficult Loves (85) 184
  Hermit in Paris (04) 339
  If on a winter's night a traveler (82) 380
  Italian Folktales (81) 450
  Marcovaldo (84) 509
  Mr. Palomar (86) 620
  Road to San Giovanni, The (94) 705
  Six Memos for the Next Millennium (89) 799
  Under the Jaguar Sun (89) 872
CAMBOR, KATHLEEN
  In Sunlight, in a Beautiful Garden (02) 404
CAMERON, PETER
  City of Your Final Destination, The (03) 151
CAMILLE, MICHAEL
  Master of Death (97) 555
CAMILLERI, ANDREA
  Snack Thief, The (04) 696
CAMPBELL, BEBE MOORE
  Your Blues Ain't Like Mine (93) 896
CAMPBELL, JAMES
  Talking at the Gates (92) 795
CAMPBELL, JEREMY
  Grammatical Man (83) 301
  Winston Churchill's Afternoon Nap (88) 964
CAMPBELL, JOSEPH
  Inner Reaches of Outer Space, The (87) 429
CAMPBELL, MARY B.
  World, The Flesh, and Angels, The (90) 921
CAMUS, ALBERT
  First Man, The (96) 268
CANETTI, ELIAS
  Torch in My Ear, The (83) 827
CANIN, ETHAN
  Emperor of the Air (89) 268
  For Kings and Planets (99) 299
  Palace Thief, The (95) 586
CANNADINE, DAVID
  Ornamentalism (02) 609
CANNON, LOUIS
  Official Negligence (99) 571
  Reagan (H-83) 362
CANTOR, JAY
  Krazy Kat (89) 445
CANTOR, MILTON
  Divided Left, The (79) 157
CANTOR, NORMAN F.
  Inventing the Middle Ages (93) 394
  Sacred Chain, The (95) 678
CANTOR, PAUL A.
  Gilligan Unbound (02) 338
CANTY, KEVIN
  Stranger in This World, A (95) 769
CAPPS, WALTER H.
  Unfinished War, The (H-83) 440
CARD, ORSON SCOTT
  Ender's Shadow (00) 226
CARDOZO, NANCY
  Lucky Eyes and a High Heart (79) 409

CAREY, PETER
  Jack Maggs (99) 432
  My Life as a Fake (04) 528
  Oscar and Lucinda (89) 626
  Tax Inspector, The (93) 775
  True History of the Kelly Gang (02) 804
CARLYLE, THOMAS, and JOHN RUSKIN
  Correspondence of Thomas Carlyle and John
    Ruskin, The (83) 153
CARO, ROBERT A.
  Years of Lyndon Johnson, Master of the Senate,
    The (03) 907
  Years of Lyndon Johnson, Means of Ascent, The
    (91) 919
  Years of Lyndon Johnson, The Path to Power, The
    (H-83) 478
CAROTENUTO, ALDO
  Secret Symmetry, A (83) 709
CARPENTER, HUMPHREY
  Benjamin Britten (94) 75
  Serious Character, A (89) 779
  Tolkien (78) 851
  W. H. Auden (82) 923
CARR, VIRGINIA SPENCER
  Dos Passos (85) 194
CARRÈRE, EMMANUEL
  Adversary, The (02) 14
CARROLL, JAMES
  American Requiem, An (97) 38
  Constantine's Sword (02) 167
  Mortal Friends (79) 462
CARROLL, LEWIS
  Letters of Lewis Carroll, 1837-1885, The
    (80) 474
CARROLL, PETER N.
  It Seemed Like Nothing Happened (H-83) 220
CARRUTH, HAYDEN
  Collected Shorter Poems, 1946-1991 (93) 171
  Scrambled Eggs and Whiskey (97) 722
CARSON, ANNE
  Autobiography of Red (99) 74
  Eros the Bittersweet (87) 248
  If Not, Winter (03) 388
  Men in the Off Hours (01) 583
CARTER, ANGELA
  Wise Children (93) 879
CARTER, JARED
  Work, for the Night Is Coming (82) 968
CARTER, JIMMY
  Keeping Faith (H-83) 239
  Why Not the Best? (77) 906
CARTER, PAUL A.
  Another Part of the Fifties (H-84) 24
CARTER, ROSALYNN
  First Lady from Plains (H-85) 146
CARTER, STEPHEN L.
  Civility (99) 177
  Culture of Disbelief, The (94) 191
  Emperor of Ocean Park, The (03) 260
  God's Name in Vain (01) 351
  Integrity (97) 456
  Reflections of an Affirmative Action Baby
    (92) 669
CARTER, WILLIAM C.
  Marcel Proust (01) 559

CARVER, RAYMOND
  All of Us (99) 28
  Cathedral (84) 143
  What We Talk About When We Talk About Love
    (82) 926
  Where I'm Calling From (89) 897
  Will You Please Be Quiet, Please? (77) 914
CASE, JOHN
  Understanding Inflation (82) 866
CASEY, JOHN
  Spartina (90) 748
  Testimony and Demeanor (80) 811
CASSEDY, STEVEN
  Flight from Eden (92) 210
CASSERLY, JACK, and BARRY M. GOLDWATER
  Goldwater (89) 321
CASSIDY, DAVID C.
  Uncertainty (93) 824
CASSIDY, FREDERIC G., editor
  Dictionary of American Regional English, Vol. I
    (86) 230
CASSILL, R. V.
  Labors of Love (81) 471
CASSITY, TURNER
  Between the Chains (92) 44
  Destructive Element, The (99) 230
  Hurricane Lamp (87) 415
CASTI, JOHN L, and WERNER DePAULI
  Gödel (01) 346
CAUDILL, HARRY M.
  Watches of the Night, The (77) 896
CAUTE, DAVID
  Great Fear, The (79) 255
CAVAFY, CONSTANTINE P.
  Before Time Could Change Them (02) 74
CAVALIERO, GLEN
  Charles Williams (84) 158
CAVALLI-SFORZA, LUIGI LUCA
  Genes, Peoples, and Languages (01) 327
CAVE BROWN, ANTHONY
  Treason in the Blood (95) 796
CEDERING, SIV
  Letters from the Floating World (85) 544
CELAN, PAUL
  Collected Prose (91) 157
  Last Poems (87) 466
  Poems of Paul Celan (90) 673
CÉSAIRE, AIMÉ
  Aimé Césaire, the Collected Poetry (84) 5
CHABON, MICHAEL
  Amazing Adventures of Kavalier and Clay, The
    (01) 19
  Model World, A (92) 514
  Mysteries of Pittsburgh, The (89) 581
  Wonder Boys (96) 831
CHAISSON, ERIC
  Cosmic Dawn (82) 130
CHALMERS, DAVID J.
  Conscious Mind, The (97) 179
CHAMBERS, JAMES
  Devil's Horsemen, The (80) 220
CHAMOISEAU, PATRICK
  Texaco (98) 755
CHANDERNAGOR, FRANÇOISE
  King's Way, The (85) 515

AUTHOR INDEX

CHANDLER, DAVID
  Waterloo (82) 912
CHANDLER, DAVID P.
  Tragedy of Cambodian History, The (93) 800
CHANDLER, RAYMOND
  Selected Letters of Raymond Chandler (82) 757
CHANG, IRIS
  Chinese in America, The (04) 113
CHANG, JUNG
  Wild Swans (92) 894
CHAPPELL, FRED
  Bloodfire (79) 60
  Earthsleep (81) 264
  Wind Mountain (80) 877
CHARTIER, ROGER
  History of Private Life, Passions of the
    Renaissance, A (90) 386
  Order of Books, The (95) 582
CHASE, JOAN
  During the Reign of the Queen of Persia
    (84) 252
CHATWIN, BRUCE
  On the Black Hill (84) 638
  Songlines, The (88) 840
  Utz (90) 835
  What Am I Doing Here (90) 874
CHAUDHURI, AMIT
  New World, A (01) 623
  Real Time (03) 643
CHÁVEZ, DENISE
  Loving Pedro Infante (02) 499
CHEEVER, JOHN
  Falconer (78) 309
  Journals of John Cheever, The (92) 393
  Letters of John Cheever, The (89) 480
  Oh What a Paradise It Seems (83) 558
  Stories of John Cheever, The (79) 713
CHEEVER, SUSAN
  Home Before Dark (85) 405
CHERNOW, RON
  House of Morgan, The (91) 432
  Titan (99) 768
CHERRY, KELLY
  Relativity (78) 700
CHESLER, PHYLLIS
  Woman's Inhumanity to Woman (03) 898
CHIAROMONTE, NICOLA
  Worm of Consciousness and Other Essays, The
    (77) 956
CHICKERING, ROGER
  We Men Who Feel Most German (H-85) 479
CHIN, MARILYN
  Rhapsody in Plain Yellow (03) 668
CHING, FRANK
  Ancestors (89) 19
CHISHOLM, ANNE, and MICHAEL DAVIE
  Lord Beaverbrook (94) 488
CHOMSKY, NOAM
  Reflections on Language (77) 668
CHRISTIAN, SHIRLEY
  Nicaragua (86) 655
CHRISTIANSON, GALE E.
  In the Presence of the Creator (H-85) 236
CHRISTIE, AGATHA
  Mousetrap and Other Plays, The (79) 470

CHUKOVSKAYA, LYDIA
  Akhmatova Journals, 1938-41, The (95) 19
CHURCHLAND, PAUL M.
  Engine of Reason, the Seat of the Soul, The
    (96) 232
CHUTE, CAROLYN
  Letourneau's Used Auto Parts (89) 460
CIARDI, JOHN
  Collected Poems of John Ciardi, The (98) 190
CISNEROS, SANDRA
  Caramelo (03) 132
  Woman Hollering Creek (92) 909
CLAMPITT, AMY
  Collected Poems of Amy Clampitt, The (98) 185
  Kingfisher, The (84) 413
  Silence Opens, A (95) 713
CLAPP, NICHOLAS
  Sheba (02) 747
CLAPP, SUSANNAH
  With Chatwin (98) 862
CLARE, JOHN
  "I Am" (04) 347
CLARK, KATERINA, and MICHAEL HOLQUIST
  Mikhail Bakhtin (86) 608
CLARK, RONALD W.
  Benjamin Franklin (H-84) 54
  Edison (78) 284
  Freud (81) 357
  Greatest Power on Earth, The (82) 343
  Life of Bertrand Russell, The (77) 423
CLARK, TOM
  Charles Olson (92) 88
CLARK, WILLIAM, and MERIWETHER LEWIS
  Lewis and Clark Journals, The (04) 442
CLARKE, ARTHUR C.
  2010 (83) 844
CLARKE, AUSTIN
  Selected Poems (77) 715
CLARKE, GERALD
  Capote (89) 135
CLARKE, JAMES W.
  American Assassins (H-83) 37
CLARY, KILLARNEY
  Who Whispered Near Me (90) 889
CLECAK, PETER
  America's Quest for the Ideal Self (H-84) 16
CLEMENS, SAMUEL LANGHORNE. See TWAIN,
    MARK
CLENDINNEN, INGA
  Aztecs (92) 30
CLIFFORD, CLARK, with RICHARD HOLBROOKE
  Counsel to the President (92) 123
CLIFTON, LUCILLE
  Generations (77) 318
CLINE, SALLY
  Zelda Fitzgerald (04) 868
CLINTON, HILLARY RODHAM
  Living History (04) 455
COCHRAN, THOMAS C.
  Frontiers of Change (82) 301
COE, JONATHAN
  Rotters' Club, The (03) 685

COETZEE, J. M.
    Age of Iron (91) 5
    Boyhood (98) 134
    Disgrace (00) 177
    Elizabeth Costello (04) 219
    Foe (88) 334
    Giving Offense (97) 335
    Life & Times of Michael K (84) 455
    Lives of Animals, The (00) 492
    Master of Petersburg, The (95) 469
    Stranger Shores (02) 764
COFER, JUDITH ORTIZ
    Latin Deli, The (94) 454
COGGINS, JACK
    Campaign for North Africa, The (81) 113
COHEN, ADAM, and ELIZABETH TAYLOR
    American Pharaoh (01) 34
COHEN, LEONARD
    Stranger Music (94) 764
COHEN, MORTON N.
    Lewis Carroll (96) 422
COHEN, STEPHEN S., and JOHN ZYSMAN
    Manufacturing Matters (88) 529
COHEN-SOLAL, ANNIE
    Sartre (88) 795
COLE, HENRI
    Middle Earth (04) 510
COLE, WAYNE S.
    Roosevelt and the Isolationists (H-84) 382
COLEBROOK, JOAN
    House of Trees, A (88) 403
COLEMAN, JAMES WILLIAM
    New Buddhism, The (02) 571
COLEMAN, WANDA
    Mercurochrome (02) 519
COLES, ROBERT
    Call of Stories, The (90) 81
    Dorothy Day (88) 252
    Flannery O'Connor's South (81) 350
    Moral Life of Children, The (87) 573
    Old and on Their Own (99) 576
    Political Life of Children, The (87) 665
COLETTE
    Collected Stories of Colette, The (84) 194
COLIN, AMY
    Paul Celan (92) 619
COLINVAUX, PAUL
    Why Big Fierce Animals Are Rare (79) 857
COLLEY, LINDA
    Britons (93) 105
COLLIER, PETER, and DAVID HOROWITZ
    Destructive Generation (90) 168
    Roosevelts, The (95) 664
COLLINS, BILLY
    Nine Horses (03) 590
    Sailing Alone Around the Room (02) 713
COLLINS, MICHAEL
    Liftoff (89) 506
COLUM, PADRAIC
    Selected Short Stories of Padraic Colum (86) 803
COLVILLE, JOHN
    Fringes of Power, The (86) 320
COMBS, JAMES E., and DAN NIMMO
    Subliminal Politics (81) 773
COMMAGER, HENRY STEELE
    Empire of Reason, The (78) 290

COMMINS, DOROTHY BERLINER
    What Is an Editor? (79) 839
COMMONER, BARRY
    Politics of Energy, The (80) 671
CONACHER, D. J.
    Aeschylus' Oresteia (88) 1
CONANT, JENNET
    Tuxedo Park (03) 848
CONGDON, LEE
    Young Lukács, The (84) 992
CONN, PETER
    Pearl S. Buck (97) 661
CONNELL, EVAN S., JR.
    Collected Stories of Evan S. Connell, The (96) 136
    Double Honeymoon (77) 242
    Saint Augustine's Pigeon (81) 703
    Son of the Morning Star (H-85) 420
    White Lantern, The (81) 916
CONNELLY, MICHAEL
    Lost Light (04) 474
CONNOLLY, CYRIL
    Selected Essays of Cyril Connolly, The (85) 793
CONNOLLY, JULIAN W.
    Nabokov's Early Fiction (93) 536
CONOT, ROBERT E.
    Justice at Nuremberg (H-84) 261
    Streak of Luck, A (80) 790
CONOVER, TED
    Newjack (01) 632
CONQUEST, ROBERT
    Harvest of Sorrow, The (87) 376
    Kolyma (79) 354
    Stalin (92) 780
CONRAD, JOSEPH
    Collected Letters of Joseph Conrad, 1861-1897,
        The (84) 178
    Collected Letters of Joseph Conrad, 1898-1902,
        The (87) 138
    Collected Letters of Joseph Conrad, 1903-1907,
        The (89) 175
CONRADI, PETER J.
    Iris Murdoch (02) 428
CONROY, FRANK
    Body and Soul (94) 100
    Midair (86) 603
CONROY, PAT
    Beach Music (96) 69
CONSTANTINE, DAVID
    Hölderlin (89) 354
CONWAY, JILL KER
    Road from Coorain, The (90) 699
    True North (95) 801
    When Memory Speaks (99) 855
COOK, BLANCHE WIESEN
    Eleanor Roosevelt, 1884-1933 (93) 253
    Eleanor Roosevelt, 1933-1938 (00) 204
COOK, ELIZABETH
    Achilles (03) 1
COOKE, HOPE
    Time Change (82) 839
COOPER, JOHN MILTON, JR.
    Walter Hines Page (78) 888
    Warrior and the Priest, The (H-84) 476
COOPER, MATTHEW
    German Army, 1933-1945, The (79) 245
    Nazi War Against Soviet Partisans, 1941-1944,
        The (80) 577

AUTHOR INDEX

COOPER, STEPHEN
Full of Life (01) 319
COOPER, WILLIAM J., JR.
Liberty and Slavery (H-84) 283
COOX, ALVIN D.
Nomonhan (87) 594
COPELAND, PETER, and DEAN HAMER
Living with Our Genes (99) 483
COPP, DEWITT S.
Forged in Fire (H-83) 145
COREN, MICHAEL
Invisible Man, The (94) 410
CORK, RICHARD
David Bomberg (88) 238
CORNELISEN, ANN
Women of the Shadows (77) 937
CORNELL, JAMES
First Stargazers, The (82) 280
CORNELL, JOSEPH
Joseph Cornell's Theater of the Mind (95) 408
CORNWELL, DAVID. See LE CARRÉ, JOHN
CORNWELL, JOHN
Hitler's Pope (00) 396
CORNWELL, PATRICIA
Blow Fly (04) 87
Body Farm, The (95) 94
CORSI, PIETRO, editor
Enchanted Loom, The (92) 183
CORTÁZAR, JULIO
Around the Day in Eighty Worlds (87) 45
Certain Lucas, A (85) 84
Change of Light, A (81) 122
Manual for Manuel, A (79) 418
We Love Glenda So Much and Other Tales
(84) 931
COSER, LEWIS A.
Refugee Scholars in America (85) 738
COSTELLO, MARK
Big If (03) 69
COSTELLO, PETER
James Joyce (94) 418
COTT, JONATHAN
Forever Young (79) 231
Wandering Ghost (92) 863
COULETTE, HENRI
Collected Poems of Henri Coulette, The (91) 152
COURTOIS, STÉPHANE, et al., editors
Black Book of Communism, The (00) 66
COWARD, NOËL
Noël Coward Diaries, The (83) 549
COWART, DAVID
Arches & Light (84) 40
COWLEY, MALCOLM
—And I Worked at the Writer's Trade (79) 24
Dream of the Golden Mountains, The (81) 249
Flower and the Leaf, The (86) 288
View from 80, The (81) 867
COX, ARCHIBALD
Court and the Constitution, The (88) 213
COZZENS, JAMES GOULD
Just Representations (79) 343
CRACE, JIM
Being Dead (01) 79
Genesis (04) 283
Gift of Stones, The (90) 294
Quarantine (99) 645

CRAFTS, HANNAH
Bondwoman's Narrative, The (03) 92
CRAIG, GORDON A.
Germans, The (H-83) 166
Germany 1866-1945 (79) 249
CRAMER, RICHARD BEN
Joe Dimaggio (01) 489
What It Takes (93) 874
CRAMPTON, MARY. See PYM, BARBARA
CRANE, ELIZABETH
When the Messenger Is Hot (04) 827
CRANKSHAW, EDWARD
Bismarck (82) 50
Shadow of the Winter Palace, The (77) 730
CRANSTON, MAURICE
Jean-Jacques (H-84) 237
Noble Savage, The (92) 583
CRAWFORD, ALAN
Thunder on the Right (81) 804
CRAWFORD, ROBERT
Devolving English Literature (93) 224
CRAY, ED
General of the Army (91) 333
CREELEY, ROBERT
Collected Essays of Robert Creeley, The
(90) 108
Collected Poems of Robert Creeley, The
(84) 189
Windows (91) 901
CREWS, FREDERICK C., ed.
Unauthorized Freud (99) 817
CRICK, FRANCIS
Life Itself (82) 462
CRISTOFER, MICHAEL
Shadow Box, The (78) 762
CRITCHFIELD, RICHARD
Those Days (87) 858
Villages (82) 879
CRITCHLEY, JULIAN
North Atlantic Alliance and the Soviet Union in the
1980's, The (H-83) 320
CRONIN, ANTHONY
No Laughing Matter (91) 629
Samuel Beckett (98) 688
CRONIN, VINCENT
Catherine, Empress of All the Russias (79) 80
CRONON, WILLIAM
Changes in the Land (H-84) 82
Nature's Metropolis (92) 554
CROSBY, ALFRED W.
Measure of Reality, The (98) 555
CROSSMAN, RICHARD
Diaries of a Cabinet Minister, The (77) 211
CROUCH, STANLEY
All-American Skin Game, The (96) 14
Always in Pursuit (99) 36
Notes of a Hanging Judge (91) 634
CROWLEY, MONICA
Nixon Off the Record (97) 622
CSIKSZENTMIHALYI, MIHALY
Flow (91) 299
CULLEN, JIM
American Dream, The (04) 26
CULLER, A. DWIGHT
Poetry of Tennyson, The (78) 665

CULVER, JOHN C., and JOHN HYDE
  American Dreamer (01) 24
CUNNINGHAM, VALENTINE
  British Writers of the Thirties (89) 130

DALE, ALZINA STONE
  Outline of Sanity (83) 582
DALLEK, ROBERT
  American Style of Foreign Policy, The (H-84) 11
  Flawed Giant (99) 286
  Franklin D. Roosevelt and American Foreign
    Policy, 1932-1945 (80) 328
  Lone Star Rising (92) 450
  Unfinished Life, An (04) 791
D'ALPUGET, BLANCHE
  Turtle Beach (84) 886
DAMASIO, ANTONIO R.
  Feeling of What Happens, The (00) 256
D'AMBROSIO, CHARLES
  Point, The (96) 589
DANGERFIELD, GEORGE
  Damnable Question, The (77) 188
DANIELEWSKI, MARK Z.
  House of Leaves (01) 417
DANIELS, DOUGLAS HENRY
  Lester Leaps In (03) 470
DANIELS, KATE
  White Wave, The (85) 1023
DANIELS, PAMELA, and SARA RUDDICK, editors
  Working It Out (78) 937
DANTE ALIGHIERI
  Inferno of Dante, The (96) 376
DANTICAT, EDWIDGE
  Krik? Krak! (96) 406
DARNELL, REGNA
  Edward Sapir (91) 245
DARNTON, ROBERT
  Great Cat Massacre and Other Episodes in French
    Cultural History, The (H-85) 183
DARR, ANN
  Cleared for Landing (79) 113
DARWIN, CHARLES ROBERT
  Charles Darwin's Letters (97) 148
DAVENPORT, GUY
  Da Vinci's Bicycle (80) 195
  Eclogues (82) 185
  Every Force Evolves a Form (88) 298
  Hunter Gracchus, The (97) 419
  Table of Green Fields, A (94) 783
DAVENPORT, JOHN, and DYLAN THOMAS
  Death of the King's Canary, The (78) 238
DAVENPORT-HINES, RICHARD
  Auden (97) 79
DAVIDSON, EUGENE
  Making of Adolf Hitler, The (78) 552
DAVIDSON, JAMES WEST, and MARK HAMILTON
  LYTLE
  After the Fact (H-83) 10
DAVIDSON, KEAY
  Carl Sagan (00) 121
DAVIE, DONALD
  Collected Poems, 1970-1983 (84) 183
  Czesław Miłosz and the Insufficiency of Lyric
    (87) 189
  These the Companions (83) 787
  Under Briggflatts (91) 833

DAVIE, MICHAEL, and ANNE CHISHOLM
  Lord Beaverbrook (94) 488
DAVIES, JOHN
  History of Wales, A (95) 309
DAVIES, NORMAN
  Europe (97) 260
DAVIES, PAUL
  Fifth Miracle, The (00) 260
DAVIES, PETER HO
  Equal Love (01) 286
DAVIES, ROBERTSON
  Cunning Man, The (96) 144
  Happy Alchemy (99) 346
  Lyre of Orpheus, The (90) 548
  Murther and Walking Spirits (92) 535
  Rebel Angels, The (83) 641
  What's Bred in the Bone (86) 939
  World of Wonders (77) 952
DAVIS, DAVID BRION
  Slavery and Human Progress (H-85) 411
DAVIS, JOHN H.
  Guggenheims (79) 260
DAVIS, KENNETH C.
  Two-Bit Culture (85) 952
DAVIS, KENNETH S.
  FDR, 1933-1937 (87) 276
  FDR, 1937-1940 (94) 278
  FDR, 1940-1943 (01) 300
DAVIS, LINDA H.
  Badge of Courage (99) 78
  Onward and Upward (88) 630
DAVIS, NATALIE ZEMON
  Women on the Margins (96) 826
DAVIS, PETER
  Hometown (83) 344
DAVIS, WILLIAM C.
  Honorable Defeat, An (02) 391
DAWIDOFF, NICHOLAS
  Catcher Was a Spy, The (95) 104
  In the Country of Country (98) 419
DAWKINS, LOUISA
  Natives and Strangers (86) 644
DAWSON, CARL
  Prophets of Past Time (89) 674
DAWSON, JOHN W., JR.
  Logical Dilemmas (98) 517
DAY, H. ALAN, and SANDRA DAY O'CONNOR
  Lazy B (03) 460
DAY, MARELE
  Lambs of God (99) 462
DAY LEWIS, C.
  Complete Poems of C. Day Lewis, The (93) 184
DAYAN, MOSHE
  Moshe Dayan (77) 513
DEAN, JOHN W., III
  Blind Ambition (77) 96
DEARBORN, MARY
  Happiest Man Alive, The (92) 266
DE BAECQUE, ANTOINE, and SERGE TOUBIANA
  Truffaut (00) 772
DE BEAUVOIR, SIMONE. See BEAUVOIR,
  SIMONE DE
DEBRECZENY, PAUL
  Other Pushkin, The (84) 657

AUTHOR INDEX

DE GALBA, MARTÍ JOAN, and JOANOT MARTORELL
Tirant lo Blanc (85) 907

DEGLER, CARL N.
In Search of Human Nature (92) 338

DE GRAND, ALEXANDER
Italian Fascism (H-83) 224

DEHAENE, STANISLAS
Number Sense, The (98) 603

DEIGHTON, LEN
Blitzkrieg (81) 88

DE JONGE, ALEX
Fire and Water (81) 335
Life and Times of Grigorii Rasputin, The (H-83) 264

DEKKER, GEORGE
American Historical Romance, The (88) 31

DELANY, PAUL
D. H. Lawrence's Nightmare (80) 223

DELANY, SAMUEL R.
Stars in My Pockets like Grains of Sand (85) 860

DELBANCO, NICHOLAS
About My Table (84) 1
Group Portrait (83) 312

DeLILLO, DON
Body Artist, The (02) 93
Libra (89) 496
Mao II (92) 479
Names, The (83) 515
Players (78) 661
Ratner's Star (77) 647
Running Dog (79) 617
Underworld (98) 791
White Noise (86) 945

DEL VECCHIO, JOHN M.
13th Valley, The (83) 791

DE MADARIAGA, ISABEL
Russia in the Age of Catherine the Great (82) 708

DEMARIA, ROBERT, JR.
Life of Samuel Johnson, The (94) 471
Samuel Johnson and the Life of Reading (98) 693

DE MILLE, AGNES
Martha (92) 485

DEMOS, JOHN PUTNAM
Entertaining Satan (H-83) 130

DENBY, DAVID
Great Books (97) 360

DENBY, EDWIN
Edwin Denby, the Complete Poems (87) 223

DENNETT, DANIEL C.
Brainchildren (99) 122
Consciousness Explained (92) 119
Darwin's Dangerous Idea (96) 148
Freedom Evolves (04) 275

DENNIS, CARL
Outskirts of Troy, The (89) 635

DENNISON, GEORGE
Luisa Domic (86) 556

DePAULI, WERNER, and JOHN L. CASTI
Gödel (01) 346

DERBYSHIRE, JOHN
Seeing Calvin Coolidge in a Dream (97) 732

DERRIDA, JACQUES
Memoirs of the Blind (95) 473

DERSHOWITZ, ALAN M.
Reversal of Fortune (87) 716

DESAI, ANITA
Clear Light of Day (81) 156

DESAI, KIRAN
Hullabaloo in the Guava Orchard (99) 396

DESCHNER, GÜNTHER
Reinhard Heydrich (82) 666

DESMOND, ADRIAN
Huxley (98) 411

DESMOND, ADRIAN, and JAMES MOORE
Darwin (93) 196

DES PRES, TERRENCE
Survivor, The (77) 797

DETZER, DAVID
Brink, The (80) 110

DE VRIES, PETER
Consenting Adults (81) 198
I Hear America Swinging (77) 372
Madder Music (78) 546
Peckham's Marbles (87) 650
Prick of Noon, The (86) 752
Sauce for the Goose (82) 742
Slouching Towards Kalamazoo (84) 796

DE VRIES, WALTER, and JACK BASS
Transformation of Southern Politics, The (77) 832

DE WAAL, FRANS
Ape and the Sushi Master, The (02) 48
Good Natured (97) 350

DEWBERRY, ELIZABETH
Sacrament of Lies (03) 699

DE WOLFE, BARBARA, with BERNARD BAILYN
Voyagers to the West (87) 917

DEXTER, PETE
Brotherly Love (92) 64
Paperboy, The (96) 565
Paris Trout (89) 644

DIAMOND, JARED
Guns, Germs, and Steel (98) 370

DiBATTISTA, MARIA
Fast-Talking Dames (02) 285

DICK, PHILIP K.
Selected Stories of Philip K. Dick (03) 737

DICKEY, JAMES
Alnilam (88) 15
Strength of Fields, The (80) 794
To the White Sea (94) 802

DICKEY, WILLIAM
Rainbow Grocery, The (79) 570

DICKINSON, CHARLES
Rumor Has It (92) 694

DICKSTEIN, MORRIS
Gates of Eden (78) 328
Leopards in the Temple (03) 465

DIDION, JOAN
After Henry (93) 1
Book of Common Prayer, A (78) 121
Democracy (85) 172
Last Thing He Wanted, The (97) 486
Miami (88) 553
Where I Was From (04) 831
White Album, The (80) 862

DIEHL, JAMES M.
Paramilitary Politics in Weimar Germany (79) 526

DIGGINS, JOHN PATRICK
Max Weber (97) 559
Promise of Pragmatism, The (95) 617

DILLARD, ANNIE
American Childhood, An (88) 25
Encounters with Chinese Writers (85) 223
For the Time Being (00) 282
Holy the Firm (78) 404
Living, The (93) 478
Living by Fiction (83) 413
Mornings Like This (96) 482
Teaching a Stone to Talk (83) 773
Writing Life, The (90) 930

DILLARD, R. H. W.
First Man on the Sun, The (84) 304
Greeting, The (83) 309

DILLON, KATHERINE V., GORDON W. PRANGE, and DONALD M. GOLDSTEIN
Miracle at Midway (H-83) 288
Pearl Harbor (86) 732

DILLON, MILLICENT
Harry Gold (01) 379
Little Original Sin, A (82) 470

DINESEN, ISAK
Carnival (78) 150
Daguerreotypes and Other Essays (80) 180

DINNERSTEIN, LEONARD
America and the Survivors of the Holocaust (H-83) 25

DITTMER, JOHN
Local People (95) 440

DIVINE, ROBERT A.
Eisenhower and the Cold War (82) 195

DIXON, STEPHEN
Stories of Stephen Dixon, The (95) 761

DJILAS, MILOVAN
Wartime (78) 894

DOBROSZYCKI, LUCJAN, editor
Chronicle of the Łódź Ghetto, 1941-1944, The (H-85) 73

DOCTOROW, E. L.
Billy Bathgate (90) 67
Lives of the Poets (85) 574
Loon Lake (81) 524
Waterworks, The (95) 849
World's Fair (86) 970

DODGE, JIM
Fup (85) 318
Stone Junction (91) 777

DOERR, HARRIET
Consider This, Señora (94) 163
Stones for Ibarra (85) 869

DOGGETT, FRANK, and ROBERT BUTTEL, editors
Wallace Stevens (81) 879

DOIG, IVAN
Dancing at the Rascal Fair (88) 228
English Creek (85) 232
Mountain Time (00) 546

DOLOT, MIRON
Execution by Hunger (86) 254

DOMINICK, RAYMOND H., III
Wilhelm Liebknecht and the Founding of the German Social Democratic Party (H-83) 467

DONALD, DAVID HERBERT
Lincoln (96) 436
Look Homeward (88) 502

DONALDSON, FRANCES
P. G. Wodehouse (83) 587

DONALDSON, SCOTT
Archibald MacLeish (93) 28
John Cheever (89) 422

DONLEAVY, J. P.
Destinies of Darcy Dancer, Gentleman, The (78) 254

DONNER, FRANK J.
Age of Surveillance, The (81) 16

DONOGHUE, DENIS
Adam's Curse (02) 5
Ferocious Alphabets (82) 271
Practice of Reading, The (99) 636
Speaking of Beauty (04) 713
Walter Pater (96) 810
Warrenpoint (91) 871
We Irish (87) 953
Words Alone (01) 925

DONOGHUE, EMMA
Hood (97) 410
Woman Who Gave Birth to Rabbits, The (03) 894

DONOVAN, ROBERT J.
Conflict and Crisis (78) 210
Tumultuous Years (H-83) 435

DOOLING, RICHARD
Brain Storm (99) 118
White Man's Grave (95) 862

DOOLITTLE, HILDA. See H. D.

DORMANDY, THOMAS
White Death, The (01) 905

DORNBERG, JOHN
Munich 1923 (H-83) 298

DORRIS, MICHAEL
Broken Cord, The (90) 76
Cloud Chamber (98) 168
Yellow Raft in Blue Water, A (88) 1004

DOSTOEVSKY, ANNA
Dostoevsky (77) 230

DOSTOYEVSKY, FYODOR
Selected Letters of Fyodor Dostoyevsky (88) 806

DOTY, MARK
Atlantis (96) 55
Heaven's Coast (97) 368
My Alexandria (94) 547

DOUGLAS, ANN
Terrible Honesty (96) 736

DOUGLAS, ELLEN
Rock Cried Out, The (80) 722

DOUGLAS, KIRK
Ragman's Son, The (89) 692

DOUGLAS, MARY
Risk and Blame (93) 687

DOVE, RITA
Grace Notes (90) 324
Mother Love (96) 486
Through the Ivory Gate (93) 792

DOVLATOV, SERGEI
Zone, The (86) 985

DOWART, JEFFREY M.
Conflict of Duty (H-84) 96

DOWER, JOHN W.
Japan in War and Peace (95) 392
War Without Mercy (87) 947

DOWNIE, LEONARD, JR., and ROBERT G. KAISER
News About the News, The (03) 577

DOYLE, RODDY
Paddy Clarke Ha Ha Ha (94) 603
Star Called Henry, A (00) 729
Woman Who Walked into Doors, The (97) 895

DRABBLE, MARGARET
Angus Wilson (97) 48
Ice Age, The (78) 431
Middle Ground, The (81) 564
Radiant Way, The (88) 720
Witch of Exmoor, The (98) 858
DRAKE, WILLIAM
Sara Teasdale (80) 741
DRAPER, THEODORE
Struggle for Power, A (97) 787
DREYFUSS, JOEL, and CHARLES LAWRENCE III
Bakke Case, The (80) 45
DRUCKER, PETER F.
Unseen Revolution, The (77) 872
DRURY, ALLEN
God Against the Gods, A (77) 332
Return to Thebes (78) 708
DRURY, TOM
End of Vandalism, The (95) 204
Hunts in Dreams (01) 437
D'SOUZA, DINESH
End of Racism, The (96) 227
DUBERMAN, MARTIN BAUML
Paul Robeson (90) 652
Visions of Kerouac (78) 878
DUBIE, NORMAN
Groom Falconer (90) 338
Selected and New Poems (84) 761
Springhouse, The (87) 818
DUBNER, STEPHEN
Turbulent Souls (99) 803
DUBOFSKY, MELVIN, and WARREN VAN TINE
John L. Lewis (78) 478
DU BOIS, W. E. B.
Writings (88) 993
DUBUS, ANDRE
Dancing After Hours (97) 196
Meditations from a Movable Chair (99) 538
Times Are Never So Bad, The (84) 873
DUBY, GEORGES, editor
History of Private Life, Revelations of the
Medieval World, A (89) 349
DUFFY, EAMON
Saints and Sinners (98) 683
DUGGER, RONNIE
Politician, The (H-83) 348
DUIKER, WILLIAM J.
Ho Chi Minh (01) 403
DUNBAR-NELSON, ALICE
Give Us Each Day (86) 349
DUNCAN, ROBERT
Ground Work (85) 329
Selected Prose, A (96) 690
DUNCAN, RUSSELL, editor
Blue-Eyed Child of Fortune (93) 91
DUNCAN-JONES, KATHERINE
Sir Philip Sidney (92) 761
DUNEIER, MITCHELL
Slim's Table (93) 744
DUNLOP, JOHN B., RICHARD S. HAUGH, and
MICHAEL NICHOLSON, editors
Solzhenitsyn in Exile (86) 843
DUNLOP, RICHARD
Donovan (H-83) 99
DUNN, STEVEN
Local Visitations (04) 465

DUNNE, GERALD T.
Hugo Black and the Judicial Revolution (78) 418
DUNNE, JOHN GREGORY
Dutch Shea, Jr. (83) 216
Harp (90) 364
DUONG THU HUONG
Paradise of the Blind (94) 607
DUPUY, T. N.
Genius for War, A (78) 332
DURANT, WILL, and ARIEL DURANT
Age of Napoleon, The (77) 33
Dual Autobiography, A (78) 280
DURAS, MARGUERITE
Lover, The (86) 547
War, The (87) 941
DUROZOI, GÉRARD
History of the Surrealist Movement (03) 370
DURRELL, LAWRENCE
Sicilian Carousel (78) 771
DYBEK, STUART
Coast of Chicago, The (91) 142
DYER, GEOFF
Yoga for People Who Can't Be Bothered to Do It
(04) 864
DYSON, FREEMAN J.
Infinite in All Directions (89) 381
DYSON, MICHAEL ERIC
I May Not Get There with You (01) 442

EAGLETON, TERRY
Literary Theory (84) 464
EARLY, GERALD
One Nation Under a Groove (96) 537
EATON, CLEMENT
Jefferson Davis (78) 464
EBAN, ABBA
Abba Eban (78) 1
New Diplomacy, The (H-84) 317
EBERHART, RICHARD
Of Poetry and Poets (80) 610
EBERSTADT, FERNANDA
Isaac and His Devils (92) 359
Low Tide (86) 551
When the Sons of Heaven Meet the Daughters of
the Earth (98) 836
EBERT, ROGER
Great Movies, The (03) 348
ECHOLS, ALICE
Scars of Sweet Paradise (00) 670
ECKHOLM, ERIK P.
Losing Ground (77) 450
ECO, UMBERTO
Baudolino (03) 56
Foucault's Pendulum (90) 277
Interpretation and Overinterpretation (93) 390
Island of the Day Before, The (96) 385
Name of the Rose, The (84) 598
Postscript to The Name of the Rose (85) 697
Search for the Perfect Language, The (96) 680
Semiotics and the Philosophy of Language
(85) 807
EDEL, LEON
Bloomsbury (80) 88
Stuff of Sleep and Dreams (83) 765
EDEN, ANTHONY
Another World, 1897-1917 (78) 59

EDEY, MAITLAND A., and DONALD C. JOHANSON
  Lucy (82) 514
EDMONDS, DAVID, and JOHN EIDINOW
  Wittgenstein's Poker (02) 875
EDMUNDS, R. DAVID
  Shawnee Prophet, The (H-84) 409
EDMUNDSON, MARK
  Nightmare on Main Street (98) 593
EDWARDS, G. B.
  Book of Ebenezer Le Page, The (82) 59
EDWARDS, MARK W.
  Homer (88) 398
EGERTON, DOUGLAS R.
  Gabriel's Rebellion (94) 325
EGGERS, DAVE
  Heartbreaking Work of Staggering Genius, A (01) 389
EHRENPREIS, IRVIN
  Swift, the Man, His Works, and the Age, Vol. III (84) 849
EHRENREICH, BARBARA
  Nickel and Dimed (02) 580
EHRLICH, GRETEL
  Islands, the Universe, Home (92) 364
  Solace of Open Spaces, The (86) 840
EHRLICHMAN, JOHN
  Witness to Power (H-83) 473
EIDINOW, JOHN, and DAVID EDMONDS
  Wittgenstein's Poker (02) 875
EIKENBAUM, BORIS
  Tolstoi in the Seventies (83) 821
  Tolstoi in the Sixties (83) 816
EINSTEIN, ALBERT
  Albert Einstein (80) 19
EISENBERG, DEBORAH
  Transactions in a Foreign Currency (87) 881
  Under the 82nd Airborne (93) 829
EISENHOWER, DAVID
  Eisenhower, at War (87) 226
EISENHOWER, DWIGHT DAVID
  Eisenhower Diaries, The (82) 199
EISENHOWER, JOHN S. D.
  Allies (H-83) 20
EISLER, BENITA
  Chopin's Funeral (04) 118
EKMAN, KERSTIN
  Blackwater (97) 119
ELDREDGE, NILES
  Dominion (96) 198
ELEY, GEOFF
  Reshaping the German Right (81) 682
ELIADE, MIRCEA
  Ordeal by Labyrinth (83) 572
ELIOT, T. S.
  Inventions of the March Hare (98) 436
  Letters of T. S. Eliot, The (89) 488
ELKIN, STANLEY
  George Mills (83) 273
  MacGuffin, The (92) 465
  Mrs. Ted Bliss (96) 469
  Pieces of Soap (93) 629
  Rabbi of Lud, The (88) 715
  Van Gogh's Room at Arles (94) 831
ELKINS, STANLEY, and ERIC McKITRICK
  Age of Federalism, The (94) 5

ELLEDGE, SCOTT
  E. B. White (85) 209
ELLIOTT, CARL
  Better than Well (04) 79
ELLIS, ALICE THOMAS
  Twenty-seventh Kingdom, The (00) 776
ELLIS, BRET EASTON
  Glamorama (00) 313
ELLIS, DAVID
  D. H. Lawrence (98) 244
ELLIS, JOHN M.
  Literature Lost (98) 512
ELLIS, JOSEPH J.
  American Sphinx (98) 55
ELLISON, RALPH
  Collected Essays of Ralph Ellison, The (96) 128
  Flying Home and Other Stories (97) 287
  Going to the Territory (87) 331
  Juneteenth (00) 457
ELLMANN, RICHARD
  a long the riverrun (90) 1
  Oscar Wilde (89) 630
ELLSBERG, DANIEL
  Secrets (03) 718
EMERSON, CARYL, and GARY SAUL MORSON
  Mikhail Bakhtin (92) 500
EMERSON, RALPH WALDO
  Emerson in His Journals (83) 224
EMERSON, STEVEN
  American Jihad (03) 23
EMERY, JANE
  Rose Macaulay (93) 693
EMMERSON, JAMES THOMAS
  Rhineland Crisis, The (78) 712
EMPSON, WILLIAM
  Argufying (89) 46
  Complete Poems of William Empson, The (02) 153
ENCHI, FUMIKO
  Masks (84) 514
ENDŌ, SHŪSAKU
  Deep River (96) 160
  Final Martyrs, The (95) 235
  Samurai, The (83) 674
  Scandal (89) 752
  Stained Glass Elegies (86) 856
  Wonderful Fool (84) 967
ENGELHARDT, TOM, and EDWARD T. LINENTHAL, editors
  History Wars (97) 400
ENGELS, FRIEDRICH, and KARL MARX
  Selected Letters (83) 722
ENGELS, JOHN
  Blood Mountain (78) 117
ENGER, LEIF
  Peace Like a River (02) 626
ENGLANDER, NATHAN
  For the Relief of Unbearable Urges (00) 277
ENRIGHT, D. J.
  Alluring Problem, The (88) 11
  Old Men and Comets (94) 577
ENZENSBERGER, HANS MAGNUS
  Europe, Europe (90) 227
EPSTEIN, HELEN
  Joe Papp (95) 396

EPSTEIN, JASON
Book Business (02) 106
EPSTEIN, JOSEPH
Familiar Territory (80) 310
Life Sentences (98) 504
Middle of My Tether, The (84) 539
Plausible Prejudices (86) 737
Snobbery (03) 784
With My Trousers Rolled (96) 818
EPSTEIN, LESLIE
King of the Jews (80) 458
Regina (83) 650
ERDRICH, LOUISE
Antelope Wife, The (99) 53
Beet Queen, The (87) 61
Bingo Palace, The (95) 76
Last Report on the Miracles at Little No Horse,
The (02) 477
Love Medicine (85) 584
Master Butchers Singing Club, The (04) 496
Original Fire (04) 579
Tales of Burning Love (97) 812
Tracks (89) 850
ERIBON, DIDIER
Michel Foucault (92) 495
ERICKSON, CAROLLY
Bloody Mary (79) 64
First Elizabeth, The (H-84) 164
Great Harry (81) 391
Mistress Anne (H-85) 319
Our Tempestuous Day (87) 620
ERICKSON, STEVE
Arc d'X (94) 47
Rubicon Beach (87) 736
Sea Came in at Midnight, The (00) 675
ERICSON, EDWARD E., JR.
Solzhenitsyn and the Modern World (94) 751
ESKIN, BLAKE
Life in Pieces, A (03) 480
ESPADA, MARTÍN
Alabanza (04) 5
Mayan Astronomer in Hell's Kitchen, A (01) 574
ESSLIN, MARTIN
Antonin Artaud (78) 68
EUGENIDES, JEFFREY
Middlesex (03) 527
EVANS, SARA
Personal Politics (80) 655
EVE, NOMI
Family Orchard, The (01) 295
EVERDELL, WILLIAM R.
First Moderns, The (98) 312
EWALD, WILLIAM BRAGG, JR.
Eisenhower the President (82) 205
EWEN, DAVID
All the Years of American Popular Music (78) 33

FADIMAN, ANNE
Ex Libris (99) 269
Spirit Catches You and You Fall Down, The
(98) 722
FAIRBANK, JOHN KING
Chinabound (H-83) 61
FAIRFIELD, CICILY. See WEST, REBECCA
FALLOWS, JAMES
Breaking the News (97) 132
Looking at the Sun (95) 451

FALUDI, SUSAN
Stiffed (00) 733
FARAGO, LADISLAS
Last Days of Patton, The (82) 428
FARAH, NURUDDIN
Secrets (99) 693
FARR, JUDITH
Passion of Emily Dickinson, The (93) 610
FARRAR, L. L., JR.
Arrogance and Anxiety (82) 22
FARRELL, JOHN A.
Tip O'Neill and the Democratic Century (02) 791
FAST, HOWARD
Second Generation (79) 648
FAULKNER, WILLIAM
Faulkner, a Comprehensive Guide to the Brodsky
Collection, Vol. II (85) 266
Uncollected Stories of William Faulkner (80) 838
FAULKS, SEBASTIAN
Birdsong (97) 110
FEILER, LILY
Marina Tsvetaeva (95) 464
FEILER, BRUCE
Walking the Bible (02) 826
FEIN, HELEN
Accounting for Genocide (80) 10
FEINSTEIN, ELAINE
Pushkin (00) 634
FELD, ROSS
Guston in Time (04) 320
FELDMAN, IRVING
All of Us Here (87) 29
Leaping Clear (77) 408
New and Selected Poems (80) 580
FELSTINER, JOHN
Paul Celan (96) 577
FENSCH, THOMAS
Steinbeck and Covici (80) 780
FENSTER, MARK
Conspiracy Theories (00) 142
FENTON, JAMES
Children in Exile (85) 96
FERGUSON, KITTY
Tycho and Kepler (04) 782
FERGUSON, NIALL
Cash Nexus, The (02) 145
Empire (04) 228
Pity of War, The (00) 609
FERGUSON, ROBERT
Enigma (88) 279
FERLING, JOHN
John Adams (93) 413
FERLINGHETTI, LAWRENCE
Endless Life (82) 229
These Are My Rivers (94) 788
FERNÁNDEZ-ARMESTO, FELIPE
Near a Thousand Tables (03) 564
FERRELL, ROBERT H.
Harry S. Truman and the Modern American
Presidency (H-84) 185
FERRIS, TIMOTHY
Coming of Age in the Milky Way (89) 199
Seeing in the Dark (03) 723
Whole Shebang, The (98) 846
FEUERLICHT, ROBERTA STRAUSS
Justice Crucified (78) 487

FEYNMAN, RICHARD P., with RALPH LEIGHTON
  "Surely You're Joking, Mr. Feynman!" (86) 868
FFORDE, JASPER
  Eyre Affair, The (03) 283
FICOWSKI, JERZY
  Regions of the Great Heresy (03) 648
FIEDLER, LESLIE
  Freaks (79) 235
  What Was Literature? (83) 884
FIELD, ANDREW
  Djuna (84) 234
  Nabokov (78) 590
  VN (87) 912
FIELD, GEOFFREY G.
  Evangelist of Race (82) 256
FIELDING, HELEN
  Bridget Jones's Diary (99) 132
FIGES, EVA
  Light (84) 459
  Waking (83) 869
FINLEY, M. I.
  Ancient Slavery and Modern Ideology (81) 43
FINNEGAN, WILLIAM
  Cold New World (99) 200
FINNEY, BRIAN
  Christopher Isherwood (80) 145
FINTAN, O'TOOLE
  Traitor's Kiss, A (99) 773
FIORI, GABRIELLA
  Simone Weil (90) 738
FIRSOV, FRIDRIKH IGOREVICH, HARVEY
  KLEHR, and JOHN EARL HAYNES, editors
  Secret World of American Communism, The
  (96) 685
FISCHER, DAVID HACKETT
  Albion's Seed (90) 24
  Paul Revere's Ride (95) 604
FISH, STANLEY
  Doing What Comes Naturally (90) 190
FISHER, CARRIE
  Delusions of Grandma (95) 162
FISHER, M. F. K.
  Sister Age (84) 792
FISHER, NIGEL
  Harold Macmillan (H-83) 185
FISHKIN, SHELLEY FISHER
  Lighting Out for the Territory (97) 521
  Was Huck Black? (94) 843
FITCH, NOËL RILEY
  Anaïs (94) 20
  Sylvia Beach and the Lost Generation (84) 854
FITOU, JEAN-FRANÇOIS, and EMMANUEL LE
  ROY LADURIE
  Saint-Simon and the Court of Louis XIV (02) 717
FITZGERALD, F. SCOTT
  Price Was High, The (80) 693
FitzGERALD, FRANCES
  Cities on a Hill (87) 121
  Way Out There in the Blue (01) 891
FITZGERALD, KEITH
  Face of the Nation, The (97) 265
FITZGERALD, PENELOPE
  Afterlife, The (04) 1
  Blue Flower, The (98) 121
  Charlotte Mew and Her Friends (89) 145

FITZGERALD, ROBERT
  Enlarging the Change (86) 244
FIUT, ALEKSANDER
  Eternal Moment, The (91) 266
FLANAGAN, RICHARD
  Gould's Book of Fish (03) 338
  Sound of One Hand Clapping, The (01) 791
FLANAGAN, THOMAS
  End of the Hunt, The (95) 200
  Tenants of Time, The (89) 826
  Year of the French, The (80) 880
FLANNER, JANET
  Darlinghissima (86) 213
FLAUBERT, GUSTAVE
  Letters of Gustave Flaubert, 1830-1857, The
  (81) 494
  Letters of Gustave Flaubert, 1857-1880, The
  (83) 395
FLAUBERT, GUSTAVE, and GEORGE SAND
  Flaubert-Sand (94) 300
FLEMING, GERALD
  Hitler and the Final Solution (H-85) 213
FLEMING, THOMAS
  Officers' Wives, The (82) 570
FLETCHER, RICHARD
  Quest for El Cid, The (91) 684
FLEXNER, JAMES THOMAS
  Young Hamilton, The (79) 922
FLINT, RONALD
  Resuming Green (84) 731
FLINT, VALERIE I. J.
  Imaginative Landscape of Christopher Columbus,
  The (93) 365
FLOWER, MILTON E.
  John Dickinson (H-84) 248
FOER, JONATHAN SAFRAN
  Everything Is Illuminated (03) 274
FOLSOM, FRANKLIN
  Impatient Armies of the Poor (92) 334
FONER, ERIC
  History of Black Americans (H-84) 202
  Politics and Ideology in the Age of the Civil War
  (81) 661
  Reconstruction (89) 697
  Story of American Freedom, The (99) 737
FOOT, M. R. D.
  Resistance (78) 704
FORBATH, PETER
  River Congo, The (78) 717
FORBIS, WILLIAM H.
  Fall of the Peacock Throne (81) 297
FORCHÉ, CAROLYN
  Angel of History, The (95) 33
  Blue Hour (04) 91
  Country Between Us, The (83) 161
  Gathering the Tribes (77) 314
FORD, ELAINE
  Missed Connections (84) 552
FORD, FORD MADOX, and EZRA POUND
  Pound/Ford, the Story of a Literary Friendship
  (83) 621
FORD, JESSE HILL
  Raider, The (77) 642

AUTHOR INDEX

FORD, RICHARD
  Independence Day (96) 372
  Multitude of Sins, A (03) 545
  Rock Springs (88) 776
  Sportswriter, The (87) 813
  Wildlife (91) 891
  Women with Men (98) 882
FORREST, LEON
  Two Wings to Veil My Face (85) 946
FORSTER, E. M.
  Selected Letters of E. M. Forster, 1879-1920
    (84) 773
  Selected Letters of E. M. Forster, 1921-1970
    (86) 793
FORSTER, MARGARET
  Daphne du Maurier (94) 204
  Elizabeth Barrett Browning (90) 203
FOSTER, MARILEE
  Dirt Under My Nails (03) 207
FOSTER, ROBERT FITZROY
  Modern Ireland (90) 573
  W. B. Yeats, 1865-1914 (98) 809
FOUCAULT, MICHEL
  Aesthetics, Method, and Epistemology (99) 15
  Ethics (98) 289
  Language, Counter-Memory, Practice (78) 504
FOWLER, WILLIAM M., JR.
  Baron of Beacon Hill, The (81) 66
  Jack Tars and Commodores (H-85) 246
FOWLES, JOHN
  Daniel Martin (78) 225
  Mantissa (83) 443
  Wormholes (99) 877
FOWLIE, WALLACE
  Sites (88) 823
FOX, RICHARD WIGHTMAN
  Reinhold Niebuhr (86) 766
FOX, ROBIN LANE. See LANE FOX, ROBIN
FOX, STEPHEN
  Mirror Makers, The (H-85) 313
FOX-GENOVESE, ELIZABETH
  Feminism Without Illusions (92) 205
FRADY, MARSHALL
  Jesse (97) 474
FRAME, JANET
  Living in the Maniototo (80) 502
FRANCIS, DICK
  Banker (84) 76
  Twice Shy (83) 841
FRANK, ELIZABETH
  Louise Bogan (86) 542
FRANK, JOSEPH
  Dostoevsky, 1821-1849 (77) 236
  Dostoevsky, 1850-1859 (84) 244
  Dostoevsky, 1860-1865 (87) 212
  Dostoevsky, 1865-1871 (96) 202
  Dostoevsky, 1871-1881 (03) 219
FRANK, KATHERINE
  Chainless Soul, A (91) 127
FRANKLIN, JOHN HOPE
  George Washington Williams (86) 332
FRANZEN, JONATHAN
  Corrections, The (02) 176
  How to Be Alone (03) 374
  Strong Motion (93) 766
FRASER, ANGUS
  Gypsies, The (93) 321

FRASER, ANTONIA
  Royal Charles (80) 732
  Weaker Vessel, The (H-85) 483
FRASER, DAVID
  Alanbrooke (H-83) 14
FRASER, GEORGE MacDONALD
  Flashman and the Dragon (87) 292
FRASER, NICHOLAS, and MARYSA NAVARRO
  Eva Perón (82) 249
FRASER, RUSSELL
  Shakespeare, The Later Years (93) 723
  Young Shakespeare (89) 933
FRAYN, MICHAEL
  Landing on the Sun, A (93) 431
FRAZIER, CHARLES
  Cold Mountain (98) 172
FRAZIER, IAN
  Family (95) 222
  Great Plains (90) 334
  Nobody Better, Better Than Nobody (88) 605
  On the Rez (01) 670
FREDRICKSON, GEORGE M.
  White Supremacy (82) 937
FREEBERG, ERNEST
  Education of Laura Bridgman, The (02) 230
FREEDMAN, RALPH
  Life of a Poet (97) 502
FREEDMAN, SAMUEL G.
  Inheritance, The (97) 451
  Jew vs. Jew (01) 480
  Small Victories (91) 750
  Upon This Rock (94) 827
FREESE, BARBARA
  Coal (04) 126
FREIDEL, DAVID, and LINDA SCHELE
  Forest of Kings, A (91) 308
FREIDENBERG, OLGA, and BORIS PASTERNAK
  Correspondence of Boris Pasternak and Olga
    Freidenberg, 1910-1954, The (83) 147
FRENCH, MARILYN
  Shakespeare's Division of Experience (82) 767
FREUD, ESTHER
  Peerless Flats (94) 618
FREUD, SIGMUND
  Complete Letters of Sigmund Freud to Wilhelm
    Fliess, The (86) 187
FRIEDAN, BETTY
  Life So Far (01) 532
  Second Stage, The (82) 752
FRIEDMAN, BRUCE JAY
  Collected Short Fiction of Bruce Jay Friedman,
    The (96) 132
FRIEDMAN, LAWRENCE M.
  Crime and Punishment in American History
    (94) 173
FRIEDMAN, MAURICE
  Martin Buber's Life and Work (H-84) 293
FRIEDMAN, THOMAS L.
  From Beirut to Jerusalem (90) 283
  Lexus and the Olive Tree, The (00) 483
FRIEDRICH, OTTO
  End of the World, The (H-83) 125
FRISCH, MAX
  Bluebeard (84) 105
  Man in the Holocene (81) 545

FROMKIN, DAVID
Peace to End All Peace, A (90) 657
Way of the World, The (00) 821
FRUM, DAVID
Right Man, The (04) 662
FRYE, NORTHROP
Great Code, The (83) 306
Northrop Frye on Culture and Literature (79) 496
Northrop Frye on Shakespeare (87) 599
FRYE, ROLAND MUSHAT
Renaissance *Hamlet*, The (85) 742
FUCHS, DANIEL
Saul Bellow, Vision and Revision (85) 776
FUCHS, LAWRENCE H.
American Kaleidoscope, The (92) 17
FUCHSER, LARRY WILLIAM
Neville Chamberlain and Appeasement (H-83) 314
FUENTES, CARLOS
Buried Mirror, The (93) 119
Burnt Water (81) 103
Campaign, The (92) 79
Christopher Unborn (90) 95
Distant Relations (83) 200
Myself with Others (89) 577
Old Gringo, The (86) 680
Terra Nostra (77) 807
Years with Laura Díaz, The (01) 935
FUGARD, ATHOL
Notebooks (85) 653
FUKUYAMA, FRANCIS
End of History and the Last Man, The (93) 262
Great Disruption, The (00) 331
Our Posthuman Future (03) 615
Trust (96) 777
FULLER, CHARLES
Soldier's Play, A (83) 751
FULLER, JACK
Fragments (85) 301
FULLER, JOHN
Flying to Nowhere (85) 292
FULLER, MARGARET
Letters of Margaret Fuller, 1817-1841, The
(84) 449
Letters of Margaret Fuller, 1842-1844, The
(85) 559
FULLER, STEVE
Thomas Kuhn (01) 820
FULTON, ALICE
Felt (02) 295
FURBANK, P. N.
Diderot (93) 229
E. M. Forster (79) 183
FURST, ALAN
Kingdom of Shadows (02) 463
Polish Officer, The (96) 593
FUSSELL, PAUL
Abroad (81) 5
Boy Scout Handbook and Other Observations, The
(83) 70
Wartime (90) 864

GABLER, NEAL
Empire of Their Own, An (89) 278
GADDIS, JOHN LEWIS
Strategies of Containment (H-83) 405
GADDIS, WILLIAM
Carpenter's Gothic (86) 96

GAGLIARDO, JOHN G.
Reich and Nation (81) 678
GAILLARD, FRYE
Watermelon Wine (79) 835
GAINES, ERNEST J.
Gathering of Old Men, A (84) 323
In My Father's House (79) 311
Lesson Before Dying, A (94) 463
GAITSKILL, MARY
Because They Wanted To (98) 104
GALBRAITH, JOHN KENNETH
Age of Uncertainty, The (78) 23
Anatomy of Power, The (H-84) 21
Life in Our Times, A (82) 458
GALEANO, EDUARDO H.
Memory of Fire, Century of the Wind (89) 548
Memory of Fire, Faces and Masks (88) 544
Memory of Fire, Genesis (86) 584
GALISON, PETER
Einstein's Clocks, Poincaré's Maps (04) 211
GALL, SALLY M., and M. L. ROSENTHAL
Modern Poetic Sequence, The (84) 570
GALLAGHER, TESS
Moon Crossing Bridge (93) 532
GALLANT, MAVIS
Across the Bridge (94) 1
Collected Stories of Mavis Gallant, The (97) 171
Home Truths (86) 431
GALLOWAY, DAVID DARRYL
Family Album, A (79) 204
GALLOWAY, JANICE
Clara (04) 122
Where You Find It (03) 882
GALLOWAY, JOSEPH L., and HAROLD G. MOORE
We Were Soldiers Once . . . and Young (93) 868
GALVIN, BRENDAN
Great Blue (91) 364
GAO XINGJIAN
One Man's Bible (03) 602
GARCIA, CRISTINA
Agüero Sisters, The (98) 14
Dreaming in Cuban (93) 249
GARCÍA LORCA, FEDERICO
Poetical Works of Federico García Lorca (93) 637
Selected Letters (84) 768
GARCÍA MÁRQUEZ, GABRIEL
Autumn of the Patriarch, The (77) 77
Chronicle of a Death Foretold (84) 163
General in His Labyrinth, The (91) 329
In Evil Hour (80) 421
Innocent Eréndira and Other Stories (79) 318
Living to Tell the Tale (04) 460
Love in the Time of Cholera (89) 521
News of a Kidnapping (98) 588
Of Love and Other Demons (96) 518
GARDAM, JANE
Crusoe's Daughter (87) 175
GARDNER, HELEN
Composition of *Four Quartets*, The (79) 128
GARDNER, JOHN
Art of Fiction, The (85) 22
Mickelsson's Ghosts (83) 475
October Light (77) 580
On Becoming a Novelist (84) 633
On Moral Fiction (79) 511
Stillness *and* Shadows (87) 822

AUTHOR INDEX

GARDNER, LLOYD C.
   Safe for Democracy (H-85) 400
GARLAND, ALEX
   Tesseract, The (00) 745
GARNETT, DAVID
   Great Friends (81) 386
GARRETT, GEORGE
   Collected Poems of George Garrett, The (85) 116
   Entered from the Sun (91) 257
   Evening Performance, An (86) 250
   James Jones (85) 484
   Luck's Shining Child (82) 509
   Succession, The (84) 842
GARRIGUE, JEAN
   Selected Poems (93) 715
GARRISON, DEBORAH
   Working Girl Can't Win, A (99) 868
GARROW, DAVID J.
   Bearing the Cross (87) 55
GARSIDE, ROGER
   Coming Alive (82) 111
GASS, WILLIAM HOWARD
   Habitations of the Word (86) 376
   On Being Blue (77) 594
   Tests of Time (03) 825
   Tunnel, The (96) 782
   World Within the Word, The (79) 913
GATES, DAVID
   Wonders of the Invisible World, The (00) 859
GATES, HENRY LOUIS, JR.
   Colored People (95) 141
   Loose Canons (93) 483
   Trials of Phillis Wheatley, The (04) 774
GATES, JOHN D.
   Du Pont Family, The (80) 240
GATHORNE-HARDY, JONATHAN
   Gerald Brenan (94) 350
GATRELL, SIMON
   Hardy the Creator (90) 348
   Thomas Hardy and the Proper Study of Mankind
      (94) 793
GATZKE, HANS W.
   Germany and the United States (81) 368
GAUKROGER, STEPHEN
   Descartes (96) 170
GAVIN, JAMES
   Deep in a Dream (03) 192
GAY, PETER
   Art and Act (77) 67
   Bourgeois Experience, Victoria to Freud, Vol. I,
      The (H-85) 53
   Freud (89) 311
   Schnitzler's Century (02) 732
GEERAERTS, JEF
   Black Ulysses (79) 55
GEERTZ, CLIFFORD
   Works and Lives (89) 923
GEIST, BENJAMIN, and MICHAEL BRECHER
   Decisions in Crisis (81) 228
GELDERMAN, CAROL
   Mary McCarthy (89) 539
GELPI, ALBERT
   Coherent Splendor, A (89) 169
GENOVESE, EUGENE D.
   Southern Tradition, The (95) 748

GENTRY, CURT
   J. Edgar Hoover (92) 369
GEOGHEGAN, THOMAS
   Which Side Are You On? (92) 885
GERBER, MERRILL JOAN
   Honeymoon (86) 440
   King of the World (91) 489
GERSTLER, AMY
   Crown of Weeds (98) 216
   Nerve Storm (95) 535
GETZLER, ISRAEL
   Kronstadt, 1917-1921 (H-84) 271
GHISELIN, BREWSTER
   Windrose (81) 935
GHOSH, AMITAV
   Glass Palace, The (02) 342
GIBBONS, KAYE
   Ellen Foster (88) 261
   On the Occasion of My Last Afternoon (99) 584
   Sights Unseen (96) 712
GIBBONS, REGINALD, editor
   Poet's Work (80) 668
GIBSON, IAN
   Federico García Lorca (90) 245
GIBSON, WILLIAM
   All Tomorrow's Parties (00) 6
   Pattern Recognition (04) 610
   Virtual Light (94) 839
GIDDINS, GARY
   Bing Crosby (02) 88
GIFFORD, DON
   Farther Shore, The (91) 287
GILBERT, ELIZABETH
   Stern Men (01) 801
GILBERT, JACK
   Monolithos (83) 484
GILBERT, MARTIN
   Israel (99) 427
   Second World War, The (90) 716
   Winston S. Churchill, 1922-1939 (78) 917
   Winston S. Churchill, 1939-1941 (H-85) 500
   Winston S. Churchill, 1941-1945 (87) 1001
   Winston S. Churchill, 1945-1965 (89) 913
GILBERT, SANDRA M., and SUSAN GUBAR
   Madwoman in the Attic, The (80) 512
   No Man's Land, Letters from the Front (95) 549
   No Man's Land, Sexchanges (90) 614
   No Man's Land, The War of the Words (89) 600
GILCHRIST, ELLEN
   Cabal and Other Stories, The (01) 168
   Victory over Japan (85) 973
GILDER, GEORGE
   Microcosm (90) 568
GILDNER, GARY
   Runner, The (79) 613
GILL, BRENDAN
   Many Masks (88) 534
GILL, STEPHEN
   William Wordsworth (90) 904
GILLIATT, PENELOPE
   Woman of Singular Occupation, A (90) 912
GILLIGAN, CAROL, and LYN MIKEL BROWN
   Meeting at the Crossroads (93) 500
GILMAN, RICHARD
   Decadence (80) 210
   Faith, Sex, Mystery (88) 303

GILMAN, SANDER L.
    Jewish Self-Hatred (87) 440
GILMAN, SANDER L., editor
    Conversations with Nietzsche (88) 199
GILMOUR, DAVID
    Last Leopard, The (92) 413
GILROY, PAUL
    Against Race (01) 10
GINSBERG, ALLEN
    Collected Poems, 1947-1980 (85) 110
    Cosmopolitan Greetings (95) 152
    Journals (78) 483
    Selected Poems 1947-1995 (97) 737
    White Shroud (87) 974
GINZBURG, EUGENIA SEMENOVA
    Within the Whirlwind (82) 963
GINZBURG, NATALIA
    Family Sayings (85) 255
GIRARD, RENÉ
    Scapegoat, The (87) 744
    Theater of Envy, A (92) 809
GITELSON, CELIA
    Biography (92) 48
GITLIN, TODD
    Media Unlimited (03) 523
GITTINGS, ROBERT and JO MANTON
    Claire Clairmont and the Shelleys (93) 157
GIVNER, JOAN
    Katherine Anne Porter (83) 376
GLADWELL, MALCOLM
    Tipping Point, The (01) 835
GLANCY, DIANE
    Flutie (99) 291
GLATTHAAR, JOSEPH T.
    Partners in Command (95) 599
GLEICK, JAMES
    Chaos (88) 132
    Faster (00) 252
    Genius (93) 308
    Isaac Newton (04) 369
GLENDINNING, VICTORIA
    Anthony Trollope (94) 29
    Edith Sitwell (82) 190
    Elizabeth Bowen (79) 179
    Jonathan Swift (00) 448
    Rebecca West (88) 732
    Vita (84) 916
GLENDON, MARY ANN
    World Made New, A (02) 884
GLENN, JOHN, with NICK TAYLOR
    John Glenn (00) 443
GLENNY, MISHA
    Balkans, The (01) 59
GLINSKY, ALBERT
    Theremin (01) 815
GLOSS, MOLLY
    Wild Life (01) 920
GLÜCK, LOUISE
    Ararat (91) 51
    ·Meadowlands (97) 564
    Seven Ages, The (02) 742
    Triumph of Achilles, The (86) 908
    Vita Nova (00) 797
GLYNN, THOMAS
    Building, The (87) 90

GODDEN, RUMER
    Five for Sorrow, Ten for Joy (80) 325
    House with Four Rooms, A (90) 396
    Peacock Spring, The (77) 614
    Time to Dance, No Time to Weep, A (89) 835
GODFREY, REBECCA
    Torn Skirt, The (03) 839
GODWIN, GAIL
    Evensong (00) 244
    Father Melancholy's Daughter (92) 201
    Finishing School, The (86) 274
    Good Husband, The (95) 275
    Mother and Two Daughters, A (83) 501
    Mr. Bedford and the Muses (84) 556
    Southern Family, A (88) 845
GOEBBELS, JOSEPH
    Final Entries, 1945 (79) 212
    Goebbels Diaries, The (H-84) 176
GOLAN, MATTI
    Secret Conversations of Henry Kissinger, The
        (77) 709
GOLD, GLEN DAVID
    Carter Beats the Devil (02) 140
GOLD, HERBERT
    Family (82) 267
    He/She (81) 426
GOLDBARTH, ALBERT
    Adventures in Egypt (98) 5
GOLDBARTH, ANDREW
    Combinations of the Universe (04) 134
GOLDBERG, MICHEL
    Namesake (83) 518
GOLDBERG, MYLA
    Bee Season (01) 74
GOLDBERG, ROBERT ALAN
    Barry Goldwater (96) 60
GOLDEN, ARTHUR
    Memoirs of a Geisha (98) 558
GOLDENSOHN, LORRIE
    Elizabeth Bishop (92) 179
GOLDHAGEN, DANIEL JONAH
    Hitler's Willing Executioners (97) 405
GOLDING, WILLIAM
    Close Quarters (88) 155
    Darkness Visible (80) 184
    Double Tongue, The (96) 206
    Fire Down Below (90) 253
    Moving Target, A (83) 506
    Paper Men, The (85) 672
    Rites of Passage (81) 690
GOLDMAN, MARSHALL I.
    U.S.S.R. in Crisis (H-84) 472
GOLDSMITH, BARBARA
    Other Powers (99) 601
GOLDSTEIN, DONALD M., GORDON W. PRANGE,
    and KATHERINE V. DILLON
    Miracle at Midway (H-83) 288
    Pearl Harbor (86) 732
GOLDSTEIN, ROBERT J.
    Political Repression in Nineteenth Century Europe
        (H-84) 342
GOLDSTEIN, THOMAS
    Dawn of Modern Science (81) 219
GOLDWATER, BARRY M., and JACK CASSERLY
    Goldwater (89) 321
GOLLOB, HERMAN
    Me and Shakespeare (03) 518

AUTHOR INDEX

GOMBROWICZ, WITOLD
  Diary, 1953-1956 (89) 236
  Diary, 1957-1961 (90) 177
  Diary, 1961-1966 (94) 225
  Trans-Atlantyk (95) 791
GONCHAROV, SERGEI N., JOHN W. LEWIS, and
    XUE LITAI
  Uncertain Partners (95) 809
GONNE, MAUD, and WILLIAM BUTLER YEATS
  Gonne-Yeats Letters 1893-1938, The (94) 368
GONZÁLEZ, JUAN
  Harvest of Empire (01) 384
GOOCH, BRAD
  City Poet (94) 128
GOODALL, JANE
  Chimpanzees of Gombe (87) 116
  Reason for Hope (00) 643
GOODMAN, ALLEGRA
  Paradise Park (02) 622
GOODMAN, CHARLOTTE MARGOLIS
  Jean Stafford (91) 471
GOODWIN, DORIS KEARNS
  Fitzgeralds and the Kennedys, The (88) 323
  Lyndon Johnson and the American Dream (77) 465
  No Ordinary Time (95) 554
GOODWIN, JASON
  Lords of the Horizons (00) 501
GOODWIN, RICHARD N.
  Remembering America (89) 703
GORBACHEV, MIKHAIL
  Perestroika (88) 677
GORDIMER, NADINE
  Burger's Daughter (80) 123
  House Gun, The (99) 387
  July's People (82) 417
  Jump (92) 398
  My Son's Story (91) 619
  None to Accompany Me (95) 564
  Pickup, The (02) 636
  Selected Stories (77) 725
  Soldier's Embrace, A (81) 745
  Something Out There (85) 844
  Sport of Nature, A (88) 850
  Writing and Being (96) 839
GORDON, CAROLINE
  Collected Stories of Caroline Gordon, The
    (82) 106
GORDON, LYNDALL
  Charlotte Brontë (96) 94
  Eliot's New Life (89) 262
  T. S. Eliot (00) 737
  Virginia Woolf (86) 927
GORDON, MARY
  Company of Women, The (82) 115
  Final Payments (79) 218
  Good Boys and Dead Girls (92) 256
  Joan of Arc (01) 485
  Men and Angels (86) 589
  Other Side, The (90) 647
  Rest of Life, The (94) 701
  Shadow Man, The (97) 749
GORDON, SUZANNE
  Lonely in America (77) 445
GORDON, W. TERRENCE
  Marshall McLuhan (98) 542
GORN, ELLIOTT J.
  Mother Jones (02) 546

GORNICK, VIVIAN
  Essays in Feminism (80) 302
  Situation and the Story, The (02) 752
GOSNELL, HAROLD F.
  Truman's Crises (81) 836
GOTTFRIED, ROBERT S.
  Black Death, The (H-84) 68
GOULD, STEPHEN JAY
  Bully for Brontosaurus (92) 69
  Dinosaur in a Haystack (97) 219
  Full House (97) 323
  Hen's Teeth and Horse's Toes (H-84) 190
  I Have Landed (03) 384
  Mismeasure of Man, The (82) 527
  Panda's Thumb, The (81) 640
  Questioning the Millennium (98) 652
  Rocks of Ages (00) 656
  Structure of Evolutionary Theory, The (03) 815
  Time's Arrow, Time's Cycle (88) 902
  Wonderful Life (90) 916
GOYEN, WILLIAM
  Had I a Hundred Mouths (86) 386
GRADE, CHAIM
  Rabbis and Wives (83) 630
GRAFTON, ANTHONY
  Footnote, The (98) 317
GRAHAM, JORIE
  Erosion (84) 279
  Errancy, The (98) 286
GRAHAM, KATHARINE
  Personal History (98) 629
GRAHAM, PETER W.
  Don Juan and Regency England (91) 227
GRAHAM, PHILIP
  How to Read an Unwritten Language (96) 347
GRAHAM-CAMPBELL, JAMES
  Viking World, The (81) 873
GRANT, JUDITH SKELTON
  Robertson Davies (96) 660
GRASS, GÜNTER
  Crabwalk (04) 138
  Flounder, The (79) 226
  Headbirths (83) 336
  Meeting at Telgte, The (82) 523
  On Writing and Politics (86) 695
GRAU, SHIRLEY ANN
  Roadwalkers (95) 656
GRAVES, RICHARD PERCEVAL
  Robert Graves, 1895-1926 (88) 770
  Robert Graves, 1926-1940 (91) 706
GRAY, ALASDAIR
  Book of Prefaces, The (01) 126
GRAY, FRANCINE DU PLESSIX
  Lovers and Tyrants (77) 455
GRAY, JOHN
  Isaiah Berlin (97) 466
GRAY, ROCKWELL
  Imperative of Modernity, The (90) 410
GRAY, WALLACE
  Homer to Joyce (86) 435
GREALY, LUCY
  Autobiography of a Face (95) 56
GREELEY, ANDREW
  Catholic Imagination, The (01) 176
GREEN, GEORGE DAWES
  Caveman's Valentine, The (95) 109

GREEN, HANNAH
Little Saint (01) 540
GREEN, JULIEN
God's Fool (86) 354
GREEN, MARTIN
Children of the Sun (77) 144
Tolstoy and Gandhi, Men of Peace
(H-84) 447
Transatlantic Patterns (78) 860
GREEN, PETER
Alexander to Actium (91) 15
GREENBERG, JOANNE
Of Such Small Differences (89) 616
GREENBLATT, STEPHEN
Hamlet in Purgatory (02) 376
GREENE, BRIAN
Elegant Universe, The (00) 208
GREENE, GRAHAM
Captain and the Enemy, The (89) 140
Doctor Fischer of Geneva or the Bomb Party
(81) 244
Getting to Know the General (H-85) 168
Human Factor, The (79) 286
Monsignor Quixote (83) 489
Ways of Escape (82) 918
World of My Own, A (95) 890
GREENE, GRAHAM, and MARIE-FRANÇOISE
ALLAIN
Other Man, The (84) 651
GREENE, MELISSA FAY
Praying for Sheetrock (92) 636
GREENSTEIN, FRED I.
Hidden-Hand Presidency, The (H-83) 190
GREER, GERMAINE
Change, The (93) 148
Obstacle Race, The (80) 600
Sex and Destiny (H-85) 406
Whole Woman, The (00) 834
GREGERSON, LINDA
Waterborne (03) 867
GREIDER, WILLIAM
One World, Ready or Not (98) 612
Secrets of the Temple (89) 766
GRIBBIN, JOHN, and MICHAEL WHITE
Stephen Hawking (93) 758
GRIFFIN, MIRIAM TAMARA
Nero (86) 650
GRIFFIN, PETER
Along with Youth (86) 16
GRIFFITH, ELISABETH
In Her Own Right (H-85) 230
GRIFFITHS, TREVOR
Comedians (77) 174
GRIGG, JOHN
1943 (81) 619
GRIMES, MARTHA
Foul Matter (04) 271
GRISHAM, JOHN
King of Torts, The (04) 417
Painted House, A (02) 618
Testament, The (00) 749
GROSS, PAUL R., and NORMAN LEVITT
Higher Superstition (95) 301
GROSSER, ALFRED
Western Alliance, The (81) 911

GROSSKURTH, PHYLLIS
Byron (98) 142
Havelock Ellis (81) 412
GROSSMAN, DAVID
Yellow Wind, The (89) 928
GROSSMAN, JUDITH
Her Own Terms (89) 345
GROSSMAN, VASILY
Life and Fate (87) 483
GRUNFELD, FREDERIC V.
Rodin (88) 780
GUBAR, SUSAN, and SANDRA M. GILBERT
Madwoman in the Attic, The (80) 512
No Man's Land, Letters from the Front
(95) 549
No Man's Land, Sexchanges (90) 614
No Man's Land, The War of the Words
(89) 600
GUERARD, ALBERT J.
Triumph of the Novel, The (77) 847
GUEST, BARBARA
Herself Defined (85) 374
Miniatures, and Other Poems (03) 536
GUEST, JUDITH
Ordinary People (77) 597
GUGLIOTTA, GUY, and JEFF LEEN
Kings of Cocaine (90) 490
GUILLERMAZ, JACQUES
Chinese Communist Party in Power, 1949-1976,
The (78) 174
GUINIER, LANI
Tyranny of the Majority, The (95) 805
GUINNESS, ALEC
Blessings in Disguise (87) 71
GUNN, THOM
Boss Cupid (01) 135
Man with Night Sweats, The (93) 495
Selected Poems, 1950-1975 (80) 750
GUPTE, PRANAY
Crowded Earth, The (H-85) 94
GURGANUS, ALLAN
Oldest Living Confederate Widow Tells All
(90) 633
GURR, ANDREW
Playgoing in Shakespeare's London (88) 696
GUSSOW, MEL
Edward Albee (00) 199
GUSTAFSSON, LARS
Sigismund (86) 816
Tennis Players, The (84) 866
GUTERSON, DAVID
East of the Mountains (00) 190
Our Lady of the Forest (04) 592
Snow Falling on Cedars (95) 729
GUTMAN, HERBERT G.
Black Family in Slavery and Freedom, 1750-1925,
The (77) 87

H. D.
End to Torment (80) 290
Gift, The (83) 278
HERmione (82) 349
HA JIN
Bridegroom, The (01) 144
HABEGGER, ALFRED
My Wars Are Laid Away in Books (02) 562

AUTHOR INDEX

HACKER, ANDREW
  Money (98) 562
HACKER, MARILYN
  Squares and Courtyards (01) 796
HACKING, IAN
  Rewriting the Soul (96) 637
HADDA, JANET
  Isaac Bashevis Singer (98) 449
HADFIELD, ALICE MARY
  Charles Williams (84) 153
HAFFENDEN, JOHN
  Life of John Berryman, The (83) 410
HAFFNER, SEBASTIAN
  Meaning of Hitler, The (80) 528
HAGEDORN, JESSICA
  Dogeaters (91) 221
HAGER, THOMAS
  Force of Nature (96) 286
HAGERTY, JAMES C.
  Diary of James C. Hagerty, The (H-84) 125
HÄGG, TOMAS
  Novel in Antiquity, The (84) 618
HAHN, KIMIKO
  Mosquito and Ant (00) 533
  Unbearable Heart, The (97) 843
HAILE, H. G.
  Luther (81) 535
HAILEY, KENDALL
  Day I Became an Autodidact, The (89) 222
HAINES, JOHN
  News from the Glacier (83) 527
  Owl in the Mask of the Dreamer, The (94) 598
HALBERSTAM, DAVID
  Children, The (99) 163
  Fifties, The (94) 292
  War in a Time of Peace (02) 834
  Playing for Keeps (00) 618
  Powers That Be, The (80) 684
  Reckoning, The (87) 695
  Summer of '49 (90) 777
  Teammates, The (04) 731
HALEY, ALEX
  Roots (77) 690
HALL, BRIAN
  I Should Be Extremely Happy in Your Company
    (04) 352
  Saskiad, The (98) 698
HALL, DAVID D.
  Worlds of Wonder, Days of Judgment (90) 925
HALL, DONALD
  Museum of Clear Ideas, The (94) 543
  Remembering Poets (79) 584
HALL, N. JOHN
  Trollope (92) 825
HALL, OAKLEY
  Bad Lands, The (79) 47
HALLE, LOUIS J.
  Out of Chaos (78) 627
HALLINAN, JOSEPH T.
  Going Up the River (02) 352
HALLIWELL, STEPHEN
  Poetics of Aristotle, The (88) 706
HALPERIN, JOHN
  Gissing (83) 283
  Life of Jane Austen, The (85) 564

HALPERN, SUE
  Migrations to Solitude (93) 513
HAMALIAN, LINDA
  Life of Kenneth Rexroth, A (92) 426
HAMER, DEAN, and PETER COPELAND
  Living with Our Genes (99) 483
HAMEROW, THEODORE S.
  Birth of a New Europe, The (H-84) 61
HAMILTON, IAN
  In Search of J. D. Salinger (89) 373
  Robert Lowell (83) 654
HAMILTON, JANE
  Disobedience (01) 242
  Map of the World, A (95) 460
  Short History of a Prince, The (99) 706
HAMILTON, NIGEL
  Brothers Mann, The (80) 119
  JFK (93) 408
  Monty (82) 531
HAMILTON, RICHARD F.
  Who Voted for Hitler? (H-83) 462
HAMILTON-PATERSON, JAMES
  Great Deep, The (93) 312
  Ghosts of Manila (95) 267
  Loving Monsters (03) 504
HAMRICK, S. J. *See* TYLER, W. T.
HAND, ELIZABETH
  Glimmering (98) 348
HANDKE, PETER
  Across (87) 6
  Afternoon of a Writer, The (90) 14
  Left-Handed Woman, The (79) 363
  Moment of True Feeling, A (78) 585
  On a Dark Night I Left My Silent House (01) 665
  Once Again for Thucydides (99) 589
  Repetition (89) 713
  Slow Homecoming (86) 830
  Weight of the World, The (85) 1013
HANDLIN, LILLIAN
  George Bancroft (H-85) 162
HANDLIN, OSCAR, and LILIAN HANDLIN
  Restless People, A (H-83) 366
HANKLA, CATHRYN
  Phenomena (84) 686
HANNAH, BARRY
  Airships (79) 5
  Hey Jack! (88) 382
  Ray (81) 674
  Yonder Stands Your Orphan (02) 894
HANSEN, BROOKS
  Chess Garden, The (96) 98
HANSEN, RON
  Assassination of Jesse James by the Coward Robert
    Ford, The (84) 54
  Hitler's Niece (00) 391
HARDWICK, ELIZABETH
  Bartleby in Manhattan (84) 82
  Sleepless Nights (80) 768
HARDY, BARBARA
  Advantage of Lyric, The (78) 11
HARJO, JOY
  How We Became Human (03) 379
  Woman Who Fell from the Sky, The (96) 822
HARMAN, CLAIRE
  Fanny Burney (02) 275
HARPER, MICHAEL S.
  Songlines in Michaeltree (01) 782

HARR, JONATHAN
   Civil Action, A (96) 116
HARRINGTON, ANNE
   Medicine, Mind, and the Double Brain (88) 539
HARRINGTON, MICHAEL
   Twilight of Capitalism, The (77) 857
HARRIS, ALEX, editor
   World Unsuspected, A (88) 984
HARRIS, KENNETH
   Attlee (H-84) 33
HARRIS, MACDONALD
   Hemingway's Suitcase (91) 390
   Yukiko (78) 942
HARRIS, MARVIN
   Cultural Materialism (80) 170
HARRIS, RICHARD
   Freedom Spent (77) 304
HARRISON, BARBARA GRIZZUTI
   Accidental Autobiography, An (97) 1
   Italian Days (90) 441
HARRISON, DAVID
   White Tribe of Africa, The (H-83) 459
HARRISON, EDWARD
   Darkness at Night (88) 233
HARRISON, GILBERT A.
   Enthusiast, The (84) 272
HARRISON, GORDON
   Mosquitoes, Malaria and Man (79) 466
HARRISON, JIM
   Dalva (89) 212
   Julip (95) 413
   Legends of the Fall (80) 462
   Selected & New Poems (83) 718
HARRISON, TONY
   Selected Poems (88) 812
HART, HENRY
   James Dickey (01) 475
HART, JOHN MASON
   Revolutionary Mexico (89) 717
HARTRICH, EDWIN
   Fourth and Richest Reich, The (81) 353
HARUF, KENT
   Plainsong (00) 614
HARVEY, NANCY LENZ
   Thomas Cardinal Wolsey (81) 800
HARWIT, MARTIN
   Cosmic Discovery (82) 135
HASAN-ROKEM, GALIT, and DAVID SHULMAN,
   editors
   Untying the Knot (97) 862
HASLIP, JOAN
   Catherine the Great (78) 155
HASS, ROBERT
   Twentieth Century Pleasures (85) 941
HASSLER, JON
   Love Hunter, The (82) 499
HASTINGS, MAX
   Korean War, The (88) 447
   Overlord (H-85) 349
HASTINGS, MAX, and SIMON JENKINS
   Battle for the Falklands, The (H-84) 43
HASTINGS, SELINA
   Evelyn Waugh (96) 237
HATCH, JAMES V.
   Sorrow Is the Only Faithful One (94) 755

HATTAWAY, HERMAN, RICHARD E. BERINGER,
   ARCHER JONES, and WILLIAM N. STILL, JR.
   Why the South Lost the Civil War (87) 980
HAUGH, RICHARD S., MICHAEL NICHOLSON, and
   JOHN B. DUNLOP
   Solzhenitsyn in Exile (86) 843
HAVEL, VÁCLAV
   Disturbing the Peace (91) 216
   Letters to Olga (89) 492
HAVELOCK, ERIC A.
   Muse Learns to Write, The (87) 590
HAVENS, THOMAS R. H.
   Valley of Darkness (79) 804
HAWKE, DAVID FREEMAN
   John D. (81) 459
HAWKES, JOHN
   Passion Artist, The (80) 644
   Travesty (77) 837
HAWKING, STEPHEN W.
   Black Holes and Baby Universes and Other Essays
     (94) 94
   Brief History of Time, A (89) 121
   Universe in a Nutshell, The (02) 818
HAYDEN, ROBERT
   Angle of Ascent (77) 48
   Collected Poems (86) 152
HAYMAN, RONALD
   Brecht (84) 118
   Kafka (83) 372
HAYNES, JOHN EARL, and HARVEY KLEHR
   Venona (00) 784
HAYNES, JOHN EARL, HARVEY KLEHR, and
   FRIDRIKH IGOREVICH FIRSOV, editors
   Secret World of American Communism, The
     (96) 685
HAYNES, STEPHEN R.
   Noah's Curse (03) 594
HAYSLIP, LE LY, with JAY WURTS
   When Heaven and Earth Changed Places (90) 879
HAYWARD, MAX
   Writers in Russia (84) 977
HAZZARD, SHIRLEY
   Great Fire, The (04) 308
   Transit of Venus, The (81) 822
HEALY, DAVID
   Creation of Psychopharmacology, The (03) 172
HEANEY, SEAMUS
   Beowulf (01) 89
   Electric Light (02) 240
   Field Work (80) 315
   Government of the Tongue, The (90) 319
   Opened Ground (99) 597
   Redress of Poetry, The (96) 624
   Seeing Things (92) 737
   Spirit Level, The (97) 777
   Station Island (85) 865
HEARON, SHELBY
   Footprints (97) 292
HEAT-MOON, WILLIAM LEAST
   Blue Highways (84) 95
   PrairyErth (92) 632
HÉBERT, ANNE
   In the Shadow of the Wind (85) 436

AUTHOR INDEX

HECHT, ANTHONY
  Hidden Law, The (94) 389
  Millions of Strange Shadows (78) 572
  Transparent Man, The (91) 825
  Venetian Vespers, The (80) 841
HECHT, JULIE
  Do the Windows Open? (98) 259
HECKMANN, WOLF
  Rommel's War in Africa (82) 700
HECKSCHER, AUGUST
  Woodrow Wilson (92) 914
HEDRICK, JOAN D.
  Harriet Beecher Stowe (95) 296
HEGI, URSULA
  Vision of Emma Blau, The (01) 877
HEILBUT, ANTHONY
  Exiled in Paradise (84) 284
HEINEMANN, LARRY
  Paco's Story (88) 651
HEINLEIN, ROBERT A.
  Cat Who Walks Through Walls, The (86) 100
  Grumbles from the Grave (91) 372
HEINRICH, BERND
  Winter World (04) 843
HELLER, ERICH
  In the Age of Prose (85) 431
HELLER, JOSEPH
  Closing Time (95) 128
  Good as Gold (80) 372
HELLER, MARK A.
  Palestinian State, A (H-84) 326
HELLMAN, LILLIAN
  Scoundrel Time (77) 702
HELPRIN, MARK
  Ellis Island and Other Stories (82) 219
  Soldier of the Great War, A (92) 770
  Winter's Tale (84) 954
HEMINGWAY, ERNEST
  Ernest Hemingway Selected Letters, 1917-1961
    (82) 245
  Garden of Eden, The (87) 313
  True at First Light (00) 768
HEMINGWAY, MARY WELSH
  How It Was (77) 362
HEMMINGS, F. W. J.
  Baudelaire the Damned (83) 49
HEMON, ALEKSANDAR
  Nowhere Man (03) 598
  Question of Bruno, The (01) 725
HEMPEL, AMY
  Tumble Home (98) 778
HENDERSON, BILL, editor
  Pushcart Prize, III, The (79) 565
HENDERSON, GREIG E.
  Kenneth Burke (90) 478
HENDRICKSON, DAVID C., and ROBERT W.
  TUCKER
  Empire of Liberty (91) 253
HENDRICKSON, PAUL
  Sons of Mississippi (04) 709
HENDRICKSON, ROBERTA
  Rise and Fall of Alexander Hamilton, The
    (82) 687
HENIG, ROBIN MARANTZ
  Monk in the Garden, The (01) 588

HENLEY, BETH
  Crimes of the Heart (83) 165
HENNESSEE, JUDITH
  Betty Friedan (00) 53
HENRY, ELISABETH
  Vigour of Prophecy, The (91) 847
HENSON, ROBERT
  Transports and Disgraces (81) 827
HENTOFF, NAT
  Boston Boy (87) 84
  Speaking Freely (98) 717
HERBERT, FRANK
  Children of Dune (77) 139
  God Emperor of Dune (82) 329
  White Plague, The (83) 900
HERBERT, ZBIGNIEW
  Elegy for the Departure and Other Poems (00) 217
  King of the Ants, The (00) 462
  Mr. Cogito (94) 530
  Still Life with a Bridle (92) 785
HERINGTON, JOHN
  Poetry into Drama (86) 742
HERM, GERHARD
  Celts, The (78) 164
HERMAN, ARTHUR
  Idea of Decline in Western History, The (98) 415
HERNÁNDEZ, FELISBERTO
  Lands of Memory (03) 451
HERR, MICHAEL
  Dispatches (78) 272
HERRING, PHILLIP
  Djuna (96) 194
HERRIOT, JAMES
  Lord God Made Them All, The (82) 480
HERRNSTEIN, RICHARD J., and CHARLES
  MURRAY
  Bell Curve, The (95) 70
HERSEY, JOHN
  Call, The (86) 91
  Walnut Door, The (78) 883
HERSH, SEYMOUR M.
  Dark Side of Camelot, The (98) 225
  Price of Power, The (H-84) 361
  "Target Is Destroyed, The" (87) 841
HERTZBERG, ARTHUR, and ARON
  HIRT-MANHEIMER
  Jews (99) 436
HERZSTEIN, ROBERT EDWIN
  War That Hitler Won, The (79) 823
HESSION, CHARLES H.
  John Maynard Keynes (H-85) 250
HEYMANN, C. DAVID
  Ezra Pound (77) 264
HIBBERT, CHRISTOPHER
  Africa Explored (H-84) 6
  Days of the French Revolution, The (81) 222
HICKEY, DES, and GUS SMITH
  Seven Days to Disaster (H-83) 387
HICKEY, DONALD R.
  War of 1812, The (90) 859
HIGGINS, AIDAN
  Flotsam and Jetsam (03) 307
HIGGINS, GEORGE V.
  Change of Gravity, A (98) 164
  Defending Billy Ryan (93) 214

HIGHAM, CHARLES
    Adventures of Conan Doyle, The (77) 22
    Trading with the Enemy (H-84) 457
HIGHWATER, JAMAKE
    Anpao (78) 63
    Journey to the Sky (79) 335
HIJUELOS, OSCAR
    Empress of the Splendid Season (00) 221
    Fourteen Sisters of Emilio Montez O'Brien, The
      (94) 308
    Mambo Kings Play Songs of Love, The (90) 553
    Mr. Ives' Christmas (96) 461
    Simple Habana Melody, A (03) 746
HILBERG, RAUL
    Perpetrators, Victims, Bystanders (93) 624
HILDESHEIMER, WOLFGANG
    Marbot (84) 498
HILL, CHRISTOPHER
    Milton and the English Revolution (79) 444
    Tinker and a Poor Man, A (90) 814
HILL, GEOFFREY
    Canaan (98) 152
    Collected Poems (87) 146
    Enemy's Country (92) 188
    New and Collected Poems, 1952-1992 (95) 540
    Orchards of Syon, The (03) 606
    Somewhere Is Such a Kingdom (77) 758
    Style and Faith (04) 718
    Triumph of Love, The (99) 791
HILL, MELVYN A., editor
    Hannah Arendt (80) 395
HILL, ROBERT A., editor
    Marcus Garvey and Universal Negro Improvement
      Association Papers, The (H-85) 283
HILLENBRAND, LAURA
    Seabiscuit (02) 737
HILLERMAN, TONY
    Thief of Time, A (89) 830
HILLESUM, ETTY
    Interrupted Life, An (85) 456
HILLGRUBER, ANDREAS
    Germany and the Two World Wars (82) 321
HILTON, TIM
    John Ruskin, The Early Years (86) 487
    John Ruskin, The Later Years (01) 499
HIMMELFARB, GERTRUDE
    Idea of Poverty, The (H-85) 219
    Marriage and Morals Among the Victorians
      (87) 525
    Poverty and Compassion (92) 627
HINEY, TOM
    Raymond Chandler (98) 665
HING, BILL ONG
    To Be an American (98) 765
HINGLEY, RONALD
    New Life of Anton Chekhov, A (77) 543
    Nightingale Fever (82) 555
    Pasternak (84) 673
HINSEY, ELLEN
    Cities of Memory (97) 152
HIRSCH, E. D., JR.
    Cultural Literacy (88) 223
HIRSCH, EDWARD
    Demon and the Angel, The (03) 197
    Lay Back the Darkness (04) 438
    On Love (99) 580

HIRT-MANHEIMER, ARON, and ARTHUR
  HERTZBERG
    Jews (99) 436
HISS, TONY
    Experience of Place, The (91) 275
HOAGLAND, EDWARD
    Balancing Acts (93) 45
    Edward Hoagland Reader, The (80) 260
    Red Wolves and Black Bears (77) 658
    Seven Rivers West (87) 760
    Tugman's Passage, The (83) 836
HOARE, PHILIP
    Noël Coward (97) 630
HOBAN, RUSSELL
    Turtle Diary (77) 852
HOBART, MICHAEL E., and ZACHARY S.
  SCHIFFMAN
    Information Ages (99) 414
HOBHOUSE, JANET
    Furies, The (94) 321
HOBSBAWM, ERIC
    Age of Empire, The (89) 14
HOBSON, FRED
    Mencken (95) 477
HODGSON, RUSSELL
    Lloyd's of London (H-85) 262
HØEG, PETER
    Smilla's Sense of Snow (94) 747
    Woman and the Ape, The (97) 890
HOFF, JOAN, and MARIAN YEATES
    Cooper's Wife Is Missing, The (01) 218
HOFFER, PETER CHARLES
    Revolution and Regeneration (H-84) 376
HOFFMAN, ALICE
    Local Girls (00) 497
    Second Nature (95) 701
    Turtle Moon (93) 820
HOFFMAN, DANIEL
    Beyond Silence (04) 83
    Hang-Gliding from Helicon (89) 340
HOFFMAN, EVA
    Lost in Translation (90) 539
HOFFMAN, IAN, and DAN STOBER
    Convenient Spy, A (03) 164
HOFFMAN, PAUL
    Man Who Loved Only Numbers, The (99) 515
HOFFMANN, PETER
    History of the German Resistance, 1933-1945, The
      (78) 388
HOFFMANN, STANLEY
    Primacy or World Order (79) 551
HOFLING, CHARLES K.
    Custer and the Little Big Horn (82) 161
HOFSTADTER, DOUGLAS R.
    Fluid Concepts and Creative Analogies (96) 277
    Gödel, Escher, Bach (80) 367
    Le Ton Beau de Marot (98) 495
HÖHNE, HEINZ
    Canaris (80) 124
HOLBROOKE, RICHARD, with CLARK CLIFFORD
    Counsel to the President (92) 123
HOLDEN, CRAIG
    River Sorrow, The (95) 652
HOLDEN, DAVID, and RICHARD JOHNS
    House of Saud, The (H-83) 195

AUTHOR INDEX

HOLLANDER, JOHN
  Blue Wine and Other Poems (80) 94
  Spectral Emanations (79) 699
HÖLLDOBLER, BERT, and EDWARD O. WILSON
  Ants, The (91) 47
HOLLERAN, ANDREW
  Beauty of Men, The (97) 100
HOLLINGHURST, ALAN
  Folding Star, The (95) 244
HOLLOWAY, DAVID
  Soviet Union and the Arms Race, The (H-84) 414
HOLMES, RICHARD
  Coleridge, Darker Reflections (00) 138
  Coleridge, Early Visions (91) 147
  Dr. Johnson and Mr. Savage (95) 176
  Footsteps (86) 297
HOLQUIST, MICHAEL, and KATERINA CLARK
  Mikhail Bakhtin (86) 608
HOLROYD, MICHAEL
  Basil Street Blues (01) 64
  Bernard Shaw, 1856-1898 (89) 89
  Bernard Shaw, 1898-1918 (90) 63
  Bernard Shaw, 1918-1950 (92) 34
  Bernard Shaw, 1950-1991 (94) 80
HOLST, SPENCER
  Spencer Holst Stories (77) 780
HOMER
  Odyssey, The (97) 640
HONAN, PARK
  Jane Austen (89) 409
  Matthew Arnold (82) 518
  Shakespeare (00) 702
HONGO, GARRETT
  River of Heaven, The (89) 741
  Volcano (96) 802
HONOUR, HUGH
  New Golden Land, The (77) 538
HOOD, ANN
  Ruby (99) 679
HOOK, SIDNEY
  Out of Step (88) 646
HOPCKE, ROBERT H.
  Guided Tour of the Collected Works of C. G. Jung, A (90) 343
HOPKINS, GERARD MANLEY
  Gerard Manley Hopkins, Selected Letters (91) 343
HORGAN, JOHN
  End of Science, The (97) 243
  Undiscovered Mind, The (00) 780
HORGAN, PAUL
  Of America East and West (H-85) 334
  Thin Mountain Air, The (78) 821
HORN, DARA
  In the Image (03) 415
HORNBY, NICK
  About a Boy (99) 1
HORNE, ALISTAIR
  Harold Macmillan, 1894-1956 (90) 352
  Harold Macmillan, 1957-1986 (90) 358
HOROWITZ, DAVID
  Radical Son (98) 661
HOROWITZ, DAVID, and PETER COLLIER
  Destructive Generation (90) 168
  Roosevelts, The (95) 664

HORWITZ, MORTON J.
  Transformation of American Law, 1870-1960, The (93) 805
HORWITZ, TONY
  Confederates in the Attic (99) 208
HOSSEINI, KHALED
  Kite Runner, The (04) 421
HOUELLEBECQ, MICHEL
  Elementary Particles, The (01) 267
HOUGH, RICHARD
  Mountbatten (82) 542
HOURANI, ALBERT
  History of the Arab Peoples, A (92) 299
HOWARD, DONALD R.
  Chaucer (88) 141
HOWARD, FRED
  Wilbur and Orville (88) 959
HOWARD, MAUREEN
  Big as Life (02) 83
  Grace Abounding (83) 296
  Natural History (93) 540
HOWARTH, DAVID
  Voyage of the Armada, The (82) 891
HOWATCH, SUSAN
  Absolute Truths (96) 1
HOWE, IRVING
  Celebrations and Attacks (80) 136
  Leon Trotsky (79) 368
  Margin of Hope, A (83) 451
  World of Our Fathers (77) 947
HOWE, MARIE
  What the Living Do (98) 832
HOWE, SUSAN
  Articulation of Sound Forms in Time (88) 63
  Birth-mark, The (94) 90
  Frame Structures (97) 311
  Nonconformist's Memorial, The (94) 568
HOWELL, ROGER, JR.
  Cromwell (78) 219
HOYT, EDWIN P.
  Closing the Circle (H-83) 75
  Improper Bostonian, The (80) 414
  Submarines at War (H-84) 430
  To the Marianas (81) 817
HRDY, SARAH BLAFFER
  Mother Nature (00) 538
HSÜ, IMMANUEL C. Y.
  China Without Mao (H-84) 87
HUDGINS, ANDREW
  After the Lost War (89) 9
  Ecstatic in the Poison (04) 207
  Saints and Strangers (86) 788
HUFF, ROBERT
  Ventriloquist, The (78) 873
HUGGAN, ISABEL
  Elizabeth Stories, The (88) 256
HUGHES, GLYN
  Rape of the Rose, The (94) 684
HUGHES, H. STUART
  Prisoners of Hope (84) 705
HUGHES, LANGSTON, and ARNA BONTEMPS
  Arna Bontemps-Langston Hughes Letters (81) 57

HUGHES, ROBERT
    American Visions (98) 59
    Barcelona (93) 49
    Culture of Complaint (94) 186
    Fatal Shore, The (88) 312
    Goya (04) 303
HUGHES, TED
    Birthday Letters (99) 109
    Moortown (81) 569
    River (85) 762
    Wolfwatching (92) 905
HUGO, RICHARD
    Making Certain It Goes On (85) 603
HULBERT, ANN
    Interior Castle, The (93) 386
    Raising America (04) 624
HULME, KERI
    Bone People, The (86) 72
HUMPHREY, WILLIAM
    Collected Stories of William Humphrey, The
    (86) 175
HUMPHREYS, DAVID, and GEORGE
WASHINGTON
    David Humphreys' "Life of General Washington"
    (92) 147
HUMPHREYS, JOSEPHINE
    Dreams of Sleep (85) 199
    Rich in Love (88) 759
HUMPHRIES, ROLFE
    Poets, Poetics, and Politics (93) 642
HUNT, GEORGE W.
    John Cheever (84) 389
HUNT, JOHN DIXON
    Wider Sea, The (83) 908
HUNTER, JANE
    Gospel of Gentility, The (H-85) 179
HUNTFORD, ROLAND
    Shackleton (87) 765
HURSTON, ZORA NEALE
    Zora Neale Hurston, Vol. I and Vol. II (96) 852
HUTTON, RONALD
    Charles the Second (91) 132
HUSTVEDT, SIRI
    What I Loved (04) 819
HUXLEY, ALDOUS
    Human Situation, The (78) 422
    Moksha (79) 451
HYDE, JOHN, and JOHN C. CULVER
    American Dreamer (01) 24
HYDE, LEWIS
    Gift, The (84) 330
    Trickster Makes This World (99) 787
HYLAND, WILLIAM G.
    Richard Rodgers (99) 658
HYNES, SAMUEL
    Growing Seasons, The (04) 312

IENAGA, SABURŌ
    Pacific War, The (79) 520
IGNATIEFF, MICHAEL
    Blood and Belonging (95) 89
IGNATOW, DAVID
    Against the Evidence (95) 10
    Tread the Dark (79) 777
    Whisper to the Earth (83) 894

ILLICH, IVAN D.
    Medical Nemesis (77) 489
INGALLS, RACHEL
    Binstead's Safari (89) 94
INGRAO, CHARLES W.
    In Quest and Crisis (80) 426
IONE, CAROLE
    Pride of Family (92) 641
IRELAND, TIMOTHY P.
    Creating the Entangling Alliance (82) 145
IRVING, DAVID
    Hitler's War (78) 398
    Trail of the Fox, The (78) 856
    War Path, The (79) 819
IRVING, DAVID, and THEODOR GILBERT
MORELL
    Secret Diaries of Hitler's Doctor, The (H-84) 398
IRVING, JOHN
    Cider House Rules, The (86) 131
    Fourth Hand, The (02) 305
    Hotel New Hampshire, The (82) 368
    Prayer for Owen Meany, A (90) 677
    Son of the Circus, A (95) 739
    Trying to Save Piggy Sneed (97) 838
    Widow for One Year, A (99) 859
    World According to Garp, The (79) 908
IRWIN, JOHN T.
    Mystery to a Solution, The (95) 519
ISAAC, RAEL JEAN, and VIRGINIA C. ARMAT
    Madness in the Streets (91) 558
ISAACSON, WALTER
    Benjamin Franklin (04) 70
    Kissinger (93) 426
ISHERWOOD, CHRISTOPHER
    Christopher and His Kind (77) 158
    Diaries (98) 249
ISHIGURO, KAZUO
    Remains of the Day, The (90) 690
    Unconsoled, The (96) 786
    When We Were Orphans (01) 900
ISKANDER, FAZIL
    Sandro of Chegem (84) 756
ISKANDER, FAZIL, et al., editors
    Metropol (84) 533
ISMAEL, TAREQ Y.
    Iraq and Iran (H-83) 216
ISRAEL, JONATHAN I.
    Radical Enlightenment (02) 679
ISSERMAN, MAURICE
    Other American, The (01) 689
ITAYA, KIKUO
    Tengu Child (84) 863

JABÈS, EDMOND
    Book of Questions, The (84) 108
JACKSON, BLYDEN
    History of Afro-American Literature, A (90) 382
JACKSON, DAVID K., and DWIGHT THOMAS
    Poe Log, The (88) 701
JACKSON, H. J.
    Marginalia (02) 507
JACKSON, HENRY F.
    From the Congo to Soweto (H-83) 155
JACKSON, JULIAN
    Fall of France, The (04) 244

AUTHOR INDEX

JACKSON, KENNETH T.
Crabgrass Frontier (87) 170

JACKSON, LAWRENCE
Ralph Ellison (03) 638

JACKSON, STANLEY
J. P. Morgan (H-84) 257

JACOB, FRANÇOIS
Statue Within, The (89) 813

JACOBS, ERIC
Kingsley Amis (99) 457

JACOBS, JANE
Cities and the Wealth of Nations (H-85) 83
Nature of Economies, The (01) 613

JACOBSEN, JOSEPHINE
Chinese Insomniacs, The (83) 110

JACOBSON, DAN
Time and Time Again (86) 883

JAKOBSON, ROMAN
Language in Literature (89) 450

JAMES, CLIVE
Unreliable Memoirs (82) 870

JAMES, D. CLAYTON
Years of MacArthur, 1945-64 (86) 980

JAMES, HENRY
Complete Notebooks of Henry James, The
(88) 179
Henry James Letters, 1883-1895 (81) 421
Henry James Letters, 1895-1916 (85) 368

JAMES, LAWRENCE
Rise and Fall of the British Empire, The (97) 696

JAMES, P. D.
Certain Justice, A (98) 160
Children of Men, The (94) 123
Death in Holy Orders (02) 185
Devices and Desires (91) 202
Murder Room, The (04) 524
Original Sin (96) 545
Time to Be in Earnest (01) 830

JAMES, ROBERT RHODES
British Revolution, 1880-1939, The (78) 145

JAMESON, FREDRIC
Brecht and Method (99) 127

JAMIESON, PERRY D., and GRADY McWHINEY
Attack and Die (H-83) 57

JANOS, LEO, and CHUCK YEAGER
Yeager (86) 974

JANOWITZ, TAMA
Slaves of New York (87) 784

JARRELL, RANDALL
No Other Book (00) 576
Randall Jarrell's Letters (86) 757

JEFFARES, A. NORMAN
W. B. Yeats (91) 876

JEFFERS, ROBINSON
Collected Poetry of Robinson Jeffers, 1920-1928,
The (89) 195
Collected Poetry of Robinson Jeffers, 1928-1938,
The (90) 122

JEN, GISH
Mona in the Promised Land (97) 595
Typical American (92) 840
Who's Irish? (00) 839

JENCKS, CHRISTOPHER
Rethinking Social Policy (93) 682

JENKINS, PHILIP
Next Christendom, The (03) 581

JENKINS, ROY
Gladstone (98) 344

JENKINS, SIMON, and MAX HASTINGS
Battle for the Falklands, The (H-84) 43

JENNINGS, FRANCIS
Ambiguous Iroquois Empire, The (H-85) 18
Empire of Fortune (89) 273

JENSEN, LIZ
Ark Baby (99) 64

JHA, RAJ KAMAL
Blue Bedspread, The (01) 108

JHABVALA, RUTH PRAWER
Heat and Dust (77) 352
Out of India (87) 626
Poet and Dancer (94) 645

JIN, HA
Crazed, The (03) 168
Waiting (00) 801

JOHANNSEN, ROBERT W.
To the Halls of the Montezumas (86) 887

JOHANSON, DONALD C., and MAITLAND A.
EDEY
Lucy (82) 514

JOHNS, ADRIAN
Nature of the Book, The (99) 547

JOHNS, RICHARD, and DAVID HOLDEN
House of Saud, The (H-83) 195

JOHNSON, CHARLES
Being and Race (89) 80
Dreamer (99) 242
Middle Passage (91) 591
Sorcerer's Apprentice, The (87) 795

JOHNSON, DAVID ALAN
Founding the Far West (93) 293

JOHNSON, DENIS
Already Dead (98) 23
Fiskadoro (86) 279
Jesus' Son (94) 427
Resuscitation of a Hanged Man (92) 679

JOHNSON, DIANE
Dashiell Hammett (84) 212
L'Affaire (04) 434
Le Divorce (98) 490
Le Mariage (01) 509
Persian Nights (88) 683
Terrorists and Novelists (83) 783

JOHNSON, ERIC A.
Nazi Terror (01) 618

JOHNSON, GEORGE
In the Palaces of Memory (92) 342

JOHNSON, JAMES WELDON
Selected Writings of James Weldon Johnson, Vol. I
and Vol. II, The (96) 694

JOHNSON, PAUL
Birth of the Modern, The (92) 52
History of the American People, A (99) 374
History of the Jews, A (88) 392
Modern Times (H-84) 306

JOHNSON, RONALD
Ark (97) 62

JOHNSON, SAMUEL
Letters of Samuel Johnson, The (93) 444

JOHNSON, WALTER
Soul by Soul (01) 787

JOHNSTON, KENNETH R.
Hidden Wordsworth, The (99) 364

1043

JOHNSTONE, ROBERT M., JR.
Jefferson and the Presidency (79) 331
JOLLEY, ELIZABETH
Foxybaby (86) 306
Well, The (87) 958
JONES, ARCHER
Civil War Command and Strategy (93) 153
JONES, ARCHER, RICHARD E. BERINGER,
HERMAN HATTAWAY, and WILLIAM N.
STILL, JR.
Why the South Lost the Civil War (87) 980
JONES, DAVID RICHARD
Great Directors at Work (87) 362
JONES, DOUGLAS C.
Arrest Sitting Bull (78) 72
JONES, EDWARD P.
Known World, The (04) 426
Lost in the City (93) 491
JONES, GAYL
Healing, The (99) 355
JONES, J. SYDNEY
Hitler in Vienna, 1907-1913 (H-84) 207
JONES, JAMES
Whistle (79) 843
JONES, LOUIS B.
California's Over (98) 147
Ordinary Money (91) 647
Particles and Luck (94) 611
JONES, MADISON
Last Things (91) 503
JONES, PRESTON
Texas Trilogy, A (77) 812
JONES, R. V.
Wizard War, The (79) 888
JONES, STANLEY
Hazlitt (91) 381
JONES, THOM
Cold Snap (96) 124
Pugilist at Rest, The (94) 676
Sonny Liston Was a Friend of Mine (00) 717
JONG, ERICA
Fanny (81) 309
How to Save Your Own Life (78) 413
JORDAN, HAMILTON
Crisis (H-83) 93
JORDAN, JUNE
Technical Difficulties (93) 779
Things That I Do in the Dark (78) 826
JOUANNA, JACQUES
Hippocrates (00) 381
JOWITT, KEN
New World Disorder (93) 559
JUDD, ALAN
Ford Madox Ford (92) 218
JUDIS, JOHN B.
William F. Buckley, Jr. (89) 908
JUDSON, HORACE FREELAND
Eighth Day of Creation, The (80) 273
JÜNGER, ERNST
Aladdin's Problem (93) 6
JUNGK, PETER STEPHAN
Franz Werfel (91) 313
JUST, WARD
American Ambassador, The (88) 20
Echo House (98) 277
Jack Gance (90) 445

KADARE, ISMAIL
General of the Dead Army, The (92) 242
KADOHATA, CYNTHIA
Floating World, The (90) 273
In the Heart of the Valley of Love (93) 374
KAEL, PAULINE
Reeling (77) 662
KAFKA, FRANZ
Letters to Friends, Family, and Editors (78) 526
Letters to Ottla and the Family (83) 401
KAGAN, DONALD
On the Origins of War and the Preservation of
Peace (96) 528
Peloponnesian War, The (04) 614
KAGAN, ROBERT
Of Paradise and Power (04) 565
KAHLO, FRIDA
Diary of Frida Kahlo, The (96) 182
KAHN, DAVID
Hitler's Spies (79) 281
KAHN, HERMAN, WILLIAM BROWN, and LEON
MARTEL
Next 200 Years, The (77) 559
KAISER, DAVID
American Tragedy (01) 39
KAISER, ROBERT G., and LEONARD DOWNIE, JR.
News About the News, The (03) 577
KALB, MADELEINE G.
Congo Cables, The (H-83) 80
KAMIN, LEON J., R. C. LEWONTIN, and STEVEN
ROSE
Not in Our Genes (H-85) 329
KAMINER, WENDY
Sleeping with Extra-Terrestrials (00) 712
Women Volunteering (H-85) 516
KAMMEN, MICHAEL
Machine That Would Go of Itself, A (87) 503
Mystic Chords of Memory (92) 545
KANFER, STEFAN
Ball of Fire (04) 49
Groucho (01) 370
KANIGEL, ROBERT
One Best Way, The (98) 607
KAPLAN, ALICE
Collaborator, The (01) 199
KAPLAN, BARRY JAY, and NICHOLAS MEYER
Black Orchid (78) 100
KAPLAN, FRED
Dickens (89) 241
Gore Vidal (00) 321
Henry James (93) 330
Thomas Carlyle (84) 869
KAPLAN, JONATHAN
Dressing Station, The (03) 238
KAPLAN, JUSTIN
Walt Whitman (81) 883
KAPLAN, ROBERT
Nothing That Is, The (00) 585
KAPLAN, ROBERT D.
Arabists, The (94) 42
Balkan Ghosts (94) 66
Coming Anarchy, The (01) 208
Empire Wilderness, An (99) 247
Ends of the Earth, The (97) 252
KAPUŚCIŃSKI, RYSZARD
Shah of Shahs (86) 811

AUTHOR INDEX

KARABELL, ZACHARY
Parting the Desert (04) 605

KARAS, THOMAS
New High Ground, The (H-84) 323

KARCHER, CAROLYN L.
First Woman in the Republic, The (96) 273

KARL, FREDERICK R.
American Fictions, 1940-1980 (84) 21
Franz Kafka (92) 227
Joseph Conrad (80) 449
William Faulkner (90) 899

KARLINSKY, SIMON
Marina Tsvetaeva (87) 520

KARNEZIS, PANOS
Little Infamies (04) 451

KARON, JAN
Out to Canaan (98) 620

KARR, MARY
Cherry (01) 181
Liar's Club, The (96) 426

KASS, LEON R.
Beginning of Wisdom, The (04) 66
Toward a More Natural Science (86) 892

KATER, MICHAEL H.
Nazi Party, The (H-84) 313

KATZ, JACOB
From Prejudice to Destruction (81) 362

KATZ, JON
Geeks (01) 323

KATZ, MICHAEL B.
Price of Citizenship, The (02) 655

KAUFFMAN, JANET
Collaborators (87) 127
Places in the World a Woman Could Walk
(85) 688

KAUFMAN, MICHAEL T.
Soros (03) 794

KAUS, MICKEY
End of Equality, The (93) 258

KAYSEN, SUSANNA
Girl, Interrupted (94) 360

KAZAN, ELIA
Elia Kazan (89) 257

KAZIN, ALFRED
American Procession, An (85) 12
God and the American Writer (98) 352
New York Jew (79) 475
Writing Was Everything (96) 843

KEANE, JOHN
Tom Paine (96) 760
Vaclav Havel (01) 863

KEARNS, DORIS. See GOODWIN, DORIS KEARNS

KEATES, JONATHAN
Stendhal (98) 726

KEEGAN, JOHN
Face of Battle, The (78) 305
First World War, The (00) 264
Second World War, The (91) 721
Six Armies in Normandy (H-83) 390

KEELEY, EDMUND
Modern Greek Poetry (85) 624

KEEN, MAURICE
Chivalry (H-85) 63

KEENE, DONALD
Dawn to the West (85) 157
Emperor of Japan (03) 255
Seeds in the Heart (94) 721
Travelers of a Hundred Years (90) 823

KEES, WELDON
Ceremony and Other Stories, The (85) 79

KEILLOR, GARRISON
Happy to Be Here (83) 326
Lake Wobegon Days (86) 500
Lake Wobegon Summer 1956 (02) 468
Leaving Home (88) 461
Love Me (04) 483
Wobegon Boy (98) 870

KEIZER, GARRET
Enigma of Anger, The (03) 265

KELLERMAN, FAYE
Stone Kiss (03) 807

KELLMAN, STEVEN G.
Translingual Imagination, The (01) 840

KELLY, LAURENCE
Lermontov (79) 373

KELLY, MICHAEL
Martyrs' Day (94) 516

KEMAL, YASHAR
They Burn the Thistles (78) 817
Undying Grass, The (79) 787

KEMP, ANTHONY
Maginot Line, The (H-83) 278

KEMP, MARTIN, and JANE ROBERTS, with PHILIP
STEADMAN
Leonardo da Vinci (90) 505

KEMPTON, MURRAY
Rebellions, Perversities, and Main Events (95) 635

KENAN, RANDALL
Let the Dead Bury Their Dead (93) 439
Walking on Water (00) 813

KENEALLY, THOMAS
American Scoundrel (03) 28
Family Madness, A (87) 265
Gossip from the Forest (77) 336
Great Shame, The (00) 336
Schindler's List (83) 684
To Asmara (90) 819
Woman of the Inner Sea (94) 860

KENNAN, GEORGE F.
Around the Cragged Hill (94) 52
At a Century's Ending (97) 71
Cloud of Danger, The (78) 183
Decline of Bismarck's European Order, The
(80) 215
Fateful Alliance, The (H-85) 135
Nuclear Delusion, The (H-83) 324
Sketches from a Life (90) 742

KENNEDY, A. L.
Everything You Need (02) 253
Original Bliss (00) 593
So I Am Glad (01) 778

KENNEDY, DENNIS
Looking at Shakespeare (94) 483

KENNEDY, EUGENE
Himself! (79) 273

KENNEDY, PAUL
Preparing for the Twenty-first Century (94) 658
Rise and Fall of the Great Powers, The (89) 735

KENNEDY, RANDALL
Nigger (03) 586

KENNEDY, ROBERT F.
  Robert Kennedy in His Own Words (89) 744
KENNEDY, ROGER G.
  Burr, Hamilton, and Jefferson (00) 112
KENNEDY, WILLIAM
  Roscoe (03) 681
KENNEDY, WILLIAM
  Flaming Corsage, The (97) 282
  Ironweed (84) 379
  Quinn's Book (89) 683
  Very Old Bones (93) 846
KENNEDY, X. J.
  Cross Ties (86) 199
KENNER, HUGH
  Chuck Jones (95) 119
  Colder Eye, A (84) 173
  Elsewhere Community, The (01) 272
  Historical Fictions (91) 400
  Joyce's Voices (79) 340
  Mechanic Muse, The (87) 536
  Sinking Island, A (89) 793
KENNEY, SUSAN
  In Another Country (85) 427
KENT, GEORGE E.
  Life of Gwendolyn Brooks, A (90) 526
KENYON, JANE
  Otherwise (97) 651
KEPEL, GILLES
  Jihad (03) 428
KER, IAN
  John Henry Newman (90) 459
KERMODE, FRANK
  Art of Telling, The (84) 49
  Shakespeare's Language (01) 769
KERMODE, FRANK, and ROBERT ALTER, editors
  Literary Guide to the Bible, The (88) 492
KERNAN, ALVIN
  Printing Technology, Letters, and Samuel Johnson
    (88) 710
KEROUAC, JACK
  Portable Jack Kerouac, The (96) 597
KERSAUDY, FRANÇOIS
  Churchill and de Gaulle (H-83) 70
KERSHAW, IAN
  Hitler, 1889-1936 (00) 386
KERT, BERNICE
  Hemingway Women, The (84) 337
KIBERD, DECLAN
  Inventing Ireland (97) 461
KIDDER, TRACY
  Among Schoolchildren (90) 34
  Home Town (00) 409
  House (86) 450
  Old Friends (94) 572
  Soul of a New Machine, The (82) 787
KIELY, BENEDICT
  Nothing Happens in Carmincross (86) 668
  State of Ireland, The (81) 766
KIERNAN, FRANCES
  Seeing Mary Plain (01) 764
KIM, MYUNG MI
  Commons (03) 155
KIM, SUJI KWOCK
  Notes from the Divided Country (04) 561
KIM, SUKI
  Interpreter, The (04) 360

KIMBALL, PHILIP
  Harvesting Ballads (85) 352
KIMMERLING, BARUCH, and JOEL S. MIGDAL
  Palestinian People, The (04) 600
KINCAID, JAMAICA
  Annie John (86) 33
  At the Bottom of the River (84) 59
  Autobiography of My Mother, The (97) 83
  Lucy (91) 549
KING, DEAN
  Patrick O'Brian (01) 707
KING, JAMES
  Virginia Woolf (96) 794
KING, MARTIN LUTHER, JR.
  Papers of Martin Luther King, Jr., January
    1929-June 1951, The (93) 601
  Papers of Martin Luther King, Jr., July
    1951-November 1955, The (95) 590
  Papers of Martin Luther King, Jr., December
    1955-December 1956, The (98) 625
KING, RICHARD H.
  Southern Renaissance, A (81) 753
KING, STEPHEN
  Bag of Bones (99) 83
  Danse Macabre (82) 171
  Dark Half, The (90) 147
  Dead Zone, The (80) 205
  Different Seasons (83) 189
  Everything's Eventual (03) 279
  Hearts in Atlantis (00) 362
  Misery (88) 569
  Needful Things (92) 564
  On Writing (01) 675
KINGSOLVER, BARBARA
  Animal Dreams (91) 38
  Bean Trees, The (89) 72
  Pigs in Heaven (94) 631
  Small Wonder (03) 779
KINGSTON, MAXINE HONG
  China Men (81) 137
  Woman Warrior, The (77) 932
KINKEAD-WEEKES, MARK
  D. H. Lawrence (97) 214
KINNELL, GALWAY
  Imperfect Thirst (95) 339
  Mortal Acts, Mortal Words (81) 582
  Past, The (86) 727
  Selected Poems (83) 726
KINNEY, HARRISON
  James Thurber (96) 389
KINSELLA, THOMAS
  Collected Poems, 1956-1994 (97) 165
KINSELLA, W. P.
  Shoeless Joe (83) 742
KIPLING, RUDYARD
  Letters of Rudyard Kipling, 1872-89, The
    (92) 421
  Letters of Rudyard Kipling, 1890-99, The
    (92) 421
KIRCH, PATRICK V., and MARSHALL SAHLINS
  Anahulu (93) 20
KIŠ, DANILO
  Hourglass (91) 427
KISSELOFF, JEFF
  Box, The (96) 77

AUTHOR INDEX

KISSINGER, HENRY
Diplomacy (95) 171
White House Years (80) 866
Years of Renewal (00) 867
Years of Upheaval (H-83) 483

KIZER, CAROLYN
Cool, Calm, and Collected (02) 172

KLAIDMAN, STEPHEN
Saving the Heart (01) 754

KLEHR, HARVEY
Heyday of American Communism, The
(H-85) 206

KLEHR, HARVEY, and JOHN EARL HAYNES
Venona (00) 784

KLEHR, HARVEY, JOHN EARL HAYNES, and
FRIDRIKH IGOREVICH FIRSOV, editors
Secret World of American Communism, The
(96) 685

KLEHR, HARVEY, and RONALD RADOSH
Amerasia Spy Case, The (97) 28

KLEIN, JOE
Natural, The (03) 554
Primary Colors (97) 679

KLEMPERER, VICTOR
I Will Bear Witness (01) 447

KLUGER, RICHARD
Simple Justice (77) 735

KNIPFEL, JIM
Buzzing, The (04) 109

KNOTT, BILL
Poems (90) 669
Selected and Collected Poems (78) 748

KNOWLES, JOHN
Peace Breaks Out (82) 621

KNOWLSON, JAMES
Damned to Fame (97) 191

KNOX, BERNARD
Essays (90) 219

KOCH, STEPHEN
Double Lives (95) 185

KOEPPEN, WOLFGANG
Hothouse, The (02) 396

KOESTLER, ARTHUR
Janus (79) 326
Thirteenth Tribe, The (77) 817

KOGAWA, JOY
Obasan (83) 554

KOLATA, GINA
Clone (99) 186
Flu (00) 268

KOMUNYAKAA, YUSEF
Neon Vernacular (94) 551
Talking Dirty to the Gods (01) 811

KONNER, MELVIN
Becoming a Doctor (88) 77

KONRÁD, GEORGE
Loser, The (83) 423

KONWICKI, TADEUSZ
Bohin Manor (91) 86
Minor Apocalypse, A (84) 547
Moonrise, Moonset (88) 579
Polish Complex, The (83) 611

KOOSER, TED
Sure Signs (81) 782

KOPELEV, LEV
Ease My Sorrows (84) 263

KORDA, MICHAEL
Charmed Lives (80) 141

KOSINSKI, JERZY
Blind Date (78) 104
Passion Play (80) 649

KOSKOFF, DAVID E.
Mellons, The (79) 434

KOSTOF, SPIRO
History of Architecture, A (86) 421

KOTLOWITZ, ALEX
Other Side of the River, The (99) 606
There Are No Children Here (92) 813

KOTT, JAN
Bottom Translation, The (88) 116
Theater of Essence, The (85) 890

KOVIC, RON
Born on the Fourth of July (77) 115

KOZOL, JONATHAN
Amazing Grace (96) 30
Rachel and Her Children (89) 687
Savage Inequalities (92) 712

KRAKAUER, JON
Under the Banner of Heaven (04) 787

KRAMER, KATHRYN
Handbook for Visitors from Outer Space, A
(85) 344

KRAMMER, ARNOLD
Nazi Prisoners of War in America (80) 573

KRAMNICK, ISAAC
Rage of Edmund Burke, The (78) 686

KRAUSS, LAWRENCE M.
Atom (02) 57

KRAUTHAMMER, CHARLES
Cutting Edges (86) 208

KREN, GEORGE M., and LEON RAPPOPORT
Holocaust and the Crisis of Human Behavior, The
(81) 439

KREYLING, MICHAEL
Eudora Welty's Achievement of Order (81) 288

KRIEGER, LEONARD
Ranke (78) 690

KRISTEVA, JULIA
Desire in Language (81) 231

KRÜGER, MICHAEL
Man in the Tower, The (94) 496

KRUGMAN, PAUL R.
Accidental Theorist, The (99) 10
Pop Internationalism (97) 666

KRUPAT, ARNOLD, and BRIAN SWANN, editors
I Tell You Now (88) 413

KUBAL, DAVID
Consoling Intelligence, The (83) 144

KUEHN, MANFRED
Kant (02) 458

KUKLICK, BRUCE
History of Philosophy in America, 1720-2000, A
(03) 366

KUMIN, MAXINE
Our Ground Time Here Will Be Brief (83) 577
Retrieval System, The (79) 593
Selected Poems, 1960-1990 (98) 707
Why Can't We Live Together Like Civilized
Human Beings? (83) 903

KUNDERA, MILAN
    Art of the Novel, The (89) 54
    Book of Laughter and Forgetting, The (81) 99
    Farewell Party, The (77) 283
    Identity (99) 410
    Ignorance (03) 392
    Immortality (92) 329
    Joke, The (83) 363
    Slowness (97) 761
    Testaments Betrayed (96) 744
    Unbearable Lightness of Being, The (85) 958
KUNITZ, STANLEY
    Collected Poems, The (01) 204
    Passing Through (96) 569
    Poems of Stanley Kunitz, 1928-1978, The (80) 665
KUNKEL, THOMAS
    Genius in Disguise (96) 303
KURALT, CHARLES
    On the Road with Charles Kuralt (86) 691
KURLAND, PHILIP B.
    Watergate and the Constitution (79) 830
KURLANSKY, MARK
    Salt (03) 708
KURTZ, MICHAEL L.
    Crime of the Century (H-83) 90
KURZWEIL, ALLEN
    Case of Curiosities, A (93) 133
    Grand Complication, The (02) 362
KUTLER, STANLEY I.
    American Inquisition, The (H-83) 41
KUTTNER, ROBERT
    Everything for Sale (98) 294
KWITNY, JONATHAN
    Man of the Century (98) 538

LACEY, ROBERT
    Ford (87) 297
LACOUTURE, JEAN
    André Malraux (77) 43
    De Gaulle, 1890-1944 (91) 192
    De Gaulle, 1945-1970 (93) 219
    Léon Blum (H-83) 253
LADER, LAWRENCE
    Power on the Left (80) 680
LADURIE, EMMANUEL LE ROY, and
JEAN-FRANÇOIS FITOU
    Saint-Simon and the Court of Louis XIV (02) 717
LaFEBER, WALTER
    Inevitable Revolutions (H-84) 232
LAGERCRANTZ, OLOF
    August Strindberg (85) 32
LA GRANGE, HENRY-LOUIS DE
    Gustav Mahler, 1892-1904 (96) 321
LAHIRI, JHUMPA
    Interpreter of Maladies (00) 430
    Namesake, The (04) 532
LAING, KOJO
    Woman of the Aeroplanes (91) 914
LAKOFF, GEORGE
    Moral Politics (97) 600
    Women, Fire, and Dangerous Things (88) 979
LAKOFF, GEORGE, and MARK TURNER
    More than Cool Reason (90) 578
LALL, ARTHUR
    Emergence of Modern India, The (82) 223
LAMB, WALLY
    I Know This Much Is True (99) 401

LAMOTT, ANNE
    Blue Shoe (03) 87
    Crooked Little Heart (98) 211
    Traveling Mercies (00) 764
L'AMOUR, LOUIS
    Jubal Sackett (86) 496
LANCHESTER, JOHN
    Mr. Phillips (01) 594
LANCHNER, CAROLYN, editor
    Paul Klee (88) 668
LANDAUER, THOMAS K.
    Trouble with Computers, The (96) 773
LANDES, DAVID S.
    Wealth and Poverty of Nations, The (99) 846
LANE, ANN J.
    To *Herland* and Beyond (91) 820
LANE, HARLAN
    When the Mind Hears (H-85) 488
    Wild Boy of Aveyron, The (77) 910
LANE FOX, ROBIN
    Pagans and Christians (88) 655
    Search for Alexander, The (81) 712
LANG, JOCHEN VON
    Secretary, Martin Bormann, The (80) 746
LANGER, ELINOR
    Josephine Herbst (85) 499
LANGER, LAWRENCE L.
    Holocaust Testimonies (92) 304
LANGGUTH, A. J.
    Saki (82) 726
LANGLAND, JOSEPH
    Any Body's Song (81) 53
LANGLEY, LESTER D.
    United States and the Caribbean, 1900-1970, The
      (81) 853
LAPIERRE, DOMINIQUE
    City of Joy, The (86) 136
LAQUEUR, WALTER
    Terrible Secret, The (82) 834
LARDNER, RING, JR.
    Lardners, The (77) 404
LARKIN, PHILIP
    Collected Poems (90) 112
    Required Writing (85) 747
    Selected Letters of Philip Larkin (94) 724
LARSON, EDWARD J.
    Evolution's Workshop (02) 258
LARSON, ERIK
    Devil in the White City, The (04) 165
LASCH, CHRISTOPHER
    Culture of Narcissism, The (80) 175
    Revolt of the Elites, The (96) 628
    True and Only Heaven, The (92) 830
    Women and the Common Life (98) 878
LASDUN, JAMES
    Delirium Eclipse and Other Stories (87) 204
    Three Evenings (93) 788
LASH, JOSEPH P.
    Roosevelt and Churchill, 1939-1941 (77) 685
LASH, JOSEPH P., editor
    World of Love, A (H-85) 521
LAUBER, JOHN
    Making of Mark Twain, The (86) 561
LAW-YONE, WENDY
    Coffin Tree, The (84) 168
    Irrawaddy Tango (95) 376

LAWRENCE, CHARLES, III, and JOEL DREYFUSS
Bakke Case, The (80) 45

LAWRENCE, D. H.
Letters of D. H. Lawrence, September 1901-May 1913, The (80) 469
Letters of D. H. Lawrence, October 1916-June 1921, The (86) 520
Letters of D. H. Lawrence, June 1921-March 1924, The (88) 466
Letters of D. H. Lawrence, March 1924-March 1927, The (90) 512
Letters of D. H. Lawrence, March 1927-November 1928, The (92) 417
Letters of D. H. Lawrence, November 1928-February 1930, The (94) 467
Mr Noon (85) 619

LAWRENCE, T. E.
T. E. Lawrence, The Selected Letters (90) 782

LAWRENCE-LIGHTFOOT, SARA
I've Known Rivers (95) 384

LAX, ERIC, and A. M. SPERBER
Bogart (98) 125

LAYE, CAMARA
Guardian of the Word, The (85) 334

LAYMAN, RICHARD
Shadow Man (82) 761

LEACH, DOUGLAS EDWARD
Roots of Conflict (87) 732

LEAKEY, RICHARD E., and ROGER LEWIN
People of the Lake (79) 535

LEAMING, BARBARA
Orson Welles (86) 709

LEAR, LINDA
Rachel Carson (98) 656

LEARS, JACKSON
Something for Nothing (04) 700

LEAVITT, DAVID
Equal Affections (90) 215
Family Dancing (85) 250
Lost Language of Cranes, The (87) 494
Place I've Never Been, A (91) 670
While England Sleeps (94) 851

LEAVY, JANE
Sandy Koufax (03) 713

LEBEAUX, RICHARD
Thoreau's Seasons (85) 895

LE CARRÉ, JOHN
Little Drummer Girl, The (84) 468
Night Manager, The (94) 559
Our Game (96) 553
Perfect Spy, A (87) 654
Russia House, The (90) 707
Secret Pilgrim, The (92) 732
Tailor of Panama, The (97) 797

LeCLAIR, TOM
Art of Excess, The (90) 49

LEDEEN, MICHAEL, and WILLIAM H. LEWIS
Debacle (82) 175

LEE, ANDREA
Russian Journal (82) 713
Sarah Phillips (85) 771

LEE, CHANG-RAE
Gesture Life, A (00) 305
Native Speaker (96) 499

LEE, DON
Yellow (02) 889

LEE, GUS
Tiger's Tail (97) 830

LEE, HERMIONE
Virginia Woolf (98) 805
Willa Cather (91) 896

LEE, J. M.
Churchill Coalition, The (81) 147

LEE, LI-YOUNG
Book of My Nights (02) 110
Winged Seed, The (96) 814

LEED, ERIC J.
Mind of the Traveler, The (92) 505

LEEMING, DAVID
James Baldwin (95) 388

LEEN, JEFF, and GUY GUGLIOTTA
Kings of Cocaine (90) 490

LEFFLAND, ELLA
Knight, Death, and the Devil, The (91) 493

LEFKOWITZ, MARY
Not Out of Africa (97) 635

LEFKOWITZ, MARY R., and GUY MacLEAN ROGERS, editors
Black Athena Revisited (97) 114

LE GOFF, JACQUES
Birth of Purgatory, The (H-85) 43

LE GUIN, URSULA K.
Always Coming Home (86) 21
Eye of the Heron, The (84) 291
Orsinian Tales (77) 601
Searoad (92) 722
Tehanu (91) 794
Unlocking the Air (97) 858

LEHMAN, DAVID
Signs of the Times (92) 752

LEHMAN, JOHN F., JR.
Command of the Seas (90) 132

LEIBOWITZ, HERBERT
Fabricating Lives (90) 236

LEIGHTON, RALPH, with RICHARD P. FEYNMAN
"Surely You're Joking, Mr. Feynman!" (86) 868

LEITHAUSER, BRAD
Hence (90) 373
Hundreds of Fireflies (83) 348

LELYVELD, JOSEPH
Move Your Shadow (86) 635

LEM, STANISLAW
Fiasco (88) 318
His Master's Voice (84) 342
Hospital of the Transfiguration (89) 357
Imaginary Magnitude (85) 421
Memoirs of a Space Traveler (83) 469
Microworlds (86) 595
One Human Minute (87) 615

LEMANN, NICHOLAS
Big Test, The (00) 57
Promised Land, The (92) 650

LENNON, J. ROBERT
Mailman (04) 487

LENTRICCHIA, FRANK
Modernist Quartet (95) 499

LEONARD, ELMORE
Bandits (88) 71
Get Shorty (91) 351
Killshot (90) 482
Tishomingo Blues (03) 834

LEONARD, THOMAS C.
Above the Battle (79) 1

LEOPARDI, GIACOMO
    Operette Morali (84) 643
LEOPOLD, JOHN A.
    Alfred Hugenberg (78) 28
LEPPMANN, WOLFGANG
    Rilke (85) 757
LERNER, GERDA
    Creation of Feminist Consciousness, The
      (94) 168
LE ROY LADURIE, EMMANUEL
    Beggar and the Professor, The (98) 108
LESSER, WENDY
    Amateur, The (00) 10
    His Other Half (92) 285
LESSING, DORIS
    Documents Relating to the Sentimental Agents in
      the Volyen Empire (84) 239
    Fifth Child, The (89) 298
    Good Terrorist, The (86) 358
    Love, Again (97) 539
    Making of the Representative for Planet 8, The
      (83) 432
    Marriages Between Zones Three, Four, and Five,
      The (81) 555
    Shikasta (80) 753
    Sirian Experiments, The (81) 737
    Stories (79) 708
    Sweetest Dream, The (03) 820
    Under My Skin (95) 814
    Walking in the Shade (98) 823
LESY, MICHAEL
    Dreamland (98) 272
LETHEM, JONATHAN
    As She Climbed Across the Table (98) 85
    Fortress of Solitude, The (04) 266
    Girl in Landscape (99) 337
    Motherless Brooklyn (00) 542
LEUCHTENBURG, WILLIAM E.
    In the Shadow of FDR (H-84) 223
LEUTZE, JAMES R.
    Bargaining for Supremacy (78) 85
LEVERICH, LYLE
    Tom (96) 756
LEVERTOV, DENISE
    Door in the Hive, A (90) 194
    Life in the Forest (79) 386
    Sands of the Well (97) 714
    Tesserae (96) 740
LEVI, PRIMO
    Drowned and the Saved, The (89) 250
    Monkey's Wrench, The (87) 564
    Periodic Table, The (85) 682
LÉVI-STRAUSS, CLAUDE
    Look, Listen, Read (98) 526
LEVIN, GAIL
    Edward Hopper (96) 214
LEVINE, GEORGE
    Realistic Imagination, The (83) 635
LEVINE, PHILIP
    Ashes (80) 35
    Mercy, The (00) 519
    What Work Is (92) 880
LEVINS, HOAG
    Arab Reach (H-84) 28
LEVIS, LARRY
    Afterlife, The (78) 17
LEVITT, NORMAN, and PAUL R. GROSS
    Higher Superstition (95) 301

LE VOT, ANDRÉ
    F. Scott Fitzgerald (84) 318
LÉVY, BERNARD-HENRI
    Who Killed Daniel Pearl? (04) 835
LEVY, LEONARD W.
    Original Intent and the Framers' Constitution
      (89) 621
LEWALSKI, BARBARA KIEFER
    Writing Women in Jacobean England (94) 869
LEWIN, ROGER
    Complexity (93) 188
LEWIN, ROGER, and RICHARD E. LEAKEY
    People of the Lake (79) 535
LEWIN, RONALD
    American Magic, The (H-83) 52
LEWIS, BERNARD
    Crisis of Islam, The (04) 142
    Islam and the West (94) 414
    Muslim Discovery of Europe, The (H-83) 303
    Race and Slavery in the Middle East (91) 692
LEWIS, C. DAY. See DAY LEWIS, C.
LEWIS, DAVID LEVERING
    W. E. B. Du Bois, 1868-1919 (94) 847
    W. E. B. Du Bois, 1919-1963 (01) 882
LEWIS, JIM
    King Is Dead, The (04) 413
LEWIS, JOHN W., SERGEI N. GONCHAROV, and
    XUE LITAI
    Uncertain Partners (95) 809
LEWIS, MERIWETHER, and WILLIAM CLARK
    Lewis and Clark Journals, The (04) 442
LEWIS, MICHAEL
    Moneyball (04) 514
    New New Thing, The (00) 571
    Next (02) 576
LEWIS, R. W. B.
    Jameses (92) 374
LEWIS, WILLIAM H., and MICHAEL LEDEEN
    Debacle (82) 175
LEWIS, WYNDHAM
    Rude Assignment (86) 778
    Snooty Baronet (85) 835
LEWIS, WYNDHAM, and EZRA POUND
    Pound/Lewis (86) 747
LEWONTIN, R. C., STEVEN ROSE, and LEON J.
    KAMIN
    Not in Our Genes (H-85) 329
LEWONTIN, RICHARD
    Triple Helix, The (01) 845
LEWY, GUENTER
    America in Vietnam (79) 14
LEYS, SIMON
    Burning Forest, The (86) 86
LHAMON, W. T., JR.
    Deliberate Speed (91) 197
L'HEUREUX, JOHN
    Desires (82) 181
LIDDY, G. GORDON
    Will (81) 928
LIEVEN, ANATOL
    Chechnya (99) 158
LIFTON, BETTY JEAN
    King of Children, The (89) 436
LIFTON, ROBERT JAY
    Destroying the World to Save It (00) 172

LIFTON, ROBERT JAY, and ERIC MARKUSEN
Genocidal Mentality, The (91) 338

LIGHTMAN, ALAN
Einstein's Dreams (94) 256

LINCOLN, W. BRUCE
In War's Dark Shadow (H-84) 227
Nicholas I (79) 479

LIND, MICHAEL
Next American Nation, The (96) 509

LINDBERG, DAVID C.
Beginnings of Western Science, The
(93) 71

LINDBERGH, ANNE MORROW
Flower and the Nettle, The (77) 294
War Within and Without (81) 890

LINDBERGH, CHARLES AUGUSTUS
Autobiography of Values (79) 43

LINDERMAN, GERALD F.
Embattled Courage (88) 271

LINDSAY, NICHOLAS VACHEL
Letters of Vachel Lindsay (80) 479

LINENTHAL, EDWARD T., and TOM
ENGELHARDT, editors
History Wars (97) 400

LINGEMAN, RICHARD
Sinclair Lewis (03) 755
Theodore Dreiser, 1871-1907 (87) 847
Theodore Dreiser, 1908-1945 (91) 798

LINGENFELTER, RICHARD E.
Death Valley and the Amargosa (87) 198

LIPKING, LAWRENCE
Samuel Johnson (99) 683

LIPSET, SEYMOUR MARTIN
American Exceptionalism (97) 33

LIPSKY, DAVID
Three Thousand Dollars (90) 801

LISCHER, RICHARD
Preacher King, The (96) 601

LISS, DAVID
Conspiracy of Paper, A (01) 213

LISS, PEGGY K.
Isabel the Queen (93) 399

LITTELL, ROBERT
Company, The (03) 159

LITTLETON, TAYLOR, editor
Time to Hear and Answer, A (78) 841

LITWACK, LEON F.
Been in the Storm So Long (80) 65
Trouble in Mind (99) 795

LIU, ERIC
Accidental Asian, The (99) 5

LIU, WU-CHI, and IRVING YUCHENG LO
Sunflower Splendor (77) 792

LIVELY, PENELOPE
Moon Tiger (89) 558
Passing On (91) 651

LIVESAY, HAROLD C.
Samuel Gompers and Organized Labor in America
(79) 641

LLERENA, MARIO
Unsuspected Revolution, The (79) 799

LLOSA, MARIO VARGAS. See VARGAS LLOSA,
MARIO

LO, IRVING YUCHENG, and WU-CHI LIU
Sunflower Splendor (77) 792

LODGE, DAVID
Nice Work (90) 603
Paradise News (93) 606
Small World (86) 835
Souls and Bodies (83) 761
Therapy (96) 748
Thinks . . . (02) 782

LOEWINSOHN, RON
Magnetic Field(s) (84) 487

LOGAN, JOHN
Only the Dreamer Can Change the Dream
(82) 599

LOGUE, CHRISTOPHER
All Day Permanent Red (04) 17
Husbands, The (96) 355
War Music (88) 954

LOMASK, MILTON
Aaron Burr, 1756-1805 (80) 6
Aaron Burr, 1805-1836 (H-83) 1

LONGENBACH, JAMES
Stone Cottage (89) 818
Wallace Stevens (92) 859

LOPATE, PHILLIP
Art of the Personal Essay, The (95) 47
Bachelorhood (82) 40

LOPEZ, BARRY
Arctic Dreams (87) 40

LORCA, FEDERICO GARCÍA. See GARCÍA
LORCA, FEDERICO.

LORD, BETTE BAO
Spring Moon (82) 806

LORD, JAMES
Giacometti (86) 343
Six Exceptional Women (95) 724

LORD, WALTER
Lonely Vigil (78) 534
Miracle of Dunkirk, The (H-83) 293

LORDE, AUDRE
Chosen Poems, Old and New (83) 113
Undersong (93) 838

LOTTMAN, HERBERT R.
Albert Camus (80) 15
Colette (92) 99
Flaubert (90) 268
Left Bank, The (83) 390

LOUIS, WM. ROGER
Imperialism at Bay (79) 305

LOURIE, RICHARD
Sakharov (03) 703

LOURY, GLENN C.
One by One from the Inside Out (96) 532

LOVELL, MARY S.
Sisters, The (03) 760
Straight on till Morning (88) 865

LOW, ALFRED D.
Jews in the Eyes of the Germans (80) 439

LOWE, SUE DAVIDSON
Stieglitz (H-84) 426

LOWE, VICTOR
Alfred North Whitehead, 1861-1910 (86) 5
Alfred North Whitehead, 1910-1947 (91) 20

LOWELL, ROBERT
Collected Poems (04) 130
Collected Prose (88) 173
Day by Day (78) 233
Selected Poems (77) 720

LOWENTHAL, DAVID
Past Is a Foreign Country, The (87) 645
LOYD, ANTHONY
My War Gone By, I Miss It So (01) 604
LUCIE-SMITH, EDWARD
Joan of Arc (78) 472
LUDINGTON, TOWNSEND
John Dos Passos (81) 464
LUKACS, JOHN
At the End of an Age (03) 37
Hitler of History, The (98) 396
1945 (79) 490
LUKAS, J. ANTHONY
Common Ground (86) 182
Nightmare (77) 565
LUMSDEN, CHARLES J., and EDWARD O. WILSON
Promethean Fire (H-84) 366
LUPTON, KENNETH
Mungo Park the African Traveler (80) 550
LURIE, ALISON
Don't Tell the Grown-ups (91) 231
Familiar Spirits (02) 271
Foreign Affairs (85) 297
Last Resort, The (99) 466
Truth About Lorin Jones, The (89) 860
LYNCH, THOMAS
Bodies in Motion and at Rest (01) 122
Undertaking, The (98) 786
LYNN, KENNETH S.
Hemingway (88) 372
LYONS, F. S. L.
Charles Stewart Parnell (78) 169
LYONS, PHYLLIS I.
Saga of Dazai Osamu, The (86) 783
LYTLE, MARK HAMILTON
After the Fact (H-83) 10

MAASS, JOACHIM
Kleist (84) 418
MAASS, PETER
Love Thy Neighbor (97) 543
McALEER, JOHN
Ralph Waldo Emerson (85) 717
McARTHUR, TOM
Worlds of Reference (87) 1015
McAULIFFE, MARY SPERLING
Crisis on the Left (79) 138
McBRIDE, JAMES
Miracle at St. Anna (03) 540
McBRIDE, JOSEPH
Frank Capra (93) 298
Steven Spielberg (98) 731
McBRIEN, WILLIAM, and JACK BARBERA
Stevie (88) 860
McCABE, PATRICK
Butcher Boy, The (94) 118
McCAGG, WILLIAM O., JR.
Stalin Embattled, 1943-1948 (79) 702
McCALL, DAN
Triphammer (91) 829
McCARRY, CHARLES
Lucky Bastard (99) 497
Second Sight (92) 727
Shelley's Heart (96) 708
McCARTHY, ABIGAIL
Circles (78) 179

McCARTHY, CORMAC
All the Pretty Horses (93) 10
Blood Meridian (86) 67
Cities of the Plain (99) 173
Crossing, The (95) 157
McCARTHY, MARY
Cannibals and Missionaries (80) 133
How I Grew (88) 407
McCARTHY, MARY, and HANNAH ARENDT
Between Friends (96) 73
McCARTHY, PATRICK
Camus (83) 96
Céline (77) 134
McCAULEY, STEPHEN
Man of the House, The (97) 546
McCLAIN, CHARLES J.
In Search of Equality (95) 351
McCLANAHAN, ED
Natural Man, The (84) 608
McCLATCHY, J. D.
Ten Commandments, The (99) 751
McCLAUGHRY, JOHN, and FRANK BRYAN
Vermont Papers, The (90) 839
McCLOSKEY, DEIRDRE N.
Crossing (00) 155
McCOMBS, DAVIS
Ultima Thule (01) 850
McCORMMACH, RUSSELL
Night Thoughts of a Classical Physicist (83) 532
McCOURT, FRANK
Angela's Ashes (97) 43
'Tis (00) 759
McCRACKEN, ELIZABETH
Giant's House, The (97) 331
MacCULLOCH, DIARMAID
Thomas Cranmer (97) 821
McCULLOUGH, COLLEEN
Thorn Birds, The (78) 831
McCULLOUGH, DAVID
John Adams (02) 444
Mornings on Horseback (82) 537
Path Between the Seas, The (78) 636
Truman (93) 810
McDERMOTT, ALICE
At Weddings and Wakes (93) 40
Charming Billy (99) 154
Child of My Heart (03) 147
That Night (88) 888
McDONALD, FORREST
Alexander Hamilton (80) 23
American Presidency, The (95) 28
Novus Ordo Seclorum (87) 604
MACDONALD, ROSS
Blue Hammer, The (77) 105
McDOUGAL, DENNIS
Privileged Son (02) 669
McDOUGALL, WALTER A.
. . . Heavens and the Earth, The (86) 396
McDOWELL, EDWIN
To Keep Our Honor Clean (81) 813
McELROY, JOSEPH
Letter Left to Me, The (89) 465
Women and Men (88) 973

AUTHOR INDEX

McEWAN, IAN
  Amsterdam (00) 14
  Atonement (03) 42
  Black Dogs (93) 79
  Child in Time, The (88) 146
  Enduring Love (99) 257
  In Between the Sheets and Other Stories (80) 417
  Innocent, The (91) 456

McFARLAND, DENNIS
  Music Room, The (91) 610

McFARLAND, PHILIP
  Sojourners (80) 771

McFEELY, ELIZA
  Zuñi and the American Imagination (02) 898

McFEELY, WILLIAM S.
  Frederick Douglass (92) 232
  Grant (82) 338
  Proximity to Death (00) 630

McGAHERN, JOHN
  Amongst Women (91) 33
  By the Lake (03) 123

McGERR, MICHAEL
  Fierce Discontent, A (04) 261

McGINLEY, PATRICK
  Red Men, The (88) 737
  Trick of the Ga Bolga, The (86) 903

McGINN, COLIN
  Mysterious Flame, The (00) 558

McGRATH, ALISTER E.
  In the Beginning (02) 408

McGRATH, PATRICK
  Asylum (98) 90

McGRATH, ROGER D.
  Gunfighters, Highwaymen, and Vigilantes (H-85) 190

McGRATH, THOMAS
  Selected Poems (89) 775

McGUANE, THOMAS
  Cadence of Grass, The (03) 128
  Keep the Change (90) 473
  Nobody's Angel (83) 544
  Nothing but Blue Skies (93) 580
  Something to Be Desired (85) 849
  To Skin a Cat (87) 863

McGUINNESS, BRIAN
  Wittgenstein, A Life (89) 918

McINERNEY, JAY
  Last of the Savages, The (97) 478

MacINTYRE, ALASDAIR
  Three Rival Versions of Moral Enquiry (91) 815
  Whose Justice? Which Rationality? (89) 902

MACK, JOHN E.
  Prince of Our Disorder, A (77) 637

MACK, MAYNARD
  Alexander Pope (87) 20

MACK SMITH, DENIS
  Cavour (86) 105
  Mussolini (H-83) 308
  Mussolini's Roman Empire (77) 520

McKAY, NELLIE Y.
  Jean Toomer, Artist (85) 489

MACKAY, JAMES
  Burns (94) 113

MacKENZIE, NORMAN
  Escape from Elba, The (H-83) 134

MACKENZIE, NORMAN, and JEANNE MACKENZIE
  Fabians, The (78) 300

McKEON, MICHAEL
  Origins of the English Novel, 1600-1740, The (88) 641

McKIBBEN, BILL
  End of Nature, The (90) 211
  Enough (04) 236

McKITRICK, ERIC, and STANLEY ELKINS
  Age of Federalism, The (94) 5

MacLAVERTY, BERNARD
  Cal (84) 132
  Secrets and Other Stories (85) 790

MACLEAN, NORMAN
  Young Men and Fire (93) 892

MacLEISH, ARCHIBALD
  Letters of Archibald MacLeish (84) 436
  New & Collected Poems, 1917-1976 (77) 534
  Riders on the Earth (79) 601

McLELLAN, DAVID
  Utopian Pessimist (91) 838

McLELLAN, DAVID S.
  Dean Acheson (77) 197

MacLEOD, ALISTAIR
  Island (02) 432

McLUHAN, MARSHALL (HERBERT)
  Letters of Marshall McLuhan (89) 484

McLYNN, FRANK
  Robert Louis Stevenson (96) 655

McMANUS, JAMES
  Positively Fifth Street (04) 619

McMICHAEL, JAMES
  Each in a Place Apart (95) 190

McMILLAN, CAROL
  Women, Reason and Nature (84) 964

McMILLAN, GEORGE
  Making of an Assassin, The (77) 470

McMILLAN, TERRY
  Waiting to Exhale (93) 860

MacMILLAN, HAROLD
  Past Masters, The (77) 610
  War Diaries (H-85) 474

McMORRIS, JENNY
  Warden of English, The (02) 838

MacMULLEN, RAMSAY
  Christianizing the Roman Empire (A.D. 100-400) (H-85) 68

McMURRY, LINDA O.
  George Washington Carver (82) 310

McMURTRY, LARRY
  Anything for Billy (89) 33
  Boone's Lick (01) 131
  Buffalo Girls (91) 110
  Cadillac Jack (83) 90
  Desert Rose, The (84) 225
  Lonesome Dove (86) 533
  Sin Killer (03) 750
  Somebody's Darling (79) 689
  Streets of Laredo (94) 769
  Texasville (88) 878
  Walter Benjamin at the Dairy Queen (00) 817

McNAMARA, ROBERT, with BRIAN VanDeMARK
  In Retrospect (96) 363

McNEILL, WILLIAM H.
  Metamorphosis of Greece Since World War II, The (79) 438
  Plagues and Peoples (77) 618
  Pursuit of Power, The (H-83) 357
McPHEE, JOHN
  Assembling California (94) 57
  Control of Nature, The (90) 137
  Founding Fish, The (03) 316
  Giving Good Weight (80) 358
  In Suspect Terrain (H-84) 218
  Irons in the Fire (98) 445
  Looking for a Ship (91) 540
  Ransom of Russian Art, The (95) 622
  Rising from the Plains (87) 722
  Table of Contents (86) 873
McPHERSON, JAMES M.
  Abraham Lincoln and the Second American Revolution (92) 1
  Battle Cry of Freedom (89) 67
  Drawn with the Sword (97) 229
McPHERSON, SANDRA
  Edge Effect (97) 234
  God of Indeterminacy, The (94) 364
  Visit to Civilization, A (03) 863
McPHERSON, WILLIAM
  Testing the Current (85) 884
MacSHANE, FRANK
  Into Eternity (86) 471
  Life of Raymond Chandler, The (77) 427
McWHINEY, GRADY, and PERRY D. JAMIESON
  Attack and Die (H-83) 57
McWHORTER, JOHN
  Power of Babel, The (03) 619
MADDEN, DAVID
  Pleasure-Dome (80) 659
  Suicide's Wife, The (79) 727
MADDOW, BEN
  Sunday Between Wars, A (80) 798
MADDOX, BRENDA
  D. H. Lawrence (95) 167
  Nora (89) 605
MADSEN, AXEL
  Hearts and Minds (78) 379
MADSEN, RICHARD, et al., editors
  Habits of the Heart (86) 380
MAECHLER, STEFAN
  Wilkomirski Affair, The (02) 861
MAIER, PAULINE
  American Scripture (98) 50
MAILER, NORMAN
  Ancient Evenings (84) 31
  Executioner's Song, The (80) 306
  Genius and Lust (77) 322
  Gospel According to the Son, The (98) 366
  Harlot's Ghost (92) 276
  Oswald's Tale (96) 549
  Pieces and Pontifications (83) 597
  Time of Our Time, The (99) 764
  Tough Guys Don't Dance (85) 912
MAILLOUX, PETER
  Hesitation Before Birth, A (90) 378
MAIRS, NANCY
  Ordinary Time (94) 594
  Voice Lessons (95) 835
  Waist High in the World (98) 814
MAKIN, PETER
  Bunting (93) 115

MAKIYA, KANAN
  Cruelty and Silence (94) 177
MALABRE, ALFRED L., JR.
  Beyond Our Means (88) 101
MALAMUD, BERNARD
  Complete Stories of Bernard Malamud, The (98) 207
  Dubin's Lives (80) 231
  God's Grace (83) 291
  People and Uncollected Stories, The (90) 661
  Stories of Bernard Malamud, The (84) 819
MALAN, RIAN
  My Traitor's Heart (91) 624
MALCOLM, JANET
  Silent Woman, The (95) 719
MALCOLM, JOYCE LEE
  To Keep and Bear Arms (95) 787
MALLON, THOMAS
  Dewey Defeats Truman (98) 239
MALONE, DUMAS
  Sage of Monticello, Vol. VI, The (82) 722
MALONE, MICHAEL
  Handling Sin (87) 366
MALOUF, DAVID
  Dream Stuff (01) 250
  Harland's Half Acre (85) 348
MALRAUX, ANDRÉ
  Lazarus (78) 515
MAMET, DAVID
  American Buffalo (78) 46
  Water Engine and Mr. Happiness, The (79) 828
MANCALL, PETER C.
  Deadly Medicine (96) 157
MANCERON, CLAUDE
  Toward the Brink, 1785-1787 (H-84) 452
  Twilight of the Old Order, 1774-1778 (78) 864
MANCHESTER, WILLIAM
  American Caesar (79) 20
  Last Lion, 1874-1932, The (H-84) 278
  Last Lion, 1932-1940, The (89) 455
MANES, STEPHEN, and PAUL ANDREWS
  Gates (94) 335
MANEY, KEVIN
  Maverick and His Machine, The (04) 501
MANFRED, FREDERICK
  Manly-Hearted Woman, The (77) 480
MANGUEL, ALBERTO
  History of Reading, A (97) 395
MANN, ROBERT
  Grand Delusion, A (02) 367
MANSFIELD, KATHERINE
  Collected Letters of Katherine Mansfield, 1903-1917, The (85) 106
  Collected Letters of Katherine Mansfield, 1918-1919, The (88) 165
MANTON, JO, and ROBERT GITTINGS
  Claire Clairmont and the Shelleys, 1798-1879 (93) 157
MANUEL, FRANK E.
  Broken Staff, The (93) 110
MARANISS, DAVID
  First in His Class (96) 263
MARCHAND, PHILIP
  Marshall McLuhan (90) 562

AUTHOR INDEX

MARCUS, GREIL
  Dead Elvis (92) 157
  Invisible Republic (98) 441
MARCUS, STEVEN
  Representations (77) 673
MARDER, NORMA
  Eye for Dark Places, An (94) 269
MARIANI, PAUL
  Broken Tower, The (00) 108
  Dream Song (91) 235
  Lost Puritan (95) 455
  William Carlos Williams (82) 946
MARÍAS, JAVIER
  Dark Back of Time (02) 181
MARIUS, RICHARD
  Martin Luther (00) 515
  Thomas More (H-85) 435
MARKSON, DAVID
  This Is Not a Novel (02) 786
MARKUS, JULIA
  Uncle (79) 783
MARKUSEN, ERIC, and ROBERT JAY LIFTON
  Genocidal Mentality, The (91) 338
MÁRQUEZ, GABRIEL GARCÍA. See GARCÍA
MÁRQUEZ, GABRIEL
MARR, DAVID
  Patrick White (93) 619
MARR, DAVID G.
  Vietnam 1945 (97) 867
MARRUS, MICHAEL R.
  Unwanted, The (86) 923
MARSDEN, GEORGE M.
  Jonathan Edwards (04) 391
  Soul of the American University, The (95) 744
MARSH, CHARLES
  God's Long Summer (98) 362
MARSH, JAN
  Christina Rossetti (96) 107
MARSHALL, P. J., and GLYNDWR WILLIAMS
  Great Map of Mankind, The (H-83) 176
MARSHALL, PAULE
  Daughters (92) 142
MARSHALL, PETER H.
  William Godwin (85) 1028
MARTEL, LEON, HERMAN KAHN, and WILLIAM BROWN
  Next 200 Years, The (77) 559
MARTEL, YANN
  Life of Pi (03) 485
MARTIN, DAVID C.
  Wilderness of Mirrors (81) 924
MARTIN, JOHN BARTLOW
  Adlai Stevenson and the World (78) 6
  Adlai Stevenson of Illinois (77) 12
MARTIN, JUSTIN
  Greenspan (01) 365
MARTIN, ROBERT BERNARD
  With Friends Possessed (86) 954
MARTIN, VALERIE
  Mary Reilly (91) 572
MARTÍN GAITE, CARMEN
  Back Room, The (84) 71
MARTINICH, A. P.
  Hobbes (00) 400

MARTORELL, JOANOT, and MARTÍ JOAN DE GALBA
  Tirant lo Blanc (85) 907
MARTY, MARTIN E.
  Modern American Religion, 1919-1941 (92) 524
  Pilgrims in Their Own Land (H-85) 358
MARX, KARL, and FRIEDRICH ENGELS
  Selected Letters (83) 722
MASEFIELD, JOHN
  Selected Poems (79) 666
MASLOW, JONATHAN EVAN
  Bird of Life, Bird of Death (87) 66
MASO, CAROLE
  Ghost Dance (87) 326
MASON, BOBBIE ANN
  Feather Crowns (94) 283
  Shiloh and Other Stories (83) 739
MASON, HAYDN
  Voltaire (82) 885
MASSIE, ROBERT K.
  Peter the Great (81) 651
MASTERS, HILARY
  Last Stands (83) 386
MATERER, TIMOTHY
  Vortex (80) 855
MATTHEWS, JAMES
  Voices (84) 921
MATTHEWS, WILLIAM
  Flood (83) 262
MATTHIESSEN, PETER
  Bone by Bone (00) 82
  Indian Country (H-85) 241
  Killing Mister Watson (91) 480
  Lost Man's River (98) 530
  Men's Lives (87) 547
  Sand Rivers (82) 737
  Snow Leopard, The (79) 685
MATUSOW, ALLEN J.
  Unraveling of America, The (H-85) 460
MAXWELL, WILLIAM
  All the Days and Nights (96) 26
  So Long, See You Tomorrow (81) 741
MAY, DERWENT
  Critical Times (03) 177
MAY, ERNEST R., and RICHARD E. NEUSTADT
  Thinking in Time (87) 853
MAYER, ARNO J.
  Persistence of the Old Regime, The (82) 626
  Why Did the Heavens Not Darken? (90) 893
MAYER, HENRY
  Son of Thunder, A (87) 789
MAYER, JANE, and JILL ABRAMSON
  Strange Justice (95) 765
MAYER, KENNETH R.
  With the Stroke of a Pen (02) 870
MAZOWER, MARK
  Dark Continent (00) 164
MEAD, MARGARET, and RHODA METRAUX
  Aspects of the Present (81) 62
MECKEL, CHRISTOPH
  Figure on the Boundary Line, The (85) 276
MEDAWAR, PETER
  Memoir of a Thinking Radish (87) 541
MEDVEDEV, GRIGORI
  Truth About Chernobyl, The (92) 835

MEDVEDEV, ROY A.
   All Stalin's Men (H-85) 12
   Khrushchev (H-84) 266
   Nikolai Bukharin (81) 614
   October Revolution, The (80) 605
MEE, CHARLES L., JR.
   End of Order, The (81) 277
   Marshall Plan, The (H-85) 292
   Ohio Gang, The (82) 575
MEHLMAN, JEFFREY
   Émigré New York (01) 277
MEHTA, VED
   Ledge Between the Streams, The (85) 539
   Remembering Mr. Shawn's "New Yorker" (99) 649
   Sound-Shadows of the New World (87) 802
   Stolen Light, The (90) 758
   Up at Oxford (94) 823
   Ved Mehta Reader, A (99) 834
MEINIG, D. W.
   Shaping of America, 1492-1800, The (87) 771
   Shaping of America, 1800-1867, The (94) 729
MEISNER, MAURICE
   Mao's China (78) 557
MELLEN, JOAN
   Kay Boyle (95) 417
MELLOW, JAMES R.
   Nathaniel Hawthorne in His Times (81) 593
   Walker Evans (00) 805
MELMAN, YOSSI, and DAN RAVIV
   Every Spy a Prince (91) 271
MENAKER, DANIEL
   Old Left, The (88) 616
   Treatment, The (99) 783
MENAND, LOUIS
   Metaphysical Club, The (02) 524
MENCKEN, H. L.
   Choice of Days, A (81) 142
   Diary of H. L. Mencken, The (91) 211
   New Mencken Letters, The (78) 603
MENDELSOHN, EZRA
   Jews of East Central Europe Between the World
      Wars, The (H-84) 243
MENDELSON, EDWARD
   Later Auden (00) 475
MENOCAL, MARÍA ROSA
   Ornament of the World, The (03) 610
MERCIER, VIVIAN
   Modern Irish Literature (95) 495
MEREDITH, MARTIN
   Elephant Destiny (04) 215
   Nelson Mandela (99) 552
MEREDITH, WILLIAM
   Cheer, The (81) 133
   Partial Accounts (88) 663
MERILLAT, HERBERT CHRISTIAN
   Guadalcanal Remembered (H-83) 181
MERK, FREDERICK
   History of the Westward Movement (79) 277
MERKIN, DAPHNE
   Enchantment (87) 238
MERRIDALE, CATHERINE
   Night of Stone (02) 588

MERRILL, JAMES INGRAM
   Changing Light at Sandover, The (84) 148
   Different Person, A (94) 234
   Divine Comedies (77) 222
   From the First Nine (84) 314
   Inner Room, The (89) 386
   Mirabell (79) 448
   Scattering of Salts, A (96) 676
   Selected Poems, 1946-1985 (93) 719
MERRY, ROBERT W.
   Taking on the World (97) 802
MERWIN, W. S.
   Compass Flower, The (78) 205
   Folding Cliffs, The (99) 295
   Regions of Memory (88) 742
   Travels (94) 811
MESSUD, CLAIRE
   Last Life, The (00) 471
METCALF, PAUL
   Collected Works, 1956-1976 (97) 175
   Collected Works, 1976-1997 (98) 199
   Where Do You Put the Horse? (87) 963
METRAUX, RHODA, and MARGARET MEAD
   Aspects of the Present (81) 62
MEYER, KARL E.
   Dust of Empire, The (04) 198
MEYER, NICHOLAS, and BARRY JAY KAPLAN
   Black Orchid (78) 100
MEYERS, JEFFREY
   D. H. Lawrence (91) 206
   Edmund Wilson (96) 210
   Hemingway (86) 406
   Robert Frost (97) 705
   Scott Fitzgerald (95) 696
MICHAELS, LEONARD
   Girl with a Monkey, A (01) 342
MICHAELS, LEONARD, and CHRISTOPHER
   RICKS, editors
   State of the Language, The (91) 773
MICHENER, JAMES A.
   Chesapeake (79) 99
   Covenant, The (81) 210
   Texas (86) 878
MICHNIK, ADAM
   Letters from Prison (87) 477
MIDDLEBROOK, DIANE WOOD
   Anne Sexton (92) 21
   Her Husband (04) 335
MIDDLEKAUFF, ROBERT
   Glorious Cause, The (H-83) 171
MIGDAL, JOEL S., and BARUCH KIMMERLING
   Palestinian People, The (04) 600
MILES, JACK
   God (96) 311
MILFORD, NANCY
   Savage Beauty (02) 722
MILLAN, GORDON
   Throw of the Dice, A (95) 782
MILLER, ANDREW
   Ingenious Pain (98) 428
MILLER, ARTHUR
   Echoes Down the Corridor (01) 263
   Theater Essays of Arthur Miller, The (79) 742
   Timebends (88) 897
MILLER, ARTHUR I.
   Einstein, Picasso (02) 235

AUTHOR INDEX

MILLER, EDWIN HAVILAND
  Salem Is My Dwelling Place (93) 702
MILLER, HEATHER ROSS
  Hard Evidence (92) 271
MILLER, J. HILLIS
  Ariadne's Thread (93) 32
  Fiction and Repetition (83) 253
MILLER, JAMES
  Passion of Michel Foucault, The (93) 614
  Rousseau (H-85) 395
MILLER, JOHN CHESTER
  Wolf by the Ears, The (78) 928
MILLER, MARY ELLEN, and LINDA SCHELE
  Blood of Kings, The (87) 75
MILLER, MERLE
  Lyndon (81) 540
MILLER, NATHAN
  FDR (H-84) 158
  Roosevelt Chronicles, The (80) 726
  Theodore Roosevelt (93) 783
MILLER, RUTH
  Saul Bellow (92) 707
MILLER, SUE
  Distinguished Guest, The (96) 186
  Family Pictures (91) 283
  For Love (94) 305
  Good Mother, The (87) 352
  While I Was Gone (00) 826
  World Below, The (02) 880
MILLER, VASSAR
  If I Had Wheels or Love (92) 319
MILLER, WILLIAM LEE
  Lincoln's Virtues (03) 490
MILLGATE, JANE
  Walter Scott (85) 989
MILLGATE, MICHAEL
  Thomas Hardy (83) 806
MILLHAUSER, STEVEN
  In the Penny Arcade (87) 424
  King in the Tree, The (04) 409
MILLIER, BRETT C.
  Elizabeth Bishop (94) 264
MILLS, HILARY
  Mailer (83) 428
MILLS, JAMES
  Underground Empire, The (87) 896
MIŁOSZ, CZESŁAW
  Bells in Winter (79) 51
  Collected Poems, The (89) 185
  Conversations with Czesław Miłosz (88) 194
  Facing the River (96) 247
  Issa Valley, The (82) 403
  Land of Ulro, The (85) 520
  Milosz's ABC's (02) 533
  Native Realm (81) 597
  New and Collected Poems, 1931-2001 (02) 567
  Provinces (92) 656
  Road-Side Dog (99) 666
  Seizure of Power, The (83) 713
  Separate Notebooks, The (85) 811
  Unattainable Earth (87) 892
  Visions from San Francisco Bay (83) 860
  Year of the Hunter, A (95) 900
  Witness of Poetry, The (84) 959
MILTON, DAVID, and NANCY DALL MILTON
  Wind Will Not Subside, The (77) 918
MILTON, JOYCE, and RONALD RADOSH
  Rosenberg File, The (H-84) 388

MIN, ANCHEE
  Becoming Madame Mao (01) 69
  Red Azalea (95) 643
MINOT, SUSAN
  Monkeys (87) 557
MINSKY, MARVIN
  Society of Mind, The (88) 828
MINTER, DAVID
  William Faulkner (81) 932
MISHIMA, YUKIO
  Acts of Worship (90) 10
MISHRA, PANKAJ
  Romantics, The (01) 741
MISTRY, ROHINTON
  Family Matters (03) 292
MITCHELL, OTIS C.
  Hitler over Germany (H-84) 213
MITCHELL, WILLIAM J.
  City of Bits (96) 112
MITFORD, JESSICA
  American Way of Death Revisited, The (99) 44
MITSUI, JAMES MASAO
  From a Three-Cornered World (98) 322
MOERS, ELLEN
  Literary Women (77) 439
MOHAMMAD REZA PAHLAVI
  Answer to History (81) 47
MOJTABAI, A. G.
  Autumn (83) 39
  Stopping Place, A (80) 785
MOLESWORTH, CHARLES
  Marianne Moore (91) 562
MOMADAY, N. SCOTT
  Man Made of Words, The (98) 534
  Names, The (78) 594
MONEGAL, EMIR RODRIGUEZ
  Jorge Luis Borges (80) 444
MONETTE, PAUL
  Becoming a Man (93) 62
  Borrowed Time (89) 112
MONK, RAY
  Bertrand Russell, 1872-1921 (97) 105
  Bertrand Russell, 1921-1970 (02) 78
MONTAGUE, JOHN
  Dead Kingdom, The (85) 167
  Mount Eagle (90) 591
MONTALE, EUGENIO
  New Poems (77) 553
  Second Life of Art, The (83) 705
MONTGOMERY, DAVID
  Fall of the House of Labor, The (88) 308
MOODY, RICK
  Demonology (02) 195
  Purple America (98) 643
MOONEY, MICHAEL MACDONALD
  Evelyn Nesbit and Stanford White (77) 260
MOORE, BRIAN
  Black Robe (86) 61
  Doctor's Wife, The (77) 226
  Lies of Silence (91) 527
  Magician's Wife, The (99) 506
  No Other Life (94) 563
  Statement, The (97) 782
MOORE, HAROLD G., and JOSEPH L. GALLOWAY
  We Were Soldiers Once . . . and Young (93) 868

1057

MOORE, JAMES, and ADRIAN DESMOND
Darwin (93) 196
MOORE, LORRIE
Birds of America (99) 105
MOORE, MARIANNE
Complete Poems of Marianne Moore, The (82) 126
Complete Prose of Marianne Moore, The (87) 165
Selected Letters of Marianne Moore, The (98) 702
MOORE, SUSANNA
Whiteness of Bones, The (90) 884
MOOREHEAD, CAROLINE
Bertrand Russell (94) 85
MORACE, ROBERT A.
Dialogic Novels of Malcolm Bradbury and David
Lodge, The (90) 173
MORAN, MARSHA, PATRICK MORAN, and
NORAH K. BARR, eds.
M. F. K. Fisher (99) 501
MORAVEC, HANS
Robot (99) 670
MORAVIA, ALBERTO
1934 (84) 613
Time of Desecration (81) 809
MORELL, THEODOR GILBERT, and DAVID
IRVING
Secret Diaries of Hitler's Doctor, The
(H-84) 398
MORGAN, EDMUND S.
Benjamin Franklin (03) 61
MORGAN, JOHN S.
Robert Fulton (78) 726
MORGAN, ROBERT
Groundwork (80) 390
MORGAN, TED
Churchill (H-83) 65
FDR (86) 269
Maugham (81) 559
MORGENTHAU, HENRY, III
Mostly Morgenthaus (92) 529
MORLEY, JOHN F.
Vatican Diplomacy and the Jews During the
Holocaust, 1939-1943 (81) 861
MORRIS, CHARLES R.
American Catholic (98) 36
MORRIS, EDMUND
Dutch (00) 185
Rise of Theodore Roosevelt, The (80) 717
Theodore Rex (02) 777
MORRIS, HERBERT
Little Voices of the Pears, The (90) 535
MORRIS, JAN
Fifty Years of Europe (98) 308
MORRIS, MARY MCGARRY
Dangerous Woman, A (92) 138
Vanished (89) 877
MORRIS, RICHARD B.
Witnesses at the Creation (86) 959
MORRIS, ROGER
Richard Milhous Nixon (90) 694
Uncertain Greatness (78) 869
MORRIS, WILLIE
Taps (02) 773
MORRIS, WRIGHT
Cloak of Light, A (86) 140
Collected Stories (87) 160

Earthly Delights, Unearthly Adornments
(79) 175
Fork River Space Project, The (78) 319
Plains Song (81) 655
Real Losses, Imaginary Gains (77) 652
Solo (84) 803
Time Pieces (90) 805
Will's Boy (82) 950
MORRISON, TONI
Beloved (88) 85
Jazz (93) 403
Love (04) 479
Paradise (99) 615
Song of Solomon (78) 789
Tar Baby (82) 828
MORRISON, WILBUR H.
Fortress Without a Roof (H-83) 150
MORROW, LANCE
Chief, The (86) 121
MORSON, GARY SAUL
Narrative and Freedom (95) 523
MORSON, GARY SAUL, and CARYL EMERSON
Mikhail Bakhtin (92) 500
MORTIMER, JOHN
Clinging to the Wreckage (83) 127
Paradise Postponed (87) 640
MOSCATI, SABATINO, editor
Phoenicians, The (90) 665
MOSLEY, LEONARD
Blood Relations (81) 93
Dulles (79) 170
Lindbergh (77) 433
Marshall (H-83) 283
MOSLEY, WALTER
Black Betty (95) 80
Little Yellow Dog, A (97) 535
Walkin' the Dog (00) 809
MOSS, HOWARD
Notes from the Castle (80) 597
MOSS, THYLIAS
Small Congregations (94) 743
MOSSE, GEORGE L.
Toward the Final Solution (79) 761
MOSSIKER, FRANCES
Madame de Sévigné (85) 595
MOTION, ANDREW
Keats (99) 449
Philip Larkin (94) 626
MOTT, MICHAEL
Seven Mountains of Thomas Merton, The (85) 815
MOYNIHAN, DANIEL PATRICK
Family and Nation (87) 259
Miles to Go (97) 581
Secrecy (99) 688
MUELLER, HERTA
Traveling on One Leg (99) 778
MUELLER, LISEL
Need to Hold Still, The (81) 603
MUKHERJEE, BHARATI
Darkness (87) 194
Desirable Daughters (03) 202
Holder of the World, The (94) 401
Jasmine (90) 450
Middleman and Other Stories, The (89) 553
MULDER, JOHN M.
Woodrow Wilson (79) 892

AUTHOR INDEX

MULDOON, PAUL
  Hay (99) 350
  Madoc (92) 469
  Poems, 1968-1998 (02) 645
MULISCH, HARRY
  Discovery of Heaven, The (97) 225
MULLEN, HARRYETTE
  Sleeping with the Dictionary (03) 775
MUNIF, ABDELRAHMAN
  Cities of Salt (89) 160
MUNRO, ALICE
  Friend of My Youth (91) 317
  Love of a Good Woman, The (99) 488
  Moons of Jupiter, The (84) 580
  Open Secrets (95) 578
  Progress of Love, The (87) 677
  Selected Stories (97) 742
MURAKAMI, HARUKI
  After the Quake (03) 5
  Elephant Vanishes, The (94) 260
  Norwegian Wood (01) 651
  South of the Border, West of the Sun (00) 721
  Underground (02) 813
MURASAKI SHIKIBU
  Tale of Genji, The (02) 769
MURAVCHIK, JOSHUA
  Heaven on Earth (03) 356
MURDOCH, IRIS
  Book and the Brotherhood, The (89) 103
  Good Apprentice, The (87) 345
  Green Knight, The (95) 279
  Message to the Planet, The (91) 587
  Metaphysics as a Guide to Morals (94) 526
  Nuns and Soldiers (81) 628
  Philosopher's Pupil, The (84) 690
MURPHY, WILLIAM M.
  Family Secrets (96) 253
MURRAY, ALBERT
  Blue Devils of Nada, The (97) 127
MURRAY, BRUCE
  Journey into Space (90) 464
MURRAY, CHARLES
  Losing Ground (H-85) 268
MURRAY, CHARLES, and RICHARD J.
  HERRNSTEIN
  Bell Curve, The (95) 70
MURRAY, JOHN
  Few Short Notes on Tropical Butterflies, A
    (04) 253
MURRAY, K. M. ELISABETH
  Caught in the Web of Words (78) 160
MURRAY, LES A.
  Conscious and Verbal (02) 163
  Daylight Moon and Other Poems, The (90) 157
  Fredy Neptune (00) 286
  Learning Human (01) 518
  Rabbiter's Bounty, The (93) 660
MURRAY, NICHOLAS
  Aldous Huxley (04) 13
  Life of Matthew Arnold, A (98) 500
  World Enough and Time (01) 930
MURRAY, PAULI
  Song in a Weary Throat (88) 835
MYERS, GERALD E.
  William James (87) 997
MYRER, ANTON
  Last Convertible, The (79) 359

NABOKOV, VLADIMIR
  Details of a Sunset and Other Stories (77) 206
  Lectures on Don Quixote (84) 427
  Lectures on Literature (81) 485
  Lectures on Russian Literature (82) 437
  Stories of Vladimir Nabokov, The (96) 724
  Strong Opinions (77) 789
  Vladimir Nabokov, Selected Letters (90) 849
NABOKOV, VLADIMIR, and EDMUND WILSON
  Nabokov-Wilson Letters, The (80) 564
NACHMAN, GERALD
  Seriously Funny (04) 679
NADLER, STEVEN
  Spinoza (00) 725
NADOLNY, STEN
  Discovery of Slowness, The (88) 247
NAFISI, AZAR
  Reading Lolita in Tehran (04) 634
NAGEL, PAUL C.
  Descent from Glory (H-84) 121
  John Quincy Adams (98) 472
NAIFEH, STEVEN, and GREGORY WHITE
  SMITH
  Jackson Pollock (91) 466
NAIPAUL, SHIVA
  Beyond the Dragon's Mouth (86) 56
NAIPAUL, V. S.
  Among the Believers (82) 6
  Bend in the River, A (80) 69
  Beyond Belief (99) 96
  Enigma of Arrival, The (88) 283
  Finding the Center (85) 281
  Half a Life (02) 372
  India (92) 346
  Return of Eva Perón, The (81) 686
  Turn in the South, A (90) 831
  Way in the World, A (95) 853
  Writer and the World, The (03) 902
NAJDER, ZDZISŁAW
  Joseph Conrad (84) 395
NARAYAN, R. K.
  Malgudi Days (83) 436
  Painter of Signs, The (77) 605
  Under the Banyan Tree (86) 918
NASAR, SYLVIA
  Beautiful Mind, A (99) 87
NASAW, DAVID
  Chief, The (01) 185
NASH, GEORGE H.
  Life of Herbert Hoover, The (H-84) 288
NATHAN, LEONARD, and ARTHUR QUINN
  Poet's Work, The (92) 623
NAVARRO, MARYSA, and NICHOLAS FRASER
  Eva Perón (82) 249
NAYLOR, GLORIA
  Linden Hills (86) 525
  Mama Day (89) 530
  Women of Brewster Place, The (83) 918
NEEDHAM, RODNEY
  Counterpoints (88) 209
  Exemplars (86) 259
NEELY, MARK E., JR.
  Last Best Hope of Earth, The (94) 449
NELSON, RAYMOND
  Van Wyck Brooks (82) 874

NEMEROV, HOWARD
    Collected Poems of Howard Nemerov, The
        (78) 200
    Figures of Thought (79) 209
NESTLE, MARION
    Food Politics (03) 311
NEUHAUS, RICHARD JOHN
    Naked Public Square, The (H-85) 324
NEUMAN, ALMA
    Always Straight Ahead (94) 11
NEUSTADT, RICHARD E., and ERNEST R. MAY
    Thinking in Time (87) 853
NEVIN, THOMAS R.
    Simone Weil (93) 736
NEWBORN, MONTY
    Kasparov Versus Deep Blue (98) 482
NEWBY, P. H.
    Kith (78) 491
NEWELL, NANCY PEABODY, and RICHARD S.
    NEWELL
    Struggle for Afghanistan, The (82) 817
NEWLOVE, DONALD
    Curranne Trueheart (87) 179
NEWMYER, R. KENT
    John Marshall and the Heroic Age of the
        Supreme Court (03) 432
NG, FAE MYENNE
    Bone (94) 105
NGOR, HAING, with ROGER WARNER
    Haing Ngor (89) 335
NICHOLL, CHARLES
    Cup of News, A (85) 147
    Reckoning, The (95) 639
NICHOLSON, GEOFF
    Female Ruins (01) 305
NICHOLSON, MICHAEL, JOHN B. DUNLOP, and
    RICHARD S. HAUGH
    Solzhenitsyn in Exile (86) 843
NICOL, CHARLES, and J. E. RIVERS, editors
    Nabokov's Fifth Arc (83) 511
NICOLSON, ADAM
    God's Secretaries (04) 295
NICOLSON, SIR HAROLD
    Harold Nicolson (81) 406
NICOSIA, GERALD
    Home to War (02) 386
NIEDECKER, LORINE
    Granite Pail, The (86) 368
NIMMO, DAN, and JAMES E. COMBS
    Subliminal Politics (81) 773
NIMS, JOHN FREDERICK
    Selected Poems (83) 730
NIN, ANAÏS
    Diary of Anaïs Nin, 1955-1966, The
        (77) 217
    Diary of Anaïs Nin, 1966-1974, The
        (81) 234
    Early Diary of Anaïs Nin, 1920-1923, The
        (83) 220
    Early Diary of Anaïs Nin, 1923-1927, The
        (84) 257
NISBET, ROBERT
    History of the Idea of Progress (81) 430
    Sociology as an Art Form (77) 753
NISBETT, RICHARD E.
    Geography of Thought, The (04) 287

NISSEN, HENRIK S., editor
    Scandinavia During the Second World War
        (H-84) 393
NISSENSON, HUGH
    Song of the Earth, The (02) 756
    Tree of Life, The (86) 896
NIVEN, JOHN
    Martin Van Buren (H-84) 298
NIXON, RICHARD M.
    In the Arena (91) 441
    Leaders (H-83) 248
    1999 (89) 595
    No More Vietnams (86) 659
    RN (79) 605
NOBLE, DAVID F.
    Forces of Production (H-85) 152
NOKES, DAVID
    Jane Austen (98) 468
NOLAN, CHRISTOPHER
    Under the Eye of the Clock (89) 868
NOLAN, TOM
    Ross Macdonald (00) 660
NOONAN, PEGGY
    What I Saw at the Revolution (91) 881
NOOTEBOOM, CEES
    Following Story, The (95) 249
NORFOLK, LAWRENCE
    Lemprière's Dictionary (93) 435
    Pope's Rhinoceros, The (97) 671
NORMAN, GEOFFREY
    Midnight Water (84) 543
NORMAN, HOWARD
    Haunting of L., The (03) 352
NORRIS, KATHLEEN
    Amazing Grace (99) 40
    Cloister Walk, The (97) 160
    Dakota (94) 200
    Little Girls in Church (96) 440
NORTON, DAVID
    History of the Bible as Literature, A (94) 397
NORTON, MARY BETH
    In the Devil's Snare (03) 405
NOSSACK, HANS ERICH
    Wait for November (83) 864
NOVAK, WILLIAM, with THOMAS P.
    O'NEILL, JR.
    Man of the House (88) 524
NOVICK, PETER
    Holocaust in American Life, The (00) 404
NOWAK, JAN
    Courier from Warsaw (H-83) 85
NOZICK, ROBERT
    Examined Life, The (90) 231
    Philosophical Explanations (82) 638
NULAND, SHERWIN B.
    How We Die (95) 324
    Lost in America (04) 469
    Mysteries Within, The (01) 609
    Wisdom of the Body, The (98) 854
NUSSBAUM, BRUCE
    World After Oil, The (H-84) 502
NUSSBAUM, MARTHA C.
    Sex and Social Justice (00) 697
NYE, NAOMI SHIHAB
    Words Under the Words (96) 835

AUTHOR INDEX

OAKES, JAMES
 Ruling Race, The (H-83) 384
OATES, JOYCE CAROL
 American Appetites (90) 29
 Angel of Light (82) 17
 Because It Is Bitter, and Because It Is My Heart
  (91) 75
 Bellefleur (81) 78
 Black Water (93) 83
 Blonde (01) 99
 Bloodsmoor Romance, A (83) 61
 Broke Heart Blues (00) 99
 Childwold (77) 149
 Faith of a Writer, The (04) 240
 Faithless (02) 267
 Foxfire (94) 313
 Heat and Other Stories (92) 281
 Last Days (85) 524
 My Heart Laid Bare (99) 542
 Mysteries of Winterthurn (85) 640
 Night-Side (78) 608
 Profane Art, The (84) 716
 Son of the Morning (79) 693
 Tattooed Girl, The (04) 727
 What I Lived For (95) 858
 You Must Remember This (88) 1009
OATES, STEPHEN B.
 Approaching Fury, The (98) 72
 Let the Trumpet Sound (H-83) 259
OBERMAN, HEIKO A.
 Luther (91) 553
O'BRIAN, PATRICK
 Blue at the Mizzen (00) 78
 Wine-Dark Sea, The (94) 856
 Yellow Admiral, The (97) 904
O'BRIEN, CONOR CRUISE
 Great Melody, The (93) 316
 Siege, The (87) 776
O'BRIEN, EDNA
 Down by the River (98) 263
 Fanatic Heart, A (85) 260
 In the Forest (03) 410
 Time and Tide (93) 796
 Wild Decembers (01) 915
O'BRIEN, GEOFFREY
 Phantom Empire, The (94) 622
O'BRIEN, GEORGE
 Village of Longing, The, *and* Dancehall Days
  (91) 851
O'BRIEN, SHARON
 Willa Cather (87) 994
O'BRIEN, TIM
 In the Lake of the Woods (95) 355
 July, July (03) 437
 Things They Carried, The (91) 803
O'CONNOR, FLANNERY
 Habit of Being, The (80) 391
O'CONNOR, FRANK
 Collected Stories (82) 100
O'CONNOR, GARRY
 Sean O'Casey (89) 757
O'CONNOR, SANDRA DAY, and H. ALAN DAY
 Lazy B (03) 460
ODETS, WALT
 In the Shadow of the Epidemic (96) 368
ŌE, KENZABURŌ
 Rouse Up O Young Men of the New Age! (03) 690

O'FAOLAIN, JULIA
 No Country for Young Men (88) 601
O'FAOLAIN, NUALA
 Almost There (04) 22
 My Dream of You (02) 554
O'FAOLAIN, SEAN
 Collected Stories of Sean O'Faolain, The (84) 198
OFFUTT, CHRIS
 Kentucky Straight (93) 422
 Out of the Woods (00) 601
 Same River Twice, The (94) 717
O'HARA, JOHN
 Selected Letters of John O'Hara (79) 656
O'HEHIR, DIANA
 I Wish This War Were Over (85) 415
OKRI, BEN
 Famished Road, The (93) 279
 Stars of the New Curfew (90) 753
OLDS, SHARON
 Blood, Tin, Straw (00) 74
 Dead and the Living, The (85) 162
 Father, The (93) 284
 Gold Cell, The (88) 353
OLIVER, MARY
 Dream Work (87) 219
 New and Selected Poems (93) 549
 Owls and Other Fantasies (04) 596
 West Wind (98) 828
 White Pine (95) 867
OLSON, CHARLES
 Maximus Poems, The (84) 519
O'MEARA, STEPHEN JAMES, and WILLIAM
 SHEEHAN
 Mars (02) 511
OMNÈS, ROLAND
 Quantum Philosophy (00) 638
O'NAN, STEWART
 Circus Fire, The (01) 194
 Names of the Dead, The (97) 615
 Prayer for the Dying, A (00) 622
ONDAATJE, MICHAEL
 Anil's Ghost (01) 44
 English Patient, The (93) 271
 Handwriting (00) 346
 In the Skin of a Lion (88) 428
O'NEILL, EUGENE
 Selected Letters of Eugene O'Neill (89) 771
O'NEILL, GERARD K.
 2081 (82) 860
O'NEILL, THOMAS P., JR., with WILLIAM NOVAK
 Man of the House (88) 524
ONG, WALTER J.
 Hopkins, the Self, and God (87) 406
 Orality and Literacy (83) 568
OPPEN, GEORGE
 Selected Letters of George Oppen, The (91) 726
OPPENHEIM, JANET
 "Shattered Nerves" (92) 742
OPPENHEIMER, JUDY
 Private Demons (89) 668
OREN, MICHAEL B.
 Six Days of War (03) 765
ORIEUX, JEAN
 Voltaire (80) 850
ORWELL, GEORGE
 Orwell, the Lost Writings (86) 715

OSBORNE, CHARLES
W. H. Auden (80) 860
OSBORNE, JOHN
Better Class of Person, A (82) 45
OSHINSKY, DAVID M.
Conspiracy So Immense, A (H-84) 100
OSTLING, RICHARD N, and JOAN K. OSTLING
Mormon America (00) 529
O'TOOLE, G. J. A.
Spanish War, The (H-85) 425
O'TOOLE, PATRICIA
Five of Hearts, The (91) 295
O'TOOLE, PETER
Loitering with Intent (98) 522
OTT, HUGO
Martin Heidegger (94) 512
OTTO, WHITNEY
How to Make an American Quilt (92) 309
OUSBY, IAN
Road to Verdun, The (03) 676
OWEN, DAVID
Balkan Odyssey (97) 95
OWEN, STEPHEN
Remembrances (87) 708
OWEN, STEPHEN, editor
Anthology of Chinese Literature, An (97) 53
OWENS, LOUIS
Sharpest Sight, The (93) 732
OZ, AMOS
Fima (94) 296
OZICK, CYNTHIA
Art & Ardor (84) 44
Bloodshed and Three Novellas (77) 101
Cannibal Galaxy, The (84) 137
Fame and Folly (97) 269
Levitation (83) 405
Messiah of Stockholm, The (88) 549
Puttermesser Papers, The (98) 648
Quarrel and Quandary (01) 721
Shawl, The (90) 734
OZMENT, STEVEN
Magdalena and Balthasar (87) 508

PACKARD, JERROLD M.
Neither Friend nor Foe (93) 545
PACKARD, VANCE
People Shapers, The (78) 649
PACKER, ANN
Dive from Clausen's Pier, The (03) 211
PACKER, ZZ
Drinking Coffee Elsewhere (04) 189
PADDOCK, LISA O., and CARL E. ROLLYSON
Susan Sontag (01) 805
PADFIELD, PETER
Armada (89) 50
Dönitz, the Last Führer (H-85) 115
PADOVER, SAUL K.
Karl Marx (79) 349
PAGE, GEORGE
Inside the Animal Mind (00) 426
PAGE, JOSEPH A.
Perón (H-84) 336
PAGELS, ELAINE
Adam, Eve, and the Serpent (89) 4
Gnostic Gospels, The (80) 363
Origin of Satan, The (96) 541

PAGELS, HEINZ R.
Cosmic Code, The (83) 156
PAINTER, GEORGE D.
Chateaubriand (1768-93) (79) 95
William Caxton (78) 909
PAINTER, NELL IRVIN
Sojourner Truth (97) 772
PAIS, ABRAHAM
Niels Bohr's Times (92) 569
PAKENHAM, THOMAS
Boer War, The (80) 97
Scramble for Africa, The (92) 717
PALEY, GRACE
Collected Stories, The (95) 133
Just as I Thought (99) 441
Later the Same Day (86) 509
PALMER, DAVE RICHARD
Summons of the Trumpet (79) 732
PAMUK, ORHAN
My Name is Red (02) 558
New Life, The (98) 583
White Castle, The (92) 890
PANCAKE, BREECE D'J
Stories of Breece D'J Pancake, The (84) 824
PANCAKE, JOHN S.
1777 (78) 757
PANTEL, PAULINE SCHMITT, editor
History of Women in the West, From Ancient
Goddesses to Christian Saints, A (93) 345
PAPALEO, JOSEPH
Italian Stories (03) 419
PAPER, LEWIS J.
Brandeis (H-84) 73
PARETSKY, SARA
Hard Time (00) 350
PARFIT, DEREK
Reasons and Persons (85) 729
PARINI, JAY
John Steinbeck (96) 398
Robert Frost (00) 651
PARKER, GEOFFREY
Grand Strategy of Philip II, The (00) 326
PARKER, HERSHEL
Herman Melville (97) 373
Reading Billy Budd (92) 665
PARKER, ROBERT DALE
Unbeliever, The (89) 864
PARKES, M. B.
Pause and Effect (94) 615
PARKIN, FRANK
Krippendorf's Tribe (87) 456
PARKINSON, ROGER
Tormented Warrior (80) 827
PARKS, GORDON
Voices in the Mirror (91) 861
PARKS, SUZAN-LORI
Getting Mother's Body (04) 291
PARKS, TIM
Destiny (01) 232
PARMET, HERBERT S.
Jack (81) 454
PARRISH, MICHAEL E.
Felix Frankfurter and His Times (H-83) 140
PARTRIDGE, FRANCES
Love in Bloomsbury (82) 504

AUTHOR INDEX

PASTAN, LINDA
Carnival Evening (99) 141
Five Stages of Grief, The (79) 222
Fraction of Darkness, A (86) 310
Imperfect Paradise, The (89) 367
PM/AM (83) 603
Waiting for My Life (82) 897
PASTERNAK, BORIS, and OLGA FREIDENBERG
Correspondence of Boris Pasternak and Olga
Freidenberg, 1910-1954, The (83) 147
PASTERNAK, BORIS, MARINA TSVETAYEVA, and
RAINER MARIA RILKE
Letters (86) 514
PASTERNAK, LEONID
Memoirs of Leonid Pasternak, The (84) 528
PATERNITI, MICHAEL
Driving Mr. Albert (01) 258
PATON, ALAN
Ah, But Your Land Is Beautiful (83) 6
Knocking on the Door (77) 396
PATTERSON, JAMES T.
Grand Expectations (97) 355
PATTERSON, ORLANDO
Freedom (92) 237
PAULEY, BRUCE F.
Hitler and the Forgotten Nazis (82) 360
PAULIN, TOM
Minotaur (93) 518
PAULOS, JOHN ALLEN
Innumeracy (90) 420
PAVIĆ, MILORAD
Dictionary of the Khazars (89) 245
PAWEL, ERNST
Labyrinth of Exile, The (90) 495
Nightmare of Reason, The (85) 645
PAYNE, STANLEY G.
Fascism (81) 314
PAZ, OCTAVIO
Collected Poems of Octavio Paz, The
(88) 169
Itinerary (01) 471
One Earth, Four or Five Worlds (86) 701
Selected Poems (85) 802
Sor Juana (89) 808
PEARL, MATTHEW
Dante Club, The (04) 156
PEARS, IAIN
Dream of Scipio, The (03) 229
Instance of the Fingerpost, An (99) 418
PEARSALL, DEREK
Life of Geoffrey Chaucer, The (93) 459
PEARSON, JOHN
Sitwells, The (80) 763
PEARSON, T. R.
Off for the Sweet Hereafter (87) 611
PEERY, JANET
River Beyond the World, The (97) 701
PELECANOS, GEORGE P.
Hell to Pay (03) 361
PELEVIN, VICTOR
Buddha's Little Finger (01) 153
PELIKAN, JAROSLAV
Jesus Through the Centuries (86) 482
Vindication of Tradition, The (H-85) 467

PENROSE, ROGER
Emperor's New Mind, The (90) 207
Shadows of the Mind (95) 705
PERCY, WALKER
Lancelot (78) 501
Lost in the Cosmos (84) 482
Second Coming, The (81) 717
Signposts in a Strange Land (92) 747
Thanatos Syndrome, The (88) 883
PEREC, GEORGES
Void, A (96) 799
PERELMAN, S. J.
Last Laugh, The (82) 433
PERL, JEFFREY M.
Skepticism and Modern Enmity (91) 746
Tradition of Return, The (85) 917
PERRETT, GEOFFREY
America in the Twenties (H-83) 33
Dream of Greatness, A (80) 226
PERROT, MICHELLE, editor
History of Private Life, From the Fires of
Revolution to the Great War, A (91) 404
PERRY, BRUCE
Malcolm (92) 474
PERRY, RICHARD
Montgomery's Children (85) 629
No Other Tale to Tell (95) 559
PERSICO, JOSEPH E.
Imperial Rockefeller, The (H-83) 206
PERSICO, JOSEPH E., with COLIN L. POWELL
My American Journey (96) 494
PETER, JOHN
Vladimir's Carrot (88) 937
PETERS, CATHERINE
King of Inventors, The (94) 440
PETERS, JOAN
From Time Immemorial (H-85) 156
PETERS, MARGOT
May Sarton (98) 551
PETERS, WILLIAM
More Perfect Union, A (88) 589
PETERSON, MERRILL D.
Great Triumvirate, The (88) 363
Lincoln in American Memory (95) 435
PETESCH, NATALIE L. M.
Duncan's Colony (83) 210
PETITFILS, PIERRE
Rimbaud (88) 765
PETROSKI, HENRY
Pencil, The (91) 656
PFAFF, WILLIAM
Wrath of Nations, The (94) 864
PHELPS, TIMOTHY M., and HELEN WINTERNITZ
Capitol Games (93) 128
PHILBRICK, NATHANIEL
In the Heart of the Sea (01) 457
PHILLIPS, ARTHUR
Prague (03) 624
PHILLIPS, CARL
Pastoral (01) 699
PHILLIPS, JAYNE ANNE
Machine Dreams (85) 589
Shelter (95) 709
PHILLIPS, JOHN A.
Eve (H-85) 130

PHILLIPS, KATE
Helen Hunt Jackson (04) 330
PHILLIPS, KEVIN
Cousins' Wars, The (00) 146
Politics of Rich and Poor, The (91) 674
Wealth and Democracy (03) 872
PHILLIPS, WILLIAM
Parisan View, A (85) 677
PIAGET, JEAN
Grasp of Consciousness, The (77) 341
PICHOIS, CLAUDE
Baudelaire (91) 70
PICKOVER, CLIFFORD A.
Time (99) 760
PIERCY, MARGE
Available Light (89) 63
Braided Lives (83) 75
Circles on the Water (83) 119
Gone to Soldiers (88) 358
Longings of Women, The (95) 446
PIERPONT, CLAUDIA ROTH
Passionate Minds (01) 694
PINCHERLE, ALBERTO. See MORAVIA,
ALBERTO
PINCKNEY, DARRYL
High Cotton (93) 335
PINKARD, TERRY
Hegel (01) 393
PINKER, STEVEN
Blank Slate, The (03) 79
How the Mind Works (98) 401
Language Instinct, The (95) 431
Words and Rules (00) 863
PINSKY, ROBERT
Explanation of America, An (81) 293
Figured Wheel, The (97) 278
History of My Heart (85) 399
Sounds of Poetry, The (99) 724
Want Bone, The (91) 866
PINSKY, ROBERT, translator
Inferno of Dante, The (96) 376
PINTER, HAROLD
Proust Screenplay, The (78) 673
PIPES, RICHARD
Property and Freedom (00) 626
PIPHER, MARY
Another Country (00) 36
PIRSIG, ROBERT M.
Lila (92) 440
PLANTE, DAVID
Accident, The (92) 5
Annunciation (95) 42
Country, The (82) 140
Woods, The (83) 923
PLATH, SYLVIA
Collected Poems, The (82) 96
Journals of Sylvia Plath, The (83) 367
PLETSCH, CARL
Young Nietzsche (92) 928
PLOWDEN, ALISON
Elizabeth Regina (81) 272
PLUMLY, STANLEY
Summer Celestial (84) 846
POCOCK, TOM
Terror Before Trafalgar, The (04) 743

PODHORETZ, NORMAN
Breaking Ranks (80) 101
POGUE, FORREST C.
George C. Marshall (88) 346
POIRIER, RICHARD
Robert Frost (78) 722
POLITI, MARCO, and CARL BERNSTEIN
His Holiness (97) 388
POLIZZOTTI, MARK
Revolution of the Mind (96) 633
POLLACK, JACK HARRISON
Earl Warren (80) 255
POLLAN, MICHAEL
Botany of Desire, The (02) 125
POLLITT, KATHA
Antarctic Traveller (83) 20
Reasonable Creatures (95) 626
POLLOCK, JOHN
Wilberforce (79) 862
POMERANCE, BERNARD
Elephant Man, The (80) 280
PONIATOWSKA, ELENA
Here's to You, Jesusa! (02) 381
POPOV, YEVGENY, et al., editors
Metropol (84) 533
PORTER, BERNARD
Britain, Europe and the World, 1850-1982
(H-84) 78
PORTER, CONNIE
All-Bright Court (92) 9
PORTER, JOSEPH C.
Paper Medicine Man (87) 636
PORTER, KATHERINE ANNE
Letters of Katherine Anne Porter (91) 517
PORTER, ROY
Greatest Benefit to Mankind, The (99) 341
PORTIS, CHARLES
Gringos (92) 262
Masters of Atlantis (86) 579
POSNER, RICHARD A.
Breaking the Deadlock (02) 130
POTOK, CHAIM
Davita's Harp (86) 217
Gift of Asher Lev, The (91) 355
POTTS, WILLARD, editor
Portraits of the Artist in Exile (80) 675
POUND, EZRA, and FORD MADOX FORD
Pound/Ford, the Story of a Literary Friendship
(83) 621
POUND, EZRA, and WYNDHAM LEWIS
Pound/Lewis (86) 747
POUND, EZRA, and DOROTHY SHAKESPEAR
Ezra Pound and Dorothy Shakespear, Their Letters,
1909-1914 (85) 243
POUND, EZRA, and WILLIAM CARLOS
WILLIAMS
Pound/Williams (97) 675
POWELL, ANTHONY
Fisher King, The (87) 287
Hearing Secret Harmonies (77) 347
Infants of the Spring (78) 447
Miscellaneous Verdicts (93) 522
O, How the Wheel Becomes It! (84) 628
Strangers All Are Gone, The (84) 833
Under Review (95) 819

POWELL, COLIN L., with JOSEPH E. PERSICO
My American Journey (96) 494
POWELL, DAWN
Diaries of Dawn Powell, 1931-1965, The
(96) 178
POWELL, PADGETT
Edisto (85) 213
Woman Named Drown, A (88) 968
POWER, SAMANTHA
"Problem from Hell, A" (03) 629
POWERS, J(AMES) F(ARL)
Wheat That Springeth Green (89) 892
POWERS, RICHARD
Gain (99) 324
Galatea 2.2 (96) 299
Gold Bug Variations, The (92) 252
Operation Wandering Soul (94) 586
Plowing the Dark (01) 711
Prisoner's Dilemma (89) 663
Time of Our Singing, The (04) 756
POWERS, RICHARD GID
Secrecy and Power (88) 801
POWERS, RON
Far from Home (92) 193
POWERS, THOMAS
Heisenberg's War (94) 380
PRAGER, DENNIS, and JOSEPH TELUSHKIN
Why the Jews? (H-84) 481
PRANGE, GORDON W.
At Dawn We Slept (82) 33
Target Tokyo (H-85) 430
PRANGE, GORDON W., DONALD M. GOLDSTEIN,
and KATHERINE V. DILLON
Miracle at Midway (H-83) 288
Pearl Harbor (86) 732
PRENSHAW, PEGGY WHITMAN, editor
Conversations with Eudora Welty
(85) 137
Eudora Welty (81) 283
PRESTON, PAUL
Franco (95) 257
PRESTON, RICHARD
Hot Zone, The (95) 319
PRICE, REYNOLDS
Blue Calhoun (93) 87
Clear Pictures (90) 104
Collected Poems, The (98) 181
Collected Stories, The (94) 150
Foreseeable Future, The (92) 222
Kate Vaiden (87) 451
Learning a Trade (99) 470
Promise of Rest, The (96) 606
Roxanna Slade (99) 675
Source of Light, The (82) 790
Three Gospels (97) 826
Whole New Life, A (95) 871
PRICE, RICHARD (1941-   )
Alabi's World (91) 10
PRICE, RICHARD (1949-   )
Breaks, The (84) 112
Clockers (93) 161
Freedomland (99) 307
PRIESTLEY, J. B.
Found, Lost, Found (78) 325
PRINCE, F. T.
Collected Poems, 1935-1992 (94) 142

PRITCHARD, WILLIAM H.
Frost (85) 312
Lives of the Modern Poets (81) 520
Randall Jarrell (91) 696
PRITCHETT, V. S.
Careless Widow and Other Stories, A (90) 86
Chekhov (89) 155
Collected Stories (83) 131
Complete Collected Essays (93) 179
Complete Collected Stories (92) 109
Gentle Barbarian, The (78) 340
Man of Letters, A (87) 512
More Collected Stories (84) 584
Myth Makers, The (80) 560
On the Edge of the Cliff (80) 627
Selected Stories (79) 669
Tale Bearers, The (81) 786
PROCTOR, ROBERT N.
Nazi War on Cancer, The (00) 562
PROFFER, ELLENDEA
Bulgakov (85) 62
PROSE, FRANCINE
Blue Angel (01) 104
Household Saints (82) 373
PROST, ANTOINE, and GÉRARD VINCENT, editors
History of Private Life, Riddles of Identity in
Modern Times, A (92) 294
PROTHERO, STEPHEN
Purified by Fire (02) 674
PROULX, E. ANNIE
Accordion Crimes (97) 5
Close Range (00) 134
Shipping News, The (94) 733
PROUST, MARCEL
Marcel Proust, Selected Letters, 1880-1903
(84) 504
Marcel Proust, Selected Letters, 1904-1909
(90) 557
On Reading Ruskin (88) 621
PRUESSEN, RONALD W.
John Foster Dulles (H-83) 229
PRYCE-JONES, DAVID
Paris in the Third Reich (82) 615
PUIG, MANUEL
Buenos Aires Affair, The (77) 129
Eternal Curse on the Reader of These Pages
(83) 235
PURDY, JAMES
In a Shallow Grave (77) 380
PUTNAM, HILARY
Renewing Philosophy (94) 696
PUTNAM, ROBERT D.
Bowling Alone (01) 139
PYM, BARBARA
Academic Question, An (87) 1
Crampton Hodnet (86) 194
No Fond Return of Love (83) 536
Some Tame Gazelle (84) 809
Unsuitable Attachment, An (83) 855
Very Private Eye, A (85) 964
PYMAN, AVRIL
History of Russian Symbolism, A (95) 305
PYNCHON, THOMAS
Mason and Dixon (98) 546
Slow Learner (85) 830
Vineland (90) 844
PYRON, DARDEN ASBURY
Southern Daughter (92) 775

QUAMMEN, DAVID
Monster of God (04) 519
QUANDT, WILLIAM B.
Decade of Decisions (78) 243
QUERRY, RON
Death of Bernadette Lefthand, The (94) 217
QUINN, ARTHUR, and LEONARD NATHAN
Poet's Work, The (92) 623
QUINN, SUSAN
Mind of Her Own, A (88) 558
QUIÑONEZ, ERNESTO
Bodega Dreams (01) 117
QUIRK, ROBERT E.
Fidel Castro (94) 287

RABAN, JONATHAN
Bad Land (97) 91
Foreign Land (86) 302
Hunting Mister Heartbreak (92) 314
Old Glory (82) 580
RABINOWITCH, ALEXANDER
Bolsheviks Come to Power, The (77) 109
RABINOWITZ, DOROTHY
New Lives (77) 549
RABY, PETER
Alfred Russel Wallace (02) 30
RADOSH, RONALD, and HARVEY KLEHR
Amerasia Spy Case, The (97) 28
RADOSH, RONALD, and JOYCE MILTON
Rosenberg File, The (H-84) 388
RAMPERSAD, ARNOLD
Jackie Robinson (98) 458
Life of Langston Hughes, 1902-1941, The
(87) 489
Life of Langston Hughes, 1941-1967, The
(89) 501
RAMPERSAD, ARNOLD, and ARTHUR ASHE
Days of Grace (94) 213
RANDALL, ALICE
Wind Done Gone, The (02) 865
RANDALL, WILLARD STERNE
Thomas Jefferson (94) 797
RANDERS-PEHRSON, JUSTINE DAVIS
Barbarians and Romans (H-84) 39
RANKIN, IAN
Resurrection Men (04) 657
RANSOM, JOHN CROWE
Selected Essays of John Crowe Ransom
(85) 797
RANSOM, ROGER L., and RICHARD SUTCH
One Kind of Freedom (78) 622
RAPPAPORT, LEON, and GEORGE M. KREN
Holocaust and the Crisis of Human Behavior, The
(81) 439
RASHID, AHMED
Jihad (03) 423
RASMUSSEN, R. KENT
Mark Twain A to Z (96) 452
RATUSHINSKAYA, IRINA
Grey Is the Color of Hope (89) 330
RAUCH, JONATHAN
Kindly Inquisitors (94) 436
RAVIV, DAN, and YOSSI MELMAN
Every Spy a Prince (91) 271

RAWLS, JOHN
Political Liberalism (94) 649
RAYFIELD, DONALD
Anton Chekhov (99) 57
RAYMOND, ANDRÉ
Cairo (02) 135
READ, PIERS PAUL
Married Man, A (80) 522
Polonaise (77) 632
READER, JOHN
Africa (99) 19
REAGAN, RONALD
American Life, An (91) 24
RECTOR, LIAM
Sorrow of Architecture, The (85) 855
REED, RALPH
Active Faith (97) 9
REED, ISHMAEL
Reckless Eyeballing (87) 690
Shrovetide in Old New Orleans (79) 681
Terrible Twos, The (83) 778
REEDER, ROBERTA
Anna Akhmatova (95) 38
REEVE, CHRISTOPHER
Still Me (99) 733
REEVES, HUBERT
Atoms of Silence (H-85) 39
REEVES, RICHARD
American Journey (H-83) 46
President Kennedy (94) 662
REEVES, THOMAS C.
Life and Times of Joe McCarthy, The (H-83) 270
Question of Character, A (92) 660
REICH, CARY
Life of Nelson A. Rockefeller, 1908-1958, The
(97) 506
REICH, ROBERT B.
Work of Nations, The (92) 919
REID, JAN
Bullet Meant for Me, The (03) 119
REID, PANTHEA
Art and Affection (97) 66
REIDEL, JAMES
Vanished Act (04) 796
REIKEN, FREDERICK
Odd Sea, The (99) 566
REILLY, ROBIN
William Pitt the Younger (80) 873
REINHARZ, JEHUDA
Chaim Weizmann (86) 111
REISCHAUER, EDWIN O.
Japanese, The (78) 459
REMINI, ROBERT V.
Andrew Jackson and His Indian Wars (02) 43
Andrew Jackson and the Course of American
Democracy, 1833-1845 (H-85) 28
Andrew Jackson and the Course of American
Empire, 1767-1821 (78) 50
Andrew Jackson and the Course of American
Freedom, 1822-1832 (82) 11
Daniel Webster (98) 221
REMNICK, DAVID
Devil Problem, The (97) 210
King of the World (99) 453
Lenin's Tomb (94) 458
Resurrection (98) 673

AUTHOR INDEX

RENDELL, RUTH
  Harm Done (00) 354
RENFREW, COLIN
  Archaeology and Language (89) 41
REUTHER, VICTOR G.
  Brothers Reuther, The (77) 124
REYNOLDS, DAVID S.
  Walt Whitman's America (96) 806
REYNOLDS, MICHAEL
  Hemingway, The American Homecoming
    (93) 325
  Hemingway, The Final Years (00) 377
  Hemingway, The 1930's (98) 379
  Hemingway, The Paris Years (90) 369
  Young Hemingway, The (87) 1021
RHODES, RICHARD
  Deadly Feasts (98) 230
  Farm (90) 240
  Hole in the World, A (91) 418
  Making of the Atomic Bomb, The (88) 517
  Masters of Death (03) 513
  Why They Kill (00) 843
RHYS, JEAN
  Letters of Jean Rhys, The (85) 554
RICE, ANNE
  Interview with the Vampire (77) 384
RICE, EDWARD
  Captain Sir Richard Francis Burton (91) 123
RICE, STAN
  False Prophet (04) 249
RICH, ADRIENNE
  Arts of the Possible (02) 53
  Atlas of the Difficult World, Poems 1988-1991, An
    (92) 25
  Collected Early Poems, 1950-1970 (94) 133
  Dream of a Common Language, The (79) 160
  Fox (02) 309
  Of Woman Born (77) 584
  On Lies, Secrets, and Silence (80) 622
  Time's Power (90) 809
  Wild Patience Has Taken Me This Far, A (82) 942
RICHARDSON, H. EDWARD
  Jesse (85) 494
RICHARDSON, JOAN
  Wallace Stevens, 1879-1923 (87) 927
  Wallace Stevens, 1923-1955 (89) 882
RICHARDSON, JOANNA
  Baudelaire (96) 65
  Sarah Bernhardt and Her World (78) 740
RICHARDSON, JOHN
  Life of Picasso, 1881-1906 (92) 431
  Life of Picasso, 1907-1917 (97) 511
RICHARDSON, ROBERT D., JR.
  Emerson (96) 222
  Henry Thoreau (87) 387
RICHLER, MORDECAI
  Solomon Gursky Was Here (91) 755
RICKELS, LAURENCE A.
  Nazi Psychoanalysis (03) 559
RICKETTS, HARRY
  Rudyard Kipling (01) 750
RICKS, CHRISTOPHER, and LEONARD
    MICHAELS, editors
  State of the Language, The (91) 773
RICKS, CHRISTOPHER B.
  Beckett's Dying Words (94) 71
  Essays in Appreciation (97) 256

RICOEUR, PAUL
  Time and Narrative, Vol. I (85) 902
RIDING, ALAN
  Distant Neighbors (86) 234
RIDLEY, JASPER
  Napoleon III and Eugénie (81) 587
  Statesman and Saint (H-84) 420
RIDLEY, JOHN
  Drift, The (03) 242
RIDLEY, MATT
  Genome (01) 332
  Nature via Nuture (04) 541
  Origins of Virtue, The (98) 616
RIFKIN, JEREMY
  Biotech Century, The (99) 100
RIGGS, DAVID
  Ben Jonson (90) 58
RILKE, RAINER MARIA
  Uncollected Poems (97) 848
RILKE, RAINER MARIA, BORIS PASTERNAK, and
    MARINA TSVETAYEVA
  Letters (86) 154
RIMBAUD, ARTHUR
  Rimbaud Complete (03) 672
RINGS, WERNER
  Life with the Enemy (H-83) 274
RÍOS, JULIÁN
  Monstruary (02) 537
RITCHIE, ROBERT C.
  Captain Kidd and the War Against the Pirates
    (87) 99
RIVERA, EDWARD
  Family Installments (83) 240
RIVERS, J. E., and CHARLES NICOL, editors
  Nabokov's Fifth Arc (83) 511
ROA BASTOS, AUGUSTO
  I the Supreme (87) 419
ROAZEN, PAUL
  Helene Deutsch (86) 402
ROBB, GRAHAM
  Balzac (95) 60
  Rimbaud (01) 736
  Victor Hugo (99) 838
ROBB, PETER
  M (01) 549
ROBBINS, CARLA ANNE
  Cuban Threat, The (H-84) 106
ROBBINS, TOM
  Half Asleep in Frog Pajamas (95) 287
ROBERTS, DAVID
  Jean Stafford (89) 414
  Newer World, A (01) 627
ROBERTS, JANE, and MARTIN KEMP, with PHILIP
    STEADMAN
  Leonardo da Vinci (90) 505
ROBERTS, JOHN MORRIS
  History of Europe, A (98) 383
ROBERTSON, JAMES I., JR.
  Stonewall Jackson (98) 736
ROBERTSON, JAMES OLIVER
  American Myth, American Reality (81) 39
ROBERTSON-LORANT, LAURIE
  Melville (97) 568
ROBINSON, DAVID
  Chaplin (86) 116

ROBINSON, JANICE S.
H. D. (83) 331

ROBINSON, KIM STANLEY
Antarctica (99) 48
Gold Coast, The (89) 316
Red Mars (94) 688
Years of Rice and Salt, The (03) 912

ROBINSON, MARILYNNE
Death of Adam, The (99) 226
Mother Country (90) 586

ROBINSON, PHYLLIS C.
Willa (84) 945

ROBINSON, ROXANA
Georgia O'Keeffe (90) 289

ROBISON, MARY
Amateur's Guide to the Night, An (84) 16
Why Did I Ever (02) 847

ROCHLIN, GENE I.
Trapped in the Net (98) 773

RODENBECK, MAX
Cairo (00) 117

RODGERS, DANIEL T.
Work Ethic in Industrial America, 1850-1920, The
(79) 904

RODRIGUEZ, ABRAHAM, JR.
Boy Without a Flag, The (93) 96
Spidertown (94) 760

RODRIGUEZ, RICHARD
Brown (03) 114
Days of Obligation (93) 204
Hunger of Memory (82) 377

ROGERS, GUY MacLEAN, and MARY R.
LEFKOWITZ, editors
Black Athena Revisited (97) 114

ROLLIN, BETTY
First, You Cry (77) 291

ROLLYSON, CARL
Lillian Hellman (89) 511
Lives of Norman Mailer, The (92) 445
Nothing Ever Happens to the Brave (91) 639
Rebecca West (97) 684

ROLLYSON, CARL E., and LISA O. PADDOCK
Susan Sontag (01) 805

ROMASCO, ALBERT U.
Politics of Recovery, The (H-84) 347

RONSON, JON
Them (03) 829

ROOKE, LEON
Shakespeare's Dog (84) 784

ROOT-BERNSTEIN, ROBERT SCOTT
Discovering (90) 186

ROREM, NED
Knowing When to Stop (95) 427

RORTY, RICHARD
Truth and Progress (99) 799

ROSE, JONATHAN
Intellectual Life of the British Working Classes,
The (02) 418

ROSE, PHYLLIS
Parallel Lives (84) 662

ROSE, STEVEN
Lifelines (98) 508

ROSE, STEVEN, R. C. LEWONTIN, and LEON J.
KAMIN
Not in Our Genes (H-85) 329

ROSEN, JONATHAN
Eve's Apple (98) 299

ROSEN, ROBERT
Nowhere Man (01) 661

ROSENBAUM, RON
Explaining Hitler (99) 273

ROSENBERG, DAVID, editor
Congregation (88) 189

ROSENBERG, TINA
Haunted Land, The (96) 330

ROSENBERG, WILLIAM G., and MARILYN B.
YOUNG
Transforming Russia and China (H-83) 426

ROSENFIELD, ISRAEL
Invention of Memory, The (89) 400

ROSENGARTEN, THEODORE, editor
Tombee (87) 875

ROSENKRANTZ, LINDA
My Life as a List (00) 554

ROSENTHAL, M. L., and SALLY M. GALL
Modern Poetic Sequence, The (84) 570
Sailing into the Unknown (79) 632

ROSS, LILLIAN
Here but Not Here (99) 360

ROSSABI, MORRIS
Khubilai Khan (89) 432

ROSSNER, JUDITH
Attachments (78) 77

ROTH, HENRY
Diving Rock on the Hudson, A (96) 190
From Bondage (97) 319
Mercy of a Rude Stream (95) 482
Requiem for Harlem (99) 654

ROTH, JACK J.
Cult of Violence, The (81) 215

ROTH, MICHAEL S., ed.
Freud (99) 311

ROTH, PHILIP
American Pastoral (98) 45
Anatomy Lesson, The (84) 26
Counterlife, The (88) 204
Deception (91) 188
Dying Animal, The (02) 217
Facts, The (89) 288
Ghost Writer, The (80) 354
Human Stain, The (01) 427
I Married a Communist (99) 406
Operation Shylock (94) 581
Patrimony (92) 615
Professor of Desire, The (78) 669
Sabbath's Theater (96) 672
Zuckerman Unbound (82) 981

ROTHENBERG, GUNTHER E.
Art of Warfare in the Age of Napoleon, The
(79) 38

ROTHMAN, ELLEN K.
Hands and Hearts (H-85) 195

ROUDINESCO, ELIZABETH
Jacques Lacan (98) 463

ROVERE, RICHARD H.
Arrivals and Departures (77) 62
Final Reports (H-85) 141

ROWAN, CARL T.
Dream Makers, Dream Breakers (94) 252

ROWLEY, HAZEL
Richard Wright (02) 703

AUTHOR INDEX

ROWLING, J. K.
Harry Potter and the Order of the Phoenix
(04) 324
ROWSE, A. L.
Eminent Elizabethans (H-84) 147
ROY, ARUNDHATI
God of Small Things, The (98) 357
RUBENFELD, FLORENCE
Clement Greenberg (99) 181
RUBIN, LOUIS D., JR., editor
History of Southern Literature, The (86) 426
RUDDICK, SARA, and PAMELA DANIELS, editors
Working It Out (78) 937
RUDMAN, MARK
Millennium Hotel, The (97) 586
RUÍZ, RAMÓN EDUARDO
Great Rebellion, The (81) 396
RUKEYSER, MURIEL
Collected Poems, The (80) 148
RUNYON, RANDOLPH PAUL
Reading Raymond Carver (93) 669
RUSH, NORMAN
Mating (92) 490
RUSHDIE, SALMAN
Fury (02) 317
Ground Beneath Her Feet, The (00) 341
Haroun and the Sea of Stories (91) 376
Imaginary Homelands (92) 324
Moor's Last Sigh, The (96) 478
Satanic Verses, The (90) 711
Shame (84) 788
Step Across This Line (03) 799
RUSK, DEAN
As I Saw It (91) 56
RUSKIN, JOHN, and THOMAS CARLYLE
Correspondence of Thomas Carlyle and John
Ruskin, The (83) 153
RUSS, JOANNA
How to Suppress Women's Writing (84) 353
RUSSELL, HERBERT K.
Edgar Lee Masters (02) 226
RUSSELL, JEFFREY BURTON
History of Heaven, A (98) 387
Lucifer (H-85) 272
Mephistopheles (87) 553
RUSSELL, SHARMAN APT
Anatomy of a Rose (02) 39
RUSSO, JOHN PAUL
I. A. Richards (90) 401
Straight Man (98) 745
RUSSO, RICHARD
Empire Falls (02) 244
Whore's Child, and Other Stories, The (03) 886
RYAN, ALAN
John Dewey and the High Tide of American
Liberalism (96) 393
RYAN, PAUL B., and THOMAS A. BAILEY
Hitler vs. Roosevelt (80) 404
RYBCZYNSKI, WITOLD
Clearing in the Distance, A (00) 126
Home (87) 402
Most Beautiful House in the World, The (90) 582
One Good Turn (01) 679
RYMER, RUSS
Genie (94) 345

SÁBATO, ERNESTO
On Heroes and Tombs (82) 585
SACHAR, HOWARD M.
Diaspora (86) 226
Dreamland (03) 233
History of the Jews in America, A (93) 340
SACKS, OLIVER
Anthropologist on Mars, An (96) 47
Island of the Colorblind and Cycad Island, The
(98) 454
Man Who Mistook His Wife for a Hat, The
(87) 516
Seeing Voices (90) 720
SAFIRE, WILLIAM
Scandalmonger (01) 759
SAFRANSKI, RÜDIGER
Martin Heidegger (99) 529
Nietzsche (02) 584
Schopenhauer and the Wild Years of Philosophy
(91) 711
SAGAN, CARL
Broca's Brain (80) 116
SAGAN, FRANÇOISE
Silken Eyes (78) 776
Unmade Bed, The (79) 791
SAGE, LORNA
Bad Blood (03) 51
SAHLINS, MARSHALL
How "Natives" Think (96) 338
SAHLINS, MARSHALL, and PATRICK V. KIRCH
Anahulu (93) 20
SAID, EDWARD W.
Culture and Imperialism (94) 181
Out of Place (00) 597
Reflections on Exile and Other Essays (02) 684
World, the Text, and the Critic, The (84) 971
ST. AUBYN, GILES
Edward VII (80) 264
ST. JOHN, DAVID
Study for the World's Body (95) 777
SAKHAROV, ANDREI
Memoirs (91) 582
SALISBURY, HARRISON E.
Journey for Our Times, A (H-84) 252
Long March, The (86) 537
New Emperors, The (93) 554
Russia in Revolution, 1900-1930 (79) 622
SALLIS, JAMES
Chester Himes (02) 149
SALTER, JAMES
Burning the Days (98) 138
Dusk and Other Stories (89) 254
SALTER, MARY JO
Henry Purcell in Japan (86) 411
SALWAK, DALE, editor
Life and Work of Barbara Pym, The (88) 471
SALYER, LUCY E.
Laws Harsh as Tigers (96) 418
SAMPSON, ANTHONY
Mandela (00) 506
SAMS, ERIC
Real Shakespeare, The (96) 619
SAMUELS, ERNEST
Bernard Berenson (80) 73
SAMUELSON, ROBERT J.
Good Life and Its Discontents, The (97) 345

SAMWAY, PATRICK H.
  Walker Percy (98) 818
SAND, GEORGE, and GUSTAVE FLAUBERT
  Flaubert-Sand (94) 300
SANDEL, MICHAEL J.
  Democracy's Discontents (97) 205
SANDERS, BARRY
  Sudden Glory (96) 728
SANDERS, DORI
  Her Own Place (94) 385
SANDERS, RONALD
  High Walls of Jerusalem, The (H-84) 197
  Lost Tribes and Promised Lands (79) 398
SANER, REG
  Climbing into the Roots (77) 164
SANFORD, JOHN
  Intruders in Paradise (98) 432
  Color of the Air, The (86) 178
SANTE, LUC
  Factory of Facts, The (99) 278
  Low Life (92) 460
SAPERSTEIN, ALAN
  Mom Kills Kids and Self (80) 541
SAPOLSKY, ROBERT M.
  Primate's Memoir, A (02) 659
SAPPHO
  If Not (03) Winter, 388
SARAMAGO, JOSÉ
  All the Names (01) 15
  Blindness (99) 114
SARDE, MICHÈLE
  Colette (81) 161
SAROYAN, WILLIAM
  Chance Meetings (79) 92
  My Name Is Saroyan (84) 588
SARRAUTE, NATHALIE
  Childhood (85) 89
SARTON, MAY
  Collected Poems (94) 137
  World of Light, A (77) 941
SARTRE, JEAN-PAUL
  Life/Situations (78) 529
  War Diaries (86) 932
SATTA, SALVATORE
  Day of Judgment, The (88) 242
SAUNDERS, FRANCES STONOR
  Cultural Cold War, The (01) 227
SAUNDERS, GEORGE
  Pastoralia (01) 703
SAVAGE, DAVID G.
  Turning Right (93) 815
SAVAGE, THOMAS
  I Heard My Sister Speak My Name (78) 427
SAVIGNEAU, JOSYANE
  Marguerite Yourcenar (94) 500
SAWYER-LAUCANNO, CHRISTOPHER
  Invisible Spectator, An (90) 424
SAYER, DEREK
  Coasts of Bohemia, The (99) 195
SAYLES, JOHN
  Anarchists' Convention, The (80) 28
SCALAPINO, LESLIE
  Zither and Autobiography (04) 872
SCALES-TRENT, JUDY
  Notes of a White Black Woman (96) 514

SCAMMELL, MICHAEL
  Solzhenitsyn (85) 839
SCHACTER, DANIEL L.
  Searching for Memory (97) 727
SCHAMA, SIMON
  Citizens (90) 99
  Dead Certainties (92) 152
  Embarrassment of Riches, The (88) 266
  History of Britain, A (01) 398
  Landscape and Memory (96) 414
  Patriots and Liberators (78) 642
SCHAPIRO, LEONARD
  Turgenev (80) 832
SCHEIN, SETH L.
  Mortal Hero, The (85) 635
SCHELE, LINDA, and DAVID FREIDEL
  Forest of Kings, A (91) 308
SCHELE, LINDA, and MARY ELLEN MILLER
  Blood of Kings, The (87) 75
SCHELL, JONATHAN
  Fate of the Earth, The (83) 244
  Time of Illusion, The (77) 822
SCHELL, ORVILLE
  Virtual Tibet (01) 873
SCHEPER-HUGHES, NANCY
  Death Without Weeping (93) 209
SCHICKEL, RICHARD
  Another I, Another You (79) 34
SCHIFF, STACY
  Saint-Exupéry (95) 683
  Véra (Mrs. Vladimir Nabokov) (00) 789
SCHIFF, ZE'EV, and EHUD YA'ARI
  Intifada (91) 461
SCHIFFMAN, ZACHARY S., and MICHAEL E.
  HOBART
  Information Ages (99) 414
SCHIFFRIN, ANDRÉ
  Business of Books, The (01) 163
SCHIFFRIN, HAROLD Z.
  Sun Yat-sen (81) 777
SCHINE, CATHLEEN
  Alice in Bed (84) 12
  Evolution of Jane, The (99) 265
  Love Letter, The (96) 448
  Rameau's Niece (94) 680
SCHLESINGER, ARTHUR M., JR.
  Cycles of American History, The (87) 183
  Life in the Twentieth Century, A (01) 527
SCHLOSSER, ERIC
  Fast Food Nation (02) 280
  Reefer Madness (04) 643
SCHNACKENBERG, GJERTRUD
  Lamplit Answer, The (86) 505
SCHNEIDER, NINA
  Woman Who Lived in a Prologue, The (81) 941
SCHNEIDER, PETER
  Wall Jumper, The (85) 978
SCHNEIDER, PIERRE
  Matisse (H-85) 303
SCHOENBRUN, DAVID
  America Inside Out (H-85) 22
  Soldiers of the Night (81) 750
SCHOLEM, GERSHOM
  Life in Letters, 1914-1982, A (03) 475

SCHOR, JULIET B.
  Overspent American, The (99) 610
  Overworked American, The (93) 597
SCHORER, MARK
  Pieces of Life (78) 657
SCHORSKE, CARL E.
  Fin-de-siècle Vienna (81) 330
SCHUCK, PETER H.
  Diversity in America (04) 174
SCHULZ, BRUNO
  Letters and Drawings of Bruno Schulz (89) 470
  Sanatorium Under the Sign of the Hourglass
    (79) 645
  Street of Crocodiles, The (78) 804
SCHUMACHER, E. F.
  Guide for the Perplexed, A (78) 364
SCHUYLER, JAMES
  Morning of the Poem, The (81) 578
SCHWARTZ, BERNARD
  Super Chief (H-84) 435
SCHWARTZ, DELMORE
  Letters of Delmore Schwartz (85) 548
SCHWARTZ, LYNNE SHARON
  Ruined by Reading (97) 710
SCHWARTZ, MAXIME
  How the Cows Turned Mad (04) 343
SCHWARTZ, STEPHEN
  From West to East (99) 319
  Two Faces of Islam, The (03) 853
SCHWARTZMAN, MYRON
  Romare Bearden (92) 684
SCHWARZ, JORDAN A.
  New Dealers, The (94) 555
  Speculator, The (82) 800
SCIASCIA, LEONARDO
  Candido (80) 129
  Open Doors and Three Novellas (93) 589
SCOTT, JOANNA
  Various Antidotes (95) 831
SCOTT, PAUL
  Staying On (78) 795
SCOTT, PETER DALE
  Coming to Jakarta (90) 127
  Deep Politics and the Death of JFK (94) 221
  Listening to the Candle (93) 469
SEABROOK, JOHN
  Deeper (98) 235
SEAGRAVE, STERLING
  Soong Dynasty, The (86) 852
SEARLE, JOHN R.
  Minds, Brains and Science (86) 614
  Rediscovery of the Mind, The (93) 673
SEATON, ALBERT
  German Army, 1933-45, The (H-83) 161
SEBALD, W. G.
  Austerlitz (02) 62
  Emigrants, The (98) 282
  On the Natural History of Destruction (04) 574
  Rings of Saturn, The (99) 662
  Vertigo (01) 868
SEBOLD, ALICE
  Lovely Bones, The (03) 499
SECORD, JAMES A.
  Victorian Sensation (02) 822

SECREST, MERYLE
  Frank Lloyd Wright (93) 303
  Stephen Sondheim (99) 728
SEE, CAROLYN
  Golden Days (87) 335
  Rhine Maidens (82) 684
SEE, LISA
  On Gold Mountain (96) 523
SEGAL, LORE
  Her First American (86) 416
  Lucinella (77) 460
SELBY, HUBERT, JR.
  Requiem for a Dream (79) 589
SELF, WILL
  How the Dead Live (01) 422
  Quantity Theory of Insanity, The (96) 615
SELINGER, SUZANNE
  Calvin Against Himself (H-85) 59
SELZER, RICHARD
  Down from Troy (93) 244
  Taking the World in for Repairs (87) 836
SEN, AMARTYA
  Inequality Reexamined (93) 382
SENN, FRITZ
  Joyce's Dislocations (85) 509
SENNETT, RICHARD
  Respect in a World of Inequality (04) 652
SERENY, GITTA
  Albert Speer (96) 5
  Cries Unheard (00) 151
SETH, VIKRAM
  Equal Music, An (00) 236
  Golden Gate, The (87) 340
  Suitable Boy, A (94) 774
SETTLE, MARY LEE
  Killing Ground, The (83) 381
  Scapegoat, The (81) 707
SEWARD, DESMOND
  Eleanor of Aquitaine (80) 277
  Hundred Years War, The (79) 291
SEXTON, ANNE
  Anne Sexton (78) 54
  Complete Poems, The (82) 120
  Words for Dr. Y (79) 897
SEYMOUR, MIRANDA
  Robert Graves (96) 650
SEYMOUR-SMITH, MARTIN
  Hardy (95) 291
  Robert Graves (84) 746
SHACHTMAN, TOM
  Day America Crashed, The (80) 200
  Phony War, 1939-1940, The (H-83) 338
SHACOCHIS, BOB
  Easy in the Islands (86) 240
  Immaculate Invasion, The (00) 413
  Swimming in the Volcano (94) 779
SHAFFER, PETER
  Amadeus (81) 27
SHAKESPEAR, DOROTHY, and EZRA POUND
  Ezra Pound and Dorothy Shakespear, Their Letters,
    1909-1914 (85) 243
SHAKESPEARE, NICHOLAS
  Bruce Chatwin (01) 148
SHAMMAS, ANTON
  Arabesques (89) 37

SHANGE, NTOZAKE
Betsey Brown (86) 52
SHANKS, BOB
Cool Fire, The (77) 180
SHANOR, DONALD R.
Soviet Triangle, The (81) 759
SHAPIRO, ALAN
Happy Hour (88) 368
Mixed Company (97) 590
SHAPIRO, BARBARA J.
"Beyond Reasonable Doubt" and "Probable Cause" (93) 75
SHAPIRO, KARL
Collected Poems, 1940-1978 (79) 124
SHARP, RONALD A.
Friendship and Literature (87) 309
SHATTUCK, ROGER
Forbidden Knowledge (97) 296
Innocent Eye, The (85) 445
SHATZ, MARSHALL S.
Soviet Dissent in Historical Perspective (82) 795
SHAW, GEORGE BERNARD
Bernard Shaw, Collected Letters, 1926-1950 (89) 84
Collected Letters, 1911-1925 (86) 145
Complete Prefaces, 1889-1913, The (95) 145
SHAW, IRWIN
Bread Upon the Waters (82) 67
SHAW, STANFORD J., and EZEL KURAL SHAW
History of the Ottoman Empire and Modern Turkey, The (78) 393
SHAWCROSS, WILLIAM
Quality of Mercy, The (H-85) 373
Shah's Last Ride, The (89) 784
Sideshow (80) 758
SHAY, JONATHAN
Achilles in Vietnam (95) 1
SHEA, LISA
Hula (95) 334
SHEED, WILFRID
Frank and Maisie (86) 313
Good Word & Other Words, The (80) 375
Transatlantic Blues (79) 772
SHEEHAN, EDWARD R. F.
Arabs, Israelis, and Kissinger, The (77) 57
SHEEHAN, NEIL
Bright Shining Lie, A (89) 125
SHEEHAN, WILLIAM, and STEPHEN JAMES O'MEARA
Mars (02) 511
SHELDEN, MICHAEL
Orwell (92) 602
SHELL, MARC, editor
American Babel (03) 19
SHELLEY, MARY WOLLSTONECRAFT
Letters of Mary Wollstonecraft Shelley, The (81) 501
SHENK, DAVID
Forgetting, The (02) 300
SHEPARD, SAM
Sam Shepard, Seven Plays (82) 731
SHERMER, MICHAEL
In Darwin's Shadow (03) 400

SHERRY, NORMAN
Life of Graham Greene, The, 1904-1939 (90) 521
Life of Graham Greene, The, 1939-1955 (96) 430
SHERWOOD, FRANCES
Vindication (94) 835
SHEVCHENKO, ARKADY N.
Breaking with Moscow (86) 81
SHI, DAVID E.
Simple Life, The (86) 820
SHIELDS, CAROL
Dressing Up for the Carnival (01) 254
Larry's Party (98) 486
Stone Diaries, The (95) 756
Unless (03) 858
SHIELDS, DAVID
Dead Languages (90) 163
SHILLER, ROBERT J.
New Financial Order, The (04) 551
SHILS, EDWARD
Portraits (98) 639
SHILTS, RANDY
And the Band Played On (88) 36
Conduct Unbecoming (94) 158
SHIMAZAKI, TSON
Before the Dawn (88) 81
SHIPLER, DAVID K.
Arab and Jew (87) 35
SHIPPEY, T. A.
J. R. R. Tolkien (02) 436
Road to Middle-Earth, The (84) 736
SHIRER, WILLIAM L.
Twentieth Century Journey, Vol. II (H-85) 451
SHLAIM, AVI
United States and the Berlin Blockade, 1948-1949, The (H-84) 469
SHORRIS, EARL
Under the Fifth Sun (81) 844
SHORT, PHILIP
Mao (01) 554
SHOSTAK, MARJORIE
Nisa (82) 559
SHOSTAKOVICH, DMITRI
Testimony (80) 808
SHOWALTER, ELAINE
Inventing Herself (02) 423
SHULMAN, ALIX KATES
On the Stroll (82) 590
SHULMAN, DAVID, and GALIT HASAN-ROKEM, editors
Untying the Knot (97) 862
SICHERMAN, BARBARA
Alice Hamilton (H-85) 6
SICK, GARY
All Fall Down (86) 10
SIEBURTH, RICHARD
Instigations (80) 431
SIGMUND, PAUL E.
Overthrow of Allende and the Politics of Chile, 1964-1976, The (78) 630
SILBER, EVELYN
Gaudier-Brzeska (98) 331
SILBER, JOAN
In the City (88) 418
SILK, LEONARD
Economists, The (77) 251

AUTHOR INDEX

SILK, LEONARD, and MARK SILK
American Establishment, The (81) 36
SILKO, LESLIE MARMON
Almanac of the Dead (92) 13
Storyteller (82) 812
SILLITOE, ALAN
Her Victory (83) 340
Lost Flying Boat, The (85) 579
Second Chance and Other Stories, The (82) 747
Widower's Son, The (78) 904
SILVERMAN, KENNETH
Edgar A. Poe (92) 174
Life and Times of Cotton Mather, The
(H-85) 256
SIME, RUTH LEWIN
Lise Meitner (97) 526
SIMIC, CHARLES
Night Picnic (02) 592
Voice at 3:00 A.M., The (04) 806
SIMMONS, CHARLES
Wrinkles (79) 918
SIMON, HERBERT
Models of My Life (92) 519
SIMON, JAMES F.
What Kind of Nation (03) 877
SIMON, JEFFREY
Cohesion and Dissension in Eastern Europe
(H-84) 91
SIMON, JOHN
Singularities (77) 742
SIMON, KATE
Bronx Primitive (83) 80
Renaissance Tapestry, A (89) 708
Wider World, A (87) 985
SIMON, LINDA
Genuine Reality (99) 329
Thornton Wilder (80) 815
SIMON, NEIL
Rewrites (97) 692
SIMPSON, EILEEN
Poets in Their Youth (83) 608
SIMPSON, HELEN
Getting a Life (02) 334
SIMPSON, LOUIS
Best Hour of the Night, The (85) 42
Collected Poems (89) 180
Revolution in Taste, A (80) 709
Searching for the Ox (77) 706
SIMPSON, MONA
Anywhere but Here (88) 42
Lost Father, The (93) 487
Regular Guy, A (97) 688
SINCLAIR, ANDREW
Jack (78) 454
SINCLAIR, CLIVE
Brothers Singer, The (84) 127
SINGAL, DANIEL JOSEPH
War Within (83) 873
William Faulkner (98) 850
SINGER, IRVING
Nature of Love, The (89) 585

SINGER, ISAAC BASHEVIS
Collected Stories of Isaac Bashevis Singer, The
(83) 135
Death of Methuselah and Other Stories, The
(89) 231
Image and Other Stories, The (86) 461
King of the Fields, The (89) 441
Lost in America (82) 485
Old Love (80) 614
Penitent, The (84) 678
Shosha (79) 677
SINGH, PATWANT
Sikhs, The (01) 774
SÎN-LEQI-UNNINNÌ
Gilgamesh (85) 324
SINYAVSKY, ANDREI. See TERTZ, ABRAM
SIRICA, JOHN J.
To Set the Record Straight (80) 822
SISMAN, ADAM
Boswell's Presumptuous Task (02) 120
SISSMAN, L. E.
Hello, Darkness (79) 264
SISSON, C. H.
Avoidance of Literature, The (80) 40
SITKOFF, HARVARD
Struggle for Black Equality, 1954-1980, The
(82) 822
SKIBELL, JOSEPH
English Disease, The (04) 232
SKIDELSKY, ROBERT
John Maynard Keynes, 1920-1937 (95) 400
John Maynard Keynes, 1937-1946 (02) 453
SKLAREW, MYRA
Science of Goodbyes, The (83) 694
SKOCPOL, THEDA
Protecting Soldiers and Mothers (94) 671
ŠKVORECKÝ, JOSEF
Bass Saxophone, The (80) 54
Engineer of Human Souls, The (85) 227
Miracle Game, The (92) 509
SLATER, LAUREN
Lying (01) 545
SLAVIN, JULIA
Woman Who Cut Off Her Leg at the Maidstone
Club and Other Stories, The (00) 855
SLAVITT, DAVID R.
Cliff, The (95) 123
Lives of the Saints (91) 530
Rounding the Horn (79) 608
Walls of Thebes, The (87) 936
SLAYTON, ROBERT A.
Empire Statesman (02) 248
SLOAN, JAMES PARK
Jerzy Kosinski (97) 470
SLOAT, WARREN
1929 (80) 591
SLOMAN, JOEL
Stops (98) 741
SLOTKIN, RICHARD
Fatal Environment, The (86) 264

1073

SMILEY, JANE
Age of Grief, The (88) 6
All-True Travels and Adventures of Lidie Newton,
The (99) 32
Good Faith (04) 299
Greenlanders, The (89) 326
Horse Heaven (01) 412
Moo (96) 473
Ordinary Love *and* Good Will (90) 642
Thousand Acres, A (92) 817
SMITH, BRADLEY F.
Reaching Judgment at Nuremberg (78) 695
Road to Nuremberg, The (82) 695
Shadow Warriors, The (H-84) 403
SMITH, BRADLEY F., and ELENA AGAROSSI
Operation Sunrise (80) 631
SMITH, DAVE
Cuba Night (91) 179
Goshawk, Antelope (80) 380
In the House of the Judge (84) 374
Roundhouse Voices, The (86) 775
SMITH, DENIS MACK. *See* MACK SMITH, DENIS
SMITH, GADDIS
Morality, Reason, and Power (87) 577
SMITH, GREGORY WHITE, and STEVEN NAIFEH
Jackson Pollock (91) 466
SMITH, GUS, and DES HICKEY
Seven Days to Disaster (H-83) 387
SMITH, HEDRICK
Power Game, The (89) 658
Russians, The (77) 694
SMITH, JOHN CHABOT
Alger Hiss (77) 38
SMITH, LEE
Last Girls, The (03) 456
Oral History (84) 647
SMITH, LILLIAN
Winner Names the Age, The (79) 879
SMITH, MARK
Death of the Detective, The (77) 202
SMITH, MARTIN CRUZ
December 6 (03) 187
Gorky Park (82) 333
SMITH, PAGE
Democracy on Trial (96) 165
New Age Now Begins, A (77) 529
Rise of Industrial America, The (H-85) 391
Trial by Fire (H-83) 431
SMITH, RICHARD NORTON
Colonel, The (98) 202
Thomas E. Dewey and His Times (H-83) 421
SMITH, STEVIE
Collected Poems of Stevie Smith, The (77) 168
Me Again (83) 458
SMITH, WALTER W. (RED)
Red Smith Reader, The (83) 645
SMITH, WILLIAM JAY
Traveler's Tree, The (81) 831
SMITH, ZADIE
Autograph Man, The (03) 46
White Teeth (01) 910
SMOUT, THOMAS CHRISTOPHER
Century of the Scottish People, 1830-1950, A
(88) 127
SMYTHE, DONALD
Pershing (87) 660

SNOW, DONALD M.
Nuclear Strategy in a Dynamic World (82) 565
SNYDER, GARY
Axe Handles (84) 65
Mountains and Rivers Without End (97) 605
No Nature (93) 565
Place in Space, A (96) 585
SOBEL, DAVA
Galileo's Daughter (00) 295
SOLBERG, CARL
Oil Power (77) 588
SOLNIT, REBECCA
River of Shadows (04) 666
Wanderlust (01) 887
SOLOMON, ANDREW
Noonday Demon, The (02) 596
SOLOMON, DEBORAH
Utopia Parkway (98) 801
SOLOMON, MAYNARD
Mozart (96) 490
SOLZHENITSYN, ALEXANDER I.
Gulag Archipelago, The (78) 370
November 1916 (00) 589
SONENSHEIN, RAPHAEL J.
Politics in Black and White (94) 654
SONG, CATHY
Picture Bride (84) 695
School Figures (95) 691
SONTAG, SUSAN
AIDS and Its Metaphors (90) 19
In America (01) 452
Illness as Metaphor (79) 295
On Photography (78) 618
Regarding the Pain of Others (04) 648
Susan Sontag Reader, A (83) 769
Under the Sign of Saturn (81) 848
Volcano Lover, The (93) 856
Where the Stress Falls (02) 842
SORIN, GERALD
Irving Howe (04) 364
SORRENTINO, GILBERT
Aberration of Starlight (81) 1
Blue Pastoral (84) 99
Mulligan Stew (80) 544
Something Said (86) 847
SOTO, GARY
New and Selected Poems (96) 504
Summer Life, A (91) 782
SOUEIF, AHDAF
In the Eye of the Sun (94) 406
SOUNES, HOWARD
Down the Highway (02) 208
SOUTHERN, R. W.
Scholastic Humanism and the Unification of
Europe, Vol. I (97) 718
SOWELL, THOMAS
Conflict of Visions, A (88) 184
Conquests and Cultures (99) 212
Marxism (86) 572
Migrations and Cultures (97) 577
SOYINKA, WOLE
Aké (83) 10
Ìsarà (90) 435
Open Sore of a Continent, The (97) 648
SPALDING, FRANCES
Roger Fry (81) 699
Vanessa Bell (84) 900

AUTHOR INDEX

SPANG, REBECCA L.
  Invention of the Restaurant, The (01) 467
SPARK, MURIEL
  Aiding and Abetting (02) 26
  Curriculum Vitae (94) 196
  Far Cry from Kensington, A (89) 293
  Loitering with Intent (82) 475
  Only Problem, The (85) 668
  Reality and Dreams (98) 670
  Stories of Muriel Spark (86) 864
  Symposium (91) 790
  Takeover, The (77) 802
  Territorial Rights (80) 804
SPEER, ALBERT
  Infiltration (82) 398
  Spandau (77) 764
SPENCE, JONATHAN D.
  Chan's Great Continent, The (99) 149
  Gate of Heavenly Peace, The (82) 305
  God's Chinese Son (97) 339
  Mao Zedong (00) 511
  Memory Palace of Matteo Ricci, The (H-85) 309
  Question of Hu, The (89) 679
  Search for Modern China, The (91) 716
  Treason by the Book (02) 800
SPENCER, ELIZABETH
  Jack of Diamonds (89) 405
  Night Travellers, The (92) 573
  Southern Woman, The (02) 760
SPENCER, SCOTT
  Endless Love (80) 294
  Ship Made of Paper, A (04) 683
  Waking the Dead (87) 922
SPENDER, MATTHEW
  From a High Place (00) 290
SPENDER, STEPHEN
  Journals, 1939-1983 (87) 446
  Thirties and After, The (79) 745
SPERBER, A. M.
  Murrow (87) 582
SPERBER, A. M., and ERIC LAX
  Bogart (98) 125
SPIELMAN, JOHN P.
  Leopold I of Austria (78) 518
SPITZ, ELLEN HANDLER
  Inside Picture Books (00) 422
SPOONER, MARY HELEN
  Soldiers in a Narrow Land (95) 733
SPRAWSON, CHARLES
  Haunts of the Black Masseur (94) 372
SPURLING, HILARY
  Ivy (85) 461
  Unknown Matisse, The (99) 826
STAFFORD, PAULINE
  Queens, Concubines, and Dowagers (H-84) 371
STAFFORD, WILLIAM
  Glass Face in the Rain, A (83) 288
  Oregon Message, An (88) 636
  Passwords (92) 612
  Stories That Could Be True (78) 799
STAGG, J. C. A.
  Mr. Madison's War (H-84) 303
STALLWORTHY, JON
  Louis MacNeice (96) 444
STANFORD, ANN
  In Mediterranean Air (78) 439
STANFORD, FRANK
  Light the Dead See, The (92) 436

STANG, SONDRA J., editor
  Presence of Ford Madox Ford, The (82) 652
STANISLAW, JOSEPH, and DANIEL YERGIN
  Commanding Heights (99) 204
STANNARD, DAVID E.
  Puritan Way of Death, The (78) 682
STANNARD, MARTIN
  Evelyn Waugh, 1903-1939 (88) 293
  Evelyn Waugh, 1939-1966 (93) 275
STANSELL, CHRISTINE
  American Moderns (01) 29
STANSKY, PETER
  Redesigning the World (86) 761
STANTON, DOUG
  In Harm's Way (02) 400
STANTON, ELIZABETH CADY, and SUSAN B.
  ANTHONY
  Elizabeth Cady Stanton, Susan B. Anthony,
    Correspondence, Writings, Speeches (82) 214
STAPLES, BRENT
  Parallel Time (95) 594
STARBUCK, GEORGE
  Argot Merchant Disaster, The (83) 25
STARK, GUY D.
  Entrepreneurs of Ideology (82) 240
STARR, KEVIN
  Dream Endures, The (98) 268
  Embattled Dreams (03) 250
  Endangered Dreams (97) 247
  Inventing the Dream (86) 477
  Material Dreams (91) 577
STARR, S. FREDERICK
  Red and Hot (84) 726
STASHOWER, DANIEL
  Teller of Tales (00) 741
STAUFFER, JOHN
  Black Hearts of Men, The (03) 74
STAVANS, ILAN
  On Borrowed Words (02) 600
STEAD, CHRISTINA
  Miss Herbert (77) 509
STEADMAN, PHILIP, with MARTIN KEMP and
  JANE ROBERTS
  Leonardo da Vinci (90) 505
STEARNS, PETER N.
  Anxious Parents (04) 35
STEEL, RONALD
  Walter Lippmann and the American Century
    (81) 886
STEELE, SHELBY
  Content of Our Character, The (91) 170
STEELE, TIMOTHY
  Color Wheel, The (96) 140
  Missing Measures (91) 601
  Sapphics Against Anger (87) 741
STEGNER, WALLACE
  Collected Stories of Wallace Stegner (91) 161
  Crossing to Safety (88) 218
  One Way to Spell Man (83) 563
  Recapitulation (80) 702
  Spectator Bird, The (77) 769
STEINBECK, JOHN
  Acts of King Arthur and His Noble Knights, The
    (77) 7

1075

STEINER, GEORGE
  Antigones (85) 17
  Errata (99) 261
  Grammars of Creation (02) 357
  No Passion Spent (97) 626
  Portage to San Cristóbal of A. H., The (83) 616
  Real Presences (90) 681
STEPHENS, JOHN RUSSELL
  Profession of the Playwright, The (93) 655
STEPHENSON, NEAL
  Cryptonomicon (00) 159
STERN, FRITZ
  Gold and Iron (78) 354
STERN, GERALD
  Bread Without Sugar (93) 101
  Lucky Life (78) 540
  Red Coal, The (82) 661
  This Time (99) 756
STERN, RICHARD
  Father's Words, A (87) 271
  Noble Rot (90) 624
  Pacific Tremors (02) 614
  Packages (81) 636
  Sistermony, A (96) 716
STERN, STEVE
  Lazar Malkin Enters Heaven (88) 457
STEVENSON, ANNE
  Bitter Fame (90) 71
STEVENSON, ELIZABETH
  Figures in a Western Landscape (95) 231
STEVENSON, WILLIAM
  Man Called Intrepid, A (77) 475
STEWART, DESMOND
  T. E. Lawrence (78) 813
STEWART, JAMES B.
  Den of Thieves (92) 162
STIGLER, STEPHEN
  History of Statistics, The (87) 397
STIGLITZ, JOSEPH E.
  Globalization and Its Discontents (03) 334
STILL, JAMES
  From the Mountain, from the Valley (02) 313
STILL, WILLIAM N., JR., RICHARD E. BERINGER,
  HERMAN HATTAWAY, and ARCHER JONES
  Why the South Lost the Civil War (87) 980
STINCHCOMBE, WILLIAM
  XYZ Affair, The (82) 972
STOBER, DAN, and IAN HOFFMAN
  Convenient Spy, A (03) 164
STOCK, R. D.
  Flutes of Dionysus, The (91) 304
STOCKING, GEORGE W., JR.
  Victorian Anthropology (88) 928
STOCKMAN, DAVID A.
  Triumph of Politics, The (87) 886
STONE, I(SIDOR) F.
  Trial of Socrates, The (89) 855
STONE, NORMAN
  Hitler (81) 434
STONE, ROBERT
  Bay of Souls (04) 54
  Bear and His Daughter (98) 99
  Children of Light (87) 112
  Damascus Gate (99) 221
  Flag for Sunrise, A (82) 284
  Outerbridge Reach (93) 593

STOPPARD, TOM
  Dirty Linen and New-Found-Land (78) 268
  Night and Day (80) 586
STOREY, DAVID
  Prodigal Child, A (84) 711
STOUTENBURG, ADRIEN
  Land of Superior Mirages (87) 461
STOWE, REBECCA
  Not the End of the World (93) 575
STRAIGHT, SUSAN
  Blacker than a Thousand Midnights (95) 85
STRAND, MARK
  Dark Harbor (94) 209
  Selected Poems (81) 723
STRATTON, JOANNA L.
  Pioneer Women (82) 642
STRAUB, PETER
  Ghost Story (80) 349
STRAUSS, WILLIAM A., and LAWRENCE M.
  BASKIR
  Chance and Circumstance (79) 88
STROGATZ, STEVEN
  Sync (04) 723
STROUSE, JEAN
  Alice James (81) 21
  Morgan (00) 524
STROUT, ELIZABETH
  Amy and Isabelle (00) 18
STUECK, WILLIAM WHITNEY, JR.
  Road to Confrontation, The (82) 690
STYRON, WILLIAM
  Darkness Visible (91) 184
  Sophie's Choice (80) 774
  This Quiet Dust and Other Writings (83) 796
SU XIAOKANG
  Memoir of Misfortune, A (02) 515
SUGDEN, JOHN
  Sir Francis Drake (92) 757
  Tecumseh (99) 746
SULLEROT, EVELYNE
  Women on Love (81) 947
SULLIVAN, ANDREW
  Love Undetectable (99) 492
SULLIVAN, WILLIAM M., et al., editors
  Habits of the Heart (86) 380
SULZBERGER, C. L.
  Such a Peace (H-83) 411
SUNDQUIST, ERIC J.
  To Wake the Nations (94) 806
SURI, MANIL
  Death of Vishnu, The (02) 190
SÜSKIND, PATRICK
  Mr. Summer's Story (94) 535
SUTCH, RICHARD, and ROGER L. RANSOM
  One Kind of Freedom (78) 622
SUTTER, ROBERT G.
  Chinese Foreign Policy After the Cultural
    Revolution, 1966-1977 (79) 108
SWAIN, CAROL M.
  New White Nationalism in America, The (03) 572
SWANBERG, W. A.
  Norman Thomas (77) 570
  Whitney Father, Whitney Heiress (81) 921
SWANN, BRIAN, and ARNOLD KRUPAT, editors
  I Tell You Now (88) 413

AUTHOR INDEX

SWEET, PAUL ROBINSON
  Wilhelm von Humboldt, 1767-1808 (79) 868
SWEETMAN, DAVID
  Mary Renault (94) 521
  Van Gogh (91) 843
SWENSON, MAY
  New & Selected Things Taking Place (79) 472
SWIDLER, ANN, et al., editors
  Habits of the Heart (86) 380
SWIFT, GRAHAM
  Last Orders (97) 482
  Light of Day, The (04) 446
  Waterland (85) 1000
SWIR, ANNA
  Happy as a Dog's Tail (86) 391
SWOFFORD, ANTHONY
  Jarhead (04) 373
SYMONS, JULIAN
  Critical Observations (82) 156
SZATMARY, DAVID P.
  Shays' Rebellion (81) 732
SZULC, TAD
  Chopin in Paris (99) 168
  Fidel (87) 282
  Illusion of Peace (79) 300
SZYMBORSKA, WISŁAWA
  View with a Grain of Sand (96) 790

TAKAKI, RONALD
  Different Mirror, A (94) 230
  Hiroshima (96) 334
  Strangers from a Different Shore (90) 772
TAKAMURA, KOTARO
  Chieko's Sky (79) 105
TALBOTT, JOHN E.
  War Without a Name, The (81) 896
TALBOTT, STROBE
  Deadly Gambits (H-85) 110
  Master of the Game, The (89) 544
TALBOTT, STROBE, and MICHAEL R.
  BESCHLOSS
  At the Highest Levels (94) 62
TALESE, GAY
  Unto the Sons (93) 842
TAN, AMY
  Bonesetter's Daughter, The (02) 102
  Hundred Secret Senses, The (96) 351
  Joy Luck Club, The (90) 468
  Kitchen God's Wife, The (92) 408
TANENHAUS, SAM
  Whittaker Chambers (98) 841
TANIZAKI, JUN'ICHIRŌ
  Naomi (86) 640
TANNER, TONY
  Jane Austen (87) 435
TARTT, DONNA
  Little Friend, The (03) 495
  Secret History, The (93) 711
TATE, JAMES
  Collected Poems, 1919-1976 (78) 188
  Constant Defender (84) 202
  Viper Jazz (77) 888
  Worshipful Company of Fletchers (95) 895
TAUBMAN, WILLIAM
  Khrushchev (04) 404
  Stalin's American Policy (H-83) 400

TAYLOR, ANNE
  Annie Besant (93) 23
  Visions of Harmony (88) 932
TAYLOR, CHARLES
  Sources of the Self (91) 763
TAYLOR, ELIZABETH, and ADAM COHEN
  American Pharaoh (01) 34
TAYLOR, GARY
  Cultural Selection (97) 187
  Reinventing Shakespeare (90) 685
TAYLOR, HENRY
  Compulsory Figures (93) 192
  Flying Change, The (86) 293
TAYLOR, INA
  Woman of Contradictions, A (91) 909
TAYLOR, NICK, with JOHN GLENN
  John Glenn (00) 443
TAYLOR, PETER
  In the Tennessee Country (95) 363
  Smoke Ring, The (H-85) 415
TAYLOR, PETER HILLSMAN
  Old Forest and Other Stories, The (86) 673
  Oracle at Stoneleigh Court, The (94) 590
  Summons to Memphis, A (87) 832
TAYLOR, TELFORD
  Munich (80) 555
TEACHOUT, TERRY
  Skeptic, The (03) 770
TELUSHKIN, JOSEPH, and DENNIS PRAGER
  Why the Jews? (H-84) 481
TEMPLETON, EDITH
  Darts of Cupid, and Other Stories, The (03) 182
TENNANT, ROBERT
  Joseph Conrad (82) 412
TERKEL, STUDS
  Good War, The (H-85) 173
TERRAINE, JOHN
  To Win a War (82) 850
TERRILL, ROSS
  Future of China After Mao, The (79) 240
  Mao (81) 549
  White Boned Demon, The (H-85) 495
TERRY, WALLACE
  Bloods (H-85) 48
TERTZ, ABRAM
  Goodnight! (90) 314
  Little Jinx (93) 473
  Strolls with Pushkin (95) 773
  Voice from the Chorus, A (77) 892
TERVALON, JERVEY
  Understand This (95) 823
TESNOHLIDEK, RUDOLF
  Cunning Little Vixen, The (86) 204
TEVETH, SHABTAI
  Ben-Gurion, 1886-1948 (88) 90
THACKARA, JAMES
  Book of Kings, The (00) 90
THANT, U
  View from the UN (79) 809
THAROOR, SHASHI
  Nehru (04) 546
THATCHER, MARGARET
  Downing Street Years, The (94) 248
  Path to Power, The (96) 573

THERNSTROM, STEPHAN, and ABIGAIL
THERNSTROM
   America in Black and White (98) 31
THEROUX, ALEXANDER
   Primary Colors, The (95) 613
THEROUX, PAUL
   Collected Stories, The (98) 194
   Consul's File, The (78) 215
   Dark Star Safari (04) 160
   Family Arsenal, The (77) 274
   Half Moon Street (85) 338
   London Embassy, The (84) 472
   Millroy the Magician (95) 491
   Mosquito Coast, The (83) 496
   Old Patagonian Express, The (80) 619
   O-Zone (87) 631
   Riding the Iron Rooster (89) 726
   Sir Vidia's Shadow (99) 711
THOLFSEN, TRYGVE R.
   Ideology and Revolution in Modern Europe
   (H-85) 225
THOMAS, D. M.
   Alexander Solzhenitsyn (99) 24
   Ararat (84) 36
   White Hotel, The (82) 932
THOMAS, DONALD
   Robert Browning (84) 741
THOMAS, DWIGHT, and DAVID K. JACKSON
   Poe Log, The (88) 701
THOMAS, DYLAN
   Collected Letters of Dylan Thomas, The (87) 132
THOMAS, DYLAN, and JOHN DAVENPORT
   Death of the King's Canary, The (78) 238
THOMAS, ELIZABETH MARSHALL
   Reindeer Moon (88) 748
THOMAS, EMORY M.
   Confederate Nation, The (80) 156
   Robert E. Lee (96) 645
THOMAS, EVAN
   John Paul Jones (04) 381
THOMAS, HUGH
   Armed Truce (88) 57
THOMAS, KEITH
   Man and the Natural World (84) 492
THOMAS, LEWIS
   Medusa and the Snail, The (80) 533
THOMAS, MERLIN
   Louis-Ferdinand Céline (81) 529
THOMPSON, E. P.
   William Morris (78) 913
THOMPSON, JEAN
   Who Do You Love (00) 830
THOMPSON, JOHN M.
   Revolutionary Russia, 1917 (82) 679
THOMPSON, KENNETH W.
   Winston Churchill's World View (H-84) 493
THOMPSON, LEONARD
   History of South Africa, A (91) 408
THOMSON, GEORGE MALCOLM
   First Churchill, The (81) 344
THOMSON, PETER
   Shakespeare's Professional Career (93) 728
THOMSON, RUPERT
   Air and Fire (95) 15
THOREAU, HENRY DAVID
   Faith in a Seed (94) 274

THORNE, CHRISTOPHER
   Allies of a Kind (79) 9
THORPE, ADAM
   Ulverton (94) 814
THORPE, NICK
   Eight Men and a Duck (03) 246
THURBER, JAMES
   Thurber Letters, The (04) 752
THURMAN, JUDITH
   Isak Dinesen (83) 358
   Secrets of the Flesh (00) 679
TIDWELL, MIKE
   Bayou Farewell (04) 58
TIERNEY, KEVIN
   Darrow (80) 188
TILGHMAN, CHRISTOPHER
   In a Father's Place (91) 437
   Mason's Retreat (97) 550
TILLMAN, SETH P.
   United States in the Middle East, The
   (H-83) 445
TILLOTSON, GEOFFREY
   View of Victorian Literature, A (79) 814
TIMERMAN, JACOBO
   Chile (88) 150
TIPTON, STEVEN M., et al., editors
   Habits of the Heart (86) 380
TOBIN, JAMES
   To Conquer the Air (04) 766
TODD, JANET
   Mary Wollstonecraft (01) 569
TODD, OLIVIER
   Albert Camus (98) 18
TODOROV, TZVETAN
   Conquest of America, The (H-85) 89
   Imperfect Garden (03) 396
   Literature and Its Theorists (89) 515
   Mikhail Bakhtin (85) 614
TOER, PRAMOEDYA ANANTA
   Girl from the Coast, The (03) 326
TÓIBÍN, COLM
   Heather Blazing, The (94) 376
TOLAND, JOHN
   Adolf Hitler (77) 17
   Infamy (H-83) 210
   No Man's Land (81) 624
TOLKIEN, J. R. R.
   Letters of J. R. R. Tolkien, The (82) 448
   Silmarillion, The (78) 780
TOLSON, JAY
   Pilgrim in the Ruins (93) 633
TOLSTAYA, TATYANA
   On the Golden Porch (90) 637
   Sleepwalker in a Fog (93) 740
TOLSTOY, LEV
   Tolstoy's Letters, Vol. I and Vol. II (79) 754
TOMALIN, CLAIRE
   Katherine Mansfield (89) 427
   Mrs. Jordan's Profession (96) 465
TOMALIN, RUTH
   W. H. Hudson (84) 935

AUTHOR INDEX

TOMLINSON, CHARLES
Annunciations (91) 43
Collected Poems (87) 151
Door in the Wall, The (94) 244
Jubilation (96) 403
Return, The (88) 753
TONE, ANDREA
Devices and Desires (02) 199
TOOLE, JOHN KENNEDY
Confederacy of Dunces, A (81) 188
Neon Bible, The (90) 596
TOOMER, JEAN
Wayward and the Seeking, The (81) 904
TORRANCE, ROBERT M.
Encompassing Nature (99) 252
TORREY, E. FULLER
Roots of Treason, The (84) 751
TOSCHES, NICK
Devil and Sonny Liston, The (01) 237
TOTH, EMILY
Kate Chopin (91) 475
TOTH, SUSAN ALLEN
Blooming (82) 55
Ivy Days (85) 466
TOTMAN, CONRAD
Japan Before Perry (82) 408
TOUBIANA, SERGE, and ANTOINE DE BAECQUE
Truffaut (00) 772
TOURNIER, MICHEL
Fetishist, The (85) 272
Four Wise Men, The (83) 267
TOUVAL, SAADIA
Peace Brokers, The (H-83) 335
TOWNSEND, KIM
Sherwood Anderson (88) 817
TRANSTRÖMER, TOMAS
For the Living and the Dead (96) 283
TRASK, DAVID F.
War with Spain in 1898, The (82) 908
TREFIL, JAMES S.
Are We Unique? (98) 76
Unexpected Vista, The (H-84) 462
TREGLOWN, JEREMY
Roald Dahl (95) 660
Romancing (02) 708
TREMAIN, ROSE
Music and Silence (01) 599
TREVELYAN, RALEIGH
Rome '44 (H-83) 372
TREVOR, WILLIAM
After Rain (97) 14
Beyond the Pale and Other Stories (83) 57
Excursions in the Real World (95) 214
Stories of William Trevor, The (84) 829
Story of Lucy Gault, The (03) 811
TRILLIN, CALVIN
Messages from My Father (97) 573
Remembering Denny (94) 692
Uncivil Liberties (83) 849
With All Disrespect (86) 950
TRILLING, LIONEL
Last Decade, The (81) 480
Speaking of Literature and Society (81) 764
TRISTAN, FLORA
Flora Tristan's London Journal, 1840 (82) 288

TROGDON, WILLIAM. See HEAT-MOON,
WILLIAM LEAST
TROW, GEORGE W. S.
Within the Context of No Context (98) 866
TROYAT, HENRI
Catherine the Great (81) 117
Chekhov (87) 105
TRUMAN, HARRY S.
Dear Bess (H-84) 117
TRUONG, MONIQUE
Book of Salt, The (04) 100
TSVETAEVA, MARINA
Art in the Light of Conscience (93) 36
TSVETAEVA, MARINA, RAINER MARIA RILKE,
and BORIS PASTERNAK
Letters (86) 514
TUCHMAN, BARBARA W.
Distant Mirror, A (79) 151
First Salute, The (89) 302
March of Folly, The (H-85) 277
Practicing History (82) 647
TUCKER, PAUL HAYES
Claude Monet (96) 120
TUCKER, ROBERT W., and DAVID C.
HENDRICKSON
Empire of Liberty (91) 253
TUCKER, WILLIAM
Progress and Privilege (H-83) 352
TUOHY, FRANK
Collected Stories, The (85) 126
TURGENEV, IVAN
Turgenev Letters (84) 879
TURNER, ELIZABETH HUTTON
Georgia O'Keeffe (00) 300
TURNER, FREDERICK
Beyond Geography (81) 82
TURNER, HENRY ASHBY, JR.
German Big Business and the Rise of Hitler
(86) 338
TURNER, MARK
Literary Mind, The (97) 530
TURNER, MARK, and GEORGE LAKOFF
More than Cool Reason (90) 578
TUROW, SCOTT
Burden of Proof, The (91) 115
Laws of Our Fathers, The (97) 490
Personal Injuries (00) 605
Pleading Guilty (94) 636
Reversible Errors (03) 663
TWAIN, MARK
Adventures of Huckleberry Finn (02) 9
Mark Twain's Letters (89) 535
TWOMBLY, ROBERT
Louis Sullivan (87) 499
TYLER, ANNE
Accidental Tourist, The (86) 1
Back When We Were Grownups (02) 66
Breathing Lessons (89) 116
Dinner at the Homesick Restaurant
(83) 194
Ladder of Years (96) 410
Morgan's Passing (81) 573
Patchwork Planet, A (99) 624
Saint Maybe (92) 703
TYLER, W. T.
Rogue's March (83) 659

TYLER-WHITTLE, MICHAEL
  Last Kaiser, The (78) 509
TYNAN, KATHLEEN
  Life of Kenneth Tynan, The (88) 482
TYNAN, KENNETH
  Letters (99) 474

UBALDO RIBEIRO, JOÃO
  Sergeant Getúlio (79) 672
UEDA, MAKOTO
  Bashō and His Interpreters (93) 53
  Modern Japanese Poets and the Nature of
    Literature (84) 566
ULAM, ADAM B.
  Dangerous Relations (H-84) 111
  In the Name of the People (78) 442
  Russia's Failed Revolutions (82) 717
ULLMAN, LESLIE
  Natural Histories (80) 569
ULRICH, LAUREL THATCHER
  Age of Homespun, The (02) 22
  Midwife's Tale, A (91) 596
UNAMUNO, MIGUEL DE
  Private World, The (85) 701
UNGAR, SANFORD J.
  FBI (77) 287
UNGER, DOUGLAS
  Leaving the Land (85) 535
UNSWORTH, BARRY
  After Hannibal (98) 9
  Hide, The (97) 378
  Sacred Hunger (93) 698
  Songs of the Kings, The (04) 705
UPDIKE, JOHN
  Afterlife and Other Stories, The (95) 6
  Bech at Bay (99) 92
  Bech Is Back (83) 53
  Brazil (95) 99
  Collected Poems, 1953-1993 (94) 146
  Coup, The (79) 133
  Early Stories, The (04) 203
  Gertrude and Claudius (01) 337
  Hugging the Shore (84) 358
  In the Beauty of the Lilies (97) 433
  Licks of Love (01) 522
  Marry Me (77) 485
  Memories of the Ford Administration
    (93) 509
  Odd Jobs (92) 588
  Problems and Other Stories (80) 697
  Rabbit at Rest (91) 688
  Rabbit Is Rich (82) 656
  Roger's Version (87) 727
  S. (89) 748
  Seek My Face (03) 727
  Self-Consciousness (90) 725
  Toward the End of Time (98) 769
  Trust Me (88) 915
  Witches of Eastwick, The (85) 1041
URIS, LEON
  Trinity (77) 842
UROFSKY, MELVIN I.
  Louis D. Brandeis and the Progressive Tradition
    (82) 488
URQUHART, JANE
  Stone Carvers, The (03) 803
  Underpainter, The (98) 782

VAILLANT, JANET G.
  Black, French, and African (91) 80
VALENSTEIN, ELLIOT S.
  Great and Desperate Cures (87) 357
VALENTINE, JEAN
  Cradle of the Real Life, The (01) 223
VAN BRUNT, LLOYD
  Poems New and Selected, 1962-1992 (94) 641
VAN CASPEL, PAUL
  Bloomers on the Liffey (87) 80
VANCE, CYRUS
  Hard Choices (H-84) 180
VanDeMARK, BRIAN, with ROBERT McNAMARA
  In Retrospect (96) 363
VANDIVER, FRANK E.
  Black Jack, Vol. I and Vol. II (78) 96
VAN TINE, WARREN, and MELVIN DUBOFSKY
  John L. Lewis (78) 478
VARGAS LLOSA, MARIO
  Aunt Julia and the Scriptwriter (83) 34
  Captain Pantoja and the Special Service (79) 75
  Cubs and Other Stories, The (80) 165
  Death in the Andes (97) 200
  Feast of the Goat, The (02) 290
  Fish in the Water, A (95) 239
  Notebooks of Don Rigoberto, The (99) 562
  Real Life of Alejandro Mayta, The (87) 685
  Storyteller, The (90) 763
  War of the End of the World, The (85) 995
  Way to Paradise, The (04) 815
VASSILIKOS, VASSILIS
  Few Things I Know About Glafkos Thrassakis,
    The (04) 257
VASSILTCHIKOV, MARIE
  Berlin Diaries, 1940-1945 (88) 95
VAUGHN, STEPHANIE
  Sweet Talk (91) 786
VENCLOVA, TOMAS
  Aleksander Wat (97) 18
VENDLER, HELEN
  Art of Shakespeare's Sonnets, The (98) 80
  Music of What Happens, The (89) 566
  Voices and Visions (88) 943
VERGHESE, ABRAHAM
  My Own Country (95) 515
VERGIL
  Eclogues of Virgil, The (00) 194
VERRIER, ANTHONY
  Through the Looking Glass (H-84) 444
VEYNE, PAUL
  History of Private Life, From Pagan Rome to
    Byzantium, A (88) 386
VICKERS, BRIAN
  Appropriating Shakespeare (94) 33
VIDAL, GORE
  At Home (89) 59
  Creation (82) 151
  1876 (77) 256
  Empire (88) 275
  Golden Age, The (01) 361
  Hollywood (91) 423
  Last Empire, The (02) 472
  Lincoln (85) 570
  Palimpsest (96) 561
  Screening History (93) 707
  Second American Revolution, The (83) 700
  United States (94) 819

AUTHOR INDEX

VIERECK, PETER
Archer in the Marrow (88) 46
VINCENT, GÉRARD, and ANTOINE PROST, editors
History of Private Life, Riddles of Identity in
Modern Times, A (92) 294
VIROLI, MAURIZIO
Niccolò's Smile (01) 641
VISSER, MARGARET
Geometry of Love, The (02) 330
VIVANTE, ARTURO
Run to the Waterfall (80) 736
VLASTOS, GREGORY
Socrates (92) 766
VOGELGESANG, SANDY
American Dream Global Nightmare (81) 31
VOLLMANN, WILLIAM T.
Atlas, The (97) 76
Fathers and Crows (93) 288
Rifles, The (95) 647
Royal Family, The (01) 745
VON ABELE, RUDOLPH
Cage for Loulou, A (79) 70
VON BAEYER, HANS C.
Rainbows, Snowflakes, and Quarks (H-85) 379
VON DREHLE, DAVID
Triangle (04) 778
VON HOFFMAN, NICHOLAS
Citizen Cohn (89) 164
VONNEGUT, KURT
Bluebeard (88) 107
Deadeye Dick (83) 174
Galápagos (86) 326
Hocus Pocus (91) 413
Jailbird (80) 436
Palm Sunday (82) 609
Slapstick (77) 749
Timequake (98) 760

WADE, BRENT
Company Man (93) 176
WAGNER-MARTIN, LINDA
Sylvia Plath (88) 874
WAGNER, BRUCE
I'm Losing You (97) 423
WAGONER, DAVID
Collected Poems, 1956-1976 (78) 197
First Light (84) 299
Who Shall Be the Sun? (79) 852
WAIN, JOHN
Pardoner's Tale, The (80) 640
Professing Poetry (79) 561
WAITE, ROBERT G. L.
Psychopathic God, The (78) 677
WAKOSKI, DIANE
Emerald City of Las Vegas, The (96) 218
Jason the Sailor (94) 422
Man Who Shook Hands, The (79) 414
WALBERT, KATE
Gardens of Kyoto, The (02) 326
WALCOTT, DEREK
Arkansas Testament, The (88) 52
Fortunate Traveller, The (82) 293
Midsummer (85) 609
Omeros (91) 643
Star-Apple Kingdom, The (80) 777
Tiepolo's Hound (01) 825
What the Twilight Says (99) 851

WALDRON, ANN
Eudora (00) 240
WALDRON, ARTHUR
Great Wall of China, The (91) 368
WALKER, ALICE
Color Purple, The (83) 139
In Search of Our Mothers' Gardens (84) 368
Meridian (77) 501
Possessing the Secret of Joy (93) 651
You Can't Keep a Good Woman Down (82) 976
WALKER, MARGARET
Richard Wright, Daemonic Genius (89) 722
WALL, STEPHEN
Trollope (90) 827
WALLACE, ANTHONY F. C.
St. Clair (88) 790
WALLACE, DAVID FOSTER
Brief Interviews with Hideous Men (00) 95
Girl with Curious Hair (90) 299
Infinite Jest (97) 446
Supposedly Fun Thing I'll Never Do Again, A
(98) 750
WALSER, MARTIN
No Man's Land (90) 619
WALSER, ROBERT
Selected Stories (83) 734
WALSH, JOHN EVANGELIST
Into My Own (89) 390
WAMBAUGH, JOSEPH
Glitter Dome, The (82) 325
WANGERIN, WALTER, JR.
Book of Sorrows, The (86) 77
WARD, GEOFFREY C.
First-Class Temperament, A (90) 258
WARD, GEOFFREY C., and KEN BURNS
Not for Ourselves Alone (00) 580
WARD, GEOFFREY C., et al.
Civil War, The (91) 137
WARNER, MARINA
From the Beast to the Blonde (96) 290
WARNER, MICHAEL
Publics and Counterpublics (03) 634
WARNER, ROGER, with HAING NGOR
Haing Ngor (89) 335
WARNER, SAM BASS, JR.
Province of Reason (H-85) 368
WARNER, SYLVIA TOWNSEND
Letters (84) 432
One Thing Leading to Another (85) 658
Scenes of Childhood and Other Stories (83) 679
WARREN, EARL
Memoirs of Earl Warren, The (78) 567
WARREN, ROBERT PENN
Being Here (81) 76
Now and Then (79) 501
Rumor Verified (82) 704
Selected Poems, 1923-1975 (78) 753
WARREN, ROSANNA
Each Leaf Shines Separate (85) 204
WASHINGTON, GEORGE, and DAVID
HUMPHREYS
David Humphreys' "Life of General Washington"
(92) 147
WASSERSTEIN, BERNARD
Secret Lives of Trebitsch Lincoln, The (89) 762

WAT, ALEKSANDER
    Lucifer Unemployed (91) 545
    My Century (89) 571
WATKINS, PAUL
    Promise of Light, The (94) 667
    Stand Before Your God (95) 752
WATSON, JAMES D., with ANDREW BERRY
    DNA (04) 179
WATSON, RICHARD
    Philosopher's Demise, The (96) 581
WATT, IAN
    Conrad (81) 193
    Myths of Modern Individualism (97) 610
WAUGH, EVELYN
    Charles Ryder's Schooldays and Other Stories
        (83) 105
    Diaries of Evelyn Waugh, The (78) 258
    Essays, Articles and Reviews of Evelyn Waugh,
        The (85) 238
    Letters of Evelyn Waugh, The (81) 489
    Little Order, A (81) 517
WEART, SPENCER R.
    Nuclear Fear (89) 610
WEBB, SIDNEY, and BEATRICE POTTER WEBB
    Letters of Sidney and Beatrice Webb, The
        (79) 378
WEBER, DAVID J.
    Spanish Frontier in North America, The (93) 749
WEBER, EUGEN JOSEPH
    Apocalypses (00) 44
WEBER, RONALD
    Hemingway's Art of Non-Fiction (91) 386
WEBSTER, GRANT
    Republic of Letters, The (80) 705
WEEKS, EDWARD
    Writers and Friends (83) 928
WEESNER, THEODORE
    Winning the City (91) 905
WEIGEL, GEORGE
    Witness to Hope (00) 847
WEIGL, BRUCE
    Circle of Hanh, The (01) 190
    Song of Napalm (89) 803
WEIGLEY, RUSSELL F.
    Eisenhower's Lieutenants (82) 210
WEIL, JIŘÍ
    Life with a Star (90) 531
WEINBERG, ARTHUR, and LILA WEINBERG
    Clarence Darrow (81) 152
WEINBERG, GERHARD L.
    World at Arms, A (95) 885
WEINBERG, STEVEN
    Facing Up (02) 263
WEINER, JONATHAN
    Beak of the Finch, The (95) 65
    Time, Love, Memory (00) 754
WEINGARTNER, JAMES J.
    Crossroads of Death (80) 162
WEINSTEIN, ALLEN
    Perjury (79) 540
WEINSTEIN, FRED
    Dynamics of Nazism, The (81) 254
WEINTRAUB, STANLEY
    Disraeli (94) 239
    London Yankees, The (80) 508

WEISBERGER, LAUREN
    Devil Wears Prada, The (04) 169
WEISS, JEFFREY
    Mark Rothko (99) 524
WEISS, THEODORE
    Views & Spectacles (80) 846
WELCH, DENTON
    Journals of Denton Welch, The (85) 504
WELCHMAN, GORDON
    Hut Six Story, The (H-83) 201
WELDON, FAY
    Puffball (81) 670
WELLEK, RENE
    History of Modern Criticism, 1750-1950, A
        (92) 290
WELLER, SHEILA
    Dancing at Ciro's (04) 151
WELLS, STANLEY
    Shakespeare (96) 704
WELLS, TOM
    War Within, The (95) 844
WELSH, IRVINE
    Glue (02) 347
WELTY, EUDORA
    Collected Stories of Eudora Welty, The (81) 178
    Eye of the Story, The (79) 200
    One Writer's Beginnings (85) 663
WERTH, BARRY
    Scarlet Professor, The (02) 727
WESCHLER, LAWRENCE
    Calamities of Exile (99) 136
WESLEY, MARY
    Imaginative Experience, An (96) 359
WEST, ANTHONY
    H. G. Wells (85) 380
WEST, DOROTHY
    Richer, the Poorer, The (96) 641
WEST, JAMES L. W., III
    William Styron (99) 864
WEST, JESSAMYN
    Life I Really Lived, The (80) 491
    Woman Said Yes, The (77) 928
WEST, PAUL
    Rat Man of Paris (87) 681
WEST, REBECCA
    Young Rebecca, The (83) 932
WESTBROOK, ROBERT B.
    John Dewey and American Democracy (92) 388
WESTLAKE, DONALD E.
    Ax, The (98) 95
WEXLER, ALICE
    Emma Goldman (H-85) 125
WHARTON, EDITH
    Letters of Edith Wharton, The (89) 475
WHARTON, WILLIAM
    Birdy (80) 79
    Dad (82) 166
    Midnight Clear, A (83) 480
WHEELOCK, JOHN HALL
    This Blessèd Earth (79) 749
WHEEN, FRANCIS
    Karl Marx (01) 504
WHELDON, DAVID
    Viaduct, The (84) 910

AUTHOR INDEX

WHETTEN, LAWRENCE L.
Germany East and West (81) 373

WHISNANT, LUKE
Watching TV with the Red Chinese (93) 864

WHITE, CHRISTOPHER
Peter Paul Rubens (88) 690

WHITE, E. B.
Essays of E. B. White (78) 295
Letters of E. B. White (77) 413

WHITE, EDMUND
Beautiful Room Is Empty, The (89) 76
Farewell Symphony, The (98) 303
Genet (94) 339
Married Man, The (01) 564
Skinned Alive (96) 720

WHITE, G. EDWARD
Earl Warren (H-83) 109
Justice Oliver Wendell Holmes (94) 431

WHITE, MICHAEL, and JOHN GRIBBIN
Stephen Hawking (93) 758

WHITE, NORMAN
Hopkins (93) 353

WHITE, PATRICK
Flaws in the Glass (83) 257
Patrick White (97) 656
Twyborn Affair, The (81) 840

WHITE, T. H.
Book of Merlyn, The (78) 126

WHITE, THEODORE H.
America in Search of Itself (H-83) 29
In Search of History (79) 314

WHITE-PARKS, ANNETTE
Sui Sin Far/Edith Maude Eaton (96) 732

WHITEHEAD, BARBARA DAFOE
Divorce Culture, The (98) 254

WHITEHEAD, COLSON
Intuitionist, The (00) 435
John Henry Days (02) 449

WHITTEMORE, REED
Feel of Rock, The (83) 250
Poet as Journalist, The (77) 623

WICKER, TOM
One of Us (92) 597

WICKWIRE, FRANKLIN, and MARY WICKWIRE
Cornwallis (81) 203

WIDEMAN, JOHN EDGAR
Brothers and Keepers (85) 57
Cattle Killing, The (97) 142
Fatheralong (95) 227
Fever (90) 249
Philadelphia Fire (91) 661
Sent for You Yesterday (84) 779
Stories of John Edgar Wideman, The (93) 762
Two Cities (99) 808

WIDENOR, WILLIAM C.
Henry Cabot Lodge and the Search for an
American Foreign Policy (81) 416

WIEBE, ROBERT H.
Opening of American Society, The (H-85) 344
Self-Rule (96) 699

WIEDER, LAURANCE
Words to God's Music (04) 851

WIENER, MARTIN J.
English Culture and the Decline of the Industrial
Spirit, 1850-1980 (82) 234

WIER, ALLEN
Blanco (80) 83

WIER, DARA
Blood, Hook & Eye (78) 112

WIESEL, ELIE
All Rivers Run to the Sea (96) 18
And the Sea Is Never Full (00) 22
Somewhere a Master (83) 756

WIESELTIER, LEON
Kaddish (99) 445

WIGGINS, MARIANNE
Bet They'll Miss Us When We're Gone (92) 39
Herself in Love and Other Stories (88) 377
John Dollar (90) 454

WILBUR, RICHARD
Catbird's Song, The (98) 156
Mayflies (01) 579
Mind-Reader, The (77) 505
New and Collected Poems (89) 590
Responses (77) 679

WILCOX, JAMES
North Gladiola (86) 664
Plain and Normal (99) 632

WILDE-MENOZZI, WALLIS
Mother Tongue (98) 567

WILDER, THORNTON
Journals of Thornton Wilder, 1939-1961, The
(86) 491

WILFORD, JOHN NOBLE
Mars Beckons (91) 568
Mysterious History of Columbus, The (92) 540

WILKINS, ROGER
Jefferson's Pillow (02) 440

WILKINSON, J. HARVIE, III
From Brown to Bakke, The Supreme Court and
School Integration (80) 334

WILLARD, CHARITY CANNON
Christine de Pizan (86) 126

WILLIAMS, C. K.
Flesh and Blood (88) 330
Tar (84) 859
With Ignorance (78) 923

WILLIAMS, GLYNDWR, and P. J. MARSHALL
Great Map of Mankind, The (H-83) 176

WILLIAMS, JOHN A.
!Click Song (83) 124

WILLIAMS, JOY
Escapes (91) 262

WILLIAMS, RAYMOND
Keywords (77) 388

WILLIAMS, SHERLEY ANNE
Dessa Rose (87) 207

WILLIAMS, T. HARRY
History of American Wars, The (82) 354

WILLIAMS, TENNESSEE
Collected Stories (86) 170
Five O'Clock Angel (91) 291
Memoirs (77) 494

WILLIAMS, TERRY TEMPEST
Leap (01) 513

WILLIAMS, THOMAS
Moon Pinnace, The (87) 568

WILLIAMS, WILLIAM CARLOS
Collected Poems of William Carlos Williams,
1909-1939, The (87) 155
Collected Poems of William Carlos Williams,
1939-1962, The (89) 190
Pound/Williams (97) 675

WILLIAMSON, JOEL
Crucible of Race, The (H-85) 99
WILLIS, CONNIE
Lincoln's Dreams (88) 487
WILLIS, JAN
Dreaming Me (02) 212
WILLMOTT, H. P.
Empires in the Balance (H-83) 119
WILLOCKS, TIM
Green River Rising (95) 283
WILLS, GARRY
Certain Trumpets (95) 114
Cincinnatus (H-85) 78
Explaining America (82) 261
Inventing America (79) 322
John Wayne's America (98) 477
Kennedy Imprisonment, The (H-83) 244
Lincoln at Gettysburg (93) 464
Necessary Evil, A (00) 567
Reagan's America (88) 725
Saint Augustine (00) 665
WILLS, JOHN E., JR.
Mountain of Fame (95) 509
WILSON, A. N.
Bottle in the Smoke, A (91) 100
C. S. Lewis (91) 175
Daughters of Albion (93) 200
Dream Children (99) 234
Gentlemen in England (87) 322
God's Funeral (00) 317
Hearing Voices (97) 364
Hilaire Belloc (85) 385
Incline Our Hearts (90) 415
Love Unknown (88) 507
Tolstoy (89) 845
Victorians, The (04) 801
Watch in the Night, A (97) 876
WILSON, ANDREW
Beautiful Shadow (04) 62
WILSON, ANGUS
Diversity and Depth in Fiction (85) 190
Setting the World on Fire (81) 727
Strange Ride of Rudyard Kipling, The (79) 717
WILSON, DICK
People's Emperor, The (81) 645
When Tigers Fight (H-83) 454
Zhou Enlai (H-85) 526
WILSON, DOUGLAS L.
Honor's Voice (99) 379
WILSON, EDMUND
Forties, The (84) 309
Letters on Literature and Politics, 1912-1972
(78) 522
Thirties, The (81) 795
WILSON, EDMUND, and VLADIMIR NABOKOV
Nabokov-Wilson Letters, The (80) 564
WILSON, EDWARD O.
Consilience (99) 216
Diversity of Life, The (93) 235
Future of Life, The (03) 321
In Search of Nature (97) 428
Naturalist (95) 528
On Human Nature (79) 506
WILSON, EDWARD O., and BERT HÖLLDOBLER
Ants, The (91) 47
WILSON, EDWARD O., and CHARLES J.
LUMSDEN
Promethean Fire (H-84) 366

WILSON, HENRY S.
Imperial Experience in Sub-Saharan Africa Since
1870, The (78) 436
WILSON, JAMES Q.
Moral Sense, The (94) 539
WILSON, JEREMY
Lawrence of Arabia (91) 512
WILSON, LANFORD
5th of July (80) 320
Talley's Folly (81) 790
WILSON, SLOAN
What Shall We Wear to This Party? (77) 901
WILSON, WILLIAM JULIUS
Truly Disadvantaged, The (88) 910
When Work Disappears (97) 880
WIMSATT, W. K.
Day of the Leopards (77) 194
WINCHELL, MARK ROYDEN
Cleanth Brooks and the Rise of Modern Criticism
(97) 156
WINCHESTER, SIMON
Krakatoa (04) 430
Map That Changed the World, The (02) 503
Meaning of Everything, The (04) 506
WINN, JAMES ANDERSON
John Dryden and His World (88) 438
WINNER, LAUREN F.
Girl Meets God (03) 330
WINTERNITZ, HELEN, and TIMOTHY M.
PHELPS
Capitol Games (93) 128
WINTERSON, JEANETTE
Passion, The (89) 654
Sexing the Cherry (91) 735
Written on the Body (94) 873
WISER, WILLIAM
Crazy Years, The (84) 207
WITCOVER, JULES
Marathon (78) 562
WOFFORD, HARRIS
Of Kennedys and Kings (81) 633
WOHL, ROBERT
Generation of 1914, The (80) 337
WOIWODE, LARRY
Born Brothers (89) 107
Indian Affairs (93) 378
Neumiller Stories, The (90) 600
Silent Passengers (94) 738
What I Think I Did (01) 896
WOJTYLA, KAROL
Love and Responsibility (82) 494
WOLF, CHRISTA
Accident (90) 6
Cassandra (85) 74
No Place on Earth (83) 540
WOLF, JOHN B.
Barbary Coast, The (80) 49
WOLFE, ALAN
Moral Freedom (02) 541
One Nation, After All (99) 593
WOLFE, TOBIAS
Night in Question, The (97) 618
WOLFE, TOM
Bonfire of the Vanities, The (88) 112
Man in Full, A (99) 511
Purple Decades, The (83) 626
Right Stuff, The (80) 713

AUTHOR INDEX

WOLFF, CHRISTOPH
  Johann Sebastian Bach (01) 494
WOLFF, CYNTHIA GRIFFIN
  Emily Dickinson (87) 233
  Feast of Words, A (78) 314
WOLFF, GEOFFREY
  Art of Burning Bridges, The (04) 45
  Black Sun (77) 91
  Duke of Deception, The (80) 236
WOLFF, TOBIAS
  Barracks Thief, The (86) 48
  In the Garden of the North American Martyrs
    (82) 392
  In Pharaoh's Army (95) 347
  Old School (04) 570
  This Boy's Life (90) 796
WOLOCH, NANCY
  Women and the American Experience (H-85) 511
WOLPERT, STANLEY
  India (92) 350
  New History of India, A (78) 598
  Roots of Confrontation in South Asia (H-83) 376
WONGAR, B.
  Track to Bralgu, The (79) 768
WOOD, GORDON S.
  Radicalism of the American Revolution, The
    (93) 665
WOOD, JAMES
  Book Against God, The (04) 96
  Broken Estate, The (00) 103
WOODALL, JAMES
  Borges (98) 130
WOODS, DONALD
  Asking for Trouble (82) 28
WOODS, GREGORY
  History of Gay Literature, A (99) 369
WOODS, JOHN
  Striking the Earth (77) 784
WOODS, RANDALL BENNETT
  Fulbright (96) 294
WOODWARD, BOB
  Veil (88) 923
WOODWARD, BOB, and SCOTT ARMSTRONG
  Brethren, The (80) 104
WOODWARD, C. VANN
  Old World's New World, The (92) 592
WOOLF, VIRGINIA
  Diary of Virginia Woolf, 1915-1919, The (78) 264
  Diary of Virginia Woolf, 1920-1924, The (79) 147
  Diary of Virginia Woolf, 1925-1930, The (81) 240
  Diary of Virginia Woolf, 1931-1935, The (83) 185
  Diary of Virginia Woolf, 1936-1941, The (85) 178
  Essays of Virginia Woolf, 1904-1912, The (88) 288
  Essays of Virginia Woolf, 1912-1918, The (89) 283
  Essays of Virginia Woolf, 1919-1924, The (90) 222
  Letters of Virginia Woolf, 1912-1922, The (77) 418
  Letters of Virginia Woolf, 1923-1928, The (79) 382
  Letters of Virginia Woolf, 1929-1931, The (80) 483
  Letters of Virginia Woolf, 1932-1935, The (80) 487
  Letters of Virginia Woolf, 1936-1941, The (81) 506
  Passionate Apprentice, A (92) 607
WOOLLEY, BRYAN
  Time and Place (78) 836
WORMSER, BARON
  Good Trembling (86) 364
  White Words, The (84) 940

WORSTER, DONALD
  Dust Bowl (80) 244
  Under Western Skies (93) 833
WORTHEN, JOHN
  D. H. Lawrence (92) 166
  Gang, The (02) 321
WOUK, HERMAN
  Inside, Outside (86) 466
WRESZIN, MICHAEL
  Rebel in Defense of Tradition, A (95) 630
WRIGHT, AUSTIN M.
  Recalcitrance, Faulkner, and the Professors
    (91) 701
WRIGHT, CHARLES
  Appalachia (99) 61
  Black Zodiac (98) 117
  Chickamauga (96) 103
  Short History of the Shadow, A (03) 741
WRIGHT, ESMOND
  Franklin of Philadelphia (87) 303
WRIGHT, J. LEITCH, JR.
  Only Land They Knew, The (82) 594
WRIGHT, JAMES
  To a Blossoming Pear Tree (78) 847
WRIGHT, JAY
  Boleros (92) 56
WRIGHT, RICHARD
  Richard Wright Reader (79) 597
WRIGHT, ROBERT
  Moral Animal, The (95) 504
  Nonzero (01) 646
WRIGHT, STEPHEN
  Going Native (95) 271
  Meditations in Green (84) 523
  M31 (89) 562
WRONG, MICHELA
  In the Footsteps of Mr. Kurtz (02) 413
WU CH'ÊNG-ÊN
  Journey to the West, Vol. IV, The (84) 401
WURTS, JAY, with LE LY HAYSLIP
  When Heaven and Earth Changed Places (90) 879
WYATT, DAVID
  Fall into Eden, The (87) 253
WYATT-BROWN, BERTRAM
  Southern Honor (H-83) 396
WYDEN, PETER
  Bay of Pigs (80) 59
  Day One (H-85) 104
  Passionate War, The (H-84) 330
WYMAN, DAVID S.
  Abandonment of the Jews, The (H-85) 1
WYND, OSWALD
  Ginger Tree, The (78) 349

XUE LITAI, SERGEI N. GONCHAROV, and
JOHN W. LEWIS
  Uncertain Partners (95) 809

YA'ARI, EHUD, and ZE'EV SCHIFF
  Intifada (91) 461
YAGODA, BEN
  About Town (01) 1
YALOM, MARILYN
  History of the Breast, A (98) 391
YANKELOVICH, DANIEL
  New Rules (82) 548

YATES, RICHARD
  Easter Parade, The (77) 247
  Liars in Love (82) 453
YEAGER, CHUCK, and LEO JANOS
  Yeager (86) 974
YEATES, MARIAN, and JOAN HOFF
  Cooper's Wife Is Missing, The (01) 218
YEATS, WILLIAM BUTLER
  Collected Letters of W. B. Yeats, 1865-1895, The
    (87) 142
  Poems, The (85) 692
YEATS, WILLIAM BUTLER, and MAUD GONNE
  Gonne-Yeats Letters 1893-1938, The (94) 368
YEHOSHUA, A. B.
  Five Seasons (90) 263
  Journey to the End of the Millennium, A (00) 453
  Late Divorce, A (85) 530
  Mr. Mani (93) 527
YERGIN, DANIEL H.
  Prize, The (92) 645
  Shattered Peace (78) 766
YERGIN, DANIEL H., and JOSEPH STANISLAW
  Commanding Heights (99) 204
YEROFEYEV, VIKTOR, et al., editors
  Metropol (84) 533
YEVTUSHENKO, YEVGENY
  Collected Poems, The (92) 104
YGLESIAS, HELEN
  Family Feeling (77) 277
YORK, HERBERT F.
  Advisors, The (77) 27
YOSHIMOTO, BANANA
  Kitchen (94) 445
YOUNG, HUGO
  Iron Lady, The (90) 429
YOUNG, MARGUERITE
  Harp Song for a Radical (00) 358
YOUNG, MARILYN B., and WILLIAM G.
  ROSENBERG
  Transforming Russia and China (H-83) 426
YOUNG, PHILIP
  Hawthorne's Secret (85) 358
YOUNG-BRUEHL, ELISABETH
  Anna Freud (89) 23
  Hannah Arendt (83) 322

YOURCENAR, MARGUERITE
  Abyss, The (77) 1
  Dark Brain of Piranesi and Other Essays, The
    (85) 152
  Fires (82) 275
  Oriental Tales (86) 706
YOVEL, YIRMIYAHU
  Spinoza and Other Heretics, Vol. I and Vol. II
    (91) 768

ZAGAJEWSKI, ADAM
  Without End (03) 890
ZAGORIN, PEREZ
  Francis Bacon (99) 303
ZAKARIA, FAREED
  From Wealth to Power (99) 315
  Future of Freedom, The (04) 279
ZEE, A.
  Old Man's Toy, An (90) 628
ZEITLIN, JUDITH T.
  Historian of the Strange (94) 393
ZERUBAVEL, EVIATAR
  Seven Day Circle, The (86) 807
ZIEGLER, PHILIP
  King Edward VIII (92) 403
  Mountbatten (86) 629
  Soldiers (03) 789
ZIFF, LARZER
  Return Passages (02) 698
  Writing in the New Nation (92) 924
ZIMMER, CARL
  At the Water's Edge (99) 69
ZIMMERMANN, WARREN
  First Great Triumph (03) 297
ZINSSER, WILLIAM
  Willie and Dwike (85) 1036
ZIOLKOWSKI, THEODORE
  German Romanticism and Its Institutions
    (91) 347
ZUBOFF, SHOSHANNA
  In the Age of the Smart Machine (89) 377
ZUKOFSKY, LOUIS
  "A" (80) 1
  Complete Short Poetry (92) 114
ZURAVLEFF, MARY KAY
  Frequency of Souls, The (97) 315
ZWEIG, PAUL
  Walt Whitman (85) 984
ZYSMAN, JOHN, and STEPHEN S. COHEN
  Manufacturing Matters (88) 529